ASPEN PUBLISHERS

# Defined Benefit Answer Book
**Fourth Edition**

*by G. Neff McGhie III*

*Defined Benefit Answer Book* provides expert guidance on the complex rules governing defined benefit pension plans. In this comprehensive resource, the author guides the subscriber, step by step, through the maze of factors that must be considered when designing and administering these plans.

## Highlights of the Fourth Edition

The Fourth Edition brings you up to date on the latest developments including:

- Complete discussion of the comprehensive changes made to defined benefit plans by the Pension Protection Act of 2006 (PPA).

- Analysis of the effects of the newly proposed Code Section 415 regulations on defined benefit plans if the regulations are finalized as originally proposed.

- Updated information regarding the requirements of the relative value regulations of Code Section 417.

- Updated information regarding amendments eliminating optional forms of benefits.

- Practical information about the uses of each type of funding method used for defined benefit plans.

- Additional information regarding multiemployer plans.

- Recent PBGC guidance and changes.

3/07

For questions concerning this shipment, billing, or other customer service matters, call our Customer Service Department at 1-800-234-1660.

For toll-free ordering, please call 1-800-638-8437.

# Defined Benefit
## Answer Book

ASPEN PUBLISHERS

# Defined Benefit Answer Book

### Fourth Edition

## G. Neff McGhie III

Wolters Kluwer
Law & Business

AUSTIN   BOSTON   CHICAGO   NEW YORK   THE NETHERLANDS

This publication is designed to provide accurate and authoritative information in regard to the subject matter covered. It is sold with the understanding that the publisher is not engaged in rendering legal, accounting, or other professional services. If legal advice or other professional assistance is required, the services of a competent professional person should be sought.

—From a *Declaration of Principles* jointly adopted by
a Committee of the American Bar Association and
a Committee of Publishers and Associations

Printed in the United States of America

ISBN 978-0-7355-6004-8

1 2 3 4 5 6 7 8 9 0

# About Wolters Kluwer Law & Business

Wolters Kluwer Law & Business is a leading provider of research information and workflow solutions in key specialty areas. The strengths of the individual brands of Aspen Publishers, CCH, Kluwer Law International and Loislaw are aligned within Wolters Kluwer Law & Business to provide comprehensive, in-depth solutions and expert-authored content for the legal, professional and education markets.

**CCH** was founded in 1913 and has served more than four generations of business professionals and their clients. The CCH products in the Wolters Kluwer Law & Business group are highly regarded electronic and print resources for legal, securities, antitrust and trade regulation, government contracting, banking, pension, payroll, employment and labor, and healthcare reimbursement and compliance professionals.

**Aspen Publishers** is a leading information provider for attorneys, business professionals and law students. Written by preeminent authorities, Aspen products offer analytical and practical information in a range of specialty practice areas from securities law and intellectual property to mergers and acquisitions and pension/benefits. Aspen's trusted legal education resources provide professors and students with high-quality, up-to-date and effective resources for successful instruction and study in all areas of the law.

**Kluwer Law International** supplies the global business community with comprehensive English-language international legal information. Legal practitioners, corporate counsel and business executives around the world rely on the Kluwer Law International journals, loose-leafs, books and electronic products for authoritative information in many areas of international legal practice.

**Loislaw** is a premier provider of digitized legal content to small law firm practitioners of various specializations. Loislaw provides attorneys with the ability to quickly and efficiently find the necessary legal information they need, when and where they need it, by facilitating access to primary law as well as state-specific law, records, forms and treatises.

Wolters Kluwer Law & Business, a unit of Wolters Kluwer, is headquartered in New York and Riverwoods, Illinois. Wolters Kluwer is a leading multinational publisher and information services company.

## ASPEN PUBLISHERS SUBSCRIPTION NOTICE

This Aspen Publishers product is updated on a periodic basis with supplements to reflect important changes in the subject matter. If you purchased this product directly from Aspen Publishers, we have already recorded your subscription for the update service.

If, however, you purchased this product from a bookstore and wish to receive future updates and revised or related volumes billed separately with a 30-day examination review, please contact our Customer Service Department at 1-800-234-1660, or send your name, company name (if applicable), address, and the title of the product to:

**ASPEN PUBLISHERS**
**7201 McKinney Circle**
**Frederick, MD 21704**

---

**Important Aspen Publishers Contact Information**

- To order any Aspen Publishers title, go to *www.aspenpublishers.com* or call 1-800-638-8437.

- To reinstate your manual update service, call 1-800-638-8437.

- To contact Customer Care, e-mail *customer.care@aspenpublishers.com*, call 1-800-234-1660, fax 1-800-901-9075, or mail correspondence to Order Department, Aspen Publishers, PO Box 990, Frederick, MD 21705.

- To review your account history or pay an invoice online, visit *www.aspenpublishers.com/payinvoices*.

Wolters Kluwer
Law & Business

# Preface

*Defined Benefit Answer Book, Fourth Edition*, is designed for professionals who need quick and authoritative answers to questions on the complex administration of defined benefit plans. It is thoroughly updated to cover all of the latest legislative developments affecting defined benefit plans, including the changes implemented by the Pension Protection Act of 2006 (PPA), the Economic Growth and Tax Relief Reconciliation Act of 2001 (EGTRRA), the Job Creation and Worker Assistance Act of 2002 (JCWAA), and the Pension Funding Equity Act of 2004. There are numerous examples of how those bills affect defined benefit plans and discussion and analysis of current laws and regulations, including how the PPA affects the future of defined benefit plan operations. Among the crucial questions answered are the following:

- Does a company's financial stability affect plan design?
- Can plans be designed to provide enhanced benefits to key employees?
- Are there ways of establishing hours of service without counting actual hours?
- Can a defined benefit plan be designed so that there is no discrimination testing each year?
- Can a defined benefit plan be designed to primarily benefit the key employees?
- Are there any advantages to having a defined contribution plan and a defined benefit plan together, and how are they administered?
- What must an employer do to satisfy minimum funding requirements?
- What distribution election forms must be provided to a participant?
- How can a QDRO be prepared for a defined benefit plan?
- How are maximum benefit limitations determined under a plan?
- How are benefits calculated and converted to alternate forms of payment?
- What administrative issues must be considered for a plan that is covered by the Pension Benefit Guaranty Corporation?
- How are cash balance plans similar and different from traditional defined benefit plans?

- How are deductible contributions determined for a defined benefit plan?
- How is a defined benefit similar and different from a defined contribution plan?
- What different administrative tasks are required for a defined benefit plan and for a defined contribution plan?
- How does a 412(i) plan operate?
- Can a 412(i) plan be more beneficial for sponsors than a regular defined benefit plan?

Some of the most useful features of *Defined Benefit Answer Book* are outlined below.

**Question-and-answer format.** The question-and-answer format effectively conveys the complex and essential subject matter of defined benefit plans, while providing quickly accessible, straightforward answers to common concerns.

**Numbering system.** The questions are numbered consecutively within each chapter.

**List of questions.** The detailed List of Questions that follows the Contents helps the reader locate areas of immediate interest. The list is similar to a detailed table of contents, providing both the question number and the page on which the question appears. A series of subheadings helps to group and organize the questions by topic within each chapter.

**Appendixes.** Valuable resource material has been provided in the appendixes that follow the last chapter. These documents include covered compensation tables, the annuity purchase rates for the applicable mortality tables, and rates of turnovers.

**Reference tables.** Reference tables keyed to question numbers are provided for Internal Revenue Code and regulations sections, revenue rulings, revenue procedures, IRS announcements and notices, court cases, PBGC regulations, ERISA regulations, and PPA sections.

**Index.** To further assist the reader in finding specific information, a detailed subject index gives comprehensive locator information for all major topics covered. All references are to question numbers.

In short, *Defined Benefit Answer Book* is designed to help readers make defined benefit plans a valuable component of their benefits and tax planning strategies.

# About the Author

**G. Neff McGhie, III,** EA, MSPA is a graduate of California State University, Fresno with a B.A. in Mathematics. He is an Enrolled Actuary, a Member of the College of Pension Actuaries (COPA) and a Member of the American Society of Pension Professionals and Actuaries (ASPPA), where he serves on the Government Affairs Committee. He has been a contributing author to various publications, including the *Journal of Pension Benefits,* and is a frequent speaker on pension issues to groups of other pension professionals locally and in national conferences.

Mr. McGhie is the owner of Sierra Pension Services, Inc. in Reno, Nevada. Sierra Pension Services, Inc. is an actuarial consulting and pension administration company specializing in creative plan design work for business owners and provides actuarial consulting to other pension administration firms. He and his wife, Carie, are the proud parents of three boys, Davone, Keegan, and Brenden. Neff's varied experiences range from having been an Eagle Scout in the Boy Scouts of America, to nearly qualifying for the Olympic Trials in the steeplechase in track and field, to serving as a Spanish-speaking missionary for the Church of Jesus Christ of Latter-day Saints in Idaho. Mr. McGhie has volunteered as a soccer coach for his sons' teams and helps his wife in her quilt shop. His hobbies include sewing machine repair (he is an authorized Bernina sewing machine technician), computer programming (he knows HTML, Perl, JavaScript, php, and VisualBasic), and Web site design (he has two sites currently up and running: www.goingbatty.com and www.mcghiefamily.com).

# Acknowledgments

In the past editions, I have acknowledged the help and direction given to me by a friend, Mr. Michael R. Deans, MSPA, of Fresno, California. He gave me my start in this business when I was a clueless college student. As a math major about to graduate, I didn't know what I wanted to do when I finished school. A friend on my cross-country team, Laura, who was also a math major, mentioned becoming an actuary. I took the first SOA exam, but didn't really know where to go from there. My wife encouraged me to find out if there were any local actuaries and ask to do an internship. I called one place, where someone suggested I call Mike.

As I look back on it, I still don't know why Mike said yes. My first day he sat me down with a copy of Aspen Publishers' *The Pension Answer Book* and told me to start reading. I didn't know anything about retirement plans, and he was going to pay me to learn. So I read for a couple of hours, asked a couple of questions, and he sent me on my way for the day. I ended up working with him for a few great months before he lined up a job for me with a firm in Reno, Nevada. He had a friend in Reno, Roy E. Arthurs, CPA, CLU, who was looking for an actuary. That's where it all began. I look back and place the blame for all of this on Mike, and after you read this book, you can blame him for it as well.

And I blame it on that old copy of *The Pension Answer Book*, too. Although *The Pension Answer Book* was a great start for learning about retirement plans, I've felt that something more was needed to teach people about defined benefit plans.

As always, I would like to recognize the efforts of the original authors of *Defined Benefit Answer Book*, Michael E. Callahan, Paul W. Denu, and Kathryn H. Smith, without whom these subsequent editions would not be possible.

If you have any suggestions about this book, I encourage you to contact me at *sierrapension@mindspring.com*. I'm always looking for ways to improve this material and help more people to understand and, ultimately, revitalize defined benefit plans. I hope that when you read this book you will be able to gain a better understanding of defined benefit plans, and be able to increase your business and help your clients achieve their goals. I dedicate this edition to my wife and boys, who sacrifice and help me find the time to update this book each year.

G. Neff McGhie, III
February 2007

# Contents

# Contents

# Contents

# Contents

# Contents

CHAPTER 19

## Minimum Funding Standards . . . . . . . . . . . . . . . . . . . . . .    19-1

# Contents

# Contents

# Contents

# List of Questions

## Chapter 1 Defined Benefit Plans: An Overview

### Basics

### Benefits

## Funding of a Defined Benefit Plan

## PBGC

## Plan Termination

# Chapter 2 Characteristics of a Defined Benefit Plan

## General Characteristics and Qualifications of Qualified Plans

### Funding

### Fiduciary Responsibilities

## Chapter 3 Plan Design

### The Basics

## Employer Objectives

## Demographics

## Plan Sponsor Structure

## Types of Defined Benefit Formulas

## Additional Limitations and Testing

## Additional Factors

# Chapter 4 Hybrid Plans

## The Basics

## Target Benefit Plans

## Eligible Combined Plans

# Chapter 5 Special Employers and Plans

## Small Businesses; Top-Heavy Plans

## Tax-Exempt Employers; Church Plans

## Governmental Plans

# Chapter 6 Eligibility—Coverage and Participation

## Eligibility

## Coverage Requirements

# Chapter 7 Measuring Service

# Chapter 8 Vesting

## Vesting

## Vesting Schedules

## Year of Service

## Protected Benefits

# Chapter 9 Plan Benefits/Accrued Benefits

## Benefit Formulas

## Accrued Benefits

## Benefit Service

## Forms of Benefit Payment

## Minimum Top-Heavy Benefits

## Compensation Used for Benefits

# Chapter 10 Safe Harbor Benefit Formulas

## Definitions

## Discrimination Tests

### Safe Harbor Methods

### Permitted Disparity

## Covered Compensation

## Adjustments and Actuarial Equivalency

## Limitations

# Chapter 11 Advanced Plan Design

## Limitations on Lump-Sum Payments

## Chapter 13 Cash Balance Plans

## Conversion from Traditional Defined Benefit Plans

## Chapter 14 412(e)(3) Defined Benefit Plans (formerly 412(i) Defined Benefit Plans)

## Medical Expense Accounts

## Deferred Retirement Option Program

# Chapter 16 Distribution of Benefits

## Administrative Requirements

## QJSA Rules

## Chapter 17 Qualified Domestic Relations Orders

## Chapter 18 Funding Methods

## Frozen Initial Liability Funding Method

## Attained Age Normal Funding Method

## Individual Level Premium (ILP) Funding Method

## Comparison of Funding Methods

## Funding Method Requirements

## Funding of Life Insurance

## Changing a Funding Method

## Consulting Issues

# Chapter 19 Minimum Funding Standards

## Funding Standard Account Prior to PPA

## Minimum Funding Standard After PPA

## Multiemployer Pension Plans

# Chapter 20 Deductibility of Employer Contributions

## Deduction Limits

## Timing of Contributions and Deductions

## Factors Affecting Deduction Limits

## Deductions for Owner-Employee Sponsored Plans

# Chapter 22 Census Data and Demographics

## Chapter 23 The Role of the Enrolled Actuary

### Definition of Actuary

### Selecting Actuarial Assumptions

### Actuarial Standards and Code of Conduct

# Chapter 24 Pension Benefit Guaranty Corporation

# Chapter 25 Plan Termination

## Termination Procedures

## Reporting to the IRS

## Standard Terminations

## PBGC Benefits and Coverage

## Surplus Assets

## Underfunded Plans

## Chapter 26 Mergers and Acquisitions

## Plan Transactions

### Plan Merger and Consolidation

### Plan Division

### Asset Allocation

## Chapter 27 Fiduciary Responsibility

# Chapter 28 Employee Communication

## Benefits and Rights Under the Plan

## Summary Plan Descriptions and Summary of Material Modifications

## Funding

## Distribution

## Plan Amendment and Termination

## Miscellaneous

# Chapter 29 Government Reporting and Disclosure

## Summary of Forms

## Due Dates

# Chapter 30 Schedule B Issues

## What Must Be Filed

## Attachments

## Line-by-Line Instructions

## Other Schedule B Issues

# Chapter 31 Financial Accounting Standards

## SFAS No. 87

# Chapter 1

# Defined Benefit Plans: An Overview

This chapter explains the basics of defined benefit plans for those who are just entering this field. This is not a complete education on defined benefit plans; that is the purpose of the rest of the book. The purpose of this chapter is to help a newcomer to the defined benefit world learn more about these plans, and be able to apply this basic knowledge to help you and your clients. The hope is that this chapter will give you a basic understanding of these types of plans and that you will want to use the rest of the book to expand your knowledge and in turn use this knowledge to increase interest in these plans and expand the number of defined benefit plans that are implemented by businesses.

## Basics

### Q 1:1   Why should you learn more about defined benefit plans?

For many years, Congress has enacted burdensome legislation for defined benefit plans, causing many employers to terminate their existing plans and driving down the number of new plans that were started. However, with the passage of the Economic Growth and Tax Relief Reconciliation Act of 2001 (EGTRRA), new life was breathed back into these plans. It has once again become advantageous to the business owner to sponsor this type of plan.

Most pension professionals agree that such plans, usually structured to replace a percentage of preretirement pay, are the only plans that provide real retirement income for employees. As more and more baby boomers move closer to retirement, the demand for defined benefit plans increases.

Defined benefit plans can be designed to solve many of today's business problems. They play an important role in attracting and retaining key employees and moving older employees into retirement smoothly. For closely held businesses, defined benefit plans provide a tremendous opportunity for favorable tax treatment for personal savings and investment and may be the only means of accumulating significant income for retirement for many business owners. Among public employers, defined benefit plans remain the predominant primary plan; almost 90 percent of full-time employees of state and local governments participate in a defined benefit plan.

Unique planning opportunities make defined benefit pension plans attractive to both large and small closely held companies. Defined benefit pension plans, which provide monthly benefits at retirement, based on a benefit formula in the plan rather than on accumulations in an account, offer employers a vehicle for serving a number of human resources needs. Owners of small companies often find defined benefit pension plans to be the best vehicle to accumulate funds for retirement.

### Q 1:2   What is the difference between a defined benefit plan and a defined contribution plan?

A defined contribution pension plan is an individual account plan. [I.R.C. § 414(i)] Annual contributions to a participant's account are based on the formula contained in the plan. Retirement benefits are based on the value of the accumulation in the account. Investment performance directly affects the value of retirement benefits. The employer's commitment is to make annual contributions, not to provide benefits. There is no guarantee as to what the value of the account will be when the participant reaches retirement. This type of plan generally favors younger employees.

There are several types of defined contribution plans. They include:

- Profit sharing
- 401(k) Cash or deferred arrangements (CODAs)
- Money Purchase Pension Plans
- Stock Bonus Plans
- Employee Stock Ownership Plans (ESOPs)
- Target Benefit Plans
- 403(b) Tax Sheltered Annuities

In addition, the way contributions are allocated can vary. Some possible allocation formulas include:

- Pro rata based on compensation

- Integrated with Social Security
- Points based on compensation, age, service, etc.
- Age-weighted
- Based on job description
- Other "new comparability" type formula requiring general discrimination testing

**Example 1.** DC Co. adopts a defined contribution pension plan that requires an annual contribution, on behalf of each eligible employee, of 10 percent of compensation. Debbie, an employee of DC Co., receives annual compensation of $50,000. DC Co. will contribute $5,000 (10 percent of $50,000) to Debbie's account in the plan. When Debbie retires, the amount in her account, increased by investment income and gains, and decreased by investment losses, will be available to provide retirement benefits.

A defined benefit pension plan is not an individual account plan, but instead a plan that promises to pay a benefit at retirement. [I.R.C. § 414(j)] Retirement benefits must be definitely determinable. The benefit payable to an employee is based on a formula set forth in the plan that often takes into consideration service and compensation. The annual contribution is determined by an actuary and can vary from year to year depending on how much is needed to fund the benefit. Benefits are generally insured by the Pension Benefit Guaranty Corporation (PBGC) in the event of plan termination with an underfunded plan. The commitment of the employer is to satisfy funding requirements to provide retirement benefits. If the plan is fully funded, no contributions may be required. The employee does not bear investment risk. There are no individual accounts; all assets must be pooled. This type of plan generally favors older employees.

**Example 2.** DB Co. adopts a defined benefit pension plan that provides an annual benefit to eligible employees of 50 percent of compensation. Debbie, an employee of DB Co., receives annual compensation of $50,000. DB Co. will contribute to the plan the amount necessary to fund the anticipated benefit as determined by the plan's actuary. When Debbie retires, she will receive a benefit equal to $25,000 per year for life (50 percent of $50,000). Debbie does not have an account under the plan; her benefit is provided regardless of the investment gains or losses of the plan.

The following table identifies the primary differences between defined contribution and defined benefit pension plans:

| | *Defined Contribution Plan* | *Defined Benefit Plan* |
|---|---|---|
| Funding | Based on formula in plan; may be discretionary (profit-sharing plan). | Based on actuarial determination of amounts needed to fund anticipated retirement benefits. |
| Benefits at retirement | Accumulation in account balance (sum of contributions, forfeitures, and investment return) provides benefit. | Based on formula in plan. |

|  | *Defined Contribution Plan* | *Defined Benefit Plan* |
|---|---|---|
| Benefit insurance | No PBGC protection. | Benefits insured by PBGC if plan terminated with insufficient assets. There are exceptions to coverage for professional employers with fewer than 25 participants, and for owner-only plans. |
| Maximum contribution | The lesser of $40,000 (as indexed) or 25 percent of compensation. | The amount necessary to fund an annuity benefit of the lesser of $160,000 (as indexed) per year or 100 percent of compensation. |
| Employer commitment | Annual funding obligation (unless profit-sharing plan); no guarantee of benefit at retirement. | Benefit obligation; funding may not be required if assets are sufficient to meet benefit obligations. |
| Employee contributions | Pre-tax employee contributions permitted in a 401(k) plan; after-tax contributions may be permitted in the plan. These contributions increase the amount in the employee's account. | Pre-tax employee contributions not permitted; after-tax contributions may be required for annual accrual of benefits. Rarely do employee contributions create an account in the plan. |
| Preretirement benefits | The value of the participant's account. | The actuarial equivalent of the accrued benefit based on the plan's formula; some plans provide early retirement subsidies. |
| Payment options | Determined by plan. Qualified joint and survivor annuities (QJSA) and qualified preretirement survivor annuities (QPSA) required except in certain profit-sharing plans. Lump-sum distributions often permitted. | Determined by plan. QJSA and QPSA required. Lump-sum distributions occasionally permitted. |

## Q 1:3   What are some of the advantages and disadvantages of defined benefit plans?

Many larger companies adopt defined benefit pension plans to attract and retain employees or provide long-term benefits to career employees. Alternatively, defined benefit plans can be structured to encourage people to retire early, providing the company with an attractive alternative to mandatory layoff. Smaller companies adopt defined benefit plans to fund retirement needs later in the business/life cycle of the owner. Defined benefit plans often offer the largest deductions for funding retirement, far exceeding the $40,000 (as indexed) limitation applicable to each individual in a defined contribution plan.

However, a defined benefit pension plan must be funded each year regardless of business profits. If a company has swings in its profitability or cash availability, a defined benefit plan's funding requirement can become burdensome, and changing the contribution can be difficult and generally requires advance planning. In some instances, where credit is given for past service, a range of contributions is allowed. Changes in interest rates, investment experience, and employer demographics can alter the funding pattern of a plan dramatically. Anticipated contribution fluctuations should be part of the planning process.

Communication of the value of the benefits earned in a defined benefit plan can be more of a challenge. A 25-year-old participant may not find much value in a $500 per month annuity that begins at age 65. For this reason, a type of defined benefit plan called a cash balance plan has become very popular, because it helps employees see the value by converting the annuity directly into a cash account.

### Q 1:4 What are some important terms to know when dealing with a defined benefit plan?

Some of the more important terms to know include:

- *Normal retirement benefit*. This is the amount the participant will begin receiving at the plan's normal retirement age, based on the plan's benefit formula, if the participant remains employed until then. This is usually expressed as a monthly annuity, payable beginning at normal retirement age until the participant dies.

- *Accrued benefit*. This is the amount of the Normal Retirement Benefit that the participant has currently earned based on past service and compensation. It is also usually expressed as a monthly life annuity.

- *Normal form of benefit*. The normal form of benefit is the default form in which the benefit is payable under the terms of the plan. In most plans, it is a Qualified Joint and Survivor Annuity (QJSA) benefit for married participants and a life annuity for unmarried participants. A QJSA pays a fixed amount for as long as the participant lives after retirement, and upon the death of the participant it will continue to pay a fixed percentage to the beneficiary of the amount that was paid while the participant was alive.

- *Optional form of benefit*. These are other forms of payment that may be offered to participants in addition to the normal form. They are usually of equal value to the normal form (they are "actuarially equivalent").

- *Actuarial equivalent*. This is an amount determined based on actuarial assumptions stated in the plan document (usually involving interest and mortality expectations) that is equivalent in value to a benefit payable in the normal form.

### Q 1:5 For what type of client could a defined benefit plan be appropriate?

There are many characteristics to look for to find those clients who could benefit from a defined benefit plan. These characteristics include age, wealth, and whether the client has employees. The older business owner, generally over age 40, will be able to contribute more to a defined benefit plan than to a defined contribution plan. Due to the required funding of a defined benefit plan, the client must be able to sustain the income necessary to fund it. Also, if the client has other employees, he or she must be aware of the benefits they will be earning in the plan and, if there are older employees, the disproportionate amount they will earn as compared to younger employees.

Therefore, some of the characteristics of a potential client could include the following, assuming the "key employee" is the person or persons that the plan is trying to benefit the most:

- The key employee is older than the staff.
- There is a desire to make larger tax-deductible contributions to the plan on behalf of the key employee than could be made to a defined contribution plan or other type of arrangement.
- The key employee has longer service than the staff.
- The business is stable and can sustain larger contributions for the duration of the plan.
- The key employee desires to attract and retain other qualified employees.

**Example.** The SPS Corporation sponsors a defined benefit plan, effective January 1, 2003, with a maximum benefit formula. The following are the costs that may be developed:

| Name | Age | Compensation | Projected Monthly Benefit | Lump Sum at Retirement | Present Value of Future Lump Sum | Annual Contribution |
|------|-----|--------------|----------------------------|-------------------------|-----------------------------------|----------------------|
| Owner | 55 | $84,000 | $7,000 | $778,540 | $434,733 | $55,723 |
| Employee 1 | 50 | $36,000 | $3,000 | $333,660 | $139,225 | $13,524 |
| Employee 2 | 30 | $36,000 | $3,000 | $333,660 | $43,411 | $2,825 |

The plan uses a 6 percent interest rate for funding and the 1971 Group Annuity Mortality (GAM) Male table, the plan's normal retirement age is 65, and the actuary uses the Individual Aggregate funding method.

Beginning in 2008, there is a new minimum funding methodology that must be employed which is based on the present value of the accrued benefits. The following are the costs that would be developed under the new rules, assuming the first year of the plan is January 1, 2008, rather than January 1, 2003:

| Name | Age | Compensation | Projected Monthly Benefit | Accrued Benefit | Present Value of Lump Sum |
|------|-----|--------------|----------------------------|------------------|----------------------------|
| Owner | 55 | $84,000 | $7,000 | $700 | $50,966 |
| Employee 1 | 50 | $36,000 | $3,000 | $200 | $10,881 |
| Employee 2 | 30 | $36,000 | $3,000 | $85.71 | $1,454 |

**Q 1:6    What is an enrolled actuary, and what is his or her role in the administration of a defined benefit plan?**

An enrolled actuary is an actuary in the field of pension plans licensed by the Joint Board for the Enrollment of Actuaries to practice before the government agencies responsible for administering the Employee Retirement Income Security Act (ERISA). In order to be licensed, an actuary must have satisfied experience and examination requirements as specified by the Joint Board. Currently, the Joint Board requires three years of experience and successful completion of three exams. [ERISA § 3042; I.R.C. § 7701(a)(35)]

The actuary's primary function is to determine the amount needed by an employer's defined benefit plan to pay future retirement benefits to participants. Assumptions and methods chosen by the actuary represent both his or her professional judgment and legislative constraints, and they affect the amount required to fund the plan. The actuary must also certify the tax-deductible amount that may be contributed to the plan. The assumptions to be selected include economic assumptions (such as interest rates and compensation scales) and demographic assumptions (such as mortality, disability, turnover, and marriage rates).

The actuary will also need to complete and certify Schedule B, part of the Form 5500 filing required for defined benefit plans. This schedule details the funding requirements for the plan.

Because actuaries will be certifying as to the costs of the benefits, they should also be consulted when designing the plan to meet the plan sponsor's goals.

## Benefits

**Q 1:7    What is the assumed form of payment from a defined benefit plan?**

In general, a defined benefit plan will offer an annuity payable monthly for the life of the participant as the default form of payment. However, a plan can offer any form of annuity or actuarially equivalent lump-sum payment to a plan participant as long as the form of payment does not extend beyond the participant's (or participant and spouse's) life expectancy. The plan is required to provide at least a life annuity to unmarried participants and a QJSA to a married participant. In general, most pension plans will provide a form of payment that is actuarially equivalent to a life annuity. The following are some common forms of benefit. Note that if the plan participant is married at the time payments commence, the spouse must consent to any form of payment other than a QJSA.

- *Life annuity.* An annuity payable for the life of the participant.
- *A period certain and life annuity.* An annuity payable for the life of a participant with payments guaranteed for a period of years (i.e., the first 5 years, 10 years, or 15 years as elected).
- *Joint and survivor annuity.* An annuity payable for the life of a participant with a potentially reduced payment continuing to the designated

beneficiary of the plan participant. The reduced payment is a percentage of the payment that was made to the plan participant based on the percentage elected (i.e., 50 percent, 69 percent, 75 percent, or 100 percent).

- *Lump-sum cash payment.* A one-time payment of the full actuarial value of the plan's monthly benefit payable as an annuity.

Plan benefits are payable in the form of benefit specified by the plan, called the normal form of benefit. The normal form of benefit is the form of payment offered to a plan participant upon becoming eligible for retirement benefits (a life annuity, 50 percent joint and survivor annuity, etc.). Generally, if a plan participant wishes to receive benefits in an alternate form of payment (e.g., a lump sum), the normal form of payment is converted to one that is either actuarially equivalent in value to the plan's normal form or adjusted using a tabular conversion factor. An actuarial equivalent benefit is one that has an equal "value" to the plan's normal form of payment at the time of the first payment.

### Q 1:8    How are benefits determined in a defined benefit plan?

There are a number of ways benefits can be calculated in defined benefit plans. Typical plan formulas include the following:

1. *Fixed benefit.* The retirement benefit for each participant is determined as a fixed percentage of compensation.
2. *Flat benefit.* The retirement benefit for each participant is determined as a flat dollar amount.
3. *Unit benefit.* The retirement benefit for each participant is determined as a fixed percentage of pay or flat dollar amount for each year of service.

### Q 1:9    What is a *flat,* or *fixed, benefit formula*?

A *flat,* or *fixed, benefit formula* defines the plan benefit at retirement as either a flat dollar amount or a fixed percentage of salary payable in monthly installments. The duration of the payment is defined by the plan's normal form of payment. In general, most plans will define the normal form of benefit as a life annuity. Usually, there is a reduction factor applied to the benefit that reduces the benefit for employees with fewer years of service at retirement. This prevents disproportionately larger benefits for older, short-service employees.

**Example 1.** The benefit formula is $1,000 per month reduced by $\frac{1}{25}$ for each year of participation to retirement less than 25. Rick is a participant with a total of 15 benefit years of service to retirement and will have his benefit reduced by $\frac{10}{25}$, for a total benefit of $600 ($1000 − ($1000 × $\frac{10}{25}$)), whereas Joan, a participant who will have 35 years of service at retirement, will receive the full benefit of $1,000.

**Example 2.** The benefit formula is 125 percent of the final 3-year average compensation reduced for participation less than 25 years to retirement. Kevin is a participant with five years of total benefit service to retirement and has average compensation of $170,000. He will have his benefit reduced by $^{20}/_{25}$, for a total of 25 percent of average compensation at retirement (125% − (125% × $^{20}/_{25}$)). Therefore, his projected benefit will be $42,500 per year ($170,000 × 25%).

### Q 1:10  What is a *unit credit formula*?

Plan benefits are typically expressed as a flat dollar amount or a percentage of average annual compensation per year of service. These unit benefit formulas are easy to understand, provide reduced benefits for short-service employees, reward long-service employees, and are flexible enough to be enhanced easily.

A *unit credit benefit formula* defines the benefit as either a flat dollar amount or percentage of average compensation multiplied by the number of years of service to retirement. The dollar amount or percentage is the unit of benefit, and these units are accumulated over the employee's working lifetime. Generally, the benefit is payable in monthly installments, and its duration of payment is defined by the plan's normal form of payment.

A typical unit benefit formula expressed as a flat dollar amount would be $15 per year of service for a maximum of 40 years. Under this formula, an employee with 10 years of service at retirement would receive $150 ($15×10) as an annuity payable under the plan's normal form of payment, which may be a life annuity; an employee with 40 years of service would receive $600 ($15×40) as an annuity. This type of formula is commonly used for employees whose compensation is paid on an hourly basis. Generally, the benefit is changed over the life of the plan to take into account the impact of inflation on the ultimate retirement benefit. It is not uncommon to see plans that have changed the flat dollar amount every two to three years.

A typical unit benefit formula expressed as a percentage of average annual compensation would be 1.25 percent of average annual compensation per year of service. Under this formula an employee with 10 years of service at retirement would receive 12.5 percent (1.25%×10) of average annual compensation as an annuity payable under the plan's normal form of payment. An employee with 40 years of service would receive 50 percent (1.25%×40) of average annual compensation as an annuity. This type of formula is commonly used for employees who are paid an annual salary and the level of the salaries follow a predictable pattern with regard to service, employment classification (i.e., sales, management, clerical, etc.), and hours worked. Notice that because benefits are a constant percentage of salary at retirement, the plan is shielded against the effects of inflation, so there is no need to increase benefits for this reason, unless the employer believes that the ultimate benefits are too low based on income objectives for the plan.

**Example.** The benefit formula is 2 percent of the final average compensation per year of service at retirement. Joan is a participant with 37 years of service at retirement and average compensation of $25,000. She would be entitled to a benefit of 74 percent (2%×37 years) of her final average compensation. Therefore, her projected benefit will be $18,500 per year ($25,000×74%).

### Q 1:11   What is an *integrated benefit formula*?

An *integrated benefit formula* takes into account the pension benefits the employer is providing to a plan participant through its contributions to Social Security. The effect of an integrated benefit formula is to provide additional benefits to those employees who derive little or no Social Security benefits from their wages in excess of certain amounts.

If a defined benefit plan ultimately will pay most benefits in the form of a lump sum, integration loses most of its leverage due to nondiscrimination regulations, which prescribe certain actuarial assumptions that must be used when calculating the lump sum. Because of this, integration has lost much of its value in the small defined benefit plan market.

### Q 1:12   How is compensation used in the benefit formula?

In a defined contribution plan, the calculation of each year's contribution is independent of every other year's calculation. This is not the case with a defined benefit plan. The benefit at retirement is generally related to what the participant's average earnings were while employed. Many employers want the benefit from the plan to provide in retirement a certain percentage of what the employee's income was while he or she was working, such as 60 percent of average compensation. Therefore, the compensation used in determining plan benefits is defined in the document as an average.

The most common way of defining the compensation average is as a final average compensation. This could be stated as "Average of the final five (or three) years of employment" or "Average of the highest three consecutive years while a participant."

Since benefits in a defined benefit plan are usually stated as monthly benefits, the compensation average is also usually computed as an average monthly compensation.

The use of an average compensation can also cause confusion with clients in understanding the plan, especially if they don't understand that contributions are not necessarily tied to benefits paid out. In the author's experience, there will always be a client that will ask why a certain participants' "contribution" stayed consistent even though he or she terminated and only earned one-half of his or her usual amount. For this reason and many others, a thorough explanation to the client that contributions in a defined benefit plan are not "allocated" to individuals but go to fund all participants' benefits can help resolve some of the confusion.

### Q 1:13   What is an *accrued benefit*?

The *accrued benefit* is the portion of the total retirement benefit earned by the plan participant as of any given date. That amount is the benefit the participant would be entitled to receive (prior to the application of a vesting schedule) if he or she were to terminate employment or retire. There are two methods a plan uses to determine the accrued benefit, either the fractional accrual method or unit credit accrual method. The fractional accrual method multiplies the total benefit at retirement by a fraction, the numerator of which is the years of benefit service at the date the determination is made and the denominator of which is the total years of benefit service at retirement. The unit credit accrual method multiplies the unit credit benefit formula by the number of years of benefit service the participant has as of the date the benefit determination is made. The accrued benefit will vary from year to year based on the participant's years of service, age, and compensation and is generally expressed as a monthly annuity payable in the plan's normal form of payment.

**Example.** The benefit formula is 2 percent of average monthly compensation times years of participation. Joan will have 35 years of participation when she reaches the plan's normal retirement age. Her average compensation is $25,000. Her accrued benefit using fractional accrual is calculated using $25,000 multiplied by 2 percent multiplied by total years of participation (35) multiplied by the accrual fraction of $\frac{1}{35}$, which results in an accrued benefit of $41.67 (.02 × 35 × $2,083.33 × $\frac{1}{35}$). According to the unit credit accrual method, Joan's accrued benefit would also be $41.67 (.02 × $2,083.33 × 1). With 35 years of participation as of her normal retirement date, her projected accrued benefit would be $1,458.33 ($2,083.33 × 2% × 35).

A plan's benefit formula must accrue a minimum level of benefits throughout the working lifetime of a plan participant. This is accomplished by meeting one of three tests, which when applied to the accrued benefit method of a plan's benefit formula ensures that at least a certain level of benefits accrues each year. These tests are known as the 3 percent rule, the 133⅓ percent rule, and the fractional accrual rule. These rules prevent a plan from providing larger benefits for service in the later years of an employee's working lifetime, also known as backloading.

## Q 1:14　How is the value of a participant's benefit calculated?

In order to determine the value of a participant's benefit, it is necessary to make assumptions concerning how long he or she will live and what interest the plan will receive on its investments in the future. Based on these assumptions, a lump-sum value is placed on the future stream of payments and then discounted to today with interest.

The value today of some amount to be paid now or in the future is known as its present value. The present value of an amount is usually calculated by multiplying its future value by a discount factor. The discount factor takes into consideration the time value of money at some assumed interest rate and may have other decrements such as turnover, death, disability, and early retirement factored into it. We will consider only a discount for the time value of money for the sake of simplicity.

**Example 1.** If a U.S. savings bond with a face value of $100 payable in 15 years is purchased for $48.10, the price paid is the present value of the bond.

The discount factor used to determine the present value is .4810 ($100 × .4810 = $48.10). Present value takes into consideration the time value of money; that is, $48.10 invested at a rate of 5 percent interest will grow to $100 in 15 years. It has the same value as $100 payable 15 years into the future.

**Example 2.** In a defined benefit plan the same concept applies, but the future value is generally a benefit payable for a lifetime. To determine the present value of $100 payable per month for life starting at age 65, an approach similar to that for determining the present value of a U.S. savings bond is used. If an enrolled actuary determines that $120 is needed at retirement for each dollar of monthly benefit, the future value of the $100 monthly benefit will be $12,000. If a plan's assets grow at a rate of 5 percent per year, the present value of the $100 monthly benefit payable in 15 years is $5,772, determined as follows:

$$\text{Future value at retirement} = \$100 \times \$120 = \$12,000$$
$$\text{Present value} = \$12,000 \times .4810 = \$5,772$$

The value of .4810 is the discount factor of the present value of $1.00 payable 15 years hence at 5 percent. If the present value of the $100 per month benefit were contributed to a trust fund that earned 5 percent per year, there would be $12,000 in the trust at the end of the 15th year. The accounting for the growth of the trust fund would be as follows:

| Year | Trust Fund at Beginning of Year | Interest of 5% | Trust Fund at End of Year |
|------|-------------------------------|----------------|---------------------------|
| 1 | $ 5,772 | $ 289 | $ 6,061 |
| 2 | $ 6,061 | $ 303 | $ 6,364 |
| 3 | $ 6,364 | $ 318 | $ 6,682 |
| 4 | $ 6,682 | $ 334 | $ 7,016 |
| 5 | $ 7,016 | $ 351 | $ 7,367 |
| 6 | $ 7,367 | $ 368 | $ 7,735 |
| 7 | $ 7,735 | $ 387 | $ 8,122 |
| 8 | $ 8,122 | $ 406 | $ 8,528 |
| 9 | $ 8,528 | $ 426 | $ 8,954 |
| 10 | $ 8,954 | $ 448 | $ 9,402 |
| 11 | $ 9,402 | $ 470 | $ 9,872 |
| 12 | $ 9,872 | $ 494 | $ 10,366 |
| 13 | $ 10,366 | $ 518 | $ 10,884 |
| 14 | $ 10,884 | $ 544 | $ 11,428 |
| 15 | $ 11,428 | $ 572 | $ 12,000 |

The amount in the beginning of each year (column 2) is increased with interest of 5 percent each year. Eventually, the assets will accumulate to the desired amount of $12,000.

### Q 1:15   What is an *annuity purchase rate*?

The factor used to determine the amount of money needed at retirement (also called the lump sum) to pay the monthly benefit is known as the *annuity purchase rate* (APR). An APR is developed from a set of actuarial assumptions, most typically a mortality table and an interest rate. Mortality tables are developed by performing historical studies of the rates of death at each age from birth. The rate of death from each successive age is measured and converted to actual numbers of lives. These hypothetical populations are then used to develop the APR for any age for which payments can be expected to be made. In general, mortality tables are identified by the year of the study and whether or not the tables contain males, females, or some combination of both. For example the 71 GAM Male table is a death study of men developed in the year 1971. Other factors such as expenses and ancillary benefits may be taken into account, but in the interest of simplicity, all the APRs used in this book are derived from interest and mortality only. APRs can vary in size based on the choice of the mortality table and interest rate as shown below. The following APRs are for single-life annuities starting at age 65:

|              | APR at 8% | APR at 6% | APR at 5% |
|--------------|-----------|-----------|-----------|
| 71 GAM Male  | 97.71     | 111.22    | 119.33    |
| 83 GAM Male  | 103.76    | 119.00    | 128.22    |

Life expectancy as compiled by the mortality table will dictate the size of the APR. The 83 GAM Male table has a longer life expectancy than the 71 GAM Male table and, as a result, a much higher APR to account for a longer payment duration. As the interest rate decreases, the APR increases. This happens in order to take into account the lower investment earnings available to help pay the cost of the benefit. Therefore, if a low interest rate and long life expectancy are assumed in retirement, then the APR will be larger, which will lead to a larger lump sum being required at retirement, increasing the amount that needs to be funded while employed. Beginning in 2008, a plan will be required to use multiple interest rates, called segment rates, to determine the present value of benefit liabilities. The *segment rate* is equal to the sum of the first, second, and third segment rates. The first segment rate is the single interest rate determined by the Treasury Department on the basis of the corporate bond yield curve with maturity during the next five years. The second segment rate is the single interest rate determined by the Treasury Department on the basis of the corporate bond yield curve with maturity between the fifth and twentieth years. The third segment rate is the single interest rate determined by the Treasury Department on the basis of the corporate bond yield curve with maturity beyond the twentieth year. [I.R.C. § 430(h)(2)(C)] The corporate bond yield curve reflects a 24-month average of the monthly yields of investment grade corporate bonds with varying maturities that are in the top three quality levels available. [I.R.C. § 430(h)(2)(D)]

### Q 1:16   How is a benefit converted to an alternate form?

Benefits are converted to actuarial equivalent forms of payment or retirement dates using the plan's interest rate and mortality table (known as actuarial equivalence assumptions). In order for a defined benefit pension plan to be qualified under Code Section 401(a), the plan must specify the actuarial assumptions that form the basis of determining a plan participant's benefits. [I.R.C. § 401(a)(25)] This requirement should not be confused with the actuarial assumptions used to determine a plan's funding requirement. Those assumptions are determined by the plan's enrolled actuary and are subject to his or her professional judgment. The actuarial equivalence assumptions specified in the plan are those assumptions used to convert one form of benefit to another. The employer may change the actuarial assumptions for determining plan benefits; however, any optional forms of benefits calculated under the new actuarial assumptions may not be less than the optional forms of benefits as calculated under the prior actuarial assumptions. [Treas. Reg. § 1.411(d)-4(a)(3)]

To make the calculation methodology clear, the plan should specify if mortality is used preretirement and postretirement or just postretirement. If one interest rate as used, then that rate is used for all retirement ages. Some plans may use a different interest rate for preretirement than they do for postretirement.

In determining actuarial equivalencies for male and female participants, a plan must use the same mortality table. The Supreme Court, in *Arizona v. Norris* [463 U.S. 1073, 1084–86 (1983)], held that the application of sex-distinct actuarial tables to employees based on their gender in calculating the amount of retirement benefits violates Title VII of the Civil Rights Act of 1964.

There are two types of actuarial equivalent benefit calculations: conversion of a benefit to an alternate form of payment and conversion of a benefit to be payable at an alternate retirement age.

*Alternate form of payment.* To determine the actuarial equivalent of the normal form of benefit payable in an alternate form, the accrued benefit is multiplied by the ratio of the APR for the normal form of benefit to the APR for the alternate form of benefit. The APRs are determined as of the age the benefit is to be paid.

> **Example.** Kevin has a $3,000 per month benefit in the plan's normal form of a straight life annuity. The APR for a straight life annuity at his retirement age under the plan's assumptions is 154.758. He would like to have a joint and 50% survivor annuity instead. The APR for this optional form using the plan's actuarial equivalence assumptions is 167.237. The benefit payable in the optional form is $2,776.14 ($3,000×154.758/167.237).

*Alternate retirement age.* To determine the actuarial equivalent of the normal form of benefit payable at an alternate retirement age, the accrued benefit is multiplied by the APR at the normal retirement age and is then decreased or increased as the case may be for interest and mortality to the age the payments are to actually commence and then divided by the APR at the age benefits commence.

> **Example.** Kevin has decided to retire early at age 58. His benefit payable at age 60 is $3,000. The APR of a straight life annuity using the plan's actuarial equivalence factors at age 58 is 161.021. First, the benefit must be discounted using interest from age 60 to age 58. If the plan's preretirement interest assumption is 8.5 percent, then this discount is .8495 ($1.085^{-2}$).

Hence, the actuarial equivalent benefit payable at age 58 is $2,449.37 (($3,000 × 154.758 × 0.8495)/161.021).

If a defined benefit plan offers a payment that is not actuarially equivalent to the accrued benefit and is of greater value than an actuarially equivalent one, that payment is considered to be subsidized by the employer. The difference between the actuarial present values of the alternate and the normal form payment is the amount of the subsidy. Since there is an increase in the value of the benefit owing to its form or timing, an additional cost is created that must be paid for by the employer. Since the cost of the benefit is contingent upon an election by the plan participant, the cost of the benefit is generally included in the plan's actuarial cost method with a discount for the probability that such a benefit will be paid.

A subsidized alternate form of payment is useful as a benefit enhancement feature and can entice employees to leave employment at an earlier date than normal retirement or can enhance benefits without increasing the benefit payable under the normal form. The advantage of a subsidized benefit feature is that not all plan participants will exercise their rights to these benefits; therefore, such a benefit feature can be more cost effective than across-the-board benefit increases.

### Q 1:17   Do defined benefit plans require discrimination testing?

Yes, unless certain benefit formulas are used. Just like in defined contribution plans, defined benefit plans have safe harbor formulas that when used will not require general testing to show nondiscrimination under Code Section 401(a)(4).

The safe harbor methods for meeting the requirements of discrimination testing are found in Treasury Regulations Section 1.401(a)(4)-3(b). A safe harbor method is a formula used for determining plan benefits that, by design, is not discriminatory in benefits. There are three design-based safe harbor methods. There is also a non-design-based safe harbor method and a safe harbor method for insurance contract plans.

### Q 1:18   What is the first safe harbor formula?

The first safe harbor is for unit credit plans. A plan satisfies the requirements of this safe harbor if the plan satisfies the 133⅓ percent accrual rule. In addition, each employee's accrued benefit under the plan as of any plan year must be determined by applying the plan's benefit formula to the employee's years of service and (if applicable) average annual compensation, both determined as of that plan year.

**Example.** The benefit and accrual formulas are 2 percent of average compensation for each of the first 10 years, plus 1.5 percent of average compensation for each of the next 10 years, plus 2 percent for each additional year of service more than 20. This plan passes the first safe harbor test because the benefits are computed in a nondiscriminatory method, since the benefits in the 21st year (2 percent) do not increase more than 133⅓ percent of the benefits in the 20th year (1.5 percent), since 2 percent is exactly 133⅓ percent more than 1.5 percent (2%/1.5%).

### Q 1:19   What is the second safe harbor formula?

The second safe harbor is for plans using a fractional accrual method to determine accrued benefits. [Treas. Reg. § 1.401(a)(4)-3(b)(4)(i)(C)(1)] A plan will satisfy the rules of this safe harbor if it satisfies each of the following requirements:

The plan meets the requirements of the fractional accrual rules if the accrued benefit computed under this method cannot be less than a fraction of the normal retirement benefit that a participant would be entitled to under the plan if the benefit was calculated as if the participant continued to earn the same rate of compensation upon which his or her normal retirement benefit is computed under the plan. The numerator of the fraction is the participant's total years of participation in the plan, and the denominator is the total years of participation the participant would have to normal retirement age if the participant continued to work to that time. If the plan provides for benefits based on average compensation in excess of 10 years (a career average pay plan), then the fractional accrual rule will not be satisfied. [I.R.C. § 411(b)(1)(C); Treas. Reg. § 1.411(b)-1(b)(3)(ii)(A)]

Under the plan, it must be impossible for any employee to accrue a portion of the normal retirement benefit that is more than one-third larger than the equivalent portion of the same benefit accrued in that or any other plan year by any other employee. When computing this test, actual and potential employees with any amount of service at normal retirement age must be taken into account (other than employees with more than 33 years of service at normal retirement age).

**Example.** The benefit formula is 4 percent of average compensation multiplied by each year of service up to 10 years and 3 percent of average compensation multiplied by years of service in excess of 10 years but not in excess of 30. Benefits are fractionally accrued over all service. This plan satisfies the second safe harbor. An employee with the maximum number of years of credited service, 30, he or she would have a benefit equal to 100 percent of his or her average annual compensation $((4\% \times 10) + (3\% \times 20))$. The greatest benefit that a participant can accrue in any year would be 4 percent for those participants with 10 or fewer years of service. Among employees who have 33 or fewer years of projected service at normal retirement age, the lowest benefit that a participant can accrue is 3.03 percent $(100\% \div 33)$. This plan passes the test since 4 percent is not more than one-third larger than 3.03 percent $(4\% \div 3.03\% = 1.32)$.

### Q 1:20   What is the third safe harbor formula?

Under the third safe harbor, the plan must meet the same fractional accrual rules as in the second safe harbor. In addition, the normal retirement benefit under the plan must be a flat benefit that requires a minimum of 25 years of service at normal retirement age in order to receive an unreduced flat benefit, determined without regard to the maximum benefits under Code Section 415. [Treas. Reg. § 1.401(a)(4)-3(b)(4)(i)(C)(2)]

**Example.** The benefit formula is 125 percent of average annual compensation reduced 1/25th for each year of participation less than 25. Kevin has average compensation of $170,000 and will have five years of participation in the plan. Kevin's projected benefit is $3,541.67/month ($170,000/ 12 × 125% × 5/25) and his accrued benefit after one year of participation is $708.33 per month ($170,000/12 × 125% × 1/25).

Joan earns $25,000 and will have 35 years of participation in the plan. Joan's projected benefit is the lesser of $2,604.17 ($25,000/12 × 125% × 25/25) or $2,083.33 ($25,000/12), or $2,083.33 since her projected benefit cannot exceed 100 percent of her average monthly compensation. However, when calculating her accrued benefit, we still use the projected benefit as calculated by the plan formula to apply the fractional accrual, which is equal to $74.40 ($2,604.17 ÷ 35).

### Q 1:21    What are the top-heavy requirements for defined benefit plans?

A defined benefit plan is top-heavy if, as of the determination date, the present value of the accrued benefits of all key employees exceeds 60 percent of the present value of the accrued benefits of all employees. [I.R.C. § 416(g)(1)(A)(i); Treas. Reg. § 1.416-1, Q&A T-1(c)]

Each non-key employee who is a participant in a top-heavy defined benefit plan and who has at least 1,000 hours of service for an accrual period must accrue a minimum benefit for that accrual computation period (there is no "last day" requirement for defined benefit plans as there is in defined contribution plans). An employee must accrue a top-heavy minimum benefit even if the employee would normally be excluded from plan participation due to compensation earned below a certain level, failure to make mandatory employee contributions, or not being employed on a certain date. [Treas. Reg. § 1.416-1, Q&A M-4] However, no top-heavy minimum need be accrued in any year in which the plan is frozen.

The accrued benefit of a non-key employee in a top-heavy plan must equal at least 2 percent of average annual compensation for each year of service with the employer, limited to 10, not to exceed a total of 20 percent. [Treas. Reg. § 1.416-1, Q&A M-2] If the non-key participant benefits under both a defined benefit plan and a defined contribution plan, each of which is subject to the top-heavy minimum benefit requirements, the defined benefit plan may provide a top-heavy minimum benefit equal to the amount described above. However, the employer may choose to provide the top-heavy minimum benefit in the defined contribution plan. In that case, the defined contribution plan must contribute at least 5 percent of the non-key participant's compensation to the account of such participant in the top-heavy plan year. [Treas. Reg. § 1.416-1, Q&A M-12]

For purposes of determining the minimum benefit in a top-heavy defined benefit plan, the average annual compensation is defined as the average annual compensation for the five consecutive years during which the employee had the highest aggregate compensation from the employer. In making this determination, years in which the employee did not earn a year of service under the rules of Code Section 411(a)(4), (5), and (6) are disregarded. [Treas. Reg. § 1.416-1, Q&A M-2(a)]

The years of service counted for purposes of the top-heavy minimum benefit are only those years during which the employee had a year of service under the rules of Code Section 411(a)(4), (5), and (6). A plan can disregard any year of service during which the plan was not top-heavy, any year of service completed in a plan year beginning before January 1, 1984, and, for plan years beginning after December 31, 2001, any year of service completed during a plan year when the plan does not benefit (within the meaning of Code Section 410(b)) any key employee or former key employee. [I.R.C. §§ 416(c)(1)(C)(ii), 416(c)(1)(C)(iii)]

If the participant, as of the date the accrued benefit is determined, has accrued at least the top-heavy minimum benefit under the regular plan formula, no additional top-heavy benefits are required. [Treas. Reg. § 1.416-1, Q&A M-2(e)]

### Q 1:22    What are the maximum benefits that can be provided in a defined benefit plan?

In general, the benefits for a participant in a defined benefit pension plan may not exceed, when expressed as an annual benefit, the lesser of $160,000 (as indexed) or 100 percent of the participant's average compensation for the highest three consecutive years. The term "annual benefit" means a benefit payable annually in the form of a straight life annuity (with no ancillary benefits) and does not include any benefits attributable to either employee contributions or rollover contributions. [I.R.C. §§ 415(b)(1), 415(b)(2); Treas. Reg. § 1.415-3(b)(1)(i)]

The $160,000 limitation is indexed each year by a cost-of-living adjustment, and the increases occur in multiples of $5,000. If the cost-of-living adjustment as applied to the $160,000 dollar limitation does not exceed $5,000, the limitation is rounded down to the next multiple of $5,000. [I.R.C. § 415(d)(1)]

The $160,000 limitation is reduced ¹⁄₁₀ for each year of plan participation less than 10. It is also adjusted if benefits to the participant begin at an age under age 62 or above age 65. [I.R.C. §§ 415(b)(5)(A), 415(b)(2)(C)]

The 100 percent of the participant's average compensation for the high-three-years limitation is reduced ¹⁄₁₀ for each year of service less than 10 years. [I.R.C. § 415(b)(5)] However, a participant will not be considered as having a benefit in excess of 100 percent of the highest three-years-average compensation if the benefit is less than or equal to $10,000 per year. However, to meet this exception, the participant must not have participated in a defined contribution plan of the employer. Furthermore, the $10,000 annual benefit is reduced for each year of service less than 10. [I.R.C. § 415(b)(4)]

> **Example.** Kevin has reached the plan's normal retirement age, which, for purposes of this example, we will assume is age 62. Kevin has a three-year-average compensation of $170,000. The plan provides a benefit of 4 percent

of highest three-year-average compensation per year of service. What is Kevin's accrued benefit as of January 1, 2005?

Accrued benefit prior to application of maximum limit:

$$\$170,000 \times .04 \times 15 \text{ years of service} = \$102,000$$

*Limit 1:* $160,000 reduced for years of participation less than 10:

$$\$160,000 \times (1-\tfrac{5}{10}) = \$80,000$$

*Limit 2:* 100% of three-year-average compensation reduced for years of service less than 10:

$$\$170,000 \times (1-\tfrac{0}{10}) = \$170,000$$

Accrued benefit equals the lesser of Limit 1 or 2, but not more than $102,000 (the benefit as calculated under the plan formula):

$$\text{Accrued benefit} = \$80,000$$

The Internal Revenue Code defines the term "average compensation for the high three years" as the three consecutive calendar years during which the participant was both an active participant in the plan and had the greatest aggregate compensation from the employer. [I.R.C. § 415(b)(3)] The Treasury Regulations define this term as the three consecutive calendar years (or the actual number of consecutive years of employment for those employees who are employed for less than three consecutive years with the employer) during which the employee had the greatest aggregate compensation from the employer. The difference between the definition in the Code and the Regulations is in what period of compensation may be used in determining the 100 percent of compensation limitation. The Code restricts the compensation to that earned while a participant, but the Regulations contain no such restriction. [Treas. Reg. § 1.415-3(a)(3)] Effective for years after December 31, 2005, Congress has clarified that compensation earned prior to plan participation may be used in determining this limit. [PPA § 832]

The plan may use any 12-month period other than the calendar year (e.g., the plan year) as long as it is uniformly and consistently applied. [Treas. Reg. § 1.415-3(a)(3)]

If the employee is self-employed as defined in Code Section 401(c)(1), "compensation from the employer" is substituted for "the participant's earned income." [I.R.C. § 415(b)(3)]

## Q 1:23  Over what period are the maximum benefits measured?

As noted, maximum annual benefits are measured during a plan's limitation year. The limitation year, with respect to any qualified retirement plan maintained by the employer, is the calendar year. However, instead of using the calendar year, an employer may elect to use any other consecutive 12-month period as the limitation year. The election is made by the adoption of a written resolution by the employer. This requirement is satisfied if the election is made in connection with the adoption of the plan or any amendments to the plan. [Treas. Reg. § 1.415-2(b)]

In the case of a group of employers that constitutes either a controlled group of corporations or trades or businesses (whether or not incorporated) under common control, the election to use a consecutive 12-month period other than the calendar year as the limitation year generally must be made by all members of the group who maintain a qualified retirement plan. [Rev. Rul. 79-5, 1979-1 C.B. 165; Ann. 95-99, 1995-48 I.R.B. 10]

Once established, the limitation year may be changed only by making the election described above. Any change in the limitation year must be a change to a 12-month period commencing with any day within the current limitation year. The limitations are applied in the normal manner to the new limitation year and are separately applied to a limitation period that begins with the first day of the current limitation year and ends on the day before the first day of the first limitation year for which the change is effective.

### Q 1:24   Is there a maximum contribution that can be made to a defined benefit plan?

NO! The contribution, per se, is not restricted. The only restriction is on the amount of benefit that can be paid from a defined benefit plan. Because the benefit is restricted, the contribution is only restricted by the amount that can be funded to achieve that benefit, within prescribed limits depending on the form of benefit.

### Q 1:25   Are there any adjustments that are required to the maximum benefits?

There are certain mandated adjustments to the maximum benefit if certain requirements are not met. The adjustment of the maximum benefit limitations to an actuarial equivalent benefit is done using certain interest rates and mortality tables. There are four different adjustments to the maximum benefit limitations that affect the use of certain actuarial assumptions. They are adjustments for the form of benefit, adjustments to the maximum dollar limitation when benefits commence prior to age 62, adjustments to the maximum dollar limitation when benefits commence after age 65, and adjustments to a form of benefit subject to Code Section 417(e)(3) (i.e., a lump-sum payment).

### Q 1:26   How are maximum benefits adjusted for a form of payment other than a life annuity?

If the benefit under the plan is payable in any form other than a life annuity, such benefit must be adjusted to the actuarial equivalent of a life annuity and, after such adjustment, must not exceed the $160,000 and 100 percent of highest three-year-average compensation limitations. However, any portion of a joint and survivor annuity that constitutes a QJSA is not to be taken into account. [I.R.C. § 415(b)(2)(B)] Treasury Regulations Section 1.401(a)-11(b)(2) defines a QJSA as an annuity for the life of the participant with a survivor annuity for the life of the spouse of a participant, which is neither less than one-half nor greater than the amount of the annuity that is payable during the joint lives of the participant and the spouse. Such an annuity must be at least the actuarial equivalent of a life annuity or any optional form of life annuity under the plan. Therefore, a plan that provides that benefits at retirement are paid in the form of a joint and survivor annuity for married participants and a life annuity for single participants will not be required to adjust a participant's joint and survivor annuity benefit if such benefit is equal to the maximum benefit limitations under Code Section 415(b). However, if a plan provides for a form of benefit other than a life annuity or a QJSA, and the participant's benefit is at the maximum limit under Code Section 415(b), that form of benefit could cause the benefit to exceed those limitations unless the benefit is reduced to one that is actuarially equivalent to a life annuity.

> **Example.** The Sierra Pension Services, Inc. Pension Plan has a 10-year certain and life annuity as its normal form of benefit. Rick is about to retire at age 60 with a benefit equal to 98 percent of his highest three-year-average salary of $50,000, or $49,000 ($50,000 × .98). However, the plan must make sure that this benefit would not exceed the maximum benefit limitations. The APR for a 10-year certain and life annuity using the plan's definition of actuarial equivalence is 159.233. The APR for a life annuity is 154.758. Hence, Rick's benefit payable as an actuarially equivalent life annuity is $50,417 (($50,000 × 98% × 159.233)/154.758). That amount exceeds his highest three-year-average salary of $50,000 by $417. Therefore, the maximum amount that can be paid as a 10-year certain and life annuity is $48,595 ($50,000 × 154.758/159.233).

### Q 1:27    How are maximum benefits adjusted if payment begins prior to age 62?

If a benefit commences prior to a participant's attaining age 62, the $160,000 annual benefit is reduced to the actuarial equivalent of a benefit payable at the earlier retirement age. The actuarial equivalent is determined as the lesser of (a) or (b) where

(a) is the amount calculated using the plan's interest rate and mortality table, or tabular reduction factors; and

(b) is the amount calculated using 5 percent and the applicable mortality table.

[Rev. Rul. 98-1, Q&A 7, step 2, 1998-2 I.R.B. 5]

The applicable mortality table is the 1994 Group Annuity Reserving mortality table, also known as the 94 GAR. Some plans that have not been updated to use this new table may still be required to use the 1983 GAM Unisex table. The applicable mortality table is used for adjusting the maximum benefit limitations under Code Section 415(b) to the actuarial equivalent of a life annuity. It is also used to determine the minimum lump-sum value payable under Code Section 417(e)(3).

The following describes the steps taken to determine this amount:

Actuarial reduction.

*Step 1.* Reduce the maximum benefit for years of participation less than 10.

If the plan provides benefits prior to age 62 using actuarial equivalent assumptions, Step 2 is used. If the plan uses a table of actuarial equivalent tabular factors, skip Step 2 and go to Step 3.

*Step 2.* Calculate the actuarial equivalent of the maximum benefit payable at the retirement age using 5 percent and the applicable mortality table and compare this amount to the actuarial equivalent of the maximum benefit payable at the retirement age using the plan interest rate and mortality table. The lesser of these two amounts is the maximum annual benefit payable at the retirement age. (Note that if no forfeiture of benefits will result upon death, mortality can be ignored in the actuarial equivalent calculation.)

*Step 3.* Apply the tabular reduction factors to the maximum benefits to determine the actuarially equivalent benefit as of the retirement age. Do the same with the applicable mortality table at an interest rate of 5 percent. The lesser of these two amounts is the actuarial equivalent of the maximum dollar limitation payable at the retirement date in the form of a life annuity or QJSA. (Note that if no forfeiture of benefits will result upon death, mortality can be ignored in the actuarial equivalent calculation.)

**Example.** Kevin is retiring at age 60, has five years of participation in the plan, and has average annual compensation of $170,000. His maximum benefit is calculated as follows:

*Step 1.* Determine the maximum dollar limitation in effect at the end of the limitation year and reduce that amount by $1/10$ for each year of plan participation less than 10.

*Result 1.* For the plan year ending in 2003, the maximum dollar limitation is $160,000. Kevin will have participated in the plan for five years, so the maximum dollar limit must be reduced by $5/10$, making it $80,000 ($160,000 × $(1 - 5/10)$). The monthly amount payable is $6,666.67 ($80,000/12).

*Step 2.* Compare the actuarial equivalent of the benefit in Step 1 payable at the retirement age using the applicable mortality table at an interest rate of 5 percent to the actuarial equivalent amount using the plan's interest rate and mortality table. The lesser of these two amounts is the maximum annual dollar benefit payable to Kevin as a life annuity starting at age 60. Although the maximum is calculated using an annual APR, we will show these steps using a monthly APR.

*Result 2.* The APR for a life annuity payable monthly at age 62 is 152.157 using 5 percent interest and the applicable mortality table. That amount is discounted from age 62 to age 60 at 5 percent interest, which results in a discount of .907 $[1.05^{-2}]$. Using 5 percent and the applicable mortality table, the APR for a life annuity payable monthly at age 60 is 159.010. Therefore, the age 60 benefit that is actuarially equivalent of the benefit in Step 1 is $5,786.07 ($6,666.67 × 152.157/159.010 × .907).

Using the plan's actuarial equivalency factors, the APR at age 62 is 148.109 and at age 60 is 154.758. The result using the plan's interest rate and mortality table is an actuarial equivalent benefit of $5,419.73 ($6,666.67 × 148.109/ 154.758 × (1.085$^{-2}$)) (the benefit is discounted using a preretirement interest rate of 8.5%).

The lesser of the two amounts is $5,419.73 and is the maximum monthly dollar benefit payable to Kevin as a life annuity starting at age 60.

*Step 3.* If the plan uses tabular reduction factors instead of using an actuarial equivalence assumption (as we used in Step 2), then apply these factors to the benefit in Step 1 to determine the actuarially equivalent benefit as of the retirement age. Compare this to the benefit determined using the applicable mortality table at an interest rate of 5 percent. The lesser of these two amounts is the maximum annual benefit payable to Kevin as a life annuity starting at age 60.

### Q 1:28   How are benefits adjusted if payment begins after age 65?

The $160,000 annual limitation is increased for benefits that begin after age 65 to the actuarial equivalent of a life annuity benefit beginning at age 65. The adjusted amount is the lesser of the amount as determined by the plan interest and mortality table or by the applicable mortality table with interest at 5 percent. If the plan uses a tabular factor in determining the actuarial equivalent late retirement benefits, the lesser of the amount determined using the tabular factors or using the applicable mortality table with interest at 5 percent is the maximum adjusted dollar limitation. [Rev. Rul. 98-1, Q&A 7, step 2, 1998-2 I.R.B. 5] In all instances, this actuarially equivalent adjustment is done without the mortality decrement.

**Example.** Assume Kevin from the previous example didn't retire and is now age 70 and wants to retire. In the year of retirement, Kevin's maximum dollar limitation at age 65 is $160,000. Using the plan's actuarial equivalencies, the APR at age 70 is 118.841 and at age 65 is 137.517. His age 70 adjusted maximum dollar limitation using the plan's postretirement interest of 5 percent and mortality table is $236,296.11 (($160,000 × (1.05)$^5$ × 137.517)/118.841). With an interest rate of 5 percent and the applicable mortality table, the APR at age 70 is 123.106 and at age 65 is 141.529. The age adjusted maximum dollar limitation using the applicable mortality table and 5 percent interest is $234,764.65 (($160,000 × (1.05)$^5$ × 141.529)/123.106). Hence the age 70 adjusted dollar limitation for Kevin is $234,764.65.

### Q 1:29   How are other benefit options adjusted from the normal form?

Recall that all defined benefit plans state that benefits are payable in the "normal form." This normal form is usually a straight life annuity for unmarried participants and a joint and survivor annuity that is the actuarial equivalent of a straight life annuity for married participants. However, documents generally allow participants to choose from a list of optional forms of benefits that are the actuarial equivalent of the normal form.

Any benefit that is in the form of a nondecreasing life annuity, including a QJSA, a QPSA, and an annuity that decreases merely because of the cessation or reduction of Social Security supplements or qualified disability payments, is not subject to Code Section 417(e)(3). In addition, a benefit that decreases during the life of the participant merely because of the death of the survivor annuitant is also exempted from the requirements of Code Section 417(e)(3), but only if the reduction is to a level not below 50 percent of the annual benefit payable before the death of the survivor annuitant. [Treas. Reg. § 1.417(e)-1(d)(6)] Therefore, an actuarial equivalent lump-sum payment of the straight life annuity would be subject to Code Section 417(e)(3).

### Q 1:30    How is an annuity benefit converted to a lump sum?

A lump-sum benefit is calculated using the plan's interest rate and mortality table for actuarial equivalence; however, a lump-sum benefit may not be less than the amount determined using the rules under Code Section 417(e)(3). That section of the Code states that for a plan in effect after December 8, 1994, the present value, in this case a lump sum, shall not be less than the value calculated using the "applicable interest rate" and "applicable mortality table." The applicable interest rate is determined by the terms of the plan document and Treasury Regulations Section 1.417(e)-1(d)(3)(i). The applicable mortality table is either the 1983 GAM Unisex table or the 94 GAR table, depending on the date of the distribution and plan provisions. [Treas. Reg. § 1.417(e)-1(d)(1)]

### Q 1:31    What is the applicable interest rate?

The applicable interest rate for a month is the annual interest rate on 30-year Treasury securities as specified by the Commissioner for that month in revenue rulings, notices, or other guidance published in the Internal Revenue Bulletin. [I.R.C. § 417(e)(3)(A)(ii)(II)] Effective for plan years beginning after December 31, 2007, the applicable interest rate will be defined as the segment rate, the same rate used for funding.

The time and method for determining the applicable interest rate for each participant's distribution must be determined in a consistent manner that is applied uniformly to all participants in the plan. In general, for distributions with annuity starting dates in plan years beginning after December 31, 1994, the applicable interest rate is determined by reference to the plan's look-back month and remains in effect for the duration of the plan's stability period. The look-back month is the month that is referenced for determining the applicable interest rate for the month (or other longer stability period) that contains the annuity starting date for the distribution. When defining a plan's look-back month and stability period, the following rules apply:

*Stability period.* This stability period may be one calendar month, one plan quarter, one calendar quarter, one plan year, or one calendar year.

*Look-back month.* The look-back month may be the first, second, third, fourth, or fifth full calendar month preceding the first day of the stability period.

[Treas. Reg. § 1.417(e)-1(d)(9)(i)]

**Example.** The look-back month and stability period for determining the applicable interest rate for the Sierra Pension Services Inc. Pension Plan is the second month preceding the first day of the plan quarter during which the annuity starting date occurs. The plan is a calendar-year plan. Joan, a terminated participant, will receive a lump-sum distribution on June 15, 2001. Since the distribution will occur in the second calendar quarter (i.e., April 1 through June 30), the look-back month in this case is the second calendar month that precedes April 1, 2001, which is February 2001. Hence, the present value of Joan's benefit will be determined using the published applicable interest rate for the month of February 2001.

A plan is permitted to use an average of the applicable interest rates instead of the applicable interest rate for a look-back month; however, such an average with respect to a stability period is an interest rate that is computed by averaging the applicable interest rates for two or more consecutive months from among the first, second, third, fourth, and fifth calendar months preceding the first day of the stability period. Furthermore, a plan must specify the manner in which the permitted average interest rate is computed. [Treas. Reg. § 1.417(e)-1(d)(4)(iv)]

**Example.** Rick terminates employment on January 1, 2001, from Sierra Pension Services, Inc. and would like to receive his benefit in a lump-sum payment. The applicable interest rate according to the plan document is determined as of the first month preceding the first day of the plan year in which the distribution occurs and is 4.92 percent. Rick's accrued benefit payable at the plan's normal retirement age of 60 is $100 per month. His lump-sum benefit is calculated as follows:

*Step 1.* Multiply the age 60 accrued benefit by the APR using the plan's actuarial equivalencies. Assume this APR is 154.758. This gives you a lump-sum amount at retirement of $15,476 ($100 × 154.758).

*Step 2.* Multiply the result in Step 1 by the discount factor calculated from the preretirement interest rate of 8.5 percent from age 60 to age 46 (14 years). This plan ignores mortality prior to retirement since the death benefit is equal to the present value of benefits (PVAB). Therefore the discount factor is the present value of $1 payable in 14 years at 8.5 percent, or 0.31914 ($1.085^{-14}$). The lump sum for Rick is $4,939 [$15,476 × 0.31914] using the plan's interest rate and mortality.

*Step 3.* Multiply the age 60 accrued benefit by the APR using the applicable mortality table (94 GAR) and applicable interest rate (4.92%). This APR is 160.237. This gives you a lump sum at retirement of $16,024 ($100 × 160.237).

*Step 4.* Multiply the result in Step 3 by the discount factor from age 60 to age 46 (14 years). In this case, the plan ignores mortality prior to retirement. Therefore, the discount factor is the present value of $1 payable in 14 years at 4.92 percent, or 0.51049 ($1.0492^{-14}$). The lump sum for Rick is $8,180 ($16,024×.51049) using the applicable interest and mortality table.

*Step 5.* The lump sum payable to Rick is the greater of the amounts in Step 2 and Step 4, in this case $8,180.

### Q 1:32   How is a distribution made from a defined benefit plan?

If a participant is eligible to receive a distribution from a defined benefit plan, either due to termination of employment or attainment of normal retirement age (in-service distributions are not allowed in a defined benefit plan unless the participant has attained normal retirement age), then certain administrative tasks must be completed. The following forms must be distributed and/or completed by the participant:

- Section 402(f) tax notice
- Participant election form
- Waiver of applicable notice periods, if allowed
- Relative value disclosures
- Qualified joint & survivor notice and waiver, if applicable

In a defined benefit plan, the participant must be made aware of the value of each of the distribution options that are available to him or her under the plan terms. This is called the "relative value disclosure." In addition to the description of each distribution option and its value, the value of each must be compared to the value of the plan's QJSA so that the participant is aware of any subsidies that any particular form has over another.

The participant must be notified at least 30 days but no more than 90 days before the distribution of these distribution options. If the participant chooses to select a distribution option other than the QJSA, then the participant and his or her spouse (if applicable) must sign a document officially waiving this form of benefit. A waiver of the minimum 30-day election period may be made if the plan document allows, but the waiting period needs to be at least nine days from the date the waiver is made.

### Q 1:33   How are maximum lump-sum benefits calculated?

In general, the accepted practice is to calculate the lump-sum payment under the plan prior to the application of the maximum benefit limitations to determine whether the actuarial equivalent (or present value) of the lump sum exceeds the lesser of (a) or (b), where

(a) equals 100 percent of the participant's average compensation for the highest-paid three years, reduced for years of service less than 10 years; and

(b) equals the age-adjusted $160,000 annual dollar limitation, as indexed, reduced for plan participation less than 10 years. When calculating the age-adjusted dollar limitation for a benefit payable before age 62 or after age 65, the adjustments to the maximum annual dollar limitation are calculated as discussed previously.

The present value of the lump sum for 2004 and 2005 is determined using a 5.5 percent interest rate for the applicable rate. Beginning with plan years after December 31, 2005, the interest rate used to convert a straight life annuity to a lump sum for purposes of determining the maximum under Code Section 415 is the lesser of 5.5 percent, the plan's interest rate, or a rate that produces a benefit of not more than 105 percent of the benefit calculated using the Code Section 417(e)(3) rate. [PPA § 303]

### Q 1:34   Are there any limitations applicable for a participant that has participated in a defined contribution plan and now participates in a defined benefit plan of the same employer?

Not any longer. Prior to year 2000 plan years, there was a special limitation called the Code Section 415(e) limitation applicable to participants that participated in both a defined benefit plan and a defined contribution plan.

A participant can now have maximum benefits in both a defined benefit plan and a defined contribution plan sponsored by the same employer. However, this repeal does not allow a participant to have maximum benefits in multiple defined benefit plans of the same employer. The only restriction applicable to an employer sponsoring both types of plans is the deduction limitation, to be discussed later.

## Funding of a Defined Benefit Plan

### Q 1:35   How is the contribution calculated each year?

The funding of a defined benefit plan is similar to the amortization of a mortgage. There is a fixed amount, that we are funding toward, at retirement age. This amount is amortized, or funded on a level basis annually, over your future working lifetime. The rules for funding will change dramatically beginning with the 2008 plan year, when the actuary will be forced to determine the minimum and maximum funding charges based on prescribed interest rates, mortality tables, and funding methods.

Prior to 2008, the funding is determined for the most part by the enrolled actuary for the plan. The actuary determines the interest rate to be used in calculating the amortization amount.

**Example 1.** Suppose that a plan sponsor wanted to know the annual contribution requirement to accumulate $5,802 in five years. If the trust earned no interest, the amount paid in equal installments over five years would be $1,160.40 ($5,802/5). Because the trust fund could be invested in an interest-bearing investment, the amount needed could be reduced to take into account the interest earned on the money. If an investment returns 5 percent per year, the present value of $5,802 is $4,546 ($5,802 × .783526). The amortization factor of $1 payable now and each year over the next four years is 4.546. Therefore, $1,000 ($4,546/4.546) contributed now and for each of the next four years would accumulate to the desired $5,802. The accounting of the trust fund would be as follows:

| Year | Trust Fund at Beginning of Year | Payment | Interest of 5% | Trust Fund at End of Year |
|------|---------------------------------|---------|----------------|----------------------------|
| 1 | $ 0 | $1,000 | $ 50 | $1,050 |
| 2 | $1,050 | $1,000 | $102 | $2,152 |
| 3 | $2,152 | $1,000 | $158 | $3,310 |
| 4 | $3,310 | $1,000 | $216 | $4,526 |
| 5 | $4,526 | $1,000 | $276 | $5,802 |
| Total | | $5,000 | $802 | |

The interest paid for $802 of the needed accumulation while the balance was paid from the $1,000 deposits.

Beginning in 2008, the interest rates to be used in determining the future liability will be prescribed by law using segment rates based on when liabilities come due. The cost attributable to a particular year is then determined pro-rata based on the amount of the benefit that accrues in that particular year, plus an amortization of any shortfall of achieving a fully funded plan.

**Example 2.** Using the information from Example 1 above, assume a benefit equal to $10 accrues each year and the total liability at the end of the five years is still $5,802. The cost each year will be based on the portion of the benefit that accrues that year, determined as follows:

| Year | Accrued Benefit | Trust Fund at Beginning of Year | Payment | Interest of 5% | Trust Fund at End of Year |
|------|-----------------|----------------------------------|---------|----------------|----------------------------|
| 1 | $10 | $ 0 | $ 909 | $ 46 | $ 955 |
| 2 | $20 | $ 955 | $ 954 | $ 96 | $2,005 |
| 3 | $30 | $2,005 | $1,002 | $151 | $3,158 |
| 4 | $40 | $3,158 | $1,053 | $210 | $4,421 |
| 5 | $50 | $4,421 | $1,105 | $276 | $5,802 |
| Total | | | $5,023 | $779 | |

## Q 1:36　What does the term *normal cost* mean?

In general, the *normal cost* is the annual contribution required to fund the plan, or also defined as the annual cost of the benefits assigned to the funding year. This cost would be paid into the plan assets in the form of a cash contribution each year until the plan is fully funded. The normal cost is adjusted each year to take into account the plan's experience with regard to participant data changes such as salary increases, terminations, deaths, and such, as well as changes in the value of the plan's assets.

### Q 1:37   What role does the enrolled actuary play in determining the amount to contribute to a defined benefit plan?

The employer will rely on the recommendation of the plan's enrolled actuary to determine how much money must be contributed to the plan each year. The enrolled actuary will generally provide the employer the minimum amount required to satisfy the minimum funding standards of the Code and ERISA, the maximum amount that could be contributed and deducted on the federal tax return of the employer, and the amount recommended by the actuary that falls within a range best suited for the plan to provide continued payments of plan benefits. Additionally, the employer will look at the availability of cash to fund the plan and whether or not contributions in the future may be limited due to a projected change in the cash flow of the business, in which case the employer may wish to contribute more now to offset future contribution requirements.

The enrolled actuary responsible for the minimum funding calculations of a defined benefit plan will take into account the following assumptions when calculating plan costs:

1. Rates at which plan participants will die either prior to or while receiving benefit payments;
2. Rates of investment return on the assets invested for the purpose of providing the benefits under the plan;
3. Rates at which the salaries increase over the working years of the participants;
4. Rates at which employees terminate prior to reaching retirement;
5. Rates at which employees become eligible for disability, early retirement, or death benefits;
6. Expenses incurred and paid out of the assets for the administration and operation of the plan; and
7. Rates at which benefits will increase after retirement as part of cost-of-living adjustments.

Based on the benefits available under the plan, the employee demographics, the plan's funding policy, and the size and general health of the employee group, the enrolled actuary may include some or all of the above assumptions to determine the plan costs.

In most small defined benefit plans, an actuary will use a pre- and postretirement interest rate and a postretirement mortality table. The actuary would not use a preretirement mortality table, since there is generally no risk of forfeiture for preretirement deaths as the plan will provide a death benefit equal to the present value of the accrued benefit. In addition, expense assumptions won't be used since many small plans pay expenses from the business as an additional deduction. The actuary may use a turnover table or salary scale depending on expected results of the small group of employees.

### Q 1:38   What are actuarial assumptions, and how do they differ from the plan's actuarial equivalence?

Recall that the actuary's primary function is to determine the amount needed by an employer's defined benefit plan to pay future retirement benefits to participants. Assumptions (such as those listed above) and methods chosen by the actuary represent both his professional judgment and legislative constraints, and affect the amount required to fund the plan. The actuary must also certify the tax-deductible amount which may be contributed to the plan.

Actuarial assumptions are different from the actuarial equivalence specified by the plan document, although they both employ the use of pre- and postretirement interest rates and mortality tables. The actuarial equivalence specified in the plan is used for the sole purpose of converting one form of benefit to another form, e.g., from a life annuity to a lump sum. The funding assumptions may be similar to the actuarial equivalence specified in the plan, but this is not required and may not be prudent. Where it may be useful to have similar assumptions is if it is assumed that all benefits will be taken in the form of a particular payment option (e.g., lump sum), then the postretirement funding assumptions chosen by the actuary may reflect the Code Section 417(e) rates and/or the plan actuarial equivalence to ensure there are sufficient funds to meet that obligation.

### Q 1:39   How does the actuary determine the funding requirement each year?

In order to determine the funding requirement for a plan, the actuary uses present value and amortization calculations.

The value today of some amount to be paid now or in the future is known as its present value. The present value of an amount is usually calculated by multiplying its future value by a discount factor. The discount factor takes into consideration the time value of money at some assumed interest rate and may have other decrements such as turnover, death, disability, and early retirement factored into it.

In order for the actuary to determine how much money is needed at retirement, he or she multiplies the projected retirement benefit at retirement by the APR. Recall that an APR is developed from a set of actuarial assumptions, most typically a mortality table and an interest rate. Mortality tables are developed by performing historical studies of the rates of death at each age from birth. The rate of death from each successive age is measured and converted to actual numbers of lives. These hypothetical populations are then used to develop the APR for any age for which payments can be expected to be made.

The amount of money the actuary determines as necessary at retirement age is then amortized over the future working lifetime of the participant. To do this, most funding methods make use of the concept of an annuity due. An annuity due is the present value of a stream of payments made at regular intervals over a specified period of time. The contribution requirement for funding methods is developed on an annual basis; hence an annuity due usually has one year as its interval when the annuity due is developed for purposes of an annual contribution. For benefits at retirement, the annuity due is usually expressed in terms of monthly intervals. The plan funding interest rate is used to discount the present value of the annuity due.

> **Example.** Joan's projected retirement benefit is $2,000/month. The APR determined using the funding assumptions is 142.854. The projected lump-sum amount at retirement for Joan is $ 285,708 ($2,000 × 142.854). She has 35 years until she reaches the plan's normal retirement age. The preretirement interest rate is 6 percent. The amount that needs to be contributed each year is determined first by discounting her projected lump sum to today. This amount is $37,172 ($285,708 × $1.06^{-35}$). This amount is then amortized over the next 35 years, which is equal to $2,419 ($37,172/15.368). In other words, if $2,419 were deposited each January 1 for the next 35 years and the trust earned exactly 6 percent, she would have $285,708 when she reached retirement age, sufficient to pay her a $2,000 a month benefit for the rest of her life as long as the postretirement mortality assumption and interest rate are also realized.

Beginning in 2008, the actuary will have much less input in determining the minimum required contribution each year. The minimum will be a prescribed amount based on methods and assumptions required to be used. The actuary may still determine a recommended amount, based on his or her professional opinion, as long as the amount falls within the minimum and maximum amounts allowed.

## Q 1:40   What is a funding method?

In order to provide the promised benefits under a defined benefit pension plan, a systematic method of allocating contributions to a pool of money (i.e., the trust fund) must be used in order to satisfy the minimum funding standards of ERISA Section 302 and Code Section 412. This systematic method is called a funding method.

Beginning in 2008, the funding method to be used in determining the minimum and maximum funding amounts is prescribed by law. It is assumed that the enrolled actuary will still be able to use other funding methods in determining the funding for the plan, as long as the contribution falls within the ranges determined by law.

In general, funding methods take into account the following:

1. *Assets.* The plan sponsor contributes money to a trust fund to provide the dollars needed to pay benefits as they come due under the terms of the plan. In general, most defined benefit plans value the assets of the plan at fair market value.

2. *Rate of return.* It will be the responsibility of the plan's fiduciary to invest the plan assets in a manner that generates additional dollars through investment earnings (i.e., interest, dividends, realized and unrealized appreciation).

3. *Mortality.* Any benefits paid to retirees will be contingent upon the survival of the retiree; therefore, life expectancy based on a mortality study will help determine the length of time that payments can be expected to be made.

4. *Benefits.* The amount of benefit is defined by the terms of the plan document; in order to determine an appropriate asset level, an estimate of the benefits that will be paid upon retirement is needed.

5. *Valuation date.* The assets and liabilities of the plan are valued as of a fixed point in time at which the recommended contribution level is calculated using these valuations.

A funding method will generally consider the benefits of all employees in the pension plan based on the current compensation and benefit formula in effect on the valuation date. The benefit at retirement is calculated for all plan participants. This calculation takes into account their service prior to the valuation date and the service they would have if they remain in the employment of the plan sponsor until the assumed retirement date. The benefit that results from this assumption is known as the projected benefit or the future benefit. Some plans have participants that have retired or terminated their employment, and, as a result, the participants will no longer earn service credits for additional benefits after their retirement or termination. In this case, the promised benefit is determined at the time of termination or retirement, and such benefit is known as their accrued benefit, which is also known as their projected benefit or future benefit. Note that active employees also have an accrued benefit; such benefit is the amount of benefit they would receive if they terminated employment prior to their retirement age and did not start collecting payment of the benefit until retirement. Therefore, the term *present value of future benefits* (PVFB) means the value today of all benefits that will be earned by each employee in the plan under the assumption of continued service to the retirement age. If decrements of turnover, death, disability, or early retirement are used by the actuary employing the funding method, the present value of the future benefits will have been adjusted to take these contingencies into account.

Once a funding method has determined the PVFB to be paid as of the valuation date, such an amount represents the total assets required to pay all benefits from the plan. Because it is not feasible for most plan sponsors to fund all the required assets in one payment, a funding method will determine an annual contribution that will eventually accumulate the PVFB. Stated another way, a plan sponsor's contribution requirement is determined by subtracting the value of any assets in the plan from the PVFB, and this difference, if any, is funded over the working years of the employee group. This funding formula is as follows:

Present value of future benefits – Assets = Present value of future contributions

("Present value of future contributions" is also known as the "present value of future normal costs (PVFNC)")

A timeline that represents the life span of a pension plan would show that the PVFB is the sum of the values of the benefits already earned for service before the valuation date and the present value of the benefits to be earned for service and compensation earned after the valuation date.

$$\begin{array}{ccc} \text{Present Value of Benefits As} \\ \text{of Valuation Date} \end{array} = \begin{array}{c} \text{Benefits earned} \\ \text{to date} \end{array} + \begin{array}{c} \text{Present Value of Benefits Projected} \\ \text{to be Earned at Retirement} \end{array}$$

| Date of Hire | Valuation Date | Date of Retirement |

The funding formula asks the question: How much money is required today, or as of the valuation date, to pay all benefits currently promised under the plan? Each funding method will develop a contribution requirement that consists of two parts: the normal cost and the amortization of the unfunded accrued liability. Some funding methods assume there is no unfunded accrued liability and fund all past and future benefits in the normal cost. Depending on the funding method used, an actuary may provide several contribution amounts based on different payment periods for the unfunded accrued liability. There are various characteristics to a funding method; the following questions detail some of these.

### Q 1:41    How does the normal cost vary by year and type of funding method chosen?

In general, the normal cost is defined as the annual cost of the benefits assigned to the funding year. This cost would be paid into the plan assets in the form of a cash contribution each year until the plan is fully funded. The normal cost is adjusted each year to take into account the plan's experience with regard to participant data changes such as salary increases, terminations, deaths, and so on, as well as changes in the value of the plan's assets.

All things being equal, each funding method will generate a different normal cost. The choice of a funding method will depend upon the size of the employee group, the employer's need for flexibility in contributions, whether or not past-service benefits are provided, the average age of the employee group, and the need for the employer to anticipate future contribution requirements.

Changes in demographics can have an effect on the normal cost. A significant number of premature terminations, deaths of employees, or lower than assumed compensation increases would lower costs. Fewer terminations, deaths, or higher than normal compensation increases could significantly increase costs.

### Q 1:42    What is an unfunded accrued liability?

In general, the unfunded accrued liability (unfunded past-service liability) is the present value of the liability assigned to benefits earned as of the valuation date, reduced by the value of the plan's assets. The unfunded accrued liability is created when an employer adopts a pension plan and recognizes service completed before the effective date of the plan and there are few or no assets in the plan to pay for this liability. Thus, an immediate liability is created for which the plan sponsor will have to pay over a period of years. In general, ERISA and the tax code require that any unfunded accrued liability be amortized in level payments of principal and interest over at least 30 years. However, the tax code also allows this liability to be paid over as early as 10 years. This difference in amortization periods creates a range of contributions that can be made each year, from the minimum that must be funded to a maximum that can be funded.

Some funding methods will add other accrued liabilities each year that serve to increase or decrease the amount of the unfunded accrued liability, such as an actuarial loss in the previous year or a liability created as a result of a plan amendment that changes benefits. In some instances, a plan may not provide for benefits prior to the effective date of the plan and still have an unfunded accrued liability. This would occur if the employer were to use a funding method that accumulates past years' theoretical contributions as the accrued liability.

Once the unfunded accrued liability is determined, it becomes the aim of the funding method to reduce that amount to zero. An enrolled actuary tries to anticipate what the unfunded accrued liability for a plan will be in the next year, based on benefits earned, benefits paid, investment earnings, and contributions made to the plan's assets.

### Q 1:43  What is the difference between an individual funding method and an aggregate funding method?

Individual funding calculates the basis of the normal cost and the amortization of the unfunded accrued liability for each participant and then adds all calculations in order to determine the total contribution for the plan.

Aggregate funding determines the value of the future benefit for each participant, but it determines the contribution for the entire plan using an averaging factor based on the future-service years or present value of the future compensation (or both) of the employee group. A plan based on future-service years uses level-dollar funding, while a plan using future compensation uses a level percentage of compensation funding. The distinction here is that under future-service years the plan's normal cost will be a flat dollar amount per plan participant, while the present value of future compensation results in a level percentage of plan compensation. Generally, plans that have a benefit based on compensation will use the present value of the future compensation. For example, assuming no increase in salary and ignoring interest, the present value of future compensation of an employee with 10 years remaining until retirement is 10 multiplied by his or her current salary. If an interest rate of 5 percent is used, the present value of the future compensation is the current salary multiplied by the present value of $1 payable for 10 years, in this case a factor of 8.11.

An individual type of funding method would generate the largest normal cost because the amortization factor under an aggregate type funding method would be smaller, since all participants are weighted equally when the factor is determined.

### Q 1:44  What is an *actuarial gain or loss*?

An *actuarial gain or loss* is the difference between what an enrolled actuary expects a plan's assets and liabilities to be on the next valuation date, according to the actuarial assumptions used, and what they are in fact. The gain or loss will serve to decrease or increase contributions in future years, as the case may be. A rate of return on a plan's assets greater than that assumed by an enrolled actuary would be an example of an asset gain attributable to the interest rate assumption; an increase in the rate of pay to the plan participants in excess of what was assumed would be an example of actuarial loss attributable to the salary scale assumption.

If the actuarial assumptions match the change in the assets and liabilities of the plan from the valuation date to the next valuation date, no adjustment is made to the contribution level. However, the change in the assets and liabilities from one valuation date to the next is rarely, if ever, identical to actuarial assumptions. The difference between expected plan assets and liabilities and the actual assets and liabilities is called an actuarial gain or loss.

There are two techniques for handling an actuarial gain or loss. The immediate-gain funding technique specifically identifies the actuarial gain or loss each year and adjusts the unfunded accrued liability by the amount of the gain or loss. The spread-gain funding technique does not explicitly identify the actuarial gain or loss but either decreases or increases the contribution over future years as a result of any gain or loss. Note that for spread-gain funding adjustments that develop an unfunded accrued liability, no adjustment is made to the unfunded accrued liability as a result of the actuarial gain or loss. The unfunded accrued liability in any year is always equal to the expected unfunded accrued liability developed from the prior year.

### Q 1:45  What are the requirements that a funding method must meet?

There are certain characteristics that all funding methods must satisfy. First, for purposes of satisfying the minimum funding requirements under Code Section 412, a funding method must be reasonable. A plan will satisfy the reasonableness requirement if it satisfies the "basic funding formula" and the normal cost is a level-dollar amount, or a level percentage of pay, that is computed from year to year on either an individual basis or an aggregate basis; or an amount equal to the PVAB accruing under the method for a particular plan year.

The basic funding formula states that the PVFB under a funding method must equal the sum of (1) the present value of normal costs (taking into account future mandatory employee contributions, within the meaning of Code Section 411(c)(2)(C), in the case of a contributory plan) over the future working lifetimes of participants (PVFNC); (2) the sum of the unamortized charge and credit bases, if any, treating credit bases under Code Section 412(b)(3)(B) as negative numbers (OB); and (3) the plan assets, decreased by a credit balance or increased by a debit balance in the funding standard account (FSA). [Treas. Reg. § 1.412(c)(3)-1(b)(1)]

$$PVFB = PVFNC + OB + Assets$$

Additionally, the funding method must satisfy the following criteria:

1. *Inclusion of all liabilities.* All liabilities of the plan for benefits, whether vested or not, must be taken into account.

2. *Production of actuarial gains and losses.* If each actuarial assumption is exactly realized under the funding method, no actuarial gains or losses are produced.

3. *The plan population must include three classes of individuals.* The three classes of participants are participants currently employed in the service of the employer; former participants who either terminated service with the employer, or retired, under the plan; and all other individuals currently entitled to benefits under the plan. However, participants who would be excluded from participation by the minimum age or service requirement of Code Section 410 but who, under the terms of the plan, participate immediately upon entering the service of the employer may be excluded until such time as they are no longer excludable. A funding method does not have to maintain in the population those participants that have left without vested benefits, even though those participants may have their benefits restored upon rehire. Additionally, a funding method must not anticipate the affiliation with the plan of future participants not employed in the service of the employer on the plan valuation date. However, a funding method may anticipate the affiliation with the plan of current employees who have not satisfied the participation requirements of the plan.

4. *Salary scale.* The use of a salary-scale assumption is not inappropriate merely because of the funding method with which it is used. Therefore, in determining whether actuarial assumptions are reasonable, a salary scale will not be considered to be prohibited merely because a particular funding method is being used. However, salary scales reflected in projected benefits must be the expected salary on which benefits would be based under the plan at the age when the receipt of benefits is expected to begin.

5. *Allocation of assets and liabilities.* Any initial allocation of assets among participants will be considered reasonable only if it is in proportion to related liabilities. Also, if a funding method allocates liabilities among different elements of past and future service, the allocation of liabilities must be reasonable.

6. *Treatment of ancillary benefit costs.* Ancillary benefit costs must be computed by using the same method used to compute retirement benefit costs under a plan. An ancillary benefit is a benefit that is paid as a result of a specified event that occurs not later than a participant's separation from service and that was detrimental to the participant's health. Benefits such as early retirement, Social Security supplements, or vesting of plan benefits more rapidly than required under the law are not subject to this

rule. If the plan uses insurance contracts to provide the ancillary benefits, regardless of the method used to compute retirement benefit costs, the cost of an ancillary benefit may equal the premium paid for that benefit under an insurance contract only if the ancillary benefit is provided under the contract and the benefit is guaranteed under the contract. Any benefits described in Code Section 401(h) for which a separate account is maintained are also not subject to this requirement.

7. *Anticipated benefit changes.* A funding method may not anticipate benefit changes that become effective, whether or not retroactively, in a future plan year or that become effective after the first day of a current plan year. However, a collectively bargained plan as described in Code Section 413(a) may, on a consistent basis, anticipate benefit increases scheduled to take effect during the term of the collective-bargaining agreement applicable to the plan. A plan's treatment of benefit increases scheduled in a collective-bargaining agreement is part of its funding method. Accordingly, a change in a plan's treatment of such benefit increases (for example, ignoring anticipated increases after taking them into account) is a change of funding method. [Treas. Reg. § 1.412(c)(3)-1]

**Example.** The sponsor of the plan adopts an amendment on January 1, 2000, that increases the plan formula from 20 percent of average compensation to 60 percent. This amendment is effective on January 1, 2001. The plan may not recognize amendments that increase benefits in the future; therefore this increase is not allowed to be recognized in the actuarial valuation done for the 2000 plan year.

### Q 1:46    What are the various funding methods called and how do they differ?

There are many different funding methods, including blends of funding methods. The basic methods are:

Unit Credit (also called the Accrued Benefit) Funding Method

Aggregate Funding Method

Individual Aggregate (also called Individual Spread Gain) Funding Method

Entry Age Normal Funding Method

Frozen Initial Liability Funding Method

Attained Age Normal Funding Method

Individual Level Premium Funding Method

Each funding method is differentiated by how the normal cost, past-service liability, and gains/losses are calculated. The following is a summary of how each funding method treats these items:

- *Individual and Aggregate Calculation of Normal Cost*

An individual method determines a contribution for each participant, and the total plan contribution is the sum of the individual contributions. In contrast, an aggregate method looks at the sum of the PVFB and determines a contribution based upon an average period of time to retirement.

The individual methods are Entry Age Normal, Individual Aggregate, Individual Level Premium, and Unit Credit.

The aggregate methods are Aggregate, Attained Age Normal, and Frozen Initial Liability.

> **Note.** An aggregate method may not be appropriate for a plan if the majority of benefits are due to be paid to the older employees. Since the contribution is determined based upon an average period of time to retirement for all participants, there may not be enough money at retirement to pay those older participants.

- *Past Service Liability*

A past-service liability is an unfunded accrued liability due to benefits based on service prior to plan inception. Funding methods that have a past-service liability have a smaller normal cost than methods without a past-service liability. Basically, the portion of the value of the benefits due to past service is amortized (paid for) separately from the regular annual contribution needed to pay for future benefits. The past-service liability must be paid off over a variable number of years. As a result, the methods that use a past-service liability have a minimum and maximum contribution, rather than a single-contribution obligation.

The methods that use a past-service liability are Attained Age Normal, Entry Age Normal, Frozen Initial Liability, and Unit Credit.

- *Spread Gain and Immediate Gain*

An immediate gain method specifically identifies the actuarial gain or loss each year and adjusts the unfunded accrued liability by the amount of the gain or loss. These gains and losses are amortized separately from the normal cost. The spread gain methods do not require a calculation of the gains or losses but either decrease or increase the contribution over future years as a result of any gain or loss. The immediate gain methods generally have a minimum and maximum contribution, rather than a single contribution obligation.

The immediate gain methods are Entry Age Normal, Individual Level Premium, and Unit Credit.

We will only consider the Individual Aggregate funding method in this chapter.

## Q 1:47   What is the individual aggregate funding method?

The allocation of plan assets on a per-participant basis is what makes the individual aggregate funding method unique. This funding method ensures that each participant will have the required assets available to him or her at retirement by allocating and tracking the contributions made to the plan on the participant's behalf. A common misconception is that the allocation of assets and contributions has bearing on the amount of assets an employee is entitled to when he or she leaves the plan before retirement. Participants are led to believe that all amounts allocated to them under the individual aggregate funding method belong to them, when in fact the amount that an individual is entitled to may be more or less. When a participant leaves prior to retirement, the value of the benefit at that time is based on the value of the accrued benefit, not on the participant's allocation of assets. The only time in the individual aggregate funding method that the assets allocated on a participant's behalf are equal to the value of the benefit is at retirement, assuming the employee remained in the employment of the plan sponsor until retirement.

### Q 1:48  How is the normal cost determined in the individual aggregate funding method?

To determine the normal cost in the individual aggregate funding method (also called individual spread gain), each employee is treated as having his or her own asset pool to fund the benefit, and the normal cost is spread over the working lifetime of each employee. The sum of the individual normal costs becomes the normal cost for the entire plan. In developing the normal cost, an allocation of the plan's assets to each participant must be determined. The allocation will depend on the status of the plan participant. For new entrants into the plan, the asset allocation is zero. For terminated and retired participants, the asset allocation is equal to the PVFB for each terminated and retired participant. Any remaining assets are allocated to each active participant in proportion to the prior-year allocation of assets plus the prior-year normal cost, both increased with interest for one year. Once the asset allocation is in place, the normal cost is determined by dividing the unfunded present value of each participant's projected benefit by an annuity factor equal to the present value of $1 to be paid over the working lifetime of the employee.

> **Example.** Rick is a participant in the SPS defined benefit plan. His projected benefit is $567 per month payable at retirement. He has 17 years until retirement. Using an APR of 142.854 and a preretirement interest rate of 6 percent, his projected benefit is $80,998.22 ($567 $\times$ 142.854). The present value of this amount is $30,079.86 (80,998.22 $\times$ 1.06$^{-17}$). The amortization of this amount over the next 17 years is $2,708.46.

### Q 1:49  Is the actuary allowed to change the plan's funding method?

Yes. However, a plan must generally obtain approval from the IRS to change its funding method. But if the proposed change of funding method meets the numerous criteria set forth in Revenue Procedure 2000-40, the plan may change its funding method without advance approval from the IRS. Additionally, in order to qualify for an automatic change in funding method, a plan must satisfy certain restrictions.

There are various changes allowed without IRS approval (provided certain requirements are met), some of which include:

Change of the valuation date to the first day of the plan year;

Changes applicable to takeover plans; and

Changes that occur when valuation software is updated.

Additionally, should a plan sponsor wish to change the funding method under a set of circumstances that does not fall within the automatic-approval guidelines, the plan may obtain approval directly from the IRS but must generally apply for approval prior to the end of the plan year.

### Q 1:50    What is the *funding standard account*?

The *funding standard account* (FSA) is the accounting tool used by the enrolled actuary to determine whether the plan has satisfied its minimum funding obligation under Code Section 412. This account is charged with money owed to the plan and credited with money paid to the plan. If the charges are equal to the credits, the plan will have satisfied its funding requirements for the plan year. If the charges exceed the credits, an accumulated funding deficiency will exist as of the end of the plan year, and the plan will not have met its funding obligation. Conversely, if the credits exceed the charges, the plan will have a credit balance at the end of the year, and this amount may be used as a credit to the account for the next plan year to help reduce the plan's future funding obligation. The FSA also maintains the equation of balance.

All plans subject to Code Section 412 must establish and maintain an FSA. [I.R.C. § 412(b)(1)]

The official record of the FSA for a plan year is the Schedule B to the IRS Form 5500, "Actuarial Information," which is completed and certified by the plan's enrolled actuary each plan year.

The FSA continues to apply in the year of plan termination; therefore a Schedule B is required to be attached to the Form 5500 filing for the year of termination. However, the charges and credits to the FSA are adjusted ratably to reflect the portion of the plan year from the first day of the plan year to the date of termination. [Treas. Reg. § 1.412(b)-(4)(b)]

### Q 1:51    What are some of the charges made to the FSA?

The charges to the FSA are the costs that are allocable to the plan's funding requirement for the plan year. Each charge represents a separate and distinct cost item. Depending on the funding method and the valuation date, the FSA may have as few as one charge or as many as six. The charges to the FSA include:

1.  The prior year's funding deficiency;
2.  The normal cost;
3.  Amortization charges;
4.  Interest on items 1, 2, and 3 above;
5.  Additional interest due to late quarterly contributions; and
6.  Additional funding charge.

All of these items are summed and represent the total charges for the plan year. The total charges less any credits, prior to any contribution, in the FSA represent the minimum contribution requirement for the plan year.

### Q 1:52   What are some of the credits made to the FSA?

The credits to the FSA are payments made that are allocable to the plan's funding requirement for the plan year. Credits are either actual money or credits to the plan through contributions, offsets against current funding requirements, actuarial liabilities that decrease funding requirements, or interest on the credits. The credits to the FSA are:

1. Prior-year credit balance;
2. Contributions;
3. Amortization credits;
4. Full-funding limitation credits;
5. Waived funding deficiencies; and
6. Amount resulting from a switch back from the alternative FSA to the regular FSA.

### Q 1:53   How are amortization charges and credits created?

Amortization charges and credits are the principal and interest portion of a level payment against an amortization base set up by either the plan actuary as a result of the funding method being used or due to a deferred pension contribution. Amortization bases are deferred liabilities (i.e., a charge base) or a deferred asset (i.e., a credit base). The amortization bases that would be created by the actuary based on the choice of a funding method would be any of the following:

1. The unfunded accrued liability (unfunded past-service liability);
2. The increase or decrease in the unfunded accrued liability due to a plan amendment that increases or decreases benefits;
3. The increase or decrease in the unfunded accrued liability due to an actuarial gain or loss;
4. The increase or decrease in the unfunded accrued liability due to a change in actuarial assumptions; and
5. The change over from the alternative FSA.

Amortization bases may also be created as a result of a funding waiver obtained by the employer in a preceding year. [I.R.C. §§ 412(b)(2), 412(b)(3)]

Each type of amortization base has its own period of time over which the plan amortizes that base in equal installments of principal and interest. The length of time depends on the type of base, the type of employer sponsoring the plan, and the date the base was created.

### Q 1:54   What are the charges and credits to be made to the FSA beginning in 2008?

For plans where the assets are less than the funding target, the minimum required contribution is equal to the sum of (1) the target normal cost, plus (2) the amortization of the funding shortfall.

For plans where assets (as defined under Code Section 430(f)(4)(A)) are greater than the funding target, the minimum required contribution is equal to the difference between (1) the target normal cost, less (2) the excess of the assets over the funding target.

The *funding target* is equal to the present value of all benefit liabilities accrued at the beginning of the plan year. [I.R.C. § 430(d)(1)] For at-risk plans, the funding target is determined using the additional actuarial assumptions and, if the plan has also been at-risk for two out of the four years, a loading factor. [I.R.C. § 430(i)(1)] In no event will the at-risk funding target be less than the regular funding target. There is a transition allowed for plans that have been in at-risk status for less than five years where a certain percentage of the deficiency is allowed to be added back in, when determining the funding target, based on the number of consecutive years the plan has been in at-risk status. [I.R.C. § 430(i)(5)]

The *target normal cost* is equal to the present value of the benefits accrued during the current year, including the increase in accrued benefits attributable to compensation increases. [I.R.C. § 430(b)] The target normal cost for a plan in at-risk status for a year is equal to the present value of the benefits accruing for the year using the additional actuarial assumptions plus, if the plan has been at-risk for two out of the last four years, a loading factor. [I.R.C. § 430(i)(2)] In no event will the at-risk target normal cost be less than the regular target normal cost determined without regard to the plan's at-risk status. There is a transition allowed for plans that have been in at-risk status for less than five years where a certain percentage of the deficiency is allowed to be added back in, when determining the target normal cost, based on the number of consecutive years the plan has been in at-risk status. [I.R.C. § 430(i)(5)]

The *funding shortfall* is equal to the excess (if any) of the applicable percent of the funding target over the assets (defined under Code Section 430(f)(4)(B) as the actuarial value of assets reduced by any prefunding balances and FSA carryover balance). [I.R.C. § 430(c)(4)]

The *funding target attainment percentage* (FTAP) is the value of plan assets (as defined under Code Section 430(f)(4)(B)) expressed as a percentage of the funding target (without adjustment for at-risk status). [I.R.C. § 430(d)(2)] There is a phase-in of this FTAP over three years. The FTAP is 92 percent for 2008, 94 percent for 2009, 96 percent for 2010, and 100 percent for 2011. [I.R.C. § 430(c)(5)] If a plan falls below the applicable percentage in any year, it will lose the transition relief and must determine the funding shortfall based on an FTAP of 100 percent. In addition, if plans is subject to the deficit reduction contribution (DRC) requirement in 2007, it is ineligible for this phase-in.

The *adjusted FTAP* is the regular FTAP adjusted by adding back in the value of any annuities purchased by the plan for non-highly compensated participants during the past two years. In addition, it is determined by adding in as an asset any security provided by the plan sponsor. [I.R.C. § 436(j)(2)]

*At-risk status* means that a plan's FTAP for the preceding year is less than 80 percent and the FTAP for the preceding year using the additional actuarial assumptions (but not the loading factor) is less than 70 percent. There is a phase-in to the 80 percent number where for 2008 it is lowered to 65 percent, for 2009 it is 70 percent, for 2010 it is 75 percent, and for 2011 and thereafter it is 80 percent. [I.R.C. § 430(i)(4)] Any plan with fewer than 500 participants on each day of the preceding plan year shall automatically be deemed not to be at-risk.

The term *additional actuarial assumptions* means that the actuary must assume that all employees who would be eligible to elect benefit payments during the next 10 years must be assumed to do so using the benefit form that produces the highest present value.

The *loading factor* is equal to the sum of $700 times the number of participants in the plan and 4 percent of the regular funding target for the plan year.

If there is no funding shortfall for a plan year, then in a later year any shortfall amortization bases and waiver amortization bases for all prior years are treated as fully amortized. There is no longer a full funding limit, but this funding shortfall acts as a full funding limit when it comes to fully amortizing existing bases. [I.R.C. §§ 430(c)(6), 430(e)(5)]

The *shortfall amortization base* is equal to the funding shortfall for the year, less the present value of future shortfall amortization installments (due to prior shortfall amortization bases), less the present value of waiver amortization installments from prior years. All gains and losses are considered in the shortfall amortization. [I.R.C. § 430(c)(3)]

The *shortfall amortization installment* is equal to the amount to amortize, with level payments, the shortfall amortization base for a plan year over seven years, amortized using the segment rates in effect in the year the base is established. [I.R.C. § 430(c)(3)]

The *segment rate* is equal to the sum of the first, second, and third segment rates. The first segment rate is the single interest rate determined by the Treasury Department on the basis of the corporate bond yield curve with maturity during the next five years. The second segment rate is the single interest rate determined by the Treasury Department on the basis of the corporate bond yield curve with maturity between the fifth and twentieth years. The third segment rate is the single interest rate determined by the Treasury Department on the basis of the corporate bond yield curve with maturity beyond the twentieth year. [I.R.C. § 430(h)(2)(C)] The corporate bond yield curve reflects a 24-month average of the monthly yields of investment grade corporate bonds with varying maturities that are in the top three quality levels available. [I.R.C. § 430(h)(2)(D)] If the plan is in existence in 2007, then the segment rates may be blended with the old current liability rates for a three-year phase-in (1/3 new to 2/3 old for 2008,

2/3 new to 1/3 old for 2009, 100 percent new in 2010). This phase-in is optional; a plan may elect not to use this transition rule. [I.R.C. § 430(h)(2)(G)]

The *effective interest rate* is the single interest rate that would produce the same funding target as the funding target produced using the segment rate. This rate is used for crediting interest on contribution requirement from plan year end to the date contribution is deposited and is also used to determine the pre-funding balance. [I.R.C. § 430(h)(2)(A)]

Liabilities are valued using the applicable segment rate that corresponds to expected benefit payments during that time period. [I.R.C. § 430(h)(2)(B)] The actuary must assume that benefits will be paid in the optional forms provided under the plan, based on the plan's experience. Optionally, the sponsor may elect to use the bond yield curve, without 24-month averaging, instead of the segment rate, but only for purposes of determining the required minimum contribution. Once this election is made, changing it would require Treasury approval. [I.R.C. § 430(h)(2)(D)]

If a plan has a funding shortfall for the preceding year, it will be subject to quarterly installments for the current year equal to 25 percent of the lesser of 90 percent of the current year's minimum required contribution or 100 percent of the prior year's minimum required contribution. If the employer fails to make a required installment, interest will be charged on the installment equal to the effective interest rate plus 5 percentage points for the period of the underpayment. [I.R.C. § 430(j)(3)]

The valuation date must be the first day of the plan year, except for small plans with 100 or fewer participants, which may use any day of the plan year. [I.R.C. § 430(g)(2)]

## Q 1:55    What is the *equation of balance*?

The *equation of balance* is a formula that is used to determine whether the FSA is in actuarial balance. The equation of balance is important for a plan that uses a funding method that develops an unfunded accrued liability. Generally, the unfunded accrued liability is equal to the outstanding balance of all amortization bases. However, if the plan has received contributions in amounts that have been more or less than required to maintain a zero credit balance in the FSA, and if certain other charges have been added to the FSA, these two amounts will no longer be equal. Therefore, an adjustment for the credit balance and the reconciliation account are needed for the equation to balance on both sides. A mathematical expression for the equation of balance is as follows:

Unfunded accrued liability = outstanding balance of all amortization bases

– credit balance – reconciliation account

For plans that do not maintain an unfunded accrued liability, the equation of balance is not maintained; however, the credit balance and the reconciliation account are accumulated each year.

The reconciliation account is the accumulation of charges to the FSA due to the additional funding charge, interest on late quarterly contributions, and the difference between the unamortized balance of a waived funding deficiency at the mandated interest rate and the outstanding balance at the plan's preretirement interest rate.

### Q 1:56   Are contributions required to be made more often than annually?

It depends. Single-employer plans that are less than 100 percent funded on a Retirement Protection Act of 1994 (RPA '94) current-liability basis are required to make quarterly contributions to the plan by the 15th day after the end of each quarter of the plan year. The 100 percent funded percentage threshold is determined as of the prior valuation date by dividing the actuarial value of the plan's assets by the RPA '94 current liability. [I.R.C. § 412(m)(1)-(4)]

The quarterly contribution is equal to 25 percent of the "required annual payment." The "required annual payment" is equal to the lesser of 90 percent of the amount required to be contributed to the plan under Code Section 412 for the current plan year (adjusted to the beginning of the plan year) or 100 percent of the amount required to be contributed to the plan for the preceding plan year. The amount required to be contributed for a plan year is the amount to avoid a funding deficiency as of the end of the plan year, without regard to any credit balance or funding waiver. (A funding deficiency, however, is included.) [Notice 89-52, Q&As 4, 7, 8]

If a quarterly contribution to the plan is not paid by the due date, the FSA is charged with additional interest. [I.R.C. § 412(m)(1)]

### Q 1:57   Can the funding requirement be limited to some smaller amount?

The minimum funding requirement of a benefit plan is sometimes limited by certain funding restrictions. If a plan has a full-funding limitation in effect for a plan year, the contribution otherwise calculated by the enrolled actuary may be reduced or eliminated. There are two full-funding limits that could come into play (both of which are eliminated beginning with the 2008 plan year):

1. *ERISA Full-Funding Limit*

The ERISA full-funding limitation is the excess (if any) of the plan's accrued liability plus normal cost (or entry age normal accrued liability plus entry age normal cost if the plan's funding method does not directly calculate an accrued liability) over the lesser of the fair market value of the plan's assets or the actuarial value of the plan's assets. The value of the assets is reduced by any credit balance existing on the first day of the plan year. The full-funding limitation is calculated as of the last day of the plan year. Therefore, if the valuation date is on the first day of the plan year, the ERISA full-funding limitation must be carried forward to the end of the plan year with interest at the funding interest rate. [I.R.C. § 412(c)(7); Prop. Treas. Reg. § 1.412(c)(6)-1]

**Note.** The following full-funding limit calculation deals with the current liability. The current liability is basically the present value of the accrued benefits using certain interest and mortality assumptions. (Actuarial assumptions to be used are defined following the description of each limit.)

*2. RPA '94 Minimum Full-Funding Limit*

The RPA '94 minimum full-funding limitation raises the full-funding limitation to a minimum level and overrides the ERISA full-funding limitation in the event it is less than the RPA '94 minimum full-funding limitation. The RPA '94 minimum full-funding limitation is the excess (if any) of 90 percent of the RPA '94 current liability (including the expected increase in RPA '94 current liability due to benefits accruing during the plan year) over the actuarial value of the plan's assets. The value of the assets is not reduced by any credit balance existing on the first day of the plan year. [I.R.C. § 412(c)(7)(E)]

### Q 1:58    What happens to the funding requirement if a full-funding limit applies?

If a plan is subject to either the ERISA or RPA '94 full-funding limitations and as a result the contribution requirement to the plan is reduced, a credit must be entered into the FSA to offset any charges in excess of the full-funding limitations. The full-funding credit is the excess (if any) of the amount of funding deficiency that would exist in the FSA at the end of the plan year if no contributions were made to the plan, and disregarding any credit balance, over the ERISA full-funding limitation. If the RPA '94 full-funding limitation is greater than the ERISA full-funding limitation, then the full-funding credit is calculated using the excess (if any) of the RPA '94 full-funding limitation over the amount of funding deficiency that would exist in the FSA at the end of the plan year if no contributions were made to the plan and disregarding any credit balance.

A full-funding credit will offset the funding deficiency prior to employer contributions and reduce the plan's contribution requirement. In general, if there is a credit balance in the FSA in the year a full-funding credit is in effect, the credit balance is preserved and carried forward to the end of the plan year with interest at the funding interest rate. There are other implications to the FSA depending on the type of full-funding credit.

### Q 1:59    Are there any additional funding charges that could be applicable?

Yes. For plans with more than 100 participants, the actuary will be required to calculate an additional funding charge that increases the contribution requirement for the year.

### Q 1:60    When are contributions due?

Contributions must be made to the plan's trust fund prior to the due date, including extensions thereon, for the contributing sponsor's federal tax return.

Contributions not made in time may be deductible in later plan years, but there may also be an excise tax for failure to meet minimum funding standards.

An employer must contribute enough money to the plan's trust fund to prevent an accumulated funding deficiency in the plan's FSA as of the last possible date to make contributions for the funding year. Generally, contributions can be credited to the FSA any time from the first day of the plan year up until 8½ months after the close of the plan year. The amount necessary to prevent an accumulated funding deficiency in the FSA is determined by the plan's enrolled actuary each year as part of the actuarial valuation report required under ERISA.

If an accumulated funding deficiency will exist in the plan's FSA without a contribution to the plan's trust fund, the employer must make a contribution regardless of profitability or obtain a funding waiver from the IRS to make up the contribution over the next few years.

Under Code Section 4971(a), there is a 10 percent excise tax (5 percent in the case of a multiemployer plan) on the amount of the accumulated funding deficiency under the plan. If the deficiency is not corrected before either a notice of deficiency is mailed by the Secretary of Labor or the date on which the 10 percent excise tax is imposed by the IRS, the IRS has the authority to impose a tax equal to 100 percent of the accumulated funding deficiency.

### Q 1:61   Could additional contributions be required even if the plan benefits are frozen?

An employer may be obligated to continue funding a plan after it is terminated or accrued benefits are frozen. An example of this is when the plan is under-funded (i.e., there are insufficient assets to meet future benefit obligations).

### Q 1:62   Is the amount deductible different from the amount that is required to be contributed to the plan?

It could be. In general, an employer can deduct contributions made to a defined benefit plan to the extent the contributions are equal to an amount no greater than one of the following limits:

1. The amount necessary to satisfy the minimum funding requirements under Code Section 412(a), if such amount is greater than item #2 or #3 below;

2. The amount necessary to provide any unfunded past and current service credits for all employees determined as a level amount, or a level percentage of compensation, over the remaining future service of each employee. In the event that 50 percent of the unfunded cost is attributable to any three employees, the unfunded cost for such employees must be distributed over at least five years; or

3. The amount of the normal cost for the plan year, plus the amount necessary to fully amortize the unfunded accrued liability in equal annual payments over 10 years.

The above amounts are subject to the full-funding limitation for the plan year determined under Code Section 412. [I.R.C. §§ 404(a)(1)(A)(i), 404(a)(1)(A)(ii), 404(a)(1)(A)(iii)]

*Rules for Limit 1.* The amount required to satisfy the minimum FSA is increased by any contributions made to satisfy the minimum FSA in the prior plan year, but were not deducted in the prior tax year solely because they were contributed to the plan's assets after the time allowed for the employer to obtain a deduction. Such contributions are known as "includible employer contributions." [Treas. Reg. § 1.404(a)-14(e)(1)(ii)]

*Rules for Limit 2.* This amount is the level amount or level percentage of compensation to fund the benefits under the aggregate, individual aggregate, or individual level premium funding methods. [Examination Guidelines for I.R.C. § 404, 1.2.1.2(1)(a)] This limit does not otherwise reduce the amount deductible under Limit 1 above (i.e., you can use less than five future years in determining the cost and it will still be deductible under Limit 1).

*Rules for Limit 3.* The normal cost plus the amount necessary to amortize the unfunded accrued liability is equal to the normal cost for the plan year plus the sum of the "limit adjustments." All amortization bases established for spread-gain funding methods amortize their bases over 10 years for deduction purposes.

The rules regarding when deposits need to be made to be deductible are the same as for defined contribution plans, that is, contributions may be deducted for a taxable year if the contribution is deposited to the plan's assets no later than the due date for filing the tax return for such taxable year (including extensions thereof). [I.R.C. § 404(a)(6)] Although the deposit may be timely for deduction purposes, it may not be timely for satisfying minimum funding standards. Conversely, a deposit may be timely for satisfying minimum funding standards and may not be timely for deduction purposes.

### Q 1:63   Are there any special deduction limits?

Yes. Subject to certain rules, a plan may, regardless of the full-funding limitations set forth above, deduct the amount required to achieve 100 percent funding using the RPA '94 current liability. This limit is increased to 150 percent of current liability for the 2006 and 2007 plan years. However, liabilities attributable to increases in benefits for highly compensated participants due to amendments within the past two years are not taken into account in determining this limit.

### Q 1:64   Are there any rules applicable to deductions when the employer sponsors both a defined benefit and a defined contribution plan?

Yes. If amounts contributed to one or more defined contribution plans and one or more defined benefit plans would otherwise be deductible except for the fact that the employer sponsors one or more defined contribution plans and one or more defined benefit plans, the total amount deductible in a taxable year under such plans may not exceed the greater of:

1. 25 percent of the compensation otherwise paid or accrued during the taxable year to the beneficiaries under such plans; or

2. The amount of contributions made to or under the defined benefit plans to the extent such contributions do not exceed the amount of employer contributions necessary to satisfy the minimum funding standard provided by Code Section 412 with respect to any such defined benefit plans for the plan year that ends with or within such taxable year (or any prior plan year).

However, the above limits do *not* apply if no employee is a beneficiary under more than one of the plans. [I.R.C. § 404(a)(7)(C)]

If the employer sponsors a 401(k) plan, such contributions made pursuant to the employee's deferral election are not counted in the deduction limitation. In other words, an employer can make a contribution to a defined benefit plan that is greater than 25 percent of compensation and can also make a deferral to a 401(k) plan.

For plan years beginning after December 31, 2005, the combined plan deduction limit of Code Section 404(a)(7) does not apply to the extent employer contributions to a defined contribution plan do not exceed 6 percent of participant compensation. [PPA § 803(a)] All contributions made to multi-employer (union) plans are ignored for purposes of Code Section 404(a)(7). [PPA § 803(b)]

# PBGC

### Q 1:65   What is the *Pension Benefit Guaranty Corporation* (PBGC)?

ERISA established the *Pension Benefit Guaranty Corporation* (PBGC) as a corporate entity within the Department of Labor (DOL). The purpose of the PBGC is to encourage the continuation and maintenance of voluntary private pension plans for the benefit of their participants, to provide for the timely and uninterrupted payment of pension benefits to participants and beneficiaries, and to maintain premiums established by the PBGC at the lowest level consistent with carrying out its obligations. The PBGC achieves these objectives by providing insurance coverage to defined benefit pension plans that meet certain criteria. In the event a plan is unable to provide the payment of benefits when due, the PBGC may take over the assets and liabilities of a plan to assure continued payment of benefits.

### Q 1:66   What types of plans are covered by the PBGC?

Only defined benefit pension plans that are qualified under Code Section 401(a) are covered by the PBGC's plan termination insurance program. However, certain defined benefit pension plans are exempted from coverage if they meet certain requirements. The two main types of plan that are exempt are:

1. A plan that benefits only "substantial owners," where a substantial owner is a sole proprietor or partner who owns 10 percent or more of the capital or profit interest in a business entity or, in the case of a corporation, a person who owns 10 percent or more of the voting stock or total stock of the corporation; and

2. A plan established and maintained by a professional service employer that did not have, at any time since the enactment of ERISA, more than 25 active participants.

A professional service employer is a sole proprietorship, partnership, or corporation that is owned or controlled by professional individuals. A professional service individual includes, but is not limited to, physicians, dentists, chiropractors, osteopaths, optometrists, other licensed practitioners of the healing arts, attorneys at law, public accountants, engineers, architects, draftsmen, actuaries, psychologists, scientists, and performing artists. [ERISA § 4021(c)(2)]

> **Example.** The Home Builders R Us defined benefit plan is wholly owned by Neff. He has two employees, his two children, Davey and Keegan, ages 25 and 30. Unfortunately, this plan is not exempt from coverage by the PBGC due to the exemption applicable to plans maintained by substantial owners. ERISA Section 4021(b)(9), which contains the exemption for plans that benefit only substantial owners, references ERISA Section 4022(b)(5) for the definition of substantial owner, which in turn references Code Section 1563(e) for attribution rules. And if the children don't have direct ownership exceeding 50 percent, then no ownership is attributed to them from their parents. Therefore, this is not a plan benefiting only substantial owners.

### Q 1:67 What is required of a plan once it is considered covered by the PBGC?

Once covered, the plan administrator must be prepared to pay premiums to the PBGC and comply with the notice and termination requirements imposed.

### Q 1:68 How are premiums to the PBGC calculated?

The amount of premium is based on the number of plan participants on the premium payment date. If the plan is not a multiemployer plan and if it has any unfunded vested benefits, the plan is subject to a variable-rate premium in addition to a flat-rate premium.

All plans, other than multiemployer plans, pay $19 per participant (this is $30 per participant beginning with the 2006 payment year). [PBGC Reg. § 4006.3(a)] The participant count is determined as of the last day of the preceding plan year and includes participants that are actively earning benefits under the plan, nonvested participants, retirees and their beneficiaries collecting benefits, and terminated participants entitled to future benefits. [PBGC Reg. § 4006.2]

The variable-rate premium is $9 for each $1,000 of unfunded vested benefits. Beginning with the 2007 premium payment year, for employers with 25 or fewer employees, the per-participant variable-rate premium may not be more than $5 multiplied by the number of plan participants in the plan at the beginning of the preceding year. Thus the maximum premium is equal to the number of participants squared times $5. For five participants, the cap is equal to $5^2 \times \$5 = \$125$. [PPA § 405]

The value of the vested benefits is determined as of the last day of the plan year that precedes the premium payment year based on the plan's provisions and population as of that date. There are two methods a plan may use for calculating the value of the unfunded vested benefits: the general rule or the alternative method. The amount of unfunded vested benefits calculated will vary depending on the method used.

A plan will not be required to pay the variable-rate portion of the premium if it meets one of the following exceptions:

*The plan has no vested participants.* A plan of any size with no vested participants as of the last day of the plan year preceding the premium payment year is exempt from the variable-rate portion of the premium as long as the plan administrator certifies to this fact.

*The plan is a plan described in Code Section 412(i).* A fully insured plan under Code Section 412(i) is exempt from the variable-rate portion of the premium as long as it is a Code Section 412(i) plan for the full plan year that precedes the premium payment year.

*Fully funded small plans.* A plan that has fewer than 500 participants may have the enrolled actuary certify (without disclosure of the computations) that the plan has no unfunded vested benefits when valued at the required interest rate. Such fully funded small plans are exempt from the variable-rate portion of the premium.

*Plans terminating in standard termination.* If the plan has filed a Notice of Intent to Terminate (NOIT) in a standard termination that has a proposed date of termination that is on or before the last day of the plan year that precedes the premium payment year, the plan administrator may certify that this requirement is met, and the plan will be exempt from the variable-rate portion of the premium. If the plan is unable to distribute benefits in a standard termination, this exemption will be revoked and the variable-rate premium owed will be due.

*Plans at the full funding limit.* A plan of any size may be exempt from the variable rate portion of the premium if, on or before the earlier of the due date for payment of the variable-rate portion of the premium or the date that portion is paid, the plan's contributing sponsor or contributing sponsors made contributions to the plan for the plan year preceding the premium payment year in an amount not less than the full funding limitation for such preceding plan year. In order for a plan to qualify for this exemption, an enrolled actuary must certify that the plan has met this requirement. [PBGC Reg. § 4006.5(a)]

### Q 1:69   When are premiums required to be paid?

For plans with fewer than 500 participants, the flat-rate and variable-rate premiums must be paid by the 15th day of the tenth full calendar month following the month in which the plan year began.

For plans with more than 500 participants, the flat-rate premium must be paid by the last day of the second full calendar month following the close of the preceding plan year. For such plans, the variable-rate premium must be paid by the 15th day of the tenth full calendar month following the month in which the plan year began.

If the filing deadline falls on a Saturday, Sunday, or federal holiday, then the deadline is extended until the next day that is not a Saturday, Sunday, or federal holiday. However, if the filing is late, interest and penalty charges are calculated including the Saturday, Sunday, or federal holiday.

The required due date for PBGC premiums for new or newly covered plans is the same regardless of the number of participants in the plan. The flat-rate and variable-rate premiums are due on or before the later of:

1. The 15th day of the tenth full calendar month following the month in which the plan year began or, if later, in which the plan became effective for benefit accruals for future service;
2. 90 days after the date of the plan's adoption; or
3. 90 days after the date on which the plan became covered by Title IV of ERISA. 3. [PBGC Reg. § 4007.11(c)]

**Example.** Home Builders R Us adopted its defined benefit plan on November 30, 1999. The first plan year began on January 1, 1999 and ended on December 31, 1999. Benefit accruals for future service began on January 1, 1999. What is the due date for the first premium payment? What is the due date for the year 2000 premium payment?

The first premium due date would be February 28, 2000 (i.e., 90 days after the plan's adoption). The due date for the year 2000 premium payment would be October 16, 2000, since October 15, 2000 was a Sunday.

### Q 1:70   What forms are required to be filed with the PBGC?

The flat-rate portion of the premium is paid with PBGC Form 1, for plans with 500 or more participants. PBGC Form 1ES is filed to pay the flat-rate portion of the premium if the plan sponsor has not yet determined the participant count or the value of the unfunded vested benefits by the due date for the flat-rate premium. PBGC Form Schedule A is used to determine the amount of the variable-rate premium, if any. If a plan is exempt from paying the variable-rate premium, then the plan files PBGC Form 1EZ.

Most plans are now required to submit these forms electronically through the PBGC's new "My Plan Administration Account" (My PAA).

### Q 1:71   Is a plan that is covered by the PBGC required to notify participants if the plan is underfunded?

Yes. If a defined benefit plan is required to pay a variable-rate premium for a year, subject to an exemption for certain plans with minimum funded ratios, the plan sponsor must provide a notice to plan participants and beneficiaries that informs them of the funded status of the plan and the limits on the PBGC's guarantee of benefits should the plan terminate while underfunded. [ERISA § 4011(a)]

In general, if a plan was not subject to the additional funding charge under Code Section 412(l) or ERISA Section 302(d) for the current or prior plan year, regardless of whether or not it has more than 100 participants, it will be exempt from the requirement to provide the participant notice in a plan year for which a variable-rate premium was paid.

In general, the additional funding charge is not applicable if the funded current liability percentage for such year is 90 percent or more.

Plans with fewer than 100 participants may make a determination as to whether or not the plan is exempt from the additional funding charge by using the OBRA '87 current liability on IRS Form Schedule B as of the beginning of the plan year.

Finally, newly covered plans will be exempt from the notice for the first premium payment year. [PBGC Reg. §§ 4011.4(a), 4011.4(b)]

The PBGC can assess a penalty of up to $1,100 per day for failure to provide the participant notice for each day that the failure continues. [PBGC Reg. § 4011.3(c)]

The PBGC has outlined in its regulations what must be contained in the notice to comply with the requirement; however, given the huge penalties that may be imposed, it may be best to use the model notice, which is found in the regulations, to meet the notice requirement.

The plan administrator must provide the notice no later than 11½ months after the end of the plan year. Generally, this date is two months after the date for filing the annual report for the plan (including extensions). [PBGC Reg. § 4011.8]

### Q 1:72   Must an employer notify the PBGC of certain events?

Yes. A reportable event is an occurrence of an event that may impact a PBGC-covered plan's ability to pay benefits or that the plan is about to terminate. Some events must be reported prior to the occurrence of the event, while others must be reported after. Generally, unless a waiver is available or certain conditions are met, the event must be reported on PBGC Form 10 for a post-event notice and PBGC Form 10-Advance for an advance notice.

## Plan Termination

### Q 1:73　Can a defined benefit plan be terminated?

Yes. In fact, in the defined benefit plan market, it is often said that you do not understand how a defined benefit plan works until you understand the termination of a plan. Defined benefit plans are designed to provide benefits to covered participants. Upon termination, all of the participants and beneficiaries are paid out their vested accrued benefits. This settlement of all benefits provides a thorough look at all features of the plan. An employer establishes a qualified retirement plan with the intention of maintaining the plan on a permanent basis. However, the law recognizes that all plans cannot last forever because the objectives and financial circumstances of employers change.

The plan document governs the provisions for terminating a plan. Unlike a defined contribution plan termination, the liquidation process for terminating a defined benefit plan has many complex features. The employer has promised that an accrued benefit will be paid, and, at plan termination, all the accrued benefits must be funded. If there is a surplus of assets, there are several rules that apply to handling the surplus. If there is a deficiency, then, in general, the employer must make up the difference. The various regulatory agencies each has its own jurisdiction over certain provisions of the plan termination.

### Q 1:74　Is it necessary to obtain a determination letter to approve the plan's termination?

No. However, with rare exceptions, obtaining a favorable determination letter for the plan termination is the best approach. A plan termination is a fulfillment of the employer's promise to the employees up until the termination date. If there are operational or document errors that are found upon an audit after all money has been distributed, the favorable tax status of the rollovers or the distributions can be jeopardized.

Ultimately, if a determination letter is not requested, the IRS will be notified of a termination, using the IRS Form 5500 series reports, indicating the return is a final return. The last actuarial report to be filed (Form 5500 Schedule B, Actuarial Information) is for the plan year in which the plan is terminated. A Schedule B is not required for years following the year of termination; however, this may not be true if the benefits are not paid out on a timely basis.

Several items should be carefully reviewed before filing for a favorable determination letter. A self-audit using the audit guidelines is essential. Reviewing operational compliance and form compliance also is important.

The decision whether or not to file for a favorable determination letter should be documented in the board of directors' resolution.

The method of handling surplus assets should be determined in advance. If additional distribution options are desired, such as lump sums, amendments should be put in place first and then notices sent to employees.

The only form that is different from that required to file for a determination letter upon termination for a defined contribution plan is Form 6088, Distributable Benefits from Employee Pension Plans. This form is required to show how much is distributable to each participant, and how that amount was calculated.

### Q 1:75  Is it necessary to notify participants of a plan's termination?

Yes. Whenever a pension plan, including a defined benefit plan, is amended to significantly reduce the rate of future benefit accruals, an ERISA Section 204(h) notice must be presented to all plan participants, beneficiaries, alternate payees under a Qualified Domestic Relations Orders (QDRO), and labor organizations at least 15 days (45 days for certain plans with more than 100 participants) prior to the effective date for the cessation of benefit accruals. [Treas. Reg. § 1.411(d)-6, Q&A 2] This notice is also required to be provided for plan terminations since future benefit accruals will end.

### Q 1:76  What steps must be taken to terminate a PBGC-covered defined benefit plan?

The following steps must be taken in order to successfully proceed with the termination of a single-employer plan in a standard termination:

1. Select a proposed termination date.
2. Issue the NOIT at least 60 days, and no more than 90 days, prior to proposed termination date.
3. Issue Notice of Plan Benefits on or before filing of PBGC Form 500.
4. File PBGC Form 500, PBGC Schedule EA-S, and PBGC Schedule REP-S on or before the 180th day after the proposed termination date.
5. Issue Notice of Annuity Information, if applicable, no later than 45 days prior to distribution date.
6. Distribute plan assets before the later of (1) 180 days after expiration of PBGC 60-day review period, or (2) 120 days after receipt of favorable DL from the IRS.
7. Follow PBGC rules for missing participants, if any.
8. Issue Notice of Annuity Contract to participants receiving benefits in the form of an annuity no later than 30 days after all plan benefits are distributed.
9. File PBGC Form 501, Post-Distribution Certification, no later than 30 days after all plan benefits are distributed.

The PBGC will notify the plan administrator in writing of the date that it received the standard termination notice. If the PBGC does not issue a notice of noncompliance during its 60-day review period, the plan administrator can proceed with the distributions and close out of the plan. The 60-day review period begins on the date the PBGC receives the complete standard termination notice. The PBGC will notify the plan sponsor, in writing, of the date that the 60-day review period begins. [PBGC Reg. § 4041.26]

Assuming the timeliest scenario, the soonest that benefits can be distributed once the termination process has begun in a standard termination filing with the PBGC is about 120 days. In a standard termination, there are at least four steps before distributions can be made from the trust: (1) Distribute the NOIT at least 60 days before the termination date; (2) distribute the Notice of Plan Benefits before the filing of the PBGC Form 500; (3) mail to the PBGC the Form 500 the day after the termination date; and (4) wait for the 60-day review period to expire after they have received the Form 500. If all goes well, the minimum waiting period will be just a few days more than 120 days, or 4 months.

The plan may be insufficient to meet projected liabilities when compared to projected assets and still be allowed to terminate in a standard termination if either the plan sponsor agrees to make a commitment to contribute any additional funds necessary or a majority owner agrees to forgo benefits until all other liabilities are met. A majority owner is anyone that owns at least 50 percent of the company.

**Example.** The Home Builders R Us defined benefit plan is terminating. Neff brought on two other owners in the prior year, and they each own 33⅓ percent of the company. The plan assets are insufficient to meet the benefit liabilities, but in order to proceed with a standard termination, Neff is willing to be the last in line to receive his benefit to the extent funded. However, Neff is no longer a majority owner and is not allowed to forgo receipt of his benefits. [PBGC Reg. § 4041.2]

### Q 1:77 What steps must be taken to terminate a PBGC-covered plan that does not have sufficient assets to pay all liabilities?

A plan that does not have sufficient assets to meet all plan benefit liabilities must file under the PBGC regulations for a distress termination. [PBGC Reg. § 4041.41] The plan sponsor or the PBGC could initiate the termination.

In order to terminate in a distress termination, the PBGC must determine that each contributing sponsor and each member of each sponsor's controlled group has substantial business hardship. There are specific regulations as to what qualifies as a substantial business hardship.

### Q 1:78 What options are available to a plan administrator when there are surplus assets in the plan?

The plan document must define how surplus assets (the excess, if any, of plan assets over liabilities) are treated in the event of a plan termination. Surplus assets are used either to increase benefits to plan participants or are reverted to the employer. If the language in the plan document allowing for a reversion to the employer has not been in the document for five years since the plan effective date, then the surplus assets must be allocated to participants in a nondiscriminatory manner. [Rev. Rul. 80-229, 1980-2 C.B. 133] If the plan permits surplus assets to revert to the employer, there is a 50 percent excise tax on the reversion.

The excise tax may be reduced to 20 percent if either the plan increases benefits prior to the reversion or the employer maintains a qualified replacement plan.

If the employer is going to reallocate the surplus to the participants, there are an infinite number of allocation methods; however, most of the considerations that are made in initial plan design must be made on the reallocation of the surplus assets. The provisions of the nondiscrimination regulations impact the design considerably. The past-service benefit accruals must be looked at carefully. In addition, maximum benefit limitations under Code Section 415, either as a percentage of pay or as a dollar amount, can become a problem. [I.R.C. § 4980(d)(1)]

### Q 1:79   What are the requirements to be considered a qualified replacement plan?

A qualified replacement plan is a qualified plan established or maintained by the employer following the termination of a defined benefit plan that meets these three requirements:

1. At least 95 percent of the active participants in the terminated plan who remain as employees of the employer after the termination are active participants in the replacement plan.
2. A direct transfer is made from the terminated plan to the replacement plan before any employer reversion. This transfer is an amount equal to the excess (if any) of 25 percent of the maximum amount the employer could receive as a reversion minus the present value of benefit increases granted to participants in the terminated defined benefit plan.
3. In the case of a defined contribution qualified replacement plan, the amount transferred is either:
   - Allocated to the accounts of plan participants in the year the transfer occurs; or
   - Credited to a suspense account and allocated over a period not to exceed seven years. [I.R.C. § 4980(d)(2)]

**Example.** The Sierra Pension Services, Inc. defined benefit plan terminates December 31, 2006. It has always had a provision allowing for a reversion of excess assets to the employer. The projected termination liabilities are $200,000 and there are assets of $240,000. If a qualified replacement plan is installed, at least 95 percent of the active participants in the terminated plan who remain as employees of the employer must be covered. Since all remain, the plan must cover all three employees. If $10,000 (25% of $40,000) is transferred to a qualified replacement plan, he reduces the excise tax to 20 percent. This would allow the plan to revert $30,000 and pay only a 20 percent excise tax on that amount, or $6,000 ($30,000 × .20).

### Q 1:80   How may benefits be increased to use up surplus assets?

The other alternative to the qualified replacement plan is that the defined benefit plan in conjunction with the termination may provide benefit increases to participants. These increases must have an aggregate present value not less than 20 percent of the maximum reversion. [I.R.C. § 4980(d)(3)] In addition, these increases must take effect immediately on the termination date.

The increase should be a pro rata increase, with each participant's accrued benefit increasing in the same proportion as the present value of his or her accrued benefit bears to the aggregate present value of accrued benefits of all participants.

The allocation of the surplus assets must not discriminate in favor of highly compensated employees and may not cause the benefits to exceed the maximum benefit provisions of Code Section 415. [I.R.C. § 4980(d)(4)(A)]

If there are surplus assets as of the date of termination, the plan will not be considered discriminatory if such excess is applied to increase benefits in a nondiscriminatory manner. One method of applying the assets to increase benefits in a nondiscriminatory manner is to amend the plan to provide a new benefit structure, such that (1) the benefit structure would not be discriminatory if the plan were not terminated and (2) the present value of the revised accrued benefits (whether or not nonforfeitable) as of the date of termination equals the value of plan assets, and to distribute assets equal to the present value of the revised accrued benefits. The new benefit structure must satisfy other requirements of the law such as Code Sections 411(d)(6) and 415.

### Q 1:81 What are the rules if a defined benefit plan that is not covered by the PBGC and has insufficient assets terminates?

A defined benefit plan that is *not* subject to PBGC coverage can terminate and pay out benefits even though there are insufficient assets to pay all calculated benefits. Code Section 411(d)(3) allows a plan to terminate and pay benefits "to the extent funded." When a plan that is not covered by PBGC terminates with insufficient assets, assets must be allocated in accordance with the priority categories established under ERISA Section 4044. [ERISA § 403(d)(1)] In addition, in order to prevent discrimination, the assets should be allocated so that the non-highly compensated employees receive from the plan at least the same proportion of the present value of their accrued benefits as highly compensated employees. [Rev. Rul. 80-229, 1980-2 C.B. 133]

# Chapter 2

# Characteristics of a Defined
# Benefit Plan

Unique planning opportunities make defined benefit pension plans attractive to both large and small closely held companies. Defined benefit pension plans, which provide monthly benefits at retirement based on a benefit formula in the plan rather than on accumulations in an account, offer employers a vehicle for serving a number of human resources needs. Owners of small companies often find defined benefit pension plans to be the best vehicle for accumulating funds for retirement. This chapter provides an overview of these plans and their funding requirements.

## General Characteristics and Qualifications of Qualified Plans

### Q 2:1  Why do employers adopt qualified plans?

A qualified plan has a number of unique tax advantages that make it attractive to companies, business owners, and employees (see Q 2:2). A defined benefit pension plan is often attractive to older owners of small businesses who want to accumulate significant sums for retirement in a relatively short period of time. These pension plans also serve a number of nontax purposes (see Q 2:3).

### Q 2:2   What are the tax advantages associated with a qualified plan?

A qualified plan provides the following tax advantages:

1. Employer contributions are deductible. [I.R.C. § 404]
2. Trust earnings are tax exempt. [I.R.C. §§ 401, 501]
3. Participants are not taxed when contributions are made or benefits become vested; taxation occurs only when benefits are received. [I.R.C. § 402]
4. Further tax deferral may be available by rolling over benefits to an individual retirement account (IRA). [I.R.C. § 402(c)]

### Q 2:3   What nontax reasons might lead an employer to select a defined benefit pension plan?

An employer might decide to adopt a defined benefit pension plan for a variety of reasons. A defined benefit plan is probably the best means of securing income for retirement. It may attract employees (although younger employees are probably more attracted by defined contribution plans, such as 401(k) plans), induce key employees to continue working, and reduce turnover. A defined benefit pension plan is the best means for an older business owner to accumulate funds for retirement. Defined benefit plans can reward long-service employees by providing income replacement at retirement.

### Q 2:4   What are the advantages to employees of having a defined benefit plan as part of their retirement benefits?

Until recently, many employees covered by a defined contribution plan believed they were accumulating abundant retirement resources due to extraordinary market returns and would be able to retire earlier than they previously anticipated. However, with the recent downturn in the financial markets and some highly publicized retirement plan losses, employees have become less confident in their ability to manage their investments. Therefore, employees are increasingly searching for retirement security. In addition, improved mortality rates have people concerned that they can outlive their retirement nest eggs.

Defined benefit plans can solve both problems, providing employees with the security of knowing that their benefits cannot be reduced due to market fluctuations and with the additional security of knowing that they will continue to receive a stream of payments no matter how long they live.

Finally, most employers provide 100 percent of the funding in a defined benefit plan, requiring no employee contributions. This allows employees to save on their own to supplement the retirement benefits provided by their employers.

### Q 2:5 What is the difference between a pension plan and a profit-sharing plan?

A pension plan must be funded each year as required to meet the minimum-funding standards. Profit-sharing plans have discretionary funding; an employer can decide from year to year whether to put money into the plan.

### Q 2:6 What is the difference between a defined contribution plan and a defined benefit plan?

A defined contribution plan is an individual account plan. [I.R.C. § 414(i)] Annual contributions to a participant's account are based on the formula contained in the plan. Retirement benefits are based on the value of the accumulation in the account. Investment performance directly affects the value of retirement benefits. The employer's commitment is to make annual contributions, not to provide benefits. The Pension Benefit Guaranty Corporation (PBGC) does not guarantee benefits in a defined contribution plan.

> **Example 1.** DC Co. adopts a money purchase pension plan (a type of defined contribution plan) that requires an annual contribution, on behalf of each eligible employee, of 10 percent of compensation. Debbie, an employee of DC Co., receives annual compensation of $50,000. DC Co. will contribute $5,000 (10 percent of $50,000) to Debbie's account in the plan. When Debbie retires, the amount in her account, increased by investment income and gains, and decreased by investment losses, will be available to provide retirement benefits.

A defined benefit pension plan is not an individual account plan. It is a plan that promises to pay a benefit at retirement. [I.R.C. § 414(j)] Retirement benefits must be definitely determinable. The benefit payable to an employee is based on a formula set forth in the plan that often takes into consideration service and compensation. The annual contribution is determined by an enrolled actuary. In general, benefits are insured by the PBGC in the event of plan termination. The commitment of the employer is to satisfy funding requirements to provide retirement benefits. If the plan is fully funded, no contributions may be required. The employee does not bear investment risk.

> **Example 2.** DB Co. adopts a defined benefit pension plan that provides an annual benefit to eligible employees of 50 percent of compensation. Debbie, an employee of DB Co., receives annual compensation of $50,000. DB Co. will contribute to the plan the amount necessary to fund the anticipated benefit as determined by the plan's actuary. When Debbie retires, she will receive a benefit equal to $25,000 per year for life (50 percent of $50,000). Debbie does not have an account under the plan; her benefit is provided regardless of the investment gains or losses of the plan.

The following table identifies the primary differences between defined contribution and defined benefit pension plans:

| | *Defined Contribution Plan* | *Defined Benefit Plan* |
|---|---|---|
| Funding | Based on formula in plan; may be discretionary (profit-sharing plan). | Based on actuarial determination of amounts needed to fund anticipated retirement benefits. |
| Benefits at retirement | Accumulation in account balance (sum of contributions, forfeitures, and investment return) provides benefit. | Based on formula in plan. |
| Benefit insurance | No PBGC protection. | Benefits insured by PBGC if plan terminated with insufficient assets. There are exceptions to coverage for professional employers with fewer than 25 participants and for owner-only plans (see chapter 24). |
| Maximum contribution | The lesser of $40,000, as indexed, or 100 percent of compensation. The deduction is limited to 25 percent of total eligible compensation. | The amount necessary to fund a benefit of the lesser of $160,000, as indexed, or 100 percent of compensation. There is no mandated dollar limitation to the amount that can be contributed. |
| Employer commitment | Annual funding obligation (unless profit-sharing plan); no guarantee of benefit at retirement. | Benefit obligation; funding may not be required if assets are sufficient to meet benefit obligations. |
| Employee contributions | Pre-tax employee contributions permitted in a 401(k) plan; after-tax contributions may be permitted in the plan. These contributions increase the amount in the employee's account. | Pre-tax employee contributions not permitted; after-tax contributions may be required for annual accrual of benefits. Rarely do employee contributions create an account in the plan. |
| Preretirement benefits | The value of the participant's account. | The present value of the accrued benefit based on the plan's formula; some plans provide early retirement subsidies. |
| Payment options | Determined by plan. Qualified joint and survivor annuities (QJSAs) and qualified preretirement survivor annuities (QPSAs) required except in certain profit-sharing plans. Lump-sum distributions often permitted. | Determined by plan. QJSA and QPSA required. Lump-sum distributions occasionally permitted. |

## Q 2:7    Why would an employer choose a defined benefit plan over another type of qualified plan?

Many larger companies adopt defined benefit pension plans to attract and retain employees or provide long-term benefits to career employees. Alternatively, defined benefit plans can be structured to encourage people to retire early, providing the company with an attractive alternative to mandatory layoff. Smaller companies adopt defined benefit plans to fund retirement needs later in the business or life cycle of the owner. Defined benefit plans often offer the largest deductions for funding retirement and can far exceed the $40,000 (as indexed)/100 percent of compensation/25 percent of compensation deduction limitations applicable to each individual in a defined contribution plan.

## Q 2:8    Is a *target benefit plan* a defined benefit plan?

No. A *target benefit plan* is a defined contribution plan that looks like a defined benefit plan. The amount of contributions to a participant's account is based on a defined benefit plan formula. Unlike the benefit in a defined benefit plan, the benefit in a target benefit plan is not a guaranteed benefit, but merely a target benefit. The actual benefit at retirement is based on accumulations in the participant's account. This plan design has great advantages for both the employer and employees, because the employer can set a benefit expectation for the employees by funding for a benefit that is representative of the employer's income objectives and the employees enjoy the convenience and ease of an account balance to review each year (see chapter 4).

## Q 2:9    What is a *cash balance plan*?

A *cash balance plan* is a defined benefit plan that looks like a defined contribution plan. The ultimate benefit payable is based on the value of a hypothetical account balance. Each year, a hypothetical account is credited with a hypothetical contribution (e.g., 3 percent of compensation), and the total accumulation is credited with a hypothetical interest rate.

The allocations under a cash balance plan are not limited to the $40,000 (as indexed) or deduction limitations generally applicable to defined contribution plans. The interest credited may be a fixed rate of interest or a formula-based rate of interest. A cash balance plan works like a defined contribution plan with a guarantee of interest by the employer (see chapters 4 and 13).

## Q 2:10    What is a *floor-offset plan*?

A *floor-offset plan* is a defined benefit plan that provides a base benefit for all participants offset by a benefit from another plan. A typical design would be a base benefit of 40 percent of average compensation offset by the benefit provided by the account balance for a defined contribution plan that provides contributions each year of 5 percent of compensation.

If the account balance in the defined contribution plan grows beyond the value of the 40 percent base benefit that would otherwise be provided under the defined benefit plan, the participant receives the greater benefit, that is, the benefit that can be provided with the account balance in the defined contribution plan. If the defined contribution plan account provides for a benefit of less than 40 percent of average annual compensation, the defined benefit plan provides a supplemental benefit so that the total benefit provided under both plans equals the 40 percent base benefit.

This type of program provides the best of both worlds to an employer's population: younger employees receive the accumulation of a defined contribution plan and have the guarantee of a minimum amount, and older employees obtain a guaranteed benefit and greater contributions (see chapter 4).

### Q 2:11   What costs should a company anticipate in establishing and maintaining a defined benefit pension plan?

In addition to the normal costs associated with funding the plan, the employer will incur some costs for professional fees. These may include any of the following:

- Legal fees to draft the plan, trust, and ancillary documents or to resolve legal issues relating to plan administration;
- Actuarial fees to determine the costs of adequately funding the plan;
- Administrative fees for handling the reporting and administrative aspects of the plan; or
- Accounting fees for financial reports and trust accounting.

### Q 2:12   What types of defined benefit pension plans are available?

There are a number of types of defined benefit plans available. The types are distinguished by the formula used to determine benefits at retirement (see chapter 11). Typical plan types include the following:

- *Fixed benefit.* The retirement benefit for each participant is determined as a fixed percentage of compensation.

**Example 1.** Each participant will receive a benefit at normal retirement equal to 40 percent of average compensation.

- *Flat benefit.* The retirement benefit for each participant is determined as a flat dollar amount.

**Example 2.** Each participant will receive a benefit at normal retirement equal to $1,000 per month.

- *Unit benefit.* The retirement benefit for each participant is determined as a fixed percentage of pay or flat dollar amount for each year of service.

**Example 3.** Each participant will receive a benefit at retirement equal to 2 percent of average compensation multiplied by years of service with the employer.

- *Cash balance.* The retirement benefit for each participant is determined by converting a hypothetical cash balance account to an annuity.

**Example 4.** Each participant will be credited with 2 percent of compensation for each year of participation. The hypothetical account will also be credited with 5 percent interest each year. The value of this hypothetical account will be converted to an annuity at retirement.

### Q 2:13   Can a plan be designed to meet specific objectives of the employer?

Yes. Often an employer considers creating a defined benefit plan for employees for several reasons:

- To provide meaningful benefits to long-service employees
- To provide a stable source of income in retirement years
- To allow for workforce transition
- To attract and retain employees
- To provide catch-up benefits for long-service employees

An employer develops a plan design to meet its specific objectives. Plan design involves developing an appropriate benefit formula and reviewing a number of other options (see Q 2:14). Chapter 3 provides details of the considerations involved in designing a successful plan.

### Q 2:14   What issues beyond basic formula design does an employer have to resolve when adopting a plan?

An employer has a number of choices to make while developing a plan to meet its needs and the needs of its employees. An employer should also consider the following:

1. *Eligibility.* What should be the terms and conditions of participation in the plan? Should participation be limited to a certain class of employees?
2. *Funding.* Should employees share the cost of funding the plan?
3. *Vesting.* How quickly should employees vest in their benefits? Is cliff vesting preferable to graduated vesting?
4. *Payment of benefits.* What annuity options should be available? Should employees be given the option of receiving benefits in a lump sum? When should benefits first be available?
5. *Ancillary benefits.* Should the plan provide for a preretirement death benefit greater than the minimum required by law? Should a disability benefit be provided? Should early retirement benefits be subsidized?

All of these elements need to be balanced against the ongoing and ultimate costs of the plan. Chapter 3 covers many of the features of designing plans.

### Q 2:15   Does a company's financial stability affect plan design?

Yes. A defined benefit pension plan must be funded each year regardless of business profits. If a company has swings in its profitability or cash availability, a profit-sharing plan (which allows completely discretionary contributions) may be preferable to a defined benefit pension plan. In some instances, where credit is given for past service, a range of contributions is allowed. Changes in interest rates, investment experience, and employer demographics can alter the funding pattern of a plan dramatically. Anticipated contribution fluctuations should be part of the planning process.

### Q 2:16   What basic requirements must be satisfied for a plan to be qualified?

A plan must satisfy a number of requirements to be qualified. Most of these are found in Internal Revenue Code (Code) Section 401(a) and the regulations thereunder. The basic requirements include the following:

1. *Formal plan.* The plan must be in writing. [I.R.C. § 401(a)(1)]
2. *Exclusive benefit.* The plan must be established for the exclusive benefit of employees and their beneficiaries. [I.R.C. § 401(a)(2)]
3. *Minimum coverage.* A plan must cover a nondiscriminatory group of employees. [I.R.C. §§ 401(a)(3), 410]
4. *General nondiscrimination.* Benefits under the plan cannot discriminate in favor of highly compensated employees (HCEs). [I.R.C. § 401(a)(4), (5), (6)]
5. *Vesting.* Benefits under the plan must vest within certain periods of time. [I.R.C. §§ 401(a)(7), 411]
6. *Benefit accrual.* Benefits must be accrued over certain periods of time. [I.R.C. §§ 401(a)(7), 411]
7. *Forfeitures.* Forfeitures cannot increase benefits. [I.R.C. § 401(a)(8)]
8. *Required distributions.* Minimum distributions must be made to certain employees after they attain age 70½. [I.R.C. § 401(a)(9)]
9. *Top-heavy rules.* Minimum benefits and accelerated vesting must be provided if the plan is top heavy. [I.R.C. §§ 401(a)(10), 416]
10. *QJSA and QPSA rules.* Benefits must be paid in the form of a QJSA or QPSA unless those forms of benefit are appropriately waived. [I.R.C. §§ 401(a)(11), 417]
11. *Mergers.* After a merger, the surviving plan must provide benefits at least equal to the benefits that would have been provided if the old plan had terminated prior to the merger. [I.R.C. §§ 401(a)(12), 414(l)]
12. *Anti-alienation.* The plan must prohibit assignment of benefits unless assignment is mandated by a qualified domestic relations order (QDRO). [I.R.C. § 401(a)(13)]
13. *Commencement of benefits.* Benefits must begin at a certain time. [I.R.C. § 401(a)(14)]

14. *Reduction for Social Security increases.* Retiree benefits cannot be reduced because of postretirement Social Security benefit increases. [I.R.C. § 401(a)(15)]

15. *Maximum benefits.* Benefits cannot exceed $160,000 (as indexed). [I.R.C. §§ 401(a)(16), 415]

16. *Maximum recognizable compensation.* Compensation taken into account in determining benefits cannot exceed $200,000 (as indexed). [I.R.C. § 401(a)(17)]

17. *Forfeiture restriction on withdrawal of contributions.* Benefits cannot be forfeited because of the withdrawal of employee contributions if the employee is 50 percent vested. [I.R.C. § 401(a)(19)]

18. *Distributions on plan termination.* A plan covered by the PBGC must notify the PBGC before it makes distributions to participants on plan termination. [I.R.C. § 401(a)(20)]

19. *Actuarial assumptions.* Actuarial assumptions must be set forth in the plan. [I.R.C. § 401(a)(25)]

20. *Minimum participation.* A minimum number or percentage of employees must participate in the plan. [I.R.C. § 401(a)(26)]

21. *Security requirement for plan amendments.* A plan that increases its liability by amendment without sufficient funding must provide security for the amendment before it will take effect. [I.R.C. § 401(a)(29)]

22. *Optional direct rollover.* A plan that permits certain nonannuity payments must allow a participant to elect a direct rollover of benefits. [I.R.C. § 401(a)(31)]

23. *Benefit increases in bankruptcy.* Amendments cannot be made to an underfunded plan that increases benefits while an employer is in bankruptcy. [I.R.C. § 401(a)(33)]

### Q 2:17  Is a trust required?

A trust is required unless all assets are held under custodial arrangements with an insurance company. A trust must be a valid trust arrangement under state law. [Rev. Rul. 69-231, 1969-1 C.B. 118; Rev. Rul. 81-114, 1981-1 C.B. 207]

### Q 2:18  Can a sole proprietor maintain a defined benefit plan?

Yes. Any business can maintain a defined benefit pension plan. Benefits are determined by reference to net income from employment for a sole proprietor (see chapter 5).

### Q 2:19  What is an *IRS determination letter*?

An *IRS determination letter* is a ruling issued by the IRS that addresses the qualified status of a plan. The IRS reviews information presented on behalf of the plan sponsor and determines whether the form of the plan satisfies the technical requirements of the Code. If the plan sponsor so requests, the IRS will also review the plan, demonstrations, and other information submitted and determine whether the design of the plan as applied to the existing employee population satisfies the Code's coverage and nondiscrimination requirements. [I.R.S. Pub. No. 794 (Rev. Apr. 1994)]

### Q 2:20   Is a plan sponsor required to obtain a determination letter from the IRS?

No. Submission of a plan to the IRS for a determination of qualification is voluntary and, in some cases, not needed. If application for a determination letter is made timely, and the IRS discovers an error in the plan on review, the plan can be corrected retroactively. [I.R.C. § 401(b); Treas. Reg. § 1.401(b)-1] A favorable determination letter provides assurance of the plan's qualified status. Certain voluntary compliance programs are available only if a recent favorable determination letter, opinion letter, or advisory letter has been issued to the plan (see Q 2:25). [Rev. Proc. 2000-16, 2000-6 I.R.B. 518]

### Q 2:21   When can a plan sponsor rely on an opinion letter or advisory letter?

Opinion letters and advisory letters are issued to plan sponsors that draft and sponsor prototype and volume submitter plans. For an individual plan sponsor to rely on an opinion letter or advisory letter, the following conditions must be satisfied:

1. The plan sponsor adopts a master or prototype (M&P) plan or volume submitter plan that has obtained a GUST opinion letter or GUST advisory letter and that has also been amended to reflect the requirements of Section 314(e) of the Community Renewal Tax Relief Act of 2000 (CRA 2000) that relate to the definition of *compensation* under Code Sections 414(s) and 415(c)(3).

2. The plan sponsor adopts the M&P plan or volume submitter plan in identical form and chooses only options permitted by the plan.

3. If the adoption of the M&P plan or volume submitter plan is the restatement of an existing plan, the plan being restated is in compliance with pre-GUST law, the plan complies with GUST in operation, and the amended plan provides the appropriate retroactive effective dates to comply with GUST.

4. The plan in operation does not continue to apply the family aggregation rules after the 1996 plan year.

5. The plan in operation does not continue to apply the Code Section 415(e) limit in post-1999 limitation years.

6. If the plan being adopted is a volume submitter plan, the plan sponsor adopts the plan after the advisory letter is issued.

7. The plan sponsor does not modify the trust agreement in a manner that would cause the plan to fail to be qualified.

If the plan sponsor maintains, or has ever maintained, another plan that covers some of the same participants, the reliance does not cover the plan for compliance with the Code Section 415 limits or the top-heavy rules of Code Section 416, except to the extent the plan is a standardized M&P plan and the other plan is a paired plan. [Announcement 2001-77]

### Q 2:22    Does a determination letter guarantee qualified plan status?

No. A determination letter does not guarantee qualified plan status. In many ways a determination letter is similar to a private letter ruling. If the information submitted to the IRS is correct and the facts and circumstances do not change, the plan sponsor can rely on the determination letter. A plan must be amended continually to comply with changes in the law, even if the changes have been made administratively, and even if the changes do not affect the plan. Errors in plan administration can affect qualified plan status. A change in employee demographics can also affect qualified status. It is important that the plan be reviewed by pension professionals to ensure continued qualified status.

### Q 2:23    What is the difference between a prototype plan, a volume submitter plan, and an individually designed plan?

Most of the plan language of a prototype plan is preapproved by the IRS. A plan sponsor has only a few options to select. Options are generally included in an adoption agreement, and the basic text of the plan is generally included in a preprinted basic plan document. If some of the options selected by an employer in the adoption agreement require demographic testing, a nonstandardized prototype is used. The IRS will provide a favorable determination letter if the options selected are within the requisite parameters. If little demographic testing is needed, a standardized prototype can be used and no IRS submission is required.

A volume submitter plan is similar to a prototype plan in that most of the plan language is preapproved by the IRS. In a volume submitter plan, however, the plan sponsor is allowed to deviate from the preapproved language on a limited basis. In addition, a volume submitter plan document does not have an adoption agreement; all required language is contained in the body of the document. A volume submitter plan can be used for plans that want to use the general test for nondiscrimination testing (see chapters 10 and 11).

If many special features are desired, an individually designed plan must be used.

### Q 2:24    How often must a pension plan be amended?

A pension plan must be amended to comply with changes in the law as of the effective dates of each law. Unfortunately, there have been substantial changes in the law affecting pension plans in almost every legislative session since the early 1980s. Most of the time, the IRS grants extensions to the time period in which a plan document must be amended for law changes by providing a remedial amendment period as allowed under Code Section 401(b). During the remedial amendment period, the plan can be amended retroactively to satisfy qualification requirements. [Treas. Reg. § 1.401(b)-1(d), (e), (f)]

### Q 2:25    Can the IRS retroactively disqualify a pension plan?

Yes. The IRS can disqualify a plan retroactively for failure to comply with current law or meet any of the conditions of qualified status (see Q 2:16). If a disqualifying plan document provision is not amended on a timely basis, the plan risks disqualification. [Mills, Mitchell & Turner v. Commissioner, T.C. Memo 1993-99 (1993)]

A plan sponsor can often take advantage of the Walk-In Closing Agreement Program (Walk-in CAP) to correct plan document failures without losing the plan's qualified status. [Rev. Proc. 2000-16, 2000-6 I.R.B. 518] The term *plan document failure* means a plan provision (or the absence of a plan provision) that, on its face, violates the requirements of Code Section 401(a). Failure to amend a plan to reflect a new qualification requirement within the plan's applicable remedial amendment period under Code Section 401(b) is a plan document failure.

## Coverage Requirements of Defined Benefit Plans

### Q 2:26    Must all employees be eligible to participate in a plan?

No. A plan can restrict eligibility to employees who have satisfied certain age and service requirements. A plan sponsor can also limit eligibility to certain classes of employees, as long as the plan satisfies minimum coverage and participation requirements (see chapter 6).

### Q 2:27    Can a plan be designed to cover just a select group of employees?

Yes. As long as the plan satisfies the minimum coverage and participation requirements of the Code and the Employee Retirement Income Security Act of 1974, (ERISA) (see chapter 6), it need not cover all employees.

### Q 2:28    Do special minimum coverage and participation rules apply when a company is part of a controlled group of corporations or businesses under common ownership?

Yes. Certain definitions work to prevent an employer from adopting a plan to cover only a limited, more highly compensated group of employees of a related entity. When companies have specified relationships, they are aggregated and treated as if they were one employer in applying the participation and coverage requirements (see chapter 6), measuring service for eligibility and vesting purposes (see chapter 7), testing for nondiscrimination in benefits (see chapters 10 and 11), funding the plan (see chapter 18), and deducting contributions (see chapter 20).

Companies that share a specified percentage of common ownership are aggregated if they are in a controlled group or under common control. [I.R.C. § 414(b), (c)] Companies are considered to be in a controlled group for pension purposes if they are part of a parent-subsidiary group or a brother-sister group (see chapter 6). [I.R.C. § 1563(a)]

Similar aggregation rules apply to the plans of unincorporated business entities, such as sole proprietorships, partnerships, and limited liability companies that have common ownership.

**Example 1.** Jeff is a health care consultant, providing services to businesses nationwide. He operates his consulting business as a sole proprietor. Jeff also owns a sporting goods store that employs 15 people. Jeff's two businesses are under common control. Jeff cannot adopt a plan just for his sole proprietorship; he must also include employees of the sporting goods store. Otherwise his plan will fail the minimum participation and coverage rules of Code Sections 401(a)(26) and 410(b).

Affiliated service groups are also treated as if they were a single employer. An affiliated service group consists of a service organization (an organization whose principal business is the performance of services, such as accounting, actuarial science, architecture, consulting, engineering, health, insurance, law, and the performing arts) and one or more related entities. The service organization is called the first service organization (FSO). The related business entity can be either an A Org or a B Org (see chapter 6). [I.R.C. § 414(m); Prop. Treas. Reg. § 1.414(m)-2]

**Example 2.** Dr. Bones operates a medical practice through his wholly owned professional corporation. Dr. Bones's corporation owns a 10 percent interest in Omnihealth LLC, a company that handles the administrative aspects of the practice and employs all administrative and medical support staff. A significant portion of these administrative and support services are provided for Dr. Bones's medical practice. Administrative and medical support services are services of a type historically performed by employees of the medical practice. The corporation set up by Dr. Bones is an FSO; Omnihealth LLC is a B Org. The corporation and the partnership constitute an affiliated service group.

## Benefits

### Q 2:29  What requirements must be satisfied for a plan to be nondiscriminatory?

Under Code Section 401(a)(4), contributions to or benefits provided under a plan cannot discriminate in favor of HCEs. Treasury regulations detail the means of satisfying these nondiscrimination requirements. Defined benefit plans must be nondiscriminatory with respect to the following:

1. The amount of benefits provided to participants;
2. The availability of all plan benefits, rights, and features; and
3. The effect of plan amendments and terminations.

Benefits provided under the plan are nondiscriminatory if the plan meets one of five design-based safe harbors or passes a general test (see chapters 10 and 11). [I.R.C. § 401(a)(4); Treas. Reg. §§ 1.401(a)(4)-1 et seq.]

### Q 2:30    Can a plan be designed so that it automatically satisfies the requirement that benefits be nondiscriminatory?

Yes. An employer can use several safe harbor plan designs either independently or in conjunction with one other. Chapter 10 provides the details of designing plans using the safe harbor nondiscrimination tests.

### Q 2:31    Is there an alternative test to prove nondiscrimination in amounts of benefits?

Yes. An employer can elect to use the general test for nondiscrimination and design a program that is more customized to the employer's needs. Plans can always discriminate in favor of one HCE over another HCE or in favor of one non-highly compensated employee (NHCE) over another NHCE, but they can never discriminate in favor of HCEs over NHCEs. The bright-line tests of Treasury Regulations Sections 1.401(a)(4)-1 et seq. define the methods to be used for nondiscrimination testing (see chapters 10 and 11).

### Q 2:32    Do any vesting standards apply to pension plans?

Yes. Almost all qualified plans must meet minimum standards concerning nonforfeitability and vesting of benefits (see chapter 8). [I.R.C. §§ 401(a)(7), 411]

### Q 2:33    What makes a plan top heavy?

A plan becomes top heavy when the accrued benefits for key employees exceed 60 percent of the accrued benefits for all employees. [I.R.C. § 416(g)(1)] If an employer sponsors more than one plan, or if other plans are sponsored by members of a controlled group or group of affiliated companies, all plans within the aggregation group (see Q 2:28) must be tested for top-heavy status (see chapter 5).

### Q 2:34    What additional requirements apply if a plan is top heavy?

If a plan is top heavy, it may be required to provide minimum benefits to all participants (see chapter 5). In addition, special, accelerated vesting schedules are required (see chapter 8). The minimum benefit requirements often make defined benefit pension plans administratively complex and rather expensive to maintain, but plan designs may be available to mitigate the costs associated with top-heavy status (see chapters 3 and 5).

### Q 2:35    What is an *accrued benefit*?

An *accrued benefit* is the benefit earned at any point in time (see Q 2:36), based on the plan formula, years of service or participation, and compensation, and payable in the normal form of payment from the plan (e.g., an annuity for the life of the participant) (see chapter 12).

### Q 2:36    How are benefits determined at any point in time?

Each participant in a defined benefit pension plan earns or accrues a portion of his or her retirement benefit over the course of plan participation (or occasionally over the course of employment). The method of accrual must meet certain requirements so that benefits are not backloaded unreasonably (see chapter 9). Often a fixed benefit is accrued over the course of participation; that is, the participant's accrued benefit at any time is determined by multiplying the projected retirement benefit by a fraction, the numerator of which is the number of years of participation in the plan at the date of determination, and the denominator of which is the number of years of participation the participant would have if he or she continued employment until retirement.

**Example.** Mark, age 45, has been a participant in the Griffen Construction Co. pension plan for 15 years. The plan provides a fixed benefit at retirement (age 65) equal to 50 percent of average compensation. Benefits accrue over plan participation. If Mark's average compensation is $50,000, his accrued benefit would be determined as follows:

$$\text{Average compensation} \times 50\% \times \frac{\text{Participation to date}}{\text{Participation at normal retirement date}}$$

$$\$50,000 \times 50\% \times \frac{15}{35} = \$10,714$$

### Q 2:37    What types of benefit formulas are typically used in a defined benefit plan?

Most formulas are a unit benefit type, expressed as a flat-dollar amount or a percentage of average annual compensation per year of service. Unit benefit formulas are easy to understand, provide reduced benefits for short-service employees, reward long-service employees, and are flexible enough to be enhanced easily.

A typical unit benefit formula expressed as a flat-dollar amount would be $15 per year of service for a maximum of 40 years. Under this formula, an employee with 10 years of service at retirement would receive $150 ($15 × 10) as an annuity payable under the plan's normal form of payment, which may be a life annuity; an employee with 40 years of service would receive $600 ($15 × 40) as an annuity. This type of formula is commonly used for employees whose compensation is paid on an hourly basis. Generally, the benefit is changed over the life of the plan to take into account the impact of inflation on the ultimate retirement benefit. It is not uncommon to see plans that have changed the flat-dollar amount every two to three years.

A typical unit benefit formula expressed as a percentage of average annual compensation would be 1.25 percent of average annual compensation per year of service. Under this formula an employee with 10 years of service at retirement would receive 12.5 percent (1.25% × 10) of average annual compensation as an annuity payable under the plan's normal form of payment. An employee with 40 years of service would receive 50 percent (1.25% × 40) of average annual compensation as an annuity. This type of formula is commonly used for employees who are paid an annual salary and whose salaries follow a predictable pattern with regard to service, employment classification (i.e., sales, management, clerical, etc.), and hours worked. Because benefits are a constant percentage of salary at retirement, the plan is shielded from the effects of inflation. Therefore, there is no need to increase benefits for this reason, unless the employer believes that the ultimate benefits are too low based on income objectives for the plan. (See chapter 9 for an in-depth discussion of plan benefits.)

### Q 2:38 Must a plan specify a normal retirement age?

Yes. Defined benefit plans must provide a definitely determinable benefit. For the plan to define the benefits payable at retirement, a normal retirement age must be part of the plan's provisions. The normal retirement age is the age at which benefits are set to begin for any participant completing the age, service, and participation requirements for normal retirement.

### Q 2:39 What ages can be used as the plan's normal retirement age?

A plan can set any reasonable normal retirement age that meets the objectives of the sponsoring employer; however, there are certain limitations on when benefits can begin and how much benefit can be received at that time. The latest date permissible for a normal retirement is the latest of the time a participant attains age 65 or the fifth anniversary of participation, or the attainment of the plan's normal retirement age if earlier. [I.R.C. § 411(b)(8)] The employer can select a normal retirement age earlier than age 65; however, certain limitations on the amount of benefits available at the younger age will apply.

### Q 2:40 What compensation can be used in determining benefits?

Generally all compensation is used to determine benefits under a compensation-related benefit formula. The plan can use alternative definitions of compensation as long as the definition does not by design discriminate in favor of HCEs and is reasonable, and as long as the average percentage of total compensation included under the alternative definition for an employer's HCEs as a group does not exceed by more than a *de minimis* amount the average percentage of total compensation included under the alternative definition for the employer's NHCEs as a group (see Q 2:41). [Treas. Reg. § 1.414(s)-1(d)] The maximum amount that can be recognized in determining plan benefits is limited by Code Section 401(a)(17) to the first $200,000 (as indexed) of compensation (see chapter 12).

### Q 2:41    Must a plan recognize all compensation in determining benefits?

No. Provided that all requirements for consistency, nondiscrimination, and reasonableness under Treasury Regulations Section 1.414(s)-1 are met, a plan can determine benefits by reference to base salary; rate of compensation; total compensation, including or excluding bonuses, vacation pay, and overtime; contributions to a 401(k), Section 125, or Section 127 plan; or any other definition of compensation that meets the objective of the employer. Any definition of compensation that falls outside the standard definitions and safe harbors of Treasury Regulations Section 1.414(s)-1 may require the plan to demonstrate that the alternative definition satisfies all requirements under the law for its use.

### Q 2:42    Must a plan recognize all service with an employer in determining benefits?

No. A plan can limit service that is recognized for benefit accrual purposes in a number of ways. Service can be recognized only for periods (computation periods) when an employee is credited with a certain number of hours of service. A plan can limit service credit to periods when the employee was an eligible participant in the plan or under a contributory plan, or to periods when the employee made the required contribution to the plan. A plan can be designed to limit the number of years of service recognized prior to the adoption of the plan. Finally, a plan can limit the number of years credited for benefit determination purposes (see chapters 3 and 7).

### Q 2:43    Can breaks in service affect benefit entitlements?

Yes. Breaks in service, generally plan years in which an employee is credited with fewer than 501 hours of service (see chapter 7), can affect benefit entitlements in a number of ways. A participant can lose vesting credit for years of service prior to the break in service (see chapter 8). Alternatively, service prior to the break in service can be included in the ultimate retirement benefit. In designing a defined benefit pension plan, turnover and rehiring patterns should be reviewed.

### Q 2:44    Are there any limits on the amount of benefits that can be provided under a defined benefit plan?

Yes. A plan cannot provide an annual benefit greater than the lesser of $160,000 (as indexed) or 100 percent of the participant's average compensation.

[I.R.C. § 415(b)(1)] This benefit limit applies to an annual benefit expressed in the form of a life annuity payable between age 62 and age 65 as long as the participant has at least 10 years of service or participation, depending on the applicable limitation (see chapter 12). If the benefits under the plan are paid in a form other than a single-life annuity, the benefit limit is adjusted actuarially. If benefits are paid in the form of a QJSA (see chapter 15), no adjustment is required [I.R.C. § 415(b)(2)(B)] If benefits begin prior to age 62, the benefit limit is reduced to the actuarial equivalent of a $160,000 annual benefit beginning at age 62. This reduction can be significant.

The Code prescribes limits on the actuarial assumptions used in adjusting the benefit limit for an alternate form of payment or early (or late) payment. [I.R.C. § 415(b)(2)(E)]

### Q 2:45   Are there additional limits that apply if a plan participant also participates in another plan sponsored by the employer?

Yes. If the employer sponsors one or more defined benefit plans, all plans are treated as one plan for purposes of applying the maximum benefit limitation. Similarly, if the employer sponsors one or more defined contribution plans, all plans are treated as one plan for purposes of applying the maximum benefit limitation. For plan years beginning before January 1, 2000, if the employee benefits are under a defined benefit plan and a defined contribution plan of the same employer, there is a limit on the total benefits that an employee could receive under each plan. (See chapter 12 for more on maximum benefits.)

### Q 2:46   Can benefits under a plan be reduced or offset by potential Social Security benefits?

A plan can offset benefits by potential Social Security benefits only under limited circumstances. A plan must follow the permitted disparity rules under Code Section 401(l) (see chapter 10), provide safe harbor offsets against the primary insurance amounts under Social Security (see chapter 10), or satisfy the general test under Code Section 401(a)(4) (see chapter 11). The employer may want to have such an arrangement to take into account the benefit levels paid for by employer contributions to each employee's Social Security benefits.

### Q 2:47   Can accrued benefits be forfeited for any reason?

Generally, no. Code Section 411(d)(6) prohibits cutbacks or reductions in accrued benefits. Vested accrued benefits generally cannot be forfeited (see chapter 8).

### Q 2:48   Must benefits be distributed in any particular form?

A plan does not have to provide benefits in any form other than a QJSA. Although most plans offer a variety of payment options for participants to choose from, benefits under a defined benefit pension plan are typically paid in the form of an annuity. An annuity provides regular monthly benefits, generally over the life of the plan participant. Lump-sum distributions are occasionally available under a defined benefit pension plan (see chapter 16).

### Q 2:49 Can an employer exercise discretion over the timing or form of benefits?

No. A plan that permits the employer, either directly or indirectly, through the exercise of discretion, to deny a participant a particular form of benefit violates Code Section 411(d)(6). [Treas. Reg. § 1.411(d)-4]

### Q 2:50 Does a participant's spouse have any rights under a plan?

Yes. Defined benefit pension plans must provide for survivor annuities for spouses of plan participants. [I.R.C. § 401(a)(11)(B)(i); Treas. Reg. § 1.401(a)-20, Q&A-3(a)] Benefits cannot be paid in any form other than a QJSA without spousal consent (see chapter 16).

### Q 2:51 Can a participant's benefit be assigned to any other party?

Generally, no. The Code and ERISA prohibit the assignment or alienation of benefits under a plan. [ERISA § 206(d)(1); I.R.C. § 401(a)(13)] There are exceptions for federal tax levies and QDROs (see chapter 15). [Treas. Reg. § 1.401(a)-13(b)(2)]

## Funding

### Q 2:52 How does an employer determine how much to contribute to a plan each year?

The employer relies on the recommendation of the plan's enrolled actuary to determine how much money to contribute to the plan each year. The enrolled actuary generally informs the employer of the minimum amount required to satisfy the minimum-funding standards of the Code and ERISA, the maximum amount that could be contributed and deducted on the federal tax return of the employer, and the amount the actuary recommends within a range best suited for the plan to provide continued payment of plan benefits. Additionally, the employer looks at the availability of cash to fund the plan and whether contributions in the future may be limited because of a projected change in the cash flow of the business, in which case the employer may want to contribute more now to offset future contribution requirements.

### Q 2:53 What assumptions does an actuary make in calculating plan costs?

The enrolled actuary responsible for the minimum-funding calculations for a defined benefit plan may take into account the following assumptions when calculating plan costs:

1. Rate at which plan participants will die either prior to or while receiving benefit payments;
2. Rate of investment return on the assets invested for the purpose of providing the benefits under the plan;
3. Rate at which salaries increase over the working years of the participants;
4. Rate at which employees terminate prior to reaching retirement;
5. Rate at which employees become eligible for disability, early retirement, or death benefits;
6. Expenses incurred and paid out of the assets for the administration and operation of the plan; and
7. Rate at which benefits will increase after retirement as part of cost-of-living adjustments.

Based on the benefits available under the plan, the employee demographics, the plan's funding policy, and the size and general health of the employee group, the enrolled actuary may take into account some or all of the above assumptions to determine plan costs (see chapter 23).

### Q 2:54    How are plan assets and liabilities determined?

In general most defined benefit plans value plan assets at fair market value. The fair market value of a plan's assets is the price at which the property would change hands between a willing buyer and a willing seller, neither being under any compulsion to buy or sell and both having reasonable knowledge of relevant facts. Several other methods can be used to determine the value of an asset; however, a value so determined must be within a range, or corridor, above and below the asset's fair market value.

Liabilities are determined by the plan's enrolled actuary. They represent the amount of assets needed at a point in time to cover either accumulated benefits or accumulated contributions. Depending on the choice of actuarial assumptions and the funding method, the liabilities of the plan may differ significantly. Therefore, any review of a plan's liabilities should include a review of the underlying actuarial assumptions. Chapter 21 outlines several methods for determining a defined benefit plan's assets and liabilities.

### Q 2:55    Can different funding methods result in different costs?

Yes. All things being equal, each funding method generates a different plan cost. The choice of a funding method depends on the size of the employee group, the employer's need for flexibility in contributions, whether past-service benefits are provided, the average age of the employee group, and the need for the employer to anticipate future contribution requirements (see chapter 18).

### Q 2:56    Can funding methods be changed after the plan is in effect?

Yes, changes in funding methods that satisfy specific criteria set forth by the IRS can be made without IRS approval, or with so-called automatic approval.

Additionally, if a plan sponsor wants to change the funding method under a set of circumstances that does not fall within the automatic-approval guidelines, the plan can obtain approval directly from the IRS (see chapter 18).

### Q 2:57   Can a change in demographics affect cost?

Yes. A significant number of premature terminations or deaths of employees or lower-than-assumed compensation increases can lower costs. Fewer terminations or deaths or higher-than-normal compensation increases can significantly increase costs (see chapter 22).

### Q 2:58   When must a contribution be made to be fully deductible?

Contributions must be made to the plan's trust fund before the due date, including extensions, for the contributing sponsor's federal tax return. Contributions not made in time may be deductible in later plan years, but there may also be an excise tax for failure to meet minimum-funding standards (see chapter 19).

### Q 2:59   What must an employer do to satisfy the minimum-funding requirements?

An employer must contribute enough money to the plan's trust fund to prevent an accumulated funding deficiency in the plan's funding standard account (see chapter 19) as of the last possible date to make contributions for the funding year. Generally, contributions can be credited to the funding standard account any time from the first day of the plan year up until eight and one-half months after the close of the plan year. The amount necessary to prevent an accumulated funding deficiency in the funding standard account is determined by the plan's enrolled actuary each year as part of the actuarial valuation report required under ERISA.

### Q 2:60   Must an employer make contributions every year regardless of profits?

If an accumulated funding deficiency will exist in the plan's funding standard account without a contribution to the plan's trust fund, the employer must either make a contribution regardless of profitability or obtain a funding waiver from the IRS to make up the contribution over the next few years (see chapter 19).

### Q 2:61   Can a plan be terminated at any time?

In general, a plan can be terminated at any time. The plan document must specify the conditions under which a plan can be terminated and how benefits will be distributed on termination.

An early termination of a plan may be challenged by the IRS to determine whether the plan was originally established to be a permanent program and not just a temporary tax shelter (see chapter 25).

### Q 2:62  Does an employer have to make contributions to a plan after it is frozen or terminated?

An employer may be obligated to continue funding a plan after it is terminated or accrued benefits are frozen. If the plan is underfunded, continued contributions may be required. Top-heavy defined benefit plans continue to have benefits accrue to non-key employees if the plan termination is not processed timely or even if all other benefits are frozen. These top-heavy accruals may cause the plan to be underfunded and require continued funding (see chapter 25).

### Q 2:63  Are there any instances when plan assets can revert to the employer sponsoring the plan?

Yes, there are limited instances when assets in a defined benefit pension plan can revert to the employer sponsoring the plan:

1. On plan termination after all plan liabilities have been satisfied. [Treas. Reg. § 1.401-2] The plan must contain a provision permitting the reversion, and this provision must have been in place for at least five years prior to the reversion event, or since the effective date of the plan if that period is shorter. [ERISA § 4044(d)(2)]. A reversion of excess assets carries an excise tax that, when combined with the income tax, can be rather confiscatory. Techniques for reducing the effective cost of the reversion are available (see chapter 25).

2. For a contribution conditioned on deductibility if the deduction is denied. [ERISA § 403(c)(2)(C)] The plan must include a provision to this effect, the contribution must be made with the express condition of deductible status, and the IRS must affirmatively deny the deduction.

3. For a contribution made under a mistake of fact if the contribution is returned to the employer within one year. [ERISA § 403(c)(2)(A)]

4. For a contribution conditioned on initial qualification if the plan was submitted to the IRS for a determination of qualification within the remedial amendment period but failed to meet qualification requirements. [ERISA § 403(c)(2)(B)]

### Q 2:64  How is the PBGC involved in defined benefit plans?

The PBGC provides benefits to the participants in a defined benefit pension plan in the event the plan is terminated and the employer is unable to make current and/or future benefit payments to the plan participants.

For a plan that has not been terminated either by the employer or by the PBGC, the involvement of the PBGC is limited to collection of premiums to provide termination insurance coverage and the review of plan funding via IRS Form 5500 and the voluntary employer notification program, which alerts the PBGC to any events that pose a threat to the PBGC's solvency (see chapter 24).

### Q 2:65    Does the PBGC protect benefits in an ongoing plan?

The PBGC protects benefits in an ongoing plan only if the plan is covered by the PBGC's plan termination program (see chapter 24). Furthermore, the PBGC has limits on the amount of benefits it protects. There are maximum dollar amounts of protection, per plan participant, at specific retirement ages, which are indexed each year, and only a portion of any benefit enhancements made in the last few years of the plan are covered. Protection of benefits for substantial owners is phased in over a 30-year period (see chapter 25).

## Fiduciary Responsibilities

### Q 2:66    Who is responsible for making decisions about the administration of a plan and the investment of plan assets?

Persons with certain powers, or functioning in a discretionary capacity with respect to the plan, are called fiduciaries. Fiduciaries are charged with a high standard of care in managing the plan and its assets and can be held personally liable for an act or omission that constitutes a breach of fiduciary responsibility (see chapter 27).

### Q 2:67    What are the primary responsibilities of a fiduciary?

A fiduciary must act solely in the interest of plan participants and beneficiaries and in the following ways (see chapter 27):

1. For the exclusive purpose of providing benefits to participants and beneficiaries and defraying reasonable expenses of administering the plan;
2. With the care, skill, prudence, and diligence that a prudent person acting in a like capacity and familiar with such matters would use;
3. To diversify the investments of the plan so as to minimize the risk of large losses; and
4. In accordance with the plan documents.

[ERISA § 404(a)(1)]

### Q 2:68    What type of information must be provided to plan participants?

Plan participants and beneficiaries have the right to receive certain information and materials relating to the plan. There are basically three types of disclosure (see chapter 28):

1. *Required disclosure.* Certain information must be provided at stated times or if certain events occur.
2. *Information on request.* Certain information and documentation must be provided on request.

3. *Document examination.* Certain materials must be available for examination at reasonable times and places.

### Q 2:69 Does a participant have a right to receive a benefit statement?

A plan is not required to provide annual benefit statements to participants. Upon the written request of a participant, however, the plan must provide a statement of the total accrued benefits and the earliest date on which benefits will become completely vested. Only one statement must be provided in any 12-month period (see chapter 28).

### Q 2:70 What penalties can be assessed for failing to satisfy reporting and disclosure requirements?

There are a number of penalties that can be assessed by the IRS, the Department of Labor (DOL), or the PBGC for specific violations of reporting and disclosure requirements, such as the following:

1. *Failure to file IRS Form 5500.* Two agencies can assess penalties for delinquent filing of a complete annual report. The IRS can impose a penalty of $25 per day up to a maximum of $15,000, and the DOL can impose a penalty of up to $1,100 per day ($1,000 prior to July 30, 1997), for failure to file a timely report. [I.R.C. § 6652(e); ERISA § 502(c)(2)]

2. *Failure to file Schedule B.* The IRS can impose a penalty of $1,000 for failure to file if the actuarial report is not filed. [I.R.C. § 6692]

3. *Failure to file Schedule SSA.* The IRS can impose a penalty of $1 per day for each participant omitted on Schedule SSA, up to a maximum of $5,000. [I.R.C. § 6652(d)(1)]

4. *Failure to provide notice of plan change.* The IRS can impose a penalty of $1 per day, up to a maximum of $1,000, if the plan administrator fails to provide notice of a plan change, such as a change in the plan name. [I.R.C. § 6652(d)(2)]

5. *Failure to provide notices to the PBGC.* The PBGC can impose a penalty of up to $1,000 per day on any party that fails to provide it with required information. [ERISA § 4071]

6. *Failure to provide summary plan description (SPD) or summary of material modifications (SMM) to the DOL.* A penalty of up to $100 per day can be imposed if the employer fails to provide a copy of the most recent SPD or SMM to the DOL within 30 days of request. [ERISA § 502(c)(6)]

7. *Failure to provide information on request.* If the plan administrator fails to comply with a request for certain information, a court can, in its discretion, require a plan administrator to pay a penalty of up to $100 per day from the date of the request. [ERISA § 502(c)(1)]

8. *Failure to provide statement of benefits to terminated vested participant.* A penalty of up to $50 per day can be imposed if the plan administrator fails to provide a statement or provides a fraudulent statement to a terminated vested participant. [I.R.C. § 6690]

9. *Failure to notify participants of failure to meet minimum-funding standards.* Penalties of up to $110 per day ($100 prior to July 30, 1997) can be imposed if the employer fails to notify a participant or beneficiary that the minimum-funding standards have not been met. [ERISA § 502(c)(3)]

10. *Failure to furnish information or maintain records of benefit entitlements.* If an employer sponsoring a plan fails to maintain records sufficient to determine the benefits due to participants, the sponsor can be assessed a penalty of $11 ($10 prior to July 30, 1997) for each affected employee. [ERISA § 209(b)]

11. *Willful violation of reporting and disclosure requirements.* Criminal fines of up to $5,000, imprisonment of up to one year, or both, for a person, or fines of up to $100,000 for any other party, can be imposed for willful violations of reporting and disclosure requirements. [ERISA § 501]

# Chapter 3

# Plan Design

Plan design is critical to a successful benefit program. This chapter provides insight into the creative thinking behind proper plan design. Each employer is different, as is each employer's workforce. Designing a plan that provides meaningful benefits to the selected group of covered employees and that meets fiscal objectives becomes an art. Compliance with the tax laws, unfortunately, takes a high priority in the design of a plan. All of the concepts discussed in this chapter are based on the assumption that the design is for a retirement plan that meets the requirements of the law and regulations. Unless specifically addressed as a limiting factor, tax compliance is assumed throughout this chapter and there are few references to the Internal Revenue Code (Code).

The retirement income policy in the United States since the 1930s has been a three-part program that anticipates that retirement benefits will come from three nearly equal sources: Social Security, an employer plan, and personal savings. Cash or deferred arrangements (401(k) plans) were initially thought of as tax-efficient tools to accumulate the personal savings portion of this program. Over the last 10 years 401(k) plans have become the cornerstone of plan design rather than the employee's personal savings program. In this chapter the employer portion of retirement planning is discussed.

## The Basics

### Q 3:1   What is meant by *plan design*?

*Plan design* means the structure of a plan with regard to the amount of benefits paid, the employee population covered, the form of benefit payments, when benefits are earned and paid, and the events that trigger payments. Each of these components can be handled in an infinite number of ways. The plan sponsor must balance each plan feature with its cost and maintenance of the program.

### Q 3:2   How is a plan design developed?

Employer objectives are identified, census and other demographic data are gathered, fiscal constraints are developed, the plan sponsor's structure is determined, and formulas are created and their application is tested for limitations and discrimination. Oftentimes, replacement ratios (see Q 3:10) are developed to determine the needed retirement benefit level for employees with a lifetime commitment to the employer (see Q 3:11). Cash-flow analysis and projections must be reviewed along with beneficial tax treatment of contributions to the plan.

## Employer Objectives

### Q 3:3   What are the primary objectives employers attempt to achieve when designing a defined benefit plan?

Employers have many objectives to balance while designing a defined benefit plan, including the following:

- To provide meaningful benefits to long-service employees
- To provide a stable source of income in retirement years for employees
- To allow for workforce transition by retiring older employees and replacing them with younger employees
- To attract and retain employees
- To receive significant tax benefits through tax deductible contributions and the tax-deferred accumulation of monetary reserves to provide the future retirement liabilities
- To provide catch-up benefits to older, longer-service employees

### Q 3:4   Can a defined benefit plan allow for catch-up of retirement benefits for employees with past service?

Yes. The catch-up provision is a key planning tool and is available only in a defined benefit plan. An employer can establish a plan that provides a past-service benefit, thereby awarding employees credit for service with the employer before the plan was established. The cost of providing the past-service benefits is spread over future years. Additionally, if an employer initially establishes a modest plan, the employer can improve benefits and provide those benefits retroactively.

### Q 3:5 Should business entities that have fluctuating or inconsistent profits or cash flow use a defined benefit plan for retirement purposes?

Careful consideration must be given to cash-flow experience. An employer should anticipate the ongoing level of required contributions to meet the minimum-funding standards. Actuaries can use various methods to determine the cost of a retirement plan each year (called actuarial cost methods). Some methods build reserves (called credit balances) to provide a funding cushion for lean years. However, beginning in 2008, with the changes implemented to the funding rules, actuaries will have much less leeway in helping an employer build this type of cushion that can be used in future years.

Defined benefit plans should be considered part of compensation. An employer should consider that a cutback in benefits is significant to employees. Additionally, consideration should be given to the fact that, depending on the number of past-service credits granted, an employer may cut back future benefits but still have considerable ongoing contribution obligations.

### Q 3:6 What are the financial implications of establishing a defined benefit plan?

Start-up costs are normally incidental compared to the contribution and accumulation amounts required in a defined benefit plan. The cost items for establishing and administering a plan include the following:

- Data collection
- Plan design
- First-year set-up fees
- Legal documents
- First-year annual administration (valuation report)
- Employee announcements and enrollments
- Participant statements
- Fiduciary and fidelity insurance premiums
- Pension Benefit Guaranty Corporation (PBGC) premiums (for covered plans)
- IRS Form 5500 preparation and audit (for plans not meeting one of the exemptions)
- Statement of Financial Accounting Standards No. 87 (a report on the financial position of the plan that must be prepared for plans that use generally accepted accounting principles (GAAP))

- Computation of benefits for participants who separate from service
- Asset management fees
- Trustee fees

These costs are in addition to the contribution amounts required for the primary and ancillary benefits under the plan. Plans are intended to be long-lived and should not be considered for short time frames (e.g., only one or two years of contributions). The tax qualification of a plan can be jeopardized if the plan is in existence for only a few years (see chapter 24). A plan sponsor should set benefit levels, and the corresponding anticipated contribution levels, within a range that it can reasonably expect to maintain in the foreseeable future.

### Q 3:7    What are the tax incentives for a plan sponsor that establishes a qualified plan?

The fees associated with establishing and maintaining a retirement plan are tax deductible under Code Section 162 as ordinary and necessary business expenses. Contributions will be considered tax deductible if they are an ordinary and necessary business expense and, therefore, must be compensation for services actually rendered. Furthermore, to be tax deductible, the contribution for an employee must be combined with the employee's regular compensation and that total must be considered reasonable. [I.R.C. §§ 162, 404; Treas. Reg. § 1.404(a)-1(b)]

Investment earnings are tax deferred and are not taxable to the plan sponsor unless they are returned as surplus because of an actuarial error. The rules covering tax deductibility and tax deferment are extensive and are covered in chapter 20.

### Q 3:8    Should an employer consider the retirement programs offered by competitors?

Yes. To attract and retain good employees, an employer must have a good idea of the compensation package that competitors provide their employees and offer programs of similar value.

### Q 3:9    How does a defined benefit plan help in the transition of an employer's aging workforce?

A defined benefit plan provides secure replacement wages for retirees. The amount of the benefit a participant has at retirement is earned over the employee's working lifetime. This provides significant security to employees and their spouses or beneficiaries. A plan can have early retirement provisions that allow participants choices regarding the timing of their retirement. Additionally, plans can provide for incentives to retain older, key employees by enhancing retirement benefits after normal retirement age.

An employer creates the opportunity of retirement through the establishment of a defined benefit pension plan. This allows the employer to replace long-service employees, who may no longer have the physical strength to fulfill job functions, with younger employees.

### Q 3:10    What are *replacement ratios*, and how do they factor into plan design?

*Replacement ratios* are calculations of the ultimate benefits that a participant receives as a percentage of final average wages. In computing replacement wages, the participant's projected Social Security benefits and other pension benefits are added to the anticipated benefits from the proposed plan and the sum is divided by the projected average salary at normal retirement age.

Traditionally, replacement ratios of 70 percent to 80 percent were considered reasonable. Recent studies have suggested that replacement ratios should be based on the participant's wages in relation to the poverty level. Participants with average salaries near the poverty level should have replacement ratios of 100 percent or more (for inflation purposes). Participants whose wages exceed seven to ten times the poverty level need replacement ratios of less than 70 percent.

**Example.** Pat has a projected final three-year average annual compensation of \$30,000. Pat's projected Social Security primary insurance amount is \$14,000 annually. Pat's projected benefit from the plan is 35 percent of average annual compensation. Pat's replacement ratio is determined as follows:

$$\$30,000 \times 35\% = \$10,500$$

($\$14,000 + \$10,500$) $\times$ \$30,000 = 0.81667, or an 81.667% replacement ratio.

### Q 3:11    How much of a benefit should an employer provide for employees?

First, an employer should determine the contribution amount that can be maintained for the foreseeable future and base the benefits on an appropriate cost range. Next, the employer should compute replacement ratios for benefiting employees to determine the level of benefits desired. Finally, the employer must balance these two items to determine the affordable range of benefits.

Recall that the retirement income policy of the United States has three equal components: Social Security, the employer plan, and personal savings. Employees must be encouraged to provide their one-third share or else a fourth leg of the policy emerges: required working past retirement.

**Example.** An employer wants to provide a 75 percent replacement ratio to its employees. If Social Security provides 25 percent and personal savings through a 401(k) plan provide another 25 percent, the employer plan should provide a benefit of 25 percent of final average compensation.

### Q 3:12   How should benefit payments be made from a defined benefit plan?

The size of the employer, the objectives of the organization, the paternalistic nature of the management team, and the funding vehicles of the plan all share in determining the types of benefit payment options available in a plan.

Benefit payments are normally made in the form of an annuity. An annuity is a periodic payment. A term-certain annuity is an annuity that begins on a specific date and ends after a specific period of time. Life annuities are paid beginning on a specific date and continue over the life of the annuitant. A life annuity with a term certain is an annuity paid over the life of the participant, but if the participant dies before the specified period ends, the payments continue to be made to the named beneficiary until the end of the certain period. For example, a 10-year certain and life monthly annuity is an annuity paid each month over the life of the participant with a guarantee of payments for 120 months (10 years). If the participant dies after 50 payments, the named beneficiary will receive the remaining 70 payments of the guaranteed 120 payments.

Defined benefit plans have a normal form of benefit payments. Optional forms of payment are calculated using the interest rate and mortality table or other factors defined in the plan. Some plans provide that all optional forms of benefit payment be the actuarial equivalent of the normal form. Other plans provide subsidies to provide a benefit of greater value at no cost to the participant. For example, a plan may provide for benefits to be paid as a life annuity for single participants and the same benefits to be paid as a 50 percent joint and survivor annuity for married participants. The joint and survivor benefit is subsidized.

Most small plans offer lump-sum distributions because of uncertainty about the continuity of the plan or about continued funding if something happens to the employer or the primary shareholder. Multiemployer and larger single-employer plans usually do not offer lump-sum options. They continue to save for their retirees and insure the annuity risk through the plan.

Plans that have early retirement ages often provide for Social Security supplements to provide level benefits to retirees before and after the retiree is eligible to receive Social Security benefits.

Other plans offer continuing benefits only to the spouse in case of the participant's death. These joint and survivor benefits are paid in a stated amount while the participant and spouse are both alive and then in some fraction of that amount to the surviving spouse. For example, the benefit might be $500 per month while the participant is alive and $250 per month to the surviving spouse on the participant's death. This form of benefit is called a 50 percent joint and survivor annuity. Other optional forms may be 66.66 percent, 75 percent, and 100 percent joint and survivor annuities.

In any event, full disclosure must be made to participants detailing the "value" of each optional form of benefit so that they may make informed elections.

## Q 3:13   Should the plan provide additional benefits such as death, postretirement medical, severance, or disability benefits?

This question should be considered in the design of a defined benefit plan, but the primary purpose of a defined benefit plan must be retirement benefits. A plan can provide for ancillary benefits, such as death benefits, postretirement medical benefits, subsidized termination benefits, or disability benefits.

Smaller plans often provide death benefits through the purchase of life insurance on the lives of each participant. If the participant pays for the cost of the insurance (PS-58 costs or one-year renewable term costs), the insurance proceeds can be paid out of the trust free from income. Larger plans normally do not offer this type of benefit. Some plans provide for the continued payment of medical premiums (coordinated with Medicare) throughout the retiree's lifetime.

Defined benefit plans must provide certain death benefits. A defined benefit plan must pay benefits in the form of a qualified joint and survivor annuity (QJSA). A QJSA is an immediate annuity for the life of the participant, with a survivor annuity for the life of the participant's spouse. The amount of the survivor annuity cannot be less than 50 percent or more than 100 percent of the amount of the annuity payable during the time that the participant and the spouse are both alive. Distributions cannot be made at any time in a form other than a QJSA unless the participant and the spouse elect otherwise. [Treas. Reg. § 1.417(e)-1(b)]

A qualified preretirement survivor annuity (QPSA) can be established to protect employees' spouses in the event a married participant dies before the annuity starting date and has vested benefits. A QPSA is an immediate annuity for the life of the surviving spouse of a participant who dies before the annuity starting date. The participant can pay the cost of this benefit by receiving a lower benefit, or the plan can subsidize the cost of this benefit.

A plan can provide a disability benefit that is: an immediate annuity at some reduced amount; continued benefit accruals until normal retirement age while a participant is disabled and no immediate annuity; or a combination of the two. Many disability policies sponsored by employers for employees outside the plan provide current benefits but stop those benefits at normal retirement age. At retirement, the accrued benefit is paid by the plan. Some employers elect to self-insure disability benefits through the defined benefit plan. Normally, employers coordinate disability benefits provided outside the plan with retirement benefits provided within the plan.

Employers also can offer employees subsidized early retirement benefits. This type of benefit targets certain employees who meet designated criteria, such as age 55 with 20 years of service, to encourage early retirement. Providing additional years of benefit service or additional percentages per year of service are two examples of enhanced benefits. The cost of these enhanced benefits can be spread out over future years, the number of which will depend on the cost method used by the actuary.

### Q 3:14 Must an optional form of benefit or ancillary benefits be nondiscriminatory?

Yes. Optional forms of benefit and ancillary benefits must be currently available to a group of employees that satisfies one of the minimum coverage tests. [Treas. Reg. § 1.401(a)(4)-4(b)]

### Q 3:15 Which employees do defined benefit plans help?

Defined benefit plans help all employees. A defined benefit plan provides a guaranteed benefit that is not based on the performance of the stock market. It provides a predetermined, level amount of benefit payments that will extend over the life of the participant or of the participant and the participant's spouse. Oftentimes, a defined benefit plan, when first installed, provides catch-up benefits to long-service employees who may not have had a retirement plan when they first went to work for the employer.

### Q 3:16 Which employees might be hurt by defined benefit plans?

Defined benefit plans spread costs throughout the employer's workforce. Costs of the plan may be 8 percent of wages on average; however, proportionately more of the contribution is needed to provide the benefit accruals for older employees. Equal contributions to each individual employee would provide greater benefits for younger employees when they reached retirement age. Consequently, some may view a defined benefit plan as favoring older employees over younger ones.

## Demographics

### Q 3:17 How do the demographics of an employer's workforce affect plan design?

The cost of a program is directly related to the demographics of the group covered as well as the amount of benefits provided. A mature population under a new plan would have much higher costs than a younger group of employees under the same plan. The cost of providing a specified replacement ratio for a group of professionals would be higher than the cost of providing the same replacement ratio to a group of unskilled laborers. The employee population should be examined to determine appropriate demographic weightings for the specific employer.

### Q 3:18 What types of compensation should be considered in determining benefits?

The employer must review its compensation policy before instituting a program. Some employers have periods when they incur high levels of overtime.

Including overtime may make the costs of the plan difficult to determine. Other plans use final three-year average compensation for determining benefits. Employees within their final three years may attempt to work as much overtime as possible, thereby inflating the benefits over what was anticipated. Some employers provide low base pay with significant performance incentives. Again, the budgeting process becomes difficult.

On the opposite end of the spectrum, if an employee receives a significant portion of compensation based on overtime or bonuses, a program that excludes the additional compensation will provide a significantly smaller replacement ratio. In this instance, plan design may fail to meet the employer's initial objectives of remaining competitive in its ability to attract and retain employees or of providing adequately for its employees in retirement.

In addition, the exclusion of some forms of compensation (e.g., overtime) may be discriminatory if significantly more of such compensation is excluded from the benefit determination for non-highly compensated employees than from the benefit determination for highly compensated employees. Discrimination issues such as this need to be analyzed in any proper plan design.

## Plan Sponsor Structure

### Q 3:19   How does the business structure of a plan sponsor affect plan design?

All forms of businesses can establish and maintain a defined benefit plan. The covered population must be reviewed in light of controlled groups, affiliated service groups, and leased employees. Qualified plans must maintain coverage and discrimination testing based on all employees of the employer, indicating those that work for members of the controlled group or affiliated service group.

In addition, the legal structure of the business can affect the plan design. For example, owners of S corporations may base benefits only on W-2 wages and cannot use the pass-through income (as reported on a Schedule K-1 as dividend income) they also receive as owners. Owners of unincorporated businesses have earned income, which is reduced by contributions for their employees and themselves, thus creating a circular equation when determining eligible compensation for benefit purposes.

### Q 3:20   Why do most governmental organizations have defined benefit plans?

Governmental organizations have a stable workforce and a steady source of income to pay for benefits. Early on, many governmental organizations paid less in wages and compensated by providing richer benefits. Many governmental organizations are now unionized, and the collective bargaining units negotiate benefit programs for their members.

### Q 3:21    Why are most multiemployer plans defined benefit plans?

By definition, a multiemployer plan is a collectively bargained plan that has more than one contributing employer. Some unionized industries have a mobile workforce. It is not uncommon for skilled union workers to move from employer to employer. Each employer contributes to a plan that allows the benefits to accumulate as long as the member stays with the union. Many unions have negotiated programs that continue the benefits of membership through retirement and to survivors. A defined benefit plan is an ideal vehicle to accommodate pension benefits provided through union membership.

### Q 3:22    What considerations should large employers take into account?

Defining the covered group, replacement ratios, costs, data collection, and data quality are key items for plan design for large employers. Large employers may have several locations. Each location may face different competition in the labor market. Each location may also have its own personnel files, payroll system, and records. As companies are acquired, the benefits of each of the companies must be reviewed in light of the new combined structure. The costs of leveraged buyouts may add financial burdens not initially anticipated when the plans were established.

### Q 3:23    What considerations should small employers take into account?

Security of benefits for all employees, volatile profit and loss, optional forms of benefit that could drain available cash, and sharp changes in asset performance are key items for small employers. Smaller companies have diversification risk such that a loss of a key client or clients or changes in legislation or the economy could lead to significant business hardship and cause future hardships, especially if it is not possible to discontinue contributions to the plan.

## Types of Defined Benefit Formulas

### Q 3:24    What is a *fixed, or flat, benefit plan*, and when is it appropriate?

A *fixed benefit plan* is a program that provides a flat-dollar benefit per year of service or after a number of years of service. For example, $15 per year of service for 30 years is a fixed benefit plan. A plan with a benefit of $200 per month reduced for each year of service less than 25 is also a fixed benefit plan, as is a plan that provides a flat benefit identified as a given percentage of compensation, for example, a benefit of 30 percent of average annual compensation.

An employer that provides compensation for piecework or has lower-paid employees, all receiving close to the same wage, might use a fixed benefit plan.

## Q 3:25   What is a *salary-related plan*, and when is it appropriate?

A *salary-related plan* is a plan that provides a benefit as a function of compensation. It could be a unit benefit plan, providing a percentage of compensation per year of service, or a fixed benefit plan.

An employer that would like to reward long-service employees over short-service employees would establish a unit benefit plan. An employer that wants to reward highly compensated employees the same level percentage of compensation as non-highly compensated employees would also establish a salary-related plan.

## Q 3:26   How can the employer protect against large benefits accruing for short-service employees?

A plan can be designed to provide for benefits based on future service or can be designed with cutbacks for shorter service periods. For example, a plan can provide that the benefit formula is 2 percent per year of service after 1998. Alternatively, a 50 percent of average compensation plan can have a service reduction of $\frac{1}{30}$ for each year of service less than 30. If an employee is hired at age 60, and the normal retirement age is 65, then the 50 percent is reduced by $\frac{25}{30}$, or 83.33 percent.

## Q 3:27   When does a larger accrual make sense in earlier years?

Vesting and benefit accruals have a significant interplay within a plan. For example, using faster accruals selectively can make the discrimination tests easier to pass.

**Example.** Lynn is a non-highly compensated employee and has a benefit accrual of 10 percent for the first year and 0 percent for the next four years in Plan *A*. Pat is a highly compensated employee and has a benefit accrual of 2 percent per year for each year for five years in Plan *B*. Pat and Lynn both end up at the end of five years with an accrued benefit of 10 percent of average annual compensation.

Both Plan *A* and Plan *B* have a five-year 100 percent cliff vesting schedule. If Pat or Lynn terminates employment in the first four years, her vested accrued benefit would be zero. For discrimination testing, especially for plans that are using the general test and the accrued-to-date method (see chapter 11), Lynn's accrual rate for the first four years exceeds Pat's accrual rate. If Lynn and Pat were the only two participants, the plans would pass the discrimination tests.

## Q 3:28   Can an employer delay accruals until service periods that are closer to retirement age?

No. Benefit accruals cannot be backloaded. A benefit accrual in a future year cannot exceed 133 percent of a benefit accrual in a prior year (see chapter 9). Preventing backloading allows for meaningful accrual of benefits throughout an employee's working lifetime. Otherwise, employees could be terminated just before earning the substantial portion of their retirement benefits.

### Q 3:29   Why are some plans integrated with Social Security?

Employers pay 50 percent of the Social Security taxes for an employee. Historically, many plan designs offset the benefits provided by the plan by a portion of the Social Security primary insurance amount to provide only one level of benefits for a range of compensation. For example, a common plan design before the Tax Reform Act of 1986 (TRA '86) was 50 percent of average annual compensation offset by 50 percent of the Social Security primary insurance amount.

Plans can now provide similar benefits as long as they pass the nondiscrimination regulations under Code Section 401(a)(4). Many plans are now designed using the permitted disparity rules under Code Section 401(l).

## Additional Limitations and Testing

### Q 3:30   How do the minimum participation requirements affect defined benefit plan design?

Under the requirements of Code Sections 410(b) and 401(a)(26), a plan must benefit a certain number of eligible employees. For example, under Code Section 401(a)(26), a defined benefit plan must benefit at least the greater of 40 percent of eligible employees or two employees. If an employer has only two eligible employees, regardless of their status as either highly compensated or non-highly compensated employees, both would be required to participate for the employer to maintain a qualified plan.

### Q 3:31   How does nondiscrimination testing affect defined benefit plan design?

Nondiscrimination testing is critical to plan design. A plan sponsor must decide whether a safe harbor design is desired or if testing based on demographics would provide a program that better meets its objectives. In a safe harbor design, the program is very basic and may require unreasonable contributions for selected employee groups. By using the general test, a plan sponsor can design benefit levels that differ for different groups, yet are deemed comparable when tested using the guidelines provided in the regulations under Code Section 401(a)(4).

### Q 3:32   What additional limitations apply to a defined benefit plan?

There are several explicit and implicit limitations within the design of a defined benefit pension plan. Explicit limitations are the Section 415 maximum dollar amount of $160,000 or the 100 percent of the high three-year average compensation limitation. There is a maximum compensation limitation under Code Section 401(a)(17) of $200,000 (as indexed for inflation), which implicitly limits benefits under a plan. Interest assumptions that must be used for actuarial equivalence limit lump-sum payouts.

### Q 3:33   When is a defined benefit plan considered top heavy?

A plan is considered top heavy under Code Section 416 when 60 percent of the present value of the accrued benefits belong to key employees. Careful attention must be paid when a company sponsors more than one plan. In most instances, all plans must be aggregated when performing the top-heavy tests. Certain distributions must be added back, and others cannot.

### Q 3:34   How does top-heavy status affect plan design?

Certain benefit improvements must be made if a plan is top heavy. In general, the non-key employees who are participants in the plan must be given a top-heavy minimum accrued benefit of 2 percent of five-year average annual compensation for a maximum period of 10 years of participation. If the normal form of benefit is other than a life annuity, the 2 percent amount is reduced to an actuarially equivalent benefit. The vesting schedule of the plan is accelerated to a minimum of 20 percent vesting after two years of service and an additional 20 percent per year thereafter. Alternatively, the vesting schedule can be 0 percent for the first two years and 100 percent on completing three years.

Top-heavy minimum benefits may accelerate benefit accruals under a plan and can be used for meeting the nondiscrimination regulations under Code Section 401(a)(4).

## Additional Factors

### Q 3:35   How does the selection of early, normal, or late retirement dates affect plan design?

Retirement ages can be selected by the plan sponsor to meet certain objectives. For example, police and fire departments traditionally have earlier retirement ages because of the hazardous and physically demanding nature of their work. Professional athletes normally have earlier retirement ages. Employers can have normal retirement ages that extend beyond the norm of age 65 as long as the benefits earned by the later of age 65 or five years of participation are fully vested and are payable to the participants on attaining the chosen normal retirement age. A plan cannot discriminate against employees on the basis of age but can limit benefit accruals after a given number of years of service. Subsidized early retirement benefits must be included in the computation of the most valuable accrual rate (see chapter 11) when performing the nondiscrimination tests under Code Section 401(a)(4). Therefore, early retirement subsidies cannot discriminate in favor of highly compensated employees. At plan termination, any subsidized benefits must be made available to eligible employees.

### Q 3:36    Can different benefits be used for various retirement ages?

Yes. Plans can be designed to provide benefits at various retirement ages as long as the benefits are available to eligible employees on a nondiscriminatory basis and the amounts payable are nondiscriminatory.

### Q 3:37    Should the plan design consider the possibility of plan termination?

Yes. Prudent plan design should address the possibility of plan termination so that benefits remain fully funded on a premature termination. Severe penalties apply and up to 30 percent of the net worth of the company can be taken to meet the obligations of the plan. Having a plan that is underfunded can also adversely affect the purchase of the business by another company, while having an overfunded plan can make the purchase of the business by another company more attractive.

# Chapter 4

# Hybrid Plans

This chapter introduces pension plans that have a combination of defined contribution and defined benefit plan features. Generally, hybrid plans are more portable than traditional defined benefit plans and therefore are easier for employees to understand. All hybrid plans provide a guarantee by the employer in the form of either benefits or contributions. Hybrid plans represent the melding of complex pension actuarial principles and concepts with the simplicity of account balances. These exciting plans are gaining the attention of employers throughout the United States in large part because of the wide interest in and convenience of account balance type defined contribution plans such as 401(k) plans. In fact, Congress recognized the importance of merging the benefits of a guaranteed account feature of a defined benefit plan with the wide interest in 401(k) features when they authorized the creation of a new plan in 2010 called an eligible combined plan.

## The Basics

### Q 4:1    What is a *hybrid plan*?

A *hybrid plan* is a retirement plan that is of one type, either defined benefit or defined contribution, but has some of the characteristics of the other type of plan (see Q 2:6). For example, a defined contribution plan generally defines contributions each year as a percentage of salary. If a particular defined contribution plan instead determines contributions based on how much money is required to purchase an annuity benefit payable at a participant's retirement, it is considered a hybrid plan because it has a characteristic typically found in defined benefit plans (see Qs 4:2–4:11). On the other hand, a hybrid defined benefit plan may, instead of calculating the annuity benefit based on attainment of normal retirement age, define hypothetical contributions to be credited to an account for the participant.

In testing a plan for discrimination in benefits or contributions, the contribution in a defined contribution plan or the benefit in a defined benefit plan can be converted to an equivalent accrued benefit or equivalent contribution, thus treating one type of plan as if it were the other type (see chapters 10 and 11).

The hybrid plans discussed in this chapter are meant to be only a sampling of some of the more common ones. There are innumerable variations, and the only limitation is that of an individual's creativity (along with the constraints of keeping a plan tax qualified).

Hybrid plans are becoming increasingly popular plan designs, with nearly 30 percent of all plans containing a type of hybrid formula (Society of Actuaries' Survey on the Prevalence of Traditional and Hybrid Defined Benefit Pension Plans, Report of Findings, March 2005).

### Q 4:2    How is an *accrued benefit* defined?

An *accrued benefit* was previously defined as the benefit payable to the participant at retirement in the plan's normal form of payment (e.g., an annuity for the life of the participant). With the passage of the Pension Protection Act of 2006 (PPA), an accrued benefit is now defined as either (1) an annuity payable at normal retirement age, (2) the balance of a hypothetical account, or (3) the current value of the accumulated percentage of the employee's final average compensation. With this change in the law, the controversy regarding whether cash balance and other hybrid plans are legal has ended, at least prospectively. It was part of this provision that this change is only to apply prospectively.

### Q 4:3    How is an accrued benefit that is defined in terms of an annuity converted to an equivalent contribution or account balance for testing purposes?

To convert an accrued benefit to an account balance, it must be converted to its actuarially equivalent lump-sum value. In converting an accrued benefit to an account balance, assumptions must be made about the mortality of the participant and the investment rate of return. (See chapter 23 for more information about how these assumptions are chosen.) It is assumed that all assumptions made for mortality and investment rate of return are exactly realized. Once a mortality table and interest rate are chosen, an annuity purchase rate (APR) (see Q 18:4) is developed and used to convert the accrued benefit to a lump sum payable at retirement. This lump sum is then discounted from retirement age to attained age using present value factors developed from the interest rate assumption selected (see Q 18:2). The resulting amount is called the "present value of the accrued benefit," which is also the actuarially equivalent account balance.

**Example.** John, age 35, is a participant in the SPS defined benefit plan and the SPS defined contribution plan. He has an accrued benefit of $3,600 per year payable at age 65 as a straight life annuity from the defined benefit plan and an account balance of $5,000 in the defined contribution plan. He wants to know which benefit is of the most value to him today. The defined benefit plan uses an APR of 12.0 and assumes 7.0 percent interest in converting benefits to their actuarial equivalent. The accrued benefit in the defined benefit plan is converted to a current account balance by first multiplying by the APR (12.0) and then discounting to today ($.1314 = 1/(1.07)^{30}$). The actuarial present value of the accrued benefit is $5,676 ($3,600 $\times$ 12.0 $\times$ .1314).

To convert the accrued benefit to an equivalent contribution, the process is the same as outlined above, with the only exception that the amount of the benefit actually accruing during that year is measured and converted to determine its actuarially equivalent "cost" or contribution.

### Q 4:4 How is a contribution in a defined contribution plan converted to an equivalent accrued benefit?

The process of converting a contribution to an equivalent accrued benefit is the exact reverse of the process outlined in Q 4:3. The contribution is accumulated to retirement age using an interest assumption and is then divided by the assumed APR to arrive at the actuarially equivalent accrued benefit.

**Example.** Assume the same facts as in the example in Q 4:3. John would like to know the equivalent accrued benefit of his account balance in the defined contribution plan. The $5,000 account balance is accumulated with 7.0 percent interest to age 65 ($7.612 = (1.07)^{30}$) and then divided by the plan's APR (12.0) to arrive at the actuarially equivalent accrued benefit of $3,172 payable annually ($5,000 $\times$ 7.612 $\div$ 12.0).

## Target Benefit Plans

### Q 4:5 What is a *target benefit plan*?

A *target benefit plan* is a money purchase type of defined contribution plan in which the amount of the contribution made to a participant's account is based on the contribution required to fund a target benefit at the plan's normal retirement age. The benefit the plan sponsor funds is based on a defined benefit pension plan formula, generally of a flat benefit or unit credit type. The contribution requirement is based on the individual level-premium funding method (see chapter 18), with the distinction that actuarial gains or losses are ignored in calculating the contribution requirement. The only promise the employer makes in such an arrangement is to fund the required contribution. If the account balance is more than necessary to pay the target benefit, the benefits will be more than anticipated. Conversely, if the account balance is less than the amount required to pay the target benefit, the benefits will be less.

### Q 4:6   Is there any limitation on the amount of the retirement benefit derived from a target benefit plan?

No. The employee's ultimate retirement benefit is based on the account balance, not the benefit formula. It is possible for an employer to fund for benefits greater than those allowed under Internal Revenue Code (Code) Section 415(b) (i.e., the lesser of 100 percent of the three-year average annual compensation or $160,000, as indexed for inflation), but the contribution is limited to the amount specified in Code Section 415(c) (i.e., the lesser of 100 percent of compensation or $40,000, as indexed for inflation), and Code Section 404 (i.e., 25 percent of total eligible compensation).

### Q 4:7   Are the services of an actuary required for a target benefit plan?

No. Although target benefit plans are subject to the minimum funding standards under Code Section 412, there is no requirement that an actuary certify that the sponsor has satisfied the minimum funding standards. It is highly recommended, however, that an actuary review the calculations to be certain that the individual level-premium funding method has been applied correctly.

### Q 4:8   What factors affect the amount of the contribution to a target benefit plan?

Contributions to a target benefit plan are affected by the amount of benefit, the age of the participant, and the number of years remaining to fund the benefit. Because the contribution is based solely on the normal cost using the individual level-premium funding method and, as stated previously, any actuarial gains or losses are ignored, the asset's rate of return has no impact on the contribution requirement. When determining the target benefit, the plan cannot use a salary scale. Older plan participants with fewer years of participation have larger contribution requirements because of the shorter time period available to fund the benefit.

### Q 4:9   What advantages does an employer gain by using a target benefit pension plan?

If, on adoption of a target benefit plan, the employer has older employees with many years of service, the contribution requirement will be a much larger percentage of compensation for the older employees than it will be for the younger employees. Therefore, if the key employees are older and have the most service with the employer, the cost of providing benefits for the key employees will be the largest percentage of the total contribution to the plan. Furthermore, the employer enjoys the promised-benefit feature of a defined benefit plan without incurring any risk due to poor investment performance, which would otherwise increase its contribution requirement to the plan. Additionally, target benefit plans are not required to pay Pension Benefit Guaranty Corporation (PBGC) insurance premiums (see chapter 23), so this cost is eliminated. Finally, employees frequently appreciate and understand an account balance better than the ultimate benefit that the formula is targeting.

### Q 4:10   How do target benefit plans satisfy the safe harbor nondiscrimination requirements?

Generally, contributions to a target benefit plan differ as a percentage of compensation for each employee and therefore may not meet the safe harbor contribution formulas for defined contribution plans. A target benefit plan can be deemed to satisfy the safe harbor requirements, however, if it meets several other criteria. If a target benefit plan complies with all the following requirements, the employer need not prove nondiscrimination using any other testing methods available:

1. The formula must provide for a straight life annuity beginning at the employee's normal retirement age under a formula that satisfies the defined benefit plan safe harbors under Treasury Regulations Section 1.401(a)(4)-3(b)(4)(i)(C)(1) or (2). The safe harbor formulas are a flat benefit formula with benefits accrued over no less than 25 years of plan participation, and a unit credit formula with benefits accrued over plan participation. The years used for determining benefits must be the same as the years over which the benefit is earned. [Treas. Reg. § 1.401(a)(4)-8(b)(3)(i)(A)] For example, an employer cannot provide for a benefit that is based on years of service with an employer and then fund the benefit over the employee's years of participation in the plan unless years of service are equal to years of participation.

2. The employer must use forfeitures to reduce contributions to the plan, and employee contributions are not permitted.

3. If the plan uses permitted disparity to determine plan benefits, the formula must follow the Social Security integration rules for defined benefit plans under Treasury Regulations Section 1.401(l)-3.

4. The plan can change the benefit formula from one year to the next with proper notification of plan participants. The law for the notice requirement can be found in Employee Retirement Income Security Act of 1974 (ERISA) Section 204(h).

5. The plan must provide postretirement benefits under the same rules as those used to determine postretirement benefits under a defined benefit plan. Generally, this means that service credit is required after retirement unless there is a service cap on the benefit formula.

6. The plan must follow the rules under Treasury Regulations Section 1.401(a)(4)-8(b)(3)(iv) through (viii) in determining the required contribution under the plan (see Q 4:11).

7. The plan must use standard mortality and interest rate actuarial assumptions (see chapter 10).

[Treas. Reg. § 1.401(a)(4)-8(b)(3)]

### Q 4:11   How are the required contributions determined for target benefit plans?

The method for determining required employer contributions is described in Treasury Regulations Section 1.401(a)(4)-8(b)(3)(iv) through (viii), and uses the individual level-premium funding method. Generally, the plan is required to fund the difference between the participant's theoretical reserve and the present value of the projected retirement benefits over the remaining years of participation as of the date the contribution is determined.

**Example.** This top-heavy plan provides 50 percent of the three-year average salary reduced for years of participation less than 25.

*Sample Plan Data*

| Participant | Projected Plan Participation | Years of Participation to Date | Age | Salary | Average Salary |
|---|---|---|---|---|---|
| Fred | 30 | 5 | 35 | $35,000 | $35,000 |
| Wilma | 10 | 0 | 55 | $40,000 | $40,000 |
| Barney | 15 | 3 | 50 | $50,000 | $50,000 |
| Betty | 5 | 7 | 67 | $25,000 | $23,500 |

*Step 1.* The target benefit is calculated for each participant. Note that Betty is working beyond her normal retirement age and that the reduction in her benefit reflects seven years of plan participation. Furthermore, she is now in an averaging period, so her benefit is based on the current three-year average. The other employees are assumed to continue earning the same rate of salary until retirement, thus creating an average salary equal to current salary.

*Target Benefit Calculation*

| | $A$ | $B$ | $C = B/25$ | $D = A \times C$ | $E = A - D$ |
|---|---|---|---|---|---|
| | 50 Percent of Average Salary | Participation Less Than 25 | Reduction Factor | Reduction In Benefit | Target Benefit |
| Fred | $17,500 | 0 | 0.00 | $    0 | $17,500 |
| Wilma | $20,000 | 15 | 0.60 | $12,000 | $ 8,000 |
| Barney | $25,000 | 10 | 0.40 | $10,000 | $15,000 |
| Betty | $11,750 | 18 | 0.72 | $ 8,460 | $ 3,290 |

*Step 2.* The regulation requires making a determination of the theoretical reserve. This is done by adding the prior year's required contribution (limited by Code Section 415(c), but without regard to any top-heavy contributions required under Code Section 416) to the prior year's theoretical reserve, increased with interest at the prior year's interest rate (we are assuming 7.5 percent interest for this example).

*Theoretical Reserve Calculation*

|  | $\underline{A}$ | $\underline{B}$ | $\begin{array}{c}C=(A+B)\\ \times\,1.075\end{array}$ |
|---|---|---|---|
|  | Prior Year's Theoretical Reserve | Prior Year's Required Contribution | Current Theoretical Reserve |
| Fred | $6,202 | $1,271 | $ 8,033 |
| Wilma | $0 | $4,248 | $ 4,566 |
| Barney | $9,500 | $4,314 | $14,850 |
| Betty | $26,000 | $ 500 | $28,488 |

*Step 3.* The present value of the target benefit at the valuation date is determined. The discount factor is the present value of $1 payable from the valuation date to the normal retirement date. For example, if Fred has 25 years until retirement, his discount factor is $(1.075)^{-25}$, or 0.164 (using a standard interest rate of 7.5 percent).

*Present Value Calculation*

|  | $\underline{A}$ | $\underline{B}$ | $\underline{C}$ | $D=A \times B \times C$ |
|---|---|---|---|---|
|  | Target Benefit | Annuity Purchase Rate | Discount Factor | Present Value |
| Fred | $17,500 | 8.50 | 0.164 | $24,395 |
| Wilma | $8,000 | 8.50 | 0.485 | $32,980 |
| Barney | $15,000 | 8.50 | 0.420 | $53,550 |
| Betty | $3,290 | 8.50 | 0.930 | $26,007 |

*Step 4.* The present value of the target benefit obtained in Step 3 is subtracted from the theoretical reserve calculated in Step 2, and the difference, otherwise known as the present value of future normal costs, is funded using a level amortization at the funding interest rate from the valuation date to the retirement date. If the amortization amount, that is, the contribution, exceeds the Section 415(c) limit, the contribution is reduced. If the plan requires a top-heavy contribution under Code Section 416, the contribution is increased.

**Note.** The regulation requires that Betty use an APR at normal retirement, not her attained age, and that her contribution be increased to the top-heavy minimum.

*Contribution Calculation*

|        | A | B | C = A − B | D | E = C/D |
|--------|---------|-------------|-------------|-------------|-------------|
|        | | Current | Present Value | | |
|        | *Present* | *Theoretical* | *of Future* | *Amortization* | *Required* |
|        | *Value* | *Reserve* | *Contributions* | *Factor* | *Contribution* |
| Fred   | $24,395 | $8,033  | $16,362  | 11.98 | $1,366 |
| Wilma  | $32,980 | $4,566  | $28,414  | 7.38  | $3,850 |
| Barney | $53,550 | $14,850 | $38,700  | 8.32  | $4,651 |
| Betty  | $26,007 | $28,488 | ($2,481) | 1.00  | $  750* |

*The $750 contribution for Betty is 3 percent of her current salary ($25,000 × 3%).

### Q 4:12  What special rules apply to target benefit plans that were in effect before September 19, 1991?

Target benefit plans that were in effect before September 19, 1991, were subject to a calculation transition, which required the recalculation of the initial theoretical reserve for the first plan year that began after this date. Only plans that satisfied nondiscrimination requirements before this date fall under this special rule. Additionally, for plan years beginning in 1994, any employer that wanted to fall under the safe harbor rules for target benefit plans and had a plan in effect prior to September 19, 1991, had to amend the plan's benefit formula to satisfy the safe harbor requirements under Treasury Regulations Section 1.401(a)(4)-8(b)(3) (see Q 4:10). The amendment had impact in two areas. The first was that participation in the plan prior to the amendment could be counted in the amended plan's benefit formula. The second was that the theoretical reserve was reestablished, using the standard mortality and interest rates (see Q 4:10). [Treas. Reg. § 1.401(a)(4)-8(b)(3)(vii)]

### Q 4:13  Are target benefit plans subject to the minimum funding standards?

Yes. Target benefit plans are treated as money purchase pension plans and are therefore subject to the minimum contribution requirements under Code Section 412. The plan must contribute the amount determined by the plan's benefit formula in effect on the valuation date using the actuarial assumptions defined in the plan document.

## Floor-Offset Plans

### Q 4:14  What is a *floor-offset plan*?

A *floor-offset plan* is a defined benefit pension plan whose benefit is reduced, or offset, by the benefits under a defined contribution plan. This arrangement allows the employer to guarantee a base, or floor, benefit regardless of the amount of benefit derived from the defined contribution plan. As a result, the employee can never get less than the benefit promised under the defined benefit plan. Alternatively, if the benefit derived under the defined contribution plan is greater than the benefit under the defined benefit plan, no benefits are paid from the defined benefit plan.

**Example.** Assume an employer sponsors a floor-offset arrangement that provides a benefit of 1 percent of the three-year average annual compensation for each year of service offset by the benefits under a defined contribution plan. An APR of $120 per $1,000 of benefit is assumed. Employee A, who retires with 30 years of service, a three-year average compensation of $40,000, and a defined contribution account balance of $130,000, receives no benefit from the defined benefit pension plan because $130,000 is $10,000 more than needed to provide the 30 percent ($1\% \times 30$ years) of average compensation benefit. The offset is calculated as follows:

| | |
|---|---|
| Benefit | $40,000 \times 0.30 \div 12 = \$1,000$ per month |
| Cash needed to provide the benefit | $120 \times \$1,000 = \$120,000$ |
| Account balance to offset the benefit | $130,000 |

The account balance is $10,000 more than required; therefore, no benefits from the offset (defined benefit) plan are due.

Employee B, who retires with 25 years of service, a three-year average compensation of $20,000, and a $35,000 account balance, receives an additional benefit worth $15,000 because the $35,000 account balance is not sufficient to provide the 25 percent ($1\% \times 25$ years) of average compensation benefit, calculated as follows:

| | |
|---|---|
| Benefit | $20,000 \times 0.25 \div 12 = \$416.67$ per month |
| Cash needed to provide benefit | $120 \times \$416.67 = \$50,000$ |
| Account balance to offset the benefit | $35,000 |

The account balance is $15,000 less than required; therefore, the lump-sum value of the benefit due from the offset plan is $15,000.

### Q 4:15    What requirements must be met for a floor-offset arrangement to be considered a safe harbor?

A floor-offset arrangement will satisfy safe harbor testing if all of the following seven criteria are met:

1. The accrued benefit that would otherwise be provided to the employee in the defined benefit plan must be reduced solely by the actuarial equivalent of all or part of the employee's account balance attributable to employer contributions under a defined contribution plan maintained by the same employer (plus the actuarial equivalent of all or part of any prior distributions from that portion of the account balance). (See Q 4:16 regarding the

determination of the actuarially equivalent benefit.) If any portion of the benefit being offset is nonforfeitable, that portion can be offset only by a benefit (or portion of benefit) that is nonforfeitable.

2. The defined benefit plan cannot be a contributory defined benefit plan, and benefits cannot be offset by any portion of an employee's account attributable to employee contributions.

3. The defined benefit plan and defined contribution plan must benefit the same employees.

4. The offset must be applied to all employees on the same terms.

5. All employees must have available to them under the defined contribution plan the same investment options and the same options with respect to the timing of preretirement distributions.

6. Either the defined benefit plan or the defined contribution plan must be a safe harbor plan; the other plan can be a safe harbor plan or not. The determination of the safe harbors is made without regard to the other plan. The defined benefit plan in all cases must satisfy certain uniformity requirements under Treasury Regulations Section 1.401(a)(4)-3(b)(2) (see Q 4:17). When the defined benefit plan is the safe harbor plan, it must be a unit credit safe harbor plan under Treasury Regulations Section 1.401(a)(4)-3(b)(3) without taking into account the offset, and the defined contribution plan must satisfy a safe harbor allocation under Treasury Regulations Section 1.401(a)(4)-2(b) or satisfy a general test under Treasury Regulations Section 1.401(a)(4)-2(c). Alternatively, if the defined contribution plan is the safe harbor plan, the defined benefit plan must satisfy either one of the safe harbor methods in Treasury Regulations Section 1.401(a)(4)-3(b) or satisfy a general test under Treasury Regulations Section 1.401(a)(4)-3(c) without taking into account the offset, and the defined contribution plan must satisfy the uniform allocation safe harbor under Treasury Regulations Section 1.401(a)(4)-2(b)(2).

7. The defined contribution plan cannot be a 401(k) or 401(m) plan.

[Treas. Reg. § 1.401(a)(4)-8(d)(1)(i)-(vii)]

### Q 4:16   How are actuarially equivalent benefits determined in a safe harbor floor-offset arrangement?

In determining the actuarial equivalent in a safe harbor floor-offset arrangement, an interest rate no higher than the standard interest rate, 8.5 percent, must be used, and no mortality rate can be assumed in determining the actuarial equivalent of any prior distribution from the defined contribution plan or for years prior to the benefit commencement date under the defined benefit plan. [Treas. Reg. § 1.401(a)(4)-8(d)(1)(i)]

### Q 4:17  What are the uniformity requirements for safe harbor floor-offset arrangements?

The following uniformity requirements must be met for floor-offset arrangements to be considered safe harbors:

1. *Uniform normal retirement benefit.* The same benefit formula must apply to all employees. The benefit formula must provide all employees with an annual benefit payable in the same form beginning at the same uniform normal retirement age. The annual benefit must be the same percentage of average annual compensation or the same dollar amount for all employees who will have the same number of years of service at normal retirement age. The annual benefit must equal the employee's accrued benefit at normal retirement age and must be the normal retirement benefit under the plan.

2. *Uniform post-normal retirement benefit.* With respect to an employee with a given number of years of service at any age after normal retirement age, the annual benefit beginning at that employee's age must be the same percentage of average annual compensation or the same dollar amount that would be payable beginning at normal retirement age to an employee who had that same number of years of service at normal retirement age.

3. *Uniform subsidies.* Each subsidized optional form of benefit available under the plan must be currently available (within the meaning of Treasury Regulations Section 1.401(a)(4)-4(b)(2)) substantially to all employees. Whether an optional form of benefit is considered subsidized for this purpose can be determined using any reasonable actuarial assumptions.

4. *No employee contributions.* The plan must not be a contributory defined benefit plan.

5. *Period of accrual.* Each employee's benefit must be accrued over the same years of service as those that are taken into account in applying the benefit formula under the plan to that employee. For this purpose, any year in which the employee benefits under the plan is included as a year of service in which a benefit accrues. Thus, for example, a plan does not satisfy the safe harbor rules for a fractional accrued method unless the plan uses the same years of service to determine both the normal retirement benefit under the plan's benefit formula and the fraction by which an employee's fractional rule benefit is multiplied to derive the employee's accrued benefit as of any plan year.

[Treas. Reg. § 1.401(a)(4)-3(b)(2)(i)-(v)]

### Q 4:18  How are the projected benefits determined in a floor-offset arrangement?

The calculation of benefits in a floor-offset arrangement requires the projection of benefits in both the defined contribution plan and the defined benefit plan. Projected benefits should be determined using the plan's funding actuarial assumptions; accrued benefits should be calculated using the plan's definition of actuarial equivalence. The distinction is that the accrued benefit is determined using the current account balance as the offset, whereas the projected benefit is determined using the current account balance plus the value of continued contributions to the defined contribution plans to retirement.

**Example.** The offset is projected using 7 percent interest and an APR of $120. Note that if the defined benefit plan is using a salary scale, the projections in the defined contribution plan should reflect the increased contribution caused by the salary scale.

*Step 1.* The defined contribution accounts are projected to the retirement date under the plan. The projection assumes continuing contributions by the employer each year until retirement.

*Determination of the Defined Contribution Plan Offset Benefit*

| | A | B | C | D | E | F = D/E |
|---|---|---|---|---|---|---|
| | | | *Years to* | | | |
| | | | *Normal* | | *Annuity* | |
| | *Account* | *Current* | *Retirement* | *Projected* | *Purchase* | *Projected* |
| | *Balance* | *Contribution* | *Date* | *Account* | *Rate* | *Offset* |
| Employee A | $50,000 | $2,000 | 10 | $127,925 | $120 | $1,066 |
| Employee B | $ 490 | $ 500 | 30 | $ 54,267 | $120 | $ 452 |

*Step 2.* The offset is applied to the projected benefit under the defined benefit plan. If the benefit remaining, after applying the offset, is zero, no benefits are provided from the defined benefit plan. Note that the benefits in column C would be the basis for the funding requirements in the defined benefit plan.

*Determination of Benefit from Defined Benefit Plan*

| | A | B | C = A + B (not less than $0) |
|---|---|---|---|
| | *Projected* | *Projected* | *Projected DB* |
| | *Benefits* | *Offset* | *Benefit* |
| Employee A | $2,000 | ($1,066) | $934 |
| Employee B | $ 350 | ($ 452) | $ 0 |

## Q 4:19   How is the accrued benefit determined in a floor-offset arrangement?

The accrued benefit under a defined contribution plan is the account balance, whereas the accrued benefit under a defined benefit plan is the benefit earned as of the valuation date. The accrued benefit in the defined benefit plan must satisfy the accrual rules of Code Section 411(b)(1), determined without regard to the offset derived from the defined contribution plan. The accrued benefit determination in a floor-offset arrangement assumes no future contributions to the defined contribution plan. All projections to the normal retirement date are done using the interest rate assumption for determining actuarial equivalence in the plan document. The plan document must also state the time (determination date) as of which the determination is made. The amount deemed provided by the account balance of the defined contribution plan is limited to the vested portion of the account balance plus any additional amount that would have been provided by a prior distribution from the account balance. [Rev. Rul. 76-259, 1976-2 C.B. 111] The projected account balance is converted to a monthly benefit that then offsets the accrued benefit under the defined benefit plan.

**Example.**

*Step 1.* Project the future value of the defined contribution plan account balance at retirement. This projection assumes no future contributions to the account balance. Divide the projected account by the APR defined in the plan document. This amount will be used to offset the accrued benefit in the defined benefit plan.

*Projection of Defined Contribution Account*

|  | A | B | C | D = B/C |
|---|---|---|---|---|
|  | Account Balance | Projected Account | Annuity Purchase Rate | Offset |
| Employee A | $50,000 | $98,358 | $120 | $820 |
| Employee B | $ 490 | $ 3,730 | $120 | $ 31 |

*Step 2.* Calculate the accrued benefit in the defined benefit pension plan without regard to any offset and then subtract the amount of benefit derived from the current account balance, that is, the offset.

*Calculation of the Accrued Benefit*

|  | A | B | C | D = (A × C)/B | E | F = D + E |
|---|---|---|---|---|---|---|
|  | Projected Benefit Prior to Offset | Total Years to Normal Retirement Date | Years to Date | Accrued Benefit Prior to Offset | Offset | Accrued Benefit |
| Employee A | $2,000 | 20 | 10 | $1,000 | ($820) | $180 |
| Employee B | $ 350 | 32 | 3 | $ 33 | ($ 31) | $ 2 |

Notice how Employee *B* has an accrued benefit in this example, but has no projected benefit in the example in Q 4:18. This occurs because the continued contributions to the defined contribution plan promised by the employer will eventually exceed the amount required to provide the floor benefit, but on a current basis, since the account balance has not yet accumulated enough funds to provide the accrued benefit; the defined benefit plan must make up the shortfall. It is for this reason that the sponsor of a floor-offset arrangement must take care to monitor the funded status of the plan. Without the ability to make future contributions to both plans the defined benefit plan may become unexpectedly insolvent unless make-up contributions are made. If this occurs, it may be possible to cease benefit accruals under the defined benefit plan and continue to fund the accounts under the defined contribution plan until all accrued benefits are fully funded under both arrangements.

### Q 4:20    How is the accrued benefit determined in a frozen defined benefit plan that is still subject to a floor-offset?

The IRS has informally indicated that the accrued benefit may not be offset by future contributions to the defined contribution plan after the defined benefit plan is frozen. Otherwise, it could be considered a violation of Code Section 411(d)(6). However, it is not entirely clear if the accrued benefit could be reduced by future, interest-only increases in the defined contribution account balance. They stated that it is the normal application when the defined benefit plan is frozen in a floor-offset arrangement to also freeze the amount of the offset that is applied. [2005 ASPPA Annual Conference, IRS Q&A 5]

## Cash Balance Plans

### Q 4:21    What is a *cash balance plan*?

A *cash balance plan* is a defined benefit pension plan that provides benefits to employees by reference to a hypothetical account balance. The hypothetical account balance is provided to the employee at retirement in the form of a lump-sum distribution or an annuity based on conversion factors defined in the plan document. The hypothetical account is credited with interest based on some outside index, such as the yield on one-year Treasury securities, or an amount defined in the plan. Hypothetical contributions to the account are based on a percentage of compensation, a multiple of age and service points, or another objective criterion.

A cash balance plan is designed to look like a defined contribution plan, in that each participant is able to see his or her hypothetical contributions, earnings, and account balance, but promises a defined benefit through the interest rate credit and contribution guarantee.

### Q 4:22    How does a cash balance plan operate?

Each year, a participant receives a hypothetical contribution to his or her hypothetical account based on the participant's compensation for that year. The account accumulates with interest each year, as defined in the plan document.

A traditional defined benefit plan can be converted to a cash balance plan. In this case, the benefit accrued under the prior formula may be converted to a lump-sum amount and becomes the opening balance of the participant's account.

However, a cash balance conversion is required to protect the accrued benefit as of the conversion date, and add to this the accrued benefit under the cash balance formula after the amendment.

At retirement, the participant can choose the accumulated account balance as a lump sum or the account can be converted to an annuity. Because a cash balance plan is a defined benefit plan, the qualified joint and survivor form of benefit is the automatic form of benefit.

### Q 4:23   What is the difference between a cash balance plan and a defined contribution plan?

The primary difference between a cash balance plan and a defined contribution plan is that increases or decreases in plan assets do not directly affect the benefit amount promised to a participant in the cash balance plan. [I.R.C. § 414(i)] In addition, Code Section 415(b) limits the ultimate benefit (see chapter 12); the defined contribution limitation under Code Section 415(c) (the lesser of $40,000 or 100 percent of pay) is not applicable to a cash balance plan. Since a cash balance plan is a defined benefit plan, benefits are generally guaranteed by the PBGC (see chapter 24).

### Q 4:24   Is the percentage of pay credited to a participant's account actually contributed to the plan by the employer?

No. As with all defined benefit plans, the contributions to the plan are actuarially determined. Since the hypothetical contributions and interest credits are guaranteed, making the plan sponsor bear all investment risk, actual contributions could be greater or less than the hypothetical contributions allocated depending on plan experience.

### Q 4:25   Are there any legal problems associated with cash balance plans?

For plans established after June 29, 2005, the law as provided under the PPA blesses cash balance plans, but makes no inference regarding cash balance plans established prior to this date. However, the appellate court judge in *IBM v. Cooper* [No. 05-3588 (7th Cir. Aug. 7, 2006)] has overturned a prior ruling that stated cash balance plans violated the accrual rules. Even with these events, opponents of cash balance plans believe that these plans violate the accrual rules as required by Code Section 411(b), fail to protect accrued benefits under Code Section 411(d)(6), and/or discriminate based on age in violation of Code Section 411(b)(1)(H). (See chapter 13 for a discussion of these issues.)

## Pension Equity Plans

### Q 4:26   What is a *pension equity plan*?

A *pension equity plan* is a hybrid defined benefit plan that provides a lump sum as the primary form of benefit payment. Participants in a pension equity plan accumulate lump-sum credits for each year of participation. These lump-sum credits are multiplied by the participant's final average compensation and years of service to determine the lump-sum benefit. Pension equity plans were also blessed by the new provisions under the PPA as they were included in the definition of an "applicable defined benefit plan." (See chapter 13 for a further discussion of this issue.)

### Q 4:27   What is the difference between a cash balance plan and a pension equity plan?

There are several key differences between a pension equity plan and a cash balance plan. The primary difference between them is that a pension equity plan defines a lump-sum benefit by direct calculation, whereas a cash balance plan provides benefits based on a hypothetical account balance and thus looks like a defined contribution plan.

Because pension equity plan balances are always defined by reference to final average pay, pension equity plan benefits will keep pace with pay increases. For example, if an employee stays with a company that has a pension equity plan, working his or her way up the corporate ladder, he or she will have a retirement benefit that will reflect his or her increased final pay times all years of service with the company. In contrast, if the company has a cash balance plan, this employee's benefit would be lower because of lower hypothetical contributions based on the employee's early years of employment.

**Example.** Ponderosa Pension Designs (PPD) has been contacted to develop a retirement program for Reverse Initiative Associates (RIA), which would provide a lump-sum retirement benefit equal to 100 percent of a participant's final year of compensation, as long as the participant has at least 10 years of service with the company. PPD proposes two different types of defined benefit plans: a cash balance plan providing a 7.25 percent hypothetical contribution with 7.0 percent hypothetical earnings, and a pension equity plan providing a lump-sum credit of 10 percent of final pay for each year of service (not to exceed 10 years). Both plans would provide a participant who had a level pay history and 10 years of service a 100-percent-of-pay lump sum at retirement. However, RIA wants to know how each plan would affect Allison, a key employee whose earnings have steadily increased over the last 10 years.

Allison has reached normal retirement age, and her compensation has increased 5 percent for each of the last 10 years. Her final year's compensation is $50,000. Her lump sum under the cash balance plan as proposed would be $39,721 (due to her lower contribution credits in earlier years when she was earning a reduced salary). In contrast, her lump sum would be $50,000 under the pension equity plan.

Therefore, the cash balance plan as proposed would not achieve the employer's stated goal (i.e., would not provide a lump-sum benefit equal to 100 percent of the final year of compensation) for employees such as Allison.

### Q 4:28  How is the benefit calculated in a pension equity plan?

Participants in a pension equity plan earn credits each year to be applied toward a lump-sum benefit at retirement. These credits are multiplied by final average compensation and can include additional credits for pay above the Social Security integration level. The credits are accumulated each year and can increase with age, service, or both. On retirement or termination, the accumulated credits are paid in the form of a lump sum or an annuity.

**Example.** George, a participant in the PEP, Inc., pension equity plan, retires at the normal retirement age of 65. The lump-sum credits for each year of participation are 10 percent of final average pay. George's final average pay is $50,000, and he has 20 years of participation. Assume that the APR is 120.0.

George can elect a lump-sum benefit equal to $100,000 (10% × $50,000 × 20 years) or a straight life annuity of $833 per month ($100,000 ÷ 120.0).

## Eligible Combined Plans

### Q 4:29  What is an eligible combined plan?

In the PPA, Congress authorized creation of a new type of plan for plan years beginning after December 31, 2009, that combines a defined benefit plan with a defined contribution plan called an eligible combined plan. In general, this type of plan is only available to small employers of 500 or fewer employees and the plan must meet certain requirements for benefits, contributions, vesting, notice, and nondiscrimination. [I.R.C. § 414(x)(2)]

This type of plan must have a single trust holding the assets of the plan, but the assets applicable to the defined benefit and defined contribution portions of the plan must be clearly identifiable and allocated to each. [I.R.C. § 414(x)(2)(iii)]

### Q 4:30  What are the benefit requirements applicable to the defined benefit portion of an eligible combined plan?

The accrued benefits for each participant from the defined benefit portion of the plan must be at least equal to the lesser of 1 percent of pay times years of service or 20 percent of pay. Pay is defined as final average pay using a period of consecutive years (not exceeding five) during which the participant had the greatest aggregate compensation with the employer. Years of service are determined under the same rules as for vesting service under Code Sections 411(a)(4)-(6).

If the defined benefit plan is a cash balance plan, or any other defined benefit plan that meets the requirements under Code Section 411(a)(13)(B), the hypothetical contribution requirements must meet the following:

| If the Participant's Age as of the Beginning of the Plan Year Is: | The Percentage of Hypothetical Contribution Needs to Be At Least: |
|---|---|
| 30 or less | 2% |
| Over 30 but less than 40 | 4% |
| Over 40 but less than 50 | 6% |
| 50 or over | 8% |

[I.R.C. § 414(x)(2)(B)]

### Q 4:31   What are the contribution requirements applicable to the defined contribution portion of the eligible combined plan?

The defined contribution portion of the plan must contain a cash or deferred arrangement (401(k)) that meets the requirements of an automatic contribution arrangement. In addition, the employer is required to make matching contributions to each eligible participating employee in an amount at least equal to 50 percent of the elective contributions of the employee up to 4 percent of the employee's compensation. The employer may also make nonelective (profit-sharing) contributions to the plan as well, but those cannot be taken into account in determining if the required match has been made. [I.R.C. § 414(x)(2)(C)]

### Q 4:32   What are the vesting requirements applicable to eligible combined plans?

For the defined benefit portion of the plan, a participant who has completed at least three years of vesting service must have a right to 100 percent of his or her accrued benefit. The matching portion of the defined contribution portion of the plan must be 100 percent vested at all times and any nonelective (profit-sharing) contributions made are subject to being 100 percent vested after a participant has completed at least three years of vesting service. [I.R.C. § 414(x)(2)(D)]

### Q 4:33   What are the nondiscrimination rules that are applicable to eligible combined plans?

There are a number of nondiscrimination rules that are applicable to these plans. First, all contributions and benefits under the defined contribution and defined benefit portions of the plan must be provided uniformly to all participants. [I.R.C. § 414(x)(2)(E)]. Second, the benefit and contribution requirements applicable to each portion of the plan must be met without taking into consideration integration with Social Security due to Code Section 401(l) and Code Sections 410(b) and 401(a)(4) requirements must be met without imputing Social Security. [I.R.C. § 414(x)(2)(F)]

In addition, the eligible combined plan must be able to meet the requirements of Code Sections 410(b) and 401(a)(4) without being aggregated with any other plan. [I.R.C. § 414(x)(2)(F)(iii)]

The actual deferral percentage test (ADP test) of Code Section 401(k)(3)(A)(ii) will not be applicable to this type of plan as long as the plan meets the requirement that it is an automatic contribution arrangement and meets the matching contribution requirements listed in Q 4:31. [I.R.C. § 414(x)(3)(A)] In order for the matching contribution to be considered nondiscriminatory, the plan must also meet an annual notice requirement. [I.R.C. § 414(x)(3)(B)]

### Q 4:34  What is an automatic contribution arrangement?

The cash or deferred arrangement (401(k)) is considered as an automatic contribution arrangement if it provides that each employee who is eligible to participate is automatically enrolled with an initial deferral election of 4 percent of pay, unless the employee specifically opts not to participate or to participate but at a different rate. The arrangement must also meet the annual notice requirement. [I.R.C. § 414(x)(5)(A)]

### Q 4:35  What is the annual notice requirement?

The eligible combined plan must notify all participants annually, within a reasonable period before the beginning of the plan year, of the following:

- Their right to elect not to have deferrals taken out of their pay;
- Their right to change the amount of deferrals taken out of their pay; and
- All other rights and obligations of the participant in the plan.

[I.R.C. § 414(x)(5)(B)

### Q 4:36  What are the top-heavy requirements applicable to an eligible combined plan?

If the plan meets all the other requirements of an eligible combined plan, it is treated as satisfying the requirements of Code Section 416 applicable to top-heavy plans. [I.R.C. § 414(x)(4)]

### Q 4:37  Can an eligible combined plan be treated as separate plans under Code Section 414(k)?

No. Code Section 414(k) is not applicable to an eligible combined plan. [I.R.C. § 414(x)(6)(A)]

### Q 4:38   What are the annual reporting requirements for an eligible combined plan?

The annual reporting requirements of Code Sections 6058 and 6059 that require the filing of Form 5500 and Schedule B are applicable to the single eligible combined plan. Therefore, only one Form 5500 filing is required each year. [I.R.C. § 414(x)(6)(B)]

### Q 4:39   What is an example of an eligible combined plan?

**Example.** The defined benefit portion of the plan has the following provisions:

- Benefit formula is 10 percent of pay times 10 years of participation;
- Accrual is unit credit;
- Vesting is a three-year cliff (100 percent vested upon completion of three years of vesting service); and
- Eligibility is age 21 with one year of service, entry on the first day of the plan year or the first day of the sixth month following completion of the eligibility requirements (whichever is nearest).

The provisions of the defined contribution plan are as follows:

- Contains a cash or deferred arrangement with an automatic contribution feature.
- Eligibility is age 21 with one year of service, entry on the first day of the plan year or the first day of the sixth month following completion of the eligibility requirements (whichever is nearest).
- Once participants have completed the eligibility requirements, they are provided a notice that details they have the right to elect out of the automatic deferral or change the amount of deferral, but if they do not, then 4 percent of pay will begin to be taken out of their pay after entry into participation.
- The matching contribution is 50 percent of the first 4 percent of pay for each participating employee. This match is 100 percent vested.
- The employer makes a profit-sharing contribution equal to 10 percent of pay for each participant. This contribution is vested based on a three-year cliff schedule.

# Chapter 5

# Special Employers and Plans

Defined benefit pension plans can be maintained by small companies, tax-exempt organizations, and governmental agencies. Many employers can contribute to the same plan pursuant to a collective bargaining agreement. This chapter discusses the rules that apply to these "special plans."

## Small Businesses; Top-Heavy Plans

### Q 5:1   Can a small business sponsor a defined benefit pension plan?

Yes. Prior to the Tax Equity and Fiscal Responsibility Act of 1982 (TEFRA), unincorporated businesses had limited opportunities to use qualified pension plans to benefit owner-employees. TEFRA attempted to create parity between incorporated and unincorporated businesses. Now any business, whether conducted through a C corporation, an S corporation, a partnership, a sole proprietorship, limited liability company (LLC), limited liability partnership (LLP), or any other form, can maintain a defined benefit pension plan for its employees, including its owner-employees. A self-employed individual or owner-employee must have earned income (see Q 5:5) to deduct contributions to a qualified plan.

### Q 5:2   What benefit can a business owner get from a defined benefit pension plan?

A defined benefit pension plan provides a unique opportunity for the small business owner to save for his or her own retirement on a tax-favored basis. The business owner receives a tax deduction for contributions made to the plan. If the business owner instead withdraws the money from the business in the form of compensation, dividends, or a distributive share of the profits in the business, the owner recognizes income and is subject to ordinary income taxes. Amounts "invested" in the plan are not taxed currently. Further, all contributions grow on a tax-deferred basis.

> **Example.** Liz designs logos for sports fans. She conducts her business through a C corporation. This year she will make $200,000 from her design work. Liz would like to save about $50,000 per year for retirement. She is 50 years old.
>
> If Liz does not establish a qualified plan, she will take home about $100,000 after taxes. If she saves $50,000 of her after-tax earnings, she will have only $50,000 for living expenses.
>
> An actuary has designed a defined benefit plan for Liz with anticipated contributions of $50,000 per year. Liz's expendable income would be increased if she adopts the plan.
>
> | | Without Plan | With Plan |
> | --- | --- | --- |
> | Potential income | $200,000 | $200,000 |
> | Pension deduction | — | ($50,000) |
> | Taxable income (W-2 wages) | $200,000 | $150,000 |
> | Income tax (35%) | ($70,000) | ($52,500) |
> | Take-home pay | $130,000 | $97,500 |
> | Savings | ($50,000) | — |
> | Expendable income | $80,000 | $97,500 |
>
> Because the pension trust pays no income taxes, the accumulation in the plan will exceed the accumulation from regular savings.
>
> If Liz has employees, she will have to extend coverage to those who meet age and service requirements. Plan design can help keep overall costs down or provide attractive benefits to important employees.

### Q 5:3   Can a defined benefit plan be designed to benefit only the owners of the business?

Maybe. A plan cannot discriminate in favor of highly compensated employees. [I.R.C. § 401(a)(4)] However, the plan benefits can be combined with benefits provided under other plans, including 401(k) profit-sharing plans, to prove nondiscrimination as long as Internal Revenue Code (Code) Section 401(a)(26) is satisfied as well. Because owners are generally more highly compensated and older than nonowners, it is often possible to design a plan (or plans) that satisfies the nondiscrimination rules and provides most of the benefits to the owner (see chapters 11 and 12).

### Q 5:4 What earnings are used to develop pension benefits and costs for a self-employed individual?

A self-employed individual's compensation for benefit and cost purposes is his or her net earned income from self-employment (see Q 5:5), taking into account the deductions attributable to the qualified plan. [I.R.C. § 404(a)(8)] This creates a circular calculation.

Because benefits under a defined benefit pension plan are generally a function of average compensation, it is possible for the cost of funding the plan to exceed the net earned income from self-employment or the available profit of a corporation. Special care must be used in developing appropriate funding methods and/or benefits (see chapter 18).

### Q 5:5 What is *earned income*?

*Earned income* is net earnings from self-employment in a trade or business in which personal services of the taxpayer are a material income-producing factor. Inactive business owners who receive income as passive investors do not have earned income that can be recognized for pension purposes. [I.R.C. § 401(c)(2); Treas. Reg. § 1.401-10(c)(3); see also I.R.S. Pub. No. 560, Retirement Plans for Small Businesses (1997)]

A shareholder of an S corporation cannot treat pass-through income reported on Schedule K-1 as net earnings from self-employment even if the shareholder performed services for the corporation. The term *employer* includes a sole proprietor or a partner in a partnership, but does not include a shareholder of an S corporation. [Durando v. United States, 70 F.3d 548 (9th Cir. 1995)] If the shareholder performs services for the corporation as an employee, however, the shareholder can participate in a pension plan sponsored by the S corporation based on his or her W-2 income as an employee of the business.

### Q 5:6 What special considerations apply to small businesses?

A small business should consider the funding obligations associated with a defined benefit pension plan. The funding of a defined benefit pension plan, unlike the funding of a profit-sharing plan, cannot be conditioned on profitability. Some small business owners confuse defined benefit plans with defined contribution plans, and expect to be able to change the amount of their contribution each year according to their business needs. In some instances, when benefit levels are high and the plan has experienced high investment returns, there may be more assets than can be used to fund the plan. If this continues, excise and income taxes may take much of the excess amount reverted to the employer. Because of the nature of the funding rules (see chapter 19), small businesses may experience significant funding swings from year to year. Finally, small businesses are often burdened by the top-heavy rules, which require minimum benefits for participants (see Q 5:16). These minimum top-heavy benefits can be expensive. Nevertheless, defined benefit plans provide the best means of funding retirement for business owners who have not been able to sponsor a plan in earlier years. The deductions available under a defined benefit plan far exceed the deductions available under a defined contribution plan.

### Q 5:7    What is a *top-heavy* plan?

A defined benefit pension plan is *top heavy* if the accrued benefits for key employees (see Q 5:12) exceed 60 percent of the accrued benefits for all employees. [I.R.C. § 416(g)(1)] If an employer sponsors more than one plan, or if other plans are sponsored by members of a controlled group or group of affiliated companies, all plans within the aggregation group (see Q 5:11) must be tested for top-heavy status.

### Q 5:8    When is top-heavy status determined?

The date for determining top-heavy status for a plan year is the last day of the preceding plan year, or in the case of the first plan year, the last day of that plan year. [I.R.C. § 416(g)(4)(C)]

### Q 5:9    How is the present value of an accrued benefit determined in a defined benefit plan?

The present value of an accrued benefit as of a determination date must be determined as of the most recent valuation date that is within a 12-month period ending on the determination date. Generally, the accrued benefit for a current employee is determined as if the individual terminated service as of such valuation date.

There are no specific prescribed actuarial assumptions that must be used for determining the present value of accrued benefits in determining top-heavy status for a plan year. The assumptions need not be the same as those used for minimum funding purposes or for purposes of determining the actuarial equivalence of optional benefits under the plan. The present value must be computed using an interest rate and a postretirement mortality assumption. [Treas. Reg. § 1.416-1, Q&A T-26]

### Q 5:10    Are distributions included in the present value calculation?

Yes. In determining top-heavy status for plan years that begin on or before December 31, 2001, benefits paid within the last five years are added back for top-heavy testing purposes. For plan years beginning after December 31, 2001, only benefits paid within the last year are added back for top-heavy testing purposes, except that distributions made to an employee while he or she is still employed are added back if made within the last five years. The following benefits, however, can be excluded:

1. *Non-key employee.* Benefit payments for a participant who was a key employee in prior plan years but ceases to be a key employee are not taken into account.

2. *Rollovers.* Rollover contributions from other qualified plans initiated and made after December 31, 1983, are not taken into account.

[I.R.C. § 416(g)(4)(A), (B), (E); Treas. Reg. § 1.416-1, Q&As T-1(d), T-32]

### Q 5:11   What plans must be included in the aggregation group?

Any plan that covers a key employee (see Q 5:12) must be included in the aggregation group (required aggregation). Additionally, any plan that is aggregated with the plan so that the latter can meet nondiscrimination and coverage rules (see chapter 6) must be included in the aggregation group. [Treas. Reg. § 1.416-1, Q&A T-6]

Occasionally, it is helpful for an employer to aggregate plans to avoid top-heavy status. Plans can be aggregated if, when considered together, the plans satisfy the nondiscriminatory benefit requirements of Code Section 401(a)(4) and the nondiscriminatory coverage requirements of Code Section 410 (permissive aggregation). [I.R.C. § 416(g)(2)(A)(ii)]

**Example.** Phantom Products maintains two plans: a defined benefit pension plan for its salaried employees and a 401(k) plan for its hourly employees. No key employees participate in the 401(k) plan. Each plan independently satisfies the requirements of Code Sections 410 and 401(a)(4). The 401(k) plan does not have to be aggregated with the defined benefit plan to determine top-heavy status. If the benefits under the 401(k) plan are comparable to those under the defined benefit plan, however, the two plans could be aggregated to determine whether or not the group consisting of both plans is top heavy. If the defined benefit plan and the 401(k) plan can be aggregated, and if the permissive aggregation group is not top heavy, then the defined benefit plan would not be considered top heavy. [Treas. Reg. § 1.416-1, Q&A T-7]

### Q 5:12   Who is a *key employee*?

A *key employee* is any employee or former employee who, at any time during the year or any of the preceding four years, is:

For plan years beginning on or before December 31, 2001:

1. *An officer.* Officers of an employer who have annual compensation greater than 50 percent of the Code Section 415(b)(1)(A) dollar limit ($45,000, as indexed);

2. *A top-ten owner of the employer.* One of the 10 employees with annual compensation in excess of the Code Section 415(c)(1)(A) dollar limit

($30,000, as indexed) and owning the largest interests in the employer (of at least 0.5 percent);

3. *A 5 percent owner.* An owner of more than 5 percent of the corporate stock or of the capital interest or profits interest in an unincorporated company; or

4. *A 1 percent owner.* An owner of more than 1 percent of the employer with annual compensation of more than $150,000.

Family members and beneficiaries of key employees are considered key employees. [I.R.C. § 416(i); Treas. Reg. § 1.416-1, Q&As T-12–T-21]

For plan years beginning after December 31, 2001:

1. *An officer.* Officers of an employer who have annual compensation greater than $130,000 (indexed in $5,000 increments, $145,000 for 2007);

2. *A 5 percent owner.* An owner of more than 5 percent of the corporate stock or of the capital interest or profits interest in an unincorporated company; or

3. *A 1 percent owner.* An owner of more than 1 percent of the employer with annual compensation of more than $150,000.

Family members and beneficiaries of key employees are considered key employees. [I.R.C. § 416(i); Treas. Reg. § 1.416-1, Q&As T-12–T-21]

### Q 5:13   How is officer status determined?

The determination of officer status is a factual determination. The test includes the source of the individual's authority, the term for which the individual is elected or appointed, and the nature and extent of the individual's duties. An employee who has the title of an officer but not the authority of an officer is not considered an officer for purposes of determining who is a key employee. An employee who does not have the title of an officer but has the authority of an officer is an officer for purposes of determining who is a key employee. [Treas. Reg. § 1.416-1, Q&A T-13]

### Q 5:14   Are all officers key employees?

No. There is a limit to the number of officers who are counted as key employees. If the number of employees (including part-time employees and counting the greatest number of employees the employer had during that plan year or any of the four preceding plan years) of all the employers aggregated under Code Section 414(b), (c), or (m) is less than or equal to 30, no more than three individuals are treated as key employees, for the plan year containing the determination date, by reason of being officers. If the number of employees is greater than 30 but less than or equal to 500, no more than 10 percent of the number of employees will be treated as key employees by reason of being officers. (If 10 percent of the number of employees is not an integer, the maximum number of individuals to be treated as key employees by reason of being officers is increased to the next integer.) If the number of employees exceeds 500, no more than 50 employees are considered key employees by reason of being officers. There is no minimum number of officers that must be taken into account. [Treas. Reg. § 1.416-1, Q&A T-14]

### Q 5:15   What happens if ownership changes during the year?

If a participant's ownership interest in the company changes during the year, status as a key employee is determined by considering the largest interest owned at any time during the year. [Treas. Reg. § 1.416-1, Q&A T-19(b)]

**Example.** Hendytax is owned equally by five individuals, *A, B, C, D,* and *E.* During the year, the five owners sell their stock to *F, G, H, I,* and *J.* In determining whether the plan is top heavy, *A, B, C, D, E, F, G, H, I,* and *J* are considered the top-ten owners of Hendytax.

### Q 5:16   What happens if a plan is top heavy?

A plan must satisfy minimum benefit requirements (see Q 5:18) and accelerated vesting requirements (see Q 5:17) if it is top heavy for a particular plan year. [I.R.C. § 416(i)(1)(A)]

### Q 5:17   What are the accelerated vesting requirements that apply to a top-heavy plan?

A top-heavy plan can select one of two alternative minimum top-heavy vesting schedules:

1. *Three-year cliff.* Under this schedule, no vesting is provided until the employee is credited with three years of service, at which time the employee becomes fully vested.

2. *Six-year graded, or 2/20.* Under this schedule, an employee must be 20 percent vested after completing two years of service, with vesting increasing in 20 percent increments until the employee is 100 percent vested after six years of service.

| Years of Service | Vesting Percentage |
|:---:|:---:|
| Less than 2 | 0% |
| 2 | 20% |
| 3 | 40% |
| 4 | 60% |
| 5 | 80% |
| 6 | 100% |

[Treas. Reg. § 1.416-1, Q&A V-1]

The top-heavy vesting schedule supersedes the plan's regular vesting schedule when the plan becomes top heavy. [I.R.C. § 416(b)] If a plan uses the six-year graded vesting schedule as its top-heavy vesting schedule and the plan becomes top heavy after an employee completes three years of service, the employee becomes 40 percent vested in his or her accrued benefit. The vesting applies to all benefits accrued as of the date the plan becomes top heavy. If the plan returns to non-top-heavy status, the non-top-heavy vesting schedule applies to all future accruals. Changes in top-heavy status create serious problems in administration, but another rule applies to ease this difficulty. Any participant with three or more years of service must be given the right to elect to continue under the old top-heavy vesting schedule as if the schedule had not been amended. [Treas. Reg. § 1.416-1, Q&A V-7]

### Q 5:18  What minimum benefits must be provided under a top-heavy plan?

A top-heavy defined benefit pension plan must provide a minimum accrued benefit equal to the product of:

1. The employee's average annual compensation for the period of consecutive years (not exceeding five) when the employee had the highest aggregate compensation from the employer; and

2. The lesser of:

    a. 2 percent per year of service with the employer, or

    b. 20 percent.

[Treas. Reg. § 1.416-1, Q&A M-2] A non-key employee will accrue the maximum top-heavy benefit after 10 years of service. A plan cannot provide a normal retirement benefit equal to the maximum top-heavy benefit with accrual based on the fractional rule of Code Section 411(b)(1)(C) (see chapter 9). [Treas. Reg. § 1.416-1, Q&A M-5]

> **Example 1.** Smallco maintains a top-heavy defined benefit pension plan. Rick, a non-key employee, is hired at age 25. After 10 years of service, Rick has fully accrued his minimum benefit of 20 percent of average compensation. The plan cannot provide a normal retirement benefit of 20 percent of average compensation because under the fractional rule, Rick's benefit at age 35, after 10 years of service, would be only 5 percent ($20\% \times {}^{10}/_{40}$) of average compensation. This accrual would not satisfy the minimum accrual requirements of Code Section 416. [Treas. Reg. § 1.416-1, Q&A M-5]

> **Example 2.** Smallco, in Example 1, decides to enhance its benefit formula to provide a normal retirement benefit of 50 percent of final average pay. The plan must calculate accrued benefits each year and provide Rick with the greater of the benefit determined using the regular formula or the benefit determined using the top-heavy formula. Under the fractional rule, Rick's benefit after 10 years of service would be 12.5 percent ($50\% \times {}^{10}/_{40}$) of average compensation using the regular formula and 20 percent ($2\% \times 10$ years) of average compensation using the top-heavy formula. The top-heavy

formula would apply. After 20 years of service, Rick's benefit would be 25 percent (50% × $^{20}/_{40}$) of average pay using the regular formula and 20 percent (2% × 10 years) of average compensation using the top-heavy formula. The regular formula would apply.

The minimum top-heavy benefit is expressed as a life annuity (with no ancillary benefits) beginning at normal retirement age. Thus, if postretirement death benefits (e.g., a joint and survivor form of benefit) are also provided, the 2 percent minimum annuity benefit can be adjusted. [Treas. Reg. § 1.416-1, Q&A M-2(d)]

### Q 5:19  How is average compensation determined in calculating the top-heavy minimum benefit?

For purposes of calculating the minimum benefit required for top-heavy plans (see Q 5:18), a participant's average compensation is determined by averaging compensation over a period of no more than five consecutive years during which the participant had the highest total compensation from the employer. [I.R.C. § 416(c)(1)(D)(iii); Treas. Reg. § 1.416-1, Q&A M-2(c)] The plan provisions establish the averaging period. Compensation is generally determined by reference to the definition contained in Treasury Regulations Section 1.415-2(d). Alternatively, Form W-2 compensation for the calendar year that ends with or within the plan year can be used. The selected definition must be used consistently for all top-heavy purposes. [Treas. Reg. § 1.416-1, Q&As M-2, T-21]

If an employee's compensation increases, the minimum benefit continues to increase even after the employee has completed 10 years of service, and, accordingly, has been credited with the maximum service.

**Example.** Jodi began participating in a top-heavy plan at age 25 with compensation of $30,000. Her compensation increased at a rate of 5 percent each year. Note the calculation of her top-heavy minimum benefit at various ages.

| | |
|---|---|
| Age 35 | $42,213 × 20% = $8,443 |
| Age 45 | $68,760 × 20% = $13,752 |
| Age 55 | $112,004 × 20% = $22,401 |

### Q 5:20  What years of service must be counted in determining the top-heavy minimum benefit?

Years of service with the employer are generally determined under the rules of Code Section 411(a)(4), (5), and (6). As a general rule, each year in which the participant completes 1,000 hours of service is counted as a year of service (see chapter 7). A plan can disregard any year of service during which the plan was not top heavy, any year of service completed in a plan year beginning before January 1, 1984, and, for plan years beginning after December 31, 2001, any year of service completed during a plan year when the plan does not benefit (within the meaning of Code Section 410(b)) any key employee or former key employee. [I.R.C. §§ 416(c)(1)(C)(ii), 416(c)(1)(C)(iii)]

The top-heavy minimum benefit requirements apply only to years in which the plan is top heavy and during which a key or former key employee benefits. Accordingly, the plan will have to keep track of the top-heavy years in calculating benefits.

**Example.** Assume the same facts as those in Example 1 in Q 5:18. The plan maintained by Smallco was top heavy only for certain years during Rick's first 10 years of employment. His accrued benefit would be determined as follows:

| Year | Top Heavy | Regular Benefit | Top-Heavy Minimum | Actual Benefit |
|------|-----------|-----------------|-------------------|----------------|
| 1 | No | 1.25% | 0% | 1.25% |
| 2 | Yes | 2.5% | 2% | 2.5% |
| 3 | Yes | 3.75% | 4% | 4% |
| 4 | No | 5% | 4% | 5% |
| 5 | No | 6.25% | 4% | 6.25% |
| 6 | No | 7.5% | 4% | 7.5% |
| 7 | Yes | 8.75% | 6% | 8.75% |
| 8 | Yes | 10% | 8% | 10% |
| 9 | Yes | 11.25% | 10% | 11.25% |
| 10 | Yes | 12.5% | 12% | 12.5% |

### Q 5:21   Who must receive a top-heavy minimum benefit?

Each non-key employee who is a participant in a top-heavy defined benefit plan and who has at least 1,000 hours of service for an accrual computation period (see chapter 7) must accrue a minimum benefit in a top-heavy defined benefit plan for that accrual computation period. [I.R.C. § 416(c)(1)]

**Example.** Mom and Pop own a small grocery store. They have decided to sponsor a defined benefit plan. Because Mom and Pop are substantially older than the rest of the employees, the value of their benefits will probably exceed 60 percent of the total plan benefits and the plan will be top heavy. Jerry, one of the clerks at the store, must receive a minimum benefit of 2 percent of compensation times his years of service at the grocery store.

### Q 5:22   If an employee is participating in a top-heavy plan but is then excluded, must the employee continue to receive the top-heavy minimum benefit?

Maybe. It is unclear whether the employee must continue to receive the top-heavy minimum benefit in this situation, although many practitioners believe the employee must, because the language in the regulations state that participants must receive the top-heavy minimum benefit. Therefore, although they are excluded from receiving further benefits under the regular benefit formula, the employee continues to be a participant in the plan.

### Q 5:23 If the employer sponsors more than one top-heavy plan, does a non-key employee have to receive the minimum benefit under each plan?

No. When an employer maintains a defined benefit plan and a defined contribution plan that are both top heavy, only one plan needs to provide minimum contributions or benefits. Because the defined benefit minimums are generally more valuable, the plans will satisfy the top-heavy minimum benefit requirements if the employee receives the minimum accrual under the defined benefit plan. Alternatively, the employer can provide a contribution to the defined contribution plan of at least 5 percent of compensation. [Treas. Reg. § 1.416-1, Q&A M-12]

### Q 5:24 What other requirements apply to top-heavy plans?

TEFRA imposed a limitation on the amount of compensation that could be recognized by top-heavy pension plans. Top-heavy plans could not consider compensation in excess of $200,000 for benefit purposes. This rule has not had any practical effect as a result of the compensation limit applicable to all plans under Code Section 401(a)(17). However, with the increase in the Code Section 401(a)(17) limit to $200,000 with indexing, it may come into consideration again.

Code Section 415(e) imposed additional limitations on key employees who participated in a top-heavy plan for plan years that began before January 1, 2000. For those prior plan years, if a plan was top heavy, the fraction used in calculating the aggregate benefit limit under Code Section 415(e) was changed to 1.0 when the dollar limit applied or 1.4 when the percentage of compensation limit applied. [I.R.C. § 416(h)(1)] Participants in plans that were not top heavy generally used a fraction of 1.25 in determining benefit limitations. The Code Section 415(e) limitation, which was a very difficult calculation involving review of benefits received over the course of an individual's employment, was further complicated by a number of transition rules. Fortunately, the Small Business Job Protection Act of 1996 (SBJPA) repealed the combined limit aggregate benefit limit under Code Section 415(e) and the further adjustment for top-heavy plans under Code Section 416(h) effective for limitation years beginning after December 31, 1999.

### Q 5:25 Are there any plan designs that minimize the cost of providing top-heavy minimum benefits when two plans are involved?

Yes. There are a variety of options available for keeping the cost of maintaining a top-heavy plan at an acceptable level (see chapter 3). Methods worth examining include the following:

1. *Defined benefit minimum only.* Because the defined benefit plan minimum benefit is considered more valuable than the defined contribution plan minimum contribution, an employer can provide only the defined benefit minimum benefit.

2. *Floor offset.* The defined benefit minimum benefit is provided in the defined benefit plan but is offset by any benefit provided under the defined contribution plan.

3. *Comparability.* The plan can show that the defined contribution minimum contribution is as valuable as the defined benefit minimum benefit using a comparability analysis set forth in Revenue Ruling 81-202 [1981-2 C.B. 93] or Treasury Regulations Section 1.401(a)(4)-8.

4. *Five-percent contribution.* The defined contribution plan can provide an enhanced contribution of 5 percent of compensation for each non-key employee.

[Treas. Reg. § 1.416-1, Q&A M-12]

## Tax-Exempt Employers; Church Plans

### Q 5:26   Can a tax-exempt entity sponsor a defined benefit plan?

Yes. A tax-exempt organization can sponsor a defined benefit pension plan for its employees.

### Q 5:27   Are there any special requirements applicable to plans sponsored by tax-exempt organizations?

For the most part, defined benefit pension plans sponsored by tax-exempt organizations are subject to the same qualification requirements as plans sponsored by for-profit businesses (see chapter 2).

Slightly different eligibility rules apply to defined benefit pension plans sponsored by educational institutions. Although plans can require employees to satisfy age and service requirements as a condition of eligibility (see chapter 6), the minimum age requirement cannot exceed age 21. A plan maintained exclusively for employees of an educational institution can require an employee to attain age 25 prior to participation if the plan provides for full vesting after one year of service. [I.R.C. § 410(a)(1)(A)(i), (ii)]

As a general rule, a participant's retirement benefit cannot exceed the lesser of (1) 100 percent of the participant's average annual compensation in the three highest-paid years of participation or (2) $160,000, as adjusted for the cost of living. [I.R.C. § 415(b)] The dollar limitation is generally expressed as a limitation on a benefit payable in the form of a life annuity beginning between age 62 and age 65. If benefits begin before age 62, limitation is reduced. The reductions applicable to benefits payable to participants in a plan sponsored by a tax-exempt organization are the same as those applicable to benefits payable by all plans prior to enactment of TEFRA: (1) the dollar limitation is reduced only if benefits begin before the participant attains age 62 and (2) the actuarial reduction cannot reduce the dollar limitation below $75,000 if benefits begin at age 55. [I.R.C. § 415(b)(2)(F)] As a result, larger early retirement benefits can often be paid to employees of tax-exempt employers.

The deduction for contributions to pension plans is generally of limited value to tax-exempt organizations, but the deduction may be valuable if the organization has unrelated business taxable income. (See chapter 20 for a discussion of deduction issues.)

A number of excise taxes can be imposed on plans and plan sponsors (see chapter 29). Under Code Section 4980, an excise tax is imposed on excess assets reverting to an employer-sponsor on plan termination (see chapter 25). Similarly, an excise tax is imposed on amounts contributed to a plan that are not deductible under Code Section 4972. If the employer sponsoring the plan has been exempt from income taxes at all times, these excise taxes do not apply. [I.R.C. § 4980(c)(1)(A)] This exemption has been construed rather strictly. The excise taxes apply if the employer has been subject to unrelated business income tax or has otherwise derived a tax benefit from the qualified plan. If any member of a controlled group participating in the plan is a for-profit organization, the excise tax applies. [I.R.C. § 4972(d)(1)(B); T.A.M. 9616003]

Church plans (see Q 5:29) that do not make a Code Section 410(d) election are exempt from a number of requirements under the Code and the Employee Retirement Income Security Act of 1974 (ERISA) (see Qs 5:30 and 5:33).

### Q 5:28   Can a church maintain a defined benefit plan?

Yes. A church or affiliated organization can maintain a defined benefit pension plan for its employees.

### Q 5:29   What is a *church plan*?

A *church plan* is "a plan established and maintained . . . for its employees (or their beneficiaries) by a church or by a convention or association of churches which is exempt from tax under Code Section 501." [I.R.C. § 414(e); ERISA § 3(33)]

### Q 5:30   Are church plans subject to ERISA?

Generally no. Church plans are exempt from the participation, vesting, funding, fiduciary responsibility, and reporting and disclosure requirements of ERISA. [ERISA § 4(b)(1)]

A church plan can waive its exemption from ERISA by making an affirmative election and notifying the Pension Benefit Guaranty Corporation (PBGC). [I.R.C. § 410(d); ERISA § 4(b)(2)] The plan administrator makes the election by filing a statement with IRS Form 5500 for the first plan year for which the election is effective or with the request for an IRS determination letter. [Treas. Reg.

§ 1.410(d)-1(c)] Once the election is made, it is irrevocable. A church plan that has never made this election is often referred to as a *nonelecting church plan.*

### Q 5:31   Are church plans covered by PBGC insurance?

Nonelecting church plans (see Q 5:30) are exempt from ERISA Title IV and are not covered by PBGC insurance. Church plans that have made the Code Section 410(d) election are fully covered by ERISA Title IV and PBGC insurance.

### Q 5:32   What qualification requirements apply to church plans?

A nonelecting church plan must satisfy the following qualification requirements:

1. Code Section 401(a)(1), formal plan and trust;
2. Code Section 401(a)(2), exclusive benefit rule;
3. Code Section 401(a)(3), minimum coverage (pre-ERISA standards);
4. Code Section 401(a)(4), general nondiscrimination rules;
5. Code Sections 401(a)(5) and 401(l), exceptions to general nondiscrimination rules and integration with Social Security;
6. Code Section 401(a)(7), vesting (pre-ERISA standards);
7. Code Section 401(a)(8), use of forfeitures;
8. Code Section 401(a)(9), minimum required distributions;
9. Code Sections 401(a)(10) and 416, top-heavy rules;
10. Code Sections 401(a)(16) and 415, maximum benefits;
11. Code Section 401(a)(17), maximum recognized compensation;
12. Code Section 401(a)(25), specified actuarial assumptions;
13. Code Section 401(a)(26), minimum participation requirements;
14. Code Section 401(a)(31), direct rollovers;
15. Code Section 401(b), retroactive amendments;
16. Code Sections 402 and 72, taxation of benefits;
17. Code Section 3405, income tax withholding on benefit payments; and
18. Code Section 6652(i), rollover notice.

(See chapter 2 for further information regarding specific requirements.)

### Q 5:33   Are church plans exempt from any Code requirements?

Yes. Nonelecting church plans are exempt from the following Code requirements:

1. Code Sections 401(a)(11) and 417 qualified joint and survivor annuity (QJSA), and qualified preretirement survivor annuity (QPSA) requirements;

2. Code Sections 401(a)(12) and 414(l), benefits after plan merger or consolidation;

3. Code Section 401(a)(13), prohibition of assignment or alienation of benefits;

4. Code Section 401(a)(14), benefit commencement date;

5. Code Section 401(a)(15), prohibition of benefit reduction due to increases in Social Security benefits;

6. Code Section 401(a)(19), benefit forfeiture after withdrawal of employee contributions;

7. Code Section 401(a)(20), distributions from a terminating plan;

8. Code Section 401(a)(29), security after plan amendment creating underfunding;

9. Code Section 410, minimum participation standards (pre-ERISA requirements);

10. Code Section 411, vesting (pre-ERISA requirements);

11. Code Section 412, minimum funding requirements and benefit commitments;

12. Code Section 414(p), qualified domestic relations order (QDRO);

13. Code Section 4971, excise tax on failure to meet minimum funding standards;

14. Code Section 4975, excise tax on prohibited transactions;

15. Code Section 4980, excise tax on reversion of plan assets; and

16. Code Sections 6057, 6058, and 6059; IRS Form 5500; Schedule B; Schedule SSA.

### Q 5:34   What minimum funding standards apply to church plans?

Nonelecting church plans are exempt from the minimum funding standards. [ERISA § 301(a); I.R.C. § 412(h)]

### Q 5:35   What filing requirements apply to church plans?

Nonelecting church plans are exempt from ERISA Title I. These church plans do not have to file IRS Form 5500 series reports; Schedule SSA, reporting terminated vested participants; or any actuarial reports. (Code Section 6057 applies only to plans subject to the vesting standards of Code Section 411(d).) [See also Ann. 82-146, 1982-47 I.R.B. 53] Nonelecting church plans are exempt from the PBGC reporting requirements and need not file Form PBGC-1 or any other reports with the PBGC. Nonelecting church plans do not have to provide notice to the IRS of a merger or spin-off. A church plan must, however, file a request for a determination of qualification with the IRS if a determination is desired. Church plans must file appropriate forms with the IRS regarding plan distributions. IRS Form 990-T must be filed to report unrelated business taxable income.

### Q 5:36   What information must church plans provide to participants?

Nonelecting church plans are exempt from ERISA Title I. These church plans do not have to provide summary plan descriptions (SPDs), summary annual reports (SARs), or benefit statements (see chapter 28). A nonelecting church plan must be communicated to employees in some fashion to be qualified. [Treas. Reg. § 1.401-1(a)(2)] Church plans must provide recipients of certain distributions with information regarding rollover rights. [I.R.C. § 402(f)] The plan must also notify a participant of withholding rights. [I.R.C. § 3405] The plan must provide participants with information regarding tax reporting on distribution on IRS Form 1099R. If a determination letter is requested, advance notice of the filing must be provided to all interested parties.

## Governmental Plans

### Q 5:37   Can a state or local government sponsor a defined benefit plan for its employees?

Yes. A state or local government or political subdivision thereof (or agency or instrumentality thereof) can sponsor a defined benefit pension plan.

### Q 5:38   What is a *governmental plan*?

Three slightly different definitions are found in the Code and ERISA. As a general rule, a *governmental plan* is a "plan established or maintained for its employees by the government of the United States, by the government of any State or political subdivision thereof, or by an agency or instrumentality of any of the foregoing." [ERISA § 3(32)] If a plan is a governmental plan as defined in ERISA Section 3(32), it is exempt from the requirements of ERISA Title I (participation, funding, vesting, fiduciary responsibility, and reporting and disclosure). Code Section 414(d), which defines governmental plans for tax purposes, contains an almost identical definition of governmental plan, except that it refers to a plan "established *and maintained*" rather than "established *or maintained.*" ERISA Section 4021(b)(2), which exempts governmental plans from plan termination insurance of ERISA Title IV, also contains the "established *and maintained*" language.

### Q 5:39   What type of entity is considered an agency or instrumentality of a government?

There is no precise test for agency or instrumentality status. The relationship between the government and the agency and the function of the agency should be evaluated. When a state government organizes an agency, controls its board, provides regular financial support, and reports operational income on its financial statement, the agency is most likely a governmental agency. If, on the other hand, the agency functions more like a private enterprise, it probably will not be considered a governmental agency. [Alley v. Resolution Trust Corp., 984 F.2d 1201 (D.C. Cir. 1993)]

The PBGC lists a number of factors to be considered in determining whether a plan is maintained by a governmental instrumentality:

1. *Control.* Is the plan or plan sponsor controlled by a governmental entity?
2. *Governance.* Are the officers or board members selected by the governmental entity?
3. *Funding.* Is the plan or plan sponsor funded by a governmental entity?
4. *Employees.* Are the employees treated as government employees?
5. *Private interests.* Are any private interests involved?

[PBGC Op. Ltr. 96-2 (June 10, 1996)]

The IRS lists similar factors. [Rev. Rul. 89-49, 1989-1 C.B. 117] A plan is not considered a governmental plan merely because the sponsor has quasi-governmental powers or a relationship with a government.

### Q 5:40  Are governmental plan documents different from plan documents used in the private sector?

Yes. The plan document often consists of a number of documents, including state or local statutes or regulations, court decisions, personnel policies, and minutes of meetings. State law may specify the precise terms of a plan or merely set broad parameters or a range of acceptable features for a plan.

### Q 5:41  Are governmental plans subject to ERISA?

No. ERISA Section 4(b)(1) exempts governmental plans from all of the provisions of ERISA Title I. Therefore, several of the participant protection provisions do not apply. A governmental plan can reduce accrued benefits, although such action would be prohibited in a private sector plan. [ERISA § 204(g)] The fiduciary responsibility requirements, reporting and disclosure requirements, and antialienation requirements do not apply to governmental plans.

### Q 5:42  Are governmental plans covered by PBGC insurance?

No. ERISA Section 4021(b)(2) and (10) exempts governmental plans from PBGC insurance and ERISA Title IV.

### Q 5:43  Can a governmental plan cover individuals who are not government employees?

The Department of Labor (DOL) has indicated that a governmental plan cannot cover more than a *de minimis* number of nongovernment employees. [DOL Op. Ltrs. 95-27A (Nov. 8, 1995), 95-14A (June 26, 1995), 95-15A (June 26, 1995)] This standard applies for purposes of ERISA Title I. The PBGC has indicated that if any nongovernment employees participate in a governmental plan, the entire plan is tainted and full involvement with ERISA Title IV and the PBGC is required. [PBGC Op. Ltr. 77-169 (Nov. 28, 1977)]

### Q 5:44 What qualification requirements apply to governmental plans?

Governmental plans must have a formal written plan and use assets exclusively for the benefit of participants and beneficiaries. Although governmental plans are exempt from many qualification requirements, they must satisfy the following requirements generally applicable to qualified plans:

1. Code Section 401(a)(1), formal plan and trust (often presents a problem in governmental plans created by statute and other assorted documents);
2. Code Section 401(a)(2), exclusive benefit rule;
3. Code Section 401(a)(3), minimum coverage (pre-ERISA standards);
4. Code Section 401(a)(4), general nondiscrimination rules (see Q 5:45);
5. Code Sections 401(a)(5) and 401(l), exceptions to general nondiscrimination rules and integration with Social Security;
6. Code Section 401(a)(7), vesting (pre-ERISA standards);
7. Code Section 401(a)(8), use of forfeitures;
8. Code Section 401(a)(9), minimum required distributions;
9. Code Sections 401(a)(16) and 415, maximum benefits and pre-Tax Reform Act of 1986 rules for limits for early and late retirement;
10. Code Section 401(a)(17), maximum recognized compensation;
11. Code Section 401(a)(25), specified actuarial assumptions;
12. Code Section 401(a)(26), minimum participation requirements (some exceptions apply; see Q 5:45);
13. Code Section 401(a)(31), direct rollovers;
14. Code Section 401(b), retroactive amendments;
15. Code Sections 402 and 72, taxation of benefits;
16. Code Section 3405, income tax withholding on benefit payments; and
17. Code Section 6652(i), rollover notice.

(See chapter 2 for further information regarding specific qualification requirements.)

### Q 5:45 Are governmental plans exempt from any Code requirements?

As a result of the Taxpayer Relief Act of 1997 (TRA '97), most governmental plans are exempt from the nondiscrimination rules generally imposed on qualified plans. For taxable years beginning on or after August 5, 1997, any governmental plan is exempt from the general nondiscrimination requirements of Code Section 401(a)(4) and the minimum participation requirement of Code

Section 401(a)(26). Governmental plans are exempt from the following Code requirements applicable to private sector plans:

1. Code Sections 401(a)(10) and 416, top-heavy rules;
2. Code Sections 401(a)(11) and 417, QJSA and QPSA requirements;
3. Code Sections 401(a)(12) and 414(l), benefits after plan merger or consolidation;
4. Code Section 401(a)(13), prohibition of assignment or alienation of benefits;
5. Code Section 401(a)(14), benefit commencement date;
6. Code Section 401(a)(15), prohibition of benefit reduction due to increases in Social Security benefits;
7. Code Section 401(a)(19), benefit forfeiture after withdrawal of employee contributions;
8. Code Section 401(a)(20), distributions from a terminating plan;
9. Code Section 401(a)(29), security after plan amendment creating underfunding;
10. Code Section 410, minimum participation standards (pre-ERISA requirements);
11. Code Section 411, vesting (pre-ERISA requirements);
12. Code Section 412, minimum funding requirements and benefit commitments;
13. Code Section 414(p), QDROs;
14. Code Section 4975, excise tax on prohibited transactions;
15. Code Section 4980, excise tax on reversion of plan assets; and
16. Code Sections 6057, 6058, and 6059; IRS Form 5500; Schedule B; Schedule SSA.

### Q 5:46  How do the pre-ERISA vesting rules apply to governmental plans?

Governmental plans must meet pre-ERISA vesting standards. An employee must be fully vested at normal retirement age. The vesting schedule cannot discriminate in operation in favor of officers, shareholders, supervisors, or highly compensated employees. On termination of the plan, full vesting of all benefits is required to the extent the participants' benefits are funded. [I.R.C. § 411(d)(3)]

### Q 5:47  Do governmental plans have limitations on the maximum benefit that can be provided to a participant?

Yes, but the limitations are more generous than the limitations under private sector plans. If benefits begin before Social Security retirement age, for private sector plans the maximum benefit limit under Code Section 415 ($160,000 as adjusted for inflation) must be adjusted actuarially; but governmental plans generally remain subject to the maximum annual benefit limits that applied before enactment of TEFRA.

The regular $160,000 limit applies to benefits paid at or after age 62. If benefits begin between age 55 and age 62, the $160,000 limit is actuarially adjusted but cannot be reduced below $75,000 (not indexed). If benefits begin before age 55, the $160,000 limit is actuarially adjusted using an actuarial equivalent of $75,000 at age 55. [I.R.C. § 415(b)(2)(F)]

### Q 5:48   What filing requirements apply to governmental plans?

Governmental plans are exempt from ERISA Title I. These plans do not have to file IRS Form 5500 series reports; Schedule SSA, reporting terminated vested participants; or any actuarial reports. (Code Section 6057 applies only to plans subject to the vesting standards of Code Section 411(d). [See also Ann. 82-146, 1982-47 I.R.B. 53]) Governmental plans are exempt from the PBGC reporting requirements and need not file Form PBGC-1 or any other reports with the PBGC. Governmental plans do not have to provide notice to the IRS of a merger or spin-off. A governmental plan must, however, file a request for a determination of qualification with the IRS if a determination is desired. Governmental plans must file appropriate forms with the IRS regarding plan distributions. IRS Form 990-T must be filed by the plan to report any unrelated business taxable income.

### Q 5:49   What information must governmental plans provide to participants?

Governmental plans are exempt from ERISA Title I. These plans do not have to provide SPDs, SARs, or benefit statements (see chapter 28). A governmental plan must be communicated to employees in some fashion to be qualified. [Treas. Reg. § 1.401-1(a)(2)] Governmental plans must provide recipients of certain distributions with information regarding rollover rights. [I.R.C. § 402(f)] The plan must also notify a participant of withholding rights. [I.R.C. § 3405] The plan must provide participants with information regarding tax reporting on distribution on IRS Form 1099R. If a determination letter is requested, advance notice of the filing must be provided to all interested parties.

### Q 5:50   What is a *pick-up contribution*?

A *pick-up contribution* is a contribution made by an employer on behalf of a government employee.

Occasionally, government employees must make contributions to the plan to accrue a benefit. Code Section 414(h)(1) generally provides that employee contributions are made with after-tax dollars. Code Section 414(h)(2) creates an exception to this rule for employee contributions to governmental plans if the employer makes, or picks up, the contribution that the employee is required to make. The pick-up contribution is treated as an employer contribution and is not subject to income tax. [Rev. Rul. 77-462, 1977-2 C.B. 358] Pick-up contributions are somewhat similar to 401(k) contributions in that they are effectively made with pre-tax dollars, but plans do not have to maintain a true account for pick-up contributions.

There are two criteria that these contributions must satisfy in order to be considered "pick-up" contributions:

1. The employer must specify that the contributions, although designated as employee contributions, are being paid by the employer in lieu of contributions by the employee; and

2. The employee must not be given the option of choosing to receive the contributed amounts directly instead of having them paid by the employer to the pension plan. [Rev. Rul. 81-35, 1981-1 C.B. 255; Rev. Rul. 81-36, 1981-1 C.B. 255]

Pick-up contributions are taken into account as wages for Federal Insurance Contributions Act (FICA) purposes. [I.R.C. § 3121(v)(1)(B)]

## Multiemployer Plans

### Q 5:51   What is a *multiemployer plan*?

A *multiemployer plan* is a plan maintained pursuant to collective bargaining agreements to which more than one employer contributes. [ERISA § 3(37)(A); I.R.C. § 414(f)] A multiemployer plan is administered by representatives from labor and management.

### Q 5:52   What is the difference between a multiemployer plan and a multiple-employer plan?

A multiple-employer plan is merely a plan maintained by more than one employer. [I.R.C. § 413(c)] Most often the participating companies are members of an affiliated or controlled group, although this is not required. [Treas. Reg. § 1.401-1(d)]

Unlike a multiemployer plan, a multiple-employer plan is not maintained pursuant to a collective bargaining agreement. Professional employer organizations (PEOs) or trade associations often use multiple-employer plans. Under a multiple-employer plan, certain qualification requirements are applied on a plan basis and others are applied on an employer basis. Each adopting employer must individually satisfy coverage, nondiscrimination, top-heavy benefits and vesting, and minimum funding requirements.

### Q 5:53   What are the advantages of a multiemployer plan?

Multiemployer plans benefit employees of a particular trade or employees working in a particular area. Under a multiemployer plan, union employees, who may be employed by different employers while working in the same trade, do not lose benefits because service in the trade with a participating employer is treated as service for benefit purposes. [DOL Reg. § 2530.210; I.R.C. § 413] Administrative costs are generally lower.

### Q 5:54   How are benefits determined under a multiemployer plan?

It is not unusual for both the benefits and the rate of contribution to be specified in the collective bargaining agreement. In other instances, the benefit levels are set by the trustees, based on the agreed level of contributions. This has led to disputes over which entity has authority to raise benefits. Multiemployer plans are often subject to pressure to increase benefits, either directly or through service credits, eligibility or vesting liberalization, cost-of-living increases, or other such devices.

### Q 5:55   Must benefits be the same for all participants?

No. Multiemployer plans can be designed to provide different levels of benefits based on region, contribution level, or a variety of other factors. Many plans, however, contain one benefit formula, and all participating employers are treated as one employer. Covered service with any participating employer is recognized for benefit accrual and vesting purposes.

### Q 5:56   Can benefits under a multiemployer plan be reduced?

Yes. In some cases, a multiemployer plan can be amended to reduce benefits retroactively, although such an action is an impermissible cutback of an accrued benefit under a single-employer plan. [I.R.C. § 411(d)(6)] A participant's *past-service benefit*, the portion of the benefit attributable to service prior to the date the employer began making contributions to the plan, can be forfeited if the employer ceases making required contributions. [ERISA § 203(a)(3)(E); I.R.C. § 411(a)(3)(E)] Benefits can be reduced in limited cases in the event of financial hardship. [I.R.C. § 412(c)(8); ERISA § 302(c)(8)]

### Q 5:57   How is an employee's share of the funding obligation calculated and allocated?

In a typical defined benefit pension plan, an actuary prepares estimates of current and projected liabilities and calculates the required contribution necessary to fund the plan based on minimum funding standards contained in Code Section 412 (see chapter 19). In a multiemployer plan, funding is often determined by the terms of the collective bargaining agreement. For example, an employer may be required to contribute $2 to the plan for each hour of service. The plan trustees often establish the benefit formula based on the level of funding. In other cases, the benefit level is established in the collective bargaining agreement, and the participating employers are obligated to contribute amounts sufficient to pay for the bargained benefits.

### Q 5:58  What funding rules apply to multiemployer plans?

For the most part, the funding rules applicable to single-employer plans apply to multiemployer plans. Accumulated funding deficiencies carry a lower excise tax, 5 percent, than that imposed on single-employer plans. [I.R.C. § 4971(a)] Because the funding level for multiemployer plans is generally mandated by the collective bargaining agreement, the mandated contribution may fall short of or exceed the amount actually needed to satisfy funding requirements. For example, contributions may be required even though the plan is fully funded under minimum funding standards (see chapter 19). In this instance, the company must continue to make the contributions required by agreement even if an excise tax might apply. [Bituminous Coal Operators' Assn v. Connors, 867 F.2d 625 (D.D.C. 1980)]

### Q 5:59  What is *withdrawal liability*?

*Withdrawal liability* is the financial liability imposed on any employer that withdraws or partially withdraws from a multiemployer plan. The liability, which can be calculated in a number of ways, is intended to ensure that a withdrawing employer pays for its share of the unfunded vested benefits (UVBs) attributable to its employees (see Q 5:65). This liability can be very significant. It may be calculated as a lump-sum payment or the employer may have to continue making contributions to the plan for a number of years.

### Q 5:60  What events trigger withdrawal liability?

Withdrawal liability is triggered when an employer withdraws, completely or partially, from a multiemployer plan. An employer completely withdraws from a multiemployer plan when it permanently ceases to have an obligation to contribute to the plan or permanently ceases all operations covered by the plan. [ERISA § 4203] A partial withdrawal occurs when:

1. There is a 70 percent decline in contribution base units (CBUs), often hours worked;

2. The employer no longer has a contractual obligation to contribute to the plan for one group of employees, but still has a contractual obligation to contribute for another group of employees; or

3. The employer no longer has a contractual obligation to contribute to the plan for work performed at one or more of its locations, but still has a contractual obligation to contribute to the plan for work performed in at least one location.

[ERISA § 4205]

### Q 5:61  Are any industries exempt from withdrawal liability?

Yes. Because of the nature of certain industries, special rules have been developed to determine whether a withdrawal that would trigger withdrawal liability has occurred. These rules and exceptions apply to the following industries:

- Building and construction
- Entertainment
- Trucking
- Household-goods moving
- Public warehousing
- Retail food

[ERISA § 4203]

### Q 5:62 Do any corporate events trigger withdrawal liability?

Not in or of themselves. Withdrawal liability is not triggered because of a mere change in identity, form, or place of organization; a liquidation of a parent; or a merger, consolidation, spin-off, or division of a company as long as the change does not change the employer's responsibility to contribute to the plan. [ERISA §§ 4069(b), 4218]

### Q 5:63 Does the sale of a company trigger withdrawal liability?

It depends. Sales of stock do not trigger withdrawal liability, even if shareholder control is completely changed, as long as there is no change in the obligation to contribute to the plan. In a typical stock sale, the buyer assumes liability for continuing company obligations. In these cases, the successor entity is treated as the original employer. [ERISA § 4218(1)] A sale of assets, in contrast, causes a withdrawal and triggers liability unless certain actions are taken (see Q 5:64).

### Q 5:64 Are there any special considerations in an asset sale?

Yes. When assets of a business are sold, the buyer need not assume liability for funding the seller's plan. Unlike the new owners in a stock sale, who assume liability for existing programs, the new owners who acquire a business through an asset sale are not generally liable for the old company's obligations unless the obligations are assumed by contract. The buyer might cease covered operations or cease to have an obligation to contribute because it no longer employs individuals under a collective bargaining agreement. Therefore, an asset sale is a withdrawal, triggering withdrawal liability.

A sale of assets is *not* treated as a withdrawal, if all of the following conditions are met:

1. *Bona fide sale.* The sale is a bona fide arm's-length transaction between unrelated parties.

2. *Assumption of obligation.* The buyer assumes the obligation to contribute to the plan at substantially the same rate as the seller.

3. *Bond.* The buyer bonds or places in escrow an amount equal to one year of the seller's contributions.

4. *Secondary liability.* The contract of sale provides that if the buyer withdraws within the next five plan years, the seller will be secondarily liable for any liability that the seller would have incurred on the sale if these actions had not been taken.

[ERISA § 4204]

If the buyer withdraws or defaults on a contribution during the five plan years after the sale, the plan receives the bond. If a withdrawal occurs within five years and the buyer does not pay the withdrawal liability, the seller is responsible for payment. [ERISA § 4204(a)(1)(B), (C)]

### Q 5:65  What is an *unfunded vested benefit?*

An *unfunded vested benefit*, or UVB, is the difference between assets and the value of benefits that are vested. [Huber v. Casablanca Indus., 916 F.2d 85 (3d Cir. 1990)]

### Q 5:66  If the plan is overfunded, can an individual employer be assessed withdrawal liability?

A few courts have upheld withdrawal liability assessments on an employer that completely withdraws from a multiemployer plan that had no UVBs. [Wise v. Ruffin, 914 F.2d 570 (4th Cir. 1990); Artistic Carton Co. v. Paper Indus. Union-Management Pension Fund, 971 F.2d 1346 (7th Cir. 1992)]

### Q 5:67  Who is liable for withdrawal liability?

All members of a controlled group of the withdrawing party (as of the appropriate liability date) may be liable for withdrawal liability. Shareholders do not generally have personal liability, absent a showing of disregard of the corporate form. Individual owners of a partnership or sole proprietorship may become liable if they are part of the controlled group with a company that has withdrawn from a multiemployer plan.

### Q 5:68  How is withdrawal liability calculated?

Employers that withdraw from a multiemployer plan are supposed to pay their "fair share" of the plan's UVBs. There are a number of options available to the plan to determine withdrawal liability. Calculation may be based on one of four statutory methods or on an alternative method approved by the PBGC.

The four statutory methods follow:

1. *The basic method, or presumptive method.* This method is usually applied to determine withdrawal liability unless the plan provides otherwise. [ERISA § 4211(b)] The basic, or presumptive, method holds an employer responsible for its allocable share of the UVBs as of December 31, 1979, based on its share of contributions over the five years prior to December 31, 1979; and for its allocable share of gains or losses in the UVBs since December 31, 1979, based on its share of contributions over the last five years prior to the withdrawal. A fraction, the numerator of which is the employer's own contributions for a five-year period prior to December 31, 1979, and the denominator of which is all employers' contributions in the same five-year period, determines the employer's allocable share. The fraction or percentage is multiplied by the UVBs of the plan as of December 31, 1979, and the result is discounted to the year of withdrawal by 5 percent per year. To this amount is added the sum of each year's allocable gain or loss (projected at 5 percent) since 1979 to the date of withdrawal. Some multiemployer plans create separate UVB pools and apply the fraction only to the affected pool. Others use different measuring periods.

2. *The modified presumptive rule, or the first alternative, or the two-pool rule.* This rule divides the UVBs into two groups or pools (prior plan liabilities and adjusted initial plan year liabilities) and applies the fraction determined under the basic method to each pool separately. [ERISA § 4211(c)(2)(B)]

   Under the modified rule, old UVBs (plan liabilities attributable to participation before September 26, 1980) are allocated and amortized over 15 years. A rolling five-year fractional allocation applies to the remainder of the UVBs. Withdrawal liability can be reduced if contributions are reduced during the five years preceding withdrawal.

3. *The rolling-five rule.* A rolling five-year allocation is applied to all UVBs. [ERISA § 4211(c)(3)] Under this rule the allocation is based on contribution levels for the current year and preceding five years.

4. *The direct attribution rule.* Under this rather complicated rule, an employer's liability is determined as the difference between the employer's share of attributable assets and its share of attributable vested benefits. [ERISA § 4211(c)(4)]

**Example 1.** Employer *N* is a participating employer in a multiemployer plan. Employer *N* withdraws from the plan on January 1, 1981. No other employers have withdrawn from the plan. The plan uses the presumptive method to allocate withdrawal liability. The value of the plan's UVB as of January 1, 1980, and January 1, 1981, is $11 million. The assumed interest rate is 5 percent. Plan contributions made for recent years are as follows:

| Year | Employer N | All Employers |
|------|-----------|---------------|
| 1975 | $10,000 | $1,000,000 |
| 1976 | $14,000 | $1,100,000 |
| 1977 | $16,000 | $1,100,000 |
| 1978 | $17,000 | $1,500,000 |
| 1979 | $19,000 | $1,500,000 |
| 1980 | $22,000 | $1,500,000 |

The sum of Employer N's contributions for the five years prior to December 31, 1979, is $76,000 and the sum of the contributions by all employers for the five years prior to December 31, 1979, is $6.2 million. Therefore, Employer N's pro rata share is 1.23 percent as of December 31, 1979. Employer N's withdrawal liability is $135,300, calculated by multiplying this percentage by the UVBs as of January 1, 1980 ($11,000,000 × 0.0123 = $135,300). This amount is discounted 5 percent from December 31, 1979, to December 31, 1980. The result is $128,535 ($135,300 × (1 − 0.05)).

The gain or loss for 1980 is calculated by comparing the expected UVBs at the end of the year, $10.45 million ($11,000,000 × 0.95), to the actual UVBs of $11 million, for a loss of $550,000 ($10,450,000 − $11,000,000). This amount is multiplied by the ratio of Employer N's contributions for the last five years to all employers' contributions for the same period, which is $88,000 ($22,000 + $19,000 + $17,000 + $16,000 + $14,000) divided by $6,700,000 ($1,500,000 + $1,500,000 + $1,500,000 + $1,100,000 + $1,100,000), or 1.31 percent. The share of the loss allocated to Employer N is $7,205 ($550,000 × 0.0131).

The total withdrawal liability is therefore $135,740 ($128,535 + $7,205).

**Example 2.** The plan information is the same as that in Example 1 except that the plan uses the modified presumptive method to determine a withdrawing employer's liability.

Employer N's share of the 1979 UVBs is calculated in the same way as it is under the presumptive method, and is $135,300. The present value of the 15-year amortization is determined as of the date of withdrawal, January 1, 1981, at the assumed interest rate of 5 percent, and equals $129,030 ($135,300 divided by the present value of a 15-year annuity, multiplied by the present value of a 14-year annuity). The allocable percentage of contributions as of December 31, 1980, is also the same as it is in Example 1, 1.31 percent. The amount of expected UVBs as of December 31, 1980, is determined by using the UVBs as of December 31, 1979, and projecting to December 31, 1980, and equals $10,490,235 ($11 million divided by the present value of a 15-year annuity, multiplied by the present value of a 14-year annuity). The loss for 1980 is equal to $509,765 ($10,490,235 − $11,000,000). Employer N's allocable share of this loss is $6,678 ($509,765 × 0.0131). Therefore, the total withdrawal liability is $135,708 ($129,030 + $6,678).

### Q 5:69   Can the employer's withdrawal liability be reduced or eliminated?

Yes. The plan can have a standard (or mandatory) *de minimis* rule, which reduces the employer's liability if its share is less than the lesser of $50,000 or 0.75 percent of the total unfunded liability of the plan. If the employer's share is between $50,000 and $150,000, it is reduced but not eliminated. The plan can also use the optional *de minimis* rule, which increases the $50,000 and $150,000 limits to $100,000 and $250,000, respectively. [ERISA § 4209]

### Q 5:70   What alternative methods are available to determine withdrawal liability?

Nonstatutory methods of determining withdrawal liability are permitted. The PBGC may approve an alternative allocation method if it determines that adoption of the method would not significantly increase the risk of loss to plan participants and beneficiaries or to the PBGC. Any alternative method must satisfy the following three conditions:

1. The method or modification allocates a plan's UVBs, both for the adoption year and for the five subsequent plan years, to the same extent as any of the statutory allocation methods.

2. The method or modification allocates UVBs to each employer on the basis of either the employer's share of contributions to the plan or the UVBs attributable to each employer. The method or modification can take into account differences in contribution rates paid by different employers and differences in benefits of different employers' employees.

3. The method or modification fully reallocates among employers that have not withdrawn from the plan all UVBs that the plan sponsor has determined cannot be collected from withdrawn employers, or that are not assessed against withdrawn employers because of ERISA Section 4209, 4219(c)(1)(B), or 4225.

[ERISA § 4211(c)(5); PBGC Reg. § 4211.13]

### Q 5:71   Can the employer contest an assessment of withdrawal liability?

Yes. An employer, following procedures specified in the plan, can contest an assessment of withdrawal liability for a variety of reasons. No later than 90 days after the employer receives the withdrawal liability notice, the employer can ask for a review of any specific matter relating to the determination of withdrawal liability. Matters for which review is typically requested include the following:

- Fact of withdrawal
- Calculation of the assessment
- Interest rate or other actuarial assumptions used
- Date of withdrawal

- Determination of assets
- Retroactive adoption of rules
- Arbitrary and capricious application or nonapplication of rules

### Q 5:72 When must withdrawal liability payments be made?

It is the plan administrator's responsibility to notify the employer of its liability "as soon as practicable" after withdrawal. This may be a few months or a few years after the withdrawal has occurred. The plan administrator then makes a demand for payment and establishes a schedule for payments. The first payment is due 60 days after demand. [ERISA § 4219(c)]

# Chapter 6

# Eligibility—Coverage and Participation

For a pension plan to maintain its qualified status it must satisfy minimum coverage and participation standards. These standards are contained in Internal Revenue Code (Code) Sections 410(b) and 401(a)(26). The coverage and participation standards are an important consideration in designing a plan and, in many instances, in testing a benefit, right, or feature for discrimination. This chapter describes the minimum coverage and participation standards and discusses their application in a defined benefit pension plan.

## Eligibility

### Q 6:1    Must all employees be covered under a defined benefit plan?

No. As long as the plan satisfies certain minimum coverage and participation requirements of the Internal Revenue Code (Code) (see Qs 6:18 and 6:37) and the Employee Retirement Income Security Act of 1974 (ERISA), it need not cover all employees. [I.R.C. §§ 401(a)(26), 410(b)]

### Q 6:2　Can an employer impose age or service requirements on employees as a condition of plan participation?

Yes. Code Section 410(a) establishes minimum age and service requirements for plan participation. Of course, a plan can allow employees to participate before they meet the Code's age and service requirements. Age and service rules place a cap on the period of service or age that can be required as a condition of participation.

A plan is permitted to limit eligibility to employees who have attained age 21 and completed one year of service (see Q 6:5). [I.R.C. § 410(a)(1); Treas. Reg. § 1.410(a)-3(a)] This rule does not prevent a plan from excluding employees on another basis unless that basis has the effect of an impermissible age or service requirement (see Q 6:9).

Prior to enactment of the Retirement Equity Act of 1984 (REA), the maximum age limit was 25. Provisions restricting eligibility to individuals who have attained age 25 must be corrected even though no employee is affected by the limit. [Basch Eng'g Inc. v. Commissioner, T.C. Memo 1990-212 (U.S. Tax Court Memos 1990)]

Although an employer generally cannot condition participation on completion of more than one year of service, a special exception to this general rule applies if a plan provides for full and immediate vesting. If a plan provides for full and immediate vesting on entry, it can condition eligibility on completion of a maximum of two years of service (see Q 6:4). [I.R.C. § 410(a)(1)(B)(i); Temp. Treas. Reg. § 1.410(a)-3T(b)]

### Q 6:3　Can an employer exclude employees who have attained a certain age from participating?

No. A qualified plan cannot exclude any employee from participation because of attainment of a specified maximum age. [I.R.C. § 410(a)(2)] Before enactment of the Tax Reform Act of 1986 (TRA '86), a defined benefit pension plan could exclude employees who were hired within five years of normal retirement age from participating in the plan. This restriction can no longer apply to any employee who completed at least one hour of service on or after January 1, 1988. [I.R.C. § 410(a)(1)(A)(ii), (B)]

### Q 6:4　Are there any advantages to the employer of extending the eligibility requirement to two years?

Yes. If employees who complete two years of service tend to remain long term, a two-year service requirement can prove beneficial to the employer—administrative costs can be lowered and benefits directed to longer-term employees. An employer may want to conduct a turnover study to determine whether costs can be reduced by including a two-year service requirement.

### Q 6:5  How are years of service generally calculated for eligibility purposes?

A year of service is generally calculated by reference to hours of service. A plan must credit an employee with a year of service for any applicable 12-consecutive-month period (see Q 6:6) during which the employee earns 1,000 or more hours of service. [I.R.C. § 410(a)(3)(A)] Because this is a minimum standard, a plan can credit an employee with a year of service for a computation period during which the employee earns less than 1,000 hours of service. Most plans credit an employee with a year of service for eligibility purposes if the employee works at least 1,000 hours during the first 12 months of employment. A number of rules apply when there are absences from work during this period.

An *hour of service* is generally any hour for which the employee is, directly or indirectly, entitled to compensation either by reason of the performance of duties or for certain reasons unrelated to the performance of duties, such as vacation or sick leave.

Occasionally years of service are measured on an elapsed-time basis (see chapter 7). [Treas. Reg. § 1.410(a)-7; Temp. Treas. Reg. § 1.410(a)-9T] Under the elapsed-time method, an employee's eligibility to participate in the plan is not based on actual hours of service. Instead, eligibility is determined by reference to the period of time that elapses while the employee is employed. This method often reduces the administrative burden of maintaining records of each employee's hours of service. The employee is credited with a year of service on the anniversary of his or her employment commencement date, irrespective of the actual hours of service completed during the year.

### Q 6:6  When does the 12-consecutive-month eligibility computation period begin?

The 12-consecutive-month eligibility computation period begins on the date the employee commences work. If the employee does not complete 1,000 hours of service during the first 12 months of employment, the next computation period begins on the anniversary of the employee's employment date, or if the plan provides, the next computation period can begin on the first day of the plan year beginning in the employee's first year of employment. [I.R.C. § 410(a)(3)(A)]

If a business employs individuals who often work less than 1,000 hours during their first year of employment, it might be helpful to have subsequent computation periods coincide with the plan year to ease the administrative burden of maintaining records of each individual's hours based on employment date.

**Example 1.** Ace Delivery maintains a pension plan that requires one year of service as a condition of eligibility. The plan year is the calendar year. Ace Delivery hires Jan in January, Marsha in March, Stephen in September, and Nancy in November. Personnel records note the following hours of service during each individual's first year of employment:

| | |
|---|---|
| Jan | 980 |
| Marsha | 750 |
| Stephen | 975 |
| Nancy | 800 |

If the plan continues to use the employee's employment commencement date as the reference for determining hours of service, and if the employee does not satisfy the 1,000 hours of service requirement during the first year of employment, time records would have to be maintained for Jan based on a January computation period, for Marsha based on a March computation period, for Stephen based on a September computation period, and for Nancy based on a November computation period. If the plan uses the plan year as the reference for determining hours of service and the employee does not satisfy the 1,000 hours of service requirement during the first year of employment, records would have to be maintained based on the calendar year for all participants.

If a plan requires two years of service as a condition of eligibility, the computation period should be based on the employee's employment commencement date to avoid double counting of overlapping service years.

**Example 2.** Dorothy is hired for full-time employment on December 15, 2001, by Ace Delivery. The Ace Delivery defined benefit plan requires two years of service for eligibility. After the initial eligibility computation period, the eligibility computation period is the plan year. Dorothy works more than 1,000 hours in her initial year of eligibility, from December 15, 2001, to December 14, 2002. The subsequent eligibility period begins January 1, 2002, and ends December 31, 2002. Within 1 year and 15 days, Dorothy is credited with two years of service and is eligible to begin participating in the plan.

If the plan had continued to use the employment year as the subsequent eligibility period, Dorothy would not have completed the two-year requirement until December 14, 2003.

### Q 6:7 Can a plan require completion of one hour of service in each of the first six months of an employee's employment as a condition of eligibility?

No. In Revenue Ruling 80-360 [1980-2 C.B. 142] the IRS held that a plan failed to meet the minimum age and service requirements of Code Section 410(a)(4) by requiring one hour of service in each of the first six months of employment. An employee could theoretically complete 1,000 hours of service within a computation period but fail to meet the plan's service requirement.

### Q 6:8 Can any years of service be disregarded for purposes of eligibility?

Yes. Under certain circumstances, a plan can disregard prior service of an employee who incurs a break in service (see chapter 7). [I.R.C. § 410(a)(5);

Treas. Reg. §§ 1.410(a)-5, 1.410(a)-6] For eligibility purposes, a plan cannot exclude years of service with an affiliated service group or with another member of a controlled group, or years of service in an ineligible class (see Q 6:17).

### Q 6:9   Can part-time employees be excluded from plan participation?

No. A plan cannot impose a provision that can in effect extend the permitted maximum service condition. Any condition that has the effect of imposing eligibility based on age or service cannot be acceptable. In a field directive issued November 22, 1994, the IRS prohibited an exclusion of part-time employees even though the plan still satisfied the coverage requirements of Code Section 410(b). In the directive, the IRS discusses Treasury Regulations Section 1.410(a)-3(e)(1) and the implicit limitations on age and service conditions. Although a plan can limit coverage to a certain business classification, problems can arise if the covered class is limited to more senior employees whose age or service typically exceeds the permitted maximums. Implicit age and service requirements are not permitted. Therefore, excluding employees based on labels such as "part-time employees" or "temporary employees," terms that suggest a built-in service component, is not permitted. [See also Ltr. Rul. 9508003]

### Q 6:10   Can an employer require employees to contribute to a defined benefit plan to become eligible?

Yes. A plan can require an employee to contribute to a plan to become a participant or to accrue a benefit in any year. If, however, the effect of mandatory contributions is discriminatory, the plan fails to meet the Code's qualification standards.

### Q 6:11   Can an employer place other conditions on eligibility?

Yes. An employer can restrict eligibility based on job classification, employment in a certain division or subsidiary or at a certain location, amount or method of compensation, or any other business classification. [Treas. Reg. § 1.410(a)-3(d)] All restrictions other than permitted age and service restrictions must be tested in operation to ensure that they do not effectively run afoul of the minimum coverage and participation rules.

In *Edes v. Verizon Communications, Inc.*, [417 F.3d 133 (1st Cir. 2005)], the First Circuit held that an employer did not violate ERISA when the company excluded employees hired and paid by a third-party payroll agency from participation in its benefit plans when the plan contained language explicitly excluding from participation those employees who were not paid directly by the company. Even though the off-payroll employees may have been considered common law employees, the exclusion in the plan document was sufficient to keep them from participating in the plans.

> **Example.** Skydivers, Inc., has 1,000 employees, 100 of whom are highly compensated employees (HCEs) (see Q 6:32). It would like to exclude its California

division from the plan. The California division has 100 employees, 10 of whom are HCEs. Without the California division the plan will still satisfy the minimum participation rule (see Q 6:37) because it covers more than 50 employees. The plan will also satisfy the minimum coverage rules (see Q 6:18) because it covers 90 percent of the non-highly compensated employees (NHCEs) (see Q 6:33) (810 out of 900) and 90 percent of the HCEs (90 out of 100). The plan's ratio percentage for the year is 100 percent (i.e., 90 percent out of 90 percent) and therefore the plan satisfies the ratio percentage test (see Q 6:20).

### Q 6:12 Can an employee waive participation in a plan?

Yes. A plan can permit an employee to waive participation. Whether it is advisable for a plan to include such a provision is another matter. In *Laniok v. Advisory Committee of the Brainerd Manufacturing Co. Pension Plan* [753 F. Supp. 1115 (W.D.N.Y. 1990)], the court reviewed a negotiated agreement waiving benefits under a defined benefit pension plan. Apparently, the employee felt coerced into signing the agreement and later attempted to void the agreement and obtain retirement benefits. The court ultimately adopted a "knowing and voluntary" standard for effective waivers. If an employee waives benefits and receives a corresponding increase in compensation, the agreement can be treated as a cash or deferred arrangement (CODA), bringing into play the various special requirements of 401(k) plans. Finally, the exclusion of employees, even if voluntary, could present problems under the minimum coverage and participation rules.

> **Example.** Dr. Goodhealth has two employees. One would like to waive participation in the pension plan so she can contribute to an individual retirement account (IRA). If she waives participation, the plan would fail the minimum coverage tests (see Q 6:18). The plan would cover 50 percent of the NHCEs (see Q 6:33) and 100 percent of the HCEs (see Q 6:32). The plan's ratio percentage for the year would be 50 percent (i.e., 50 percent out of 100 percent) and therefore the plan would fail the ratio percentage test (see Q 6:20) and possibly be disqualified.

### Q 6:13 When must an eligible employee enter the plan?

A plan does not have to make an employee a participant in the plan on the day the employee satisfies the eligibility criteria. Participation can be deferred until the next entry date. Certain rules in the Code provide outside entry dates.

Once an otherwise eligible employee satisfies the minimum age and service requirements, he or she must become a participant in the plan no later than the earlier of:

1. The first day of the first plan year beginning after the date the employee satisfies the requirements unless the employee is no longer employed; or

2. Six months after the date the employee satisfies the requirements unless the employee is no longer employed.

[I.R.C. § 410(a)(4); Treas. Reg. § 1.410(a)-4(b)(1)]

**Example 1.** A plan requires one year of service as a condition of eligibility. The plan has a calendar year as its plan year. Elizabeth begins employment on April 1, 2001. If Elizabeth is employed on a basis such that she will be credited with at least 1,000 hours of service, she will have satisfied the minimum service requirement on March 31, 2002. She must become a participant in the plan no later than the earlier of January 1, 2003 (the first day of the plan year beginning after satisfaction of the service requirement) or October 1, 2002 (six months after satisfaction of the eligibility requirement).

A plan cannot delay participation to the first day of the plan year beginning after the requirements are satisfied. In Revenue Ruling 80-360 [1980-2 C.B. 142], the IRS indicated that the plan's single annual entry date violated the minimum age and service requirements of the Code. Under this provision an employee would not always be eligible to participate in the plan within six months after meeting the age and service requirements.

**Example 2.** Assume the plan from Example 1 specifies one annual entry date, corresponding to the first day of the plan year beginning after the eligibility requirement is satisfied. The plan will not satisfy the age and service requirements of Code Section 401(a) because it is possible that its entry date rules could delay an employee's admission longer than the age and service rules allow. For instance, although Elizabeth completes the service requirement on March 31, 2002, she would not be admitted until January 1, 2003, which is later than the earlier of six months after she has satisfied the maximum allowable service requirement (October 1, 2002) or the first day of the next plan year (January 1, 2003). Providing for two annual entry dates, for example, on the first day of the plan year and six months thereafter, would cure this problem.

**Practice Pointer.** Many plans are drafted to satisfy the entry and participation requirements by providing at least two entry dates for an employee who has satisfied the eligibility requirements. If only two entry dates are provided, the first should be the first day of the plan year and the second should be the first day of the seventh month of the plan year. Use of a single entry date eases administration but generally results in earlier participation than use of two entry dates. If a single entry date is desirable, employees must enter on the first day of the plan year *nearest* the date the service requirement is satisfied or on the first day of the plan year *in which* the service requirement is satisfied. If the first day of the plan year *after* the date the service requirement is satisfied is used as the entry date, the service requirement must be shortened to six months.

### Q 6:14   Is there a limit on the number of entry dates a plan can have?

No. An employee can have daily, monthly, quarterly, or semiannual entry dates, or entry dates based on any other period as long as the minimum requirements are satisfied. A limited number of entry dates, however, reduces the recordkeeping and administrative burden on a plan. Once an employee enters a plan and becomes a plan participant, the employee must receive a summary plan description and other information regarding the plan (see chapter 28), and benefit accruals are often based on entry date.

### Q 6:15   Must a plan cover an employee who leaves employment before the scheduled entry date?

No. An employee who terminates employment before the scheduled entry date need not be covered. A temporary absence due to vacation, sickness, strike, or seasonal layoff does not constitute termination of employment, and an employee who has satisfied the eligibility criteria cannot be denied participation merely because he or she is absent on the scheduled entry date. [I.R.C. §§ 410(a)(4), 410(a)(5)(E)]

### Q 6:16   If an employee terminates employment, will that employee automatically become a participant on rehire?

No. A plan can disregard an employee's prior service under the break-in-service rules (see chapter 7). [I.R.C. § 410(a)(4)] Special rules apply, however, in the case of vested employees and returning nonparticipants with prior service, and another set of rules applies in the case of a plan that measures service on an elapsed-time basis (see chapter 7).

*Former vested employees.* If an employee who was a vested participant in the plan returns to work, he or she must generally participate immediately on rehire. [See Rev. Rul. 80-360, 1980-2 C.B. 142] In Revenue Ruling 80-360 the IRS was asked to consider when a former participant renewed participation after return to employment. The plan had two semiannual entry dates. The IRS indicated that entry on one of the next scheduled entry dates was insufficient to satisfy the requirements of Treasury Regulations Section 1.410(a)-4(b).

*Returning nonparticipants.* A returning employee who had satisfied eligibility requirements but left employment before the entry date must begin participation immediately after returning to service unless the plan's break-in-service rules preclude consideration of the prebreak service. [I.R.C. § 410(a)(5); Treas. Reg. § 1.410(a)-4(b)(1)]

*Elapsed-time service measurement.* If a plan measures service on an elapsed-time basis, an employee with a period of absence beginning before the scheduled entry date must begin participation as of the entry date if he or she satisfied the age and service requirements before the period of absence. [Treas. Reg. § 1.410(a)-4(b)(1)] Participation must begin immediately after the absence ends unless the plan's break-in-service rules preclude consideration of the prebreak service. [I.R.C. § 410(a)(4); Treas. Reg. § 1.410(a)-4(b)(1)]

### Q 6:17   What are eligible and ineligible classes of employees, and what happens to an employee who transfers out of the eligible class?

An *eligible class of employees* is a group of employees eligible to participate in the plan based on business criteria established by the employer (see Q 6:11). An *ineligible class of employees* is a group of employees who do not meet the criteria and are thus ineligible to participate in the plan.

An employee who transfers out of an eligible class and then returns to covered employment becomes eligible to participate immediately on return to the eligible class.

**Example.** Hotshots Inc. maintains a plan exclusively for its salaried employees working at its New Haven location. The plan requires two years of service as a condition of eligibility and has entry dates of January 1 and July 1. Sharon has participated in the plan for a number of years. She is transferred to the Denver location to work on a project for six months. When she transfers, she is no longer an active participant in the plan because she is not in the eligible class under the plan. When she returns to New Haven in August she becomes a participant in the plan immediately. She does not have to wait until the next scheduled entry date.

## Coverage Requirements

### Q 6:18 Are there minimum coverage requirements for defined benefit plans?

Yes. Under Code Section 410(b), a plan must meet one of the following coverage tests as a condition of qualification:

1. *Ratio percentage test.* The ratio percentage test is an objective test that compares the percentage of NHCEs (see Q 6:33) covered under the plan to the percentage of HCEs (see Q 6:32) covered under the plan. If the ratio percentage test is satisfied (see Q 6:20), the plan meets the coverage requirements. [I.R.C. § 410(b)(1)]

2. *Average benefit test.* The average benefit test is really a two-part test that has a subjective component. First, the plan must benefit a nondiscriminatory class of employees—the classification test (see Q 6:24). Then the benefits provided to NHCEs are compared to the benefits provided to HCEs—the average benefit percentage test (see Q 6:27). If both of these tests are satisfied, the plan meets the coverage requirements. [I.R.C. § 410(b)(2)]

### Q 6:19 Do any plans automatically satisfy the minimum coverage requirements?

Yes. The following plans automatically satisfy the minimum coverage requirements:

1. Plans maintained by employers with no NHCEs (see Q 6:33) [Treas. Reg. § 1.410(b)-2(b)(5)];

2. Plans benefiting no HCEs (see Q 6:32) [Treas. Reg. § 1.410(b)-2(b)(6)]; and

3. Plans benefiting collectively bargained employees [Treas. Reg. § 1.410(b)-2(b)(7)].

### Q 6:20   How is the ratio percentage test satisfied?

The ratio percentage test is satisfied if the percentage of NHCEs who benefit under the plan is at least 70 percent of the percentage of HCEs who benefit under the plan (see Q 6:21). For these purposes, percentages are rounded to the nearest 0.01 percent. [I.R.C. § 410(b)(1); Treas. Reg. § 1.410(b)-2(b)(2)]

> **Example.** ABC Corp. has 100 employees, 10 of whom do not meet the one-year minimum service requirement. Of the otherwise eligible 90 employees, all 10, or 100 percent, of the HCEs are covered under the plan. To meet minimum coverage requirements the plan must cover at least 70 percent (70 percent of 100 percent) of the 80 NHCEs who have met the age and service requirements, or 56 NHCEs. If four of the otherwise eligible HCEs were excluded, thereby reducing the percentage of HCEs covered to 60 percent, the plan would have to cover at least 42 percent (70 percent of 60 percent) of the 80 NHCEs who have met the age and service requirements, or 34 NHCEs.

### Q 6:21   How are the percentages of covered employees calculated?

First, the employer must determine the total number of employees. For these purposes, the term *employee* includes all entities in the controlled group (see Q 6:43) as well as in any affiliated service group (see Q 6:44) or entity aggregated with the primary employer under Code Section 414(b) or 414(m). For example, if the sole proprietor of a restaurant also owns a corporation that runs a radio station, the total number of employees in the employer universe would include both restaurant and radio station employees.

> **Example 1.** Steno LLC provides secretarial services to numerous dentists in a medical building, and each dentist maintains his or her own practice. JoLynne Dentist owns 20 percent of Steno LLC and accounts for 20 percent of its gross receipts. JoLynne Dentist and Steno LLC constitute an affiliated service group. Accordingly, if JoLynne Dentist adopts a defined benefit pension plan, she must take into account all employees in her employer universe—employees of her practice and employees of Steno LLC.

The next step is to exclude employees who can be excluded by statute (the *excludable employees*). These include employees who have not satisfied the age and service requirements set forth in the plan, and employees whose employment is covered by a collective bargaining agreement if retirement benefits were the subject of good-faith bargaining (see Q 6:22).

The ratio percentage test is then applied to the remaining nonexcludable employees. First, the number of NHCEs benefiting under the plan (see Q 6:31) is divided by the total number of nonexcludable NHCEs. This fraction is the coverage percentage for NHCEs. Second, the number of HCEs benefiting under the plan is divided by the total number of nonexcludable HCEs. This fraction is the coverage percentage for HCEs. Finally, the coverage percentage for NHCEs is divided by the coverage percentage for HCEs. If the resulting ratio percentage is greater than 70 percent, the ratio percentage test is satisfied.

**Example 2.** The facts are the same as those in the example in Q 6:20. The coverage percentages for ABC Corp. are calculated as follows:

| | | |
|---|---|---|
| 1. | Total employees | 100 |
| 2. | Excludable employees | 10 |
| 3. | Nonexcludable employees | 90 |
| 4. | Number of nonexcludable NHCEs | 80 |
| 5. | Number of NHCEs in line 4 benefiting under the plan | 70 |
| 6. | NHCE coverage percentage line 5 ÷ line 4 | 87.5% |
| 7. | Number of nonexcludable HCEs | 10 |
| 8. | Number of HCEs in line 7 above benefiting under the plan | 10 |
| 9. | HCE coverage percentage line 8 ÷ line 7 | 100% |
| 10. | Ratio percentage line 6 ÷ line 9 | 87.5% |

## Q 6:22   Can any employees be excluded from the coverage tests?

Yes. The following employees can be excluded from both the coverage and participation tests:

1. Employees who failed to meet the plan's age and service requirements (see Q 6:2);
2. Nonresident aliens with no U.S. source earned income;
3. Employees whose employment is covered by a collective bargaining agreement if retirement benefits were the subject of good-faith bargaining;
4. Employees of separate lines of business (see Q 6:45); and
5. Employees who terminated employment during the year with no more than 500 hours of service (see chapter 7).

[I.R.C. § 410(b)(3), (4); Treas. Reg. § 1.410(b)-6]

## Q 6:23   What is the average benefit test?

The average benefit test, an alternative to the ratio percentage test for meeting the minimum coverage requirements (see Q 6:18), separately tests the following two aspects of benefits coverage:

1. *Classification.* The plan must provide benefits based on a reasonable classification (see Q 6:24) of employees. The classification must also be nondiscriminatory based on an objective safe harbor rule (see Q 6:25) or a subjective facts-and-circumstances test (see Q 6:26).
2. *Average benefit percentage.* The average benefit percentage for NHCEs must equal at least 70 percent of the average benefit percentage for HCEs (see Q 6:28).

[I.R.C. § 410(b)(2); Treas. Reg. §§ 1.410(b)-2(b)(3), 1.410(b)-4, 1.410(b)-5]

**Caution.** To meet the minimum coverage requirements, both prongs of the average benefit test [Treas. Reg. § 1.410(b)-2(b)(3)]—the nondiscriminatory classification test [Treas. Reg. § 1.410(b)-4] and the average benefit percentage test [Treas. Reg. § 1.410(b)-5]—must be satisfied.

### Q 6:24   What is a reasonable classification for purposes of the average benefit test?

The classification established by the employer must be reasonable and based on objective business criteria. Reasonable classifications include specified job categories, nature of compensation, geographic location, and other similar bona fide business criteria. [Treas. Reg. § 1.410(b)-4(c)] The classification must also satisfy an objective safe harbor rule (see Q 6:25) or a subjective facts-and-circumstances test (see Q 6:26).

### Q 6:25   What is the objective safe harbor rule?

Under the safe harbor rule, a plan's classification is nondiscriminatory for purposes of the average benefit test if the plan's ratio percentage is not less than the applicable safe harbor percentage. The ratio percentage used in the objective safe harbor rule is similar to that used in the basic ratio percentage test under Code Section 410(b)(1) (see Q 6:20), except that significantly lower ratio percentages are permitted. Under the safe harbor approach, the acceptable ratio percentage is based on the employer's NHCE concentration. The higher the concentration of NHCEs in the employer's workforce, the lower the permitted ratio percentage. The safe harbor test is satisfied, and the plan's classification is nondiscriminatory, if the ratio percentage (NHCEs (see Q 6:33) benefiting under the plan divided by HCEs (see Q 6:32) benefiting under the plan) equals or exceeds the specified safe harbor. If the ratio percentage is below the specified unsafe harbor, the plan is discriminatory; if it is between the unsafe and safe harbor amounts, the subjective facts-and-circumstances test (see Q 6:26) must be satisfied.

Safe harbor and unsafe harbor percentages corresponding to each concentration percentage are set forth below.

| NHCE Concentration (%) | Safe Harbor (%) | Unsafe Harbor (%) |
|:---:|:---:|:---:|
| 0-60 | 50.00 | 40.00 |
| 61 | 49.25 | 39.25 |
| 62 | 48.50 | 38.50 |
| 63 | 47.75 | 37.75 |
| 64 | 47.00 | 37.00 |
| 65 | 46.25 | 36.25 |
| 66 | 45.50 | 35.50 |
| 67 | 44.75 | 34.75 |

| NHCE Concentration (%) | Safe Harbor (%) | Unsafe Harbor (%) |
| --- | --- | --- |
| 68 | 44.00 | 34.00 |
| 69 | 43.25 | 33.25 |
| 70 | 42.50 | 32.50 |
| 71 | 41.75 | 31.75 |
| 72 | 41.00 | 31.00 |
| 73 | 40.25 | 30.25 |
| 74 | 39.50 | 29.50 |
| 75 | 38.75 | 28.75 |
| 76 | 38.00 | 28.00 |
| 77 | 37.25 | 27.25 |
| 78 | 36.50 | 26.50 |
| 79 | 35.75 | 25.75 |
| 80 | 35.00 | 25.00 |
| 81 | 34.25 | 24.25 |
| 82 | 33.50 | 23.50 |
| 83 | 32.75 | 22.75 |
| 84 | 32.00 | 22.00 |
| 85 | 31.25 | 21.25 |
| 86 | 30.50 | 25.50 |
| 87 | 29.75 | 20.00 |
| 88 | 29.00 | 20.00 |
| 89 | 28.25 | 20.00 |
| 90 | 27.50 | 20.00 |
| 91 | 26.75 | 20.00 |
| 92 | 26.00 | 20.00 |
| 93 | 25.25 | 20.00 |
| 94 | 24.50 | 20.00 |
| 95 | 23.75 | 20.00 |
| 96 | 23.00 | 20.00 |
| 97 | 22.25 | 20.00 |
| 98 | 21.50 | 20.00 |
| 99 | 20.75 | 20.00 |

[Treas. Reg. § 1.410(b)-4(c)(4)(iv)]

**Example.** Sweatshop, Inc., maintains a defined benefit pension plan for its salaried employees and a separate defined benefit pension plan for its hourly employees. There are no age or service requirements under either plan. Each plan covers 100 employees. The salaried plan covers all 20 of the HCEs.

To meet the coverage requirements of Code Section 410(b), the plan must satisfy the ratio percentage test or the average benefit test (see Q 6:23).

The salaried plan fails the ratio percentage test (see Q 6:20) because 100 percent of the HCEs benefit under the plan but only 44.44 percent (80 out of 180) of the NHCEs benefit under the plan.

The plan may, however, be able to pass the average benefit test (see Q 6:23). The classification is reasonable and established under objective business criteria. The NHCE concentration is 90 percent (180 out of 200 employees). Under the table, the safe harbor percentage for a 90 percent NHCE concentration is 27.50 percent. Because the plan covers 44.44 percent of NHCEs, the plan satisfies the objective safe harbor.

The plan will satisfy the coverage requirements if it also satisfies the second prong of the average benefit test (see Qs 6:27–6:30).

### Q 6:26    How is the subjective facts-and-circumstances option applied?

The facts-and-circumstances option is available only if the plan's ratio percentage is at least equal to the unsafe harbor percentage set forth in the table in Treasury Regulations Section 1.410(b)-4(c)(4)(iv) (see Q 6:25). If the plan's ratio percentage falls below the unsafe harbor, the classification is considered discriminatory. If the plan's ratio percentage exceeds the unsafe harbor, the plan can attempt to show that the coverage classification is, under the facts and circumstances, nondiscriminatory. Although no one factor is determinative, the following factors are relevant in determining whether a classification is nondiscriminatory:

1. The business reason for the classification;
2. The percentage of employees benefiting under the plan;
3. Whether the number of employees benefiting under the plan in each salary range is representative of the number of employees in that salary range in the workforce;
4. The difference between the ratio percentage and the safe harbor; and
5. The extent to which the plan's average benefit percentage test exceeds 70 percent.

[Treas. Reg. § 1.410(b)-4(c)(3)]

### Q 6:27    How does a plan satisfy the average benefit percentage test?

A plan satisfies the average benefit percentage test of Treasury Regulations Section 1.410(b)-5 if and only if the average benefit percentage for the plan year (see Q 6:28) is at least 70 percent.

### Q 6:28    How is the average benefit percentage determined?

The average benefit percentage for a plan is the percentage determined by dividing the actual benefit percentage (see Q 6:29) of the NHCEs (see Q 6:33) in all plans in the testing group for the testing period by the actual benefit percentage of the HCEs (see Q 6:32) in all plans in the testing group for the testing period. [Treas. Reg. § 1.410(b)-5(b)]

### Q 6:29   How is an employee's actual benefit percentage calculated?

The actual benefit percentage for an individual employee is determined in the same manner as the rate is determined for purposes of applying the general test for nondiscrimination in Treasury Regulations Section 1.401(a)(4)-2, 1.401(a)(4)-3, 1.401(a)(4)-8, or 1.401(a)(4)-9, by aggregating all plans of the employer (see chapter 10). All nonexcludable employees of the employer are taken into account, even if they are not covered under any plan being considered in the test. [Treas. Reg. § 1.410(b)-5(b), (c); Prop. Treas. Reg. § 1.410(b)-5(d), (e)]

Employee benefit percentages can be determined on either a contributions or a benefits basis, and permitted disparity can be imputed in the calculation of these percentages. In addition, either an annual method or accrued-to-date method can be used in the calculation of the normal accrual rate. [Treas. Reg. § 1.410(b)-5(d)] (See chapters 10 and 11 for discussion of the calculation of normal accrual and allocation rates.)

**Example.** The Horney Frog defined benefit plan is performing the average benefit percentage test on an annual basis without imputing permitted disparity in 2000. Pinky, the sole owner of the company, has accrued an additional $1,000 monthly benefit and has monthly compensation of $14,000. Greeney, the only NHCE of the company, has accrued an additional $160 monthly benefit this year and has monthly compensation of $3,000 in 2000. Pinky's normal accrual rate on an annual basis and without imputing permitted disparity is 0.0714 ($1,000 ÷ $14,000); Greeney has a normal accrual rate of 0.0533 ($160 ÷ $3,000). Because the normal accrual rate for Greeney is at least 70 percent of the normal accrual rate for Pinky (0.0533 ÷ 0.0714 = 74.65%), the plan passes the average benefit percentage test.

### Q 6:30   Must an employer include employees covered under its other plans in determining actual benefit percentages for purposes of the average benefit percentage test?

Yes. All employees other than those excludable by statute (i.e., those who fail to meet age or service requirements) must be included in the average benefit percentage test. Generally, benefits accrued under an employer's other plans are considered for purposes of the average benefit percentage test. Employee benefit percentages can, however, be determined under plans of one type (i.e., defined benefit or defined contribution) by treating all plans of the other type as if they were not part of the testing group. [Treas. Reg. § 1.410(b)-5(e)(3)]

### Q 6:31  When does a participant benefit under a defined benefit pension plan?

Generally, an employee is treated as benefiting under a defined benefit pension plan only if he or she is accruing a benefit under the plan. If, however, an employee fails to accrue a benefit during a particular year solely because of the Section 415 limits or uniformly applicable benefit limits, the employee is deemed to be benefiting under the plan. Additionally, if a current accrual is offset by a benefit provided under another plan sponsored by the employer, the employee is deemed to be benefiting under the plan. Finally, if the employee has attained normal retirement age (see chapter 9) and fails to accrue a benefit because of actuarial adjustments applicable to the deferred benefit, the employee is still deemed to benefit under the plan. [Treas. Reg. § 1.410(b)-3(a)(1), (2)(i)–(iv); Rev. Proc. 93-42, 1993-2 C.B. 540]

### Q 6:32  Who is a *highly compensated employee*?

For years beginning with 1997 and after, a *highly compensated employee* is any employee who:

1. Is a 5 percent owner of the employer (see Q 6:34) during the current year or the preceding year; or
2. Received at least $80,000 ($100,000 as indexed for 2006 and 2007) in compensation from the employer during the preceding year.

**Note.** The compensation and amount used are for the preceding year. Therefore, the $100,000 will first be used for the 2007 plan year to look back at the compensation earned in the 2006 plan year.

[I.R.C. § 414(q)]

An employer can elect to limit employees identified in item #2 to those in the *top-paid group*, that is, employees included in the top 20 percent of the workforce when employees are ranked on the basis of compensation. [Temp. Treas. Reg. § 1.414(q)-1T, Q&A 9]

### Q 6:33  Who is a *non-highly compensated employee*?

Any employee who is not a highly compensated employee (see Q 6:32) is considered a *non-highly compensated employee*, or NHCE.

### Q 6:34  Who is a *5 percent owner*?

A *5 percent owner* is any person who owns (or is considered as owning within the meaning of Code Section 318) more than 5 percent of the outstanding stock of the company or more than 5 percent of the combined voting power of all stock during the year. If the employer is not a corporation, a 5 percent owner is any employee who owns more than 5 percent of the capital or profits interest in the employer. [I.R.C. §§ 414(q)(2), 416(i)(1); Treas. Reg. § 1.416-1, Q&A T-17]

### Q 6:35 Does family relationship affect an individual's classification as an HCE or NHCE?

Yes. In many instances, an individual's ownership in the business entity is attributed to other family members, making them HCEs even if they take no role in management and are paid significantly less than the $80,000 (as indexed) threshold generally required for HCE status. [I.R.C. §§ 414(q)(3), 416(i)(1)(B)(i)] Family attribution applies in determining 5 percent ownership. Therefore, a person is considered to own the shares of stock or the profit of capital interests owned by his or her children, spouse, grandchildren, and parents. [Temp. Treas. Reg. § 1.414(q)-1T, Q&A 8]

> **Example.** Frank, a cook at a local diner, earns $25,000 a year. He marries Wanda, the owner of the diner. Wanda's stock is attributed to Frank for pension purposes, and he becomes an HCE.

### Q 6:36 What happens if a plan does not satisfy the minimum coverage requirements?

A plan that does not satisfy the minimum coverage requirements can take remedial action by the 15th day of the 10th month following the close of the plan year by amending the plan retroactively to increase benefits or coverage as needed to satisfy the coverage tests. The amendment must satisfy Code Section 401(a)(4) (relating to nondiscrimination in benefits) and Code Section 410(b) (relating to coverage) standing alone. Benefits cannot be reduced in violation of Code Section 411(d)(6). [Treas. Reg. § 1.401(a)(4)-11(g)(2), (3)(iv)] A plan that fails to make timely correction can be able to take corrective action under one of the voluntary correction programs described in Revenue Procedure 2001-17. [2001-7 I.R.B. 589] If the plan is disqualified, the value of vested accrued benefits will be included in the income of the HCEs. [I.R.C. § 402(b)(2)]

## Participation

### Q 6:37 Is there a minimum participation requirement for defined benefit plans?

Yes. Under Code Section 401(a)(26), as a condition of qualification, a plan must benefit at least the lesser of the following:

1. 50 employees; or
2. The greater of 40 percent of all employees, or two employees.

[I.R.C. § 401(a)(26)]

**Example.** Two physicians maintain a small medical practice. The older of the two would like to set up a defined benefit pension plan; the younger physician does not want to participate in the plan. If they are the only two employees of the practice, a plan cannot be established. A defined benefit plan must always benefit at least two employees unless there is only one employee. If the physicians hire another employee who is eligible under the proposed plan, the plan could be set up to benefit just one physician and the employee. The plan would then satisfy the minimum participation requirement because it would cover two employees, constituting 66.66 percent of the workforce.

### Q 6:38  Do any plans automatically satisfy the minimum participation rule?

Yes. The following plans automatically satisfy the minimum participation rule even if the requisite number or percentage of employees do not benefit from the plan:

1. A plan that benefits only NHCEs (see Q 6:33) and is not aggregated with any other plan to help the other plan meet the minimum coverage requirements of Code Section 410(b) [Treas. Reg. § 1.401(a)(26)-1(b)(1)];

2. Multiemployer plans (see chapter 5) [Treas. Reg. § 1.401(a)(26)-1(b)(2)];

3. Certain underfunded defined benefit plans (i.e., plans with insufficient assets to meet all liabilities and under which all benefit accruals have ceased) [Treas. Reg. § 1.401(a)(26)-1(b)(3)];

4. Certain plans of an employer involved in an acquisition or disposition (see chapter 25) [Treas. Reg. § 1.401(a)(26)-1(b)(5)]; and

5. Frozen defined benefit plans that satisfied the prior benefit structure rules (see Q 6:40) (i.e., plans under which there are no employee benefits and under which at least 50 employees or 40 percent of the employer's employees or former employees have meaningful accrued benefits) [Treas. Reg. §§ 1.401(a)(26)-2(b), 1.401(a)(26)-3].

### Q 6:39  Can plans be aggregated for purposes of meeting the minimum participation rule?

No. Each plan of the employer must satisfy the minimum participation requirement of Code Section 401(a)(26) independently, even if comparable benefits are being provided. [Treas. Reg. §§ 1.401(a)(26)-1(a), 1.401(a)(26)-2(a)]

### Q 6:40  What special rules apply to prior benefit structures?

A prior benefit structure, that is, all benefits accrued to a certain point in time, satisfies the minimum participation requirement if at least 50 employees or 40 percent of the workforce currently accrue meaningful benefits. The determination about whether a prior benefit structure provides meaningful benefits is a facts-and-circumstances determination that considers:

1. The level of current accruals;

2. Comparative rate of new accruals to prior accruals;

3. A comparison of the projected accrued benefits as of the current year and immediately preceding year;

4. The length of time the current benefit formula has been in effect;

5. The number of employees with accrued benefits; and

6. The length of time the plan has been in effect.

[Treas. Reg. § 1.401(a)(26)-3(c)]

### Q 6:41  What criteria are used to determine if a benefit is meaningful?

The determination as to whether a prior benefit structure provides meaningful benefits is a facts-and-circumstances determination that considers:

1. The level of current accruals;

2. The comparative rate of new accruals to prior accruals;

3. A comparison of the projected accrued benefits as of the current year and the immediately preceding year;

4. The length of time the current benefit formula has been in effect;

5. The number of employees with accrued benefits; and

6. The length of time the plan has been in effect.

[Treas. Reg. § 1.401(a)(26)-3(c)]

The IRS has stated in a field memorandum that an accrued benefit equal to 0.5 percent of total compensation times years of participation (or a current accrual rate of 0.5 percent of total compensation per year of participation) payable at normal retirement age would generally be considered meaningful. It is not clear at this time if an accrued benefit payable at a different retirement age (such as age 65) that is the actuarial equivalent of a 0.5 percent of pay benefit commencing at normal retirement age would also be considered meaningful. The IRS also stated in the memorandum that an accrued benefit or current accrual less than this would not necessarily fail to be meaningful; the facts and circumstances of each case would need to be considered.

## The Employer

### Q 6:42  Are related companies included for coverage testing purposes?

Generally, yes. In reviewing the minimum coverage and participation tests, all employees of corporations that are in the same controlled group must be treated as if employed by the same single employer. Similar requirements apply to affiliated service groups and other businesses under common control. [Treas. Reg. § 1.410(b)-9; I.R.C. § 414(b), (c), (m), (o)] There is an exception to this general rule for qualified separate lines of business (see Q 6:45).

### Q 6:43  What is a *controlled group*?

The controlled group rules follow the basic tests established under Code Section 1563. [I.R.C. § 414(b)] A *controlled group* of corporations exists for pension purposes if there is:

1. A parent-subsidiary controlled group with at least 80 percent common ownership (these groups are generally chains of subsidiaries with a common parent); or
2. A brother-sister controlled group in which:
   a. Five or fewer people own 80 percent or more of the stock of each corporation (considering value or voting power); and
   b. The same five or fewer people together own more than 50 percent of the stock (by value or voting power) when taking into consideration stock ownership only to the extent that it is identical with respect to each organization.

[I.R.C. §§ 414(b), 1563; United States v. Vogel Fertilizer Co., 102 S. Ct. 821 (1982)]

Before *Vogel Fertilizer*, the IRS maintained that a person did not need to own stock in all members of the controlled group to have that person's stock counted in the 80 percent test. Now the IRS has agreed that stock is counted only if the individual maintains ownership interests in each corporation in the purported controlled group.

**Example 1.** Tech 2000, Inc., is a wholly owned subsidiary of Omnitech Limited, a Canadian company, which is in turn an 80 percent-owned subsidiary of Omni Limited, also a Canadian corporation. Omni Limited has two direct U.S. subsidiaries, both of which are wholly owned: Omnifilm USA, Inc., and Omnisport USA Inc. Omnisport own 60 percent of Mulligans, Inc., another U.S. company. A parent-subsidiary group exists when 80 percent of the stock of each subsidiary is owned by companies in the group and the parent corporation owns at least 80 percent of one of the companies in the group. In this example, 80 percent of the stock of all of the companies except Mulligans Inc. is owned by companies in the group and Omni Limited, the parent, owns at least 80 percent in Omnifilm USA Inc., Omnisport USA Inc., and Omnitech Limited. The controlled group consists of all of the companies except Mulligans, Inc., because only 60 percent of Mulligans, Inc. is owned by the group.

**Example 2.**

*Stock Ownership (%)*

| Shareholders | Corp A | Corp B | Corp C | Identical Stock Ownership (%) |
|:---:|:---:|:---:|:---:|:---:|
| X | 40% | 26% | 45% | 26% |
| Y | 25% | 40% | 45% | 25% |
| Z | 20% | 30% | 1% | 1% |
| Total | 85% | 96% | 91% | 52% |

Corp *A*, Corp *B*, and Corp *C* comprise a brother-sister controlled group because both the 80 percent and the 50 percent tests are satisfied.

If *Z* did not own any stock in *C*, *C* would not be included in the controlled group because 80 percent or more of the stock of each corporation would not have been held by the same three shareholders.

**Example 3.**

*Stock Ownership (%)*

| Shareholders | Corp A | Corp B | Corp C | Identical Stock Ownership (%) |
|---|---|---|---|---|
| X | 45% | 26% | 45% | 26% |
| Y | 20% | 40% | 45% | 20% |
| Z | 20% | 30% | 1% | 1% |
| Total | 85% | 96% | 91% | 47% |

A brother-sister controlled group does not exist among any of the corporations because identical stock ownership is 47 percent and thus the 50 percent test is not satisfied.

## Q 6:44 What is an *affiliated service group*?

Affiliated service groups exist when two or more business entities are connected operationally. An *affiliated service group* consists of a first service organization (FSO) and one or more of the following organizations:

1. Another service organization (A-ORG) that is an owner of the FSO and regularly performs services for the FSO or is regularly associated with the FSO in performing services for third parties; or

2. Any other organization (B-ORG) when a significant portion of its business is the performance of services for the FSO or the A-ORG and services are of a type usually performed by employees, and when 10 percent or more of the interests in the B-ORG are held by individuals who are HCEs of the FSO or the A-ORG.

[I.R.C. § 414(m); Prop. Treas. Reg. § 1.414(m)-2(c)(1); Rev. Rul. 81-105, 1981-1 C.B. 256]

**Example 1.** Attorney William Wise has incorporated his practice as William Wise P.C. The corporation is a partner in a large law firm. Attorney Wise and his corporation are regularly associated with the firm in performing legal services for third parties.

Both the law firm and William Wise P.C. are service organizations. Consider the law firm as the FSO. The professional corporation would be A-ORG because it is a partner in the firm and is regularly associated with the law firm in providing services for third persons. The law firm and attorney Wise's professional corporation constitute an affiliated service group. [Treas. Reg. § 1.414(m)-2(b)(3), Ex. (1)]

**Example 2.** Morris owns one third of an employee benefit consulting firm and one third of an insurance agency. A significant portion of the consulting firm's business involves assisting the insurance agency in developing employee benefit packages for sale to others and providing services to the insurance agency in connection with these programs. The insurance agency routinely refers its clients to the consulting firm to assist them in designing plans. About 20 percent of the consulting firm's revenues are a result of services for the insurance agency.

The insurance agency is the FSO. The consulting firm is a B-ORG because a significant portion of its business is the performance of services of a type historically performed by employees in the insurance field and more than 10 percent of the interests in the consulting firm are held by HCEs of the insurance agency. (A 5 percent owner of a business is an HCE (see Q 6:32).) The two companies constitute an affiliated service group. [Prop. Treas. Reg. § 1.414(m)-2(c)(8), Ex. (4)]

### Q 6:45   What is a *separate line of business*?

A *separate line of business* (SLOB) is an entity affiliated with a controlled group that is organized and operated independently from others in the group. A number of criteria must be satisfied for an entity to qualify as a SLOB (see Q 6:46). Once an employer is classified as a SLOB, it can be considered independently of other entities in its controlled group for purposes of applying the minimum coverage and participation rules.

### Q 6:46   What must an employer do to qualify as a SLOB?

An employer must show that it has two or more lines of business existing for bona fide business reasons, each of which employs at least 50 employees and is organized and operated separately from the other. A SLOB must satisfy a statutory safe harbor (which considers participation of HCEs), meet one of a number of administrative safe harbors, or obtain a ruling from the IRS. The flowchart in Proposed Treasury Regulations Section 1.414(r)-0(c) presents the various steps necessary to secure SLOB status (see Figure 6-1).

Figure 6-1. Qualified Separate Lines of Business (QSLOB)

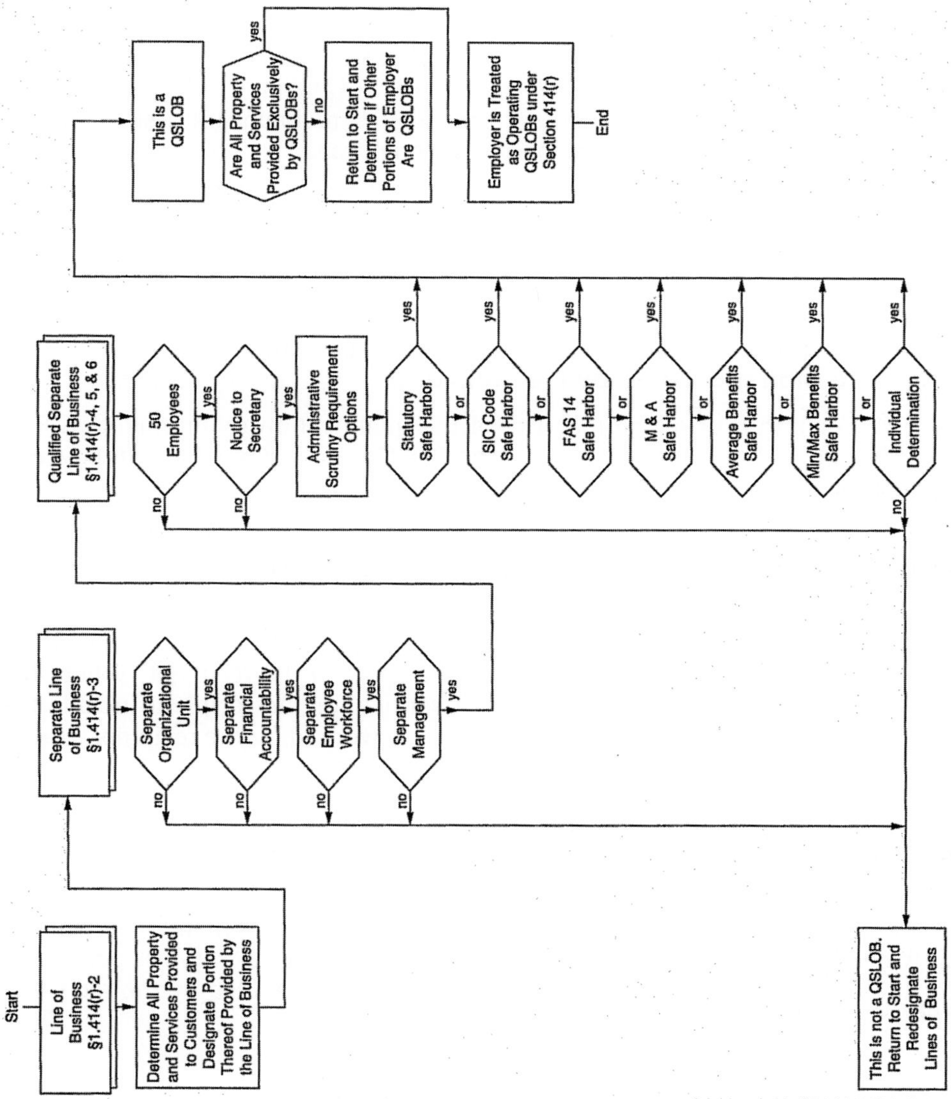

[Treas Reg § 1.414(r)-0(c)]

## Leased Employees

### Q 6:47  Who is a *leased employee*?

A *leased employee* is any person who is not an employee of the recipient and who provides services to the recipient if all of the following conditions are met:

1. The services are provided based on an agreement between the recipient and the leasing organization.
2. The person has performed services for the recipient on a substantially full-time basis for a period of at least one year.
3. The services are performed under the primary direction or control of the recipient.

[I.R.C. § 414(n)(2)]

### Q 6:48  Is a leased employee required to be covered by a plan sponsored by the recipient?

Yes. For purposes of the majority of the qualification requirements [I.R.C. § 414(n)(1), (3)], a leased employee (see Q 6:47) is considered an employee of the recipient.

### Q 6:49  When is a leased employee first considered an employee of the recipient?

A leased employee is first considered an employee of the recipient when he or she first becomes a leased employee with respect to the recipient. When that happens, the leased employee's years of service for the recipient include the entire period during which the leased employee worked for the recipient. [I.R.C. § 414(n)]

### Q 6:50  Can a leased employee participate in a qualified plan sponsored by the leasing organization?

Yes. If the leasing organization sponsors a qualified retirement plan, benefits provided by the leasing organization that are attributable to services performed for the recipient are treated as if they were actually provided by the recipient. [I.R.C. § 414(n)(1)]

### Q 6:51  Are there any circumstances under which a leased employee is not treated as an employee of the recipient?

Yes. If the leasing organization sponsors a safe harbor money purchase plan and leased employees make up no more than 20 percent of the recipient's non-highly compensated workforce, the leased employee is not treated as an employee of the recipient for most qualification requirements. The safe harbor plan must meet all of the following requirements:

1. It must be a money purchase pension plan (see chapter 2).

2. It must contribute at least 10 percent of compensation for each leased employee.

3. It must provide for full and immediate vesting (see chapter 8).

4. It must provide for immediate participation on hire.

[I.R.C. § 414(n)(5)]

If the leasing organization does not sponsor a safe harbor money purchase plan as described above, leased employees can be excluded from participation in the recipients defined benefit plan only if the minimum coverage requirements (see Q 6:18) and the minimum participation requirements (see Q 6:37) are satisfied.

# Chapter 7

# Measuring Service

Service is a very important concept in defined benefit pension plans. An individual's eligibility to participate in a plan often depends on length of service. Vesting also depends on service, and service is typically a factor in determining a participant's benefit under a plan. This chapter reviews the various elements of service and illustrates how they work in a defined benefit pension plan.

## The Importance of Service

### Q 7:1  Why is the concept of service important in defined benefit pension plans?

An individual's service is measured to determine eligibility (see chapter 6) and vesting (see chapter 8). If less service is credited than required, a plan risks disqualification for failing to satisfy the minimum age and service standards of Internal Revenue Code (Code) Section 410(a). Most benefits under defined benefit plans are determined by reference to years of service with the employer or years of participation in the plan (see chapter 9).

### Q 7:2  How is service generally measured?

Service is generally measured by one of two methods: the *general* method or the *elapsed-time* method. Under the general method, which is used by most plans, an individual is credited with a year of service (see Q 7:17) if he or she has been credited with a certain number of hours of service (see Q 7:4) during a computation period (see Q 7:10). Under the elapsed-time method, an individual is credited with years of service for periods of service (see Q 7:39) that have elapsed during a given period of time without regard to the number of hours of service during the period.

## Hour of Service

### Q 7:3  What is the significance of an hour of service?

An hour of service is the fundamental unit for computing service under most plans. Unless a plan has adopted the elapsed-time method of crediting service or has selected an acceptable equivalency (see Q 7:8), service is determined by reference to actual hours of service performed during a specified computation period. The concept of an hour of service forms the basis of the definitions of the following:

1. Years of service;
2. Years of participation for benefit accrual;
3. Break in service; and
4. Employment commencement date.

All of these concepts are used for purposes of applying eligibility and minimum vesting standards. [DOL Reg. § 2530.200b-2(a)] Unless the plan provides more generous standards, an employee who performs 1,000 hours of service during a 12-month computation period is credited with a year of service, and an employee who performs less than or equal to 500 hours of service during a 12-month computation period is charged with a break in service. An employee who is credited with between 501 and 999 hours of service during a 12-month computation period neither receives credit for a year of service nor is charged with a break in service.

### Q 7:4  What is an *hour of service*?

An *hour of service* is:

1. Any hour for which the employee is paid, or entitled to payment, for the performance of duties for the employer;
2. Each hour for which the employee is paid, or entitled to payment, by the employer on account of a period during which no duties are performed (regardless of whether the employment relationship has terminated)

because of vacation, holiday, illness, incapacity (including disability), layoff, jury duty, military duty, or leave of absence; and

3. Each hour for which back pay, irrespective of mitigation of damages, is either awarded or agreed to by the employer.

[DOL Reg. § 2530.200b-2(a)]

### Q 7:5 Must an employee receive credit for an hour of service when the employee is not actually at work?

Up to a point. Credit must be given for specified periods when the employee is not actually at work because of:

- Vacation
- Holiday
- Illness
- Disability
- Layoff
- Jury duty
- Military duty
- Leave of absence

[DOL Reg. § 2530.200b-2(a)(2)]

Plans have to credit only 501 hours for any single continuous period during which the employee performs no duties for the employer. [DOL Reg. § 2530.200b-2(a)(2)(i)] Plans can exclude periods when an employee receives payment under workers' compensation, unemployment compensation, or disability insurance. [DOL Reg. § 2530.200b-2(a)(2)(ii)] Plans are not required to provide service credit for hours relating to a payment that reimburses an employee solely for medical expenses incurred. [DOL Reg. § 2530.200b-2(a)(2)(iii)]

### Q 7:6 How are hours of service counted when no duties are performed?

An individual who has a regular work schedule must receive credit for the regularly scheduled work hours included in the period for which payment is made. [DOL Reg. § 2530.200b-2(b)(1)(i)]

**Example 1.** If Elizabeth regularly works a 37.5-hour workweek and takes a two-week paid vacation, she would be credited with 75 hours of service (two weeks at 37.5 hours per week) even though she did not perform any services during those two weeks.

**Example 2.** Sam becomes disabled and is absent from work for 11 weeks. The company pays his normal weekly salary for the first eight weeks of the disability. The company's long-term disability policy pays Sam 65 percent of his regular weekly salary for the remaining three weeks.

Sam's normal workweek is 40 hours. Sam receives credit for 440 hours of service (11 weeks × 40 hours) even though he received less than full salary and was not paid directly by the company.

If an employee does not have a regular work schedule, the plan can provide a reasonable method of calculating the number of hours associated with a period or can use an 8 hour per day or 40 hour per week convention. [DOL Reg. § 2530.200b-2(b)(1)(i)] If payment does not correspond to a period of time, the plan must divide the amount of payment by the employee's most recent hourly rate of pay. [DOL Reg. § 2530.200b-2(b)(2)(ii)]

### Q 7:7   Are there ways of establishing hours of service without counting actual hours?

Yes. Any plan that measures years of service by reference to hours of service can use an equivalency method instead of counting actual hours (see Q 7:8). [DOL Reg. § 2530.200b-3(c)] Use of equivalencies or the elapsed-time method for determining service often reduces administrative costs. Under these methods, a plan does not have to keep detailed records of actual hours of service. Equivalencies are particularly helpful when detailed records are unavailable or difficult to maintain. Equivalencies are also helpful when employees have irregular work hours. Even if the employer maintains detailed hour records, the plan can adopt an equivalency for determining periods of service and breaks in service. The plan must specifically identify the equivalency used. Generally, equivalencies are based on units of working time, periods of employment, or earnings. A plan can use different equivalency methods for different classifications of employees as long as there is a reasonable business reason for the different treatment and the method is consistently applied and does not result in discrimination. [DOL Reg. § 2530.200b-3(c)(2)]

### Q 7:8   What types of equivalencies can be used instead of calculating actual hours of service?

Equivalencies are usually based on working time, periods of employment, or earnings.

*Working time.* Hours can be determined on the basis of actual hours worked or regular-time hours. [DOL Reg. § 2530.200b-3(d)] Under the hours-worked equivalency, only hours for which service was performed are counted. The plan can ignore vacation, sick leave, and other periods when the employee did not perform duties for the employer. Because this method will result in fewer credited hours than the general method (see Q 7:2), 870 hours must be treated as equivalent to 1,000 hours, and 435 hours must be treated as equivalent to 500 hours. [DOL Reg. § 2530.200b-3(d)(1)] If hours are determined by reference to regular-time hours (i.e., excluding hours when a premium rate is due), 750 hours must be treated as 1,000 hours, and 375 hours must be treated as 500 hours. [DOL Reg. § 2530.200b-3(d)(2)] The working-time equivalency can be advantageous when employees have different work schedules and are compensated on an hourly basis.

**Example 1.** The plan uses the working-time equivalency to determine years of service. Alex actually works 870 hours during the year. He must be credited with one year of service for eligibility and vesting under the plan. If Alex had completed only 869 hours during the year, he would not receive credit for a year of service.

*Period equivalencies.* An employer can adopt (in the plan document) an equivalency based on shifts, days, weeks, semimonthly periods, or months. The following general rules apply:

1. *Shifts.* The employee must be credited with the number of hours normally in a shift if the employee is credited with 1 hour of service during the shift.
2. *Days.* The employee must be credited with 10 hours of service for each day in which 1 hour of service is performed.
3. *Weeks.* The employee must be credited with 45 hours of service for each week in which at least 1 hour of service is performed.
4. *Semimonthly periods.* The employee must be credited with 95 hours of service for each semimonthly payroll period in which at least 1 hour of service is performed.
5. *Months.* The employee must be credited with 190 hours of service for each month in which at least 1 hour of service is performed.

[DOL Reg. § 2530.200b-3(e)]

**Example 2.** The plan uses an equivalency based on shifts worked. There are three eight-hour shifts in a workday. Each employee generally works one shift per day. On a given day, Beatrice works one entire shift and one hour during the next shift. Beatrice must be credited with 16 hours of service: 8 hours for the first full shift and 8 hours for the second shift, since she completed at least 1 hour of service during the shift. [DOL Reg. § 2530.200b-3(e)(3), Ex. (vii)]

*Equivalencies based on earnings.* If employees are paid on an hourly basis, a plan can credit hours based on earnings. [DOL Reg. § 2530.200b-3(f)] The number of hours credited to an individual during any computation period is simply the employee's compensation during that period divided by the hourly rate. The hourly rate can be the actual rate paid to the employee, or a uniform rate can be applied for a group of employees. If a uniform rate of pay is used, it must be the lowest rate of compensation payable to an employee in the same or similar job classification. If equivalency is based on actual earnings, 870 hours must be treated as equivalent to 1,000 hours, and 435 hours must be treated as equivalent to 500 hours. [DOL Reg. § 2530.200b-3(f)(1)(i)]

Earnings equivalencies can also be used if an employee's compensation is not determined by reference to an hourly rate. The number of hours credited to an individual during any computation period is equal to the employee's total earnings during the period divided by the lowest computed hourly rate for that period. [DOL Reg. § 2530.200b-3(f)(2)(i)] The computed hourly rate depends on whether the employee has a regular work schedule. For employees with a regular work schedule, the hourly rate is determined by dividing the employee's lowest rate of pay during the period by the number of the employee's regularly scheduled hours during the period. If an employee does not have a regular work schedule, a plan can calculate hours by assuming a 40-hour workweek or an 8-hour workday. [DOL Reg. § 2530.200b-3(e), (f)(3)(i)]

> **Example 3.** Carl receives total earnings of $4,350 during the computation period. The lowest hourly rate received during the period was $5. The plan uses the earnings equivalency for determining hours of service. Carl is credited with 870 hours of service ($4,350 ÷ $5 per hour) during the computation period, which is treated as the equivalent of 1,000 hours of service. [DOL Reg. § 2530.200b-3(f)(4)(ii)]

*Elapsed time.* Under the elapsed-time method (see Q 7:35), an employee's hours of service are disregarded and the plan credits service based on the total period for which the employee is employed. Service is counted from the time the employee first completes one hour of service to the date the employee severs employment. [DOL Reg. § 2530.200b-9]

### Q 7:9   What credit must a veteran receive for service in the military?

The Uniformed Services Employment and Reemployment Rights Act of 1994 (USERRA) and Code Section 414(u) clarified pension rights for reemployed veterans. An old case, *Alabama Power Co. v. Davis* [431 U.S. 581 (1977)], required a plan to include an employee's World War II military service of 30 months for benefit accrual purposes under a defined benefit pension plan. Under 38 U.S.C. Section 4318, periods of service in the military must be counted as service with the employer when determining vesting and benefit accrual. Reemployed veterans do not incur breaks in service because of military service.

## Computation Periods

### Q 7:10   What is a *computation period?*

A *computation period* is a period of 12 consecutive months selected by the employer and identified in the plan document. A plan must designate a computation period for measuring years of service for eligibility, vesting, and benefit accrual purposes unless the elapsed-time method is selected. [DOL Reg. § 2530.200b-1(a)] The years of service actually credited to an employee depend on the hours of service credited to an employee during the plan's computation period.

Generally, a plan can designate any 12-consecutive-month period as the computation period if it is uniformly applied to all participants. [DOL Reg. § 2530.203-2(a)]

### Q 7:11  Is the plan year the best computation period?

The availability of records often dictates the computation period. If hour records are maintained on a calendar-year basis and it is difficult to adjust records to correspond to another 12-month period, the calendar year can be the best computation period. Most plans use the plan year as the computation period.

### Q 7:12  What computation period must be used for eligibility purposes?

A plan must credit an employee with one year of service for eligibility purposes if the employee is credited with 1,000 hours of service during an eligibility computation period. [I.R.C. § 410(a)(3)(A)] The initial computation period for determining eligibility must be the 12-month period beginning on the employment commencement date. After the initial computation period, a plan can continue to use each anniversary of the employment commencement date as the start of subsequent computation periods or shift the computation period to the plan year. If the computation period shifts to the plan year, however, the first plan year computation period must begin with the plan year that includes the first anniversary of the employee's employment commencement date. This results in double counting of certain periods of service.

> **Example.** A plan requires two years of service as a condition of eligibility. After the initial computation period, the computation period changes to the plan year, which is the calendar year. Drew begins employment on November 15, 2001. His initial computation period is November 15, 2001, to November 14, 2002. The next computation period would be the plan year that includes the first anniversary of Drew's employment commencement date (November 15, 2002), which is January 1, 2002, through December 31, 2002. Service between January 1, 2002, and November 14, 2002, is counted twice. If Drew is credited with 1,000 hours of service during the initial computation period (November 15, 2001, through November 14, 2002) and during the next computation period (January 1, 2002, through December 31, 2002), he is credited with two years of service for eligibility purposes.

### Q 7:13  What computation periods are generally used for vesting purposes?

A plan must credit an employee with a year of service for vesting purposes when an employee is credited with 1,000 hours of service in a vesting computation period. [I.R.C. § 411(a)(5)] A plan can designate any 12-month period as the computation period for vesting purposes if the computation period applies uniformly to all employees. A plan can use the 12-consecutive-month period beginning with an employee's employment commencement date as the computation period. [DOL Reg. § 2530.203-2(a)] For administrative ease, many plans use the plan year as the computation period for vesting purposes. A plan cannot use a computation period that unreasonably postpones credit. For example, the regulations prohibit a computation period measured by reference to a period beginning four months after an employee's employment commencement date. [DOL Reg. § 2530.203-2(a)] The selection of the computation year may have a significant effect on vesting.

**Example.** A plan uses the five-year cliff vesting schedule, that is, an employee remains 0 percent vested until completion of five years of service (see chapter 8). Emily began employment in July 2002. She works 40-hour weeks and completes 960 hours of service during 2002. She terminates employment in June 2007 after 800 hours of service. Note the difference in years of service recognized for vesting purposes, and the resultant vesting percentage determined with computation periods based on the calendar year and employment year:

| Calendar Year | | Employment Year | |
|---|---|---|---|
| *Year* | *Year of Service* | *Year* | *Year of Service* |
| 2002 | No | 7/02–6/03 | Yes |
| 2003 | Yes | 7/03–6/04 | Yes |
| 2004 | Yes | 7/04–6/05 | Yes |
| 2005 | Yes | 7/05–6/06 | Yes |
| 2006 | Yes | 7/06–6/07 | Yes |
| 2007 | No | N/A | |

If the plan uses the calendar year as the vesting computation period, Emily is credited with only four years of service and is 0 percent vested. If the employment year is used as the computation period, Emily would be credited with five years of service and would therefore be 100 percent vested.

### Q 7:14   What computation period is generally used for benefit accrual purposes?

A defined benefit pension plan has a great deal of flexibility in establishing computation periods for purposes of benefit accrual. Accrual service can be determined on any reasonable basis that considers all service while an employee is participating in the plan. [DOL Reg. § 2530.204-3(a)] Any 12-month period can be used as an accrual computation period. A plan must specify the number of hours required to earn credit for a full year of service. An employee who has at least 1,000 hours of service during a computation period must be credited with at least a partial year of service for benefit accrual purposes. [ERISA § 204(a)(4)(C); I.R.C. § 411(b)(4)]

### Q 7:15   Must the same computation period apply for eligibility and vesting?

No. A plan does not have to use the same computation period for eligibility and vesting purposes. [DOL Reg. § 2530.200b-1(a)] If the plan uses different computation periods for vesting and eligibility purposes, the plan has to maintain separate hours records unless an equivalency method is selected (see Q 7:7).

### Q 7:16 What credit must be given to an employee if there is a change in the computation period?

With regard to eligibility, a change in the computation period generally has little effect. The initial computation period is measured by reference to the employment commencement date. In a plan requiring two years of service as a condition of eligibility, however, the employee will receive double credit for the overlapping period when the computation period changes to the plan year (see Q 7:12).

Vesting computation periods may change because of a plan amendment or an employee's reemployment after a break in service. With regard to vesting, when a plan changes its computation period and an employee is credited with a year of service in each of the overlapping years, double credit must be given. If the vesting computation period is changed:

1. The new computation period must begin before the old vesting period ends; and
2. An employee who is credited with 1,000 hours of service in each of the old and new vesting computation periods must be credited with two years of service for vesting purposes.

[DOL Reg. § 2530.203-2(c)(1)]

**Example.** A plan measures vesting on the basis of its plan year. The plan year ends on March 31. The employer changes its fiscal year to the calendar year and amends its pension plan to change the plan year to conform to the employer's new fiscal year. The change becomes effective on April 1, 2002. One computation period would be the period from April 1, 2001, to March 31, 2002. The second computation period would be the period from January 1, 2002, to December 31, 2002. The period from January 1, 2002, to March 31, 2002, is double counted for purposes of determining years of service for vesting purposes.

## Year of Service

### Q 7:17 When must an employee be credited with a year of service?

*Eligibility.* For eligibility purposes, an employee must be credited with a year of service if he or she completes at least 1,000 hours of service during the 12-consecutive-month period (computation period) beginning with the date employment begins. [I.R.C. § 410(a)(3)(A)] After the initial computation period, the employee must be credited with a year of service if he or she completes at least 1,000 hours of service during the applicable computation period. The computation period can be changed to the plan year. A shift to the plan year may, however, produce unintended results in a plan that requires two years of service as a condition of eligibility.

> **Example.** Fantasy Incorporated's plan requires two years of service as a condition of eligibility. The plan year is the calendar year. Frank is hired on December 15, 2001. He completes more than 1,000 hours of service during the 12-month computation period from December 15, 2001, to December 14, 2002, and is credited with one year of service. If the plan changes the computation period to the plan year and Frank is credited with at least 1,000 hours of service during the 12-month period from January 1, 2002, to December 31, 2002, (the plan year beginning within his first employment year), Frank will receive credit for another year of service. He will accordingly be credited with two years of service as of December 31, 2002 (although he really has completed only 1 year and 15 days of service) and will become a participant on January 1, 2003. If, instead, subsequent computation periods are determined by reference to employment dates, Frank will not be credited with two years of service until December 14, 2003, the second anniversary of his employment commencement date, and will not become a plan participant until January 1, 2004.

*Vesting.* For vesting purposes, an employee must be credited with a year of service if he or she completes at least 1,000 hours of service during the 12-month computation period. [I.R.C. § 411(a)(5)]

*Benefit accrual.* ERISA does not provide a threshold hour of service requirement for benefit accrual purposes. A plan does not have to credit an employee with a year of service for any 12-month computation period during which the employee is credited with less than 1,000 hours of service. [DOL Reg. § 2530.203-2(c)]

### Q 7:18   Is a year of participation the same as a year of service?

No. A year of participation is generally a year of service during which the employee was eligible and participating in the plan. A year of participation is often used for benefit accrual purposes.

### Q 7:19   Must an employee be employed on a certain date to receive credit for a year of service?

No. An employee need not be present on any particular day within the computation period to be credited with a year of service during that computation period for purposes of eligibility, vesting, or benefit accrual. Credit for a year of service is determined solely by reference to the number of hours (or other units of service) credited to the employee within the computation period. [DOL Reg. § 2530.200b-1(b)] For eligibility purposes, however, if an employee is not employed on the entry date, a plan can exclude an employee from participation even if the service requirement is satisfied (see chapter 6).

## Q 7:20   Must an employee receive credit for a partial year of service?

With regard to eligibility and vesting, generally, an employee either receives credit for a year of service or does not. If the employee completes 1,000 hours of service during the applicable computation period, he or she must be credited with a full year of service for eligibility and vesting purposes even if he or she has been employed for less than 12 months. Similarly, if the employee falls short of the 1,000-hour threshold, he or she receives no credit for service during that computation period even if he or she has been employed for the full 12 months. [DOL Reg. § 2530.200b-1]

With regard to benefit accrual, if an employee has at least 1,000 hours of service during the computation period, the employee must receive credit for at least a partial year of service. Partial-year credit is generally determined by a fraction, the numerator of which is the credited hours of service and the denominator of which is the number of hours of service required to accrue a full year of service. [DOL Reg. § 2530.204-2(c)(1)]

## Q 7:21   How can a partial year of service be counted?

Partial years of service are rarely counted for vesting or eligibility purposes. If an employee has at least 1,000 hours of service during the computation period, the plan credits the employee with a year of service. If the employee has less than 1,000 hours of service, no credit is usually given. If a participant has at least 1,000 hours of service but less than the number required for a full year of service for benefit accrual purposes, the plan can credit the employee with a portion of a year of service, or a full year of service even though the service is less than that required for full credit, as long as the method of credit is reasonable and consistent. [DOL Reg. § 2530.204-2(c)(2)] It should be noted, however, that using hours as a basis for prorating benefit accrual may result in discrimination prohibited under Code Section 401(a)(4).

If the plan prorates benefit accruals as explained above and, in addition, defines benefits on a basis that has the effect of prorating benefits to reflect less than full-time employment or less than maximum compensation, and does not adjust less-than-full-time service to reflect the equivalent of full-time hours or compensation, then this is considered double proration and is prohibited. [DOL Reg. § 2530.204-2(d)(1)]

> **Example 1.** A plan requires 2,000 hours of service to receive credit for a full year of service for benefit accrual purposes. Under the plan, an employee with more than 1,000 hours of service but less than 2,000 hours of service is credited with a partial year of service for benefit accrual purposes. The partial-year credit is determined by dividing the number of hours of service by 2,000. If Jake completes 1,800 hours of service, he would be credited with nine-tenths of a year of service (1,800 ÷ 2,000 = 0.9) for benefit accrual purposes.

> **Example 2.** The Going Batty defined benefit plan (the Plan) formula provides that the annual retirement benefit will be 2 percent of the average

compensation in all years of participation multiplied by the number of years of participation. Laura is a full-time employee who has completed 2,000 hours during each of 20 accrual computation periods. Laura's average hourly rate was $5 an hour. Therefore, Laura's average compensation for each year during participation in the plan is $10,000 ($5 per hour × 2,000 hours). If the plan states that a full year of participation is 2,000 hours, then Laura's annual retirement benefits, if she retired at that time, would be $4,000 ($10,000 per year of compensation × .02 × 20 years of participation).

Teri, however, is a part-time employee who completes 1,000 hours of service during each of 20 accrual computation periods. Like Laura, Teri's average hourly rate is $5 per hour. Teri's average compensation for her total years of participation is $5,000 ($5 per hour × 1,000 hours). Thus, the plan's benefit formula, by basing benefits on an employee's average compensation in all years of participation, in effect prorates benefits to reflect the fact that during Teri's participation in the plan, she has earned less than the maximum compensation that a full-time employee paid at the same rate could earn during the same period of participation in the plan. However, the plan also states that a full year of participation is 2,000 hours, which is double proration, in effect reducing Teri's years of service by half. (If double proration were permitted, Teri's total years of participation would be only 10 since she would be credited with only one-half of a year of participation during each of the accrual computation periods (1,000/2,000). Thus, Teri's annual retirement benefit would be $1,000—i.e., $5,000 average compensation × .02 × 10 years of participation.) The plan is not permitted to use double proration to prorate Teri's years of participation to reflect her less than full-time employment throughout the time she participated in the plan. Therefore, Teri's annual retirement benefit would be $2,000 ($5,000 average compensation × .02 × 20 years of participation). If, however, the plan adjusts the average compensation during plan participation to reflect full compensation, then the plan may prorate years of participation. Thus, the average full annual compensation for Teri would be $10,000 rather than the $5,000 actually paid. Teri's annual retirement benefit would then be $2,000 ($10,000 average full compensation × .02 × 10 years of participation).

### Q 7:22    Can an employee be required to make contributions to a plan to receive service credit?

Yes. A plan can require employee contributions to earn a year of service credit for vesting and benefit accrual purposes.

### Q 7:23    Can any years of service be excluded?

*Eligibility.* Generally, all years of service must be counted in determining years of service for eligibility purposes. Plans requiring two years of service, however, can disregard service before a break in service under certain conditions (see Q 7:28). [I.R.C. § 410(a)(5)]

*Vesting.* Generally, all years of service must be counted in determining years of service for vesting purposes; however, a plan can permit the following years to be disregarded:

1. Years before the employee attained age 18;
2. Years during which the employee failed to make required contributions;
3. Years before the plan (or a predecessor plan) became effective;
4. Years that can be disregarded under the break-in-service rules;
5. Pre-1971 service if the participant did not complete three years of post-1970 service; and
6. Pre-ERISA service if the plan could have disregarded such service under the pre-ERISA break-in-service rules.

[I.R.C. § 411(a)(4)]

*Benefit accrual.* If a terminated employee receives a distribution of his or her entire vested benefit (even if $0) and is later reemployed, the plan can disregard the employee's prior service for benefit accrual purposes unless the employee repays the prior distribution with interest within a prescribed period of time. [I.R.C. § 411(a)(7)(B)] A plan can also offset future benefits by the value of any prior distribution that is not repaid. A benefit formula can limit the number of years of service that are taken into account in determining an employee's benefit (see chapter 9). The plan can, for example, disregard years of service in excess of 35 years. A plan cannot, however, cease accruals or reduce the rate of accruals because the employee has attained a certain age. [I.R.C. § 411(b)(1)(H); Prop. Treas. Reg. § 1.411(b)-2]

### Q 7:24 Under what circumstances should a plan be drafted to exclude some years of service?

*Service before age 18* (for vesting purposes). When an employer's workforce has a number of employees under age 18, using the rule that disregards service before age 18 can keep costs down without jeopardizing employee relations significantly, because retirement benefits are rarely of concern to very young employees.

*Rule of parity* (for eligibility and vesting purposes) (see Q 7:28). This option is generally helpful only in a plan that provides cliff vesting or no vesting in the employee's first few years of employment. Since enactment of the Retirement Equity Act of 1984 (REA), years of service completed after five consecutive one-year breaks in service can be disregarded. This rule can be invoked, however, only when an employee has not attained any level of vesting in the plan. If a plan provides 20 percent vesting after two years of service, this rule applies only to employees who have not completed two years of service.

*One-year holdout* (for eligibility and vesting purposes) (see Q 7:28). The one-year holdout rule may be useful when employees terminate before completing one year of service. Under the one-year holdout rule, after an employee incurs a one-year break in service, prebreak service is not counted until the employee completes a year of service after reemployment. After the new year is completed, the employee must receive retroactive credit for all prior years of service.

*Noncovered service* (for benefit accrual purposes only). If the employer has several divisions or employee classifications, some of which are not covered under the plan, or if the employer is a member of a controlled group of corporations, benefit accrual should be limited to service within the eligible class to avoid significant liabilities associated with transferees.

## Break in Service

### Q 7:25    What is a *break in service*?

A *break in service* occurs when an employee does not complete at least 501 hours of service (see Q 7:4) during the 12-consecutive-month computation period (see Q 7:10) specified in the plan. [I.R.C. §§ 410(a)(5)(C), 411(a)(6)(A); DOL Reg. § 2530.200b-4] If an employee has a break in service, he or she can lose credit for service performed before the break in service (see Q 7:28).

### Q 7:26    Does an absence due to a maternity or paternity leave count as a break in service?

For both eligibility and vesting purposes, an employee who is on a maternity or paternity leave of absence is credited with the number of hours of service he or she normally would have completed, up to a maximum of 501 hours, to prevent a break in service. The hours are credited in the year the absence begins, if necessary, to prevent a break in service. If the credit is not needed to prevent a break in service in the year the absence begins, hours are credited in the next year. The hours are credited only to prevent a break in service; the plan need not credit the employee with a year of service for such period. Accordingly, the rules have a neutral effect: the employee is neither charged with a break in service nor credited with an additional year of service. [I.R.C. §§ 410(a)(5)(E), 411(a)(6)(E)]

**Example.** Granite Construction Co. maintains a defined benefit pension plan and uses the monthly equivalency for determining hours of service (see Q 7:8). Under the equivalency method selected, each employee is credited with 190 hours of service for each month in which at least one hour of service is performed. The plan uses the calendar year as its computation period. Gloria leaves on a maternity leave on March 15 and does not return until the following year. She has already been credited with at least 501 hours of service (190 × 3 months). Accordingly, Gloria will not have a break in service and will not receive additional service credit for the maternity leave. If Gloria had left in February, she would have been credited with only 380 hours of service (190 × 2 months). In that case, the plan would credit her with an additional 121 hours to bring her up to 501 hours, sufficient to avoid a break in service.

## Q 7:27   Does an absence due to layoff or authorized leave of absence count as a break in service?

Although an employee must receive credit for hours of service for specified periods when the employee is not actually at work because of vacation, holiday, illness, disability, layoff, jury duty, military duty, or leave of absence (see Q 7:5), no more than 501 hours of service need to be credited if no duties are performed. [DOL Reg. § 2530.200b-2(a)(2), (3)] Because up to 501 hours will be credited for an absence due to layoff or leave of absence, the employee will not suffer a break in service.

## Q 7:28   Under what conditions can an employee lose credit for service before a break in service?

With regard to eligibility, plans that require more than one year of service as a condition of eligibility can include a provision to disregard years of service before a break in service if the employee has not yet satisfied the eligibility criteria. [I.R.C. §§ 410(a)(1)(B), 410(a)(5)(B)]

**Example 1.** Healthworks Co.'s plan requires two years of service as a condition of eligibility. Harry begins employment on January 1, 2001, and terminates employment on January 15, 2002. He is reemployed on January 1, 2003. Because Harry did not complete at least 500 hours of service during the 2002 computation period (January 1, 2002, through December 31, 2002), he has incurred a break in service. All of his service before the break is disregarded. The plan will calculate Harry's service from the January 1, 2003, reemployment commencement date, as if he were a new hire. If Harry had terminated employment later in the 2002 year after completing at least 500 hours of service, he would receive credit for his prior service when he was reemployed.

**Example 2.** Art, Burt, and Curt have been employed at Healthworks Co. (see Example 1) for a number of years. The following table illustrates when each will be eligible to participate in the plan:

|          | Hours of Service Completed During Plan Year | | |
| Plan Year | Art | Burt | Curt |
| --- | --- | --- | --- |
| 2001 | 1,000 | 1,000 | 1,000 |
| 2002 | 1,000 | 999 | 400 |
| 2003 | 1,000 | 1,000 | 1,000 |
| 2004 | 400 | 1,000 | 999 |
| 2005 | 1,000 | 1,000 | 1,000 |

Art satisfied the eligibility criteria at the end of the 2002 plan year and enters the plan in 2003. Although he has a break in service in 2004, his years of service before the break cannot be disregarded for eligibility purposes because he was a former plan participant. He continues to be eligible under the plan.

Burt satisfies the eligibility criteria at the end of the 2003 plan year and enters the plan in 2004. Although he does not receive credit for one year of service for 2002 because he worked fewer than 1,000 hours, he did not incur a break in service and therefore all prior years of service are counted.

Curt will not satisfy the eligibility requirements until 2005 and will enter the plan in 2006. He loses credit for the first year of employment because he had a break in service in 2002. Although he was not credited with a year of service in 2004, he did not incur a break in service and his one-year credit for 2003 is not lost.

With regard to vesting, a plan that includes break-in-service provisions can disregard prebreak service under any of the following conditions:

1. *One-year holdout.* If an employee has a one-year break in service, prebreak service can be disregarded for vesting purposes until the employee has completed a year of service after his or her return. [I.R.C. § 411(a)(6)(B)]
2. *Rule of parity.* A nonvested employee's prebreak service must be counted if the number of consecutive one-year breaks in service is less than the greater of:
   a. Five; or
   b. The number of years of service credited to the employee before the break in service.

Prebreak service that does not have to be counted under the rule of parity can be disregarded. [I.R.C. § 411(a)(6)(D)]

Because an employee must generally have at least a partially vested benefit if he or she has been credited with at least five years of service (see chapter 8), the rule of parity effectively disregards prebreak service only for nonvested employees who have five or more consecutive break-in-service years.

**Example 3.** Stepco Inc.'s plan provides for vesting under the seven-year graduated vesting schedule (i.e., an employee remains 0 percent vested until completion of three years of service; thereafter, vesting increases by 20 percent each year) (see chapter 8). Jenna completes three years of service before she terminates employment. Jake completes two years of service before he terminates employment. If Jenna returns to covered employment, she must receive credit for her three prebreak years of service regardless of when she returns. Her prebreak service cannot be disregarded. Because she had completed three years of service, she had a nonforfeitable interest before her break in service, that is, she was 20 percent vested before termination of employment. Jake must receive credit for his prebreak service if he returns to employment before he has five consecutive break-in-service years. Because he had not completed three years of service, he was 0 percent vested before termination of employment. Therefore, Jake's prebreak service can be disregarded if he does not return to employment within five years.

**Example 4.** Alice, Bette, and Carol have been employed at Stepco (see Example 3) for a number of years. The following table illustrates how service is credited for vesting purposes under the plan:

| Plan Year | Hours of Service Completed During Plan Year | | |
|---|---|---|---|
| | Alice | Bette | Carol |
| 2001 | 1,000 | 1,000 | 1,000 |
| 2002 | 1,000 | 1,000 | 400 |
| 2003 | 1,000 | 999 | 0 |
| 2004 | 400 | 500 | 0 |
| 2005 | 1,000 | 1,000 | 0 |
| 2006 | 1,000 | 0 | 0 |
| 2007 | 1,000 | 1,000 | 1,000 |

Alice changes to part-time status in 2004 and returns to work on a full-time basis in 2005. Although she has a break in service in 2004, her years of service before the break cannot be disregarded for vesting purposes, because she has a vested benefit in the plan (she has completed three years of service and is 20 percent vested). After 2007, Alice will be credited with six years of service for vesting purposes.

Bette changes to part-time status in 2003 and returns to work on a full-time basis in 2005. Although she has a break in service in 2004, her years of service before the break cannot be disregarded for vesting purposes, because the number of her consecutive one-year breaks in service (one) is less than the number of years of credited service before the break (two). After completing her one year of service in 2005, Bette will be credited with three years of service. Because she now has a vested benefit in the plan (she has completed three years of service and is 20 percent vested), her subsequent break in service in 2006 will not cause Bette to lose credit for any prebreak service. After 2007, Bette will be credited with four years of service for vesting purposes.

Carol terminates employment in 2002 and does not return until 2007. She has five consecutive one-year breaks in service; hence, her one-year credit for 2001 is lost. Under the rule of parity, prebreak service is disregarded for a nonvested participant if the number of consecutive one-year breaks in service equals or exceeds five. After 2007, Carol will be credited with one year of service for vesting purposes.

## Q 7:29 When must prebreak service be counted for eligibility purposes?

With regard to eligibility, prebreak service must be counted if:

1. The employee was a prior participant;

2. The plan requires one year of service (or less) as a condition of eligibility; or

3. The employee did not incur a one-year break in service.

[I.R.C. § 410(a)(5)]

### Q 7:30  When must prebreak service be counted for vesting purposes?

With regard to vesting, prebreak service must be counted if:

1. The employee had any vested interest in the plan before the break;

2. The number of consecutive one-year breaks in service is less than five; or

3. The number of consecutive one-year breaks in service is less than the number of years of prebreak service.

[I.R.C. § 411(a)(6)]

### Q 7:31  When will postbreak service affect prebreak benefits?

When service is disregarded under the break-in-service rules (see Q 7:28), it is disregarded for purposes of determining the amount of benefits earned before the break and the amount of benefits earned after the break.

> **Example.** Bungie Manufacturing Co. maintains a plan that provides for five-year cliff vesting. Under five-year cliff vesting, an employee is 0 percent vested until he or she has completed five years of service (see chapter 8). Ben incurs a break in service after completing four years of service. At the time of termination of employment Ben had accrued a benefit of $100 per month. Ben returns to work and accrues another benefit of $200 per month. If Ben's return to work is six years after his initial termination (i.e., he has incurred six consecutive one-year breaks in service), the plan could disregard his prior four years of service, since the number of consecutive one-year breaks in service (six) would equal or exceed the greater of Ben's total years of prebreak service (four) and five. In that case, he would lose the four years of prebreak service for purposes of determining his vested percentage in the original $100 benefit and the new $200 benefit. If, however, Ben's return is within four years of his original termination date (i.e., he had incurred only four consecutive one-year breaks in service), Ben's four years of prebreak service would have to be aggregated with his postbreak service for vesting purposes. In this case, he would be fully vested in the original $100 benefit as well as the new $200 benefit.

### Q 7:32  Can a plan require an employee to complete a year of service after rehire before recognizing prebreak service?

With regard to eligibility, a plan can require an employee to complete one year of service after a break in service before prebreak service is counted under the one-year holdout rule (see Q 7:33). [I.R.C. § 410(a)(5)(C); Treas. Reg. § 1.410(a)-5(c)(3)]

With regard to vesting, if a participant has a break in service and the rule of parity requires that the prebreak service be taken into account, the plan can provide that the prebreak service will not be counted until the employee completes another year of service after returning to employment under the one-year holdout rule (see Q 7:33). [I.R.C. § 411(a)(6)(B)]

### Q 7:33   What is the *one-year holdout rule*?

Under the *one-year holdout rule*, a plan can disregard (i.e., not count) service rendered before a break in service until the employee returns to work and completes one year of service. [I.R.C. § 410(a)(5)(C); Temp. Treas. Reg. § 1.410(a)-8T(c)(3)] The one-year holdout rule allows an employer to wait and see if the employee is going to remain employed before restoring him or her to active participant status. Until the employee completes one year of service after reemployment, the employee does not accrue benefits or earn additional vesting credit. Once the employee completes one year of service subsequent to reemployment, all prior years of service must be restored to his or her credit.

**Example.** ABC Co. maintains a plan that requires an employee to complete one year of service as a condition of eligibility. The plan contains a one-year holdout provision. Kevin satisfies the plan's eligibility requirement and becomes a participant in the plan on January 1, 2001. Three years later, on December 30, 2003, he terminates employment. Kevin returns to work for the employer on January 1, 2005, after incurring a one-year break in service (he was not credited with the minimum required 501 hours of service during 2004). After Kevin completes a year of service in 2005, he must be readmitted to the plan and receive credit for his three years of prior service for vesting and benefit accrual purposes.

### Q 7:34   What is the *rule of parity*?

Under the *rule of parity*, when the number of consecutive one-year breaks in service (see Q 7:25) equals or exceeds the greater of five or the total number of years of service (see Q 7:17) before the break, and the employee has not attained any level of vesting in his or her accrued benefit derived from employer contributions, prebreak service can be disregarded. [I.R.C. § 411(a)(6)(D)]

**Example.** Parasail Manufacturing Co. maintains a plan that provides for vesting under the five-year cliff vesting schedule. Under five-year cliff vesting, an employee is 0 percent vested until he or she has completed five years of service (see chapter 8). Brian incurs a break in service after completing four years of service. If Brian does not return to work for six years (i.e., he has incurred six consecutive one-year breaks in service), the plan could disregard his prior four years of service, because the number of consecutive one-year breaks in service (six) would equal or exceed the greater of Brian's total years of prebreak service (four) and five. If, however, Brian returns within four years of his termination date (i.e., incurs only four consecutive one-year breaks in service), Brian's four years of prebreak service cannot be disregarded under the rule of parity and is aggregated with his postbreak service for vesting purposes.

## Elapsed Time

### Q 7:35   What is the elapsed-time method of determining service?

The elapsed-time method is an alternative to the general method of measuring service (see Q 7:2). Service is determined by reference to the time that elapses during employment, regardless of the number of hours completed. For example, if three years have elapsed from an employee's employment commencement date to his or her date of severance from service, the employee is credited with three years of service regardless of the number of hours worked during that three-year period.

> **Example.** Lynn began employment on January 15, 2001. She terminates employment on March 15, 2003. Using the elapsed-time method, she is credited with two years and two months of service.

### Q 7:36   How is a year of service calculated on an elapsed-time basis?

Under the elapsed-time method service is measured while the employee is employed by the employer maintaining the plan. The period of service, rather than years of service, is used in determining service to be taken into account under the plan. The employee's period of service (see Q 7:39) is measured from the date the employee first performs an hour of service (see Q 7:4) and ends when the employee severs from service. Because the endpoint of the period of service is the date the employee severs from service, the employee is credited with time during any absence (other than voluntary termination, retirement, discharge, or death) that is less than 12 months. Under these service-spanning rules, many periods of severance (see Q 7:43) between periods of service are disregarded. Records must be kept showing employment commencement date, reemployment commencement date (if applicable), and date of severance from service. Years of service are determined by aggregating periods of service and then adjusting for periods of severance. The elapsed-time method can be used to measure service for eligibility, vesting, and benefit accrual purposes. [I.R.C. §§ 410(a)(3), 411(a)(2), (b)(4)]

For vesting purposes, the employee is credited with the whole years of an employee's period of service. The total number of whole years of service is determined by aggregating all periods of service. [Treas. Reg. § 1.410(a)-7(d)(1)(i)] In this case, a period of service is not disregarded merely because it is less than a one-year period of service. After aggregating periods of less than a whole year, only the integer portion is considered, and the remaining period of service is disregarded for vesting purposes (see Q 7:38).

### Q 7:37 How does the elapsed-time method apply in determining eligibility to participate?

An employee who completes a one-year period of service on the first anniversary of his or her employment commencement date is credited with a year of service under the elapsed-time method. [Treas. Reg. § 1.410(a)-7(c)(2)(i)] An intervening absence during the first 12 months of employment is not treated as an absence if the employee returns to employment before a break in service has occurred. [Treas. Reg. § 1.410(a)-7(a)(2)(iii)] An employee can be treated as satisfying the service requirement during a period of severance that is taken into account under the service-spanning rules. [Treas. Reg. § 1.410(a)-7(c)(2)(iii), (3)(ii)(B)]

If an employee does not satisfy the service requirement during his or her initial year of employment, successive periods of service are aggregated. A one-year period of service is credited when the employee completes 12 months of service. Thirty days of service are deemed to be a month; 365 days are treated as a one-year period of service. [Treas. Reg. § 1.410(a)-7(c)(2)(i)]

### Q 7:38 How does the elapsed-time method apply in counting service for purposes of vesting?

When a plan uses the elapsed-time method to calculate service, the plan must credit the employee with the number of whole years of the employee's period of service. For these purposes, the employee's periods of service are aggregated. A period of service is not disregarded merely because it is less than a whole year. Twelve months are deemed to be a whole year; 30 days are deemed to be a whole month. If a plan aggregates on a daily basis, 365 days are deemed to be a whole year of service. [Treas. Reg. § 1.410(a)-7(d)(1)(ii)] After aggregation is complete, the plan disregards periods of less than whole years.

> **Example.** A plan uses the elapsed-time method for calculating service for vesting purposes. The plan aggregates on a daily basis. Matt has a period of service of 400 days, another of 600 days, and a third of 400 days. None of these periods of service can be disregarded. Matt's total periods of service are aggregated; he has 1,400 days of service and must be credited with three years of service ($1,400 \div 365 = 3.84$). The fractional year of service is disregarded.

### Q 7:39 What is a *period of service*?

A *period of service* is the period used under the elapsed-time method for purposes of determining eligibility, vesting, and benefit accrual. For eligibility and vesting purposes, an employee's period of service begins on the employment commencement date (or reemployment commencement date) and ends on the severance from service date. [Treas. Reg. § 1.410(a)-7(b)(6)] For benefit accrual purposes, an employee's period of service generally begins on the date the employee begins participation in the plan and ends on the date of severance from service (or transfer out of the eligible class). [Treas. Reg. § 1.410(a)-7(a)(3)(iv)] Periods of service of less than one year are aggregated unless they can be excluded.

### Q 7:40    What periods of service must be counted in an elapsed-time plan?

*Eligibility.* An employee's entire period of service must be taken into account unless a specific exclusion permits the plan to disregard service. [I.R.C. § 410(a)(5)]

*Vesting.* For vesting purposes, absences of less than 12 consecutive months are not treated as absences. [Treas. Reg. § 1.410(a)-7(a)(2)(iii)] Generally, all service must be included in determining periods of service for vesting purposes. [I.R.C. § 411(a)(5); Treas. Reg. § 1.410(a)-5(a)] For vesting purposes, however, a plan can exclude:

1. Service before age 18 [Treas. Reg. §§ 1.410(a)-7(d), 1.411(a)-5(b)(1)(iii)];
2. Service while an employee declines to make mandatory contributions [Treas. Reg. § 1.410(a)-7(d)(2)(ii)(B)];
3. Service before the date the employer adopted the plan or a predecessor plan [Treas. Reg. § 1.410(a)-7(d)(2)(ii)(C)]; and
4. Service disregarded under the break-in-service rules (see Q 7:41).

*Benefit accrual.* The regulations permit a plan to credit service for benefit accrual purposes on any reasonable and consistent basis that takes into account the period of service the employee participates in the plan. [I.R.C. § 410(a)(5); Treas. Reg. § 1.410(a)-7(e)(2)] The plan can determine years of service for benefit accrual purposes without regard to computation periods. In this instance, the plan cannot exclude a period of service merely because the employee has been credited with less than 1,000 hours of service. [I.R.C. § 411(b)(4)(C); Treas. Reg. § 1.410(a)-7(e)(2)]

A plan need not take into account an employee's absence in calculating service for purposes of benefit accrual. [Treas. Reg. § 1.410(a)-7(a)(2)(iv)]

### Q 7:41    How is a break in service determined on an elapsed-time basis?

*Eligibility.* A one-year break in service occurs under an elapsed-time plan when an employee incurs a one-year period of severance. A one-year period of severance occurs if an employee fails to complete one hour of service during the 12-consecutive-month period beginning on the date of severance from service and ending on the first anniversary of that date. If an employee is credited with one hour of service during that 12-consecutive-month period, a one-year period of severance, and accordingly a break in service, does not occur. [Treas. Reg. § 1.410(a)-7(c)(4)]

*Vesting.* A one-year break in service occurs under an elapsed-time plan when an employee incurs a one-year period of severance. A one-year period of severance occurs if an employee does not complete one hour of service during the 12-consecutive-month period beginning on his or her date of severance from service and ending on the first anniversary of that date. [Treas. Reg. § 1.410(a)-7(d)(4)] If a one-year period of severance (break in service) occurs, service before the break in service can be disregarded under either the one-year holdout rule or the rule of parity.

Under the one-year holdout rule, periods of service before the break in service can be disregarded until the employee completes a one-year period of service after reemployment. [Treas. Reg. § 1.410(a)-7(d)(5)] Under the rule of parity, prebreak service can be disregarded for a nonvested employee who returns to work after a break in service of at least five years if the consecutive period of severance is at least equal to the prior periods of service (whether or not consecutive). [Treas. Reg. § 1.410(a)-7(d)(7)]

### Q 7:42    When does severance from service occur?

Severance from service occurs on the earlier of:

1. The date the employee quits, retires, is discharged, or dies; or
2. The first anniversary of the date the employee was absent for another reason.

[Treas. Reg. § 1.410(a)-7(b)(2)]

### Q 7:43    What is a *period of severance*?

A *period of severance* is a period of time during which the employee was not employed by the employer. A period of severance begins with the date of severance from service and ends when the employee returns to work. Breaks in service are determined by reference to periods of severance. [Treas. Reg. § 1.410(a)-7(a)(3)(v)] If a period of severance does not constitute a break in service, the period of severance can be treated as a period of service for eligibility and vesting purposes.

### Q 7:44    What are the service-spanning rules?

Service-spanning rules apply to tie together periods of employment under the elapsed-time method. There are basically two spanning rules provided in the regulations:

1. *Severance before an absence.* Under the first rule, service is aggregated if an employee severs from service because of voluntary termination, discharge, or retirement and returns to employment within 12 months after the original severance date. In this case, the period of severance is disregarded, and the plan must credit the period of absence as a period of service.
2. *Absence before severance.* Under the second rule, service is aggregated if an employee is absent for a period of at least two days for reasons other

than voluntary termination, discharge, or retirement and later incurs a severance from service because of voluntary termination, discharge, or retirement but returns to employment before the first anniversary of the first day of absence.

[Treas. Reg. § 1.410(a)-7(a)(3)(v)]

**Example.** Walt completes six months of service and is laid off. After a two-month layoff, Walt quits. Five months later, Walt returns to service. For eligibility purposes, Walt must be credited with 13 months of service (8 months of service and 5 months of severance). If Walt had not returned to service within the first 10 months of severance (i.e., within 12 months after the first day of layoff), Walt would have been credited with only 8 months of service. [Treas. Reg. § 1.410(a)-7(c)(2)]

### Q 7:45   Under what conditions can an employee lose credit for service before a period of severance?

*Eligibility.* A plan cannot exclude any periods of service that are less than one year until the employee incurs a one-year period of severance (break in service). [Treas. Reg. § 1.410(a)-7(c)(6)(ii)] Under the one-year holdout rule, if an employee incurs a one-year period of severance, a plan can disregard the employee's period of service before the period of severance until the employee completes a one-year period of service after the period of severance.

**Example 1.** TimeOut, Inc., maintains a plan with a minimum service requirement of one year. George completes a 7-month period of service, quits, and returns to work 15 months later, thereby incurring a one-year period of severance. After working four months, George is laid off for nine months and then returns to work. The plan can "hold out" George from participation until he completes a one-year period of service after the one-year period of severance. George satisfies the one-year holdout requirement as of the eighth month of layoff and is entitled to participate immediately on return to service.

Under the rule of parity, a plan can disregard a period of service if a participant does not have any nonforfeitable interest (i.e., the participant is not even partially vested) and the employee's latest period of severance equals or exceeds his or her prior periods of service, whether or not consecutive, completed before the latest period of severance. [Treas. Reg. § 1.410(a)-7(c)(6)] The regulations do not reflect the requirement that the period of severance equal or exceed five years. This requirement should be added (see Q 7:34).

**Example 2.** The plan requires one year of service for eligibility purposes and contains the rule of parity. Joe works for 3 months, quits, and then is rehired 10 months later. Joe is entitled to receive 13 months of credit for eligibility purposes. Although the period of severance exceeds the period of service, the three months of service cannot be disregarded, because no one-year period of severance occurred. [Treas. Reg. § 1.410(a)-7(c)(6)]

*Vesting.* A plan that determines service on an elapsed-time basis must credit employees with a number of years of service equal to the whole years of the employee's period of service, whether or not the periods of service are completed consecutively. A plan can disregard periods of service before a severance of service under the one-year holdout rule or the rule of parity.

Under the one-year holdout rule, a period of service completed before a period of severance is not required to be taken into account until the employee has completed a one-year period of service after his or her return to service (see Q 7:33).

Under the rule of parity, periods of service before a period of severance for a nonvested employee can be disregarded if the consecutive period of severance exceeds the prior periods of service, whether or not consecutive, completed before the period of severance. [Treas. Reg. § 1.410(a)-7(d)] The regulations should include the five-year minimum for the rule of parity as found in Code Section 410(a)(5)(D) (see Q 7:34).

### Q 7:46   How does the rule of parity apply to an elapsed-time plan?

Under the rule of parity, the pre-severance period of service is compared to the most recent period of severance. If the most recent period of severance exceeds the preceding periods of service and the period of severance is at least five years, the plan can disregard periods of service before the most recent period of severance. This rule applies only to nonvested participants. [Treas. Reg. §§ 1.410(a)-7(c)(6)(i), 1.410(a)-8]

### Q 7:47   Why would an employer consider an elapsed-time basis for calculating years of service?

Recordkeeping and administrative costs are generally reduced significantly under the elapsed-time method. The elapsed-time method often favors permanent part-time employees and employees with intermittent work schedules who do not have an absence long enough to be treated as a separation from service. Absences between start point and end point are generally disregarded unless they are of sufficient duration to constitute a break in service.

## Affiliated Employers and Transfers in and out of Covered Service

### Q 7:48   Who is the employer for purposes of calculating years of service?

Service with any member of a controlled group of corporations, businesses under common control, and affiliated service groups must be counted for eligibility and vesting purposes (see chapter 6). [I.R.C. § 414, (b), (c), (m)]

Businesses that have common ownership are usually aggregated and treated as one employer. [DOL Reg. § 2530.210(d)] A plan maintained by one member of the aggregated group must count service with each other member of the group unless the service could have been disregarded if rendered by one employer. [DOL Reg. § 2503.210(d)] Covered service for benefit accrual purposes generally means service with the employer or employers maintaining the plan while the employee is in the eligible class under the plan. [DOL Reg. § 2530.210(c)(3)(ii)]

### Q 7:49  Can a plan recognize service with a former employer?

For many purposes, service with a predecessor of the employer or service with an affiliated employer must be counted.

For eligibility purposes, if the employer adopts and maintains the plan of a predecessor, service with the predecessor employer is counted. A plan can count service with a predecessor for eligibility purposes even if the successor employer does not adopt the predecessor's plan or the predecessor had no plan. [Farley Funeral Homes, Inc. v. Commissioner, 62 T.C. 150 (1974)]

For vesting purposes, if an employer adopts the plan of a predecessor organization (e.g., if a sole proprietor incorporates his or her business and continues the plan), service with the predecessor employer must be counted. Even if the new entity does not maintain the predecessor's plan, service with the predecessor employer can be recognized for vesting purposes. [I.R.C. § 414(a); Ltr. Rul. 7742003] Because service credit with a predecessor employer is discretionary in this case, the plan has some flexibility in determining the manner of crediting predecessor service.

**Example.** Newco recently acquired the assets and employees of Oldco. Newco will be establishing a pension plan for its employees. The plan has a five-year cliff vesting schedule under which an employee is 0 percent vested until he or she completes five years of service. Newco would like to recognize some service with Oldco for vesting purposes. Newco drafts the plan to give Oldco employees credit for one year of service for vesting purposes for every two years of service completed before the acquisition. A former Oldco employee who had 10 years of service before the acquisition would be credited with 5 years of service for vesting purposes. If this provision is not discriminatory in practice, it is permitted because the proposed method is more generous than required. Newco could have disregarded all prior service with Oldco for vesting purposes.

### Q 7:50  How is service counted when an employee transfers from one plan of the employer to another because of a change in employment classification?

Generally, all years of service with the employer or employers maintaining the plan must be taken into account for eligibility and vesting purposes. [DOL Reg. § 2530.210(a)(1)] Only periods of covered service must be taken into account for purposes of benefit accrual. [DOL Reg. § 2530.210(a)(2)]

## Q 7:51   How is service counted when an employee transfers from one employer to another employer that sponsors the same plan?

In a multiple-employer plan, if an employee has covered service and contiguous noncovered service, the employee's eligibility to participate is determined by aggregating all service. [DOL Reg. § 2530.210(c)(1)] In determining service for vesting purposes, covered service and contiguous noncovered service must be aggregated. [DOL Reg. § 2530.210(c)(1)] A plan can, however, exclude noncontiguous noncovered service. [DOL Reg. § 2530.210(f)(1)] For benefit accrual purposes, plans can calculate service only for periods when the employee is employed in covered service. [DOL Reg. § 2530.210(c)(1)]

**Example.** Aerobics R Us and Moe's Massage contribute to a multiple-employer plan for their salaried employees. Allison completes one year of service as an hourly employee of Aerobics R Us and then transfers to salaried status. Bertha quits service as an hourly employee with Aerobics R Us and begins salaried employment with Moe's Massage. Chris transfers from salaried employment with Aerobics R Us to salaried employment with Moe's Massage. Dean is transferred from a salaried position to an hourly position with Moe's Massage.

*Noncovered to covered service with the same employer.* Allison completes one year of noncovered service and immediately begins four years of covered service for Aerobics R Us. No voluntary termination, discharge, or other service break interrupts the covered and noncovered service. Allison's noncovered service is contiguous. The plan must credit Allison with five years of service for eligibility and vesting purposes.

*Noncovered service to covered service with another employer.* After two years of hourly employment with Aerobics R Us, Bertha quits and is hired as a salaried employee of Moe's Massage. Bertha's noncovered service is not contiguous, because of the voluntary termination between noncovered and covered employment. The plan need not count the service with Aerobics R Us for any purposes under the plan.

*Covered service with one employer to covered service with another employer.* Chris completes three years of salaried service with Aerobics R Us and then transfers to Moe's Massage, where he completes another three years of covered service. The plan must count all of Chris's service.

*Covered service to noncovered service with the same employer.* After completing three years of salaried service with Moe's Massage, Dean is transferred to an hourly position where he completes another three years of service. No voluntary termination, discharge, or other service break interrupts the transition between covered and noncovered employment. The plan must credit Dean with all service with Moe's Massage for eligibility and vesting purposes.

[DOL Reg. § 2530.210(c)(3)(iv)(B)]

### Q 7:52   What is contiguous service?

Service is contiguous if:

1. The noncovered service precedes or follows a period of covered service; and

2. No voluntary termination, retirement, or discharge occurs between covered and noncovered service.

[DOL Reg. § 2530.210(c)(3)(a)]

# Chapter 8

# Vesting

If a participant in a defined benefit pension plan is not vested and the participant's employment terminates before retirement, his or her benefit can be forfeited. This chapter describes how benefits become vested. It also describes benefits, rights, and features of a plan that are protected benefits, that is, benefits that cannot be eliminated.

## Vesting

### Q 8:1  What are *vested benefits*?

*Vested benefits* are benefits that are no longer subject to risk of forfeiture. Benefits are forfeitable if they can be lost.

ERISA requires a qualified plan to give participants a vested right to benefits, that is, a right that cannot be taken away or forfeited. A plan must provide a schedule under which an employee whose employment is terminated before normal retirement age will vest in a portion of his or her benefit. [I.R.C. § 411(a)] The extent to which an employee is vested depends on the number of years of service with the employer (see chapter 7) and the vesting schedule set forth in the plan (see Q 8:9). After the employee completes the required years of service, the employee acquires a vested, nonforfeitable right to all or a percentage of his or her accrued benefit.

**Example.**  Amos has accrued a benefit of $1,000 per month payable at age 65. Amos has been employed by the company sponsoring the plan for four years. The company's pension plan has a five-year cliff vesting schedule; that is, an employee is 0 percent vested until completion of five years of service. At this time, Amos has not completed the requisite five years of service and is 0 percent vested. If he terminates employment before he completes five years of service, Amos will be 0 percent vested in his accrued benefit and will forfeit his right to receive a benefit at retirement ($1,000 × 0% = $0). After five years of service, he will become 100 percent vested in his accrued benefit. If he leaves employment after five years of service, Amos will be entitled to his vested accrued benefit of $1,000 ($1,000 × 100%) at age 65.

### Q 8:2   To what qualified plans do the vesting standards apply?

All qualified plans must meet the minimum vesting standards [I.R.C. § 401(a)(7)], except for the following plans:

1. Governmental plans, as long as they meet pre-ERISA vesting requirements;
2. Church plans that do not make the election provided by Internal Revenue Code (Code) Section 410(d) (see chapter 5);
3. Plans that have not provided for employer contributions since September 2, 1974; and
4. Plans established by a society or association described in Code Sections 501(c)(8) or (9) if no part of any contribution is made by employers of plan participants.

[I.R.C. § 411(e)(1); Treas. Reg. § 1.411(a)-1(c)(1)]

### Q 8:3   Must all benefits be vested at normal retirement age regardless of years of service?

Yes. An employee who is a participant at normal retirement age must be 100 percent vested in the normal retirement benefit regardless of pre-normal retirement age, service, or vesting level. [Treas. Reg. § 1.411(a)-1(a)(1)] *Normal retirement age* is defined as the earlier of the following designated ages:

1. Normal retirement age as specified in the plan; or
2. The later of age 65 or the fifth anniversary of the date participation began.

[I.R.C. § 411(a)(8)]

**Caution.** A plan that provides that an employee's benefit becomes vested on his or her normal retirement date fails to meet this qualification requirement if the normal retirement date falls after normal retirement age as defined in Code Section 411(a)(8). [Rev. Rul. 81-211, 1981-2 C.B. 98] This may happen inadvertently if, for example, the plan defines the normal retirement date as the first day of the month following the calendar month of the employee's 65th birthday.

**Q 8:4   Are there any other circumstances under which an employee must become 100 percent vested even if the employee has not satisfied the service requirements for full vesting?**

Yes. An employee must be 100 percent vested in his or her accrued benefit in the following instances regardless of the number of years of service completed:

1. The plan terminates (fully or partially) (see Q 8:43) [I.R.C. § 411(d)(3)]; or
2. Eligibility for plan participation requires more than one year of service (see chapter 6) [I.R.C. § 410(a)(1)(B)(i)].

**Q 8:5   Must benefits payable because of death or disability be fully vested?**

No. Although a plan may provide for 100 percent vesting if the employee dies or becomes disabled, full vesting is not required.

**Q 8:6   Can a plan require an employee to satisfy eligibility requirements and participate in the plan for a number of years before full vesting?**

As a general rule, no. A plan will not meet minimum vesting requirements unless it provides for vesting of benefits after the service requirements are satisfied, even if the service is rendered while the employee is ineligible to participate in the plan. For example, an employee whose employment is covered by a collective bargaining agreement (a union employee) can be excluded from participation in the nonunion plan of the employer, but his or her years of service count for vesting purposes if his or her status as a union employee changes in the future. A plan can, however, use a vesting schedule that recognizes service only while an employee is in covered employment as long as one of the statutory schedules for vesting based on all service is satisfied (see Q 8:9). For example, a plan can provide for 100 percent vesting after five years of service (thereby satisfying the minimum vesting standards), but permit accelerated vesting if the employee works in a particular division for at least two years or actually participates in the plan for at least three years. In *Ferrara v. Allentown Physician Anesthesia Associates, Inc.* [711 F. Supp. 206 (E.D. Pa. 1989)], a vesting schedule based on years of participation was permitted.

If a plan requires employee contributions, the plan can disregard any years in which the employee fails to make a contribution (see Q 8:21).

**Q 8:7   Must an early retirement benefit be fully vested?**

No. A plan does not have to provide for special accelerated vesting on attainment of early retirement age. However, a plan may provide for accelerated vesting on attainment of early retirement age if the sponsor wants to do this.

### Q 8:8   Can an employer place a vesting schedule on benefits attributable to employee contributions?

No. Benefits derived from employee contributions, whether mandatory or voluntary, must be 100 percent vested at all times and not subject to forfeiture. [I.R.C. § 411(a)(1); Treas. Reg. §§ 1.411(a)-1(a)(2), 1.411(c)-1]

## Vesting Schedules

### Q 8:9   What vesting schedules are permitted?

Benefits derived from employer contributions must generally vest within the period set forth in either one of two statutorily defined vesting schedules. These schedules are based on the employee's years of service (see Qs 8:18 and 8:19) with the employer. In general, an employee is credited with a year of service when the employee completes 1,000 hours of service during a computation period (see chapter 7). The basic vesting rules are set forth in Code Section 411(a). If the plan is top heavy, however, the more rapid vesting schedules of Code Section 416(b) apply (see Q 8:10). If the plan is an applicable defined benefit plan, such as a cash balance or pension equity plan, the plan will be subject to a three-year cliff vesting schedule (see Q 8:11).

The two statutory minimum vesting schedules are described below:

1. *Five-year cliff vesting.* An employee who is credited with five years of service must be 100 percent vested. [I.R.C. § 411(a)(2)(A); Temp. Treas. Reg. § 1.411(a)-3T(b)]

   | Years of Service | Required Vesting |
   |:---:|:---:|
   | Less than 5 | 0% |
   | 5 or more | 100% |

   Under cliff vesting, an employee has no vested interest in benefits for several years and then becomes fully vested. An employee who terminates employment before full vesting occurs, falls off the "cliff" and loses all rights to a benefit under the plan.

   The potential for forfeiture is great under cliff vesting. If a pattern of vesting abuse exists, such as dismissal of employees just before full vesting, the plan may not be qualified. [I.R.C. §§ 401(a)(4), 411(d); Treas. Reg. § 1.401(a)(4)-11(c)]

   > **Example 1.** Precision Blades Company maintains a computer program with codes identifying each employee's benefit and vesting level. Employees approaching benefit vesting are identified and targeted for layoff. Such terminations would constitute a vesting abuse. [McLendon *Co.* Continental Can Co., 908 F.2d 1171 (3d Cir. 1990)]

2. *Seven-year graded, or 3/20, vesting.* An employee who is credited with three years of service must be 20 percent vested. The vesting percentage must increase by 20 percent for each additional year of service. [I.R.C. § 411(a)(2)(B); Temp. Treas. Reg. § 1.411(a)-3T(c)]

| Years of Service | Required Vesting |
|------------------|------------------|
| Less than 3      | 0%               |
| 3                | 20%              |
| 4                | 40%              |
| 5                | 60%              |
| 6                | 80%              |
| 7                | 100%             |

Under a graded vesting schedule, an employee gradually vests in benefits over years of service.

A plan can have a more liberal vesting schedule than the two schedules identified in Code Section 411 as long as the vested percentage in any given year is at least as favorable as that permitted under one of the statutory schedules. A plan cannot satisfy one schedule in one year and another in a later year; it must satisfy the same schedule for all years. [Temp. Treas. Reg. § 1.411(a)-3T(a)(2)]

**Example 2.** The vesting schedule under ABC Co.'s pension plan is as follows:

| Years of Service | Vesting Percentage |
|------------------|--------------------|
| Less than 4      | 0%                 |
| 4                | 25%                |
| 5                | 50%                |
| 6                | 75%                |
| 7                | 100%               |

The plan does not satisfy the minimum vesting standards. Under the seven-year graded vesting schedule, an employee must be at least 20 percent vested after completion of three years of service. Even though the vesting percentages are greater than the vesting percentages required for later years, failure to meet required minimum for any one year constitutes a violation of the minimum vesting standards. The plan cannot use one permitted schedule for some years and the other for other years. If the plan sponsor wants to use a vesting schedule that provides less than 20 percent vesting for employees with three years of service, the plan has to satisfy the required vesting minimums under the five-year cliff vesting schedule for all years.

## Q 8:10  How does top-heavy status affect the vesting schedule?

If a plan is top heavy (see chapter 5) for any plan year, it must provide for more rapid vesting than is otherwise required. A plan can select one of two alternative top-heavy minimum vesting schedules:

1. *Three-year cliff.* Under this schedule, no vesting is provided until the employee is credited with three years of service, at which time the employee becomes fully vested.

2. *Six-year graded, or 2/20.* Under this schedule, an employee must be 20 percent vested after completing two years of service, with vesting increasing in 20 percent increments until the employee is 100 percent vested after six years of service.

| Years of Service | Vesting Percentage |
|---|---|
| Less than 2 | 0% |
| 2 | 20% |
| 3 | 40% |
| 4 | 60% |
| 5 | 80% |
| 6 | 100% |

The top-heavy vesting schedule supersedes the plan's regular vesting schedule when the plan becomes top heavy. [I.R.C. § 416(b)] If a plan uses the six-year graded vesting schedule as its top-heavy vesting schedule and the plan becomes top heavy after an employee completes three years of service, the employee becomes 40 percent vested in his or her accrued benefit. The vesting applies to all benefits accrued as of the date the plan becomes top heavy. If the plan returns to non-top-heavy status, the non-top-heavy vesting schedule applies to all future accruals. Despite this rule, however, any participant with three or more years of service must be given the right to elect to continue under the old top-heavy vesting schedule as if the schedule had been amended (see Q 8:17). [Treas. Reg. § 1.416-1, Q&A V-7]

**Example.** Cliffside Manor maintains a defined benefit pension plan for its employees. The plan has a five-year cliff vesting schedule; that is, an employee does not become vested until he or she completes five years of service. If the plan becomes top heavy, however, the six-year graded vesting schedule applies. Cliffside Manor hires Shannon in 1997. Under the terms of the plan, Shannon will accrue a benefit of $100 for each year of service. The plan is top heavy for the 1999 plan year. Shannon's vested accrued benefit is determined as follows:

| Year | Accrued Benefit | Vesting | Vested Accrued Benefit (Regular Schedule) | Vesting | Vested Accrued Benefit (Top-Heavy Schedule) |
|---|---|---|---|---|---|
| 1998 | $100 | 0% | $ 0 | 0% | $ 0 |
| 1999* | $200 | 0% | $ 0 | 20% | $ 40 |
| 2000 | $300 | 0% | $ 0 | 40% | $ 120 |
| 2001 | $400 | 0% | $ 0 | 60% | $ 240 |
| 2002 | $500 | 100% | $ 500 | 80% | $ 400 |

*Top-heavy year

When the plan became top heavy in 1999, Shannon's accrued benefit became vested under the top-heavy vesting schedule. After two years of service, benefits are 20 percent vested under the top-heavy vesting schedule. Accordingly, Shannon has a vested accrued benefit of $40 ($200 × 20%) in 1999. In 2000, when the plan is no longer top heavy, the non-top-heavy vesting schedule would generally apply; however, any participant with three years of service can elect to continue under the top-heavy schedule. Shannon's benefit will vest under the top-heavy schedule even though the plan was top heavy only for one year.

### Q 8:11   What vesting schedule applies to an applicable defined benefit plan?

As part of the Pension Protection Act of 2006 (PPA), an applicable defined benefit plan, such as a cash balance plan or pension equity plan (see chapter 13), is required to use a three-year cliff vesting schedule. Under this schedule, no vesting is provided until the employee is credited with three years of service, at which time the employee becomes fully vested.

This is effective immediately for plans commencing after June 29, 2006. Plans in existence on June 29, 2006, have a permissible delayed effective date until plan years beginning after December 31, 2007.

### Q 8:12   Can a vesting schedule consider both age and service?

No. Before the enactment of Tax Reform Act of 1986 (TRA '86), plans could adopt an age-related vesting schedule known as the rule of 45. Under this schedule, when a participant's age plus years of service equaled 45, the participant became entitled to 50 percent vesting in his or her benefit derived from employer contributions. Thereafter, the participant became vested in an additional 10 percent for each increment of two years, that is, one year of age plus one year of service. When age plus service equaled 55, the participant was 100 percent vested. This schedule is no longer permitted.

### Q 8:13   Can an employer apply a separate vesting schedule for new benefits as they accrue?

No. Certain profit-sharing and money purchase plans were permitted to treat each year's employer contribution as a separate class. Under these class-year plans, a contribution for a given year became 100 percent vested within five years after the year for which it was made. Class-year vesting was eliminated by TRA '86. Class-year vesting was never permitted for defined benefit plans.

### Q 8:14   Can an employer use different vesting schedules for different groups of employees?

Yes. A plan can provide different vesting schedules for different classes of employees. The manner in which employees vest in their accrued benefits under the vesting schedules in Code Section 411(a)(2)(A) and (B) and Code Section 416 (b)(1)(A) and (B) are treated as equivalent to one another. [Treas. Reg. § 1.401 (a)(4)-11(c)(2)] The plan must, however, apply one schedule to all of the employee's years of service. [Temp. Treas. Reg. § 1.411(a)-3T(a)(2)]

### Q 8:15   Can an employer apply different vesting schedules based on the reason for termination of employment?

Yes. If a plan offers a more liberal vesting schedule than that required by statute (see Q 8:9), accelerated vesting can be taken away. For example, if an employee is terminated for misconduct or violation of a noncompete agreement, the plan does not have to vest benefits faster than the rules require. This is commonly referred to as a "bad boy" clause. A law firm provided for complete vesting after 5 years of service subject to a clause forfeiting benefits for participants with fewer than 10 years of service who entered competing employment. The dual vesting schedules were acceptable because the plan met the 10-year cliff standard in effect at that time. [Lojek v. Thomas, 716 F.2d 675 (9th Cir. 1983)] A plan can provide a five-year cliff vesting schedule for employees dismissed for cause and a three-year graded schedule for other employees. [Rev. Rul. 85-31, 1985-1 C.B. 153; Temp. Treas. Reg. § 1.411(a)-4T]

### Q 8:16   Can a vesting schedule be changed?

Yes. Most plans permit an employer to make amendments to a plan at any time. An employer can change a vesting schedule, as it can change any other plan provision.

### Q 8:17   What rights do participants have if the vesting schedule is changed?

Under Proposed Treasury Regulations Section 1.411(d)-3(a)(3), if a vesting schedule is changed, a participant must be given the greater of the two vesting schedules. This was a result of the *Central Laborers' Pension Fund v. Heinz* [541 U.S. 739 (2004)] decision rendered by the Supreme Court in 2004. The Treasury Department has provided two examples of this effect in Proposed Treasury Regulations Section 1.411(d)-(3)(a)(4), example 3 and 4. Previously, if a vesting schedule was changed, each participant with at least three years of service (determined without regard to the exclusions permitted under Code Section 411(a)(4); see Q 8:21) must have been able to elect to have his or her vested percentage determined on the basis of the vesting schedule in effect before the amendment. [I.R.C. § 411(a)(10); Temp. Treas. Reg. § 1.411(a)-8T] A change in vesting schedule cannot result in a forfeiture of previously vested benefits. [I.R. C. § 411(a)(10); Temp. Treas. Reg. § 1.411(a)-8T(b)(1)]

> **Practice Pointer.** Pursuant to the PPA, the vesting schedule for all cash balance plans that were in existence on June 29, 2006, will be required to use a three-year cliff vesting schedule beginning with plan years after

December 31, 2007. Therefore, this rule that provides participants with the greater of two vesting schedules may come into play. For example, if the plan was using a six-year graded vesting schedule, the plan will have the following vesting schedule for existing participants on the first day of the 2008 plan year:

| Years of vesting service | Vesting Percentage |
|:---:|:---:|
| Less than 2 | 0% |
| 2 | 20% |
| 3 | 100% |

## Year of Service

### Q 8:18   How is a year of service calculated?

A year of service for vesting purposes is similar to a year of service for purposes of eligibility and benefit accrual. Unless a plan provides a more liberal definition, a participant, for vesting purposes, must be credited with a year of service for each 12-consecutive-month period during which the employee is credited with at least 1,000 hours of service. [I.R.C. § 411(a)(5)] The employer has discretion in selecting the 12-month computation period, but has to maintain additional records or use an equivalency if it uses a computation period different from that used for benefit accrual purposes. When the plan changes its vesting computation period, double credit must be given when an employee earns a year of service in each of the overlapping years (see Q 8:20). All years of an employee's service with the employer are counted for vesting purposes except those specifically excluded under the plan as permitted under Code Section 411(a) (see Q 8:21). [Treas. Reg. §§ 1.411(a)-5, 1.411(a)-6]

### Q 8:19   How is service counted for vesting purposes in an elapsed-time plan?

Under the elapsed-time method, service is measured by reference to the period of time that elapses while the employee is employed by the employer, regardless of the number of hours completed during the period. The employee's periods of service are aggregated. After aggregation is complete, the plan disregards periods less than whole years (see chapter 7).

**Example.** Keri's Kennel uses the elapsed-time method for calculating service for vesting purposes under its plan. Nick begins employment on July 4, 2000. He terminates employment on January 4, 2003. Under the elapsed-time method, Nick is credited with two years and six months of service regardless of the number of hours completed during the period. Because periods of service that are less than whole years are disregarded, Nick is credited with two years of service for vesting purposes.

### Q 8:20   What vesting rules apply in a change of plan year or a short plan year?

When the vesting computation period is changed, the following rules apply:

1. A new computation period is established before the old vesting period ends.

2. An employee who is credited with a year of service in each of the two overlapping computation periods must be credited with two years of service for vesting purposes (see chapter 7).

[DOL Reg. § 2530.203-2(c)(1)]

> **Example.** Havoc and Chaos Inc. maintains a pension plan. The plan has a six-year graduated vesting schedule and measures years of service by reference to the plan year. The plan year ends on June 30. As of January 1, 2002, Havoc and Chaos Inc. changes its plan year to the calendar year. Mike, who was employed on October 1, 2001, will be credited with two years of service for vesting purposes by the first anniversary of his date of employment. He will be credited with one year of service for the period October 1, 2001, through June 30, 2002, because he completed 1,000 hours of service during the plan year ending June 30, 2002. He will be credited with a second year of service for the period January 1, 2002, through October 1, 2002, because he completed 1,000 hours of service during the plan year ending December 31, 2002.

### Q 8:21   Can any years of service be disregarded for vesting purposes?

Yes. A plan can disregard the following years of service for vesting purposes:

1. Years of service rendered before the employee attained age 18;

2. Years of service during which the employee declined to make mandatory contributions (if any) (see Q 8:22);

3. Years of service during which the employer did not maintain the plan or a predecessor plan (see Q 8:23);

4. Years of service that can be disregarded under the break-in-service rules (see Q 8:25);

5. Pre-1971 service if the participant did not complete three years of post-1970 service;

6. Pre-ERISA years of service if such service could be disregarded under the pre-ERISA break-in-service rules; and

7. For multiemployer plans (see chapter 5), service rendered after the participant's employer completely withdraws from the plan, service rendered after decertification, and service after the plan has terminated.

[I.R.C. § 411(a)(4)]

These years can be disregarded *only* if the plan expressly provides for the exclusion.

### Q 8:22   Can service be disregarded for vesting purposes if an employee does not make required contributions?

Yes. If a plan requires an employee to make contributions it can disregard all years of service during which the employee declined to make contributions, for vesting purposes. [I.R.C. § 411(a)(4)(B)]

### Q 8:23   What is a *predecessor plan*?

A *predecessor plan* is a qualified retirement plan that was terminated within a five-year period preceding or following the establishment of a new qualified retirement plan. If a new defined benefit plan is established within five years following the termination of another qualified plan of the employer, the new defined benefit plan cannot exclude years of service before the effective date of the defined benefit plan for purposes of calculating an employee's vested percentage. [Treas. Reg. § 1.411(a)-5(b)(3)]

**Example.** The Ginger Root Inc. money purchase plan terminated on January 1, 1998. Ginger Root Inc. established a defined benefit plan on January 1, 2002. The money purchase plan is a predecessor plan with respect to the defined benefit plan because the defined benefit plan was established within the five-year period immediately following the date the money purchase plan terminated. Therefore, the defined benefit plan can only exclude service before the establishment of the money purchase plan when calculating an employee's vested percentage in his or her accrued benefit.

### Q 8:24   Is a partial termination considered a termination for purposes of excluding service for vesting purposes?

No. Code Section 411(a)(4) and Treasury Regulations Section 1.411(a)-5(a) provide that, in computing the period of service under a plan for purposes of determining the nonforfeitable percentage under Code Section 411(a)(2), all of an employee's years of service with the employer or employers maintaining the plan are taken into account subject to certain exceptions. These include an exception for years of service with an employer during any period for which the employer did not maintain the plan or a predecessor plan. In particular, Treasury Regulation Section 1.411(a)-5(b)(3)(iii) provides that the period for which a plan is not maintained by an employer includes the period after the plan is terminated. For purposes of Treasury Regulations Section 1.411(a)-5, a plan is terminated at the date there is a termination of the plan within the meaning of Code Section 411(d)(3)(A) and the regulations thereunder. Treasury Regulations Section 1.411(d)-2(c) provides rules for determining when a plan has undergone a termination. Treasury Regulations Section 1.411(d)-2(b) provides rules for determining when a plan has undergone a partial termination. A partial termination of a plan is not a termination. For vesting purposes, Treasury Regulations Section 1.411(a)-5(b)(3)(iii) excludes service after a plan has been terminated but does not exclude service after a partial termination. The freezing of accruals under a qualified retirement plan so that a partial termination of the plan occurs, does not constitute a plan termination, for purposes of determining whether service for the plan sponsor after the plan was established may be disregarded toward vesting, if accruals resume under the plan. Accordingly, all years of service for the plan sponsor following the establishment of the previously frozen plan must be taken into account for purposes of vesting. [Rev. Rul. 2003-65, 2003-25 I.R.B. 1035]

### Q 8:25   What is a *break in service*?

A participant who does not work enough hours during a computation period (see chapter 7) is considered to have a *break in service*. Generally, a *break in service* occurs when an employee is credited with fewer than 501 hours of service during the plan year or other specified computation period.

**Example.** Jeremy's Chocolate Emporium maintains a plan that uses the six-year graduated vesting schedule. An employee who completes at least 1,000 hours of service during the plan year is credited with one year of service for vesting purposes. The plan also provides that an employee who does not complete more than 500 hours of service during the plan year incurs a one-year break in service. Jonathan begins employment with Jeremy's Chocolate Emporium on January 1, 1997. His employment history for the 1997-2002 plan years is as follows:

| Year | Hours of Service Completed |
|------|---------------------------|
| 1997 | 2,000 |
| 1998 | 750 |
| 1999 | 1,500 |
| 2000 | 400 |
| 2001 | 0 |
| 2002 | 1,000 |

Jonathan has incurred a break in service in the 2000 and 2001 plan years.

In the case of a plan that uses the elapsed-time method to measure service (see chapter 7), a break in service occurs when 12 months have elapsed after an employee's severance from service during which the employee did not complete any hours of service.

### Q 8:26   Can an employee's benefit be forfeited after a break in service?

It depends. A nonvested participant's benefit derived from employer contributions can be forfeited when the number of consecutive one-year breaks in service (see Q 8:25) exceeds the greater of the following:

1. The number of prebreak years of service; or
2. Five.

[I.R.C. § 411(a)(6)(D)]

**Example.** Consider the Example in Q 8:25. Jonathan had completed two years of service before his break in service (1,000 hours of service in 1997 and 1999). He is 20 percent vested in his accrued benefit. Because Jonathan had a vested benefit, his benefit cannot be forfeited because of his subsequent breaks in service. If Jonathan had not completed 1,000 hours of service in 1997, he would be credited with only one year of service and therefore would not be vested when he terminated employment in 2000. In this instance, his benefit could not be forfeited because the number of consecutive one-year breaks in service (two, for 2000 and 2001) is less than five.

A plan can force a distribution of a participant's vested benefit in certain circumstances. If a plan distributes the present value of the participant's accrued benefit to the participant in a single sum, the employee's nonvested benefit can be forfeited immediately. This involuntary cash-out is permitted only for a participant who terminates employment when the present value of the vested accrued benefit is $5,000 or less. The plan must, however, give the employee the opportunity to restore (buy back) forfeited amounts if the employee resumes covered employment within a certain period (see Q 8:29).

### Q 8:27   If an employee returns to work after a break in service, is his or her prebreak service recognized for vesting purposes?

It depends. Under limited circumstances, service before a break in service (see Q 8:25) can be disregarded for vesting purposes (see chapter 7). Prebreak service must be counted for a participant who has any vested benefit under the plan. A nonvested participant's prebreak service must be counted if the number of consecutive one-year breaks in service is less than the greater of the following:

1. Five; or
2. The number of years of service credited to the employee before the break in service.

[I.R.C. § 411(a)(6)(D)]

In application, the break-in-service rules effectively allow employers to disregard prebreak service only for nonvested employees who have five or more consecutive break-in-service years.

**Example.** Stepco Inc.'s plan provides for vesting under the seven-year graded vesting schedule (see Q 8:9). Barbara completes three years of service before termination of employment. Bob completes two years of service before termination of employment. If Barbara returns to covered employment, she must receive credit for the three prebreak years of service regardless of when she returns. Her prebreak service cannot be disregarded, because she had a nonforfeitable interest before her break in service. Bob must receive credit for his prebreak service only if he returns to employment before he has five consecutive break-in-service years.

**Q 8:28 If an employee who received full benefits returns to work, is the employee credited with his or her old service?**

It depends. The plan can disregard service associated with the benefits distributed if the employee receives either of the following distributions:

1. An involuntary distribution of the present value of the accrued benefit because it was less than $5,000; or

2. A voluntary distribution of the present value of his or her vested accrued benefit.

[I.R.C. § 411(a)(7)(B), (11); Treas. Reg. § 1.411(a)-7(d)(4)]

The plan must, however, give the employee the opportunity to restore (buy back) forfeited amounts if the employee resumes covered employment under certain circumstances (see Q 8:29). [I.R.C. § 411(a)(7)(C); Treas. Reg. § 1.411 (a)-7(d)(4)]

**Q 8:29 What buy-back rights must a plan provide to an employee who receives a distribution from the plan?**

If an employee receives a distribution of the present value of his or her vested accrued benefit and subsequently resumes covered employment, the employee must have the opportunity to repay the amount distributed and buy back his or her forfeited benefits. Repayment must occur before the employee has five consecutive one-year breaks in service (see Q 8:25) beginning after the distribution, or before five years after reemployment if earlier. A former participant who has five or more consecutive one-year breaks in service does not have a buy-back right. [I.R.C. § 411(a)(7)(C)]

Most plans require interest to be paid on the amount of the prior distribution. Interest is computed on the amount of the distribution from the date of the distribution to the date of repayment, compounded annually from the date of the distribution. Interest can be charged at a rate equal to or less than 120 percent of the federal midterm rate in effect on the first day of the plan year during which the repayment occurs. [I.R.C. § 411(a)(7)(C), (c)(2)(C); Treas. Reg. § 1.411(a)-7(d)(2) (ii)(B)]

**Q 8:30 Is service with related employers counted for vesting purposes?**

Yes. With limited exceptions, in computing years of service for vesting purposes, all of the employee's years of service with the employer maintaining the plan must be taken into account, even service during years when the employee was not eligible to participate in the plan. [I.R.C. § 411(a)(5); Treas. Reg. § 1.411(a)-5] Service with the members of the controlled group and trades or businesses under common control (see chapter 6) must be counted for vesting purposes. Also, a participant's service with different employers maintaining the same plan (a multiple-employer plan) must be counted for vesting purposes under the plan. [Treas. Reg. § 1.413-2(d)] Certain service with predecessor employers must also be counted (see chapter 7). [DOL Reg. § 2530.210; I.R.C. § 414(a)]

**Example.** International Sporting Goods Inc. has two wholly owned subsidiaries, What A Racket Inc. and Tee Time Inc. Therefore, the companies are all members of a controlled group. Tee Time Inc. has a defined benefit pension plan that covers its salaried employees only. Anne completes one year of service as an hourly employee of Tee Time Inc. and then transfers to salaried status. Jan completes five years of service as a salaried employee of What A Racket Inc. and then transfers to salaried employment with Tee Time Inc. The Tee Time Inc. pension plan must give Anne credit for her one year of service for vesting purposes even though she was not eligible to participate in the plan. The Tee Time Inc. pension plan must also give Jan credit for her five years of service with What A Racket Inc. for vesting purposes even though she was not an employee of Tee Time Inc., because employment with any member of the controlled group must be counted for vesting purposes.

## Forfeiture

### Q 8:31  Are there any instances when a participant can lose benefits?

Yes. The following events, which can cause a participant to lose benefits, are not considered impermissible forfeitures:

1. *Preretirement death.* Benefits (other than those required to be paid to a surviving spouse) can be forfeited if not paid or distributed before death (see Q 8:32).

2. *Suspension of benefits on reemployment.* Benefits can be suspended when a retiree returns to active employment (see Q 8:33).

3. *Retroactive plan amendment.* Benefits can be reduced retroactively as permitted under Code Section 412(c)(8). Code Section 412(c)(8) allows certain retroactive amendments decreasing accrued benefits when it appears that the plan will not be able to continue to operate unless it receives the IRS's permission to reduce retroactively benefits accrued in the most recent plan year.

4. *Withdrawal of mandatory contributions.* Retirement benefits can be forfeited if a participant withdraws his or her mandatory contributions (see Q 8:35).

5. *Lost participant; escheat.* Benefits can be forfeited if the plan is unable to find the participant or beneficiary, provided that if a claim is subsequently made, the benefit must be reinstated.

[Treas. Reg. § 1.411(a)-4(b)]

### Q 8:32  Can a plan provide for forfeiture at death?

Yes. Benefits payable in the form of a life annuity terminate on the death of the participant. Such a termination does not constitute an impermissible forfeiture. The vesting rules do not require accelerated vesting on death before retirement. A benefit is not treated as forfeited in violation of the vesting rules solely because the plan provides that benefits will not be payable if the employee dies. [I.R.C. § 411(a)(3)(A)] Minimum survivor death benefits, however, must be provided to a participant's surviving spouse under Code Section 417 (see chapter 16).

### Q 8:33    Can vested benefits be suspended?

Yes. If a retired employee resumes employment with the employer sponsoring the plan, benefits can be suspended while the employee is employed. [I.R.C. § 411(a)(3)(B); DOL Reg. § 2530.203-3; Rev. Rul. 81-140, 1981-01 C.B. 180; Notice 82-23, 1982-2 C.B. 752] The suspension does not change vesting, but merely delays the payment of vested accrued benefits.

### Q 8:34    Can employee mandatory contributions be forfeited?

No. An employee's rights to benefits attributable to employee contributions must be nonforfeitable. [I.R.C. § 411(a)(1)]

### Q 8:35    What happens to an employee's retirement benefit if the employee withdraws his or her mandatory contributions?

A plan that requires participants to contribute can provide that participants who are less than 50 percent vested will forfeit their rights to the benefit derived from employer contributions if they withdraw any amount attributable to the mandatory contributions. The plan cannot allow such a forfeiture, however, unless it provides that the forfeited benefit will be restored if the participant repays the full amount of the withdrawal, plus interest. Repayment must be made by the earlier of five years after reemployment or the close of the fifth consecutive one-year break in service (see chapter 7) following withdrawal. [I.R.C. § 411(a)(3)(D)]

### Q 8:36    Are benefit reductions due to offsets considered forfeitures?

No. Many plans offset or reduce benefits by all or a percentage of the amounts payable under Social Security (generally referred to as primary insurance amount or PIA), workers' compensation, or another plan sponsored by the employer. Any such offset must satisfy the nondiscrimination requirements of Code Section 401(a)(4) (see chapters 10 and 11). A pension plan can offset benefits by amounts payable under a profit-sharing plan if the following requirements are satisfied:

1. The accrued benefits without regard to the offset satisfy the vesting requirements; and

2. The offset is equal to all or a portion of the vested account balance in the profit-sharing plan.

[Rev. Rul. 76-259, 1976-2 C.B. 111]

An otherwise nonforfeitable right is not treated as forfeitable merely because it can be reduced or eliminated under permitted disparity rules. [I.R.C. § 401(a) (5), (l); Temp. Treas. Reg. § 1.411(a)-4T(a)]

**Example 1.** Elliott's Emporium maintains a defined benefit plan that provides a benefit of 50 percent of final average compensation minus 25 percent of a participant's PIA under Social Security. This type of plan is often referred to as a *defined benefit offset plan*. The reduction in benefits does not constitute an impermissible forfeiture.

**Example 2.** Fabulous Floors LLC maintains a defined benefit plan and a defined contribution plan. Under the defined contribution plan, each participant's account is credited with a contribution equal to 5 percent of compensation for each year of participation. Under the defined benefit plan, each participant will receive a retirement benefit equal to 40 percent of final average compensation reduced by, or offset by, the actuarial equivalent of the participant's account balance in the defined contribution plan. This type of plan is often referred to as a *floor-offset plan* (see chapter 4). The potential reduction in benefits under the defined benefit plan does not constitute an impermissible forfeiture.

### Q 8:37   Can benefits be forfeited even if they are fully vested?

No. Once an employee has satisfied the service requirements needed for full vesting under one of the statutory vesting schedules, benefits cannot be forfeited for any reason. ERISA requires vesting despite misconduct of an employee who satisfied minimum vesting standards. [Guidry v. Sheet Metal Workers Nat'l Pension Fund, 493 U.S. 365 (1990)]

Benefits derived from employer contributions can be forfeited only if the forfeiture is permitted under one of the statutory vesting schedules.

**Example.** Goodbodies Inc. maintains a plan that provides for graduated vesting under the following vesting schedule:

| Years of Service | Vesting Percentage |
|:---:|:---:|
| 1 | 20% |
| 2 | 40% |
| 3 | 60% |
| 4 | 80% |
| 5 | 100% |

The plan can provide that benefits will be forfeited for conviction of drug use, driving under the influence, or any reason before year 5, because even with the forfeiture, the plan's vesting schedule would provide at least as great a vested benefit as the five-year cliff vesting schedule.

### Q 8:38   When does a nonvested participant lose benefits?

Forfeiture of benefits occurs when an employee terminates employment before being 100 percent vested. The nonvested benefit is generally forfeited at the earlier of the following two events:

1. The date the employee receives a distribution of his or her entire vested accrued benefit; or

2. After the employee incurs five consecutive one-year breaks in service (see Q 8:25).

[I.R.C. § 411(a)(6)(C)]

> **Example.** Jonah terminates employment with a monthly accrued benefit of $1,000. He has completed three years of service and is 20 percent vested under the plan. Accordingly, he has a monthly vested accrued benefit of $200 ($1,000 × 20%). The nonvested benefit of $800 will be forfeited after Jonah has five consecutive one-year breaks in service. If, however, the plan provides a cash-out option and Jonah receives the value of his accrued benefit immediately in a lump sum, the $800 nonvested benefit will be forfeited immediately on distribution of the single-sum benefit.

### Q 8:39   Can benefits be forfeited for cause?

Yes. Benefits in excess of those required to be vested under a statutory minimum vesting schedule can be forfeited because of certain acts, such as violation of a noncompete agreement or a crime against the employer. [Rev. Rul. 85-31, 1985-1 C.B. 153; Temp. Treas. Reg. § 1.411(a)-4T]

"Bad boy" clauses, provisions that create forfeiture of benefits for an employee who commits a criminal act against the employer, are not generally permitted. Courts have permitted the imposition of "bad boy" clauses, however, when the vesting provided in the plan was more generous than that required under one of the two statutorily defined vesting schedules (see Q 8:9).

> **Example.** ABC has a seven-year graduated vesting schedule. The plan provides a forfeiture of benefits for an employee fired for cause within five years of employment. This could be a prohibited forfeiture, but because the provision is limited to employees who have completed less than five years of service and the plan could have used the five-year cliff vesting schedule and still have complied with minimum vesting standards, the provision is acceptable. [Temp. Treas. Reg. § 1.411(a)-4T(c); Treas. Reg. § 1.411(d)-4, Q&A 6; Rev. Rul. 85-31, 1985-1 C.B. 153]

### Q 8:40   Can a participant waive vested benefits?

No, employees generally cannot waive vested benefits. [Treas. Reg. § 1.411(d)-4, Q&A 3(a)(3); T.A.M. 9146005] In *Bruchac v. Universal Cab Co.* [580 F. Supp. 295 (D. Ohio 1984)], participant waivers of retirement benefits in exchange for severance pay were voided.

## Q 8:41  Can a change in actuarial assumptions cause a violation of the vesting rules?

Yes. A change in actuarial assumptions that decreases benefits can result in a violation of the minimum vesting standards and anti-cutback rules of Code Section 411(d)(6).

Some plans use variable standards, such as a floating interest rate, for computing actuarial equivalencies. In the case of a variable standard, any change in actuarial factors consistent with the standard does not violate the minimum vesting standards. If the basis or standard for computing actuarial equivalence is changed, however, the plan must generally specify the means of ensuring that a participant's accrued benefit will be protected.

**Example 1.** A plan has a lump-sum payment option. Actuarial equivalence is determined on the basis of the applicable mortality table and the applicable interest rate as of the first day of the plan year in which the annuity starting date occurs. The applicable interest rate changes from 6 percent to 6.25 percent, resulting in a reduction in lump-sum value. Because the basis of determining actuarial equivalence (the applicable interest rate) did not change, the mere change in the calculation rate does not result in a violation of the minimum vesting standards even though the actual amount payable may be reduced.

One method of avoiding an impermissible reduction in a participant's accrued benefit is to provide that the actuarial equivalent of the accrued benefit on or after the date of the change in equivalencies will be determined as the sum of (1) the actuarial equivalent of the accrued benefit as of the date of change computed on the old basis and (2) the actuarial equivalent, computed on the new basis, of the excess of (a) the total accrued benefit over (b) the accrued benefit as of the date of change.

Another acceptable method is to provide that the actuarial equivalent of the accrued benefit on or after the date of the change will be determined as the greater of (1) the actuarial equivalent of the accrued benefit as of the date of change computed on the old basis or (2) the actuarial equivalent of the total accrued benefit computed on the new basis. [Rev. Rul. 81-12, 1981-1 C.B. 228]

The Retirement Protection Act of 1994 (RPA '94), which was part of the General Agreement on Tariffs and Trade of 1994 (GATT), revised the rules for valuing lump-sum distributions. Under GATT, the value of lump-sum payments must be determined by using the applicable mortality table and the applicable interest rate, unless plan actuarial equivalencies provide a greater value. The applicable mortality table and the applicable interest rate often produce lower lump-sum values than those required under Code Section 417(e)(3) before GATT. Under Treasury Regulations Section 1.417(e)-1(d)(10)(ii), a participant's accrued benefit is not considered reduced in violation of Code Section 411(d)(6) merely because of a plan amendment that changes any interest rate or mortality assumption used to calculate the present value of a participant's benefit under the plan if the following conditions are satisfied:

1. The amendment replaces the Pension Benefit Guaranty Corporation (PBGC) interest rate (or an interest rate or rates based on the PBGC interest

rate) as the interest rate used under the plan in determining the present value of a participant's benefit.

2. The present value of a participant's benefit under the plan is not less than the amount calculated using the applicable mortality table and the applicable interest rate for the first full calendar month preceding the calendar month that contains the annuity starting date.

If the time for determining the interest rate used in determining lump-sum values is changed and that results in a reduction in lump-sum values, Code Section 411(d)(6) is not violated as long as the applicable interest rate is determined for the calendar month that contains the date as of which the PBGC interest rate was determined immediately before the amendment, or for one of the two calendar months immediately preceding that month.

In all other events, a plan amendment changing the time for determining the applicable interest rate will not be treated as reducing accrued benefits in violation of Code Section 411(d)(6) if distributions made during the next 12-month period are calculated using both interest rates and the larger value is available to the participant as a lump-sum distribution.

**Example 2.** On December 31, 1994, Plan *A* provided that all single-sum distributions were to be calculated using the UP-1984 Mortality Table and 100 percent of the PBGC interest rate for the date of distribution. Plan *A* was amended to provide that all single-sum distributions are to be calculated using the applicable mortality table and the applicable interest rate for the first full calendar month preceding the calendar month that contains the annuity starting date. This amendment of Plan *A* is not considered to reduce the accrued benefit of any participant in violation of Code Section 411(d)(6). [Treas. Reg. § 1.417(e)-1(d)(10)(ii)]

Adjustments that exceed reasonable actuarial adjustments may result in impermissible forfeiture. [Temp. Treas. Reg. § 1.411(a)-4T(a)] For example, an excessive discount might divest an employee of accrued benefits.

### Q 8:42   What happens to forfeited benefits?

In a defined benefit plan, a forfeiture reduces the expected liabilities of the plan and either will be treated as an actuarial gain or will reduce the present value of future normal costs in a spread gain funding method. Forfeitures, therefore, reduce the employer's contribution to the plan. Forfeitures cannot be allocated to other plan participants or applied to increase benefits. [I.R.C. § 401(a)(8)]

## Plan Termination

### Q 8:43   What vesting requirements apply on plan termination?

On full or partial plan termination (see chapter 25), all benefits accrued to the date of termination must be nonforfeitable (100 percent vested) to the extent that they are funded. [I.R.C. § 411(d)(3); Treas. Reg. § 1.411(d)-2] This means that if the plan has sufficient assets to cover accrued benefits, each affected participant becomes 100 percent vested in his or her accrued benefit. A plan must include language to this effect as a condition of qualification. [Tionesta Sand and Gravel, Inc. v. Commissioner, 73 T.C. 758 (1980)]

### Q 8:44   When does a partial termination occur?

A partial termination occurs when a group of employees who were previously covered by the plan lose coverage because of a plan amendment or severance (a vertical partial termination; see Q 8:45).

Whether a partial plan termination has occurred is a facts and circumstances determination. [Treas. Reg. § 1.411(d)-2(b)] Generally, the occurrence of a significant corporate event is indicative of a partial termination. For example, the closing of a plant or division or layoffs and terminations as a result of downsizing or corporate restructuring constitute such corporate events. Probably the most crucial factor in determining whether a vertical partial termination has occurred is the size of the reduction in plan participation. In this regard, the IRS has suggested two tests.

Under the first test, often referred to as the *significant number test*, a partial termination is deemed to occur when a significant number of participants terminate, regardless of the size of the plan. [Rev. Rul. 81-27, 1981-1 C.B. 228]

The second test, the *significant percentage test*, considers the percentage reduction in participation. [Rev. Rul. 72-439, 1972-2 C.B. 223] The significant decrease in participation does not require causes within the employer's control or adverse economic conditions. [Halliburton Co. v. Commissioner, 16 Employee Benefits Cas. (BNA) 1929 (4th Cir. 1994)] Reductions of 34 percent or more have been treated as partial terminations, whereas reductions of up to 15 percent have been considered insignificant. [Tipton & Kalmbach, Inc. v. Commissioner, 83 T.C. 154 (1984); Kreis v. Charles O Townley, M.D. & Assocs., P.C., 833 F.2d 74 (6th Cir. 1987)] The IRS has indicated that it will scrutinize reductions of 20 percent or more. [IRM ch. 6, nn. 13-15]

### Q 8:45   What are *vertical* and *horizontal partial terminations*?

Two types of partial terminations are generally recognized. Each type of partial termination requires 100 percent vesting for all affected employees. [I.R.C. § 411(d)(3)]

*Vertical partial terminations,* or reductions in force, occur when an employee group that was covered under the plan loses coverage by amendment or severance. Because a vertical partial termination affects nonvested terminated employees, nonvested terminated employees must be fully vested in their accrued benefits.

*Horizontal partial terminations,* or reductions in benefits, occur when a plan curtails benefits and increases a potential reversion or creates a potential reversion. Because a horizontal partial termination affects current employees, current employees must be fully vested in their accrued benefits.

**Example 1.** As a result of a corporate reorganization, Pinkslip Ltd. terminates 35 percent of its employees. A vertical partial termination has occurred. The accrued benefits of all employees terminated by the company must be fully vested.

**Example 2.** Big Bucks, Inc., maintains a defined benefit pension plan with assets of $40 million. Plan liabilities for benefits are $35 million; liabilities for vested benefits are $25 million. Big Bucks, Inc., ceases accruals in the plan in an attempt to freeze liabilities. Big Bucks, Inc., assumes some participants will terminate employment with less than full vesting. Any forfeitures would probably cause plan assets to exceed the value of liabilities by more than they already do. A horizontal termination may have occurred. In such case, the accrued benefits of all active employees must be fully vested.

[Treas. Reg. § 1.411(d)-2(b)(2)]

The IRS's internal guidelines on partial terminations are included in the Internal Revenue Manual.

### Q 8:46   Does a plan have to vest unaccrued benefits on termination?

No. On plan termination, participants are entitled to benefits accrued as of the date of termination. Retirement benefits do not include benefits attributable to future service. [Blessitt v. Retirement Plan for Employees of Dixie Engine Co., 848 F.2d 1164 (11th Cir. 1988); May v. Houston Post Pension Plan, 898 F.2d 1068 (5th Cir. 1990)]

### Q 8:47   Can a former employee buy-back rights on plan termination?

Generally a participant who was partially vested does not become 100 percent vested on plan termination if he or she was paid out in full before the date of termination. If, however, a participant has not been paid his or her vested accrued benefit, the participant must become 100 percent vested on plan termination (see chapter 25).

## Protected Benefits

### Q 8:48   What benefits are protected by Code Section 411(d)(6)?

Code Section 411(d)(6) prohibits plan amendments that have the effect of decreasing accrued benefits. The elimination of certain benefits (or features) is treated as an impermissible cutback of accrued benefits under Code Section 411(d)(6). Protected benefits include the following:

1. Accrued benefits;
2. Early retirement benefits and retirement-type subsidies; and
3. Optional forms of benefit.

[Treas. Reg. §§ 1.411(d)-3, 1.411(d)-4, Q&A 1(a)]

### Q 8:49  What plan provisions are taken into account in determining whether there is a reduction in a participant's accrued benefit?

For purposes of determining whether a participant's accrued benefit is decreased, all of the amendments to the provisions of a plan affecting, directly or indirectly, the calculation of accrued benefits are taken into account. Plan provisions indirectly affecting the calculation of accrued benefits include, for example, provisions relating to years of service and compensation.

In addition, two or more amendments with the same effective date are treated as one amendment and combined to determine the net effect on the accrued benefit. If there are multiple amendments within a three-year period, they will be looked at together to determine if they have the effect of reducing or eliminating protected accrued benefits.

[Treas. Reg. § 1.411(d)-3(2)]

### Q 8:50  Can an amendment be made to the plan by only changing the plan in operation without changing plan provisions?

No. In *Frommert v. Conkright* [433 F.3d 254 (2d Cir. 2006)], the Second Circuit court found no merit in Xerox's claim that an amendment may be made by plan administrators by simply changing the operation of the plan, but held that the change implemented in a summary plan description (SPD) was sufficient.

### Q 8:51  Can an employer place a greater restriction or condition on a participant's right to a protected benefit through amendment?

No. In accordance with *Central Laborers' Pension Fund v. Heinz* [541 U.S. 739 (2004)], an employer may not impose a greater restriction or condition on a participant's rights to protected benefits that have already accrued.

Under Revenue Procedure 2005-23, the IRS imposed a requirement that all plans that were in violation of the Supreme Court's decision in *Central Laborers' Pension Fund* were required to be amended and comply in operation. Revenue Procedure 2005-76 extended the time by which a plan must be in compliance to January 1, 2007.

[Prop. Treas. Reg. § 1.411(d)-(3)(a)(3)]

### Q 8:52  What plan features are not considered Section 411(d)(6) protected benefits?

The regulations cite the following as benefits that are not Section 411(d)(6) protected benefits and accordingly are not subject to the anti-cutback prohibition:

1. Ancillary life insurance protection;
2. Accident or health insurance benefits;
3. Social Security supplements;

4. Loans;

5. The right to make after-tax employee contributions;

6. The right to direct investments;

7. The right to a particular form of investment;

8. Allocation dates for earnings and forfeitures; and

9. Administrative procedures relating to benefit distribution.

[Treas. Reg. § 1.411(d)-4, Q&A 1(d)]

### Q 8:53  Do defined benefit plans have any special protected benefits?

The defined benefit feature of a guaranteed benefit unaffected by investment loss is a Section 411(d)(6) protected benefit. [Treas. Reg. § 1.411(d)-4, Q&A 3(a)(2)] Transfers of nondistributable benefits from a defined benefit plan to a defined contribution plan violate the anti-cutback rules if the defined contribution plan's terms expose the transferred benefits to risk of loss not present in the defined benefit plan.

### Q 8:54  To what extent are early retirement subsidies protected benefits?

Early retirement benefits and retirement-type subsidies are protected benefits that cannot be eliminated or cut back by plan amendment to the extent they have accrued, but applies only to a participant who satisfies (either before or after the amendment) the preamendment conditions for the subsidy. [I.R.C. § 411(d)(6)(B); Treas. Reg. § 1.411(d)-4]

In *Lindsay v. Thiokol Corp.* [20 Employee Benefits Cas. (BNA) 2793 (10th Cir. 1997)], the company amended its defined benefit plan to eliminate early retirement subsidies prospectively. Accrued benefits were preserved. Several employees who took early retirement received less than they would have before the amendment eliminating the subsidy. The prospective elimination of the subsidy was upheld.

In Revenue Ruling 85-6 [1985-1 C.B. 133], the IRS stated that the exception to the prohibition against reduction of benefits is not applicable to a terminated plan, that is, the plan must provide the early retirement benefit whether or not the participant has satisfied the conditions for the subsidy upon plan termination.

ERISA requires advance written notice of an amendment to a pension plan that would significantly reduce the rate of future benefit accrual. [ERISA § 204(h)] Under prior regulations, an amendment that did not affect the annual benefit beginning at normal retirement age was not considered to affect the rate of future benefit accrual. According to this approach under prior law, an amendment affecting early retirement benefits would not require advance notice. [Treas. Reg. § 1.411(d)-6. But see Normann v. Amphenol Corp., 956 F. Supp. 158 (N.D. N.Y. 1997)]

Effective with the enactment of the Economic Growth and Tax Relief Reconciliation Act of 2001 (EGTRRA), amendments that affect early retirement benefits and retirement-type subsidies are considered to reduce the rate of future benefit accrual and do require an ERISA Section 204(h) notice. [I.R.C. § 4980F(f)(3)]

### Q 8:55  Are cost-of-living adjustments protected benefits?

In *Hickey v. Chicago Truck Drivers, Helpers and Warehouse Workers Union* [980 F.2d 1080 (7th Cir. 1992)], the court held that the elimination of a cost-of-living adjustment (COLA) provision violated the anti-cutback requirements of Code Section 411(d)(6). The COLA had been eliminated in connection with plan termination. The issue as to whether the termination of the plan qualified as an amendment to the plan was, unfortunately, not addressed.

### Q 8:56  Are Section 411(d)(6) benefits preserved when plan assets and liabilities are transferred to another plan?

Yes. If plan assets and liabilities are transferred to another plan through a merger or consolidation (see chapter 26), each participant must be entitled to receive benefits that are at least equal to the benefits to which the participant would have been entitled if the plan had been terminated before the merger. [I.R.C. § 401(a)(12); Treas. Reg. §§ 1.401(a)-12, 1.414(l)-1] Section 411(d)(6) protected benefits cannot be eliminated by plan merger.

### Q 8:57  Can an employee waive a Section 411(d)(6) protected benefit?

No. A Section 411(d)(6) protected benefit cannot be eliminated, even with the consent of the employee.

### Q 8:58  Are there any instances when accrued benefits can be reduced?

Yes. A plan amendment that has the effect of reducing accrued benefits is permissible in the following instances:

1. The amendment was necessary as a condition of qualification, and the qualification requirement could not be satisfied by any other means.
2. The plan has three or more joint and survivor annuity payment options. In this case any option other than the ones with the largest and smallest survivor percentages can be eliminated.
3. The plan terminates. In this case the plan can substitute cash for in-kind distributions in certain instances.
4. The amendment eliminates the involuntary cash-out provision or reduces the threshold amount below the statutory level.
5. The amendment eliminates provisions requiring execution on an account used to secure a loan in default.
6. The amendment changes the timing on payment of benefits, but payment is available within two months of the original payment date.

[Treas. Reg. § 1.411(d)-4, Q&A 2(b)]

### Q 8:59 Can a defined benefit plan eliminate certain optional forms of distribution?

Yes, subject to certain rules. Treasury Regulations Section 1.411(d)-3 allows a plan to reduce or eliminate early retirement benefits, retirement-type subsidies, and optional forms of benefit that create significant burdens or complexities for the plan and plan participants, unless such amendment adversely affects the rights of any participant in more than a *de minimis* manner.

### Q 8:60 What rules must be followed for a plan to reduce an optional form of benefit?

Any plan amendment eliminating optional forms of benefits must satisfy either the "redundancy" rules of paragraph (c) of Treasury Regulations Section 1.411(d)-3 or the "core option" rules of paragraph (d). However, all such amendments must also comply with the "burdensome" and "*de minimis*" rules of paragraph (e). In addition, a plan amendment that increases a payment amount is not considered as an elimination of an optional form of benefit (e.g., changing a 90 percent QJSA to a 91 percent QJSA). Each is described below.

### Q 8:61 What are the redundancy rules?

Plan amendments comply with the redundancy rules of these proposed regulations if they meet a three-prong test:

1. They eliminate optional forms of benefits that are redundant with retained options;
2. They eliminate optional forms of benefits that have annuity starting dates at least 90 days (equal to the number of days in the maximum QJSA explanation period) after the amendment adoption date; and
3. They satisfy the requirements of paragraph (e) in that they are "burdensome and of a *de minimis* value."

[Treas. Reg. § 1.411(d)-3(c)(1)]

Under the regulations, an optional form of benefit that is being eliminated is "redundant" with a retained optional form if:

1. The retained optional form is available to the participant;
2. The retained optional form is in the same "family";
3. There are no materially greater restrictions for the participant on the retained optional form; and
4. If it is a "core option," then the eliminated optional form and the retained optional form are identical, not considering actuarial factors, annuity starting dates, pop-up provisions, and cash refund features. [Treas. Reg. § 1.411(d)-3(c)(3)]

[Treas. Reg. § 1.411(d)-3(c)(2)]

The regulations define six "families" of optional forms of benefit and indicate that any optional form of distribution that is not in this closed list represents its own family. Therefore, as long as one optional form of benefit from within the family is retained, then other optional forms of benefit from within the family may be eliminated by a plan amendment. The six families are:

1. A 50 percent to 100 percent joint and survivor annuity (regardless of term certain provisions, pop-up provisions, or cash refund features);
2. A 1 percent to 49 percent joint and survivor annuity;
3. A 1-year to 10-year certain and life annuity;
4. An 11-year or higher term certain and life annuity;
5. A 1-year to 10-year installment payment; and
6. An 11-year or higher term installment payment.

[Treas. Reg. § 1.411(d)-3(c)(4)]

Additionally, there are rules on eliminating options that have Social Security leveling, return of employer contributions, and retroactive annuity date features. If an optional form of benefit that is being eliminated includes either a Social Security leveling feature or a refund of employee contributions feature, the retained optional form of benefit must also include that feature, and, to the extent that the optional form of benefit that is being eliminated does not include a Social Security leveling feature or a refund of employee contributions feature, the retained optional form of benefit must not include that feature. For purposes of applying this paragraph (c), to the extent an optional form of benefit that is being eliminated does not include a retroactive annuity starting date feature, the retained optional form of benefit must not include the feature. [Treas. Reg. § 1.411(d)-3(c)(5)]

**Example.** The MD defined benefit plan allows distributions at any time after age 55. At each potential annuity starting date, a participant can elect a straight life annuity or any number of actuarially equivalent forms of benefits, including a straight life annuity with a COLA and a joint and survivor benefit with any continuation percentage from 1 percent to 100 percent and the ability to name any beneficiary. The plan is amended (adopted September 2, 2004 to be effective January 1, 2005) to delete all continuation percentages in the J&S option other than 25 percent, 50 percent, 75 percent, and 100 percent.

There are four "families" of optional forms of benefits before the amendment: (1) a straight life annuity; (2) a straight life annuity with COLA; (3) all joint and survivor annuities with a continuation percentage of 0 percent to 49 percent; and (4) all joint and survivor annuities with a continuation percentage of 50 percent to 100 percent. The amendment affects only the third and fourth families.

The amendment is allowed because it satisfies the three requirements under paragraph (c) of Treasury Regulations Section 1.411(d)-3:

1. The retained 25 percent J&S annuity is redundant with all other options in the third family and the retained 50 percent, 75 percent, and 100 percent

J&S annuities are each redundant with all other options in the fourth family. In addition, neither the eliminated options nor the retained options include Social Security leveling, return of employee contributions, or retroactive annuity starting date features. Furthermore, the amendment does not eliminate any of the core options, including the most valuable option for a participant with a short life expectancy;

2. The amendment is not effective with respect to annuity starting dates that are less than 90 days from the date of the amendment; and

3. Since the retained optional forms of benefit are available on the same annuity starting date and have the same actuarial present value as the optional forms that are being eliminated, then the amendment does not need to comply with the "burdensome" and "*de minimis*" requirements of paragraph (e).

### Q 8:62   What are the core option rules?

Plan amendments eliminating noncore optional forms of benefits where other "core" forms are offered comply with these regulations if they meet a different three-prong test:

1. If after the amendment, each of the "core" options is still available to the participant with respect to benefits accrued both before and after the amendment;

2. If the plan amendment does not eliminate an optional form of benefit with an annuity starting date that is less than four years after the amendment adoption date; and

3. If they satisfy the requirements of paragraph (e) in that they are "burdensome and of a *de minimis* value."

[Treas. Reg. § 1.411(d)-3(d)(1)]

The "core" options, as defined in paragraph (g), are generally:

1. A straight life annuity;

2. A 75 percent joint and survivor annuity (or alternatively, the plan may offer both a joint and 50 percent survivor annuity and a joint and 100 percent survivor annuity);

3. A 10-year certain and life annuity; and

4. The most valuable benefit option for a participant with a short life expectancy.

Item #4 above generally means the optional form of benefit, for each annuity starting date, that is reasonably expected to result in payments that have the largest actuarial present value in the case of a participant who dies shortly after the annuity starting date, taking into account payments due to the participant both prior to the participant's death and also any payments due after the participant's death. The plan can assume that the participant's spouse is the same age as the participant, and that a most valuable option (MVO) for any age beyond age 70½ is the MVO payable at age 70½, and that a MVO for any age earlier than age 55 is the MVO payable at age 55.

There are three safe harbors for plans to use in defining "the most valuable option for a participant with a short life expectancy":

1. If a single-sum distribution option is available that is more valuable than any of the optional forms being eliminated by the plan amendment, then the plan can treat that single-sum distribution as the MVO for all participants;

2. If the plan does not have a single-sum distribution option, then a 75 percent joint and survivor option can be treated as the MVO as long as it is available at all annuity starting dates; and

3. If the plan offers neither a single-sum distribution nor a 75 percent joint and survivor option, then a 15-year certain and life annuity option may be treated as the MVO as long as it is available at all annuity starting dates.

[Treas. Reg. § 1.411(d)-3(g)(5)]

In order to utilize this method to eliminate certain optional forms of benefit, the following criteria must be satisfied:

1. The eliminated forms of benefit must be retained for those participants with annuity starting dates within four years of the amendment date;

2. No optional form may be eliminated if it provides for a lump sum of at least 25 percent of the participant's total present value of accrued benefit;

3. Core forms must have essentially the same annuity commencement dates (i.e., within six months of each other);

4. The core forms must not be less valuable than the eliminated forms of benefit by more than a *de minimis* amount, or the amendment must have a delayed effective date equal to the amount of time it would take for the eliminated form of benefit to be subsumed by the retained form of benefit;

5. No further changes may occur to the core benefit options for at least seven years from the amendment date;

6. If the eliminated form of benefit contains either a Social Security leveling feature or a refund of employee contributions feature, at least one of the core forms must have this feature as well. And if the eliminated form does not contain either a Social Security leveling feature or a refund of employee contributions feature, each of the core options must be available without that feature; and

7. If the form of benefit being eliminated does not contain a retroactive annuity starting date feature, each of the core forms must also not contain this feature.

**Example.** The Preserve All defined benefit plan offers *all participants* the following actuarially equivalent standard distribution options: a straight life annuity; a 50 percent, 75 percent, or 100 percent J&S annuity; or a 5-year, 10-year, and 15-year certain and life annuity. Each annuity payable to a participant under age 65 is available with or without a Social Security leveling feature where the participant selects an assumed age of Social Security benefit commencement between 62 and 67. The employer, who has sponsored this plan for over 30 years, has merged over 20 plans into this plan, many of which have preserved optional forms only for those affected participants (such as certain insurance carrier annuity options and single-sum distributions). Specifically, in the one merger, lump sums available to those participants at the date of the merger were frozen, and as of April 1, 2005, each such single-sum distribution option applies to less than 25 percent of the acquired participants' accrued benefits. As a result of its merger practices of preserving the nonstandard optional forms of benefits only for the participant's premerger service, as of April 1, 2005, there are a large number of optional forms of benefit, which are not members of a "family," but which do not provide any early retirement subsidies to any participant because any subsidies have been subsumed by the actuarially reduced accrued benefit. On April 1, 2005, the plan is amended, effective with annuity starting dates on or after May 1, 2009, to eliminate all of the nonstandard options, including the single-sum options for the XYZ acquired participants.

The amendment is permissible for three reasons:

1. The only single-sum distributions that are eliminated are less than 25 percent of the affected participant's total accrued benefit on the date of elimination (May 1, 2009) and furthermore, the amendment retains core options, including the MVO for a participant with a short life expectancy (here, the 100 percent J&S annuity; note the retained single-sum distribution options are NOT the most valuable options for a participant with a short life expectancy because only a portion of the accrued benefit is payable as a single sum), and at least one of the retained core options contains the Social Security leveling, refund of employee contribution, and/or retroactive annuity starting date features of the eliminated options;

2. The amendment is not effective with respect to annuity starting dates that are less than four years after the amendment is adopted; and

3. Since the retained optional forms of benefit are available on the same annuity starting dates and have the same actuarial present value as the optional forms that are being eliminated, the amendment does not need to comply with the "burdensome" and *de minimis* requirements of paragraph (e).

### Q 8:63   What are the rules for determining whether optional forms of benefits are burdensome and affect participants in no more than a *de minimis* manner?

Paragraph (e) of Treasury Regulations Section 1.411(d)-3 discusses the additional necessary requirements for all plan amendments that either eliminate optional forms of benefits that are redundant (as described in paragraph (c)) or that eliminate noncore optional forms of benefit where "core" options are offered (as described in paragraph (d)).

Plan amendments that comply with these regulations can eliminate only those optional forms of benefit that:

1. Create significant burdens or complexities for the plan and its participants; and

2. Do not adversely affect the rights of any participant in a more than *de minimis* manner.

[Treas. Reg. § 1.411(d)-3(e)(1)]

As to the significant burdens, there is a facts and circumstances analysis. If the plan amendment eliminates an early retirement benefit, relevant factors include the complexity and burdensomeness of the annuity starting dates and whether the amendment results in a reduction in the number of categories of early retirement benefits. On the other hand, if the plan amendment eliminates a retirement-type subsidy or if it changes the actuarial factors, the relevant factors include the complexity and burdensomeness of the actuarial factors and whether the amendment results in a reduction in the number of categories of retirement-type subsidies or other actuarial factors. However, in a plan amendment that, in effect, either eliminates an annuity starting date and replaces it with another annuity starting date, or eliminates one set of actuarial factors and replaces it with another set of actuarial factors, but which does not reduce the number of categories of optional forms of benefits, then the plan amendment did not really relieve the burdensomeness and complexity of the plan and therefore does not comply with these proposed regulations. Additionally, a plan amendment that adds burdensomeness and complexity to a plan so that a future amendment can eliminate other optional forms of benefits will violate these proposed regulations.

[Treas. Reg. § 1.411(d)-3(e)(2)]

As to the *de minimis* effect, the retained optional forms of benefit for each participant must:

1. Have substantially the same annuity commencement date as the optional form being eliminated (i.e., within six months of each other); and

2. Either have no more than a "*de minimis* difference in the actuarial present value" than that of the optional form being eliminated *or* have a "delayed effective date."

[Treas. Reg. § 1.411(d)-3(e)(3)]

The regulations define "*de minimis* difference in actuarial present value" as not more than the greater of: 2 percent of the present value of the retirement-type subsidy under the eliminated optional form of benefit prior to the amendment, or 1 percent of the greater of the participant's Section 415(c)(5) compensation for the prior plan year or the participant's average compensation for his or her highest three years. [Treas. Reg. § 1.411(d)-3(e)(5)]

The regulations define "delayed effective date" as an expected transition period (limited to those participants who continue to accrue benefits under the plan through the end of the expected transition period) that begins when the amendment is adopted and ends when it is reasonable to expect that the form being eliminated would be subsumed by another optional form of benefit (based on reasonable actuarial assumptions, about the future, that are likely to result in the longest period of time until the optional form of benefit would be subsumed and after taking into account expected future accruals). [Treas. Reg. § 1.411(d)-3 (e)(6)]

### Q 8:64    Are future accruals in a defined benefit plan a protected benefit?

No. A plan's benefit formula can be changed at any time. If the change results in a significant reduction in future benefit accruals or eliminates or significantly reduces an early retirement benefit or retirement-type subsidy, the amendment will not be allowed unless, after adoption of the amendment and within a reasonable time before the amendment's effective date, the plan administrator provides a written notice setting forth the plan amendment and its effect (written in a manner to be understood by the average plan participant), as well as its effective date, to each plan participant, each alternate payee under an applicable qualified domestic relations order (see chapter 17), and each employee organization representing plan participants. [ERISA § 204(h)]

### Q 8:65    What is an amendment that affects the rate of future benefit accrual for purposes of ERISA Section 204(h)?

An amendment to a defined benefit plan affects the rate of future benefit accrual only if it is reasonably expected to change the amount of the future annual benefit beginning at normal retirement age in the plan's normal form of payment (generally a straight life annuity) or that eliminates or reduces an early retirement benefit or retirement-type subsidy. The rate of future benefit accrual is determined without regard to optional forms of benefit, ancillary benefits, or other rights or features. [I.R.C. § 4980F(f)(3); ERISA § 204(h); Treas. Reg. § 54.4980F, Q&A 6]

### Q 8:66    What plan provisions are taken into account in determining whether there has been a reduction in the rate of future benefit accrual?

All plan provisions that may affect the rate of future accrual of benefits must be taken into account in determining whether an amendment provides for a significant reduction in the rate of future benefit accrual. Such provisions include the dollar amount or percentage of compensation on which benefit accruals are based; in the case of a plan using permitted disparity under Code Section 401(l), the amount of disparity between the excess benefit percentage or excess contribution percentage and the base benefit percentage or base contribution percentage (all as defined in Code Section 401(l)); the definition of service or compensation taken into account in determining an employee's benefit accrual; the method of determining average compensation for calculating benefit accruals; the definition of normal retirement age in a defined benefit plan; the exclusion of current participants from future participation; benefit offset provisions; and minimum benefit provisions. Plan provisions that may affect early retirement benefits or retirement-type subsidies include the right to receive payment of benefits after severance from employment and before normal retirement age and actuarial factors used in determining optional forms for distribution of retirement benefits.

Plan provisions that do not affect the rate of future accrual of benefits are not taken into account in determining whether there has been a reduction in the rate of future benefit accrual. For example, vesting schedules and optional forms of benefit are not taken into account. [Treas. Reg. § 54.4980F, Q&A 7]

### Q 8:67   What is the basic principle used in determining whether an amendment provides for a significant reduction in the rate of future benefit accrual for purposes of ERISA Section 204(h)?

An amendment to a defined benefit plan reduces the rate of future benefit accrual only if it is reasonably expected to reduce the amount of the future annual benefit commencing at normal retirement age for benefits accruing for a year. For this purpose, the annual benefit commencing at normal retirement age is the benefit payable in the normal form of the plan.

The determination of a significant reduction in the rate of future benefit accrual is made based on reasonable expectations taking into account the relevant facts and circumstances at the time the amendment is adopted. This is done by comparing the amount of the annual benefit beginning at normal retirement age under the terms of the plan as amended with the amount of the annual benefit beginning at normal retirement age under the terms of the plan before amendment. [Treas. Reg. § 54.4980F, Q&A 6, 8]

### Q 8:68   Is an ERISA Section 204(h) notice required to be given to employees who have not yet become participants in the plan?

No. Employees who have not yet become participants in a plan at the time an amendment to the plan is adopted are not taken into account in applying ERISA Section 204(h) with respect to the amendment. Thus, if an ERISA Section 204(h) notice is required with respect to an amendment, the plan administrator need not provide the ERISA Section 204(h) notice to such employees. [Treas. Reg. § 54.4980F, Q&A 10]

### Q 8:69   If an ERISA Section 204(h) notice is required with respect to an amendment, must such notice be provided to participants whose rate of future benefit accrual is not reduced by the amendment?

No. A plan administrator need not provide an ERISA Section 204(h) notice to any participant whose rate of future benefit accrual is reasonably expected not to be reduced by the amendment, nor to any alternate payee under an applicable qualified domestic relations order whose rate of future benefit accrual is reasonably expected not to be reduced by the amendment. A plan administrator need not provide an ERISA Section 204(h) notice to an employee organization unless the employee organization represents a participant to whom an ERISA Section 204(h) notice is required to be provided. [Treas. Reg. § 54.4980F, Q&A 10]

### Q 8:70 What information is the ERISA Section 204(h) notice required to contain?

An ERISA Section 204(h) notice must include sufficient information to allow applicable individuals to understand the effect of the plan amendment, including the approximate magnitude of the expected reduction. If the effect of the amendment is different for different participants, the notice must either identify the general classes of participants to whom the reduction is expected to apply, or include sufficient information to allow each applicable individual receiving the notice to determine which reductions are expected to apply to that individual.

The information must be written in a manner calculated to be understood by the average plan participant and to apprise the applicable individual of the significance of the notice. If the amendment reduces the rate of future benefit accrual, the notice must include a description of the benefit or allocation formula before the amendment, a description of the benefit or allocation formula under the plan as amended, and the effective date of the amendment. If the amendment reduces an early retirement benefit or retirement-type subsidy (other than as a result of an amendment reducing the rate of future benefit accrual), the notice must describe how the early retirement benefit or retirement-type subsidy is calculated from the accrued benefit before the amendment, how the early retirement benefit or retirement-type subsidy is calculated from the accrued benefit after the amendment, and the effective date of the amendment.

**Example.** The Changes, Inc., plan has a normal retirement age of 65 but provides for an unreduced normal retirement benefit at age 55. The plan is amended to provide an unreduced normal retirement benefit at age 60 for benefits accrued in the future, with an actuarial reduction to apply for benefits accrued in the future to the extent that the early retirement benefit begins before age 60. The ERISA Section 204(h) notice states that and specifies the factors that apply in calculating the actuarial reduction (e.g., a 5 percent per year reduction applies for early retirement before age 60).

If the magnitude of the changes that result from the amendment are not reasonably apparent from the description provided by a narrative, additional narrative information may be required, as well as illustrative examples. Further narrative explanation of the effect of the difference between the old and new formulas or benefit calculation may be provided to make the approximate magnitude of the reduction apparent. In addition, if the magnitude of the reduction is still not reasonably apparent from the descriptions provided, the notice must include one or more illustrative examples showing the approximate magnitude of the reduction in the example. Thus, illustrative examples are required for a change from a traditional defined benefit formula to a cash balance formula or a change that results in a period of time during which there are no accruals (or minimal accruals) with regard to normal retirement benefits or an early retirement subsidy (a wear-away period).

These examples must illustrate the ranges of the reductions by showing examples that bound the possibilities. In addition, the examples generally may be based on any reasonable assumptions (e.g., about the representative participant's age, years of service, and compensation; any interest rate and mortality table used in the illustrations; and salary scale assumptions used in the illustrations for amendments that alter the compensation taken into account under the plan), but the ERISA Section 204(h) notice must identify those assumptions. If a plan's benefit provisions, however, include a factor that varies over time (such as a variable interest rate), the determination of whether an amendment is reasonably expected to result in a wear-away period must be based on the value of the factor applicable under the plan at a time that is reasonably close to the date the ERISA Section 204(h) notice is provided, and any wear-away period that is solely a result of a future change in the variable factor may be disregarded. For example, to determine whether a wear-away occurs as a result of a Section 204(h) amendment that converts a defined benefit plan to a cash balance pension plan that will credit interest based on a variable interest factor specified in the plan, the future interest credits must be projected based on the interest rate applicable under the variable factor at the time the Section 204(h) notice is provided. [Treas. Reg. § 54.4980F, Q&A 11]

### Q 8:71   Will an ERISA Section 204(h) notice that contains false or misleading information be considered valid?

No. A notice that includes materially false or misleading information (or omits information to cause the information provided to be misleading) does not constitute a valid ERISA Section 204(h) notice. Therefore, it will not be considered as having been provided and all associated penalties will apply (see Q 8:75). [Treas. Reg. § 54.4980F, Q&A 11]

### Q 8:72   Must the same ERISA Section 204(h) notice be provided to all applicable individuals?

No. If an amendment by its terms affects different classes of participants differently (e.g., one new benefit formula will apply to Division *A* and another to Division *B*), the notice requirements apply separately with respect to each general class of participants. In addition, the notice must include sufficient information to enable a participant to identify his or her class.

If an amendment affects different classes of applicable individuals differently, the plan administrator may provide a different ERISA Section 204(h) notice to each affected class. This notice may omit information that does not apply to the individuals to whom it is furnished, but it must identify the class or classes of applicable individuals to whom it is provided. [Treas. Reg. § 54.4980F, Q&A 11]

### Q 8:73 How can an ERISA Section 204(h) notice be provided?

A plan administrator (including a person acting on behalf of the plan administrator, such as the employer or plan trustee) can use any method reasonably calculated to ensure actual receipt of the ERISA Section 204(h) notice. First-class mail to the last known address of the party is an acceptable delivery method. Hand delivery is also acceptable, as is electronic delivery. However, posting the notice is not considered to be actually providing the notice. The ERISA Section 204(h) notice can be combined with other notices required to be provided to the participants, such as a notice of intent to terminate under ERISA Title IV. [Treas. Reg. § 54.4980F, Q&A 13]

EGTRRA specifically authorizes the IRS to provide regulations to allow delivery of the notice by using new technologies. [ERISA § 204(h)(7)] In Private Letter Ruling 200407021, the IRS ruled that a plan sponsor's Microsoft PowerPoint presentation at employee meetings satisfied the written notice requirement of ERISA Section 204(h). Although a letter ruling may not be relied upon by other taxpayers, it does show that the IRS is willing to accept this form of delivery. Some key points in the approval were that the plan sponsor did make available printed copies of the presentation, multiple employee meetings were held, and the plan sponsor took appropriate steps to ensure that all affected parties received the Section 204(h) notice.

### Q 8:74 How can the timing-of-notice requirement be satisfied?

An ERISA Section 204(h) notice must be provided within a reasonable time before the effective date of the amendment. In general, the notice must be provided at least 45 days before the effective date of any Section 204(h) amendment. In the case of a small plan or a multiemployer plan, however, the ERISA Section 204(h) notice must be provided at least 15 days before the effective date of any Section 204(h) amendment. A small plan is one that the plan administrator reasonably expects to have, on the effective date of the Section 204 (h) amendment, fewer than 100 participants who have an accrued benefit under the plan.

There is also an exception to the general timing rule for amendments made in connection with an acquisition or disposition of a business. In such case, the ERISA Section 204(h) notice must be provided at least 15 days before the effective date of the Section 204(h) amendment. In addition, if the amendment is made in connection with certain plan transfers, mergers, or consolidations and reduces only an early retirement benefit or retirement-type subsidy but does not significantly reduce the rate of future benefit accrual, the notice must be provided no later than 30 days after the effective date of the Section 204(h) amendment. [Treas. Reg. § 54.4980F, Q&A 9]

**Q 8:75   Are there any penalties for failure to provide the ERISA Section 204(h) notice?**

Yes. An excise tax equal to $100 per day per individual is applied to any failure to provide the ERISA Section 204(h) notice properly. There are limited exceptions to the application of the excise tax:

1. The excise tax will not be imposed if the plan administrator was not aware of the failure and exercised reasonable diligence in trying to satisfy the notice requirements.

2. The excise tax will not apply if the plan administrator exercised reasonable diligence in trying to satisfy the notice requirements and provides the ERISA Section 204(h) notice within 30 days of finding such failure.

3. The Secretary has the authority to waive the excise tax in full or in part for any failure that was due to reasonable cause to the extent that the payment of the tax would be excessive or be otherwise inequitable relative to the failure involved.

If the plan administrator exercised reasonable diligence in providing the ERISA Section 204(h) notice, the total excise tax imposed during the fiscal year of the plan sponsor will not exceed $500,000. [I.R.C. § 4980F]

If the failure to provide the ERISA Section 204(h) notice is egregious, all applicable individuals will be entitled to receive the greater of the benefits under the old or new plan formula. An egregious failure is defined as:

1. An intentional failure; or

2. A failure, whether or not intentional, to provide most of the individuals with most of the information they are entitled to receive.

[ERISA § 204(h)(6); Treas. Reg. § 54.4980F, Q&A 14]

If the failure to provide the notice is not egregious, the amendment may become effective with respect to all individuals.

**Q 8:76   How does ERISA Section 204(h) apply to the sale of a business?**

Whether an ERISA Section 204(h) notice is required in connection with the sale of a business depends on whether a plan amendment that significantly reduces the rate of future benefit accrual or significantly reduces an early retirement benefit or retirement-type subsidy is adopted. [Treas. Reg. § 54.4980F, Q&A 16]

**Q 8:77   How are amendments to cease accruals and terminate a plan treated under ERISA Section 204(h)?**

Amendments providing for the cessation of benefit accruals on a specified future date and for the termination of a plan are subject to ERISA Section 204(h). [Treas. Reg. § 54.4980F, Q&A 17]

**Example.** The GNM Construction Company adopts an amendment to its defined benefit plan that provides for the cessation of benefit accruals on December 31, 2002, and for the termination of the plan pursuant to ERISA Title IV as of a proposed termination date that is also December 31, 2002. As part of the notice of intent to terminate required under ERISA Title IV, the plan administrator gives the ERISA Section 204(h) notice of the amendment ceasing accruals to all affected participants; the notice states that benefit accruals will cease "on December 31, 2002." Because of an oversight by the plan actuary, however, all the requirements of ERISA Title IV for a plan termination are not satisfied, and the plan cannot be terminated until a date that is later than December 31, 2002.

Nonetheless, because the ERISA Section 204(h) notice was given stating that the plan was amended to cease accruals on December 31, 2002, the amendment to cease accruals is still effective on December 31, 2002. If the ERISA Section 204(h) notice had merely stated that benefit accruals would cease "on the termination date" or "on the proposed termination date," the cessation of accruals would not be effective on December 31, 2002.

# Chapter 9

# Plan Benefits/Accrued Benefits

The term *benefit* in *defined benefit pension plan* refers to the amount of money a participant can expect to receive at retirement. There are several types of benefit formulas and methods for earning benefits while one is a plan participant. Once the amount of the benefit is determined, the method of payment must be selected by the plan participant. This chapter provides detailed calculations of various types of benefits and actuarially equivalent benefits.

## Benefit Formulas

### Q 9:1 Why is the benefit formula an important part of determining the employee's accrued benefit?

An *accrued benefit* is the portion of the total retirement benefit earned by the plan participant as of any given date. Therefore, it is often necessary to know the employee's projected benefit (calculated under the plan's benefit formula) to determine the accrued benefit.

### Q 9:2  What is a *projected benefit*?

A *projected benefit* is the benefit calculated under the plan's benefit formula payable at the plan's normal retirement date (see chapter 8) in the normal form of benefit (see Q 9:18). The benefit formula is usually either a flat or fixed formula, unit credit formula, or integrated formula. There are also other unique benefit formulas, such as cash balance plans and floor offset plans.

### Q 9:3  What is a *flat, or fixed, benefit formula*?

A *flat, or fixed, benefit formula* is a benefit formula that defines the plan benefit at retirement, as either a flat dollar amount or a fixed percentage of salary, payable in monthly installments. The duration of the payment is defined by the plan's normal form of payment. In general, most plans will define the normal form of benefit as a life annuity. Usually, there is a reduction factor applied to the benefit that reduces the benefit for employees with fewer years of service at retirement. This prevents disproportionately larger benefits for older, short-service employees.

**Example 1.** The Reese Company Pension Plan provides a flat dollar benefit of $1,000 per month payable at retirement. The benefit is reduced by $\frac{1}{25}$ for each year of service to retirement less than 25. Dane, a participant with a total of 10 benefit years of service to retirement, will have his benefit reduced by $\frac{15}{25}$, for a total benefit of $400 ($1,000 − ($1,000 × $\frac{15}{25}$)). Brittany, a participant who will have 30 years of service at retirement, will receive the full benefit of $1,000.

**Example 2.** The Robby Company Pension Plan has a benefit formula that provides 75 percent of the final three-year average compensation reduced for service to retirement less than 30 years. Reese, a participant with 10 years of total benefit service to retirement, will have his benefit reduced by $\frac{20}{30}$, for a total of 25 percent of three-year average compensation at retirement (75% − (75% × $\frac{20}{30}$)).

### Q 9:4  What is a *unit credit benefit formula*?

A *unit credit benefit formula* is a benefit formula that defines the benefit as either a flat dollar amount or percentage of average compensation multiplied by the number of years of service to retirement. The dollar amount or percentage is the unit of benefit, and these units are accumulated over the employee's working lifetime. Generally, the benefit is payable in monthly installments, and the duration of payment is defined by the plan's normal form of payment.

**Example 1.** The Dane Company Pension Plan uses a unit credit benefit formula of 2 percent of the final three-year average compensation per year of service at retirement. Reese, a participant with 10 years of service at retirement, would be entitled to a benefit of 20 percent (2% × 10 years) of his final three-year average compensation.

**Example 2.** The Brittany & Associates Retirement Plan uses a unit credit benefit formula of $25 per month per year of service at retirement. Robby, a participant with 35 years at retirement, would be entitled to a benefit of $875 ($25 × 35 years).

### Q 9:5  What is an *integrated benefit formula*?

An *integrated benefit formula* is a benefit formula that takes into account the pension benefits the employer is providing to a plan participant through its contributions to Social Security. The effect of an integrated benefit formula is to provide additional benefits to employees who derive little or no Social Security benefits from their wages in excess of certain amounts.

Currently, the employer pays a tax of 6.2 percent of any employee's wages up to the taxable wage base ($97,500 in 2007). The taxable wage base is used to develop the benefit a participant will receive at Social Security retirement age. Each year the taxable wage base is increased for changes in the cost of living. At retirement, the average of the taxable wage bases over a participant's working lifetime is used to determine his or her Social Security retirement benefit.

The average of the taxable wage bases is known as *covered compensation*. The year of a participant's birth and the date the benefit is calculated determine the amount of covered compensation (see Appendix A for covered compensation tables for various years). An integrated benefit formula can be a fixed benefit (see Q 9:3) or a unit credit benefit (see Q 9:4) formula that provides a percentage of benefits above and below covered compensation. The Internal Revenue Code (Code) uses the term *permitted disparity* to describe this method of providing benefits. Chapter 11 outlines the permitted disparity rules under Code Section 401(l).

There are two methods of integrating a benefit with Social Security: an excess benefit or an offset benefit. Each method can use either a fixed percentage formula or a unit credit formula. The following example illustrates these methods.

**Example.** The employee, Frank, has average compensation in his last three years with the employer of $80,000, covered compensation of $45,000, and 25 years of service at retirement.

*Excess fixed benefit.* The Ken Company Pension Plan has an integrated excess fixed benefit formula that provides a retirement benefit of 20 percent of average compensation up to covered compensation plus 40 percent of average compensation in excess of covered compensation. The entire benefit is reduced for years of service less than 35. Frank's benefit at retirement is the sum of 20 percent of his average compensation up to his covered compensation, in this case $9,000 (20% × $45,000) and 40 percent of his average compensation in excess of his covered compensation, or $14,000 (40% × ($80,000 − $45,000)), for a total of $23,000 ($9,000 + $14,000). Because Frank has 25 years of service at retirement, and the plan requires a reduction in the benefit for each year of service less than 35, Frank's total benefit is reduced by $^{10}/_{35}$, or $6,571 ($23,000 × $^{10}/_{35}$). Hence, Frank's net benefit is $16,429 ($23,000 − $6,571), or $1,369 payable as a monthly benefit ($16,429 ÷ 12).

*Excess unit credit benefit.* The Hugh Company Pension Plan provides a retirement benefit of 1 percent of average compensation per year of service up to covered compensation plus 1.65 percent of average compensation per year of service in excess of covered compensation. The maximum number of years considered for determining a benefit is 35. One percent of Frank's average compensation up to his covered compensation is $450 (1% × $45,000), and 1.65 percent of his excess compensation is $578 (1.65% × ($80,000 − $45,000)). The sum of these two amounts is $1,028 ($450 + $578). Frank has 25 years at retirement; hence, his benefit will be $25,700 ($1,028 × 25), or $2,142 as a monthly benefit ($25,700 ÷ 12).

*Offset fixed benefit.* The Ken Company Pension Plan has an offset fixed benefit formula that provides a retirement benefit of 40 percent of average compensation reduced by 20 percent of average compensation below covered compensation. The entire benefit is reduced for years of service less than 35 at retirement. Forty percent of Frank's average compensation is $32,000 (40% × $80,000). That amount is reduced by 20 percent of Frank's average compensation up to his covered compensation, or $9,000 (20% × $45,000). Frank's net benefit before the service reduction is $23,000 ($32,000 − $9,000). Because he has 25 years of service at retirement, the entire benefit is reduced by $^{10}/_{35}$, or $6,571 ($23,000 × $^{10}/_{35}$). Hence, Frank's net benefit is $16,429 ($23,000 − $6,571), or $1,369 payable as a monthly benefit ($16,429 ÷ 12).

*Offset unit credit benefit.* The Hugh Company Pension Plan provides a retirement benefit of 1.65 percent of average compensation per year of service reduced by 0.65 percent of average compensation per year of benefit service for compensation below covered compensation. The maximum years of service for a benefit is 35, and 1.65 percent of Frank's average compensation is $1,320 (1.65% × $80,000). That amount is reduced by 0.65 percent of Frank's compensation up to his covered compensation, or $293 (0.65% × $45,000). The result of the subtraction is $1,027 ($1,320 − $293). Frank has 25 years of service at retirement; hence his benefit will be $25,675 ($1,027 × 25), or $2,140 as a monthly benefit ($25,675 ÷ 12).

### Q 9:6    What is a *Social Security primary insurance amount offset benefit formula*?

A *Social Security primary insurance amount offset benefit formula* is a benefit formula that reduces the projected retirement benefit at retirement by a portion of a participant's Social Security benefit, otherwise known as the primary insurance amount (PIA). Such a benefit formula works much like an integrated benefit formula using permitted disparity; however, in the case of a Social Security PIA offset benefit formula, the benefit is directly reduced by the benefits provided by Social Security. Such a formula can be a flat benefit or unit credit formula.

## Accrued Benefits

### Q 9:7   What is an *accrued benefit?*

An *accrued benefit* is the portion of the total retirement benefit earned by the plan participant as of any given date. Under revisions made by the Pension Protection Act of 2006 (PPA), the accrued benefit may, under the terms of the plan, be expressed as an annuity payable at normal retirement age, the balance of a hypothetical account, or the current value of the accumulated percentage of the employee's final average compensation. [I.R.C. § 411(b)(5)(A)(iv)] That amount is the benefit the participant would be entitled to receive (before the application of a vesting schedule) if he or she were to terminate employment or retire. There are two methods a plan can use to determine the accrued benefit: the fractional accrual method (see Q 9:8) or the unit credit accrual method (see Q 9:10). The accrued benefit will vary from year to year based on the participant's years of service, age, and compensation and is generally expressed as a monthly annuity payable in the plan's normal form of payment (see Q 9:18).

### Q 9:8   What is the *fractional accrual method?*

Under the *fractional accrual method* the projected retirement benefit is multiplied by a fraction, the numerator of which is benefit service as of the date the accrued benefit is calculated, and the denominator of which is the total benefit service the participant will have at retirement. This method accrues the benefits in equal portions over the participant's total years of benefit service.

> **Example.** If Andrew, a plan participant, has completed 20 of 30 years of total benefit service as of the date the accrued benefit is calculated, he will have accrued $20/30$ of his total projected pension benefit. If the plan benefit formula is 50 percent of the final three-year average compensation, the accrued benefit would be calculated using the average compensation over the last three years multiplied by 50 percent multiplied by the accrual fraction of $20/30$. This results in an accrued benefit of 33.33 percent (50% × $20/30$) of the final three-year average compensation.

Defined benefit plans have the option of defining benefit service for the accrual fraction to be total years of service with the employer, known as a *service accrual*; total years of participation in the plan, known as *participation accrual*; or total years of participation plus some number of years before participation in the plan.

### Q 9:9   How is the accrued benefit calculated under the fractional accrual method when there has been a partial year of participation?

Under the fractional accrual method, the entire benefit must be accrued at normal retirement age. In the years following an accrual computation period in which the participant was not credited with a full year of participation, the participant must accrue the fractional rule benefit that is attributable to the new continuous period of participation, at least ratably, over the new period. The IRS has stated that the accrued benefit must be at least equal to the "fractional rule benefit" (computed in accordance with Treasury Regulations Section 1.411(b)-1(b)(3)(ii)(A)) times an "accrual ratio." The accrual ratio is equal to the sum of:

1. The prior accrual ratio at the end of the last computation period (N) in which the participant was not credited with a full year of participation; and

2. The product of:

   a. One minus the prior accrual ratio determined in item #1 above; and

   b. The fraction equal to the number of years of participation subsequent to N divided by the number of years of participation that the participant would have participated in the plan after N if the participant separated at normal retirement age.

**Example 1.** Fred commenced participation in the Going Batty defined benefit plan at age 25. The normal retirement age under the plan is 65 and his projected benefit at normal retirement age is $1,000. The plan uses the fractional rule for determining a participant's accrued benefit. During the first four accrual computation periods that Fred participated in the plan, full years of participation were earned. Fred's "accrual ratio" at the end of the fourth accrual computation period was .1 (4/40, the number of years of participation divided by the total number of years of participation Fred would have participated in the plan if he separated from service at normal retirement age under the plan), and his accrued benefit is $100 (.1 × $1000).

During the fifth accrual computation period, Fred earned one-half of a year of participation. Consequently, his "accrual ratio" at the end of this accrual computation period was .1125 (4.5/40) and his accrued benefit is $112.50 (.1125 × $1000).

In the sixth accrual computation period, Fred earned a full year of participation. At the end of this accrual computation period, his "accrual ratio" was .1379 (.1125 + (1 − .1125) 1/35). His accrued benefit is calculated as $137.90 ($112.50 + ($887.50 × 1/35)). Thus, if he completed 35 years of participation after the year in which a full year of participation was not earned, he would accrue the fractional rule benefit that is attributable to the new period of continuous participation ((1 − .1125) times the fractional rule benefit) ratably over the 35-year period, and at normal retirement age the entire fractional rule benefit would be accrued. Consequently, the accrual rule under this plan produces the lowest accrued benefit permissible under the fractional rule.

It is also permissible, in lieu of the above method, to define the numerator as the number of actual credited years of participation (including the partial years) and adjust the denominator to be equal to the sum of the numerator as of the end of the prior accrual computation period and the number of years from such time to normal retirement age.

**Example 2.** The facts are the same as in Example 1, but the plan uses the method as described above for dealing with a partial year of participation. In the sixth accrual computation period, the accrual ratio would be 5.5/39.5, or

.1392. Therefore, Fred's accrued benefit using this method would be $139.20, which is more than under Example 1, satisfying the requirement that the accrued benefit must be at least the amount as calculated using the method from Example 1. [Rev. Rul. 81-11, 1981-1 C.B. 227]

### Q 9:10   What is the *unit credit accrual method*?

Under the *unit credit accrual method*, the unit benefit formula in the plan is applied to service as of the date the benefit is determined. For example, if a plan provides 1 percent of the three-year average compensation for each year of benefit service, the accrued benefit for any participant in the plan is equal to 1 percent times the three-year average compensation times the number of years of service completed as of the date the accrued benefit is determined.

**Example 1.** Frank, a plan participant, currently has a three-year average compensation of $30,000 and 20 years of benefit service as of the date the accrued benefit is calculated. The plan provides 1 percent of three-year average compensation per year of service. Frank's accrued benefit would be $6,000 ($30,000 × 1% × 20). If Frank is projected to have 40 years of benefit service as of his normal retirement date, his projected accrued benefit would be $12,000 ($30,000 × 1% × 40).

**Example 2.** If Frank was a participant in a plan that provided $10 per month per year of service, Frank would have an accrued benefit of $200 per month ($10 × 20) and a projected accrued benefit of $400 ($10 × 40).

### Q 9:11   Is there a minimum level of benefits that must accrue under a plan's benefit formula?

Yes. A plan's benefit formula must accrue a minimum level of benefits throughout the working lifetime of a plan participant. This is accomplished by meeting one of the three tests, which when applied to the accrued benefit method of a plan's benefit formula ensures that at least a certain level of benefits accrues each year. These rules prevent a plan from providing larger benefits for service in the later years of an employee's working lifetime, a practice known as *back-loading*.

### Q 9:12   What are the three accrual tests?

The three tests are known as the 3 percent rule, the 133s⅓ percent rule, and the fractional accrual rule.

*Three percent rule.* A plan's benefit formula and accrual method will satisfy the 3 percent rule if, as of the close of any plan year, the accrued benefit to which each participant is entitled is not less than the product of 3 percent and the maximum projected benefit and the number of years of participation as of the date of determination. The *maximum projected benefit* is the benefit a participant would be entitled to under the plan if the participant entered the plan at the earliest permissible entry age (age 0 if none is specified in the plan) and remained continuously in the plan until the earlier of normal retirement or age 65. [Treas. Reg. § 1.411(b)-1(b)(1)]

**Example 1.** The Dane Company would like to provide a benefit formula that rewards its long-service employees. In designing the plan, it asked its retirement plan consultant if the following benefit formula would be acceptable: a unit credit accrued benefit of 1 percent of the highest three-year average compensation per year of service for the first 15 years plus 1.4 percent for the next 5 years, and 1.65 percent for the last 5 years. Employees can enter the plan on completion of 1 year of service and attainment of age 21 and can retire at the earlier of completion of 25 years of service or attainment of age 65. To prove that this formula satisfies the 3 percent rule, the following chart, which reviews the accrued benefits for an employee entering the plan at age 21, was prepared:

| _A_ | _B_ | _C_ | _D_ | _E_ |
|---|---|---|---|---|
| | | | *3 Percent of Projected* | |
| *Benefit* | *Additional* | *Accrued Benefit* | *Benefit Times Benefit* | *3 Percent* |
| *Service* | *Accrued Benefit* | *Close of Year* | *Service* | *Rule Test* |
| 1 | 1.00% | 1.00% | 0.91% | Pass |
| 2 | 1.00% | 2.00% | 1.82% | Pass |
| 3 | 1.00% | 3.00% | 2.72% | Pass |
| 4 | 1.00% | 4.00% | 3.63% | Pass |
| 5 | 1.00% | 5.00% | 4.54% | Pass |
| 6 | 1.00% | 6.00% | 5.45% | Pass |
| 7 | 1.00% | 7.00% | 6.35% | Pass |
| 8 | 1.00% | 8.00% | 7.26% | Pass |
| 9 | 1.00% | 9.00% | 8.17% | Pass |
| 10 | 1.00% | 10.00% | 9.08% | Pass |
| 11 | 1.00% | 11.00% | 9.98% | Pass |
| 12 | 1.00% | 12.00% | 10.89% | Pass |
| 13 | 1.00% | 13.00% | 11.80% | Pass |
| 14 | 1.00% | 14.00% | 12.71% | Pass |
| 15 | 1.00% | 15.00% | 13.61% | Pass |
| 16 | 1.40% | 16.40% | 14.52% | Pass |
| 17 | 1.40% | 17.80% | 15.43% | Pass |
| 18 | 1.40% | 19.20% | 16.34% | Pass |
| 19 | .40% | 20.60% | 17.24% | Pass |
| 20 | 1.40% | 22.00% | 18.15% | Pass |
| 21 | 1.65% | 23.65% | 19.06% | Pass |
| 22 | 1.65% | 25.30% | 19.97% | Pass |
| 23 | 1.65% | 26.95% | 20.87% | Pass |
| 24 | 1.65% | 28.60% | 21.78% | Pass |
| 25 | 1.65% | 30.25% | 22.69% | Pass |

Column C is the accrued benefit as a percentage of the highest three-year average compensation as of the close of every plan year that the employee could work from year 1 to year 25. The amount in column D is calculated by multiplying the ultimate retirement benefit, 30.25 percent, by 3 percent and then multiplying that result by the amount in column A (benefit service). The amount in column C must be greater than the amount in column D in each year for the plan to satisfy the 3 percent rule. Column E indicates whether the accrued benefit in column C is greater than or equal to the amount in column D and thus whether the formula satisfies the 3 percent rule test. The plan accrues at least the minimum benefit for all years of service and therefore satisfies the 3 percent rule.

*133⅓ percent rule.* The 133⅓ percent rule requires (1) that the accrued benefit payable at normal retirement age be equal to the normal retirement benefit and (2) the annual rate at which any individual who is or could be a participant can accrue the normal retirement benefit for any later plan year be not more than 133⅓ percent of the annual rate at which the individual can accrue benefits for any prior year. This includes increases for consecutive and nonconsecutive prior years. If the plan reduces benefits in later years, the reduction in the accrual rate does not apply to the 133⅓ percent rule. [Treas. Reg. § 1.411(b)-1(b)(2)]

**Example 2.** The Reese Company provides 1 percent of the highest three-year average compensation per year of service for the first 20 years and 1.33 percent for each year of service after 20. It would like to replace the 1.33 percent with 1.50 percent. The retirement plan consultant noticed that the increase in the accrued benefit from the 20th year to the 21st year would be 150 percent of the accrued benefit in the 20th year. This is more than 133⅓ percent and is not allowed under the 133⅓ rule.

*Fractional accrual rule.* Under the fractional accrual rule, the accrued benefit as of the close of any year must be at least equal to the participant's projected retirement benefit multiplied by a fraction whose numerator is the total number of years of participation as of the close of the year and whose denominator is the total number of years of participation the participant will have at the normal retirement age under the plan. The projected retirement benefit is determined as if the participant had retired as of the close of the plan year, with the benefit based on the current rate of compensation, which is assumed to continue until normal retirement. If the plan provides for benefits based on average compensation in excess of 10 years (i.e., in a career-average-pay plan), the fractional rule will not be satisfied. [Treas. Reg. § 1.411(b)-1(b)(3)]

**Example 3.** The KDB & S Company has installed a defined benefit with a unit credit formula of 2 percent of pay for the first 10 years plus 4 percent of pay for the next 20 years. Although this formula would fail the 3 percent rule and 133⅓ percent rule if the accrual was also unit credit, the accrued benefit can instead be defined using the fractional accrual rule and would then pass. This would mean that an employee with 30 years of service would have a 100-percent-of-pay benefit and would accrue ¹⁄₃₀ of the benefit during each year for a rate of accrual of 3.33 percent per year.

### Q 9:13   May an accrued benefit ever decrease?

No. An accrued benefit may never decrease on account of increasing age or service [I.R.C. § 411(b)(1)(G)] (see Q 9:14) or by plan amendment [I.R.C. § 411 (d)(6)] (see chapter 8).

### Q 9:14   May an accrued benefit decrease if the compensation average decreases in a final average pay plan?

No. The current IRS view appears to be that a participant's compensation average cannot decrease without an additional year of service; therefore, the accrued benefit cannot decrease without violating Code Section 411(b)(1)(G). [2001 ASPPA Annual Conference, IRS Q&A 21]

## Benefit Service

### Q 9:15   What is a *past-service credit*?

A *past-service credit* is a method of providing benefits to plan participants for years they worked for the employer before the effective date of a defined benefit pension plan. Generally, past-service credits are granted to employees to take into account the years they worked for the employer when the employer had no pension plan in place. A past-service credit is also a grant of service for periods in the past vis-á-vis a plan amendment. If an employer wants to provide for a past-service credit to plan participants in excess of five years, the plan must prove that a grant of service in excess of five years does not discriminate in favor of the highly compensated employees (HCEs) in the plan. Furthermore, if a pattern of amendments has the effect of discriminating in favor of the plan's HCEs, the five-year safe harbor is not available. [Treas. Reg. § 1.401(a)(4)-5(a)(3)]

### Q 9:16   Can a plan limit the number of years of service used to determine a benefit?

Yes. A plan can provide that the years of service be limited so as to limit the amount of plan benefit. For plans that use a unit credit formula (see Q 9:4), the limit on the years of service would be the largest such number that the benefit formula would take into account when determining a benefit.

**Example 1.** The Ken Company provides a benefit of 1 percent of the participant's highest three-year average compensation for each year of service to a maximum of 25 years. Jamie will have 35 years of service at the time she retires. Although she will accrue no new benefits after her 25th year with Ken Company, her benefit will increase as her average compensation increases in the last 10 years of her employment.

A plan that uses a flat benefit formula (see Q 9:3) can require benefits to accrue fractionally over the participant's working lifetime, except that in no event will the denominator of the fraction exceed a limited number of years.

**Example 2.** The Lisa Company provides a benefit of 30 percent of the participant's highest three-year average compensation. The benefit is reduced by $\frac{1}{30}$ for each year of service less than 30. The benefit is fractionally accrued over the employee's service with Lisa Company; however, in no event will the denominator of the fraction exceed 30 years. Ken, a plan participant, will have 40 years of service at the time he retires. Although he will accrue no new benefits after his 30th year with Lisa Company, his benefit will increase as his average compensation increases in the last 10 years of his employment. The following illustrates Ken's accrued benefit in 10-year intervals with Lisa Company.

| Year | Accrued Benefit as a Percentage of Average Compensation |
|------|------------------------------------------|
| 10 | 30% × 10 ÷ 30 = 10% |
| 20 | 30% × 20 ÷ 30 = 20% |
| 30 | 30% × 30 ÷ 30 = 30% |
| 40 | 30% × 30 ÷ 30 = 30% |

### Q 9:17   Can a plan use a date that will exclude benefit service?

Yes. A plan can provide that for purposes of calculating a benefit, service before a date selected by the employer will not be counted. In doing so, however, the plan must apply this service limitation on a nondiscriminatory basis. It is very common for plans to exclude service before the effective date when calculating a benefit. The effect is to reduce the benefit to a lower level than it would have been if the employer had counted all or a portion of an employee's service before the effective date of the plan.

## Forms of Benefit Payment

### Q 9:18   What is meant by the plan's *normal form of benefit?*

The *normal form of benefit* is the form of payment offered to a plan participant on becoming eligible for retirement benefits (e.g., a life annuity, 50 percent joint and survivor annuity, or any other benefit payment form). Generally, if a plan participant wants to receive benefits in an alternate form of payment, the normal form of payment is converted to one that is either actuarially equivalent in value to the plan's normal form or adjusted using a tabular conversion factor. An *actuarially equivalent benefit* is a benefit that has an actuarial present value equal to the plan's normal form of payment at the time of the first payment.

**Example.** Nick, a 65-year-old participant in his employer's pension plan, has reached retirement. He can receive his payment in the form of a life annuity or he can elect to receive his payment in the form of a 10-year certain and life annuity. Nick's retirement benefit is $1,000 per month as a life annuity. The plan's actuarially equivalent benefit is calculated using 7 percent interest and the 1983 Male Group Annuity Mortality (GAM) Table. The annuity purchase rates (APRs) for a life annuity and for a 10-year certain and life annuity using that table are 110.905 and 118.708, respectively. This means that the present value of the life annuity for Nick's benefit is $110,905 ($1,000 × 110.905). A 10-year certain and life annuity for Nick with a present value of $110,905 is $934.27, determined by dividing $110,905 by the 10-year certain and life factor of 118.708. If Nick elects the 10-year certain annuity, his monthly benefit will be $934.27.

### Q 9:19   How is a normal form of benefit converted to an actuarially equivalent benefit?

Two types of calculations are used to determine actuarially equivalent benefits: conversion of a benefit to an alternate form of payment and the conversion of a benefit to be payable at an alternate retirement age. Benefits are converted to actuarially equivalent forms of payment or retirement dates using the plan's interest rate and mortality table (known as *actuarial equivalence assumptions*). To make the calculation methodology clear, the plan should specify if mortality is used preretirement and postretirement or just postretirement. If one interest rate is used, that rate is used for all retirement ages. Some plans may use a different interest rate for preretirement than they do for postretirement.

*Alternate form of payment.* To determine the actuarial equivalent of the normal form of benefit payable in an alternate form, the accrued benefit is multiplied by the ratio of the APR for the normal form of benefit to the APR for the alternate form of benefit. (See chapter 18 for a definition of APR.) The APRs are determined as of the age the benefit is to be paid.

> **Example 1.** The MS Pension Plan provides a life annuity at age 65 based on the 1983 Male Individual Annuity Mortality (IAM) table with interest at 6 percent. The APR for the life annuity is 126.910; the joint and 50 percent survivor APR for a 65-year-old beneficiary is 138.394. Jeff is about to retire with a benefit of $1,000 per month and has elected a joint and 50 percent survivor annuity, which is $917.02 per month on an actuarially equivalent basis (($1,000 × 126.910) ÷ 138.394).

*Alternate retirement age.* To determine the actuarial equivalent of the normal form of benefit payable at an alternate retirement age, the accrued benefit is multiplied by the APR at the normal retirement age and adjusted for interest and mortality to the age the payments are to begin, and the result is divided by the APR at the age benefits begin.

> **Example 2.** The MS Pension Plan provides a life annuity at age 65 based on the 1983 Male IAM table with interest at 6 percent. The APR for the life annuity is 126.910 at age 65, and 141.335 at age 60. Jeff has an accrued benefit of $1,000 per month payable at age 65 and has elected to retire early, at age 60, with an actuarially equivalent benefit. According to the plan's definition of actuarial equivalence, mortality is ignored before retirement. The discount for interest only from age 65 to age 60 is the present value of $1 payable in five years at 6 percent interest, or 0.747258 $(1.06^{-5})$. Hence, the actuarially

equivalent benefit payable at age 60 is $670.99 ($1,000 × 126.910 × 0.747258) ÷ 141.335).

When benefits are paid at an alternate retirement age and in an alternate form of payment, the calculation of an actuarially equivalent benefit consists of first converting to a benefit payable at the alternate retirement age and then to a benefit payable in the alternate form of payment.

### Q 9:20   Can a plan use different mortality tables for males and females in determining actuarially equivalent benefits?

No. A plan must use the same mortality table in determining actuarial equivalencies for male and female participants. The Supreme Court, in *Arizona v. Norris* [463 U.S. 1073, 1084–10 (1983)], held that the application of sex-distinct actuarial tables to employees in calculating the amount of retirement benefits violates Title VII of the Civil Rights Act of 1964.

### Q 9:21   What alternate forms of benefit payment are available?

A defined benefit pension plan can offer any form of annuity or actuarially equivalent lump-sum payment to a plan participant as long as the form of payment does not extend beyond the participant's life expectancy. The plan is required to provide at least a life annuity to unmarried participants and a qualified joint and survivor annuity to married participants. In general, most pension plans will provide a form of payment that is actuarially equivalent to a life annuity. The following are some common forms of benefit:

1. *Life annuity.* An annuity payable for the life of the participant.
2. *A period certain and life annuity.* An annuity payable for the life of a participant with payments guaranteed for a period of years (i.e., the first 5, 10, or 15 years as elected).
3. *Joint and survivor annuity.* An annuity payable for the life of a participant with a reduced payment continuing to the designated beneficiary of the plan participant. The reduced payment is a percentage of the payment that was made to the plan participant based on the percentage elected (i.e., 50 percent, 69 percent, 75 percent, or 100 percent).
4. *Lump-sum cash payment.* A one-time payment of the full actuarial value of the plan's monthly benefit payable as an annuity.

If the plan participant is married at the time payments begin, the spouse must consent to any form of payment other than a qualified joint and survivor annuity.

### Q 9:22   Is a defined benefit pension plan required to specify the actuarial assumptions used in determining plan benefits?

Yes. For a defined benefit pension plan to be qualified under Code Section 401(a), the plan must specify the actuarial assumptions that form the basis of determining a plan participant's benefits. [I.R.C. § 401(a)(25)] This requirement should not be confused with the actuarial assumptions used to determine a plan's funding requirement. Those assumptions are determined by the plan's enrolled actuary and are subject to his or her professional judgment. The actuarial assumptions specified in the plan are the assumptions used to convert one form of benefit to another. The employer can change the actuarial assumptions for determining plan benefits; however, any optional form of benefit calculated under the new actuarial assumptions cannot be less than the optional form of benefit calculated under the prior actuarial assumptions. [Treas. Reg. § 1.411(d)-4(a)(3)]

> **Example.** During the 2000 plan year, Kelly, a 64-year-old plan participant in the Acme Pension Plan, has an accrued benefit of $1,000 per month. At that time, the plan provided that any optional form of payment would be the actuarial equivalent of a life annuity using the 1983 Male IAM table set back five years with interest at 6 percent. For the 2001 plan year, the plan is amended to use the 1984 Unisex Mortality Table. The optional forms of payment are a life annuity, a 10-year certain and life annuity, and a joint and 50 percent survivor annuity. The following table lists the actuarially equivalent benefits for Kelly at age 65 under the old assumptions and the new assumptions using her accrued benefit at age 64 and her accrued benefit at age 65, which will be $1,030 per month:

|  | Optional Forms of Payment at Age 65 | | |
|---|---|---|---|
|  | *Life Annuity* | *10-Year Certain & Life* | *Joint & 50 Percent Survivor* |
| Accrued benefit at age 64 | $1,000 | $950.04 | $917.02 |
| Accrued benefit at age 65 | $1,030 | $938.93 | $927.08 |

> Although the life annuity under the new assumptions is greater than the life annuity under the prior assumptions, not all of the optional forms of payment are. Therefore, the actuarial assumptions cannot be reduced by the plan amendment. If Kelly elects to retire at age 65, the plan must offer her a life annuity of $1,030, a 10-year certain and life annuity of $950.04, or a joint and 50 percent survivor annuity of $927.08.

### Q 9:23    What is a *subsidized optional form of benefit*?

A *subsidized optional form of benefit* is a payment that is not actuarially equivalent to the accrued benefit and is of greater value than an actuarially equivalent benefit. The difference between the actuarial present values of the alternate and the normal forms of payment is the amount of the employer's subsidy. Because there is an increase in the value of the benefit due to its form or timing, an additional cost is created and must be paid for by the employer.

Because the cost of the benefit is contingent on an election by the plan partici-pant, the cost of the benefit is generally included in the plan's actuarial cost method with a discount for the probability that such a benefit will be paid.

**Example 1.** The D&R Pension Plan has a life annuity as its normal form of benefit at retirement. If a plan participant is married at retirement, the partici-pant can receive monthly payments in the form of a joint and 50 percent survivor annuity, reduced according to a table of reduction factors. All other optional forms of benefit are the actuarial equivalents of a life annuity using the 1983 Male GAM table with interest at 6 percent. Sheila, age 65, has a spouse who is 62 years old. Her monthly benefit at retirement is $1,500. According to the table of reduction factors, Sheila could receive a joint and 50 percent survivor annuity of 96 percent of the life annuity, or a monthly benefit of $1,440 ($1,500 × 96%). The actuarial equivalent of the life annuity payable as a joint and 50 percent survivor annuity using the plan's actuarial assumptions is $1,287 per month. The difference between these monthly benefits is $153 per month and has an actuarial present value of $21,224, which represents the subsidy.

**Example 2.** The D&R Pension Plan offers an early retirement benefit starting at age 55 for participants with at least 10 years of service. The plan's normal retirement benefit is payable at age 65. The early retirement benefit is the age 65 accrued benefit at the time early retirement is elected reduced by a table of reduction factors. Tammy, age 57, has an accrued benefit of $2,000 and elects early retirement. According to the table, Tammy is entitled to 73 percent of her accrued benefit on her early retirement date, or $1,460. The plan defines actuarially equivalent benefits using the 1983 Male GAM table with interest at 6 percent, which, if used to determine early retirement benefits, would pro-duce a benefit at early retirement of $1,041. The difference between these monthly benefits is $419 per month and has an actuarial present value of $60,114, which represents the subsidy.

A subsidized alternate form of payment is useful as a benefit enhancement feature and can entice employees to leave employment before normal retirement age or can enhance benefits without increasing the benefit payable under the normal form of payment. The advantage of a subsidized benefit feature is that not all plan participants will exercise their rights to these benefits; therefore, such a benefit feature can be more cost effective than across-the-board benefit increases.

## Minimum Top-Heavy Benefits

### Q 9:24 When is a defined benefit plan top heavy?

A defined benefit plan is top heavy when, as of the determination date, the present value of the accrued benefits of all key employees exceeds 60 percent of the present value of the accrued benefits of all employees. [I.R.C. § 416(g)(1)(A)(i); Treas. Reg. § 1.416-1, Q&A T-1(c)] (See chapter 5 for further discussion of the definition of a top-heavy plan.)

### Q 9:25  What is the defined benefit plan minimum benefit for a top-heavy plan?

The accrued benefit of a non-key employee in a top-heavy plan must equal at least 2 percent of average annual compensation (see Q 9:26) for each year of service with the employer, not to exceed a total of 20 percent. [Treas. Reg. § 1.416-1, Q&A M-2]

### Q 9:26  How is *average annual compensation* defined for purposes of the top-heavy minimum benefit?

For purposes of determining the minimum benefit in a top-heavy defined benefit plan, *average annual compensation* is defined as the average annual compensation for the five consecutive years during which the employee had the highest aggregate compensation from the employer. In making this determination, years in which the employee did not earn a year of service under the rules of Code Section 411(a)(4), (5), and (6) are disregarded. [Treas. Reg. § 1.416-1, Q&A M-2(a)]

### Q 9:27  What years are counted as years of service for purposes of the top-heavy minimum benefit?

For purposes of the top-heavy minimum benefit, only those years during which the employee had a year of service under the rules of Code Section 411(a)(4), (5), and (6) are counted as years of service. A plan can disregard any year of service during which the plan was not top heavy; any year of service completed in a plan year beginning before January 1, 1984; and, for plan years beginning after December 31, 2001, any year of service completed during a plan year when the plan does not benefit (within the meaning of Code Section 410(b)) any key employee or former key employee. [I.R.C. § 416(c)(1)(C)(ii), (iii)]

The top-heavy minimum benefit requirements apply only to years in which the plan is top heavy and during which a key or former key employee benefits. Accordingly, the plan will have to keep track of the top-heavy years in calculating benefits.

### Q 9:28  Can benefits already accrued under the plan satisfy the top-heavy minimum requirement?

Yes. If the participant, as of the date the accrued benefit is determined, has accrued at least the top-heavy minimum benefit under the plan, no additional top-heavy benefits are required. [Treas. Reg. § 1.416-1, Q&A M-2(e)]

**Example.** Nick has accrued a benefit of 30 percent of his highest five-year-average annual compensation as of December 31, 1998. Nick has five years of top-heavy service with the employer as of that date. Nick's top-heavy minimum benefit must be at least 10 percent (2% × 5) of his highest five-year-average annual compensation. In this case it is 30 percent and therefore no additional top-heavy benefits are required.

### Q 9:29 What is the form of benefit payment for the top-heavy minimum benefit?

The top-heavy minimum benefit must be paid in the form of a single life annuity (with no ancillary benefits) beginning at the plan's normal retirement age. If the plan provides an alternate form of payment at retirement, that form must be the actuarial equivalent of the single life annuity. If the benefit begins after normal retirement age, the payment of the top-heavy minimum benefit at the later age must be the actuarial equivalent of the single life annuity payable at the normal retirement age. The actuarial assumptions for the conversions to actuarially equivalent benefits are not mandated by law and are determined by the terms of the plan; however, the actuarial assumptions must be reasonable. [Treas. Reg. § 1.416-1, Q&A M-3]

### Q 9:30 Which employees must accrue a minimum top-heavy benefit?

Each non-key employee who is a participant in a top-heavy defined benefit plan and who has at least 1,000 hours of service for an accrual period must accrue a minimum benefit for that accrual computation period. An employee must accrue a top-heavy minimum benefit even if the employee would normally be excluded from plan participation because of compensation earned below a certain level, failure to make mandatory employee contributions, or not being employed on a certain date. [Treas. Reg. § 1.416-1, Q&A M-4]

### Q 9:31 What is the top-heavy minimum benefit if the employer maintains a defined benefit plan and a defined contribution plan, both of which are top heavy?

For non-key participants who benefit under the defined benefit plan only, the minimum benefit is at least 2 percent of average annual compensation (see Q 9:26) for each year of service with the employer, not to exceed a total of 20 percent. If the non-key participant benefits under both a defined benefit plan and a defined contribution plan, each of which is subject to the top-heavy minimum benefit requirements, the defined benefit plan can provide a top-heavy minimum benefit equal to the amount described above, but the employer can choose to provide the top-heavy minimum benefit in the defined contribution plan. If the employer chooses to provide the top-heavy minimum benefit in the defined contribution plan, the defined contribution plan must contribute at least 5 percent of the non-key participant's compensation to that participant's account in the top-heavy plan year. [Treas. Reg. § 1.416-1, Q&A M-12]

## Compensation Used for Benefits

### Q 9:32 Why is the definition of compensation used by a plan to determine benefits important?

Throughout the Code and the Employee Retirement Income Security Act of 1974 (ERISA), the term *compensation* is used in the description of plan requirements, such as maximum benefit limitations, top-heavy minimum bene-fits, nondiscrimination in benefits, and so forth. If the plan uses a definition of compensation to determine benefits other than the definition used to meet certain provisions of the law, the plan may fail to comply with those provisions. Admin-istratively, it is helpful to use the definition of compensation in Treasury Regulations Section 1.414(s)-1, which applies to many provisions in the Code, for purposes of determining plan benefits and compliance with applicable require-ments under the law. If the plan fails to meet the applicable provision of the law, it is easier to take corrective action because the compensation used for benefit pur-poses is the same as the compensation used for applying a provision of the law.

### Q 9:33   What are the safe-harbor definitions of plan compensation under Code Section 414(s)?

There are four safe-harbor definitions of compensation that will satisfy Code Section 414(s):

1. A definition that includes all compensation for purposes of Code Section 415(c)(3) (see chapter 12) and excludes all other compensation.

2. The Section 415(c)(3) definition for compensation (see chapter 12).

3. A definition of compensation within the meaning of Code Section 3401(a) and all other payments of compensation to an employee by his or her employer for which the employer is required to furnish the employee a written statement under Code Sections 6041(d), 6051(a)(3), and 6052. This definition can exclude amounts paid or reimbursed by the employer for moving expenses incurred by an employee, but only to the extent that, at the time of the payment, it is reasonable to believe that these amounts are not deductible by the employee under Code Section 217. Compensa-tion must be determined without regard to any rules under Code Section 3401(a) that limit the remuneration included in wages based on the nature or location of the employment or nature of the services rendered.

4. A definition of compensation within the meaning of Code Section 3401(a) but determined without regard to any rules that limit the remuneration included in wages based on the nature or location of the employment or nature of the services rendered.

[Treas. Reg. § 1.414(s)-1(c)(2)]

In general, Code Section 3401(a) defines *wages* as all remuneration for services performed by an employee for his or her employer, including the cash value of all remuneration (including benefits) paid in any medium other than cash. The term *wages* does not include remuneration for numerous other amounts. The list is long and contains many exceptions that are not usually found in pension practice, such as remuneration paid for combat pay to armed services personnel, agricultural labor, or domestic service; remuneration paid in amounts less than $50 in any calendar quarter; and remuneration paid by a foreign government to a nonresident alien. [I.R.C. § 3401(a)]

### Q 9:34   Is there any maximum limitation on the amount of annual compensation that can be considered for benefit purposes?

Yes. Code Section 401(a)(17) provides that a defined benefit pension plan cannot base benefit accruals on compensation in excess of the maximum compensation limitation. This limit is not applicable, however, in determining a participant's maximum benefit for purposes of the Code Section 415(b)(1)(B) 100 percent of three-year average compensation limitation. In general, the annual compensation limit is $200,000, adjusted as provided by the commissioner. The adjusted dollar amount of the annual compensation limit is determined by adjusting the $200,000 amount for changes in the cost of living (see Q 9:35). Any increase in the annual compensation limit is effective as of January 1 of a calendar year and applies to any plan year beginning in that calendar year. For example, if a plan has a plan year beginning July 1, 1994, and ending June 30, 1995, the annual compensation limit in effect on January 1, 1994 ($150,000), applies to the plan for the entire plan year. [Treas. Reg. § 1.401(a)(17)-1(a)(3)(i)]

### Q 9:35   What are the maximum compensation limitations for each plan year since the limitation went into effect?

The maximum compensation limitation went into effect for all plans for the plan year beginning on or after January 1, 1989. At that time, however, the maximum limitation on compensation was $200,000 and was indexed to its highest level of $235,840 in 1993. Starting in 1994 the limitation was reduced to $150,000. Then again, the limitation was increased for plan years beginning after December 31, 2001, back to $200,000. The following table lists the maximum compensation limitations for each year since the limitation took effect. The limitation applies to the plan year that begins in the calendar year.

| Plan Year That Begins in the Calendar Year | Compensation Limitation in Effect |
|---|---|
| Before 1989 | Deemed to be $200,000 |
| 1989 | $200,000 |
| 1990 | $209,200 |
| 1991 | $222,220 |
| 1992 | $228,860 |
| 1993 | $235,840 |
| 1994 | $150,000 |
| 1995 | $150,000 |
| 1996 | $150,000 |
| 1997 | $160,000 |
| 1998 | $160,000 |
| 1999 | $160,000 |
| 2000 | $170,000 |
| 2001 | $170,000 |

| Plan Year That Begins in the Calendar Year | Compensation Limitation in Effect |
|:---:|:---:|
| 2002 | $200,000 |
| 2003 | $200,000 |
| 2004 | $205,000 |
| 2005 | $210,000 |
| 2006 | $220,000 |
| 2007 | $225,000 |

### Q 9:36   How is the annual compensation limit adjusted each year for the cost of living?

*Plan years beginning on or before December 31, 2001.* The $150,000 amount is adjusted for changes in the cost of living by the commissioner at the same time and in the same manner as the limitations under Code Section 415(d), except that the base period for the annual adjustment is the quarter ending September 30 of the calendar year preceding the year for which the limitation is being determined. When $150,000, as adjusted by the index, exceeds the annual compensation limit for the prior calendar year by $10,000 or more, the annual compensation limit will be increased by the amount of such excess, rounded down to the next lowest multiple of $10,000. [Treas. Reg. § 1.401(a)(17)-1(a)(3)(ii), (iii)]

*Plan years beginning after December 31, 2001.* The $200,000 amount is adjusted for changes in the cost of living by the commissioner at the same time and in the same manner as the limitations under Code Section 415(d), except that the base period for the annual adjustment is the quarter ending June 30 of the calendar year preceding the year for which the limitation is being determined. When $200,000, as adjusted by the index, exceeds the annual compensation limit for the prior calendar year by $5,000 or more, the annual compensation limit will be increased by the amount of such excess, rounded down to the next lowest multiple of $5,000.

### Q 9:37   How is an increase in the annual compensation limit applied to accrued benefits in a defined benefit pension plan?

When the maximum compensation limitation increases due to a cost-of-living adjustment, the limitation in effect for the current plan year applies only to the compensation for that year that is taken into account in determining plan allocations or benefit accruals for the year. Therefore, when a cost-of-living adjustment occurs, compensation for any prior plan year taken into account in determining an employee's allocations or benefit accruals for the current plan year is subject to the applicable annual compensation limit in effect for that prior year. Thus, increases in the annual compensation limit apply only to compensation taken into account for the plan year in which the increase is effective.

However, if the maximum compensation limitation is changed due to a change in law, the change in the compensation due to the law change is effective for prior years as well. Therefore, if compensation for any plan year beginning before January 1, 1994 (i.e., the effective date of the Omnibus Budget Reconciliation Act of 1993 (OBRA '93)), is used for determining allocations or benefit accruals in a plan year beginning on or after January 1, 1994, but before January 1, 2002, the annual compensation limit for that prior year is $150,000. [Treas. Reg. § 1.401(a)(17)-1(b)(2)] If compensation for any plan year beginning before January 1, 2002 (the effective date of the law change due to the Economic Growth and Tax Relief Reconciliation Act of 2002 (EGTRRA)) is used for determining allocations or benefit accruals in a plan year beginning on or after January 1, 2002, the annual compensation limit for that prior year may be increased to $200,000. However, the employer through completion of the plan document, chooses whether or not to make the increase retroactive. [Notice 2001-56, 2001-38 I.R.B. 277]

In Revenue Ruling 2003-11 [I.R.B. 285], the IRS allowed an amendment to a defined benefit plan that would apply the new $200,000 compensation limit to recalculate accrued benefits for former HCEs. In addition, this increase will not have an effect on nondiscrimination [I.R.C. § 401(a)(4)] or coverage [I.R.C. § 410(b)] requirements. However, Code Section 401(a)(26) still remains to be satisfied, and the lesser of 40 percent or 50 former employees must have an actual increase in benefits due to the amendment in order to satisfy this Code Section.

**Example 1.** The R&D Pension Plan has a calendar-year plan year and bases benefits on the average of an employee's high three-consecutive-year compensation. The OBRA '93 effective date for the plan is January 1, 1994. Reese, an employee in the plan, has a high three-consecutive-year compensation of $160,000 (1994), $155,000 (1993), and $135,000 (1992). His average compensation as of December 31, 1994, may not exceed $145,000, determined as follows:

| Compensation | Year | Limit | Compensation Considered |
|---|---|---|---|
| $160,000 | 1994 | $150,000 | $150,000 |
| $155,000 | 1993 | $150,000 | $150,000 |
| $135,000 | 1992 | $150,000 | $135,000 |
| Average: | | | $145,000 |

For purposes of determining Reese's 1994 accrual, each year (1994, 1993, and 1992), not the average of the three years, is subject to the 1994 annual compensation limit of $150,000.

**Example 2.** The R&D Pension Plan has a calendar-year plan year and bases benefits on the average of an employee's high three-consecutive-year compensation. Dane, an employee in the plan, has a high three-consecutive-year compensation before the application of the limits of $185,000 (1997), $175,000 (1996), and $165,000 (1995). R&D cannot base plan benefits for Dane in 1997 on compensation in excess of $153,333, determined as follows:

| Compensation | Year | Limit | Compensation Considered |
|---|---|---|---|
| $185,000 | 1997 | $160,000 | $160,000 |
| $175,000 | 1996 | $150,000 | $150,000 |
| $165,000 | 1995 | $150,000 | $150,000 |
| Average: | | | $153,333 |

For purposes of determining Dane's 1997 accrual, each year (1997, 1996, and 1995), not the average of the three years, is subject to its annual compensation limit—$150,000 for 1995 and 1996, and $160,000 for 1997. [Treas. Reg. § 1.401(a)(17)-1(b)(6)]

**Example 3.** The R&D Pension Plan in Example 2 is determining the maximum compensation limitation for Dane in 2002. Her compensation for the last three years is as follows: $190,000 (2001), $180,000 (2000), and $170,000 (1999). The Code Section 401(a)(17) limitations in effect for those years were $160,000 for 1999, and $170,000 for 2000 and 2001. Thus, the participant's highest three-year average compensation for benefit accrual purposes in the plan year ending December 31, 2001, is $166,667 (($160,000 + $170,000 + $170,000) ÷ 3). For 2002, this participant's compensation is $200,000. To determine this participant's maximum compensation limitation for the 2002 plan year, the plan has the following two choices with respect to the effective date of the increased compensation dollar limit. Option 1 is to apply the new $200,000 compensation limit not only to 2002, but also to prior plan years. Option 2 is to apply the new $200,000 compensation limit only to compensation periods beginning in 2002 and later, and continue to apply the compensation limits that were in effect in prior years, as determined under prior law.

*Option 1.* Under this approach, the participant's compensation for 2000 and 2001, which are the two years included with 2002 to determine her highest three-year average, is also limited to $200,000 per year. This results in an average compensation of $190,000 for the 2002 plan year (($200,000 + $190,000 + $180,000) ÷ 3).

*Option 2.* Under this approach, the participant's compensation for 2000 and 2001, which are the two years included with 2002 to determine her highest three-year average, remain limited to $170,000 per year (which reflects the Code Section 401(a)(17) limit in effect in each of those years). This results in an average compensation of $180,000 for the 2002 plan year (($200,000 + $170,000 + $170,000) ÷ 3).

### Q 9:38     How is the accrued benefit determined for an employee whose benefit is subject to the maximum compensation limitations for the years in which the limitations became effective?

There are three dates during which the maximum annual compensation limitations changed, the statutory effective date, the OBRA '93 effective date, and the EGTRRA effective date.

In determining a participant's accrued benefit as of either of first two dates, the benefit is calculated as if the plan had been frozen the day before those dates using the compensation, benefit formula, and compensation limitation then in effect. The accrued benefit as determined on the statutory effective date is known as the *Section 401(a)(17) frozen accrued benefit*. The accrued benefit as determined on the OBRA '93 effective date is known as the *OBRA '93 frozen accrued benefit*. The first day following the determination of the Code Section 401(a)(17) frozen accrued benefit or the OBRA '93 frozen accrued benefit is known as the *Section 401(a)(17) fresh-start date* or the *OBRA '93 fresh-start date*, respectively. To determine the benefit on and after the fresh-start dates, one of the following three fresh-start formulas defined in Treasury Regulations Section 1.401(a)(4)-13(c)(4) can be used.

*Method 1: Without wear-away.* Under this method an employee's accrued benefit under the plan is equal to the sum of (1) the employee's Code Section 401(a)(17) frozen accrued benefit or OBRA '93 frozen accrued benefit, as the case may be, and (2) the employee's accrued benefit determined under the formula applicable to benefit accrual in the current plan year using the current formula as applied to the employee's years of service after the fresh-start date.

> **Example 1.** The D&R Pension Plan is a calendar-year defined benefit plan providing an annual benefit for each year of service equal to 2 percent of compensation averaged over an employee's highest three consecutive calendar years' compensation. The statutory effective date under Code Section 401(a)(17) applies to the D&R Pension Plan in 1989. As of the close of the 1988 plan year, Dane, an employee with five years of service and an average annual compensation of $250,000, had accrued a benefit of $25,000 (2% × 5 × $250,000). D&R decides to make an amendment effective for plan years beginning on or after January 1, 1989, and uses December 31, 1988, as the Code Section 401(a)(17) fresh-start date. The amendment uses the fresh-start formula without wear-away. Therefore, Dane's accrued benefit as of December 31, 1989, is $29,000, which is equal to the sum of $25,000 (Dane's accrued benefit as of December 31, 1988) and $4,000 (2% × 1 year since fresh-start date × $200,000). [Treas. Reg. § 1.401(a)(17)-1(e)(5)]

*Method 2: With wear-away.* Under this method an employee's accrued benefit under the plan is equal to the greater of (1) the employee's Code Section 401(a)(17) frozen accrued benefit or OBRA '93 frozen accrued benefit, as the case may be, or (2) the employee's accrued benefit determined under the formula applicable to benefit accrual in the current plan year using the current formula as applied to the employee's total years of service before and after the fresh-start date.

> **Example 2.** The D&R Pension Plan is a calendar-year defined benefit plan providing an annual benefit for each year of service equal to 2 percent of compensation averaged over an employee's highest three consecutive calendar years' compensation. The statutory effective date under Code Section 401(a)(17) applies to the D&R Pension Plan in 1989. As of the close of the 1988 plan year, Dane, an employee with five years of service and an average annual compensation of $250,000, had accrued a benefit of $25,000 (2% × 5 × $250,000). D&R decides to make an amendment effective for plan years beginning on or

after January 1, 1989, and uses December 31, 1988, as the Code Section 401(a)(17) fresh-start date. The amendment uses a fresh-start formula with wear-away. Therefore, Dane's accrued benefit at the end of 1989 remains $25,000, which is the greater of her accrued benefit as of the last day of the 1988 plan year ($25,000), and $24,000, which is her benefit based on the plan's benefit formula applied to total years of service (2% × 6 × $200,000).

*Method 3: Extended wear-away.* Under this method an employee's accrued benefit under the plan is equal to the greater of (1) the employee's accrued benefit determined using the *without wear-away method* and (2) the employee's accrued benefit determined using the *with wear-away method.* [Treas. Reg. § 1.401(a)(17)-1(e)(5)]

In determining accrued benefits after the EGTRRA effective date, the maximum compensation limitation is determined using either the current dollar limit in effect as applied to prior years, or using each dollar limit that was in effect in prior years.

**Example 3.** The facts are the same as in Example 3 in Q 9:37. The R&D Pension Plan uses a benefit formula of 1 percent of average annual compensation times years of participation. Dane has four years of participation. The plan has two options in determining the accrued benefit for Dane in 2002:

*Option 1.* The plan determines Dane's accrued benefit by applying the $200,000 dollar limit to all prior years. Dane's average annual compensation is $190,000. Her accrued benefit as of December 31, 2002, is $7,600 per year.

*Option 2.* The plan determines Dane's accrued benefit by applying each dollar limitation that was in effect in each year. Her average annual compensation is $180,000. Her accrued benefit as of December 31, 2002, is $7,200 per year.

### Q 9:39   Can an employee's Code Section 401(a)(17) frozen accrued benefit or OBRA '93 frozen accrued benefit be increased after the fresh-start dates?

Yes, but the plan must provide for such an adjustment. The adjustment is made by multiplying the Code Section 401(a)(17) or OBRA '93 frozen accrued benefit by a fraction. The numerator of the fraction is the employee's current average compensation after the fresh-start date using the limitations in effect at that time, and the denominator is the annual compensation that was used to determine the fresh-start accrued benefit under Code Section 401(a)(17) or OBRA '93, as the case may be. [Treas. Reg. § 1.401(a)(17)-1(c)(4)(iii)]

## Employee Contributions

### Q 9:40   How are benefits attributable to mandatory employee contributions determined under a defined benefit plan?

If a plan requires mandatory employee contributions, a portion of the accrued benefit is attributable to the mandatory employee contributions. The employee portion of the accrued benefit is equal to the employee's accumulated contributions (as of the determination date) expressed as an annual benefit, beginning at normal retirement age, using an interest rate prescribed in Code Section 417(e)(3). [I.R.C. § 411(c)(2)(B)]

*Mandatory employee contributions* are amounts contributed to the plan by the employee that are required as a condition of employment, as a condition of participation in the plan, or as a condition of obtaining benefits under the plan attributable to employer contributions. [I.R.C. § 411(c)(2)(C)]

### Q 9:41   How are accumulated contributions determined?

Accumulated contributions are the sum of the following amounts:

1. All mandatory contributions made by the employee;
2. Interest compounded annually at 5 percent for periods before the first plan year beginning after December 31, 1987;
3. Interest compounded annually at 120 percent of the federal midterm rate for years beginning with the first plan year beginning after December 31, 1987, and ending with the date on which the employee receives a distribution; and
4. Interest compounded at the Code Section 417(e) interest rates from the determination date to the date the employee attains normal retirement age. If the plan has been amended for the Retirement Protection Act of 1994 (RPA '94), the interest rate is the applicable interest rate.

[I.R.C. § 411(c)(2)(C)]

**Example.** Diane, a participant in the DFH, Inc., contributory defined benefit plan, terminates employment in 1999 and elects a lump-sum distribution. She reaches normal retirement age in 2005. The plan was amended to use the applicable interest rate and mortality table in 1995, and the plan year runs from January 1 to December 31.

For 1986 and 1987, a 5 percent interest rate is used for accumulation purposes. For 1988 through 1999, 120 percent of the federal midterm rate is used. For 2000 through 2005, the Code Section 417(e) interest rate of 6.35 percent is used. The accumulated mandatory contributions are calculated as shown in the following table:

| Year | Mandatory Contribution Amounts | Interest Rate | Interest Credit | Accumulated Balance |
|------|------|------|------|------|
| 1986 | $500 | 5.00% | $ 25 | $ 525 |
| 1987 | $550 | 5.00% | $ 54 | $1,129 |
| 1988 | $650 | 10.61% | $189 | $1,967 |
| 1989 | $700 | 11.11% | $296 | $2,964 |
| 1990 | $750 | 9.57% | $355 | $4,069 |

| Year | Mandatory Contribution Amounts | Interest Rate | Interest Credit | Accumulated Balance |
|------|------|------|------|------|
| 1991 | $ 800 | 9.78% | $ 476 | $ 5,345 |
| 1992 | $ 850 | 8.10% | $ 502 | $ 6,697 |
| 1993 | $ 900 | 7.63% | $ 580 | $ 8,177 |
| 1994 | $ 950 | 6.40% | $ 584 | $ 9,711 |
| 1995 | $1,000 | 9.54% | $1,022 | $11,733 |
| 1996 | $1,000 | 6.89% | $1,877 | $13,610 |
| 1997 | $1,000 | 7.34% | $1,072 | $15,683 |
| 1998 | $1,000 | 7.13% | $1,189 | $17,872 |
| 1999 | $1,000 | 5.59% | $1,055 | $19,927 |
| 2000 | $   0 | 6.35% | $1,265 | $21,192 |
| 2001 | $   0 | 6.35% | $1,346 | $22,538 |
| 2002 | $   0 | 6.35% | $1,431 | $23,969 |
| 2003 | $   0 | 6.35% | $1,522 | $25,491 |
| 2004 | $   0 | 6.35% | $1,619 | $27,110 |
| 2005 | $   0 | 6.35% | $1,721 | $28,832 |

The accumulated contributions for Diane as of her normal retirement date are $28,832.

### Q 9:42   How are the accumulated contributions converted into an accrued benefit?

The accumulated contributions are converted into an accrued benefit by using the actuarial equivalence factors as stated in the plan document, but the converted benefit can never be less than the benefit computed using the applicable Code Section 417(e) rates. [Treas. Reg. § 1.417(e)-1(d)(1)]

**Example.** The facts are the same as those in the example in Q 9:41. Diane's accrued benefit from the mandatory employee contributions is determined by dividing the accumulated balance of the mandatory contributions calculated at her normal retirement age by the APR using the applicable Code Section 417(e) rates. This APR is 124.366 and her monthly accrued benefit is $231.83 ($28,832 ÷ 124.366).

### Q 9:43   How does the accrued benefit derived from employee mandatory contributions affect the accrued benefit from employer contributions?

An employee's accrued benefit derived from employer contributions as of any applicable date is the excess, if any, of the accrued benefit for the employee determined under the terms of the plan as of the applicable date over the accrued benefit derived from mandatory employee contributions as of that date. [I.R.C. § 411(c)(1)]

**Example.** The facts are the same as those in the example in Q 9:42. In addition, assume Diane has an accrued benefit based on the provisions of the DFH Inc. defined benefit plan of $500 per month. The accrued benefit derived from employer contributions is determined by subtracting the accrued benefit derived from mandatory contributions from the total accrued benefit. This amount is $268.17 ($500.00 − $231.83).

Only the portion of the accrued benefit derived from employer contributions is subject to the plan's vesting schedule.

## Benefit Accruals After Normal Retirement Age

### Q 9:44 Can a defined benefit plan reduce the rate of benefit accrual due to the plan participant's attaining any age?

No. A defined benefit plan's benefit formula may not reduce or eliminate the accrual of additional benefits as a result of the participant's attaining any age, nor may it ignore compensation used in determining the benefit that may have been paid after attaining any age. [Prop. Reg. § 1.411(b)-2(b)(1)(i)(A)&(B)] This is not the same as imposing a service limitation, which is allowable (see Q 9:16).

**Note.** The maximum benefit limitations of Code Section 415 (i.e., the 100 percent of three-year average compensation limit or maximum annual dollar benefit limitation) will preclude any increase in accrued benefits beyond normal retirement if such increases in benefits would cause the benefit to exceed those limitations.

### Q 9:45 How is the accrued benefit determined for a plan participant working beyond the normal retirement date?

There are three options available, each of which has its own record keeping and reporting requirements. Some of these options require complex actuarial calculations for determining the accrued benefit paid at the time the employee actually retires.

*Option 1: Additional accruals with suspended benefit payments.* The plan could provide additional accrued benefits to the participant working beyond normal retirement and suspend any payment of benefits that would otherwise be payable at normal retirement (see Q 9:46).

*Option 2: Provide the greater of additional accruals or the actuarial equivalent of the normal retirement benefit.* This option requires the plan to track the actuarial equivalent of the normal retirement benefit to the delayed retirement date and the accrued benefit with additional accruals as of the delayed retirement date. Upon actual retirement of the employee, the larger of the two benefits is paid (see Q 9:54).

*Option 3: Additional accruals offset by benefits paid.* Using this option, the plan commences payment of the normal retirement benefit to the participant at the normal retirement date while he or she continues employment with the employer. At the end of each year, until the employee actually retires, the plan calculates the accrued benefit with additional accruals for service after the normal retirement date and then offsets that benefit by the actuarial equivalent of the retirement benefits paid prior to actual retirement (see Q 9:55).

### Q 9:46  How is the accrued benefit determined when the plan opts to provide additional accruals with suspended benefit payments?

In such a case, the employer would suspend payment of benefits and continue to accrue benefits for the employee as the plan would prior to normal retirement. In order to suspend benefit payments, the plan must comply with certain notice requirements (see Q 9:47).

**Example.** The Warrior Helmet Company maintains a defined benefit plan that provides a normal retirement benefit of $20 per month multiplied by the participant's years of credited service. The plan contains no limit on the number of years of credited service taken into account for purposes of determining the normal retirement benefit provided by the plan. Brenden attains normal retirement age of 65 and continues working full-time for Warrior Helmet. At age 65, Brenden has 30 years of credited service under the plan and could receive a normal retirement benefit of $600 per month ($20 × 30 years) if he retires. The plan provides for the suspension of Brenden's normal retirement benefit (in accordance with ERISA Section 203(a)(3)(B)) during the period of Brenden's continued employment with Warrior Helmet. Accordingly, the plan does not provide adjustment of his benefit because of delayed payment, nor does it pay benefits while Brenden remains employed. If Brenden retires at age 67, after completing two additional years of credited service for Warrior Helmet, he must receive additional accruals for the two years of credited service completed after attaining age 65. Accordingly, he is entitled to receive a normal retirement benefit of $640 per month ($20 × 32 years). [Prop. Treas. Reg. § 1.411(b)-2(b)(4)(iv), Ex. 1]

### Q 9:47  What are the rules for suspending payment of benefits?

A plan may suspend payment of an employee's accrued benefits under the following circumstances:

1. The employee continues in employment with the employer by either working 40 or more hours (or working eight or more days) per month. [DOL Reg. § 2530.203-3(c)(1)(i), (ii)]

2. The employer issues a timely notice to the employee explaining the suspension of benefit rules. [DOL Reg. § 2530.203-3(b)(4)]

### Q 9:48  What is the notice requirement for suspension of benefits?

The plan must notify the employee in writing by personal delivery or first-class mail during the first calendar month or payroll period in which the plan withholds payments that the employee's benefits are suspended. The notice must contain the following:

- A description of the specific reasons why benefit payments are being suspended;
- A general description of the plan provisions relating to the suspension of payments;
- A copy of such provisions; and
- A statement to the effect that applicable DOL regulations may be found in Section 2530.203-3 of the Code of Federal Regulations.

In addition, the suspension notice must inform the employee of the plan's procedure for affording a review of the suspension of benefits. Requests for such reviews may be considered in accordance with the claims procedure adopted by the plan pursuant to ERISA Section 503 and applicable regulations. In the case of a plan that requires the filing of a benefit resumption notice in order to resume payment of benefits, the suspension notification must also describe the procedure for filing such notice and include the forms (if any) that must be filed. Furthermore, if a plan intends to offset any suspendible amounts actually paid during the periods of employment, the notification must identify the specific periods of employment, the suspendible amounts that are subject to offset, and the manner in which the plan intends to offset such suspendible amounts. Where the plan's summary plan description (SPD) contains information that is substantially the same as information required in the notice, the suspension notification may refer the employee to relevant pages of the SPD for information, provided the employee is told how to obtain a copy of the SPD and that such a request must be made within a reasonable period of time, not to exceed 30 days. [DOL Reg. § 2530.203-3(b)(4)]

### Q 9:49  If a plan has suspended payments to a retiree, when should payments resume?

After benefit payments have been suspended, payments must resume no later than the first day of the third calendar month after the calendar month in which the employee ceases to be employed. However, the employee must have complied with any reasonable procedure adopted by the plan for notifying the plan that he or she has ceased such employment. The initial payment upon resumption must include the payment scheduled to occur in the calendar month when payments resume and any amounts withheld during the period between the cessation of employment and the resumption of payments, less any amounts that are subject to offset. [DOL Reg. § 2530.203-3(b)(2)]

### Q 9:50  If a retired participant is collecting benefits and continues to work, can the plan recover the suspendible benefit during the time the retiree was working for the employer?

Yes. A plan that provides for the suspension of benefits may deduct payments made during those calendar months or pay periods in which the employee was employed from benefit payments to be made subsequently. However, such deduction or offset may not exceed (in any one month) 25 percent of that month's total benefit payment which would have been due but for the offset. [DOL Reg. § 2530.203-3(b)(3)]

### Q 9:51 May a plan require an employee to notify the plan of employment?

Yes. A plan may require an employee to notify the plan of any employment that may cause benefits to be suspended. A plan may request from an employee access to reasonable information for the purpose of verifying such employment. Furthermore, a plan may provide that an employee must, as a condition to receiving future benefit payments, either certify that he or she is unemployed or provide factual information sufficient to establish that any employment does not constitute service that would cause benefits to be suspended. Once an employee has furnished the required certification or information, the plan must forward, at the next regularly scheduled time for payment of benefits, all payments that had been withheld. [DOL Reg. § 2530.203-3(b)(5)]

### Q 9:52 Should a plan have a procedure for helping retirees determine what constitutes employment that would cause their benefits to be suspended?

Yes. If a plan provides for suspension of benefits, the plan must adopt a procedure to inform employees of how they may request a determination of whether specific contemplated employment will cause a suspension of benefits. The explanation must be provided by the plan administrator in a reasonable amount of time. Requests for status determinations may be considered in accordance with the claims procedure adopted by the plan pursuant to ERISA Section 503 and applicable regulations. [DOL Reg. § 2530.203-3(b)(6)]

### Q 9:53 If a retiree has not reported employment that would cause his or her benefits to be suspended, can the plan presume the employment and suspend payments?

Yes, provided the plan adopted employment verification requirements and complies with the suspension of benefits notice requirements. If the plan fiduciaries become aware of a retiree employed in work that would cause his or her benefits to be suspended and the retiree has not complied with the plan's reporting requirements with regard to that employment, the plan fiduciaries may, unless it is unreasonable under the circumstances to do so, act on the basis of a rebut table presumption that the retiree had worked a period exceeding the plan's minimum number of hours for that month. [DOL Reg. § 2530.203-3(b)(7)]

### Q 9:54 How is the accrued benefit determined when the plan opts to provide the greater of the additional accruals or the actuarial equivalent of the normal retirement benefit?

When the plan opts to provide benefits under this method, there is no need to provide the employee with a suspension of benefits notice. The plan is, in effect, accumulating the unpaid benefit and providing it to the employee upon the actual retirement date. If the withheld payments are less than the accrued benefit determined with additional accruals, the larger accrued benefit is paid upon actual retirement.

**Example 1.** Brenden, an employee of the Warrior Helmet Company, has a pension plan that provides a benefit at retirement age and each year thereafter that will be actuarially increased for delayed retirement. The plan will provide Brenden with a benefit of $20 per month for each year of credited service. Upon reaching his normal retirement age, Brenden has 30 years of credited service for a benefit of $600 per month ($20 × 30). The plan will provide at least $620 per month after Brenden completes 31 years of credited service ($20 × 31); however, the actuarial equivalent of the age 65 benefit of $600 per month is $672 of monthly benefit. Since that amount is greater than the $620 per month of benefit when considering 31 years of credited service at age 66, the plan will pay Brenden $672 per month at age 66 should he elect to retire at that time. [Prop. Treas. Reg. § 1.411(b)-2(b)(4)(iv), Ex. 2]

**Example 2.** Brenden's plan provides a benefit equal to 2 percent of the highest three-year average compensation for each year of service. Brenden's normal retirement benefit would be equal to the greater of his normal retirement benefit (adjusted actuarially under the plan from the benefit to which he was entitled at the close of the prior plan year) determined at the close of the plan year and the normal retirement benefit determined at the close of the plan year by taking into account his years of credited service and benefit accruals after attaining normal retirement age. The following table tracks the accrued benefit for Brenden from age 65 (normal retirement) to age 70 (actual retirement).

| *A* | *B* | *C* | *D* | *E* | *F* |
|---|---|---|---|---|---|
| *Age* | *Credited Service* | *3-Year Average Compensation* | *Normal Benefit with Additional Accrual* | *Increase of Column F Benefit Prior Year* | *Accrued Benefit End of Year* |
| 65 | 10 | $20,000 | $ 4,000 | N/A | $ 4,000 |
| 66 | 11 | $21,000 | $ 4,620 | $ 4,482 | $ 4,620 |
| 67 | 12 | $29,000 | $ 6,960 | $ 5,192 | $ 6,960 |
| 68 | 13 | $30,000 | $ 7,800 | $ 7,848 | $ 7,848 |
| 69 | 14 | $33,000 | $ 9,240 | $ 8,880 | $ 9,240 |
| 70 | 15 | $35,000 | $10,500 | $10,494 | $10,500 |

The benefit in column F is the benefit payable at each age and is the benefit to which the actuarial increase for the next year applies. For example, $5,192 in column E is the $4,620 benefit at age 66 increased actuarially for one year delayed retirement. [Prop. Treas. Reg. § 1.411(b)-2(b)(4)(iv), Ex. 5]

**Q 9:55    How is the accrued benefit determined when the plan opts to provide additional accruals offset by any benefits paid?**

In such a case, a plan would commence payment of the retirement benefits due at the plan's normal retirement age. At the time the participant actually retires, the plan would determine the additional accrued benefit after normal retirement and offset that amount by the actuarial equivalent benefit paid since the normal retirement date. The resulting amount, if any, would be added to the benefit currently being paid to the participant.

A plan using such an option would not be required to issue a notice of suspended benefits, since payments would actually commence even though the participant had yet to actually retire.

**Example 1.** Brenden, an employee of the Warrior Helmet Company, has a pension plan that provides benefit payments at retirement age even though he continues to work for the company beyond that date. The plan will provide Brenden with a benefit of $20 per month for each year of credited service. Upon reaching his normal retirement age, Brenden has 30 years of credited service for a benefit of $600 per month ($20 × 30). When Brenden actually retires at age 67, he has received 24 monthly benefit payments of $600. The total monthly benefit payments of $14,400 have an actuarial value at age 67 of $15,839 (reflecting interest and mortality), which produces a monthly benefit payment of $156 commencing at age 67. The benefit accrual for the two years of credited service Brenden completed after attaining normal retirement age is $40 per month ($20 × 2 years). Because the actuarial value (determined as a monthly benefit of $156) of the benefit payments made during the two years of credited service after his normal retirement age exceeds the benefit accrual ($20 × 2 years = $40), the plan is not required to accrue benefits on his behalf for the first and second year of credited service he completed after attaining normal retirement age. Hence, the plan is not required to increase his current monthly benefit payment of $600. [Prop. Treas. Reg. § 1.411(b)-2(b)(4)(iv), Ex. 3]

**Example 2.** Suppose Brenden's plan provides a benefit equal to 2 percent of the highest three-year average compensation for each year of service. Brenden has elected to continue in the full-time service of his employer. Upon his attainment of age 70, the plan commences benefit payments. The annual benefit paid to Brenden in the first plan year is $10,500 ($35,000 × .02 × 15 years). In determining the annual benefit payable to him in each subsequent plan year, the plan offsets the value of benefit distributions made to the participant by the close of the prior plan year against benefit accruals in plan years during which such distributions were made. Accordingly, for each subsequent plan year, Brenden is entitled to receive benefit payments based on his benefit (at the close of the prior plan year) determined under the plan formula by taking into account all of his years of credited service, reduced (but not below $10,500) by the value of total benefit distributions made to him by the close of the prior plan year. The following table illustrates the recalculation of Brenden's retirement benefit payable in each year following the year in which payments began.

| A | B | C | D | E | F | G | H |
|---|---|---|---|---|---|---|---|
| | | | | | | Excess of Increase | |
| | | | | | | Accrued | |
| | | | | | Actuarial | Benefits | |
| | | | Normal | | Equivalent | over | |
| | | | Benefit | | of | | Accrued |
| | Credited | 3-Year | with | Increase | Payments | Payments | Benefit |
| | Paid | Average | Additional | Accrued | Made to | Made to | End of |
| Years | Service | Compensation | Accrual | Benefit | Date | Date | Year |
| N/A | 15 | $35,000 | $10,500 | $      0 | $      0 | $      0 | $10,500 |
| 1 | 16 | $35,000 | $11,200 | $   700 | $ 1,472 | $      0 | $10,500 |
| 2 | 17 | $45,000 | $15,300 | $ 4,800 | $ 3,209 | $ 1,591 | $12,091 |
| 3 | 18 | $50,000 | $18,000 | $ 7,500 | $ 5,510 | $ 1,990 | $12,490 |

For the first two full years Brenden receives a benefit of $10,500. By the beginning of the third year his payment is increased to $12,091, while in the beginning of the fourth year his payment increases to $12,490. [Prop. Treas. Reg. § 1.411(b)-2(b)(4)(iv), Ex. 6]

# Chapter 10

# Safe Harbor Benefit Formulas

Defined benefit plans can have many different types of benefit formulas. However, the Treasury regulations provide for certain safe harbor plan designs that when used require no, or minimal, specific discrimination tests. Discrimination testing in defined benefit plans is complex and has many variables. This chapter discusses the features of safe harbor plan benefit formulas. The next chapter, Advanced Plan Design, provides more examples and expands on the options available.

## Definitions

### Q 10:1  Are defined benefit plans subject to discrimination rules?

Yes, defined benefit plans are subject to discrimination testing under Internal Revenue Code (Code) Section 401(a)(4) and (5). In general, the provisions of Code Section 401(a)(4) state that to remain qualified a plan cannot discriminate in providing benefits or contributions in favor of highly compensated employees (HCEs). A plan must satisfy the discrimination rules in both form and in operation.

Plans are tested for discrimination between two groups of an employer's employees: HCEs and non-highly compensated employees (NHCEs). The criteria for assigning employees to one group or the other are dictated by Code Section 414(q) and are a critical aspect of the discrimination testing process.

### Q 10:2  On what criteria are defined benefit plans tested for discrimination?

First, the benefits under the plan must be nondiscriminatory in amount. The primary tests for testing defined benefit plans with regard to benefit amounts are found in Treasury Regulations Section 1.401(a)(4)-3. Alternatively, a defined benefit plan can be tested on the basis of the amount of contributions under Treasury Regulations Section 1.401(a)(4)-8(c). Second, a plan must be nondiscriminatory in coverage. That is, all benefits, rights, and features must be made available on a nondiscriminatory basis. [Treas. Reg. § 1.401(a)(4)-4] Third, the timing of plan amendments must not have the effect of discriminating in favor of HCEs. [Treas. Reg. § 1.401(a)(4)-5]

### Q 10:3  What is the difference between discrimination in benefits and discrimination in coverage?

Discrimination in coverage addresses the provisions for eligibility for receiving a benefit, whereas discrimination in benefits addresses the amount of benefits received by participants. Coverage requirements are defined in Code Sections 410 and 401(a). For example, if an employer excluded all part-time employees regardless of the number of hours worked, there would be discrimination in coverage. If a plan provided a benefit of $1 per year of service for NHCEs and 100 percent of compensation for HCEs, there would most likely be discrimination in the amount of benefits (subject to the tests provided under Code Section 401(a)(4)).

### Q 10:4  What is meant by the requirement that a plan cannot discriminate with regard to benefits, rights, and features?

First, it is helpful to know what is included in the term *benefits, rights, and features*. In general, all optional forms of benefit, ancillary benefits (such as life insurance), features such as plan loans, and rights such as the right to make voluntary after-tax contributions are included. For a benefit, right, or feature to be nondiscriminatory, it must be currently available. Current availability is demonstrated by satisfying the coverage requirements of Code Section 410(b). In addition, the benefit, right, or feature must be effectively available on a nondiscriminatory basis. This last requirement is a demographics test that can be best explained through an illustration.

**Example.** Acme Cleaners, Inc., sponsors a defined benefit plan with a normal retirement age of 65 and an early retirement benefit available at age 55 for any participant with 30 years of service. The owners of Acme Cleaners, Inc., both started the business at age 25, so they will have 30 years of service at age 55. They have 10 employees. Eight of the employees were hired after they attained age 25. Two of the employees were hired before age 25. Because the group that can benefit from the early retirement option includes only HCEs, this benefit feature is in effect discriminatory. If the number of employees hired before age 25 was eight instead of two, the feature would not be discriminatory.

There are many conditions and rules that apply in determining whether a plan discriminates with regard to benefits, rights, and features. The regulations should be reviewed in detail. [Treas. Reg. § 1.401(a)(4)-4] See also chapter 11 for further discussion.

### Q 10:5   When is a participant considered to benefit under a plan?

Though the answer seems obvious, there are several items that must be considered. Under Treasury Regulations Section 1.410(b)-3, an employee benefits under a plan when the employee meets any of the following criteria:

- The employee receives an allocation under a defined contribution plan other than a 401(k) or 401(m) plan for more than a *de minimis* amount.
- The employee is eligible for making a salary deferral under a 401(k) or 401(m) plan.
- The employee has an increase in his or her accrued benefit in a defined benefit plan.

Additionally, an employee is treated as benefiting under a plan if the employee would have benefited but for meeting any of the following criteria:

- The employee's accrued benefit exceeds a plan limit (on service, benefit, or compensation).
- The employee's prior accrued benefit is greater than the accrued benefit otherwise determined.
- A floor-offset arrangement eliminates the increase in the employee's accrued benefit.
- The theoretical reserve is larger than the actuarial present value of the employee's retirement benefit in a target benefit safe harbor.
- The actuarial increase for delayed retirement is larger than the benefit that would otherwise have accrued to the employee.

If they are ignored in the Code Section 401(a)(4) testing, a defined benefit plan can ignore the effects of the Code Section 415 limit when determining whether an accrued benefit has increased. [Treas. Reg. § 1.410(b)-3(a)(2)(ii)]

### Q 10:6   Who is considered an HCE?

To distinguish which active employees are highly compensated and which are not, two time periods, called determination periods, must be examined. The first period is the current year, also called the determination year. The second period is the look-back year, or the preceding year. An employee who satisfies the criteria of either of these determination periods is considered an HCE for the determination year.

*Determination year.* For the determination (current) year period, an employee is a highly compensated active employee only if, at any time during the determination year, the employee is a 5 percent owner (see Q 10:7).

*Look-back year.* For the look-back (preceding) year period, a highly compensated active employee is an employee who performs service for the employer during the determination year, and who during the look-back year meets either of the following two criteria:

1. The employee was a 5 percent owner at any time (see Q 10:7); or

2. The employee received compensation from the employer of more than $80,000 ($100,000 for 2006 and 2007, as indexed) and is part of the top-paid group (see Q 10:8), provided the employer elects to use the top-paid group.

**Note.** The compensation and amount used are for the preceding year. Therefore, the $100,000 will be first used for the 2007 plan year to look back at the compensation earned in the 2006 plan year. [I.R.C. § 414(q)(1)]

The process for identifying the HCE group can be summarized in three steps:

*Step 1.* Identify all employees categorized as highly compensated in accordance with the determination-year period criteria.

*Step 2.* Identify all employees categorized as highly compensated in accordance with the look-back year period criteria.

*Step 3.* Add the preceding two groups together to obtain the complete highly compensated active employee group.

### Q 10:7   What is a *5 percent owner?*

A *5 percent owner* is a person who owns, directly or indirectly at any time during the determination year or the look-back year, more than 5 percent of the shares of stock of a corporation. If the employer is not a corporation, ownership is determined based on profit or capital interest in the employer. Family attribution applies in determining 5 percent ownership. Therefore, a person is considered to own the shares of stock or the profit or capital interests owned by his or her children, spouse, grandchildren, and parents. [Temp. Treas. Reg. § 1.414(q)-1T, Q&A 8]

### Q 10:8   What is the *top-paid group?*

The *top-paid group* is the group of employees who fall within the top 20 percent of all active employees of the employer when the employees are ranked on the basis of compensation received from the employer for the look-back year. Employees who perform no services are not included. An employer can elect to use this 20 percent computation, and its election can be advantageous if the employer has a high percentage of employees earning more than $80,000 ($100,000 for 2006 and 2007, as indexed). As a result of making this election, some employees earning more than this limit can be considered non-highly compensated. Having such employees classified as non-highly compensated can make it easier to satisfy the nondiscrimination tests. [Temp. Treas. Reg. § 1.414 (q)-1T, Q&A 9]

### Example

| Participant | Compensation | Ownership %<br>2000 and<br>2001 | 2002 |
|---|---|---|---|
| President | $120,000 | 75% | 65% |
| Senior Vice President | $ 90,000 | 25% | 25% |
| Office Manager | $ 85,000 | 0% | 10% |
| Salesperson A | $100,000 | 0% | 0% |
| Salesperson B | $ 65,000 | 0% | 0% |
| Comptroller | $ 65,000 | 0% | 0% |
| Secretary C | $ 30,000 | 0% | 0% |
| Secretary D | $ 30,000 | 0% | 0% |

*For 2001.* The employer elects to use the top-paid group.

President and Senior Vice President are HCEs because of their ownership interest. There are four people earning in excess of $80,000; however, only two people need to be included in the top-paid group (20% × 8 = 1.6, which is rounded up to 2). President and Senior Vice President fall within the top-paid group. There are only two HCEs for 2001.

*For 2002.* The employer does not elect to use the top-paid group.

There are three HCEs by ownership: President, Senior Vice President, and Office Manager. In addition, Salesperson A is considered an HCE because of the election not to use the top-paid group.

Not all employees have to be counted when determining the top-paid group. At the option of the employer, the following groups of employees can be excluded:

- Employees with less than six months of service at the end of the year;
- Employees who normally work fewer than 17½ hours a week during the year;
- Employees who normally work six months or less during the year;
- Employees who have not attained age 21 by the end of the year;
- Certain nonresident aliens; and
- Union employees if the plan covers only nonunion people and the union makes up 90 percent of the employer's workforce.

There is a significantly more complicated determination for years before 1997.

### Q 10:9 How is the determination of the top-paid group affected if an employee is classified as an HCE on more than one basis?

Employees can be assigned HCE status by virtue of ownership or compensation. An employee can be classified as an HCE because he or she is a 5 percent owner in the determination year or was a 5 percent owner in the look-back year (see Qs 10:6 and 10:7). Additionally, an employee can be classified as an HCE because he or she is in the top-paid group of the look-back year as determined by compensation (see Qs 10:6 and 10:8). Occasionally, an employee falls within both categories. If an employee is both a 5 percent owner in either the current year or the look-back year and is in the top-paid group for the look-back year, he or she will be included in the determination of the top-paid group for the determination year. [Temp. Treas. Reg. § 1.414(q)-1T, Q&A 3(d)] This means that the employee can be counted twice. That is, the employee will be an HCE by virtue of being a 5 percent owner and will be counted as one of the top-paid group. This has the effect of reducing the total number of HCEs by one. (See the three-step process for determining the total number of HCEs in Q 10:6.)

> **Example.** Paul is a 10 percent owner of Pensions, Inc., Paul's compensation for the look-back year was $90,000, and he was in the top-paid group. If there were ten people in the group of employees for the look-back year, the top-paid group for the determination year consists of two people (10 employees × 20%). Suppose employees Mary and Sherry earned $90,000 and $85,000, respectively, in the look-back year. The top-paid group for the determination year includes Paul ($90,000) and Mary ($90,000). Sherry is not an HCE.

### Q 10:10   Who is considered a *non-highly compensated employee*?

Any employee who is not an HCE is considered a *non-highly compensated employee,* or NHCE.

### Q 10:11   Who is a *highly compensated former employee*?

A *highly compensated former employee* is any former employee who separated from service while being classified as an HCE or any employee who was a highly compensated active employee for any determination year on or after the HCE's 55th birthday. [Temp. Treas. Reg. § 1.414(q)-1T, Q&A 4]

### Q 10:12   What is and who is considered a *nonexcludable employee*?

A *nonexcludable employee* is an employee who is not excluded from discrimination testing. A nonexcludable employee can be either an HCE or an NHCE.

The following employees may be excluded for the following reasons:

- Employees who do not meet the minimum age and service rules under Code Section 410(a);
- Employees who fail all of the plan's age and service requirements;
- Certain nonresident aliens;
- Collectively bargained employees;
- Terminated employees if they do not benefit under the plan and the participant was eligible to participate in the plan; if the plan has a minimum

period of service for a participant to accrue a benefit and the participant did not meet the minimum period of service; or if the employee terminates employment with fewer than 500 hours of service during the plan year; and

- Generally, all former employees not currently benefiting under the plan.

[Treas. Reg. § 1.410(b)-6]

### Q 10:13   Who is considered an *employee* or a *former employee*?

An *employee* is an individual who performs services for the employer and who is a common-law employee of the employer, a self-employed individual (see chapter 5), or a leased employee who is treated as an employee of the employer recipient (see chapter 6). A *former employee* is an individual who was, but has ceased to be, an employee of the employer. An employee who has separated from service is both an employee and a former employee in the year of separation. An individual is considered an employee if the individual worked more than 500 hours during the plan year or the plan defined the individual as an employee.

## Discrimination Tests

### Safe Harbor Methods

### Q 10:14   What are the safe harbor discrimination methods?

The safe harbor methods for meeting the requirements of discrimination testing are found in Treasury Regulations Section 1.401(a)(4)-3(b). A *safe harbor method* is a formula used for determining plan benefits that, by design, is not discriminatory. There are three design-based safe harbor methods, one non-design-based safe harbor method, and one safe harbor for insurance contract plans.

### Q 10:15   What basic provisions must a plan contain to use the design-based safe harbor methods?

To use the design-based safe harbor methods, a plan must meet the following requirements:

1. *Uniform normal retirement benefit.* The plan's benefit formula must provide all employees with an annual benefit payable in the same form beginning at the same uniform normal retirement age (see Q 11:10).
2. *Uniform post-normal retirement benefit.* The plan must continue to credit service for benefit purposes after a participant has attained normal retirement age.
3. *Uniform subsidies.* Any subsidized optional form of benefit must be available to all employees.

4. *No employee contributions.* The plan must not be a contributory defined benefit plan.

5. *Period of accrual.* Each employee's benefit must be accrued over the same years of service that are taken into account in applying the benefit formula under the plan to that employee.

6. *Average annual compensation.* The plan must determine benefits either as a dollar amount unrelated to an employee's compensation or as a percentage of each employee's average annual compensation (see Q 10:32).

[Treas. Reg. § 1.401(a)(4)-3(b)]

### Q 10:16   What features do not disqualify a plan from using the safe harbors?

A plan can have any of the following features and continue to use the safe harbors:

1. A plan can have one or more entry dates.

2. A plan can provide that a participant work at least 1,000 hours to accrue a benefit, with exceptions allowed for retirement, death, and disability.

3. A plan can have provisions that limit the number of years of service used in determining plan benefits.

4. A plan can provide for maximum benefit limitations as a percentage of compensation or a flat dollar amount.

5. A plan can provide for lower benefits to one or more HCEs than would otherwise be provided to a participant in the plan.

6. The plan can provide that a participant's benefit under the plan is the greater of the benefits determined under two or more formulas or is the sum of benefits determined under two or more formulas as long as the benefit formulas are safe harbor formulas.

7. A plan can provide top-heavy minimum benefits solely to all non-key employees eligible to receive the top-heavy minimum benefits in top-heavy years. If the plan only provides top-heavy minimum benefits to non-key employees and the plan would not meet the coverage test under Code Section 410(b) without the top-heavy minimum benefits, then a safe harbor formula cannot be used.

8. The provisions listed above can be used more than once. For example, a participant's benefit can be determined based on the greater of two benefits and one of those benefits can be the sum of two other benefits.

[Treas. Reg. § 1.401(a)(4)-3(b)(6)]

### Q 10:17   What is the *first safe harbor*?

The *first safe harbor* is for unit credit plans and is found in Treasury Regulations Section 1.401(a)(4)-3(b)(3). A plan satisfies the requirements of this safe harbor if the plan satisfies the 133⅓ percent rule of Code Section 411(b)(1)(B) (see chapter 9). In addition, each employee's accrued benefit under the plan as of any plan year must be determined by applying the plan's benefit formula to the employee's years of service (see Q 11:8) and (if applicable) average annual compensation (see Q 10:32), both determined as of that plan year.

**Example.** Plan A provides that the accrued benefit for each participant as of any plan year is equal to the participant's average compensation multiplied by a percentage that depends on the participant's years of service as follows:

- 2 percent for each of the first 10 years; plus
- 1.5 percent for each of the next 10 years; plus
- 2 percent for each additional year of service more than 20.

Plan *A* passes the first safe harbor test because the benefits are computed in a nondiscriminatory manner; that is, the benefits in the 21st year (2 percent) are not more than 133⅓ percent of the benefits in the 20th year (1.5 percent), because 2 percent is exactly 133⅓ percent of 1.5 percent (2% ÷ 1.5%).

### Q 10:18   What is the *second safe harbor*?

The *second safe harbor* is for plans using a fractional accrual method to determine accrued benefits. [Treas. Reg. § 1.401(a)(4)-3(b)(4)(i)(C)(1)] A plan satisfies the rules of this safe harbor if it meets both of the following requirements:

1. The plan determines accrued benefits according to the fractional accrual rules under Code Section 411(b)(1)(C), which specify that the accrued benefit computed under a fractional accrual method cannot be less than a fraction of the normal retirement benefit that a participant would be entitled to under the plan if the benefit were calculated as if the participant continued to earn the same rate of compensation as that on which his or her normal retirement benefit is computed under the plan. The numerator of the fraction is the participant's total years of participation in the plan, and the denominator of the fraction is the total years of participation the participant would have up to normal retirement age if the participant continued to work until that time. If the plan provides for benefits based on average compensation in excess of 10 years (a career-average-pay plan), the fractional accrual rules are not satisfied. [I.R.C. § 411(b)(1)(C); Treas. Reg. § 1.411(b)-1(b)(3)(ii)(A)]

2. It must be impossible under the plan for any employee to accrue a portion of the normal retirement benefit that is more than one-third larger than the equivalent portion of the same benefit accrued in that or any other plan year by any other employee. When performing this test, actual and potential employees with any amount of service at normal retirement age must be taken into account (other than employees with more than 33 years of service at normal retirement age). If a plan is a Code Section 401(l) plan, the rate of accrual is either the excess benefit percentage or the gross benefit percentage. [Treas. Reg. § 1.401(a)(4)-3(b)(4)(i)(C)(1)]

**Example.** Plan *A* has a normal retirement benefit of 4 percent of average compensation multiplied by each year of service up to 10 years and 3 percent of average compensation multiplied by years of service in excess of 10 years but not in excess of 30 years. The accrued benefit of the participant is computed by multiplying the participant's projected normal retirement benefit by a fraction, the numerator of which is the employee's years of service as of the plan year and the denominator of which is the employee's projected years of service as of the normal retirement age. An employee with the maximum number of years of credited service, 30, would have a benefit equal to 100 percent of his or her average annual compensation $((4\% \times 10) + (3\% \times 20))$.

The greatest benefit that a participant can accrue in any year would be 4 percent for participants with no more than 10 years of service. Among employees who have 33 or fewer years of projected service at normal retirement age but more than 10 years of service, the lowest benefit that a participant can accrue is 3.33 percent $(100\% \div 33)$. This plan passes the test, because 4 percent is not more than one-third larger than 3.33 percent $(4\% \div 3.33\% = 1.201\%)$.

### Q 10:19    What is the *third safe harbor*?

Under the *third safe harbor*, a plan must meet the same fractional accrual rules as a plan must meet under the second safe harbor (see Q 10:18). In addition, the normal retirement benefit under the plan must be a flat benefit and the plan must require a minimum of 25 years of service at normal retirement age for a participant to receive an unreduced flat benefit, determined without regard to the maximum benefits under Code Section 415. [Treas. Reg. § 1.401(a)(4)-3(b) (4)(i)(C)(2)]

**Example 1.** Plan Sponsor *A* wants to provide a 100 percent of pay benefit to plan participants and use the third safe harbor. Participant Pat is 55 years old and earns $160,000 per year. The normal retirement age is 65, so Pat will only have 10 years of participation. To meet the safe harbor and to provide Pat with a benefit of 100 percent of pay when he reaches normal retirement age, the plan's formula must be 250 percent of average annual compensation reduced by $\frac{1}{25}$ for each year of service less than 25 $(250\% \times 10 \times \frac{1}{25} = 100\%)$. The net effect of this formula is an acceleration of benefit accruals for younger participants because the reduction for years of service less than 25 will have no effect on their benefit percentage because they have in excess of 25 years of service until attainment of the plan's normal retirement age. Participant Sam is 40 years old and therefore the reduction for years of service less than 25 has no effect on his benefit. To determine Sam's accrued benefit, his average annual compensation is multiplied by 250 percent. This benefit is accrued fractionally over Sam's remaining years of participation (with his accrued benefit each year appropriately limited by the requirements of Code Section 415).

**Example 2.** Plan *B* has a projected normal retirement benefit of 50 percent of average compensation reduced by $\frac{1}{30}$ for each year of service less than 30.

This plan passes the third safe harbor test because the plan provides a flat benefit of 50 percent of average compensation and requires more than 25 years of service for a full benefit.

### Q 10:20 Why is the fourth safe harbor called a non-design-based safe harbor and what does that mean?

The fourth safe harbor must pass a simplified accrual rate test each year; therefore, it is not a design-based safe harbor. If a plan satisfies the requirements for the third safe harbor (see Q 10:19) except that the minimum number of years of service required for a participant to receive the unreduced flat benefit is not at least 25 years, the plan must meet an average benefit test too. If the plan also passes the average benefit test, it is considered a safe harbor. To pass the average benefit test, the average of the normal accrual rates (see chapter 11) for all NHCEs must be at least 70 percent of the average of the normal accrual rates for all the HCEs. The averages are determined using all nonexcludable employees (see Q 10:12) even if they are not participating in the plan or benefiting under the plan. Any other benefits or contributions from other plans are excluded from computation of the averages. [Treas. Reg. § 1.401(a)(4)-3(b)(4)(i)(C)(3)]

> **Example 1.** Plan *B* has a formula of 50 percent of average compensation reduced for each year of service less than 20. Assume further that the average of the normal accrual rates for the NHCEs is 2.5 percent and the average of the normal accrual rates for the HCEs is 3.5 percent. This plan satisfies the requirement for a non-design-based safe harbor, because 70 percent of 3.5 percent is less than 2.5 percent (3.5% × 0.70 = 2.45%).

> **Example 2.** The Semi-Safe Harbor, Inc., defined benefit plan provides a formula of 125 percent of average annual compensation reduced by 5 percent for each year of service less than 25 that a participant has at normal retirement age. If the 70 percent test is not met, limiting the amount of selected benefits payable to HCEs would lower the average of the normal accrual rates for the HCEs. Alternatively, a minimum benefit made payable to a group of NHCEs would raise the average of the normal accrual rates for the NHCEs. A plan could provide for minimum benefits to participants who worked less than 1,000 hours, earned less than a selected compensation level, and so forth. Such additional benefits might cost little and yet be meaningful benefits to lower-compensated employees.

### Q 10:21 What is the safe harbor for insurance contract plans (the fifth safe harbor)?

Insurance contract plans, or fully insured plans, must meet the following requirements to satisfy the fifth safe harbor:

1. The accrued benefit must be equal to the cash value of the insurance contracts. [I.R.C. § 411(b)(1)(F)]

2. The plan must be funded exclusively by the purchase of individual insurance contracts and such contracts must provide for level annual premium

payments extending no later than the retirement age of the participant and beginning no earlier than when the individual becomes a participant in the plan; the benefits provided by the plan are equal to the benefits provided under each contract, all premiums must be timely paid, and there must be no policy loans outstanding. [I.R.C. § 412(i); under the PPA, this section has been renumbered to § 412(e)(3)]

3. The plan formula must meet the requirements of the third safe harbor for plans using the fractional accrual rules (see Q 10:19). [Treas. Reg. § 1.401(a)(4)-3(b)(5)(vi)]

4. Experience gains or losses must be used to reduce premiums.

5. The benefits must be funded through the same series of contracts.

6. If the benefits provided take into account permitted disparity, the rules of permitted disparity under Treasury Regulations Section 1.401(l)-3 must be met.

[Treas. Reg. § 1.401(a)(4)-3(b)(5)]

### Q 10:22  What happens if a plan does not satisfy any of the five safe harbors?

If a plan does not satisfy any of the safe harbors, it must satisfy the general test for nondiscrimination (see chapter 11).

### Q 10:23  How do the safe harbor methods differ from the general test?

The safe harbor methods, with the exception of the fourth safe harbor (see Q 10:20), are design-based methods. As long as the plan is structured (i.e., the plan document is written) according to the safe harbor, and complies with the terms of the plan in operation, no testing is necessary.

The general test is very flexible and provides for creative plan design. If the plan does not satisfy one of the safe harbors, then the general test must be performed each year to measure compliance with the nondiscrimination rules. Plan benefits for NHCEs must be increased if the plan fails the test after benefits have accrued. Plan provisions must be reviewed each year when performing the test. Retroactive plan amendments made after the end of the plan year, unless crafted carefully, may apply automatically to two plan years—the year of correction and the current plan year.

### Q 10:24  When is a safe harbor method most appropriate?

If the results of a safe harbor method either meet or come close to the objectives of the plan sponsor, the safe harbor method should be used over the more complicated and time-consuming general test. This can require a trial-and-error determination until the administrator understands the effect each type of plan design has on costs and benefits with different employee groups.

## Q 10:25  What is the two-step unit credit benefit formula?

This plan design can often be the most advantageous safe harbor formula for an older key employee with younger employees. To determine if the safe harbor method is advantageous, use the parameters of the targeted employee group and work backward. This benefit formula uses the fractional accrual rules under the second safe harbor method for unit credit plans.

The first step is to determine the maximum benefit accrual rate desired for the key employee. As required by the rules of the safe harbor for fractional accruals, divide this rate by 133⅓ percent to get the lowest allowable accrual rate. Next, multiply the lowest allowable accrual rate by 33.

Remove the desired benefit of the key employee to get the increase in benefit for the other employees. Then subtract the number of total years of service that the preferred employee will have at retirement from 33 to obtain the additional years of benefit accruals for the other employees. Finally, divide the required increase in benefits during the additional years by the number of additional years. The result will be the lowest design-based accrual rate for employees other than the key employee.

**Example.** Car Sales, Inc., has a key employee with 11 years of service to normal retirement and wants a benefit of 44 percent of average annual compensation. The formula would be determined as follows:

| | | | |
|---|---|---|---|
| Accrual rate for key employee | 44% ÷ 11 yrs | = | 4% |
| 133% rule | 4% ÷ 133% | = | 3% |
| Maximum benefit | 3% × 33 yrs | = | 99% |
| Remaining benefit | 99% − 44% | = | 55% |
| 33 years less key employee years of service | 33 yrs − 11 yrs | = | 22 yrs |
| Lowest accrual rate | 55% ÷ 22 yrs | = | 2.5% |

The formula, therefore, is 4 percent for the first 11 years of service plus 2.5 percent for the next 22 years of service times average annual compensation. The maximum benefit for a participant with 33 years of service would be 99 percent of average annual compensation, requiring benefit accruals of 3 percent of average annual compensation per year of service.

## Permitted Disparity

## Q 10:26  What is *permitted disparity*?

*Permitted disparity* is the allowable use of supplementing or offsetting Social Security benefits in a pension plan. The Treasury regulations under Code Section 401(l) permit disparate rates of benefit accruals if certain requirements are met, and it prescribes methods for computing such rates. Additional rules under Code Section 401(a)(5) allow for other safe harbor methods of computing disparate rates of benefit accruals.

Each plan that provides for permitted disparity has a plan formula that either (1) provides for benefits above the integration level (see Q 10:27) that are greater than benefits below that level (see maximum excess allowances in Q 10:29), or (2) provides for benefits based on total average annual compensation that are offset, or reduced, by benefits based on average annual compensation up to an offset level (see Q 10:28) (see also maximum offset allowance in Q 10:30).

Disparity in a benefit, right, or feature within a plan must be provided on a uniform basis. For plans using the maximum excess amount, any benefits, rights, or features of a plan provided to average annual compensation above the integration level must also be provided to average annual compensation below the integration level. Similarly, for plans using the maximum offset amounts, benefits, rights, and features provided to gross benefits must be provided on the same terms as to net benefits after the offset. If the benefits, rights, or features provided to excess or gross benefits are provided on different terms than to the base or net benefits, the value of the benefits, rights, or features provided must be inherently equal. [Treas. Reg. § 1.401(l)-3(f)]

**Example.** Wacky Widgets sponsors a defined benefit plan that uses a formula of 0.75 percent of average annual compensation, plus 0.65 percent of average annual compensation in excess of $10,000, multiplied by the number of years of service up to 35 years. The plan provides a death benefit of 100 times the projected benefit computed on the maximum excess amount. The death benefit is a benefit, right, or feature that does not meet the uniformity requirements because it is provided only to those participants with compensation above the integration level of $10,000. Therefore, this plan would not be considered a Code Section 401(l) qualified plan.

### Q 10:27   What is an *integration level*?

*Integration level* means the dollar amount specified in an excess plan at or below which the rate of benefits up to the specified dollar amount is less than the rate of benefits above the specified dollar amount. [Treas. Reg. § 1.401(l)-1(c)(20)]

### Q 10:28   What is an *offset level*?

*Offset level* means the dollar limit specified in the plan of which each employee's final average compensation is taken into account in determining the offset under an offset plan. [Treas. Reg. § 1.401(l)-1(c)(23)]

### Q 10:29   What is the *maximum excess allowance*?

The *maximum excess allowance* is the maximum excess benefit percentage that can be used in determining benefits with respect to a participant's average annual compensation above the plan's integration level. This is generally equal to the lesser of 0.75 percent or the base benefit percentage. (See Q 10:30 for when this maximum percentage must be adjusted.)

In a plan using permitted disparity based on the maximum excess allowance, the benefit is made up of two parts. The first portion is calculated using the *base benefit percentage*, which is the percentage of total average annual compensation that is to be multiplied by years of service. The second portion is calculated using the maximum excess allowance for any plan year.

**Example.** Waveriders, Inc.'s defined benefit plan uses the following formula to determine the benefits under the plan. The base benefit percentage of 1 percent is multiplied by average annual compensation, and the product is added to the product of the maximum excess allowance of 0.75 percent multiplied by average annual compensation in excess of the integration level. This formula meets the requirements of Treasury Regulations Section 1.401(l)-3.

If, instead, the base benefit percentage were 0.5 percent, the maximum excess allowance would be limited to 0.5 percent. [Treas. Reg. § 1.401(l)-3(b)(2)]

## Q 10:30   What is the *maximum offset allowance*?

The *maximum offset allowance* is the maximum percentage of the participant's final average compensation that can be used to reduce or offset a participant's benefit under an offset plan. This is generally equal to the lesser of 0.75 percent or half of the *gross benefit percentage* multiplied by a fraction, the numerator of which is the employee's annual compensation and the denominator of which is the employee's final average compensation up to the offset level. The gross benefit percentage means the rate at which benefits are determined under an offset plan (before application of the offset) with respect to a participant's average annual compensation (expressed as a percentage of average annual compensation).

In a plan using permitted disparity based on the maximum offset allowance, the benefit is made up of two parts. The first portion is the gross benefit, that is, the portion before any offset is applied. The second portion is the amount that is used to reduce, or offset, the gross benefit.

**Example.** Reg-reader Company sponsors a defined benefit plan that uses the following formula to determine benefits under the plan: gross benefit percentage of 2 percent multiplied by final average annual compensation, minus 0.75 percent multiplied by final average annual compensation up to the offset level, for each year up to 35 years of service. This plan satisfies the requirements of the regulations because the offset percentage of 0.75 percent does not exceed the lesser of 0.75 percent or 1 percent (half of the gross benefit percentage of 2 percent).

If, instead, the formula was gross benefit percentage of 1 percent of final average annual compensation, minus 0.75 percent of final average annual compensation up to the offset level for each year of service up to 35 years of service, the plan would not meet the requirements of this section of the regulations because the maximum offset allowance would exceed half of the gross benefit percentage (0.5 percent). [Treas. Reg. § 1.401(l)-3(b)(3)]

### Q 10:31   What is the purpose of the safe harbor plan designs for permitted disparity?

The safe harbor plan designs for permitted disparity allow for simple formulas using the maximum excess allowance or the maximum offset allowance, and using a life annuity form of benefit with no lump-sum options (see Qs 10:29 and 10:30) and normal retirement age of 65. No variations in definitions of compensation, offset or excess amount, or forms of benefits are allowed without adjustments to the excess or offset amounts. [Treas. Reg. § 1.401(l)-3(c)(2)]

## Covered Compensation

### Q 10:32   What is *covered compensation*?

*Covered compensation* is the average (without indexing) of the Social Security taxable wage bases in effect for each calendar year during the 35-year period ending with the last day of the calendar year in which an employee attains the Social Security retirement age (SSRA). A 35-year period is used regardless of the employee's date of birth. [Treas. Reg. § 1.401(l)-1(a)(7)]

To determine this average for a plan year before an employee's attainment of the SSRA, the current taxable wage base is used to project future taxable wage bases. Covered compensation for a participant who remains employed after attainment of his or her SSRA remains the same as it was when he or she attained the SSRA. For employees participating in the plan before the beginning of the 35-year period, covered compensation equals the taxable wage base in effect during such year.

Each year, the Social Security Administration adjusts (for the cost of living) the level of covered compensation used to determine Social Security benefits. The maximum amount used to compute Social Security benefits in any year is the Social Security taxable wage base for that year. Additionally, covered compensation changes each year because prior taxable wage bases are replaced by new taxable wage bases as each new group of employees attains SSRA.

### Q 10:33   What is the *covered compensation table* and must a plan change it annually?

A *covered compensation table* is a table that is developed by rounding the actual amounts of covered compensation for different years of birth. In lieu of using actual covered compensation, a plan may use a covered compensation table. [Treas. Reg. § 1.401(l)-1(a)(7)(ii)(A)]

Generally a plan must provide that an employee's covered compensation is automatically adjusted for each plan year; however, a plan may maintain a covered compensation table from an earlier year for up to five years. [Treas. Reg. § 1.401(l)-1(a)(7)(iii)]

## Q 10:34  Must a plan use covered compensation for its integration level or its offset level?

No. Several alternate amounts can be used. [Treas. Reg. § 1.401(l)-3(d)(3)] A plan can use (1) a single dollar amount, (2) a uniform percentage of the covered compensation amount, or (3) some intermediate amount.

If an alternative is used, the maximum excess or offset allowance must be adjusted. If the integration level or the offset level is each employee's covered compensation as of the plan year, no adjustments are required. If the plan specifies an integration level or an offset level that exceeds an employee's covered compensation level, the maximum excess or offset allowance must be reduced. For a plan that uses a single dollar amount as an integration or offset level, that amount cannot exceed the greater of $10,000 or half of the covered compensation of an individual who attains the SSRA in the calendar year in which the plan year begins.

If a plan specifies an integration level or an offset level that is a uniform percentage (in excess of 100 percent) of each employee's covered compensation, it must reduce the maximum excess or offset allowance (also known as the permitted disparity factor) to the following amounts:

**Table 10-1. Integration or offset level and its permitted disparity factor**

| *Integration or Offset Level* | *Permitted Disparity Factor* |
|---|---|
| 100% of covered compensation | 0.75% |
| 125% of covered compensation | 0.69% |
| 150% of covered compensation | 0.60% |
| 175% of covered compensation | 0.53% |
| 200% of covered compensation | 0.47% |
| The taxable wage base or final average compensation | 0.42% |

If the plan uses an integration or offset level that is between the percentages of covered compensation in the table, the permitted disparity factor applicable to the plan can be determined either by a straight-line interpolation between the permitted disparity factors in the table or by rounding the integration or offset level up to the next highest percentage of covered compensation in the table.

**Example 1.** Clocks, Inc., sponsors a defined benefit plan that uses the following plan formula: 1 percent of final average compensation, plus 0.69 percent of average compensation in excess of 120 percent of the covered compensation table.

The plan meets the requirements of Treasury Regulations Section 1.401(l)-3(d)(9)(iv) because the integration level is between 100 percent and 125 percent of the covered compensation level, and the maximum excess allowance is reduced according to the table above by rounding up to the next highest percentage of covered compensation.

Finally, for a plan that uses an intermediate amount different from the amounts indicated above, special tests are applied. Tests under Treasury Regulations Section 1.401(l)-3(d)(8) specify that the following two requirements must be met:

1. The average attained age of the NHCEs cannot be greater than the greater of age 50 or five plus the average attained age of the HCEs.

2. At least one of the following tests must be satisfied:

    a. *Minimum percentage test.* Fifty percent of the NHCEs in the plan must have average compensation at least equal to 120 percent of the integration level or offset level.

    b. *Ratio test.* The percentage of the non-highly compensated, nonexcludable employees who are in the plan and who have average annual compensation at least equal to 120 percent of the integration level or offset level is at least 70 percent of the percentage of the highly compensated, nonexcludable employees who are in the plan.

    c. *High dollar amount test.* The integration level or offset level exceeds 150 percent of the covered compensation of an individual who attains the SSRA in the calendar year in which the plan year begins.

    d. *Individual disparity reductions.* The offset plan uses an offset level of each employee's final average compensation and makes individual disparity reductions, pursuant to Table 10-1, for each employee whose covered compensation is less than the offset level.

For a plan that uses an intermediate amount as the integration level, the applicable reduction must be determined on either a plan-wide or individual basis. If a plan-wide reduction is used, the single dollar amount is compared to the covered compensation for an individual attaining the SSRA in the calendar year in which the plan year begins. If the reduction is made on an individual basis, the covered compensation for each individual is compared to the single dollar amount for the year and the permitted disparity factor is reduced for each participant as applicable.

**Example 2.** Waveriders Inc. sponsors a defined benefit plan that uses a single dollar integration level of $30,000 and a plan-wide reduction. Participant Pat has a covered compensation amount of $20,000. The maximum excess or offset allowance is reduced for the entire plan to 0.60 percent (see Table 10-1) because $30,000 is more than 125 percent of the covered compensation amount but not more than 150 percent of the covered compensation amount.

If the plan used individual reductions instead, participant Pat's maximum excess or offset percentage allowance would have to be reduced. The maximum excess or offset percentage amount of any participant with covered compensation at least equal to $30,000 would not have to be reduced.

**Example 3.** Krazy Kiltz sponsors a defined benefit plan that uses the Social Security taxable wage base as the single dollar amount integration level. The 0.75 percent factor must reduce to 0.42 percent if the reduction is computed on a plan-wide basis. [Treas. Reg. § 1.401(l)-3(d)(9)(iv)]

## Q 10:35    How is the integration or offset level affected by a short plan year?

If there is a short plan year the integration level or the offset level must be reduced by a fraction, the numerator of which is the number of months in the plan year and the denominator of which is 12. [Treas. Reg. § 1.401(l)-3(d)(7)]

# Adjustments and Actuarial Equivalency

## Q 10:36    What adjustments are required for benefits that commence on a date other than a participant's SSRA?

Adjustments to the maximum excess or offset allowance are required for benefits that commence on a date other than the participant's SSRA. The reductions or increases are based on the factors provided in the tables 6.3A, 6.3B, 6.3C, and 6.3D of Treasury Regulations Section 1.401(l)-3(e)(3), a composite of which is presented below.

### Table 10-2. Benefit plan for the participant's SSRA

| Age at Which Benefits Commence | A  SSRA 67 | B  SSRA 66 | C  SSRA 65 | D  Simplified Table |
|:---:|:---:|:---:|:---:|:---:|
| 70 | 1.002 | 1.101 | 1.209 | 1.048 |
| 69 | 0.908 | 0.998 | 1.096 | 0.950 |
| 68 | 0.825 | 0.907 | 0.996 | 0.863 |
| 67 | 0.750 | 0.824 | 0.905 | 0.784 |
| 66 | 0.700 | 0.750 | 0.824 | 0.714 |
| 65 | 0.650 | 0.700 | 0.750 | 0.650 |
| 64 | 0.600 | 0.650 | 0.700 | 0.607 |
| 63 | 0.550 | 0.600 | 0.650 | 0.563 |
| 62 | 0.500 | 0.550 | 0.600 | 0.520 |
| 61 | 0.475 | 0.500 | 0.550 | 0.477 |
| 60 | 0.450 | 0.475 | 0.500 | 0.433 |
| 59 | 0.425 | 0.450 | 0.475 | 0.412 |
| 58 | 0.400 | 0.425 | 0.450 | 0.390 |
| 57 | 0.375 | 0.400 | 0.425 | 0.368 |
| 56 | 0.344 | 0.375 | 0.400 | 0.347 |
| 55 | 0.316 | 0.344 | 0.375 | 0.325 |

**Example.** The BPM defined benefit plan is an excess benefit plan that provides a normal retirement benefit of 0.75 percent of average annual compensation up to the integration level, plus 1.5 percent of average annual compensation in excess of the integration level, for each year of service up to 35. The plan does not provide any benefits, other than normal retirement benefits at age 65. Brenden, born in 1947, has an SSRA of 66. Because the plan provides for the distribution of normal retirement benefits before Brenden's SSRA, the 0.75 percent factor in the maximum excess allowance applicable to Brenden must be reduced to 0.70 percent in accordance with Table 10-2, Column B. Accordingly, the disparity provided to Brenden under the plan exceeds the maximum excess allowance because the excess benefit percentage (1.5 percent) exceeds the base benefit percentage (0.75 percent) by more than the maximum excess allowance of 0.70 percent.

### Q 10:37    Does permitted disparity require the use of specific actuarial assumptions by a plan?

No. Permitted disparity does not require specific actuarial assumptions to be used for funding or valuation purposes. If, however, interest rates or mortality tables other than those prescribed by Treasury Regulations Section 1.401(a)(4)-12 (see definition of reasonable interest and mortality assumptions) are used to determine actuarial equivalence for a form of benefit other than a level annuity, the maximum excess or offset allowances must be reduced.

### Q 10:38    What assumptions are considered reasonable when normalizing the benefits for comparing the factors developed under actuarial equivalence?

If a plan provides for a form of benefit other than a straight life annuity or an annuity that decreases only because of the death of the employee or the employee's beneficiary, that form of benefit must be normalized by computing the actuarial equivalent of the benefit provided as a straight life annuity (even if the plan does not allow for life annuities). The normalized benefits must be limited to the maximum excess allowance or maximum offset allowance. The interest rates and mortality tables under Treasury Regulations Section 1.401(a)(4)-12 are considered reasonable. The interest rates must be between 7.5 percent and 8.5 percent and a standard mortality table must be used. [Treas. Reg. § 1.401(l)-3(b)(4)(iii)(C)]

Because the benefits must be normalized, the advantage of using permitted disparity to achieve disparity in benefits for a small plan that provides for a lump-sum provision at the Code Section 415 maximum limit is nearly eliminated if the rules under Code Section 401(l) are followed.

### Q 10:39    How does the form of benefit affect the maximum excess or offset allowance?

The maximum excess or offset allowance must be reduced for any accrued benefits paid in a form other than a straight life annuity. Any other benefit forms must be "normalized" under Treasury Regulations Section 1.401(a)(4) to a life annuity using the allowable actuarial assumptions. [Treas. Reg. § 1.401(a)(4)-12] The resultant annuity is reduced to the maximum permitted amount. [Treas. Reg. § 1.401(l)-3(b)(3)(iii)]

**Example.** Millie's Milk sponsors a defined benefit plan that is an excess plan. It provides for a normal retirement benefit of 1 percent of average annual compensation up to the integration level, plus 1.7 percent of average annual compensation in excess of the integration level for each year of service up to 35 years payable in the form of a joint and survivor annuity. The plan also allows participants to receive the benefit in the form of an actuarial equivalent straight life annuity. The actuarial equivalent straight life annuity equals 1.09 percent of average annual compensation up to the integration level, plus 1.85 percent of average annual compensation in excess of the integration level for each year of service up to 35 years. The permitted disparity provided under the Millie's Milk plan with regards to a straight life annuity (1.85% − 1.09% = 0.76%) exceeds the maximum excess allowance of 0.75 percent. Therefore, the maximum excess allowance must be reduced.

### Q 10:40   Is an adjustment required to the maximum excess or offset allowance if the plan provides for ancillary benefits?

No. If the plan provides for ancillary benefits such as qualified disability benefits or preretirement death benefits, no adjustment is required to be made to the maximum excess or offset allowance merely because of these additional benefits.

### Q 10:41   Can a plan use permitted disparity in its design but not in its formula?

Yes. For example, a plan could provide a formula of 20 percent of average annual compensation for NHCEs and 35 percent of average annual compensation for HCEs, each reduced 1/25 for each year of service less than 25. If the demographics are such that the plan uses the general test to satisfy the nondiscrimination rules under Treasury Regulations Section 1.401(a)(4)-3(c)(1), the plan can impute permitted disparity [Treas. Reg. § 1.401(a)(4)-3(b)(6)(ii)] but not have it in the formula. This means that when the discrimination tests are computed, each participant's accrual rate (see chapter 11) is increased by the maximum excess allowance without the participant's actually accruing the benefit. When a defined benefit plan is combined with a defined contribution plan for discrimination testing purposes [I.R.C. § 401(a)(4)], permitted disparity can be used only once, that is, either in the defined benefit plan or in the defined contribution plan, but not in both.

## Limitations

### Q 10:42   What are the limitations for defined benefit plans that use a fractional accrual method to determine a participant's accrued benefit?

Some plans define a normal retirement benefit and then accrue the benefit on a fractional basis. Under these plans, the maximum excess allowance or the maximum offset allowance is a percentage of average annual compensation multiplied by years of service. To use permitted disparity in a plan that uses the fractional accrual rules, the normal retirement formula must be converted to a unit credit formula (see chapter 18) using a period of at least 35 years. If a plan provides for fractional accrual and uses permitted disparity for 35 years, for each year of service up to 35, the benefit formula must use the same base benefit percentage and the same excess benefit percentage for all employees in the case of an excess plan, or the same gross benefit percentage and the same offset percentage in the case of an offset plan. For each additional year of service, the benefit formula for all the employees must use a uniform percentage of all average annual compensation that is no greater than the excess benefit percentage or the gross benefit percentage, whichever is applicable. [Treas. Reg. § 1.401 (l)-3(c)(2)(ii)]

If a plan provides for fractional accruals and uses disparity for a period of less than 35 years, the plan must provide for the same excess benefit percentage and the same base benefit percentage for each year of service in the employee's initial period of service that comprises less than 35 years. For each year of service after the initial period and up to at least 35 years, the benefit formula must use a uniform percentage of all average compensation that is equal to the excess benefit percentage or the gross benefit percentage. For each year of service after 35 years, the benefit formula must use uniform percentage of all average annual compensation that is no greater than the excess benefit percentage or the gross benefit percentage. [Treas. Reg. § 1.401(l)-3(c)(2)(iii)]

> **Example.** The CAM pension plan is an offset plan that provides a normal retirement benefit of 2 percent of average annual compensation for each year of service up to 35, minus 0.75 percent of final average compensation up to the offset level for each year of service up to 25. The plan determines an employee's accrued benefit under the fractional accrual method. Because the formula under the plan uses the same gross benefit percentage and the same offset percentage for 25 years of service, and for years of service after 25 and up to 35 the plan provides a benefit at a uniform rate (equal to the gross benefit percentage) of all average annual compensation, and the plan accrues the benefit ratably, the disparity under the plan is deemed to be uniform.

### Q 10:43  How do employee contributions affect the maximum excess or offset allowance?

In general, the benefits derived from employee contributions cannot be used to compute the maximum excess or offset allowance. If, for example, after computing the value of the benefit derived from employee contributions, the net employer contribution is zero, the plan cannot provide for a maximum excess or offset allowance. [Treas. Reg. § 1.401(l)-3(h)] This is because the maximum excess allowance cannot exceed the lesser of 0.75 percent or the base benefit percentage and the maximum offset allowance cannot exceed the lesser of 0.75 percent or half the gross benefit percentage. In this instance, the employer's base or gross benefit percentage is 0 percent in either case.

## Q 10:44 What is the annual permitted disparity limit for an employee who benefits under more than one plan of an employer using permitted disparity?

When two or more plans of one employer are combined and permitted disparity is used, the aggregate permitted disparity for an employee who benefits under those plans is limited to the maximum excess or maximum offset allowance (see Qs 10:29 and 10:30). *Disparity* is defined as either the amount by which the excess benefit percentage exceeds the base benefit percentage or, in the case of an offset plan, the offset percentage. The annual permitted disparity limit is the disparity provided for the plan year divided by the maximum excess or offset allowance for the year. Thus, a participant in a plan that provides for the maximum excess or offset allowance will have an annual permitted disparity limit of one for the year because the excess or offset percentage provided is divided under the terms of the plan (which is at the maximum) by itself. If a plan that wants to comply with Code Section 401(l) is combined with another plan that imputes permitted disparity when testing for discrimination under the general test of Treasury Regulations Section 1.401(a)(4)-3(c) and the overall aggregate limits are exceeded, the imputed computation is considered to be at the maximum excess or offset allowance limit. [Treas. Reg. § 1.401(l)-5)]

## Q 10:45 What is the *cumulative permitted disparity limit* for an employee?

The *cumulative permitted disparity limit* for an employee is equal to the sum of the annual permitted disparity limits for each year of participation. The cumulative disparity limit may not exceed 35. [Treas. Reg. § 1.401(l)-5(c)(1)]

> **Example.** The Davone Corporation Pension Plan is a defined benefit excess plan that provides a normal retirement benefit of 0.75 percent of average annual compensation up to covered compensation, plus 1.25 percent of average annual compensation above covered compensation, for each year of service up to 45. The plan contains no provision that would require a reduction in the 0.75 percent factor. The disparity provided under the plan for the plan year is 0.5 percent, the excess benefit percentage of 1.25 percent minus the base benefit percentage of 0.75 percent. The maximum excess allowance for the plan year is 0.75 percent. Thus, each employee's annual permitted disparity limit under the plan for each plan year is 0.67 (0.5 percent ÷ 0.75 percent). Because the plan limits the years of service taken into account under the plan to 45, the sum of the total annual permitted disparity limits for an employee is 30 (0.67 × 45). The plan therefore satisfies the cumulative permitted disparity limit.

## Q 10:46 What is the permitted disparity limit if an employee receives compensation from more than one employer sponsoring a plan?

Related employers, such as controlled groups or affiliated service groups, must combine the compensation of employees who work for the various related entities. Only one maximum excess or offset allowance is allowed.

## Past-Service Credits

### Q 10:47   What are the safe harbor rules that apply to past-service grants?

There are three safe harbor methods for granting past service:

1. A five-year grant [Treas. Reg. § 1.401(a)(4)-5(a)(3)];

2. The provision that all employees affected by the grant would satisfy Treasury Regulations Section 1.410(b)-4 in all prior years and that the grants are the same or equivalent for all HCEs and NHCEs [Treas. Reg. § 1.401(a)(4)-5(a)(4), Ex. 5]; and

3. The provision that no NHCE would receive a higher benefit if the amendment had occurred in the year the past-service grant is extending credit to and no NHCE ever terminated. [Treas. Reg. § 1.401(a)(4)-5(a)(4), Ex. 8]

### Q 10:48   Do the structure of the plan and the testing method have to match when testing past-service grant discrimination?

No. The plan formula, fresh-start dates, testing methods, testing parameters, and accrued benefit methods are all separate and do not have to correspond to each other.

# Chapter 11

# Advanced Plan Design

The art of discrimination testing is to determine the most efficient testing method that meets the objectives of the plan sponsor within a reasonable cost and time frame. Testing results can always discriminate against highly compensated employees (HCEs), discriminate in favor of one HCE over another, and discriminate in favor of one non-highly compensated employee (NHCE) over another. The difficulty is in proving that a plan formula that may otherwise look like it unfairly benefits HCEs is in fact nondiscriminatory. The previous chapter should be reviewed before reading this chapter. This chapter will provide examples of solutions to illustrate the testing techniques, with an emphasis on providing the most benefits to HCEs. These testing techniques can also be helpful when multiple plans of an employer are required to be aggregated to prove that the various benefits provided are nondiscriminatory.

## The General Test

### Q 11:1 What is the general test for nondiscrimination?

The general test for nondiscrimination in the amount of benefits is a complex series of categorizations and calculations. It is used by all plans that do not qualify for a safe harbor by virtue of plan design. Under the general test, all nonexcludable employees are assigned to rate groups (see Q 11:2) based on both normal accrual rates (see Q 11:5) and most valuable accrual rates (MVARs) (see Q 11:6).

The general test for nondiscrimination in amount of benefits is satisfied if each rate group satisfies the minimum coverage requirements of Internal Revenue Code (Code) Section 410(b). Generally, the minimum coverage requirements for these rate groups are the same requirements as those used to determine a plan's eligibility for qualified status (see chapter 6). This means that to be nondiscriminatory, each rate group must satisfy one of the eligibility tests—either the ratio percentage test or the average benefit test (see chapter 6).

### Q 11:2 What is a *rate group*?

A *rate group* consists of one HCE and all other employees, both HCEs and NHCEs, who have a normal accrual rate (see Q 11:5) and a most valuable accrual rate (see Q 11:6) greater than or equal to the HCE's normal and most valuable accrual rates, respectively. An employee can be in many rate groups. An employee will be in the rate group of each HCE who has a lower normal or most valuable accrual rate.

**Example.** Pension Inc. has a defined benefit plan. Each of the covered participants has the following rates (assume the normal accrual rate is equal to the MVAR for each employee):

|  | Compensation | Accrual Rate |
| --- | --- | --- |
| President (75% owner) | $120,000 | 4.0 |
| Senior Vice President (19% owner) | $100,000 | 4.0 |
| Office Manager (6% owner) | $ 80,000 | 3.62 |
| Administrator *A* | $ 50,000 | 5.0 |
| Administrator *B* | $ 50,000 | 5.0 |
| Administrator *C* | $ 40,000 | 3.8 |
| Administrator *D* | $ 40,000 | 3.8 |
| Administrator *E* | $ 35,000 | 4.0 |
| Secretary *F* | $ 25,000 | 5.0 |
| Secretary *G* | $ 25,000 | 3.2 |

There are three HCEs. Each one has a rate group.

President's rate group consists of all employees who have an accrual rate that is greater than or equal to her rate. Therefore, President's rate group is as follows:

| Employee | Accrual Rate |
|----------|:---:|
| President | 4.0 |
| Senior Vice President | 4.0 |
| Administrator *A* | 5.0 |
| Administrator *B* | 5.0 |
| Administrator *E* | 4.0 |
| Secretary *F* | 5.0 |

Senior Vice President has the same rate group.

The Office Manager rate group consists of all employees except Secretary *G*.

## Q 11:3   How is the ratio percentage test applied to a rate group?

The ratio percentage test of Code Section 410(b)(1) is used to test each rate group for discrimination as illustrated in the following example.

**Example.** Assume a plan has the following demographics:

- HCE1 has a MVAR of 4 percent.
- HCE2 through HCE5 have MVARs of 3 percent.
- NHCE1 through NHCE10 have MVARs of 2.5 percent.
- NHCE11 through NHCE15 have MVARs of 3.5 percent.
- NHCE16 through NHCE25 have MVARs of 4.5 percent.

The ratio percentage test for HCE1 is performed as follows:

- HCE1 represents one-fifth of all HCEs, or 20 percent.
- NHCEs 16 through 25 represent two-fifths of all NHCEs, or 40 percent.
- The percentage of NHCEs who have a MVAR greater than HCE1's MVAR is 200 percent (40% ÷ 20%).

The threshold of Code Section 410(b)(1) is 70 percent. Therefore, HCE1's rate group passes the ratio percentage test. If the average benefit percentage test of Code Section 410(b) is passed for the plan at a 70 percent ratio, the ratio of NHCEs to HCEs that is required in each rate group can be reduced significantly.

## Q 11:4   What is the ratio of NHCEs to HCEs that needs to be achieved for each rate group if the average benefit percentage test of Code Section 410(b) is passed for the plan?

A plan satisfies the average benefit percentage test of Code Section 410(b) for a plan year if the average benefit percentage of the plan for the plan year is at least 70 percent. [Treas. Reg. § 1.410(b)-5(a)] The average benefit percentage of a plan for a plan year is the percentage determined by dividing the actual benefit percentage of the NHCEs in the plan by the actual benefit percentage of the HCEs. [Treas. Reg. § 1.410(b)-5(b)] The actual benefit percentage of a group of employees for a testing period is the average of the employee benefit percentages, calculated separately with respect to each of the employees in the group for the testing period. All nonexcludable employees of the employer are taken into account for this purpose, even if they are not benefiting under any plan that is taken into account. [Treas. Reg. § 1.410(b)-5(c)] The employee benefit percentage is determined for purposes of Code Section 410(b) in the same manner as it is calculated for purposes of Code Section 401(a)(4) when calculating the normal accrual rate (see Q 11:5). [Treas. Reg. § 1.410(b)-5(d)]

If the plan passes the average benefit percentage test of Code Section 410(b), then the ratio necessary for each rate group is reduced below the 70 percent threshold that would ordinarily be required. In determining the ratio that is required, it is necessary to know the non-highly compensated concentration percentage that is used to determine the midpoint between the safe and unsafe harbor percentages of Treasury Regulations Section 1.410(b)-4(c). The ratio percentage of the rate group must exceed this midpoint in order to pass the modified Code Section 410(b) test.

The NHCE concentration percentage of an employer is the percentage of all the employees of the employer who are NHCEs. Employees who are excludable employees for purposes of the average benefit test are not taken into account. [Treas. Reg. § 1.410(b)-4(c)(4)(iii)] The following table shows the midpoint between the safe and unsafe harbor percentages that is determined based on the NHCE concentration percentage:

| NHCE Concentration Percentage | Safe Harbor Percentage | Unsafe Harbor Percentage | Midpoint |
|---|---|---|---|
| 0-60 | 50 | 40 | 45 |
| 61 | 49.25 | 39.25 | 44.25 |
| 62 | 48.5 | 38.5 | 43.5 |
| 63 | 47.75 | 37.75 | 42.75 |
| 64 | 47 | 37 | 42 |
| 65 | 46.25 | 36.25 | 41.25 |
| 66 | 45.5 | 35.5 | 40.5 |
| 67 | 44.75 | 34.75 | 39.75 |
| 68 | 44 | 34 | 39 |
| 69 | 43.25 | 33.25 | 38.25 |
| 70 | 42.5 | 32.5 | 37.5 |
| 71 | 41.75 | 31.75 | 36.75 |
| 72 | 41 | 31 | 36 |

| NHCE Concentration Percentage | Safe Harbor Percentage | Unsafe Harbor Percentage | Midpoint |
|---|---|---|---|
| 73 | 40.25 | 30.25 | 35.25 |
| 74 | 39.5 | 29.5 | 34.5 |
| 75 | 38.75 | 28.75 | 33.75 |
| 76 | 38 | 28 | 33 |
| 77 | 37.25 | 27.25 | 32.25 |
| 78 | 36.5 | 26.5 | 31.5 |
| 79 | 35.75 | 25.75 | 30.75 |
| 80 | 35 | 25 | 30 |
| 81 | 34.25 | 24.25 | 29.25 |
| 82 | 33.5 | 23.5 | 28.5 |
| 83 | 32.75 | 22.75 | 27.75 |
| 84 | 32 | 22 | 27 |
| 85 | 31.25 | 21.25 | 26.25 |
| 86 | 30.5 | 20.5 | 25.5 |
| 87 | 29.75 | 20 | 24.875 |
| 88 | 29 | 20 | 24.5 |
| 89 | 28.25 | 20 | 24.125 |
| 90 | 27.5 | 20 | 23.75 |
| 91 | 26.75 | 20 | 23.375 |
| 92 | 26 | 20 | 23 |
| 93 | 25.25 | 20 | 22.625 |
| 94 | 24.5 | 20 | 22.25 |
| 95 | 23.75 | 20 | 21.875 |
| 96 | 23 | 20 | 21.5 |
| 97 | 22.25 | 20 | 21.125 |
| 98 | 21.5 | 20 | 20.75 |
| 99 | 20.75 | 20 | 20.375 |

**Example.** Plan D has two HCEs and eight NHCEs. The NHCE concentration percentage for plan D is 80 percent (8 NHCEs/10 total employees). Based on this percentage, the midpoint between the safe and unsafe harbor percentages of Code Section 410(b) is 30 percent. If the plan passes the average benefit percentage test, each of the rate groups that is created when performing the general test only requires to be passed at a 30 percent ratio. If there is one HCE in the first rate group, the number of NHCEs that are required to be in that rate group is 2 since 2 divided by 8 is 0.25 and 1 divided by 2 is 0.50; therefore the ratio percentage of the rate group is 0.25/0.50, or 50 percent.

### Q 11:5   What is the *normal accrual rate*?

The *normal accrual rate* for an employee, generally speaking, is the increase in the employee's accrued benefit during the measurement period (see Q 11:7) divided by the employee's testing service (see Q 11:8) during the measurement period, and is expressed either as a dollar amount or as a percentage of the employee's average annual compensation (see Q 11:11).

The accrued benefit must be expressed in terms of an annual benefit beginning at normal retirement age. If the accrued benefit is expressed in any other form, it must be converted to a single-life annuity using reasonable interest rate and mortality assumptions (see Q 11:14).

### Q 11:6   What is the *most valuable accrual rate*?

The *most valuable accrual rate* for an employee for a plan year is the increase in the employee's most valuable optional form of payment of the accrued benefit during the measurement period (see Q 11:7) divided by the employee's testing service during the measurement period (see Qs 11:7 and 11:8), and is expressed either as a dollar amount or as a percentage of the employee's average annual compensation (see Q 11:11). The employee's most valuable optional form of payment of the accrued benefit is determined by calculating for the employee the normalized (see Q 11:14) qualified joint and survivor annuity (QJSA) associated with the accrued benefit that is potentially payable in the current or any future plan year at any age under the plan and selecting the largest (per year of testing service). The Internal Revenue Service (IRS) in Technical Advice Memoranda 2006_05_30_07_28_26 confirmed that the QJSA was used for the calculation of the MVAR even though using the lump sum would have produced a higher equivalent benefit accrual rate (EBAR).

The MVAR reflects the value of the most valuable optional form of benefit accrued, or treated as accrued under the anti-cutback provisions of Code Section 411(d)(6), that is payable in any form and at any time under the plan. It includes early retirement benefits, retirement-type subsidies, early retirement window benefits, and so forth. The MVAR must consider any such benefit that is available during the year even if the benefit ceases to be available before the end of the year or in some future year. [Treas. Reg. § 1.401(a)(4)-3(d)(1)(ii)]

### Q 11:7   What is the *measurement period*?

The *measurement period* is the time period used in performing discrimination tests. The measurement period can be the current plan year; the current plan year and all prior plan years; or the current plan year, all prior plan years, and all future plan years. The measurement period can be changed from year to year. [Treas. Reg. § 1.401(a)(4)-3(d)(1)(iii)]

A measurement period that includes future plan years cannot be used if the pattern of accruals discriminates in favor of HCEs. For example, a plan that front-loads benefit accruals for HCEs but not for NHCEs would be considered discriminatory and would not be allowed. Testing is based on relevant facts and circumstances. If an employee terminates employment, future plan years cannot be included in that employee's measurement period. [Treas. Reg. § 1.401(a)(4)-3(d)(2)(iii)]

### Q 11:8    How is *testing service* determined?

*Testing service* means an employee's years of service as defined in the plan for purposes of applying the benefit formula under the plan, or any year in which the employee benefits under the plan. Alternatively, testing service can be determined in any reasonable manner that does not discriminate in favor of HCEs. For example, including only years of participation in the plan is an acceptable definition of testing service. [Treas. Reg. § 1.401(a)(4)-3(d)(1)(iv)(A)]

In the case of a measurement period that is the current plan year, testing service for the plan year equals one. [Treas. Reg. § 1.401(a)(4)-3(d)(1)(iv)(B)(2)]

Testing service can also include years of service with a prior employer, as long as such service is included for all similarly situated employees, there is an acceptable business reason for including such service, and there is no significant discrimination in favor of HCEs. [Treas. Reg. § 1.401(a)(4)-11(d)(3)]

### Q 11:9    What is the *testing age*?

*Testing age* means the following:

1. If the plan provides the same uniform normal retirement age (see Q 11:10) for all employees, the testing age is the employee's normal retirement age.
2. If the plan provides for different uniform normal retirement ages for different employees or different groups of employees, the employee's testing age is the latest normal retirement age under any uniform normal retirement age under the plan, regardless of whether that age applies to the particular employee. For example, suppose a plan has the following uniform normal retirement ages:

| | |
|---|---|
| Executives | age 60 |
| Salaried employees | age 62 |
| Hourly employees | age 63 |

The testing age for all employees in this example would be age 63.

3. If the plan does not provide a uniform normal retirement age, the employee's testing age is 65.
4. If an employee is beyond the testing age otherwise determined for the employee under items #1 through #3, the employee's testing age is the employee's current age.

[Treas. Reg. § 1.401(a)(4)-12]

### Q 11:10   What is the *uniform normal retirement age*?

*Uniform normal retirement age* means a single normal retirement age under the plan that does not exceed the maximum age (generally age 65) and that is the same for all of the employees in a given group. The plan will also have a uniform normal retirement age if the plan provides that the normal retirement age of all employees in the group is the later of a stated age (not exceeding the maximum age) or a stated anniversary no later than the fifth anniversary of the time each employee commenced participation (or service) in the plan.

To have a uniform normal retirement age, the difference between the normal retirement date and the uniform normal retirement age cannot exceed six months for any employee.

> **Example 1.** Plan A's definition of normal retirement date is the last day of the plan year nearest attainment of age 65 or the anniversary of completing five years of participation in the plan. Jane became a participant at age 63. The plan can use age 65 as the testing age for some employees and age 68 as the testing age for Jane.

> **Example 2.** Plan B's definition of normal retirement date is the last day of the plan year nearest attainment of age 55 or the 10th anniversary of participation in the plan. This plan does not have a uniform definition of normal retirement and would be required to use age 65 as the testing age.

> **Example 3.** Plan C's definition of normal retirement date is the last day of the plan year coincident with or following attainment of age 62 or the fifth anniversary of participation in the plan. This plan does not have a uniform definition of normal retirement and would be required to use age 65 as the testing age.

### Q 11:11   What definition of compensation must be used for discrimination testing purposes?

Average annual compensation must be used for purposes of determining benefits under a safe harbor method or for purposes of determining accrual rates under the general test. An employee's *average annual compensation* is the average of the employee's annual Section 414(s) compensation as determined over the averaging period in the employee's compensation history during which the average of the employee's annual Section 414(s) compensation is the highest. The averaging period must consist of three or more consecutive 12-month periods, but need not be longer than the employee's period of employment. An employee's compensation history must be continuous, can begin at any time, must be no shorter than the averaging period, and must end in the current year. [Treas. Reg. § 1.401(a)(4)-3(e)(2)(i)]

If the measurement period for determining accrual rates is the current plan year, plan year compensation can be used instead of average annual compensation. [Treas. Reg. § 1.401(a)(4)-3(e)(2)(ii)(A)]

Compensation earned in the year an employee terminates does not need to be included in determining the employee's average annual compensation if it is also not used in determining benefits. [Treas. Reg. § 1.401(a)(4)-3(e)(2)(ii)(B)]

If a plan is not a Section 401(l) plan and does not impute Social Security in the testing, the consecutive years requirement does not apply. [Treas. Reg. § 1.401(a)(4)-3(e)(2)(ii)(E)]

**Planning Pointer.** The definition of compensation for benefit accrual purposes does not have to be the same as the definition of compensation for discrimination testing purposes if the general test is used. For example, a plan can use a one-year average compensation for computation of the benefit accrual and still pass the discrimination tests as long as the correct average annual compensation is used when performing those tests. [Treas. Reg. § 1.401(a)(4)-3(e)(1)]

### Q 11:12    How are normal accrual rates calculated?

In general, there are three methods for calculating an employee's normal accrual rate: the annual method, the accrued-to-date method, and the projected method.

*Annual method.* Under the annual method, benefit accrual rates are calculated using a measurement period of the current year only and either current plan year compensation or average annual compensation. The annual method computes the difference between the accrued benefit as of the last day of the prior year and the accrued benefit as of the last day of the current year. Past-service grants can skew the results of this computation.

**Example 1.** Henry's compensation for 2002 is $28,000, and the increase in his accrued benefit for the 2002 plan year is $1,400. His annual normal accrual rate, expressed as a percentage of compensation for the measuring period, is $1,400 (accrued benefit for the measuring period) divided by $28,000 (compensation for the measurement period), or 5 percent.

*Accrued-to-date method.* Under the accrued-to-date method, benefit accrual rates are calculated using a measurement period of the current year and prior plan years and average annual compensation.

**Example 2.** Henry's average annual compensation is $25,000 for the 2002 plan year. Henry has been a participant in the plan for five years, and his accrued benefit to date is $5,000 per year. Henry's accrued-to-date normal accrual rate is $5,000 (accrued benefit) divided by five years (the testing service period), or $1,000 per year. Expressed as a percentage of average annual compensation for the measuring period, Henry's accrued-to-date normal accrual rate is 4 percent ($1,000 per year ÷ $25,000 average annual compensation).

*Projected method.* Under the projected method, benefit accrual rates are calculated using a measurement period of the current year, all prior years, and all future years. Projected plan benefits, testing service, and average annual compensation must be determined in a reasonable manner, reflecting actual or projected service and compensation only through the end of the measurement period. The determination of projected plan benefits is not reasonable if it incorporates an assumption that in future years, an employee's compensation will increase or the employee will terminate employment before the employee's testing age. Future years beginning after an employee's attainment of the employee's testing age cannot be included in the measurement period. [Treas. Reg. § 1.401(a)(4)-3(d)(2)]

> **Example 3.** Assume that Henry has 10 years of future participation until reaching normal retirement age. Assume further that Henry's projected normal retirement benefit (i.e., the benefit accrued at normal retirement age) is $15,000. His compensation for the 1998 measurement period is $28,000, and this is projected to continue until Henry's normal retirement age. Henry's projected normal accrual rate is $15,000 (accrued benefit) divided by 15 years (testing service period), or $1,000. Expressed as a percentage of compensation for the measuring period, Henry's projected normal accrual rate is 3.57 percent ($1,000 per year ÷ $28,000 compensation for the measuring period).

### Q 11:13   How are MVARs calculated?

MVARs, like normal accrual rates, are calculated using an annual, accrued-to-date, or projected method. The difference is that the most valuable benefit possible is calculated for each age between the current age and the testing age. The most valuable benefit is usually the qualified joint and survivor benefit. It is helpful to set up a table that shows the normalized qualified joint and survivor benefit for each age and the associated accrual rate for each age. The MVAR for the employee is the highest accrual rate listed in the table. The table will look something like this:

| Each Age from Current Age to Testing Age | Accrued Benefit | Accrued Benefit Payable in the Form of a QJSA | Normalized QJSA Benefit | Testing Service | Compensation | Accrual Rate Equal to the Normalized QJSA Divided By Testing Service Times Compensation |
|---|---|---|---|---|---|---|

The MVAR is then equal to the highest number in the last column of the table.

## Normalizing a Benefit

### Q 11:14   What does it mean *to normalize* a benefit?

*To normalize* a benefit is to convert a benefit to the actuarially equivalent straight life annuity beginning at the employee's testing age. [Treas. Reg. § 1.401(a)(4)-12]

Conversions to the same testing age, same form of benefit, or actuarially equivalent values must use a reasonable interest rate and mortality table, and be gender neutral. A standard interest rate and a standard mortality assumption are considered reasonable. A *standard interest rate* is an interest rate that is neither less than 7.5 percent nor more than 8.5 percent, compounded annually. *Standard mortality table* means one of the following tables:

- UP-1984 Mortality Table (Unisex)
- 1983 Group Annuity Mortality Table (Female)
- 1983 Group Annuity Mortality Table (Male)
- 1983 Individual Annuity Mortality Table (Female)
- 1983 Individual Annuity Mortality Table (Male)
- 1971 Group Annuity Mortality Table (Female)
- 1971 Group Annuity Mortality Table (Male)
- 1971 Individual Annuity Mortality Table (Female)
- 1971 Individual Annuity Mortality Table (Male)

In order to normalize the benefit, the following items are needed:

- Reasonable preretirement interest rate
- Reasonable postretirement interest rate
- Reasonable mortality table
- Plan's benefit form
- Benefit payment age
- Testing age
- Annuity rate based on plan's benefit form, using the reasonable interest and mortality, payable at the plan's benefit payment age (plan annuity rate)
- Annuity rate based on straight life annuity, using the reasonable interest and mortality, payable at the testing age (401a4 annuity rate)
- Benefit to normalize

The normalized benefit is equal to the benefit to normalize times the plan annuity rate times the interest increase from benefit payment age to testing age (using the reasonable preretirement interest rate) divided by the 401a4 annuity rate.

**Example.**

> Reasonable preretirement interest rate = 8.5%
>
> Reasonable postretirement interest rate = 8.5%
>
> Reasonable mortality table = 1983 IAM female table
>
> Plan's benefit form = life annuity with 10 years certain
>
> Benefit payment age = 60
>
> Testing age = 62
>
> Annuity rate based on plan's benefit form, using the reasonable interest and mortality, payable at the plan's benefit payment age (plan annuity rate) = 125.56

Annuity rate based on straight life annuity, using the reasonable interest and mortality, payable at the testing age (401a4 annuity rate) = 120.52

Benefit to normalize = $1,000/mo.

Normalized benefit = $1000 × 125.56 × $(1.085)^2$ ÷ 120.52 = $1,226.46

### Q 11:15  How can normalizing a benefit help a plan pass the discrimination tests?

Normalizing a benefit is converting the benefit to the actuarially equivalent straight life annuity beginning at the employee's testing age. [Treas. Reg. § 1.401(a)(4)-12] This conversion must be done using a reasonable interest rate and mortality table. Standard interest rates (neither less than 7.5 percent nor more than 8.5 percent) and standard mortality tables (see Q 11:14) are considered reasonable.

The interest rate assumption makes a big difference in determining the present value of benefits. If the definition of actuarial equivalence uses an interest rate less than the standard assumptions (see Q 11:14), using the lowest possible uniform normal retirement age and providing actuarially increased postretirement benefits available for all employees can increase the disparity in benefits between HCEs and NHCEs by approximately 30 percent.

**Example.** TV Repairs Inc. has an HCE who needs a benefit of 75 percent of average annual compensation (which is $160,000) to retire at age 65. The annual normal retirement benefit would therefore be $120,000 ($160,000 × 75%). The HCE is aged 60 and has 10 years of past service and 5 years of future service. The benefit accrual rate would be 5 percent per year of service (75% ÷ (10 + 5)). NHCE1 has one year of service and at the end of the year would be age 26 and have an accrued benefit of 5 percent of average annual compensation (which is $20,000). Her accrued benefit is $1,000 per year ($20,000 × 5%). Using 5 percent interest and the 1983 Group Annuity Mortality Table (female) as the definition of actuarial equivalence, the present value of NHCE1's accrued benefit would be $1,893.

Instead, assume the plan uses an age 55 uniform normal retirement age and an actuarial increase for delayed retirement based on 8.5 percent interest and the 1971 Group Annuity Mortality Table (female). To provide the HCE with a $120,000 annual benefit at age 65, the plan must provide a benefit of $44,000 annually at age 55 (an annual benefit of $44,000 increased actuarially to age 65 would be $120,000). An annual benefit of $44,000 represents 27.5 percent of the HCE's compensation of $160,000. Therefore, the HCE would only need an accrual rate of 1.834 percent per year of service (27.5% ÷ 15). NHCE1 would have an annual accrued benefit of $367. The present value of the accrued benefit would be $1,380. The decrease in the present value of NHCE1's accrued benefits is 27 percent ($1,893 − $1,380 = $513; $513 ÷ $1,893 = 27%). Therefore, by normalizing a benefit for delayed retirement using a standard interest rate and standard mortality table, the plan is still able to be within the parameters of a nondiscriminatory benefit and increase the disparity in benefits provided to the HCE by 27 percent.

### Q 11:16   How does a subsidized early retirement benefit affect the computation of the benefit accrual?

Subsidized early retirement benefits under safe harbor conditions (benefits must be currently and effectively available) can provide greater disparity between benefits payable to those employees closer to the early retirement age (generally the HCEs) than to those who are further from the early retirement age (generally the NHCEs). If a plan has a fully subsidized early retirement benefit at 55, and a uniform normal retirement age of 65, benefit payments for employees not yet eligible for early retirement will be based on the retirement age. If an HCE wants to retire at age 55, providing a subsidized benefit can significantly increase the benefits to the HCE without increasing the benefits to any other participants. Caution should be used when contemplating the use of this feature. On plan termination, the fully subsidized benefits generally must be included in the value of the payouts. [Rev. Rul. 85-6, 1985-1 C.B. 133] This feature is advantageous only for safe harbor designs because when computing the MVARs in the general test, the value of the subsidized early retirement benefit must be included.

### Q 11:17   Can the testing age be forced when normalizing a benefit?

Yes. By defining the normal retirement age so it does not conform to the definition of a uniform normal retirement age (see Q 11:10), the testing age is forced to be age 65 or the Social Security normal retirement age independent of the plan's normal retirement age. Each year of difference in testing ages causes a 10 percent change in the accrual rates. This method can be effective when the HCEs have a normal retirement age greater than that of the NHCEs. The disparity between a normal retirement age of 65 and testing at Social Security normal retirement age can also be effective for increasing some of the younger participants' benefit accrual rates.

## Miscellaneous Testing Concerns

### Q 11:18   Does the plan document need to specify the methods, assumptions, or values to be used for discrimination testing?

No. Operational compliance with the nondiscrimination rules must be demonstrated each year according to the regulations, but the methods, assumptions, and values do not have to be specified in the plan document. Because the tests can be changed from year to year based on the plan's demographics, they do not have to meet the definitely determinable standards that apply to provisions on vesting, benefit accruals, and plan formulas.

### Q 11:19   Who has to be counted in the tests?

In general, all nonexcludable employees must be counted in the tests (see chapter 10).

### Q 11:20   Can a plan always discriminate against an HCE?

Yes. To the extent that the discrimination is not based on age, disability, sex, creed, or other illegal criteria, a plan can provide less of a benefit for one HCE than for another HCE or an NHCE.

### Q 11:21   How does a change in the projected benefit affect discrimination testing?

A change in the projected benefit may or may not affect the testing results, depending on the accrued benefit method and the method used for computing the benefit accrual rates.

**Example.** Plan A has a formula of 2 percent of average compensation multiplied by years of service. It changes the formula to 2 percent of average compensation up to 25 years plus 2.25 percent of average compensation for years of service exceeding 25. The accrual rates for participants who have fewer than 25 years of service to date, using either the annual or the accrued-to-date method, will not change for the year of the amendment. If the projected method is used, their accrual rates will change.

### Q 11:22   How does the Age Discrimination in Employment Act affect discrimination tests?

There are no specific provisions of the Age Discrimination in Employment Act (ADEA) that directly relate to the discrimination tests under Code Section 401(a)(4).

### Q 11:23   What is *snapshot testing*?

*Snapshot testing* is testing the workforce on a single day for compliance with the nondiscrimination rules. The provisions for snapshot testing are provided in Revenue Procedure 93-42. [1993-2 C.B. 540] Snapshot testing generally uses "substantiation quality data." Use of substantiation quality data is allowed for employers that do not have precise data available at a reasonable expense, but only if there is a high likelihood that using this data will provide similar results as using precise data. The employer tests the amount of benefits or contributions and the current availability of benefits, rights, and features using substantiation quality data for the snapshot population. Generally, it will be practical for the employer to select a snapshot day that is the same day for which the employer has substantiation quality data, but this need not necessarily be the case. If the plan excludes participants from benefiting if they do not work 1,000 hours and the snapshot day is early in the plan year, employees who terminate after the snapshot day may have been treated as benefiting even when they may not in fact benefit. Therefore, the employer must account for the effect of the minimum service requirement by making an adjustment to the ratio percentage or non-discriminatory classification percentage of Code Section 410(b) to reflect terminations. For this purpose, an adjustment of 5 percent (i.e., 70 percent becomes 73.5 percent) for a 1,000-hour rule will be treated as a safe harbor.

Using snapshot testing can be advantageous in cases where compiling census data continuously is very difficult. This type of testing method is generally more appropriate for larger plans.

## Fresh Starts

### Q 11:24   What is a *fresh-start date*?

A *fresh-start date* is the date on which the past accrual of benefits is frozen and future accruals will be earned according to a new method. The fresh-start date is normally the last day of the plan year but could be another date, such as the date employees with a frozen accrued benefit were transferred to the plan that is being tested. Fresh-start dates are very important in providing optional methods of passing the discrimination tests. There are three fresh-start formulas:

- *Without wear-away.* The participant's accrued benefit is equal to the participant's frozen accrued benefit as of the fresh-start date plus the participant's accrued benefit determined using (1) the formula applicable to the current year and (2) the years of service of the participant after the fresh-start date.
- *With wear-away.* The participant's accrued benefit is equal to the greater of the participant's accrued benefit as of the fresh-start date or the participant's accrued benefit computed using (1) the current formula and (2) the participant's total years of service that are taken into account under the current formula.
- *With extended wear-away.* The participant's accrued benefit is equal to the greater of the participant's accrued benefit determined using the fresh-start formula without wear-away or the participant's accrued benefit computed using (1) the current benefit formula and (2) the participant's total years of service that are taken into account under the formula.

### Q 11:25   How can a fresh-start date help a plan pass the discrimination tests?

A fresh-start date freezes the past nondiscriminatory benefit accruals for purposes of testing and allows a plan to use a different method to test benefit accruals after the fresh-start date. The method of accruing future benefits should be coordinated with the testing. The choice of a formula without wear-away, with wear-away, or with extended wear-away is important to the testing results (see Q 11:24).

### Q 11:26   When should a fresh-start date be used?

A fresh-start date can be very helpful when plan demographics change. As the demographics of a plan change, patterns of benefit accruals may become discriminatory. Benefit accruals that satisfied the discrimination tests in the past and met the objectives of the plan can be frozen and a fresh-start date chosen to establish a new benefit accrual pattern based on the new demographics.

**Example.** Assume a plan initially targeted a group of employees within five years of normal retirement age. Five years have passed, and the plan no longer passes the discrimination tests because the employees have retired. The company now wants to target all employees in its Northeast location. Selecting a fresh-start date provides a new plan formula with existing benefit accruals locked in. As long as the new benefit accruals are nondiscriminatory, what happened in the past no longer affects the testing procedure.

### Q 11:27   What demographic data determine whether a fresh-start date will help?

A fresh-start date will help if a component of the plan's benefit formula decreases. In that case, past benefit accruals can be frozen at the fresh-start date and additional benefit accruals can be added for future years (fresh-start without wear-away).

**Example.** Baskets Inc. sponsors a plan that provides a benefit of 2 percent of average annual compensation per year of service. On December 31, 1993, participant Pat has an average annual compensation of $200,000 and five years of service. For plan years beginning after December 31, 1993, compensation over $150,000 cannot be taken into account. Using a fresh-start date of December 31, 1993, and a fresh-start method of without wear-away, past benefit accruals are frozen using a $200,000 average salary and future benefit accruals are computed at the new compensation amounts and added to the frozen benefit to determine the total accrued benefit for Pat.

Fresh-start without wear-away can be effective whenever an HCE's compensation is reduced, especially when the compensation is defined to be the average annual compensation computed as of a final averaging period. Note that all participants with compensation below the new limit are not affected, but those above the new limit are protected.

Remember that fresh-start dates are a function of testing and not necessarily of the plan formula. Similarly, use of the annual method, projected method, or accrued-to-date method is also independent of the plan formula (see chapter 10). In testing for discrimination, the accrued-to-date method can be used in coordination with the fresh-start date, using the measurement period from the fresh-start date instead of all years.

### Q 11:28   Can a defined benefit plan have a *tiered benefit formula*?

Yes, and a *tiered benefit formula,* that is, a plan formula applied to one segment of service and another formula applied to a subsequent segment of service, can help a plan pass the discrimination tests.

**Example 1.** The Donut Inc. Defined Benefit Plan was established on January 1, 1989, and provided 2 percent of average annual compensation. On January 1,

1994, the plan was amended to reflect the new compensation limits. HCE Pat had an average annual compensation of $200,000 on December 31, 1993, and five years of participation. Using a fresh-start date of December 31, 1993, Pat has a frozen accrued benefit of $20,000 ($200,000 × 2% × 5), which is 13.33 percent of $150,000; the new compensation limit can be obtained when there are compensation increases for the NHCEs but compensation remains frozen for the HCEs. Using the annual method, the difference between the accrued benefit from the beginning of the year to the end of the year can be divided into two segments: the first segment is the additional accrual amount based on the plan benefit formula, and the second segment is the increase in the accrued benefit based on the average compensation increase that occurs during the year. The computed accrual rate will be greater than the plan benefit formula for the NHCEs.

**Example 2.** Chris is an NHCE in the Donut Inc. Defined Benefit Plan, described in Example 1, with annual compensation, for each prior year, of $20,000. Chris received an increase of $4,000 in compensation during the year. Chris has three years of past service at the beginning of the year. The accrued benefit at the beginning of the year is $1,200 ($20,000 × 0.02 × 3). At the end of the year, Chris's average annual compensation is $21,000 (($20,000 + $20,000 + $20,000 + $24,000) ÷ 4) and his accrued benefit is $1,680 ($21,000 × 0.02 × 4).

The additional year accrual provided an increase of $400 ($20,000 × 0.02), and the compensation increase provided an $80 increase ($4,000 × 0.02). The accrual rate on an annual basis is 2.28 percent (($1,680 – $1,200) ÷ $21,000).

This means that the plan could provide Pat, the HCE in Example 1, with a benefit accrual of 2.28 percent of average annual compensation for the year without failing the discrimination tests.

## Past-Service Grants

### Q 11:29 Can past-service accruals cause a plan to discriminate currently?

Yes. If past-service grants that would substantially affect the benefits for HCEs more than the benefits for NHCEs are given, the grant of past-service credits will be discriminatory. [Treas. Reg. § 1.401(a)(4)-5] Chapter 10 discusses advanced methods of performing the discrimination tests and avoiding such problems.

### Q 11:30 When can a plan provide for a past-service grant in excess of five years?

A plan can provide for a past-service grant in excess of five years at any time that such a grant of past service does not significantly discriminate in favor of the plan's highly compensated participants. The rule of thumb is that if the ratio of HCEs to former HCEs receiving the past-service grant is significantly higher than the ratio of current NHCEs to former NHCEs receiving the past-service grant, the past-service grant will probably be considered discriminatory. The definition of *significantly higher* is not clear; however, if the ratio for NHCEs is equal to or greater than that for the HCEs, the past-service grant is probably nondiscriminatory.

> **Example.** Acme Company currently provides that participants in its pension plan receive a benefit of 1.5 percent of the highest three-year average compensation for each year of service with the employer. Acme wishes to increase the benefit to 2 percent, and the plan has been in effect for 15 years. Over the last 15 years, Acme had five former HCEs participate in the plan under the 1.5 percent benefit feature. Acme currently has two HCEs who will receive the 2 percent benefit. Over that same period, 35 former NHCEs have benefited at the 1.5 percent rate, and Acme currently has 20 employees who will receive the 2 percent benefit. A comparison of the current employees to former employees grouped by HCEs and NHCEs is shown below:

| | Current | Former | Ratio |
|---|---|---|---|
| HCEs | 2 | 5 | 0.40 |
| NHCEs | 20 | 35 | 0.57 |

Because the ratio for NHCEs is greater than the ratio for HCEs, the past-service grant is probably nondiscriminatory. If the ratio for the NHCEs falls below that for the HCEs, it would be advisable to obtain a determination from the IRS that the grant of the past-service credit is nondiscriminatory.

## Compensation Issues

### Q 11:31   What compensation periods should be used to maximize the discrimination tests?

If the compensation levels of the NHCEs have decreased over the last few years, the years to average should be restricted to those last few years. If the compensation levels of the HCEs have decreased over the last few years, the testing averaging period should be extended to include past years of high compensation. The objective in testing is to obtain the lowest benefit accrual rate for HCEs and the highest benefit accrual rate for NHCEs. Compensation does not have to be annualized. If a plan participant receives a full benefit accrual for the plan year but worked only part of the year, not annualizing the compensation and adding a minimum flat-dollar-benefit can be a very effective way to increase the accrual rate of NHCEs over what their accrual rate might otherwise be under the regular plan formula.

### Q 11:32   Can different compensation averaging periods be used in the testing method?

Yes. Plans can be restructured (see Q 11:42) to test groups with different compensation averaging periods. For example, it is possible to select a group of

HCEs with the lowest compensation average and a group of NHCEs with the highest compensation average as one component plan using a particular definition of average compensation that is different from the definition used in a separate component plan.

### Q 11:33   What years are optional in computing average salary?

The year of hire (if the eligibility requirements include a year of service) or the year of termination (if the plan excludes it in determining benefits) can be included or excluded. Compensation for those years does not have to be included in the computation of plan benefits. Remember, testing compensation is different from plan compensation.

**Example.** Chris, who was hired on December 1, 1999, earns $1,000 per month and has never had a compensation increase. The company sponsors a calendar-year plan. For testing purposes, all years are included. Chris has been with the company for two years and one month and the average compensation for testing must be determined as of December 31, 2001.

If the year of hire is excluded, the average compensation is $12,000.

If the year of hire is included, the average compensation for testing purposes is

$$\$1,000/mo. \times 25 \text{ mo.} = \$25,000$$

$$\$25,000 \div 3 \text{ yrs.} = \$8,333$$

If Chris accrued a benefit of $240, the benefit accrual rate under each option would be:

Excluding year of hire $240 ÷ $12,000 = 0.02 or 2%

Including year of hire $240 ÷ $8,333 = 0.0288 or 2.88%

**Planning Pointer.** If an HCE has fluctuating compensation, use nonconsecutive years for the averaging period. If nonconsecutive years are used, however, permitted disparity cannot be imputed (see Q 11:34).

## Optional Testing Items

### Q 11:34   Can permitted disparity be imputed?

Permitted disparity (see chapter 10) can be imputed into the computation of the accrual rates at the option of the plan sponsor. [I.R.C. § 401(a)(5)(C)] Permitted disparity amounts must meet the requirements of Code Section 401(l). Permitted disparity can be imputed even if the plan is not a Code Section 401(l) plan or the plan formula does not contain any permitted disparity amounts. For example, permitted disparity can be added to the accrual rate in a plan formula of 1 percent per year of service multiplied by average compensation even though permitted disparity is not in the formula. The accrual rate could be 1.75 percent if the Social Security normal retirement age is 65 and the normal and most valuable accrual rates are equal. In general, it is favorable to impute permitted disparity when the HCE is older and highly paid. If the employer has young, lower paid HCEs, such as a 5 percent owner, imputing permitted disparity may not help the plan pass the discrimination tests.

### Q 11:35    Will imputing permitted disparity always help?

No. Using nonconsecutive years for average compensation may be more advantageous than imputing permitted disparity. Adding the additional benefits is more helpful when the HCEs have significant excess compensation above the covered compensation amounts and when there is no lump-sum option that has to be normalized.

### Q 11:36    What is an *adjusted accrual rate*, and how is it calculated?

An *adjusted accrual rate* is the regular accrual rate adjusted for permitted disparity. To calculate the adjusted accrual rate, the normalized accrual rate, the employer-provided accrual for the year, the average compensation, the testing compensation, the covered compensation from a covered compensation table in effect at the beginning of the plan year, and the permitted disparity factor for the employee must have already been calculated (see chapter 10).

The adjusted accrual rate with imputed permitted disparity for employees with testing compensation that exceeds covered compensation is the lesser of (1) the employer-provided accrual divided by the difference between the testing compensation and half of the covered compensation and (2) the sum of the employer-provided accrual plus the product of the permitted disparity factor and covered compensation, all divided by the testing compensation. [Treas. Reg. § 1.401(a)(4)-7(c)(3)]

The adjusted accrual rate with imputed permitted disparity for employees with testing compensation that does not exceed the covered compensation is the lesser of (1) two times the unadjusted accrual rate and (2) the unadjusted accrual rate plus the permitted disparity factor for the employee. [Treas. Reg. § 1.401(a)(4)-7(c)(2)]

> **Example.** Joe is a participant in the Jones defined benefit plan. The plan is using the annual method to compute the normal accrual rate with imputed permitted disparity. Joe's accrual for 2002 is $300 and he has monthly compensation, in that year, of $10,000. Therefore, his unadjusted normal accrual rate is 3 percent ($300 ÷ $10,000). His permitted disparity factor is 0.65 percent and his monthly covered compensation is $3,000. The normal accrual rate with permitted disparity is the lesser of (1) $300 divided by the difference between $10,000 and half of $3,000 ($1,500), or 3.53 percent ($300 ÷ ($10,000 − (0.5 × $3,000))) and (2) $300 plus the product of 0.65 percent and covered compensation, all divided by $10,000, or 3.2 percent (($300 + (0.0065 × $3,000)) ÷ $10,000). Therefore, Joe's adjusted normal accrual rate after imputing permitted disparity is the lesser of 3.53 percent and 3.2 percent, or 3.2 percent.

## Q 11:37   What is *grouping of accrual rates*?

*Grouping of accrual rates* is the practice of treating all employees who have accrual rates within a specified range above and below a midpoint rate chosen by the employer as having an accrual rate equal to the midpoint rate within that range. Accrual rates within a given range cannot be grouped if the accrual rates of HCEs within the range generally are significantly higher than the accrual rates of NHCEs within the range. The specified ranges may not overlap and must be within 5 percent (not 5 percentage points) of the midpoint of the range. In the case of MVARs, the lowest and highest accrual rates in the range must be within 15 percent (not 15 percentage points) of the midpoint rate. The lowest and highest accrual rates need not be within 5 percent (or 15 percent) of the midpoint rate if they are no more than 0.05 of a percentage point above or below the midpoint rate and accrual rates are determined as a percentage of average annual compensation. [Treas. Reg. § 1.401(a)(4)-3(d)(3)(ii)]

> **Example.** If midpoint chosen is 3.0 percent, the range is 2.85 percent to 3.15 percent for normal accrual rates and 2.55 percent to 3.45 percent for MVARs.

## Q 11:38   When does benefit rate grouping help?

When testing for discrimination, certain HCEs may almost pass. If these HCEs are grouped with other HCEs whose rate groups are close in amount, there may be enough NHCEs to allow the HCEs to pass. The benefit accrual rates for the HCEs within the rate group cannot be significantly higher than the benefit accrual rates for the NHCEs within the rate group. This is a fact-and-circumstances test, so no bright-line rules can be applied.

## Q 11:39   Can plans be aggregated when performing discrimination tests?

Yes. The coverage tests of Treasury Regulations Section 1.410(b)-7 are used for determining the plans that can or must be aggregated under the tests of Code Section 401(a)(4). Certain plans or portions of a plan must be disaggregated. Mandatory disaggregation must occur for the following plans or portions of a plan:

- Plans subject to Code Section 401(k) or 401(m)
- Plans that have separate asset pools for different sets of participants under Treasury Regulations Section 1.414(l)-1(b)
- Employee stock ownership plans (ESOPs) or portions of a plan
- Plans benefiting separate lines of business under Code Section 414(r) that are treated for Code Section 410(b) purposes as separate plans
- Plans or portions of a plan benefiting employees under a collectively bargained agreement
- Multiple-employer plans of separate employers (i.e., not controlled groups or affiliated service groups)

Some plans have many features. For example, a profit-sharing plan can have an ESOP component, a 401(k) component, a matching component, and a discretionary employer contribution component. Each component would be a portion of the plan.

All other plans of the same employer, whether they are defined benefit plans or defined contribution plans, can be permissively aggregated. The methods of Treasury Regulations Section 1.401(a)(4)-8 must be used to test the aggregated plans on either a benefits basis or a contributions basis. To do so, the plan years must be the same, and all other factors must be consistent to the extent reasonable (e.g., the same interest rate, measurement period, and mortality table must be used). A profit-sharing plan may have a lump-sum distribution alternative and a defined benefit plan may not, and the plans can still be aggregated, however, as long as the aggregation does not result in discrimination in favor of HCEs.

### Q 11:40   Can a plan be disaggregated for discrimination testing?

Yes. Participants who are younger than age 21 or have less than one year of service can be disaggregated and tested separately from participants who meet the statutory eligibility requirements.

### Q 11:41   Must a plan use one test consistently?

No. A plan can change the method of testing annually, and through restructuring can use different tests in the same plan year.

### Q 11:42   What is *restructuring*?

*Restructuring* is the practice of treating a plan as consisting of two or more component plans for purposes of determining if the plan is discriminatory. If each plan satisfies the requirements of Code Sections 401(a)(4) and 410(b) as if it were a separate plan, the plan is treated as satisfying Code Section 401(a)(4).

A plan can be restructured into component plans, each consisting of all of the allocations, accruals, and other benefits, rights, and features provided to a selected group of employees. The employer can select the group of employees used for this purpose in any manner, and the composition of the groups can be changed from plan year to plan year. Every employee must be included in one and only one component plan under the same plan for a plan year.

The rules applicable in determining whether component plans satisfy Code Section 410(b) are generally the same as those applicable in determining whether the whole plan satisfies Code Section 410(b). A component plan is deemed to satisfy the average benefit percentage test, however, if the plan of which it is a part satisfies the test. [Treas. Reg. § 1.401(a)(4)-9(c)]

Component plans can be established for each HCE. Each component plan must satisfy Code Section 410(b). Therefore, the component plan must either cover a reasonable classification of employees or have a ratio percentage of at least 70 percent. Some component plans can use one method of testing (e.g., the annual method), and other component plans can use other methods of testing (e.g., the accrued-to-date method).

### Q 11:43   Why is restructuring used?

In general, plans are restructured to associate one group of HCEs with the most advantageous group of NHCEs for a particular testing method, and the balance of the HCEs with the balance of the NHCEs for testing under a different testing method.

Terminated employees test better under the annual method; active employees often test better under an accrued-to-date method. There are many ways to restructure a plan. For example, there are 672 ways to restructure a plan with two HCEs and ten NHCEs based on component plans that satisfy the 70 percent ratio percentage test of Code Section 410(b).

### Q 11:44   How can front-loading of benefit accruals help a plan pass the discrimination tests?

Front-loading of benefits provides for larger benefit accruals for HCEs each year and allows NHCEs to catch up to where they would have been if they had had a level benefit accrual pattern. Front-loading means that a participant obtains larger benefit accruals in the earlier years of employment.

**Example.** The Donut Inc. Defined Benefit Plan has a formula of 6 percent of average annual compensation for the first year of service, 0 percent of average annual compensation for the next two years of service, and 2 percent of average annual compensation per year of service thereafter for NHCEs. The benefit formula for HCEs is 3 percent of average annual compensation per year of service. For the first two years of service, the NHCEs' accrual rate would be greater than or equal to the HCEs' accrual rate. If Donut Inc. has high turnover, there may be enough new employees to meet the testing requirements.

## Cross-Testing

### Q 11:45   Can a defined benefit plan be shown to be nondiscriminatory by testing it as if it were a defined contribution plan?

Yes. Equivalent allocations can be determined under a defined benefit plan and shown to be nondiscriminatory in amount for a plan year if the plan would satisfy Code Section 401(a)(4) for the plan year if equivalent normal and most valuable allocation rates were substituted for each employee's normal and most valuable accrual rates, respectively, in the determination of rate groups. [Treas. Reg. § 1.401(a)(4)-8(c)] This is known as *cross-testing.*

A safe harbor cash balance plan (see chapter 13) generally satisfies Code Section 401(a)(4) through cross-testing.

### Q 11:46    How is an equivalent allocation rate calculated in a defined benefit plan?

An employee's equivalent normal and most valuable allocation rates for a plan year are equal to the actuarial present value of the increase over the plan year in the benefit that would be taken into account in determining the employee's normal and most valuable accrual rates for the plan year, respectively. The allocation rate is expressed either as a dollar amount or as a percentage of the employee's plan year compensation. [Treas. Reg. § 1.401(a)(4)-8(c)(2)(i)]

The actuarial present value of the increase in an employee's benefit must be determined using a standard interest rate and a standard mortality table, with no assumption of preretirement mortality. [Treas. Reg. § 1.401(a)(4)-8(c)(2)(ii)]

> **Example.** Carie, age 30, is a participant in the Home School Defined Benefit Plan. The plan has a normal retirement age of 65. The plan sponsor is using the annual method to determine accrual rates, and Carie's normal accrual rate is 3 percent, determined by dividing the increase in her monthly benefit over the 2002 plan year of $30 by her monthly compensation of $1,000. The sponsor wants to convert this accrual rate to an equivalent allocation rate using a standard preretirement and postretirement interest rate of 8 percent and the 1983 Group Annuity Mortality Table (male). Using that interest rate and that mortality table gives an annuity purchase rate of 103.76, and a lump-sum value at retirement, of Carie's accrual, of $3,112.80 ($30 × 103.76). The present value of this lump-sum amount is $210.53 ($3,112.80 × $1.08^{-35}$). Carie's equivalent allocation rate is 1.75 percent ($210.53 ÷ $12,000).

> Permitted disparity can be imputed in the calculation of the equivalent allocation rates.

[Treas. Reg. § 1.401(a)(4)-8(c)(2)(iii)]

### Q 11:47    Is there a minimum accrual necessary to pass discrimination?

Possibly. Under Code Sections 410(b) and 401(a)(4), generally any accrual, no matter how small, is used in the testing. However, under Code Section 401(a)(26), which tests minimum participation requirements, an accrual must be considered meaningful. [Treas. Reg. § 1.401(a)(26)-3(c)] This rule is intended as an anti-abuse rule to prevent employers from maintaining plans the primary purpose of which is to function as individual plans for a few employees or for the employer. Therefore, the question of whether a plan has meaningful accrued benefits or is providing meaningful benefit accruals is one of facts and circumstances. The IRS has stated in a Field Memo that an accrued benefit equal to 0.5 percent of total compensation times years of participation (or a current accrual rate of 0.5 percent of total compensation per year of participation) would generally be considered meaningful. However, they also stated that an accrued benefit or current accrual less than this would not necessarily fail to be meaningful. The factors to consider are the level of current accruals, comparative rates of accruals under the current and prior formulas, currently projected accrued benefits versus benefits accrued as of the beginning of the year, how long the current formula has been in effect, how long the plan has been in effect, and the number of employees with accrued benefits under the plan.

### Q 11:48    Will a defined benefit plan pass the discrimination tests if the majority of the non-highly compensated participants receiving benefits are short-service employees?

Possibly not. On October 22, 2004, Carol Gold, Director of Employee Plans, issued a memorandum to the EP Examinations stating that some plans have sought to satisfy the requirements of Code Sections 410(b), 401(a)(4), and 401(a)(26) by allocating benefits to the sponsor's lowest paid employees, who may also have been hired for a very short time period, possibly for the sole purpose of distorting the discrimination testing for the plan. The intent, according to the memo, of these allocations is to create large EBAR's based on these relatively small benefits. She believes that this plan design does not interpret Treasury Regulations Section 1.401(a)(4)-8 in a "reasonable manner consistent with the purpose of preventing discrimination in favor of highly compensated employees" as required by Treasury Regulations Section 1.401(a)(4)-1(c)(2), because the results of the general test are distorted through the use of allocation rates produced by the allocation of small amounts to NHCEs hired temporarily for short periods of time.

This memo was later clarified by Ms. Gold in a letter dated February 4, 2005, sent to various groups. In this subsequent letter, Ms. Gold said that the intent of the IRS program is to focus on designs that provide allocations to the lowest paid employees who also happen to be short-service employees.

## Combination Defined Benefit/Defined Contribution Plans

### Q 11:49    How are combination plans tested for nondiscrimination?

First, each plan must satisfy one of the coverage tests of Code Section 410(b), either by itself or in combination with one or more plans. Then, any plans that are combined to meet Code Section 410(b) must also be combined when applying the rules for nondiscrimination under Code Section 401(a)(4). All of the normal rules are followed, including possibly restructuring a plan into two or more component plans (see Q 11:42).

In addition, there is a gateway requirement for combination defined benefit/defined contribution plans that must be satisfied (see Q 11:50).

**Q 11:50   Can allocations made in a defined contribution plan be combined with accruals in a defined benefit plan when testing for discrimination?**

Yes. It may be advantageous to the testing results to combine plans when testing for discrimination. To combine the plans, it is necessary to convert either the defined contribution allocations to equivalent accruals or to convert the defined benefit accruals to equivalent allocations before combining the plans. Once combined, the discrimination testing is done in the same manner as if there were a single plan. To be combined, the plans must also satisfy one of the following gateway tests:

1. The combined plan must be primarily defined benefit in character;

2. The combined plan consists of broadly available separate plans; or

3. The combined plan satisfies a minimum allocation gateway.

A safe harbor floor-offset arrangement should also be considered when an employer wants to combine a defined contribution plan with a defined benefit plan because these are not subject to the gateway provisions.

**Q 11:51   How is a combined plan considered primarily defined benefit in character?**

A combined plan is primarily defined benefit in character if, for more than 50 percent of the NHCEs benefiting under the plan, the normal accrual rate attributable to benefits provided under defined benefit plans for the NHCE exceeds the equivalent accrual rate attributable to contributions under defined contribution plans for the NHCE.

**Example.** Ranch Inc. has established a profit-sharing plan and a defined benefit plan that cover all employees. The company wants to combine the two plans for discrimination testing. John is an HCE, all other employees are NHCEs. The EBARs for the employees are as follows:

|  | EBAR Profit-Sharing Plan | EBAR Defined Benefit Plan |
|---|---|---|
| John | 3.70% | 14.4% |
| Fred | 5.60% | .30% |
| George | 4.60% | .60% |
| Ray | 2.00% | 2.50% |
| Lynn | 2.00% | 3.00% |
| Brad | 3.00% | 3.10% |

Because the EBAR for the NHCEs in the defined benefit plan is greater than the EBAR in the profit-sharing plan for more than 50 percent of the NHCEs ($\frac{3}{5} = 60\%$), the combined plan is primarily defined benefit in character.

### Q 11:52   How does a combined plan consist of broadly available separate plans?

A combined plan consists of broadly available separate plans if the defined contribution plan and the defined benefit plan, tested separately, would each satisfy the requirements of Code Section 410(b) and the nondiscrimination requirements, but for this purpose assuming satisfaction of the average benefit percentage test. Similarly, the defined benefit plan must separately satisfy the nondiscrimination requirements, assuming for this purpose satisfaction of the average benefit percentage test. In conducting the required separate testing, all plans of a single type (defined contribution or defined benefit) within the combined plan are aggregated, but those plans are tested without regard to plans of the other type.

This alternative is useful, for example, when an employer maintains a defined contribution plan that provides a uniform allocation rate for all covered employees at one business unit and a safe harbor defined benefit plan for all covered employees at another unit, and when the group of employees covered by each of those plans is a group that satisfies the nondiscriminatory classification requirement of Code Section 410(b). Because the employer provides broadly available separate plans, it may continue to aggregate the plans and test for nondiscrimination on the basis of benefits, as an alternative to using the qualified separate line of business rules or separately demonstrating satisfaction of the average benefit percentage test.

### Q 11:53   How does a combined plan satisfy the minimum aggregate allocation gateway?

First, each employee's aggregate normal allocation rate must be determined. The employee's aggregate normal allocation rate is determined by adding the employee's allocation rate under the defined contribution plan to the employee's equivalent allocation rate under the defined benefit plan. This aggregation allows an employer that provides NHCEs with both a defined contribution and a defined benefit plan to take both plans into account in determining whether the minimum aggregate allocation gateway is met.

Under this gateway, if the aggregate normal allocation rate of the HCE with the highest aggregate normal allocation rate under the plan (HCE rate) is less than 15 percent, the aggregate normal allocation rate for all NHCEs must be at least $\frac{1}{3}$ of the HCE rate. If the HCE rate is between 15 percent and 25 percent, the aggregate normal allocation rate for all NHCEs must be at least 5 percent. If the HCE rate exceeds 25 percent, the aggregate normal allocation rate for each NHCE must be at least 5 percent plus one percentage point for each five-percentage-point increment (or portion thereof) by which the HCE rate exceeds 25 percent (e.g., the NHCE minimum is 6 percent for an HCE rate that exceeds 25 percent but not 30 percent, and 7 percent for an HCE rate that exceeds 30 percent but not 35 percent). However, a plan is deemed to satisfy this minimum aggregate allocation gateway if the aggregate normal allocation rate for each NHCE is at least 7.5 percent of compensation within the meaning of Code Section 415(c)(3).

In determining the equivalent allocation rate for an NHCE under a defined benefit plan, a plan is allowed to treat each NHCE who benefits under the defined benefit plan as having an equivalent allocation rate equal to the average of the equivalent allocation rates under the defined benefit plan for all NHCEs benefiting under that plan. This averaging rule recognizes the grow-in feature inherent in traditional defined benefit plans (i.e., the defined benefit plan provides higher equivalent allocation rates at higher ages).

**Example.** The employer in the example in Q 11:51, Ranch Inc., wants to use the minimum aggregate allocation gateway to combine the two plans for discrimination testing. The equivalent allocation rates are as follows:

| | EBAR Profit-Sharing Plan | EBAR Defined Benefit Plan | Total |
|---|---|---|---|
| John | 7.00% | 50.00% | 57.00% |
| Fred | 7.00% | .55% | 7.55% |
| George | 7.00% | .75% | 7.75% |
| Lynn | 7.00% | .60% | 7.60% |
| Ray | 7.00% | .85% | 7.85% |
| Brad | 7.00% | .90% | 7.90% |

Because each NHCE has an aggregate normal allocation rate that exceeds 7.5 percent, the minimum aggregate allocation gateway is satisfied and the combined plan may proceed with the nondiscrimination testing.

## Case Study

### Q 11:54    What is the optimal plan design?

A determination of what is optimal is up to the employer to decide. However, often the employer is presented with various examples of the maximum that can be provided to the HCEs and the minimum that will be provided to the NHCEs for their particular group. The plan advisor should have answers to the following questions before beginning this process:

1. What are the employer's goals for benefiting the key employees?
2. What are the employer's goals for benefiting the rank-and-file employees?
3. What is the goal retirement age?
4. What is the employer's desire for eligibility and vesting?

Once these answers are known and different options are presented that address the answers, the employer can always choose to increase benefits to the NHCEs or decrease benefits to the HCEs without having to worry about the discrimination regulations.

In the following examples, the employer's goal is to maximize the benefits to the oldest shareholder and minimize benefits for the rank-and-file participants.

The employer would like to have at least 60 percent of the total cost be due to the benefit provided to HCE1.

When trying to find the optimal plan design, it is important to also keep the following design principles in mind to avoid future problems:

- Revisit often the client's goals to ensure the plan is meeting these. Keep the plan as simple as possible and make sure the client understands how his plan operates.

- It is preferable to base benefits on future participation rather than past service to avoid problems with unfunded liabilities in the early years of the plan. This helps as well to possibly decrease premiums required to be paid to the PBGC.

- Use a reasonable funding method that will keep funding in line with termination liabilities each year.

- Try to keep funding in line with Code Section 417(e) minimum lump sums as well, so that the employer understands his liabilities better and the plan stays adequately funded.

For purposes of the case study, only the normal accrual rates are used to show whether a plan design passes discrimination testing. It is assumed that the MVARs follow the same pattern as the normal accrual rates.

The census used to illustrate this process is as follows:

**Sample Data Plan**

| Participant Name | Compensation | Age |
|---|---|---|
| HCE1 | $200,000 | 55 |
| HCE2 | $200,000 | 50 |
| NHCE1 | $ 40,000 | 45 |
| NHCE2 | $ 30,000 | 40 |
| NHCE3 | $ 25,000 | 35 |
| NHCE4 | $ 20,000 | 30 |
| NHCE5 | $ 20,000 | 25 |
| NHCE6 | $ 20,000 | 21 |

Plan effective date: January 1, 2002.

Normal retirement age: End of year nearest to attainment of age 62 with five years of participation.

Actuarial equivalence and funding assumptions: 6.0 percent interest Pre & Post Retirement; 1983 GAM Unisex Post Retirement.

Maximum dollar limit for oldest HCE: $9,333.10 ($13,333.00 (7 × 10)).

The HCEs were hired in 1995, the NHCEs were all hired in early 2001. There were no NHCEs before 2001.

### Q 11:55   What is the first step in the process of determining optimal plan design?

Once the employer's goals are known, the first step is usually to generate a plan design using a simple safe harbor plan formula. If the safe harbor formula meets the employer's goals, then the process is complete.

For the simple safe harbor formula, a fixed benefit safe harbor formula is used of 200 percent of average monthly compensation, reduced for years of participation less than 25 using fractional accrual. The following are the results:

| | Accrued Benefit | PVAB | Normal Cost | 401(a)(4) EBAR |
|---|---|---|---|---|
| HCE1 | $1,333.29 | $128,836.00 | $152,411.00 | 8.00 |
| HCE2 | $1,333.30 | $ 96,276.00 | $108,335.00 | 8.00 |
| NHCE1 | $ 266.65 | $ 14,388.00 | $ 16,195.00 | 8.00 |
| NHCE2 | $ 200.00 | $ 8,064.00 | $ 7,897.00 | 8.00 |
| NHCE3 | $ 154.33 | $ 4,650.00 | $ 4,483.00 | 7.41 |
| NHCE4 | $ 104.16 | $ 2,345.00 | $ 2,514.00 | 6.25 |
| NHCE5 | $ 90.08 | $ 1,516.00 | $ 1,795.00 | 5.40 |
| NHCE6 | $ 81.29 | $ 1,083.00 | $ 1,384.00 | 4.88 |
| Total: | | $257,158.00 | $295,014.00 | |

The percentage of the normal cost provided to HCE1 is 51.7 percent ($152,411 ÷ $295,014). However, the total cost ($295,014) is more than sufficient to cover the benefits due ($257,158), which is a plus in this design's favor.

### Q 11:56   Should the advisor look at any other safe harbor formulas?

Absolutely! All of them should be tried to make sure the advisor has exhausted all possibilities. Following is a unit credit safe harbor formula of 8 percent of average monthly compensation times years of participation, limited to seven years with unit credit accrual.

| | Accrued Benefit | PVAB | Normal Sample Plan Data Cost | 401(a)(4) EBAR |
|---|---|---|---|---|
| HCE1 | $1,333.00 | $128,810.00 | $152,411.00 | 8.00 |
| HCE2 | $1,333.00 | $ 96,254.00 | $ 75,834.00 | 8.00 |
| NHCE1 | $ 267.00 | $ 14,407.00 | $ 9,071.00 | 8.01 |
| NHCE2 | $ 200.00 | $ 8,064.00 | $ 4,423.00 | 8.00 |
| NHCE3 | $ 167.00 | $ 5,032.00 | $ 2,511.00 | 8.02 |
| NHCE4 | $ 133.00 | $ 2,995.00 | $ 1,407.00 | 7.98 |
| NHCE5 | $ 133.00 | $ 2,238.00 | $ 1,005.00 | 7.98 |
| NHCE6 | $ 133.00 | $ 1,772.00 | $ 775.00 | 7.98 |
| Total: | | $259,572.00 | $247,437.00 | |

Under this plan design, the percentage of the cost provided to HCE1 is 61.6 percent. This meets one of the goals to have at least 60 percent of the total cost be due to the benefit provided to HCE1. However, the present value of accrued benefit (PVAB) is greater than the cost generated and may cause the plan to be underfunded upon termination.

### Q 11:57 Would a non-design-based safe harbor formula be advantageous in this case?

Yes, it would. A non-design-based safe harbor formula still requires some discrimination testing (see chapter 10), but it is much less complicated than the general test. The formula chosen was 56 percent of average monthly compensation because that is what is needed to provide HCE1 with the maximum benefit ($200,000 ÷ 12 × .56 ÷ 7 = $1,333.33). This benefit is fractionally accrued over participation, not to exceed 12 years.

| | Accrued Benefit | PVAB | Normal Cost | 401(a)(4) EBAR |
|---|---|---|---|---|
| HCE1 | $1,333.29 | $128,836.00 | $152,411.00 | 8.00 |
| HCE2 | $ 777.75 | $ 56,160.00 | $ 75,834.00 | 4.67 |
| NHCE1 | $ 155.58 | $ 8,395.00 | $ 9,071.00 | 4.67 |
| NHCE2 | $ 116.67 | $ 4,704.00 | $ 4,423.00 | 4.67 |
| NHCE3 | $ 97.25 | $ 2,930.00 | $ 2,511.00 | 4.67 |
| NHCE4 | $ 77.75 | $ 1,751.00 | $ 1,407.00 | 4.67 |
| NHCE5 | $ 77.75 | $ 1,308.00 | $ 1,005.00 | 4.67 |
| NHCE6 | $ 77.75 | $ 1,036.00 | $ 775.00 | 4.67 |
| Total: | | $205,120.00 | $247,437.00 | |

To do the discrimination testing, a table should be set up showing the average normal accrual rates for the HCEs and the NHCEs. The average rate for the NHCEs (4.67%) should be at least 70 percent of the average rate for the HCEs ((8.00% + 4.67%) ÷ 2 = 6.34%). Seventy percent of the HCE rate is 4.44 percent, so this plan passes.

Under this plan formula, the cost is the same as with the safe harbor unit credit formula because the projected benefits are the same, 56 percent of average monthly compensation (8% × 7 years = 56%). However, under the unit credit formula, the benefit is accrued ratably over 7 years, whereas under this formula, it is spread out over 12 years. Therefore, because the accruals are smaller, the total cost more than matches the total PVABs. However, care should be taken in future years as the cost remains the same but the PVABs increase.

### Q 11:58 Are there any other safe harbor formulas that can be used?

Yes. The two-step unit credit safe harbor is a unit credit formula that allows fractional accruals. This formula would be 8 percent times years of participation, limited to 7 years, plus 5.47 percent times each of the next 26 years of participation. (See chapter 10 for the details on how this formula was calculated.)

| | Accrued Benefit | PVAB | Normal Cost | 401(a)(4) EBAR |
|---|---|---|---|---|
| HCE1 | $1,333.29 | $128,836.00 | $152,411.00 | 8.00 |
| HCE2 | $1,157.67 | $ 83,594.00 | $108,335.00 | 6.95 |
| NHCE1 | $  217.06 | $ 11,712.00 | $ 16,195.00 | 6.51 |
| NHCE2 | $  156.86 | $  6,325.00 | $  7,897.00 | 6.27 |
| NHCE3 | $  127.63 | $  3,846.00 | $  4,483.00 | 6.13 |
| NHCE4 | $  100.41 | $  2,261.00 | $  2,514.00 | 6.02 |
| NHCE5 | $   89.30 | $  1,502.00 | $  1,795.00 | 5.36 |
| NHCE6 | $   80.59 | $  1,074.00 | $  1,384.00 | 4.84 |
| Total: | | $239,150.00 | $295,014.00 | |

This safe harbor formula decreases the accruals for the NHCEs over the other safe harbor plan designs but does not do anything in this instance to improve the cost ratio because the projected benefits for the NHCEs turn out to be very high. This plan design tends to work best when a safe harbor formula is desired, or perhaps when a safe harbor formula is going to provide the best results (e.g., when there is only one HCE).

### Q 11:59   Can a tiered benefit formula be beneficial for this client?

Yes, very. A tiered benefit formula was chosen that also has a minimum benefit. The formula is 8 percent of compensation times years of participation for HCE1, 2 percent of compensation times years of participation, limited to 10 years, for all others. A minimum benefit and accrual of $133.33 times years of participation limited to seven years is provided.

| | Accrued Benefit | PVAB | Normal Cost | 401(a)(4) EBAR |
|---|---|---|---|---|
| HCE1 | $1,333.29 | $128,836.00 | $152,416.00 | 8.00 |
| HCE2 | $  333.33 | $ 24,069.00 | $ 27,084.00 | 2.00 |
| NHCE1 | $  133.33 | 47,194.00 | $  4,535.00 | 4.00 |
| NHCE2 | $  133.33 | $  5,376.00 | $  2,948.00 | 5.33 |
| NHCE3 | $  133.33 | $  4,017.00 | $  2,008.00 | 6.40 |
| NHCE4 | $  133.33 | $  3,002.00 | $  1,408.00 | 8.00 |
| NHCE5 | $  133.33 | $  2,243.00 | $  1,005.00 | 8.00 |
| NHCE6 | $  133.33 | $  1,777.00 | $    775.00 | 8.00 |
| Total: | | $176,514.00 | $192,179.00 | |

Average benefit percentage test:

NHCE    6.62%

HCE    5.00%

Is the NHCE average at least 70 percent of the HCE average?

Yes, so it passes.

Concentration percentage: 75%

Midpoint between safe and unsafe harbor percentage: 33.75%

Rate group 1: (⅜) ÷ (½) = 100%

Rate group 2: (%) ÷ (⅔) = 100%

Are the rate groups at least 33.75 percent?

Yes, so they pass.

Under this plan design, HCE1's share of the total cost is 79.3 percent, and the total cost covers the PVABs. Care should be taken, however, to ensure that there are enough assets to cover benefits in future years. If this is a concern, the plan could be funded using a unit credit funding method instead.

### Q 11:60   Is it possible under this tiered formula to provide a greater benefit to the other HCE (HCE2) as well?

Yes. To do this, a tiered benefit formula with a flat dollar accrual for the NHCEs is used. This would be 8 percent of compensation times years of participation for HCEs, flat-dollar-benefit of $133.33 times years of participation for NHCEs.

| | Accrued Benefit | PVAB | Normal Cost | 401(a)(4) EBAR |
|---|---|---|---|---|
| HCE1 | $1,333.29 | $128,836.00 | $152,416.00 | 8.00 |
| HCE2 | $1,333.33 | $ 96,278.00 | $108,338.00 | 8.00 |
| NHCE1 | $ 133.33 | $ 7,194.00 | $ 4,535.00 | 4.00 |
| NHCE2 | $ 133.33 | $ 5,376.00 | $ 2,948.00 | 5.33 |
| NHCE3 | $ 133.33 | $ 4,017.00 | $ 2,008.00 | 6.40 |
| NHCE4 | $ 133.33 | $ 3,002.00 | $ 1,408.00 | 8.00 |
| NHCE5 | $ 133.33 | $ 2,243.00 | $ 1,005.00 | 8.00 |
| NHCE6 | $ 133.33 | $ 1,777.00 | $ 775.00 | 8.00 |
| Total: | | $248,723.00 | $273,433.00 | |

Average benefit percentage test:

NHCE    6.62%

HCE    8.00%

Is the NHCE average at least 70 percent of the HCE average?

Yes (6.62% ÷ 8% = 82.75%), so it passes.

Concentration percentage: 75%

Midpoint between safe and unsafe harbor percentage: 33.75%

Rate group 1: (¾) ÷ (½) = 100%

Rate group 2: (¾) ÷ (²⁄₄) = 50%

Are the rate groups at least 33.75 percent?

Yes, so they pass.

This type of formula does not do anything more for HCE1; it just helps bring HCE2 up to a level formula.

### Q 11:61    Is there a way to provide the same benefit using a grant of past-service credit?

Yes. Because there were no NHCEs in prior years, past-service credit can be given all the way to original date of hire. Therefore, the formula can be 4 percent of compensation times years of service, not to exceed 20.

| | Accrued Benefit | PVAB | Normal Cost | 401(a)(4) EBAR |
|---|---|---|---|---|
| HCE1 | $1,333.30 | $128,836.00 | $152,411.00 | 4.00 |
| HCE2 | $1,333.30 | $ 96,276.00 | $102,924.00 | 4.00 |
| NHCE1 | $ 267.00 | $ 14,407.00 | $ 11,661.00 | 4.00 |
| NHCE2 | $ 200.00 | $ 8,064.00 | $ 6,318.00 | 4.00 |
| NHCE3 | $ 167.00 | $ 5,032.00 | $ 3,587.00 | 4.00 |
| NHCE4 | $ 133.00 | $ 2,995.00 | $ 2,010.00 | 4.00 |
| NHCE5 | $ 133.00 | $ 2,238.00 | $ 1,436.00 | 4.00 |
| NHCE6 | $ 133.00 | $ 1,772.00 | $ 1,107.00 | 4.00 |
| Total: | | $259,620.00 | $281,454.00 | |

This is a safe harbor formula, except for the grant of past service. Once that is shown to be nondiscriminatory (which it is because there were no NHCEs who could have benefited during the time the past-service grant covers), there is no further testing involved.

### Q 11:62    Can a cash balance plan be beneficial for this employer?

Yes, if the benefits are general tested and the safe harbors for cash balance plans are not used. The formula used here provides allocations of $125,000 for

HCE1, $91,419 for HCE2, and $2,500 for each NHCE (increased for top heavy, if required). The plan is funded unit credit.

| | Accrued Benefit | PVAB | Normal Cost | 401(a)(4) EBAR |
|---|---|---|---|---|
| HCE1 | $1,330.62 | $125,000.00 | $125,000.00 | 8.16 |
| HCE2 | $1,333.30 | $ 91,419.00 | $ 91,419.00 | 8.51 |
| NHCE1 | $ 66.67 | $ 3,337.00 | $ 3,337.00 | 2.50 |
| NHCE2 | $ 68.44 | $ 2,500.00 | $ 2,500.00 | 3.24 |
| NHCE3 | $ 93.77 | $ 2,500.00 | $ 2,500.00 | 5.00 |
| NHCE4 | $ 128.48 | $ 2,500.00 | $ 2,500.00 | 8.21 |
| NHCE5 | $ 176.02 | $ 2,500.00 | $ 2,500.00 | 11.06 |
| NHCE6 | $ 226.45 | $ 2,500.00 | $ 2,500.00 | 14.09 |
| Total: | | $232,256.00 | $232,256.00 | |

Average benefit percentage test:

$$NHCE \quad 7.35\%$$

$$HCE \quad 8.33\%$$

Is the NHCE average at least 70 percent of the HCE average?

Yes (7.35% ÷ 8.33% = 88.24%), so it passes.

Concentration percentage: 75%

Midpoint between safe and unsafe harbor percentage: 33.75%

Rate group 1: (%) ÷ (½) = 66.7%

Rate group 2: (%) ÷ (%) = 50%

Are the rate groups at least 33.75 percent?

Yes, so they pass.

This plan only provides 53.8 percent of the total cost of the plan to HCE1, but has the added benefit of the cost exactly matching the benefits owed (as long as the plan is designed to avoid the whipsaw of Code Section 417(e)). The cost for HCE1 is lower in this design because of the unit credit funding, and will increase each year as HCE1 nears retirement age.

### Q 11:63    Can a safe harbor plan design be used that also takes advantage of restructuring?

Yes. When a plan is restructured, each component plan must satisfy the 70 percent test of Code Section 410(b). Any employees can be selected for a component plan; in this case, the three youngest NHCEs are put with HCE1 and all other employees are put in the other component plan. The plan design is as follows: 8 percent of average monthly compensation times years of participation, limited to 10, for HCE1, NHCE4, NHCE5, NHCE6; 2 percent of average monthly compensation times years of participation, limited to 10, for all others.

|  | Accrued Benefit | PVAB | Normal Cost | 401(a)(4) EBAR |
|---|---|---|---|---|
| HCE1 | $1,333.29 | $128,836.00 | $152,416.00 | 8.00 |
| HCE2 | $ 333.33 | $ 24,069.00 | $ 27,084.00 | 4.00 |
| NHCE1 | $ 67.00 | $ 3,615.00 | $ 3,241.00 | 2.01 |
| NHCE2 | $ 50.00 | $ 2,016.00 | $ 1,580.00 | 2.00 |
| NHCE3 | $ 42.00 | $ 1,265.00 | $ 897.00 | 2.02 |
| NHCE4 | $ 133.33 | $ 3,002.00 | $ 2,011.00 | 8.00 |
| NHCE5 | $ 133.33 | $ 2,243.00 | $ 1,436.00 | 8.00 |
| NHCE6 | $ 133.33 | $ 1,777.00 | $ 1,107.00 | 8.00 |
| Total: | | $166,823,00 | $189,772,00 | |

Average benefit percentage test:

NHCE      5.01%

HCE      5.00%

Is the NHCE average at least 70 percent of the HCE average?

Yes (5.01% ÷ 5.00% = 100%), so it passes.

Concentration percentage: 75%

Midpoint between safe and unsafe harbor percentage: 33.75%

Rate group 1: (⅜) ÷ (½) = 100%

Rate group 2: (%) ÷ (²⁄₂) = 100%

Are the rate groups at least 33.75 percent?

Yes, so they pass.

Although this plan passes the general test, it is still considered a safe harbor because each component plan is also considered a safe harbor. This design provides HCE1 with 80.3 percent of the total cost and the costs cover the PVABs.

### Q 11:64   Would a combination defined benefit/defined contribution plan be beneficial for this client?

Yes. However, the Code Section 404(a)(7) 25 percent of pay deduction limit will come into play if there are overlapping participants in the plans. Therefore, the participants are separated into two different plans to avoid this limit. HCE2 and NHCE5 and NHCE6 will be in the defined contribution plan, while the others will be in the defined benefit plan. HCE1 will get a maximum benefit in the defined benefit plan, while the others will get top heavy only. The participants in the defined contribution plan need to have a 5 percent allocation to pass the discrimination test. The combination plan passes the gateway by providing benefits that are primarily defined benefit in character (more than 50 percent of the participants have a greater defined benefit EBAR than a defined contribution EBAR).

| | Defined Benefit Normal Cost | Defined Contribution | Defined Benefit EBAR | Defined Contribution EBAR | 401(a)(4) EBAR |
|---|---|---|---|---|---|
| HCE1 | $152,416.00 | $ 0.00 | 8.00 | 0.00 | 8.00 |
| HCE2 | $ 0.00 | $10,000.00 | 0.00 | 1.13 | 1.13 |
| NHCE1 | $ 3,239.00 | $ 0.00 | 2.00 | 0.00 | 2.00 |
| NHCE2 | $ 1,580.00 | $ 0.00 | 2.00 | 0.00 | 2.00 |
| NHCE3 | $ 897.00 | $ 0.00 | 2.00 | 0.00 | 2.00 |
| NHCE4 | $ 503.00 | $ 0.00 | 2.00 | 0.00 | 2.00 |
| NHCE5 | $ 0.00 | $ 1,000.00 | 0.00 | 8.66 | 8.66 |
| NHCE6 | $ 0.00 | $ 1,000.00 | 0.00 | 12.01 | 12.01 |
| Total: | $158,635.00 | $12,000.00 | | | |

Total contributions to both plans: $170,635

Average benefit percentage test:

$$\text{NHCE} \quad 4.78\%$$

$$\text{HCE} \quad 4.57\%$$

Is the NHCE average at least 70 percent of the HCE average?

Yes (4.78% ÷ 4.57% = 105%), so it passes.

Concentration Percentage: 75%

Midpoint between safe and unsafe harbor percentage: 33.75%

Rate group 1: (⅔) ÷ (½) = 66.67%

Rate group 2: (%) ÷ (⅔) = 100%

Are the rate groups at least 33.75 percent?

Yes, so they pass.

HCE1 gets 89.3 percent of the contribution, which is the highest percentage of all the plan designs shown so far. The administration costs, however, will be much greater in this type of design due to the complexity and the fact that there are now two plans to administer.

### Q 11:65    Can a safe harbor floor-offset arrangement work for this client?

Yes. There are some points to remember when designing a safe harbor floor-offset plan, though (see also chapter 5 for more information). First, the plans are subject to the Code Section 404(a)(7) deduction rules for combined plans, limiting the total deduction to 25 percent of eligible compensation. Second, the defined contribution plan cannot have a last-day-of-plan-year requirement in order to satisfy the rule that all employees benefiting in a defined benefit plan must also benefit in the defined contribution plan. And lastly, a general tested defined benefit plan, such as a cash balance plan, can be used in combination with a safe harbor defined contribution plan. A 5 percent allocation formula will be used in the defined contribution plan in order to satisfy top-heavy requirements. The cash balance design passes the general test on its own. The allocations could look like this:

| | DB Cost Prior to Offset | DB Accrued Benefit | Defined Contribution/ Allocation | DC Offset | DB Benefit After Offset | DB Cost After Offset |
|---|---|---|---|---|---|---|
| HCE1 | $72,500 | $12,195 | $10,000 | $2,862 | $ 9,333 | $55,485 |
| HCE2 | $72,500 | $16,320 | $10,000 | $4,384 | $12,017 | $53,382 |
| NHCE1 | $ 1,700 | $    512 | $ 2,000 | $1,294 | $ 0.00 | $      0 |
| NHCE2 | $ 1,700 | $    685 | $ 1,500 | $1,460 | $ 0.00 | $      0 |
| NHCE3 | $ 1,700 | $    917 | $ 1,250 | $1,829 | $ 0.00 | $      0 |
| NHCE4 | $ 1,700 | $ 1,227 | $ 1,000 | $2,200 | $ 0.00 | $      0 |
| NHCE5 | $ 1,700 | $ 1,642 | $ 1,000 | $3,308 | $ 0.00 | $      0 |
| NHCE6 | $ 1,700 | $ 2,073 | $ 1,000 | $4,584 | $ 0.00 | $      0 |
| Total: | | | $27,750 | | | $108,867 |

Total contributions to both plans: $136,617

25 percent of eligible pay: $138,750

Since this is a safe harbor design and both plans pass on their own prior to offset, no further discrimination testing is required. However, being subject to the 25 percent deduction limitation severely curtails the contributions for the owners. If the HCE2 does not want such a high contribution, he can elect to receive a smaller contribution in the defined benefit plan, which would allow the HCE1 to receive a greater contribution in the plan.

# Chapter 12

# Maximum Plan Benefits

The term *benefit* in defined benefit pension plan refers to the amount of money a participant can expect to receive at retirement. The Employee Retirement Income Security Act of 1974 (ERISA) and the Internal Revenue Code (Code) limit the minimum and maximum benefit that can be earned each year and define the service and compensation used to determine the amount of the benefit earned. This chapter outlines these limitations and definitions.

## Limitations on Annual Benefits

### Q 12:1    What is a *limitation year*?

A *limitation year* is the measuring period for determining the maximum amount of annual benefit. The limitation year, with respect to any qualified retirement plan maintained by the employer, is the calendar year. Instead of using the calendar year, however, an employer can elect to use any other consecutive 12-month period, including the plan year, as the limitation year. The election is made by the adoption of a written resolution by the employer. This requirement is satisfied if the election is made in connection with the adoption of the plan or any amendments to the plan. [Treas. Reg. § 1.415-2(b)]

In the case of a group of employers that constitutes either (1) a controlled group of corporations or (2) trades or businesses (whether or not incorporated) under common control (see chapter 6), the election to use a consecutive 12-month period other than the calendar year as the limitation year generally must be made by all members of the group that maintain a qualified retirement plan. [Rev. Rul. 79-5, 1979-1 C.B. 165; Ann. 95-99, 1995-48 I.R.B. 10]

### Q 12:2    Can the limitation year be changed?

Yes. However, once established, the limitation year can be changed only by written resolution of the employer. Any change in the limitation year must be a change to a 12-month period beginning with any day within the current limitation year. The limitations are applied in the normal manner to the new limitation year and are separately applied to a limitation period that begins with the first day of the current limitation year and ends on the day before the first day of the first limitation year for which the change is effective. This change creates a "limitation period," which begins with the first day of the current limitation year and ends on the day before the first day of the new limitation year. [Treas. Reg. § 1.415-2(b)(4)]

> **Example.** In 2002, an employer with a plan using the calendar year as the limitation year elects to change the limitation year to a limitation year commencing on July 1 and ending on June 30. The plan must satisfy the requirements of Code Section 415 for both the current limitation period commencing on January 1, 2002, and ending on June 30, 2002, and the next limitation year commencing on July 1, 2002, and ending on June 30, 2003.

### Q 12:3    What is the maximum amount of annual benefit that can be paid from a defined benefit pension plan?

In general, the benefits for a participant in a defined benefit pension plan cannot exceed, when expressed as an annual benefit during the limitation year, the lesser of $160,000 (as indexed) or 100 percent of the participant's average compensation for the high three years. The term *annual benefit* means a benefit payable annually in the form of a straight life annuity (with no ancillary benefits), and does not include any benefits attributable to either employee contributions or rollover contributions. [I.R.C. § 415(b)(1), (2); Treas. Reg. § 1.415-3(b)(1)(i)]

The $160,000 limitation is indexed each year by a cost-of-living adjustment, and the increases occur in multiples of $5,000. If the cost-of-living adjustment as applied to the $160,000 limitation does not exceed $5,000, the limitation is rounded down to the next multiple of $5,000. [I.R.C. § 415(d)(1)] The following table lists the maximum dollar limitation in effect for each limitation year that ended in that calendar year.

| Limitation Year Ending in the Calendar Year | Maximum Annual Dollar Limitation |
|:---:|:---:|
| 1987 | $ 90,000 |
| 1988 | $ 94,023 |
| 1989 | $ 98,064 |
| 1990 | $102,582 |
| 1991 | $108,963 |
| 1992 | $112,221 |

| Limitation Year Ending in the Calendar Year | Maximum Annual Dollar Limitation |
|---|---|
| 1993 | $115,641 |
| 1994 | $118,800 |
| 1995 | $120,000 |
| 1996 | $120,000 |
| 1997 | $125,000 |
| 1998 | $130,000 |
| 1999 | $130,000 |
| 2000 | $135,000 |
| 2001 | $140,000 |
| 2002 | $160,000 |
| 2003 | $160,000 |
| 2004 | $165,000 |
| 2005 | $170,000 |
| 2006 | $175,000 |
| 2007 | $180,000 |

### Q 12:4  Are there any reductions to the annual maximum benefit limitations?

Yes. The $160,000 limitation is reduced $\frac{1}{10}$ for each year of plan participation less than 10 years. It is also adjusted if benefits to the participant begin at an age other than the participant's Social Security retirement age; for limitation years ending in 2002 and later, the adjustment is made if benefits begin before age 62 or after age 65 (see Q 12:17). [I.R.C. § 415(b)(2)(C), (5)(A)]

The limitation of 100 percent of the participant's average compensation for the high three years is reduced $\frac{1}{10}$ for each year of service less than 10 years. [I.R.C. § 415(b)(5)] The Code Section 401(a)(17) compensation limit is not applicable in determining a participant's maximum benefit for purposes of the Code Section 415(b)(1)(B) 100 percent of three-year average compensation limitation. This limitation may be increased for cost of living after separation of service in the same manner and percentage as the dollar limitation is increased. The Internal Revenue Service (IRS) has released these percentages recently:

| Year | Percentage |
|---|---|
| 2003 | 1.0159 |
| 2004 | 1.022 |
| 2005 | 1.0273 |
| 2006 | 1.0383 |
| 2007 | 1.0334 |

[I.R.C. § 415(d)(1)(B)]

**Example 1.** Brenden is the owner of Kids Play A Lot Inc. and earned $400,000 for 2000, $100,000 for 2001, and $100,000 for 2002. His three-year average compensation for Code Section 415 purposes for these three years is $200,000. However, the plan may only recognize at the most $133,333 as the average annual compensation. Therefore, to take advantage of the higher Code Section 415 average, the benefit formula will need to be increased to 150 percent ($133,333 × 150% = $200,000) of average annual compensation in order to provide a benefit equal to 100 percent of the Code Section 415 average annual compensation.

**Example 2.** Jan has participated in the JJ Pension Plan for 7 years and has worked for the employer for 25 years. Her Social Security retirement age is the same as the plan's normal retirement age. Jan has a three-year average compensation of $145,000 and wants to understand her accrued benefit in the plan as of December 31, 2001. The plan provides a benefit of 3 percent of the highest three-year average compensation per year of service. Jan anticipated that her benefit would be $108,750 as of December 31, 2001, but she is told that her benefit is only $98,000. Jan is presented with the following calculations, which illustrate the impact of the maximum benefit limitations on her benefit.

Accrued benefit before application of maximum limit:

$$\$145,000 \times 0.03 \times 25 \text{ years of service} = \$108,750$$

Limit 1—$140,000 reduced for years of participation less than 10 years:

$$\$140,000 \times (1 - \tfrac{3}{10}) = \$98,000$$

Limit 2—100% of three-year average compensation reduced for years of service less than 10 years: $145,000 × $(1 - \tfrac{9}{10})$ = $145,000

Accrued benefit equals the lesser of limit 1 or limit 2, but no more than $108,750:

$$\text{Accrued benefit} = \$98,000$$

### Q 12:5   Are there any exceptions to the 100 percent of high three-year average compensation limit?

Yes. A plan that benefits employees under a collective bargaining agreement is not required to limit a participant's annual benefit to 100 percent of the highest three-year average compensation; however, the participant's maximum dollar limitation is reduced from $160,000 to one-half of the indexed dollar limitation in the year of retirement. To have these alternate limitations, the plan must meet the following criteria:

- The plan is maintained for the year of retirement pursuant to a collective bargaining agreement between employee representatives and one or more employers.
- The plan at all times during the year of retirement has at least 100 participants.

- The plan determines benefits solely by reference to length of service, the particular years during which the service was rendered, age at retirement, and date of retirement.
- The plan provides that a participant with four years of service is 100 percent vested in his or her accrued benefit.
- The plan allows an employee to participate in the plan before the completion of 60 consecutive days of service with the employer or employers maintaining the plan.

These limitations are not available to a participant who either (1) terminates service with the employer if such participant had compensation in 3 out of the last 10 years preceding termination that exceeded the three-year average compensation to all such participants in those years or (2) received benefits from another plan maintained by the same employer that was subject to the alternative maximum annual benefit limitations described above. [I.R.C. § 415(b)(7)]

### Q 12:6   Is there a minimum benefit that may be provided?

Yes. A participant is not considered to have a benefit in excess of 100 percent of average compensation for the high three years if the benefit is less than or equal to $10,000 per year. To meet this exception, however, the participant must not have ever participated in a defined contribution plan of the employer. Furthermore, the $10,000 annual benefit is reduced for each year of service less than 10 years. [I.R.C. § 415(b)(4)]

This $10,000 *de minimis* benefit may only be paid out in an amount not to exceed $10,000 per year. In other words, if there is an optional form of payment allowed under the plan that would provide for a payment within the limitation year in excess of $10,000, the Code Section 415 limit for this participant will be exceeded. Therefore, a lump-sum benefit that is the actuarial equivalent would most likely not be allowed. In addition, the IRS has said in its Code Section 415 proposed regulations that if the benefit payment is limited in order to comply with the Code, then this is considered an impermissible forfeiture of benefits and the plan could be disqualified.

### Q 12:7   What is a *year of service*?

A *year of service* is generally determined by plan provisions on a reasonable and consistent basis. [Treas. Reg. § 1.415-3(g)(1)(ii)]

Years of service can include years of service with businesses that were in existence before an existing corporation when the corporation is a mere formal or technical change in the form of business entity, but the business operations of the corporation and the previous entity remain substantially the same. Thus, the period during which a doctor operated his practice as a sole proprietorship before the business's incorporation and its sponsorship of a defined benefit plan constituted years of service with the employer. [Lear Eye Clinic, Ltd. v. Commissioner, 106 T.C. 418 (1996)] However, in a consolidated case [Brody Enters, Inc. v. Commissioner, 106 T.C. 418 (1996)], an attorney who was the sole shareholder and employee of a corporation that adopted a defined benefit plan in which he participated could not include as years of service with the employer the period during which he conducted a part-time private law practice while working full time for the IRS. The practice was located in a different city, the corporation failed to show that the attorney conducted a private law practice, and the attorney maintained no records of the hours that he spent on the practice. In addition, the attorney could not include the five-year period during which he worked for a law firm that was also located in a different city. He had no ownership interest in the law firm and there was no relationship between the corporation's business operations and those of the law firm.

### Q 12:8 What is a participant's *average compensation for the high three years*?

The Code defines *average compensation for the high three years* as the three consecutive calendar years during which the participant was both an active participant in the plan and had the greatest aggregate compensation (see Q 12:39) from the employer. [I.R.C. § 415(b)(3)] The Pension Protection Act of 2006 (PPA) amended the Code to provide that the Code Section 415(b)(3) limit is based on all years of service with the employer, including years prior to the effective date of the plan. This change is applicable to plan years beginning after December 31, 2005. The Treasury regulations define this term as the three consecutive calendar years (or the actual number of consecutive years of employment for employees who are employed for less than three consecutive years with the employer) during which the employee had the greatest aggregate compensation from the employer. [Treas. Reg. § 1.415-3(a)(3)] The PPA changed the wording in the Code and there is now no difference between what the Code and Regulations provide (e.g., the Code Section 415 limit for a participant can be based on that individual's highest three consecutive years of service with the employer).

The plan can use any 12-month period other than the calendar year (e.g., the plan year) as long as it is uniformly and consistently applied. [Treas. Reg. § 1.415-3(a)(3)]

If the employee is self-employed as defined in Code Section 401(c)(1), "the participant's earned income" is substituted for "compensation from the employer." [I.R.C. § 415(b)(3)]

### Q 12:9 Is any adjustment to the annual maximum benefit limitations required if the form of benefit is different from a life annuity?

Maybe. If the benefit under the plan is payable in any form other than a life annuity, it must be adjusted to the actuarial equivalent of a life annuity, and after such adjustment, it must not exceed the $160,000 (as indexed) and 100 percent of highest three-year average compensation limitations. Any portion of a joint and survivor annuity that constitutes a qualified joint and survivor annuity (QJSA) is not to be taken into account, and does not need to be adjusted. [I.R.C. § 415(b)(2)(B)] Treasury Regulations Section 1.401(a)-11(b)(2) defines a *qualified joint and survivor annuity* as an annuity for the life of the participant with a survivor annuity for the life of the spouse of a participant that is neither less than half nor greater than the amount of the annuity that is payable during the joint lives of the participant and the spouse. Such an annuity must be at least the actuarial equivalent of a life annuity or any optional form of life annuity under the plan. Therefore, a plan that provides that benefits at retirement are paid in the form of a joint and survivor annuity for married participants and a life annuity for single participants will not be required to adjust a participant's joint and survivor annuity benefit if such benefit is limited to the maximum benefit limitations under Code Section 415(b). If, however, a plan provides for a form of benefit other than a life annuity or a QJSA, and the participant's benefit is at the maximum limit under Code Section 415(b), that form of benefit could cause the benefit to exceed those limitations unless the benefit is reduced to one that is actuarially equivalent to a life annuity.

> **Example.** The CTKD Pension Plan has a 10-year certain and life annuity as its normal form of benefit. Jose is about to retire with a benefit equal to 97 percent of his highest three-year average salary of $55,000. The plan's definition of actuarial equivalence is the 1983 Group Annuity Mortality (GAM) Table, blended using 50 percent of the male mortality rates and 50 percent of the female mortality rates, with interest at 5 percent. The monthly annuity purchase rate (APR) for a life annuity is 138.408; for a 10-year certain and life annuity the APR is 144.949. Hence, Jose's benefit payable as an actuarially equivalent straight life annuity is $55,871 (($55,000 × 97% × 144.949) ÷ 138.408). That amount exceeds his highest three-year average salary of $55,000 by $871 and must be reduced to avoid exceeding that limitation.

### Q 12:10    What impact does Code Section 417(e)(3) have on the maximum benefit limitations?

Code Section 417(e)(3) requires certain payments from defined benefit plans to be converted from a life annuity to the particular form of payment using certain interest rates and mortality tables. This amount, however, may not exceed the maximum payment allowed under Code Section 415.

### Q 12:11    What forms of benefits are not subject to Code Section 417(e)(3)?

Any benefit that is in the form of a nondecreasing life annuity, including a QJSA, a qualified preretirement survivor annuity, and an annuity that decreases merely because of the cessation or reduction of Social Security supplements or qualified disability payments, is not subject to Code Section 417(e)(3). A benefit that decreases during the life of the participant merely because of the death of the survivor annuitant is also exempted from the requirements of Code Section 417(e)(3), but only if the reduction is to a level not below 50 percent of the annual benefit payable before the death of the survivor annuitant. [Treas. Reg. § 1.417(e)-1(d)(6)] Therefore, an actuarial equivalent lump-sum payment of the straight life annuity would be subject to Code Section 417(e)(3).

### Q 12:12    Is there any limitation on the actuarial assumptions used to calculate the actuarial equivalent of the maximum benefit limitations?

Yes. The adjustment of the maximum benefit limitations to an actuarially equivalent benefit is done using certain interest rates and mortality tables. Four adjustments to the maximum benefit limitations affect the use of certain actuarial assumptions. They are adjustments for the form of benefit (see Q 12:13), adjustments to the maximum dollar limitation when benefits begin before a certain age (see Q 12:17), adjustments to the maximum dollar limitation when benefits commence after a certain age (see Q 12:19), and adjustments to a form of benefit subject to Code Section 417(e)(3) (e.g., a lump-sum payment) (see Q 12:20).

### Q 12:13    How are the adjustments to the maximum benefit limitation done when the benefit is paid in a form other than a life annuity that is not subject to the requirements of Code Section 417(e)(3)?

When converting the maximum benefit limitations to a form of payment that is the actuarial equivalent of a life annuity, the plan's interest rate and mortality table or table of reduction factors are used; however, the adjusted amount cannot exceed the actuarially equivalent amount calculated using 5 percent interest and the applicable mortality table (see Q 12:14). [Rev. Rul. 98-1, Q&A 7, 1998-2 I.R.B. 5]

**Example 1.** The Ken Company Pension Plan provides a monthly life annuity benefit of 100 percent of the participant's highest three-year average compensation as its normal form of benefit. The plan's definition of actuarial equivalence is the 1983 Male Group Annuity Mortality Table with interest at 6 percent. The monthly APR for a life annuity is 118.999; for a 10-year certain and life annuity, the APR is 127.309. Jamie is about to retire in 2005 with a benefit of $15,000 payable in monthly installments. The actuarially equivalent 10-year certain and life annuity is $14,021 ($15,000 × 118.999 ÷ 127.309). That amount and form of payment may be paid to Jamie as long as the amount does not exceed the actuarially equivalent amount using the applicable mortality table and 5 percent interest, $14,348 ($15,000 × 11.992 ÷ 12.537). These APRs are expressed annually, because the maximum benefit limitations are based on annual benefits.

If the plan uses a table of conversion factors, the actuarially equivalent benefit is determined using the table of conversion factors. The resulting amount is compared to the actuarially equivalent benefit using 5 percent interest and the applicable mortality table (see Q 12:14). The lesser of these two amounts is the maximum benefit payable in the plan's alternate form.

**Example 2.** The facts are the same as those in Example 1 except that the plan uses a table of conversion factors to determine the actuarially equivalent benefit and the table produces an actuarially equivalent 10-year certain and life annuity of $14,500. This amount cannot be paid because it exceeds the actuarially equivalent amount calculated using the applicable mortality table and 5 percent interest, $14,348 ($15,000 × 11.992 ÷ 12.537).

### Q 12:14   What is the *applicable mortality table*?

The *applicable mortality table* is the table found in Revenue Ruling 95-6 [1995-1 C.B. 80] (the 83 GAM-U table) for payments made on or before December 30, 2002, and is the table found in Revenue Ruling 2001-62 [2001-53 I.R.B. 1] (the 94 GAR table) for payments made after December 30, 2002, and is prescribed by the Secretary of the Treasury. Both tables are based on a fixed blend of 50 percent of the male mortality rates and 50 percent of the female mortality rates from the underlining mortality rates from the 1983 GAM table and the 1994 Group Annuity Reserving Table projected in 2002, respectively. They are both considered gender neutral. These tables are used for adjusting the maximum benefit limitations under Code Section 415(b) to the actuarial equivalent of a life annuity. They are also used to determine the minimum lump-sum value payable under Code Section 417(e)(3). The 94 GAR table may be used as early as January 1, 2002, if plan provisions provide for such use. The Treasury Department is required to issue a new applicable mortality table for plan years beginning in 2007.

### Q 12:15   What is the *applicable interest rate*?

The *applicable interest rate* for a month is the annual interest rate on 30-year Treasury securities as specified by the Commissioner for that month in revenue rulings, notices, or other guidance published in the Internal Revenue Bulletin. For plan years beginning after December 31, 2007, the PPA requires the use of segment rates as the applicable interest rate. The adjusted first, second, and third segment rates are the first, second, and third segment rates that would be determined under Code Section 430(h)(2)(C), except that these rates are determined based on the average yields for the distribution period and there is a five-year phase-in. The five-year phase-in requires 20 percent of the segment rates to be used in determining the applicable interest rate for 2008 and increases by 20 percent per year until 2012 when 100 percent of the segment rates will be required. [I.R.C. § 417(e)(3)(A)(ii)(II)]

### Q 12:16   What is the time for determining the applicable interest rate for purposes of the maximum benefit limitations?

The Retirement Protection Act of 1994 (RPA '94) changed the rules under Code Section 417(e)(3) for determining the present value of a lump-sum payment. A plan must use the same date for applying the applicable interest rate to a distribution subject to the requirements of Code Section 417(e)(3) (i.e., minimum lump sums) as it does for applying the applicable interest rate to a distribution subject to the requirements of Code Section 415(b) (i.e., maximum benefits). Until the plan is amended to reflect the changes to Code Section 417(e), however, it can use any date that is permitted under Treasury Regulations Section 1.417(e)-1(d)(4). In addition, a plan can implement these rules at different times for purposes of Code Sections 415 and 417. [Rev. Rul. 98-1, 1998-1 C.B. 249]

**Q 12:17    What adjustments must be made to the $90,000 annual limitation (as indexed; $160,000 for limitation years ending in 2002 or later) if benefits begin before Social Security retirement age (or age 62 for limitation years ending in 2002 or later) and the benefit is payable in a form that is not subject to Code Section 417(e)(3)?**

**For limitation years ending on or before December 31, 2001:**

If a benefit begins before a participant's Social Security retirement age, the $90,000 ($160,000 for limitation years ending in 2002 or later) annual benefit is reduced to the actuarial equivalent of a benefit payable at the earlier retirement age. The actuarial reduction is done using a formula if the age at which the participant's benefits begin is age 62 or older. If the benefits begin before age 62, the actuarial equivalent is determined under the formula until age 62 and is actuarially reduced thereafter to the lesser of (1) the amount calculated using the plan's interest rate and mortality table, or tabular reduction factors and (2) the amount calculated using 5 percent and the applicable mortality table (see Q 12:14). [Rev. Rul. 98-1, Q&A 7, Step 2, 1998-1 C.B. 249]

The following describes the steps taken to determine the Code Section 415 limit. The term *retirement age* as it appears in the following means the age at which the benefits begin before the participant's Social Security retirement age.

*Actuarial reduction from Social Security retirement age to age 62.*

*Step   1.*   Determine the participant's Social Security retirement age:

1.  If a participant is age 62 before January 1, 2000, the Social Security retirement age is 65.

2.  If a participant is age 62 after December 31, 1999, and before January 1, 2017, the Social Security retirement age is 66.

3.  If a participant is age 62 after December 31, 2016, the Social Security retirement age is 67.

*Step   2.*   Calculate the number of months from the participant's Social Security retirement age to the later of the retirement age or age 62.

*Step   3.*   Calculate the reduction factor from Social Security retirement age to the later of the retirement age or age 62. The reduction is $\frac{5}{9}$ of 1 percent for the first 36 months and $\frac{5}{12}$ of 1 percent for each additional month greater than 36 to a maximum of 24 additional months.

*Step   4.*   Determine the maximum dollar limitation in effect at the end of the limitation year, and reduce that amount by $\frac{1}{10}$ for each year of plan participation less than 10 years.

*Step   5.*   Apply the reduction factor in Step 3 to the amount in Step 4. If the benefit is payable at age 62 or later, no further adjustments are required and the amount in Step 5 is the maximum dollar limitation for the participant payable at the retirement age in the form of a life annuity or QJSA. If the benefit is payable before age 62, continue to Step 6 below.

*Actuarial reduction below age 62.* If the plan provides benefits before age 62 using actuarially equivalent assumptions, Step 6 is used. If the plan uses a table of actuarially equivalent factors, skip Step 6 and go to Step 7.

*Step 6.* Calculate the actuarial equivalent of the age 62 benefit in Step 5 payable at the retirement age using 5 percent interest and the applicable mortality table (see Q 12:14) and compare this amount to the actuarial equivalent of the age 62 benefit in Step 5 payable at the retirement age using the plan interest rate and mortality table. The lesser of these two amounts is the maximum annual benefit payable at the retirement age. (If no forfeiture of benefits will result upon death, mortality can be ignored in the calculation of actuarially equivalent benefits.)

*Step 7.* Apply the tabular reduction factors to the benefits in Step 5 to determine the actuarially equivalent benefit as of the retirement age. Do the same with the applicable mortality table at an interest rate of 5 percent. The lesser of these two amounts is the actuarial equivalent of the maximum dollar limitation payable at the retirement date in the form of a life annuity or QJSA. (If no forfeiture of benefits will result upon death, mortality can be ignored in the calculation of actuarially equivalent benefits.)

**Example 1.** Frank, a participant in a defined benefit pension plan, was born on April 1, 1940. The plan year is August 1 to July 31, and the calculation of the maximum dollar limitation is being made as of April 1, 2000. The plan's normal retirement age is 60, the normal form of benefit is a life annuity, and the limitation year is the same as the plan year. Frank has participated in the plan for five years. His maximum dollar limitation is calculated as follows:

*Step 1.* Determine the participant's Social Security retirement age.

*Result 1.* Frank's Social Security retirement age is 67.

*Step 2.* Calculate the number of months from the participant's Social Security retirement age to the later of the retirement age or age 62.

*Result 2.* Frank's age is 60, which is less than 62; therefore, the number of months is calculated from age 67 to age 62. There is a total of 60 months between those ages.

*Step 3.* Calculate the reduction factor from Social Security retirement age to the later of the participant's projected retirement age or age 62.

*Result 3.* The reduction is $\frac{5}{9}$ of 1 percent for the first 36 months, or 20 percent ($\frac{5}{9}\% \times 36$) plus $\frac{5}{12}$ of 1 percent for the next 24 months, or 10 percent ($\frac{5}{12}\% \times 24$). Frank's total reduction to his maximum dollar limitation is 30 percent.

*Step 4.* Determine the maximum dollar limitation in effect at the end of the limitation year and reduce that amount by $\frac{1}{10}$ for each year of plan participation less than 10.

*Result 4.* According to the chart in Q 12:3, for the plan year ending in 2000, the maximum dollar limitation is $135,000. Frank has participated in the plan for five years. Therefore, the maximum dollar limitation must be reduced by $5/10$, to $67,500 ($135,000 × (1 − $5/10$)).

*Step 5.* Apply the reduction factor in Step 3 to the amount in Step 4.

*Result 5.* A 30 percent reduction to $67,500 results in a maximum dollar limitation of $47,250 ($67,500 × (100% − 30%)).

*Actuarial reduction below age 62.* For purposes of Step 6, the plan's interest rate is 5 percent and the mortality table is the 1983 Individual Annuity Male Mortality Table. For purposes of Step 7, the tabular reduction is 2 percent for each year that benefits begin before age 65.

*Step 6.* Compare the actuarial equivalent of the age 62 benefit in Step 5 payable at the retirement age using the applicable mortality table (see Q 12:14) at an interest rate of 5 percent to the actuarially equivalent amount using the plan's interest rate and mortality table. The lesser of these two amounts is the maximum annual benefit payable to Frank as a life annuity starting at age 60.

*Result 6.* The APR for a life annuity payable annually at age 62 is 12.914 using 5 percent interest and the applicable mortality table. That amount is discounted from age 62 to age 60 at 5 percent interest. This results in an APR of 11.713 (12.914 × $1.05^{-2}$). The APR for a life annuity payable annually at age 60 using 5 percent and the applicable mortality table is 13.496. Therefore, the age 60 benefit that is actuarially equivalent to the benefit in Step 5 is $41,008 ($47,250 × (11.713 ÷ 13.496)).

The result using the plan's interest rate and mortality table is an actuarial equivalent benefit of $41,080 ($47,250 × (11.611 ÷ 13.355)). (The APR at age 62, discounted two years at 5 percent interest is 11.611; the APR at age 60 is 13.355.)

The lesser of the two amounts is $41,008 and is the maximum annual benefit payable to Frank as a life annuity starting at age 60.

*Step 7.* If the plan used tabular reduction factors to the benefit in Step 5 to determine the actuarially equivalent benefit as of the retirement age, the same is done with the applicable mortality table at an interest rate of 5 percent. The lesser of these two amounts is the maximum annual benefit payable to Frank as a life annuity starting at age 60.

*Result 7.* The plan's reduction in the benefit at age 62 would be 94 percent (100% − (2% × 3)) and at age 60 would be 90 percent (100% − (2% × 5)). The actuarial equivalent of the age 62 benefit at age 60 is the ratio of the reduction factors, 95.7 percent (90% ÷ 94%). Therefore, the actuarial equivalent of the age 62 maximum dollar limitation at age 60 using the tabular reduction is $45,218 ($47,250 × 95.7%).

The APR for a life annuity payable annually at age 62 using 5 percent and the applicable mortality table is 12.914. That amount is discounted from age 62 to age 60 at 5 percent interest. This results in an APR of 11.713 (12.914 × $1.05^{-2}$). The APR for a life annuity payable annually at age 60 using 5 percent and the applicable mortality table is 13.496. Therefore, the age 60 benefit that is actuarially equivalent to the benefit in Step 5 is $41,008 ($47,250 × (11.713 ÷ 13.496)). That amount is less than Frank's maximum annual benefit for the plan using tabular reduction factors.

**For limitation years ending after December 31, 2001:**

The maximum benefit of $160,000 is adjusted for payments beginning before age 62. If the benefits begin before age 62, the actuarial equivalent is determined by reducing from age 62 to the age of payment using the lesser of (1) the amount calculated using the plan's interest rate and mortality table, or tabular reduction factors and (2) the amount calculated using 5 percent and the applicable mortality table (see Q 12:14). [Rev. Rul. 98-1, Q&A 7, Step 2, 1998-1 C.B. 249; Rev. Rul. 2001-51, Q&A 3, 2001-45 I.R.B. 427]

The following describes the steps taken to determine the Code Section 415 limit. The term *retirement age* as it appears in the following means the age at which the benefits begin before age 62.

*Step 1.* Determine the maximum dollar limitation in effect at the end of the limitation year, and reduce that amount by ¹⁄₁₀ for each year of plan participation less than 10 years. If the plan's normal retirement age is between age 62 and age 65, this is the maximum dollar limitation for the year.

*Actuarial reduction below age 62.* If the plan provides benefits before age 62 using actuarially equivalent assumptions, Step 2 is used. If the plan uses a table of actuarially equivalent factors, skip Step 2 and go to Step 3.

*Step 2.* Calculate the actuarial equivalent of the age 62 benefit in Step 1 payable at the retirement age using 5 percent interest and the applicable mortality table (see Q 12:14) and compare this amount to the actuarial equivalent of the age 62 benefit in Step 1 payable at the retirement age using the plan interest rate and mortality table. The lesser of these two amounts is the maximum annual benefit payable at the retirement age. (If no forfeiture of benefits will result upon death, mortality can be ignored in the calculation of actuarially equivalent benefits.)

*Step 3.* Apply the tabular reduction factors to the benefits in Step 1 to determine the actuarially equivalent benefit as of the retirement age. Do the same with the applicable mortality table at an interest rate of 5 percent. The lesser of these two amounts is the actuarial equivalent of the maximum dollar limitation payable at the retirement date in the form of a life annuity or QJSA. (If no forfeiture of benefits will result upon death, mortality can be ignored in the calculation of actuarially equivalent benefits.)

**Example 2.** Joe, a participant in a defined benefit pension plan, was born on July 1, 1957. The plan year is August 1 to July 31, and the calculation of the maximum dollar limitation is being made as of April 1, 2002. The plan's normal retirement age is 60, the normal form of benefit is a life annuity, and the limitation year is the same as the plan year. Joe has participated in the plan for five years. His maximum dollar limitation is calculated as follows:

*Step 1.* Determine the maximum dollar limitation in effect at the end of the limitation year and reduce that amount by $\frac{1}{10}$ for each year of plan participation less than 10 years.

*Result 1.* According to the chart in Q 12:3, for the plan year ending in 2002, the maximum dollar limitation is $160,000. Joe has participated in the plan for five years. Therefore, the maximum dollar limitation must be reduced by $\frac{5}{10}$, to $80,000 ($160,000 $\times$ $(1 - \frac{5}{10})$).

*Actuarial reduction below age 62.* For purposes of Step 2, the plan's interest rate is 5 percent and the mortality table is the 1983 Individual Annuity Male Mortality Table. For purposes of Step 3, the tabular reduction is 2 percent for each year that benefits begin before age 65.

*Step 2.* Compare the actuarial equivalent of the age 62 benefit in Step 1 payable at the retirement age using the applicable mortality table (see Q 12:14) at an interest rate of 5 percent, to the actuarially equivalent amount using the plan's interest rate and mortality table. The lesser of these two amounts is the maximum annual benefit payable to Joe as a life annuity starting at age 60.

*Result 2.* The APR for a life annuity payable annually at age 62 is 12.914 using 5 percent interest and the applicable mortality table. That amount is discounted from age 62 to age 60 at 5 percent interest. This results in an APR of 11.713 (12.914 $\times$ $1.05^{-2}$). The APR for a life annuity payable annually at age 60 using 5 percent and the applicable mortality table is 13.496. Therefore, the age 60 benefit that is actuarially equivalent to the benefit in Step 5 is $69,431 ($80,000 $\times$ (11.713 $\div$ 13.496)).

The result using the plan's interest rate and mortality table is an actuarial equivalent benefit of $69,553 ($80,000 $\times$ (11.611 $\div$ 13.355)). (The APR at age 62, discounted two years at 5 percent interest is 11.611; the APR at age 60 is 13.355.)

The lesser of the two amounts is $69,431 and is the maximum annual benefit payable to Joe as a life annuity starting at age 60.

*Step 3.* If the plan used tabular reduction factors to the benefit in Step 2 to determine the actuarially equivalent benefit as of the retirement age, the same is done with the applicable mortality table at an interest rate of 5 percent. The lesser of these two amounts is the maximum annual benefit payable to Joe as a life annuity starting at age 60.

*Result 3.* The plan's reduction in the benefit at age 62 would be 94 percent (100% $-$ (2% $\times$ 3)) and at age 60 would be 90 percent (100% $-$ (2% $\times$ 5)). The actuarial equivalent of the age 62 benefit at age 60 is the ratio of the reduction factors, 95.7 percent (90% $\div$ 94%). Therefore, the actuarial equivalent of the age 62 maximum dollar limitation at age 60 using the tabular reduction is $76,560 ($80,000 $\times$ 95.7%).

The APR for a life annuity payable annually at age 62 using 5 percent and the applicable mortality table is 12.914. That amount is discounted from age 62 to age 60 at 5 percent interest. This results in an APR of 11.713 (12.914 × $1.05^{-2}$). The APR for a life annuity payable annually at age 60 using 5 percent and the applicable mortality table is 13.496. Therefore, the age 60 benefit that is actuarially equivalent to the benefit in Step 5 is $69,431 ($80,000 × (11.713 ÷ 13.496)). That amount is less than Joe's maximum annual benefit for the plan using tabular reduction factors.

### Q 12:18   What considerations must be made for a plan that has a normal retirement age less than 65?

In the case of a plan with a normal retirement age less than 65, the requirements for nonforfeitability of benefits and actuarial increase for delayed retirement of Code Section 411 (see chapter 8) must be coordinated with the requirements of Code Section 415. Under Code Section 411, if benefits are not paid to a participant after the participant attains the plan's normal retirement age, and the plan's terms do not provide for the "suspension" of the participant's benefits in accordance with Code Section 411(a)(3)(B) and DOL Regulation 2530.203-3, the participant's benefit must be actuarially increased for late retirement to avoid any forfeiture of the participant's benefit.

Under Code Section 415 as amended by the Economic Growth and Tax Relief Reconciliation Act of 2001 (EGTRRA), however, the dollar limitation applicable to a participant does not increase between age 62 and age 65. If a participant continues to work past a plan's normal retirement age that is less than 65, and the participant's benefit equals the Code Section 415 dollar limitation at an age between 62 and 65, any actuarial increase to the participant's benefit after that age and before age 65 would violate Code Section 415. In such a case, to satisfy Code Sections 415 and 411, the terms of the plan must either provide for the in-service payment of the participant's benefit (where the participant has attained normal retirement age and has a benefit that cannot be actuarially increased without violating Code Section 415), or provide for the suspension of benefits in accordance with Code Section 411(a)(3)(B) and 29 C.F.R. Section 2530.203-3 (see chapter 28). [Rev. Rul. 2001-51, 2001-45 I.R.B. 427]

### Q 12:19   What adjustments are required to the $90,000 annual dollar limitation if benefits begin after Social Security retirement age (age 65 for limitation years ending after December 31, 2001)?

**For limitation years ending on or before December 31, 2001:**

The $90,000 annual limitation is increased for benefits that begin after the Social Security retirement age to the actuarial equivalent of a life annuity benefit beginning at the Social Security retirement age. The adjusted amount is the lesser of the amount as determined by the plan interest rate and mortality table or by the applicable mortality table with interest at 5 percent. If the plan uses a tabular factor in determining the actuarially equivalent late retirement benefits, the lesser of the amount determined using the tabular factors or using the applicable mortality table with interest at 5 percent is the maximum adjusted dollar limitation. [Rev. Rul. 98-1, Q&A 7, Step 2, 1998-1 C.B. 249] In all instances, this actuarially equivalent adjustment is done without the mortality decrement.

**Example 1.** Frank is age 71 with a Social Security retirement age of 65. His pension plan determines actuarially equivalent benefits using the 1983 Male Individual Annuity Mortality Table with interest at 6 percent. In the year of retirement, Frank's maximum dollar limitation at age 65 is $135,000. His age 71 adjusted maximum dollar limitation using the plan's interest and mortality table is $224,335 (($135,000 $\times$ $(1.06)^6$ $\times$ 11.034) $\div$ 9.419). The age-adjusted maximum dollar limitation using the applicable mortality table and 5 percent interest is $216,147 (($135,000 $\times$ $(1.05)^6$ $\times$ 11.993)/10.038). Hence, the age 71 adjusted dollar limitation for Frank is $216,147.

**For limitation years ending after December 31, 2001:**

The $160,000 annual limitation is increased for benefits that begin after age 65 to the actuarial equivalent of a life annuity benefit beginning at age 65. The adjusted amount is the lesser of the amount as determined by the plan interest rate and mortality table or by the applicable mortality table with interest at 5 percent. If the plan uses a tabular factor in determining the actuarially equivalent late retirement benefits, the lesser of the amount determined using the tabular factors or using the applicable mortality table with interest at 5 percent is the maximum adjusted dollar limitation. [Rev. Rul. 98-1, Q&A 7, Step 2, 1998-1 C.B. 249; Rev. Rul. 2001-51, Q&A 3, 2001-52 I.R.B. 427] In all instances, this actuarially equivalent adjustment is done without the mortality decrement.

**Example 2.** Joe is age 71. His pension plan determines actuarially equivalent benefits using the 1983 Male Individual Annuity Mortality Table with interest at 6 percent. In the year of retirement, Joe's maximum dollar limitation at age 65 is $160,000. His age 71 adjusted maximum dollar limitation using the plan's interest and mortality table is $265,879 (($160,000 $\times$ $(1.06)^6$ $\times$ 11.034) $\div$ 9.419). The age-adjusted maximum dollar limitation using the applicable mortality table and 5 percent interest is $256,174 (($135,000 $\times$ $(1.05)^6$ $\times$ 11.993) $\div$ 10.038). Hence, the age 71 adjusted dollar limitation for Joe is $256,174.

## Limitations on Lump-Sum Payments

### Q 12:20    How are the maximum benefit limitations applied to a benefit payable in a form subject to Code Section 417(e)(3)?

Under Code Section 415(b)(2)(B), if the benefit under the plan is payable in any form other than a straight life annuity, the determination as to whether the limitations of Code Section 415(b) have been satisfied is made by adjusting the participant's benefit so that it is equivalent to a straight life annuity.

Code Section 415(b)(2)(E) provides limitations on the actuarial assumptions that must be used to adjust a benefit payable in a form other than a straight life annuity to determine the annual benefit for this purpose. Prior to its amendment by the Pension Funding Equity Act of 2004 (PFEA '04) Section 415(b)(2)(E)(ii) provided that, for purposes of adjusting any benefit payable in a form that is subject to the minimum present value requirements of Code Section 417(e)(3), the interest rate assumption must not be less than the greater of the applicable interest rate (as defined in Code Section 417(e)(3)) or the rate specified in the plan. Code Section 415(b)(2)(E)(v) also prescribes a specific mortality table to be used, the 94 GAR (see Q 12:14).

Revenue Ruling 98-1 [1998-1 C.B. 249, Q&A 8] provides that the actuarially equivalent straight life annuity for a benefit that is paid in a form that is subject to the minimum present value requirements of Code Section 417(e)(3) is the greater of (1) the actuarially equivalent straight life annuity computed using the plan rate and plan mortality table or plan tabular factor specified in the plan for actuarial equivalence for the particular form of benefit payable and (2) the actuarially equivalent straight life annuity computed using the applicable interest rate and the applicable mortality table under Code Section 417(e)(3).

Section 101(b)(4) of PFEA '04 amended Code Section 415(b)(2)(E)(ii) to provide that, for purposes of adjusting any benefit payable in a form that is subject to the minimum present value requirements of Code Section 417(e)(3), the interest rate assumption must not be less than the greater of the applicable interest rate (as defined in Code Section 417(e)(3)) or the rate specified in the plan, except that in the case of plan years beginning in 2004 or 2005, 5.5 percent is used in lieu of the applicable interest rate. (See Q 12:25.) However, there was a transition rule for 2004 providing that the maximum benefit subject to these rules cannot be less than the lump sum that would have been calculated using the applicable interest rate in effect under the plan as of the last day of the 2003 plan year. This change does require a plan amendment prior to the last day of the 2006 plan year, but the legislation provides Code Section 411(d)(6) relief to allow plans to implement this change to reduce distributions in plan operation even though the plan may not be amended until a later date. [Notice 2004-78, 2004-48 I.R.B. 879]

The PPA amended this section once again to provide that for plan years beginning after December 31, 2005, the interest rate cannot be less than the greatest of:

1. 5.5 percent,
2. the rate that provides a benefit of not more than 105 percent of the benefit that would be provided if the applicable interest rate (as defined in Code Section 417(e)(3)) were the interest rate assumption, or
3. the rate specified under the plan.

**Example 1.** Dane, whose Social Security retirement age is 65, retires at age 62 from the D&R Pension Plan and elects to receive a distribution in the form of a lump sum. The lump-sum payment using the plan's benefit formula and the rules under Code Section 417(e)(3) is $1,175,000.

At the time of the distribution (and as defined by the terms of the plan) the applicable interest rate is 6.5 percent. The APR at age 62 for the applicable mortality table using an interest rate of 6.5 percent is 11.420. Hence, the actuarially equivalent annual benefit using that rate is $102,890 ($1,175,000 × 11.420).

The actuarially equivalent annual benefit is now compared to Dane's highest three-year average annual compensation and his age-adjusted dollar limitation at age 62.

Dane's highest three-year average annual compensation is $113,000; therefore, the $102,890 actuarially equivalent annual benefit paid as a lump sum does not exceed that limitation.

If Dane were to receive payment in 1997, the maximum dollar limitation is $125,000 at Dane's Social Security retirement age. There is a 20 percent reduction in the dollar limitation from age 65 to age 62 (5/9% × 36 months), or a reduction of $25,000 ($125,000 × 20%), for a maximum annual benefit at age 62 of $100,000. Therefore, Dane's age-adjusted dollar limitation at age 62 is $100,000. The actuarial equivalent of the lump-sum benefit, $102,890, exceeds Dane's age-adjusted dollar limitation of $100,000 by $2,890. Therefore, the plan must reduce the lump-sum payment to the actuarial equivalent of $100,000, or $1,142,000 ($100,000 × 11.420).

If, instead, Dane were to receive payment during 2002, the maximum dollar limitation is $160,000, payable at age 62. The actuarial equivalent of the lump-sum benefit, $102,890, does not exceed Dane's dollar limitation, and he can receive the full value of his lump-sum distribution.

**Example 2.** Jim is retiring at age 62 in 2006 with an accrued benefit of $14,583 per month. His highest three-year average annual compensation is $17,500. The maximum benefit limitation in 2006 is $14,583.33 (175,000/12). The plan's definition of actuarial equivalence is 5 percent and the 1983 IAM, Female table. The applicable interest rate is 4.65 percent. The Code Section 415 maximum lump sum is determined as the smallest of the following three amounts:

1. Using 5.5 percent and the applicable mortality table. The monthly APR using these assumptions is 145.47063, and the maximum lump sum is $2,121,398 ($14,583 × 145.47063).

2. Using the rate that provides a benefit of not more than 105 percent of the benefit that would be provided if the applicable interest rate (as defined in Code Section 417(e)(3)) were the interest rate assumption. The monthly APR using the 4.65 percent interest rate assumption is 157.16080, and the maximum lump sum is $2,406,470 ($14,583 × 157.16080 × 1.05).

3. Using the rate as specified under the plan. The monthly APR using these assumptions is 163.64122, and the maximum lump sum is $2,386,380 ($14,583 × 163.64122).

Therefore, the maximum lump sum is determined as the lesser of the above limits, or $2,121,398.

**Q 12:21   What is the effect of PFEA '04 on the maximum benefit limitations?**

PFEA '04 changed how maximum benefits under Code Section 415(b)(2) subject to Code Section 417(e)(3) are calculated. Under the changes to Code Section 415(b)(2) made by Section 101(b)(4) of PFEA '04, if a defined benefit plan provides a benefit in a form that is subject to the minimum present value requirements of Code Section 417(e)(3) in a plan year beginning in 2004 or 2005, the actuarially equivalent straight life annuity (that is used for demonstrating compliance with Code Section 415) is the greater of the straight life annuity determined using the plan rate and plan mortality table and the straight life annuity determined using 5.5 percent and the applicable mortality table.

> **Example.** The Abbott pension plan has an actuarial equivalence interest rate of 5 percent, the applicable interest rate under Code Section 417(e)(3) is 5.25 percent, and the plan uses the applicable mortality table for determining actuarial equivalence. Costello, age 65, has an accrued benefit equal to the maximum dollar limit for 2004 of $13,750. PFEA '04 requires the conversion of a single-sum distribution paid during the plan year beginning in 2004 to an equivalent straight life annuity using 5.5 percent rather than the applicable interest rate of 5.25 percent as under prior law. In Costello's case, to satisfy the limitations of Code Section 415, the maximum single-sum distribution for him in 2004 would be $1,866,645 calculated using 5.5 percent as required by PFEA '04 rather than $1,905,638 calculated using 5.25 percent as required under prior law. However, a higher distribution may be permitted in certain situations during 2004 pursuant to the transition rule of PFEA '04 Section 101(d)(3). [Notice 2004-78, Q&A 1, 2004-48 I.R.B. 879]

The changes made by PFEA '04 must be adopted by a plan prior to the last day of the first plan year beginning on or after January 1, 2006 (December 31, 2006, for a calendar year plan), as long as the plan is operated as though the amendment were in effect during the period beginning on the date the amendment is effective. [Notice 2004-78, Q&A 6, 2004-48 I.R.B. 879] This date was extended by the PPA to the last day of the 2009 plan year.

**Q 12:22   What is the effective date of the changes to Code Section 415 made by PFEA '04?**

The changes to Code Section 415(b)(2) made by PFEA '04 apply to all distributions during the 2004 and 2005 plan years; however, the changes do not apply to plans that terminated prior to April 10, 2004, the date of enactment of PFEA '04, and there is a special transition rule for 2004. [Notice 2004-78, Q&A 2, 2004-48 I.R.B. 879]

**Q 12:23   What is the transition period allowed by PFEA '04 and how does it affect the calculation of the maximum benefit?**

The transition period begins on the first day of the first plan year beginning on or after January 1, 2004. The transition period ends on December 31, 2004. Thus, the transition rule of PFEA '04 Section 101(d)(3) applies to a distribution if the distribution has an annuity starting date that is on or after the first day of the first plan year beginning in 2004, but only if the annuity starting date is before December 31, 2004. [Notice 2004-78, Q&A 5, 2004-48 I.R.B. 879]

The transition amount is the otherwise determined benefit that—when converted to an actuarially equivalent straight life annuity determined using the plan rate and the plan mortality table—is within the limitations of Code Section 415 and—when converted to an actuarially equivalent straight life annuity determined using the transition rate and the applicable mortality table—is within the limitations of Code Section 415. For this purpose, the transition rate is the applicable interest rate determined under the plan terms that are adopted and in effect on the last day of the last plan year beginning before January 1, 2004 (i.e., the applicable interest determined under the plan for the 2003 plan year that is applicable for 2004).

> **Example.** Using the same information as in the example in Q 12:21, if the transition rate (the applicable interest rate for 2004) is 5.25 percent when a plan provides a single-sum distribution, then the effect of the transition rule would be to allow the conversion of the single-sum distribution to an equivalent straight life annuity using the transition rate of 5.25 percent (the greater of the transition rate and the plan rate) rather than 5.5 percent, which was required by PFEA '04. So for Costello, his maximum single-sum distribution in 2004 would be $1,905,638.

### Q 12:24  How were distributions that are subject to Code Section 417(e)(3) supposed to be calculated for the 2006 plan year for the period between the first day of the plan year and the date of enactment of the PPA?

This is a question that has not yet been answered by the IRS. When the PPA was enacted on August 17, 2006, the section of the law that affected this Code Section 415 benefit limit was made retroactive to the beginning of the 2006 plan year. However, during that time period before the bill became law, the law said that the maximum benefit limit was based on pre-PFEA '04 limits of the smallest benefit based on the plan rate and plan mortality table or the applicable interest rate and applicable mortality table. If the lump sum was determined based on these rates, it most likely was greater than what would have been determined using the new rates under the PPA and so the plan has failed to comply with Code Section 415—a tax disqualifying event. Informally, representatives of the IRS have stated that relief will be given for those plans that made distributions during that time period based on old law.

> **Example.** Richard, a participant in the Flying High defined benefit plan, retires on April 1, 2006, at age 62 with a monthly retirement benefit of $14,583. The plan actuarial equivalence assumptions are 5 percent and the 1983 GAM, unisex mortality table. As calculated in Example 2 in Q 12:20, the maximum lump sum under the new law is $2,121,398. Under old law, the maximum is $2,291,876 ($14,583 × 157.16080). Therefore, a lump sum was paid on that date of $2,291,876. When the PPA became law, this lump sum

paid was in excess of Code Section 415 and the plan could be disqualified even though the provisions of the new law were not known at the time of the payment, unless the IRS grants relief for this scenario.

### Q 12:25 How is the present value of the maximum dollar limitation calculated for participants receiving benefits before Social Security retirement age in a form subject to Code Section 417(e)(3)?

A lump-sum payment in a defined benefit pension plan is subject to the calculation requirements of Code Section 417(e)(3) and therefore must use the applicable interest rate and applicable mortality table for calculating the present value of the lump-sum payment. The adjustments to the maximum annual dollar limitation are calculated as they are in Qs 12:17 and 12:19, with the exception that the lump sum is determined by multiplying the age-adjusted dollar limit by the APR using the applicable interest rate and applicable mortality table. For 2004 and 2005, PFEA '04 has changed the interest rate used in converting benefits subject to Code Section 417(e)(3) to the greater of 5.5 percent or the rate specified in the plan for actuarial equivalence calculations. For plan years beginning after 2005, the PPA changed the interest rate used in converting benefits subject to Code Section 417(e)(3) to the greater of 5.5 percent, the rate that provides a benefit of not more than 105 percent of the benefit that would be provided if the applicable interest rate (as defined in Code Section 417(e)(3)) were the interest rate assumption, or the rate specified under the plan. This rate is only used when converting the age-adjusted dollar limit to a lump-sum value (or other forms subject to Code Section 417(e)(3)), and not in the conversion from age 62 to the plan's normal retirement age. There is a transition rule providing that for 2004 the maximum benefit subject to these rules cannot be less than the lump sum that would have been calculated using the applicable interest rate in effect under the plan as of the last day of the 2003 plan year. This change does require a plan amendment prior to the last day of the 2006 plan year, but the legislation provides Code Section 411(d)(6) relief to allow plans to implement this change to reduce distributions in plan operation, even though the plan may not be amended until a later date.

> **Example 1.** Frank is age 60 and would like to retire with a lump-sum payment of his pension benefit during 2000. Frank's highest three-year average compensation is $200,000. Because Frank has participated in his employer's pension plan for 5 years, his age-adjusted dollar limitation is half of what it would have been if he had 10 years of plan participation. (For a fully detailed calculation of Frank's age-adjusted maximum dollar limitation, see Q 12:17.) It has been determined that Frank's maximum annual age-adjusted dollar limitation at age 60 is $41,008, which is less than his plan benefit without regard to this limitation; therefore, his plan benefit is reduced to this amount. The plan defines the applicable interest rate as of the first day of the plan year in which the distribution occurs. In this case the interest rate is 6.5 percent, which produces an annual APR of 11.860. Therefore, Frank's maximum lump-sum payment is $486,355 ($41,008 × 11.860).

**Example 2.** Joe is age 60 and would like to retire with a lump-sum payment of his pension benefit during 2002. Joe's highest three-year average compensation is $200,000. Because Joe has participated in his employer's pension plan for 5 years, his age-adjusted dollar limitation is half of what it would have been if he had had 10 years of plan participation. (For a fully detailed calculation of Joe's age-adjusted maximum dollar limitation, see Q 12:17.) It has been determined that Joe's maximum annual age-adjusted dollar limitation at age 60 is $69,431, which is less than his plan benefit without regard to this limitation; therefore, his plan benefit is reduced to this amount. The plan defines the applicable interest rate as of the first day of the plan year in which the distribution occurs. In this case the interest rate is 6.5 percent, which produces an annual APR of 11.860. Therefore, Joe's maximum lump-sum payment is $823,452 ($69,431 × 11.860).

**Example 3.** Rich is age 62 and would like to retire with a lump-sum payment of his pension benefit during 2004. Rich's highest three-year average compensation is $200,000, and he has participated in his employer's plan for 10 years. His accrued benefit under the plan is $165,000. The plan rate is 5 percent, and the plan's APR is 13.0, the applicable interest rate is 5.07 percent, and the APR based on this rate and the applicable mortality table is 12.8, while the APR based on 5.5 percent and the applicable mortality table is 12.4. The lump-sum distribution based on Code Section 417(e)(3) is $2,112,000. The lump-sum distribution based on plan rates is $2,145,000. The lump-sum distribution based on 5.5 percent is $2,046,000. Since this distribution is occurring in 2004, the transition rule applies, which provides that the distribution may not be less than the amount provided under old rules. The maximum under the new law as amended by PFEA is the lesser of the lump sum using plan rates or 5.5 percent and is $2,046.000. However, due to the transition rule, the maximum for 2004 may not be less than $2,112,000.

### Q 12:26   How were the maximum benefit limitations calculated for a participant receiving annual benefits from a defined benefit pension plan before December 8, 1994 (the enactment of the RPA '94)?

The maximum annual benefit limitations before December 8, 1994, were the same as they are under current law (i.e., the lesser of 100 percent of the participant's average compensation for the highest-paid three years or $90,000, as indexed). The difference in the limitations is the adjustment of the annual benefit for an alternate form of payment, including lump-sum payments, or for benefits that begin before Social Security retirement age. To determine the maximum benefit limitation for lump-sum payments before Social Security retirement age, the interest rate assumption must not be less than the greater of 5 percent or the actuarial equivalence rate specified in the plan. When adjusting benefits beginning after Social Security retirement age, the interest rate assumption must not be greater than the lesser of 5 percent or the actuarial equivalence rate specified in the plan. In all cases, plan mortality is used. [I.R.C. § 415(b)(2)(E)]

### Q 12:27 How are the maximum benefit limitations calculated for a participant receiving annual benefits from a defined benefit pension plan on or after December 8, 1994, for a plan that was in effect before December 8, 1994?

In general, the new applicable interest and mortality table must be used to determine the maximum benefit limitations to all benefits under a plan on or after the first day of the first limitation year beginning in 1995. This date is known as the RPA '94 Section 415 effective date. A plan can, however, apply the maximum benefit limitations under Code Section 415(b) using the limitations that were in effect on December 7, 1994 (without regard to amendments made after December 7, 1994), with respect to the portion of the benefits accrued on or before the earlier of (1) the later of the date a plan amendment applying the new actuarial assumption requirements using the applicable mortality table and applicable interest rate is adopted or made effective or (2) the first day of the first limitation year beginning after December 31, 1999.

The date that this amendment is made effective is known as the *final implementation date.* Any accrued benefit determined using the provisions in effect on December 7, 1994, on a specific date on or after December 7, 1994, and before the final implementation date is known as an *old-law benefit.*

A participant's old-law benefit is determined as of a date specified in the plan for the participant (known as the *participant's freeze date*) that is before the final implementation date. The plan can provide that the freeze date for all participants is the day before the final implementation date for the plan. Alternatively, the plan can specify an earlier date as the freeze date for some or all participants. The participant's old-law benefit is determined for each possible annuity starting date and optional form of benefit based on the participant's accrued benefit under the terms of the plan as of the participant's freeze date, after applying Code Section 415 as in effect on December 7, 1994 (old-law limitations). [Rev. Rul. 98-1, Q&A 13, 1998-2 I.R.B. 5]

To determine the old-law benefit, the Code Section 415(b) limitations must be applied using the plan's mortality table as, in effect, on December 7, 1994, and for benefits that begin before Social Security retirement age, an interest rate that is no less than the greater of 5 percent or the plan rate used to determine actuarial equivalence, in effect, on December 7, 1994. If, as of December 7, 1994, the plan rate for a particular optional form of benefit was a variable interest rate, the plan rate that would be comparable to 5 percent is the value of the variable rate at the time the old-law limitations are applied, not the value of the variable rate on December 7, 1994. [Rev. Rul. 98-1, Q&A 13, 1998-2 I.R.B. 5]

Plan amendments that are adopted after the participant's freeze date are not taken into account in determining the old-law benefit, and the old-law benefit is determined without regard to cost-of-living adjustments that become effective under Code Section 415(d) after the participant's freeze date. [Rev. Rul. 98-1, Q&A 13, 1998-2 I.R.B. 5]

> **Example.** Kevin, a participant in the KJD Pension Plan, retires at age 60 in 2000 and elects a lump-sum distribution. The plan's normal retirement age is age 65. The plan is amended on December 31, 1999, for the changes made to Code Section 415(b)(2)(E), and the amendment specifies a December 31, 1999, freeze date and January 1, 2000, final implementation date. The plan was effective January 1, 1989, and the actuarial equivalence assumptions specified in the plan document on December 7, 1994, were 5 percent interest and UP-1984 mortality. No amendments have been made to the actuarial equivalence assumptions and the plan has a preretirement death benefit. Kevin's accrued benefit payable at age 65 is $110,000.
>
> The lump-sum amount is calculated as the product of the accrued benefit and the APR using the plan's actuarial equivalence assumptions. The APR at age 65 is 10.036. The lump-sum benefit payable at age 60 is $864,982 ($110,000 × 10.036 × (1 ÷ $(1.05)^5$)). The old-law lump-sum benefit is $864,982.

### Q 12:28    What methods are available to make the transition to the new RPA '94 Section 415 limitations?

In determining a participant's maximum benefit, whether it is paid in the form of an annual payment or a lump sum, the plan can use one of three methods for determining the limitations.

*Method 1.* Under this method, the plan applies the annual benefit limitations as it normally would, except that, if the benefit is not payable in the form of a life annuity or QJSA, the equivalent annual benefit is computed separately with respect to the old-law benefit (not to exceed the total plan benefit) and the portion of the total plan benefit that exceeds the old-law benefit. The annual benefit that is actuarially equivalent to the old-law benefit is determined in accordance with Code Section 415(b)(2)(E) as in effect on December 7, 1994 (see Q 12:26). The determination of the annual benefit that is equivalent to the portion of the plan benefit that is in excess of the old-law benefit must reflect the maximum annual benefit limitations under current law. The results of these two separate computations are added together to determine the equivalent annual benefit.

If the determination is being made before the final implementation date, the plan rate and the plan mortality table used to determine the annual benefit that is equivalent to the old-law benefit are based on the plan provisions in effect on December 7, 1994. If the determination is being made on or after the final implementation date, however, the plan rate and the plan mortality table used to determine the annual benefit that is equivalent to the old-law benefit are based on the plan provisions in effect on the date of determination.

In some cases, the use of the applicable mortality table in adjusting the maximum annual dollar limitation for a benefit that begins before or after Social Security retirement age can result in an age-adjusted maximum dollar limitation lower than the age-adjusted maximum dollar limitation used in determining the old-law benefit. A plan using Method 1 can provide that in any event the participant will receive no less than the old-law benefit.

*Method 2.* A plan can apply the maximum annual benefit limitation to the total plan benefit under current law, but provide that in no event will the participant receive less than the old-law benefit.

*Method 3.* A plan can apply the maximum annual benefit limitation by limiting a benefit only to the extent needed to satisfy either Method 1 or Method 2.

[Rev. Rul. 98-1, Q&A 14, 1998-2 I.R.B. 5]

**Example.** David retired from DML Industries on December 31, 2002, and is requesting a lump-sum distribution from the DML pension plan as of January 1, 2003. The DML pension plan uses Method 3 to determine maximum lump-sum distributions. David's accrued benefit is at the 100 percent of the highest three-year average compensation limit. His accrued benefit as of the freeze date of December 31, 1999, was $5,800. His accrued benefit as of December 31, 2002, was $7,800. The APR under the plan's actuarial equivalence assumptions in effect on December 7, 1994, was 170. The APR using the plan's Code Section 417(e) actuarial equivalence assumptions for 2003 is 140.

Under Method 1, David's lump sum is calculated as the old-law accrued benefit times the old-law APR plus the new-law accrued benefit times Code Section 417(e) APR. His lump-sum amount under old-law provisions is $5,800 × 170 = $986,000. His lump-sum amount under new-law provisions is $2,000 (($7,800 − $5,800) × 140 = $280,000). Therefore, his lump-sum amount as calculated under Method 1 is $1,266,000 ($986,000 + $280,000).

Under Method 2, David's lump sum is calculated entirely under new law, but with the lump sum being no less than that as calculated under old law. His lump-sum amount under the new-law provisions is $7,800 × 140 = $1,092,000. This is greater than the lump-sum amount calculated under old law of $986,000. Therefore, his lump sum under Method 2 is $1,092,000.

Under Method 3, David's lump sum is calculated as the greater of Method 1 or Method 2 and is, therefore, equal to $1,266,000.

### Q 12:29 Can a participant's old-law benefit change after the freeze date?

Yes. Under certain circumstances a participant's old-law benefit can be reduced; however, it can never increase. The following events illustrate situations that could cause a reduction in a participant's old-law benefit:

*Code Section 415(e) decrease.* A plan may be required to reduce an old-law benefit because of the required reductions under Code Section 415(e) for participants who receive benefits from a defined benefit plan and defined contribution plan. After the last plan year that begins in 1999, however, the limitation under Code Section 415(e) no longer applies.

*Post-final implementation date decrease.* After the final implementation date, the determinations of actuarial equivalence under Code Section 415 that apply with respect to the old-law benefit must take into account any changes in the plan's terms that occurred after December 7, 1994, and are relevant in applying the old-law limitations. If the equivalent annual benefit determined in this manner exceeds the age-adjusted maximum annual dollar limitation, the old-law benefit must be limited accordingly.

*Old-law benefit limited before applying Code Section 415.* The total plan benefit may be less than the old-law benefit before the application of the Code Section 415 limitations if the plan is amended to apply Code Section 417(e)(3) in a way that would reduce a participant's total plan benefit, even if the amendment occurs after the participant's freeze date.

[Rev. Rul. 98-1, Q&A 15, 1998-2 I.R.B. 5]

### Q 12:30    How are the maximum annual benefit limitations affected if the employer maintains both a defined benefit plan and a defined contribution plan for plan years beginning before the first plan year after December 31, 1999?

The maximum annual benefits and contributions for a plan participant who participates in both a defined contribution plan and a defined benefit plan of the same employer are limited by Code Section 415(e). For plan years that begin after December 31, 1999, Code Section 415(e) is repealed and no longer applies to any plan.

The limitation under Code Section 415(e) is exceeded if the sum of the defined benefit plan fraction and a defined contribution plan fraction in any limitation year exceeds 1.0. The calculation of each of these fractions is as follows:

*Defined benefit plan fraction* $= A \div B$

where

$A$ = the projected annual benefit of the plan participant as of close of the limitation year.

$B$ = the lesser of 1.25 times the participant's defined benefit dollar limitation as of the close of the limitation year, or 1.40 times 100 percent of the participant's highest three-year average compensation as defined by Code Section 415.

*Defined contribution fraction* $= C \div D$

where

$C$ = the sum of the annual additions to the participant's account as of the close of the limitation year.

$D$ = the sum of the lesser of 1.25 times the participant's defined contribution dollar limitation as of each such limitation year, or 1.40 times 25 percent of the participant's compensation (as defined by Code Section 415) as of the limitation year and determined as of the close of the limitation year, each such limitation year for each year of service with the employer.

[I.R.C. § 415(e)]

### Q 12:31 How are the maximum annual benefit limitations affected if the employer maintains both a defined benefit plan and a defined contribution plan for plan years beginning after December 31, 1999?

After that date, the limitations of Code Section 415(e) no longer apply, but there are restrictions as to who is affected by the repeal (see Q 12:32), how benefits are calculated after the repeal (see Q 12:33), when plan amendments need to be adopted to recognize the repeal (see Qs 12:33 and 12:34), and how the repeal affects the funding of a defined benefit plan (see Q 12:34) and the minimum participation requirements (see Q 12:35).

### Q 12:32 Who is affected by the repeal of Code Section 415(e)?

The general principle is that the repeal is effective for all defined benefit plan participants who have not begun receiving benefits as of the first day of the first limitation year following December 31, 1999 (the effective date); however, the plan sponsor can continue to impose the limit (e.g., to not incur a large increase in cost). If the sponsor continues to impose this limit and the defined contribution fraction continues to increase, there may be problems satisfying the nondiscrimination tests of Code Section 401(a)(4) or the anti-cutback rules of Code Section 411(d)(6). [Notice 99-44, Q&A 2, 1999-35 I.R.B. 326]

Participants who have begun to receive annuity distributions from the defined benefit plan can also have their benefits increased prospectively as long as they still have an accrued benefit under the plan on the effective date. Participants who have received a complete distribution of their benefit would not be eligible to receive increased benefits unless they accrued additional benefits following the effective date. [Notice 99-44, Q&A 3, 1999-35 I.R.B. 326]

### Q 12:33 How are benefits determined following the repeal of Code Section 415(e) for those who have begun receiving benefits before the effective date of the repeal?

For any limitation year beginning on or after the effective date of the repeal of Code Section 415(e) for the plan, the benefit payable to any current or former employee who has begun receiving benefits under the plan before that date in a form not subject to Code Section 417(e)(3) can be increased to a benefit that is no greater than the benefit that would have been permitted for that year under Code Section 415(b) for the employee if Code Section 415(e) had not limited the benefit at the time of commencement. Thus, the annual benefit for limitation years beginning on or after the effective date of the repeal of Code Section 415(e) for the plan is limited to the Section 415(b) limitation for the employee based on the employee's age at the time the employee began receiving benefits.

In the case of a form of benefit that is subject to Code Section 417(e)(3), the benefit payable for any limitation year beginning on or after the effective date of the repeal of Code Section 415(e) for the plan can be increased by an amount that is actuarially equivalent to the amount of increase that could have been provided if the benefit had been paid in the form of a straight life annuity.

Whether the form of benefit is subject to Code Section 417(e)(3), benefits attributable to limitation years beginning before January 1, 2000, cannot reflect benefit increases that could not be paid for those years because of Code Section 415(e). In addition, any plan amendment to provide an increase as a result of the repeal of Code Section 415(e) can be effective no earlier than the effective date of the repeal of Code Section 415(e) for the plan. [Notice 99-44, Q&A 4, 1999-35 I.R.B. 326]

**Example 1.** The Flint Rock defined benefit plan has a calendar plan year and limitation year. The plan is not a top-heavy plan during any relevant period. Under the plan, participants can elect to receive benefit distributions either in the form of an annuity or a lump sum. The plan provides that benefits for retirees are increased as the dollar limitation is indexed under Code Section 415(d). To reflect the Code Section 417(e)(3) change made by the General Agreement on Tariffs and Trade of 1994 (GATT), the plan was amended on January 1, 1995, effective as of that date, to substitute the applicable interest rate and the applicable mortality table for the original plan rate and the UP-1984 Mortality Table, respectively, to compute lump-sum benefits under the plan. Additionally, the plan was amended on July 1, 1998, effective as of January 1, 1995, to apply the Code Section 415(b)(2)(E) changes made by GATT and the Small Business Job Protection Act of 1996 (SBJPA) to all benefits under the plan on or after the RPA '94 Section 415 effective date, as defined in Revenue Ruling 98-1. [1998-2 I.R.B. 5] Under the plan, early retirement benefits and other optional forms of benefit are determined as the actuarial equivalents of a straight life annuity at normal retirement age using the applicable interest rate and applicable mortality table. For purposes of this example, the applicable interest rate for all relevant periods is 6 percent.

Sabrina was a participant both in the Flint Rock defined benefit plan and the Flint Rock defined contribution plan before retiring at the end of 1995. Sabrina was born on January 1, 1940, and is unmarried. Her Social Security retirement age is 66. She began receiving distributions from the defined benefit plan in the form of a single life annuity on January 1, 1996, at age 56. The dollar limitation of Code Section 415(b)(1)(A) for 1996 was $120,000. Sabrina's compensation-based limitation under Code Section 415(b)(1)(B) was $150,000 for all relevant periods. Accordingly, the Code Section 415(b) limitation for her benefit in 1996 was $54,753 ($120,000 reduced for early retirement at age 56).

Sabrina's defined contribution fraction for 1996 was 0.36. Therefore, to comply with Code Section 415(e), Sabrina's benefit in the defined benefit plan was limited so that her defined benefit fraction was equal to 0.64 (1−0.36). Thus, Sabrina's benefit in 1996 was limited to $43,802 (0.64 × the lesser of 1.25 × $54,753, or 1.4 × $150,000).

The dollar limitation under Code Section 415(b)(1)(A) increased to $125,000 in 1997 and to $130,000 in 1998 and 1999. Therefore, in 1997 Sabrina's benefit increased to $45,628. Similarly, in 1998, Sabrina's benefit increased to $47,453. In 1999, because the dollar limitation was unchanged from 1998, Sabrina's benefit continued to be limited to $47,453. (The Code Section 415(b)(1)(A) dollar limitation will be $135,000 in 2000.)

As of January 1, 2000, Sabrina's annuity payments under the defined benefit plan could increase to a maximum annuity benefit of $61,597 ($135,000 reduced for early retirement at age 56) and no increase in Sabrina's benefit is permitted to reflect the difference between the limitation of Code Section 415(b) and the limitation of Code Section 415(e) in prior limitation years.

Alternatively, if the Flint Rock defined benefit plan had not provided that benefits for retirees are increased as the dollar limitation is indexed under Code Section 415(d), but was amended to provide for such increases effective for the limitation year beginning January 1, 2000, Sabrina's benefit could be increased from $43,802 (the benefit without adjustment for increases in the Code Section 415(b)(1)(A) dollar limitation) to $61,597, plus the annual amount that is actuarially equivalent to the $9,128 that could have been paid in the prior limitation years ($1,826 for 1997, and $3,651 each for 1998 and 1999) if the plan had provided for benefit increases to reflect the cost-of-living increases under Code Section 415(d).

**Example 2.** Assume the same facts as those in Example 1 except that the Flint Rock defined benefit plan does not provide that benefits for retirees are increased as the dollar limitation is indexed under Code Section 415(d), and Sabrina began receiving distributions from the defined benefit plan in the form of 10 equal annual installments on January 1, 1996. Accordingly, the Code Section 415(b) limitation for Sabrina's benefit in 1996 was $89,635 ($120,000 reduced for early retirement at age 56 and adjusted for the install-ment option). To comply with Code Section 415(e), Sabrina's installment payment in 1996 was limited to $71,707. Similarly, for 1997 through 1999, Sabrina received installment payments of $71,707. As of January 1, 2000, Sabrina had six installment payments remaining. Because the defined benefit plan does not provide for cost-of-living adjustments under Code Section 415(d), Sabrina's six remaining installment payments under the defined benefit plan could be increased, effective January 1, 2000, by the actuarial equivalent (spread over a period of six years) of the value of the increases in the single life annuity that would have been payable beginning on January 1, 2000 (i.e., the increase from $43,802 to $54,753), if Sabrina had elected a single life annuity rather than the installment payment option.

If the Flint Rock defined benefit plan was amended to provide for cost-of-living adjustments under Code Section 415(d), effective January 1, 2000, Sabrina's six remaining installment payments could be increased by the actuarial equivalent (spread over a period of six years) of the value of the increases in the single life annuity that would have been payable beginning on January 1, 2000 (i.e., the increase from $43,802 to $61,597), if Sabrina had elected a single life annuity rather than the installment payment option. Furthermore, the defined benefit plan could provide that each of Sabrina's six remaining installment payments under the defined benefit plan is increased by the actuarial equivalent (spread over six years) of the value of the increases in the prior installment payment that would have been paid in the prior limitation years if the plan had provided for increases in the installment payments to reflect the increases under Code Section 415(d).

### Q 12:34    How is the repeal of Code Section 415(e) treated under the plan for purposes of the minimum funding requirements of Code Section 412?

For purposes of Code Section 412, any increase in the liabilities of a plan as a result of the repeal of Code Section 415(e) must be treated as occurring pursuant to a plan amendment effective no earlier than the first day of the first limitation year beginning on or after January 1, 2000 (whether the increase in liabilities under the terms of the plan arises pursuant to a plan amendment, or pursuant to existing plan provisions, for example, where benefits automatically increase as of the effective date of the repeal of Code Section 415(e) for the plan). Accordingly, any amortization base that is established under Code Section 412 for an increase in liabilities under a plan resulting from the repeal of Code Section 415(e) must have an amortization period of 30 years. A plan amendment that makes the repeal of Code Section 415(e) effective for a plan cannot be taken into account for purposes of Code Section 412 before the effective date of the repeal of Code Section 415(e) for the plan. [Notice 99-44, Q&A 11, 1999-35 I.R.B. 326]

### Q 12:35    How are the minimum participation requirements of Code Section 401(a)(26) affected by the repeal of Code Section 415(e)?

Treasury Regulations Section 1.401(a)(26)-4 requires certain defined benefit plans that benefit former employees to benefit at least the lesser of 50 former employees or 40 percent of all employees. In testing whether a plan will satisfy this requirement after the repeal of Code Section 415(e), there are three different types of plans to consider:

1. *Safe harbor plans.* This type of plan, which provides for uniformly applicable benefit increases due to the Code Section 415(e) repeal, will not fail to pass the minimum participation requirements because the Code Section 415 limits are ignored for this purpose under Treasury Regulations Section 1.410(b)-3(a)(2)(ii)(A).

2. *General test plans that do not take Code Section 415 limits into account under Code Section 401(a)(4).* This type of plan will also not fail to pass the minimum participation requirements.

3. *General test plans that do take Code Section 415 limits into account under Code Section 401(a)(4).* This type of plan will need to be tested to make sure that the minimum participation test is satisfied.

[IRS Memorandum, Dec 23, 1999, Technical Guidance on Code Section 401(a)(26) Testing]

### Q 12:36 May a plan provide for benefit increases to reflect the increased Code Section 415 limitations under EGTRRA for a current or former employee who began receiving benefits under the plan before the effective date of EGTRRA?

Yes, but only if the employee or former employee is a participant in the plan on or after that effective date. An employee or former employee for this purpose is a participant in the plan on a date if the employee or former employee has an accrued benefit (other than an accrued benefit resulting from a benefit increase that arises solely as a result of the increases in the Code Section 415 limitations under EGTRRA) on that date. Thus, benefit increases to reflect the increases in the Code Section 415 limitations under EGTRRA cannot be provided to current or former employees who do not have accrued benefits under the plan on or after the effective date of the Code Section 415 increases under EGTRRA for the plan. If a current or former employee, however, accrues additional benefits under the plan that could have been accrued without regard to the increased Code Section 415 limitations under EGTRRA (including benefits that accrue as a result of a plan amendment) on or after the effective date of the increased Code Section 415 limitations under EGTRRA for the plan, the current or former employee may receive a benefit arising from the increased Code Section 415 limitations under EGTRRA. [Rev. Rul. 2001-51, Q&A 5, 2001-45 I.R.B. 427]

### Q 12:37 How is the maximum permissible benefit increase calculated for a current or former employee who began receiving benefits in a form not subject to Code Section 417(e)(3) before the effective date of EGTRRA?

For any limitation year beginning on or after the effective date for the plan of the increased Code Section 415 limitations under EGTRRA, the benefit payable to any current or former employee who has commenced benefits under the plan before such effective date in a form not subject to Code Section 417(e)(3) may be increased to a benefit that is no greater than the benefit that could have been provided had the provisions of EGTRRA been in effect at the time of the commencement of benefit. Thus, the annual benefit for limitation years beginning on or after the effective date for the plan of the increased Code Section 415 limitations under EGTRRA is limited to the Code Section 415(b) limitation for the employee (increased for cost-of-living adjustments, if the plan provides for such adjustments) based on the employee's age at the time of commencement. Benefits attributable to limitation years beginning before the effective date for the plan of the increased Code Section 415 limitations under EGTRRA cannot reflect benefit increases that could not be paid for those years because of Code Section 415(b). In addition, any plan amendment to provide an increase as a result of the increased Code Section 415 limitations under EGTRRA can be effective no earlier than the effective date of the increased Code Section 415 limitations under EGTRRA for the plan.

> **Example.** Sam is a participant in the Sturgeon Inc. defined benefit plan, which has a calendar year limitation year, and provides that retiree benefits limited by Code Section 415 are increased as cost-of-living adjustments are made under Code Section 415(d). Sam retired in 2000 at age 60, with 20 years of participation. Sam's Social Security retirement age is 66. Sam's annual benefit under the plan formula before limitation for Code Section 415 was $180,000, and this benefit was limited by the defined benefit dollar limit to $85,252 (the applicable mortality table and 6 percent are used under the plan for early retirement purposes). The defined benefit compensation limitation applicable to Sam was $200,000 and, thus, did not limit Sam's benefit. Following the increase in the Code Section 415(b) dollar limit on January 1, 2001, to $140,000, Sam's benefit was increased to $88,409 ($85,252 × ($140,000 ÷ $135,000)). Following the Code Section 415(b) increase in the dollar limit under EGTRRA on January 1, 2002, Sam's annual benefit may be increased to an amount equal to the annual benefit commencing at age 60 that is actuarially equivalent (calculated using actuarial assumptions that satisfy Code Section 415(b)(2)(E)) to an annual benefit of $160,000 payable at age 62. In other words, Sam's benefit may be increased to an amount equal to the benefit that a 60-year-old could receive if the defined benefit dollar limit is $160,000 (with no reduction in the dollar limit for benefits that commence before age 65 and on or after age 62, but reduced actuarially for benefits that commence before age 62). Sam's annual benefit may be increased to $134,720, which Sam is eligible to receive on January 1, 2002.

[Rev. Rul. 2001-51, Q&A 6, 2001-45 I.R.B. 427]

### Q 12:38    How is the maximum permissible benefit increase calculated for a current or former employee under a plan whose benefit is payable in a form subject to Code Section 417(e)(3) before the effective date of EGTRRA?

In the case of a form of benefit that is subject to Code Section 417(e)(3), the benefit payable for any limitation year beginning on or after the effective date for the plan of the increased Code Section 415 limitations under EGTRRA may be increased by an amount that is actuarially equivalent to the amount of increase that could have been provided had the benefit been paid in the form of a straight life annuity. Benefits attributable to limitation years beginning before the effective date for the plan of the increased Code Section 415 limitations under EGTRRA cannot reflect benefit increases that could not be paid for those years because of Code Section 415(b). In addition, any plan amendment to provide an increase as a result of the increased Code Section 415 limitations under EGTRRA can be effective no earlier than the effective date of the increased Code Section 415 limitations under EGTRRA for the plan.

> **Example.** Jana is another participant in the Sturgeon Inc. defined benefit plan, which has a calendar year limitation year and plan year. Jana retires on

January 1, 2001—her 64th birthday—with 25 years of service and participation. Jana's Social Security retirement age is 65. The terms of the plan provide for increases in retiree benefits (that are limited by Code Section 415(b)) as the Code Section 415 limits are increased for cost-of-living adjustments under Code Section 415(d). On retirement, Jana's annual benefit in the form of an annuity under the plan formula, before limitation for Code Section 415, is $200,000. Jana's accrued benefit under the plan in the form of an annuity is limited to $130,667 ((140,000) × (1 − (⁵⁄₉)(12)(.01)) to satisfy Code Section 415(b). Jana's benefit is payable in the form of 10 equal annual installments commencing January 1, 2001. For purposes of actuarial equivalence for early commencement and optional forms, the plan provides for the use of the applicable mortality table and the applicable interest rate (assumed to be 6 percent for purposes of this example). When Jana's benefits began, the benefit was calculated as a straight life annuity of $130,667 per year, adjusted for payment as 10 annual payments. The annuity benefit of $130,667 was multiplied by an age 64 annuity factor (calculated using the applicable mortality table and the applicable interest rate), and the resulting amount was spread over 10 years, using the applicable interest rate.

Jana has an accrued benefit under the plan when EGTRRA becomes effective for the plan on January 1, 2002. If the plan is amended to provide for such increases to retired participants, Jana's benefit, if payable in the form of a straight life annuity, could be increased to a straight life annuity of $160,000 in the limitation year beginning January 1, 2002. As of January 1, 2002, Jana has nine remaining installment payments. The remaining nine installment payments could be increased by the actuarial equivalent (spread over a period of nine years) of the value of the increase in the straight life annuity that would have been payable beginning January 1, 2002, if Jana had elected a straight life annuity on retirement rather than the installment payment option. That is, the maximum increase that Jana is permitted to receive in 2002 as a result of the Code Section 415(b) increase under EGTRRA is the amount equal to the product of $29,333 ($160,000 − $130,667) times an age 65 annuity factor (derived using the applicable mortality table and the applicable interest rate), spread over nine years at an assumed interest rate equal to the applicable interest rate.

[Rev. Rul. 2001-51, Q&A 7, 2001-45 I.R.B. 427]

## Compensation Limitations

**Q 12:39**    **What does compensation include for purposes of determining the maximum benefit limitations under Code Section 415?**

For purposes of applying the maximum benefit limitations under Code Section 415, *compensation* includes the following amounts:

1. The employee's wages, salaries, fees for professional services (without regard to whether an amount is paid in cash), and fees for personal services

actually rendered in the course of employment with the employer maintaining the plan to the extent that the amounts are includible in gross income (including, but not limited to, commission paid to salespersons, compensation for services on the basis of a percentage of the profits, commissions on insurance premiums, fringe benefits, and reimbursements or other expense allowances under a nonaccountable plan);

2. In the case of a self-employed person as defined in Code Section 401(c)(1), such employee's earned income;

3. Taxable accident or health insurance benefits to the extent such amounts are includible in the gross income of the employee;

4. Amounts paid or reimbursed by the employer for moving expenses incurred by an employee, but only to the extent that, at the time of the payment, it is reasonable to believe that these amounts are not deductible by the employee under Code Section 217;

5. The value of a nonqualified stock option granted to an employee by an employer, but only to the extent that the value of the option is includible in the gross income of the employee for the taxable year in which it is granted;

6. The amount includible in the gross income of an employee upon making the election described in Code Section 83(b) (i.e., payment for services rendered through the transfer of property); and

7. Contributions made by the employer to a plan of deferred compensation to the extent such contributions are not included in the taxable income of the employee, including elective deferrals under a 401(k) arrangement, a salary reduction simplified employee pension (SEP), or a Code Section 125 arrangement (i.e., a cafeteria plan or dependent care program), or a SEP. (**Note.** These amounts are excluded from the definition of Code Section 415 compensation for plan years beginning before January 1, 1998.)

[Treas. Reg. § 1.415-2]

Excluded from the definition of compensation are the following amounts:

1. Distributions from a deferred compensation plan (i.e., a defined benefit pension plan or defined contribution plan); however, distributions from an unfunded nonqualified plan are permitted to be considered part of Code Section 415 compensation in the year the amounts are includible in the gross income of the employee;

2. Amounts realized from the exercise of a nonqualified stock option or when restricted stock (or property) held by an employee either becomes freely transferable or is no longer subject to risk of forfeiture;

3. Amounts realized from the sale, exchange, or other disposition of stock acquired under a qualified stock option; and

4. Other amounts that receive special tax benefits, such as premiums for group term life insurance (but only to the extent that the premiums are not includible in the gross income of the employee) or contributions made by an employer (whether or not under a salary reduction agreement)

toward the purchase of an annuity contract described in Code Section 403(b).

[Treas. Reg. § 1.415-3]

### Q 12:40   Can accrued compensation be used for purposes of Code Section 415?

No. The compensation actually paid or made available to an employee within the limitation year is the compensation used for purposes of applying the limitations of Code Section 415, unless the amount is considered *de minimis*. An employer may include in compensation amounts earned but not paid in a year because of the timing of pay periods and paydays, if these amounts are paid during the first few weeks of the next year, the amounts are included on a uniform and consistent basis with respect to all similarly situated employees, and no compensation is included in more than one limitation period. No formal election is required to include the accrued compensation permitted under this *de minimis* rule.

### Q 12:41   What compensation is included when an employee is a member of a controlled group?

In the case of an employee of two or more corporations that are members of a controlled group of corporations (as defined in Code Section 414(b) and as modified by Code Section 415(h)), the term *compensation* for such employee includes compensation from all employers that are members of the group, regardless of whether the employee's particular employer participates in that plan or even has a qualified plan. This special rule is also applicable to an employee of two or more trades or businesses (whether or not incorporated) that are under common control (as defined in Code Section 414(c) and as modified by Code Section 415(h)), to an employee of two or more members of an affiliated service group as defined in Code Section 414(m), and to an employee of two or more members of any group of employers who must be aggregated and treated as one employer pursuant to Code Section 414(o).

### Q 12:42   Is compensation limited under Code Section 401(a)(17) for purposes of determining the maximum benefit limitations under Code Section 415?

No. Code Section 401(a)(17) limits only the compensation that can be recognized in calculating accrued benefits determined under the plan's benefit formula, but not the maximum allowable benefits under Code Section 415.

**Example.** Kyle, the owner and an employee of Hancock Inc., earns $600,000 in 2002. Kyle has over 10 years of service with this company, but this is the only year in which he takes any compensation. In determining his maximum benefit payable at normal retirement age, the full amount of compensation he earned in 2002 is divided by three years to determine his highest three-year average. Therefore, his highest three-year average compensation for purposes of Code Section 415 is $200,000 ($600,000 ÷ 3). However, his average annual compensation for purposes of applying the benefit formula is limited to $66,667 ($200,000 ÷ 3) because his 2002 compensation is limited to the Code Section 401(a)(17) limit in effect that year ($200,000). However, the benefit formula could be 300 percent of compensation ($66,667 × 300% = $200,000), to circumvent this limitation and provide Kyle with his maximum benefit.

### Q 12:43    Can a non-compensation-related benefit formula cause an accrued benefit to exceed the maximum annual benefit limitations for a participant?

Yes. A non-compensation-related benefit formula can cause a participant's benefit to exceed the annual benefit limitations under Code Section 415(b) when the employer has low-wage earners who have worked for the employer for most of their working lifetimes.

**Example.** The Widgets Inc. Pension Plan provides a monthly benefit at retirement equal to $25 per year of service with the employer. Widgets Inc. hired Ron at age 18, and he has worked for the company his entire working lifetime. At age 65, Ron's benefit is $1,175 per month ($25 × 47) or $14,100 annually. In his final three years of employment, Ron averaged $6 per hour and worked 40 hours per week. This equated to a highest three-year average annual income of $12,480. Unless the plan meets certain criteria, Ron's benefit will exceed the maximum annual benefits allowable under Code Section 415(b).

# Chapter 13

# Cash Balance Plans

Over the last several years, cash balance plans have received a great deal of attention in the mainstream media. Employee groups were very concerned about their benefits under these types of plans and elicited the support of government representatives and reporters to help protect their benefits. Press articles have accused employers of trying to save money and hide reductions in benefits through the use of these plans. In the House and the Senate, lawmakers introduced legislation that would prohibit these cash balance plans, increase disclosure requirements, or even prohibit employers from ever reducing future benefits. The Internal Revenue Service (IRS) even issued proposed regulations to provide guidance to employers sponsoring this type of plan, but the IRS had to later withdraw the regulations. Finally, in August 2006 two separate incidents occurred that combined would help protect and advance the concept of cash balance pension plans. This chapter explores the many issues involved in the administration of a cash balance plan.

## Overview

### Q 13:1   What is a *cash balance plan*?

A *cash balance plan* is a defined benefit plan that tries to look like a defined contribution plan by providing benefits to employees in the form of a hypothetical account balance. The hypothetical account balance is provided to the employee at retirement as a lump-sum distribution or an annuity based on conversion factors defined in the plan document. The hypothetical account is credited with interest based on some outside index, such as the yield on one-year Treasury securities, or an amount defined in the plan. Contributions to the account are based on a percentage of compensation, a multiple of age and service points, or other objective criteria.

A cash balance plan is designed to look like a defined contribution plan, with contributions and earnings credited to a participant's account, but has the promised-benefit feature of a defined benefit plan through the interest rate credit and benefit guarantee.

### Q 13:2    How does a cash balance plan operate?

Each year, a participant receives a hypothetical contribution to his or her account based on his or her compensation for that year. The account accumulates with interest each year, as defined in the plan document.

**Example.** Debbie is a participant in the Cookie Cutter cash balance plan, which provides hypothetical contributions each year of 5 percent of pay and hypothetical interest credits of 8 percent. Debbie's hypothetical account balance will grow as follows:

| Year | Salary | Contribution | Interest | Balance |
|------|--------|--------------|----------|---------|
| 1997 | $ 20,000 | $ 1,000 | $ 0 | $ 1,000 |
| 1998 | $ 23,000 | $ 1,150 | $ 80 | $ 2,230 |
| 1999 | $ 25,000 | $ 1,250 | $ 178 | $ 3,658 |
| 2000 | $ 28,000 | $ 1,400 | $ 293 | $ 5,351 |
| 2001 | $ 30,000 | $ 1,500 | $ 428 | $ 7,279 |
| 2002 | $ 33,000 | $ 1,650 | $ 582 | $ 9,511 |
| 2003 | $ 40,000 | $ 2,000 | $ 761 | $ 12,272 |

Traditional defined benefit plans are often converted to cash balance plans. In such cases, the benefit accrued under the prior formula is generally converted to a lump-sum amount, which becomes the opening balance of the participant's account, subject to certain conversion protections (see Q 13:28).

### Q 13:3    What is the difference between a cash balance plan and a traditional defined benefit plan?

A traditional defined benefit plan typically defines the benefit at retirement as a function of average monthly compensation or service, or both. This benefit is usually payable for the participant's lifetime on attainment of the plan's normal retirement age. In contrast, a cash balance plan defines the benefit at retirement as an accumulation of contribution credits and interest credits at retirement age, which is usually payable as a lump sum.

**Example.** The Rubber Stamping Supplies defined benefit plan has a benefit formula of 2 percent of final three-year average pay times years of service. Carie has 35 years of service and $20,000 average compensation. Under this defined benefit plan, Carie will receive $14,000 a year on reaching retirement age (2% × $20,000 × 35). An actuarially equivalent lump-sum benefit would be approximately $138,226.

If instead Carie was employed by the Crystal Products R Us company and participated in its cash balance plan, which would give her a 5 percent of compensation credit for each of her 35 years of service, she would have an account balance at retirement of $147,913 (assuming a 7 percent interest credit). The actuarially equivalent life annuity benefit calculated using the same actuarial assumptions as those used under the other plan would be approximately $14,981, payable for the rest of her lifetime.

### Q 13:4    What are the similarities between a traditional defined benefit plan and a cash balance plan?

A cash balance plan is a defined benefit plan. Therefore, it has many of the characteristics of a traditional defined benefit plan. For instance, benefits must be definitely determinable, that is, the participant's benefit at retirement age must be determined by the plan. This is accomplished in a cash balance plan by defining the contribution credits and interest credits in the plan document.

Like the plan sponsor of any defined benefit plan, the plan sponsor of a cash balance plan assumes the plan's investment risks. Because the interest credits to a participant's hypothetical account are defined in the plan document, the trust investment risk is borne by the employer.

There are various other similarities, including the benefit protection guarantees of the Pension Benefit Guaranty Corporation (PBGC) as long as the plan is considered a covered plan (see chapter 24). Actual contributions are determined actuarially (not by the contribution credits to the individual participant accounts). Both types of plans must offer the qualified joint and survivor annuity (QJSA) as the normal form of payment.

### Q 13:5    Why would an employer choose a cash balance plan over a traditional defined benefit plan?

An important part of any retirement program is helping employees understand the value of the plan, and many individuals who change jobs frequently do not receive a significant benefit from a traditional defined benefit plan. A cash balance plan helps employees see something they are already familiar with, an account balance. Many do not understand the value associated with a monthly benefit payable at retirement age.

Another benefit for employers is having the option of a lump-sum payout, which reduces the administrative burden of keeping track of former employees.

Under a traditional defined benefit plan, benefits are often not payable until the participant reaches normal retirement age, and then payable only in the form of an annuity. It can be costly for an employer to find past participants once they reach the plan's normal retirement age.

A cash balance plan also gives employers the chance to equalize contribution credits to equally valuable participants who happen to be of different ages. One of the problems inherent under a traditional defined benefit plan is that an equal accrued benefit earned by participants may have very different values simply because of the difference in ages of the participants. A cash balance plan can be used to equalize this disparity.

Despite some of the potential legal issues surrounding cash balance plans in the past (see the Legal Issues section later in this chapter), cash balance plans were becoming a popular option for plan sponsors. According to a recent survey by the Society of Actuaries (Society of Actuaries' Survey on the Prevalence of Traditional and Hybrid Defined Benefit Pension Plans, Report of Findings, March 2005), 23 percent of public-sector participants and 35 percent of private-sector participants are covered under some type of cash balance plan.

### Q 13:6   How can a cash balance plan be more valuable for a participant?

Employees want cash balance plans for many of the same reasons employers do. Many employees appreciate the ability to receive a lump-sum distribution on termination of employment, which allows them to direct the use of the money to their best interest. They can, for example, continue the tax deferral of the money by rolling it over into an individual retirement account (IRA).

In addition, because a cash balance plan is a defined benefit plan, it has many of the protections associated with defined benefit plans, including protection from loss due to poor performance of investments, and the protection of the PBGC if the plan is covered.

For individuals who change jobs frequently, a cash balance plan may ultimately provide a greater retirement benefit. In a traditional defined benefit plan, the accruals are inherently more valuable as the employee grows older with the company. Although the percentage of pay may stay constant, the corresponding lump-sum value of the accrual increases. Under a cash balance plan, the lump-sum value of the accrual may stay constant. This provides a younger employee with a greater benefit in the earlier years of his or her career.

**Example.** Diane is 30 years old and earns $20,000 a year working for Plans R Us Inc. The company is considering adopting a defined benefit plan and is choosing between a traditional plan that provides a benefit equal to 2 percent of compensation times years of service and a cash balance plan that provides hypothetical contributions to an account each year equal to 5 percent of each participant's compensation. The plan actuary prepares the following comparison of benefits for Diane. It shows the accumulated lump-sum values at different ages:

| Age | Traditional | Cash Balance |
|---|---|---|
| 35 | $ 3,482 | $ 5,975 |
| 40 | $ 9,320 | $ 13,972 |
| 50 | $ 33,381 | $ 38,993 |
| 60 | $ 89,671 | $ 83,802 |
| 65 | $ 140,000 | $ 118,121 |

(The interest credit and discount factor are 6 percent, the age 65 annuity purchase rate is 10.0.)

The cash balance accumulation is greater for younger and shorter-service employees. The traditional defined benefit plan has a greater value at retirement for longer-service employees.

## Nondiscrimination Requirements

### Q 13:7   What are the requirements for a cash balance plan to be considered nondiscriminatory?

Cash balance plans, like all other defined benefit plans, must satisfy the nondiscrimination requirements of Internal Revenue Code (Code) Section 401(a)(4). Satisfaction of these rules can be made by testing the contributions or testing the equivalent accruals (see chapter 11 for more information regarding these testing methods), or by means of a specific safe harbor for cash balance plans. There are specific guidelines in the safe harbor rules with regard to the following:

- Hypothetical allocations (see Q 13:8)
- Hypothetical interest adjustments (see Q 13:12)
- Accumulation of allocations and interest adjustments (see Q 13:13)
- Determination of the accrued benefit (see Q 13:15)
- Optional forms of benefit (see Q 13:20)
- Past-service credits (see Q 13:23)
- Post-normal retirement age benefits (see Q 13:24)
- Certain uniformity requirements (see Q 13:25)
- Changes in the plan's benefit formula (see Q 13:26)

[Treas. Reg. § 1.401(a)(4)-8(c)(3)]

The following questions deal only with the rules applicable to these safe harbors. For more information on cash balance plans that do not satisfy the safe harbor testing method, see chapter 11.

### Q 13:8    How can an employer determine the amount of the hypothetical allocations to an account in a cash balance plan?

The hypothetical allocations provided under a cash balance plan's benefit formula either (1) must be determined according to a uniform hypothetical allocation formula and be considered a design-based safe harbor (see Q 13:9) when so determined or (2) must satisfy a modified general test (see Q 13:10). [Treas. Reg. § 1.401(a)(4)-8(c)(3)(iii)]

### Q 13:9    What conditions must be satisfied for a cash balance plan formula to be considered a uniform hypothetical allocation formula?

For a plan's benefit formula to be considered a uniform hypothetical allocation formula, it must provide for hypothetical allocations for all employees in the plan for all plan years as if the hypothetical allocations were the only allocations under a defined contribution plan for the employees for those plan years. The plan's benefit formula must provide for hypothetical allocations for all employees in the plan for all plan years that are the same percentage of plan year compensation or the same dollar amount. In determining whether the hypothetical allocations are uniform, the plan can provide for any of the following provisions on a uniform basis to all employees:

1. Integrate with Social Security as part of the allocation formula.
2. Allow for dual entry dates for plan participation.
3. Provide that the allocation will be conditioned on the employees' employment on the last day of the plan year or the employees' completion of a minimum number of hours of service (not to exceed 1,000).
4. Limit allocations to a maximum dollar limit or percentage of compensation.
5. Provide for a dollar allocation per uniform unit of service.

[Treas. Reg. § 1.401(a)(4)-8(c)(3)(iii)(B)]

### Q 13:10    How does a cash balance plan satisfy the modified general test?

For a cash balance plan to satisfy the modified general test, the plan's benefit formula must provide for hypothetical allocations for all employees in the plan for the plan year that would satisfy the general test in Treasury Regulations Section 1.401(a)(4)-2(c) as if the hypothetical allocations were the only allocations for the employees taken into account under a defined contribution plan for the plan year. [Treas. Reg. § 1.401(a)(4)-8(c)(3)(iii)(C)]

The general test under Treasury Regulations Section 1.401(a)(4)-2(c) states that contributions allocated under a defined contribution plan are nondiscriminatory in amount if each rate group under the plan satisfies Code Section 410(b) (i.e., each rate group has a ratio greater than 70 percent or each rate group's ratio is within the safe and unsafe harbor percentages and the plan satisfies the average benefit test). The calculation of the allocation rates for an employee takes into account the sum of the allocations to an employee's account for the plan year, expressed either as a percentage of plan year compensation or as a dollar amount. In determining the allocation rate, allocations of income, expenses, gains, and losses attributable to the account are not taken into account; permitted disparity under Code Section 401(l) can be imputed in accordance with the rules of Treasury Regulations Section 1.401(a)(4)-7; and the employer can treat all employees who have allocation rates within a specified range above and below a midpoint as having an allocation rate equal to the midpoint within that range.

### Q 13:11   How does a cash balance plan satisfy Code Section 401(a)(26)?

A cash balance plan, like a traditional defined benefit plan, must benefit at least the lesser of (1) 50 employees of the employer or (2) the greater of 40 percent of all employees of the employer, or two employees (or if there is only one employee, such employee). In addition, the plan must provide these employees with meaningful benefits.

A field memorandum published by the IRS stated that if employees in a cash balance plan do not accrue at least 0.5 percent of compensation per year of participation or service, then the plan should be reviewed to see whether it satisfies Code Section 401(a)(26).

> **Example.** Joe, the owner of C&L, participates in the C&L cash balance plan. He earns $200,000 in 2003 and has an allocation in the plan of $45,000, which corresponds to an accrued benefit of $1,000 per month payable at normal retirement age. Joe has one employee, Gail. Gail earns $30,000 and receives a cash balance allocation of $100, which corresponds to an accrued benefit of $10 per month. This accrued benefit provides only 0.4 percent ($10×$30,000×12) accrual rate and, therefore, this plan may not satisfy Code Section 401(a)(26).

### Q 13:12   How are the interest rate adjustments made to a hypothetical account in a cash balance plan?

The plan benefit formula must provide that the dollar amount of the hypothetical allocation for each employee for a plan year is automatically adjusted using an interest rate that satisfies certain conditions (see Q 13:13) and that the interest is compounded no less frequently than annually, for a period that begins with a date in the plan year and ends at normal retirement age. This requirement is not satisfied if any portion of the interest rate adjustment to a hypothetical allocation is contingent on the employee's satisfaction of any requirement. Thus, for example, interest adjustments to a hypothetical allocation must be provided through normal retirement age even though the employee terminates employment or begins receiving benefits before that age. [Treas. Reg. § 1.401(a)(4)-8(c)(3)(iv)(A)]

### Q 13:13　What conditions must the interest rate adjustment satisfy in a cash balance plan?

The interest rate must be a single rate specified in the plan that is the same for all employees in the plan for all plan years. It can be either a standard or variable interest rate. If the interest rate is a variable interest rate, the plan must specify the variable interest rate, the method for determining the current value of the variable interest rate, and the period (not to exceed one year) for which the current value of the interest rate applies. The following are permissible variable interest rates:

1. The rate on three-month Treasury bills;
2. The rate on six-month Treasury bills;
3. The rate on one-year Treasury bills;
4. The yield on one-year Treasury constant maturities;
5. The yield on two-year Treasury constant maturities;
6. The yield on five-year Treasury constant maturities;
7. The yield on 10-year Treasury constant maturities;
8. The yield on 30-year Treasury constant maturities; and
9. The single interest rate such that, as of a single age specified in the plan, the actuarial present value of a deferred straight life annuity of an amount beginning at the normal retirement age under the plan, calculated using that interest rate and a standard mortality table but assuming no mortality before normal retirement age, is equal to the actuarial present value, as of the single age specified in the plan, of the same annuity calculated using the Code Section 417(e) rates applicable to distributions in excess of $25,000 (determined under Treasury Regulations Section 1.417(e)-1(d)), and the same mortality assumptions.

The current value of the variable interest rate for a period must be either the value of the variable interest rate determined as of a specified date in the period or the immediately preceding period, or the average of the values of the variable interest rate as of two or more specified dates during the current period or the immediately preceding period. The value as of a date of the rate on a Treasury bill is the average auction rate for the week or month in which the date falls, as reported in the Federal Reserve Bulletin. The value as of a date, of the yield on a Treasury constant maturity is the average yield for the week, month, or year in which the date falls, as reported in the Federal Reserve Bulletin. The plan can limit the current value of the variable interest rate to a maximum (not less than the highest standard interest rate), a minimum (not more than the lowest standard interest rate), or both. [Treas. Reg. § 1.401(a)(4)-8(c)(3)(iv)(B), (C)]

According to the Pension Protection Act of 2006 (PPA), the hypothetical interest rate must also not exceed a "market rate of return" or else the plan will be considered as failing ERISA Section 204(b)(1)(H) (which refers to the section prohibiting reductions in the rate of benefit accruals) and Code Section 411(b)(1)(H). The Treasury Department has yet to specify what is a "market rate of return." The market rate of return can be a reasonable guaranteed rate of return or the greater of a fixed or variable rate of return. There is an additional requirement that the hypothetical account balance may never be less than the accumulated contributions credited to the account, which insinuates that the interest crediting rate may at times be negative. In addition, if the cash balance plan is terminated, the interest credit that must be applied to each participant's account will be equal to the average of the interest crediting rates under the plan for the last five years ending on the plan's termination date. [I.R.C. § 411(b)(5)(B)]

### Q 13:14   What is the value of an employee's hypothetical account in a cash balance plan?

The value of an employee's hypothetical account as of a particular date must equal the sum of all hypothetical allocations and the interest adjustments to each such hypothetical allocation provided through that date for the employee under the plan's benefit formula (without regard to any interest adjustments provided under the plan's benefit formula for periods after that date). [Treas. Reg. § 1.401(a)(4)-8(c)(3)(v)(A)]

The value of an employee's hypothetical account must be determined as of normal retirement age to determine the employee's accrued benefit as of any date at or before normal retirement age. As of any date at or before normal retirement age, the value of an employee's hypothetical account as of normal retirement age must equal the sum of each hypothetical allocation provided through that date for the employee under the plan's benefit formula, plus the interest adjustments provided through normal retirement age on each of those hypothetical allocations for the employee under the plan's benefit formula (without regard to any hypothetical allocations that might be provided after that date under the plan's benefit formula). If the interest rate specified in the plan is a variable interest rate, the plan must specify that the determination in the preceding sentence is made by assuming that the current value of the variable interest rate for all future periods is either the current value of the variable interest rate for the current period or the average of the current values of the variable interest rates for the current period and one or more periods immediately preceding the current period (not to exceed five years in the aggregate). [Treas. Reg. § 1.401(a)(4)-8(c)(3)(v)(B)] If the plan is terminating, and if the interest crediting rate is a variable rate, the interest crediting rate that must be used to project the current account balance to normal retirement age is the average of the interest crediting rates under the terms of the plan for the last five years ending on the plan's termination date. [I.R.C. § 411(b)(5)(B)(v)]

### Q 13:15   How is the accrued benefit determined in a cash balance plan?

The plan must provide that at any date at or before normal retirement age the accrued benefit may, under the terms of the plan, be expressed as an annuity payable at normal retirement age, the balance of a hypothetical account, or the current value of the accumulated percentage of the employee's final average compensation. [I.R.C. § 411(b)(5)(A)(iv)] In determining the accrued benefit, the subsidized portion of any early retirement benefit or retirement-type subsidy is disregarded. However, a plan will be treated as failing to meet the requirement under Code Section 411(b)(1)(H)(i) that requires the rate of benefit accrual shall not decrease on account of age unless a participant's accrued benefit, as determined as of any date under the terms of the plan, would be equal to or greater than that of any similarly situated, younger individual who is or could be a participant. A participant is considered to be similarly situated to any other individual if such participant is identical to such other individual in every respect (including period of service, compensation, position, date of hire, work history, and any other respect) except for age.

### Q 13:16    What is the normal form of benefit for a cash balance plan?

The normal form of benefit must be an annuity payable in the same form at the same uniform normal retirement age for all employees in the plan. The annual benefit must be the normal retirement benefit under the plan (within the meaning of Code Section 411(a)(9)). [I.R.C. § 411(a)(7); Treas. Reg. § 1.401(a)(4)-8(c)(3)(vi)(B)]

### Q 13:17    How are actuarially equivalent benefits determined under a cash balance plan?

Actuarially equivalent benefits must be determined using a standard mortality table and either a standard interest rate or the interest rate specified in the plan for making interest adjustments to hypothetical allocations. If the interest rate used is the interest rate specified in the plan and that rate is a variable interest rate, the assumed value of the variable interest rate for all future periods must be the same value that would be assumed in determining the value of the hypothetical account at normal retirement age (see Q 13:14). The same actuarial assumptions must be used for all employees in the plan. [Treas. Reg. § 1.401(a)(4)-8(c)(3)(vi)(C)]

### Q 13:18    Do Code Sections 415 (maximum benefits) and 416 (top-heavy minimum benefits) apply to a cash balance plan?

Yes. Therefore, the accrued benefit of an employee must be adjusted to take into account these maximum and minimum benefit requirements without causing the plan to improperly calculate the accrued benefit of an employee according to the rules in Treasury Regulations Section 1.401(a)(4)-8(c)(3)(vi)(A) (see Q 13:15).

> **Example.** Seth, age 25, and Pamela, age 55, are new entrants into the top-heavy CP Inc. cash balance plan and earn $20,000 each. The contribution credit under this plan is 4 percent of pay, the interest credit is 5 percent, and the plan's annuity purchase rate is 10.0. Seth's and Pamela's accrued benefits are calculated as follows:

|                                          | Seth        | Pamela      |
|------------------------------------------|-------------|-------------|
| 1. Account balance                       | $ 800.00    | $ 800.00    |
| 2. Projected to 65 at 5%                 | $ 5,632.00  | $ 1,303.00  |
| 3. Accrued benefit (line 2 ÷ 10.0)       | $ 563.20    | $ 130.30    |
| 4. Top-heavy minimum (2% × $20,000)      | $ 400.00    | $ 400.00    |

Because the accrued benefit for Seth is greater than the top-heavy minimum, no change needs to be made to the hypothetical contribution allocated to his account. For Pamela, however, the hypothetical contribution needs to be increased to satisfy the top-heavy requirements. Pamela's hypothetical contribution would be $2,456 ($400.00 × 10.0 × $(1.05)^{-10}$)

### Q 13:19   What are the vesting requirements applicable to cash balance plans?

For plans that were not in existence on June 29, 2005, the requirement is that participants fully vest in their accrued benefits in three years or less. For cash balance plans in existence on June 29, 2005, the requirement to fully vest accrued benefits in three years or less is not effective until plan years beginning after December 31, 2007. However, this delayed application is linked to the new interest crediting rules of the PPA, which require the use of a market rate of return. [PPA § 701(e)(3)] Prior to the enactment of the PPA, the vesting rules were the same as for other types of defined benefit plans.

**Practice Pointer.** This new vesting rule combined with the IRS interpretation in the *Central Laborers* decision (see chapter 8) requires plans that are currently on a six-year graded vesting schedule and wanting to go to a three-year cliff vesting schedule will now, for current participants, have the following schedule:

| Years of Service  | Vested Percent |
|-------------------|----------------|
| 1 year of less    | 0%             |
| 2 years           | 20%            |
| 3 or more years   | 100%           |

Once the vesting schedule is amended, any new participants who have not ever been on the six-year graded schedule will only be on the three-year cliff schedule.

### Q 13:20   Are there any restrictions on optional forms of benefit in a cash balance plan for forms of benefit other than a lump sum?

Yes. A cash balance plan must provide that all subsidized optional forms of benefit satisfy the uniform subsidies requirement of Treasury Regulations

Section 1.401(a)(4)-3(b)(2)(iv). Furthermore, unless hypothetical allocations are determined under a uniform hypothetical allocation formula (see Q 13:9), the actuarial present value of any QJSA provided under the plan must not be greater than the single-sum distribution to the employee that would be calculated using the greater of the vested hypothetical account balance (see Q 13:14) or the actuarial present value (calculated in accordance with Treasury Regulations Section 1.417(e)-1(d)) of the employee's accrued benefit (see Q 13:21) if it is assumed that the benefit was distributed to the employee on the date of commencement of the QJSA. [Treas. Reg. § 1.401(a)(4)-8(c)(3)(vii)(A)-(C)]

### Q 13:21    Are lump-sum forms of benefit for cash balance plans determined under the rules restricting interest rates under Code Section 417(e)?

Sort of. The PPA added Code Section 411(a)(13)(A) that provides that for distributions on or after June 29, 2005, an applicable defined benefit plan does not fail to satisfy Code Section 411(c) or 417(e) if the present value of the accrued benefit for a participant is equal to the balance in the hypothetical account. An *applicable defined benefit plan* is a defined benefit plan under which the accrued benefit (or any portion thereof) is calculated as the balance of a hypothetical account maintained for the participant (a cash balance plan) or as an accumulated percentage of the participant's final average compensation (a pension equity plan). [I.R.C. § 411(a)(13)(C)]

Prior to this amendment to the Code, if a cash balance plan provided for a distribution alternative that is subject to the interest rate restrictions under Code Section 417(e) (e.g., a lump-sum distribution), the actuarial present value of the benefit paid to the employee under the distribution alternative must equal the nonforfeitable percentage (determined under the plan's vesting schedule) of the greater of the current value of the employee's hypothetical account as of the date the distribution begins or the actuarial present value (calculated in accordance with Treasury Regulations Section 1.417(e)-1(d)) of the employee's accrued benefit. Thus, it was possible for an employee to receive a distribution in an amount greater than his or her hypothetical account balance. This was applicable to distributions from cash balance plans prior to June 29, 2005.

Treasury Regulations Section 1.417(e)-1(d) outlines the restrictions and valuations of distributions subject to Code Sections 411(a)(11) and 417. Notice 96-8 [1996-1 C.B. 359] contained proposed guidance on the application of Code Sections 411(a)(11) and 417(e) to single-sum distributions under cash balance plans. The notice required cash balance plans to develop a normal retirement annuity by projecting the account balance to normal retirement age using the plan's interest crediting rate, and then convert that amount to an annuity. The annuity benefit must then be discounted to the date of distribution using the Code Section 417(e) applicable interest rate. [Lyons v. Georgia-Pacific Corp. Salaried Employees Ret. Plan, 221 F.3d 1235 (11th Cir. 2000)] The Seventh Circuit ruled in a cash balance case that the use of a preretirement mortality discount when there is a death benefit is "unfathomable" and denied such use. [Berger v. Xerox Corp. Ret. Income Guarantee Plan, 2003 U.S. App. LEXIS 19374

(7th Cir. 2003)] If the projection rate used by the plan was greater than the discount rate under Code Section 417(e), the plan would have to pay a lump-sum distribution greater than the account balance, to remain qualified. This result has often been called a "whipsaw."

**Example.** Diane, age 45, has a hypothetical account balance in her employer's cash balance plan of $50,000 as of her date of termination, June 1, 2005. The plan uses an interest rate of 8 percent for the hypothetical interest credits. Diane requests an immediate lump-sum distribution. The lump-sum amount under the plan is equal to the greater of the hypothetical account balance or the single sum as calculated under Code Section 417(e) (assuming that the current applicable rate under Code Section 417(e) is 6.5 percent). Under Code Section 417(e), the single-sum amount is calculated as follows:

| | |
|---|---:|
| Hypothetical account balance | $ 50,000 |
| Years to age 65 | 20 |
| Projected to age 65 at 8% | $ 233,048 |
| Present value at Section 417(e) rate | $ 66,138 |

Therefore, the plan must pay Diane $66,138, $16,138 more than the hypothetical account balance.

If this distribution occurred on July 1, 2005, the amount required to be distributed would have only been her account balance under the terms of the plan, $50,000.

Generally, if the hypothetical interest credit is greater than the Code Section 417(e) applicable rate, the plan will be "whipsawed" into paying a lump sum that is greater than the participant's hypothetical account balance. A way to eliminate this is by defining the plan rate to be equal to the Code Section 417(e) rate, which is currently the 30-year rate for Treasury securities.

In addition, courts have ruled that it is an improper forfeiture of benefits for a plan to use a lower interest rate in projecting a terminated employee's account balance to normal retirement age than the rate used in determining interest credits for active employees. [Esden v. Bank of Boston, 229 F.3d 154 (2d Cir. 2000)]

**Practice Pointer.** In order to avoid the "whipsaw" problem, many plans defined the interest crediting rate in their plan documents as the 30-year rate for Treasury securities. Therefore, this law change doesn't change the amount of distributions for these plans. However, those plans that had a different interest crediting rate and paid out distributions during the period from June 29, 2005, to the date of enactment of the PPA, are awaiting guidance from the IRS as to how they need to treat the excess distributions that occurred. This law change will have a great effect in the future as well when the Code Section 417(e) rate changes to the new segment rates (see chapter 16) and also on how minimum required contributions will be determined for cash balance plans for plan years beginning after December 31, 2007 (see chapter 19).

### Q 13:22   Are there any restrictions on the interest rate and mortality assumptions for determining optional forms of benefit?

Yes. For purposes of calculating optional forms of benefit, any actuarial present value must be determined using a reasonable interest rate and mortality table. A standard interest rate and a standard mortality table are considered reasonable for this purpose. (For a definition of *standard mortality tables* and *standard interest rate,* see chapter 10.)

[Treas. Reg. § 1.401(a)(4)-8(c)(3)(vii)(D)]

### Q 13:23   Can a cash balance plan provide for past-service credit?

Yes, it can, provided certain requirements are satisfied with regard to any hypothetical allocation that takes into account past-service credit. The benefit formula under the plan cannot provide for hypothetical allocations in the current plan year that are attributable to years of service before the current plan year, unless each of the following requirements is satisfied:

1. The years of past-service credit are granted on a uniform basis to all current employees in the plan. [Treas. Reg. § 1.401(a)(4)-8(a)(3)(viii)(A)]

2. Hypothetical allocations for the current plan year are determined under a uniform hypothetical allocation formula (see Q 13:9). [Treas. Reg. § 1.401(a)(4)-8(a)(3)(viii)(B)]

3. The hypothetical allocations attributable to the years of past service would have satisfied the uniform hypothetical allocation formula requirement (see Q 13:9), and the interest adjustments to those hypothetical allocations would have satisfied Treasury Regulations Section 1.401(a)(4)-8(c)(3)(iv)(A) (see Q 13:12), if the plan provision granting past service had been in effect for the entire period for which years of past service are granted to any employee. To satisfy this requirement, the hypothetical allocation attributable to a year of past service must be adjusted for interest for the period (including the retroactive period) beginning with the year of past service to which the hypothetical allocation is attributable and ending at normal retirement age. If the interest rate specified in the plan is a variable interest rate, the interest adjustments for the period before the current plan year either must be based on the current value of the variable interest rate for the period in which the grant of past service first becomes effective or must be reconstructed based on the then current value of the variable interest rate that would have applied during each prior period. [Treas. Reg. § 1.401(a)(4)-8(a)(3)(viii)(C)]

### Q 13:24   Must employees working beyond normal retirement age continue to accrue benefits in a cash balance plan?

Yes. In the case of an employee who continues to work beyond normal retirement age, the plan must provide that interest adjustments continue to be made to the employee's hypothetical account until the employee actually retires. In the case of such an employee, the employee's accrued benefit is defined as an annuity that is the actuarial equivalent of the employee's hypothetical account as of the date of benefit commencement. [Treas. Reg. § 1.401(a)(4)-8(a)(3)(ix)]

### Q 13:25    What are the uniformity requirements for a cash balance plan?

In order to satisfy the safe harbor requirements and in addition to the uniformity requirements for hypothetical interest adjustments and allocation (see Qs 13:8-13:14), a cash balance plan must uniformly provide vesting and service credits to all employees. Furthermore, a cash balance plan cannot provide for employee contributions.

### Q 13:26    Can a cash balance plan be amended to change the interest rate adjustment?

Yes. A plan can be amended to change the interest rate used to adjust hypothetical allocations for plan years after a fresh-start date, provided that the accrued benefits for plan years beginning after the fresh-start date are determined without wear-away (see chapter 11). For example, the accrued benefit after an interest rate change must equal the sum of the accrued benefit determined before the fresh-start date plus the accrued benefit after the fresh-start date using the new interest rate adjustment. [Treas. Reg. § 1.401(a)(4)-13(f)(3)(ii)]

### Q 13:27    Can a cash balance plan be amended to change the allocation formula?

Yes. A change to the allocation formula of a cash balance plan can be made on a prospective basis only and any benefits accrued as of the date of the amendment must be preserved. The plan must provide that benefits at the time of the amendment be equal to the greater of the accrued benefit before the amendment or the accrued benefit after the amendment. [ERISA § 204(h)]

## Conversion from Traditional Defined Benefit Plans

### Q 13:28    How are accrued benefits calculated when a traditional defined benefit plan is converted to a cash balance plan?

As of June 29, 2005, a defined benefit plan that is converted to a cash balance plan must provide that the employee's accrued benefit be equal to the frozen accrued benefit on the date of conversion. [I.R.C. § 411(b)(5)(B)(ii)] For conversions that occurred prior to this date, the plan sponsor had three choices in determining the employee's accrued benefit under the terms of the plan prior to the conversion. It could be the greater of:

1. The frozen accrued benefit on the date of conversion;

2. The opening hypothetical account balance (see Q 13:29); or

3. The amount the hypothetical account would have had if the cash balance plan had always been in existence, provided the plan satisfies the past-service credit rules applicable to cash balance plans (see Q 13:23).

### Q 13:29    How is the opening hypothetical account balance determined in a cash balance plan?

For conversions that occur after June 29, 2005, the employee's accrued benefit for years of service before the effective date of the amendment must be defined as the accrued benefit determined under the terms of the plan as in effect prior to the amendment converting the traditional defined benefit plan to a cash balance plan. [I.R.C. § 411(b)(5)(B)(iii)] This accrued benefit must also include any early retirement benefit or retirement-type subsidy if, when the employee terminates employment, he or she meets the age, years of service, and any other requirements under the plan for entitlement to such benefit or subsidy. [I.R.C. § 411(b)(5)(B)(iv)]

For conversions that occurred prior to June 29, 2005, an employee's opening hypothetical account balance equaled the actuarial present value of the employee's frozen accrued benefit as of the conversion date. For this purpose, if the plan provides for a single-sum distribution as of the conversion date, the actuarial present value of the employee's frozen accrued benefit as of the conversion date equals the amount of a single-sum distribution payable under the plan on that date if it is assumed that the employee terminated employment on the conversion date, the employee's accrued benefit was 100 percent vested, and the employee satisfied all eligibility requirements under the plan for the single-sum distribution. If the plan does not offer a single-sum distribution as of the conversion date, the actuarial present value of the employee's frozen accrued benefit as of the conversion date must be determined using a standard mortality table and the applicable Code Section 417(e) rates, as defined in Treasury Regulations Section 1.417(e)-1(d). [Treas. Reg. § 1.401(a)(4)-13(f)(2)(iii)(A)]

### Q 13:30    Can a participant's accrual under an old traditional defined benefit plan be frozen after conversion to a cash balance plan?

Yes. Prior to June 29, 2005, the employer had three choices in calculating accrued benefits after the date of conversion:

*Method 1. Without wear-away.* Under this method the employee's accrued benefit under the plan is equal to the sum of (1) the employee's accrued benefit as of the date of conversion under the prior formula and (2) the employee's accrued benefit determined under the formula applicable to benefit accrual in the current plan year using the current formula and the employee's years of service after the conversion date.

**Example 1.** The D&B pension plan is a calendar-year defined benefit plan providing an annual benefit for each year of service equal to 2 percent of compensation averaged over an employee's highest three consecutive calendar years of compensation. As of the close of the 2001 plan year, Forrest, an employee with five years of service and an average annual compensation of $20,000, had accrued a benefit of $2,000 ($2\% \times 5 \times \$20,000$). D&B decides to convert the plan to a cash balance plan effective January 1, 2002. Contribution credits equal 5 percent per year of service after December 31, 2001, and the rate of interest credit is 7 percent for each year. The amendment uses the formula without wear-away. Therefore, Forrest's accrued benefit as of December 31, 2002, is his accrued benefit under the old formula converted to a hypothetical account balance plus the contribution credit for 2002. The lump-sum value of Forrest's old benefit as of December 31, 2001, is $10,000, the hypothetical interest credit is $1,000, and the interest credit is $700. Therefore, Forrest's total account balance under this method is $11,700.

*Method 2. With wear-away.* Under this method the employee's accrued benefit under the plan is equal to the greater of (1) the employee's accrued benefit under the prior benefit formula and (2) the employee's accrued benefit determined under the formula applicable to benefit accrual in the current plan year using the current formula and the employee's total years of service before and after the date of amendment. Under this "greater of" technique of transitioning from an old benefit formula to a new benefit formula, the benefit under the old formula is generally "frozen," or fixed as of the amendment date. This results in "wear-away" as the participant's frozen benefit under the old formula is initially greater than the benefit under the new formula. Under these circumstances, the participant's benefit is, for some period of time, the frozen benefit under the old formula. However, as the participant continues to work and earn additional benefits under the new formula, the participant's benefit under the new formula will eventually catch up and exceed the benefit under the old formula. When this will occur depends on each participant's circumstances and the benefit levels under the new formula.

**Example 2.** The facts are the same as those in Example 1 except that the plan uses wear-away in calculating future benefits. The lump-sum value of the old benefit on December 31, 2002, is $10,700 ($10,000 \times 1.07$). The present value of the cash balance account, if hypothetical contributions and interest credits for all years of service are assumed, is $6,153. Therefore, under this method, Forrest's total account balance as of December 31, 2002, is $10,700.

*Method 3. Extended wear-away.* Under this method the employee's accrued benefit under the plan is equal to the greater of (1) the employee's accrued benefit determined using the without wear-away method and (2) the employee's accrued benefit determined using the with wear-away method.

[Treas. Reg. § 1.401(a)(4)-13(c)(4)]

For conversions occurring after June 29, 2005, the plan must use Method 1 above, without wear-away, to determine the accrued benefit after the amendment to a cash balance plan. [I.R.C. § 411(b)(5)(B)(iii)]

### Q 13:31 Is wear-away legal?

Yes. The Treasury regulations under Code Section 401(a)(4) specifically allow for determining a participant's benefit using wear-away. [Treas. Reg. § 1.401(a)(4)-13(c)(4)(ii)] In addition, the First Circuit, in *Campbell v. BankBoston, N.A.* [327 F.3d 1 (1st Cir. 2003)], ruled that the freezing of accruals under an old formula and protection of that amount was legal under current regulations.

### Q 13:32 Is the conversion of a traditional defined benefit plan to a cash balance plan a breach of fiduciary duty?

No. In *Lockheed v. Spink* [517 U.S. 882 (1996)], the Supreme Court held that "the act of amending a pension plan does not trigger ERISA's fiduciary provisions." Other courts, however, have held that employers have an affirmative obligation to inform affected participants when the company is seriously considering changing its plan. In addition, lying or misleading employees about benefit plan changes is a breach of the employer's fiduciary duties. [Varity Corp. v. Howe, 516 U.S. 911 (1996)]

### Q 13:33 What disclosures need to be made to employees when the employer is converting a traditional defined benefit plan to a cash balance plan?

The required disclosure is contained in ERISA Section 204(h) and the Treasury Regulations contained in Code Section 4980F. These sections state that employees must receive proper notice (called an ERISA Section 204(h) notice) of any amendment that significantly reduces the rate of future benefit accruals or eliminates or significantly reduces an early retirement benefit or retirement-type subsidy.

However, the conversion, in and of itself, is not necessarily considered a reduction of future benefit accruals. In *Engers v. AT&T* [2006 U.S. Dist. LEXIS 23028 (D.N.J. 2006)], the federal judge ruled that AT&T did not need to provide employees with advance notice of the conversion of a traditional defined benefit plan to a cash balance plan because after comparing the rates of future benefits there was no reduction in the rate of future benefit accruals.

### Q 13:34 How are participants to be notified of a significant reduction in the rate of future benefit accruals?

The ERISA Section 204(h) notice must be provided in writing in a manner calculated to be understood by the average plan participant. In addition, it must provide sufficient information to allow applicable individuals to understand the effect of the plan amendment. [ERISA § 204(h)(2)]

The ERISA Section 204(h) notice must be provided within a reasonable time before the effective date of the plan amendment. Generally, this is 45 days before the effectivedate of the plan amendment but is reduced to 15 days for multiemployer plans and small plans that expect to have fewer than 100 participants in the plan as of the effective date. [Treas. Reg. § 54.4980F, Q&A 9]

Generally, the notice cannot be distributed until after the adoption of the amendment but can be distributed before adoption as long as there is no material modification of the amendment before it is adopted. [ERISA § 204(h)(5)]

### Q 13:35   What information is required to be provided in the ERISA Section 204(h) notice?

In general, the ERISA Section 204(h) notice must include sufficient information to allow participants to understand the effect of the plan amendment, including the approximate magnitude of the expected reduction. If the amendment is not uniformly applicable to all participants, the notice must either identify the general classes of participants to whom the reduction is expected to apply or include sufficient information to allow each participant receiving the notice to determine which reductions are expected to apply to that individual. The type and amount of information necessary will vary depending on the nature of the change resulting from the amendment.

For a conversion from a traditional defined benefit plan to a cash balance plan, it is necessary for the notice to include the following:

- A description of the benefit or allocation formula before the amendment, a description of the benefit or allocation formula under the plan as amended, and the effective date of the amendment; and
- One or more illustrative examples showing the approximate magnitude of the reduction in the example.

[Treas. Reg. § 54.4980F, Q&A 11]

### Q 13:36   What requirements apply to the examples that must be provided in the ERISA Section 204(h) notice?

For a cash balance conversion, most likely the amendment will result in reductions that vary; therefore, the illustrative examples must show the approximate range of the reductions.

For a reduction that varies from small to large depending on service or other factors, two illustrative examples may be provided showing the smallest likely reduction and the largest likely reduction. However, any reductions that are likely to occur in only a *de minimis* number of cases are not required to be taken into account in determining the range of the reductions if a narrative statement is included to that effect and examples are provided that show the approximate range of the reductions in other cases. Amendments for which the maximum reduction occurs under identifiable circumstances, with proportionately smaller reductions in other cases, may be illustrated by one example illustrating the maximum reduction, with a statement that smaller reductions also occur.

The examples are not required to be based on any particular form of payment (such as a life annuity or a single sum) but may be based on whatever form that appropriately illustrates the reduction. The examples may generally be based on any reasonable assumptions (e.g., assumptions relating to the representative participant's age, years of service, and compensation; any interest rate and mortality table used in the illustrations; and salary scale assumptions used in the illustrations for amendments that alter the compensation taken into account under the plan), but the notice must identify those assumptions. However, if a plan's benefit provisions include a factor that varies over time (such as a variable interest rate), the determination of whether an amendment is reasonably expected to result in a wear-away period must be based on the value of the factor applicable under the plan at a time that is reasonably close to the date the notice is provided, and any wear-away period that is solely a result of a future change in the variable factor may be disregarded.

If the notice includes materially false or misleading information (or omits information to cause the notice to be misleading) it will not be considered to be an ERISA Section 204(h) notice.

**Example.** John Boy plan is a defined benefit plan under which each participant accrues a normal retirement benefit as a life annuity beginning at the normal retirement age of 65, equal to the participant's number of years of service times 1.5 percent times the participant's average pay over the three consecutive years for which the average is the highest.

The John Boy plan is amended, effective July 1, 2005, to change the formula for all future accruals to a cash balance formula under which the opening account balance for each participant on July 1, 2005, is zero, hypothetical pay credits equal to 5 percent of pay are credited to the account thereafter, and hypothetical interest is credited monthly based on the applicable interest rate under Code Section 417(e)(3) at the beginning of the quarter. Any participant who terminates employment with vested benefits can receive an actuarially equivalent annuity (based on the same reasonable actuarial assumptions that are specified in the John Boy plan) commencing at any time after termination of employment and before the plan's normal retirement age of 65. The benefit resulting from the hypothetical account balance is in addition to the benefit accrued on June 30, 2005 (taking into account only service and highest three-year pay before July 30, 2005), so it is reasonably expected that no wear-away period will result from the amendment. John Boy's plan administrator expects that, as a general rule, depending on future pay increases and future interest rates, the rate of future benefit accrual after the conversion is higher for participants who accrue benefits before age 50 and after age 70, but is lower for participants who accrue benefits between age 50 and age 70.

The plan administrator of the John Boy plan announces the conversion to a cash balance formula on May 16, 2005. The announcement is delivered to all participants and includes a written notice that describes the old formula, the new formula, and the effective date. In addition, the notice states that the formula before the conversion provided a normal retirement benefit equal to the product of a participant's number of years of service times 1.5 percent times the participant's average pay over the three years for which the average is the highest (highest three-year pay). The notice includes an example showing the normal retirement benefit that will be accrued after June 30, 2005, for a participant who is age 49 with 10 years of service at the time of the conversion. The plan administrator believes that such a participant is representative of the participants whose rate of future benefit accrual will be reduced as a result of the amendment. The example estimates that, if the participant continues employment to age 65, the participant's normal retirement benefit for service from age 49 to age 65 will be $657 per month for life. The example assumes that the participant's pay is $50,000 at age 49. The example states that the estimated $657 monthly pension accrues over the 16-year period from age 49 to age 65 and that, based on assumed future pay increases, this amount annually would be 9.1 percent of the participant's highest three-year pay at age 65, which over the 16 years from age 49 to age 65 averages 0.57 percent per year times the participant's highest three-year pay. The example also states that the sum of the monthly annuity accrued before the conversion in the 10-year period from age 39 to age 49 and the $657 monthly annuity estimated to be accrued over the 16-year period from age 49 to age 65 is $1,235. In addition, the example states that, based on assumed future increases in pay, this would be 17.1 percent of the participant's highest three-year pay at age 65, which over the employee's career from age 39 to age 65 averages 0.66 percent per year times the participant's highest three-year pay.

The notice also includes two other examples with similar information, one that shows the circumstances in which a small reduction may occur and one that shows the largest reduction that is likely to occur. The notice states that the estimates are based on the assumption that pay increases annually after June 30, 2005, at a 4 percent rate. The notice also specifies that the applicable interest rate under Code Section 417(e) for hypothetical interest credits after June 30, 2005, is assumed to be 6 percent, which is the Code Section 417(e) applicable interest rate under the plan for 2005. [Treas. Reg. § 54.4980F, Q&A 11]

### Q 13:37    What happens if the ERISA Section 204(h) notice is not provided to all participants?

An excise tax equal to $100 per day per individual is applied to any failure to properly provide the ERISA Section 204(h) notice. There are limited exceptions to the application of the excise tax, enumerated below:

1. The excise tax will not be imposed if the plan administrator was not aware of the failure and exercised reasonable diligence in trying to satisfy the notice requirements.

2. The excise tax will not apply if the plan administrator exercised reasonable diligence in trying to satisfy the notice requirements and provides the ERISA Section 204(h) notice within 30 days of finding such failure.

3. The Treasury Secretary has the authority to waive the excise tax in full or in part for any failure that was due to reasonable cause to the extent that the payment of the tax would be excessive or be otherwise inequitable relative to the failure involved.

If the plan administrator exercised reasonable diligence in providing the ERISA Section 204(h) notice, the total excise tax imposed during the fiscal year on the plan sponsor will not exceed $500,000. [I.R.C. § 4980F]

If the failure to provide the ERISA Section 204(h) notice is egregious, all applicable individuals will be entitled to receive the greater of the benefits under the old or new plan formula. An egregious failure is defined as

1. An intentional failure;
2. A failure to provide most of the individuals with most of the information they are entitled to receive; or
3. A failure that is determined by the Treasury Secretary to be egregious under the regulations.

[ERISA § 204(h)(6)]

## Legal Issues

### Q 13:38   Are there any legal problems associated with a cash balance plan?

Currently, no. The PPA settled this issue for new plans by making amendments and clarifications to certain ERISA sections, Code sections, and ADEA (Age Discrimination in Employment Act) sections. However, for plans that existed prior to enactment of the PPA, this issue is unsettled. In PPA Section 701(d), Congress specifically stated that there was no inference to be made by the amendments contained in the Act to the treatment of cash balance plans under prior regulations. This leaves prior cash balance plans open to litigation. However, on August 7, 2006, the Seventh Circuit in *Cooper v. IBM Personal Pension Plan* [274 F. Supp. 2d 1010 (S.D. Ill. 2003)] reversed the district court's holding that the IBM cash balance plan was discriminatory (see Q 13:42). With this ruling, the legal atmosphere surrounding older plans has gotten much clearer.

### Q 13:39   Do cash balance plans fail to satisfy the accrual rules of Code Section 411(b)?

No. The Seventh Circuit ruled in the *Cooper* case that cash balance plans are not age discriminatory. The accrual rule that cash balance plans satisfy is the 133⅓ rule of Code Section 411(b)(1)(B). A defined benefit plan satisfies the requirements of this Code section for a particular plan year if under the plan the accrued benefit payable at normal retirement age is equal to the normal retirement benefit and the annual rate at which any individual who is or could be a participant can accrue the retirement benefits payable at normal retirement age under the plan for any later plan year is not more than 133⅓ percent of the annual rate at which he or she can accrue benefits for any plan year beginning on or after such particular plan year and before such later plan year. [I.R.C. § 411(b)(1)(B)]

This rule prevents back-loading, that is, preventing discrimination in rates of accrual by increasing the accrual rate for those who work longer with the company by greater than 133⅓ percent. Most cash balance plans are front-loaded; that is, the accruals in earlier years are inherently worth more (see the example in Q 13:6). If the cash balance plan has contribution credits and interest credits that increase with age and/or service, the plan has the potential of failing the 133⅓ rule.

### Q 13:40 Does a conversion from a traditional defined benefit plan to a cash balance plan fail to protect accrued benefits?

A defined benefit plan is required to protect accrued benefits and any optional form of the accrued benefit. [I.R.C. § 411(d)(6)] If the opening account balance in a cash balance plan conversion is not at least the actuarial equivalent of the accrued benefit under the traditional defined benefit plan formula, the cash balance plan does not satisfy this rule and can be disqualified.

### Q 13:41 Is a plan required to protect future accruals of benefits?

No. A plan can change the plan benefit structure, reduce future benefits, or even terminate the plan with proper notice. [ERISA § 204(h)] There is no obligation to guarantee future benefits.

### Q 13:42 Do cash balance plans discriminate on the basis of age?

All courts have now ruled that cash balance plans do not discriminate based on age. In the case of *Eaton v. Onan Corp.* [117 F. Supp. 2d 812 (S.D. Ind. 2000)], a federal court in Indiana concluded that the cash balance plan did not violate the ADEA because, based on the ADEA's legislative history, the ADEA was intended only to protect participants beyond the age of normal retirement under the plan. Furthermore, the court determined that even if the ADEA intended to protect participants younger than normal retirement age, a cash balance plan still does not violate the ADEA's protection against declining rates of benefit accrual.

The court cited Code Section 411(b)(1)(H)(i), which states that a plan will be discriminatory if the rate of an employee's benefit accrual is reduced because of the attainment of any age. Under a typical cash balance plan that provides for uniform contribution and interest credits, the value of each year's accrual is less than the prior year's accrual because there are fewer future years to compound the contribution with interest.

However, the court ruled that this prohibition in the Code that states that accruals cannot be decreased "because of" the attainment of any age does not prohibit plan designs in which a reduction in accruals is correlated to some extent with the age of the participants. For example, a plan does not fail this requirement solely because the plan imposes a limitation on the number of years of service that are taken into account for purposes of determining benefit accrual under the plan. [I.R.C. § 411(b)(1)(H)(ii)] In fact, the preamble to the 1991

Treasury regulations under Code Section 401(a)(4) stated, "The fact that interest adjustments through normal retirement age are accrued in the year of the related hypothetical allocation will not cause a cash balance plan to fail to satisfy the requirements of section 411(b)(1)(H), relating to age-based reductions in the rate at which benefits accrue under a plan." [56 Fed. Reg. 47,528 (Sept. 19, 1991)]

In addition, the proposed Treasury regulations under Code Section 411(b)(1)(H) state, "A defined benefit plan is not considered to discontinue benefit accruals or reduce the rate of benefit accrual on behalf of a participant because of the attainment of any age in violation of section 411(b)(1)(H) . . . solely because of a positive correlation between increased age and a reduction or discontinuance in benefit accruals or account allocations under a plan." [Prop. Treas. Reg. § 1.411(b)-2(a)]

Likewise, in *Tootle v. ARINC* [2004 U.S. Dist. LEXIS 10629 (D. Md. 2004)], a federal court in Maryland ruled that cash balance plans do not discriminate against older participants. In that case, the court determined that "the more sensible approach" to evaluating whether age discrimination occurs in cash balance plans is to examine the rate of increase to the participant's notional account balance. The court ruled that a "potential claim of age discrimination arises only by applying a definition for accrued benefits which does not fit with the way cash balance plans are structured." Rather, the court determined that age discrimination should be tested by "examining the rate at which amounts are allocated and the changes over time to an individual's account balance."

In another case, the U.S. District Court in Philadelphia sided with the *Eaton* and *Tootle* courts in favor of cash balance plans, dismissing all charges of discrimination in *Register v. PNC Financial Services Group, Inc.* [36 Employee Benefits Cas. (BNA) 1321(D. Pa. 2005)] This court sided with Eaton's interpretation that the accrual rate should be "the change in the employee's cash balance account from one year to the next." Therefore, "this Court cannot find any reason that ERISA § 204(h)(1)(H) should be construed otherwise. Since this Court finds that rate of an employee's benefit accrual does not necessarily refer to the accrued benefit at age 65, PNC's cash balance plan is not age discriminatory."

However, in *Cooper v. IBM Personal Pension Plan* [274 F. Supp. 2d 1010 (S.D. Ill. 2003)], the position taken by the district court was that the reference in ERISA Section 204(b)(1)(H) to the "rate of benefit accrual" should be read in the same manner as the reference to "accrued benefit" in ERISA Section 204(b)(1)(G), in that the relevant comparison is the benefit expressed as an annual benefit at normal retirement age. The Seventh Circuit overturned this ruling stating that "it is important to separate age discrimination from other characteristics that may be correlated with age . . . [A] plaintiff alleging age discrimination must demonstrate that the complained-of effect is actually on account of age. One need only look at IBM's formula to rule-out a violation. It is age neutral."

# Chapter 14

# 412(e)(3) Defined Benefit Plans (formerly 412(i) Defined Benefit Plans)

Under the Pension Protection Act of 2006 (PPA), Internal Revenue Code (Code) Section 412(i) was moved to Code Section 412(e)(3). A 412(i) plan is now referred to a 412(e)(3) plan. A 412(e)(3) defined benefit plan is a regular defined benefit plan with special funding rules. This type of plan has existed for many years, but was not very popular in the past. In recent years, specifically since the enactment of the Economic Growth and Tax Relief Reconciliation Act of 2001 (EGTRRA), 412(e)(3) plans have reemerged in the headlines. Unfortunately, there were some 412(e)(3) arrangements that were purported to be able to circumvent traditional limitations, and the IRS has moved to shut those abusive arrangements down. However, a valid 412(e)(3) plan may still fit within an employer's goals, and this chapter explains how it works. (Throughout this chapter, an insurance contract plan that meets the requirements of Code Section 412(e)(3) is referred to as a 412(e)(3) plan.)

## Basics of 412(e)(3)

### Q 14:1   What is a *412(e)(3) plan*?

A *412(e)(3) plan* is, simply, a defined benefit plan that meets the requirements of Code Section 412(e)(3). It refers to defined benefit pension plans that are funded exclusively through insurance contracts (life and/or annuity).

### Q 14:2   What are the requirements of Code Section 412(e)(3)?

A plan meets the requirements of Code Section 412(e)(3) if:

1. The plan is funded exclusively by the purchase of individual insurance contracts (see Q 14:3);

2. Such contracts provide for level annual premium payments to be made extending not later than the retirement age for each individual participating in the plan, and commencing with the date the individual became a participant in the plan (or, in the case of an increase in benefits, commencing at the time such increase becomes effective) (see Q 14:4);

3. Benefits provided by the plan are equal to the benefits provided under each contract at normal retirement age under the plan and are guaranteed by an insurance carrier (licensed under the laws of a state to do business with the plan) to the extent premiums have been paid;

4. Premiums payable for the plan year, and all prior plan years, under such contracts have been paid before lapse or there is reinstatement of the policy (see Q 14:5);

5. No rights under such contracts have been subject to a security interest at any time during the plan year (see Q 14:6); and

6. No policy loans are outstanding at any time during the plan year (see Q 14:7).

A plan can be funded exclusively by the purchase of group insurance contracts, but only if the contracts have the same characteristics as contracts described above (see Q 14:8).

### Q 14:3   How does a 412(e)(3) plan meet the requirements for being funded exclusively through the purchase of individual contracts?

According to Code Section 412(e)(3), the plan must be funded exclusively by the purchase from an insurance company or companies (licensed under the law of a state or the District of Columbia to do business with the plan) of individual annuity or individual insurance contracts, or a combination thereof. The purchase may be made either directly by the employer or through the use of a custodial account or trust.

A plan will not be considered to be funded otherwise than exclusively by the purchase of individual annuity or individual insurance contracts merely because the employer makes a payment necessary to comply with the provisions of Code Section 411(c)(2) (relating to accrued benefit from employee contributions). [Treas. Reg. § 1.412(i)-1(b)(2)(i)]

### Q 14:4   How does a 412(e)(3) plan meet the level premium requirements?

The individual annuity or individual insurance contracts issued under the plan must provide for level annual (or more frequent) premium payments to be made under the plan for the period beginning with the date each individual began participating in the plan and ending not later than the normal retirement age for that individual or, if earlier, the date the individual ceases his or her participation in the plan.

Premium payments may be considered to be level even though items such as experience gains and dividends are applied against premiums.

In the case of an increase in benefits, the contracts must provide for level annual payments with respect to such increase to be paid for the period beginning at the time the increase becomes effective. If payment commences on the first payment date under the contract occurring after the date an individual becomes a participant or after the effective date of an increase in benefits, the level premium requirements will be satisfied even though payment does not commence on the date on which the individual's participation commenced or on the effective date of the benefit increase, whichever is applicable.

If an individual accrues benefits after his or her normal retirement age, the level premium requirements are satisfied if payment is made at the time such benefits accrue.

If the provisions for level premiums are set forth in a separate agreement with the issuer of the individual contracts, they need not be included in the individual contracts. [Treas. Reg. § 1.412(i)-1(b)(2)(ii)]

### Q 14:5   When must reinstatement occur if there was a lapse of a policy?

In general, all premiums payable for the plan year, and for all prior plan years, under the insurance or annuity contracts must have been paid before lapse. If a lapse has occurred during the plan year, the plan will still be considered to meet the requirements of Code Section 412(e)(3) if reinstatement of the insurance policy, under which the individual insurance contracts are issued, occurs during the year of the lapse and before distribution is made or benefits commence to any participant whose benefits are reduced because of the lapse.

### Q 14:6   May a contract under a 412(e)(3) plan be subject to a security interest?

No. No rights under the individual contracts may have been subject to a security interest at any time during the plan year. This requirement does not apply to contracts that have been distributed to participants if the security interest is created after the date of distribution.

### Q 14:7   May a 412(e)(3) plan allow loans?

No. No policy loans, including loans to individual participants, on any of the individual contracts may be outstanding at any time during the plan year. This requirement does not apply to contracts that have been distributed to participants if the loan is made after the date of distribution.

An application of funds by the issuer to pay premiums due under the contracts shall be deemed not to be a policy loan if the amount of the funds so applied, and interest thereon, is repaid during the plan year in which the funds are applied and before distribution is made or benefits commence to any participant whose benefits are reduced because of such application.

### Q 14:8   Can a 412(e)(3) plan be funded with a group insurance or annuity contract?

Yes. A 412(e)(3) plan can be funded with a group insurance or annuity contract instead of individual insurance or annuity contracts as long as the same requirements are met for the group contracts as are listed for the individual contracts (i.e., funding from a licensed insurer, level premiums, and so forth). In addition, the following requirements must be satisfied by the group contracts:

1. If the plan is funded by a group annuity contract, the value of the benefits guaranteed by the insurance company issuing the contract under the plan with respect to each participant under the contract must not be less than the value of such benefits which would be provided by the cash surrender value for that participant under any individual annuity contract plan.

2. If the plan is funded by a group insurance contract, the value of the benefits guaranteed by the insurance company issuing the contract under the plan with respect to each participant under the contract must not be less than the value of such benefits which would be provided by the cash surrender value for that participant under any individual insurance contract plan.

3. Under the group annuity or group insurance contract, premiums or other consideration received by the insurance company (and, if a custodial account or trust is used, the custodian or trustee thereof) must be allocated to purchase individual benefits for participants under the plan.

A plan maintaining unallocated funds in an auxiliary trust fund or providing that an insurance company will maintain unallocated funds in a separate account (e.g., a group deposit administration contract) does not satisfy the requirements of Code Section 412(e)(3).

### Q 14:9   May a 412(e)(3) plan be funded with a combination of individual and group contracts?

Yes. A plan that is funded by a combination of individual contracts and a group contract does meet the requirements of Code Section 412(e)(3) if the combination, in the aggregate, satisfies the requirements of this Code section for the plan year.

### Q 14:10    Must a 412(e)(3) plan meet the other requirements of Code Section 412?

No. If the plan meets the requirements of Code Section 412(e)(3), it is exempt from the rest of the requirements of Code Section 412. [I.R.C. § 412(h)(2); Treas. Reg. § 1.412(i)-1(a)]

### Q 14:11    From what requirements of Code Section 412 is a 412(e)(3) plan exempt?

Since a 412(e)(3) plan is not subject to the rest of the requirements of Code Section 412, the following are not applicable:

- Full-funding limitations
- Quarterly contribution requirements
- Additional funding charges
- Current liability testing
- Schedule B requirement or enrolled actuary certifications (unless there is an additional contribution needed to meet top-heavy requirements)
- Investment risk

### Q 14:12    Is a 412(e)(3) plan subject to the Pension Benefit Guaranty Corporation (PBGC) requirements?

Yes, in part. A 412(e)(3) plan is subject to the per participant premium of $19, but is exempt from the variable rate premium.

### Q 14:13    What Code requirements are still applicable to a 412(e)(3) plan?

Since a 412(e)(3) plan is a regular defined benefit plan that has special funding rules, the rest of the Code sections applicable to any qualified defined benefit plan remain applicable to 412(e)(3) plans. These include the maximum benefit limitations of Code Section 415, the minimum coverage rules of Code Section 410, the nondiscrimination regulations of Section 401(a)(4), the minimum participations rules of Code Section 401(a)(26), the minimum vesting rules of Code Section 411, the deduction rules of Code Section 404 (excluding Code Section 404(a)(1)(A)(i)), and the top-heavy regulations of Code Section 416.

## Nondiscrimination Requirements

### Q 14:14    How is the accrued benefit determined in a 412(e)(3) plan?

A participant's accrued benefit in a 412(e)(3) plan must be no less than the cash surrender value of his or her insurance contract. [I.R.C. § 411(b)(1)(F)]

### Q 14:15   Does Code Section 417 apply to 412(e)(3) plans in determining lump-sum payments?

Generally, no. If the 412(e)(3) plan defines the accrued benefit as the cash surrender value of the insurance contract, then no, there is no requirement to apply Code Section 417 to the distribution of the annuity, including avoiding the GATT interest rate and mortality assumptions of Code Section 417(e). However, if the plan defines the accrued benefit using the fractional rule, the provisions of Code Section 417 do apply. In addition, if there are top-heavy minimums in the 412(e)(3) plan, the participant will have a portion of the accrued benefit defined as an annuity that is subject to Code Section 417 provisions. [IRS Q&A 2005 ASPPA Annual Conference]

### Q 14:16   Is the accrued benefit under a 412(e)(3) plan definitely determinable?

Yes. Treasury Regulations Section 1.401-1(b)(1)(i) provides that a plan designated to provide benefits to be paid upon retirement will, for purposes of Code Section 401(a), be considered a pension plan if the employer contributions under the plan can be determined actuarially on the basis of definitely determinable benefits. In a 412(e)(3) plan, an employee's accrued benefit cannot be less than the cash surrender value of the individual's contracts. This is considered definitely determinable.

However, it is the practice of some life insurance companies to provide a larger retirement benefit if, at the time the cash surrender value of the insurance policy (or annuity contract) is applied to purchase an annuity, the company's then-current annuity purchase rate is more favorable than the annuity purchase rate guaranteed in the policy. Many policies contain a provision that specifies how the calculations of the larger benefit would be made in such circumstances. Where no such provision is incorporated in the policy, the insurance company will provide the larger benefit administratively based on the established practice of the company at the time the cash surrender value is so applied. In either case, the increased benefit arises simply by the substitution of one (lower) purchase rate for the guaranteed rate, and the amount of the increased benefit is thereby uniquely determinable at the time the benefit is to be purchased. In Revenue Ruling 78-56 [1978-1 C.B. 116], the IRS ruled that, if this is the case, the fact that the cash value of a participant's policy may provide a benefit in excess of the benefit intended by the plan document will not necessarily mean that the benefit is not definitely determinable. The benefit will be considered to be definitely determinable so long as:

1. The participant's accrued benefit at all times is determinable under the insurance contract;

2. A plan benefit is uniquely determinable, based on (a) such accrued benefit, (b) the procedures stated in the insurance contract or established

insurance company practice, and (c) the current annuity purchase rate offered by the insurance company;

3. The current annuity purchase rate is not affected by forfeitures under the plan; and

4. None of these factors is within the discretion of the employer (other than by plan amendment).

### Q 14:17   Is there a special safe harbor rule for nondiscrimination testing of 412(e)(3) plans?

Yes. Under Treasury Regulations Section 1.401(a)(4)-3(b)(5), a plan satisfies the safe harbor for 412(e)(3) plans if it satisfies each of the following requirements:

1. The accrued benefit must be no less than the cash surrender value of each participant's contract as required under Code Section 411(b)(1)(F).

2. The plan must meet all of the requirements of Code Section 412(e)(3).

3. The benefit formula under the plan must be one that would satisfy the requirements of the fractional accrual rule of Treasury Regulations Section 1.401(a)(4)-3(b)(4), using only participation as plan service. Thus, the benefit formula may not recognize years of service before an employee commenced participation in the plan because, otherwise, the definition of years of service for determining the normal retirement benefit would differ from the definition of years of service for determining the accrued benefit. Notwithstanding the foregoing, a 412(e)(3) plan adopted and in effect on September 19, 1991, may continue to recognize years of service prior to an employee's participation in the plan for an employee who is a participant in the plan on that date to the extent provided by the benefit formula in the plan on such date.

4. The scheduled premium payments under an individual or group insurance contract used to fund an employee's normal retirement benefit must be level annual payments to normal retirement age. Thus, payments may not be scheduled to cease before normal retirement age.

5. The premium payments for an employee who continues benefiting after normal retirement age must be equal to the amount necessary to fund additional benefits that accrue under the plan's benefit formula for the plan year.

6. Experience gains, dividends, forfeitures, and similar items must be used solely to reduce future premiums.

7. All benefits must be funded through contracts of the same series. Among other requirements, contracts of the same series must have cash values based on the same terms (including interest and mortality assumptions) and the same conversion rights. A plan does not fail to satisfy this requirement, however, if any change in the contract series or insurer applies on the same terms to all employees. However, an amendment to the plan to

change the insurer may need to be tested to make sure it does not discriminate. [Treas. Reg. § 1.401(a)(4)-5(a)(4), Ex. 12]

8. If permitted disparity is taken into account, the normal retirement benefit stated under the plan's benefit formula must satisfy Treasury Regulations Section 1.401(l)-3. For this purpose, the 0.75-percent factor in the maximum excess or offset allowance in Treasury Regulations Section 1.401(l)-3(b)(2)(i) or (b)(3)(i), respectively, adjusted in accordance with Treasury Regulations Section 1.401(l)-3(d)(9) and (e), is reduced by multiplying the factor by 0.80.

### Q 14:18    Can a 412(e)(3) plan meet the nondiscrimination rules in any manner other than using the safe harbor?

Yes. As with other defined benefit plans, a 412(e)(3) plan may meet the general testing requirements of Code Section 401(a)(4). However, this can be problematic due to a 412(e)(3) plan's definition of accrued benefit being the cash surrender value of the insurance. Under general testing requirements of Code Section 401(a)(4), compliance is tested by comparing the normal and most valuable benefit accrual rates of the non-highly compensated employees to the highly compensated employees. Therefore, the surrender values will need to be converted to an annuity in order to determine the accrual rates. Common practice in determining the normal accrual rate under the annual method appears to be using the guaranteed rates under the contract in order to project the increase in the cash surrender value for the current plan year to the testing age. In determining the most valuable accrual rate, the increase in the cash surrender value is projected to the earliest permissible annuity starting date using the contract rates and then normalized to testing age using standard assumptions. Similar methodology is used for the accrued-to-date method or for testing involving fresh-starts.

### Q 14:19    Are there any other nondiscrimination rules that need to be considered?

Yes. Under Treasury Regulations Section 1.401(a)(4)-5(a), a change in the insurance company providing the contracts for the plan is an amendment to the plan that must be tested to make sure it does not discriminate in favor of highly compensated employees. [Treas. Reg. § 1.401(a)(4)-5(a)(4), Ex. 12]

**Example 1.** The Play It Safe defined benefit plan is a 412(e)(3) plan. For all plan years before 2002, the plan purchases insurance contracts from the Insural insurance company. In 2002, the plan shifts future purchases of insurance contracts to Insural At Any Cost insurance company. The shift in insurance companies is a plan amendment subject to testing for nondiscrimination.

In addition, if the benefits, rights, or features of the life insurance contracts held by highly compensated employees are of inherently greater value than the benefits, rights, or features of contracts held by non-highly compensated employees, then the plan is considered discriminatory. [Rev. Rul. 2004-21, 2004-10 I.R.B. 544]

These benefits, rights, or features can include optional forms of benefit, ancillary benefits, and other rights and features that can be expected to have meaningful value. Differences in insurance contracts, including differences in cash value growth terms or different exchange features that may be purchased from a plan can create distinct other rights or features even if the terms under which the contracts are purchased from the plan are the same. [Rev. Rul. 2004-21, 2004-10 I.R.B. 544]

> **Example 2.** The PayAllLess defined benefit plan provides an incidental death benefit for each participant (this is not necessarily a 412(e)(3) plan). The plan holds a life insurance contract on the life of each participant to fund this incidental death benefit. Prior to distributions from the plan, each participant is offered the opportunity to purchase his or her contract for the cash surrender value in accordance with Prohibited Transaction Exemption 92-6 [57 Fed. Reg. 5,189 (Feb. 12, 1992)]; thus the purchase is not a prohibited transaction under Code Section 4975. The contracts for the highly compensated participants are different from the ones for the non-highly compensated participants in that the cash values grow faster and the other purchase rights are different. Since the benefits, rights, or features of the contract are of inherently greater value to the highly compensated employees and are not currently made available in a nondiscriminatory manner to the non-highly compensated employees, this plan fails the requirements of Code Section 401(a)(4).

### Q 14:20   How is an employee considered as benefiting under Code Section 410(b)?

Under Code Section 410(b), a participant in a 412(e)(3) plan is considered benefiting only if a premium is paid on behalf of the participant for the plan year. However, an employee is treated as benefiting under a 412(e)(3) plan for a plan year if the sole reason that a premium is not paid on behalf of the employee is one of the following:

1. The employee's benefit would otherwise exceed a limit that is applicable on a uniform basis to all employees in the plan.

2. The benefit previously accrued by the employee is greater than the benefit that would be determined under the plan if the benefit previously accrued were disregarded.

3. The plan offsets the employee's current benefit accrual under an offset arrangement described in Treasury Regulations Section 1.401(a)(4)-3(f)(9) (without regard to whether the offset is attributable to pre-participation service or past service).

4. The employee has attained normal retirement age under a deemed benefit plan and fails to accrue a benefit because of the provisions of Code Section 411(b)(1)(H)(iii) regarding adjustments for delayed retirement.

5. The insurance contracts that have previously been purchased on behalf of the employee guarantee to provide for the employee's projected normal retirement benefit without regard to future premium payments.

## Top-Heavy Requirements

### Q 14:21    How does a 412(e)(3) plan meet the top-heavy requirements of Code Section 416?

Under Code Section 416, a top-heavy defined benefit plan requires a minimum accrual of 2 percent per year of service (limited to 10 years) for each non-key employee (see chapter 5). Unfortunately, the accrued benefits provided for a non-key employee under most level premium insurance contracts might not provide a benefit satisfying this defined benefit minimum because of the lower cash values in early years under most level premium insurance contracts, and because such contracts normally provide for level premiums until normal retirement age. Therefore, in order to satisfy the requirements of Code Section 416, a 412(e)(3) plan may be required to provide either an auxiliary fund or deferred annuity contracts to provide extra benefits to those employees whose current benefits are not sufficient to satisfy the top-heavy minimum. However, a plan will not be considered to violate the requirements of Code Section 412(e)(3) merely because it funds these extra benefits in this manner if the following conditions are met:

1. The targeted benefit at normal retirement age under the level premium insurance contract is determined, taking into account the defined benefit minimum that would be required assuming the current top-heavy (or non top-heavy) status of the plan continues until normal retirement age; and

2. The benefits provided by the auxiliary fund or deferred annuity contracts do not exceed the excess of the defined benefit minimum benefits over the benefits provided by the level premium insurance contract.

If the above conditions are satisfied, then the portion of the plan funded by the level premium annuity contract is still exempt from the minimum funding requirements under Code Section 412 and may still utilize the special accrued benefit rule in Code Section 411(b)(1)(F) (see Q 14:13); however, the portion funded by an auxiliary fund is subject to Code Section 412. Thus, a funding standard account must be maintained, and a Schedule B must be filed with the annual report. The accrued benefit for any participant may be determined using the rule in Code Section 411(b)(1)(F), but must not be less than the defined benefit minimum as required under Code Section 416.

## Conversions

### Q 14:22    Can a regular defined benefit plan be converted into a 412(e)(3) plan?

Yes. One of the requirements of Code Section 412(e)(3) is that a plan must provide for level annual premium payments to be made commencing with the date the individual became a participant in the plan (or, in the case of an increase in benefits, commencing at the time the increase becomes effective) and extending not later than the retirement age for each individual participating in the plan. [I.R.C. § 412(e)(3)(B)] If an existing defined benefit plan is converted to a plan under which future accruals are funded in the manner prescribed by Code Section 412(e)(3), level premium payments will begin with the year of conversion. The level annual premium payments will, therefore, start after the dates on which existing participants became participants in the plan. Therefore, the plan would not satisfy Code Section 412(e)(3)(B) following the conversion and would not be exempt under Code Section 412(h)(2) from the minimum funding requirements of Code Section 412. However, Revenue Ruling 94-75 [1994-2 C.B. 59] provides an exception to the requirement that premiums commence with participation by deeming defined benefit plans that have not been 412(e)(3) plans to satisfy Code Section 412(e)(3)(B) if certain requirements are met.

An existing defined benefit plan subject to Code Section 412 that, in accordance with the requirements specified below, is converted to a plan funded in the manner prescribed by Code Section 412(e)(3) will not be deemed to fail the requirements of Code Sections 412(e)(3)(B), 403(a), and 404(a)(2) merely because of the conversion, or merely because of participation in the plan before level annual premiums commence. The date on which the conversion is deemed to occur (the conversion date) is the first day of the first plan year for which the plan satisfies these requirements:

1. The plan otherwise satisfies the requirements of Code Sections 412(e)(3), 403(a), and 404(a)(2) for the plan year containing the conversion date.

2. All benefits accruing for each participant on and after the conversion date are funded by level annual premium contracts that satisfy the requirements of Code Section 412(e)(3)(B).

3. All benefits accrued for each participant before the conversion date are guaranteed through insurance or annuity contracts, the purchase price of which equals the minimum amount required by the life insurance company for a contract that guarantees, on and after the conversion date, to provide the participant's accrued benefits, including any optional forms of payment at each retirement age available under the plan.

4. There are meaningful continuing benefit accruals under the plan after the conversion date. A plan is considered to satisfy this requirement if there are meaningful benefit accruals under the plan for at least three plan years ending after the conversion date. [See Letter Ruling 9234004 for an example of a plan that did not satisfy this requirement and the minimum funding requirements continued to apply.]

5. The following actions are taken on or before the conversion date: (a) contracts are purchased guaranteeing the benefits accrual before the conversion date; (b) any remaining plan assets are applied to the payment or prepayment of premiums for level annual premium contracts described in item #2 above; and (c) any plan amendments necessary to satisfy these requirements for conversion and the requirements of Code Sections 412(e)(3), 403(a), and 404(a)(2) are adopted and made effective. Contracts purchased within one month after the first day of a plan year are

deemed to be purchased on the first day of the plan year for purposes of this requirement.

If these requirements for conversion are not satisfied on or before the first day of a plan year, the minimum funding requirements and funding standard account of the plan continue to apply to the plan for that plan year.

### Q 14:23 Are any contributions made that are necessary to fund existing benefits under a conversion deductible?

Yes. When a defined benefit plan that has been subject to Code Section 412 is deemed converted to a 412(e)(3) plan, the deduction limitations under Section 404(a)(1)(A) with respect to plan years ending prior to the conversion date are derived from the funding standard account requirements. Accordingly, with respect to any plan year ending prior to the conversion date, the deductible limit under Code Section 404(a)(1)(A) with respect to the plan is the greater of (1) the amount necessary to satisfy the minimum funding requirement under Code Section 412, as provided in Code Section 404(a)(1)(A)(i), or (2) the deductible limit calculated under Code Section 404(a)(1)(A)(ii) or (iii), whichever applies to the plan.

Except for the funding of any additional top-heavy benefits, for the conversion year and succeeding plan years in which the plan is deemed a Code Section 412(e)(3) plan, Code Section 404(a)(1)(A)(i) no longer applies because the minimum funding requirements of Code Section 412 no longer apply to the plan.

After a defined benefit plan is deemed converted to a 412(e)(3) plan, all benefits accrued as of the conversion date will have been guaranteed through contracts issued by an insurance company without any required future premiums. Therefore, only the costs of future benefit accruals (including future benefit increases) are allocated to future service. All other costs are allocated to prior years. This type of allocation is consistent with the cost allocation under a reasonable funding method for a defined benefit plan that is subject to Code Section 412, with an accrued liability equal to the actuarial present value of accrued benefits and to which Code Section 404(a)(1)(A)(iii) applies. Therefore, to determine the deductible limit with respect to plan years beginning on or after the conversion date, Code Section 404(a)(i)(A)(iii) is applicable.

The employer's deductible limit with respect to the conversion year and succeeding plan years, other than for any contribution to fund additional top-heavy benefits is the sum of (1) the normal cost for a 412(e)(3) plan established on the conversion date for post-conversion benefit accruals; (2) the limit adjustments, if any, for any 10-year amortization bases remaining unamortized as of the conversion date that are maintained for purposes of Code Section 404(a)(1)(A)(iii); and (3) the limit adjustment, if any, for any 10-year amortization base created on account of treating the plan as if terminated for purposes of Code Section 412 as of the last day of the plan year immediately preceding the conversion year (pre-conversion year). Normal cost under Code Section

404(a)(1)(A) and Treasury Regulations Section 1.404(a)-14 is based on the annual premiums for level annual premium contracts providing for the post-conversion benefit accruals (and any increases in benefits) that are reasonable in view of the funding medium and reasonable expectations as to the effects of mortality, interest, and other pertinent factors. Ten-year amortization bases under Treasury Regulations Section 1.404(a)-14 remain or are established based on treating the conversion as a change to the unit credit funding method (if that was not the funding method of the plan for the pre-conversion year), with the accrued liability as of the conversion date deemed to be equal to the reasonable cost of single premium contracts guaranteeing benefits accrued prior to the conversion date (conversion accrued liability).

If, as of the conversion date, there are no unamortized 10-year amortization bases under Code Section 404(a)(1)(A)(iii) and Treasury Regulations Section 1.404(a)-14 with respect to the plan, a new 10-year amortization base is established on conversion equal to the excess, if any, of (1) the conversion accrued liability over (2) the value of plan assets minus the sum of (a) any carryover under Code Section 404(a)(1)(E) from the prior taxable year plus (b) any contribution made for the current taxable year that is included in plan assets. The sum of (a) and (b) is referred to as *undeducted contributions*.

If, as of the conversion date, there is at least one unamortized 10-year amortization base under Code Section 404(a)(1)(A)(iii) and Treasury Regulations Section 1.404(a)-14 with respect to the plan and the conversion accrued liability is greater than the value of plan assets minus any undeducted contributions, a new 10-year amortization base is established on conversion equal to (1) the conversion accrued liability minus (2) the sum of (a) the value of plan assets less any undeducted contributions and (b) the net unamortized balance of any existing 10-year amortization bases under Code Section 404(a)(1)(A)(iii) (treating negative bases as having negative unamortized amounts). This new 10-year amortization base may be negative. Any existing 10-year amortization base under Code Section 404(a)(1)(A)(iii) for a plan that remains unamortized as of the conversion date must continue to be maintained. These new and existing 10-year amortization bases are maintained in the same manner as bases maintained following the termination of a plan subject to Code Section 412. The bases may be combined or replaced in accordance with the general method or the fresh-start alternative under Treasury Regulations Section 1.404(a)-14(i).

If, as of the conversion date, a plan's conversion accrued liability is not greater than the value of plan assets minus any undeducted contributions, no new base is established and all existing bases are considered fully amortized.

**Example.** The COM pension plan is a qualified defined benefit pension plan and trust with a calendar plan year and a valuation date of January 1. The plan is maintained by a calendar year taxpayer. As of January 1, 2004, the fair market value of the plan's assets was $1 million. There were no outstanding loans to participants under the plan. The plan is not a top-heavy plan. Before 2004, the plan was not a 412(e)(3) plan.

On December 10, 2003, the plan was amended effective as of January 1, 2004, to become a 412(e)(3) plan. Under these amendments, the terms of the plan satisfy the requirements of Code Sections 412(e)(3)(A), (C), (D), (E), and (F) beginning on January 1, 2004. Under the plan as amended, all benefit accruals on and after January 1, 2004, will be funded exclusively by insurance or annuity contracts that provide for level annual premium payments. The plan provides that level annual premium payments for each participant are to be paid for the period commencing with the later of the 2004 plan year or the first plan year of the participant's participation in the plan and ending with the plan year the participant attains normal retirement age. Benefit accruals after normal retirement age are to be funded by insurance or annuity contracts as they accrue.

On January 1, 2004, a single premium deferred annuity contract was purchased for each plan participant. Beginning on January 1, 2004, each contract was guaranteed by a life insurance company to provide the payment of the participant's benefits accrued prior to January 1, 2004, including any optional forms of payment at each retirement age available under the plan. The premium for each participant's single premium contract was the minimum amount required by the insurer to guarantee the payment of that participant's accrued benefit, beginning on January 1, 2004. The total purchase price of the single premium contracts was $1,300,000.

In addition, a level annual premium deferred annuity contract was purchased for each plan participant on January 1, 2004, to provide for the excess, if any, of the participant's projected normal retirement benefit over the portion of the normal retirement benefit provided by the single premium contract purchased for that participant. For purposes of determining the projected normal retirement benefit, it was assumed that the amount of each participant's current compensation would not change before the participant's normal retirement age. For 2004, the total of the level annual premiums needed to provide the additional normal retirement benefits under the terms of the plan (post-conversion benefit accruals) was $50,000.

The costs of the single premium annuity contracts purchased to fund participants' benefits accrued prior to January 1, 2004, and the level annual premium contracts purchased to fund participants' post-conversion benefit accruals, were reasonable in view of the funding medium and reasonable expectations as to the effects of mortality, interest, and other pertinent factors.

On January 1, 2004, in addition to the $1 million in existing plan assets that was paid to the insurance company, the employer paid a plan contribution of $350,000 (the total premium due of $1,350,000 less plan assets of $1 million) to the insurer to meet the 2004 premium requirement for all annuity contracts.

As of January 1, 2004, no additional amounts contributed to the plan could be deducted by the employer for the 2003 plan year. As of the end of 2003, there were no unamortized 10-year amortization bases with respect to the plan for purposes of Code Section 404(a)(1)(A), and no nondeductible contributions were carried over to 2004 under Code Section 404(a)(1)(E).

The single premium deferred annuity contracts guaranteeing the payment of prior benefit accruals were purchased for $1,300,000 during the first month of the 2004 plan year; all remaining plan assets ($50,000) were applied to purchase level annual premium contracts during the first month of that plan year; and plan amendments were made before and effective on the first day of that plan year. The plan meets the requirements to be converted to a 412(e)(3) plan, and January 1, 2004 is, therefore, the conversion date. Accordingly, the minimum funding requirements of Code Section 412 do not apply to the plan for the 2004 plan year and later years. This is based on the assumption that the plan will continue to provide meaningful continuing benefit accruals after the conversion date and that the plan will satisfy all the requirements of Code Sections 403(a), 404(a)(2), and 412(e)(3)(A), (C), (D), (E), and (F) on and after the conversion date.

In determining how the extra contribution is to be deducted, it is important to note that the plan was deemed converted to a 412(e)(3) plan as of the first day of the 2004 plan year. Accordingly, the funding standard account for the plan was terminated as of December 31, 2003. In connection with the conversion of the plan, the employer contributed $350,000 to the plan on January 1, 2004. This amount, combined with existing plan assets of $1 million, was used to purchase single premium deferred annuity contracts for $1,300,000 and to pay the level annual premium of $50,000 for 2004.

The deductible limit under Code Section 404(a)(1)(A) with respect to the plan for the conversion year and thereafter is determined under Code Section 404(a)(1)(A)(iii). The conversion process is treated under Code Section 404(a)(1)(A)(iii) and Treasury Regulations Section 1.404(a)-14 as creating a 10-year amortization base of $300,000. This is equal to (1) the conversion accrued liability ($1,300,000) minus (2) the sum of (a) the value of plan assets less any undeducted contributions ($1,350,000 in plan assets, less $350,000 in undeducted contributions) and (b) the net unamortized balance of any existing 10-year amortization bases under Code Section 404(a)(1)(A)(iii) ($0). This 10-year amortization base of $300,000 is maintained under Code Section 404(a)(1)(A)(iii) and Treasury Regulations Section 1.404(a)-14 in the same manner as a base would be maintained following the termination of a plan subject to Code Section 412.

The deductible limit under Code Section 404(a)(1) with respect to the plan was calculated solely under Code Section 404(a)(1)(A).

The contributions paid by the employer as premiums for the annuity contracts that are not deductible under Code Section 404(a)(1)(A) for the 2004 taxable year are nondeductible contributions for 2004 and are subject to the excise tax on nondeductible contributions under Code Section 4972. However, they will become deductible as the 10-year base continues to be amortized. In addition, the excise tax on nondeductible contributions will apply only for the 2004 plan year. [Rev. Rul. 94-75, 1994-2 C.B. 59]

### Q 14:24   Can a 412(e)(3) plan be converted to a traditional defined benefit plan?

Yes. It is necessary to break only one of the requirements of Code Section 412(e)(3) to force it back into following the funding requirements of Code Section 412.

## Advantages and Disadvantages

### Q 14:25   What are some of the advantages proponents offer from a 412(e)(3) plan?

Proponents of 412(e)(3) plans offer the following as advantages of these arrangements:

1. Retirement benefit is fully guaranteed.
2. Insurance company bears all investment risk.
3. Investments are not subject to market fluctuation.
4. There is no full-funding limitation or current liability test to limit deductions.
5. There can be no over funding, and thus no reversion penalty (assuming annuity payouts).
6. There can be no under funding.
7. No enrolled actuary is required, since there is no Schedule B (Form 5500) to file (as long as there is no top-heavy accumulation fund).
8. There are no quarterly contribution requirements.
9. Generally, much larger contributions (deductions) are available.
10. Employer funding of the plan can be more readily understood.
11. Administration fees may be lower.

### Q 14:26   What are some of the disadvantages of 412(e)(3) plans?

Some of the disadvantages of these arrangements are:

1. No flexibility in investments.
2. It is not possible to take advantage of any market gains.
3. Premiums must be paid as they come due.
4. There is no flexibility in timing or amount of contributions.
5. Premiums are determined by insurance company rates.
6. No policy loans are allowed.
7. No participant loans are allowed.
8. Plan can become over funded if a lump sum is desired.

### Q 14:27  How can a 412(e)(3) plan become over funded?

If a 412(e)(3) plan is funded to the maximum assuming an annuity payout, the low interest rate assumptions used by the insurance company may cause there to be more money in the plan than is necessary, and allowed, if the principal retires and selects a lump-sum payout.

**Example.** Dr. Freddy installs a 412(e)(3) plan at age 60 with a retirement age of 65. The insurance company uses a guaranteed rate of return of 3 percent, both preretirement and postretirement. Dr. Freddy is excited that he will be able to fund nearly $229,000 into the plan for each of the next five years—which is much more than the $150,000 that he received as a proposal under a traditional defined benefit plan. At Dr. Freddy's retirement, the 412(e)(3) plan has assets of $1,250,000 to pay his annuity benefit. However, Dr. Freddy believes he can do a better job of managing the money during his retirement than the insurance company and decides he would like a lump-sum distribution. The Code Section 415 maximum lump sum based on his annuity payment is only $925,000, leaving $325,000 as excess assets in the plan.

### Q 14:28  Can a lump sum be paid from a 412(e)(3) plan and the plan not be over funded?

Yes. However, planning is required in order to avoid this problem. Three different approaches are suggested:

1. Make an assumption as to what the 30-year Treasury rate will be at the principal's retirement date. Then use the insurance company's guaranteed rate to determine what the equivalent guaranteed annuity amount of the GATT maximum would be. Use this lower monthly amount in determining the formula for the 412(e)(3) plan.

2. Fund for the maximum annuity, but fund for only a certain number of years until the maximum lump-sum amount is reached based on a projected 30-year Treasury rate. Freeze the plan at that time. (The plan becomes subject to Code Section 412.)

3. Fund for the maximum annuity, as in option 2, but terminate the plan once the maximum lump-sum amount is reached.

### Q 14:29  Can death benefits be provided in a 412(e)(3) plan?

Yes, subject to the same limitations as in a traditional defined benefit plan. Therefore, the death benefit provided by the insurance must be incidental to the primary purpose of providing retirement income and may not exceed the greater of the following two limits:

1. The face amount cannot exceed 100 times the projected monthly benefit; or

2. The premium used to purchase the policy may not be more than 25 percent of the total cost of providing retirement benefits in the case of term insurance, or 50 percent in the case of ordinary life insurance.

[Rev. Rul. 74-307, 1974-2 C.B. 126]

Death benefits are often added to a 412(e)(3) plan to provide insurance coverage and increase the tax deduction.

### Q 14:30   How should a life insurance contract be valued when distributed to a participant?

The IRS previously ruled in Notice 89-25, Q&A 10 [1981-1 C.B. 662] that the cash surrender value may not always be the best way to value an insurance policy when determining taxable income of a participant. Treasury Regulations Section 1.402(a)-1(a)(1)(iii) provides that the amount includible in a plan participant's gross income by reason of the distribution of property by the plan shall be the fair market value of such property. Life insurance contracts constitute property within the meaning of this section. Treasury Regulations Section 1.402(a)-1(a)(2) provides that a distributee must include in gross income the cash value of any retirement income, endowment, or other life insurance contract at the time of the distribution. Treasury Regulations Section 1.72-16(c)(2)(ii) indicates that the reserve accumulation in a life insurance contract constitutes the source of and approximates the amount of such cash value.

Individuals who receive an insurance policy as a distribution from a qualified plan use the stated cash surrender value of the policy as its fair market value for purposes of determining the amount includible in their gross income under Code Section 402(a). However, the IRS stated that this practice is not appropriate where the total policy reserves, including life insurance reserves (if any) computed under Code Section 807(d), together with any reserves for advance premiums, dividend accumulations, and so forth, represent a much more accurate approximation of the fair market value of the policy than does the policy's stated cash surrender value.

The IRS has issued proposed regulations [Prop. Treas. Reg. § 1.402(a)-1(a)(1)(iii) and (a)(2)] to clarify that, where the Code Section 402(a) regulations refer to *entire cash value* of a contract, such terms should be interpreted as fair market value. Thus, when a qualified plan distributes a life insurance contract, retirement income contract, endowment contract, or other contract providing life insurance protection, the fair market value of such contract is to be included in the distributee's income, not merely the cash value as defined in the contract. Fair market value for this purpose is defined as the value of all rights under the contract, including any supplemental agreements thereto, whether or not guaranteed.

In addition, the IRS issued Revenue Procedure 2004-16 [2004-10 I.R.B 559], prescribing an interim method of valuing insurance contracts, pending the issuance of the proposed regulations in final form. The IRS is issuing this procedure in recognition that, under its current guidance regarding the valuation of insurance contracts distributed from a plan, taxpayers may have difficulty in determining fair market value of these contracts.

Under the interim valuation method, the cash value (without reduction for surrender charges) may be treated as the fair market value of a contract, provided the cash value is no less than the amount determined under the following formula:

$$-x + y - z$$

where $x$, $y$ and $z$ are determined as follows:

- $x$ equals the premiums paid from the date of issue through the date of determination.

- $y$ equals any amounts credited (or otherwise made available) to the policyholder with respect to those premiums, including interest, dividends, and similar income items (whether under the contract or otherwise). In the case of variable contracts, $y$ equals all adjustments made with respect to the premiums paid from the date of issue through the date of determination (whether under the contract or otherwise) that reflect investment return and the current market value of segregated asset accounts.

- $z$ equals reasonable mortality charges and other reasonable charges that are actually charged on or before the date of determination and are expected to be paid.

The *date of determination* is the date of a distribution, in the case of valuing a contract distributed from a qualified plan.

> **Example.** Dr. John is a participant in the John's defined benefit plan. On January 1, 2001, $400,000 of plan assets was used to purchase an insurance policy. The policy was distributed to John on January 1, 2003, two years after the date of purchase. The policy provides a stated cash surrender value for each of the first five policy years, as set forth in the table below. The total end-of-year reserves held by the insurance company for the policy also are set forth in the table. These reserves may include life insurance reserves and any other reserves such as for advance premiums and dividend accumulations. Life insurance reserves, if any, are calculated using the rules in Code Section 807(d), which provides rules for determining the amount of those reserves for purposes of calculating the tax liability of the insurance company issuing the policy.
>
> | Year | Surrender Value | Reserves |
> |------|-----------------|----------|
> | 1 | $106,000 | $406,949 |
> | 2 | $112,360 | $426,596 |
> | 3 | $119,102 | $447,052 |
> | 4 | $126,248 | $468,178 |
> | 5 | $489,908 | $489,908 |

As the total reserves for the policy at the end of year two, $426,597, substantially exceed the policy's cash surrender value, $112,360, the reserves represent a much more accurate approximation of the fair market value of the policy when distributed than does the policy's cash surrender value. Accordingly, the amount includible in John's gross income by reason of the distribution of the policy at the end of year two is an amount equal to the $426,597 reserve, not the $112,360 stated cash surrender value at that date.

In the case of a distribution in excess of John's accrued benefit, as defined in Treasury Regulations Section 1.411(a)-7(a)(1), resulting from valuing the policy at $112,360 rather than $426,547, the distribution would not be treated as a distribution to John from a qualified plan and, depending upon the facts and circumstances of the case, could be treated as a reversion to the employer. Of course, depending on the facts and circumstances, such distributions could disqualify the plan for exceeding the limitations of Code Section 415.

### Q 14:31   Can a death benefit for a participant be provided in excess of the incidental limitations?

Yes, but pursuant to Revenue Ruling 2004-20, the amount of the contribution used to fund the death benefit in excess of plan limits is not deductible in the current year, is most likely subject to a 10 percent excise tax, and will only be deductible in future years pursuant to the rules of Code Section 404(a)(1)(E). This ruling serves to shut down another abusive arrangement that was being sold on the basis of being able to provide a death benefit well in excess of the incidental limitations, but whereby the beneficiary would receive only the amount that is considered incidental. Any remaining death benefit would remain in the pension plan. This extra money would be used to fund other participants' benefits, or would revert to the employer at substantial excise taxes.

However, the goal of this plan was to distribute the policy to the participant at a depressed value (see Q 14:30), which later grew to a very large value without additional funding. Then, since this is an insurance contract, the policyholder could borrow from the policy up to the cash value tax free. This option has now been closed down as a result of Revenue Ruling 2004-20 [2004-10 I.R.B. 550] and Revenue Procedure 2004-16 [2004-10 I.R.B. 559].

Revenue Ruling 2004-20 also designates any transaction where the face amount of a policy exceeds the participant's death benefit under the plan by more than $100,000 as a "listed transaction." If a plan is involved in a "listed transaction," the plan sponsor must notify the IRS that it is involved in such a transaction by including a statement with its income tax return.

**Example.** Dr. Brown is a doctor who operates her medical practice as a solely owned corporation. She participates in the 412(e)(3) pension plan maintained by her corporation. The pension plan provides a $1,000,000 death benefit, payable upon the death of Dr. Brown, to her beneficiaries. Although the death benefit is equal to $1,000,000, the plan purchased a life insurance policy with a face value of $5,000,000. The plan provides that if she dies while she is employed by the corporation, $1,000,000 is payable to her beneficiaries but the remaining $4,000,000 is to be applied to pay premiums under the plan for other participants. This is considered a "listed transaction" and as such the corporation must include a statement with its tax return detailing this transaction. In addition, any premiums paid in excess of what are needed to cover the $1,000,000 death benefit are nondeductible to the corporation.

**Q 14:32    Are there any other possible consequences
             if the sponsor pays more for the premium than
             what is necessary to provide for the retirement benefit?**

Yes. Pursuant to Revenue Ruling 2004-20, if the insurance policies are structured within what purports to be a "fully-insured" plan, and:

1. If premiums are paid through a participant's normal retirement age;

2. If the annuity purchase rates guaranteed under the contract are applied; and

3. If the benefits payable at normal retirement age under the contract as a result of item #1 or #2 above will exceed the participant's benefit under the terms of the plan

then the plan fails to satisfy the requirement of Code Section 412(e)(3)(C) and is not treated as a fully-insured plan. Code Section 412(e)(3)(C) requires that: "benefits provided by the plan are equal to the benefits provided under each contract at normal retirement age under the plan and are guaranteed by an insurance carrier (licensed under the laws of a State to do business with the plan) to the extent premiums have been paid." Therefore, if a contract provides for premiums that, when guaranteed rates are applied, create benefits that exceed plan stated benefits, this requirement is not satisfied.

If a plan does not satisfy this requirement, then it is no longer a 412(e)(3) plan and certain exceptions that apply to 412(e)(3) plans are no longer applicable. These exceptions include minimum funding exceptions, special nondiscrimination testing options, PBGC exceptions, etc. (See Q 14:25 for a more complete list.) Thus, the plan is subject to the minimum funding requirements of Code Section 412, with charges and credits to the funding standard account determined using the reasonable funding method selected for the plan and using reasonable actuarial assumptions. The actuarial method and assumptions so determined also affect the deductibility of employer contributions under Code Section 404. In addition, the special accrual rule permitted under Code Section 411(b)(1)(F), which deems a fully-insured plan to satisfy the minimum accrual requirements under Code Section 411(b), is not applicable (see Qs 14:14–14:22).

# Chapter 15

# Ancillary Benefits

In addition to providing normal retirement benefits, a defined benefit plan can provide additional benefits to participants to cover preretirement death and disability contingencies and provide the opportunity to retire before normal retirement age. A plan's choice of ancillary benefits is generally based on the objectives of the employer in providing and communicating its benefits package to its employees. In certain plans, such as those for union employees, ancillary benefits and retirement benefits are equally important.

## General Restrictions

### Q 15:1  Can a plan provide for benefits other than those received at normal retirement?

Yes. Subject to certain restrictions and limitations, a defined benefit plan can provide for disability, preretirement death, early retirement, and medical expense account benefits. Ancillary benefits, like any other benefit, right, or feature, must not discriminate in favor of the plan's highly compensated employees (HCEs). [Treas. Reg. § 1.401(a)(4)-4(a)]

### Q 15:2   When is an ancillary benefit nondiscriminatory?

An ancillary benefit does not discriminate in favor of a plan's HCEs when the benefit is both "currently available" and "effectively available" as defined in the following paragraphs.

*Currently available.* The group of employees to whom an ancillary benefit is currently available must satisfy the ratio percentage test under Internal Revenue Code (Code) Section 410(b) (ignoring the average benefit percentage test). [Treas. Reg. § 1.401(a)(4)-4(b)(1)] The determination of whether an ancillary benefit is currently available to a current employee is based on current facts and circumstances with respect to that employee. Any age, service, or other condition required to receive an optional form of benefit is ignored, except for time-limited age or service conditions, such as a limited-time offer for an early retirement benefit. [Treas. Reg. § 1.401(a)(4)-4(b)(2)(i), (ii)(A)(1), (2)]

A plan can place specified conditions on the availability of a benefit, right, or feature, and these are disregarded in determining the employees to whom the benefit, right, or feature is currently available. These conditions include: requiring a specified percentage of the employee's accrued benefit to be nonforfeitable, termination of employment, death, satisfaction of a specified health condition (or failure to meet such condition), disability, hardship, family status, default on a plan loan secured by a participant's account balance, execution of a covenant not to compete, application for benefits or similar ministerial or mechanical acts, election of a benefit form, execution of a waiver of rights under the Age Discrimination in Employment Act (ADEA) or other federal or state law, or absence from service. In addition, if a multiemployer plan includes a reasonable condition that limits eligibility for an ancillary benefit, or other right or feature, to those employees who have recent service under the plan (e.g., a condition on a death benefit that requires an employee to have a minimum number of hours credited during the last two years) and the condition applies to all employees in the multiemployer plan (including the collectively bargained employees) to whom the ancillary benefit, or other right or feature, is otherwise currently available, then the condition is disregarded in determining the employees to whom the ancillary benefit, or other right or feature, is currently available. [Treas. Reg. § 1.401(a)(4)-4(b)(2)(ii)(B)]

> **Example 1.** Keegan is a participant in his employer's defined benefit pension plan. The plan provides a disability benefit on completion of 10 years of service and attainment of age 55, subject to an employee's becoming disabled as defined under Social Security. Although Keegan has not satisfied any of the age, service, or disability conditions required to receive the benefit, it is currently available to him if the age, service, and disability conditions are disregarded.

*Effectively available.* Based on all the relevant facts and circumstances, the group of employees to whom an ancillary benefit is effectively available must not substantially favor the plan's HCEs. In determining whether a benefit is effectively available, any conditions required to receive the benefit are considered, and if it is not possible for an employee to satisfy the conditions for receipt of the benefit, the benefit is not considered effectively available to that employee. [Treas. Reg. § 1.401(a)(4)-4(c)(1)]

> **Example 2.** Jacob is a participant in his employer's defined benefit pension plan. The plan provides an early retirement benefit on completion of 30 years of service and attainment of age 55. Jacob was hired at age 50 and will never have the 30 years of service required to receive the early retirement benefit. Hence, the benefit is not effectively available to him. [Treas. Reg. § 1.401(a)(4)-4(c)(1)]

### Q 15:3   Can an employer impose restrictions on the availability of ancillary benefits?

Yes. Subject to certain rules (see Q 15:2), a plan can impose certain eligibility requirements that may restrict the availability of an ancillary benefit. Most plans will make an ancillary benefit available based on the employer's objective in providing the benefit.

## Disability Benefits

### Q 15:4   Can a plan provide for payment of benefits when an employee becomes disabled?

Yes. Disability benefits can be provided in many different amounts and over many different periods. The cost of the benefits differs based on the benefit structure selected. In general, any disability benefit that exceeds the present value of the vested accrued benefit creates additional costs to the plan.

### Q 15:5   What criteria can an employer use for purposes of defining disability?

A wide range of criteria can be used to determine eligibility for disability benefits. Some plans provide that if a participant is eligible to receive Social Security disability benefits, the participant is eligible for the disability benefits of the plan. Other plans require a physician's certification of full disability. Still others require two independent physicians to certify to the disability, with a third physician, picked by the employer, as the deciding physician in case of a dispute.

### Q 15:6   Can a plan have an age or service requirement for disability benefits?

Yes. Since disability benefits are ancillary to the primary purpose of a defined benefit pension plan, the eligibility requirements for disability benefits can be different from the eligibility requirements for other plan benefits. Ancillary benefits cannot, however, be made available on a discriminatory basis (see Q 15:2).

### Q 15:7  Can a plan cease payment of disability benefits?

Yes. The duration of the benefit payments can be limited. Benefits in pay status, however, are accrued and must be maintained until the limit in the plan document is reached or the benefit is scheduled to cease. Hence, a terminated plan must have adequate assets to cover liabilities for those benefits.

### Q 15:8  Can a plan pay disability benefits to terminated participants who subsequently become disabled?

Yes. Eligibility requirements, however, normally exclude all but active participants.

## Preretirement Death Benefits

### Q 15:9  Must a defined benefit plan provide preretirement death benefits?

Yes. A defined benefit plan at the very least must provide for a qualified preretirement survivor annuity (QPSA). (See chapter 16 for discussion of these benefits.) Any benefit in excess of a QPSA is considered an ancillary benefit. Furthermore, a death benefit under a defined benefit pension plan must be incidental and cannot exceed certain limitations. A death benefit in a defined benefit plan is considered incidental as long as the primary purpose of the plan is to provide retirement benefits (see Q 15:13). [Treas. Reg. § 1.401-1(b)(1)(i)]

### Q 15:10  Does a death benefit in excess of a QPSA result in additional cost to the plan?

It depends. Several factors affect the cost of a death benefit that is greater in value than the required QPSA. In general, typical preretirement death benefits that result in additional cost to the plan include the following:

- A 100 percent survivor annuity
- A lump-sum benefit equal to the present value of the accrued benefit
- A benefit that is 100 times the projected monthly retirement benefit

If the death benefit is rather generous, such as 100 times the projected monthly retirement benefit, a small plan will purchase life insurance to cover the benefit, and a large plan (typically more than 1,000 participants) generally will self-insure the risk by adding the cost of the death benefit to the plan's funding requirement and depositing that amount in the plan's trust fund.

### Q 15:11  Can a plan use life insurance to fund death benefits?

Yes. A plan can use life insurance to provide the funding for preretirement death benefits. The use of life insurance can protect the plan from a large reduction in the plan's assets as a result of a premature death. The proceeds of the policy can be used to fund the QPSA and benefits in excess of the QPSA. A plan cannot, however, provide the QPSA plus a death benefit from life insurance if the total amount of the QPSA plus the life insurance death benefit exceeds 100 times the projected monthly retirement benefit. [Rev. Rul. 85-15, 1985-1 C.B. 132]

### Q 15:12   Are there any nondiscrimination provisions applicable to the provision of life insurance protection?

Yes. Pursuant to Treasury Regulations Section 1.401(a)(4)-1(b)(3), a plan can satisfy the requirements of Code Section 401(a)(4) only if all benefits, rights, or features provided under the plan are made available under the plan in a nondiscriminatory manner. In order to do so, the benefits, rights, or features must satisfy the current availability requirement and effective availability requirement (see Q 15:2). The plan is considered discriminatory if the benefits, rights, or features of the life insurance contracts held by HCEs are of inherently greater value than the benefits, rights, or features of contracts held by non-highly compensated employees (NHCEs). [Rev. Rul. 2004-21, 2004-1 C.B. 544] These benefits, rights, or features can include optional forms of benefit, ancillary benefits, and other rights and features that can be expected to have meaningful value. Differences in insurance contracts, including differences in cash value growth terms or different exchange features that may be purchased from a plan, can create distinct other rights or features even if the terms under which the contracts are purchased from the plan are the same. [Rev. Rul. 2004-21, 2004-1 C.B. 544]

### Q 15:13   What is the maximum preretirement death benefit a defined benefit plan can provide?

Generally, for a preretirement death benefit to be considered incidental to a plan's primary purpose of providing retirement benefits, the death benefit cannot exceed 100 times the projected monthly retirement benefit. The proceeds of the life insurance policy are considered incidental, however, if the premium used to purchase the policy is no more than 25 percent of the total cost of providing retirement benefits in the case of term insurance or 50 percent in the case of ordinary life insurance. [Rev. Rul. 74-307, 1974-2 C.B. 126]

A defined benefit plan can use as much as 33 percent and 66 percent, instead of 25 percent and 50 percent, of the employer contribution that would be required under the individual level-premium funding method to fund the benefits under the plan. The death benefit from such a policy purchased by the plan could not exceed the value of the QPSA plus the policy proceeds plus the theoretical reserve under the individual level-premium funding method minus the cash value of the policy.

**Example.** Antony is a participant in his employer's defined benefit pension plan, and the employer provides that a policy will be purchased using 66 percent of the amount of the participant's contribution as determined under the individual level-premium funding method. In the fifth year, Antony's normal cost under that funding method is $10,000. Therefore, $6,666 is used to purchase an ordinary life insurance policy for Antony. If Antony dies in the next year, his maximum death benefit can be the value of the QPSA plus the proceeds of the policy plus the theoretical accumulation of the normal costs using the individual level-premium funding method minus the cash value of the policy.

### Q 15:14   Who is the beneficiary of death benefits?

The spouse is the beneficiary of the QPSA. Any death benefits in excess of that amount can be paid to an alternate beneficiary of the participant's choosing without spousal consent. Pursuant to a waiver of the QPSA by the spouse, the proceeds of the QPSA and any additional death benefits can be paid to any beneficiary of the participant's choosing.

### Q 15:15   Is there any requirement about how preretirement death benefits are to be paid?

Yes. A death benefit must be paid under either the five-year rule or the alternative rule. The five-year rule requires that the participant's death benefit be distributed within five years after his or her death. The alternative rule requires that within one year of the participant's death, the benefit must be paid over the beneficiary's life expectancy or a period not to exceed the beneficiary's life expectancy. [I.R.C. § 401(a)(9)(B)]

## Early Retirement Benefits

### Q 15:16   What is an *early retirement benefit*?

An *early retirement benefit* is a benefit payable before the plan's normal retirement age, the amount of which is based on the plan's normal retirement benefit and age. A plan can provide for an early retirement benefit that is based on the plan's projected normal retirement benefit or the benefit that has accrued as of the early retirement date. The following are examples of an early retirement benefit:

- The actuarial equivalent of the normal retirement benefit or accrued benefit
- A fixed percentage or formula reduction of the accrued benefit
- An amount that exceeds the actuarial equivalent of the normal retirement or accrued benefit
- Additional years of service credit granted to increase the accrued benefit on early retirement

There are as many types of early retirement benefits as imagination allows; however, all such benefits must not discriminate in favor of the plan's HCEs. [Treas. Reg. § 1.401(a)(4)-4(a)]

### Q 15:17   How does an early retirement benefit meet the availability requirements?

For an early retirement benefit not to discriminate in favor of the plan's HCEs, it must be currently and effectively available on a nondiscriminatory basis.

For an early retirement benefit to be currently available on a nondiscriminatory basis, the group of NHCEs and HCEs who can receive the benefit must satisfy the ratio percentage test under Code Section 410(b). [Treas. Reg. § 1.401(a)(4)-4(b)(1)] In general, any age or service conditions required to receive the early retirement benefit are disregarded for purposes of determining whether a benefit is currently available. If the age and service conditions must be satisfied within a certain period of time, however, the age and service conditions cannot be disregarded in determining current availability.

> **Example.** The Black Rock defined benefit plan allows participants to retire after age 55 with 15 years of service and receive their accrued benefit without actuarial reduction. The plan requires that participants elect to retire within the period beginning January 1, 2001, and ending December 31, 2002. If this requirement were not part of the benefit, the benefit would be currently available to all employees, because age and service requirements are ignored in determining current availability.

In determining whether an early retirement benefit is effectively available on a nondiscriminatory basis, the conditions needed to receive the benefit must be taken into account. Based on the facts and circumstances relating to the plan's participants, the early retirement benefit must not substantially favor the HCEs.

### Q 15:18   Can a terminated employee who has satisfied the service requirements for early retirement benefits receive an early retirement benefit on meeting the age requirement?

For a defined benefit plan that offers an early retirement benefit to be qualified, a participant who satisfies the service requirements for the early retirement benefit but terminates before satisfying the age requirement for the early retirement benefit must be entitled on satisfaction of the age requirement to receive no less than the actuarially reduced benefit to which he or she would be entitled at normal retirement age.

An employer that wants to provide an early retirement benefit for active employees to encourage them to leave the employer before they reach normal retirement age can do so through the use of an early retirement benefit that is greater than the actuarial equivalent of the normal retirement benefit. To reduce the cost associated with such a benefit, the plan can offer only the actuarial equivalent benefit to terminated employees that have not met the age requirement.

### Q 15:19   Are there any restrictions on the age and service conditions that can be placed on an early retirement benefit?

No. As long as the age and service conditions placed on the right to receive an early retirement benefit are nondiscriminatory, there are no other constraints on the age and service conditions that an employer can place on the availability of an early retirement benefit.

### Q 15:20    When does an early retirement benefit increase the cost to the employer?

Anytime an early retirement benefit is greater than the actuarial equivalent of the accrued benefit at the age of retirement, an early retirement benefit may result in additional cost to the employer. The plan's enrolled actuary, in assessing the probability that an early retirement will occur, may or may not add a cost for early retirement benefits. If no cost is added and no one ever elects early retirement, the benefit feature will not result in additional cost.

### Q 15:21    Are there any limitations on the amount of early retirement benefits?

Yes. Early retirement benefits are subject to the limitations of Code Section 415 (see chapter 12).

### Q 15:22    Can a plan provide a one-time incentive to entice employees to opt for early retirement, otherwise known as an early retirement window?

Yes. A plan can provide an employee the opportunity to retire before normal retirement age through the use of an incentive that produces an early retirement benefit that has a greater value than it would absent the incentive. Because the incentive is a limited-time offer and will end after a stated period of time, it is often referred to as an *early retirement window.* If the early retirement window benefits are greater than the actuarial equivalent of the accrued benefit, the window must meet the current availability requirements of Treasury Regulations Section 1.401(a)(4)-4.

> **Example.** The D&R pension plan provides that any employee with 10 years of service who has attained age 55 between January 1, 2001, and December 31, 2002, can retire with 110 percent of his or her accrued benefit if early retirement is elected during that period. The D&R pension plan has 2 nonexcludable HCEs and 10 nonexcludable NHCEs. Only one HCE is eligible for the early retirement benefit. For the current availability requirement to be satisfied, the window must pass the ratio percentage test of Code Section 410(b); that is, the percentage of NHCEs who are eligible to receive the benefit divided by the percentage of HCEs who are eligible to receive the benefit must at least equal 70 percent. In this case, 70 percent of one out of two HCEs is 35 percent ($70\% \times \frac{1}{2}$), and 35 percent of 10 NHCEs is 3.5, which must be rounded to the next highest integer. Therefore, at least four of the NHCEs must satisfy the age and service requirements between January 1, 2001, and December 31, 2002.

### Q 15:23    What is a *qualified Social Security supplement?*

Commonly referred to as a QSUPP, a *qualified Social Security supplement* is a supplemental payment to a plan participant on retiring from the employer that continues until the date that Social Security benefits begin, at which time total payments are reduced by the amount of the Social Security supplement. This form of benefit allows the plan participant to enjoy a level pension benefit throughout retirement.

For such a benefit to be deemed a QSUPP, the amount of the supplement must equal the lesser of the employee's old-age insurance benefit, unreduced on account of age, under Social Security Act Title II, or the accrued supplement determined under one of the following methods:

1. In the case of a defined benefit excess plan (see chapter 10), the accrued supplement equals the employee's average annual compensation up to the integration level multiplied by the disparity provided by the plan for the employee's years of service used in determining the employee's accrued benefit.

2. In the case of an offset plan (see chapter 10), the accrued supplement equals the offset accrued for the employee under the plan.

3. In the case of a primary insurance amount (PIA) offset plan (see chapter 10), the accrued supplement equals the dollar amount of the offset accrued for the employee. A *PIA offset plan* is a plan that reduces an employee's benefit by an offset based on a stated percentage of the employee's PIA under the Social Security Act.

4. In the case of a plan other than those in items #1, 2, and 3 above, any supplement defined by the plan must accrue ratably over the time the supplement became effective to the earliest date the supplement could be paid.

Furthermore, (1) any QSUPP must be nonforfeitable as if it were an early retirement benefit; (2) the plan must impose the same eligibility conditions on receipt of the early retirement benefit as it imposes on receipt of the Social Security supplement; (3) the QSUPP must provide payment in the form of a qualified joint and survivor annuity (QJSA); and (4) the QSUPP must be a protected form of benefit, that is, one that cannot be eliminated. [Treas. Reg. § 1.401(a)(4)-12]

# 414(k) Accounts

### Q 15:24   What is a *414(k) account?*

A *414(k) account* is a separate account within a defined benefit plan that is derived from employer contributions and from which some benefits are paid.

Code Section 414(k) allows a defined benefit plan to provide benefits in part from a separate account balance derived from employer contributions. The portion of the plan that provides benefits from the separate account balance is treated as a defined contribution plan for purposes of satisfying the minimum participation and vesting standards, maximum contribution limitations, nondiscrimination tests for matching and employee contributions, and treatment of employee contributions as a separate contract. [I.R.C. § 414(k)]

Generally, contributions to a 414(k) account are in addition to the contributions that fund the basic retirement benefits provided by the plan and are used to enhance retirement benefits.

### Q 15:25　How is a 414(k) account created?

Code Section 414(k) states that if a defined benefit plan provides a benefit from employer contributions that is based partly on the balance of a separate account, this account is *treated* as if it were a defined contribution plan for many of the qualification requirements. The IRS stated in Revenue Ruling 79-259 [1979-2 C.B. 197], however, that for a separate account within a defined benefit plan to satisfy the provisions of Code Section 414(k), the plan provisions regarding a participant's separate account must satisfy the requirements of a defined contribution plan. Therefore, to create a 414(k) account, the plan document provisions describing this separate account must contain language similar to the language of other defined contribution plans.

### Q 15:26　How is a 414(k) account tested under the minimum participation standards of Code Section 410(b)?

A 414(k) account is treated as a separate plan. Therefore, it is tested separately and must satisfy Code Section 410(b) as if it were a separate defined contribution plan of the employer. [Treas. Reg. §§ 1.410(b)-9, 1.410(b)-7(b)]

### Q 15:27　How are the maximum contribution limitations under Code Section 415 determined for a 414(k) account?

Employer contributions to a 414(k) account are tested under Code Section 415(c) as if they were contributed to a defined contribution plan of the employer. Thus, they are subject to the annual addition limitation of the lesser of $40,000 (as indexed) or 100 percent of compensation.

### Q 15:28　Can a 414(k) account be used to transfer excess earnings in a defined benefit plan on an ongoing basis?

No. If a defined benefit plan transfers to a 414(k) account each year the actual trust earnings in excess of the valuation rate used in the valuation of the costs of providing the defined benefit, the allocation is considered not definitely determinable and therefore the plan is disqualified. [Rev. Rul. 78-403, 1978-2 C.B. 153]

### Q 15:29　Can assets already in a defined benefit plan that are in excess of the amount required to fund current defined benefits on a termination basis be used to fund a 414(k) account?

The IRS considers a 414(k) account to be a separate defined contribution account and has stated that any transfer of assets from the defined benefit plan to the 414(k) account would be considered a violation of the exclusive benefit rule and be subject to income and excise taxes. [See 1995 Enrolled Actuaries Meeting Gray Book, Q&A 51.] In addition, the IRS ruled in Letter Ruling 9723033 that a transfer of excess assets in a defined benefit plan to a 414(k) account to fund a matching contribution under Code Section 401(m) would cause the employer to recognize income for federal income tax purposes. Further, the allocation will be a deemed or actual reversion of plan assets that will subject the employer to an excise tax, as stated in Code Section 4980. [Ltr. Rul. 9723033]

### Q 15:30   Is a participant's separate account in a 414(k) account credited with actual trust earnings?

Yes. The IRS stated in Revenue Ruling 79-259 [1979-2 C.B. 197] that a 414(k) account must satisfy the requirements of a defined contribution plan under Code Section 414(i). Code Section 414(i) defines a *defined contribution plan* as a plan providing for an individual account for each participant and for benefits based solely on the amounts contributed to the account and any income, expenses, gains, losses, or forfeitures that may be allocated to the participant's account.

### Q 15:31   Can a participant's defined benefit be transferred or distributed to a 414(k) account?

Maybe. Some IRS officials have opined that a participant's benefit in the defined benefit portion of a plan cannot be transferred to a 414(k) account. They believe that such a transfer or distribution must be from one plan to a different plan to eliminate the protected defined benefit characteristic, as defined under the regulations to Code Section 411(d)(6), of the participant's benefit. Therefore, a transfer or distribution within the same plan would not eliminate that characteristic and the benefit would remain subject to all defined benefit limits, including the Code Section 415 limit. Accordingly, this could not even be done in a voluntary manner with full participant and spousal consent (as in a distribution) because a Section 411(d)(6) protected benefit cannot be waived. [Treas. Reg. § 1.411(d)-4, Q&A 3(a)(3)]

Others believe, however, that because a 414(k) account is treated as a separate defined contribution plan for other purposes, it should be treated as such for this purpose as well. This position would effectively allow a distribution from the defined benefit plan to the 414(k) account as long as all other requirements for receiving a distribution from the plan are met.

If a plan sponsor wants to allow such a transfer, it is recommended that a determination letter or other official ruling be sought regarding the plan language and procedure.

### Q 15:32   Can matching contributions as defined under Section 401(m) be made to a 414(k) account?

Yes. A 414(k) account is treated as a defined contribution plan for purposes of receiving matching and employee after-tax contributions. Excess assets in the defined benefit plan, however, cannot be used to fund the matching contribution allocated to the 414(k) account (see Q 15:29).

## Medical Expense Accounts

### Q 15:33 What is a *medical expense account* under Code Section 401(h)?

A *medical expense account* under Code Section 401(h) is an account within a defined benefit pension plan for the payment of the sickness, accident, hospitalization, and medical expenses of retired employees and the spouses and dependents of retired employees. [Treas. Reg. § 1.401-14(a)] The term *retired* for purposes of eligibility to receive medical benefits under Code Section 401(h) means that the employee is eligible to receive retirement benefits under the plan or is treated as retired by the employer by reason of the employee's permanent disability. An employee who must terminate employment with the employer as a condition of receiving retirement benefits is not considered retired. [Treas. Reg. § 1.401-14(b)(1)]

### Q 15:34 What requirements must a plan satisfy with respect to a Section 401(h) arrangement?

A plan must satisfy the following requirements with respect to a Section 401(h) arrangement:

*Nondiscrimination.* A Section 401(h) arrangement cannot discriminate in favor of officers, shareholders, supervisory employees, or HCEs with respect to coverage or with respect to contributions and benefits. The determination of whether a Section 401(h) arrangement so discriminates is made with reference to the retirement portion of the defined benefit plan as well as the Section 401(h) arrangement. [Treas. Reg. § 1.401-14(b)(2)]

*Benefits.* A Section 401(h) arrangement must specify the medical benefits that will be available and must contain provisions for determining the amount that will be paid. Furthermore, such benefits, when added to any life insurance protection provided under the defined benefit plan, must be subordinate to the retirement benefits provided by the plan (see Q 15:35). [Treas. Reg. § 1.401-14(c)(1)]

*Separate account.* A separate account must be established for the contributions used to fund the Section 401(h) benefits. The separation is for recordkeeping purposes only; therefore, the plan can invest the contributions to the 401(h) account in the same manner as it invests funds used to provide retirement benefits. [Treas. Reg. § 1.401-14(c)(2)]

*Reasonable and ascertainable contributions.* The contributions to fund medical benefits must be reasonable and ascertainable. The employer must, at the time it makes a contribution, designate the portion of the contribution allocable to funding medical benefits. [Treas. Reg. § 1.401-14(c)(3)]

*Impossibility of diversion prior to satisfaction of all liabilities.* It must be impossible at any time prior to the satisfaction of all liabilities under the plan for any part of the corpus or income of the medical benefits account to be used for, or diverted to, any purpose other than providing medical benefits under the plan. The payment of necessary or appropriate expenses attributable to the administration of the medical benefits account, however, does not affect the qualification of the plan. [Treas. Reg. § 1.401-14(c)(4)]

*Reversion on satisfaction of all liabilities.* The plan must provide that any amounts that are contributed to fund the 401(h) account and that remain in the account after satisfaction of all liabilities arising out of the operation of the Section 401(h) arrangement are returned to the employer. [Treas. Reg. § 1.401-14(c)(5)]

*Forfeiture.* The plan must expressly provide that if an individual's interest in the medical benefits account is forfeited prior to termination of the plan, an amount equal to the amount of the forfeiture will be applied as soon as administratively possible to reduce employer contributions to fund the 401(h) account. [Treas. Reg. § 1.401-14(c)(6)]

### Q 15:35   When are benefits provided under a Section 401(h) arrangement considered subordinate to retirement benefits?

The medical benefits provided under a Section 401(h) arrangement are considered subordinate to the plan's retirement benefits if at all times the aggregate contributions made to provide the medical benefits and any life insurance protection do not exceed 25 percent of the aggregate contributions (made after the date that the plan first includes the medical benefits) exclusive of contributions to fund past-service credits. [Treas. Reg. § 1.401-14(c)(1)(i)]

**Example.** The Landscaping and Rock Company amended its defined benefit pension plan to provide medical benefits as described in Code Section 401(h) effective for the 2000 plan year. The total contributions under the plan (excluding those for past-service credits) for the 2000 plan year are $125,000, of which $100,000 is for retirement benefits, $10,000 for life insurance, and $15,000 for medical benefits. The medical benefits described in Code Section 401(h) are considered subordinate to the retirement benefits because the portion of the contributions allocated to the medical benefits ($15,000) and to life insurance ($10,000), or $25,000, does not exceed 25 percent of $125,000.

For the 2001 plan year, the company contributes $140,000 (exclusive of past-service credits), of which $100,000 is for retirement benefits, $10,000 for life insurance protection, and $30,000 for medical benefits. The medical benefits described in Code Section 401(h) are still considered subordinate to the retirement benefits because the aggregate contributions allocated to the medical benefits ($45,000) and to life insurance ($20,000), or $65,000, do not exceed 25 percent of $265,000, the aggregate contributions made in 2000 and 2001.

### Q 15:36    Can excess assets in a defined benefit plan be used to fund medical benefits described in Code Section 401(h)?

Yes. Employers are permitted to transfer excess assets from a defined benefit plan to an account for the payment of medical benefits described in Code Section 401(h). A plan is deemed to have excess assets for this purpose if assets exceed 125 percent (120 percent for transfers occurring after August 17, 2006, if the employer chooses to make a qualified future transfer) of the plan's current liability. In addition, there are several rules that must be followed:

1. The transferred amount can be used to pay medical benefits for either the year of the transfer or the year of transfer and the future transfer period, called a qualified future transfer (see Q 15:37).

2. The transferred amount must approximate the amount of medical expenses anticipated for the year of transfer or the year of transfer and future years during the transfer period.

3. An employer can make only one such transfer in a year.

4. All accrued benefits of participants in the defined benefit plan must be fully vested.

5. The employer must commit to a "maintenance of effort" requirement (see Q 15:39) with respect to the medical benefits.

[I.R.C. § 420]

This provision that allows for the transfer of excess assets to a 401(h) account is set to expire on December 31, 2013. [I.R.C. § 420(b), as amended by the Pension Funding Equity Act of 2004]

For plan year beginning after December 31, 2006, multiemployer plans may also transfer excess pension assets to 401(h) accounts, subject to the same rules as single employer plans. [I.R.C. § 420(e)(5)]

### Q 15:37    What is a qualified future transfer?

In lieu of a regular qualified transfer during a tax year, an employer may elect to make a qualified future transfer. A qualified future transfer is equal to the sum of:

1. If the transfer period includes the taxable year of the transfer, the amount determined under a regular qualified transfer (as determined under Code Section 420(b)(3)) for such taxable year; and

2. In the case of all other taxable years in the transfer period, the sum of the qualified current retiree health liabilities which the plan reasonably estimates (to be determined in accordance with guidance yet to be issued) will be incurred for each of such years.

[I.R.C. § 420(f)(2)(C)]

The qualified future transfer may transfer excess pension assets from the defined benefit plan to the 401(h) account based on the plan being funded with assets equal to at least 120 percent of current liability rather than a 125 percent of current liability level as required for regular qualified transfers. [I.R.C. § 420(f)(2)(B)(i)] However, the sponsor must also track the funded status of the defined benefit plan during the transfer period and if the current liability ever drops below the 120 percent funded level as of any valuation date during the transfer period, then the employer must either (1) contribute additional funds to the defined benefit plan in order to increase the assets above the 120 percent of current liability, or (2) transfer funds back to the defined benefit plan from the 401(h) account. [I.R.C. § 420(f)(2)(B)(ii)]

Except as stated above, a qualified future transfer must meet all the other requirements applicable to regular qualified transfers.

### Q 15:38   What is a *transfer period*?

The *transfer period* means, with respect to any transfer, a period of consecutive taxable years (not less than two) specified in the qualified future transfer election which begins and ends during the 10-taxable-year period beginning with the taxable year of the transfer.

### Q 15:39   What is the maintenance of effort requirement?

*Maintenance of cost.* For transfers occurring before December 8, 1994, or after December 17, 1999, an employer is required to continue to pay for a specified level of retiree medical benefits for the year of the asset transfer and the following four years. For qualified future transfers, this period is extended to the fourth year following the end of the transfer period. [I.R.C. § 420(f)(2)(D)] This minimum level is based on average per capita retiree health costs for the higher-cost year of the two years preceding the asset transfer. [I.R.C. § 420(c)(3)] In addition, if the employer decreases coverage by a total of more than 20 percent during the cost maintenance period (or by more than 10 percent in any one year for taxable years after January 1, 2002), this requirement is not met. [Treas. Reg. § 1.420-1(b)]

**Example.** ACE maintains a defined benefit pension plan that includes a 401(h) account and permits qualified transfers that satisfy Code Section 420. The number of individuals receiving coverage for applicable health benefits as of the day before the first day of Year 1 is 100. In Year 1, ACE makes a qualified transfer under Code Section 420. There is no change in the number of individuals receiving health benefits during Year 1. As of the last day of Year 2, applicable health benefits are provided to 99 individuals, because 2 individuals became eligible for coverage due to retirement and 3 individuals died in Year 2. During Year 3, ACE amends its health plan to eliminate coverage for five individuals, one new retiree becomes eligible for coverage, and an additional three individuals are no longer covered due to their own decision to drop coverage. Thus, as of the last day of Year 3, applicable health benefits are provided to 92 individuals. During Year 4, ACE amends its health plan to eliminate coverage under its health plan for 8 more individuals, so that as of the last day of Year 4, applicable health benefits are provided to

84 individuals. During Year 5, ACE amends its health plan to eliminate coverage for eight more individuals.

There is no significant reduction in retiree health coverage in either Year 1 or Year 2, because there is no reduction in health coverage as a result of employer action in those years. There is no significant reduction in Year 3. The number of individuals whose health coverage ended during Year 3 by reason of employer action (amendment of the plan) is five. Because the number of individuals receiving coverage for applicable health benefits as of the last day of Year 2 is 99, the employer-initiated reduction percentage for Year 3 is 5.05 percent ($\frac{5}{99}$), which is less than the 10 percent annual limit. There is no significant reduction in Year 4. The number of individuals whose health coverage ended during Year 4 by reason of employer action is eight. Because the number of individuals receiving coverage for applicable health benefits as of the last day of Year 3 is 92, the employer-initiated reduction percentage for Year 4 is 8.70 percent ($\frac{8}{92}$), which is less than the 10 percent annual limit. The sum of the employer-initiated reduction percentages for Year 3 and Year 4 is 13.75 percent, which is less than the 20 percent cumulative limit. In Year 5, there is a significant reduction. The number of individuals whose health coverage ended during Year 5 by reason of employer action (amendment of the plan) is eight. Because the number of individuals receiving coverage for applicable health benefits as of the last day of Year 4 is 84, the employer-initiated reduction percentage for Year 5 is 9.52 percent ($\frac{8}{84}$), which is less than the 10 percent annual limit. However, the sum of the employer-initiated reduction percentages for Year 3, Year 4, and Year 5 is 23.27 percent (5.05% + 8.70% + 9.52%), which exceeds the 20 percent cumulative limit, and the requirement is not met.

## Deferred Retirement Option Program

### Q 15:40   What is a *deferred retirement option program (DROP)*?

A *DROP* is a deferred retirement option feature within a defined benefit plan. It is used to encourage those employees who are eligible for retirement benefits to remain employed for a specific period. It is generally a contractual agreement between the employee and the employer that enables the participant to receive his or her regular compensation while the retirement benefits the participant would have received are added to the DROP account.

### Q 15:41   What types of employers can have a DROP?

Because of the restrictions due to certain Code sections (see Q 15:43), generally only government plans can use a DROP feature.

### Q 15:42   What is a DROP account?

Generally, if an employee elects to work past retirement age, the monthly benefit he or she would have received is contributed to the DROP account.

During this period, the employee continues to work and receive compensation, but not service credit. This account is then credited with interest at some specified rate. This account usually can be distributed as a lump sum upon actual retirement from employment. The lump-sum distribution is eligible for rollover. [Ltr. Rul. 200038055]

A DROP can also be used to provide additional late retirement accruals, where the value of the accrual is added to the account.

> **Example.** Jimmy has 20 years of participation in the Mile High defined benefit pension plan, which has a DROP feature that credits interest at 6 percent. He has reached the plan's normal retirement age of 60 but has agreed to remain employed for five more years and will have his regular pension payments made to the DROP account. He has accrued the maximum benefit allowed under the plan of $2,000 per month (the plan formula provides a $100 per month benefit times years of participation, not to exceed 20). Therefore, monthly deposits of $2,000 will be credited to the DROP account, and at the end of five years, Jimmy can elect to receive a lump-sum distribution from the DROP account in the amount of $139,648 (the $2,000 per month accumulated with interest) and can also begin receiving his regular pension payment of $2,000 per month.

### Q 15:43 What are the drawbacks to implementing a DROP?

Private sector employers will generally not be able to implement a DROP because this feature currently violates many Code provisions. For example, a participant who agrees to a DROP is electing to begin retirement benefits at a later date in a specified form, which may violate the 90-day election period for the QJSA. In addition, the Section 417 requirements applicable to lump sums may cause a "whipsaw" effect, just as is the case for cash balance plans. The Section 401(a)(4) nondiscrimination requirements would have to be dealt with as well because the DROP would be considered a benefit, right, or feature. Code Section 415 may also limit the accumulation of the DROP account.

# Chapter 16

# Distribution of Benefits

When a participant attains normal retirement age, or becomes entitled to a distribution from the plan, the participant generally will have choices about how benefits are to be paid. Although benefits normally are payable in the form of a qualified joint and survivor annuity (QJSA), other forms of benefit payment may be available under the plan. The plan administrator must provide information about benefit payment options and tax consequences.

This chapter discusses when benefits can and must be paid and typical payment options. It also explains the QJSA and qualified preretirement survivor annuity (QPSA) requirements and reviews how benefits are taxed.

## Administrative Requirements

### Q 16:1   What events can trigger a plan distribution?

A number of events can trigger a distribution or payment from the plan:

1. *Employment termination with* de minimis *benefit.* A participant who terminates employment with a vested deferred benefit that has a present

value less than $5,000 may be entitled to a distribution of benefits. If the plan includes a cash-out provision (see Q 16:9), benefits are immediately distributable.

2. *Employment termination with lump-sum immediate option.* Some defined benefit plans, primarily cash balance plans and plans maintained by small employers, may include a provision permitting a terminated vested participant to receive an immediate distribution of benefits after termination of employment in the form of a single lump-sum payment.

3. *Early retirement.* A plan participant who has satisfied the conditions for early retirement can elect to receive benefits after termination of employment.

4. *Normal retirement.* A plan participant who has satisfied the conditions for normal retirement can elect to receive benefits after termination of employment.

5. *Attaining age 70.* Minimum benefits must be paid to certain employees who have attained age 70½ (see Q 16:89).

6. *Receipt of a QDRO.* Payments can be directed to an alternate payee pursuant to a qualified domestic relations order, or QDRO (see chapter 17).

7. *Disability.* A plan may provide for payment of retirement benefits to a participant who becomes disabled.

8. *Death.* The spouse of a participant must receive a QPSA (see Q 16:68) unless the participant has waived the benefit and the spouse has consented to the waiver. Additional death benefits may be payable under the plan.

### Q 16:2    What information must a participant receive regarding benefit distribution rights?

All plan participants should receive information about distribution options and tax rules. Distribution options must be described in the plan document and the summary plan description (see chapter 28).

Each participant who separates from service with a vested benefit that is payable at a later date (a deferred vested participant) must receive a benefit statement. The statement must include the following information:

1. Plan name;

2. Name and address of the plan administrator;

3. Description of the amount and normal form of payment of the deferred vested benefit; and

4. Description of the benefit that may be forfeited if the participant dies.

This statement must be provided by the time Schedule SSA of Internal Revenue Service (IRS) Form 5500 is filed for the plan year following the plan year in which the participant separated from service. [ERISA § 105(c)]

A plan must generally provide participants with notice of their benefit distribution rights no less than 30 days and no more than 90 days (180 days for annuity starting dates after December 31, 2006) before the annuity starting date (see Q 16:27).

The notice must contain a general description or explanation of the QJSA (see Q 16:47), the circumstances in which the QJSA will be provided, the availability of any election to have benefits paid in another form, and the relative financial effect on a participant's annuity of the alternative elections (see Q 16:50). [Treas. Reg. § 1.401(a)-11(c)(3)(i)] It is important that a participant have sufficient information to make knowing and voluntary elections. A plan can be liable if it provides materially misleading information to a plan participant or if the information supplied is insufficient to enable a participant to make an informed decision. [Larsen v. NMU Pension Plan Trust, 14 Employee Benefits Cas. (BNA) 1421 (S.D.N.Y. 1991); Estate of Becker v. Eastman Kodak Co., 21 Employee Benefits Cas. (BNA) 1384 (2d Cir. 1997)] The notice should explain that benefit elections are irrevocable and that the designation of a spouse as the surviving spouse for purposes of the QJSA cannot be changed because of subsequent divorce, death of the spouse, or any other reason. [Jordan v. Fed. Express Corp., 116 F.3d 1005 (3d Cir. 1997)] A participant's consent to a distribution is not valid unless the participant has received a general description of the material features—and an explanation of the relative values—of the optional forms of benefit available under the plan in a manner that would satisfy the notice requirements of Internal Revenue Code (Code) Section 417(a)(3). [Treas. Reg. § 1.417(e)-1(b)(2)(i); Franklin v. Thornton, 16 Employee Benefits Cas. (BNA) 1433 (9th Cir. 1993)]

Distributions from pension plans have certain tax implications. If a distribution qualifies as an eligible rollover distribution (see Q 16:118), the plan administrator must provide a notice to the participant explaining the potential tax consequences of the distribution.

### Q 16:3   May a participant's accrued benefit be reduced to pay for the fees associated with preparing the forms necessary to distribute the benefit?

In the author's opinion, the answer to this question is no. This question has been answered in the affirmative for defined contribution plans (see DOL Field Assistance Bulletin 2003-3), but has never been specifically addressed in official guidance as it pertains to distributions from defined benefit plans. However, following general principles, when a defined benefit plan pays fees, it only reduces the overall investment return of the plan, but does not reduce participants' benefits. In addition, reducing participants' benefits for fees would be an impermissible violation of Code Section 411(d)(6).

### Q 16:4   Do any special notice rules apply if the participant can elect to receive benefits in a lump sum?

Yes. Participants who receive eligible rollover distributions (see Q 16:118) must be notified of the potential tax consequences. Within a reasonable time before making the eligible rollover distribution, the plan administrator must provide the participant or spousal beneficiary with a written explanation of tax consequences associated with the distribution and the direct rollover rules. The notice, often referred to as a *Section 402(f) notice*, must explain the following:

1. The rules under which the distributee can elect to have the distribution paid to an eligible retirement plan in the form of a direct rollover;
2. The rules requiring tax withholding if the distribution is not paid in the form of a direct rollover;
3. The rules that permit the distributee to defer taxes by rolling over a distribution to an eligible retirement plan within 60 days of distribution;
4. Other taxation rules that may be applicable; and
5. Any default provisions that apply if the distributee does not make an election.

[I.R.C. § 402(f); Treas. Reg. §§ 1.402(f)-1, 1.401(a)(31)-1] (See chapter 28.)

The IRS has published a model Section 402(f) notice. [Notice 2002-3, 2002-2 I. R.B. 289]

### Q 16:5   When must information regarding benefit payment options be given to an employee?

Information regarding the QJSA (see Q 16:47) and any benefit options must be communicated to plan participants within specified times:

1. A plan must generally provide participants with a written explanation of the QJSA and the right to waive this form of payment in favor of another form of benefit payment provided in the plan (see Q 16:59) no less than 30 days and no more than 90 days (180 days for years beginning after December 31, 2006) before the annuity starting date (see Q 16:27). [Temp. Treas. Reg. § 1.417(e)-1T(b)(3)(ii)]
2. The plan administrator must provide a written explanation of the direct rollover and withholding rules (see Q 16:118) no less than 30 days and no more than 90 days (180 days for years beginning after December 31, 2006) before the date of distribution.

If the distributee, after having received the notices, affirmatively elects a distribution, the plan will not fail to satisfy the 30-day-minimum rule merely because the distribution is made less than 30 days after the notice was provided to the participant, provided the participant received information clearly advising him or her of the right to consider the decision for at least 30 days. [Treas. Reg. §§ 1.402(f)-1, Q&A-2, 1.411(a)-11(c)(2)(iii)] Distributions cannot begin, however, before the expiration of a seven-day period that begins on the day after the explanation of the QJSA is provided to the participant. [Treas. Reg. § 1.417(e)-1(b)(3)(ii)] Because the seven-day period does not begin until the day *after* the day the notice is provided, and because distribution cannot occur until *after* the seven-day period has expired, there is effectively a nine-day wait from the date notice is given to the date benefits can begin.

**Example.** Curt is a participant in a cash balance plan that permits lump-sum distributions on termination of employment. Curt has just quit his job and would like to roll over his benefits into his individual retirement account (IRA) as soon as possible. The plan administrator provides Curt with the QJSA explanation and the Section 402(f) notice on April 15, 2002. Even if Curt waives the 30-day waiting period and returns his election forms to the plan administrator the next day, the rollover distribution cannot occur before April 23 (after seven days have expired since the explanation of the QJSA was provided to Curt).

Revenue Procedure 93-47 [1993-2 C.B. 578] provides model language for waiver of the 30-day period.

## Form of Benefits

### Q 16:6   In what form are benefits normally paid?

The normal form of benefit under a defined benefit pension plan generally is a benefit payable in the form of an annuity. The amount of the payment may be fixed or may change based on a cost-of-living index. The total amount payable is determined by the benefit formula in the plan. The benefit will be calculated on the basis of factors including years of service, compensation, and/or Social Security benefits (see chapter 12).

Plans do not have to provide any form of benefit other than the QJSA (see Q 16:47). The two general types of distributions are annuities and lump sums. An *annuity* provides regular monthly benefits, generally over the life of the plan participant. A *lump sum* is a single-sum payment that extinguishes liability for further benefit payment under the plan.

The most common forms of benefit payment available under a defined benefit pension plan are the following:

1. *Single-life or straight-life annuity.* Benefits are paid over the life of the participant. When the participant dies, no further benefits are payable. This annuity is often selected by unmarried participants. The single-life annuity usually provides the largest monthly annuity payment.
2. *Term-certain and life annuity.* Benefits are paid over the life of the participant but are guaranteed for a certain period of time (5 years and 10 years are typical term-certain payment options). If the participant dies before the term-certain period, benefits continue to the designated beneficiary for the remainder of the term. The term-certain and life annuity usually provides a monthly benefit of about 90 percent of the single-life annuity.
3. *QJSA.* Benefits are paid over the life of the participant, and after the participant's death, they are paid to the participant's surviving spouse for his or her life. The benefits paid to the surviving spouse are often 50 percent, 66⅔ percent, or 100 percent of the amount paid to the participant. Payments end at the death of the surviving spouse. Plan participants married at least

one year at retirement must receive this annuity unless it is appropriately waived. The QJSA usually provides smaller payments than the single-life annuity because benefits are based on two life expectancies. The relative value of the monthly payments depends on the percentage benefit provided to the surviving spouse and the age of the surviving spouse.

4. *Joint and survivor annuity (JSA) or contingent annuity.* Benefits are paid over the life of the participant, and after the participant's death, they are paid over the life of the participant's designated beneficiary, who can be someone other than the participant's spouse. The benefits paid to the beneficiary are often 50 percent, 66⅔ percent, or 100 percent of the amount paid to the participant. Benefits end at the death of the surviving beneficiary. The JSA usually provides smaller payments than the single-life annuity because benefits are based on two life expectancies. The relative value of the monthly payments depends on the percentage benefit provided to the beneficiary and the age of the beneficiary.

5. *Lump sum.* The present value of the participant's benefits are calculated and a lump-sum payment is made of the participant's entire interest in the plan. No further benefits are payable under the plan.

The normal and automatic form of benefit for married participants is a QJSA. The normal form of benefit for a single participant is a single-life annuity. To waive either of these benefit forms, the participant must waive the automatic form of payment, and if the participant is married, the participant's spouse must consent to the participant's election (see Q 16:59).

Plan documents and summary plan descriptions (see chapter 28) must describe the distribution options available to plan participants.

### Q 16:7   How is the amount of the monthly benefit affected by choosing an optional form of payment?

The monthly benefit must be adjusted actuarially to reflect the potentially longer payment period and the life expectancy of the beneficiary if a joint benefit is elected. For example, if an employee is entitled to $100 per month for life and the payment is guaranteed for 10 years, he or she would receive a smaller monthly benefit and benefits would be paid to a beneficiary after the participant's death. Benefits cannot be paid in an optional benefit form unless certain actuarial equivalency rules are complied with. If a benefit is paid in a different form than the normal form specified in the plan, or is paid at a different age than normal retirement age, the benefit payable to the participant must be the actuarial equivalent of the benefit payable in the normal form at normal retirement age. [I.R.C. § 411(c)(3); Treas. Reg. § 1.411(c)-1(e)] Actuarial equivalencies must be stated in the plan. The Code provides rules to be used in determining lump-sum present values (i.e., actuarial equivalence) for this purpose (see Q 16:10).

A plan can also subsidize optional benefit forms by not adjusting them to their actuarially equivalent value (see Q 16:37). This is possible only if the limitation under Code Section 415 is still satisfied. The payment of a QJSA (see Q 16:47) does not need to be adjusted to the actuarial equivalent of a straight-life annuity to meet the limitations of Code Section 415. [Treas. Reg. § 1.415-3(c)]

### Q 16:8   Can an employee ever receive a lump-sum distribution from a defined benefit plan?

The answer depends on the plan provisions. Many plans provide for lump-sum payments if the present value of the accrued benefits does not exceed a certain dollar amount. The Code permits a cash-out of an employee if the value of the benefits does not exceed $5,000. Some plans, particularly cash balance plans (see chapters 4 and 13) and plans sponsored by small employers, may offer lump-sum options for larger benefits. Many plans permit lump-sum payments on plan termination (see chapter 25).

### Q 16:9   Can an employee be forced to take a lump-sum payment?

It depends. If the value of a participant's benefit is $5,000 or less at the time of payment (called a mandatory distribution), even if the balance has exceeded $5,000 at a previous distribution date, the plan can provide for a cash-out of the value of the participant's benefit without the participant's consent. [Treas. Reg. § 1.411(a)-11(c)(3)]

EGTRRA provides that mandatory distributions of more than $1,000 to a plan participant must automatically be rolled over into an IRA, unless the participant elects to have the distribution rolled over to another retirement plan or to take it in cash. This rule does not apply to a surviving spouse, to a former spouse who is an alternate payee, or to involuntary cash-outs made at the later of age 62 or normal retirement age under the plan. [Notice 2005-5, 2005-3 I.R.B. 1]

If the present value of a participant's vested accrued benefit exceeds $5,000, or if the present value is less than $5,000 but the annuity starting date (see Q 16:27) has already passed, the plan must obtain the participant's written consent to distribute any part of the benefit before the later of the date the participant attains age 62 or normal retirement age. [I.R.C. § 411(a)(11)(A); Treas. Reg. §§ 1.411(a)-11(c)(4), 1.417(e)-1(b)(2)]

Consent of the participant is not required for payments to an alternate payee under a QDRO (see chapter 17) unless the order expressly provides for consent. In addition, consent is not required to satisfy the required minimum distribution rules (see Q 16:87). [Treas. Reg. § 1.411(a)-11(c)]

### Q 16:10   Are there special ways of calculating lump-sum amounts?

Code Section 417(e)(3) provides rules for determining the present value of plan benefits for purposes of the cash-out rules (see Q 16:9).

The value of lump-sum payments cannot be less than the present value determined by using the applicable mortality table and the applicable interest rate. However, in the case of a cash balance or pension equity plan, the plan may define the present value of the accrued benefit (without failing any qualification requirements) equal to the amount expressed as the balance in the hypothetical account (for cash balance plans) or as an accumulated percentage of the participant's final average compensation (for pension equity plans).

The *applicable mortality table* prescribed by the IRS is based on the "prevailing commissioners' standard table" used to determine reserves for group annuity contracts issued on the date as of which the present value is determined. For distributions occurring before December 31, 2002, the 1983 Group Annuity Mortality (GAM) Table, blended 50 percent for male mortality rates and 50 percent for female mortality rates (83 GAM-U or GATT table) is used. For distributions occurring after December 30, 2002, the 1994 Group Annuity Reserving (94 GAR) Table projected to 2002 based on a fixed blend of 50 percent of the unloaded male mortality rates and 50 percent of the unloaded female mortality rates underlining the mortality rates is used. [I.R.C. § 417(e)(3)(A)(ii)(I); Rev. Rul. 95-6, 1995-1 C.B. 80; Rev. Rul. 2001-62, 2001-53 I.R.B. 1] This mortality table is to change for the 2007 plan year.

The *applicable interest rate* is the annual interest rate on 30-year Treasury securities as specified by the Commissioner for that month (called the GATT rate). [I.R.C. § 417(e)(3)(A)(ii)(II); Treas. Reg. § 1.417(e)-1(d)(3)] For plan years beginning after December 31, 2007, the Pension Protection Act of 2006 (PPA) requires the use of segment rates as the applicable interest rate. The adjusted first, second, and third segment rates are the first, second, and third segment rates which would be determined under Code Section 430(h)(2)(C), except that these rates are determined based on the average yields for the distribution period and there is a five-year phase-in. The five-year phase-in requires 20 percent of the segment rates to be used in determining the applicable interest rate for 2008 and increases by 20 percent per year until 2012 when 100 percent of the segment rates will be required to be used.

### Q 16:11   How are the first, second, and third segment rates determined?

The term *first segment rate* means, with respect to any month, the single rate of interest which shall be determined by the Secretary of Treasury for such month on the basis of the corporate bond yield curve for such month, taking into account only that portion of such yield curve which is based on bonds maturing during the five-year period commencing with such month.

The term *second segment rate* means, with respect to any month, the single rate of interest which shall be determined by the Secretary of Treasury for such month on the basis of the corporate bond yield curve for such month, taking into account only that portion of such yield curve which is based on bonds maturing during the 15-year period beginning at the end of the period used for the first segment rate.

The term *third segment rate* means, with respect to any month, the single rate of interest which shall be determined by the Secretary of Treasury for such month on the basis of the corporate bond yield curve for such month, taking into account only that portion of such yield curve which is based on bonds maturing during periods beginning after the period used for the second segment rate.

### Q 16:12 How will the lump-sum distribution be calculated in a defined benefit pension plan in years beginning after December 31, 2007?

This is subject to future regulations yet to be issued by the Treasury Department. However, the author believes this is how the calculation will work: First, determine the first, second, and third segment rates that are applicable to the distribution. Second, apply these interest rates to the annuity stream beginning on the annuity starting date, calculating a present value for each payment. Once each of these separately calculated present values is known, add them together to determine the current present value. This is the current lump sum.

**Example.** Assume Sandy is retiring at age 68 with an accrued benefit equal to $12,000 per month payable in the form of a straight-life annuity. The first segment rate is 5.50 percent, the second segment rate is 6.0 percent, and the third segment rate is 6.5 percent. Assume the applicable mortality table is the 1994 GAR table. A spreadsheet would be set up similar to the following to determine the present value of each payment stream.

|   | Year | Age | Payment Amount | Vn | Lx | Discount | APR | Value |
|---|------|-----|----------------|------|------|----------|---------|-------|
| 1 | 2008 | 68 | $12,000.00 | 1.0000000 | 869328.9 | 1 | 125.725 | $1,508,698.25 |
| 2 | 2013 | 73 | $12,000.00 | 0.7651344 | 791373.8 | 0.6965227 | 107.737 | $ 900,492.74 |
| 3 | 2013 | 73 | $12,000.00 | 0.7472582 | 791373.8 | 0.6802495 | 104.374 | $ 852,004.77 |
| 4 | 2028 | 88 | $12,000.00 | 0.3118047 | 334821.6 | 0.1200914 | 52.173 | $ 75,186.13 |
| 5 | 2028 | 88 | $12,000.00 | 0.2837970 | 334821.6 | 0.1093043 | 51.338 | $ 67,337.41 |

Vn is the discount using interest only.

Lx is the discount using mortality only.

Discount is the discount for interest and mortality combined.

APR = Annuity Purchase Rate.

Line 1 is the value of the payment stream at the first segment rate through death (equal to the payment times discount times APR). Line 2 is used to determine the value of the payment stream at the first segment rate after Year 5 through date of death. Line 3 then determines the value of the payment stream at the second segment rate from Year 5 through death. Line 4 determines the value of the payment stream at the second segment rate after Year 20 through date of death. Line 5 determines the value of the payment stream after Year 20 through date of death using the third segment rate. The total present value is line 1 minus line 2 plus line 3 minus line 4 plus line 5, or $1,452,361 ($1,508,698 − $900,493 + $852,005 − $75,186 + $67,337).

### Q 16:13   How is the lump-sum benefit calculated in a defined benefit pension plan prior to January 1, 2008?

A lump-sum benefit is calculated using the plan's interest rate and mortality table for actuarial equivalence; however, a lump-sum benefit cannot be less than the amount determined using the rules under Code Section 417(e)(3). That section of the Code states that for a plan in effect after December 8, 1994, the present value, in this case a lump sum, shall not be less than the value calculated using the applicable interest rate and applicable mortality table.

**Example.** The Joanne & Associates Pension Plan, a traditional defined benefit plan, provides that the present value of a lump-sum payment shall be the actuarial equivalent of the amount determined using the 1983 Male Individual Annuity Mortality Table and an interest rate of 6 percent. In no event is the lump sum to be less than the amount calculated using the applicable interest rate and applicable mortality table. The applicable interest rate according to the plan document is determined as of the first day of the plan year in which the distribution occurs. David, a plan participant, terminates his employment during 2002 at the age of 45 and would like to receive his benefit in a lump-sum payment. David's accrued benefit payable at age 65 is $500 per month. Assume for purposes of this example that the applicable interest rate is 5 percent.

*Step 1.*  Multiply the age 65 accrued benefit by the APR using the plan mortality table with interest at 6 percent. In David's case that amount is $63,455 ($500 × 126.910).

*Step 2.*  Multiply the result in Step 1 by the discount factor from age 65 to age 45 (20 years). In this case, the plan ignores mortality before retirement. Therefore, the discount factor is the present value of $1 payable in 20 years at 6 percent, or 0.311805 ($1.06^{-20}$). The lump sum for David is $19,786 ($63,455 × 0.311805) using the plan's interest rate and mortality.

*Step 3.*  Multiply the age 65 accrued benefit by the APR using the applicable mortality table with interest at 5 percent (the applicable interest rate). In David's case that amount is $69,204 ($500 × 138.407).

*Step 4.*  Multiply the result in Step 3 by the discount factor from age 65 to age 45 (20 years). In this case, the plan ignores mortality before retirement. Therefore, the discount factor is the present value of $1 payable in 20 years at 5 percent, or 0.3768895 ($1.05^{-20}$). The lump sum for David is $26,082 ($69,204 × 0.3768895) using the applicable interest and mortality table.

*Step 5.*  The lump sum payable to David is the greater of the amounts in Step 2 and Step 4, $26,082.

### Q 16:14   How is the lump-sum benefit calculated in a defined benefit pension plan that was in effect before December 8, 1994?

For a plan that was in effect before December 8, 1994, the plan is not required to use the applicable interest rate and mortality table for purposes of determining the minimum present value (i.e., the lump sum) until the earlier of the later of the date a plan amendment applying the applicable interest rate and mortality table is adopted or made effective, or the first day of the plan year beginning after December 31, 1999.

Until the earlier of those dates, a plan can use the interest rate determined under the regulations of the Pension Benefit Guaranty Corporation (PBGC) in effect on September 1, 1993, and use the provisions of the plan in effect on December 7, 1994, provided the plan met the requirements of Code Section 417(e)(3) and Treasury Regulations Section 1.417(e)-1(d) on that date. [I.R.C. § 417(e)(3); Treas. Reg. § 1.417(e)-1(d)(8)]

In general, for lump-sum distributions that were made in plan years beginning after December 31, 1986, and before January 1, 1995, the interest rate or rates were determined on either the annuity starting date or the first day of the plan year that contains the annuity starting date (the plan must provide which date is applicable) and there was no applicable mortality table specified in the calculation. The mortality table used is the actuarial equivalence table if no other table is specified.

The applicable interest rate for a distribution that occurs during the above time period is the rate or rates that would be used by the PBGC for a trusteed single-employer plan to value the participant's (or beneficiary's) vested benefit (PBGC interest rate) if the present value of such benefit does not exceed $25,000; or 120 percent of the PBGC interest rate if such present value exceeds $25,000. In no event shall the present value determined by use of 120 percent of the PBGC interest rate result in a present value less than $25,000. [Treas. Reg. § 1.417(e)-1(d)(9)]

The PBGC interest rate may be a series of interest rates for any given date. For example, the PBGC interest rate for immediate annuities for November 1994 is 6 percent, and the PBGC interest rates for the deferral period for that month are as follows: 5.25 percent for the first seven years of the deferral period, 4 percent for the following eight years of the deferral period, and 4 percent for the remainder of the deferral period. For November 1994, 120 percent of the PBGC interest rate is 7.2 percent (1.2 × 6%) for an immediate annuity, 6.3 percent (1.2 × 5.25%) for the first seven years of the deferral period, 4.8 percent (1.2 × 4%) for the following eight years of the deferral period, and 4.8 percent (1.2 × 4%) for the remainder of the deferral period. The PBGC interest rates are the interest rates that would be used (as of the date of the distribution) by the PBGC for purposes of determining the present value of that benefit on termination of an insufficient funded trusteed single-employer plan.

**Example.** The D&R Pension Plan provides that the present value of a lump-sum payment shall be the actuarial equivalent of the amount determined using the 1983 Male Individual Mortality Table and the PBGC interest rate in effect on the annuity start date. Dane, a plan participant, terminated his employment during 1994 at age 45 and would like to receive his benefit in a lump-sum payment. Dane's accrued benefit payable at age 65 is $500 per month. His annuity start date falls in the month of November. His lump-sum payment is determined as follows:

*Step 1.*   Multiply the age 65 accrued benefit by the APR using the plan mortality table with interest at the immediate interest rate of 6 percent. In Dane's case that amount is $63,455 ($500 × 126.910).

*Step 2.*   Multiply the result in Step 1 by the discount factor from age 65 to age 45 (20 years). In this case, the plan ignores mortality before retirement. For the first seven years of the deferral period, the interest rate is 5.25 percent, with 4 percent used for the next eight years and 4 percent for any period thereafter. Therefore, the discount factor is the present value of $1 payable in 20 years at those rates, or 0.41977 $[(1.0525^{-7}) \times (1.04)^{-8} \times (1.04)^{-5}]$. The lump sum for Dane using the PBGC interest rate is $26,636 ($63,455 × 0.41977).

*Step 3.*   Dane's lump sum exceeds $25,000 using 100 percent of the PBGC interest rates and so must be now determined using 120 percent of the PBGC interest rates. To do so, multiply the age 65 accrued benefit by the APR using 120 percent of the November 1994 PBGC interest rate. In Dane's case that amount is $57,990 ($500 × 115.979).

*Step 4.*   Multiply the result in Step 3 by the discount factor from age 65 to age 45 (20 years). In this case, the plan ignores mortality before retirement. For the first seven years of the deferral period, the interest rate is 6.3 percent, with 4.8 percent used for the next eight years and 4.8 percent for any period thereafter. Therefore, the discount factor is the present value of $1 payable in 20 years at those rates, or 0.3544627 $[(1.0630^{-7}) \times (1.048)^{-8} \times (1.048)^{-5}]$. The lump sum for Dane is $20,555 ($57,990 × 0.3544627) using 120 percent of PBGC interest rates. Because this amount is less than $25,000, Dane's lump-sum payment is increased to a minimum of $25,000.

The plan can provide for the use of any other time for determining the PBGC interest rate or rates if such time is determined in a consistent manner, is applied uniformly to all participants, and is not more than 120 days before the annuity starting date. [Temp. Treas. Reg. § 1.417(e)-1(d)(9)]

## Q 16:15   When and how is the applicable interest rate determined?

The time and method for determining the applicable interest rate for each participant's distribution must be determined in a consistent manner that is applied uniformly to all participants in the plan. In general, for distributions with annuity starting dates in plan years beginning after December 31, 1994, the applicable interest rate is determined by reference to the plan's look-back month and remains in effect for the duration of the plan's stability period. The look-back month is the month that is referenced for determining the applicable interest rate for the month (or other longer stability period) that contains the annuity starting date for the distribution. When defining a plan's look-back month and stability period, the following rules apply:

*Stability period.* The stability period can be one calendar month, one plan quarter, one calendar quarter, one plan year, or one calendar year.

*Look-back month.* The look-back month can be the first, second, third, fourth, or fifth full calendar month preceding the first day of the stability period. [Treas. Reg. § 1.417(e)-1(d)(9)(i)]

A plan can use an average of the applicable interest rates instead of the applicable interest rate for a look-back month; however, such an average with respect to a stability period is an interest rate that is computed by averaging the applicable interest rates for two or more consecutive months from among the first, second, third, fourth, and fifth calendar months preceding the first day of the stability period. Furthermore, a plan must specify the manner in which the permitted average interest rate is computed. [Treas. Reg. § 1.417(e)-1(d)(4)(iv)]

> **Example.** The D&R Pension Plan is a calendar-year plan. D&R wants to amend the plan so that the applicable interest rate will remain fixed for each plan quarter and so the applicable interest rate for distributions made during each plan quarter can be determined approximately 80 days before the beginning of the plan quarter. The plan is amended to provide that the applicable interest rate is the annual interest rate on 30-year Treasury securities as specified by the Commissioner for the fourth calendar month preceding the first day of the plan quarter during which the annuity starting date occurs (i.e., the look-back month). Reese, a terminated plan participant, is going to receive his distribution on May 1, 2003. The distribution will occur in the second calendar quarter (i.e., April 1, 2003, through June 30, 2003) and the look-back month in this case is the fourth calendar month that precedes April 1, 2003, that is, December 2002. Hence, the present value of Reese's benefit will be determined using the published applicable interest rate for December 2002.

### Q 16:16    Can a preretirement mortality decrement be applied in determining a lump-sum distribution?

It depends. In general, a preretirement mortality decrement is only used in determining a lump-sum distribution if there is a risk of forfeiture of the benefit on death. In other words, if there is no death benefit defined in the plan document, then it is appropriate to decrease the lump-sum benefit by the preretirement mortality. However, if there is a death benefit, the IRS has ruled that for some purposes (like determining the Code Section 415 maximum benefit) it is not appropriate to apply a preretirement mortality decrement. The Seventh Circuit agreed with this interpretation as it applies to determining the lump sum for both plan and Section 417 purposes as well. The court stated in *Berger v. Xerox* the following, "... Xerox complains that the district judge refused to discount the pension benefit by the probability that the employee would actually live till age 65. This complaint ... is unfathomable, since the plan provides that if the employee dies before reaching retirement age his spouse or other designated beneficiary steps into his shoes and is entitled to his entire pension benefit." [Berger v. Xerox Corp. Ret. Income Guarantee Plan, 388 F.3d 755 (7th Cir. 2003)]

### Q 16:17 What is the annuity starting date for a plan that is terminating?

The annuity starting date for a lump-sum distribution is the date of distribution, regardless of whether the plan is terminating. In *Pension Benefit Guaranty Corp. v. Wilson N. Jones Memorial Hospital* [374 F.3d 362 (5th Cir. 2004)], the hospital argued that the annuity starting date was the date that its defined benefit plan terminated (i.e., December 31, 1995). However, distributions were not made until November 1996. The PBGC won this case in court, and the hospital was required to recalculate benefits using November 1996 as the annuity starting date.

### Q 16:18 What are the potential time frames that a plan could use to transition the present value requirements under RPA '94?

A plan that was adopted and in effect on December 7, 1994, has three optional dates for implementing the present value requirements under Code Section 417(e)(3).

1. Implement the changes for the first plan year that begins after December 31, 1994. This date is referred to as the *effective date* of the Retirement Protection Act of 1994 (RPA '94) rules.
2. Implement the changes for any plan year that begins after December 31, 1994, and before the first plan year that begins after December 31, 1999. The dates that fall within this range are referred to as the *optional delayed effective date* of the RPA '94 rules.
3. Implement the changes for any distribution that begins after December 7, 1994. This date is known as the *optional accelerated effective date* of the RPA '94 rules.

[Treas. Reg. § 1.417(e)-1(d)(8)(i), (ii), (iii)]

The optional delayed effective date, or the optional accelerated effective date, whichever is applicable, is the date plan amendments applying both the applicable mortality table and the applicable interest rate are adopted, or if later, are made effective. [Treas. Reg. § 1.417(e)-1(d)(8)(iv)]

**Example.** The R&D Pension Plan, a calendar-year plan, adopted an amendment to implement the optional delayed effective date of the RPA '94 rules on October 10, 1997. This amendment is to be effective for distributions beginning on or after January 1, 1998. In this case the optional delayed effective date is January 1, 1998.

### Q 16:19 How are the present value requirements under the RPA '94 rules transitioned for a plan that was in effect on December 7, 1994?

The minimum present value requirements under RPA '94 are transitioned through a plan amendment that incorporates the new applicable interest rate, mortality table, stability period, and look-back month. A plan amendment that changes the interest rate, the time for determining the interest rate, or the mortality assumptions used for purposes of computing a present value is normally subject to Code Section 411(d)(6) and cannot be eliminated; however, a plan amendment that implements the new present value requirements will not be in violation of Code Section 411(d)(6), provided the amendment meets certain requirements. Furthermore, Code Section 411(d)(6) relief does not apply to a plan amendment that replaces an interest rate other than the PBGC interest rate (or an interest rate or rates based on the PBGC interest rate) as an interest rate used under the plan in determining the present value of a participant's benefit. Thus, the accrued benefit determined using that interest rate and the associated mortality table is protected under Code Section 411(d)(6). An interest rate is based on the PBGC interest rate if the interest rate is defined as a specified percentage of the PBGC interest rate, the PBGC interest rate minus a specified number of basis points, or an average of such interest rates over a specified period. Three common methods are used to make the transition to the new present value requirements through the use of a plan amendment. Each method and corresponding plan amendment must meet certain requirements.

*Method 1. Interest rate one month before annuity start date.* Under Method 1, these requirements must be met:

- The amendment replaces the PBGC interest rate (or an interest rate or rates based on the PBGC interest rate) as the interest rate used under the plan in determining the present value of a participant's benefit.
- After the amendment is effective, the present value of a participant's benefit under the plan cannot be less than the amount calculated using the applicable mortality table and the applicable interest rate for the first full calendar month preceding the calendar month that contains the annuity starting date.

[Treas. Reg. § 1.417(e)-1(d)(10)(iii)(A), (B)]

**Example 1.** On December 31, 1994, the D&R Pension Plan provided that all single-sum distributions were to be calculated using the UP-1984 Mortality Table and 100 percent of the PBGC interest rate for the date of distribution. On January 4, 1995, and effective on February 1, 1995, the plan was amended to provide that all single-sum distributions are calculated using the applicable mortality table and the annual interest rate on 30-year Treasury securities for the first full calendar month preceding the calendar month that contains the annuity starting date. [Treas. Reg. § 1.417(e)-1(d)(10)(vii), Ex. 1]

*Method 2. Interest rate determined concurrent with, or one or two months before, PBGC interest rate date.* The following requirements must be met under Method 2:

- The amendment replaces the PBGC interest rate (or an interest rate or rates based on the PBGC interest rate) as the interest rate used under the plan in determining the present value of a participant's benefit.
- After the amendment is effective, the present value of a participant's benefit under the plan cannot be less than the amount calculated using

the applicable mortality table and the applicable interest rate, but only if the applicable interest rate is the annual interest rate on 30-year Treasury securities for the calendar month that contains the date as of which the PBGC interest rate (or an interest rate or rates based on the PBGC interest rate) was determined immediately before the amendment, or for one of the two calendar months immediately preceding such month.

[Treas. Reg. § 1.417(e)-1(d)(10)(iv)(A), (B)]

**Example 2.** On December 31, 1994, the D&R Pension Plan provided that all single-sum distributions were to be calculated using the UP-1984 Mortality Table and an interest rate equal to the lesser of 100 percent of the PBGC interest rate for the date of distribution or 6 percent. On January 4, 1995, and effective on February 1, 1995, the plan was amended to provide that all single-sum distributions are calculated using the applicable mortality table and the annual interest rate on 30-year Treasury securities for the second full calendar month preceding the calendar month that contains the annuity starting date. For the amendment to satisfy the requirements of Code Section 411(d)(6), the plan must provide that the single-sum distribution payable to any participant must be no less than the single-sum distribution calculated using the UP-1984 Mortality Table and an interest rate of 6 percent, based on the participant's benefits under the plan accrued through January 31, 1995, and based on the participant's age at the annuity starting date. This result is due to the fact that the amendment replaced an interest rate other than the PBGC interest rate. [Treas. Reg. § 1.417(e)-1(d)(10)(vii), Ex. 2]

*Method 3. Interest rate determined on alternate date.* If the plan is to use a determination date for the interest rate that is other than those in Method 1 or 2, the plan will not be considered to reduce a participant's accrued benefit as long as the plan provides as follows:

- The amendment replaces the PBGC interest rate (or an interest rate or rates based on the PBGC interest rate) as the interest rate used under the plan in determining the present value of a participant's benefit.

- After the amendment is effective, the present value of a participant's benefit under the plan cannot be less than the amount calculated using the applicable mortality table and the applicable interest rate.

- The plan amendment satisfies either the "Section 411(d)(6) relief for change in time for determining interest rate rule" or the "special early transition interest rate rule" as follows:

*Section 411(d)(6) relief for change in time for determining interest rate rule.* If the plan amendment is effective on or after the adoption date, any distribution for which the annuity starting date occurs in the one-year period beginning at the time the amendment is effective must be determined using the interest rate provided under the plan determined at either the date for determining the interest rate before the amendment or the date for determining the interest rate after the amendment, whichever results in the larger distribution. If the plan amendment is adopted retroactively (i.e., the amendment is effective before the adoption date), the plan must use the interest rate determination date resulting in the larger distribution for the period beginning with the effective date and ending one year after the adoption date.

*Special early transition interest rate rule.* Any distribution for which the annuity starting date occurs in the one-year period beginning at the time the plan amendment is effective is determined using whichever of the following two interest rates results in the larger distribution:

1. The interest rate as provided under the terms of the plan after the effective date of the amendment, but determined at a date that is either one month or two months (as specified in the plan) before the date for determining the interest rate used under the terms of the plan before the amendment; or

2. The interest rate as provided under the terms of the plan after the effective date of the amendment, determined at the date for determining the interest rate after the amendment.

[Treas. Reg. § 1.417(e)-1(d)(10)(v)(A), (B), (C)]

The following example makes use of the Section 411(d)(6) relief for change in time for determining interest rate rule:

**Example 3.** On December 31, 1994, the D&R Pension Plan, a calendar-year plan, provided that all single-sum distributions were to be calculated using the UP-1984 Mortality Table and an interest rate equal to the PBGC interest rate for January 1 of the plan year. On March 1, 1995, and effective on July 1, 1995, the plan was amended to provide that all single-sum distributions are calculated using the applicable mortality table and the annual interest rate on 30-year Treasury securities for August of the year before the plan year that contains the annuity starting date. The plan amendment provides that each distribution with an annuity starting date after June 30, 1995, and before July 1, 1996, is calculated using the 30-year Treasury rate for August of the year before the plan year that contains the annuity starting date, or the 30-year Treasury rate for January of the plan year that contains the annuity starting date, whichever produces the larger benefit. The amendment in this example has an effective date after the adoption of the amendment and provides that for one year from the effective date, the distribution will be the larger amount that results from the amendment or the interest rate determination date used before the amendment. [Treas. Reg. § 1.417(e)-1(d)(10)(vii), Ex. 3]

The following example makes use of the special early transition interest rate rule:

**Example 4.** On December 31, 1994, the D&R Pension Plan, a calendar-year plan, provided that all single-sum distributions were to be calculated using the UP-1984 Mortality Table and an interest rate equal to the PBGC interest rate for January 1 of the plan year. On March 1, 1995, and effective on July 1, 1995, the plan was amended to provide that all single-sum distributions are calculated using the applicable mortality table and the annual interest rate on 30-year Treasury securities for August of the year before the plan year that contains the annuity starting date. The plan amendment provides that each distribution with an annuity starting date after June 30, 1995, and before July 1, 1996, is calculated using the 30-year Treasury rate for August of the year before the plan year that contains the annuity starting date, or the 30-year Treasury rate for November of the plan year preceding the plan year that contains the annuity starting date, whichever produces the larger benefit. [Treas. Reg. § 1.417(e)-1(d)(10)(vii), Ex. 5]

### Q 16:20   How does a plan change the time for determining the interest rate under Code Section 417(e)?

In general, a plan amendment that changes the time for determining the applicable interest rate (including an indirect change as a result of a change in plan year) will not be treated as reducing accrued benefits in violation of Code Section 411(d)(6) merely on account of this change if the plan amendment is effective on or after the adoption date. Any distribution for which the annuity starting date occurs in the one-year period beginning at the time the amendment is effective must be determined using the interest rate provided under the plan determined at either the date for determining the interest rate before the amendment or the date for determining the interest rate after the amendment, whichever results in the larger distribution. If the plan amendment is adopted retroactively (i.e., the amendment is effective before the adoption date), the plan must use the interest rate determination date resulting in the larger distribution for the period beginning with the effective date and ending one year after the adoption date; however, in limited circumstances this rule does not apply (see Q 16:19, Methods 1 and 2). [Treas. Reg. § 1.417(e)-1(d)(10)(ii)]

### Q 16:21   Can the plan provide for a gradual transition to the RPA '94 rules under Code Section 417(e)?

Yes. A plan amendment is not considered to reduce a participant's accrued benefit in violation of Code Section 411(d)(6) even if the plan amendment provides for temporary additional benefits to accommodate a more gradual transition from the plan's old interest rate to the new rules. [Treas. Reg. § 1.417(e)-1(d)(10)(ii)]

**Example.** The D&R Pension Plan is a calendar-year plan. As of December 7, 1994, the plan provided for single-sum distributions to be calculated using the PBGC interest rate as of the annuity starting date for distributions not greater than $25,000, and 120 percent of that interest rate (but not an interest rate producing a present value less than $25,000) for distributions over $25,000. D&R wants to delay the effective date of the RPA '94 rules for a year and to provide for an extended transition from the use of the PBGC interest rate to the new applicable interest rate under Code Section 417(e)(3). On December 1, 1995, and effective on January 1, 1996, D&R amends the plan to provide that single-sum distributions are determined as the sum of (1) the single-sum distribution calculated using the applicable mortality table and the annual interest rate on 30-year Treasury securities for the first full calendar month preceding the calendar month that contains the annuity starting date, and

(2) a transition amount. The transition amount is a transition percentage of the excess, if any, of the amount that the single-sum distribution would have been under the plan provisions in effect before this amendment over the amount of the single sum that is determined in (1) above. The transition percentages are 80 percent for 1996, decreasing to 60 percent for 1997, 40 percent for 1998, and 20 percent for 1999. The amendment also provides that the transition amount is zero for plan years beginning on or after January 1, 2000. [Treas. Reg. § 1.417(e)-1(10)(d)(vii), Ex. 4]

### Q 16:22  Can the plan administrator have discretion over when and how benefits are paid?

Generally no. A plan that permits the employer, either directly or indirectly, through the exercise of discretion, to deny a participant a particular form of benefit payment violates the provisions of Code Section 411(d)(6). [Treas. Reg. § 1.411(d)-4] A plan cannot provide a cash-out option to participants at the discretion of the plan administrator.

A plan can permit limited discretion with respect to the ministerial or mechanical administration of the plan, including the application of objective plan criteria specifically set forth in the plan. For example, Code Section 411(d)(6) is satisfied even if the plan provides administrative discretion with respect to the following:

1. *Timing.* Commencement of benefits as soon as administratively feasible;
2. *Objective criteria.* Authority to determine whether objective criteria (e.g., objective criteria used to determine whether an employee has a permanent and total disability) have been satisfied; and
3. *Guidelines.* Authority to determine, pursuant to specific guidelines set forth in the plan, whether a participant or spouse is dead or cannot be located.

[Treas. Reg. § 1.411(d)-4, Q&A 4]

### Q 16:23  Can an employer eliminate an optional form of benefit?

No. An optional form of benefit is a protected benefit under Code Section 411(d)(6). It cannot be eliminated by the employer. [Treas. Reg. § 1.411(d)-4, Q&A 2] A plan that provides three or more actuarially equivalent joint and survivor options can, however, be amended to eliminate options other than the options with the largest and smallest survivor payment percentages. [Treas. Reg. § 1.411(d)-4, Q&A 2(b)(2)(ii)] In addition, the Department of Treasury has issued proposed regulations at Section 1.411(d)-3 to allow for eliminating benefits that are redundant or burdensome. (See chapter 8 for more information regarding these proposed regulations.)

**Example.** JS Consulting Group Inc. maintains a plan that provides four different joint and survivor options. Under these optional forms, survivor benefits of 100 percent, 75 percent, 66⅔ percent, or 50 percent of the amount payable to the participant will be paid to the participant's surviving spouse. The options with 75 percent and 66⅔ percent survivor benefits can be eliminated without violating Code Section 411(d)(6).

## Time of Payment

### Q 16:24  Are there specific rules governing when payments can be distributed from a plan?

The Code contains rules governing when a participant's benefits under a qualified retirement plan can be distributed (see Q 16:25) and when they must be distributed (see Q 16:26). In certain situations, a participant's consent is required for benefits to begin. For required minimum distributions, however, a participant cannot delay the commencement of benefits (see Q 16:87).

### Q 16:25  When can an employee elect to receive benefits from the plan?

A plan must permit a participant to receive benefits at his or her earliest retirement age. *Earliest retirement age* is the earliest date on which the participant could elect to receive benefits under the plan. [I.R.C. § 417(f)(3); Treas. Reg. § 1.401(a)-20, Q&A 17(b)] Earliest retirement age is not necessarily the early retirement date specified in the plan. A participant may be entitled to receive a benefit on termination of employment or in the event of disability. The plan document and summary plan description will identify the earliest date benefits can be paid from the plan.

> **Example 1.** Evergreen Co. maintains a plan that permits a vested participant to receive benefits on separation from service, actuarially reduced to reflect payment before normal retirement date. Earliest retirement age is the date of separation from service.

> **Example 2.** Redwood Co. maintains a plan that provides benefits at normal retirement age (age 65) only. Ralph terminates employment at age 55 with 25 years of service. Ralph's earliest retirement age occurs when he attains age 65.

A participant who satisfies the service requirement for an early retirement benefit but separates from service before satisfying the age requirement can receive the early retirement benefit on attainment of early retirement age. [Treas. Reg. § 1.401(a)-14(c)]

> **Example 3.** Redwood Co. maintains a plan that provides benefits at normal retirement age (age 65) or when a participant has attained age 55 and completed 10 years of service. Ralph terminates employment after completing eight years of service. Earliest retirement age occurs when Ralph attains age 65. If Ralph had completed 10 years of service as of the date of termination, his earliest retirement age would be the date he attains age 55. [Treas. Reg. § 1.401(a)-20, Q&A 17(b)(4)]

## Q 16:26   When must benefits begin to be paid from a plan?

Unless a participant elects otherwise, he or she must begin to receive benefits from the plan within 60 days after the close of the plan year in which the *last* of the following occurs:

1. The participant attains age 65, or the plan's normal retirement age if it is earlier than age 65;

2. The 10th anniversary of the year in which the participant began plan participation; or

3. The participant terminates employment with the employer.

[I.R.C. § 401(a)(14); Treas. Reg. § 1.401(a)-14; ERISA § 206]

Most plans require a participant to file a claim for benefits before benefits will begin. If filing a claim for benefits is a prerequisite to receiving benefits, the plan can postpone benefit payment until a claim is made. [Treas. Reg. § 1.401(a)-14(a)]

If it is impossible to make a payment because the plan administrator has been unable to locate the participant after making reasonable efforts, payment, retroactive to the required date, must be made no later than 60 days after the participant is located. [Treas. Reg. § 1.401(a)-14(d)]

Whether or not all three triggering events have occurred and regardless of a participant's election to defer a distribution to a later date, benefits may have to begin when the participant reaches age 70½ (see Q 16:87).

## Q 16:27   What is an *annuity starting date*?

An *annuity starting date* is the first day of the first period for which an amount is payable as an annuity (regardless of when or whether payment is actually made), or in the case of benefits not payable in the form of an annuity, the date by which all events that entitle the participant to the benefit have occurred. [I.R.C. § 417(f)(2); Treas. Reg. § 1.401(a)-20, Q&A 10(b)(2)]

**Example.** The plan provides for retirement benefits to begin on the first day of the month following retirement. Alice attains age 65 on January 15, 2002, and retires on her birthday. Because of administrative delays, her first payment is not sent until April 1, 2002. Alice's annuity starting date is February 1, 2002, the first day of the month in which the payment was due and payable as an annuity. [Treas. Reg. § 1.401(a)-20, Q&A 10(b)(2)]

## Q 16:28   What is *normal retirement age*?

*Normal retirement age* is the date specified in the plan for benefits to begin. A plan cannot provide a normal retirement age later than the later of the date the participant attains age 65 or the fifth anniversary of the date the participant began plan participation. [I.R.C. § 411(a)(8)] A participant must be 100 percent vested at normal retirement age (see chapter 8).

### Q 16:29   What is the importance of the annuity starting date?

The annuity starting date is important in determining when notices must be provided to a participant. For example, a participant cannot waive a QJSA form of benefit (see Q 16:47) more than 90 days before his or her annuity starting date. A participant's spouse's consent to a waiver of the QJSA must also be obtained within 90 days of the annuity starting date. To provide the participant the opportunity to make these elections, the plan must provide information to a participant within the same time period.

If the participant is married as of the annuity starting date, the QJSA is the normal form of benefit and the participant's spouse as of the annuity starting date is the party who will receive benefits after the participant's death under the QJSA unless an alternate beneficiary is properly designated.

### Q 16:30   Can the QJSA notice be provided after the annuity starting date?

Yes. Code Section 417(a)(7)(A) provides that the notice and explanation of the QJSA may be provided after the annuity starting date as long as the participant is given at least 30 days after the explanation is provided to waive the QJSA form of benefit. The first date of actual payment is substituted for the annuity starting date in applying the timing rules for notice and consent. This date is called a "retroactive annuity starting date."

Spousal consent would also be required even if the QJSA is the form of payment elected by the participant if the survivor portion of the annuity is less than the minimum permissible survivor annuity (i.e., less than 50 percent) under a QJSA that has an annuity starting date after the date the explanation is provided. [Treas. Reg. § 1.417(e)-1(b)(3)(v)(A)]

### Q 16:31   Can all defined benefit plans provide for a retroactive annuity starting date?

Yes. The IRS issued proposed regulations (effective for plan years beginning on or after January 1, 2002) that allow a plan document to provide for a retroactive annuity starting date, but only if the participant elects to use the retroactive annuity starting date. The final regulations are effective for all plan years beginning on or after January 1, 2004.

The regulations do not require plans to provide for a retroactive annuity starting date. Instead, plans can continue to stipulate that the QJSA explanation is to be provided before the annuity starting date under the rules of Code Section 417(a) without regard to Code Section 417(a)(7)(A). In addition, if a plan is amended to provide for a retroactive annuity starting date, the plan can impose additional restrictions on availability not imposed under the regulations, provided that the additional restrictions do not violate any of the rules applicable to qualified plans. For example, plans that generally provide benefit options that include annuities and lump-sum payments can provide that retroactive annuity starting dates are available only for participants who elect annuities. [Treas. Reg. § 1.417(e)-1(b)(3)(iv)(A)]

### Q 16:32 How does a retroactive annuity starting date affect a participant's payments?

The election under the regulations place the participant in approximately the same situation in which he or she would have been had benefit payments actually commenced on the retroactive annuity starting date. Therefore, the future periodic payments for a participant who elects a retroactive annuity starting date must be the same as the periodic payments that would have been paid to the participant had payments actually begun on the retroactive annuity starting date, and the participant must also receive a make-up amount to reflect the missed payments (with an appropriate adjustment for interest from the date the payments would have been made to the date of actual payment).

In addition, because the purpose of a retroactive annuity starting date is to place the participant in approximately the same situation that he or she would have been in had benefits commenced on the retroactive date, the retroactive benefit payments are required to be based upon the terms of the plan in effect as of the retroactive annuity starting date (taking into account plan amendments executed after the retroactive annuity starting date but made effective on or before that date). Accordingly, the retroactive annuity starting date cannot be earlier than the date the participant could have started receiving benefits if the payments had commenced at the earliest date permitted under the terms of the plan (e.g., the retroactive annuity starting date cannot be before the earlier of the date of the participant's termination of employment or attainment of normal retirement age), and the amount of the benefit must satisfy Code Sections 415 and 417 as of the retroactive annuity starting date.

[Treas. Reg. § 1.417(e)-1(b)(3)(iv)(B)]

### Q 16:33 Are there any additional limitations imposed on the amount of benefit that can be paid when there is a retroactive annuity starting date?

Yes. The regulations have an additional limit on the permissible amount of the distribution under Code Sections 417(e)(3) (if applicable) and 415. The present value of the distribution (including determining the applicable interest rate and the applicable mortality table) will have to be determined as of the date of distribution to satisfy Code Section 417(e)(3), and the amount of the benefit cannot exceed the Section 415 limitation, also as of the date of actual distribution. [Treas. Reg. § 1.417(e)-1(b)(3)(v)(B)]

### Q 16:34 Can a participant elect to defer benefits until a later date?

It depends on the plan. Many plans permit a terminated vested participant who is eligible to receive early retirement benefits to defer payment until his or her normal retirement age. Many participants choose this option if there is a significant benefit reduction for early payment or if there is no current need for income. Some plans permit a former employee who has attained normal retirement age to defer benefits until a later date. Deferral beyond normal retirement age, for an inactive employee, rarely makes economic sense.

### Q 16:35    When can a terminated vested employee elect to receive retirement benefits?

If the plan permits benefits to begin after a participant reaches an early retirement age specified in the plan, a participant who terminates service at an earlier age must be permitted to elect commencement of benefits on attainment of the specified early retirement age, but the benefit can be actuarially reduced for commencement before the normal retirement age specified in the plan. [Treas. Reg. § 1.401(a)-14(c)]

### Q 16:36    How are benefits adjusted for early retirement?

Most plans contain an actuarial adjustment that reduces the monthly retirement payment to take into account the longer period of time that benefits are likely to be payable. The early retirement adjustment factor is often 5 percent per year for each year payment precedes normal retirement.

**Example.** Acme Products offers early retirement at age 50 with 25 years of service. Doris, who has been with the company for 25 years, is considering early retirement. Her monthly accrued benefit at age 65 is $1,000. The plan document specifies that benefits will be reduced 5 percent for each year benefits begin before age 65. If Doris retires at age 50, her benefit will be reduced by 75 percent (5% × 15 years). She would be entitled to a benefit of $250 per month if she elected to receive benefits beginning at age 50.

### Q 16:37    What is an *early retirement subsidy*?

An *early retirement subsidy* is a benefit payable at an earlier retirement date whose value is greater than the actuarial equivalent of the normal retirement benefit. Subject to nondiscrimination rules under Code Section 401(a)(4), employees who work until a plan's early retirement age may receive a subsidized early retirement benefit that need not be available to employees who terminate before the plan's early retirement age. A subsidized early retirement benefit may be the same as the retirement benefit payable at normal retirement age, or it may be somewhat less than the normal retirement benefit, but not as low as the normal retirement benefit reduced to an actuarially equivalent benefit. Many employers offer early retirement subsidies to encourage employees to retire early.

**Example.** The facts are the same as those in the example in Q 16:36 except that Acme Products is offering an early retirement window for employees whose age plus years of service equals at least 75. Employees accepting the offer and retiring during the early retirement window will receive the same benefit they would receive if they retire at age 65, the plan's normal retirement age. If Doris decides to retire under this program, she would receive a subsidized benefit equal to $1,000 per month beginning at age 50, although the actuarial equivalent of her normal retirement benefit would be $250 per month.

### Q 16:38    Can benefits be paid while an employee is actively employed?

Generally, no. A pension plan cannot make in-service distributions unless it is terminating; however, a plan can provide for distributions to be made after the participant's normal retirement age or after attainment of age 62 (for plan years beginning after December 31, 2006), even if the participant is actively employed. [I.R.C. § 401(a)(36); Treas. Reg. § 1.401-1(b)(1)(i); Rev. Rul. 71-24, 1971-1 C.B. 114] In-service distributions, however, cannot be made at early retirement date.

### Q 16:39    Can a participant receive benefits from a defined benefit plan in the event of hardship?

No. In-service distributions for hardship are not permitted in a defined benefit pension plan (see Q 16:38).

### Q 16:40    Are there instances when an employee can be involuntarily cashed out?

Yes. If the value of a participant's benefit is $5,000 or less, the plan can provide for a cash-out of the value of the participant's benefit without the participant's consent. (See Q 16:10 for discussion of the rules for calculating the present value of a participant's benefit.) If the present value of a participant's vested accrued benefit exceeds $5,000, the plan must obtain the participant's written consent to distribute any part of the benefit before the later of the date the participant attains age 62 or normal retirement age. [I.R.C. § 411(a)(11)(A); Treas. Reg. § 1.411(a)-11(c)(4)]

### Q 16:41    Are there instances when a participant cannot receive retirement benefits in the form of a lump sum even though the participant may otherwise be eligible to receive a lump-sum payment?

Yes. There are two separate limits, one based on minimum-funding requirements (see Q 16:42) and another that is part of the nondiscrimination regulations (see Q 16:43).

### Q 16:42    What are the distribution limitations if certain minimum-funding requirements are not met?

Under new rules created by the PPA, there are restrictions applicable to benefits if a plan does not meet certain funding guidelines. If the adjusted funding target attainment percentage (adjusted FTAP; see chapter 19 for the definition of FTAP) is more than 60 percent but less than 80 percent, the plan may only make a prohibited payment of the lesser of 50 percent of the present value of the total benefit or the amount of the PBGC guaranteed benefit. In addition, the participant may only receive one such payment during consecutive years while this restriction is in effect. [I.R.C. § 436(d)(3)]

If the plan sponsor is in bankruptcy or if the plan has an adjusted FTAP of less than 60 percent, the plan may not make prohibited payments. It appears this applies to all plans, including one-participant plans. [I.R.C. § 436(d)] In addition, unpredictable contingent event benefits (UCEBs) may not be paid either. [I.R.C. § 436(b)] Benefit accruals must also cease as of the beginning of the plan year in which the adjusted FTAP is less than 60 percent, unless there is an additional contribution sufficient to make the adjusted FTAP at least 60 percent. [I.R.C. § 436(e)] After a benefit accrual restriction is removed due to an improved funding status, the plan does not need to provide the missed accruals. [I.R.C. § 436(i)]

If a plan was subject to a restriction in the prior plan year, the plan will remain restricted in the current plan year until the actuary certifies to the current adjusted FTAP. If the actuary has not certified to the current FTAP by the first day of the 10th month of the current plan year, the plan will remain restricted through the end of that plan year. Even if a plan was not restricted from making benefit payments in the prior plan year, but was within 10 percentage points of being restricted, and if the actuary has not certified by the first day of the fourth month of the current plan year, the plan will be considered restricted until the actuary certifies otherwise. The actuary has up until the first day of the 10th month to make this certification, otherwise the plan will remain restricted until the end of that plan year. [I.R.C. § 436(h)]

A *prohibited payment* is a benefit payment whose value is (1) in excess of the monthly amount of a straight-life-only annuity, (2) the amount of the payment to purchase an irrevocable commitment from an insurer, or (3) anything else determined by the Treasury. [I.R.C. § 436(d)(5)]

Restrictions on benefit payments do not apply during the first five years of a plan. [I.R.C. § 436(g)]

Participants must be given a notice within 30 days of when a benefit becomes restricted. There is a monetary sanction under ERISA Section 502(c)(4) for failure to provide the notice. [ERISA § 101(j)]

### Q 16:43    What are the distribution limitations if certain nondiscrimination requirements are not met?

The nondiscrimination regulations limit the amount that can be distributed to certain highly compensated employees if a plan does not meet certain funding levels. A payment in excess of the single-life annuity amount cannot be made to any of the 25 highest paid employees unless, after the distribution is made, the value of plan assets is at least 110 percent of current liabilities as defined in Code Section 412(l)(7). If these restrictions apply, the maximum amount that can be paid equals the payment that would be made to the employee under a single-life annuity that is the actuarial equivalent of all of the employee's benefits under the plan. [Treas. Reg. § 1.401(a)(4)-5(b)(3)]

There is some leeway in calculating the current liability for this purpose. It does not have to use the same interest rate as is used for minimum-funding purposes for the year. Any reasonable and consistent method may be used for determining the value of the current liabilities and the value of plan assets. The IRS has interpreted the consistency requirement to mean that the current liability must be calculated on a consistent basis within the plan year for any lump-sum distributions during the plan year. The methodology for the calculation of the current liability may be changed from year to year. [2005 Grey Book, Q&A 32]

Exceptions to the restriction on distribution are available if the value of the benefit payable to the restricted employee is negligible or if adequate security is established (called an *escrow account*) for repayment of the restricted amounts in case the plan is terminated with insufficient assets. [Rev. Rul. 92-76, 1992-2 C.B. 76] Rollovers of the restricted amounts to IRAs have been permitted when a pledge or bond secured repayment of the restricted amount. [Ltr. Rul. 9631031] Rollovers of the restricted amounts to IRAs have also been permitted if there was an agreement to transfer into the IRA amounts from other retirement plans of the participant in order to satisfy the requirement that there be at least 125 percent of the restricted amount in the account. [Ltr. Rul. 200606051]

The IRS has ruled that, in the case of a multiple employer plan, the 25 highest paid employees are determined based on each participating employer on an individual basis. However, if the plan assets are available to pay benefits of all participants, then the determination of the current liability is based on all plan assets. [Ltr. Rul. 200449043]

### Q 16:44    How is the security in an escrow account determined?

Under Revenue Ruling 92-76 [1992-2 C.B. 76], if a restricted employee receives a lump-sum distribution, he or she must enter into an agreement to secure the repayment obligation with property having a fair market value of at least 125 percent of the restricted amount. This restricted amount is redetermined each year. The nonrestricted limit is equal to the payments that could have been made to the employee, commencing when distribution commenced to the employee, had the employee received payments in the annuity form. An accumulated amount is determined as the amount of a payment increased by a reasonable amount of interest from the date the payment was made (or would have been made) until the date for determination of the restricted amount. The restricted amount is then the total paid, less the amount that could have been paid in the form of an annuity.

**Example.** John, a restricted employee, has an accrued benefit in the form of a straight-life annuity of $2,000 per month. His lump-sum distribution has a value of $283,059, using GATT rates (5 percent) and mortality. The following table shows the restricted amounts:

| Year | Unrestricted Amount | Unrestricted Amount with Interest | Total | Restricted Amount |
|------|------|------|------|------|
| 1 | $ 24,000 | $ 24,600 | $ 283,059.00 | $ 258,459 |
| 2 | $ 48,000 | $ 50,430 | $ 297,212.00 | $ 246,782 |
| 3 | $ 72,000 | $ 77,552 | $ 312,073.00 | $ 234,521 |
| 4 | $ 96,000 | $ 106,030 | $ 327,677.00 | $ 221,647 |
| 5 | $ 120,000 | $ 135,932 | $ 344,061.00 | $ 208,129 |
| 6 | $ 144,000 | $ 167,329 | $ 361,264.00 | $ 193,935 |
| 7 | $ 168,000 | $ 200,295 | $ 379,327.00 | $ 179,032 |
| 8 | $ 192,000 | $ 234,910 | $ 398,293.00 | $ 163,383 |
| 9 | $ 216,000 | $ 271,256 | $ 418,208.00 | $ 146,952 |
| 10 | $ 240,000 | $ 309,419 | $ 439,118.00 | $ 129,699 |
| 11 | $ 264,000 | $ 349,490 | $ 461,074.00 | $ 111,584 |
| 12 | $ 288,000 | $ 391,565 | $ 484,128.00 | $ 92,563 |
| 13 | $ 312,000 | $ 435,743 | $ 508,334.00 | $ 72,591 |
| 14 | $ 336,000 | $ 482,130 | $ 533,751.00 | $ 51,621 |
| 15 | $ 360,000 | $ 530,837 | $ 560,439.00 | $ 29,602 |
| 16 | $ 384,000 | $ 581,979 | $ 588,461.00 | $ 6,482 |
| 17 | $ 408,000 | $ 635,678 | $ 617,884.00 | — |
| 18 | $ 432,000 | $ 692,062 | $ 648,778.00 | — |
| 19 | $ 456,000 | $ 751,265 | $ 681,217.00 | — |
| 20 | $ 480,000 | $ 813,428 | $ 715,278.00 | — |

For John, 125 percent of the restricted amount must remain in the account as security to repay the plan if needed upon plan termination. Any amounts above that 125 percent value may be distributed to John.

### Q 16:45   Can a distribution be paid from a restricted participant's account to satisfy a QDRO?

No. If a participant is subject to the distribution restrictions of Treasury Regulations Section 1.401(a)(4)-5, then payments may not be made to satisfy a QDRO unless there is compliance with the full requirements of the regulation. [1995 Grey Book, Q&A 45]

## QJSA Rules

### Q 16:46    Does a participant's spouse have any right to benefits under a defined benefit pension plan?

Generally, yes. When a married participant reaches his or her annuity starting date (see Q 16:27), benefits must be paid in the form of a QJSA (see Q 16:47). This form of benefit payment provides a survivor annuity to a surviving spouse after the participant's death. The QJSA can be waived and an alternate form of benefit payment can be selected by the participant only with the consent of the participant's spouse (see Q 16:59).

Some plans require a participant to be married for one year for the participant's spouse to gain these rights. A plan is not required to treat a participant as married unless the participant and the participant's spouse have been married throughout the one-year period ending on the participant's annuity starting date. If the one-year marriage convention is used, however, a few unusual rules apply. A participant and the participant's spouse must be treated as married throughout the one-year period ending on the participant's annuity starting date, even though they are married to each other for less than one year before the annuity starting date, if they remain married to each other for at least one year. If a plan adopts the one-year marriage convention, the plan must treat the participant and spouse who are married on the annuity starting date as married and must provide benefits that are to begin on the annuity starting date in the form of a QJSA unless the participant (with spousal consent) elects another form of benefit. No additional elections are required when the one-year period is satisfied. If the participant and the spouse have not remained married for at least one year, the plan can treat the participant as having not been married on the annuity starting date. Although survivor benefits are lost, no retroactive correction of the amount paid to the participant is required.

**Example.** Couples Corporation maintains a plan that requires a participant to be married for one year before the participant's spouse is treated as the spouse under the plan, and as such is afforded the protection of the QJSA rules. Jack and Jill married six months before Jack's annuity starting date. Couples Corporation's pension plan must treat Jack as married and must begin payments to Jack in the form of a QJSA unless Jack elects another form of benefit with Jill's consent. If Jack and Jill are divorced before they have been married for one year, Jill will lose her survivor rights under the annuity. If Jack and Jill stay married and Jack dies within the one-year period, the plan will treat Jack as unmarried and Jill will lose the survivor benefits that would have been payable to her. [Treas. Reg. § 1.401(a)-20(b), Q&A 25(b)]

### Q 16:47    What is a *qualified joint and survivor annuity*?

Defined benefit plans must provide for survivor annuities for spouses of plan participants. [I.R.C. § 401(a)(11)(B)(i); Treas. Reg. § 1.401(a)-20, Q&A 3(a)]

If a participant dies and is survived by a spouse, benefits continue (usually at a reduced amount) to the participant's spouse. The payment to the spouse is referred to as a *survivor annuity*.

A *qualified joint and survivor annuity* is a form of annuity under which payments are made over the participant's lifetime and, after the participant's death, payments continue to the participant's spouse over his or her lifetime. [I.R.C. §§ 401(a)(11)(A)(i), 417(b)] The surviving spouse's payments from a QJSA cannot be less than 50 percent of, and not more than 100 percent of, the amount of the payments to the participant while both spouses were alive. [I.R.C. § 417(b)(1)] In addition, the PPA added another QJSA option, called a qualified optional survivor annuity (QOSA). This provides that if the QJSA is less than 75 percent, then the QOSA needs to be 75 percent. If the QJSA is greater than or equal to 75 percent, then the QOSA is 50 percent. The QOSA is actuarially equivalent to a straight-life annuity for a single participant. This is effective for plan years beginning after December 31, 2007. [I.R.C. § 417(g)]

> **Example 1.** Fred has retired and elected a 50 percent QJSA. Under the QJSA, Fred will receive $400 per month for his life. If Fred's wife, Wilma, is still living after Fred's death, she will receive $200 (50 percent of $400) for her life. If Wilma dies before Fred, Fred's monthly benefit will not change.

> **Example 2.** The facts are the same as in Example 1, but this distribution is occurring in the 2008 plan year. Therefore, since the QJSA under the plan is a 50 percent JSA, then the QOSA is required to be a 75 percent JSA. Fred will need to choose between a 50 percent JSA and a 75 percent JSA, both of which may be actuarially equivalent to the normal form of payment under the plan.

An unmarried participant who retires must receive his or her benefit in the form of a single-life annuity, also called a QJSA. In this instance, annuity payments are made over the participant's lifetime and stop at the participant's death. [Treas. Reg. § 1.401(a)-20, Q&A 25(a)]

The QJSA must be the actuarial equivalent of a single-life annuity for the life of the participant. [I.R.C. § 417(b)(2)] By definition, the QJSA must be at least as valuable as any other optional form of benefit payable at the same time. [Treas. Reg. § 1.401(a)-20, Q&A16] However, use of the Code Section 417(e)(3) actuarial assumptions can cause the value of a lump-sum distribution to exceed the actuarial present value of a QJSA, especially when the participants are younger. Accordingly, regulations for this section have been issued modifying this requirement to provide that a plan will not fail to satisfy this requirement merely because the amount payable under an optional form of benefit that is subject to Code Section 417(e)(3) is calculated using the applicable interest rate and applicable mortality table under Code Section 417(e)(3). [Treas. Reg. § 1.401(a)-20, Q&A 16] Plans can have multiple JSAs and designate the most valuable as the QJSA.

Unless a participant elects otherwise, and the participant's spouse consents to the election, retirement benefits will be paid in the form of a QJSA.

### Q 16:48   Can a plan pay benefits in the form of a QJSA without the participant's consent?

Generally, no. Plans cannot begin benefit payments without the participant's consent. If, however, the participant receives notice of the QJSA and other distribution options no less than 30 days nor more than 90 days (180 days for annuity starting dates after December 31, 2006) before the annuity starting date (or retroactive starting date; see Q 16:30), a QJSA can be distributed without the participant's consent after the participant reaches the later of normal retirement age or age 62. [Treas. Reg. §§ 1.417(e)-1(b), 1.411(a)-11(c)(2)]

The consent of the participant's spouse is not required for a benefit payable in the form of a QJSA. Consent is required for payment in any form other than a QJSA unless the present value of the QJSA is *de minimis* (see Q 16:57).

### Q 16:49   Is a QJSA payable only at normal retirement age?

No. A QJSA is payable when the participant attains the earliest retirement age under the plan (see Q 16:25). [Treas. Reg. § 1.401(a)-20, Q&A 17] If the plan allows the participant to elect to receive the present value of his or her accrued benefit in a lump sum on termination of employment, the plan cannot give a participant the option of an immediate lump-sum distribution or a JSA payable at normal retirement age. If a plan provides an immediate lump-sum option, an immediate QJSA option must be available.

**Example.** Thomas, whose age is 45, has terminated employment. The plan cannot offer him a choice only between a single-sum distribution at termination of employment and a JSA that satisfies all of the requirements of a QJSA except that it begins at normal retirement rather than at termination of employment. If the plan offers an immediate single-sum payment, it must also offer an immediate QJSA. Thomas could elect to have annuity payments begin (albeit at a significantly lower amount) at age 45.

[Treas. Reg. § 1.417(e)-1(b)(1)]

### Q 16:50   What information must be provided to a participant regarding the QJSA?

The plan must provide the participant a written explanation of the following:

1. The terms and conditions of the QJSA;
2. The participant's right to make, and the effect of, an election to waive the QJSA;
3. The rights of the participant's spouse to consent or not to consent to a waiver of a QJSA; and
4. The right and the effect of revocation of an election to waive a QJSA.

[I.R.C. § 417(a)(3)(A); ERISA § 205(c)(3)(A)]

The participant must also receive a general description of the eligibility conditions and other material features of the optional forms of benefit and sufficient additional information to explain the relative values of the optional forms of benefit available under the plan. [Treas. Reg. § 1.401(a)-20, Q&A 36] The regulations suggest various means of satisfying the information requirements for describing the relative financial effect of various optional forms of benefit payment. The notice should include the dollar amount of the annuity under the available options or an illustration of the percentage reduction from the straight-life annuity. The participant must be informed that additional information can be obtained regarding benefit options. [Treas. Reg. § 1.401(a)-11(c)(3)(ii)]

### Q 16:51   What information must be provided to a participant to explain optional forms of benefits?

Each defined benefit plan must provide to eligible participants an explanation with respect to each of the optional forms of benefit presently available to the participant (i.e., optional forms of benefit for which the QJSA explanation applies that have an annuity starting date after the providing of the QJSA explanation and optional forms of benefit with retroactive annuity starting dates that are available with payments commencing at that same time) describing (1) all available optional benefit forms, (2) eligibility conditions, (3) the financial effect of electing or not electing the QJSA form (i.e., the amounts and timing of payments to the participant under the form of benefit during the participant's lifetime, and the amounts and timing of payments after the death of the participant), (4) the relative value of the optional form compared to the value of the QJSA, and (5) other material features. Generally, plans have met this requirement under existing rules by describing only a form of payment and the amount of each payment. [Treas. Reg. § 1.417(a)(3)-1(c)(1)]

### Q 16:52   How is the comparison of the relative value of optional forms to the value of the QJSA to be disclosed?

The description of the relative value of an optional form of benefit compared to the value of the QJSA must be expressed to the participant in a manner that provides a meaningful comparison of the relative economic values of the two forms of benefit without the participant's having to make calculations using interest or mortality assumptions. Thus, in performing the calculations necessary to make this comparison, the benefits under one or both optional forms of benefit must be converted, taking into account the time value of money and life expectancies, so that the values of both optional forms of benefit are expressed in the same form. Treasury Regulations Section 1.417(a)(3)-1, finalized in late 2003, clarifies what information needs to be disclosed with respect to the financial effect of choosing among available distribution forms and imposed a requirement to disclose the relative value of optional forms. These regulations were originally to be effective for distributions with annuity starting dates after September 2004. However, in IRS Announcement 2004-58 [2004-29 I.R.B. 66], the IRS has extended the effective date for these new disclosure requirements to February 2006. Importantly, this extension is not applicable to distributions if

(1) they are subject to the requirements of Code Section 417(e)(3) (like lump sums), and (2) their actuarial present value is less than the actuarial present value of the plan's QJSA. In effect, the extension will not be applicable to distributions where subsidized annuity options are available, but the lump sum is based on the normal form of benefit. In addition, Treasury Regulations Section 1.417(a)(3)-1 includes a special rule that would enable a plan to use the delayed effective date rule even if there are minor differences between (1) the value of an optional form and (2) the value of the QJSA for a married participant, where those minor differences are caused by the calculation of the amount of the optional form of benefit based on the life annuity, rather than on the QJSA. [Treas. Reg. § 1.417(a)(3)-1(f)] The IRS has announced, however, that a reasonable, good-faith effort to comply with the final regulations is acceptable for QJSA explanations subject to the February 2006 extension if the explanations are provided before January 1, 2007.

The regulations permit plans to use either the QJSA for married participants or the QJSA for unmarried participants (i.e., a single-life annuity) as the uniform basis for comparing relative values for all plan participants, regardless of their marital status. Such a comparison may be expressed to the participant using any of the following techniques:

1. Expressing the actuarial present value of the optional form of benefit as a percentage or factor of the actuarial present value of the QJSA;
2. Stating the amount of the annuity that is the actuarial equivalent of the optional form of benefit and that is payable at the same time and under the same conditions as the QJSA; or
3. Stating the actuarial present value of both the optional form of benefit and the QJSA.

[Treas. Reg. § 1.417(a)(3)-1(c)(2)(i)]

When providing a numerical comparison, the following rules apply:

1. Any comparison of the value of the optional form subject to Code Section 417(e)(3) (e.g., a lump sum) to the QJSA must be made using the applicable mortality table and the applicable interest rate (see Q 16:10). All other optional forms must be compared using a single set of interest rates and mortality tables that are reasonable and applied uniformly. For this purpose, the reasonableness of interest and mortality assumptions is determined without regard to the circumstances of the individual participant. In addition, the applicable mortality table and the applicable interest rate as defined in Code Section 417(e) are considered reasonable actuarial assumptions for this purpose and are permitted (but not required) to be used.
2. The notice is required to explain that the relative value comparison is intended to allow the participant to compare the total value of distributions paid in different forms, that the relative value comparison is made by converting the value of optional forms currently available to a common form (such as the QJSA or lump sum), and that this conversion uses interest and life expectancy assumptions.

3. The interest rate used to develop any numerical comparison must be disclosed. In addition, there must be a general statement that all numerical comparisons are based on average life expectancies and that the relative value of payments ultimately made under the annuity optional form will depend on actual longevity.

4. The explanation must be written in a manner to be understood by the average plan participant. It is suggested that the plan may want to add further explanation of the effects of ill health or other factors influencing expected longevity on the desirability of electing annuity forms of distribution.

5. The explanations must be provided in writing by first-class mail or hand delivery. Posting is not an acceptable means of delivery.

[Treas. Reg. § 1.417(a)(3)-1(c)(2)(iii) & (iv)]

**Example.** Tina is a participant in the Going Batty Defined Benefit Plan. Under the plan, the QJSA is a joint and 100 percent survivor annuity, which is actuarially equivalent to the single-life annuity determined using 6 percent interest and the Code Section 417(e)(3) applicable mortality table that applies as of January 1, 1995. On January 1, 2005, Tina will terminate employment at age 55. When Tina terminates employment, she will be eligible to elect an unreduced early retirement benefit, payable as either a life annuity or the QJSA. Tina will also be eligible to elect a single-sum distribution equal to the actuarial present value of the single-life annuity payable at normal retirement age (age 65), determined using the applicable mortality table and the applicable interest rate under Code Section 417(e)(3) (5.5 percent).

Tina is provided with a QJSA explanation that describes the single-life annuity, the QJSA, and single-sum distribution option under the plan, and any eligibility conditions associated with these options. The explanation indicates that, if Tina commenced benefits at age 55 and had a spouse age 55, the monthly benefit under an immediately commencing single-life annuity is $3,000, the monthly benefit under the QJSA is estimated to be 89.96 percent of the monthly benefit under the immediately commencing single-life annuity, or $2,699, and the single sum is estimated to be 74.7645 times the monthly benefit under the immediately commencing single-life annuity, or $224,293.

The QJSA explanation indicates that the single-life annuity and the QJSA are of approximately the same value, but that the single-sum option is equivalent in value to a QJSA of $1,215. (This amount is 45 percent of the value of the QJSA at age 55 ($1,215 ÷ (89.96% × $3,000) = 45%).) The explanation states that the relative value comparison converts the value of the single-life annuity and the single-sum options to the value of each if paid in the form of the QJSA and that this conversion uses interest and life expectancy assumptions. The explanation specifies that the calculations relating to the single-sum distribution were prepared using 5.5 percent interest and average life expectancy, that the other calculations were prepared using a 6 percent interest rate, and that the relative value of actual annuity payments for an individual can vary depending on how long the individual and spouse live. The explanation notes that the calculation of the QJSA assumed that the spouse was age 55, that the amount of the QJSA will depend on the actual age of the spouse (for example, annuity payments will be significantly lower if the spouse is significantly younger than the participant), and that the amount of the single-sum payment will depend on the interest rates that apply when the participant actually takes a distribution. The explanation also includes an offer to provide a more precise calculation to the participant, taking into account the spouse's actual age.

Tina requests a more precise calculation of the financial effect of choosing a QJSA, taking into account the actual age of her spouse. Based on the fact that Tina's spouse is age 50, the plan determines that the monthly payments under the QJSA are 87.62 percent of the monthly payments under the single-life annuity, or $2,628.60 per month, and provides this information to her. The plan is not required to provide an updated calculation of the relative value of the single sum because the value of single sum continues to be 45 percent of the value of the QJSA.

### Q 16:53    Are there ways of simplifying the information that must be provided?

Yes. There are three ways this disclosure may be simplified:

1. Through the use of estimates, as long as the notice clearly indicates that the numerical comparisons are estimates and the participant has the right to request a more precise calculation;
2. By using banding; and
3. By using generally applicable information.

Estimates may be used for purposes of providing a description of the relative value of an optional form of benefit compared to the value of the QJSA (and also for purposes of comparing the financial effect of the distribution forms available to a participant) based on data as of an earlier date than the annuity starting date, an estimate of the spouse's age, or an estimated applicable interest rate under Code Section 417(e)(3). If estimates are used, the participant has a right to a more precise calculation upon request. [Treas. Reg. § 1.417(a)(3)-1(c)(3)]

Another way to simplify this disclosure is by using a banding rule under which two or more optional forms of benefit that have approximately the same value could be grouped for purposes of disclosing relative value. Under Treasury regulations, two or more optional forms of benefit would be treated as having approximately the same value if they vary in relative value in comparison to the value of the QJSA by five percentage points or less when the relative value comparison is made by expressing the actuarial present value of each of those optional forms of benefit as a percentage of the actuarial present value of the QJSA. For such a group of optional forms of benefit, the requirement relating to disclosing the relative value of each compared to the value of the QJSA could be satisfied by disclosing the relative value of any one of the optional forms in the group compared to the value of the QJSA, and disclosing that the other optional forms of benefit in the group are of approximately the same value. If a single-sum distribution is included in such a group of optional forms of benefit, the single-sum distribution must be the distribution form that is used for purposes of this comparison.

Under the proposed regulations, there were two other special grouping rules. The final regulations repeal these rules effective December 31, 2006. Under the first rule, the relative value of all optional forms of benefit that have an actuarial present value that is at least 95 percent of the actuarial present value of the QJSA may be described by stating that those optional forms of benefit are of approximately equal value to the value of the QJSA. Under the second rule, any optional form with a present value of at least 95 percent, but not more than 102.5 percent, of the present value of a single-life annuity can be described as approximately equal to the value of a single-life annuity. The final regulations apply a different grouping rule. Beginning January 1, 2007, plan sponsors may describe all optional forms of benefit whose actuarial present value falls between 95 percent and 105 percent of the current actuarial value of the benchmark QJSA or single-life annuity as approximately equal in value.

Thus, these rules would permit a plan that provides no subsidized forms of benefit to state the comparison of relative values simply by stating that all distribution forms are approximately equal in value to the QJSA. If, under the banding rule, two or more optional forms of benefit are grouped, a representative relative value for all of the grouped options could be used as the approximate relative value for all of the grouped options, in lieu of using the relative value of one of the optional forms of benefit in the group. [Treas. Reg. § 1.417(a)(3)-1(c)(2)(iii)]

If the actuarial assumptions used in calculating the estimates are not provided in the notice, then this information must be made available upon request.

The regulations also permit the disclosure of the financial effect and relative value of optional forms of benefit to be made in the form of generally applicable information rather than information specific to the participant, provided that information specific to the participant regarding the optional form of benefit is furnished at the participant's request. In lieu of providing a QJSA explanation that describes each optional form available to the participant, the generalized QJSA explanation would need to reflect only the generally available optional forms of benefits, along with a reference to where to find the information for any other optional forms of benefits (such as optional forms from prior benefit structures for limited groups of employees) available to the participant. In addition, the generalized QJSA explanation may include a chart or other comparable device showing a series of examples of financial effects and relative value comparisons for hypothetical participants. The examples in the chart should reflect a representative range of ages for the hypothetical participants and use reasonable assumptions for the age of the hypothetical participant's spouse and any other variable that affects the financial effect, or relative value, of the optional form of benefit. Reasonable estimates are permitted only if the plan follows the requirements for using reasonable estimates as provided under the participant-specific method. [Treas. Reg. § 1.417(a)(3)-1(d)(2)(ii)] The chart must be accompanied by a general statement describing the effect of significant variations between the assumed ages or other variables on the financial effect of electing the optional form of benefit and the comparison of the relative value of the optional form of benefit to the value of the QJSA. A generalized QJSA explanation that includes a chart must also include the amount payable to the participant under the normal form of benefit, either at normal retirement age or payable immediately. A generalized QJSA explanation may also contain items of participant-specific information in place of the corresponding generally applicable information. [Treas. Reg. § 1.417(a)(3)-1(d)(5)] In addition, the chart must be accompanied by a statement that includes an offer to provide, upon the participant's request, a statement of financial effect along with a comparison of relative values that is specific to the participant for one or more available optional forms of benefit, and a description of how a participant may obtain this additional information. Thus, with respect to those optional forms of benefit for which additional information is requested, the participant must receive a QJSA explanation specific to the participant that is based on the participant's actual age and benefit. [Treas. Reg. § 1.417(a)(3)-1(d)(2)]

> **Example.** The facts are the same as in the example in Q 16:52, except that under the Going Batty Defined Benefit Plan, the single-sum distribution is determined as the actuarial present value of the immediately commencing single-life annuity. In addition, the plan provides a joint and 75 percent survivor annuity that is reduced from the single-life annuity, and that is the QJSA under the plan. For purposes of determining the amount of the QJSA, the reduction is only half of the reduction that would normally apply under the actuarial assumptions specified in the plan for determining actuarial equivalence of optional forms.
>
> In lieu of providing information specific to Tina in the QJSA notice, the plan satisfies the QJSA explanation requirement by providing Tina with a statement that her monthly benefit under an immediately commencing single-life annuity (which is the normal form of benefit under the plan, adjusted for immediate commencement) is $3,000, along with the following chart showing the financial effect and the relative value of the optional forms of benefit compared to the QJSA for a hypothetical participant with a $1,000 benefit and a spouse who is three years younger than the participant. For each optional form generally available under the plan, the chart shows the financial effect and the relative value, using grouping rules. Separate charts are provided for ages 55, 60, and 65.

### Age 55 Commencement

| Optional Form | Amount of Distribution per $1,000 of Immediate Single-Life Annuity | Relative Value |
|---|---|---|
| Life Annuity | $1,000 per month | Approximately the same value as the QJSA |
| QJSA (Joint and 75% Survivor Annuity) | $956 per month | N/A |
| Joint and 100% Survivor Annuity | $886 per month | Approximately the same value as the QJSA |
| Lump Sum | $165,959 | Approximately the same value as the QJSA |

### Age 60 Commencement

| Optional Form | Amount of Distribution per $1,000 of Immediate Single-Life Annuity | Relative Value |
|---|---|---|
| Life Annuity | $1,000 per month | Approximately 94% of the value as the QJSA |
| QJSA (Joint and 75% Survivor Annuity) | $945 per month | N/A |
| Joint and 100% Survivor Annuity | $859 per month | Approximately 94% of the value as the QJSA |
| Lump Sum | $151,691 | Approximately the same value as the QJSA |

### Age 65 Commencement

| Optional Form | Amount of Distribution per $1,000 of Immediate Single-Life Annuity | Relative Value |
|---|---|---|
| Life Annuity | $1,000 per month | Approximately 93% of the value as the QJSA |
| QJSA (Joint and 75% Survivor Annuity) | $932 per month | N/A |

*Age 65 Commencement*

| Optional Form | Amount of Distribution per $1,000 of Immediate Single-Life Annuity | Relative Value |
|---|---|---|
| Joint and 100% Survivor Annuity | $ 828 per month | Approximately 93% of the value as the QJSA |
| Lump Sum | $ 135,759 | Approximately 93% of the value as the QJSA |

The chart disclosing the financial effect and relative value of the optional forms specifies that the calculations were prepared assuming that the spouse is three years younger than the participant, that the calculations relating to the lump-sum distribution were prepared using 5.5 percent interest and average life expectancy, that the other calculations were prepared using a 6 percent interest rate, and that the relative value of actual payments for an individual can vary depending on how long the individual and spouse live. The explanation states that the relative value comparison converts the QJSA, the single-life annuity, the joint and 100 percent survivor annuity, and the single-sum options to an equivalent present value and that this conversion uses interest and life expectancy assumptions. The explanation notes that the calculation of the QJSA depends on the actual age of the spouse (e.g., annuity payments will be significantly lower if the spouse is significantly younger than the participant) and that the amount of the lump-sum payment will depend on the interest rates that apply when the participant actually takes a distribution. The explanation also includes an offer to provide a calculation specific to the participant upon request.

Tina requests information regarding the amounts payable under the QJSA, the joint and 100 percent survivor annuity, and the single sum. Based on the information about the age of Tina's spouse, the plan determines that her QJSA is $2,856.30 per month, the joint and 100 percent survivor annuity is $2,628.60 per month, and the single sum is $497,876. The actuarial present value of the QJSA (determined using the 5.5 percent interest and the Code Section 417(e)(3) applicable mortality table, the actuarial assumptions required under Code Section 417) is $525,091. Accordingly, the value of the lump-sum distribution available to Tina on January 1, 2004, is 94.8 percent of the actuarial present value of the QJSA. In addition, the actuarial present value of the life annuity and the 100 percent JSA are 95.0 percent of the actuarial present value of the QJSA.

The plan provides Tina with a QJSA explanation that incorporates these more precise calculations of the financial effect and relative values of the optional forms for which she requested information.

### Q 16:54    Is there a way to simplify the presentation of information, especially when there are a multitude of similar optional benefit forms?

Yes. Simplified presentations of financial effect and relative values are permitted for disclosure of a significant number of substantially similar optional forms. This is extremely helpful when, for example, a plan offers an array of joint and survivor annuities with survivor payments available at any whole number percentage between 50 percent and 100 percent. In order to avoid overwhelming the participant, the plan is permitted to provide a simplified description of a range of substantially similar benefits the features of which vary linearly. The simplified description must provide a representative range of examples, one at each end of the range plus at least one in the middle of the range if that is sufficient to adequately describe the values. The participant must be notified that they can request additional information regarding the other optional benefits. [Treas. Reg. § 1.417(a)(3)-1(c)(5)]

If the plan permits the participant to make separate benefit elections with respect to two or more portions of the participant's benefit, the description of the financial effect and relative values of optional forms of benefit can be made separately for each such portion of the benefit, rather than for each optional form of benefit (i.e., each combination of possible elections).

### Q 16:55    Has the IRS or Department of Labor released any guidance on QJSA notice requirements?

Yes. The IRS issued Notice 97-10 [1997-1 C.B. 370], which provides sample language for plan administrators to use in preparing spousal consent forms that meet the statutory requirements. Appendix A and Appendix B of the notice contain sample language to be used in defined benefit pension plans.

### Q 16:56    What happens to the QJSA election if the participant's marital status changes after benefits begin?

After the annuity starting date (see Q 16:27), the participant's designation of the party to receive survivor benefits under a QJSA is fixed. [Jordan v. Fed. Express Corp., 116 F.3d 1005 (3d Cir. 1997)] The spouse to whom the participant was married on the annuity starting date is entitled to the survivor benefits provided under the QJSA unless the QJSA had been waived at the appropriate time with the consent of the participant's spouse. If the spouse and the participant divorce, the spouse cannot revoke his or her right to a survivor annuity. The survivor benefit is still payable to the former spouse, even if the participant and spouse are not married at the time of participant's death, unless a QDRO provides otherwise (see chapter 17). If, after the participant's death, the spouse remarries, the plan must continue to pay survivor benefits to the person who was the participant's spouse as of the annuity starting date. The critical factor is the marital status as of the annuity starting date. [Treas. Reg. § 1.401(a)-20, Q&A 25]

**Example.** Ricky and Lucy have been married for a number of years. When Ricky retires, he elects to receive his benefits in the form of a QJSA. Under the

QJSA, Ricky will receive benefits of $1,000 per month for his lifetime, and after his death, Lucy will receive benefits of $500 per month for her lifetime. One year after Ricky's retirement, he and Lucy divorce. Ricky marries Suzy. Ten years later, Ricky dies. Lucy, not Suzy, will receive a survivor annuity of $500 per month for her lifetime.

**Planning Pointer.** It is critical that the participant receives all information necessary to make an informed decision about the form of benefit payment (see Q 16:2).

### Q 16:57  Are there any instances when the QJSA election and notification requirements do not apply?

Yes. There are a few circumstances when the QJSA election and notification requirements do not apply:

1. *Plan subsidizes cost.* Notice of the right to waive the QJSA is not required if the plan fully subsidizes the cost of the benefit and the plan does not permit a participant to waive the benefit or designate another beneficiary. A plan fully subsidizes the cost of a benefit if the participant's benefit is not reduced because of the QJSA. [I.R.C. § 417(a)(5); Treas. Reg. § 1.401(a)-20, Q&A 37]

   **Example 1.** A plan provides a life annuity of $100 per month and a joint and 100 percent survivor annuity of $99 per month. The plan does not fully subsidize the joint and survivor benefit because the participant's benefit is reduced from $100 to $99.

   **Example 2.** A plan provides a single-sum optional form of benefit payment. Regardless of the actuarial value of the QJSA, the plan does not fully subsidize the QJSA. In the event of the participant's early death, the participant would have received less under the QJSA than he or she would have received under the single-sum option. [Treas. Reg. § 1.401(a)-20, Q&A 38]

2. *Short marriage.* A plan can provide that no QJSA will be provided to a married participant unless the participant has been married for at least a one-year period ending on the earlier of the participant's annuity starting date or date of death. [I.R.C. § 417(d); Treas. Reg. § 1.401(a)-20, Q&A 25]

3. *Lost spouse.* The plan can distribute benefits in a form other than the QJSA without the otherwise required spousal consent when it is established to the satisfaction of a plan representative that:

   a. There is no spouse;

   b. The spouse cannot be located; or

   c. The participant is legally separated or the participant has been abandoned (within the meaning of local law), and the participant has a court order to that effect. [I.R.C. § 417(a)(2)(B); Treas. Reg. § 1.401(a)-20, Q&A 27]

4. De minimis *benefit.* The QJSA does not have to be provided if the present value of the participant's vested accrued benefit is $5,000 or less.

### Q 16:58    Can a participant waive the QJSA?

Yes. Each participant must have the opportunity to waive the QJSA. The time for waiving the QJSA, called the *applicable election period* [I.R.C. § 417(a)(1); ERISA § 205(c)(1)], is the 90-day (180 days for annuity starting dates after December 31, 2006) period ending on the annuity starting date. [I.R.C. § 417(a)(6); ERISA § 205(c)(7)] The waiver must occur within this period to be valid. [Jacobs v. Reed College TIAA-CREF Ret. Plan, 12 Employee Benefits Cas. (BNA) 2826 (D. Or. 1990)] An exception is permitted for explanations provided after the annuity starting date as long as the applicable election period is extended for 30 days after the date on which the explanation is provided (see Q 16:30). [I.R.C. § 417(a)(7)(A)]

### Q 16:59    How does the participant waive the QJSA?

The plan participant can elect a nonsurvivor benefit, or if the plan permits, a survivor benefit payable to someone other than the participant's spouse. To do this, the participant must affirmatively waive the QJSA and specify the particular optional form of benefit payment and the specific nonspouse beneficiary elected. [Treas. Reg. § 1.401(a)-20(b), Q&A 31] The waiver must be informed (see Q 16:50). Further, the participant's waiver of the automatic qualified joint and survivor benefit is valid only if the participant's spouse consents to the waiver and to the form of benefit elected by the participant.

The Code and Treasury regulations focus on the conditions necessary for valid spousal consent to a participant's choice of an alternative form of benefit payment. A spouse's consent to the participant's election to waive a QJSA is not valid unless:

1. The spouse consents in writing to the election;
2. The election designates a form of benefit that cannot be changed without spousal consent; and
3. The spouse's consent acknowledges the effect of the election and is witnessed by a plan representative or a notary public.

[I.R.C. § 417(a)(2)(A); ERISA § 205(c)(2)(A)]

Notice 97-10 [1997-2 I.R.B. 41] provides information that should be included in spousal consent forms.

The waiver of the QJSA and the spouse's consent must be informed, about material features of all forms of benefit available as well as their relative values (see Q 16:50). An alternative form of payment cannot be elected without notice of the QJSA and waiver rights. Further, the election and spousal consent are not valid if given more than 90 days (180 days for annuity starting dates after December 31, 2006) before the date the distribution begins. [Treas. Reg. § 1.411(a)-11(c)(2)]

All benefit election forms must be signed and acknowledged in accordance with the regulations. For example, a spouse's consent to her husband's waiver of the QJSA and election of an alternative form of benefit payment was considered invalid because it had not been witnessed by a plan representative or notary public, even though she had confirmed that she had given her consent to the participant's election. [Lasche v. George W. Lasche Basic Profit Sharing Plan, 21 Employee Benefits Cas. 1001 (BNA) (11th Cir. 1997)]

A consent form that was signed by a surviving spouse before the start of the 90-day election period was similarly considered invalid. [Jacobs v. Reed College TIAA-CREF Ret. Plan, 12 Employee Benefits Cas. (BNA) 2826 (D. Or. 1990)]

### Q 16:60    What if a spouse cannot be located?

The plan can distribute benefits in a form other than the QJSA without the otherwise required spousal consent when it is established to the satisfaction of a plan representative that:

1. There is no spouse;
2. The spouse cannot be located; or
3. The participant is legally separated or the participant has been abandoned (within the meaning of local law), and the participant has a court order to that effect.

[I.R.C. § 417(a)(2)(B); Treas. Reg. § 1.401(a)-20, Q&A 27]

### Q 16:61    For QJSA purposes, at what point in time is a participant's marital status (and spouse) determined?

An individual's marital status is determined as of the annuity starting date (see Q 16:27). Accordingly, a QJSA is not required if a participant is not married on the annuity starting date. Payments to be made under a QJSA do not change because the participant divorces after the annuity starting date. [Treas. Reg. § 1.401(a)-20, Q&A 25(b)(3)]

Consent by one spouse is binding only with respect to the consenting spouse and does not bind any subsequent spouse of the same participant. [Treas. Reg. § 1.401(a)-20, Q&A 29]

### Q 16:62    What if the spouse is legally separated from the participant?

Spousal consent rules can be waived if the participant is legally separated or the participant has been abandoned, and the participant has a court order to that effect, unless a QDRO requires otherwise. [Treas. Reg. § 1.401(a)-20, Q&A 27]

### Q 16:63    Will a spouse lose survivor benefits if he or she murders the participant?

Courts, often applying state "killer" laws, have denied survivor benefits to spouses and other beneficiaries who murder plan participants. [Mendez-Bellido v.

Board of Trs. of Div. 1181, 709 F. Supp. 329 (E.D.N.Y. 1989)] In General Counsel Memorandum 39000 [Jan. 1983], the IRS suggested that denial of benefits might be appropriate after consideration of state law. Murder can be considered an abandonment within the meaning of Treasury Regulations Section 1.401(a)-20, Q&A 27. [New Orleans Elec. Pension Fund v. Newman, 14 Employee Benefits Cas. (BNA) 2747 (E.D. La. 1992); see also Ltr. Ruls. 8908063, 8905058]

### Q 16:64  Is a prenuptial agreement waiving retirement benefits valid under the Code?

No. A prenuptial agreement, or similar agreement entered into before marriage, does not satisfy the consent requirements necessary to waive the QJSA or the QPSA. [Treas. Reg. § 1.401(a)-20, Q&A 28] A waiver must come from a spouse (not a future spouse) and must satisfy the specific requirements in the Code with respect to disclosure, form, and timing. [Hurwitz v. Sher, 982 F.2d 778 (2d Cir. 1992); Pedro Enters., Inc. v. Perdue, 998 F.2d 491 (7th Cir. 1993)] A participant may have a claim under state law, however, if a spouse is unwilling to comply with a prenuptial agreement.

### Q 16:65  When must an employer provide QJSA notice to a disabled employee who is entitled to disability benefits under the plan?

Notification requirements for disability benefits depend on whether the disability benefit is a regular disability retirement benefit or an auxiliary benefit. A disability benefit is an auxiliary benefit if on attainment of early or normal retirement age, a participant receives a retirement benefit that satisfies the accrual and vesting rules of Code Section 411 without taking into account the disability benefit payments up to that date. If the benefit is a nonauxiliary benefit, the normal notice and consent requirements apply. Auxiliary disability benefits can be paid in the form provided under the plan without regard to the QPSA rules.

> **Example 1.** David, age 45, is entitled to a vested accrued benefit of $100 per month beginning at age 65 in the form of a JSA under the plan. If David receives a disability benefit under the plan before he reaches age 65 and the payment of his disability benefit does not reduce the amount of his $100 monthly retirement benefit beginning at age 65, the disability benefit payments made to David between ages 45 and 65 are auxiliary benefits. In that case, David's annuity starting date does not occur until he attains age 65. David's spouse would be entitled to receive a QPSA if David died before he attained age 65. At age 65, David's annuity commencement date, he would have the opportunity to waive the QJSA and elect an alternative form of benefit, subject to his wife's consent.

> **Example 2.** If in Example 1 David's benefit payable at age 65 is reduced to $99 per month because a disability benefit was provided to him before age 65, the disability benefit would not be an auxiliary benefit. Accordingly, the date

disability benefits begin is treated as David's annuity starting date, and any benefit paid to David would be required to be paid in the form of a QJSA (unless waived by David with the consent of his spouse).

[Treas. Reg. § 1.401(a)-20, Q&A 10(c)]

## Death Benefits and the QPSA Rules

### Q 16:66   Must a plan provide preretirement death benefits to married participants?

A QPSA (see Q 16:68) must be provided to the surviving spouse of a participant if the participant dies with a vested benefit before his or her annuity starting date. [I.R.C. § 401(a)(11)(A)(ii)]

### Q 16:67   Must a plan provide preretirement death benefits to an unmarried participant?

No. Although some defined benefit plans provide additional death benefits if a participant dies before his or her annuity starting date, there is no required death benefit for an unmarried participant.

### Q 16:68   What is a *qualified preretirement survivor annuity*?

A *qualified preretirement survivor annuity,* is a survivor annuity for the life of the surviving spouse of the participant in the event the participant dies before the annuity starting date. [I.R.C. § 417(c)] The QPSA tries to put the surviving spouse in the same position as he or she would have been in if the participant had retired and elected to receive a QJSA (see Q 16:47). The QPSA is payable to the surviving spouse unless the participant has waived (with the spouse's consent) the right to have the death benefit paid in that form. [ERISA § 205(e)(12)(A); Treas. Reg. § 1.401(a)-20, Q&A 18]

> **Example.** Fred has accrued a benefit, payable in the form of a QJSA, of $400 per month for his life and after his death, $200 per month continuing to his wife, Wilma. Fred has not yet retired. If Fred dies while still employed, Wilma will receive a survivor annuity of $200 per month for her lifetime.

### Q 16:69   Does the QPSA apply to all benefits payable under the plan by reason of a participant's death?

No. The QPSA applies only to the benefits in which the participant was vested immediately before death. If a plan provides for full vesting at death, the portion of the death benefit that was not vested before death does not have to be paid in the form of a QPSA. [Treas. Reg. § 1.401(a)-20, Q&A 12] A QPSA does not apply to enhanced death benefits. If, for example, the plan provides a lump-sum death benefit equal to the present value of the accrued benefit, the excess value over the value of the QPSA need not be paid in the form of a QPSA. As a practical matter, however, many plans apply the QPSA to the total benefit to ease administration.

### Q 16:70   When must QPSA benefits begin?

The plan must permit the surviving spouse to receive survivor benefit payments under the QPSA no later than the month in which the participant would have attained the earliest retirement age (see Q 16:25). [I.R.C. § 417(c)(1)(B), (f)(3); Treas. Reg. § 1.401(a)-20, Q&A 22]

### Q 16:71   How is the survivor annuity under a QPSA determined?

Payments to a surviving spouse cannot be less than the amount that would have been payable as a survivor annuity under a QJSA (see Q 16:47) if the participant had retired with an immediate QJSA on the day before the date of death. [I.R.C. § 417(c)(1)(B)(i); Treas. Reg. § 1.401(a)-20, Q&A 18] The QPSA survivor annuity to the spouse must be the amount of the payments that would have been made under the QJSA if:

1. The participant had retired with an immediate QJSA on the day before his or her death (in the case of a participant who dies after attaining the earliest retirement age under the plan); or
2. The participant had:
   a. Separated from service on the date of death;
   b. Survived to the earliest retirement age;
   c. Retired with an immediate QJSA at the earliest retirement age; and
   d. Died on the day after the day on which he or she would have attained the earliest retirement age.

In the case of a participant who separates from service before his or her death, the amount of a QPSA is to be calculated by reference to the actual date of separation and not from the date of the participant's death. [I.R.C. § 417(c)(1)(A)]

> **Example.** Fred died while actively employed. If he had retired and elected a QJSA before death, he would have been entitled to an annuity for life equal to $400, with a survivor benefit payable to his wife equal to $200, starting at age 65. His wife, Wilma, is entitled to a QPSA equal to $200 starting when Fred would have attained age 65. If the plan provided for an earlier retirement date, Wilma could receive survivor benefits at that time, but the actual amount of the benefit would be reduced for early payment.

### Q 16:72   What happens if a surviving spouse dies before the QPSA is scheduled to begin?

The QPSA may be forfeited if the spouse does not survive until the date survivor benefits are to begin. [Treas. Reg. § 1.401(a)-20, Q&A 19]

### Q 16:73   Must a plan provide a preretirement death benefit to a nonvested participant?

The survivor annuity requirements apply only to benefits that were vested immediately before death. The QPSA rules do not cover benefits that vest solely because of a participant's death. [Treas. Reg. § 1.401(a)-20, Q&A 12(a)]

### Q 16:74   What other death benefits can be provided under a defined benefit pension plan?

A number of enhanced benefits can be provided under a defined benefit pension plan. A plan can purchase life insurance on the lives of plan participants and pay a death benefit equal to the proceeds of the insurance. Some plans provide a death benefit equal to the present value of the accrued benefit. Plans can provide a widow's benefit, similar to the QPSA, but with no reduction for early payment. Some plans provide benefits to dependent children. These enhanced benefits are often conditioned on service for a number of years. Special benefits, such as enhanced death benefits, must not be available only to highly compensated employees. [Treas. Reg. § 1.401(a)(4)-4] In all events, however, a QPSA must be provided under the plan.

### Q 16:75   Can an employee waive QPSA coverage?

A plan participant can waive the QPSA if his or her spouse consents in writing to the waiver (see Q 16:77). A participant may choose to waive the QPSA if there is a charge for preretirement death benefit coverage (see Q 16:82) or if the plan provides additional death benefits and the participant would like to name other individuals, such as children, as beneficiaries. To be effective, the spouse's consent must satisfy certain conditions (see Q 16:77).

### Q 16:76   What is required to waive the QPSA?

The participant's waiver of the QPSA and the spouse's consent (see Q 16:77) must identify the beneficiary who will receive the preretirement death benefit. The participant cannot change the beneficiary without the consent of his or her spouse. If, however, the beneficiary is a trust, the participant's spouse need only consent to the designation of the trust as the beneficiary and need not consent to any changes in the terms of the trust or the beneficiaries of the trust. A participant's waiver of a QPSA and the spouse's consent do not have to specify the optional form of any preretirement death benefit. [Treas. Reg. § 1.401(a)-20, Q&A 31]

### Q 16:77   Is a spouse's consent required to waive the QPSA?

Yes. A participant's waiver of the QPSA is not valid unless:

1. The spouse consents to the waiver in writing;

2. The election designates a beneficiary that cannot be changed without spousal consent;

3. The spouse's consent acknowledges the effect of the election; and

4. The spouse's consent is witnessed by a plan representative or notary public.

[I.R.C. § 417(a)(2)]

The spouse's consent can permit the participant to change beneficiaries in the future without additional spousal consent. This broad general consent is not valid unless the consent acknowledges that the spouse has the right to limit his or her consent to a specific beneficiary and that he or she voluntarily elects to relinquish that right. [Treas. Reg. § 1.401(a)-20, Q&A 31]

### Q 16:78 When can an employee waive QPSA coverage?

A participant can waive the QPSA at any time after the first day of the first plan year in which he or she attains age 35, or if it is earlier, at any time after he or she separates from service. [I.R.C. § 417(a)(6)(B)] A plan can provide a temporary waiver of a QPSA benefit to a participant before the participant attains age 35. Such a waiver, however, becomes invalid on the beginning of the plan year in which the participant reaches age 35. [Treas. Reg. § 1.401(a)-20, Q&A 33(b)]

**Planning Pointer.** Many plans, other than plans that provide enhanced death benefits, do not permit pre-age 35 waivers.

### Q 16:79 When can the plan pay death benefits in a form other than the QPSA?

A plan does not have to provide death benefits in the form of a QPSA in any of the following instances (if provided in the plan):

1. *Single participant.* A QPSA is payable only to a surviving spouse.

2. *Short marriage.* A QPSA does not have to be provided to the surviving spouse of a married participant unless the participant and the spouse had been married for at least one year as of the date of death. The plan must contain language requiring a marriage of at least one year as a condition to treatment as a surviving spouse.

3. De minimis *benefit.* A QPSA does not have to be provided if the value of the QPSA is $5,000 or less. In such case, the surviving spouse would receive death benefits in a single lump sum.

4. *Subsidized benefit.* A plan does not have to give participants the option to waive the QPSA if it fully subsidizes the cost of the benefit and does not permit the participant to designate another beneficiary. [I.R.C. § 417(a)(5)]

5. *Waiver.* A QPSA does not have to be provided if the participant, with the consent of his or her spouse, has validly waived the QPSA.

### Q 16:80   Can a QDRO affect benefit payments?

Yes. A QDRO can require the plan to treat a former spouse as the participant's surviving spouse for all or a portion of the participant's benefits. In such case, benefits payable by reason of a participant's death are payable to the former spouse. The former spouse's consent will also be required for waiver of the QPSA (see chapter 17).

### Q 16:81   Can a participant name a person other than his or her spouse as the QPSA beneficiary?

No. The QPSA is payable only to a surviving spouse (or former spouse under a QDRO) (see chapter 17).

> **Example.** With her husband's consent, Celia named her daughter as the QPSA beneficiary. After Celia died, the plan refused to pay a survivor's benefit to her daughter, saying the plan provided QPSAs only for surviving spouses. The court upheld the plan administrator's determination. [Butler v. Encyclopedia Brittanica Inc, 18 Employee Benefits Cas. (BNA) 2589 (7th Cir. 1994)]

### Q 16:82   Can a plan charge for QPSA coverage?

Yes. A plan is permitted to charge a participant for the cost of providing a QPSA. A charge that reasonably reflects the cost of providing the survivor benefit is allowed even though the charges may reduce the accrued benefit. [Treas. Reg. § 1.401(a)-20, Q&A 21] A plan cannot charge the participant for the cost of the survivor benefit before the participant is eligible for the benefit or before the participant is notified of the benefit and has the opportunity to waive coverage. [Treas. Reg. § 1.401(a)-20, Q&A 21]

> **Example.** Steve is a participant in the Spa Time Inc. pension plan. Under the terms of the plan, he is entitled to a benefit equal to $1,000 per month at normal retirement age. If he does not waive QPSA coverage, his normal retirement benefit will be reduced by 0.5 percent (in his case, $5 per month) for each year the QPSA coverage is in force. Steve, who is age 45, does not waive the QPSA coverage. His monthly benefit at his normal retirement age will be $900 ($1,000 − ($5 × 20 years)).

## Suspension of Benefits

### Q 16:83   Do benefits stop if a retiree returns to work?

They can. If an employee retires and is then reemployed, a plan can suspend retirement benefit payments during employment. On eventual retirement, benefits must be actuarially increased for the period of suspension unless special notice requirements are met (see chapter 28; see Q 16:84). [I.R.C. § 411(a)(3)(B); D.O.L. Reg. § 2530.203-3(b)]

### Q 16:84   What is a *suspension of benefits notice*?

A *suspension of benefits notice* is a notice informing an employee who previously had retired and is receiving benefits under the plan that his or her retirement benefits are being suspended and identifying the plan provisions that authorize the suspension of benefits. Many times an explanation of the suspension of benefits rules is contained in the summary plan description. In this case, the suspension of benefits notice can refer to the relevant portions of the summary plan description (see chapter 28).

### Q 16:85   When must a suspension of benefits notice be given to a plan participant?

Reemployed employees who will have benefits suspended during a period of reemployment must be notified during the first payroll period or month of reemployment that their benefits are being suspended. Notification must be accomplished by personal delivery or first-class mail. [ERISA § 203(a)(3)(B); D.O.L. Reg. § 2530.203-3(b)(4)]

### Q 16:86   What happens if a suspension of benefits notice is not provided when required?

If a suspension of benefits notice is not provided to a reemployed participant previously in pay status, his or her ultimate retirement benefits must be actuarially increased to reflect benefits lost during suspension.

## Required Minimum Distributions

### Q 16:87   Do any rules mandate distribution of benefits during a participant's lifetime?

Yes. Code Section 401(a)(9) was enacted to ensure that income from retirement plans was actually used for retirement. Under Code Section 401(a)(9), minimum distributions must be made during the participant's life, beginning by the participant's required beginning date (see Q 16:88).

### Q 16:88   What is the *required beginning date*?

Code Section 401(a)(9) provides that, for a plan to be qualified under Code Section 401(a), distributions of each participant's interest in the plan must begin no later than the required beginning date for the participant. A participant's *required beginning date* is April 1 of the calendar year following the later of

1. The year the participant attains age 70½, or
2. The year the participant (other than a 5 percent owner) retires.

For owners of more than 5 percent of the stock of a corporate employer or more than 5 percent of the capital or profits interest of an unincorporated employer, the required beginning date is April 1 of the calendar year following the year the participant owner attains age 70½. [I.R.C. § 401(a)(9)(C); Treas. Reg. § 1.401(a)(9)-2, Q&A 2]

An individual attains age 70½ six months after the individual's 70th birthday. [Treas. Reg. § 1.401(a)(9)-2, Q&A 3)]

**Example.** Calvin works for Hobbson Enterprises Inc. He and his boss, Hobbs (who owns 100 percent of the company), are participants in the Hobbson Enterprises Inc. defined benefit pension plan. Calvin and Hobbs were both born on October 10, 1930. Both are still actively employed in the 2002 calendar year. The required beginning date for each is determined as follows:

Calvin—April 1 of the calendar year following the later of the following:

1. The year Calvin attains age 70½ (2001; October 10, 1930, plus 70 years and six months is April 10, 2001); or

2. The year Calvin retires.

Because Calvin is actively employed, he has not yet reached his required beginning date even though he has attained age 70. If Calvin quits in 2002, his required beginning date would be April 1, 2003—April 1 of the calendar year following the year he retires.

Hobbs—April 1 of the calendar year following the year Hobbs attains age 70½ (2001; October 10, 1930, plus 70 years and 6 months is April 10, 2001).

Because Hobbs is a 5 percent owner, his employment status is irrelevant to the determination of his required beginning date. His required beginning date is April 1, 2002—April 1 of the calendar year following April 10, 2001, the date he attained age 70½.

For years beginning before January 1, 1997 (before the amendment made by the Small Business Job Protection Act of 1996 (SBJPA)), the required beginning date was April 1 of the calendar year following the year the participant attained age 70½ regardless of employment status, the same rule that remains for 5 percent owners. This meant that a participant who had attained age 70½ was required to begin receiving distributions from the plan during the following calendar year, even if the employee had not retired from employment with the employer maintaining the plan. Unless the plan makes an optional election described in Notice 97-75 [1997-2 C.B. 337] (see Q 16:89), a participant (other than a 5 percent owner) who attained age 70½ before January 1, 1997, has a new required beginning date.

An active employee (other than a 5 percent owner) who attained age 70½ in 1996 and who, before SBJPA, had a required beginning date of April 1, 1997, was not required to begin receiving minimum distributions by April 1, 1997. [Notice 96-67, 1996-2 C.B. 235]

### Q 16:89    Do any special rules apply to participants who attained age 70½ before 1997?

Yes. A minimum distribution does not have to be made by April 1, 1997, for a participant (other than a 5 percent owner) who attains age 70½ in 1996 but has not retired from employment. The participant's required beginning date is April 1 of the calendar year following the year in which the participant actually retires. [Notice 96-67, 1996-2 C.B. 235]

> **Example.** Kermit, who is not a 5 percent owner, attained age 70½ in 1996. He is still actively employed. Before SBJPA, his required beginning date was April 1, 1997. His new required beginning date will be the April 1 after he retires.

Plan sponsors had several options regarding participants who attained age 70½ before the law changed and who now have a different required beginning date. Employers could have allowed active employees who attained age 70½ before 1997 to elect to stop receiving benefits from the plan until retirement. [Notice 97-75, 1997-2 C.B. 337] Elections were subject to the qualified joint and survivor notice requirements. Employers can offer active employees who attain age 70½ after 1995 the option to defer receiving in-service pension plan distributions even if the plan administrator has not amended the plan to provide such a choice. [Ann. 97-24, 1997-11 I.R.B. 24]

The elimination of the right of participants to receive in-service distributions at age 70½ presents a problem because this right is considered an optional form of benefit that cannot be reduced under Code Section 411(d)(6). Under a transitional rule, however, plans can stop in-service distributions to active employees over the age of 70½ without violating the anti-cutback rules. Employees must be offered an option to defer the distribution, and elect to defer, or be offered a make-up distribution. If the employer offers the deferral option, the employee must have made the election by December 31, 1997. Plans must pay a make-up distribution to employees who decide not to defer.

Treasury regulations allow plans to eliminate in-service distributions after age 70½ for employees who attain age 70½ after calendar year 1998. An amendment eliminating the in-service distribution option will apply only to employees attaining age 70½ after December 31, 1998, or the date the amendment is adopted if it is later. [Treas. Reg. § 1.411(d)-4, Q&A 10]

### Q 16:90    How much must be distributed at the required beginning date?

To satisfy the minimum distribution rules, if the entire benefit is not paid in a single sum, benefits must be paid

1. Over the employee's life;
2. Over the lives of the employee and a designated beneficiary;
3. For a period not exceeding the employee's life expectancy; or
4. For a period not exceeding the joint and survivor life expectancies of the employee and a designated beneficiary.

[I.R.C. § 401(a)(9)(A); Treas. Reg. § 1.401(a)(9)-2, Q&A 1]

## Q 16:91 How are minimum distributions satisfied in a defined benefit plan?

On June 15, 2004, the IRS issued final regulations addressing how the minimum distribution requirements of Code Section 401(a)(9) are satisfied in a defined benefit plan. These final regulations apply to distributions on or after January 1, 2003. However, distributions that satisfy any of the following prior regulations will be deemed to satisfy the final regulations for the 2003, 2004, and 2005 calendar distribution years:

- 2002 Final and Temporary Regulations Section 1.401(a)(9)-6T, A-1;
- 2001 Proposed Regulations Section 1.401(a)(9)-6, A-1; or
- 1987 Proposed Regulations Section 1.401(a)(9)-1, F-3A.

This transition period allows defined benefit plans to continue calculating required minimum distributions using the "account balance method" (or any other allowable method under prior regulations) as allowed under the 1987 proposed regulations (see Q 16:92).

The final regulations retain the basic rules of the temporary regulations. The general rule is that distributions of an employee's entire interest must be paid in the form of periodic annuity payments for the employee's or beneficiary's life (or the joint lives of the employee and beneficiary) or over a comparable period certain. The payments must be nonincreasing or only increase as provided in the regulations. Annuity payments must also satisfy the minimum distribution incidental benefit (MDIB) requirements. [Treas. Reg. § 1.401(a)(9)-6, Q&A 1(a)]

The period certain cannot exceed the applicable distribution period for the employee as determined in accordance with the Uniform Life Table for the calendar year that contains the annuity starting date. If the beneficiary is the employee's spouse, then the period certain is permitted to be as long as the joint life and last expectancy of the employee and spouse, if longer than the life expectancy of the employee. For a single employee age 70 as of the annuity starting date, the life expectancy used for the period certain cannot exceed 27.4 years; however, if the employee is married and the spouse is more than 10 years younger than the employee, then the distribution period can be greater.

> **Example.** The accrued benefit for an employee is $1,000 per year. The employee is required to begin taking minimum required distributions, and has elected to begin distribution in the form of a term certain. The employee is single and age 70, and has elected a distribution over 27 years. The present value of the accrued benefit is $12,000 and the interest rate used is 5 percent. The minimum required distribution is the actuarial equivalent of the accrued benefit spread over 27 years at 5 percent interest, or $819.50.

## Q 16:92 How are minimum distributions satisfied in a defined benefit plan in the event of a total lump-sum distribution?

In the case of a lump-sum distribution of an employee's entire accrued benefit during a distribution calendar year, the amount that is the required minimum distribution for the distribution calendar year (and thus not eligible for rollover under Code Section 402(c)) is determined using either of the following methods:

1. The portion of the single-sum distribution that is a required minimum distribution is determined by treating the single-sum distribution as a distribution from an individual account plan and treating the amount of the single-sum distribution as the employee's account balance as of the end of the relevant valuation calendar year. If the single-sum distribution is being made in the calendar year containing the required beginning date and the required minimum distribution for the employee's first distribution calendar year has not been distributed, the portion of the single-sum distribution that represents the required minimum distribution for the employee's first and second distribution calendar years is not eligible for rollover.

2. The portion of the single-sum distribution that is a required minimum distribution may be determined by expressing the employee's benefit as an annuity that would satisfy this section with an annuity starting date as of the first day of the distribution calendar year for which the required minimum distribution is being determined and treating one year of annuity payments as the required minimum distribution for that year, and, therefore, not eligible for rollover. If the single-sum distribution is being made in the calendar year containing the required beginning date and the required minimum distribution for the employee's first distribution calendar year has not been made, the benefit must be expressed as an annuity with an annuity starting date as of the first day of the first distribution calendar year, and the payments for the first two calendar years would be treated as required minimum distributions, and not eligible for rollover.

**Example 1.** Juan is retiring in 2004 and turned 70½ during 2003. His required beginning date is April 1, 2004, and no minimum required distribution has yet been made for the first distribution calendar year. His lump-sum distribution will be $50,000. Under option #1 (above), his minimum distribution is $1,824.82 ($50,000 ÷ 27.4) for 2004 and $1,817.93 ($48,175.18 ÷ 26.5) for 2005. Therefore, $3,642.75 ($1,824.82 + $1,817.93) must be distributed to Juan and the remainder ($46,357.25) may be rolled over to an IRA.

**Example 2.** The facts are the same as in Example 1, but this time Juan's minimum required distribution is calculated under option #2 (above). Juan's accrued benefit is $450 per month. Therefore, his minimum required distribution for 2004 is $5,400 ($450 × 12) and $5,400 for 2005. Therefore, $10,800 must be distributed to Juan and the remainder ($39,200) may be rolled over to an IRA.

According to final regulations, a participant's benefit in a defined benefit plan is no longer eligible to be treated as an individual account for purposes of calculating ongoing minimum required distributions. However, the plan sponsor may use the old 1987 proposed regulations until after the 2005 calendar year. [Notice 2003-2, 2003-2 I.R.B. 257]

[Treas. Reg. § 1.401(a)(9)-6, Q&A 1(d)]

**Q 16:93    What increases are permitted to be made to the annuity payments and still satisfy Code Section 401(a)(9)?**

There are various methods of providing allowable increases in payments, as follows:

1. Plans may provide annual increases that do not exceed the increase in an eligible cost-of-living index for a 12-month period.

2. Plans can provide annuity payments with percentage adjustments based on the increase in compensation for the position held by the employee at the time of retirement, *but only if* the increase was provided under the terms of the plan in effect on April 17, 2002 (there are special rules for governmental plans).

3. Increases in payments that solely reflect better than assumed investment performance (due to actuarial gains) are permitted, but only if the interest rate for calculating the initial level of payments is at least 3 percent.

4. Fixed rate increases may be provided, but only if the rate of increase is less than 5 percent.

5. The regulations also allow a payment at death to the extent that the annu-itized payments are less than the present value of the employee's accrued benefit as of the annuity starting date, using the interest and mortality assumptions prescribed under Code Section 417(e).

6. Any increase in benefits pursuant to a plan amendment.

7. A pop-up in payments in the event of the death of the beneficiary or the divorce of the employee and spouse.

8. To allow a beneficiary to convert the survivor portion of a JSA into a single-sum distribution upon the employee's death.

[Treas. Reg. § 1.401(a)(9)-6, Q&A 14]

**Example.** Use the same facts as in the example in Q 16:91, but this time the plan allows for a fixed annual increase of 4.5 percent per year. The minimum required distribution for the first year is now $476.23, but will increase by 4.5 percent per year thereafter.

**Q 16:94    Do the regulations allow changes in distribution form once distributions have commenced?**

Yes, upon satisfaction of certain conditions. Annuity payments may be reamortized if the annuity payment period is changed and the annuity payments are modified in association with that change. This is applicable only if the reason for the change is one of the following:

1. The employee retires or the plan terminates;

2. The annuity is a period certain without life contingencies; or

3. The employee elects a QJSA after becoming married.

In order to modify a stream of annuity payments, the following conditions must be satisfied:

1. The future payments under the modified stream satisfy Code Section 401(a)(9) (determined by treating the date of the change as a new annuity starting date and the actuarial present value of the remaining payments prior to modification as the entire interest of the participant);

2. For purposes of Code Sections 415 and 417, the modification is treated as a new annuity starting date;

3. After taking into account the modification, the annuity stream satisfies Code Section 415 (determined at the original annuity starting date, using the interest rates and mortality tables applicable to such date); and

4. The end point of the period certain, if any, for any modified payment period is not later than the end point available under Code Section 401(a)(9) to the employee at the original annuity starting date.

[Treas. Reg. § 1.401(a)(9)-6, Q&A 13]

> **Example.** Mike is a participant in the Deans Defined Benefit Plan (the Plan), who has 10 years of participation in a frozen defined benefit plan (The Plan), attains age 70½ in 2005. Mike is not retired and elects to receive distributions from The Plan in the form of a straight-life (i.e., level payment) annuity with annual payments of $240,000 per year beginning in 2005 at a date when Mike has attained age of 70. The Plan offers nonretired employees in pay status the opportunity to modify their annuity payments due to an associated change in the payment period at retirement. The Plan treats the date of the change in payment period as a new annuity starting date for the purposes of Code Sections 415 and 417. Thus, for example, the plan provides a new qualified and joint survivor annuity election and obtains spousal consent.
>
> The Plan determines modifications of annuity payment amounts at retirement such that the present value of future new annuity payment amounts (taking into account the new associated payment period) is actuarially equivalent to the present value of future pre-modification annuity payments (taking into account the pre-modification annuity payment period). Actuarial equivalency for this purpose is determined using the applicable interest rate and the applicable mortality table as of the date of modification.
>
> Mike retires in 2009 at the age of 74 and, after receiving four annual payments of $240,000, elects to receive his remaining distributions from The Plan in the form of an immediate final lump-sum payment (calculated at 4 percent interest) of $2,399,809.
>
> Because payment of retirement benefits in the form of an immediate final lump-sum payment satisfies (in terms of form) Code Section 401(a)(9), condition #1 above is met.
>
> Because The Plan treats a modification of an annuity payment stream at retirement as a new annuity starting date for purposes of Code Sections 415 and 417, condition #2 is met.

After taking into account the modification, the annuity stream determined as of the original annuity starting date consists of annual payments beginning at age 70 of $240,000, $240,000, $240,000, $240,000, and $2,399,809. This benefit stream is actuarially equivalent to a straight-life annuity at age 70 of $250,182, an amount less than the Code Section 415 limit determined at the original annuity starting date, using the interest and mortality rates applicable to such date. Thus, condition #3 is met.

Thus, because a stream of annuity payments in the form of a straight-life annuity satisfies Code Section 401(a)(9), and because each of the conditions are satisfied, the modification of annuity payments to Mike described in this example satisfies the conditions for increasing benefit payments.

### Q 16:95    What is the MDIB requirement for defined benefit plans?

Annuity distributions under a defined benefit plan that are paid in the form of a life annuity for the life of the employee automatically satisfy the MDIB requirement. In addition, a joint and survivor life annuity (with spousal beneficiary) automatically will satisfy the minimum distribution rule. [Treas. Reg. § 1.401(a)(9)-6, Q&A 2] If the benefit is being paid in the form of a JSA and the beneficiary is not the participant's spouse, the survivor annuity cannot exceed a certain percentage of the amount that was payable to the employee. This percentage depends on the excess of the age of the employee over the age of the beneficiary according to the following table:

| *Adjusted Employee/Beneficiary Age Difference* | *Applicable Percentage* |
|:---:|:---:|
| 10 years or less | 100 |
| 11 | 96 |
| 12 | 93 |
| 13 | 90 |
| 14 | 87 |
| 15 | 84 |
| 16 | 82 |
| 17 | 79 |
| 18 | 77 |
| 19 | 75 |
| 20 | 73 |
| 21 | 72 |
| 22 | 70 |
| 23 | 68 |
| 24 | 67 |
| 25 | 66 |

| Adjusted Employee/Beneficiary Age Difference | Applicable Percentage |
|:---:|:---:|
| 26 | 64 |
| 27 | 63 |
| 28 | 62 |
| 29 | 61 |
| 30 | 60 |
| 31 | 59 |
| 32 | 59 |
| 33 | 58 |
| 34 | 57 |
| 35 | 56 |
| 36 | 56 |
| 37 | 55 |
| 38 | 55 |
| 39 | 54 |
| 40 | 54 |
| 41 | 53 |
| 42 | 53 |
| 43 | 53 |
| 44 and greater | 52 |

[Treas. Reg. § 1.401(a)(9)-6, Q&A 2(c)]

### Q 16:96   How is the minimum distribution requirement satisfied when the employee continues to work and accrue benefits after distributions have commenced?

An active participant will continue to accrue benefits under the plan after his or her required beginning date. Each annual accrual must be treated as a separate component benefit or benefit block, with required minimum distributions due in the next year. Accordingly, the required minimum distribution for an active employee can be a series of annuity blocks, increasing the total payment until actual retirement. [Treas. Reg. § 1.401(a)(9)-6, Q&A 5] Nonvested benefits are treated as not having accrued until they vest. [Treas. Reg. § 1.401(a)(9)-6, Q&A 6]

**Example 1.** John, who has attained age 70½ in 2002, has accrued a monthly benefit of $500 payable as a life annuity with 10 years certain. To meet the minimum distribution requirements, John must receive a payment of $500 on or before April 1, 2003, and continuing monthly payments of $500 thereafter for life or the 10-year certain period.

**Example 2.** The facts are the same as those in Example 1. In 2003, John accrues an additional monthly benefit of $15 payable as a life annuity with 10 years certain. To meet the minimum distribution requirements, John must receive a benefit of $515 payable on or before December 31, 2004.

**Example 3.** Miguel was born on March 1, 1936, and retires at age 65. Distributions commence on January 1, 2002. Miguel's daughter, Luz, born on February 5, 1966, is Miguel's beneficiary. The distributions are in the form of a 100 percent JSA for the lives of Miguel and Luz with payments of $500 a month. There is no provision under the option for a change in the projected payments to Luz as of April 1, 2007, Miguel's required beginning date. Consequently, as of January 1, 2002, the date annuity distributions commence, the plan does not satisfy the MDIB requirement in operation because, as of such date, the distribution option provides that, as of Miguel's required beginning date, the monthly payment to Luz upon Miguel's death will exceed 60 percent of Luz's monthly payment (the maximum percentage for a difference of ages of 30 years).

### Q 16:97  Are minimum distributions required after a participant's death?

Yes. Distributions must continue to the participant's beneficiary. For post-death distributions, the required minimum distribution depends on whether the participant died after or before his or her required beginning date. When an employee dies *after* his or her required beginning date, the general rule is that the participant's remaining interest in the plan must be distributed at least as rapidly as it would have been distributed under the distribution method that was being used at the time of the employee's death.

**Example 1.** Barney has retired and elected to receive his benefits in the form of a life annuity with a 10-year certain term. On January 1, 2003, annuity distributions begin to him in the amount of $1,000 per month. After Barney's death, the annuity payments must continue over the remaining years in the 10-year certain period.

**Example 2.** Barney has retired and elected to treat his benefit as an individual account for purposes of determining the required minimum distribution. As permitted under the plan, he elects not to recalculate his life expectancy. He has not named a beneficiary, but, as allowed under the 2001 proposed Treasury Regulations, he calculates his life expectancy as if he has a beneficiary who is 10 years younger. [2001 Prop. Treas. Reg. § 1.401(a)(9)-5, Q&A 4] Barney's life expectancy under the MDIB table is 26.2 years. After Barney's death, the required minimum distributions must continue over the remaining years in the 26.2-year period. [Treas. Reg. § 1.401(a)(9)-5, Q&A 5(c)]

For years before 2001, the general rule is that if the participant dies *before* his or her required beginning date, the participant's entire interest must be distributed by the last day of the fifth calendar year following the participant's death. Optionally for 2001, and required for 2002 and thereafter, the general rule is that if the participant dies before or after the required beginning date, the default method of distribution is the life expectancy method (unless there is no beneficiary, in which case the default method is the five-year rule). In other words, any amount payable to a designated beneficiary can be distributed over the life, or a period not extending beyond the life expectancy, of that beneficiary as long as the distributions begin on or before December 31 of the calendar year following the calendar year of the employee's death. [I.R.C. § 401(a)(9)(B)(iii); Treas. Reg. § 1.401(a)(9)-3, Q&A 1] If the designated beneficiary is the surviving spouse of the employee, commencement of the distribution can be postponed until the employee would have reached age 70½. [I.R.C. § 401(a)(9)(B)(iv); Treas. Reg. § 1.401(a)(9)-3, Q&A 3(b)]

A plan can include provisions specifying whether the five-year rule or the life expectancy method is the distribution method to be used for benefits payable in the event of the death of an active employee. Few plans provide for all of the distribution options available under the law.

> **Example 3.** Ray dies on April 15, 1998, while actively employed. The plan provides a lump-sum death benefit of $100,000. His son Ralph, the designated beneficiary, is 26 years old and has a life expectancy of 56 years. Under the five-year rule, the entire death benefit must be distributed to Ralph by December 31, 2003. Under the life expectancy method, payments can be made over Ralph's 56-year life expectancy, as long as distributions begin by December 31, 1999.

### Q 16:98  Must benefits be adjusted for employees over the age of 70½ who do not receive in-service distributions?

Yes. If a participant who has attained age 70½ does not receive distributions until retirement, his or her retirement benefit must be actuarially increased to reflect the period during which he or she did not receive benefits from the plan. [I.R.C. § 401(a)(9)(C)(ii); Temp. Treas. Reg. § 1.401(a)(9)-6T, Q&A 7(a)] The period for which the actuarial increase must be provided ends when benefits actually begin to be distributed in an amount sufficient to satisfy Code Section 401(a)(9). [Temp. Treas. Reg. § 1.401(a)(9)-6T, Q&A 7(b)] The actuarial increase is not required if the plan uses the pre-SBJPA required beginning date (April 1 of the calendar year following the calendar year in which the employee attained age 70½, regardless of whether the employee is a 5 percent owner) *and* the plan makes distributions in an amount sufficient to satisfy Code Section 401(a)(9) using that required beginning date. [Notice 97-75, 1997-2 C.B. 337; Temp. Treas. Reg. § 1.401(a)(9)-6T, Q&A 7(c)]

### Q 16:99  What is the amount of the actuarial increase required to be provided if distributions are postponed?

To satisfy Code Section 401(a)(9)(C)(iii), the retirement benefits payable with respect to an employee as of the time minimum required distributions commence must be no less than

1. The actuarial equivalent of the employee's retirement benefits that would have been payable as of the date the actuarial increase must commence if benefits had commenced on that date;
2. Plus the actuarial equivalent of any additional benefits accrued after that date; and
3. Reduced by the actuarial equivalent of any distributions made with respect to the employee's retirement benefits after that date.

Actuarial equivalence is determined using the plan's assumptions for determining actuarial equivalence for purposes of satisfying Code Section 411. [Temp. Treas. Reg. § 1.401(a)(9)-6T, Q&A 8] This actuarial increase must be provided even during the period during which an employee's benefit has been suspended in accordance with ERISA Section 203(a)(3)(B) and is generally the same as, and not in addition to, the actuarial increase required for the same period under Code Section 411 to reflect any delay in the payment of retirement benefits after normal retirement age. [Temp. Treas. Reg. § 1.401(a)(9)-6T, Q&A 9]

### Q 16:100　What is a *TEFRA Section 242(b) election*?

A *TEFRA Section 242(b) election* is an election to defer distributions from the plan until retirement. Before the Tax Equity and Fiscal Responsibility Act of 1982 (TEFRA), a participant in a pension plan did not have to take minimum distributions while actively employed. An election could be made, before January 1, 1984, to defer distributions from the plan until retirement. Additionally, the amounts payable over a participant's lifetime could be paid at a lower rate. [TEFRA § 242(b)(2); Treas. Reg. § 1.401(a)(9)-8, Q&A 13] If a distribution inconsistent with the TEFRA election is made, or a change to the election is made (other than a change in beneficiary that does not affect the distribution period), the election is deemed revoked, and payments must be made in accordance with Code Section 401(a)(9). [Treas. Reg. § 1.401(a)(9)-8, Q&A 16] The TEFRA election is still valuable to 5 percent owners, and the implications of revocation should be considered in the context of a rollover or transfer of plan assets to another plan.

## Assignment and Alienation of Benefits

### Q 16:101　Can retirement benefits be assigned to another party?

No. The Code and ERISA prohibit the assignment or alienation of benefits. [ERISA § 206(d)(1); I.R.C. § 401(a)(13)]

There are a few exceptions to this general rule. Benefits can be assigned to an alternate payee under a QDRO (see chapter 17). [I.R.C. § 401(a)(13)(B)] In addition, if a participant commits a breach of fiduciary duty or commits a criminal act with respect to the plan, the participant's benefits can be assigned to others affected by the participant's bad acts. [I.R.C. § 401(a)(13)(C)]

A number of cases have addressed the issue of recovery of a participant's benefits in the case of personal bankruptcy. As a general rule, a participant's benefits are protected from a participant's creditors in bankruptcy. [Patterson v. Shumate, 112 S. Ct. 2242 (1992)]

### Q 16:102    Are there any protections provided by a defined benefit plan in the event of bankruptcy?

A number of cases have addressed the issue of recovery of a participant's benefits in the case of personal bankruptcy. As a general rule, a participant's benefits in an ERISA qualified plan are protected from a participant's creditors in bankruptcy. [Patterson v. Shumate, 112 S. Ct. 2242 (1992)] Under the Bankruptcy Abuse Prevention and Consumer Protection Act of 2005 (BAPCPA) , all qualified plan assets are exempt from the bankruptcy estate as long as the retirement plan is qualified under Code Section 401. Qualification is presumed if:

- There is a current favorable determination letter for the plan, or
- Neither the IRS nor a court has made a prior determination that the plan is not qualified, or
- The plan is in substantial compliance with Code Section 401, or
- The plan is not in substantial compliance with Code Section 401, but the debtor is not materially responsible for that failure.

### Q 16:103    Can the IRS levy against a retirement benefit?

Yes. The anti-alienation rules do not apply to a federal tax levy or to the collection by the United States of a judgment resulting from unpaid taxes. [Treas. Reg. § 1.401(a)-13(b)(2)] In addition, under a federal criminal procedure rule [18 U.S.C. § 3613(c)], a fine imposed as part of either (1) a criminal sentence or (2) an order of restitution is a lien in favor of the federal government on all property of the person fined, as if the liability of the person fined were a tax liability. Therefore, several courts and the IRS have held that qualified retirement plans will not be disqualified for paying a participant's benefits to satisfy his or her criminal fines under garnishment orders relating to federal criminal statutes. [Ltr. Rul. 200426027; United States v. Tyson, 265 F. Supp. 2d 788 (D. Mich. 2003); United States v. Clark, 2003 U.S. Dist. LEXIS 26441 (E.D. Mich. 2003)]

The IRS has ruled that any distribution in satisfaction of a federal tax levy is not an eligible rollover distribution and therefore is not subject to mandatory 20 percent withholding or the Code Section 402(f) written notice requirements. In addition, relying on the tax court's decision in *Murillo v. Commissioner* [T.C.Memo 1998-13 (1998)], the IRS has held that these payments are not subject to the 10 percent additional tax under Code Section 72(t)(1). [Ltr. Rul. 200426027]

### Q 16:104 Can an employer recover embezzled money from the undistributed funds from a pension account of the employee who committed the crime?

No. ERISA Section 206(d)(1) states, "Each pension plan shall provide that benefits provided under the plan may not be assigned or alienated." Based on this, the Supreme Court has ruled out "any generalized equitable exception—either for employee malfeasance or for criminal misconduct—to ERISA's prohibition on the assignment or alienation of pension benefits." [Guidry v. Sheet Metal Workers Nat'l Pension Fund, 493 U.S. 365, 376 (1990)] In addition, the U.S. Court of Appeals for the Ninth Circuit ruled in *United States v. James Jackson* [229 F.3d 1223 (9th Cir. 2000)] that a union could not recover funds (from a pension fund balance covered by ERISA) that were embezzled from the employer by an employee.

### Q 16:105 Can a participant's benefit be attached once it is distributed from the plan?

Yes. A first circuit court has held that the anti-alienation provision of ERISA Section 206(d)(1) does not apply once the funds have been distributed from a qualified plan. The court held that the anti-alienation provision governs only the plan itself and is not a prohibition against creditors reaching the pension benefits once they have left the hands of the plan administrator. [Hoult v. Hoult, 373 F.3d 47 (1st Cir 2004)]

## Taxation of Distributions

### Q 16:106 What general income tax rules apply to distributions from defined benefit plans?

As a general rule, distributions from defined benefit pension plans are taxed under Code Section 72. [I.R.C. § 402(a)(1)] Single-sum distributions, however, may be eligible for favorable income averaging (see Q 16:112). If a plan is funded solely by employer contributions, amounts received from the plan are generally subject to tax as ordinary income. The tax consequences of benefit payments depend on the form of distribution, the reason for the distribution, and the age of the participant.

1. *Return of employee contributions.* When employee contributions are returned to a participant, the portion of the distribution attributable to the previously taxed contributions is tax free.

2. *Annuity payments.* Periodic payments are taxed as the payments are received.

3. *Annuity contracts.* When a participant receives an annuity contract to provide for benefit payment, taxes are due as payments are received.

4. *Lump-sum distributions.* Certain single-sum payments may qualify for favorable tax treatment.

5. *Eligible rollover contributions.* When benefits are paid in a single sum or another form that qualifies for rollover, a participant can defer taxes through a direct rollover.

6. *Disability payments.* Disability benefits may be tax free in limited situations.

7. *Death benefits.* Payments to beneficiaries generally carry over the tax treatment available to the participant. Only a spouse, however, can roll over a lump-sum death benefit into an IRA.

8. *QDROs.* If the alternate payee is the former spouse of the participant, benefits are taxable to the alternate payee as if he or she were the participant. If the alternate payee is a child, the participant is taxed on benefit payments.

### Q 16:107 How are annuity payments taxed?

If the participant has not made any contributions to the plan and has no basis in his or her interest in the plan, each annuity payment is fully taxed as ordinary income. [I.R.C. §§ 72,402(a); Treas. Reg. § 1.72-4(d)(1)] If the participant has a basis, or investment, in the contract, a portion of each annuity payment is excludable from income. The recovery of the participant's investment in the contract is determined by using the exclusion ratio if the annuity starting date (see Q 16:27) is before November 19, 1996 (see Q 16:108), or the simplified recovery rules if the annuity starting date is after November 18, 1996 (see Q 16:109). Before July 1, 1996, basis could be recovered on a pro rata basis or under the three-year rule. If the annuity payments payable over three years equaled or exceeded the participant's basis, the participant would recover basis first, that is, early payments were tax free.

A participant may not increase the tax-free basis in the contract to account for inflation. [Nordtvedt v. Commissioner, 116 T.C. 165 (T.C. 2001)]

### Q 16:108 What is the *exclusion ratio* used in determining a participant's investment in an annuity contract?

The *exclusion ratio,* which applies if the annuity starting date is after June 30, 1986, and before November 19, 1996, is equal to the after-tax employee contributions divided by the life expectancy of the employee (and spouse if the benefit is to be paid as a JSA). It represents the percentage of each payment that is a tax-free recovery of investment in the contract, and is determined as follows:

1. The numerator of the exclusion ratio is the employee's *investment in the contract,* basically the amount of after-tax employee contributions to the plan.

2. The denominator of the exclusion ratio is the *expected return* under the contract, which is determined by multiplying the annual annuity payment by the number of years of the participant's life expectancy according to annuity tables contained in the regulations.

**Example.** Mona retired in 1995, at the age of 65. She will receive retirement benefits of $15,000 per year for her life. Over the course of her employment, Mona contributed $20,000 to the plan. The life expectancy for a 65-year-old is 20 years (Table V of Treasury Regulations Section 1.72-9). The expected return on the contract is $300,000 ($15,000 × 20). Accordingly, Mona's exclusion ratio is $20,000/$300,000, or 6.67 percent. Each year she will exclude $1,334 (6.67% × $20,000) of her benefit payment from income. The remainder of the annuity payment is taxed as ordinary income.

If the annuity starting date is before January 1, 1987, the exclusion ratio applies to all payments received under the annuity contract. After December 31, 1986, the total exclusion is limited to the investment in the contract. If a participant dies before recovering the full amount of nontaxable employee contributions, the unrecovered amounts can be deducted on his or her final income tax return. [I.R.C. § 72(b)(3), (c)(1), (c)(3); Treas. Reg. §§ 1.72-1(c), 1.72-4, 1.72-5(b), 1.72-6(a), 1.72-8]

A simplified safe harbor (see Q 16:109) can be used in lieu of the exclusion ratio if annuity payments are based on the life of the employee or the joint lives of the employee and a beneficiary. [Notice 88-118, 1988-2 C.B. 450]

### Q 16:109    What are the simplified recovery rules used in determining a participant's investment in an annuity contract?

The simplified method of determining the taxable and nontaxable portions of annuity payments uses the participant's age rather than the life expectancy tables in the regulations. The simplified method is not available to participants age 75 or older unless fewer than five years of payments are guaranteed. [Notice 88-118, 1988-2 C.B. 450] The expected number of monthly payments, based on the participant's age at the annuity starting date, are taken from the following table:

| Age | Payments |
|---|---|
| 55 and under | 360 |
| 56-60 | 310 |
| 61-65 | 260 |
| 66-70 | 210 |
| 71 and over | 160 |

The investment in the contract is divided by the expected number of monthly payments to determine the nontaxable amount of each monthly annuity payment. The remainder of each monthly payment is taxable.

The nontaxable level-dollar amount of each monthly annuity payment determined at the annuity starting date remains unchanged even though the dollar amount of the payment increases because of a cost-of-living factor or decreases because of a reduced survivor annuity. If, in a reduced survivor annuity, the nontaxable level-dollar amount of each monthly annuity payment exceeds the actual monthly annuity, the payment is fully excludable. As is the case under the exclusion ratio recovery method, annuity payments received following recovery of the entire investment in the contract are fully taxable. Any unrecovered investment in the contract (because annuity benefits cease before completion of the applicable number of expected payments from the foregoing table) is allowed as a deduction on the recipient's final income tax return. [IRS Pub. No. 575; Notice 88-118, 1988-2 C.B. 450]

The simplified method is not as favorable as the exclusion ratio recovery method. Longer anticipated life expectancies result in a higher number of expected payments, spreading recovery over a longer time.

> **Example.** Mona retired in 1995, at the age of 65. She will receive retirement benefits of $15,000 per year ($1,250 per month) for life. Over the course of her employment, Mona contributed $20,000 to the plan. The expected number of monthly payments for a 65-year-old is 260. Each month Mona will exclude $76.92 ($20,000 ÷ 260) from income. The remainder of the annuity payment is taxed as ordinary income.

The SBJPA modified the simplified method of determining the nontaxable portion of annuity payments. If the annuity is payable over one life, the number of anticipated payments is based on the table applicable for annuity starting dates after November 18, 1996. If payment is made over two lives, the excludable portion of each monthly payment is determined by dividing the investment in the contract by the number of payments as determined by the table set forth below:

| Combined Ages | Payments |
|---|---|
| 110 and under | 410 |
| 111-120 | 360 |
| 121-130 | 310 |
| 131-140 | 260 |
| 141 and over | 210 |

[I.R.C. § 72(d)(1)(B)(iv)]

## Q 16:110 How are tax consequences reported to the party receiving benefit payments?

Annuity distributions are generally reported on IRS Form 1099-R. Taxable and nontaxable amounts must be reported. The plan administrator or benefit payer must provide a notice to annuity recipients explaining that the simplified method is being used on the form and that the taxable portion computed under the simplified method may vary from that computed under the general exclusion ratio method. [Notice 88-118, 1988-2 C.B. 450]

## Q 16:111   What special rules apply to lump-sum distributions from a plan?

Nonannuity payments are included in gross income to the extent they are allocable to income and excluded to the extent they are allocable to the investment in the contract. [I.R.C. § 72(e); Treas. Reg. § 1.72-11] The plan administrator must provide a notice explaining special tax rules, including the rollover and withholding rules (see chapter 28). [Treas. Reg. § 1.402(c)-2, Q&A 1(b)(2)]

## Q 16:112   Can taxes be reduced by using income averaging?

Yes. Some defined benefit pension plans permit participants to take a lump-sum distribution instead of periodic or annuity distributions. A single-sum payment of a participant's entire interest in a qualified retirement plan within the same taxable year may qualify for income averaging. To qualify for averaging, the distribution must occur because of the employee's

1. Death;
2. Disability;
3. Separation from the employer's service; or
4. Attainment of age 59½.

[I.R.C. § 402(d)(4); Treas. Reg. § 1.402(e)-2(d)]

Self-employed individuals do not qualify for forward averaging treatment for distributions on separation from service, but do qualify if the triggering event is disability. For other employees, separation from service, but not disability, is a qualifying event.

In addition, a distribution will not qualify for averaging if the participant did not participate in the plan for at least five years before the distribution.

Effective for tax years beginning after December 31, 1999, five-year averaging is repealed for lump-sum distributions. [I.R.C. § 402(d)]

Individuals who attained age 50 before January 1, 1986, can still use 10-year averaging as long as the prior (pre-1986) tax rates are used. An individual can elect forward averaging only once.

**Example.** Waldo terminated his employment and received a lump-sum payment equal to the present value of his accrued benefits under the plan in 1999. The lump-sum payment was $100,000. Waldo satisfied all of the conditions for five-year averaging. Because he was born before 1936, he is also eligible for 10-year averaging. The tax on the distribution is calculated as follows:

*Five-Year Tax Option*

| | |
|---|---|
| (a) Total distribution | $100,000 |
| (b) ⅕ of total distribution | $20,000 |
| (c) Tax on (b) from five-year table | $3,000 |
| (d) Multiply tax by 5 | $15,000 |

*Ten-Year Tax Option*

| | |
|---|---:|
| (a) Total distribution | $ 100,000 |
| (b) ¹⁄₁₀ of total distribution | $ 10,000 |
| (c) Tax on (b) from ten-year table | $ 1,447 |
| (d) Multiply tax by 10 | $ 14,470 |

Waldo will complete Form 4972 and attach it to his federal income tax return.

Detailed instructions for the calculation of taxes due on lump-sum distributions and the tax rate schedules are included in IRS Form 4972 and the instructions to the form.

### Q 16:113  What other taxes may apply to distributions from pension plans?

Two events may trigger additional taxes: premature distributions and late distributions.

*Premature distributions* (lump-sum or non-life annuity distributions made before the participant attains age 59½) carry an additional tax burden. An additional 10 percent tax applies to distributions from qualified retirement plans unless the distributions are made:

1. After the participant attains age 59½;
2. On account of the death or disability of the employee;
3. In annuity form for the participant's life;
4. To an employee after separation from service after reaching age 55; or
5. As payment to an alternate payees under QDRO.

[I.R.C. § 72(t)]

*Late distributions* (distributions made after the required beginning date) are subject to an excise tax if an insufficient amount is paid to the participant or beneficiary. The excise tax is 50 percent of the shortfall from the minimum required distribution. [I.R.C. § 4974]

### Q 16:114  Is there an additional tax if a distribution from the plan is too large?

Before January 1, 1997, a 15 percent penalty tax was imposed on excess distributions from plans. This tax, often referred to as the *success tax*, was repealed by the Taxpayer Relief Act of 1997 (TRA '97). [I.R.C. § 4980A]

### Q 16:115  Can a distribution be too small, and if so, is there an additional tax on it?

Yes. If an actual distribution amount falls short of the required minimum distribution, an excise tax equal to 50 percent of the amount by which the distribution was underpaid is imposed on the participant, beneficiary, or estate entitled to the benefits. [I.R.C. § 4974]

### Q 16:116   Are beneficiaries subject to income taxes?

Yes. Single-sum death benefit payments to beneficiaries (other than life insurance proceeds) in excess of the employee's basis in the contract are taxed as ordinary income unless averaging rules are available. The beneficiary may be entitled to an income tax deduction (the income in respect of decedent (IRD) deduction) for any federal estate taxes attributable to the pension distribution. Annuity or installment payments are fully taxable as ordinary income if the participant had no basis, or investment, in the contract. If the payments do not come from life insurance, the beneficiary is taxed in the same manner as the participant would have been taxed, taking into consideration the participant's investment in the contract.

**Example.** As her uncle's beneficiary, Audrey received $100,000 from a pension plan. Her uncle's estate paid substantial estate taxes, and the federal estate taxes attributable to the pension were $50,000. Audrey is entitled to a deduction for the estate taxes paid even though she did not pay them personally. Only $50,000 ($100,000 − $50,000) of the pension benefit is subject to tax. Audrey will include the IRD deduction on Schedule A of her federal tax return.

### Q 16:117   Are life insurance benefits taxable?

No. As long as the PS-58 costs have been taxed to the employee or premiums were paid with after-tax contributions, the face amount of the death benefit payable from life insurance is excluded from income. [Treas. Reg. § 1.72-16(c)(4)] The balance is taxed as any other distribution is taxed.

### Q 16:118   Can distributions from defined benefit plans be rolled over into another qualified plan or an IRA by the participant?

Yes. Occasionally, payments from defined benefit pension plans can be rolled over into an IRA or other qualified plan. An *eligible rollover distribution* is any distribution of all or any part of the participant's benefit in the plan received by the participant or the surviving spouse, or by a spouse or former spouse as an alternate payee under a QDRO, except the following:

1. *Installment payment.* Any distribution that is one of a series of substantially equal periodic payments made either over a life expectancy or for a period of at least 10 years;

2. *Mandatory payment.* Any required minimum distribution under Code Section 401(a)(9); or

3. *Nontaxable payment.* Any distribution that is not includible in the recipient's gross income.

[I.R.C. § 402(c)(4), (9), (e)(1); Temp. Treas. Reg. § 1.402(c)-2T]

If the distribution is directly rolled over, it is exempt from withholding and is not includible in the participant's or other distributee's income.

### Q 16:119   What plans can receive a rollover from a defined benefit plan?

Although plans must offer participants the option to roll over distributions directly into qualified plans or IRAs, they are not required to accept these rollovers. If plans are amended to accept rollovers, they can limit their acceptance to similar plan types. For example, a defined benefit pension plan can choose to accept only rollovers from other defined benefit pension plans.

A plan that accepts a direct rollover will not be disqualified if the distributing plan was not qualified but the receiving plan reasonably thought the distributing plan was qualified. The distributing plan does not have to have a determination letter with respect to its qualified status. [Prop. Treas. Reg. § 1.401(a)(31)-1, Q&A 14]

## Lost Participants

### Q 16:120   What can a plan administrator do if a participant cannot be located?

The IRS has established a procedure to help plan administrators find lost participants. The employer sponsoring the plan sends the IRS a letter to the participant, which the IRS then forwards to the participant. The cover letter to the IRS must include the participant's Social Security number and explain the reason that letter forwarding by the IRS is desired. [Rev. Proc. 94-22, 1994-1 C.B. 608]

Requests for letter-forwarding assistance involving 49 or fewer participants and beneficiaries are sent to the disclosure officer at the IRS's district office nearest the requester. There is no charge for this service.

Requests involving 50 or more potential participants and beneficiaries are processed under Project 753, Computerized Mailout Program. Generally, it will take 90 days from the IRS's acknowledgment of the request before the mailing can be performed. The charge for Project 753 requests is subject to change but currently is approximately a flat $1,750 fee per request, plus 1 cent per address search and 50 cents per letter forwarded. Requests for service under Project 753 are sent to:

Internal Revenue Service Director

Office of Disclosure CP:EX:D—Room 1603

1111 Constitution Avenue NW

Washington, DC 20224

The letter to the participant must be generic (i.e., not drafted specifically for a particular party) and include the following disclaimer language: "In accordance with current policy the Internal Revenue Service has agreed to forward this letter because we do not have your current address. The Service has not disclosed your address or any other tax information and has no involvement in the matter aside from forwarding this letter."

The Social Security Administration (SSA) also provides a letter-forwarding service for advising participants of benefits. The SSA, like the IRS, will not confirm whether the participant has actually received the letter. The SSA program accepts up to 200 letters for forwarding at a charge of $3 per participant. Requests are made in writing to:

Social Security Administration

Freedom of Information Branch

4th Floor

Annex Building

6401 Security Boulevard

Baltimore, MD 21235

The request should include the participant's name, Social Security number, and reason for the letter.

In addition, there are several private firms that provide participant and beneficiary search services.

### Q 16:121    If a plan is terminated, are additional options available with regard to lost participants?

For a plan that is subject to the requirements of ERISA Title IV, under ERISA Section 4050 the plan administrator can either:

1. Transfer the participant's benefit to the PBGC; or

2. Purchase an irrevocable commitment from an insurer.

Before requesting PBGC assistance, the plan administrator must conduct a diligent search for the lost parties. The PBGC considers the following to be a diligent search:

1. The search begins not more than six months before notices of intent to terminate are issued and is carried on in such a manner that if the individual is found, distribution to the individual can reasonably be expected to be made on or before the deemed distribution date.

2. The search includes inquiry of any plan beneficiaries (including alternate payees) of the missing participant whose names and addresses are known to the plan administrator.

3. The search includes use of a commercial locator service.

[PBGC Reg. § 4050.4]

The plan administrator must provide the PBGC with information and certifications regarding the benefit or irrevocable commitment. After assets have been transferred to the PBGC, the PBGC assumes responsibility for the distribution to a missing participant. [PBGC Reg. § 4050]

# Chapter 17

# Qualified Domestic Relations Orders

Pension benefits can be assigned to a spouse, former spouse, or child pursuant to a special type of court order, called a qualified domestic relations order (QDRO). Because defined benefit pension plans provide benefits at retirement rather than an account balance, it is often difficult to divide the benefits in an appropriate manner. This chapter explains how the QDRO rules apply to defined benefit pension plans.

## General Rules and Considerations

### Q 17:1   What is a *qualified domestic relations order*?

A *qualified domestic relations order* is a court order relating to child support, alimony, or property rights often issued in connection with a divorce. The order assigns to the plan participant's spouse, former spouse, child, or other dependents (the alternate payee) the right to receive all or a portion of the benefits payable to the participant under the plan. [I.R.C. § 414(p)(1)(A)]

### Q 17:2   Why are QDROs necessary?

As a general rule, the Employee Retirement Income Security Act of 1974 (ERISA) and the Internal Revenue Code (Code) prohibit a participant from assigning his or her benefits in the plan to any other person. [I.R.C. § 401(a)(13); ERISA § 206(d)(1)] Before the Retirement Equity Act of 1984 (REA), it was unclear whether retirement benefits could be assigned to a former spouse pursuant to a court order, because of these rules. An early case, which may have been the impetus for the QDRO exception to the anti-assignment rules, permitted the plan administrator to garnish and set aside a portion of a participant's accrued pension benefits to satisfy postdivorce alimony and support obligations to a former wife. [American Tel & Tel Co. v. Merry, 592 F.2d 118 (2d Cir. 1979)] In general, however, there were significant inconsistencies in the treatment of orders attempting to divide pension benefits in the context of divorce. REA created an exception to the anti-assignment rules to establish consistent guidelines for the assignment of benefits to a former spouse. If a QDRO is obtained, benefits can be assigned to an alternate payee.

### Q 17:3 Can a prenuptial agreement form the basis for the division of pension assets on divorce?

No. A prenuptial agreement is not a QDRO. Probably the most a prenuptial agreement can do is establish a contractual obligation for the parties to agree to settlement terms that would be incorporated in a QDRO at a later date. A prenuptial agreement in which a wife relinquished her right to a death benefit in the event of her husband's preretirement death was not an effective waiver of a surviving spouse's right to a qualified preretirement survivor annuity (QPSA; see chapter 16). [Hurwitz v. Sher, 982 F.2d 788 (2d Cir. 1992); National Automobile Dealers and Assocs. Ret. Trust v. Arbeitman, 89 F.3d 496 (8th Cir. 1996)]

In addition, a postnuptial agreement may not be valid. One court has held that a postnuptial agreement was a prohibited alienation of benefits, and the agreement could not be considered a QDRO because no divorce or other action involving the domestic relations court existed at the time of the agreement. [Merchant v. Kelly, Haglund, Garnsey & Kahn, 874 F. Supp. 300 (D. Colo. 1995)]

### Q 17:4 Are all qualified plans subject to the QDRO rules?

No. Certain types of plans are not subject to the anti-assignment rules of the Code and ERISA and therefore do not need a QDRO to assign benefits to a spouse in the context of divorce. Governmental plans, church plans, plans that have not provided for employer contributions since September 2, 1974, and certain plans maintained by tax-exempt entities are not subject to the anti-assignment rules. Local law, however, may deny the assignment of a participant's benefits under these plans even if a QDRO is presented.

### Q 17:5 What aspects of QDROs are particularly important in defined benefit pension plans?

Defined benefit pension plans are more complex than defined contribution pension plans, and many family law practitioners are unfamiliar with the concepts of benefit accrual, actuarial equivalents, and annuitization of benefits.

The practitioner drafting a QDRO for a defined benefit pension plan should consider the following five sets of questions:

1. How should benefits be divided? Is the division intended to be more in the nature of a property settlement or a support payment?

2. Should the alternate payee's share of benefits be set apart, or should the alternate payee's share of benefits be dovetailed with benefits provided to the participant? What options are available in the plan?

3. Should the alternate payee's share of benefits be based on current benefit levels or on a portion of future benefits? Should future benefit increases or subsidies be shared?

4. Should survivorship benefits be provided in the event of the participant's death?

5. When should the alternate payee begin to receive benefits? How does early payment affect the level of benefits payable to the alternate payee?

### Q 17:6  Must defined benefit plans include language describing the rights and options afforded alternate payees under QDROs?

No. Qualified plans do not have to include provisions that describe the rules regarding QDROs. [Treas. Reg. § 1.404(a)-13(g)(2)] The plan must, however, include language prohibiting the assignment or alienation of benefits as a condition of qualification. [I.R.C. § 401(a)(13)] QDROs are usually recognized as an exception to the anti-assignment rules in the plan document.

Each plan must "establish reasonable procedures to determine the qualified status of a domestic relations order and to administer distributions under such qualified orders." [I.R.C. § 414(p)(6)(B)] The procedures can be included in the plan document or be part of an administrative policy (see Q 17:59). The procedures must:

1. Be in writing;

2. Be reasonable;

3. Provide that each person specified in a domestic relations order (DRO) received by the plan as entitled to payment of benefits under the plan will be notified (at the address specified in the DRO) of the plan's procedures for making QDRO determinations on receipt of a DRO; and

4. Permit an alternate payee to designate a representative for receipt of copies of notices and plan information that are sent to the alternate payee with respect to a DRO.

[ERISA § 206(d)(3)(G)(ii)]

## Elements of a QDRO

### Q 17:7  What are the essential elements of a QDRO?

For an order to be properly treated as a QDRO, it must contain a number of features. First, the order must be a DRO (see Q 17:8). Second, the order must create or recognize the right of an alternate payee (see Q 17:14) to receive all or a portion of the benefits otherwise payable to the participant under the plan. Third, the order must specifically identify the parties and plan involved and provide complete directions regarding the assigned benefits (see Q 17:11). Finally, the QDRO must not contain a disqualifying defect (see Q 17:13).

The Pension Protection Act of 2006 (PPA) contained language stating that the Treasury Department is to issue regulations under Code Section 414(p) to clarify that a DRO otherwise meeting the requirements to be a QDRO, including the requirements of Code Section 414(p)(3), shall not fail to be treated as a QDRO solely because—

(A) the order is issued after, or revises, another DRO or QDRO, or

(B) of the time at which it is issued. [PPA § 1001]

### Q 17:8   What is a *domestic relations order*?

A *domestic relations order* (DRO) is a judgment, decree, or order (including the approval of a property settlement agreement) that:

1. relates to the provision of child support, alimony payments, or marital property rights to a spouse, former spouse, child, or other dependent of a participant; and
2. is made pursuant to a state domestic relations law.

[I.R.C. § 414(p)(1)(B); ERISA § 206(d)(3)(B)(ii)]

Unless the order is issued pursuant to a state domestic relations law, it is not a DRO. An order issued by a state's probate court would not generally qualify as a DRO. [D.O.L. Adv. Ops. 90-46A, 90-47A (Dec. 1990); Boggs v. Boggs, 520 U.S. 833 (1997); Ablamis v. Roper, 937 F.2d 1450 (9th Cir. 1991)]

### Q 17:9   Is a settlement agreement a DRO?

No. A property settlement agreement signed by the parties, or any other agreement between the parties, does not constitute a DRO. A state authority, usually a court, must issue a judgment or order, or otherwise formally approve an agreement before it can be a DRO. [D.O.L. QDRO Guidance Q 1-2 (July 1997)]

### Q 17:10   Can a temporary restraining order be a DRO?

Possibly. A court order prohibiting certain action for a limited period of time, such as a temporary restraining order, often satisfies several of the criteria of a DRO:

1. It is an order.
2. It could specifically relate to the provision of child support, alimony, or marital property rights because it may restrain payments that would otherwise be paid to the participant and could be used to satisfy those rights.
3. It could relate to the rights of a spouse, former spouse, or child of the participant.

Temporary restraining orders, however, are often made under the general rules of civil procedure rather than under state domestic relations law.

### Q 17:11    What must a DRO contain to be a qualified DRO, or QDRO?

A DRO must specifically answer the questions *who, what, how,* and *where* to be treated as a QDRO. The DRO must clearly specify all of the following:

1. The name and the last known address of the participant and alternate payee;

2. The amount or percentage of the participant's benefit to be paid to the alternate payee, or the manner in which the amount or percentage is to be determined;

3. The number of payments or period to which the order applies; and

4. Each plan to which the order applies.

[I.R.C. § 414(p)(2)]

### Q 17:12    Must all of the requirements be included in a DRO for it to qualify as a QDRO?

No. The plan administrator should not reject a DRO if the order fails to include factual identifying information that is easily obtainable by the plan administrator. [D.O.L. QDRO Guidance Q 2-9 (July 1997)] An order does not fail to qualify as a QDRO merely because the order does not specify the current mailing address of the participant and the alternate payee if the plan administrator has reason to know the addresses independently of the order. [S. Rep. No. 98-575, at 2148 (1984)] Some courts have upheld orders that were in "substantial compliance" with the statutory requirements of Code Section 414(p). [Metropolitan Life Ins. Co. v. Wheaton, 42 F.3d 1080 (7th Cir. 1994)] Another decision emphasized that a marital settlement agreement that provided direction but did not meet the statutory requirements was not a QDRO. Simply identifying the pension plan in the settlement agreement did not "create or recognize an alternate payee's right to, or assign to an alternate payee the right to, plan benefits with respect to a plan participant." [Hawkins v. Commissioner, 102 T.C. 61 (1994)]

### Q 17:13    Are there any restrictions on what can be required under a QDRO?

Yes. A QDRO cannot require:

1. Payment of "any type or form of benefits, or any option, not otherwise provided under the plan." [I.R.C. § 414(p)(3)(A)] For example, a QDRO cannot mandate a lump-sum distribution if that form of payment is not provided in the plan.

2. Increased benefits determined on the basis of actuarial value. [I.R.C. § 414(p)(3)(B)] For example, a QDRO cannot require a payment of $100 per month for a child's lifetime if the participant has only accrued a benefit of

$100 per month for his or her lifetime. Such a payment to a child would have a higher actuarial value because a child has a longer life expectancy than his or her parent.

3. Payment of benefits to an alternate payee that are required to be paid to another alternate payee under another order previously determined to be a QDRO. [I.R.C. § 414(p)(3)(C)] For example, if a previous QDRO has awarded all of a participant's benefits to an alternate payee, a current QDRO could not award additional benefits to a different alternate payee.

## Alternate Payees

### Q 17:14   Who is an *alternate payee*?

An *alternate payee* is the spouse, former spouse, child, or other dependent of a participant who is recognized by a QDRO as having a right to receive all or a portion of the participant's benefits payable under a pension plan. [I.R.C. § 414(p)(8)] Benefits can be assigned only to a person who qualifies as an alternate payee.

### Q 17:15   Can attorneys' fees be paid under a QDRO?

No. Benefits can be paid only to an alternate payee. An attorney is not an alternate payee. [AT&T Management Pension Plan v. Tucker, 902 F. Supp. 1168 (C.D. Cal. 1995)] Of course, benefits payable to an alternate payee can be used by the alternate payee to pay legal fees.

### Q 17:16   Is an alternate payee considered a participant for Pension Benefit Guaranty Corporation purposes?

No. An alternate payee is not treated as a participant in determining Pension Benefit Guaranty Corporation (PBGC) premiums. [ERISA § 206(d)(3)(J)]

## Amount of Assigned Benefit

### Q 17:17   What portion of an individual's benefit can be assigned?

The amount that can be assigned is generally dictated by state law, the terms of the settlement agreement, and the parties' negotiations. A DRO is not qualified, however, if it requires the plan to provide increased benefits (determined on the basis of actuarial value) to the alternate payee. [I.R.C. § 414(p)(3)(B)]

**Example.** Assume that the plan participant, Ian, has attained the early retirement age of 62 and is entitled to an immediate annuity of $1,000 per month for life. A QDRO cannot assign a monthly benefit of $1,000 per month for the life of the alternate payee 51-year-old Elaine because Elaine is younger than Ian. In this case, the value of the assigned benefit would exceed the value of

Ian's accrued benefit because the younger alternate payee, Elaine, has a longer life expectancy.

### Q 17:18   What is an *accrued benefit*?

Defined benefit pension plans provide a benefit payable at normal retirement age. A participant does not become eligible for the full benefit immediately. Instead, the participant earns, or accrues, the benefit over time. An *accrued benefit* represents the benefit, payable at normal retirement age, that has been earned as of a particular date (see chapter 9).

**Example.** TJ Shoes Inc. maintains a defined benefit plan that provides a normal retirement benefit of $1,000 per month beginning at age 65. The plan provides for fractional accrual of benefits over years of participation. Jenna becomes a participant at age 45. Because she has 20 years to normal retirement, she will accrue a monthly normal retirement benefit of $50 ($\frac{1}{20}$ of the $1,000 normal retirement benefit) for each year she participates in the plan. If Jenna remains in the plan until age 65, she will have a fully accrued monthly normal retirement benefit of $1,000. Tyler becomes a participant at age 25. Because he has 40 years to normal retirement, he will accrue a monthly normal retirement benefit of $25 ($\frac{1}{40}$ of the $1,000 normal retirement benefit) for each year he participates in the plan. After three years of partici-pation, Tyler will have accrued a monthly normal retirement benefit of $75 ($\frac{3}{40}$ of the $1,000 normal retirement benefit).

### Q 17:19   What is the *present value of the accrued benefit*?

The *present value of the accrued benefit* is the number that represents the current value of a stream of annuity payments in the future. An actuary converts this stream of future payments into a single sum using a number of assumptions, including interest rates and mortality.

**Example.** Assume Ben has an accrued benefit of $1,000 per month payable for life beginning at age 65. Ben is currently age 45. The actuary needs to determine what pool of funds is necessary to provide this benefit beginning at age 65. If the mortality table used in the determination is a recent table, the life expectancies may be longer, and a larger pool of funds would therefore be required to provide the retirement benefit. If the interest rate used in the determination is higher, the anticipated return and growth of the fund will be greater, and therefore a smaller initial pool of funds would be required. Assume the pool of funds needed to provide the benefit at age 65 is $120,000. Unfortunately, this is not the end of the analysis. Ben is age 45, 20 years from normal retirement age. The next inquiry is what pool of funds is needed today so that 20 years hence there will be a $120,000 pool of assets to provide a benefit of $1,000 per month for life. Again, the actuary considers interest rates (the higher the assumed rate, the lower the present value) and, perhaps, the chance that Ben will die before retirement (referred to as *preretirement mortality*). If the assumed interest rate is 7 percent, and no preretirement mortality is assumed, the present value of the accrued benefit would be $31,010.

Under these assumptions, the $31,010 would grow to the $120,000 needed to provide a monthly benefit of $1,000 per year for the participant's life beginning at retirement at age 65.

### Q 17:20 How can benefits be assigned to an alternate payee in a defined benefit plan?

There are as many ways of dividing benefits as creative family law practitioners can devise. Most formulas, however, fall within two basic categories:

1. A shared-payment, or piggyback, QDRO; or

2. A separate-interest QDRO.

*Shared-payment, or piggyback, QDRO.* Under a shared-payment, or piggyback, QDRO, the alternate payee is assigned a portion of the participant's retirement income benefit when (and if) it becomes payable to the participant. The assigned benefit is completely dependent on the existence and continuation of the benefit payable to the participant.

> **Example 1.** A QDRO assigns to Clyde, Bonnie's husband, 50 percent of each of her monthly benefit payments. When Bonnie retires, she becomes eligible for a monthly retirement benefit of $100 for life. Clyde will receive 50 percent of that retirement benefit, or $50 per month, when Bonnie's payments begin.

Generally these types of arrangements give the participant absolute control over the timing and form of benefit payment. If a participant is already receiving retirement benefits, QDROs must be structured as shared-payment QDROs, because the form and timing of the benefit payments cannot be changed once the participant is in pay status. A shared-payment QDRO could then assign all or a portion of the participant's retirement benefit to the alternate payee for the remaining term based on the benefit form previously selected by the participant. The alternate payee cannot modify the form of payment or elect to defer or accelerate benefit payments. The QDRO can indicate when payments to the alternate payee will begin and end. [D.O.L. QDRO Guidance Q 3-7 (July 1997)]

*Separate-interest QDRO.* A separate-interest, or separate-share, QDRO divides the value of the benefit and creates a separate interest for the alternate payee. This type of arrangement is more typically found in defined contribution plans, under which the participant's account balance can be divided and treated as two separate account balances. A division into shares of appropriate values is more difficult in a defined benefit plan. In a separate-interest QDRO, the value of the assigned benefit is effectively carved out for the benefit of the alternate payee.

> **Example 2.** A QDRO assigns to Jack, Jill's husband, 50 percent of the value of Jill's accrued benefit as of the date of divorce. As of the date of divorce, the present value of Jill's accrued benefit under the plan is $20,000. Fifty percent of that value, or $10,000, is apportioned to Jack. The apportioned value is eventually converted to an immediate or deferred benefit for Jack.

In most instances, the alternate payee can elect to receive benefits paid at the time and in the form directed by the alternate payee. The amount of the benefit payable to the alternate payee is the actuarial equivalent of the separate share established under the QDRO. Under a separate-interest QDRO, the alternate payee can elect to begin payment before the participant retires. Although it is rare, occasionally an alternate payee can be "cashed out" of the assigned benefit on entry of the QDRO.

**Caution.** Some defined benefit pension plans do not recognize separate-interest QDROs and will not accept a DRO that attempts to treat alternate payees as quasi-participants. The PBGC will recognize separate-interest QDROs as long as the participant has not begun to receive payments from the plan. [PBGC, "Divorce Orders & PBGC" (Aug. 2000), p. 4]

### Q 17:21 How is the portion of the pension benefit that is subject to division determined?

Many times state law dictates how the pension benefit is to be divided. For example, the alternate payee's benefit may be based on the benefit accrued during the marriage, the current accrued benefit, or the total accrued benefit payable at retirement.

### Q 17:22 What is the difference between a QDRO based on the current accrued benefit and one based on the accrued benefit payable at retirement?

A QDRO that divides benefits based on the *current accrued benefit* determined as of the date of divorce treats pension entitlements like a fixed property right. The value of the benefits at the time of divorce is divided (or swapped) like any other asset. A QDRO based on the accrued benefit as of the date of divorce can be valued immediately.

If the QDRO divides benefits based on the *accrued benefit payable at retirement*, the alternate payee is sharing in future accruals under the plan that may occur after the divorce. A QDRO based on the accrued benefit at retirement does not have a fixed value, but is contingent on future compensation, credited service, and benefit formula changes.

**Example.** Assume a plan provides a unit benefit equal to 2 percent of the final five years of average pay multiplied by years of service. At the time of divorce, the employee, Ken, had been married for 12 years and had 10 years of service and an average pay of $40,000. Therefore, his accrued benefit at the time of divorce would be $8,000 (2% × $40,000 × 10). Fifteen years later, when Ken reaches retirement age, his average pay is $75,000. Ken's accrued benefit at actual retirement would be $37,500 (2% × $75,000 × 25). The share of the benefits payable to Barbie, the alternate payee, is to be 50 percent of the marital share. The *marital share* is based on the number of years of marriage while Ken was accruing benefits divided by the total years of plan participation at the time of determination. Under the current accrued benefit method, Barbie would receive $4,000 (50% × $8,000 × $^{10}/_{10}$). Under the accrued benefit payable at retirement method, Barbie would receive $7,500 (50% × $37,500 × $^{10}/_{25}$). This method is more valuable to an alternate payee when the participant's compensation or the benefit formula is expected to increase.

### Q 17:23    What method of dividing pension benefits is typically used?

Usually the alternate payee's share of benefits is defined in terms of a percentage of the participant's benefit or a percentage of the value of the benefit. In many states, a marital share is calculated by multiplying 50 percent of the benefit by a coverture fraction (see Q 17:24). For purposes of property settlement, the value of the pension may be used to offset property passing to the other spouse.

### Q 17:24    What is a *coverture fraction*?

A *coverture fraction*, sometimes called the marital share, is a fraction, the numerator of which is the number of years of marriage for which credited service under the plan was earned and the denominator of which is the total years of credited service under the plan.

> **Example.** Jill has been a participant in the Sew Forever defined benefit plan for the last 20 years. She was married to Jack for 15 years before their divorce. Her accrued benefit is currently $3,000 per month payable at age 65. Jack and Jill agree that Jack is entitled to 50 percent of Jill's benefit she earned while married. Jack will receive 50 percent of $2,250 ($3,000 × 15 ÷ 20), or $1,125.

### Q 17:25    How does an actuary calculate the value of an individual's retirement benefits in divorce proceedings?

Many times the parties will want to know the value of the accrued pension benefit for purposes of property settlement if this asset is to be used to offset other assets in the community. The pension plan asset is a stream of payments, an annuity, to be received in the future. The present value of this annuity should reflect current market replacement costs of the annuity. The valuation hinges on whether the value is a fair one.

Actuarial Standards of Practice (ASOP) No. 34 provides guidance to the actuary who performs professional services concerning retirement plan benefits in domestic relations actions. This ASOP provides specific guidance relating to performing an actuarial valuation and preparing the related report, participating in adversarial proceedings, providing information on the division of retirement plan benefits, assisting in drafting a court order, and reviewing or implementing a court order.

### Q 17:26    What guidance is provided by ASOP No. 34 to assist the actuary in performing the actuarial valuation and preparing a related report?

An actuarial valuation is required to determine the value of benefits payable from a defined benefit pension plan that may be included in marital property.

The goal of performing an actuarial valuation is to provide a reasonable and objective assessment of the value of retirement plan benefits that are marital property. To prepare an actuarial valuation, the actuary should do the following: identify and collect the information required to determine the covered party's retirement plan benefits; select an allocation method, unless prescribed; select nonprescribed actuarial assumptions; and perform the computations. Each of these steps is described in more detail below.

### Q 17:27   What information is generally required to be collected by the actuary in performing a valuation?

Typically, information that must be collected by the actuary will include the following:

1. The identity of the retirement plan(s) relevant to the engagement and each plan's circumstances—such as ongoing, frozen, or terminated; qualified, nonqualified, or governmental.

2. Relevant retirement plan provisions—including benefit formulas, eligibility for participation and for benefit entitlement, ancillary benefits, early retirement subsidies, and optional forms of payment.

3. Covered party and spouse information—such as employment and plan participation status (active, terminated, vested, disabled, retired); compensation history; dates of birth, hire, plan participation, marriage, separation, and other relevant dates; accrued retirement plan benefits; prior DROs; and any special circumstances that might materially affect the valuation results.

4. Measurement date—when the measurement date is selected by the actuary, such date should be reasonable and the actuary should be prepared to justify the date selected.

The actuary may rely on information supplied by the attorney, plan sponsor, plan administrator, covered party, spouse, or plan record keeper, but the actuary is responsible for reviewing, when practicable, the reasonableness of the applicable data. The actuary should disclose the data used, the source of the data, and any data deficiencies that might materially affect the results. [ASOP No. 34, 3.3.1]

### Q 17:28   What allocation method should the actuary use in performing the valuation?

The actuary is bound first to following what is required by local law. When the actuary is responsible for selecting an allocation method, the allocation method should be reasonable, and the actuary should be prepared to justify the selection. The acceptability of a given allocation method may depend on the legal jurisdiction applicable to the parties involved in the action. There are two allocation methods prescribed by the ASOP, direct tracing and fractional rule methods:

1. *Direct tracing.* The portion of the retirement benefit that is marital property is equal to the actual benefit accrued during the allocation period. For

example, in applying direct tracing to a defined benefit pension plan, the portion of the retirement benefit included in marital property would generally be the increase from the accrued (or vested) benefit, if any, at the marriage date to the accrued (or vested) benefit at the allocation date.

2. *Fractional rule.* The retirement benefit is allocated by multiplying the retirement benefit by a fraction. The numerator and denominator of the fraction may be based on compensation, contributions, benefit accrual service, plan participation, employment, or other relevant data that are used directly in the determination of the accrued benefit. The numerator is equal to the selected measure accrued during the allocation period. The denominator is equal to the selected measure accrued during the total period in which the benefit is earned. When the selected measure is an elapsed time period, this method is commonly referred to as the *time rule.*

Variations of these basic methods exist. The actuary should provide a complete description of the method(s) used. [ASOP No. 34, 3.3.2(a)]

**Example.** The plan provides a retirement plan benefit equal to 1 percent of the final year's compensation multiplied by years of service. Accrued benefits vest after five years of service, and participants are eligible to retire early at age 55 if they have completed 10 years of service. Normal retirement is at age 65. The covered party joined the plan at age 25, was married at age 29, and is age 40 at the allocation date. The covered party's historical service, compensation, accrued benefit, and vested accrued benefit are shown in the following table.

| Age | Completed Years of Service | Prior Plan Year's Compensation | Accrued Benefit | Vested Accrued Benefit |
|-----|-----|-----|-----|-----|
| 26 | 1 | $11,500 | $ 115 | $ 0 |
| 27 | 2 | $12,500 | $ 250 | $ 0 |
| 28 | 3 | $14,500 | $ 420 | $ 0 |
| 29 | 4 | $14,500 | $ 580 | $ 0 |
| 30 | 5 | $15,000 | $ 750 | $ 750 |
| 31 | 6 | $15,500 | $ 930 | $ 930 |
| 32 | 7 | $16,750 | $1,173 | $1,173 |
| 33 | 8 | $18,000 | $1,440 | $1,440 |
| 34 | 9 | $19,000 | $1,710 | $1,710 |
| 35 | 10 | $20,000 | $2,000 | $2,000 |
| 36 | 11 | $23,500 | $2,585 | $2,585 |
| 37 | 12 | $25,000 | $3,000 | $3,000 |
| 38 | 13 | $27,500 | $3,575 | $3,575 |
| 39 | 14 | $29,000 | $4,060 | $4,060 |
| 40 | 15 | $33,000 | $4,950 | $4,950 |

*Direct tracing allocation method.* In the direct tracing method, the portion of the retirement plan benefit that is often considered to be marital property is equal to the actual benefit accrued during the allocation period (typically the period from the date of marriage to the allocation date). For example, in applying direct tracing to a defined benefit pension plan, the portion of the retirement plan benefit included in marital property would generally be the increase from the accrued benefit, if any, at the marriage date to the accrued benefit at the allocation date. If the direct tracing method were applied to the data given in the table above, subtracting the $580 accrued benefit at the date of marriage from the $4,950 accrued benefit at the allocation date would yield the portion of the accrued benefit that is marital property: $4,370.

Alternatively, the direct tracing method could be applied to the covered party's vested accrued benefit. Under this approach, the entire $4,950 is marital property because the vested accrued benefit was $0 at the date of marriage.

*Fractional rule allocation method.* The fractional rule method allocates the retirement plan benefit by multiplying the retirement plan benefit by a fraction. The fraction may be based on compensation, contributions, benefit accrual service, plan participation, employment, or other relevant historical data. The numerator is equal to the selected measure accrued during the allocation period (typically the period from the date of marriage to the allocation date). The denominator is equal to the selected measure accrued during the total period in which the retirement plan benefit is earned. When the selected measure is an elapsed time period, this method is commonly referred to as the *time rule.*

If the fractional rule method based on benefit accrual service were applied to the data in the table above, the $4,950 accrued benefit at the allocation date would be multiplied by the fraction ($11/15$) because the covered party was married for 11 of the 15 years over which the benefit was accrued. The portion of the accrued benefit that is marital property is $3,630.

If the fractional rule method were based on compensation instead, the numerator of the fraction would be compensation earned from the date of marriage to the allocation date ($242,250), and the denominator would be the covered party's total compensation earned from employment date to the allocation date ($294,750). When the $4,950 accrued benefit is multiplied by the fraction ($242,250/$294,750), the portion of the accrued benefit that is considered to be marital property is $4,068. [ASOP No. 34, Appendix 2]

### Q 17:29    How does the valuation change if there are age or service conditions applicable to benefits?

If the covered party has not satisfied the applicable age or service conditions for certain benefits provided in the plan but remains employed by the plan sponsor at the allocation date, the actuary should determine how to allocate the age or service-dependent benefit. Unless otherwise required by applicable law, acceptable approaches include the immediate termination approach, which values the benefit as if the covered party terminated on the allocation date; and the continued employment approach, which reflects continued covered employment in accordance with selected retirement, turnover, mortality, or disability assumptions.

**Note.** Different types of allocation methods can produce significantly different results. An actuary working in situations where different methods are used should educate his or her client as to the differences between the methods and the general financial impact of those differences.

**Example.** The Quilt Shop retirement plan provides that the benefit payable upon early retirement at age 55 is 100 percent of the accrued benefit if the participant has completed at least 25 years of service, and 50 percent of the accrued benefit otherwise. If the covered party has not satisfied the eligibility requirements at the allocation date but remains employed by the plan sponsor, alternative approaches are available. One approach would exclude from marital property any age or service-dependent benefit that is available only if the covered party remains employed after the allocation date. A second approach would include such benefits in marital property under the assumption that the covered party will remain employed by the plan sponsor until eligibility conditions for the higher benefit level are satisfied. These two approaches may produce quite different results. The early retirement provision described above, including the value of the 25-years-of-service subsidy in marital property, could double the value of the retirement plan benefit. [ASOP No. 34, 3.3.2(b)]

### Q 17:30 What factors must the actuary consider when choosing actuarial assumptions?

When selecting assumptions for an actuarial valuation of retirement plan benefits in a domestic relations action, the actuary should consider limitations imposed by applicable law and the facts and circumstances of the valuation, including each relevant retirement plan's circumstances and provisions; information about the covered party and spouse; and past experience and future expectations for the group of which the covered party is a member.

Each assumption selected by the actuary should be individually reasonable and consistent with every other assumption selected by the actuary. The actuary should be prepared to justify each assumption selected.

The following sections (1-10) describe assumptions commonly used in valuing retirement plan benefits and factors that the actuary should consider in selecting assumptions for valuing such benefits in domestic relations actions. This list is not intended to be all-inclusive; additional assumptions may be required depending on the provisions of the retirement plan being valued, specific circumstances of the covered party or spouse, and unique requirements of the jurisdiction.

1. *Discount rate.* Unless another assumption is clearly warranted by the facts and circumstances, the discount rate selected for valuing retirement plan benefits in domestic relations actions should be a low-risk rate of investment return, determined as of the measurement date and based on the cash-flow pattern of benefits being valued (for example, the current or a recent average yield to maturity on U.S. Treasury bonds of comparable duration, or a published index reflecting yield rates for high-quality corporate bonds).

2. *Mortality assumption.* A mortality table that is generally accepted for valuing annuities or pension benefits, or a table that reflects the expected mortality experience of plan participants, is generally appropriate. However, in some cases it may be appropriate to adjust the mortality assumption to reflect the health of the covered party or spouse.

3. *Annuity purchase.* As an alternative to selecting a discount rate under section #1, and a mortality assumption under section #2, the actuary may assume the cost of the purchase of an immediate or deferred annuity contract, as appropriate, from an insurance carrier. Typically, this may be done by using an actual insurance survey or by reference to published tables that are derived from such surveys.

4. *Retirement assumption.* The retirement assumption may be a single assumed retirement age or a table of retirement rates by age. The retirement assumption should reflect the applicable facts and circumstances, such as the following:

   • The plan's normal retirement age;
   • The ages at which the covered party is first eligible to retire, to receive subsidized early retirement plan benefits, to receive unreduced retirement plan benefits, to receive Social Security benefits, and to receive Medicare benefits;
   • Plan participants' average retirement age and retirement rates by age (if known to the actuary) or norms as to retirement age in the covered party's industry or profession;
   • The availability of medical and other postretirement plan benefits;
   • The level of total retirement plan benefits; or
   • The covered party's income level, job position, and family circumstances.

   Statements made by the covered party or spouse as to anticipated retirement age may also be considered, but should not be given undue weight because such statements may be self-serving and the domestic relations action itself may alter retirement planning decisions.

5. *Cost-of-living adjustments.* If the retirement plan automatically adjusts benefits for increases in the cost of living, the actuarial valuation should generally reflect expected future increases in benefits attributable to such cost-of-living adjustments. In some cases, it may be appropriate to make an assumption about future ad hoc cost-of-living adjustments.

6. *Disability assumption.* A disability assumption may be required if the plan provides special benefits upon disability and if including a disability assumption would materially affect the valuation results. A disability table that is generally accepted for use in valuing annuities or pension benefits, or a table that reflects the expected disability experience of plan participants, is generally appropriate. However, in some cases it may be appropriate to adjust the disability assumption to reflect the health of the covered party.

7. *Turnover assumption.* An assumption as to the rate of participant termination may be required if the benefit is not yet vested or the benefit amount depends on future service. However, some jurisdictions permit

only involuntary termination to be reflected when valuing retirement plan benefits in domestic relations actions. The turnover assumption should reflect the specific facts and circumstances, such as the following:

- The actual or expected turnover experience of plan participants (if known to the actuary);
- The covered party's age and service;
- The covered party's job position; and
- Plan provisions such as the age and service required to receive subsidized early retirement plan benefits.

8. *Compensation scale.* While it is common for the actuarial valuation of retirement plan benefits in domestic relations actions to reflect compensation through the allocation date only, some methods, and some jurisdictions, require the actuary to consider future levels of compensation. For example, a compensation scale may be appropriate when the retirement plan automatically adjusts accrued retirement plan benefits based on compensation increases for the covered party's last position, title, or pay grade, regardless of whether the covered party remains employed.

9. *Growth of individual account balances.* Some retirement plan benefits have components directly related to the accumulation of real or hypothetical individual account balances (including defined contribution plans, floor offset arrangements, and cash balance pension plans). An assumption regarding the future investment return earned by the actual or hypothetical accounts may be required to value benefits under such plans. Unless another assumption is clearly warranted, this assumed rate of investment return should generally equal the discount rate.

10. *Variable conversion factors.* Valuing certain retirement plan benefits may require converting from one payment form to another (e.g., converting a projected individual account to an annuity or converting an annuity to a lump sum). If the conversion basis is variable (e.g., recalculated each year based on a stated mortality table and an interest rate equal to the yield on 30-year Treasury bonds), an assumption regarding future conversion rates may be required.

[ASOP No. 34, 3.3.3]

### Q 17:31   What process should the actuary use in performing the valuation?

An actuarial valuation should generally involve the following steps:

1. Identify the measurement date, the allocation date, the allocation period, potential retirement plan benefits, the contingencies that may affect payment of those benefits, and any special requirements of the applicable legal jurisdiction;

2. Project the timing and amounts of potential benefit payments, applying the selected or prescribed allocation method and applicable economic assumptions, and assuming that any required contingencies are met;

3. Calculate expected payments by multiplying each potential benefit payment determined in item #2 by the probability that the required contingencies are met, and applying the selected or prescribed demographic and other assumptions; and

4. Discount the expected payments determined in item #3 back to the measurement date, using the selected or prescribed discount rate.

[ASOP No. 34, 3.3.4]

### Q 17:32  Can a QDRO assign benefits that have not been earned yet?

Only indirectly. A QDRO cannot require the plan to pay benefits that are greater than the amount payable to the participant. [I.R.C. § 414(p)(3)(B)] A QDRO can, however, assign a percentage of the benefit ultimately payable to the participant to the alternate payee. If the participant's compensation and credited service increase, the amount ultimately payable to the alternate payee may be greater than the accrued benefit of the participant at the time of divorce.

**Example 1.** Marge has accrued a benefit of $50 per month as of the date of divorce. A QDRO assigns to Homer, Marge's husband, 50 percent of each of her monthly benefit payments. When Marge retires, she becomes eligible for a monthly retirement benefit of $100 for life. Homer will receive 50 percent of that retirement benefit, or $50 per month for Marge's life.

**Example 2.** Bambi was employed on January 1, 1983, by GB Enterprises. She married Thumper on January 1, 1993. They divorced as of January 1, 2003, when she had an accrued benefit of $666.67 per month. Her normal retirement date is January 1, 2013. She has a projected benefit at retirement of $1,250 per month. The present value of the benefit as of January 1, 2003, is $44,672. The coverture fraction is 10 years of marriage divided by 20 total years of service, or 50 percent. Therefore, the amount of the benefit subject to division is $22,336 ($44,672 ÷ 50%). The spouse is currently entitled to one-half of this amount, or $11,168. On the other hand, the present value at January 1, 2013, of Bambi's benefit is $149,850. If a QDRO is prepared to provide that the benefit will be equitably divided upon Bambi's retirement, then she will be entitled to 10/30's (the coverture fraction) of the present value at January 1, 2013, which is $49,950 ($149,850 × 10 ÷ 30). Thumper's share will be one-half of this amount, or $24,975, on January 1, 2013. The decision for the two parties then becomes whether to divide the benefit now, when Thumper will receive only $11,168, or 10 years from now, when Thumper will receive $24,975.

### Q 17:33  Can a QDRO require payment of a flat monthly benefit to the alternate payee?

Yes. A QDRO can establish a flat dollar amount, a percentage of the benefit payable to the participant, or a percentage of the accrued benefit as of a particular date.

### Q 17:34    Can a QDRO be effective after a retiree is in pay status?

Yes. A QDRO entered after a retiree is in pay status can assign a portion of the amount payable to the retiree to the alternate payee. In this case, the QDRO must be structured as a shared-payment QDRO. The alternate payee cannot change the form of benefits already elected. In addition, the QDRO can assign only benefits otherwise payable to the participant. For example, if the participant has elected to receive benefits in the form of a qualified joint and survivor annuity (QJSA) and designated his or her new spouse as the party to receive survivor benefits in the event of the participant's death, the alternate payee has limited access to benefits. The QDRO cannot treat the former spouse as the surviving spouse and therefore provide survivor benefits to the former spouse in the event of the participant's death. A former spouse can preserve his or her interest in survivor benefits only by obtaining the QDRO before the participant retires and elects the form of benefit payment. [Hopkins v. AT&T Global Information Solutions Co., 914 F. Supp. 1362 (D. W.Va. 1996)]

### Q 17:35    Can QDRO benefit payments be front-end loaded?

Generally, no. A QDRO cannot provide for increased benefits "up front" unless the plan provides an optional form of benefit that contains such a feature. Occasionally, practitioners will draft QDROs to provide additional benefits to "catch up" for benefits lost during the pendancy of the QDRO. It can be argued that a DRO that contains a catch-up provision is not qualified, because it requires payment in a form not permitted under the plan, in violation of Code Section 414(p)(3)(A).

Some QDROs require payment for a limited period of time. It can be argued that if a plan provides benefits only in the form of an annuity, a QDRO that requires payments for a limited period of time has requested a form of benefit that is not provided in the plan in violation of Code Section 414(p)(3)(A). Guidance provided by the Department of Labor (DOL) states that QDROs can specify an ending date as long as notice is given to the plan administrator of the occurrence of the event triggering termination of payment. [D.O.L. QDRO Guidance Q 3-3 (July 1997)] Rarely do plans accept QDROs with termination dates that can be perceived as discretionary.

**Example.** George is currently receiving monthly retirement benefits of $1,500. A DRO assigns to his former spouse, Penelope, $1,000 per month until their daughter graduates from college, and $100 per month thereafter. This DRO would probably not qualify as a QDRO.

### Q 17:36    How can actuarial equivalencies and reductions affect QDRO benefits?

Benefits payable to an alternate payee in a form other than the normal form, or at a time other than the participant's normal retirement date, will be adjusted to produce actuarially equivalent benefits. Even though values may be actuarially equivalent, benefits payable over the life of a younger alternate payee will be less than those payable to the participant over his or her lifetime, because there is a greater likelihood that benefits will be paid over a longer period. Similarly, benefits payable before the normal retirement date will be reduced to account for the longer payout expectancy. These reductions can be significant.

**Example.** Harry has accrued a benefit of $500 per month beginning at normal retirement, age 65. Sally, his wife, has obtained a separate-interest QDRO assigning 50 percent of the accrued benefit to her. She would like to begin receiving her share of the benefits as soon as possible. Because Harry has reached age 55, the earliest retirement age under the plan, Sally is permitted to begin receiving benefit payments. Her first check is for $125, rather than the $250 she anticipated. Because she has requested accelerated payment, her $250 benefit is actuarially reduced (5 percent per year, in this case).

### Q 17:37   What is an *early retirement subsidy*?

An *early retirement subsidy* is a benefit whose actuarial equivalent value is greater than the value of the normal retirement benefit reduced to the early retirement age. When a participant retires before the plan's normal retirement date, the accrued benefit payable at the normal retirement date is actuarially reduced to account for the longer period of time over which benefits are likely to be paid. A plan provides an early retirement subsidy if benefits payable at an early retirement date are not reduced as much as they would have been using actuarial equivalencies.

### Q 17:38   Can a QDRO be drafted to give an alternate payee the benefit of any employer-provided subsidies, such as an early retirement subsidy?

No. Payments made to an alternate payee that begin before the participant separates from service must be calculated as if the participant had retired on the date payments are to begin under the QDRO. The Code and ERISA state that the calculation must be done based only on the benefits that have accrued and not on any early retirement subsidy. [I.R.C. § 414(p)(4)(A)(iii)] This is because the early retirement subsidy is usually available only if and when the participant actually retires. A QDRO can be drafted to increase the benefits payable to the alternate payee in the event a participant retires and takes advantage of an early retirement window or an early retirement subsidy. [REA of 1984, 130 Cong. Rec. H8761, Ex. 2 (comments of Rep. Clay)]

**Example.** Under the Huge Aircraft Company pension plan, a participant can retire early, at age 55, without actuarial reduction for early payment if the participant's age plus years of service equals at least 75 (the "rule of 75"). Under a QDRO, Mary is awarded a share of James's retirement benefits under the plan. The QDRO requires Mary's benefits to be determined as if James had retired at age 55. At the time of the order James is still working. Although James would have been eligible for unreduced retirement benefits if he had retired, these unreduced benefits are an employer subsidy that cannot be paid to Mary while James is still working. A QDRO ordering unreduced benefits is invalid. [In re Marriage of Oddino, 16 Cal. 4th 67 (1997)]

### Q 17:39    Can a QDRO provide a security interest in an account?

Yes. Under the facts of Private Letter Ruling 200252093, a security interest in a spouse's account can be created if the assignment is pursuant to a QDRO. In this ruling, Taxpayer *A* received a portion of the spouse's account pursuant to a QDRO and the balance was to remain as the spouse's sole and separate property. However, Taxpayer *A* was to receive a security interest in the spouse's remaining interest in the plan to secure the spouse's obligation under the judgment for dissolution of marriage between the parties. The IRS ruled that this was an allowable assignment under Code Section 401(a)(13)(B).

## Form of Payment

### Q 17:40    In what forms can QDRO benefits be paid?

The statute does not address distribution options; it merely states that an alternate payee cannot "require a plan to provide any . . . form of benefit, or any option, not otherwise provided under the plan." [I.R.C. § 414(p)(3)(A)] Some plans do not give an alternate payee any distribution options. In other words, the alternate payee has no choice but to take benefits in the form selected by the participant.

As a general rule, when a piggyback, or shared-payment, QDRO is in place, the form of benefits payable to the alternate payee is usually the form elected by the participant (see Q 17:20). For example, if a life annuity is selected, both the participant and the alternate payee will receive benefits over the life of the participant.

If a separate-interest QDRO is in place, the alternate payee may be allowed to select the form of payment (see Q 17:20). A benefit payable before the participant retires may be paid in any form in which "benefits may be made under the plan to the participant (other than in the form of a joint and survivor annuity with respect to the alternate payee and his or her subsequent spouse)." [I.R.C. § 414(p)(4)(A)(iii)] If the participant can elect to receive benefits in a lump sum or in one of many annuity options, the QDRO can direct payment of the alternate payee's assigned benefits in a lump sum or in one of the annuity options.

### Q 17:41    Is it possible for a QDRO to pay benefits over the alternate payee's lifetime?

Yes. Generally, assigned benefits are paid by reference to the participant's age and life. Many plans, however, permit the value of the benefits assigned to an alternate payee to be paid to the alternate payee as if he or she were the participant. In this case, the actuarial equivalent of the value of the assigned benefit is converted to an annuity for the life of the alternate payee. Not all plans permit this option.

### Q 17:42   Can a QDRO stop benefit payments to an alternate payee on the alternate payee's remarriage?

No. A QDRO cannot require a form of benefit that is not permitted under the plan. [I.R.C. § 414(p)(3)(A)] A QDRO cannot provide for benefits to be paid to the alternate payee until remarriage unless the plan provides an optional form of benefit that is contingent on being unmarried.

### Q 17:43   Under a defined benefit plan, can an alternate payee receive benefits under a QDRO in a lump sum?

It depends on the plan. If the plan permits lump-sum distributions, a QDRO can generally be drafted to permit the alternate payee to receive the actuarially equivalent value of the assigned benefits in a lump sum.

### Q 17:44   If benefits are paid to an alternate payee under a separate-interest QDRO, how are actuarially equivalent values determined?

Benefit equivalencies are calculated by reference to the interest rates and mortality tables specified in the plan. If no rate is specified, an interest rate of 5 percent is used. [I.R.C. § 414(p)(4)(A); ERISA § 206(d)(3)(E)(i)]

### Q 17:45   Can QDROs be affected by the QJSA and qualified preretirement survivor annuities rules?

Yes. Pending finalization of the divorce, the participant's spouse has by law certain protections against divestiture by a plan participant. If the participant dies while married to the potential alternate payee, a QPSA (see chapter 16) may be payable to the surviving spouse.

A QDRO can be written to treat the alternate payee as the surviving spouse for purposes of the QPSA and QJSA rules. If the alternate payee is treated as the surviving spouse for purposes of the QJSA rules, the participant cannot elect to receive retirement benefits in any form other than the QJSA with the alternate payee as the surviving spouse without the alternate payee's consent. If the alternate payee is designated as the surviving spouse for purposes of the QPSA rules, the alternate payee will be entitled to all or a portion of the QPSA if the participant dies before retirement.

## Timing of QDRO Benefit Payment

### Q 17:46   When can the alternate payee first begin receiving benefits?

Many alternate payees expect payment immediately on entry of the QDRO. Although it is possible, it is very unlikely that benefits can be paid immediately unless the participant has terminated employment and reached his or her earliest retirement age (see Q 17:48). A plan cannot be forced to pay benefits before the date the participant attains earliest retirement age.

There are few absolute rules defining when benefits must begin under a QDRO. In large part, benefit timing is dependent on the terms of the QDRO, the plan, and the participant's age and employment status.

In a shared-payment QDRO, the alternate payee generally does not receive benefits until the participant retires and elects benefit commencement. In a separate-interest QDRO, the alternate payee often has the right to direct the timing of benefit commencement, subject to the earliest retirement age restriction (see Q 17:47).

Some plans create an early retirement age exclusively for QDRO purposes. This is more frequently found in defined contribution plans.

### Q 17:47   Can a QDRO require benefits to be paid to an alternate payee before the participant separates from service?

Yes. Although a DRO is not generally qualified if it provides benefits to an alternate payee not otherwise provided to a participant, a QDRO can require benefits to be paid to an alternate payee at a time when no benefit is payable to the participant. [I.R.C. § 414(p)(3)(A), (4)] Benefits can be paid to an alternate payee before a participant has separated from service on or after the date on which the participant attains (or would have attained if the participant were still living) the earliest retirement age under the plan. [I.R.C. § 414(p)(4)(A)(i)] Preseparation benefit payment to an alternate payee does not violate the prohibition against requiring a plan to provide benefits not provided to a participant even though the participant could not have elected to receive benefits while actively employed.

### Q 17:48   What is the *earliest retirement age*?

For purposes of the rules permitting distribution of benefits to an alternate payee, the *earliest retirement age* is the earlier of two dates:

1. The date on which the participant is entitled to a distribution under the terms of the plan; or
2. The later of the following:
   a. The date the participant attains age 50; or
   b. The earliest date on which the participant could begin receiving benefits under the plan if the participant has separated from service.

[I.R.C. § 414(p)(4)(A)]

**Example.** Assume that normal retirement age under the plan is age 65. The plan also provides for a "rule of 80" normal retirement when the sum of the participant's age plus credited service equals 80. The plan allows an early retirement benefit payable at the election of an employee who has terminated employment at age 55 with 10 years of credited service. If a participant terminates employment before attaining early or normal retirement age, he or she can receive a deferred vested benefit beginning at either one of these times.

Also assume that the DRO requires payment to the alternate payee at the earliest time permitted by law. The participant is currently 48 years old with 20 years of service. Under this scenario, the earliest retirement age, and therefore the earliest date benefits can begin to an alternate payee, is the earlier of the following dates:

1. The date on which the participant is entitled to a distribution under the terms of the plan, which would be at age 54 with 26 years of service under the "rule of 80"; or

2. The later of the following:

   a. The date the participant attains age 50; or

   b. The earliest date on which the participant could begin receiving benefits under the plan if the participant has separated from service (no distribution can be made to the participant until age 55 if he or she terminates employment before normal retirement age).

The earliest date a distribution can be made to the alternate payee is when the participant reaches age 54 if the participant remains employed for six more years. If the participant terminated employment before completing six more years of service, the earliest date a distribution can be made to the alternate payee is when the participant attains age 55.

### Q 17:49   Under a defined benefit plan, can an alternate payee receive benefits under a QDRO immediately?

Sometimes. If the participant is in pay status or has attained earliest retirement age, and immediate payment is directed in the QDRO, benefits payable to an alternate payee can begin immediately. A QDRO that requires a plan to make payments "as soon as administratively possible" will fail to qualify in many instances because it would require a plan to distribute benefits to the alternate payee before the participant's earliest retirement date. [Dickerson v. Dickerson, 803 F. Supp. 127 (E.D. Tenn. 1992)]

> **Caution.** An alternate payee who elects to receive benefits early should be aware that the amount payable may be significantly less than the amount payable at normal retirement.

> **Planning Pointer.** A limited number of defined benefit plans provide a lump-sum payment option. If this option is available, an alternate payee may be able to receive the value of the assigned benefit in a lump sum immediately upon entry of the QDRO.

### Q 17:50   If a plan permits immediate payment to an alternate payee, can the employer amend the plan to eliminate this feature?

It depends. Generally, employers can amend plans at any time. If, however, a plan is amended to defeat an alternate payee's claim or to make it more difficult to receive benefits, an alternate payee can bring an action against the employer.

[Stephen Allen Lynn P.C. Employee Profit Sharing Plan and Trust v. Stephen Allen Lynn P.C., 25 F.3d 280 (5th Cir. 1994)]

### Q 17:51   Can an alternate payee opt to accelerate payment if there is an early retirement window?

Yes, but only if the participant also has the optional benefit. An order is not qualified if it requires a plan to provide any type or form of benefit, or any option, not otherwise provided under the plan. [I.R.C. § 414(p)(3)(A)] To gain the benefits of an early retirement subsidy or early retirement window, the participant must actually retire. An order that requires the plan to pay an early retirement subsidy or to recognize the benefits available under an early retirement window before the participant satisfies the requirements of the benefit, that is, actually retires, would require the plan to provide a type of benefit not provided under the plan and, therefore, would not be valid. A QDRO could be drafted to accelerate payment (or increase the alternate payee's benefit) if the participant takes advantage of the early retirement window or any other subsidy.

### Q 17:52   What is the impact of a QDRO on the distribution restrictions for underfunded plans?

Under the nondiscrimination Treasury Regulations Section 1.401(a)(4)-5(b), a payment may not be made over a certain amount to a highly compensated employee unless certain requirements are met (see chapter 16). The IRS has opined that the restrictions on distributions under the regulation are applied on a pro-rata basis to the benefit of the restricted employee and the alternate payee. [1995 Grey Book, Q&A 45]

If the payment is limited due to the plan having an adjusted funding target attainment percentage (see chapter 19) of more than 60 percent but less than 80 percent, then the amount that is allowed to be distributed is allocated in proportion to the amount of the accrued benefit that is allocated to each alternate payee, unless the QDRO specifies otherwise. [I.R.C. § 436(d)(3)(B)(ii)]

## Death of Parties

### Q 17:53   Why are survivorship issues of importance in a QDRO?

A participant's spouse has a number of protections under ERISA and the Code. A married participant must receive retirement benefits in the form of a QJSA, which continues to pay all or a portion of the retirement benefits previously payable to the participant to his or her spouse after the participant's death, unless a participant elects another form of benefit payment and the spouse consents (in writing) to the form of benefit elected by the participant. In addition, if a participant dies before retirement, a plan must provide a minimum survivor annuity to a surviving spouse (QPSA; see chapter 16). When a divorce is finalized, the former spouse loses all rights to these survivor benefits. If the participant remarries, the new spouse will acquire these rights. QDROs can be drafted to treat the former spouse as the participant's surviving spouse for all or part of the benefits payable by reason of the participant's death. This may be the only way to provide benefits to the former spouse in the event of the participant's death. [D.O.L. QDRO Guidance Q 3-5 (July 1997)]

### Q 17:54    What happens to the assigned benefits if the participant dies before benefits begin?

The disposition of benefits is generally governed by the terms of the QDRO, the plan, and the marital status of the parties at the time of the death of the participant. Many family law practitioners do not include provisions in a QDRO to deal with benefits in the case of preretirement death.

If the QDRO is structured as a shared-payment QDRO and the participant dies before benefits begin, no benefits are generally payable to the alternate payee unless the QDRO specifically assigns a portion of the preretirement death benefit to the alternate payee. If a QDRO assigns to the alternate payee a specified percentage of benefits payable to the participant, no amounts will be payable to the alternate payee because no amounts are payable to the participant.

> **Example.** A QDRO assigns to the alternate payee 50 percent of the amount payable to the participant. The participant dies. Therefore, nothing is payable to the participant. The alternate payee is entitled to 50 percent of nothing, which is nothing.

If the QDRO is structured as a separate-interest QDRO and the alternate payee is treated as a quasi-participant, the amount allocable to the alternate payee may be protected.

A defined benefit pension plan must pay a survivor benefit to a surviving spouse for the spouse's lifetime when a married participant dies before retirement (see chapter 16). [I.R.C. § 401(a)(11)] An individual loses this protection on divorce; however, a QDRO can be drafted to treat the alternate payee as the surviving spouse for purposes of the QPSA rules. In such case, the alternate payee will receive at least the minimum preretirement survivor annuity required under Code Section 417 (see chapter 16) unless he or she consents to the participant's waiver of the QPSA.

Some plans provide preretirement death benefits in excess of the QPSA. In this event, the QDRO can name the alternate payee as the beneficiary of all or part of the preretirement death benefit. If the plan provides preretirement death benefits in excess of the minimum QPSA, the participant can be precluded from designating any other person as the beneficiary of the assigned benefit without the consent of the alternate payee.

> **Planning Pointer.** To preserve benefits for an alternate payee in the event of the death of the participant before retirement, the QDRO should be structured as a separate-interest QDRO or the QDRO should require the alternate payee to be treated as the surviving spouse for all or a portion of the benefit. The plan should be reviewed carefully to determine death benefit options.

### Q 17:55   Can an alternate payee receive a QPSA?

Yes. A QDRO can designate the alternate payee as the surviving spouse for purposes of the QPSA rules. [I.R.C. § 414(p)(5)(A)] If this designation is made in the QDRO and the participant dies before retirement, the alternate payee will receive a QPSA. Model language designating the alternate payee as the surviving spouse is included in Notice 97-11. [1997-1 C.B. 379]

### Q 17:56   What happens to the assigned benefit if the participant dies after benefits begin?

A QDRO cannot change the form of benefit provided under the plan. [I.R.C. § 414(p)(3)(A)] Therefore, if the participant dies after retirement benefits begin, benefits continue in the form chosen. If a life annuity is chosen, all benefits cease on the death of the participant. If the QDRO is structured as a shared-payment order (see Q 17:20), benefit payments will continue based on the participant's elected benefit form and the terms of the QDRO.

> **Example.** Assume the participant, John, retired and elected to receive monthly benefits for life with 10 years certain. A QDRO provided for the alternate payee, Debbie, to receive 50 percent of the benefit amount payable at John's retirement. If John dies eight years after retirement, Debbie would continue receiving her share of benefits for two more years. At that time benefits would cease. If John dies 13 years after retirement, the assigned benefit would cease at John's death.

### Q 17:57   What happens if the alternate payee dies?

If the alternate payee dies after the alternate payee is in pay status and if the QDRO so directs, remaining benefits can be paid to the alternate payee's designated beneficiary. Many times, QDROs are structured to revert benefits to the participant in the event of the alternate payee's death.

> **Caution.** There is some difference of opinion over what happens to assigned benefits if the alternate payee dies before the benefit is in pay status. Although there does not appear to be express authority for this position, some plan administrators will not accept a QDRO if the alternate payee's share of benefits is directed to a third party in the event of the alternate payee's death before benefits are in pay status.

### Q 17:58   Can an interim survivorship order protect a spouse going through a divorce?

Yes. Some attorneys prepare interim survivorship QDROs pending ultimate distribution of the pension benefits. The interim order can name the alternate payee as the beneficiary in the event of the participant's death before finalization of the agreement on the division of the assets.

# QDRO Policy and Procedure

### Q 17:59   What must a plan administrator do when a QDRO is received?

Each plan must "establish reasonable procedures to determine the qualified status of a domestic relations order and to administer distributions under such qualified orders." [I.R.C. § 414(p)(6)(B)] The plan administrator must follow the written procedures or risk liability for acts or omissions that are not addressed in the written policy. [Schoonmaker v. Employee Sav. Plan of Amoco Corp., 987 F.2d 410 (7th Cir. 1993)]

The statute specifically requires the following steps:

1. *Acknowledge receipt.* The plan administrator must notify the participant and the alternate payee of receipt of a DRO. [I.R.C. § 414(p)(6)(A)(i)]

2. *Send QDRO policy.* The plan administrator must mail a copy of the written QDRO policy to the participant and alternate payee. [I.R.C. § 414(p)(6)(A)(i)]

3. *Segregate accounts.* During the period in which a determination of whether a DRO is a QDRO is being made, the plan administrator must separately account for the amounts that would have been payable to the alternate payee during the period if the order had been determined to be qualified. [I.R.C. § 414(p)(7)(A)]

4. *Determine status.* The plan administrator must determine whether the order qualifies as a QDRO within a reasonable period of time after the order is received. [I.R.C. § 414(p)(6)(A)(ii)]

5. *Notify parties of determination.* The plan administrator must notify the participant and the alternate payee (or their representatives) whether the order qualifies as a QDRO. [I.R.C. § 414(p)(6)(A)(ii)]

### Q 17:60   Can the plan administrator delay payment of a retiree's pension if a QDRO is imminent?

Occasionally, draft QDROs are presented to the plan administrator. Because they have not been entered by the court, however, they do not technically qualify as QDROs. Many QDRO procedures allow for the preapproval of DROs. During the review process, the plan administrator can place a hold on the account or segregate amounts that would be payable to the alternate payee. Any actions taken must follow the written QDRO policy.

A plan administrator should be extremely cautious about taking any action that is not explicitly provided for under the QDRO policy, particularly an anticipatory action when no order has been presented. In one case, a plan administrator placed a hold on a participant's account after it had been informed that a divorce had occurred and a QDRO was imminent. The written QDRO procedure required a hold on a participant's account when the plan received a DRO. The court held that the plan administrator was liable for investment losses suffered by the participant because its action, although consistent with a long-standing informal practice, did not follow the written QDRO policy. [Schoonmaker v. Employee Sav. Plan of Amoco Corp., 987 F.2d 410 (7th Cir. 1993)]

### Q 17:61   Does an alternate payee have a right to receive any information regarding the plan?

The DOL's position is that prospective alternate payees—spouses, former spouses, children, and other dependents of the participant—should be afforded access to information sufficient to prepare a QDRO. As a beneficiary, the alternate payee must be provided with copies of the summary plan description, latest annual report, plan document, and a number of other materials on request (see chapter 28). [D.O.L. QDRO Guidance Q 2-16 (July 1997)]

### Q 17:62   Can a fee be charged to review and handle a QDRO?

No. An advisory opinion issued by the DOL prohibits the plan from charging fees for processing or administering a QDRO. [PWBA Op. Ltr. 94-32A (Aug. 4, 1994)] To do so would "constitute an impermissible encumbrance on the exercise of the right of an alternate payee, under Title I of ERISA, to receive benefits under a QDRO."

### Q 17:63   What notification must be provided if the proposed QDRO is not qualified?

If a proposed QDRO is not qualified, the plan administrator cannot merely provide a rejection notice to counsel for the alternate payee. The notice should include the following information:

1. The reasons why the order is not qualified;
2. References to plan provisions on which the decision is based;
3. An explanation of any relevant time limits that may affect the alternate payee's or the participant's rights under the plan; and
4. A description of additional material or modifications necessary for the order to be qualified.

[D.O.L. QDRO Guidance Q 2-14 (July 1997)]

### Q 17:64   What are the tax consequences of a QDRO?

When a distribution is made to a spouse or former spouse pursuant to a QDRO, the distribution is included in the gross income of the alternate payee as if the alternate payee had been the participant. Recovery of after-tax contributions to the plan is tax free. If the distribution is made to a child or other dependent of the participant, the distribution is included in the gross income of the participant.

An agreement or arrangement regarding division of retirement benefits can have unexpected tax implications in the absence of a QDRO. [Hawkins v. Commissioner, 86 F.3d 982 (10th Cir. 1996)] The participant and alternate payee cannot change tax obligations or shift tax responsibilities in a manner that is contrary to the express language of the Code, even by agreement or through a QDRO. [Clawson v. Commissioner, T.C. Memo 1996-446 (1996)]

Mandatory 20 percent income tax withholding applies if an eligible rollover distribution (see chapter 16) is made to a spouse unless the distribution is rolled over directly into an individual retirement account (IRA). [I.R.C. § 402(c)]

A distribution made pursuant to a QDRO is not subject to the 10 percent early distribution tax, regardless of the payee. [I.R.C. § 72(t)]

### Q 17:65    Has the IRS issued any sample QDRO language?

The IRS and the DOL have issued materials that may be helpful in drafting or reviewing QDROs. Notice 97-11 [1997-1 C.B. 379] includes sample language for inclusion in the QDRO and identifies a number of issues that should be considered in drafting a QDRO. Information regarding the rights of participants and spouses to benefits under a defined benefit pension plan can be found in IRS Publication 1566. The DOL has released a booklet entitled "QDROs: The Division of Pensions Through Qualified Domestic Relations Orders" (1997), which provides an overview of the QDRO provisions and discusses, in question-and-answer format, a number of issues relating to the administration and drafting of QDROs. This booklet is available on the Internet at http://www.dol.gov/ebsa/publications/qdros.html, or by calling the Pension and Welfare Benefits Administration Publication Hotline at 1-800-998-7542.

### Q 17:66    Can a QDRO be issued for a plan that is taken over by the PBGC?

Yes. Sometimes a defined benefit plan that does not have enough money to pay benefits may be terminated if the employer responsible for the plan faces severe financial difficulty, such as bankruptcy, and is unable to maintain the plan. In such an event, the PBGC becomes trustee of the plan and pays pension benefits, subject to legal limits, to plan participants and beneficiaries.

If this occurs, a participant's accrued benefits under the plan may be reduced to the legal limit that can be provided by the PBGC. In addition, the PBGC may allow different forms of payment than could have been provided by the plan before it was taken over by the PBGC. It is important for the participant and alternate payee to understand these differences before a DRO is submitted (see chapter 25).

### Q 17:67    What is the procedure for submitting a DRO to the PBGC?

The PBGC will review a submitted DRO to determine whether the order is qualified before paying benefits to an alternate payee. The DRO should be submitted to:

PBGC QDRO Coordinator

P.O. Box 19153

Washington, DC 20036-0153

The PBGC will informally review a DRO to determine whether it will satisfy qualification requirements but will generally not take any other action on an informal review other than to notify the party requesting the review of its opinion.

Once the certified or authenticated DRO is received, the PBGC will suspend any payments that are currently being received by the participant until a review of the DRO is completed. In no event will this suspension last for more than 18 months.

If the PBGC determines that the order is not a QDRO, the PBGC will explain the reason for its decision, along with its procedures for appealing the determination. An appeal, or a request for an extension of time to appeal, must be filed within 45 days after the date of the PBGC's determination. In addition, the PBGC will lift the suspension and make any back payments to the participant.

If the PBGC determines that the order is a QDRO, it will begin making payments (including any suspended payments) to the alternate payee under the order after the 45-day appeal period has elapsed. The alternate payee must also complete an application as required by the PBGC that provides necessary personal data. [PBGC, "Divorce Orders & PBGC" (Aug. 2000), pp. 22, 23]

### Q 17:68    How should a QDRO with the PBGC be drafted?

The PBGC requires the following:

1. The QDRO must specify the name and last known mailing address of the plan participant and each alternate payee, and the formal name of each plan to which the order applies;

2. The QDRO must specify or allow the alternate payee to choose when payments to the alternate payee begin and the form of payments, and should be clear on how much is to be paid to the alternate payee; and

3. A QDRO should specify when benefits to the alternate payee stop, whether benefits are to be paid to the alternate payee upon the death of the participant (and the amount), whether the alternate payee is to be treated as the participant's spouse for purposes of any survivor benefits, and what happens when the alternate payee dies.

The PBGC will reject a DRO if it requires the PBGC to:

1. Provide any type or form of benefit, or any option, not otherwise provided by the PBGC, ERISA, or the Code;

2. Pay benefits with a value in excess of the value of benefits that would otherwise be payable by the PBGC or allowed by ERISA or the Code; or

3. Pay benefits to an alternate payee when those benefits are required to be paid to another alternate payee under an order previously determined to be a QDRO.

[PBGC, "Divorce Orders & PBGC" (Aug. 2000), pp. 2, 3]

The PBGC has also published model language for use by participants and alternate payees. Two model QDROs have been published: PBGC Model Separate-Interest QDRO and PBGC Model Shared-Payment QDRO. These may be obtained from a publication of the PBGC called "Divorce Orders & PBGC" (Aug. 2000), or at its Web site at http://www.pbgc.gov/docs/Divorce_Orders _and_PBGC.pdf.

# Chapter 18

# Funding Methods

To provide the promised benefits under a defined benefit pension plan and to satisfy the minimum funding standards of the Employee Retirement Income Security Act of 1974 (ERISA) Section 302 and Internal Revenue Code (Code) Section 412 for plan years beginning prior to January 1, 2008, a systematic method of allocating contributions to a pool of money (i.e., the trust fund) must be used. The principles of life contingencies, compound interest, and capital accumulation are combined in various ways to produce generally accepted funding methods and to achieve a financially sound pension program. This chapter introduces the basic requirements of the accepted funding methods and examples of their application. The explanations of the funding methods in this chapter ignore the application of preretirement decrements such as turnover, death, and disability, which are beyond the scope of this text. Furthermore, salary scales are not used in any methods other than the unit credit funding method. With the passage of the Pension Protection Act of 2006 (PPA), the ability and utility of using these funding methods for plan years beginning after December 31, 2007 are not yet known. The PPA has changed everything in this regard. Many actuaries feel that they will still be able to use these funding methods, as long as the method generates a cost somewhere between the minimum and maximum that the PPA requires (see chapters 19 and 20 for a discussion of these). However, others believe that actuaries may become little more than technicians who have no professional expertise in developing proper funding for a plan and instead, merely apply the regulations, and the employer picks a contribution number somewhere between the minimum and maximum that the actuary calculates. This chapter lists the funding method required under the PPA and describes it as the PPA funding method so that the reader can readily find the differences that are required now.

## Funding Method Basics

### Q 18:1    What characteristics must all funding methods have?

A funding method is a budgeting tool for a defined benefit plan's enrolled actuary and its plan sponsor that assists with the systematic accumulation of money to provide benefits under the plan. There are three basic components to a funding method:

1. The cost method (also referred to, unfortunately, as the funding method);
2. The valuation date; and
3. The asset value.

In general, funding methods take into account the following:

1. *Assets.* The plan sponsor contributes money to a trust fund to provide the dollars needed to pay benefits as they come due under the terms of the plan.
2. *Rate of return.* It is the responsibility of the plan's fiduciary to invest the plan assets in a manner that generates additional dollars through investment earnings (i.e., interest, dividends, and realized and unrealized appreciation).
3. *Mortality.* Any benefits paid to retirees are contingent on the survival of the retiree; therefore, life expectancy based on a mortality study helps to determine the length of time over which payments can be expected to be made.
4. *Benefits.* The amount of benefit is defined by the terms of the plan document; to determine an appropriate asset level, an estimate of the benefits that will be paid on retirement is needed.
5. *Valuation date.* The assets and liabilities of the plan are valued as of a fixed point in time at which the recommended contribution level is calculated using these valuations.

A funding method will generally consider the benefits of all employees in the pension plan based on the current compensation and benefit formula in effect on the valuation date. The benefit at retirement is calculated for all plan participants. This calculation takes into account their service before the valuation date and the service they would have if they remain in the employment of the plan sponsor until the assumed retirement date. The benefit that results from this assumption is known as the *projected benefit* or the *future benefit*. Some plans have participants who have retired or terminated their employment, and, as a result, they no longer earn service credits for additional benefits. In this case the promised benefit is determined at the time of termination or retirement and is known as the *accrued benefit*, which is also known as the *projected benefit* or *future benefit*. Active employees also have an accrued benefit; it is the amount of benefit they would receive if they terminated employment before their retirement age and did not start collecting payment of the benefit until retirement. Therefore, the term *present value of future benefits* means the value today, or as of valuation date, of all benefits that will be earned by each employee in the plan under the assumption of continued service to the retirement age. If decrements of turnover, death, disability, or early retirement are used by the actuary employing the funding method, the present value of the future benefits is adjusted to take these contingencies into account.

The present value (see Q 18:2) of future benefits to be paid as of the valuation date represents the total assets required to pay all benefits from the plan. Because it is not feasible for most plan sponsors to fund all the required assets in one payment, a funding method will determine an annual contribution that will eventually accumulate the present value of future benefits. In other words, a plan sponsor's contribution requirement is determined by subtracting the value of any assets in the plan from the present value of future benefits. This difference, if any, is funded over the working years of the employee group. This funding formula is expressed as follows:

$$\text{Present value of future benefits} \div \text{Assets} = \text{Present value of future contributions}$$

(*Present value of future contributions* is also known as the *present value of future normal costs*.)

A timeline that represents the life span of a pension plan would show that the present value of future benefits is the sum of the value of the benefits already earned for service before the valuation date and the present value of the benefits to be earned for service and compensation earned after the valuation date.

Present Value of Benefits as of Valuation Date Equals

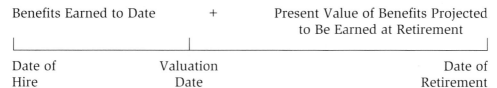

| Benefits Earned to Date | + | Present Value of Benefits Projected to Be Earned at Retirement |
|---|---|---|
| Date of Hire | Valuation Date | Date of Retirement |

The funding formula asks the question: How much money is required today, or as of the valuation date, to pay all benefits currently promised under the plan? Each funding method will develop a contribution requirement that consists of two parts: the normal cost (see Q 18:5) and the amortization of the unfunded accrued liability (see Q 18:7). Some funding methods assume there is no unfunded accrued liability and fund all past and future benefits in the normal cost. Depending on the funding method used, an actuary may provide several contribution amounts based on different payment periods for the unfunded accrued liability.

### Q 18:2   What is *present value*?

The value today of some amount to be paid now or in the future is known as its *present value*. The present value of an amount is usually calculated by multiplying its future value by a discount factor. The discount factor takes into consideration the time value of money at some assumed interest rate and may have other decrements such as turnover, death, disability, and early retirement factored into it. All present values in this book simply take into account a discount for the time value of money.

**Example 1.** If a U.S. savings bond with a face value of $100 payable in 15 years is purchased for $48.10, the price paid is the present value of the bond. The discount factor used to determine the present value is 0.4810 ($100 × 0.4810 = $48.10). Present value takes into consideration the time value of money; that is, $48.10 invested at a rate of 5 percent interest will grow to $100 in 15 years. It has the same value as $100 payable 15 years into the future.

**Example 2.** In a defined benefit plan the same concept applies, but the future value is generally a benefit payable for a lifetime. To determine the present value of $100 payable per month for life starting at age 65, an approach similar to that for determining the present value of a U.S. savings bond is used. If an enrolled actuary determines that $120 is needed at retirement for each dollar of monthly benefit, the future value of the $100 monthly benefit will be $12,000. If a plan's assets grow at a rate of 5 percent per year, the present value of the $100 monthly benefit payable in 15 years is $5,772, determined as follows:

$$\text{Future value at retirement} = \$100 \times \$120 = \$12,000$$

$$\text{Present value} = \$12,000 \times 0.4810 = \$5,772$$

The value of 0.4810 is the discount factor of the present value of $1 payable 15 years hence at 5 percent. If the present value of the $100 per month benefit were contributed to a trust fund that earned 5 percent per year, there would be $12,000 in the trust at the end of the 15th year. The accounting for the growth of the trust fund would be as follows:

| Year | Trust Fund Beginning of Year | Interest 5% | Trust Fund End of Year |
|------|------------------------------|-------------|------------------------|
| 1    | $ 5,772                      | $289        | $ 6,061                |
| 2    | $ 6,061                      | $303        | $ 6,364                |
| 3    | $ 6,364                      | $318        | $ 6,682                |
| 4    | $ 6,682                      | $334        | $ 7,016                |
| 5    | $ 7,016                      | $351        | $ 7,367                |
| 6    | $ 7,367                      | $368        | $ 7,735                |
| 7    | $ 7,735                      | $387        | $ 8,122                |
| 8    | $ 8,122                      | $406        | $ 8,528                |
| 9    | $ 8,528                      | $426        | $ 8,954                |
| 10   | $ 8,954                      | $448        | $ 9,402                |
| 11   | $ 9,402                      | $470        | $ 9,872                |
| 12   | $ 9,872                      | $494        | $10,366                |
| 13   | $10,366                      | $518        | $10,884                |
| 14   | $10,884                      | $544        | $11,428                |
| 15   | $11,428                      | $572        | $12,000                |

The amount in the beginning of each year (the second column) is increased with interest of 5 percent each year. Eventually, the assets will accumulate to the desired amount of $12,000.

## Q 18:3  What is an *annuity due*?

Most funding methods make use of the concept of an annuity due. An *annuity due* is the present value of a stream of payments made at regular intervals over a specified period of time. The contribution requirement for funding methods is developed on an annual basis; hence, an annuity due usually has one year as its interval when the annuity due is developed for purposes of an annual contribution. For benefits at retirement, the annuity due is usually expressed in terms of monthly intervals. The plan funding interest rate is used to discount the present value (see Q 18:2) of the annuity due.

**Example.** Suppose that a plan sponsor wanted to know the annual contribution requirement to accumulate $5,802 in five years. If the trust earned no interest, the present value would be $5,802. That amount paid in equal installments over five years would be $1,160.40 ($5,802 ÷ 5) for the first payment plus $1,160.40 more each year over the next four years. Because the trust fund could be invested in an interest-bearing investment, the present value could be discounted to take into account the interest earned on the money. If an investment returns 5 percent per year, the present value of $5,802 is $4,546 ($5,802 × 0.783526). The value of an annuity due of

$1 payable now and each year over the next four years is 4.546. Therefore, $1,000 ($4,546 ÷ 4.546) contributed now and for each of the next four years would accumulate to the desired $5,802. The accounting of the trust fund would be as follows:

| Year | Trust Fund Beginning of Year | Payment | Interest 5% | Trust Fund End of Year |
|------|------------------------------|---------|-------------|------------------------|
| 1 | $ 0 | $1,000 | $ 50 | $1,050 |
| 2 | $1,050 | $1,000 | $102 | $2,152 |
| 3 | $2,152 | $1,000 | $158 | $3,310 |
| 4 | $3,310 | $1,000 | $216 | $4,526 |
| 5 | $4,526 | $1,000 | $276 | $5,802 |
| Total | | $5,000 | $802 | |

The interest paid for $802 of the needed accumulation; the $1,000 deposits paid for the balance.

Funding methods that use mortality, turnover, and other decrements will calculate the annuity due using commutation functions and are beyond the scope of this book. All annuity due calculations herein use interest only. The formula for an annuity due is as follows:

$$\text{Annuity due} = \frac{1-(1+i)^{-n} \times (1+i)}{i}$$

$$\text{where } i = \text{rate of interest}$$
$$n = \text{the number of payments or intervals}$$

## Q 18:4   What is the *annuity purchase rate*?

The factor used to determine the amount of money needed at retirement to pay the monthly benefit is known as the *annuity purchase rate* (APR). An APR is developed from a set of actuarial assumptions, most typically a mortality table and an interest rate. Mortality tables are developed by performing historical studies of the rates of death at each age from birth. The rate of death from each successive age is measured and converted to actual numbers of lives. These hypothetical populations are then used to develop the APR for any age for which payments can be expected to be made. In general mortality tables are identified by the year of the study and whether they are for males, females, or some combination of both. For example, the 71 GAM Male table is a death study of men developed in 1971. Other factors such as expenses and ancillary benefits may be taken into account, but in the interest of simplicity, all the APRs in this chapter are derived from interest and mortality only. APRs can vary in size based on the choice of the mortality table and interest rate as shown below. The following APRs are for single-life annuities starting at age 65.

| Table | APR at 8% | APR at 6% | APR at 5% |
|-------|-----------|-----------|-----------|
| 71 GAM Male | 97.71 | 111.22 | 119.33 |
| 83 GAM Male | 103.76 | 119.00 | 128.22 |

Life expectancy as compiled by the mortality table will dictate the size of the APR. The 83 GAM Male table has a longer life expectancy than the 71 GAM Male table and, as a result, a much higher APR to account for a longer payment duration. As the interest rate decreases, the APR increases. This happens to take into account the lower investment earnings available to help pay the cost of the benefit.

The development of an APR for the PPA funding method is more complicated as there are multiple interest rates called segment rates to consider. The first segment rate will be applicable for the first 5 years after retirement, the second segment rate will be applicable for the next 15 years and the third segment rate will be applicable for all years after the 20th. (See Q 16:12 for an example of this calculation.)

### Q 18:5  What is the *normal cost*?

In general, the *normal cost* is defined as the annual cost of the benefits assigned to the funding year. This cost would be paid into the plan in the form of a cash contribution each year until the plan is fully funded. The normal cost is adjusted each year to take into account the plan's experience with regard to participant data changes such as salary increases, terminations, deaths, and so forth, as well as changes in the value of the plan's assets.

### Q 18:6  What is the *accrued liability*?

ERISA Section 3(29) defines the term *accrued liability* as the excess of the present value measured as of a particular point in time (usually the valuation date) of the projected future benefit costs and administrative expenses for all plan participants and beneficiaries over the present value of future contributions (also known as the present value of future normal costs) of all applicable plan participants and beneficiaries.

### Q 18:7  What is the *unfunded accrued liability*?

In general, the *unfunded accrued liability* (*unfunded past-service liability*) is the present value (see Q 18:2) of the liability assigned to benefits earned as of the valuation date, reduced by the value of the plan's assets. The unfunded accrued liability is created when an employer adopts a pension plan that recognizes service completed before the effective date of the plan and there are little or no assets in the plan to pay for this liability. Thus, an immediate liability is created for which the plan sponsor will have to pay over a period of years. In general, ERISA and the Tax Code require that any unfunded accrued liability be amortized in level payments of principal and interest over at least 30 years. (See chapter 19 for an explanation of the required amortization periods.) Some funding methods add other accrued liabilities each year that serve to increase or decrease the amount of the unfunded accrued liability, such as an actuarial loss in the previous year or a liability created as a result of a plan amendment that changes benefits. In some instances, a plan may not provide for benefits before the effective date of the plan and still have an unfunded accrued liability. This occurs when the employer uses a funding method that accumulates past years' theoretical contributions as the accrued liability.

### Q 18:8 What is the difference between individual funding and aggregate funding?

Individual funding calculates the basis of the normal cost (see Q 18:5) and the amortization of the unfunded accrued liability (see Q 18:7) for each participant and then adds all calculations to determine the total contribution for the plan.

Aggregate funding determines the value of the future benefit for each participant but determines the contribution for the entire plan using an averaging factor based on the future-service years or present value of the future compensation (or both) of the employee group. A plan based on future-service years uses level-dollar funding; a plan using future compensation uses level percentage of compensation funding. The distinction here is that under future-service years the plan's normal cost will be a flat dollar amount per plan participant, whereas the present value of future compensation results in a level percentage of plan compensation. Generally, plans that have a benefit based on compensation will use the present value of the future compensation. For example, if there is no increase in salary and interest is ignored, the present value of future compensation of an employee with 10 years remaining until retirement is 10 multiplied by his or her current salary. If an interest rate of 5 percent is used, the present value of the future compensation is the current salary multiplied by the present value of $1 payable for 10 years, in this case a factor of 8.12.

### Q 18:9 What is an *actuarial gain or loss*?

An *actuarial gain or loss* is the difference between what an enrolled actuary expects a plan's assets and liabilities to be on the next valuation date and what they are in fact. The gain or loss will serve to decrease or increase contributions in future years, as the case may be. A rate of return on a plan's assets greater than that assumed by an enrolled actuary would be an example of an asset gain attributable to the interest rate assumption; an increase in the rate of pay to the plan participants in excess of what was assumed would be an example of actuarial loss attributable to the salary-scale assumption.

### Q 18:10 What is an immediate-gain adjustment to an actuarial gain or loss, and what is a spread-gain adjustment to an actuarial gain or loss?

Funding methods use actuarial assumptions to develop the normal cost (see Q 18:5) and the unfunded accrued liability (see Q 18:7). If the actuarial assumptions match the change in the assets and liabilities of the plan from the valuation date to the next valuation date, no adjustment is made to the contribution level. The change in the assets and liabilities from one valuation date to the next, however, is rarely, if ever, identical to actuarial assumptions. The difference between expected plan assets and liabilities and the actual assets and liabilities is called an actuarial gain or loss (see Q 18:9).

There are two techniques for handling an actuarial gain or loss. The immediate-gain funding technique specifically identifies the actuarial gain or loss each year and adjusts the unfunded accrued liability (see Q 18:7) by the amount of the gain or loss. The spread-gain funding technique does not explicitly identify the actuarial gain or loss, but either decreases or increases the contribution over future years as a result of any gain or loss. For spread-gain funding adjustments that develop an unfunded accrued liability, no adjustment is made to the unfunded accrued liability as a result of the actuarial gain or loss. The unfunded accrued liability in any year is always equal to the expected unfunded accrued liability developed from the prior year.

**Example.** A plan's actuarial assumption is that the salary for each participant will increase by 4 percent. The actual increase is only 2 percent. There is an actuarial gain because of smaller than anticipated benefits. The immediate-gain method would quantify this loss, add it to the unfunded accrued liability, and amortize the part of the unfunded accrued liability due to the gain or loss in equal installments of principle and interest, generally over a period of five years. The spread-gain method would adjust the normal cost in the next year to account for the anticipated decrease in projected benefits, thus spreading the gain over the remaining working lifetime of the plan participants.

### Q 18:11   How is the expected unfunded accrued liability calculated?

Once the unfunded accrued liability is determined (see Q 18:7), it becomes the aim of the funding method to reduce that amount to zero. An enrolled actuary tries to anticipate what the unfunded accrued liability for a plan will be in the next year based on benefits earned, benefits paid, investment earnings, and contributions made to the plan's assets. The expected unfunded accrued liability is calculated as follows:

Expected unfunded accrued liability $= (\text{UFAL} + \text{NC}) \times (1 + i) - \text{C} - \text{Ci}$

where UFAL is the unfunded accrued liability (last year)

   NC is normal cost (last year)
   $(1 + i)$ is one year of interest at the funding interest rate
   C is contributions made to the plan since last year
   Ci is interest earned on the contribution at the funding interest rate

### Q 18:12   How are unfunded accrued liabilities paid?

Unfunded accrued liabilities must be paid off over a period sufficient to accumulate enough assets to pay benefits as they come due. They are paid off in the same manner as a home mortgage, in level payments, generally over 30 years. In some instances 30 years is too long, and the actuary may determine that a shorter payment period would be needed to fund the plan adequately. Code Section 404 generally allows amortization over as short a period as 10 years. (See chapters 19 and 20 for a discussion on the differences between minimum and maximum contributions.)

> **Example.** Perfect Plumbing Inc. has a pension plan with two participants: Glen, age 65, and Bryce, age 25. The plan credits past service, with the result that on plan inception, benefits are $1,000 per month for Glen and $0 per month for Bryce. The plan's enrolled actuary determines that the unfunded accrued liability is $120,000, attributable solely to Glen. Because Glen can retire immediately, the contribution to the plan in the first year must be sufficient to pay at least $1,000 per month over the next year to cover Glen's benefit payments, that is, $12,000 (without an assumption for interest). If the plan's funding interest rate is 5 percent, an amount as of the beginning of the year equal to a 30-year amortization of $120,000 (i.e., $7,435) would not be enough to cover Glen's benefits. (The 30-year amortization factor (annuity due) at 5 percent is 16.141; $120,000 ÷ 16.141 = $7,435.) Perfect Plumbing therefore will have to pay off the unfunded accrued liability much sooner. Perfect Plumbing can, as of the beginning of the plan year, contribute an amount equal to a 10-year amortization of $120,000, that is, $14,800 ($120,000 ÷ 8.108 = $14,800), and have enough money to pay Glen's benefits for the first year.

### Q 18:13   What are the various funding methods used?

There are seven basic types of funding methods, each distinguished by how they handle the normal cost, unfunded accrued liability (past-service liability), and actuarial gains and losses. The seven types are:

- Aggregate (see Q 18:24)
- Attained Age Normal (see Q 18:42)
- Entry Age Normal (see Q 18:39)
- Frozen Initial Liability (see Q 18:38)
- Individual Aggregate (Individual Spread Gain) (see Q 18:28)
- Individual Level Premium (see Q 18:47)
- Unit Credit (Accrued Benefit) (see Q 18:15)
- PPA Funding Method (see Q 18:21)

### Q 18:14   What are the characteristics of each funding method?

There are four basic characteristics of a funding method:

- Projected versus Accrued benefit methods
- Individual versus Aggregate methods
- Immediate-gain versus Spread-gain methods
- Past-service liability versus No past-service liability

Each funding method will calculate the normal cost by either funding for the projected benefit at retirement age or by funding for the amount accrued in each year. They will fund for these benefits either on an individual basis or by aggregating all participants. Gains and losses will either be funded immediately by amortizing them over a certain number of years or they will be spread over the funding of the plan. And finally, some funding methods will separately determine and fund for a past-service liability while others will not.

## Unit Credit/Accrued Benefit Funding Method

### Q 18:15  How is the normal cost determined in the unit credit funding method?

To understand the unit credit funding method, it is important to understand the concept of an accrued benefit. The *accrued benefit* is the amount of benefit earned by the participant based on service and compensation, if applicable, earned as of a point in time. The accrued benefit increases each year as new benefits are earned. The unit credit funding method looks at the accrued benefit as of the valuation date and the amount of the benefit that will be added to the accrued benefit one year from the valuation date. The normal cost is the present value (see Q 18:2) of the amount of benefit added to the accrued benefit during the plan year; in other words, the normal cost is the present value of the increase in the accrued benefit during the year. A mathematical expression for the normal cost would be as follows:

Normal cost = Increase in accrued benefit × Cost of benefit at retirement
× Discount factor

where the cost of the benefit is established by the plan's postretirement mortality table as an APR (see Q 18:4) and the discount factor expresses the cost of the benefit at retirement in terms of today's dollars on the valuation date (i.e., a present value). In addition to interest, the discount factor may take into account other decrements such as turnover, death, and early retirement. If such decrements other than interest are used, the cost of any benefits that may be received for such events are added to the normal cost. Such techniques for handling these benefits can be found in actuarial texts that provide detailed discussion and analysis on the cost of these benefits.

**Example.** The accrued benefits for the Real Rock Co. are illustrated in the following table. The plan provides a benefit of 1 percent of average monthly salary for each year of service with Real Rock Co. Average salary is defined as the highest three-year average salary while an employee with Real Rock Co. The plan's funding method is unit credit, the APR at retirement is $120 for each dollar of benefit, and all benefits are valued at 5 percent interest.

| | A | B | C | D | E | F |
| | | | | Accrued Benefits | | |
| Name | Past Service | Accrual Rate | Monthly Salary | Beginning of Year | Increase | End of Year |
|---|---|---|---|---|---|---|
| Fred | 10 | 1% | $3,750 | $ 375 | $38 | $ 413 |
| Barney | 15 | 1% | $8,333 | $1,250 | $83 | $1,333 |
| Wilma | 0 | 1% | $2,083 | $ 0 | $21 | $ 21 |
| Betty | 5 | 1% | $6,250 | $ 313 | $63 | $ 376 |

Real Rock Co. would like to know the plan's normal cost for the benefits illustrated above. Fred has 10 years of service for an accrued benefit of 10 percent of his current average monthly salary, or $375 (found in column D). During the year Fred will earn another 1 percent of monthly salary, or $38. By the end of the year, Fred will have an accrued benefit of 11 percent of average monthly salary, or a $413 monthly benefit. The normal cost for the plan will be the present value (see Q 18:2) of the amounts in column E. The enrolled actuary has assumed that the APR (see Q 18:4) for this plan will be $120 and that interest on the trust fund assets will be 5 percent. The normal cost for each participant is determined, and the resulting sum of those amounts becomes the normal cost for the plan.

| Name | A Accrued Benefit Increase | B APR | C Years to Retirement | D Discount for Interest | E Normal Cost |
|---|---|---|---|---|---|
| Fred | $38 | 120 | 20 | 0.377 | $ 1,719 |
| Barney | $83 | 120 | 5 | 0.784 | $ 7,809 |
| Wilma | $21 | 120 | 35 | 0.181 | $ 456 |
| Betty | $63 | 120 | 25 | 0.295 | $ 2,230 |
| Total | | | | | $12,214 |

To determine the present value of the amount in column A, the benefit is multiplied by the APR and a discount factor, in this case the present value of $1 with interest at 5 percent from the participant's current age to retirement. The sum of column E represents the normal cost, which is equal to $12,214. This amount will be added to the amortization of the unfunded accrued liability to determine the funding requirement.

### Q 18:16 How is the unfunded accrued liability determined in the unit credit funding method?

In the unit credit funding method, the *unfunded accrued liability* is the present value (see Q 18:2) of the accrued benefits minus the value of the plan's assets. The present value of the accrued benefits is determined in the same manner as the normal cost (see Q 18:15), but, instead of multiplying the benefit earned during the year by a discount for interest and an APR, the total accrued benefit is used. A mathematical expression for the total unfunded accrued liability is as follows:

Total unfunded accrued liability = (Sum total for each participant
of (Accrued benefit × Cost of benefit
at retirement × Discount factor)) −
Plan assets

where the cost of the benefit is established by the plan's postretirement mortality table as an APR (see Q 18:4) and the discount factor expresses the cost of the benefit at retirement in terms of today's dollars on the valuation date (i.e., a present value). The plan's assets are valued as of the valuation date before any contributions made for the current plan year. In addition to interest, the discount factor may take into account other decrements such as turnover, death, and early retirement. If such decrements other than interest are used, the cost of any benefits that may be received for such events are added to the normal cost. Such techniques for handling these benefits can be found in actuarial texts that provide detailed discussion and analysis on the cost of these benefits.

**Example.** The accrued benefits for the Real Rock Co. are illustrated in the following table. The plan provides a benefit of 1 percent of average monthly salary for each year of service with Real Rock Co. Average salary is defined as the highest three-year average salary while an employee with Real Rock Co. The plan's funding method is unit credit; the APR at retirement is $120 for each dollar of benefit; the plan's assets are valued at $50,000; and all benefits are valued at 5 percent interest.

| | A | B | C | D | E |
|---|---|---|---|---|---|
| | *Accrued* | | *Years to* | *Discount for* | *Accrued* |
| *Name* | *Benefit* | *APR* | *Retirement* | *Interest* | *Liability* |
| Fred | $   375 | 120 | 20 | 0.377 | $  16,965 |
| Barney | $1,250 | 120 | 5 | 0.784 | $117,600 |
| Wilma | $     0 | 120 | 35 | 0.181 | $          0 |
| Betty | $   313 | 120 | 25 | 0.295 | $  11,080 |
| Total | | | | | $145,645 |
| Assets | | | | | ($  50,000) |
| Unfunded accrued liability | | | | | $  95,645 |

Real Rock Co. would like to know the unfunded accrued liability as of the valuation date. Column A is the total accrued benefit as of the valuation date. This amount is multiplied by the APR and a discount factor, in this case the present value of $1 with interest at 5 percent from the participant's current age to retirement age. The accrued liability is $145,645, of which the employer has accumulated $50,000 in assets, leaving an unfunded accrued liability of $95,645.

### Q 18:17  How is the net actuarial gain or loss determined in the unit credit funding method?

The net actuarial gain or loss is determined by subtracting the actual unfunded accrued liability (see Q 18:16) from the expected unfunded accrued liability (see Q 18:11). If the result is a positive number, the plan had an actuarial gain; whereas a negative result would indicate an actuarial loss. The *actual unfunded accrued liability* in the unit credit funding method is the accrued liability less the value of the plan's assets on the valuation date.

> **Example.** In the year before the current valuation date, Real Rock Co. had an actual unfunded accrued liability of $100,000 and normal cost of $10,500. Real Rock Co. contributed $15,000 to the plan's trust fund, which was deposited midyear. At 5 percent, a half year's interest on the contribution is $375. As of the current valuation date, the plan's unfunded accrued liability is $95,645. The actuarial gain or (loss) will be the expected unfunded accrued liability minus the actual unfunded accrued liability of $95,645. By applying the formula from Q 18:11 ((UFAL + NC) × (1 + i) − C − Ci), the expected unfunded accrued liability for the Real Rock plan is calculated as $100,650 (($100,000 + $10,500) × 1.05 − $15,000 − $375). The net actuarial gain is ($100,650 minus $95,645) $5,040. The term *net actuarial gain* is used because which factors caused the actuarial gain over the preceding plan year has not been determined. Finding the source of the actuarial gain is done by comparing the expected liability and assets under each of the plan's actuarial assumptions to the actual result.

### Q 18:18  How does the use of a salary scale affect the calculations of normal cost and unfunded accrued liability in unit credit funding?

An enrolled actuary may choose to anticipate increases in salary over the future working years of an employee's employment. Based on the practices of an employer, the enrolled actuary may decide to project the retirement benefits based on a level increase in compensation from the valuation date to retirement. Such increases are derived from a salary scale. The scale may be a level increase per year, such as 3 percent, or the plan may develop its own increases based on age or service. The use of a salary scale in unit credit funding has the effect of increasing the normal cost and the unfunded accrued liability. When a salary scale is used in unit credited funding, it is sometimes referred to as *projected unit credit funding*. Instead of using the current accrued benefits to develop the normal cost and the accrued unfunded liability, an actuarial assumption projecting benefits that may result from future salary increases is used.

**Example.** The enrolled actuary for the Real Rock Co. has decided that a salary scale of 3 percent per year should be used as part of the plan's funding method. The projected average salaries and accrued benefits are calculated and illustrated in the following table. The plan's funding method is unit credit; the APR at retirement is $120 for each dollar of benefit; the plan's assets are valued at $50,000; and all benefits are valued at 5 percent interest. Real Rock Co. would like to know the normal cost and the unfunded accrued liability as of the valuation date.

| | A | B | C | D | E | F |
| | | | | | Accrued Benefits | |
| Name | Past Service | Accrual Rate | Projected Average Salary | Beginning of Year | Increase | End of Year |
|---|---|---|---|---|---|---|
| Fred | 10 | 1% | $ 6,578 | $ 658 | $ 66 | $ 724 |
| Barney | 15 | 1% | $ 9,382 | $1,407 | $ 94 | $1,501 |
| Wilma | 0 | 1% | $ 5,692 | $ 0 | $ 57 | $ 57 |
| Betty | 5 | 1% | $12,709 | $ 635 | $127 | $ 762 |

Fred has 10 years of service for an accrued benefit of 10 percent of his projected average monthly salary, or $658 (found in column D). During the year Fred will earn another 1 percent of projected monthly salary, or $66. By the end of the year, Fred will have a projected accrued benefit of 11 percent of average monthly salary, or a $724 monthly benefit. The normal cost for the plan will be the present value (see Q 18:2) of the amounts in column E. The normal cost for each participant is determined, and the sum of those amounts becomes the normal cost for the plan.

| | A | B | C | D | E |
| Name | Accrued Benefit Increase | APR | Years to Retirement | Discount for Interest | Normal Cost |
|---|---|---|---|---|---|
| Fred | $ 66 | 120 | 20 | 0.377 | $ 2,986 |
| Barney | $ 94 | 120 | 5 | 0.784 | $ 8,844 |
| Wilma | $ 57 | 120 | 35 | 0.181 | $ 1,238 |
| Betty | $127 | 120 | 25 | 0.295 | $ 4,496 |
| Total | | | | | $17,564 |

To determine the present value of the amount in column A, the benefit is multiplied by the APR and a discount for interest, in this case the present value of $1 with interest at 5 percent from the participant's current age to retirement. The sum of column E represents the normal cost, which is equal to $17,564. The unfunded accrued liability is the present value of the projected accrued benefits on the valuation date less the value of the assets on the valuation date. The following table calculates that amount for the Real Rock Co. Pension Plan:

| Name | A Projected Accrued Benefit | B APR | C Years to Retirement | D Discount for Interest | E Accrued Liability |
|------|------|-----|------|------|------|
| Fred | $ 658 | 120 | 20 | 0.377 | $ 29,768 |
| Barney | $1,407 | 120 | 5 | 0.784 | $132,371 |
| Wilma | $ 0 | 120 | 35 | 0.181 | $ 0 |
| Betty | $ 635 | 120 | 25 | 0.295 | $ 22,479 |
| Total | | | | | $184,618 |
| Assets | | | | | ($ 50,000) |
| Unfunded accrued liability | | | | | $134,618 |

Column A is the total projected accrued benefit as of the valuation date. This amount is multiplied by the APR and a discount factor, in this case the present value of $1 with interest at 5 percent from the participant's current age to retirement age. The accrued liability is $184,618, of which the employer has accumulated $50,000 in assets, leaving an unfunded accrued liability of $134,618.

Note the difference in the normal cost and accrued liability calculations for Real Rock Co. with a salary scale (this example) versus without a salary scale (examples in Qs 18:15 and 18:16):

| | Salary Scale | No Salary Scale |
|------|------|------|
| Normal cost | $ 17,564 | $ 12,214 |
| Accrued liability | $184,618 | $145,645 |

## Q 18:19  What makes the unit credit funding method different from other funding methods?

Unit credit funding uses the accrued benefit to develop all costs and liabilities. Many practitioners call such a strategy a *plan termination funding method* because the accrued liability in this method represents the amount of assets needed to terminate the pension plan if the employer elects to close out the plan and pay the value of the benefits. Unit credit funding is the only funding method that uses the accrued benefit to develop the normal cost and the unfunded accrued liability. The attained age normal (AAN) funding method makes use of the accrued benefit only for purposes of developing the unfunded accrued liability in the first year. All other funding methods generally calculate the total projected benefit at retirement and fund that benefit over the future working lifetime of the employee, or over the average working lifetime of the employee group in the case of an aggregate funding method.

### Q 18:20   When is the unit credit funding method generally used?

This funding method is used generally by plans that use a unit benefit type of formula such as $100 times years of service. This type of funding method is also recommended, or required, for terminating or frozen plans that have no future accruals (see Qs 18:66 and 18:68). A variation of this funding method, called the projected unit credit (PUC) funding method, is generally used by plans that provide a benefit based on a percentage of pay times years of service. The PUC funding method is required to be used in calculating the pension expense and liability under the FASB 132 guidelines (see chapter 31).

## PPA Funding Method

### Q 18:21   How is the normal cost determined in the PPA funding method?

The normal cost, now called the target normal cost under the PPA, is calculated in the PPA funding method in a similar manner to the PUC funding method. The PPA funding method looks at the accrued benefit as of the valuation date and the amount of the benefit that was added to the accrued benefit since the last valuation date. The normal cost is the present value (see Q 18:2) of the amount of benefit added to the accrued benefit during the plan year; in other words, the normal cost is the present value of the increase in the accrued benefit during the year. A mathematical expression for the normal cost would be as follows:

Normal cost = Increase in accrued benefit × Cost of benefit at retirement
× Discount factor

where the cost of the benefit is NOT established by the plan's postretirement mortality table but by the applicable mortality table yet to be issued by the Treasury Department and using the segment rates that are applicable as of the valuation date and the discount factor is the cost of the benefit at retirement in terms of today's dollars on the valuation date (i.e., a present value) using these same segment rates. In addition, the accrued benefit used in determining the target normal cost includes all benefits that are expected to be paid with a proper decrement reflecting the probability of each being paid. If any accrued benefit attributable to services performed in a preceding plan year is increased by reason of any increase in compensation during the current plan year, the increase in this benefit is treated as having accrued during the current plan year. [I.R.C. § 430(b)]

**Example.** Bob has an increase in his accrued benefit during 2008 of $300 which is payable at his attainment of normal retirement age of age 65 in 2015. The target normal cost for Bob is based on a first segment rate of 5.5 percent, a second segment rate of 6 percent, and a third segment rate of 6.5 percent. We will assume that the applicable mortality table in 2008 will be the 1994 GAR table. The normal cost can best be shown on a spreadsheet as follows:

|   | Year | Age | Accrued Benefit | Vn | Lx | Discount | APR | Value |
|---|------|-----|---------|-----------|----------|-----------|---------|-----------|
| 1 | 2015 | 65 | 300.00 | 0.6874368 | 937546.4 | 0.6874368 | 134.913 | 27,823.21 |
| 2 | 2015 | 65 | 300.00 | 0.6874368 | 937546.4 | 0.6874368 | 134.913 | 27,823.21 |
| 3 | 2015 | 65 | 300.00 | 0.6650571 | 937546.4 | 0.6650571 | 129.632 | 25,863.87 |
| 4 | 2028 | 78 | 300.00 | 0.3118047 | 766648.4 | 0.2549683 | 84.145 | 6,436.32 |
| 5 | 2028 | 78 | 300.00 | 0.2837970 | 766648.4 | 0.2320659 | 82.066 | 5,713.39 |

Vn is the discount using interest only.

Lx is the discount using mortality only.

Discount is the discount for interest and mortality combined.

APR = Annuity Purchase Rate.

Line 1 is the value of the payment stream at the first segment rate through death (equal to the accrued benefit times discount times APR). Line 2 is used to determine the value of the payment stream at the first segment rate after year 5 through date of death (line 2 is equal to line 1 because he is more than five years away from retirement age). Line 3 then determines the value of the payment stream at the second segment rate from year 5 through death. Line 4 determines the value of the payment stream at the second segment rate after year 20 through date of death. Line 5 determines the value of the payment stream after year 20 through date of death using the third segment rate. The total present value is line 1 minus line 2 plus line 3 minus line 4 plus line 5, or $25,141 (27,823 − 27,823 + 25,864 − 6,436 + 5,713). This is the target normal cost for Bob.

## Q 18:22   How is the unfunded accrued liability determined in the PPA funding method?

In the PPA funding method, what was once called an *unfunded accrued liability* is now called a funding shortfall. The *funding shortfall* is equal to the excess of the funding target over the assets. In general, the funding target is equal to the present value (see Q 18:2) of all accrued benefit liabilities as of the beginning of the plan years minus the value of the plan's assets. The funding target is determined in a similar manner as the normal cost (see Q 18:15), but, instead of multiplying the benefit earned during the year by a discount for interest and an APR, the total accrued benefit is used.

The assets to be used in this determination are the actuarial value of assets reduced by all credit balances.

**Q 18:23   How is the net actuarial gain or loss determined in the PPA funding method?**

Under the PPA funding method, gains or losses are no longer separately determined per se. All gains and losses are netted together and included in what is called the shortfall amortization base, which is equal to the funding shortfall (see Q 18:22) for the year.

## Aggregate Funding Method

**Q 18:24   How is the normal cost determined in the aggregate funding method?**

The aggregate funding method calculates the normal cost by dividing the unfunded present value of future benefits by a temporary annuity factor equal to the present value of salaries to be paid over the working lifetime of all employees divided by the current salary. This method spreads the normal cost over the working lifetime of all employees and calculates the normal cost on an aggregate basis as opposed to an individual basis (see Q 18:8). In other words, the normal cost is not calculated per individual; it is calculated for the group. A mathematical expression for the normal cost is as follows:

Normal cost = (Present value of future benefits – assets)
              ÷ (Present value of future salaries ÷ Current salaries)

The present value of future salaries divided by current salaries is a temporary annuity factor; thus, there is an alternative expression for the normal cost:

Normal cost = (Present value of future benefits – assets)
              ÷ Temporary annuity factor

**Example.** The projected benefits for the Real Rock Co. are illustrated in the following table. The plan provides a benefit of 1 percent of average monthly salary for each year of service with Real Rock Co. Average salary is defined as the highest three-year average salary while an employee with Real Rock Co.

|  | A | B | C | D | E |
|---|---|---|---|---|---|
|  |  |  |  |  | Total |
|  | Past | Future | Accrual | Monthly | Monthly |
| Name | Service | Service | Rate | Salary | Benefit |
| Fred | 10 | 20 | 1% | $3,750 | 30% |
| Barney | 15 | 5 | 1% | $8,333 | 20% |
| Wilma | 0 | 35 | 1% | $2,083 | 35% |
| Betty | 5 | 25 | 1% | $6,250 | 30% |

The past-service and future-service years are added and then multiplied by the accrual rate to arrive at the projected monthly benefit at retirement (column E). To determine the projected benefit in terms of actual dollars, the percentage in column E is multiplied by the monthly salary.

| | A | B | C | D | E |
|---|---|---|---|---|---|
| | | | | | Present Value |
| | Projected | | | | of Projected |
| | Monthly | | Years to | Discount | Monthly |
| Name | Benefit | APR | Retirement | for Interest | Benefit |
| Fred | $1,125 | 120 | 20 | 0.377 | $ 50,895 |
| Barney | $1,667 | 120 | 5 | 0.784 | $156,831 |
| Wilma | $ 729 | 120 | 35 | 0.181 | $ 15,834 |
| Betty | $1,875 | 120 | 25 | 0.295 | $ 66,375 |
| Total | | | | | $289,935 |

Column A reflects the projected monthly benefit in terms of actual dollars, and its present value is determined by multiplying by the APR at the participant's retirement age and then discounting for interest. The temporary annuity factor is calculated by summing the present value of the total salary to be paid over the working lifetimes of all participants and dividing that result by the total of the current salaries.

| | A | B | C |
|---|---|---|---|
| | Present Value | | Present Value |
| | Annuity Due of | | of Monthly Salary |
| | $1 over Future | Monthly | Paid over |
| Name | Years | Salary | Future Years |
| Fred | 13.085 | $ 3,750 | $ 49,069 |
| Barney | 4.546 | $ 8,333 | $ 37,882 |
| Wilma | 17.193 | $ 2,083 | $ 35,813 |
| Betty | 14.799 | $ 6,250 | $ 92,494 |
| Total | | $20,416 | $215,258 |

The present value of the monthly salary to be paid over the working lifetime of each participant is calculated by multiplying the monthly salary in column B by the present value of an annuity due over the participant's future years in column A. The temporary annuity factor is the total of column C ($215,258) divided by column B ($20,416), or 10.544. This factor will be used to spread the cost over the average working lifetimes of the plan participants. If the plan has assets on the valuation date, they must be subtracted from the present value of future benefits because the only concern is funding for unfunded future benefits. The value of the assets in this example is $50,000 and is subtracted from the present value of future benefits of $289,935. That result, $239,935, is divided by the temporary annuity factor of 10.544 for a funding contribution amount (i.e., normal cost) of $22,756 (($289,935 − $50,000) ÷ 10.544).

**Q 18:25   How is the unfunded accrued liability determined in the aggregate funding method?**

There is no unfunded accrued liability in the aggregate funding method. The assumption is that the unfunded accrued liability is zero and all costs for the funding method are part of the normal cost.

**Q 18:26   When is the aggregate funding method generally used?**

The aggregate funding method is recommended for larger plans due to its simplicity. It is not appropriate for small plans if there is a large benefit coming due soon for an older employee such as an owner. For plans using either the frozen initial liability (FIL) or AAN methods, a change to the aggregate funding method is recommended after the full-funding limit becomes applicable. (See Qs 18:74 and 18:75.)

**Q 18:27   What makes the aggregate funding method different from other methods?**

Because there is no unfunded accrued liability to maintain, aggregate funding is considered by many to be the simplest of the funding methods.

## Individual Aggregate Funding Method

**Q 18:28   How is the normal cost determined in the individual aggregate funding method?**

Individual aggregate funding (also called *individual spread gain*) works just like aggregate funding except that each employee is treated as having his or her own asset pool to fund the benefit and the normal cost is spread over the working lifetime of each employee. The sum of the individual normal costs becomes the normal cost for the entire plan. In developing the normal cost, an allocation of the plan's assets to each participant must be determined. The allocation depends on the status of the plan participant. For new entrants into the plan, the asset allocation is zero. For terminated and retired participants, the asset allocation is equal to the present value of future benefits for each terminated and retired participant. Any remaining assets are allocated to each active participant in proportion to the prior year's allocation of assets plus the prior year's normal cost, both increased with interest for one year. Once the asset allocation is in place, the normal cost is determined by dividing the unfunded present value of each participant's projected benefit by an annuity factor equal to the present value of $1 to be paid over the working lifetime of the employee.

**Example.** The projected benefits for the Real Rock Co. are illustrated in the following table. The plan provides a benefit of 1 percent of average salary for each year of service with Real Rock Co. Average salary is defined as the highest three-year average salary while an employee with Real Rock Co. The plan's funding method is individual aggregate; the APR at retirement is $120 for each dollar of benefit; the plan's assets are valued to be $50,000; and all benefits are valued at 5 percent interest. Real Rock Co. would like to know the normal cost for the current year.

| | A | B | C | D | E | F |
| | | | | | Total | |
| | Past | Future | Accrual | Monthly | Monthly | Projected |
| Name | Service | Service | Rate | Salary | Benefit | Benefit |
| Fred | 10 | 20 | 1% | $3,750 | 30% | $1,125 |
| Barney | 15 | 5 | 1% | $8,333 | 20% | $1,667 |
| Wilma | 0 | 35 | 1% | $2,083 | 35% | $ 729 |
| Betty | 5 | 25 | 1% | $6,250 | 30% | $1,875 |

The past-service and future-service years are added and then multiplied by the accrual rate to arrive at the total monthly benefit at retirement (column E). To determine the projected benefit in terms of actual dollars, the percentage in column E is multiplied by the monthly salary. Column F reflects the projected benefit in terms of actual dollars.

| | Projected | | | | Present Value |
| | Monthly | | Years to | Discount | of Projected |
| Name | Benefit | APR | Retirement | for Interest | Benefit |
| Fred | $1,125 | 120 | 20 | 0.377 | $ 50,895 |
| Barney | $1,667 | 120 | 5 | 0.784 | $156,831 |
| Wilma | $ 729 | 120 | 35 | 0.181 | $ 15,834 |
| Betty | $1,875 | 120 | 25 | 0.295 | $ 66,375 |
| Total | | | | | $289,935 |

The present value of the projected benefit is determined by multiplying the projected benefit by the APR at the participant's retirement age and by a discount for interest factor. The plan's assets can now be allocated to each participant according to the allocation percentages. The unfunded projected benefits are determined by subtracting each participant's share of the assets from the present value of the projected benefit.

The following table illustrates the basis of the asset allocation for the current year.

| Name | A Prior-Year Asset Allocation | B Prior-Year Normal Cost | C Interest | D Current-Year Basis | E Percentage of Allocation |
|------|------|------|------|------|------|
| Fred | $ 4,100 | $ 3,400 | $ 375 | $ 7,875 | 12.58% |
| Barney | $23,000 | $20,000 | $2,150 | $45,150 | 72.15% |
| Wilma | $ 0 | $ 0 | $ 0 | $ 0 | 0.00% |
| Betty | $ 5,000 | $ 4,100 | $ 455 | $ 9,555 | 15.27% |
| Total | | | | $62,580 | 100.00% |

Column A reflects the allocation of the plan's assets in the prior year; column B reflects the normal cost in the prior year. Column C is the sum of 5 percent interest on the amounts in column A and column B. Column D, the sum total of columns A, B, and C for each participant, reflects the basis for the current year's asset allocation. Based on the results, Fred will have 12.58 percent ($7,875 ÷ $62,580) of the assets in the current year allocated to him to determine his normal cost. The assets are $50,000 on the valuation date and are allocated according to the percentages in the table that follows:

| Name | A Present Value of Projected Benefit | B Percentage of Asset Allocation | C Asset Allocation | D Present Value Unfunded Projected Benefit |
|------|------|------|------|------|
| Fred | $ 50,895 | 12.58% | $ 6,290 | $ 44,605 |
| Barney | $156,831 | 72.15% | $36,075 | $120,756 |
| Wilma | $ 15,834 | 0.00% | $ 0 | $ 15,834 |
| Betty | $ 66,375 | 15.27% | $ 7,635 | $ 58,740 |
| Total | $289,935 | 100.00% | $50,000 | $195,335 |

After the assets in column C are allocated, they are subtracted from the present value of projected benefits in column A to arrive at the present value of the unfunded projected benefits in column D. That amount is funded over the future working years of each employee by dividing it by the present value of $1 paid over the working lifetime of the employee. The following table develops the normal cost.

| Name | A Present Value Annuity Due of $1 over Future Years | B Present Value Unfunded Projected Benefit | C Normal Cost |
|------|------|------|------|
| Fred | 13.085 | $ 44,605 | $ 3,409 |
| Barney | 4.546 | $120,756 | $26,563 |

| Name | A Present Value Annuity Due of $1 over Future Years | B Present Value Unfunded Projected Benefit | C Normal Cost |
|---|---|---|---|
| Wilma | 17.193 | $15,834 | $ 921 |
| Betty | 14.799 | $58,740 | $ 3,969 |
| Total | | | $34,862 |

Column A is the present value of an annuity due (see Q 18:3) of $1 from the valuation date to normal retirement age. The normal cost is the present value of the unfunded projected benefit in column B divided by column A. Fred's normal cost is $3,409 ($44,605 ÷ 13.085). The total normal cost for Real Rock Co. is $34,862.

**Note.** When a salary scale is part of the funding assumptions, the projected average salary is calculated using the scale. The present value of the annuity due is determined at a blended rate that takes into account the salary scale and the interest rate. Please consult actuarial texts on funding methods for further discussion.

### Q 18:29 How is the unfunded accrued liability determined in the individual aggregate funding method?

There is no unfunded accrued liability in the individual aggregate funding method.

### Q 18:30 What makes individual aggregate funding different from other funding methods?

The allocation of plan assets on a per-participant basis is what makes the individual aggregate funding method unique. This funding method ensures that each participant will have the required assets available to him or her at retirement by allocating and tracking the contributions made to the plan on the participant's behalf. A common misconception is that the allocation of assets and contributions has bearing on the amount of assets an employee is entitled to when he or she leaves the plan before retirement. Participants are led to believe that all amounts allocated to them under the individual aggregate funding method belong to them, when in fact the amount to which an individual is entitled may be more or less. When a participant leaves before retirement, the value of the benefit at that time is based on the value of the accrued benefit, not on the participant's allocation of assets. The only time in the individual aggregate funding method that the assets allocated on a participant's behalf are equal to the value of the benefit is at retirement (if it is assumed that the employee remains in the employment of the plan sponsor until retirement).

**Q 18:31  When is the individual aggregate funding method generally used?**

The individual aggregate funding method is popular with small plans due to its simplicity. However, in exchange for simplicity employers sacrifice flexibility in contributions compared to some other methods (usually no range in contributions). Also, the cost generated by this method does not always match the present value of the benefit accrual, giving employers a false impression of how much they may owe a participant.

## Entry Age Normal Funding Method

**Q 18:32  How is the normal cost determined in the entry age normal funding method?**

The entry age normal funding method develops the normal cost by calculating what the contribution would have been starting from the earliest age at which the employee could have participated in a plan of the employer (generally, the employee's date of hire) if the plan had always been in existence. This method is similar to the individual aggregate funding method (see Q 18:28) except that the normal cost is determined without regard to the amount of plan assets and the normal cost is determined from an employee's date of hire.

The mathematical expression for the normal cost for each participant would be as follows:

Normal cost = Present value of future benefits at date of hire
÷ Present value of annuity due of $1 over future working years

The plan's normal cost is the sum of the normal costs for each participant.

**Example.** The projected benefits for the Real Rock Co. are illustrated in the following table. The plan provides a benefit of 1 percent of average monthly salary for each year of service with Real Rock Co. Average monthly salary is defined as the highest three-year average salary while an employee with Real Rock Co. The plan's funding method is entry age normal; the APR at retirement is $120 for each dollar of benefit; and all benefits are valued at 5 percent interest. Real Rock Co. would like to know the normal cost for the current year.

|  | A | B | C | D | E | F |
|---|---|---|---|---|---|---|
|  |  |  |  |  | *Total* | *Projected* |
|  | *Past* | *Future* | *Accrual* | *Monthly* | *Monthly* | *Monthly* |
| *Name* | *Service* | *Service* | *Rate* | *Salary* | *Benefit* | *Benefit* |
| Fred | 10 | 20 | 1% | $3,750 | 30% | $1,125 |
| Barney | 15 | 5 | 1% | $8,333 | 20% | $1,667 |
| Wilma | 0 | 35 | 1% | $2,083 | 35% | $ 729 |
| Betty | 5 | 25 | 1% | $6,250 | 30% | $1,875 |

The past-service and future-service years are added and then multiplied by the accrual rate to arrive at the projected monthly benefit at retirement (column E). To determine the projected benefit in terms of actual dollars, the percentage in column E is multiplied by the monthly salary. Column F reflects the projected benefit in terms of actual dollars.

The first step in determining the normal cost in entry age normal funding is to determine the present value of the projected benefit as of the date the employee first could have entered the plan.

| | A | B | C | D | E | F |
|---|---|---|---|---|---|---|
| Name | Age at Date of Hire (EA) | Years to Retirement | Projected Benefit | APR | Discount for Interest | Present Value of Projected Benefit at Hire |
| Fred | 35 | 30 | $1,125 | 120 | 0.231 | $31,185 |
| Barney | 45 | 20 | $1,667 | 120 | 0.377 | $75,415 |
| Wilma | 30 | 35 | $ 729 | 120 | 0.181 | $15,834 |
| Betty | 35 | 30 | $1,875 | 120 | 0.231 | $51,975 |

The age at the time an employee is hired is referred to as the *entry age,* or EA. Column A uses the employee's entry age to determine the number of working years from entry age to retirement, which is shown in column B. The projected benefit in column C is multiplied by the APR (see Q 18:4) and a discount for interest to arrive at the present value of the projected benefit at the time the employee was hired. That amount is illustrated in column F and is also known as the *present value of future normal costs at date of hire.* The normal cost is the level amount to fund the benefit over the employee's working lifetime from the date of hire. The normal cost is determined by dividing the present value of projected benefits by the present value of an annuity due of $1 to be paid over the future working lifetime of the employee.

| | A | B | C |
|---|---|---|---|
| Name | Present Value Annuity Due of $1 over Future Years | Value Projected Benefit at Hire | Normal Cost |
| Fred | 16.141 | $31,185 | $ 1,932 |
| Barney | 13.085 | $75,415 | $ 5,763 |
| Wilma | 17.193 | $15,834 | $ 921 |
| Betty | 16.141 | $51,975 | $ 3,220 |
| Total | | | $11,836 |

The annuity due of $1 from the entry age to retirement is shown in column A. The normal cost in column C is column B divided by column A. Fred's normal cost is $1,932 ($31,185 ÷ 16.141). The amount in column C is the annual contribution required each year to accumulate the cash needed at retirement to fund the projected benefit if that contribution was made each year from the employee's date of hire.

**Note.** If a salary scale is part of the actuarial assumptions, the normal cost is developed as a percentage of the current salary. This is done by projecting the current salary backwards to the entry age and calculating the annuity due of $1 using a blended interest rate that takes into account the salary scale and the interest rate. For further discussion consult actuarial texts on funding methods.

### Q 18:33  Is the aggregate entry age normal funding method a reasonable funding method?

No. The IRS has ruled that using an aggregate form of the entry age normal funding method is unreasonable because it can generate experience gains or losses, even though all assumptions are exactly realized. [Rev. Rul. 2003-83, 2003-30 I.R.B. 128]

### Q 18:34  How is the unfunded accrued liability determined in the entry age normal funding method?

The accrued liability in the entry age normal funding method is what the value of the normal costs would be if the normal cost had been contributed to the plan each year from the employee's date of hire. If the present value of projected benefits is known as of the valuation date and the present value of all normal costs to be made to the plan in the future is subtracted from that amount, the remainder is how much money would have accumulated since the contributions began at each employee's hire date. The mathematical expression for the accrued liability is as follows:

Accrued liability = Present value of future benefits
                          – Present value of future normal costs

The unfunded accrued liability is the accrued liability minus the plan's assets.

**Example.** Real Rock Co. as of the valuation date has the following normal costs using the entry age normal funding method for its plan participants and is now prepared to determine the accrued liability of the plan using that funding method. The plan's funding method is entry age normal; the APR at retirement is $120 for each dollar of benefit; and all benefits are valued at 5 percent interest. The present value of an annuity due of $1 paid over the employee's working lifetime from the valuation date multiplied by the normal cost equals the present value of future normal costs. In the following table the amount in column A multiplied by the amount in column B equals the present value of future normal costs for each participant. The total of all amounts in column C is equal to the present value of future normal costs for the entire plan; in this case that amount is $114,967.

|        | A<br>Present Value<br>Annuity Due of<br>$1 over Future<br>Years | B<br><br><br><br>Normal Cost | C<br>Present Value of<br>Future Normal<br>Cost |
|--------|-------------------|-------------|--------------|
| Name   |                   |             |              |
| Fred   | 13.085            | $ 1,932     | $ 25,280     |
| Barney | 4.546             | $ 5,763     | $ 26,199     |
| Wilma  | 17.193            | $   921     | $ 15,835     |
| Betty  | 14.799            | $ 3,220     | $ 47,653     |
| Total  |                   | $11,836     | $114,967     |

In the table that follows, the present value of projected benefits is calculated by determining the present value of all benefits to be paid at retirement. Column A is the number of working years to retirement from the valuation date. The projected benefit in column B is multiplied by the APR ( see Q 18:4) and a discount for interest over the number of years in column A to arrive at the present value of the projected benefits.

|        | A<br>Years to<br>Retirement | B<br>Projected<br>Benefits | C<br><br>APR | D<br>Discount<br>for Interest | E<br>Present Value<br>of Projected<br>Benefits |
|--------|-------------|------------|-----|-------------|--------------|
| Name   |             |            |     |             |              |
| Fred   | 20          | $1,125     | 120 | 0.377       | $ 50,895     |
| Barney | 5           | $1,667     | 120 | 0.784       | $156,831     |
| Wilma  | 35          | $ 729      | 120 | 0.181       | $ 15,834     |
| Betty  | 25          | $1,875     | 120 | 0.295       | $ 66,375     |
| Total  |             |            |     |             | $289,935     |
| Less present value future normal cost |  |  |  |  | ($114,967) |
| Equals accrued liability |  |  |  |  | $174,968 |
| Assets |             |            |     |             | ($ 50,000) |
| Equals unfunded accrued liability |  |  |  |  | $124,968 |

The total of column E is equal to the present value of projected benefits for the entire plan and is reduced by the present value of future normal costs. That reduced amount is the plan's accrued liability. The accrued liability reduced by the plan's assets is the unfunded accrued liability.

### Q 18:35   How is the actuarial gain or loss determined using entry age normal funding?

The net actuarial gain or loss is determined by comparing the expected unfunded accrued liability (see Q 18:11) to the actual unfunded accrued liability.

The term *net actuarial gain or loss* means the total result from all gains and losses that occurred under each assumption that was not realized over the one-year period for which the determination is being made. Finding the source of these actuarial gains or losses is done by comparing each expected liability and asset under the plan's actuarial assumptions to the actual result.

> **Example.** In the year before the current valuation date, Real Rock Co. had an unfunded accrued liability of $135,000 and normal cost of $10,500 using the entry age normal funding method. Real Rock Co. contributed $15,000 to the plan's trust fund, which was deposited midyear. A half year's interest at 5 percent on the contribution is $375. As of the current valuation date the plan's unfunded accrued liability is $124,968. The actuarial gain or (loss) will be the expected unfunded accrued liability minus the actual unfunded accrued liability of $124,968. By applying the formula from Q 18:11 ((UFAL + NC) × (1 + i) − C − Ci), the expected unfunded accrued liability for the Real Rock plan is calculated as $137,400 (($135,000 + $10,500) × 1.05 − $15,000 − $375). The net actuarial gain is $12,432 ($137,400 − $124,968). This result is a gain, because the plan's actual unfunded accrued liability is less than expected under the plan's actuarial assumptions. In other words, the plan's funding has improved over what was assumed.

### Q 18:36  What makes entry age normal funding different from other funding methods?

The factor that makes entry age normal funding different from other funding methods is the development of an accrued liability that is based on what the level of assets in the plan would be if the sponsor had been making contributions on the participant's behalf from his or her date of hire. Such liability looks very different from other liabilities that are calculated based on accrued benefits. As a result, the term *liability* when used in the context of entry age normal funding can be quite misleading. The unfunded accrued liability under this method represents a contribution shortfall over the life of the plan; whereas an unfunded accrued liability using an accrued method such as unit credit funding is a total asset shortfall.

### Q 18:37  When is the entry age normal funding method generally used?

This method would generally be used to provide funding flexibility, generating a range of possible contributions. But it is rarely used for small plans.

## Frozen Initial Liability Funding Method

### Q 18:38  How is the normal cost developed in the *frozen initial liability* funding method?

The *frozen initial liability* (FIL) funding method is identical to the aggregate funding method (see Q 18:24) except that the entry age normal accrued liability (see Q 18:39) is used to develop the unfunded accrued liability. That unfunded accrued liability is amortized over a period of at least 30 years. Then the amortized unfunded accrued liability, along with the plan assets, is subtracted from the present value of projected benefits. The remainder is divided by a temporary annuity factor equal to the present value of salaries to be paid over the future working lifetimes of all employees divided by current salaries. This method spreads the normal cost over the working lifetimes of all employees and calculates the normal cost on an aggregate basis as opposed to an individual basis. The unfunded accrued liability is reduced each year by calculating the expected unfunded accrued liability (see Q 18:11) and maintaining that amount as the unfunded accrued liability in the next year. The mathematical expression for the FIL normal cost is as follows:

Normal cost = (Present value of future benefits − Unfunded accrued liability
        − Assets) ÷ (Present value of future salaries
        ÷ Current salaries)

The denominator of this fraction is the temporary annuity factor; therefore, an alternative expression for the normal cost is as follows:

Normal cost = (Present value of future benefits − Unfunded accrued liability
        − Assets) ÷ Temporary annuity factor

**Example.** The projected benefits for the Real Rock Co. are illustrated in the following table. The plan provides a benefit of 1 percent of average salary for each year of service with Real Rock Co. Average salary is defined as the highest three-year average salary while an employee with Real Rock Co. The plan's funding method is FIL; the APR at retirement is $120 for each dollar of benefit; and all benefits are valued at 5 percent interest. The plan has assets of $50,000, and the unfunded accrued liability is $75,000.

|  | A | B | C | D | E |
|---|---|---|---|---|---|
| Name | Past Service | Future Service | Accrual Rate | Monthly Salary | Total Monthly Benefit |
| Fred | 10 | 20 | 1% | $3,750 | 30% |
| Barney | 15 | 5 | 1% | $8,333 | 20% |
| Wilma | 0 | 35 | 1% | $2,083 | 35% |
| Betty | 5 | 25 | 1% | $6,250 | 30% |

The past-service and future-service years are added and then multiplied by the yearly benefit formula to arrive at the projected monthly benefit at retirement (column E). To determine the projected benefit in terms of actual dollars, the percentage in column E is multiplied by the monthly salary. The following table calculates the present value of the projected benefits.

| | A | B | C | D | E |
|---|---|---|---|---|---|
| | Projected | | Years to | Discount | Present Value of Projected |
| Name | Benefit | APR | Retirement | for Interest | Benefit |
| Fred | $1,125 | 120 | 20 | 0.377 | $ 50,895 |
| Barney | $1,667 | 120 | 5 | 0.784 | $156,831 |
| Wilma | $ 729 | 120 | 35 | 0.181 | $ 15,834 |
| Betty | $1,875 | 120 | 25 | 0.295 | $ 66,375 |
| Total | | | | | $289,935 |

Column A reflects the projected benefit in terms of actual dollars, and its present value is determined by multiplying the projected benefit by the APR at the participant's retirement age and by a discount for interest to the valuation date. The temporary annuity factor is calculated by summing the present value of the total salary to be paid over the working lifetimes of all participants and dividing that result by the total of the current salaries.

| | A | B | C |
|---|---|---|---|
| | Present Value Annuity Due of $1 | | Present Value of Monthly Salary Paid |
| Name | over Future Years | Monthly Cost | over Future Years |
| Fred | 13.085 | $ 3,750 | $ 49,069 |
| Barney | 4.546 | $ 8,333 | $ 37,882 |
| Wilma | 17.193 | $ 2,083 | $ 35,813 |
| Betty | 14.799 | $ 6,250 | $ 92,494 |
| Total | | $20,416 | $215,258 |

The present value of the monthly salary to be paid over the working lifetime of each participant is calculated by multiplying the salary in column B by the present value of an annuity due over the participant's future years in column A. The temporary annuity factor is equal to the total of column C ($215,258) divided by the total of column B ($20,416, or 10.544). This factor will be used to spread the cost over the average working lifetimes of the plan participants after the unfunded accrued liability using the entry age normal method and the plan's assets are subtracted from the present value of projected benefits. Expressed mathematically, the result is as follows:

Normal cost = ($289,935 − $75,000 − $50,000) ÷ 10.544 = $15,643

### Q 18:39   How is the accrued liability determined in FIL funding?

The accrued liability in FIL funding is established on plan inception and is equal to what the entry age normal accrued liability would be using that funding method (see Q 18:34). Because there are no plan assets on plan inception, the unfunded accrued liability is equal to the accrued liability. This liability is amortized over a period of at least 30 years.

### Q 18:40   How does FIL funding account for the unfunded accrued liability?

FIL funding uses a spread-gain adjustment for actuarial gain or loss, so no actuarial gain or loss is identified when determining the actual unfunded accrued liability. Therefore, the actual unfunded accrued liability is equal to the expected unfunded accrued liability (see Q 18:11). The actuarial gain or loss is spread out in the normal cost. If there is a plan amendment changing the level of benefits, the unfunded accrued liability adjustment is accounted for by the change in the entry age normal accrued liability, which is a direct result of the benefit formula change.

> **Example.** The Real Rock Co. Pension Plan amends the plan's benefit formula to increase past and future benefits. Before the amendment, the accrued liability using the entry age normal funding method was $150,000. As a result of the amendment, the entry age normal accrued liability increases to $175,000. The unfunded accrued liability before the amendment was $100,000; after the amendment it is $125,000 ($100,000 + ($175,000 − $150,000)).

### Q 18:41   When is the FIL funding method generally used?

This method is used when simplicity is necessary because it doesn't separately calculate gains and losses. It also has the advantage of generating ranges of contributions due to the amortization of the past-service liability, allowing flexibility in contributions. However, if the lower end of the range is consistently chosen, there may not be enough assets to pay out larger lump-sum benefits, especially in the earlier years of the plan.

## Attained Age Normal Funding Method

### Q 18:42   How is the normal cost determined in the *attained age normal* funding method?

The *attained age normal* (AAN) funding method is identical to the aggregate funding method (see Q 18:24) except that the unit credit unfunded accrued liability (see Q 18:12) is made part of the normal cost calculation. That unfunded accrued liability is amortized over a period of at least 30 years. Then the amortized unfunded accrued liability, along with the plan's assets, is subtracted from the present value of projected benefits. The remainder is divided by a temporary annuity factor equal to the present value of salaries to be paid over the future working lifetimes of all employees divided by current salaries. This method spreads the normal cost over the working lifetimes of all employees and calculates the normal cost on an aggregate basis as opposed to an individual basis. The unfunded accrued liability is reduced each year by calculating the expected unfunded accrued liability (see Q 18:11) and maintaining that amount as the unfunded accrued liability in the next year. The mathematical expression for the AAN normal cost is as follows:

Normal cost = (Present value of future benefits − Unfunded accrued liability
 − Assets) ÷ (Present value of future salaries
 ÷ Current salaries)

The denominator of this fraction is the temporary annuity factor: therefore, an alternative expression for the normal cost is as follows:

Normal cost = (Present value of future benefits − Unfunded accrued liability
 − Assets) ÷ Temporary annuity factor

**Example.** The projected benefits for the Real Rock Co. are illustrated in the following table. The plan provides a benefit of 1 percent of average salary for each year of service with Real Rock Co. Average salary is defined as the highest three-year average salary while an employee with Real Rock Co. The plan's funding method is attained age normal; the APR at retirement is $120 for each dollar of benefit; and all benefits are valued at 5 percent interest. The plan has assets of $50,000 and an unfunded accrued liability using the unit credit funding method of $100,000.

| | A | B | C | D | E |
|---|---|---|---|---|---|
| Name | Past Service | Future Service | Accrual Rate | Monthly Salary | Total Monthly Benefit |
| Fred | 10 | 20 | 1% | $3,750 | 30% |
| Barney | 15 | 5 | 1% | $8,333 | 20% |
| Wilma | 0 | 35 | 1% | $2,083 | 35% |
| Betty | 5 | 25 | 1% | $6,250 | 30% |

The past-service and future-service years are added and then multiplied by the accrual rate to arrive at the projected monthly benefit at retirement (column E). To determine the projected benefit in terms of actual dollars, the percentage in column E is multiplied by the monthly salary.

The following table calculates the present value of the projected benefits.

| | A | B | C | D | E |
|---|---|---|---|---|---|
| Name | Projected Benefit | APR | Years to Retirement | Discount for Interest | Present Value of Projected Benefit |
| Fred | $1,125 | 120 | 20 | 0.377 | $ 50,895 |
| Barney | $1,667 | 120 | 5 | 0.784 | $156,831 |
| Wilma | $ 729 | 120 | 35 | 0.181 | $ 15,834 |
| Betty | $1,875 | 120 | 25 | 0.295 | $ 66,375 |
| Total | | | | | $289,935 |

Column A reflects the projected benefit in terms of actual dollars, and its present value is determined by multiplying the projected benefit by the APR at the participant's retirement age and by the discount for interest to the valuation date. The temporary annuity factor is calculated by summing the present value of the total salary to be paid over the working lifetimes of all participants and dividing that result by the total of the current salaries.

| Name | A<br>Present Value<br>Annuity Due of<br>$1 over Future<br>Years | B<br><br><br><br>Monthly Cost | C<br><br>Present Value of<br>Monthly Salary Paid<br>over Future Years |
|---|---|---|---|
| Fred | 13.085 | $ 3,750 | $ 49,069 |
| Barney | 4.546 | $ 8,333 | $ 37,882 |
| Wilma | 17.193 | $ 2,083 | $ 35,813 |
| Betty | 14.799 | $ 6,250 | $ 92,494 |
| Total | | $20,416 | $215,258 |

The present value of the monthly salary to be paid over the working lifetime of each participant is calculated by multiplying the salary in column B by the present value of an annuity due over the participant's future years in column A. The temporary annuity factor is equal to the total of column C ($215,258) divided by the total of column B ($20,416, or 10.544). This factor will be used to spread the cost over the average working lifetimes of the plan participants after the unfunded accrued liability using the unit credit funding method and the plan's assets are subtracted from the present value of projected benefits. Expressed mathematically, the result is as follows:

Normal cost = ($289,935 − $100,000 − $50,000) ÷ 10.544 = $13,272

### Q 18:43 How is the unfunded accrued liability determined in AAN funding?

The accrued liability in AAN funding is established on plan inception and is equal to what the unit credit accrued liability would be under that funding method (see Q 18:16). Because there are no plan assets on plan inception, the unfunded accrued liability is equal to the accrued liability.

### Q 18:44 How is the unfunded accrued liability accounted for in AAN funding?

AAN funding uses a spread-gain adjustment for actuarial gains or losses, so no actuarial gain or loss is identified when determining the actual unfunded accrued liability. Instead, the actuarial gain or loss is spread out over the future normal costs. If there is a plan amendment changing the level of benefits, the unfunded accrued liability adjustment is accounted for by the change in the unit credit accrued liability, which is a direct result of the benefit formula change.

**Example.** The Real Rock Co. Pension Plan amends the plan's benefit formula to increase past and future benefits. Before that amendment, the accrued liability using the unit credit funding method was $150,000. As a result of the amendment, the unit credit accrued liability increases to $175,000. The unfunded accrued liability before the amendment was $100,000; after the amendment it is $125,000 ($100,000 + ($175,000 − $150,000)).

### Q 18:45   What makes the FIL and AAN funding methods different from other methods that use spread-gain adjustments and the aggregate basis?

FIL and AAN funding use an unfunded accrued liability that must be accounted for each year, but instead of calculating the actuarial gain or loss from the expected and the actual unfunded accrued liabilities, the actuarial gain or loss is spread out through the normal cost. Both FIL and AAN funding operate very similarly. The only difference is that FIL funding uses entry age normal funding to determine the accrued liability, whereas AAN funding uses unit credit funding to determine the accrued liability.

### Q 18:46   When is the AAN funding method generally used?

The advantages and disadvantages of this funding method are similar to those of the FIL funding method.

## Individual Level Premium (ILP) Funding Method

### Q 18:47   How is the normal cost determined under the ILP funding method?

The ILP funding method calculates each participant's normal cost as a level amount from the date the participant enters a plan to the retirement date. Such a strategy is similar to the individual aggregate funding method (see Q 18:28) except that the plan develops the total normal cost each year based on the prior years' accumulated normal costs plus the normal cost in the current year for any change in plan benefit. Additionally, the ILP funding method calculates an actuarial gain and loss each year, since assets are not allocated to the individual plan participants as they are in the individual aggregate funding method.

**Example 1.** The projected benefits for the Real Rock Co. are illustrated in the following table. The plan provides a benefit of 1 percent of average monthly salary for each year of service with Real Rock Co. Average salary is defined as the highest three-year average salary while an employee with Real Rock Co. The plan's funding method is ILP; the APR at retirement is $120 for each dollar of benefit; and all benefits are valued at 5 percent interest. This is the first year the plan is in effect, and Real Rock wants to know the normal cost.

| Name | A<br>Past<br>Service | B<br>Future<br>Service | C<br><br>Rate | D<br>Accrual<br>Rate | E<br>Total<br>Monthly<br>Salary | F<br>Projected<br>Benefit |
|---|---|---|---|---|---|---|
| Fred | 10 | 20 | 1% | $3,750 | 30% | $1,125 |
| Barney | 15 | 5 | 1% | $8,333 | 20% | $1,667 |
| Wilma | 0 | 35 | 1% | $2,083 | 35% | $ 729 |
| Betty | 5 | 25 | 1% | $6,250 | 30% | $1,875 |

The past-service and future-service years are added and then multiplied by the accrual rate to arrive at the total monthly benefit at retirement (column E). To determine the projected benefit in terms of actual dollars, the percentage in column E is multiplied by the monthly salary. Column F reflects the projected benefit for each employee in terms of actual dollars.

The following table calculates the present value of the projected benefits.

| Name | A<br>Projected<br>Benefit | B<br><br>APR | C<br>Years to<br>Retirement | D<br>Discount<br>for Interest | E<br>Present Value<br>of Projected<br>Benefit |
|---|---|---|---|---|---|
| Fred | $1,125 | 120 | 20 | 0.377 | $ 50,895 |
| Barney | $1,667 | 120 | 5 | 0.784 | $156,831 |
| Wilma | $ 729 | 120 | 35 | 0.181 | $ 15,834 |
| Betty | $1,875 | 120 | 25 | 0.295 | $ 66,375 |
| Total | | | | | $289,935 |

The present value of the projected benefit is determined by multiplying the projected benefit by the APR at the participant's retirement age and by a discount factor for interest. This is the amount to be funded over the future working lifetime of each employee.

The following table develops the normal cost.

| Name | A<br>Present Value<br>Annuity Due of $1<br>over Future Years | B<br>Present Value<br>Projected Benefit | C<br>Normal<br>Cost |
|---|---|---|---|
| Fred | 13.085 | $ 50,895 | $ 3,890 |
| Barney | 4.546 | $156,831 | $34,499 |
| Wilma | 17.193 | $ 15,834 | $ 921 |
| Betty | 14.799 | $ 66,375 | $ 4,485 |
| Total | | $289,935 | $43,795 |

The normal cost is the present value of the unfunded projected benefits (column B) divided by the present value of an annuity due of $1 from the valuation date to normal retirement age (column A). Fred's normal cost is $3,890 ($50,895 ÷ 13.085). The total normal cost for Real Rock Co. is $43,795.

**Note.** When a salary scale is part of the funding assumptions, the projected average salary is calculated using the scale. The present value of the annuity due is determined at a blended rate that takes into account the salary scale and the interest rate. Please consult actuarial texts on funding methods for further discussion.

In the second plan year, the change in the projected plan benefits is determined based on the new salaries paid for that plan year. Generally, when an employee is within three years of retirement, the average of the highest three years of salary will be used to determine the projected benefit.

**Example 2.** The facts are the same as those in Example 1, except that Real Rock Co. now wants to know the normal cost for the second year of plan operation. Because each of the employees is more than three years from retirement, their current monthly salaries, instead of their average salaries of the last three years, are used to develop the projected benefits.

| Name | A Total Monthly Benefit | B Projected 1st Year | C Monthly Salary 2d Year | D Projected Benefit 2d Year | E Change in Projected Benefit |
|---|---|---|---|---|---|
| Fred | 30% | $1,125 | $4,000 | $1,200 | $ 75 |
| Barney | 20% | $1,667 | $9,000 | $1,800 | $133 |
| Wilma | 35% | $ 729 | $3,000 | $1,050 | $321 |
| Betty | 30% | $1,875 | $7,000 | $2,100 | $225 |

The table above calculates the new projected benefit in column D and compares that amount to the projected benefit from the first year (column B). Column E is the change in the projected benefit, and the additional normal cost will be determined based on this benefit change.

| Name | A Projected Benefit | B APR | C Years to Retirement | D Discount for Interest | E Present Value of Projected Benefit |
|---|---|---|---|---|---|
| Fred | $ 75 | 120 | 19 | 0.396 | $ 3,564 |
| Barney | $133 | 120 | 4 | 0.823 | $13,135 |
| Wilma | $321 | 120 | 34 | 0.190 | $ 7,319 |
| Betty | $225 | 120 | 24 | 0.310 | $ 8,370 |
| Total | | | | | $32,388 |

The present value of the change in projected benefit is determined by multi-plying the change in projected benefit by the APR at the participant's retire-ment age and by a discount factor for interest. This amount is to be funded over the future working years of each employee. The following table develops the normal cost in the second plan year.

| | A | B | C |
|---|---|---|---|
| | Present Value Annuity Due of $1 over Future | Present Value Change in Projected | |
| Name | Years | Benefit | Normal Cost |
| Fred | 12.690 | $ 3,564 | $ 281 |
| Barney | 3.723 | $13,135 | $3,528 |
| Wilma | 17.003 | $ 7,319 | $ 430 |
| Betty | 14.489 | $ 8,370 | $ 578 |
| Total | | | $4,817 |

The normal cost attributed to the change in the projected benefit is the present value of the change in projected benefits in column B divided by the present value of an annuity due of $1 from the valuation date to normal retirement age (column A). Fred's additional normal cost is $281 ($3,564 ÷ 12.690). The accumulated normal cost from the prior year is now added to the normal cost attributed to the change in projected benefit to determine the plan's total current normal cost.

| Name | Change in Projected Benefit Normal Cost | Prior Years' Accumulated Normal Cost | Current Year's Accumulated Normal Cost |
|---|---|---|---|
| Fred | $ 281 | $ 3,890 | $ 4,171 |
| Barney | $3,528 | $34,499 | $38,027 |
| Wilma | $ 430 | $ 921 | $ 1,351 |
| Betty | $ 578 | $ 4,485 | $ 5,063 |
| Total | $4,817 | $43,795 | $48,612 |

### Q 18:48　How is the unfunded accrued liability determined in the ILP funding method?

The accrued liability in ILP funding is the accumulation of the past normal costs to the plan. At plan inception the accrued liability is equal to zero because this method calculates the normal cost from plan inception. In future years, the actual accrued liability is equal to the accrued liability from the previous year plus the normal cost increased with interest. The unfunded accrued liability is the accrued liability less the value of the plan's assets.

**Example.** The normal costs for the first and second years for Real Rock Co. Pension Plan were $43,795 (see Example 1 in Q 18:47) and $48,612 (see Example 2 in Q 18:47), respectively, using the ILP funding method. All benefits are valued at 5 percent. The plan's assets were $0 in the first year, $45,000 beginning in the second year, and $105,000 beginning in the third year. The accrued liability beginning in the first year is $0; beginning the second year, it would be $45,985 (43,795 × 1.05); and beginning in the third year, it would be $99,327 ((45,985 + 48,612) × 1.05). The unfunded accrued liability beginning in the first year is $0 ($0 − $0); beginning in the second year, it would be $985 ($45,985 − $45,000); and beginning in the third year, it would be ($5,673) ($99,327 − $105,000). The parentheses around $5,673 indicate a negative number.

### Q 18:49   How is the actuarial gain or loss determined in the ILP funding method?

The net actuarial gain or loss is determined by subtracting the expected unfunded accrued liability (see Q 18:11) from the actual unfunded accrued liability (see Q 18:7).

**Example.** In the year before the current valuation date, Real Rock Co. had an actual unfunded accrued liability of $985 and a normal cost of $48,612. Real Rock Co. contributed $50,000 to the plan's trust fund, which was deposited midyear. A half year's interest at 5 percent on the contribution is $1,250. As of the current valuation date, the plan's actual unfunded accrued liability is ($5,673). The actuarial gain or loss will be the expected unfunded accrued liability minus the actual unfunded accrued liability of ($5,673). By applying the formula in Q 18:11 ((UFAL + NC) × (1 + i) − C − Ci), the expected unfunded accrued liability for the Real Rock plan is calculated as ($827) (($985 + $48,612) × 1.05 − $50,000 − $1,250). The net actuarial gain is $827 minus ($5,673), or $6,500. Because the result is positive, there is a gain.

### Q 18:50   What makes ILP funding different from other funding methods?

ILP funding develops the accrued liability from plan inception starting at zero and adjusts the normal cost based on the change in projected benefit from year to year. It funds for the change in projected benefit in every year after the first.

### Q 18:51   When is the ILP funding method generally used?

ILP funding is rarely used, except for target benefit plans where it is the generally accepted funding method.

## Comparison of Funding Methods

### Q 18:52   Which funding methods are considered individual methods?

An individual method determines a contribution for each participant and the total plan contribution is the sum of the individual contributions. In contrast, an aggregate method looks at the sum of the present value of future benefits and determines a contribution based on an average period of time to retirement.

The individual methods are entry age normal, individual aggregate, ILP, unit credit, and the PPA funding method.

The aggregate methods are aggregate, AAN, and FIL. (See Table 1 at end of this section.)

**Note.** An aggregate method may not be appropriate for a plan if the majority of benefits are due to be paid to the older employees. Because the contribution is determined based on an average period of time to retirement for all participants, there may not be enough money at retirement to pay those older participants.

### Q 18:53   Which funding methods use a past-service liability?

A *past-service liability* is an unfunded accrued liability due to benefits based on service before plan inception. Funding methods that have a past-service liability have a smaller normal cost than methods without a past-service liability. Basically, the portion of the value of the benefits due to past service is amortized (paid for) separately from the regular annual contribution needed to pay for future benefits. The past-service liability must be paid off over a variable number of years. As a result, the methods that use a past-service liability have a minimum and maximum contribution, rather than a single contribution obligation.

The methods that use a past-service liability are AAN, entry age normal, FIL, unit credit, and the PPA funding method. (See Table 1 at end of this section.)

### Q 18:54   Which funding methods are immediate-gain methods?

An immediate-gain method specifically identifies the actuarial gain or loss each year and adjusts the unfunded accrued liability by the amount of the gain or loss (see Q 18:9). These gains and losses are amortized separately from the normal cost. The spread-gain methods do not require a calculation of the gains or losses, but either decrease or increase the contribution over future years as a result of any gain or loss. The immediate-gain methods generally have a minimum and maximum contribution, rather than a single contribution obligation.

The immediate-gain methods are entry age normal, ILP, unit credit, and the PPA funding method. (See Table 1 at end of this section.)

### Q 18:55   Which funding methods directly calculate an accrued liability?

An accrued liability can be directly calculated under the funding method used for the plan if the following three conditions are met:

1. The accrued liability may be determined solely from the computations with respect to the liabilities (without reference to plan assets);
2. The accrued liability is an integral part of the funding method used; and
3. The accrued liability satisfies the definition of ERISA Section 3(29).

For the accrued liability to be an integral part of the funding method used for the plan, such accrued liability or both the present value of future benefits and the present value of future normal costs must be calculated as part of the funding method and must be used to determine plan costs. Further, for the accrued liability to satisfy the definition of ERISA Section 3(29), it must be equal to the present value of future benefits less the present value of future normal costs. The normal costs that are so used are the plan's anticipated future normal costs under the funding method as of the valuation date. [Rev. Rul. 81-13, 1981-1 C.B. 229]

**Example.** The MLB defined benefit plan uses the ILP method. Under this funding method, experience gains and losses are separately determined and amortized, and the accrued liability is the present value of future benefits less the present value of future normal costs, thus satisfying the requirement of ERISA Section 3(29). Because the accrued liability is determined solely from the computations with respect to the liabilities, is an integral part of the ILP funding method, and satisfies the definition of ERISA Section 3(29), such accrued liability is directly calculated within the meaning of Code Section 412(c)(7) and ERISA Section 302(c)(7). (See Table 1 at end of this section.)

### Table 1. Comparison of various funding methods

| Actuarial Cost Method | Accrued or Projected | Individual or Aggregate | Immediate or Spread Gain | Past-Service Liability |
|---|---|---|---|---|
| Individual Level Premium | Projected | Individual | Immediate | No |
| Aggregate | Projected | Aggregate | Spread | No |
| Attained Age Normal | Projected | Aggregate | Spread | Yes |
| Entry Age Normal | Projected | Individual | Immediate | Yes |
| Frozen Initial Liability | Projected | Aggregate | Spread | Yes |
| Individual Aggregate | Projected | Individual | Spread | No |
| Unit Credit | Accrued | Individual | Immediate | Yes |
| PPA Funding Method | Accrued | Individual | Immediate | Yes |

## Funding Method Requirements

### Q 18:56  What requirements must be met for a funding method to be used in a qualified defined benefit pension plan?

For purposes of satisfying the minimum funding requirements under Code Section 412, a funding method must be reasonable. A plan funding method satisfies the reasonableness requirement if it satisfies the basic funding formula (see Q 18:57) and the normal cost is a level-dollar amount, or a level percentage of pay, that is computed from year to year on either an individual basis or an aggregate basis, or an amount equal to the present value of benefits accruing under the method for a particular plan year. Additionally, the funding method must satisfy the following criteria:

1. *Inclusion of all liabilities.* All liabilities of the plan for benefits, whether vested or not, must be taken into account.

2. *Production of actuarial gains and losses.* If each actuarial assumption is exactly realized under the funding method, no actuarial gains or losses are produced.

3. *The plan population must include three classes of individuals.* The three classes of participants are participants currently employed in the service of the employer; former participants who either terminated service with the employer, or retired, under the plan; and all other individuals currently entitled to benefits under the plan. However, participants who would be excluded from participation by the minimum age or service requirement of Code Section 410 but who, under the terms of the plan, participate immediately on entering the service of the employer may be excluded until such time as they are no longer excludable. A funding method does not have to maintain in the population participants who have left without vested benefits even though those participants may have their benefits restored on rehire. Additionally, a funding method must not anticipate the affiliation with the plan of future participants not employed in the service of the employer on the plan valuation date. However, a funding method may anticipate the affiliation with the plan of current employees who have not satisfied the participation requirements of the plan.

4. *Salary scale.* The use of a salary-scale assumption is not inappropriate merely because of the funding method with which it is used. Therefore, in determining whether actuarial assumptions are reasonable, a salary scale will not be considered to be prohibited merely because a particular funding method is being used. However, salary scales reflected in projected benefits must be the expected salary on which benefits would be based under the plan at the age when the receipt of benefits is expected to begin.

5. *Allocation of assets and liabilities.* Any initial allocation of assets among participants will be considered reasonable only if it is in proportion to related liabilities. In addition, if a funding method allocates liabilities among different elements of past and future service, the allocation of liabilities must be reasonable. The IRS ruled in Revenue Ruling 85-131 [1985-2 C.B. 138] that a plan that uses the unit credit funding method must provide a reasonable allocation of liabilities to past and current service in determining the portion of the accrued benefit that is amortized as an initial liability and the portion that represents the current normal cost.

6. *Treatment of ancillary benefit costs.* Ancillary benefit costs must be computed by using the same method used to compute retirement benefit costs under a plan, with an exception to allow the use of the one-year term

method to fund for the ancillary benefits and an additional exception to use the premium paid for that benefit under an insurance contract. [Treas. Reg. § 1.412(c)(3)-1(f)] An *ancillary benefit* is a benefit that is paid as a result of a specified event that occurs not later than a participant's separation from service and that was detrimental to the participant's health. Benefits such as early retirement, Social Security supplements, or vesting of plan benefits more rapidly than required under the law are not subject to this rule. If the plan uses insurance contracts to provide ancillary benefits, regardless of the method used to compute retirement benefit costs, and if only an ancillary benefit is provided under an insurance contract and the benefit is guaranteed under an insurance contract, the cost of the ancillary benefit may equal the premium paid for that benefit under the insurance contract. Any benefits described in Code Section 401(h) for which a separate account is maintained are also not subject to this requirement.

7. *Anticipated benefit changes.* A funding method may not anticipate benefit changes that become effective, whether or not retroactively, in a future plan year or that become effective after the first day of a current plan year. However, a collectively bargained plan as described in Code Section 413(a) is required to anticipate benefit increases scheduled to take effect during the term of the collective bargaining agreement applicable to the plan. [I.R.C. § 412(c)(12); Rev. Rul. 77-2, 1977-1 C.B. 120]

[Treas. Reg. § 1.412(c)(3)-1]

### Q 18:57  What is the basic funding formula?

The *basic funding formula* states that the present value of future benefits under a funding method must equal the sum of (1) the present value of normal costs (taking into account future mandatory employee contributions, within the meaning of Code Section 411(c)(2)(C), in the case of a contributory plan) over the future working lifetimes of participants; (2) the sum of the unamortized charge and credit bases, if any, treating credit bases under Code Section 412(b)(3)(B) as negative numbers; and (3) the plan assets, decreased by a credit balance or increased by a debit balance in the funding standard account. [Treas. Reg. § 1.412(c)(3)-1(b)(1)]

### Q 18:58  Are plans that use the unit credit funding method subject to special rules for its use to be considered reasonable?

Yes. In determining a plan's normal cost and accrued liability for a particular plan year, the projected benefits of the plan must be allocated between past years and future years. Except in the case of a career-average-pay plan, this allocation must be in proportion to the applicable rates of benefit accrual under the plan. Thus, the allocation to past years is effected by multiplying the projected benefit by a fraction. The numerator of the fraction is the participant's credited years of service. The denominator is the participant's total credited years of service at the anticipated benefit commencement date. Adjustments are made to account for changes in the rate of benefit accrual. An allocation based on compensation is not permitted. In the case of a career-average-pay plan, an allocation between past-service and future-service benefits must be reasonable. [Treas. Reg. § 1.412 (c)(3)-1(e)(3)]

## Funding of Life Insurance

### Q 18:59   Can the cost of life insurance protection increase the total contributions to the plan?

Yes. Life insurance with cash values can be handled one of two ways in the funding of a plan. Because the cash value can be used to pay for the benefit at retirement, it must be considered in the funding method for the plan. The two methods are known as *split funding* and *envelope funding*. These are not actuarial funding methods, but ways of dealing with the insurance.

### Q 18:60   How is the plan's normal cost affected by split funding?

Split funding treats the insurance policy as an investment separate from the rest of the plan. In this case, the cash value that will be accumulated in the policies at retirement can be used to pay for the benefit at retirement. Because the policy is being treated as a separate investment, the normal cost needs to take into account only the benefit not being paid for by the insurance policy.

> **Example.** Fred, the sole participant in the Real Rock Co. Defined Benefit Plan, has an insurance policy that has an annual premium of $100 and that will have $5,000 in cash value at retirement. The Real Rock Co. plan is funded using the individual aggregate funding method. Fred's projected monthly benefit will be $1,125, with a lump-sum value at retirement of $135,000. With split funding, the cash value of the life insurance at retirement is subtracted from the lump-sum value of the retirement benefits, leaving a lump-sum value of $130,000. Fred has 20 years until attainment of his normal retirement age. The discount factor for this many years using 5 percent interest is 0.377; therefore, the present value of Fred's projected benefit is $48,996. The assets this year are $3,400. The normal cost is determined by dividing the present value of the unfunded projected benefit of $45,596 ($48,996 − $3,400) by the temporary annuity factor of 13.085. Fred's normal cost to fund the retirement benefit is therefore $3,485. This is referred to as the *side fund normal cost*.

The total normal cost is equal to the side fund normal cost ($3,485) plus the insurance premium ($100), or $3,585.

### Q 18:61   How is the plan's normal cost affected by envelope funding?

Envelope funding is a method of dealing with the insurance on a term-cost basis. *Term cost* is the cost to provide the death benefit portion of the insurance if the participant dies during the next year.

Under this method, the plan treats the cash value of the insurance policy as a plan asset. The normal cost is calculated much like the normal cost of a plan with no insurance, by including the current cash value of the insurance in the asset value. The total normal cost is equal to the side fund normal cost plus a one-year term cost of the insurance.

**Example.** Assume the same facts as those in the example in Q 18:60, but the insurance for Fred has a current cash value of $500 and a term cost of $48. Recall that the lump-sum value of the benefit at retirement is $135,000. The present value of this benefit is therefore equal to $50,895 ($135,000 × 0.377). From this is subtracted the allocated assets, which consist of the side fund assets of $3,400 and the current cash value of the life insurance of $500, for a total of $3,900. The present value of future normal costs is therefore equal to $46,995 ($50,895 − $3,900). The normal cost is determined by dividing the present value of future normal costs of $46,995 by the temporary annuity factor of 13.085. Therefore, Fred's normal cost to fund the retirement benefit is $3,592. Because total normal cost must include the term-cost portion of the premium, the total normal cost is $3,640 ($3,592 + $48).

## Changing a Funding Method

### Q 18:62   What is a change in funding method?

The term *funding method*, when used for purposes of Code Section 412, has the same meaning as the term *actuarial cost method* in ERISA Section 3(31). In these contexts, the funding method of a plan includes not only the specific type of funding method (cost method) used by the plan but also all underlying computations used in applying the overall method. The funding method of a plan, in this context, includes three basic components:

1. The valuation date (the date on which assets and liabilities are valued);
2. The cost method; and
3. The asset valuation method.

The cost method includes the definition of compensation that is used to determine the normal cost or accrued liability.

When there is a "change in funding method" for a plan, the term refers to a change in one of the three basic components to a funding method. Furthermore, a change from one accepted cost method to another does not change the other components of the funding method such as the current valuation date or asset valuation method used for the plan. [Rev. Proc. 2000-40, 2000-42 I.R.B. 357, § 2.02]

Treasury Regulations Section 1.412(c)(2)-1 provides that a change in the actuarial valuation method used to value the assets of a plan is also a change in funding method. (See chapter 21 for the various asset valuation methods available.)

Revenue Ruling 81-215 [1981-2 C.B. 106] adds as a part of the funding method the plan's treatment of scheduled increases in the maximum dollar benefit under Code Section 415. A plan is allowed to reflect in the whole year's funding the dollar benefit in effect as of the last day of the plan year. Because this is part of the funding method, a change in the treatment of such scheduled increases is a change in funding method.

### Q 18:63   Under what circumstances may a plan change its funding method?

Generally a plan must obtain approval from the IRS to change its funding method. If, however, the proposed change of funding method meets the numerous criteria set forth in Revenue Procedure 2000-40 [2000-42 I.R.B. 357], the plan can change its funding method without advance approval from the IRS. Additionally, to qualify for an automatic change in funding method, a plan must satisfy certain restrictions (see Q 18:64).

### Q 18:64   What are the restrictions that apply to eligibility for automatic approval of a change in funding method?

Any plan considering the use of automatic approval for a change in funding method must satisfy all of the following criteria:

1. Schedule B of IRS Form 5500 has not been filed for the plan year in which the changes are to be made, using some other funding method, or the due date (including extensions) for such Schedule B has not passed.

2. The plan administrator (within the meaning of Code Section 414(g)) or an authorized representative of the plan sponsor indicates as part of the series Form 5500 for the plan year for which the change is effective that the plan administrator or plan sponsor agrees to the change in funding method. In the case of one of the following changes in funding method, however, the plan administrator or authorized representative does not need to agree to the request:

   a. Correction of unreasonable allocation of costs (see Qs 18:73–18:75);

   b. Takeovers (see Q 18:76); and

   c. Changes in valuation software (see Q 18:80).

   In these cases, the requirement that the plan administrator or authorized representative of the plan sponsor agree to the change is satisfied if the plan administrator or authorized representative of the plan sponsor is made aware of the change before the Schedule B is filed.

3. The plan has not requested a minimum funding waiver under the plan year of the change [I.R.C. § 412(d)], and a funding waiver is not being amortized.

4. The plan has not requested an extension of an amortization period under Code Section 412(e), or such an extension is not currently applicable for computing the minimum funding requirements for the plan.

5. The plan is not under an IRS Employee Plans examination (audit) for any plan year; or the plan sponsor, or a representative, has not received verbal or written notification from the IRS Employee Plans Exempt Organization Division of an impending IRS Employee Plans examination (audit) or of an impending referral from another part of the IRS for an Employee Plans examination; or the plan has been under such an examination and is in appeal or in litigation for issues raised in an Employee Plans examination.

6. The plan has not been terminated in the plan year of the change. If, however, a plan is fully funded and meets certain other criteria, the plan can change its funding method to the unit credit funding method (see Q 18:67).

7. A plan using the shortfall method must continue to use the shortfall method after any change in funding method.

8. If a plan uses universal life insurance products, all plan benefits, including those provided by the universal life insurance policies, are considered liabilities in calculating costs and are funded using the same method as used for retirement costs (however, ancillary benefits, within the meaning of Treasury Regulations Section 1.412(c)(3)-1(f)(2), may be funded on a reasonable one-year term funding method); and the cash value as of the valuation date of such contracts is treated the same as all other assets of the plan in calculating costs.

9. A plan cannot automatically change the asset valuation method if the asset valuation method was changed in any of the four preceding plan years.

10. A plan cannot automatically change the valuation date if the valuation date was changed in any of the four preceding plan years.

11. A plan cannot automatically change the funding method if the funding method was changed in any of the four preceding plan years. Changes in asset valuation methods and valuation dates are not considered funding method changes for purposes of this requirement. Thus, a plan may have changed its valuation date and asset valuation method in one of the last four preceding plan years and still change its funding method. This restriction is also not applicable to a change in funding method due to (a) anticipation of scheduled benefit increases, (b) correction of an unreasonable allocation of costs, (c) a fully funded terminating plan, or (d) takeover plans.

12. A plan cannot automatically change its funding method if under the new method the liabilities are adjusted to reflect the performance or expected performance of the assets.

13. A plan cannot automatically change its funding method if, as a result of the change in method, a negative normal cost or a negative unfunded liability is produced.

14. A plan cannot automatically change its funding method if, in connection with the change, the plan is involved in a spin-off or merger, unless the change follows prescribed guidelines (see Q 18:76).

15. A plan cannot automatically change its funding method if such change was required by Treasury Release R-2697 dated May 24, 1984, concerning the reversion of assets from a terminated plan. Furthermore, if in the 15 years preceding the date of change, a plan was involved in a transaction described in that Treasury release after May 24, 1984, the plan cannot automatically change its funding method.

[Rev. Proc. 2000-40, 2000-42 I.R.B. 357, § 6]

### Q 18:65 When can a plan's funding method automatically be changed to the unit credit funding method?

A change in funding method to the unit credit funding method is allowed provided that the plan and funding method meet the following criteria:

1. The plan is not a cash balance plan.
2. The normal cost is the sum of the individual normal costs for all active participants.
3. The accrued liability under the method is the sum of the individual accrued liabilities for each participant.
4. The unfunded liability equals the total accrued liability less the actuarial value of plan assets, and all present values are determined as of the valuation date.
5. The projected retirement benefit is determined under the plan's benefit formula considering projected compensation. The portion allocated to the current plan year is the difference between the benefit calculated using credited service through the end of the current plan year and the benefit calculated through the end of the prior plan year. The accrued benefit determined in this manner for funding purposes cannot be less than the accrued benefit determined under the terms of the plan document, including top-heavy minimum benefits.

[Rev. Proc. 2000-40, 2000-42 I.R.B. 357, § 3.01]

(See Qs 18:64 and 18:77 regarding the general rules and restrictions on funding method changes.)

### Q 18:66 Can a frozen defined benefit plan automatically change to the unit credit funding method?

If a plan provides that no participant can accrue a benefit as of a date that is no later than the first day of the plan year, the plan can change to the unit credit funding method. [Rev. Proc. 2000-40, 2000-42 I.R.B. 357, § 4.01(5)]

**Note.** No automatic approval is provided for any method other than the unit credit funding method under the above circumstances. [Rev. Proc. 2000-40, 2000-42 I.R.B. 357, § 6.02(5)] (See Qs 18:64 and 18:77 regarding the general rules and restrictions on funding method changes.)

### Q 18:67   Can a plan that is terminating change its funding method to the unit credit funding method in the year of plan termination?

Yes, it can, provided that the normal cost for the plan year is the present value of the benefits accruing in the plan year, and the accrued liability is the present value of the benefits accrued as of the first day of the plan year. Furthermore, the plan must be fully funded on the termination date. This means that the fair market value of the assets of the plan (exclusive of contributions receivable) must not be less than the present value of all benefit liabilities (whether or not vested). If the plan is covered by the Pension Benefit Guaranty Corporation (PBGC) termination insurance program, a timely notice of intent to terminate must have been filed with the PBGC.

As part of the change in method, the valuation date can be changed to the date of termination or the first day of the plan year, and the asset valuation method can be changed to value plan assets at fair market value. [Rev. Proc. 2000-40, 2000-42 I.R.B. 357, § 4.02]

These are the only preapproved changes allowed for a plan in the year of termination. [Rev. Proc. 2000-40, 2000-42 I.R.B. 357, § 6.01(5)]

### Q 18:68   Can a plan change the valuation date?

Yes, it can, provided that it is changed to the first day of the plan year. If the plan is terminating, the actuary has the additional option of changing the valuation date to the date of termination, as long as the funding method is also changed to the unit credit method. [Rev. Proc. 2000-40, 2000-42 I.R.B. 357, § 3.13]

**Example.** The termination date for the Real Rock Co. Defined Benefit Plan, a calendar-year plan, is January 31, 2003. The actuary has projected that the plan's liabilities are fully funded as of December 31, 2002; however, the valuation date for the plan has always been January 1. In calculating the normal cost for 2002, the actuary has determined that under the appropriate funding assumptions, there is a $100,000 required contribution. Using a valuation date of December 31 would mean that no contribution would be required. The plan does not have automatic approval to change the valuation date to December 31.

### Q 18:69   When can a plan's funding method automatically be changed to the aggregate funding method?

A plan can change to the aggregate funding method when the normal cost is determined either as a level percentage of compensation for compensation-related benefit plans or a level-dollar amount for non-compensation-related benefit plans.

A change to the level percentage of compensation aggregate funding method is allowed provided that the following conditions are met:

1. The plan provides for compensation-related benefits (i.e., the benefit is equal to a percentage of compensation).
2. The normal cost is calculated in the aggregate as the normal cost accrual rate multiplied by the total compensation of all active participants; where

the normal cost accrual rate is the total present value of future benefits of all participants and beneficiaries, less adjusted assets, divided by the total, for all active participants, of the present value of the compensation expected to be paid to each participant for each year of the participant's anticipated future service, determined as of the participant's attained age.

A change in funding method to the level-dollar aggregate funding method is allowed provided that the following conditions are met:

1. The normal cost is calculated in the aggregate as the normal cost per active participant multiplied by the number of active participants.

2. The normal cost per active participant is the total present value of future benefits of all participants and beneficiaries, less adjusted assets, divided by the total, for all active participants, of the present value of an annuity of $1 per year for every year of a participant's anticipated future service, determined as of the participant's attained age.

[Rev. Proc. 2000-40, 2000-42 I.R.B. 357, §§ 3.02, 3.03]

(See Qs 18:64 and 18:77 regarding the general rules and restrictions on funding method changes.)

### Q 18:70  When can a plan's funding method be automatically changed to the individual aggregate funding method?

A plan can change to the individual aggregate funding method when the normal cost is determined either as a level percentage of compensation for compensation-related benefit plans or a level-dollar amount for non-compensation-related benefit plans. If, however, the actuarial value of the plan's assets is less than the present value of benefits of terminated vested participants, retired participants, and beneficiaries, the automatic change is not allowed. Furthermore, if the adjusted value of the plan's assets is less than zero, an automatic change to this method is not allowed. In this case the *adjusted value* of the plan's assets means the actuarial value of the assets, plus the sum of the outstanding balances of the amortization bases established on account of (1) the current liability full-funding limitation if any; (2) funding waivers under Code Section 412(b)(2)(C); (3) a switch-back to the regular funding standard under Code Section 412(b)(2)(D); (4) use of the shortfall method under Treasury Regulations Section 1.412(c)(1)-2; and (5) the transition under Treasury Regulations Section 1.412(c)(3)-2(d); minus the credit balance (or plus the funding deficiency), if any, in the funding standard account; minus any liabilities retained by the plan for any of the terminated vested participants, retired participants, and beneficiaries.

If the requirements above are satisfied, a plan can change its funding method to the level percentage of compensation individual aggregate funding method as described below:

1. The plan provides for compensation-related benefits (i.e., the benefit is equal to a percentage of compensation).

2. The normal cost is the sum of the individual normal costs for each active participant.

3. The normal cost for an active participant is the present value of future benefits for the participant, less the allocated adjusted value of the plan's assets, divided by the ratio of the present value of the compensation expected to be paid to the participant for each year of the participant's anticipated future service, determined as of the participant's attained age, to the participant's current compensation.

4. In the first year in which the method is used, the allocated adjusted value of the assets for an active participant is calculated by allocating the adjusted value of the assets in proportion to the present value of accrued benefits, or in proportion to the accrued liability determined under the unit credit or individual entry age normal funding method.

5. For years after the first year in which the method is used, the adjusted value of the assets is allocated to an active participant in the proportion that the sum of the allocated adjusted assets and calculated normal cost as of the valuation date for the prior year for that active participant bears to the total of the amounts for all active participants.

A plan can change its funding method to the level-dollar individual aggregate funding method described below:

1. The normal cost is the sum of the individual normal costs for each active participant.

2. The normal cost for an active participant is the present value of future benefits for the participant, less the allocated adjusted value of the plan's assets, divided by the present value of an annuity of $1 per year for every year of the participant's anticipated future service, determined as of the participant's attained age.

3. In the first year in which the method is used, the allocated adjusted value of assets for an active participant is calculated by allocating the adjusted value of the assets in proportion to the present value of accrued benefits, or in proportion to the accrued liability determined under the unit credit or individual entry age normal funding method.

4. For years after the first year in which the method is used, the adjusted value of the assets is allocated to an active participant in the proportion that the sum of the allocated adjusted assets and calculated normal cost as of the valuation date for the prior year for that active participant bears to the total of the amounts for all active participants.

[Rev. Proc. 2000-40, 2000-42 I.R.B. 357, §§ 3.04, 3.05]

(See Qs 18:64 and 18:77 regarding the general rules and restrictions on funding method changes.)

### Q 18:71   When can a plan's funding method automatically be changed to the FIL funding method?

A plan can change to the FIL funding method when the normal cost is determined either as a level percentage of compensation for compensation-related benefit plans or a level-dollar amount for non-compensation-related benefit plans.

A plan can change its funding method to the level percentage of compensation FIL funding method as described below:

1. The plan provides for compensation-related benefits.

2. The normal cost is calculated in the aggregate for every year the method is used, including the first, as the normal cost accrual rate multiplied by the total compensation of all active participants.

3. The normal cost accrual rate is the total present value of future benefits of all participants and beneficiaries, less the sum of the actuarial value of assets and the unfunded liability, divided by the total, for all active participants, of the present value of the compensation expected to be paid to each participant for each year of the participant's anticipated future service, determined as of the participant's attained age.

4. On the date of change, the unfunded liability is set equal to the unfunded accrued liability determined under the level percentage of compensation individual entry age normal funding method.

5. For years after the plan year of the change in method, the unfunded liability equals the unfunded liability for the prior plan year, plus the normal cost for the prior plan year (the result adjusted with appropriate interest to the valuation date), minus the actual contribution or contributions for the prior plan year (adjusted with appropriate interest to the valuation date).

6. Increases or decreases are made to the unfunded liability in the amount of any base established on the valuation date that results from a plan amendment or a change in assumptions. Such bases are amortized over the period or periods described in Code Section 412(b)(2)(B) or (3)(B), as applicable.

A plan can change its funding method to the level-dollar FIL funding method as described below:

1. The normal cost is calculated in the aggregate for every year the method is used, including the first, as the normal cost per active participant multiplied by the number of active participants.

2. The normal cost per active participant is the total present value of future benefits of all participants and beneficiaries, less the sum of the actuarial value of assets and the unfunded liability, divided by the total, for all active participants, of the present value of an annuity of $1 per year for every year of a participant's anticipated future service, determined as of the participant's attained age.

3. On the date of change, the unfunded liability is set equal to the unfunded accrued liability determined under level-dollar individual entry age normal funding.

4. For years after the plan year of the change in method, the unfunded liability equals the unfunded liability for the prior plan year, plus the normal cost for the prior plan year (the result adjusted with appropriate interest to

the valuation date), minus the actual contribution or contributions for the prior plan year (adjusted with appropriate interest to the valuation date).

5. Increases or decreases are made to the unfunded liability by the amount of any base established on the valuation date that results from a plan amendment or a change in assumptions. Such bases are amortized over the period or periods described in Code Section 412(b)(2)(B) or (3)(B), as applicable.

[Rev. Proc. 2000-40, 2000-42 I.R.B. 357, §§ 3.06, 3.07]

(See Qs 18:64 and 18:77 regarding the general rules and restrictions on funding method changes.)

### Q 18:72 When can a plan's funding method automatically be changed to the individual entry age normal funding method?

A plan can change to the individual entry age normal funding method when the normal cost is determined either as a level percentage of compensation for compensation-related benefit plans or a level-dollar amount for non-compensation-related benefit plans. The approval does not apply, however, if the alternative minimum funding standard account is used at any time within the five-year period commencing with the first day of the plan year for which the change is made.

If the requirement above with regard to the alternative minimum funding standard account is met, a plan can change its funding method to the level percentage of compensation individual entry age normal funding method as described below:

1. The plan provides for compensation-related benefits.

2. The normal cost is the sum of the individual normal costs for all active participants. For an active participant, the normal cost is the participant's normal cost accrual rate multiplied by the participant's current compensation.

3. The normal cost accrual rate equals the present value of future benefits for the participant, determined as of the participant's entry age, divided by the present value of the compensation expected to be paid to the participant for each year of the participant's anticipated future service, determined as of the participant's entry age.

4. When determining the present value of future compensation, the salary scale must be applied both retrospectively and prospectively to estimate compensation in years before and subsequent to the valuation year based on the compensation used for the valuation.

5. The accrued liability is the sum of the individual accrued liabilities for all participants and beneficiaries. A participant's accrued liability equals the present value, at the participant's attained age, of future benefits less the present value, at the participant's attained age, of the individual normal costs payable in the future. A beneficiary's accrued liability equals

the present value, at the beneficiary's attained age, of future benefits. The unfunded accrued liability equals the total accrued liability less the actuarial value of assets.

6. The entry age used for each active participant is the participant's age at the time he or she would have commenced participation if the plan had always been in existence under current terms or the age as of which he or she began to earn service credits for purposes of benefit accrual under the current terms of the plan.

If the requirement above with regard to the alternative minimum funding standard account is met, a plan can change its funding method to the level-dollar individual entry age normal funding method as described below:

1. The normal cost is the sum of the individual normal costs for all active participants.

2. For an active participant, the individual normal cost equals the present value of future benefits for the participant, determined as of the participant's entry age, divided by the present value of an annuity of $1 per year for every year of the participant's anticipated future service, determined as of the participant's entry age.

3. The accrued liability is the sum of the individual accrued liabilities for all participants and beneficiaries. A participant's accrued liability equals the present value, at the participant's attained age, of future benefits, less the present value, at the participant's attained age, of the individual normal costs payable in the future. A beneficiary's accrued liability equals the present value, at the beneficiary's attained age, of future benefits. The unfunded accrued liability equals the total accrued liability less the actuarial value of the plan assets.

4. The entry age used for each active participant is the participant's age at the time he or she would have commenced participation if the plan had always been in existence under current terms or the age as of which he or she began to earn service credits for purposes of benefit accrual under the current terms of the plan.

[Rev. Proc. 2000-40, 2000-42 I.R.B. 357, §§ 3.08, 3.09]

(See Qs 18:64 and 18:77 regarding the general rules and restrictions on funding method changes.)

### Q 18:73　Can the allocation of assets to a participant in a plan using the individual aggregate funding method automatically be changed?

Yes. If a plan uses an individual aggregate funding method and an individual normal cost becomes negative for a participant, any assets in excess of the present value of future benefits for that participant can be reallocated to the remaining active participants in proportion to the present value of accrued benefits, or in proportion to the accrued liability determined under the unit credit funding method or the entry age normal funding method (either the level percentage of compensation or level-dollar basis depending on whether plan benefits are salary related), or in proportion to the allocated adjusted assets before the reallocation. [Rev. Proc. 2000-40, 2000-42 I.R.B. 357, § 4.01(1)] (See Qs 18:64 and 18:77 regarding the general rules and restrictions on funding method changes.)

### Q 18:74   If the normal cost and/or unfunded accrued liability for a plan using the FIL or the AAN funding method becomes negative, what options are available?

If a plan uses the FIL or the AAN funding method and the normal cost and/or unfunded liability become negative, the plan can reestablish the unfunded liability using the method that originally established the unfunded liability before its becoming negative. If, after reestablishing the unfunded liability, the result is still negative, the plan can use the aggregate funding method as either a level percentage of compensation amount for compensation-related plans or a level-dollar amount for non-compensation-related plans. [Rev. Proc. 2000-40, 2000-42 I.R.B. 357, § 4.01(2)] (See Qs 18:64 and 18:77 regarding the general rules and restrictions on funding method changes.)

### Q 18:75   If a plan using the FIL or the AAN funding method becomes fully funded, what option is available?

If a plan uses the FIL or the AAN funding method and the plan becomes fully funded under Code Section 412(c)(6) (without taking into account Code Section 412(c)(7)(A)(i)(I)), the plan can use the aggregate funding method as either a level percentage of compensation amount for compensation-related plans or a level-dollar amount for non-compensation-related plans. In this case *fully funded* means the old full-funding limitation, not the current liability full-funding limitation. [Rev. Proc. 2000-40, 2000-42 I.R.B. 357, § 4.02(3)] (See Qs 18:64 and 18:77 regarding the general rules and restrictions on funding method changes.)

### Q 18:76   If a new enrolled actuary takes over a plan and the contribution calculations are different from the prior actuary's calculations, is this a change of funding method and as such does it require IRS approval?

Yes. If the following conditions are satisfied, however, IRS approval is not required:

1. There has been a change in both the enrolled actuary for the plan and the business organization providing actuarial services to the plan.

2. The method used by the new actuary is substantially the same as the method used by the prior actuary and is consistent with the information contained in the prior actuarial valuation reports or prior Schedules B of Form 5500. In addition, the method used by the new actuary must be applied to the prior year (using the assumptions of the prior actuary)

and the absolute value of each resulting difference in normal cost, accrued liability (if directly computed under the method), and actuarial value of assets that is attributable to the change in cost method must not exceed 5 percent of the respective amounts calculated by the prior actuary for that year.

3. The change in costs due to the change in method is treated in the same manner as an actuarial gain or loss, unless the actuarial assumptions are being changed, in which case the change in method is treated as part of the change in assumptions.

[Rev. Proc. 2000-40, 2000-42 I.R.B. 357, § 4.03]

If the funding method used by the new actuary is not substantially the same as that used by the prior actuary, this approval cannot be used and the actuary would need to satisfy the conditions for automatic approval for a change in funding method pursuant to a different section of Revenue Procedure 2000-40 [2000-42 I.R.B. 357] or apply for approval pursuant to Revenue Procedure 2000-41 [2000-42 I.R.B. 371]. [2001 Enrolled Actuaries Meeting Gray Book Q&A 20] (See Qs 18:64 and 18:77 regarding the general rules and restrictions on funding method changes.)

### Q 18:77  What are the general rules regarding amortization bases that must be followed when changing a funding method?

When a funding method is changed under the automatic approvals, certain amortization bases must be maintained and a change in funding method base can be required. If this is so, the base established due to the change in funding method must be amortized over 10 years. Furthermore, an amortization base is not established for a change due solely to a change in valuation date. [Rev. Proc. 2000-40, 2000-42 I.R.B. 357, § 5.01(4)] In all instances, the following amortization bases must be maintained:

1. A funding waiver base as described in Code Section 412(b)(2)(C);
2. A base due to a switchback to the regular funding standard account as described in Code Section 412(b)(2)(D);
3. A shortfall base as described in Treasury Regulations Section 1.412(c)(1)-2(g);
4. A transition base as described in Treasury Regulations Section 1.412(c)(3)-2(d); and
5. A base that was established to amortize a credit in the funding standard account due to the current liability full-funding limitation.

[Rev. Proc. 2000-40, 2000-42 I.R.B. 357, § 5.01(1)]

For a change in funding method to unit credit funding, individual entry age normal funding, or FIL funding, all existing bases must be maintained and an amortization base must be established equal to the difference between the unfunded accrued liability under the new method and an amount equal to the net sum of the outstanding balances of all amortization bases (including, when the preceding method was an immediate-gain method, the gain or loss base for the immediately preceding period) treating credit bases as negative bases, less the credit balance (or plus the funding deficiency), if any, in the funding standard account; less the sum of any existing accumulation of additional funding charges for prior plan years due to Code Section 412(l), any existing accumulation of additional interest charges due to late or unpaid quarterly installments for prior plan years, and any existing accumulation of additional interest charges due to the amortization of prior funding waivers, all adjusted for interest at the valuation rate to the valuation date in the plan year for which the change is made. If this difference is a positive or negative number, the resulting base will be a charge base or a credit base, respectively. A base established in accordance with these requirements is to be amortized over 10 years. If a plan's funding method is changed to the individual aggregate funding or the aggregate funding method, all amortization bases other than those described in items 1 through 5 above must be considered fully amortized. [Rev. Proc. 2000-40, 2000-42 I.R.B. 357, § 5.01(3)]

### Q 18:78   How does the maximum compensation limitation affect the calculation of the present value of the future compensation?

Compensation must be limited in accordance with Code Section 401(a)(17) in determining benefits to be valued; however, it may or may not be so limited in determining the present value of future compensation. Whichever alternative is used becomes part of the funding method and any change in such practice is a change in funding method. [Rev. Proc. 2000-40, 2000-42 I.R.B. 357, § 5.02]

### Q 18:79   If a plan has used a funding method that determines the normal cost as a level percentage of compensation or level-dollar amount per participant, can the level percentage or per-participant cost be applied to employees not included in the original determination?

No. Sometimes a plan can neglect to include certain participants in the determination of the normal cost and correct the omission by increasing the normal cost based on the compensation for the omitted participants or by the dollar cost per participant. Such a practice is not permitted for the funding methods with automatic approval. [Rev. Proc. 2000-40, 2000-42 I.R.B. 357, § 5.03]

### Q 18:80   Can a change in the computer software used in calculation of costs and liabilities be considered a change in funding method?

According to the IRS, yes. Treasury Regulations Section 1.412(c)(1)-1(b) defines the funding method of a plan to include not only the specific type of funding method used by the plan but also all underlying computations used in applying the overall method. Therefore, for example, a change in rounding conventions would be considered a change in funding method. Certain other changes, however, including updates to software to use the actual Social Security taxable wage base, are not considered changes in the funding method. In addition, if any of the results of each specific computation are the same after the change in valuation software, there is no change in funding method.

Approval is granted for a change in funding method that results from a change in valuation software as long as the following conditions are satisfied:

1. There has been a modification to the computations in the valuation software or a different valuation system has been used.

    **Note.** Determining whether a computational change has been made can be problematic with an updated version of the software, because vendors may not disclose this information.

2. The underlying method is unchanged and consistent with the information contained in the prior actuarial reports and prior year's Schedule B.

3. The modifications made to the software or the use of a different valuation system is designed to produce results that are no less accurate than the results produced before the change.

4. The net charge to the funding standard account for the current year, or for the prior year, determined using the new software does not differ from the net charge to the funding standard account determined using the old software (all other factors being held constant) by more than 2 percent.

    **Note.** This requires either that the old software used for the prior year's valuation be maintained or that the prior year's valuation be rerun on the new system for comparison purposes.

5. A change in valuation software requiring approval was not made for the prior year.

6. The automatic approval for takeover plans is not applicable to the change.

7. The effect of the change in method is treated in the same manner as an experience gain or loss, unless the actuarial assumptions are also changed, in which case the effect of the change in method is treated as part of the change in assumptions.

[Rev. Proc. 2000-40, 2000-42 I.R.B. 357, § 4.04]

### Q 18:81  Can a change in funding method be made when two defined benefit plans merge?

Yes. Approval has been granted on satisfaction of certain requirements depending on the type of merger. The following types of mergers have approved methods of changing the funding method:

1. *De minimis* mergers;
2. Mergers with the same plan year where the merger occurred on either the first or the last day of the plan year;
3. Mergers with a transition period of no more than 12 months; and
4. Mergers with a transition period of more than 12 months.

**Q 18:82  What is the approved method for changing a funding method in the event of a *de minimis* merger?**

A *de minimis merger* for this purpose is defined as provided under Treasury Regulations Section 1.414(1)-1(h), which involves the merger of a small plan with a much larger plan. If such a merger takes place, the actuary has automatic approval to allow for the merged plans to use the funding method of the larger plan. For the period before the date of the merger, the credits and charges to the funding standard account for the smaller plan are determined without regard to the merger. If the date of the merger is before the last day of a full 12-month plan year, there is a short plan year for the smaller plan up to the date of the merger. Many of the rules applicable to short plan years will apply, including determination of charges and credits for Section 412 and Section 404 purposes [see Rev. Rul. 79-237, 1979-2 C.B. 190; Rev. Proc. 87-27, 1987-1 C.B. 769] and computation of the period allowed for crediting contributions to the funding standard account (eight and one-half months after the date of merger). The Section 4971(b) excise tax will not apply, but the Section 4971(a) excise tax may apply.

For the larger plan, if the valuation date is before the date of merger, the Section 412 and Section 404 costs are determined without regard to the merger. If the valuation date is coincident with or follows the date of the merger, the funding method used is that of the larger plan and the smaller plan's method is disregarded. The change in assets and liabilities that occurs because of the merger is treated in the same manner as any other gain or loss experienced by the larger plan. All amortization bases, credit balances, and funding deficiencies with respect to the smaller plan cease to exist following the merger. [Rev. Proc. 2000-40, 2000-42 I.R.B. 357, § 4.05]

**Q 18:83  What is the approved method of changing the funding method with a merger of two plans that have the same plan year where the merger occurs on either the first or the last day of the plan year?**

For this approval to apply the funding method used for each plan must be one of those listed in Section 3 of Revenue Procedure 2000-40 [2000-42 I.R.B. 357], both plans must have the same plan year and valuation date (being either the first or last day of the plan year), the date of merger must be either the first or last day of the plan year, and neither plan can have a funding deficiency for the plan year just before the date of merger.

If the date of the merger is the first day of the plan year, the Section 412 and Section 404 costs are determined for the merged plans for the entire year. In determining these charges and credits, the asset valuation methods must either be the same for each of the two plans or be changed to one of the methods described in Section 3 of Revenue Procedure 2000-40. [2000-42 I.R.B. 357] The remaining components of the funding method to be used for the merged plan will be the same as those used by the ongoing plan. In addition, the amortization bases that were in existence for each plan before the merger will continue to be maintained (as long as the surviving funding method maintains bases) and any credit balances will be carried forward and combined. Any unfunded liability will be determined after any change in actuarial assumptions and methods, and for spread-gain methods, the unfunded liability will be redetermined in the same manner as it was originally computed for the ongoing plan.

If the date of the merger is the last day of the plan year, the Section 412 and Section 404 costs will be separately determined for each plan without regard to the merger. For the plan year following the merger, the Section 412 and Section 404 costs will be determined as if the merger occurred on the first day of such following plan year. [Rev. Proc. 2000-40, 2000-42 I.R.B. 357, § 4.06]

### Q 18:84    What is the approved method of changing the funding method if the plan has a *transition period* of no more than 12 months?

A *transition period* is the period from the first day of the plan year of the plan that is not the ongoing plan to the end of the plan year of the ongoing plan in which the merger takes place. For the approval discussed in this question to apply, the transition period as defined here cannot exceed 12 months.

In addition, the funding method used for each plan must be one of those listed in Section 3 of Revenue Procedure 2000-40 [2000-42 I.R.B. 357], both plans must not have the same plan year and valuation date (being either the first or last day of the plan year), or if they do, the date of merger must not be either the first or the last day of the plan year, and neither plan can have a funding deficiency for the plan year just before the date of merger.

The merger creates two valuation periods for the plan that is *not* the ongoing plan: the short plan year (which is the period from the beginning of the plan year to the date of the merger), and the interim period (which is the period from the date of the merger to the end of the plan year of the ongoing plan). The valuation for this plan during these periods is handled as follows:

*Short plan year.* The charges and credits to the funding standard account are determined without regard to the merger. The charges and credits to the funding standard account are ratably adjusted using the principles of Revenue Ruling 79-237 [1979-2 C.B. 190] in the same manner as if the date of the merger was the date of plan termination of that plan, and a Schedule B of Form 5500 is filed for the short plan year. Any contributions made for that plan after the date of the merger, but not later than eight months after the date of the merger, are credited to the funding standard account of that plan for the short plan year.

*Interim period.* Charges and credits are determined without regard to the merger. Accordingly, the charges and credits are determined based on the funding method, actuarial assumptions, and valuation results used for purposes of the short plan year, and are ratably adjusted to reflect the length of the interim period. Such charges and credits should include interest to reflect the period from the valuation date to the date of the merger, as well as interest for the interim period. The credit balance, if any, at the end of the short plan year is carried forward to the beginning of the interim period.

The funding standard account for the ongoing plan in the plan year in which the merger occurs is determined in three steps (unless the date of the merger is the first day of the plan year of the ongoing plan):

1. The funding standard account for the ongoing plan is determined without regard to the merger.

2. Charges and credits attributable to the plan that is not the ongoing plan are determined for the interim period as described above.

3. The charges and credits from the first two steps are combined in a manner similar to the treatment for separate plans under Code Section 413(c)(4)(A), except that the credit balance or funding deficiency for each plan at the end of the year are combined to determine an overall credit balance or funding deficiency. Schedule B of Form 5500 is filed for the ongoing plan for the plan year in which the merger occurred with the combined entries to the funding standard account as described above. The other entries on the Schedule B (e.g., lines dealing with accrued liability) should be those for the ongoing plan without regard to the merger.

For the plan year of the ongoing plan following the plan year in which the merger occurs, the funding method for the ongoing plan is determined in accordance with the following rules:

1. If the same asset valuation method (in all respects) is used for each of the two plans, it is continued as the asset valuation method of the merged plan. If the same asset valuation method (in all respects) is not used for each of the two plans (e.g., the smoothing period is three years for one of the plans and five years for the other plan), the asset valuation method used for the merged plan must be an asset valuation method described in Section 3 of Revenue Procedure 2000-40. [2000-42 I.R.B. 357]

2. If the funding method (without regard to the asset valuation method) used for each of the two plans is the same, that funding method is continued for the plan after the merger. If the funding method (without regard to the asset valuation method) used for each of the two plans is not the same, then the funding method used for the ongoing plan is continued after the merger. The funding method used for the plan that is not the ongoing plan is disregarded.

3. An experience gain or loss is determined separately for each of the two plans, for the period before the valuation date for the plan year following the plan year in which the merger occurred, without regard to the merger and any associated changes (i.e., changes in funding method, actuarial assumptions, or plan benefits). The preceding sentence applies only to the extent that an experience gain or loss would have been determined under the methods used for the plans before the merger.

4. All amortization bases that were maintained for the two plans continue to be maintained for the ongoing plan to the extent they would be maintained under the funding method used for the ongoing plan. If an unfunded liability is determined under the funding method used for the ongoing plan, it must be determined after any change in actuarial assumptions

and methods (including a change in asset valuation method as described above). In the case of a funding method that is a spread-gain method, the unfunded liability is redetermined in the same manner that the unfunded liability was originally determined for the ongoing plan. Therefore, the amortization base established pursuant to the rules of Section 5.01(2) of Revenue Procedure 2000-40 [2000-42 I.R.B. 357] will reflect any change of actuarial assumptions and methods.

The deductible limit under Code Section 404 for the plan that is not the ongoing plan for the short plan year is determined, without regard to the merger, by ratably reducing the otherwise deductible amount for a 12-month plan year in proportion to the number of months in the short plan year. [Rev. Proc. 87-27, 1987-1 C.B. 769] The deductible limit under Code Section 404 for the plan that is the ongoing plan is determined for the plan year in which the merger occurs as the sum of the limit determined for the plan without regard to the merger plus the limit determined with respect to the plan that is not the ongoing plan for the interim period (as described above).

If the date of the merger is the first day of the plan year of the ongoing plan, the minimum funding standard and the deductible limit under Code Section 404 are determined as follows:

1. The minimum funding standard and deductible limit under Code Section 404 are determined for the short plan year as described above (by ratably reducing the applicable amounts) as if the merger occurred on the last day of the preceding plan year of the ongoing plan.

2. As there is no interim period, the calculations applicable to the interim period as described above are not made. Instead, the minimum funding standard and deductible limit under Code Section 404 for the plan year of the merger will fully reflect the merger as described above.

[Rev. Proc. 2000-40, 2000-42 I.R.B. 357, § 4.07]

### Q 18:85   What is the approved method of changing the funding method if the plan has a *transition period* of more than 12 months?

The definition of *transition period* is the same as in Q 18:84. The restrictions for use of this approval are the same as those listed in Q 18:84, but the transition period is more than 12 months.

In this case, the merger creates four valuation periods for the plan that is *not* the ongoing plan: the short plan year (which is the period from the beginning of the plan year to the date of the merger); the interim period (which is the period from the date of the merger to the end of the plan year of the ongoing plan); the first partial period (which is the period from the date of the merger to the date that would have been the end of the plan year of the plan that is not the ongoing plan had there been no merger); and the second partial period (which is the period from the date that would have been the end of the plan year of the plan that is not the ongoing plan had there been no merger to the end of the plan year of the ongoing plan in which the merger occurs). The valuation for this plan during these periods is handled as follows:

*Short plan year.* The charges and credits to the funding standard account are determined without regard to the merger. The charges and credits to the funding standard account are ratably adjusted using the principles of Revenue Ruling 79-237 [1979-2 C.B. 190] in the same manner as if the date of the merger was the date of plan termination of that plan, and a Schedule B of Form 5500 is filed for the short plan year. Any contributions made for that plan after the date of the merger, but not later than eight months after the date of the merger, are credited to the funding standard account of that plan for the short plan year.

*Interim period.* Charges and credits are determined without regard to the merger. Accordingly, the charges and credits are determined based on the funding method, actuarial assumptions, and valuation results used for purposes of the short plan year.

*First partial period.* The charges and credits to the funding standard account are determined by ratably adjusting the charges and credits determined during the short plan year to reflect the length of the first partial period. Such charges and credits should include interest to reflect the period from the valuation date (of the plan that is not the ongoing plan) to the date of the merger, as well as interest for the interim period. The credit balance at the end of the short plan year is carried forward to the beginning of the first partial period.

*Second partial period.* The charges and credits to the funding standard account are determined based upon the expected normal cost amortization charge, and amortization credit from the valuation used for purposes of the short plan year, and are ratably adjusted to reflect the length of the second partial period. Such charges and credits should include interest for the second partial period. In addition, if the funding method used for the plan that is not the ongoing plan is a funding method that directly calculates an accrued liability within the meaning of Revenue Ruling 81-13 [1981-1 C.B. 229], an amortization base is developed to reflect the gain or loss with respect to assets for the short plan year by comparing the expected and actual value of the assets. For this purpose, the expected value of the assets is computed as the market value of the assets determined for purposes of the short plan year, plus contributions made for the short plan year, minus disbursements (i.e., benefit payments and expenses determined on either an actual or expected basis), with all items adjusted for expected interest at the valuation rate for the period to the date of the merger. The actual value of the assets is set to the market value of the assets of the plan that is not the ongoing plan (that become part of the assets of the ongoing plan) on the date of the merger. The amortization charge or credit (whichever is the case) is determined for such base and is ratably adjusted to reflect the length of the interim period.

The funding standard account for the ongoing plan for the plan year in which the merger occurs is determined in the following three steps:

1. The funding standard account for the ongoing plan is determined without regard to the merger.

2. The funding standard account for the plan that is not the ongoing plan is determined for the interim period by adding together the charges and credits for the first and second partial periods described above.

3. The charges and credits from the first two steps are combined in a manner similar to the treatment for separate plans under Code Section 413(c)(4)(A), except that the credit balance or funding deficiency for each plan at the end of the year are combined to determine an overall credit balance or funding deficiency. Schedule B of Form 5500 is filed for the ongoing plan for the plan year in which the merger occurred with the combined entries to the funding standard account as described above. The other entries on the Schedule B (e.g., lines dealing with accrued liability) should be those for the ongoing plan without regard to the merger.

For the plan year following the plan year in which the merger occurs, the funding method for the ongoing plan is determined in the same manner as for a merger with a transition period of no more than 12 months (see Q 18:84).

The deductible limit under Code Section 404 for the plan that is not the ongoing plan for the short plan year is determined, without regard to the merger, by ratably reducing the otherwise deductible amount for a 12-month plan year in proportion to the number of months in the short plan year. [Rev. Proc. 87-27, 1987-1 C.B. 769] The deductible limit under Code Section 404 for the plan that is the ongoing plan is determined for the plan year in which the merger occurs as the sum of the limit determined for the plan without regard to the merger plus the limit determined with respect to the plan that is not the ongoing plan for the interim period. [Rev. Proc. 2000-40, 2000-42 I.R.B. 357, § 4.07]

### Q 18:86  Can the funding method be changed if it does not satisfy the requirements for automatic approval?

Yes. Under Revenue Procedure 2000-41 [2000-42 I.R.B. 371], the plan administrator, plan sponsor, or authorized representative can apply for approval for any other change that does not meet the requirements for automatic approval. The request should normally be made before the last day of the plan year for which the change is to be effective, but requests made no later than two and one-half months after the close of the plan year will generally be considered. The request should disclose in detail the plan information and the effect the change will have on the plan. (See Exhibit 18-1 for suggested information to enclose with the submission.) There is a $2,800 filing fee required for such requests. [Rev. Proc. 2006-8, I.R.B. 2006-1]

The request should be mailed to:

Internal Revenue Service
Commissioner, TE/GE
Attention: T:EP:RA
P.O. Box 27063, McPherson Station
Washington, DC 20038

There are generally three elements to a funding method, the asset valuation method, the valuation date, and the cost method. A request to change a specific element of a funding method will usually not be considered if a recently approved change was made to that same element.

A class ruling can also be requested by an enrolled actuary on behalf of an insurance company, consulting firm, or software vendor. The change desired must be identical for more than 40 plans, and at least 30 of the plans covered by the ruling must adopt that change in funding method. The approval will generally be effective for no longer than 36 months.

**EXHIBIT 18-1**

**CHANGE IN FUNDING METHOD REQUEST CHECKLIST IS YOUR SUBMISSION COMPLETE?**

Instructions

The Service will be able to respond more quickly to your change in funding method request if it is carefully prepared and complete. To ensure your request is in order, use this checklist. Answer each question in the checklist by inserting Y for yes, N for no, or N/A for not applicable, as appropriate, in the blank next to the item. Sign and date the checklist (as taxpayer or authorized representative) and place it on top of your request.

You must submit a completed copy of this checklist with your request. If a completed checklist is not submitted with your request, substantive consideration of your submission will be deferred until a completed checklist is received. However, this checklist need not be submitted if the request involves a class ruling.

1. If you want to designate an authorized representative or a third party contact, have you included a properly executed Form 2848 (Power of Attorney and Declaration of Representative) or Third Party Contact Authorization Form?

2. Have you satisfied all the requirements of Rev. Proc. 2000-4 or its successors (especially concerning signatures and penalties of perjury statement)? (See sections 2.05 and 4.03.)

3. Have you included the user fee required under Revenue Procedure 2000-8 or its successors? (See section 2.06.)

4. Have you included the employer identification number, the plan name and number, and the name and address of the plan administrator or plan sponsor? (See section 4.04(1).)

5. Have you included a copy of the actuarial valuation report for the plan year preceding the year of change, and, if available, a draft of the actuarial valuation report for the year of change? (See section 4.04(2).)

6. Have you included a copy of the last Schedule B (Actuarial Information) of Form 5500, including attachments thereto (for requests involving mergers, a copy of the last Schedule B for each of the merging plans)? (See section 4.04(3).)

7. Have you included a statement of the plan year first affected by the proposed change? (See section 4.04(4).)

8. Have you included a complete description of the current and proposed funding methods, including asset valuation methods? (See section 4.04(5).)

9. Have you included a brief statement of the reason for the proposed change and a statement why automatic approval under Revenue Procedure 2000-40 cannot be used to make the change? (See section 4.04(6).)

10. Have you included a statement whether a change in funding method was previously requested? (See section 4.04(7).)

11. Have you included a statement of other changes being made for the year of change, such as a change in plan year or change in actuarial assumptions? (See section 4.04(8).)

12. Have you included a worksheet prepared by the enrolled actuary for the plan, showing a "before and after" list of the amortization bases, the unfunded liability of the plan, and the basic funding formula (or equation of balance) using the proposed method? Have you included the calculation of the full-funding limitation for the plan year before the plan year of change and for the plan year of change? (See section 4.04(9).)

13. Have you included a statement of whether a waiver of the minimum funding standard is currently in effect and whether a request for a waiver is currently pending or is expected to be submitted in the near future? (See section 4.04(10).)

               Signature                       Date

               Title or Authority

Typed or printed name of person signing checklist

## Consulting Issues

### Q 18:87   What considerations should be taken into account when selecting a funding method?

The main consideration is assuring that assets are sufficient to pay benefits as they come due. However, when multiple methods will satisfy this criterion, then other considerations will come into play including (1) plan design, (2) plan sponsor objectives, and (3) other administrative considerations.

The design of the plan benefits will often determine which funding method is the most appropriate for the plan. For example, if the benefit formula grants credit for past service, then a funding method that allows quicker funding of this credit may be appropriate. Other considerations to take into account when making a choice in funding methods include (1) determining when the principal participants will retire, (2) determining whether the formula is based on final average compensation or on a career average, (3) determining whether there is another plan that will cause the deduction limits under Code Section 404(a)(7) to be exceeded, and (4) finding out if the plan is top heavy.

The objectives of the plan sponsor could also be taken into consideration in determining an appropriate funding method. For example, if the sponsor knows that its income will be greater over the next couple of years than later on, then a funding method that generates the largest current contributions may be most appropriate. If the sponsor knows that its income is cyclical, then a funding method that allows some flexibility (ranges) in annual contributions may work better.

Finally, there are other administrative concerns that must be considered. For example, it may be desirable to limit the amount of PBGC variable-rate premiums to be paid. If the plan will be terminating in the next 5 to 10 years, then it will be necessary to assure that the plan will be adequately funded by that time.

### Q 18:88   Is there an appropriate funding method for cash balance plans?

Since a cash balance plan is just a defined benefit plan, any reasonable funding method may be used. However, if there is a change in funding method, the actuary does not have automatic approval to change to the unit credit funding method (see Q 18:65).

By using the unit credit funding method, the normal cost will equal the annual cash balance credits. However, the total annual contribution requirement may be different due to the amortization of gains or losses. In addition, the plan could easily hit the ERISA full-funding limit since it is based on the present value of the accrued benefit under this funding method.

Other methods may provide more flexibility in contributions than the unit credit funding method. If there is credit for past service, the entry age normal or FIL funding methods may provide the most flexibility in contributions due to the range of contributions between the Section 412 minimum and the Section 404 maximum. However, even if there is a range of contributions, it is advisable to set the recommended contribution at a level that keeps the plan fully funded even in the event of a termination.

Using the individual aggregate funding method may be advisable when the owners are closer to retirement age to assure that the plan is fully funded (preventing any unamortized balances from past-service liabilities or gains/losses). In addition, this method will, more likely, not be subject to full-funding limitations like the unit credit funding method.

# Chapter 19

# Minimum Funding Standards

The Employee Retirement Income Security Act of 1974 (ERISA) and the Internal Revenue Code (Code) require that a qualified defined benefit pension plan satisfy certain minimum funding standards. As part of the law, the funding standard account (FSA) was developed to determine the contribution required each year based on the results of the plan's funding method. With the passage of the Pension Protection Act of 2006 (PPA), there will be only one funding method used for determining the minimum required contribution. The PPA has completely changed the mode of how the funding is calculated for a defined benefit plan for plan years beginning after December 31, 2007. This chapter explains the various actuarial, technical, and accounting rules associated with the minimum funding standards, including updates for the new rules due to the PPA. The official record of a plan's compliance with the minimum funding standards is Internal Revenue Service (IRS) Form 5500, Schedule B, Actuarial Information, which is completed and certified by the plan's enrolled actuary each plan year. This chapter not only covers the minimum funding standards but also provides explanations and interpretations of the major items disclosed on Schedule B.

## Funding Standard Account Prior to PPA

### Q 19:1   What is the *funding standard account*?

The *funding standard account* (FSA) is the accounting tool used by an enrolled actuary to determine if a plan has satisfied its minimum funding obligation under Code Section 412. The FSA is charged with money owed by the sponsor to the plan and credited with money paid to the plan. If the charges are equal to the credits, the plan will have satisfied its funding obligation for the plan year. If the charges exceed the credits, an accumulated funding deficiency will exist as of the end of the plan year, and the plan will not have met its funding obligation. Conversely, if the credits exceed the charges, the plan will have a credit balance at the end of the year, and this amount can be used as a credit to the account for the next plan year to help reduce the plan's future funding obligation. The FSA also maintains the equation of balance (see Q 19:11).

All plans subject to Code Section 412 must establish and maintain a FSA. [I.R.C. § 412(b)(1)]

### Q 19:2   What are the *charges to the FSA*?

The *charges to the FSA* are the costs that are allocable to the plan's funding requirement for the plan year. Each charge represents a separate and distinct cost item. Depending on the funding method and the valuation date, the FSA may have only one charge or as many as six charges. The charges to the FSA are

1. The prior year's funding deficiency;
2. The normal cost;
3. Amortization charges (see Q 19:4);
4. Interest on items 1, 2, and 3 above;
5. Additional interest due to late quarterly contributions (see Qs 19:13–19:16); and
6. The additional funding charge (see Q 19:32).

The sum of these items represents the total charges for the plan year. The total charges less any credits in the FSA, before any contribution, represent the minimum contribution requirement for the plan year.

**Example.** The RM Company Pension Plan has been told by the plan's enrolled actuary that the total charges in the FSA are $100,000 as of the end of the plan year. Before any contributions, the plan has a credit balance of $10,000. The plan's funding interest rate is 7 percent. Therefore, the interest on the credit balance is $700, for a total credit of $10,700 ($10,000 + $700). The minimum required contribution is $100,000 less the credit balance with interest, or $89,300.

### Q 19:3   What are the *credits to the FSA*?

The *credits to the FSA* are payments made that are allocable to the plan's funding requirement for the plan year. Credits are either actual money or credits to the plan through contributions, offsets against current funding requirements, actuarial liabilities that decrease funding requirements, or interest on the credits. The credits to the FSA are

1. The prior year's credit balance;
2. Contributions;
3. Amortization credits (see Q 19:4);
4. Full-funding limitation credits (see Q 19:25);
5. Waived funding deficiencies; and
6. The amount resulting from a switch back from the alternative FSA to the regular FSA.

**Example.** The RM Company Pension Plan has been told by the plan's enrolled actuary that the total charges in the FSA are $100,000 as of the end of the plan year. Before any contributions, the plan has a credit balance of $10,000 and a full-funding limitation credit of $50,000. The plan's funding interest rate is 7 percent. Therefore, the interest on the credit balance is $700, for a total credit balance of $10,700 ($10,000 + $700). The minimum required contribution is $100,000 less the credit balance with interest less the full-funding limitation credit, or $39,300 ($100,000 − $10,700 − $50,000).

### Q 19:4   What are the *amortization charges and credits* in the FSA?

*Amortization charges and credits* are the principal and interest portion of a level payment against an amortization base set up by the plan actuary either as a result of the funding method being used or as a result of a deferred pension contribution. *Amortization bases* are deferred liabilities (i.e., a charge base) or deferred assets (i.e., a credit base). The amortization bases that would be created by the actuary based on the choice of a funding method are any of the following:

1. The unfunded accrued liability (unfunded past-service liability);
2. The increase or decrease in the unfunded accrued liability due to a plan amendment that increases or decreases benefits;
3. The increase or decrease in the unfunded accrued liability due to an actuarial gain or loss;
4. The increase or decrease in the unfunded accrued liability due to a change in actuarial assumptions;
5. The amount resulting from a changeover from the alternative FSA; or
6. The amount resulting from a change in funding method. [Rev. Proc. 2000-40, 2000-42 I.R.B. 357, § 5.01(2)]

Amortization bases are also created as a result of the plan's reaching the Omnibus Budget Reconciliation Act of 1987 (OBRA '87) fullfunding limitation or as a result of a funding waiver obtained by the employer in a preceding year. [I.R.C. § 412(b)(2), (3)]

**Example.** The RM Company Pension Plan is a newly established, defined benefit pension plan. RM Company has been told by its plan's enrolled actuary that the plan has an unfunded accrued liability of $1.5 million and a normal cost for the first plan year of $200,000. An amortization base for the unfunded accrued liability is created and amortized over 30 years. The plan's funding interest rate is 7 percent. The 30-year amortization factor is 13.278. Therefore, the amortization charge of principal and interest for the unfunded accrued liability is $112,969 ($1,500,000 ÷ 13.278). Seven percent interest on the amortization charge and the normal cost is $21,908 (7% × ($112,969 + $200,000)). That amount plus the normal cost and the amortization charge equals the plan's total charges in the FSA, $334,877 ($21,908 + $200,000 + $112,969).

### Q 19:5   Are all amortization bases amortized over the same period of time?

No. Each amortization base is amortized over a different period of time in equal installments of principal and interest. The length of time depends on the type of base, the type of employer sponsoring the plan, and the date the base was created. The following tables outline the amortization periods available:

**Single-Employer Plans**

| Base | Created Before 1989 | Created After 1988 |
|---|---|---|
| Unfunded past-service liability before January 1, 1974 | 40 | N/A |
| Unfunded past-service liability on or after January 1, 1974 | 30 | 30 |
| Plan amendment | 30 | 30 |
| Actuarial gain or loss | 15 | 5 |
| Change in actuarial assumptions | 30 | 10 |
| Waived funding deficiency | 15 | 5 |
| Switch back | 5 | 5 |
| Shortfall gain or loss | 15 | 15 |
| Due to OBRA '87 full-funding limit before 1999 | N/A | 10 |
| Due to OBRA '87 full-funding limit after 1998 | N/A | 20 |
| Change in funding method | N/A | 10 |

## Multiemployer Plans

| Base | In Effect Before 9/26/1980 | In Effect After 9/25/1980 |
|---|---|---|
| Unfunded past-service liability before January 1, 1974 | 40 | N/A |
| Unfunded past-service liability on or after January 1, 1974 | 40 | 30 |
| Plan amendment | 40 | 30 |
| Actuarial gain or loss | 20 | 15 |
| Change in actuarial assumptions | 30 | 30 |
| Waived funding deficiency | 15 | 15 |
| Switch back | 5 | 5 |
| Shortfall gain or loss | 20 | 20 |
| Due to OBRA '87 full-funding limit before 1999 | N/A | 10 |
| Due to OBRA '87 full-funding limit after 1998 | N/A | 20 |
| Change in funding method | N/A | 10 |

[I.R.C. § 412(b)(2), (3), (6); Rev. Proc. 2000-42, IRB 357; Ann. 96-25, 1996-17 I.R.B. 13]

### Q 19:6 Can the length of time for amortizing a charge or credit base be extended beyond the required time periods?

Yes, it can, provided the plan sponsor satisfies certain conditions and obtains approval from the IRS. The IRS may extend the period of time to amortize an unfunded past-service liability for a period of time not to exceed 10 years. The IRS in making the determination to extend an amortization period must consider whether the extension would carry out the purposes of ERISA and provide adequate protection for plan participants and their beneficiaries. The extension will be granted only if the IRS believes that failure to grant it would result in a substantial risk to the voluntary continuation of the plan, or a substantial curtailment of pension benefit levels or employee compensation, and be adverse to the interests of the plan participants in the aggregate. [I.R.C. § 412(e)]

### Q 19:7 Is the interest rate the same for all amortization bases?

In general, yes, the interest rate for all amortization bases is the plan's preretirement funding interest rate. [I.R.C. § 412(b)(5)(A)] A waived funding deficiency or a base that has had its amortization period extended is amortized at the greater of the plan's interest rate or 150 percent of the federal midterm rate (as in effect under Code Section 1274 for the first month of such plan year). If the plan is a multiemployer plan, the interest on a waived funding deficiency or extended amortization period is the rate under Code Section 6621(b). [I.R.C. § 412(d)(1)(A), (B), (E)]

**Q 19:8  How are the amortization bases accounted for?**

Three methods are available to account for the amortization bases:

1. Maintain each base separately and amortize the base with principal and interest over the required amortization period.
2. Combine all charge bases and all credit bases. This results in one charge base and one credit base for the plan.
3. Combine all charge bases and all credit bases and then offset both amortization bases into one base with its own amortization period.

Note, however, that bases established because of a waived funding deficiency must be maintained and accounted for separately and therefore cannot be combined or offset with other amortization bases.

**Example 1.** *Method 1—Maintain separate amortization bases.* The plan has the following bases as of the valuation date. These bases are being amortized separately, at an interest rate of 7 percent, over the required periods. Therefore, each has its own amortization base and amortization amount.

| Type of Amortization Base | Amortization Base | Amortization Payment | Years Remaining |
|---|---|---|---|
| *Credit Bases* | | | |
| Unfunded past-service liability | $469,560 | $ 37,657 | 25.00 |
| Amendment | $ 72,447 | $  5,649 | 27.00 |
| Actuarial loss | $ 24,783 | $  6,838 | 4.00 |
| *Charge Bases* | | | |
| Actuarial gain | ($   6,400) | ($   2,279) | 3.00 |
| Change in assumptions | ($ 68,014) | ($ 10,645) | 8.00 |

**Example 2.** *Method 2—Combine amortization bases.* The plan can combine the charge bases and the credit bases separately and amortize both the total charge base and the total credit base over the remaining years using the total base and total payment. In this example, the combined charge base of $566,790 is amortized over 19.88 years based on a combined payment of $50,144. Alternatively, the amortization payment can be recalculated by amortizing the charge base over the remaining years rounded down to the nearest integer, and the amortization payment for the credit base can be based on years rounded to the next highest integer. This alternative allows for amortization over full years and eliminates fractional periods.

| Type of Amortization Base | Amortization Base | Amortization Payment | Years Remaining |
|---|---|---|---|
| *Charge Bases* | | | |
| Unfunded past-service liability | $ 469,560 | $ 37,657 | 25.00 |
| Amendment | $ 72,447 | $ 5,649 | 27.00 |
| Actuarial loss | $ 24,783 | $ 6,838 | 4.00 |
| Combined base and payment | $ 566,790 | $ 50,144 | 19.88 |
| Alternative base and payment | $ 566,790 | $ 51,251 | 19.00 |
| *Credit Bases* | | | |
| Actuarial gain | ($ 6,400) | ($ 2,279) | 3.00 |
| Change in assumptions | ($ 68,014) | ($ 10,645) | 8.00 |
| Combined base and payment | ($ 74,414) | ($ 12,924) | 6.99 |
| Alternative base and payment | ($ 74,414) | ($ 12,905) | 7.00 |

**Example 3.** *Method 3—Combine and offset amortization bases.* To simplify the accounting of charge and credit bases even further, the plan can offset the charge and credit bases to arrive at one base for the plan. Offsetting is done after all bases have been combined as they are in Method 2. The greater of the absolute values of the two bases is subtracted from the lesser. The resulting amount is amortized over the remaining years for the larger of the two bases. Alternatively, the amortization payment can be recalculated by amortizing the offset base over the remaining years of the greater base, rounded down to the nearest integer if the greater base was a charge base or to the next highest integer if the greater base was a credit base.

| | Amortization Base | Amortization Payment | Years Remaining |
|---|---|---|---|
| Combined charge base and payment | $566,790 | $50,144 | 19.88 |
| Combined credit base and payment | ($ 74,414) | ($12,924) | 6.99 |
| Offset base and payment | $492,376 | $43,560 | 19.88 |
| Alternative offset base and payment | $492,376 | $44,522 | 19.00 |

[Prop. Treas. Reg. § 1.412(b)-1]

### Q 19:9   What happens to the existing amortization bases and their charges and credits if the preretirement interest rate assumption is changed?

If the plan's preretirement interest rate is changed, the charges and credits of all existing amortization bases are redetermined at the new interest rate. The new charges and credits are the amount necessary to amortize the outstanding balance of the amortization base over the remaining years needed to amortize the base in full before the change in the interest rate. See Q 19:10 for which plans must establish a new base when an actuarial assumption is changed.

> **Example.** The RM Company Pension Plan has two amortization bases, both of them charges. As of the 2001 valuation, the outstanding balance of the first base was $1,467,129, its amortization payment at 7 percent was $112,972, and there were 28 payments remaining. The second base was $200,000, its amortization payment was $26,613 at 7 percent interest, and there were 10 payments remaining. As of the 2002 valuation, the plan's enrolled actuary decreased the preretirement interest rate to 6 percent. The amortization bases as of 2001 are carried forward to the 2002 valuation date at the old interest rate of 7 percent. The outstanding balances are $1,448,948 ($1,467,129 − $112,972 + $94,791) and $185,524 ($200,000 − $26,613 + $12,137) with 27 and 9 payments remaining, respectively. For 2002, the outstanding balances of the amortization bases will be amortized in 27 and 9 years at 6 percent. The new charges are $103,473 and $25,732.

### Q 19:10   How does a change in actuarial assumptions affect the amortization bases?

Plans that use the unit credit, entry age normal, frozen initial liability (FIL), attained age normal (AAN), or individual level-premium funding method, must establish a new amortization base in any year the actuarial assumptions are changed. The new base is equal to the difference between the accrued liability under the new assumptions and the accrued liability under the old assumptions. The new base is amortized over a period of 10 years for single-employer plans.

> **Example.** The RM Company Pension Plan's funding method is unit credit with an accrued liability of $7,639,673 and assets of $6 million. Its unfunded accrued liability is therefore $1,639,673 ($7,639,673 − $6,000,000). The pre-retirement interest rate for funding purposes is 7 percent. The enrolled actuary changes the plan's postretirement mortality table, causing the accrued liability to decrease to $7,156,868. A new base is added to the unfunded accrued liability of $1,639,673 in an amount equal to $7,639,673 minus $7,156,868, or ($482,805). That amount amortized over 10 years at 7 percent is ($64,244) and is added to any existing amortization credits in the FSA. Because the change in the method resulted in a negative amortization

base, the base and the amortization payment are considered a credit base and an amortization credit in the FSA.

## Q 19:11   What is the *equation of balance*?

The *equation of balance* is a formula used to determine if the FSA is in actuarial balance. The equation of balance is important for a plan that uses a funding method that develops an unfunded accrued liability. Generally, the unfunded accrued liability is equal to the outstanding balance of all amortization bases. If, however, the plan has received contributions in amounts that have been more or less than required to maintain a zero credit balance in the FSA, and certain other charges have been added to the FSA, these two amounts will no longer be equal. Therefore, an adjustment for the credit balance and the reconciliation account is needed for the equation to balance. A mathematical expression for the equation of balance is as follows:

$$\text{unfunded above accured above liability} = \text{Outstanding balance of all amortization bases} - \text{Credit balance} - \text{Reconciliation account}$$

(See Q 19:12.)

> **Example.** The RM Company Pension Plan has two amortization bases whose sum total is $1,644,873. The plan's funding method is FIL with an accrued liability of $7,639,673 and assets of $6 million. The plan has a credit balance of $5,000 and a total reconciliation account of $200. Using the equation of balance proves that the plan is in balance: The unfunded accrued liability, $1,639,673 ($7,639,673 − $6,000,000) is equal to the outstanding balance of the amortization bases reduced by the credit balance and the reconciliation account ($1,644,873 − $5,000 − $200 = $1,639,673).

For plans that do not maintain an unfunded accrued liability, the equation of balance is not maintained; however, the credit balance and the reconciliation account are accumulated each year.

## Q 19:12   What are the components of the *reconciliation account*?

The *reconciliation account* is the accumulation of charges to the FSA due to the additional funding charge (see Q 19:32), interest on late quarterly contributions, and the difference between the unamortized balance of a waived funding deficiency at the mandated interest rate and the outstanding balance at the plan's preretirement interest rate.

> **Example.** The RM Company Pension Plan has the following in the reconciliation account from the 2001 plan year: $150,000 in additional funding charges and $2,500 of interest on late quarterly contributions. In that same year, the plan had a $175,000 additional funding charge, $3,000 of interest because of late quarterly contributions, and a $48,358 charge for a waived

funding deficiency of $200,000. For 2001 the preretirement interest rate was 7 percent and the waived funding deficiency was amortized at 10.5 percent over a period of five years. Based on this information, the 2001 reconciliation account would be calculated as follows:

| | |
|---|---|
| Additional funding charges | ($150,000 + $175,000) × 1.07 = $347,750 |
| Interest on late quarterly contributions | ($2,500 + $3,000) × 1.07 = $5,885 |
| Waived funding deficiency | ($200,000 – $48,358) × 1.105 – ($200,000 – $48,358) × 1.07 = $5,307 |

The total reconciliation account as of 2001 is therefore $358,942 ($347,750 + $5,885 + $5,307).

## Q 19:13    When is the employer required to make contributions to the plan?

To satisfy the FSA, the plan must not have an accumulated funding deficiency as of the last day of the plan year. [I.R.C. § 412(a)] Contributions for a plan year made by the employer during the period beginning on the day after the last day of such plan year and ending on the day which is eight and a half months after the close of the plan year are deemed to have been made on such last day. [I.R.C. § 412 (c)(10)] Due to the terrorist attack of September 11, 2001, the due date for contributions that would ordinarily have been made between this date and September 23, 2001, was extended for all employers to September 24, 2001. For those employers directly affected by the attacks, the due date for contributions that would ordinarily have been required between September 11, 2001, and February 11, 2002, was extended to February 12, 2002. [Notice 2002-7, 2002-6 I.R.B. 489]

Single-employer plans that are less than 100 percent funded on a Retirement Protection Act of 1994 (RPA '94) current-liability basis are required to make quarterly contributions to the plan by the 15th day after the end of each quarter of the plan year. The 100 percent funded percentage threshold is determined as of the prior valuation date by dividing the actuarial value of the plan's assets by the RPA '94 current liability. [I.R.C. § 412(m)(1)–(4)] Due to the changes made by the Pension Funding Equity Act of 2004 (PFEA), sponsors may (but are not required to) use the new permissible range (see Q 19:28) for determining whether they are required to make quarterly contributions for the 2004 plan year. However, the installment amount will still be based on what the required funding amount was for the prior year, using the "permissible range" as defined under the old law.

**Example.** The RM Company Pension Plan has a plan year that begins August 1 and ends July 31. As of the August 1, 2001, valuation date, the plan was 90 percent funded on the RPA '94 current-liability basis. The quarterly contributions for the RM Company Pension Plan must be made by November 15, 2001, February 15, 2002, May 15, 2002, and August 15, 2002, for the plan year that began August 1, 2001.

### Q 19:14   How much is the *required quarterly contribution*?

The *required quarterly contribution* is equal to 25 percent of the required annual payment. The *required annual payment* is equal to the lesser of 90 percent of the amount required to be contributed to the plan under Code Section 412 for the current plan year (adjusted to the beginning of the plan year) or 100 percent of the amount required to be contributed to the plan for the preceding plan year. The amount required to be contributed for a plan year is the amount required to avoid a funding deficiency as of the end of the plan year, without regard to any credit balance or funding waiver. (A funding deficiency, however, is included.) [Notice 89-52, 1989-1 C.B. 692, Q&As 4, 7, 8]

> **Example.** The RM Company Pension Plan's FSA would have had a funding deficiency of $65,000 in the preceding plan year without the credit balance, employer contributions, or waived funding deficiency. The funding requirement for the current plan year is $60,000 as of the end of the plan year. Interest to the FSA is credited at 7 percent; therefore, 90 percent of the current year's funding requirement as of the beginning of the year is $50,467 ((90% × $60,000) ÷ 1.07). The required annual payment is $12,617, which is 25 percent of the lesser of $50,467 and $65,000.

For plan years before 1989, the quarterly contribution requirement did not exist, and for plan years beginning in 1989, 1990, and 1991, 25 percent was replaced with 6.25 percent, 12.5 percent, and 18.75 percent, respectively. [I.R.C. § 412(m)(4)(C)]

### Q 19:15   Does the employer's failure to make a required quarterly contribution to the plan create a charge to the FSA?

Yes. If a quarterly contribution to the plan is not paid by the due date, the FSA is charged with interest at the greater of (1) 175 percent of the federal midterm rate under Code Section 1274 for the first month of such plan year, (2) the rate of interest used to determine the RPA '94 current liability, or (3) the valuation rate. [I.R.C. § 412(m)(1); Instructions to Schedule B (Form 5500), line 9e; Ann. 90-67, 1990-20 I.R.B. 19]

### Q 19:16   How is the interest charge to the FSA calculated when a required quarterly contribution is paid late?

When a plan subject to quarterly contributions is credited with contributions after the due date, contributions are credited against the past-due payments in the order of oldest first. [I.R.C. § 412(m)(1)(C)] Therefore, when calculating the interest charge on late quarterly contributions, it is helpful to track the unpaid balance of any required payment. The interest charge on a late payment runs from the due date of the payment to the date the payment is actually made. Payments made during the plan year are offset by interest that would have been credited to the FSA if the contribution had been made on the due date.

**Example.** The RM Company made the following contributions to its pension plan for the plan year that began January 1, 2000:

| Payment Date | Contribution |
|---|---|
| June 30, 2000 | $10,000 |
| Dec. 31, 2000 | $40,000 |
| May 15, 2001 | $20,000 |
| Sep. 15, 2001 | $30,000 |

The quarterly payments were to have been $25,000 due on April 15, 2001, July 15, 2001, October 15, 2001, and January 15, 2002. The actual payments were credited according to the following schedule and any balances remaining were recorded as shown. The interest owing to late quarterly payments for this plan is determined by tracking each payment, in the order received, against the required payments and calculating the number of days by which the payment is late. In the following payment schedule, as of June 30, 2001, $15,000 of the April 15, 2001, required payment was still outstanding and was not paid in full satisfaction until December 31, 2001. Similarly, on May 15, 2001, only $20,000 was deposited against the October 15, 2001, contribution. As a result, the unpaid balance of $5,000 was late until full payment was made on September 15, 2001.

| Due Date | Date Made | Balance Owed | Actual Payment | Balance Owed |
|---|---|---|---|---|
| Apr. 15, 2000 | June 30, 2000 | $25,000 | $10,000 | $15,000 |
| Apr. 15, 2000 | Dec. 31, 2000 | $15,000 | $15,000 | $    0 |
| July 15, 2000 | Dec. 31, 2000 | $25,000 | $25,000 | $    0 |
| Oct. 15, 2000 | May 15, 2000 | $25,000 | $20,000 | $ 5,000 |
| Oct. 15, 2000 | Sept. 15, 2001 | $ 5,000 | $ 5,000 | $    0 |
| Jan. 15, 2001 | Sept. 15, 2001 | $25,000 | $25,000 | $    0 |

The amount of interest charged to the FSA for late payment of required quarterly contributions will depend on the number of months by which the payment was late and how many months any payment would have been in the FSA until the date of deposit if it had been made on time. The following table details the number of months by which each payment was late. For any payment made before December 31, 2001, the table counts the number of months from the due date to the payment date, whereas for any payment after that date, it counts the number of months from the due date to the last day of the plan year.

| Due Date | Date Made | Actual Payment | Number of Months Late | Months of FSA Credit |
|---|---|---|---|---|
| Apr. 15, 2000 | June 30, 2000 | $ 10,000 | 2.50 | 2.50 |
| Apr. 15, 2000 | Dec. 31, 2000 | $ 15,000 | 8.50 | 8.50 |
| July 15, 2000 | Dec. 31, 2000 | $ 25,000 | 5.50 | 5.50 |
| Oct. 15, 2000 | May 15, 2001 | $ 20,000 | 7.00 | 2.50 |
| Oct. 15, 2000 | Sept. 15, 2001 | $  5,000 | 11.00 | 2.50 |
| Jan. 15, 2001 | Sept. 15, 2001 | $ 25,000 | 8.00 | 0.00 |
| Total | | $100,000 | | |

Interest is calculated on the dollar amount of the late payment at the greater of (1) the RPA '94 current-liability rate of interest, (2) 175 percent of the federal midterm rate, or (3) the valuation rate. The RPA '94 current-liability rate is 6 percent, the valuation rate is 7 percent, and the federal midterm rate is 12 percent; therefore, the late interest charge is calculated at the 12 percent rate. The plan rate of interest for FSA purposes is 7 percent. Interest is calculated by multiplying the late payment by the following expression:

$$((1 + \text{interest rate})^{(\text{months}/12)}) \div 1$$

In the following table each payment is multiplied by this expression, which is based on the number of months used for the interest calculation. For example, the late interest for the $10,000 payment is $239, determined as follows:

$$\$10,000 \times (1.12^{(2.5/12)} \div 1)$$

Because the $10,000 payment was made before the end of the plan year, interest for the FSA that would have been earned if the payment had been made on time, $142, is subtracted from $239 to arrive at a late charge of $97. The $142 is determined as follows:

$$\$10,000 \times (1.07^{(2.5/12)} \div 1)$$

| A | B | C | D | E | F |
|---|---|---|---|---|---|
| | 12.00% | 7.00% | (A × B) | (A × C) | (D − E) |
| Actual Payment | Late Interest | FSA Interest | Late Interest | FSA Interest | Late Charge |
| $10,000 | 2.39% | 1.42% | $ 239 | $142 | $ 97 |
| $15,000 | 8.36% | 4.91% | $1,254 | $737 | $ 517 |
| $25,000 | 5.33% | 3.15% | $1,333 | $788 | $ 545 |
| $20,000 | 6.83% | 1.42% | $1,367 | $284 | $1,083 |
| $ 5,000 | 10.95% | 1.42% | $ 547 | $ 71 | $ 476 |
| $25,000 | 7.85% | 0.00% | $1,962 | $ 0 | $1,962 |
| Total | | | $6,702 | $2,022 | $4,680 |

The late charges in column F are added to get the total late charge to the FSA, $4,680.

[Notice 89-52, 1989-1 C.B. 692]

### Q 19:17   Does a plan have any additional funding requirements if it has a liquidity shortfall?

Yes. Plans that are subject to quarterly contribution requirements and that have more than 100 participants on any day of the prior plan year are subject to the liquidity requirements of Code Section 412(m)(5). If the plan has a liquidity shortfall, it must increase the quarterly contribution to a level sufficient to meet the shortfall. If any contribution is insufficient to cover the shortfall, the plan is treated as failing to pay the full amount of any required installment (see Qs 19:55–19:71). [Rev. Rul. 95-31, Q&As 7-9, 1995-1 C.B. 76]

### Q 19:18   Does the FSA apply in the year of plan termination?

Yes; however, the charges and credits to the FSA are adjusted ratably to reflect the portion of the plan year from the first day of the plan year to the date of termination. [Prop. Treas. Reg. § 1.412(b)-4(b); Rev. Rul. 79-237, 1979-2 C. B. 190]

The date contributions are due for purposes of meeting the minimum FSA deadline does not change merely because the date of termination precedes the last day of the plan year. [Rev. Rul. 79-237, 1979-2 C.B. 190]

### Q 19:19   How is the FSA affected in the event of a short plan year?

A short plan year is treated similarly to a plan that has terminated (i.e., certain charges and credits are ratably adjusted to reflect the portion of the plan year before the change in plan year). However, the amount necessary to amortize a waived funding deficiency from a prior year, contributions to the trust, the amount of a waived funding deficiency for the current year, and the amount of any credit applicable to a switch back from the alternative minimum FSA are not adjusted. [Prop. Treas. Reg. § 1.412(b)-4(b)]

### Q 19:20   How is the FSA affected by plan amendments that occur after the valuation date?

A change in the benefit structure that becomes effective in a subsequent plan year cannot be considered in determining the charges or credits to the FSA for a previous plan year.

In the case of a change in the benefit structure that becomes effective as of a date during a plan year (but subsequent to the first day in such plan year), the charges and credits to the FSA shall be ratably adjusted to reflect the portion of the plan year for which the change is effective. [Rev. Rul. 77-2, 1977-1 C.B. 120] An exception to this rule is provided in Code Section 412(c)(8).

Code Section 412(c)(8) allows the plan administrator to elect to consider an amendment that is adopted after the close of a plan year, but within two and one-half months after the close of such plan year, as having been made as of the first day of such plan year. The amendment, however, cannot reduce the accrued benefit of any participant determined as of the beginning of the first plan year to which the amendment applies nor as of the time of adoption. This allows the amendment to be considered in determining the charges and credits to the FSA for that year to which it applies. [I.R.C. § 412(c)(8)] Pursuant to Revenue Ruling

79-235 [1979-2 C.B. 190] and Revenue Procedure 94-42 [1994-1 C.B. 717], Code Section 412(c)(8) also applies to plan amendments adopted during the plan year to which the amendment relates, not just to amendments adopted after the end of the plan year. This interpretation was confirmed by the IRS at the 2005 ASPPA Annual Conference in the IRS Q&A 25.

## Full-Funding Limitations Prior to PPA

### Q 19:21   What is the effect of a full-funding limitation?

The minimum funding requirement of a benefit plan is sometimes limited by certain funding restrictions. If a plan has a full-funding limitation in effect for a plan year, the contribution otherwise calculated by the enrolled actuary may be reduced or eliminated.

### Q 19:22   What is the *ERISA full-funding limitation*?

The *ERISA full-funding limitation* is the excess (if any) of the plan's accrued liability plus normal cost (or entry age normal accrued liability plus entry age normal cost if the plan's funding method does not directly calculate an accrued liability) [Rev. Rul. 81-13, 1981-1 C.B. 229] (see chapter 18) over the lesser of the fair market value of the plan's assets or the actuarial value of the plan's assets. The value of the assets is reduced by any credit balance existing on the first day of the plan year but is not adjusted for any funding deficiency that exists at the beginning of the plan year. The ERISA full-funding limitation is calculated as of the last day of the plan year, and therefore, if the valuation date is the first day of the plan year, the ERISA full-funding limitation must be carried forward to the end of the plan year with interest at the funding interest rate. [I.R.C. § 412(c)(7); Prop. Treas. Reg. § 1.412(c)(6)-1]

**Example.** The following is an example of the ERISA full-funding limitation calculation:

| | | |
|---|---|---|
| 1. | Accrued liability | $450,000 |
| 2. | Normal cost | $ 35,000 |
| 3. | Total | $485,000 |
| 4. | Credit balance | $   5,000 |
| 5. | Market value of assets | $435,000 |
| 6. | Actuarial value of assets | $440,000 |
| 7. | Lesser of line 5 or line 6, reduced by line 4 | $430,000 |
| 8. | ERISA full-funding limitation at beginning of year: line 3 – line 7 | $ 55,000 |
| 9. | Interest to end of year: line 8 × 0.07 | $   3,850 |
| 10. | ERISA full-funding limitation at end of year: line 8 + line 9 | $ 58,850 |

### Q 19:23   What is the *OBRA '87 full-funding limitation*?

This limitation is not applicable for plan years beginning in 2004 and thereafter. [I.R.C. § 412(c)(7)(A)(i)(I)]

The *OBRA '87 full-funding limitation* is the excess (if any) of the applicable percentage (see below) of the plan's OBRA '87 current liability (see Q 19:27) (including the expected increase in current liability due to benefits accruing during the plan year) over the lesser of the fair market value of the plan's assets or the actuarial value of the plan's assets. The value of the assets is reduced by any credit balance existing on the first day of the plan year but is not adjusted for any funding deficiency that exists at the beginning of the plan year. The OBRA '87 full-funding limitation is calculated as of the last day of the plan year. As a result, if the valuation date is the first day of the plan year, the OBRA '87 full-funding limitation must be carried forward to the end of the plan year with interest at the funding interest rate for the plan's assets and the current-liability rate for the OBRA '87 current liability. [I.R.C. § 412(c)(7); Prop. Treas. Reg. § 1.412(c)(6)-1] If the employer has elected to disregard certain service in determining the plan's RPA '94 current liability for other purposes [I.R.C. § 412(l)(7)(D)], such service must be part of the RPA '94 current liability for purposes of determining this limitation. [I.R.C. § 412(c)(7)(E)]

The applicable percentage for this purpose is as follows:

| In the Case of Any Plan Year Beginning in | The Applicable Percentage Is |
|:---:|:---:|
| 1999 or 2000 | 155 |
| 2001 | 160 |
| 2002 | 165 |
| 2003 | 170 |
| 2004 | N/A |

[I.R.C. § 412(c)(7)(A), (F)]

**Example.** The following is an example of the OBRA '87 full-funding limitation calculation for a 1999 plan year. The OBRA '87 current liability is valued at 7.5 percent; the interest rate for the plan's assets is 7 percent.

| | | |
|:---|:---|---:|
| 1. | OBRA '87 current liability | $300,000 |
| 2. | Expected increase in OBRA '87 current liability | $ 15,000 |
| 3. | Interest to end of year: (line 1 + line 2) × 0.075 | $ 23,625 |
| 4. | 155 percent of OBRA '87 current liability at end of year: (line 1 + line 2 + line 3) × 1.55 | $524,869 |
| 5. | Credit balance | $  5,000 |
| 6. | Market value of assets | $435,000 |
| 7. | Actuarial value of assets | $440,000 |
| 8. | Lesser of line 6 or line 7, reduced by line 5 | $430,000 |
| 9. | Interest to end of year: line 8 × 0.07 | $ 30,100 |
| 10. | OBRA '87 full-funding limitation at end of year: line 4 − line 8 − line 9, if any | $ 64,769 |

### Q 19:24   What is the *RPA '94 minimum full-funding limitation*?

The *RPA '94 minimum full-funding limitation* raises the full-funding limitation to a minimum level and overrides the ERISA and OBRA '87 full-funding limitations in the event they are less than the RPA '94 minimum full-funding limitation. The RPA '94 minimum full-funding limitation is the excess (if any) of 90 percent of the RPA '94 current liability (see Q 19:28) (including the expected increase in RPA '94 current liability due to benefits accruing during the plan year) over the actuarial value of the plan's assets. The value of the assets is not reduced by any credit balance existing on the first day of the plan year but is not adjusted for any funding deficiency that exists at the beginning of the plan year. If the employer has elected to disregard certain service in determining the plan's RPA '94 current liability for other purposes [I.R.C. § 412(l)(7)(D)], such service must be part of the RPA '94 current liability for purposes of determining this limitation. [I.R.C. § 412(c)(7)(E)]

> **Example.** The following is an example of the RPA '94 minimum full-funding limitation calculation. The OBRA '87 current liability is valued at 7.5 percent; the interest rate for the plan's assets is 7 percent.

| | | |
|---|---|---:|
| 1. | RPA '94 current liability | $375,000 |
| 2. | Expected increase in RPA '94 current liability | $ 18,750 |
| 3. | Interest to end of year: (line 1 + line 2) × 0.075 | $ 29,531 |
| 4. | 90 percent of RPA '94 current liability at end of year: (line 1 + line 2 + line 3) × 0.90 | $380,953 |
| 5. | Actuarial value of assets | $325,000 |
| 6. | Interest to end of year: line 5 × 0.07 | $ 22,750 |
| 7. | Actuarial value of assets at end of year: line 5 + line 6 | $347,750 |
| 8. | RPA '94 minimum full-funding limitation: line 4 – line 7, if any | $ 33,203 |

### Q 19:25   How is the full-funding credit determined?

If a plan is subject to the ERISA, OBRA '87, or RPA '94 full-funding limitation and as a result the contribution requirement to the plan is reduced, a credit must be entered into the FSA to offset any charges in excess of the full-funding limitation. The full-funding credit is the excess (if any) of the amount of funding deficiency that would exist in the FSA at the end of the plan year (including any funding deficiency that exists as of the beginning of the plan year) if no contributions were made to the plan and disregarding any credit balance over the lesser of the ERISA full-funding limitation or the OBRA '87 full-funding limitation. [I.R.C. § 412(c)(6)(A)] If the RPA '94 full-funding limitation is greater than both the ERISA and OBRA '87 full-funding limitations, the full-funding credit is calculated using the excess (if any) of the amount of funding deficiency that would exist in the FSA at the end of the plan year if no contributions were made to the plan and disregarding any credit balance over the RPA '94 full-funding limitation. [I.R.C. § 412(c)(7)(E)(i)]

The following examples illustrate the full-funding credit under different scenarios.

**Example 1.** *ERISA full-funding limitation.* The ERISA full-funding limitation is in effect. Therefore, the credit to the FSA is based on the excess of this limitation over the funding deficiency before the employer contributions and the FSA credit balance. As a result, the employer will satisfy the minimum funding requirement by contributing $50,000 to the plan.

| | | |
|---|---|---:|
| 1. | Funding deficiency before employer contributions and disregarding the credit balance | $130,000 |
| 2. | ERISA full-funding limitation | $ 50,000 |
| 3. | OBRA '87 full-funding limitation | $140,000 |
| 4. | RPA '94 minimum full-funding limitation | $     0 |
| 5. | Full-funding limitation in effect: lesser of line 2 or line 3 but no less than line 4 | $ 50,000 |
| 6. | Full-funding credit: line 1 – line 5 | $ 80,000 |

**Example 2.** *OBRA '87 full-funding limitation.* Sometimes the OBRA '87 full-funding limitation is substantially less than the ERISA full-funding limitation, and as a result, the employer's contribution requirement is cut back dramatically. In this example, the actuary has determined that this plan should have a $130,000 contribution; however, the OBRA '87 full-funding limitation reduces the requirement by $100,000. The credit does not eliminate the employer's obligation to contribute the $100,000. The contribution is simply deferred and must be amortized in equal installments of principal and interest over the next 20 years for FIL and immediate gain funding methods (10 years for plan years before 1999 [Rev. Rul. 2000-20, 2000-16 I.R.B. 880]). This situation generally occurs when the plan's accrued benefits are quite small in comparison to the projected benefits.

| | | |
|---|---|---:|
| 1. | Funding deficiency before employer contributions and disregarding the credit balance | $130,000 |
| 2. | ERISA full-funding limitation | $150,000 |
| 3. | OBRA '87 full-funding limitation | $ 30,000 |
| 4. | RPA '94 minimum full-funding limitation | $     0 |
| 5. | Full-funding limitation in effect: lesser of line 2 or line 3 but no less than line 4 | $ 30,000 |
| 6. | Full-funding credit: line 1 – line 5 | $100,000 |

**Example 3.** *RPA minimum full-funding limitation.* When the RPA '94 minimum full-funding limitation is greater than both the ERISA and OBRA '87 full-funding limitations, the full-funding credit is reduced and the employer will have to make a larger contribution to the plan. In this example the full-funding credit is $60,000 as opposed to $110,000 without regard to the RPA '94 minimum limit.

| | | |
|---|---|---|
| 1. | Funding deficiency before employer contributions and disregarding the credit balance | $130,000 |
| 2. | ERISA full-funding limitation | $ 20,000 |
| 3. | OBRA '87 full-funding limitation | $ 30,000 |
| 4. | RPA '94 minimum full-funding limitation | $ 70,000 |
| 5. | Full-funding limitation in effect: lesser of line 2 or line 3 but no less than line 4 | $ 70,000 |
| 6. | Full-funding credit: line 1 – line 5 | $ 60,000 |

**Example 4.** *ERISA and OBRA '87 full-funding limitations.* If both the ERISA and OBRA '87 full-funding limitations are less than the funding deficiency before employer contributions and the OBRA '87 limitation is less than the ERISA limitation, the plan develops two credits to the FSA. The first is based on the ERISA full-funding limitation; the second is no greater than the difference between the ERISA and OBRA '87 full-funding limitations.

| | | |
|---|---|---|
| 1. | Funding deficiency before employer contributions and disregarding the credit balance | $130,000 |
| 2. | ERISA full-funding limitation | $ 80,000 |
| 3. | OBRA '87 full-funding limitation | $ 70,000 |
| 4. | RPA '94 minimum full-funding limitation | $ 0 |
| 5. | Full-funding limitation in effect: lesser of line 2 or line 3 but no less than line 4 | $ 70,000 |
| 6. | Full-funding credit: line 1 – line 5 | $ 60,000 |
| 7. | First credit due to ERISA full-funding: line 6 – (line 2 – line 3) | $ 50,000 |
| 8. | Second credit due to OBRA '87 full-funding limitation: line 6 – line 7 | $ 10,000 |

## Q 19:26  What impact does a full-funding credit have on the plan's FSA?

A full-funding credit offsets the funding deficiency before employer contributions and reduces the plan's contribution requirement. If there is a credit balance in the FSA in a year the full-funding limit is equal to zero, the credit balance is preserved and carried forward to the end of the plan year with interest at the funding interest rate. Depending on the type and amount of full-funding credit, the FSA (including the credit balance) can be affected in other ways.

If the full-funding credit was a result of the ERISA full-funding limitation, amortization charges and credit bases due to past-service liabilities, plan amendments, actuarial gains or losses, and funding waivers are considered fully amortized. In addition, any balance in the accumulated reconciliation account is eliminated. If there was a credit balance in the FSA and the plan uses a funding method that recognizes actuarial gains and losses immediately, the credit balance is treated as an actuarial loss in the subsequent plan year and an amortization base is created equal to the credit balance at the end of the prior plan year. [I.R.C. § 412(c)(6); Rev. Rul. 81-213, 1981-2 C.B. 101]

Section 7.02 of Revenue Ruling 81-213 prohibits negative unfunded accrued liabilities for minimum funding purposes. In other words, if the assets ever exceed the accrued liability, then the unfunded accrued liability should be stated as $0. Therefore, if the plan has an ERISA full-funding credit in the prior year (causing the elimination of the amortization bases) and has a negative unfunded accrued liability (assets exceed liabilities) on the current valuation date, then the unfunded accrued liability will be stated as $0 and the plan will have no amortization bases.

If the full-funding credit was due solely to the OBRA '87 full-funding limitation, any amortization bases are not considered fully amortized. In the subsequent plan year, a charge base is created equal to the amount of the full-funding credit for spread gain funding methods that use an unfunded liability in determining the normal cost (generally, this will be the FIL funding methods and immediate gain funding methods). This base is amortized in equal installments of principal and interest over 20 years. Before 1999, any charge base created as a result of this credit was amortized over 10 years for all funding methods. If this charge base is in existence in 1999, spread gain funding methods that use an unfunded liability in determining the normal cost must amortize this base in equal annual installments over 20 years reduced by the number of years that have passed since the amortization base was established. [I.R.C. § 412(b)(2)(E); Rev. Rul. 2000-20, 2000-16 I.R.B. 880]

The IRS has provided that the 1999 plan year can be a transition year for spread gain funding methods that do not use an unfunded liability in determining the normal cost (such as aggregate and individual aggregate) which were previously amortizing this credit. For the 1999 plan year, instead of eliminating (or not establishing) the charge base, the plan's actuary may follow the same rules that apply for immediate gain funding methods. However, if this transition is used, the actuary must fully amortize this base in the 2000 plan year.

### Q 19:27    What is a plan's OBRA '87 current liability?

This limitation is not applicable for plan years beginning in 2004 and thereafter. [I.R.C. § 412(c)(7)(A)(i)(I)]

The *OBRA '87 current liability* is the sum total of all liabilities under a plan for all participants and their beneficiaries. The OBRA '87 current liability is valued as if the plan had terminated using the plan's funding assumptions; however, this liability must be valued using an interest rate within the permissible range as defined in Code Section 412(b)(5)(B). The *permissible range* is a rate of interest that is between 90 percent and 110 percent of the weighted average of the rates of interest on 30-year Treasury securities during the four-year period ending on the last day before the beginning of the plan year. If the plan's funding interest rate is not in the permissible range, the plan must use an interest rate within this range. The permissible interest rate range is published in IRS notices each month.

Before plan years beginning in 1995, the OBRA '87 current liability was the only current liability used to determine the plan's full-funding limitation under

Code Section 412(c)(7) and the additional funding charge under Code Section 412(l). Beginning with the 1995 plan year, the OBRA '87 current liability is calculated only for the purpose of determining the plan's OBRA '87 full-funding limitation under Code Section 412(c)(7)(A)(i). The RPA '94 current liability (see Q 19:28) is used to determine the minimum full-funding limitation under Code Section 412(c)(7)(E) and the additional funding charge (see Q 19:32) under Code Section 412(l).

### Q 19:28   What is a plan's *RPA '94 current liability*?

For plan years beginning in 1995, a plan must determine its *RPA '94 current liability*, which is the sum total of all liabilities under the plan for all participants and their beneficiaries. The RPA '94 current liability is valued as if the plan had terminated using interest and mortality assumptions prescribed by Code Section 412(l)(7)(C). The interest rate for the RPA '94 current liability must be within the permissible range as defined in Code Section 412(b)(5)(B). The *permissible range* is a rate of interest that is not more than 5 percent above, and not more than 10 percent below, the weighted average of the rates of interest on 30-year Treasury securities during the four-year period ending on the last day before the beginning of the plan year. The Job Creation and Worker Assistance Act of 2002 temporarily increased the upper end of the permissible range to 120 percent of the weighted average. This change is effective only for plan years beginning in 2002 and 2003. If the plan's funding interest rate is not in the permissible range, the plan must use an interest rate within this range. There is a phase-in of the 5 percent threshold above the 30-year Treasury rate. If the plan year begins in any of the following years, the 5 percent threshold is replaced with a phase-in percentage:

| Plan Years Beginning | Phase-in Percentage |
|---|---|
| 1995 | 9% |
| 1996 | 8% |
| 1997 | 7% |
| 1998 | 6% |
| 1999, 2000, 2001, 2006, and thereafter | 5% |
| 2002 and 2003 | 20% |

The PFEA changed the permissible range temporarily for the 2004 and 2005 plan years to 90 percent and 100 percent of the four-year weighted average composite corporate bond rate.

The mortality table used for purposes of calculating the RPA '94 current liability is prescribed by the Treasury Department and is subject to review every five years, starting in 2000, to determine if a change in the table is necessary to reflect the actual experience of pension plans and projected trends in such experience. The table in effect for 1995 through 1999 is the 1983 Group Annuity Mortality Table found in Revenue Ruling 95-28. [1995-1 C.B. 74] This mortality table continues to be in effect for this purpose for years since the year 2000.

Pursuant to proposed regulations, this table is scheduled to change effective for plan years beginning on or after January 1, 2007, to the RP-2000 Mortality Table, using Projection Scale AA. [Prop. Treas. Reg. § 1.412(l)(7)-1]

The mortality tables used for purposes of calculating the RPA '94 current liability for individuals who are entitled to benefits on account of disabililty are also prescribed by the Treasury Department. These tables can be found in Revenue Ruling 96-7. [1996-1 C.B. 59]

The permissible interest rate range is published in IRS notices each month.

### Q 19:29   Is there any requirement that certain actuarial assumptions be identical when calculating the RPA '94 current liability and the OBRA '87 current liability?

Yes, the interest rate must be identical, except when the employer elects to use the highest allowable interest rate for calculating the OBRA '87 current liability. In that case, the RPA '94 current-liability interest rate must be the highest allowable, and as a result, the interest rates will not be identical. All other assumptions, except the mortality tables required for RPA '94 current liability, must be identical and should reflect the same assumptions used for calculating costs for the FSA. If a plan uses a salary scale for determining plan costs, the salary scale should not be used in computing any current liability, with the exception of the increase in the current liability due to benefits accruing during the plan year. This amount can reflect one year's salary scale. [Rev. Rul. 96-21, 1996-1 C.B. 64; Notice 90-11, 1990-1 C.B. 319]

### Q 19:30   What is *preparticipation service*, and how is it disregarded in the current-liability calculations?

*Preparticipation service* is the years of service before an employee becomes a participant in the plan.

When calculating current liability for purposes of the additional funding charge under Code Section 412(l) (see Q 19:32), the plan sponsor can make a one-time election to exclude a percentage of the benefits accrued before the time the participant entered the plan. The percentage that can be excluded is based on the number of years the participant has participated in the plan, as follows:

| Years of Participation | Percentage Excluded |
|:---:|:---:|
| 1 | 80% |
| 2 | 60% |
| 3 | 40% |
| 4 | 20% |
| 5 or more | 0% |

For the plan sponsor to disregard preparticipation service, the participant at the time of becoming a participant must:

1.  Not have accrued any benefits under any other defined benefit plan (whether or not terminated) maintained by the employer or a member of the same controlled group of which the employer is a member;

2.  Not have participated in the plan before December 31, 1987; and

3.  Have years of service greater than the minimum years of service necessary for eligibility to participate in the plan.

[I.R.C. § 412(l)(7)(D)]

**Example.** Margot meets the criteria above and has three years of participation in the plan, and her accrued benefit is based on six years of service. The plan's benefit formula is 1 percent of average compensation per year of service. Her employer has elected to disregard preparticipation service for purposes of the current-liability calculations. Margot's monthly accrued benefit based on current average monthly compensation of $2,000 is $120 per month ($2,000 × 6 × 0.01). The benefit based on service before her participation in the plan is $60 per month ($2,000 × 3 × 0.01). The plan would exclude 40 percent of this benefit based on her years of participation, or $24 per month ($60 × 40%). The total benefit used for purposes of calculating the plan's current liability for Margot is $96 per month ($120 − $24).

It would be useful for a plan to calculate two current liabilities for any participant who is affected by this election. In the example above, the plan would apply the current-liability present value factor to the $120 benefit and the $24 benefit. This way the plan would have the total current liability, which is needed to calculate the full-funding limitations under Code Section 412(c)(7), and the amount of current liability that may be excluded from the total for purposes of calculating the additional funding charge under Code Section 412(l).

### Q 19:31   How is the *expected increase in the current liability* calculated?

The *expected increase in the current liability* is the actuarial present value of the amount of current liability that will result as additional benefits are earned over the plan year. This increase can take into account one year's salary scale.

## Additional Funding Charges Prior to PPA

### Q 19:32   What is the *additional funding charge*?

For plan years that begin after December 31, 1987, the *additional funding charge* is an amount added to the FSA equal to the excess, if any, of the deficit reduction contribution (DRC) (see Q 19:35) over the sum of various charges and credits in the FSA, plus the unpredictable contingent event amount, if any, for the plan year.

The additional funding charge cannot exceed the amount that, after taking into account the charges and credits in the FSA other than the additional funding charge, would increase the funded current-liability percentage to 100 percent. For purposes of determining the funded current-liability percentage, current liability includes the benefits expected to accrue during the current plan year. Furthermore, if the employer has more than 100 but fewer than 150 participants in the plan, the additional funding charge is reduced 2 percent for each participant less than 150. [I.R.C. § 412(l)(1)]

**Example.** The Jodi Company has 300 employees participating in its defined benefit pension plan. The plan's funded current-liability percentage for the plan year beginning in 2000 was 75 percent. The plan is required to calculate an additional funding charge in 2001. The DRC is calculated to be $500,000, which is then reduced by the normal cost and various amortization charges and credits. The plan has a normal cost and net charges and credits of $230,000 and no unpredictable contingent event amount. As a result, the plan is required to add $270,000 to the charges in the FSA for 2001. The following illustrates how each component of the FSA offsets the DRC:

| | | |
|---|---|---|
| 1. | Deficit reduction contribution | $500,000 |
| 2. | Normal cost | $150,000 |
| 3. | Amortization of past-service liability | $ 75,000 |
| 4. | Net amortization of actuarial losses | $ 20,000 |
| 5. | Net amortization of actuarial gains | ($ 15,000) |
| 6. | Net offset: the sum of lines 2 through 5 | $230,000 |
| 7. | Unpredictable contingent event amount | $    0 |
| 8. | Additional funding charge: line 1 − line 6 + line 7 | $270,000 |

### Q 19:33  What plans are subject to the additional funding charge?

Any plan (other than a multiemployer plan) that has more than 100 participants on any day of the preceding plan year and in the current year has a funded current-liability percentage of less than 90 percent is subject to the additional funding charge under Code Section 412(l). For a plan that has been spun off from another plan, the number of participants in the parent plan for the prior year is analyzed to determine whether there were more than 100 participants on any day of the preceding plan year. There is no adjustment made to this figure to account for the spinoff. [2001 Enrolled Actuaries Meeting Gray Book, Q&A 5] Even though a plan may be less than 90 percent funded in a preceding plan year, it may not be subject to the additional funding charge if the funded current-liability percentage was at least 90 percent in the second and third preceding plan years. The PFEA changed how the RPA '94 current liability is calculated for the 2004 and 2005 plan years, and also permits recalculation of prior year's funded current-liability percentages based on the new rules in determining whether the plan will be subject to the additional funding charge for 2004 or 2005.

For plan years beginning before January 1, 1995, a special rule treats the plan as having a funded current-liability percentage of at least 90 percent in that plan year if the plan met one of the following requirements:

1. The full-funding limitation was zero.
2. The plan was not subject to the additional funding requirement in the year or would not have been subject to the additional funding requirement if the current liability of the plan was calculated at the highest allowable interest rate and the assets were not adjusted for the credit balance.
3. The plan's additional funding requirement in that year did not exceed the lesser of 0.5 percent of current liability or $5 million.

For plan years beginning in 1995 and 1996, the plan can be treated as having a funded current-liability percentage of at least 90 percent in the second and third preceding years if the plan met any of the requirements in items #1 through #3 above in any of the two years beginning in 1992, 1993, or 1994 (whether or not consecutive). [I.R.C. § 412(l)(9)]

### Q 19:34    How was the calculation of the additional funding charge changed for plan years beginning after December 31, 1994?

The calculation of the additional funding charge was changed for plan years beginning in 1995 and later. There were changes in the calculation of the current liability, the determination of the DRC, the amortization of the charges and credits used to offset the contribution, the calculation of the unfunded new liability amount, and the unfunded old liability amount.

Options were made available to the plan to ease the transition to the new additional funding charge calculations.

### Q 19:35    What is the *deficit reduction contribution*?

For plan years beginning after December 31, 1994, the *deficit reduction contribution* is the sum of the unfunded old liability amount, the unfunded new liability amount, the expected increase in the RPA '94 current liability due to benefits accruing during the plan year, and the aggregate of the unfunded mortality increase amounts. [I.R.C. § 412(l)(2); Rev. Rul. 96-20, 1996-1 C.B. 62]

For plan years that began after December 31, 1987, and before January 1, 1995, the DRC was the unfunded new liability amount plus the unfunded old liability amount.

The PFEA allows certain employers to elect an "alternative DRC" for the 2004 and 2005 plan years.

### Q 19:36    What is the alternative DRC?

Code Section 412(l)(12) was added by the PFEA, providing for an alternative DRC. This section allows "applicable employers" to elect a reduced amount of additional required contribution under the DRC rules for certain plans and applicable plan years. An applicable plan year is one beginning after December 27, 2003, and before December 28, 2005. The election must be made by the end of the first quarter of the plan year for which the employer is making the election. However, if an employer makes an election on or before June 30, 2004, the election will be deemed timely for the plan year that begins before April 1, 2004. [Ann. 2004-51, 2004-23 I.R.B. 1041]

The amount of the alternative DRC for an applicable plan year is the greater of:

1. 20 percent of the amount of the additional contribution that would otherwise be required (the regular DRC), or

2. the additional contribution that would be required if the DRC for the plan year were determined as the expected increase in current liability due to benefits accruing during the plan year.

This election may only be made if the plan was not subject to the DRC rules for the plan year beginning in 2000.

An applicable employer that may qualify for this relief is one that is:

1. a commercial passenger airline, or

2. primarily engaged in the production or manufacture of a steel mill product, or the processing of iron ore pellets, or

3. an organization described in Code Section 501(c)(5) that established the plan for which an alternative DRC is elected on June 30, 1955.

During a plan year for which the employer is electing DRC relief amendments increasing liabilities or changing accruals or vesting may not be made unless:

1. an enrolled actuary certifies that the amendment provides for an increase in annual contributions that exceed the increase in annual charges to the FSA attributable to the amendment, or

2. the amendment is required by a collective bargaining agreement that is in effect on the date of enactment of PFEA.

If the employer elects an alternative DRC for any year, the employer must provide written notice of the election to participants, beneficiaries, and the Pension Benefit Guaranty Corporation (PBGC) within 30 days of filing the election.

The employer making the election must file the following election form with the IRS:

### ELECTION OF ALTERNATIVE DEFICIT REDUCTION CONTRIBUTION

**A.** As an officer of the employer maintaining the plan, I hereby elect an alternative deficit reduction contribution under Section 412(l)(12) of the Code and Section 302(d)(12) of ERISA and include the following information:

1. The employer is:

     a. a commercial passenger airline,

     b. primarily engaged in the production or manufacture of a steel mill product or the processing of iron ore pellets, or

    c. an organization described in Section 501(c)(5) of the Code and which established a plan on June 30, 1955, to which Section 412 now applies.

2. The name and EIN of the employer:

3. The name and plan number of the plan:

4. The plan year to which the election relates:

5. Specify the plan year beginning in 2000 for which the additional contributions under Section 412(l) did not apply:

6. If any of the information in items 2 or 3 is different from the name of the employer or the plan, etc., than in the plan year for which the election is being made, enter the plan name, plan number, and name and EIN of the employer for the 2000 plan year:

7. Signature of employer and Date

The election must be signed by an officer of the employer maintaining the plan. An authorized representative of the employer, plan administrator, or enrolled actuary may not sign this election on behalf of the employer.

**B.** This election must be filed at the following address:

Internal Revenue Service
Commissioner, Tax Exempt and Government Entities Division
Attention: SE:T:EP:RA:T
Alternative DRC Election
P.O. Box 27063
McPherson Station
Washington, DC 20224

[Notice 2004-59, 2004-36 I.R.B. 447; Ann. 2004-38, 2004-18 I.R.B. 878]


### Q 19:37 What must the notice to participants contain when electing the alternative DRC?

In order for an applicable employer to satisfy the requirements for electing the alternative DRC under Code Section 412(l)(12), the employer must provide plan participants and beneficiaries a written notice within 30 days of filing for the election. This notice must contain the following information:

- The amount of the required minimum contribution for the effected plan year, calculated after taking into account the alternative DRC election.
- The amount of the required minimum contribution for the plan year, calculated without taking into account the alternative DRC election.
- The due date of the required minimum contribution for the plan year.
- The aggregated amount of any required quarterly contributions for the plan year, calculated after taking into account the alternative DRC.
- A description of the benefits under the plan that are eligible for guarantee by the PBGC, including an explanation of the limitations on these guarantees. This requirement may be satisfied by including in the notice

the portion from the Model Participant Notice of Underfunded Plans that is found under the heading "PBGC Guarantees."

In addition, the employer may also include information regarding contributions made for the plan year prior to issuing the notice. The employer is permitted to estimate the amounts required to be included in the notice.

This notice is considered delivered if mailed to the last known address of the participant or beneficiary.

The employer may be liable for a penalty for failure to provide the required notice on a timely basis of up to $100 per day payable to the participant or beneficiary, or such other relief as the court deems proper. [Ann. 2004-43, 2004-21 I.R.B. 955]

### Q 19:38   What must the notice to the PBGC contain when electing the alternative DRC?

In order for an applicable employer to satisfy the requirements for electing the alternative DRC under Code Section 412(l)(12), the employer must provide the PBGC with a written notice within 30 days of filing for the election. However, if the employer issues a PBGC notice for a plan year on or before June 5, 2004, the PBGC will treat the notice as timely issued. This notice must contain the following information:

- The amount of the required minimum contribution for the effected plan year, calculated after taking into account the alternative DRC election.
- The amount of the required minimum contribution for the plan year, calculated without taking into account the alternative DRC election.
- The due date of the required minimum contribution for the plan year.
- The aggregated amount of any required quarterly contributions for the plan year, calculated after taking into account the alternative DRC.
- The number of years it will take to restore the plan to full funding if the employer only makes the required minimum contributions. A plan is fully funded for this purpose if it is subject to the full-funding limitation.
- The amount by which the plan is underfunded, including the plan's termination liability as of a date within the most recent plan year and the market value of plan assets as of that date.
- The capitalization of the employer.

In determining the number of years it will take the employer to restore the plan to full funding, the projection must be based on reasonable actuarial assumptions, must reflect the regular interest rate rules for plan years beginning after 2005, and include the required minimum contributions that form the basis of the projections for the current plan year and each of the subsequent four plan years.

In determining the capitalization of the employer, if the employer's stock is publicly traded, the capitalization is equal to the product of the number of outstanding shares of stock and the market price per share. Other information is applicable if the stock is not publicly traded.

The employer may be liable for a penalty for failure to provide the required notice on a timely basis of up to $100 per day payable to the PBGC, or such other relief as the court deems proper. [Ann. 2004-43, 2004-21 I.R.B. 955]

### Q 19:39   What is the *unfunded old liability amount?*

The *unfunded old liability amount* is the amount needed to amortize the unfunded current liability of a plan for the first plan year that began after December 31, 1987, using equal installments of principal and interest over 18 years. The unfunded current liability on that date is known as the *unfunded old liability*. The unfunded current liability on that date was the current liability using the provisions of the plan in effect on October 16, 1987, less the actuarial value of the plan's assets. The interest rate used to amortize the unfunded old liability is the interest rate used for determining the plan's current liability. If the current-liability interest rate is changed in any plan year, a new unfunded old liability amount is determined using the new interest rate.

> **Example 1.** D&R Inc. had an unfunded old liability valued at 8 percent as of January 1, 1988, in the amount of $1 million. Using an 8 percent amortization factor, the unfunded old liability amount was $98,798 ($1,000,000 ÷ 10.121638). For the plan year beginning January 1, 1989, the actuary changed the interest rate for determining the plan's current liability to 7.5 percent. The recalculated unfunded old liability amount is the unamortized unfunded old liability as of January 1, 1989, amortized over 17 years using a 7.5 percent amortization factor of 10.1415. The 1989 unfunded old liability is the 1988 unfunded old liability increased with interest at the 1988 interest rate (($1,000,000 − $98,798) × 1.08 = $973,298). Based on the unfunded old liability of $973,298, the unfunded old liability amount for 1989 will be $95,972 ($973,298 ÷ 10.1415).

If the plan is sponsored by an employer as a result of a collective-bargaining agreement and if amendments to the plan that increased benefits were ratified before October 29, 1987, the liability for such increase in benefits is amortized over 18 years beginning with the year in which such increase takes effect, or if the employer elects, the plan year beginning after December 31, 1988. Liabilities attributable to such amendments are known as *existing benefit increase liabilities* and are equal to the current liability attributable to such benefits reduced by the excess, if any, of the actuarial value of the plan's assets over the current liability determined without regard to the amendment.

> **Example 2.** D&R Inc. is a collectively bargained plan that ratified an increase in the plan's benefit formula of 10 percent starting with the first plan year that begins in 2002. The employer elected to defer the amortization of this liability until that date. For the plan year that began in 2002, the plan's actuarial value of its assets was $1.5 million. The current liability without regard to the amendment was $1.8 million. The existing benefit increase liability would be equal to $180,000, which was determined by increasing the current

liability by 10 percent, or $180,000, and subtracting the excess, if any, of $1.5 million over $1.8 million, or zero.

[I.R.C. § 412(l)(3)]

### Q 19:40 What adjustments are made to the unfunded old liability amount for plan years beginning after December 31, 1994?

For the first plan year that begins after December 31, 1994, the plan's current liability for purposes of determining the additional funding charge was required to be calculated using the RPA '94 current liability rather than the OBRA '87 current liability. If the RPA '94 current-liability assumptions were more conservative than the OBRA '87 current-liability assumptions, the plan's unfunded current liability would be greater than expected. To account for this, a plan was required to increase the unfunded old liability amount by the amount necessary to amortize, in equal installments of principal and interest, this additional unfunded old liability over a period of 12 years. [I.R.C. § 412(l)(3)(D)(i)]

The *additional unfunded old liability* was established for the first plan year that began after December 31, 1994, and is the excess, if any, of the RPA '94 current liability over the OBRA '87 current liability valued on that date; however, the OBRA '87 current liability must be valued using the same assumptions that were used with respect to the first plan year that began after December 31, 1992, with the exception that the interest rate must be the same percentage of the weighted average current-liability interest rate used for the first plan year that began after December 31, 1992. [I.R.C. § 412(l)(3)(D)(ii)]

> **Example 1.** As of January 1, 1995, D&R Inc. Pension Plan was required to determine the additional unfunded old liability. The 1993 OBRA '87 current-liability assumptions must be used to determine the 1995 OBRA '87 current liability for this calculation. The interest rate used in 1993, however, was 100 percent of the weighted average, or 7.5 percent. For the 1995 plan year, 100 percent of the weighted average was 7.25 percent. As a result, the OBRA '87 current liability is valued at 7.25 percent instead of 7.5 percent. All other 1993 OBRA '87 current-liability assumptions remain the same.

Under the optional rule, in lieu of calculating the additional unfunded old liability amount by amortizing the difference in the RPA '94 and OBRA '87 current liabilities as stated above, the plan sponsor could calculate the additional unfunded old liability as the difference between the unfunded RPA '94 current liability and the unamortized portion of the unfunded old liability under the plan as of the first day of the plan year beginning after December 31, 1994. This election, once made, was irrevocable. Furthermore, if the additional funding charge that resulted from making this election is less than the additional funding charge that would have resulted using the additional funding charge rules in effect for plan years that began before January 1, 1995, the plan's additional funding charge must be increased to the amount that would have resulted using those rules (see Q 19:34). This minimum additional funding charge must be calculated until the plan year that begins on or after January 1, 2002. [I.R.C. § 412(l)(3)(E)]

**Example 2.** For the January 1, 1995, plan year, the sponsor of the D&R Inc. Pension Plan is subject to an additional funding charge, and it has been determined that the plan could calculate its additional funding charge using an additional unfunded old liability of $1.05 million, under the optional rule, or $800,000. These amounts can be amortized at 7.5 percent interest over a 12-year period in the amounts of $126,271 and $96,207, respectively. The plan has been presented with the following options by the plan's actuary:

|  |  | Option 1 | Option 2 |
|---|---|---|---|
| 1. | Actuarial value of the plan's assets | $2,750,000 | $2,750,000 |
| 2. | RPA '94 current liability | $4,550,000 | $4,550,000 |
| 3. | OBRA '87 current liability | $3,500,000 | $3,500,000 |
| 4. | Unamortized unfunded old liability | $1,000,000 | $1,000,000 |
| 5. | Unfunded old liability amount | $ 120,259 | $ 120,259 |
| 6. | Additional unfunded old liability Option 1: line 2 − line 3 | $1,050,000 | — |
| 7. | Additional unfunded old liability Option 2: line 2 − line 1 − line 4 | — | $ 800,000 |
| 8. | Additional unfunded old liability amount | $ 126,271 | $ 96,207 |
| 9. | New unfunded old liability amount: line 5 + line 8 | $ 246,530 | $ 216,466 |

Option 1 funds the increase in the plan's current liability over the next 12 years and continues to amortize the unfunded liability that existed on January 1, 1989. Option 2 amortizes the plan's unfunded RPA '94 current liability on the date of election. Option 2 allows the plan sponsor to take into account the plan's assets; whereas Option 1 considers only the change in liability. Therefore, it may have been advantageous for an employer to make the Option 2 election if the plan's investment performance since 1989 has been well above expectations.

## Q 19:41   What is the *unfunded new liability amount?*

The increase or decrease in the unfunded current liability of the plan is known as the *new unfunded liability* and is equal to the unfunded current liability in excess of the sum of the unamortized portions of the old unfunded current liability, the additional unfunded old liability, each unfunded mortality increase, the existing benefit increase liability, and the liability for any unpredictable contingent event benefits. The *unfunded new liability amount* is a percentage of the unfunded new liability. The percentage used is based on a formula that takes into account the plan's funded status (i.e., assets divided by current liability). For a plan that is less than 60 percent funded, the unfunded new liability amount is 30 percent of the unfunded new liability. For plans with a funded ratio greater than 60 percent, 30 percent is decreased by the product of 0.40 and the amount by which the funded ratio exceeds 60 percent. For example, a plan with a funded ratio of 70 percent would multiply 26 percent (30% − (0.40 × (70% − 60%))) by the unfunded new liability to determine the unfunded new liability amount.

For plan years that began before December 31, 1994, the unfunded new liability was determined by subtracting the outstanding balance of the unfunded old liability and the liability attributable to any unpredictable contingent event benefit from the unfunded current liability. The percentage of the unfunded new liability used to determine the unfunded new liability amount was 30 percent for a plan with a funded current-liability percentage that was less that 35 percent. For plans with a funded ratio greater than 35 percent, 30 percent was decreased by the product of 0.25 and the amount by which the funded ratio exceeded 35 percent. For example, a plan with a funded ratio of 70 percent would multiply 21.25 percent $(30\% - (0.25 \times (70\% - 35\%)))$ by the unfunded new liability to determine the unfunded new liability amount. [I.R.C. § 412(l)(4)]

### Q 19:42   What is the *unfunded mortality increase amount?*

The *unfunded mortality increase amount* is the 10-year amortization in equal payments of principal and interest of the change in a plan's RPA '94 current liability due to a change in the prescribed mortality table. Starting with the first plan year beginning after December 31, 1999, the IRS will review the mortality table used for calculating the RPA '94 current liability. If a change takes place, the additional funding charge will add the 10-year amortization of the excess of the RPA '94 current liability using the new table over the RPA '94 current liability using the old table. [I.R.C. § 412(l)(10)]

### Q 19:43   What is the *unpredictable contingent event amount?*

A typical unpredictable event would be the layoff of several employees, who as a result of the layoff begin receiving retirement benefits. These benefits and resulting liabilities must be isolated to determine the *unpredictable contingent event amount*, which is the greatest of the following:

1. The contingent event benefits paid during the plan year (including a payment for the purchase of an annuity contract) multiplied by the product of (a) 100 percent reduced by the unfunded current-liability percentage, and (b) the applicable percentage from the chart below:

| For Plan Year Beginning | Applicable Percentage |
|:---:|:---:|
| 1989 | 5% |
| 1990 | 5% |
| 1991 | 10% |
| 1992 | 15% |
| 1993 | 20% |
| 1994 | 30% |
| 1995 | 40% |
| 1996 | 50% |
| 1997 | 60% |
| 1998 | 70% |
| 1999 | 80% |
| 2000 | 90% |
| 2001 and thereafter | 100% |

2. The seven-year amortization of the unpredictable contingent event liabilities; or

3. For plans with a funded ratio of less than 60 percent, 30 percent of the contingent event liabilities (for plans with a funded ratio greater than 60 percent, 30 percent is decreased by the product of 0.40 and the amount by which the funded ratio exceeds 60 percent).

[I.R.C. § 412(l)(5)]

**Example 1.** In 1997, the Wolf Pack Company paid $100,000 in unpredictable contingent event benefits. The liability for these benefits, valued at 7.5 percent, was $1.2 million. The plan was 65 percent funded on the valuation date, and the employer is subject to the additional funding charge. The unpredictable contingent event amount is the greatest of the following:

1. $100,000 \times 60\% \times (100\% - 65\%) = \$21,000$;

2. $1,200,000 amortized for 7 years at 7.5\% = \$210,754$; or

3. $1,200,000 \times (30\% - (0.40 \times (65\% - 60\%))) = \$336,000$.

Therefore, the unpredictable contingent event amount is $336,000.

**Example 2.** Instead of paying $100,000 in unpredictable contingent event benefits, the plan in Example 1 purchased an annuity contract for these benefits at a price of $1 million. As a result of the purchase, there is no unpredictable contingent event benefit liability for the plan. The unpredictable contingent event amount would then be 21 percent of $1 million, or $210,000, because items #2 and #3 in Example 1 would be eliminated as a result of the annuity purchase.

### Q 19:44   How is the current-liability funded percentage determined for purposes of the additional funding charge requirements?

The current-liability funded percentage is equal to the actuarial value of the plan's assets without reduction for the credit balance in the FSA, divided by the plan's RPA '94 current liability calculated at the highest allowable interest rate. Due to the Job Creation and Worker Assistance Act of 2002 the upper limit of the permissible range for determining the highest allowable interest rate for plan years beginning in 2002 and 2003 was increased to 120 percent. However, as a result of the PFEA, the upper limit was modified to be 100 percent of the four-year weighted average composite corporate bond rate. [I.R.C. § 412(l)(9)(C)]

### Q 19:45   What is the *transition rule election*, and how does it affect the additional funding charge?

A plan that was in effect before 1995 can use the transition rule in any year until 2001. The *transition rule election* allows the additional funding charge to equal an amount (the *target amount*) that will bring the plan's funded ratio to a target percentage based on the plan year in which the determination is made. In no event may the additional funding charge be less than it would be under the rules in effect before 1995 or greater than the amount under current law. Therefore, the transition rule election is helpful if it results in an amount less than required under current law and the plan sponsor wants to minimize the additional funding charge for a year.

The target amount is equal to the excess, if any, of the product of the *target percentage* and the *adjusted current liability* of the plan, over the *adjusted assets* of the plan.

*Target Percentage.* For a plan that was less than 75 percent funded for the first plan year that began after December 31, 1994, the funded current-liability percentage on that date becomes the plan's initial funded percentage. The target funded percentage is the sum of the initial funded percentage and an additional amount from the following table:

| Plan Year | Amount Added to Initial Funded Percentage |
|-----------|-------------------------------------------|
| 1995 | 3% |
| 1996 | 6% |
| 1997 | 9% |
| 1998 | 12% |
| 1999 | 15% |
| 2000 | 19% |
| 2001 | 24% |

For plans with an initial funded percentage of more than 75 percent, the target percentage is based on the following formula:

$$\text{Target percentage} = 2\% + \text{Prior year's additional percentage} + (10\% \times (85\% - (\text{Prior year's percentage} + \text{Initial funded percentage})))$$

**Note.** For plan years beginning in 2000, 2 percent is replaced with 3 percent, and for plan years beginning in 2001, 3 percent is replaced with 4 percent.

If a plan has an initial year funded percentage of less than 75 percent and adding the percentages in the table above produces a total greater than 75 percent, the plan should use the formula for calculating its target percentage and treat its initial year funded percentage as the sum of the initial year funded percentage plus the corresponding amount in the table above. [I.R.C. § 412(l) (11)(B); Rev. Rul. 96-21, Q&A 6, 1996-1 C.B. 64]

*Adjusted Current Liability.* The *adjusted current liability* is equal to the excess of (1) the RPA '94 current liability of the plan for the plan year, including the expected increase in current liability due to benefits accruing during the plan year, over (2) the expected release from current liability on account of disbursements (including single-sum distributions) from the plan expected to be paid after the valuation date but before the end of the plan year. The components of this calculation are determined as of the valuation date, and each is appropriately adjusted with interest to the end of the plan year using the RPA '94 current-liability interest rate. [Rev. Rul. 96-21, Q&A 7, 1996-1 CB 64]

*Adjusted Assets.* The *adjusted assets* are equal to the actuarial value of assets for the plan year adjusted by (1) subtracting any credit balance (or adding any debit balance) in the plan's FSA as of the end of the prior plan year, adjusted with interest to the valuation date at the valuation interest rate, (2) subtracting the disbursements from the plan (including single-sum distributions) expected to be paid after the valuation date but before the end of the plan year, (3) adding the charges to the FSA for the plan year (other than the additional funding charge under Code Section 412(l)), and (4) subtracting the credits to the FSA for the plan year (other than credits for contributions and waived funding deficiencies). The actuarial value of assets and the adjustments described above are determined as of the valuation date, and each is appropriately adjusted with interest to the end of the plan year at the valuation interest rate. The result of this calculation may be a negative number, which would increase the *target amount.* [Rev. Rul. 96-21, Q&A 8, 1996-1 C.B. 64]

**Example.** The employer of the Jimmy's defined benefit plan elects the transition rule for the 2000 plan year. The plan year is the calendar year, and the valuation date is January 1, 2000. The valuation interest rate is 8 percent, and the interest rate used to determine the RPA '94 current liability is 6 percent.

The valuation results are as follows:

| | |
|---|---:|
| Initial funded current-liability percentage | 54% |
| RPA '94 current liability | $1,000,000 |
| Expected increase in current liability due to benefits accruing during the plan year | $ 70,000 |
| Actuarial value of assets | $ 720,000 |
| Prior year credit balance | $ 20,000 |
| Expected disbursements (expected to be paid on December 31, 2000) | $ 50,000 |
| Expected release from current liability as a result of expected disbursements (valued as of January 1, 2000) | $ 40,000 |
| Charges (other than the additional funding charge), including interest to December 31, 2000 | $ 100,000 |
| Credits, including interest to December 31, 2000 | $ 75,000 |

Because the initial funded current-liability percentage was less than 75 percent, the *target percentage* for the plan is the plan's *initial funded current-liability percentage* plus the applicable number of percentage points under Code Section 412(l)(11)(B). Thus, the *target percentage* is 73 percent (54 percent + 19 percent, the applicable number of percentage points under Code Section 412(l)(11)(B)(i)).

The *adjusted current liability* of the plan is equal to the excess of $1,070,000 (the sum of $1,000,000 + $70,000) over $40,000, each adjusted with interest to the end of the plan year at the RPA '94 current-liability interest rate. The

$1,070,000 is adjusted with a full year's interest ($1,070,000 × 1.06, or $1,134,200) and the $40,000 is adjusted with a full year's interest at the same rate ($40,000 × 1.06, or $42,400). The resulting *adjusted current liability* is $1,091,800 ($1,134,200 − $42,400).

The *adjusted assets* of the plan are equal to $720,000 minus $20,000, minus $50,000, plus $100,000, minus $75,000, each adjusted with interest from the appropriate date to the end of the plan year at the valuation interest rate. The $720,000 and $20,000 as adjusted with a full year's interest at the valuation interest rate equals $756,000 ($720,000 − $20,000 × 1.08). The $50,000 receives no interest adjustment, as benefit payments are expected to be paid at the end of the year. The charges and credits already are calculated with interest to the end of the year. The resulting *adjusted assets* equal $731,000 ($756,000 − $50,000 + $100,000 − $75,000).

Therefore, the *target amount* is equal to the excess of the product of 73 percent (the *target percentage*) and $1,091,800 (the *adjusted current liability*), over $731,000 (the *adjusted assets*), or $66,014 ((0.73 × $1,091,800) − $731,000).

## Funding Deficiencies Prior to PPA

### Q 19:46  When does an *accumulated funding deficiency* occur?

An *accumulated funding deficiency* occurs when for any plan year the total charges to the FSA for all plan years exceed the total credits calculated for such years. If the alternative minimum FSA (see Q 19:47) is utilized and the deficiency is less than that as calculated under the FSA, the accumulated funding deficiency is the excess of the total charges to the alternative minimum FSA for all plan years over the total credits to such account for such years. [I.R.C. § 412(a)] This is determined as of the end of the plan year ending with or within the employer's taxable year. [I.R.C. § 4971(a)]

### Q 19:47  What is the *alternative minimum FSA*?

The *alternative minimum FSA* is an optional way of calculating the minimum contribution required to avoid an accumulated funding deficiency for any plan year. This can only be utilized by plans that use the entry age normal funding method.

Plans that use the entry age normal funding method (see chapter 16), can reduce the contribution required to avoid an accumulated FSA deficiency by adding the following amounts to determine charges. The alternative minimum FSA is charged with the sum of

1. The lesser of the normal cost determined under the unit credit or entry age normal funding method;
2. The excess of the present value of the accrued benefits (PVAB) under the plan over the fair market value of the assets (FMVA); and

3. The excess, if any, of credits to the alternative minimum FSA for all prior plan years over charges to such account for all such years.

The only credits to this account are contributions made by the employer for the plan year. [I.R.C. § 412(g)]

Assets are not adjusted for any credit balance or deficiency, and the plan cannot apply any credit balance to the alternative minimum FSA deficiency.

The alternative minimum FSA (and items therein) shall be charged and credited with interest from the valuation date to the end of the plan year. [I.R.C. § 412(g)(3)]

**Example.** The Red Rock Defined Benefit Plan uses the entry age normal funding method. It elects to determine charges and credits using the alternative minimum FSA for 1998. The valuation interest rate is 7 percent, the unit credit funding method would generate a normal cost of $60,000, and the excess of the PVAB over the market value of assets (MVA) is $20,000: all as of January 1, 1998. Regular charges are as follows:

| | |
|---|---|
| Normal cost | $ 70,000 |
| Amortization of past-service liability | $ 20,000 |
| Amortization of experience loss | $ 10,000 |
| Total | $100,000 |

Charges under the alternative minimum FSA are as follows:

| | |
|---|---|
| Normal cost | $60,000 (lesser of $70,000 or $60,000) |
| PVAB – MVA | $20,000 |
| Total | $80,000 |

Therefore, the minimum required contribution for 1998 to avoid an accumulated FSA deficiency is $80,000 plus interest to the end of the plan year, or $85,600 ($80,000 × 1.07).

## Q 19:48   Can a plan switch back to the regular FSA?

Yes. Although the alternative minimum FSA is used to determine the amount required to avoid an accumulated funding deficiency for a particular funding method, the plan continues to maintain the regular FSA. In the year following usage of the alternative minimum FSA, the regular FSA is credited with the excess of the regular FSA charges over the alternative minimum FSA charges for the prior year and charged with a five-year amortization of such credit.

**Example.** The Red Rock Defined Benefit Plan had total charges under the regular FSA for 1998 of $107,000, and charges under the alternative minimum FSA of $85,600. In 1999, the regular FSA is credited with $21,400 ($107,000 – $85,600) and charged with a five-year amortization of the $21,400 computed at the valuation interest rate, which is $4,878.

### Q 19:49　Are there any penalties if a plan has an accumulated FSA deficiency?

Yes. Under Code Section 4971(a), there is a 10 percent excise tax (5 percent for a multiemployer plan) on the amount of the accumulated funding deficiency under the plan.

### Q 19:50　Can additional penalties be imposed if the deficiency is not corrected?

Yes. If the deficiency is not corrected before either a notice of deficiency is mailed by the Secretary of Labor or the date on which the 10 percent excise tax is imposed by the IRS, the IRS has the authority to impose a tax equal to 100 percent of the accumulated funding deficiency.

### Q 19:51　What is the statute of limitations period if the excise taxes for an accumulated funding deficiency are not paid?

If the Form 5330 is filed disclosing the accumulated funding deficiency, but the tax is not paid with the form, the statute of limitations for collecting the tax expires three years after the filing of the form. If the Form 5330 is filed for other reasons and the funding deficiency is not disclosed, then the statute of limitations on assessment of the excise tax is six years. If the Form 5330 is not filed for a year in which an accumulated funding deficiency occurs, then the tax may be assessed at any time after the date prescribed for filing the return. The filing of the Form 5500 does not start the running of the statute of limitations in the event of an accumulated funding deficiency. [Rev. Rul. 2003-88, 2003-32 I.R.B. 292]

### Q 19:52　Does the 10 percent excise tax continue to apply in plan years after a plan is terminated?

No. According to Revenue Ruling 79-237 [1979-2 C.B. 190], the penalty applicable to funding deficiencies does not continue to apply after the plan year of termination because, for funding purposes, there is no new plan year after the plan year of termination. It should be noted, however, that a termination does not relieve the employer of the obligation to fund the accumulated funding deficiency as of the end of the plan year in which the plan is terminated. If this deficiency is not reduced to zero, the 100 percent penalty tax imposed by Code Section 4971(b) will apply.

If the plan is not terminated timely (thus voiding the prior termination date), the 10 percent excise tax would continue to apply. [Rev. Rul. 89-87, 1989-2 C.B. 81]

### Q 19:53　Are there any conditions under which the 100 percent excise tax may be waived?

Yes. The employer can request a waiver of the additional 100 percent excise tax if it can show that the tax would be a substantial business hardship and would be adverse to the interests of plan participants. [Rev. Proc. 81-44, 1981-2 C.B. 618]

In addition, the IRS has provided an automatic waiver for plans with termination dates after December 31, 1999, if the following conditions are satisfied:

1. The plan is subject to ERISA Title IV and is terminated in a standard termination under ERISA Section 4041.

2. Plan participants are not entitled to any portion of residual assets remaining after all liabilities of the plan to participants and their beneficiaries have been satisfied.

3. Excise taxes that have been or could be imposed under Code Section 4971 (a) have been paid for all taxable years, including the taxable year related to the year of plan termination.

4. All applicable forms in the IRS Form 5500 series, including Schedules B, Actuarial Information, have been filed for the plan for all plan years, including the year of plan termination.

[Rev. Proc. 2000-17, 2000-11 I.R.B. 1]


## Shortfall Funding Method Prior to PPA

### Q 19:54   What is the *shortfall funding method*?

The *shortfall funding method* is a funding method that adapts a plan's underlying funding method solely for purposes of determining charges under Code Section 412. A plan can use the shortfall funding method only if it is a collectively bargained plan described in Code Section 413(a) and contributions to the plan are made at a rate specified under the terms of a legally binding agreement applicable to the plan.

### Q 19:55   How are charges to the FSA computed using the shortfall funding method?

Charges using the shortfall funding method are computed on the basis of an estimated number of units of service or production (for which a certain amount per unit is to be charged). The *estimated unit charge* is equal to the total charges under the plan's underlying funding method for the year divided by the estimated units of service or production. The *net shortfall charge* is then computed as the product of the estimated unit charge and the actual units for the year.

**Example.** The Red Rock Defined Benefit Plan uses the entry age normal funding method. For 1999, total charges to the FSA under this method are $100,000. Estimated hours for the year are 200,000. Actual hours are 180,000. The estimated unit charge is $0.50 ($100,000 ÷ 200,000). The actual charge to the FSA for the year is $90,000 ($0.50 × 180,000).

### Q 19:56   Are there any other charges or credits under the shortfall funding method?

Yes. The difference between the net amount charged under this method and the net amount that otherwise would have been charged under Code Section 412 for the same period is a shortfall gain or loss and is to be amortized over certain subsequent plan years.

The other items that may be credited, if applicable, are a waived funding deficiency and the alternative minimum funding standard credit adjustment.

### Q 19:57   How are shortfall gains or losses amortized?

Shortfall gains or losses are amortized over 15 years (20 years for a multiemployer plan). The amortization of this gain or loss begins in the earlier of the fifth year following the plan year in which the shortfall gain or loss arose, or the first plan year beginning after the latest scheduled expiration date of a collectively bargained agreement in effect with respect to the plan during the plan year in which the shortfall gain or loss arose. If a collective-bargaining agreement is expiring on the last day of a plan year in which the gain or loss arose, the contract is deemed to be renewed on that last day for the same period of years as the contract that succeeds the expiring contract.

The amortization of a shortfall gain or loss must end in the 15th plan year (20th for a multiemployer plan) following the plan year in which the shortfall gain or loss arose.

**Example.** The Red Rock Union Defined Benefit Plan has a shortfall loss for the plan year ending December 31, 1997, equal to $40,000. The collective-bargaining agreement then in effect expires December 31, 1999. Beginning in the 2000 plan year, this loss is amortized over 13 years and has been increased with interest for the two intervening years at the valuation rate of 7 percent. The amortization payment as of January 1, 2000, is $5,121.

## Liquidity Requirement Prior to PPA

### Q 19:58   What plans are subject to the liquidity requirement of Code Section 412(m)(5)?

Defined benefit plans that are subject to the quarterly contribution requirement for a plan year and that have more than 100 participants on any day of the preceding plan year are subject to the liquidity requirement of Code Section 412 (m)(5). Thus, multiemployer plans, plans with funded current-liability percentages of 100 percent or more for the preceding plan year, and plans that on every day of the preceding plan year had 100 or fewer participants (considering all defined benefit plans of the employer, including controlled groups) are not subject to the liquidity requirement. [Rev. Rul. 95-31, Q&A 7, 1995-1 C.B. 76]

### Q 19:59   What steps must be taken to satisfy the liquidity requirement?

For plans subject to the liquidity requirement, the amount of the liquidity shortfall must be determined as of the end of each quarter for which there is a required quarterly installment. If a plan has a liquidity shortfall equal to zero, the liquidity requirement is satisfied. If a plan has a liquidity shortfall greater than zero, the employer must make a contribution to the plan in the form of liquid assets equal to no less than the amount of the liquidity shortfall. In addition, this contribution must be made to the plan on or before the due date of the required quarterly installment. [Rev. Rul. 95-31, Q&A 8, 1995-1 C.B. 76]

### Q 19:60   What are some of the consequences if an employer fails to satisfy the liquidity requirement?

If the employer fails to satisfy the liquidity requirement, the employer is treated as failing to make a required installment under Code Section 412(m) and ERISA Section 302(e). Thus, there is an additional interest charge to the FSA under Code Section 412(m)(1), and the employer is treated as failing to make a required installment for purposes of Code Section 412(n)(1)(A). In addition, a 10 percent excise tax under Code Section 4971(f) is applicable, and fiduciaries are prohibited from making certain payments from the plan under ERISA Section 206(e). [Rev. Rul. 95-31, Q&A 9, 1995-1 C.B. 76]

### Q 19:61   How is the *liquidity shortfall* determined for a quarter?

The *liquidity shortfall* for a quarter is the amount equal to the excess (if any) of (1) the *base amount* with respect to such quarter, over (2) the value of the plan's *liquid assets* with respect to such quarter. However, the liquidity shortfall for a quarter is limited to the amount that, when added to prior installments for the plan year, is necessary to increase the funded current-liability percentage for the current plan year (taking into account the expected increase in current liability due to benefits accruing during the plan year) to 100 percent. [Rev. Rul. 95-31, Q&A 10, 1995-1 C.B. 76]

### Q 19:62   How is the *base amount* determined with respect to any quarter?

The *base amount* with respect to any quarter is the amount equal to three times the sum of the *adjusted disbursements* from the plan for the 12 months ending on the last day of that quarter. Adjusted disbursements are all disbursements from the trust, including benefit distributions under the plan (whether paid in the form of annuities, single-sum distributions, or other forms of benefit), purchases of annuities under which insurers provide irrevocable commitments for the payment of benefits, and payments of administrative expenses, adjusted as described in Revenue Ruling 95-31, Q&A 12. [Rev. Rul. 95-31, Q&As 11, 12, 1995-1 C.B. 76]

### Q 19:63   How are the disbursements adjusted for purposes of calculating the base amount?

The disbursements are adjusted by reducing those disbursements by the product of (1) the plan's funded current-liability percentage defined under Code Section 412(l)(8) as of the valuation date for the plan year and (2) the sum of the purchases of annuity contracts and the payments of single-sum distributions that were included in the disbursements. For this purpose, the funded current-liability percentage is computed without subtracting any credit balance in the plan's FSA from the plan's actuarial value of assets. [Rev. Rul. 95-31, Q&A 12, 1995-1 C.B. 76]

### Q 19:64   Is there a special rule for determining the base amount if disbursements are attributable to nonrecurring circumstances?

A special rule under Code Section 412(m)(5)(E)(ii)(II) permits the adjusted disbursements to be determined without regard to nonrecurring circumstances. However, this rule is available for the quarter only if the base amount (determined without regard to this special rule) exceeds an amount equal to two times the sum of the adjusted disbursements from the plan for the 36-month period ending on the last day of that quarter, and the enrolled actuary for the plan certifies to the satisfaction of the Treasury Secretary that the excess amount is the result of nonrecurring circumstances (by attaching a certification to the Schedule B). [Rev. Rul. 95-31, Q&A 13, 1995-1 CB 76]

### Q 19:65   What are the *liquid assets* of a plan?

For purposes of Code Section 412(m)(5)(E)(v), the *liquid assets* of a plan are cash, marketable securities, and certain other assets. For this purpose, marketable securities include financial instruments such as stocks and other equity interests, evidences of indebtedness (including certificates of deposit), options, futures contracts, and other derivatives, for which there is a liquid financial market, and other interests in entities (such as partnerships, trusts, or regulated investment companies) for which there is a liquid financial market. A *liquid financial market* is an established financial market described in Treasury Regulations Section 1.1092(d)-1(b) (other than an interbank market or an inter-dealer market described in Treasury Regulations Section 1.1092(d)-1(b)(v) and (vi), respectively). Any security that is issued or guaranteed by the government of the United States or an agency or instrumentality thereof for which there is an established financial market described in Treasury Regulations Section 1.1092(d)-1(b) is a marketable security. Finally, any financial instrument or other interest in an entity that, under its terms, contains a right by which the instrument or other interest may immediately be redeemed, exchanged, or converted into cash or a marketable security, is a marketable security, provided that there are no restrictions on the exercise of that right. [Rev. Rul. 95-31, Q&A 14, 1995-1 C.B. 76]

### Q 19:66   What other assets besides cash and marketable securities are treated as liquid assets of a plan?

Until such time as regulations are issued, other assets that are treated as liquid assets of a plan are insurance, annuity, or other contracts issued by an insurance company that is licensed to do business under the laws of any state, but only if any such insurance, annuity, or other contract (1) would be treated as a marketable security (if it were a financial instrument), (2) provides for substantially equal monthly disbursements, or (3) is benefit responsive. Thus, for example, an insurance contract is a liquid asset if the contract contains a right by which the contract may be immediately redeemed for cash. If the contract provides for substantially equal monthly disbursements (e.g., an annuity contract in pay status), the only portion of the contract that may be treated as liquid assets is the amount equal to 36 times the monthly disbursement (in the month containing the last day of the quarter) which is available under the terms of the contract, provided that there are no restrictions on the disbursements. A contract is considered benefit responsive if, under applicable law and contractual provisions, the plan has the right to receive, without restrictions, disbursements from the contract in order to pay plan benefits for any participant in the plan. For the purposes of determining whether an asset is a liquid asset, a restriction on a redemption, exchange, or conversion right, or a restriction on a disbursement, may result not only from applicable law or contractual provisions, but also from rehabilitation, conservatorship, receivership, insolvency, bankruptcy, or similar proceedings. [Rev. Rul. 95-31, Q&A 15, 1995-1 C.B. 76]

### Q 19:67   How are assets valued for purposes of determining the value of a plan's liquid assets?

The value of a plan's liquid assets with respect to a quarter is the fair market value of the plan's liquid assets as of the last day of the quarter. If an asset of a plan is considered liquid solely as a result of a redemption, exchange, or conversion right provided under the terms of the financial instrument, other interest, or contract, the FMVA must be determined assuming that that right has been exercised. The value of a plan's liquid assets must be reduced by the amount of any liability or other obligation of the plan (other than liabilities of the plan for benefits payable under the plan). The value of the plan's liquid assets as of the last day of any quarter must also be reduced by subtracting contributions (adjusted with interest to the last day of the quarter at the plan's valuation interest rate) that were made in the form of liquid assets during the quarter, provided that they were not taken into account as a contribution toward a required quarterly installment for a prior quarter and were not made for a prior plan year. [Rev. Rul. 95-31, Q&A 16, 1995-1 C.B. 76]

> **Example.** The Creative Designs defined benefit plan has a calendar-year plan year. The plan has a required quarterly installment of $300,000 that is due April 15, 2002. The plan's valuation interest rate is 8 percent. The base amount and liquid assets (before adjustment) as of March 31, 2002, are $1 million and $900,000, respectively. A contribution of $250,000 in the form of liquid assets is made on February 1, 2002, as a payment made for the first quarter of the 2002 plan year. A contribution of $75,000 in the form of liquid assets

is made on February 20, 2002, as a payment made for the plan year ended December 31, 2001. For purposes of determining the liquidity shortfall, the liquid assets as of March 31, 2002, are equal to $646,773 and are calculated by subtracting the contribution (adjusted with interest) made February 1, 2002 from the fair market value of the liquid assets as of March 31, 2002 ($900,000 – $253,227 = $646,773).

The liquidity shortfall as of March 31, 2002, is $353,227 and is equal to the base amount minus the adjusted liquid assets ($1,000,000 – $646,773 = $353,227).

Because a contribution of $250,000 in liquid assets has already been made on February 1, 2002, as a payment made for the first quarter of the 2002 plan year, the additional payment that is necessary to satisfy the liquidity requirement is $100,000, where $100,000 is equal to the excess of the liquidity shortfall for the quarter ($353,227), over the amount of such shortfall that has been paid for the quarter in the form of liquid assets (adjusted for interest to the last day of the quarter) ($253,227). The additional payment of $100,000 (in the form of liquid assets) must be paid on or before April 15, 2002, in order to satisfy the liquidity requirement for the first quarter of the plan year.

### Q 19:68   Is a credit balance in the plan's FSA treated as a contribution that may be used for purposes of satisfying the liquidity requirement?

No. A credit balance in the plan's FSA may not be treated as a contribution that may be used to satisfy the liquidity requirement. Actual contributions in the form of liquid assets must be made to the plan in order to satisfy the liquidity requirement. [Rev. Rul. 95-31, Q&A 17, 1995-1 C.B. 76]

## Multiple Employer Plans Prior to PPA

### Q 19:69   What is a *multiple employer plan*?

A *multiple employer plan* is a plan maintained by more than one employer and is not a plan maintained pursuant to a collective-bargaining agreement between employee representatives and one or more employers. [I.R.C. § 413(a), (c)] In addition, one or more of the participating employers is not aggregated with the others to form a controlled group, an affiliated service group, or a management function group. [I.R.C. § 414(b), (c), (m)]

### Q 19:70   How is the FSA maintained in the case of a multiple employer plan?

In the case of a plan established after December 31, 1988, each employer shall be treated as maintaining a separate plan for purposes of Code Section 412. Therefore, all charges and credits to the FSA are determined separately for each participating employer. This is the case unless the funding of the plan is computed in such a way that all employers are considered together, but the plan uses a method for determining required contributions that provides that any employer contributes not less than the amount, which would be required if such employer maintained a separate plan. [I.R.C. § 413(c)(4)(A)]

The assets and liabilities of the plan are also required to be segregated and accounted for each participating employer as they would be, if the employer withdrew from the multiple employer plan. [I.R.C. § 413(c)(7)(B)]

If the plan was established before December 31, 1988, and the plan administrator did not elect before the close of the first plan year of the plan beginning after the date of enactment of the Technical and Miscellaneous Revenue Act of 1988 to treat each participating employer as having a separate plan, then the requirements of Code Section 412 shall be determined as if all participants in the plan were employed by a single employer. The election of the plan sponsor under this rule can be revoked only with the consent of the IRS. [I.R.C. § 413(c)(4)(B)]

### Q 19:71  Which employers are responsible for the excise tax when there is an accumulated funding deficiency?

If there is an accumulated funding deficiency in a multiple employer plan, the liability for the excise tax is allocated first on the basis of each employer's deficiency and then on the basis of the employers' respective liabilities for contributions under the plan. [I.R.C. § 413(c)(5)]

## Multiemployer Plans Prior to PPA

### Q 19:72  What is a *multiemployer plan*?

A *multiemployer plan* is a plan maintained pursuant to a collective-bargaining agreement between employee representatives (for example, a union) and one or more employers. [I.R.C. §§ 413(a), 414(f)]

### Q 19:73  How are the participation and discrimination rules applied to a multiemployer plan?

Code Sections 410 and 401(a)(4) are applied as if all employees of each of the employers who are parties to the collective-bargaining agreement and who are subject to the same benefit computation formula under the plan were employed by a single employer.

### Q 19:74  How are the vesting rules applied to a multiemployer plan?

The vesting rules under Code Section 411 are applied as if all employers who have been parties to the collective-bargaining agreement constituted a single employer. Therefore, if an employee terminates employment with one employer and goes to work for another employer that is a part of the same collective-bargaining agreement and in the same defined benefit plan, vesting service will continue for this employee with the new employer. In addition, service with two or more employers by the same employee covered by the same collective-bargaining agreement will be combined for vesting purposes.

### Q 19:75   How are the funding rules applied to a multiemployer plan?

The minimum funding standard provided by Code Section 412 is determined as if all participants in the plan were employed by a single employer. However, there are some differences in rules as compared to a single employer plan. Actuarial gains or losses and waived funding deficiencies are amortized over 15 years rather than 5, gains or losses resulting from a change in actuarial assumptions are amortized over 30 years rather than 10, and a shortfall gain or loss is amortized over 20 years rather than 15.

In addition, the PFEA provided a special rule allowing multiemployer plans to defer a portion of experience gains or losses for a certain time period. [See Q 19:76; I.R.C. § 412(b)(7)(F)]

### Q 19:76   How did the PFEA affect the funding requirements for multiemployer plans?

The PFEA provides an election for certain multiemployer plans to defer up to 80 percent of the amortization charge arising from the net experience loss for the first plan year beginning after December 31, 2001, with respect to plan years beginning after June 30, 2003, and before July 1, 2005, and can apply to more than one plan year.

Under PFEA Section 104(b), an eligible multiemployer plan is a plan that satisfies all of the following conditions:

1. The plan had a new investment loss of at least 10 percent for the 2002 plan year;

2. The plan's enrolled actuary has certified that the plan is projected to have an accumulated funding deficiency for any plan year beginning after June 20, 2003, and before July 1, 2006; and

3. The plan has not:

   a. Failed to timely pay an excise tax under Code Section 4971 with respect to that plan for any taxable year beginning during the 10-year period preceding the particular plan year, or

   b. For any plan year beginning after June 20, 1993, and before the particular plan year:

     (i) The average contribution required to be made to the plan by all employers did not exceed 10 cents per hour,

     (ii) No employer contributions were required,

    (iii) A waiver of the minimum funding standards was granted, or

    (iv) An extension of the amortization period under Code Section 412(e) was granted.

A plan is considered to have had a net investment loss of at least 10 percent for the 2002 plan year if the plan's net investment return for that plan year was less than or equal to negative 10 percent, measured using the same formula as used to measure the rate of return on the Schedule B (Form 5500): $2I/(A + B - I)$.

In order for the enrolled actuary to certify that the plan will have an accumulated funding deficiency for a specific plan year, he or she must project all charges and credits to the end of the specific year using valuation data and results from the most recent completed valuation. The actuary must assume that there will be no new entrants and no new plan amendments and must disregard the effect of any election to defer a net experience loss charge.

This election allows a plan to defer up to 80 percent of the otherwise applicable amortization charge with respect to the 2002 plan year. The amount deferred is increased with interest at the federal short-term rate under Code Section 6621(b). The amount deferred must be charged to the FSA for either of the two plan years that immediately succeed the plan year for which the election is made.

If a deferral election is in effect, the plan is restricted from adopting any plan amendment that increases benefit liabilities unless (1) the amendment is the result of a collective-bargaining agreement in effect on April 10, 2004, or (2) the actuary certifies that the amendment is a fully funded amendment.

[I.R.C. § 412(b)(7)(F); Notice 2005-40, 2005-21 I.R.B. 1088]

### Q 19:77 How does a plan make a deferral election under Section 412(b)(7)(F)?

The joint board of trustees of an eligible multiemployer plan makes the deferral election for a plan year by filing with the IRS prior to the end of the plan year or June 30, 2005, if later.

Each participant, beneficiary, union, employer, and the PBGC must be notified within 30 days of filing the election with the IRS. There is a penalty of not more than $1,000 per day for each violation of the notice requirement.

[I.R.C. § 412(b)(7)(F); Notice 2005-40, 2005-21 I.R.B. 1088]

### Q 19:78 How is the liability determined for a failure to meet minimum funding standards?

If a liability under Code Section 4971 for a plan year exists, the liability of each employer who is a party to the collective-bargaining agreement is determined as follows:

1. First, on the basis of their respective delinquencies in meeting required employer contributions under the plan; and

2. Next, on the basis of their respective liabilities for contributions under the plan.

An employer's withdrawal liability under Title IV of ERISA is not treated as a liability for contributions under the plan.

### Q 19:79   How are the deduction limitations determined for a multiemployer plan?

Each applicable limitation provided by Code Section 404(a) is determined as if all participants in the plan were employed by a single employer. The amounts contributed to or under the plan by each employer for the portion of its taxable year which is included within such a plan year, are considered not to exceed such a limitation if the anticipated employer contributions for such plan year (determined in a manner consistent with the manner in which actual employer contributions for such plan year are determined) do not exceed such limitation.

### Q 19:80   Is there an annual funding notice that must be provided by a multiemployer plan?

Yes. The PFEA added subsection (f) to ERISA Section 101, requiring the administrator of a multiemployer defined benefit plan to provide plan participants, beneficiaries, unions, each employer obligated to contribute to the plan, and the PBGC, with an annual funding notice. The notice must include the following:

1. The name of the plan;
2. The address and phone number of the plan administrator and the plan's principal administrative officer (if different from the plan administrator);
3. The plan sponsor's employer identification number;
4. The plan number;
5. A statement as to whether the plan's funded current-liability percentage (as defined in Section 302(d)(8)(B)) for the plan year to which the notice relates is at least 100 percent (and, if not, the actual percentage);
6. A statement of the market value of the plan's assets (and valuation date), the amount of benefit payments, and the ratio of the assets to the payments for the plan year to which the notice relates;
7. A summary of the rules governing insolvent multiemployer plans, including the limitations on benefit payments and any potential benefit reductions and suspensions (and the potential effects of such limitations, reductions, and suspensions on the plan);
8. A general description of the benefits under the plan which are eligible to be guaranteed by the PBGC, along with an explanation of the limitations on the guarantee and the circumstances under which such limitations apply; and
9. Any additional information that the plan administrator elects to include, provided that such information is necessary or helpful to understanding the mandatory information in the notice.

[Labor Reg. § 2520.101-4(b)]

The notice must be given in plan years beginning after December 31, 2004, and must be provided within nine months after the end of the plan year (or two months after the end of the Form 5500 extension period). The Department of Labor has provided a model notice that can be used to satisfy this requirement:

**Annual Funding Notice for [Insert name of pension plan]**

**Introduction**

This notice, which federal law requires all multiemployer plans to send annually, includes important information about the funding level of [insert name, number, and EIN of plan] (Plan). This notice also includes information about rules governing insolvent plans and benefit payments guaranteed by the PBGC, a federal agency. This notice is for the plan year beginning [insert beginning date] and ending [insert ending date] (Plan Year).

**Plan's Funding Level**

The Plan's "funded current-liability percentage" for the Plan Year was [insert percentage-see instructions below]. In general, the higher the percentage, the better funded the plan. The funded current-liability percentage, however, is not indicative of how well a plan will be funded in the future or if it terminates. Whether this percentage will increase or decrease over time depends on a number of factors, including how the plan's investments perform, what assumptions the plan makes about rates of return, whether employer contributions to the fund increase or decline, and whether benefit payments from the fund increase or decline.

(Instructions: For purposes of computing the "funded current-liability percentage," insert ratio of actuarial value of assets to current liability, as of the valuation date, expressed as a percentage. If the percentage is equal to or greater than 100 percent, you may insert "at least 100 percent.")

**Plan's Financial Information**

The market value of the Plan's assets as of [insert valuation date] was [insert amount]. The total amount of benefit payments for the Plan Year was [enter amount]. The ratio of assets to benefit payments is [enter amount calculated by dividing the value of plan assets by the total benefit payments]. This ratio suggests that the Plan's assets could provide for approximately [enter amount calculated above] years of benefit payments in annual amounts equal to what was paid out in the Plan Year. However, the ratio does not take into account future changes in total benefit payments or plan assets.

**Rules Governing Insolvent Plans**

Federal law has a number of special rules that apply to financially troubled multiemployer plans. Under so-called "plan reorganization rules," a plan with adverse financial experience may need to increase required contributions and may, under certain circumstances, reduce benefits that are not eligible for the PBGC's guarantee (generally, benefits that have been in effect for less than 60 months). If a plan is in reorganization status, it must provide notification that the plan is in reorganization status and that, if contributions are not increased, accrued benefits under the plan may be reduced or an excise tax may be imposed (or both). The law requires the plan to furnish this notification to each contributing employer and the labor organization.

Despite the special plan reorganization rules, a plan in reorganization nevertheless could become insolvent. A plan is insolvent for a plan year if its available financial resources are not sufficient to pay benefits when due for the plan year. An insolvent plan must reduce benefit payments to the highest level that can be paid from the plan's available financial resources. If such resources are not enough to pay benefits at a level specified by law (see Benefit Payments Guaranteed by the PBGC, below), the plan must apply to the PBGC for financial assistance. The PBGC, by law, will loan the plan the amount necessary to pay benefits at the guaranteed level. Reduced benefits may be restored if the plan's financial condition improves.

A plan that becomes insolvent must provide prompt notification of the insolvency to participants and beneficiaries, contributing employers, labor unions representing participants, and PBGC. In addition, participants and beneficiaries also must receive information regarding whether, and how, their benefits will be reduced or affected as a result of the insolvency, including loss of a lump-sum option. This information will be provided for each year the plan is insolvent.

### Benefit Payments Guaranteed by the PBGC

The maximum benefit that the PBGC guarantees is set by law. Only vested benefits are guaranteed. Specifically, the PBGC guarantees a monthly benefit payment equal to 100 percent of the first $11 of the Plan's monthly benefit accrual rate, plus 75 percent of the next $33 of the accrual rate, times each year of credited service. The PBGC's maximum guarantee, therefore, is $35.75 per month times a participant's years of credited service.

> **Example 1.** If a participant with 10 years of credited service has an accrued monthly benefit of $500, the accrual rate for purposes of determining the PBGC guarantee would be determined by dividing the monthly benefit by the participant's years of service ($500/10), which equals $50. The guaranteed amount for a $50 monthly accrual rate is equal to the sum of $11 plus $24.75 (.75 × $33), or $35.75. Thus, the participant's guaranteed monthly benefit is $357.50 ($35.75 × 10).

> **Example 2.** If the participant in Example 1 has an accrued monthly benefit of $200, the accrual rate for purposes of determining the guarantee would be $20 (or $200/10). The guaranteed amount for a $20 monthly accrual rate is equal to the sum of $11 plus $6.75 (.75 × $9), or $17.75. Thus, the participant's guaranteed monthly benefit would be $177.50 ($17.75 × 10).

In calculating a person's monthly payment, the PBGC will disregard any benefit increases that were made under the plan within 60 months before the earlier of the plan's termination or insolvency. Similarly, the PBGC does not guarantee pre-retirement death benefits to a spouse or beneficiary (e.g., a qualified pre-retirement survivor annuity) if the participant dies after the plan terminates, benefits above the normal retirement benefit, disability benefits not in pay status, or non-pension benefits, such as health insurance, life insurance, death benefits, vacation pay, or severance pay.

**Where to Get More Information**

For more information about this notice, you may contact [enter name of plan administrator and, if applicable, principal administrative officer], at [enter phone number and address]. For more information about the PBGC and multi-employer benefit guarantees, go to PBGC's Web site, *www.pbgc.gov*, or call PBGC toll-free at 1-800-400-7242 (TTY/TDD users may call the Federal relay service toll free at 1-800-877-8339 and ask to be connected to 1-800-400-7242).

[Appendix to Labor Reg. § 2520.101-4]

## Funding Waivers Prior to PPA

### Q 19:81  May an employer request a waiver from the minimum required funding charges?

Yes. If an employer is unable to satisfy the minimum funding standard for a plan year without temporary substantial business hardship and if application of the standard would be adverse to the interests of plan participants in the aggregate, the IRS may waive the minimum funding requirements of Code Section 412(a) for a plan year with respect to all or any portion of the minimum funding standard other than the amortization amounts from any previous funding waivers.

In the case of a multiemployer plan, 10 percent or more of the number of employers contributing to or under the plan would need to prove substantial business hardship, rather than temporary substantial business hardship. [I.R.C. § 412(d)(1)]

### Q 19:82  How often may an employer request a waiver from the funding requirements?

The IRS will not waive the minimum funding standard with respect to a plan for more than three of any 15 (5 of any 15 in the case of a multi-employer plan) consecutive plan years. [I.R.C. § 412(d)(1)]

### Q 19:83  Is an employer required to restore the amount of the funding that was waived?

Yes. The amount of the funding requirement that was waived is charged to the FSA in equal annual installments (until fully amortized) beginning in the year following the year of the waiver over a period of five plan years (15 plan years in the case of a multiemployer plan). [I.R.C. § 412(b)(2)(C)]

The interest rate used for purposes of computing the amortization charge is (1) in the case of a plan other than a multiemployer plan, the greater of

150 percent of the federal midterm rate (as in effect under Code Section 1274 for the first month of such plan year), or (2) the valuation rate used by plan in determining costs, and (3) in the case of a multiemployer plan, the rate determined under Code Section 6621(b). [I.R.C. § 412(d)(1)]

### Q 19:84    How is the determination of business hardship made?

The factors taken into account in determining temporary substantial business hardship (substantial business hardship in the case of a multiemployer plan) include (but are not be limited to) whether or not:

1. The employer is operating at an economic loss;
2. There is substantial unemployment or underemployment in the trade or business and in the industry concerned;
3. The sales and profits of the industry concerned are depressed or declining; and
4. It is reasonable to expect that the plan will be continued only if the waiver is granted.

[I.R.C. § 412(d)(2)]

If an employer is a member of a controlled group (within the meaning of Code Section 414(b), (c), (m), or (o)), the temporary substantial business hardship requirements will be treated as met only if such requirements are met:

1. With respect to such employer; and
2. With respect to the controlled group of which that employer is a member (determined by treating all members of the group as a single employer).

Evidence of business hardship will depend on the individual facts and circumstances of each case. However, the IRS requests that the following information be submitted:

1. General facts concerning the employer, including (a) the history of the employer and its primary business, (b) the ownership of the employer and any recent or contemplated changes, and (c) whether the employer belongs to any controlled groups and whether those members also participate in the plan.
2. The financial condition of the employer, including the annual financial report of the employer for the current and prior two tax years. This will include at least the balance sheet, profit and loss statement, cash flow statement, and notes to the financial statement.
3. Any executive compensation arrangements that have been made with any officers or directors of the employer during the previous 36 months.
4. The nature and extent of the business hardship, including discussion of the reasons for the current situation, how likely the possibility for a recovery is, how the employer plans to recover, when increased contributions to the plan will resume, and projected financial statements for the next 5 years.

5. Facts concerning the pension plan.

6. Facts concerning any other retirement plans the employer maintains.

7. Any other pertinent information.

[Rev. Proc. 2004-15, 2004-7 I.R.B. 490]

An analysis of a trade or business or industry of a member may not need to be conducted if the IRS determines that such an analysis would not significantly affect the determination. [I.R.C. § 412(d)(5)]

### Q 19:85   When must the application for a funding waiver be submitted?

In the case of a plan other than a multiemployer plan, no waiver may be granted under Section 412 with respect to any plan for any plan year unless an application is submitted to the IRS no later than two and a half months after the close of the plan year for which the waiver is requested. For a multiemployer plan, the application generally needs to be made no later than the close of the plan year following the plan year for which the waiver is requested. [IRC § 412(d)(4); Ann 96-25, 1996-17 IRB 13; Rev Proc 2004-15, 2004-7 IRB 490]

### Q 19:86   What procedures must be followed in requesting a waiver of the minimum funding standards?

There are four procedures that must be followed:

1. The request must be signed by the taxpayer or authorized representative of the applicant.

2. A penalty of perjury statement signed by the taxpayer must accompany the request.

3. Compliance with Code Section 6110 is required, including payment of the applicable user fee. The user fee for waiver requests of less than $1,000,000 is $2,290. If the waiver is for more than $1,000,000, the fee is $5,415. [Rev. Proc. 2004-8, 2004-1 I.R.B. 240]

4. A copy of the notice to participants must be included.

The request for waiver of the minimum funding standard must be submitted to:

Employee Plans
Internal Revenue Service
Commissioner, TE/GE
Attention: SE:T:EP:RA
P.O. Box 27063
McPherson Station
Washington, DC 20038

[Rev. Proc. 2004-15]

## Q 19:87   May an employer request an extension of the amortization period?

Yes. The period of years required to amortize any unfunded liability, other than a funding waiver, may be extended for a period of time (not in excess of 10 years) if the IRS determines that such extension would carry out the purposes of ERISA and would provide adequate protection for participants and their beneficiaries. Further considerations are whether the failure to permit such extension would (1) result in (a) a substantial risk to the voluntary continuation of the plan or (b) a substantial curtailment of pension benefit levels or employee compensation, and (2) be adverse to the interests of plan participants in the aggregate.

In the case of a plan other than a multiemployer plan, the interest rate applicable for any plan year under any extension granted will be the greater of (1) 150 percent of the federal midterm rate (as in effect under Code Section 1274 for the first month of such plan year) or (2) the rate of interest used under the plan in determining costs. In the case of a multiemployer plan, the rate is determined under Code Section 6621(b).

## Q 19:88   What rules must the employer abide by if an extension or waiver is to be granted?

The following requirements are applicable to any waiver or extension request:

1. Benefits may not be increased during the waiver or extension period. No amendment of the plan which increases the liabilities of the plan by reason of any increase in benefits, any change in the accrual of benefits, or any change in vesting under the plan may be adopted if a waiver or an extension of time is in effect. If a plan is amended in violation of this requirement, the waiver or extension of time will not apply to any plan year ending on or after the date on which the amendment is adopted. However, this will not be applicable if the IRS determines that the amendment is reasonable and provides for only *de minimis* increases in the liabilities of the plan, or is required as a condition of qualification.

2. In general, the Secretary may require an employer maintaining a single-employer defined benefit plan to provide security as a condition for granting or modifying a waiver or an extension. Any security provided may be perfected and enforced only by the PBGC, or at the direction of the PBGC, by a contributing sponsor, or a member of such sponsor's controlled group.

3. The IRS will, before granting or modifying a waiver or an extension, provide the PBGC with:

   a. A notice of the completed application for the waiver, extension, or modification, and

   b. An opportunity to comment on the application within 30 days after receipt and to consider any comments of the PBGC, as well as any employee organization (union) representing participants in the plan, which are submitted in writing to the IRS.

4. The employer must also provide evidence to the IRS that the applicant has provided notice of the filing of the application for waiver or extension to each employee organization representing employees covered by the affected plan, and each participant, beneficiary, and alternate payee (within the meaning of Section 414(p)(8)). The notice must include a description of the extent to which the plan is funded for benefits that are guaranteed and for benefit liabilities. The notice must be provided within 14 days prior to the date of the application. (There is a model notice provided in Revenue Procedure 2004-15 [2004-7 I.R.B. 490] which may be used for this purpose.)

**Note.** The requirement for security and consultation with the PBGC (items #2 and #3 above) will not apply to any plan if the sum of the accumulated funding deficiencies, the outstanding balance of the amount of the waived funding deficiencies, and the outstanding balance of the amount of decreases in the minimum funding standard allowed is less than $1,000,000.

[I.R.C. § 412(f)]

### Q 19:89  What is the procedure the employer must follow to request an extension of an amortization period?

Only a plan administrator, plan sponsor, or an authorized representative of either may submit a request for approval to extend the period of years required to amortize any unfunded liability. The request must be signed by the taxpayer maintaining the plan or an authorized representative of the applicant (including an enrolled actuary) who submits a Power of Attorney Form 2848 with the request. For multiemployer plans, the request must be made by the Board of Trustees (which shall be deemed to be the applicant) or by an authorized representative of the Board of Trustees. An individual is not an authorized representative of the applicant merely on account of being an administrator or trustee of the plan.

Requests for approval to extend an amortization period must be submitted to:

Employee Plans
Internal Revenue Service
Commissioner, TE/GE
Attention: SE:T:EP:RA
P.O. Box 27063
McPherson Station
Washington, DC 20038

The user fee for this request is currently $2,570 and must be sent with the request. [Rev. Proc. 2004-8, 2004-1 I.R.B. 240]

All extension requests should be submitted by the last day of the plan year for which the extension is intended to take effect. The IRS will consider applications for extensions submitted after this date only upon a showing of good cause. In seeking an extension of an amortization period with respect to a plan year which has not yet ended, the applicant may have difficulty in furnishing sufficient current evidence in support of the request. For this reason, it is generally advised that a request not be submitted earlier than 180 days prior to the end of the plan year for which the extension is requested.

The IRS has provided a checklist (see end of this question) for the convenience of the taxpayer submitting the request. This checklist should be signed by the taxpayer or authorized representative, dated, and placed on top of the request.

A request must contain the following information:

1. Penalty of Perjury Statement: "Under the penalties of perjury, I declare that I have examined this request, including accompanying documents, and to the best of my knowledge and belief, the facts presented in support of the request are true, correct, and complete." This declaration must be signed by the applicant (e.g., an authorized officer of a corporation). The signature of an individual with a power of attorney will not suffice for the declaration.

2. Because a request for an extension constitutes a request for a ruling, compliance with Code Section 6110 is also required. Section 601.201 of the Statement of Procedural Rules sets forth the requirements applicable to requests for rulings and determination letters which are subject to Section 6110. Section 601.201(e) furnishes specific instructions to applicants.

The applicant must provide with the request either a statement of proposed deletions and the statutory basis for each proposed deletion, or a statement that no information other than names, addresses, and taxpayer identifying numbers need be deleted.

3. The applicant must provide a copy of a written notification to each employee organization representing employees covered by the plan, and each participant, beneficiary, and alternate payee of the plan, that an application for an extension of the amortization period under § Section 412(e) has been submitted to the Service. The original of the written notification must bear a signature by an appropriate officer of the applicant and must be substantially in the form set forth in the Model Notice A (see end of question). The Service does not require the applicant to furnish any information in addition to that required by the Model Notice in the Appendix A to plan participants, beneficiaries, alternate payees, or employee organizations as part of the extension application process, but additional information may, of course, be provided by the applicant pursuant to the collective bargaining process or otherwise.

The application must state that such notice was hand delivered or mailed to the last known address of each employee organization, participant, beneficiary, and alternate payee within 14 days prior to the date of the application. If the applicant makes a reasonable effort to carry out the provisions of this paragraph, failure of an employee organization, participant, beneficiary, or alternate payee to receive the notice will not cause the applicant to fail the notice requirement. However, merely posting the notice on a bulletin board is not sufficient to satisfy this requirement.

The applicant must furnish appropriate evidence that the extension of the amortization period is needed to continue the plan or to prevent a substantial curtailment of pension benefit levels or employee compensation, and that a denial of the extension would be adverse to the interests of the plan participants in the aggregate. The IRS has stated that what constitutes appropriate evidence will depend on the facts and circumstances of each case. A response must be furnished for each of the paragraphs (1) through (6) below. In certain cases, some of the material described in paragraphs (1) through (6) may be inapplicable, unavailable, inappropriate, or burdensome to furnish. In such cases, the applicant should furnish a statement indicating why the material for a particular paragraph is inapplicable, unavailable, inappropriate, or burdensome.

1. General facts concerning the employer.

A brief statement should be submitted concerning: (a) the history of the employer and its primary business; (b) the ownership of the employer and any recent or contemplated changes (such as acquisitions, mergers, discontinuances of operations) which might have a bearing on the employer's organization or financial condition; (c) whether the employer is aggregated with any other entity for purposes of Code Section 414(b), (c), (m), or (o); and (d) whether the plan is also maintained by employers described in (c) above or any other employers.

2. The financial condition of the employer.

For plans other than multiemployer plans, the latest available annual financial report of the employer and each of the other entities included within the controlled group of which the employer is a member. This submission must include at least the balance sheet, profit and loss statement, cash flow statement, and notes to the financial statement. Recent interim financial reports for each of the controlled group members, if available, should also be submitted along with an interim financial report covering the corresponding period for the previous year. If the employer submits financial reports to the Securities and Exchange Commission, these reports should be submitted for the same period as the annual financial report. Preferably, the financial report should include certified financial statements. If certified financial statements have not been prepared, an uncertified report is acceptable. If neither certified nor uncertified reports are available, a copy of the company's latest available federal income tax return, including all of the supporting schedules, must be submitted.

For multiemployer plans, the financial information described in the above paragraph must only be submitted for employers who either (1) are represented on the Board of Trustees or (2) made or were required to make 5 percent or more of the total required contributions under the collective bargaining agreements relating to the plan for which the extension is requested. In addition, the applicant must submit a general description of the financial state of the industry in which employees covered by the plan are employed. Regardless of whether any employer makes more than 5 percent of the total contributions, a general description of the financial state of the industry in which employees covered by the plan are employed is required. For purposes of this paragraph, a multiple employer plan for which the plan administrator did not make an election under

Code Section 413(c)(4)(B) is required to submit the same information as a multiemployer plan. Financial information of employers contributing to a multiemployer plan (identified by name of plan and plan number) must be submitted directly from the contributing employers to the Service at the same time that the submission is made to the following address:

Employee Plans
Internal Revenue Service
Commissioner, TE/GE
Attention: SE:T:EP:RA
P.O. Box 27063
McPherson Station
Washington, DC 20038

3. Information concerning the extension of the amortization period. Information concerning the extension of the amortization period should include the following.

    a. The unfunded liability for which an extension of the amortization period is requested.

    b. The reasons why an extension of the amortization period is needed.

    c. The length of the extension of the amortization period desired (up to a maximum of 10 years).

    d. Information concerning the actions taken by the applicant to reduce the plan's unfunded liability before the request for an extension has been made. Such actions would include the reduction of future plan benefit accruals and increases in employer contribution rates. Also describe any benefit reductions, contribution rate increases, or other actions that are intended to be taken in the future.

    e. Projections of (i) FSA credit balance/accumulated funding deficiencies, (ii) actuarial value of assets and market value of assets, (iii) current liabilities, and (iv) funding ratios, for the length of the extension of the amortization period requested and for the period ten (10) years afterwards. For example, if the applicant requests an extension of ten (10) years, the projections should be for a 20-year period. These projections must be prepared by an enrolled actuary.

    f. The plan year for which the extension is requested, that is, the first plan year for which the extension of the amortization period will be reflected in the determination of the minimum funding standard for the plan (e.g., 1/1/2004–12/31/2004).

The Service may request additional information as needed.

4. Facts concerning the pension plan. For each pension plan for which an extension is requested, the following information should be supplied.

    a. The name of the plan, the plan's identification number, and file folder number (if any).

    b. The date the plan was adopted.

c. The effective date of the plan.

d. The classes of employees covered.

e. The number of employees covered.

f. A copy of the current plan document and the most recent summary plan description.

g. A copy of the most recent determination letter issued to the plan.

h. A brief description of all plan amendments adopted during the year for which the extension is requested and the previous four years which affect plan costs, including the approximate effect of each amendment on such costs.

i. The most recent actuarial report, plus any available actuarial reports for the preceding two plan years. Also, if not shown in that report, the PVAB, present value of vested benefits, and fair market value of assets (excluding contributions not yet paid).

j. A description of how the plan is funded (i.e., trust fund, individual insurance policies, etc.).

k. A list of the contributions actually paid in each month, from the 24th month prior to the beginning of the plan year for which the extension is requested through the date of the request and the plan year to which the contributions were applied, with the employee contributions and the employer contributions listed separately.

l. The approximate contribution required to meet the minimum funding standard. For defined benefit plans, this amount should be determined by the plan's enrolled actuary.

m. A copy of the most recently completed *Annual Return/Report of Employee Benefit Plan* (Form 5500 series, as applicable) and in the case of a defined benefit plan, a copy of the corresponding *Actuarial Information* schedule (Schedule B of Form 5500).

n. A copy of each ruling letter that waived the minimum funding standard during the last 15 plan years, a statement of the amount waived for each plan year, and a statement of the outstanding balance of the amortization base for each waived funding deficiency. The outstanding balance of the amortization base for each waiver is to be calculated as of the first day of the plan year for which an extension is being requested.

o. A copy of each ruling letter that granted, under § Code Section 412(e) and Section 304(a) of ERISA, an extension of time to amortize any unfunded liability which became applicable at any time during the last 15 plan years.

5. Other pension, profit-sharing, or stock bonus plans. If the employer maintains more than one plan, an outline of the essential facts for each such plan should be submitted. This should include:

a. A brief description of the plan, including the name of the plan and its plan year.

b. The number of employees covered.

c. The classes of employees covered.

d. The approximate annual contribution required.

e. The amount of contributions that have been made, or are intended to be made, for any plan year of such other plan commencing in, or ending in, the plan year for which the extension is requested.

f. A statement as to whether a request for a waiver of the minimum funding standard or an extension of an amortization period is contemplated for the plan.

6. Other information.

a. Describe the nature of any matters pertaining to the plan which are currently pending or are intended to be submitted to the Service, the Department of Labor or the PBGC.

b. Furnish details of any existing arbitration, litigation, or court procedure which involves the plan.

**Model Notice A**

**MODEL NOTICE OF APPLICATION FOR AN EXTENSION OF AN AMORTIZATION PERIOD TO EMPLOYEE ORGANIZATIONS (UNIONS), PARTICIPANTS, BENEFICIARIES, AND ALTERNATE PAYEES**

This notice is to inform you that an application for an extension of an amortization period for unfunded liability under § Section 412(e) of the Internal Revenue Code (Code) and Section 304 of the Employee Retirement Income Security Act of 1974 (ERISA) has been submitted by [**INSERT APPLICANT'S NAME**] to the Internal Revenue Service (Service) for the [**INSERT PLAN NAME**] for the plan year beginning [**INSERT DATE**].

Under Code Section 412(f)(4)(B) and Section 304(a) of ERISA, the Service will consider any relevant information submitted concerning this application for an extension of the amortization period for unfunded liability. You may send this information to the following address:

Director, Employee Plans
Internal Revenue Service
Attn: SE:T:EP:RA:T:A
1111 Constitution Avenue, N.W.
Washington, DC 20224

Any such information should be submitted as soon as possible after you have received this notice. Due to the disclosure restrictions of Code Section 6103, the Service can not provide any information with respect to the extension request itself.

In accordance with Section 104 of ERISA and Section 2520.104b-10 of the Department of Labor Regulations (29 C.F.R. Part 2520), annual financial reports for this plan, which include employer contributions made to the plan for any plan year, are available for inspection at the Department of Labor in Washington, D.C. Copies of such reports may be obtained upon request and upon payment of copying costs from the following address:

Public Disclosure Room
Room N-5507
Employee Benefits Security Administration
U.S. Department of Labor
200 Constitution Avenue, N.W.
Washington, DC 20210

As required by Section 104(b)(2) of ERISA, copies of the latest annual plan report are available for inspection at the principal office of the plan administrator, who is located at [**INSERT ADDRESS**]. Copies of the annual report may be obtained upon request and upon payment of a copying charge of [**INSERT CHARGE**] by writing to the plan administrator at the above address.

The following information is provided pursuant to Code Section 412(f)(4)(A) and Section 303(e)(1) of ERISA:

Present Value of Vested Benefits $_____

Present Value of Benefits, calculated as though the plan terminated $_____

Fair Market Value of Plan Assets $_____

The above present values were calculated using an interest rate or rates of [**INSERT INTEREST RATE(S)**].

[**SIGNATURE OF APPROPRIATE OFFICER OF THE PLAN SPONSOR**]

[**INSERT NAME**]

[**INSERT TITLE**]

## Checklist

**REQUEST FOR EXTENSION OF AN AMORTIZATION PERIOD CHECKLIST IS YOUR SUBMISSION COMPLETE?**

*Instructions*

The Service will be able to respond more quickly to your request for an extension of an amortization period if it is carefully prepared and complete. To ensure your request is in order, use this checklist. Answer each question in the checklist by inserting Y for yes, N for no, or N/A for not applicable, as appropriate, in the blank next to the item. ***Sign and date the checklist (as taxpayer or authorized representative) and place it on top of your request.***

You must submit a completed copy of this checklist with your request. If a completed checklist is not submitted with your request, substantive consideration of your submission will be deferred until a completed checklist is received.

| | | |
|---|---|---|
| _____ | 1. | If you want to designate an authorized representative, have you included a properly executed Form 2848 (*Power of Attorney and Declaration of Representative*)? |
| _____ | 2. | Have you satisfied all the requirements of Rev. Proc. 2004-4 or its successors (especially concerning signatures and penalties of perjury statement)? (See section 3.03(1)) |
| _____ | 3. | Have you included statement of proposed deletions? (See section 3.03(2)) |
| _____ | 4. | Have you included the user fee required under Rev. Proc. 2004-8 or its successors? (See section 3.02) |
| _____ | 5. | Have you included a copy of the written notification that an application for an extension of an amortization period has been submitted and a statement that such notice was hand delivered or mailed to each employee organization, participant, beneficiary and alternate payee? (See section 3.03(3) and Appendix A) |

| | | |
|---|---|---|
| _____ | 6. | Have you included the general facts concerning the employer? (See section 3.04(1)) |
| _____ | 7. | Have you included a description of the employer's financial condition? (See section 3.04(2)) |
| _____ | 8. | Have you included information concerning the extension of the amortization period? (See section 3.04(3)) |
| _____ | 9. | Have you included information concerning the pension plan? (See section 3.04(4)) |
| _____ | 10. | Have you included information concerning other pension, profit-sharing, or stock bonus plans of the employer? (See section 3.04(5)) |
| _____ | 11. | Have you included information concerning other matters pertaining to the plan? (See section 3.04(6)) |

| | |
|---|---|
| Signature | Date |

Title or Authority

Typed or printed name of person signing checklist

[Rev. Proc. 2004-44, 2004-31 I.R.B. 134]

## Minimum Funding Standard After PPA

### Q 19:90   What is the minimum funding standard after PPA?

The PPA, which is effective for funding requirements for plan years beginning after December 31, 2007, eliminated what was formerly called the FSA and completely rewrote Code Section 412. The PPA also added Code Section 430 (minimum funding standards for single-employer defined benefit plans) for single-employer plans and Code Sections 431 (minimum funding standards for multiemployer plans) and 432 (additional funding rules for multiemployer plans in endangered status or critical status) for multiemployer plans.

Under Code Section 412, in order for a plan to satisfy the minimum funding standard, a single-employer plan must contribute sufficient to meet the minimum required contribution determined under Code Section 430. A multiemployer plan must contribute sufficient to meet the requirements of Code Section 431. [I.R.C. § 412 (a)(2)] There is no longer a specific funding standard "account" as in prior years.

### Q 19:91   What is now contained in Code Section 412?

Code Section 412 now specifically references separate sections to determine if a plan has met the minimum funding requirements, Code Section 430 for a single-employer plan and Code Section 431 for a multiemployer plan. [I.R.C. § 412(a)] In addition, Code Section 412(b) states who is responsible to make contributions and Code Section 412(c) contains any allowable variance from this standard. Code Section 412(d) states that permission is required to change the plan's funding method, valuation date, or plan year [I.R.C. § 412(d)(1)], and how certain retroactive plan amendments are treated. [I.R.C. § 412(d)(2)] Code Sections 412(e)(1) and 412(e)(2) state which plans must comply with the minimum funding requirements and Code Section 412(e)(3) now contains the funding requirements for insurance contract plans (formerly called the 412(i) plan). This is all that is now contained in the amended Code Section 412, which is applicable for plan years beginning after December 31, 2007, a marked difference from the prior Code Section 412.

### Q 19:92  Who is responsible to make contributions under a defined benefit plan?

In general, the amount of any contribution required by Code Sections 412 and 430 must be paid by the employer responsible for making contributions to or under the plan. If the employer is a member of a controlled group, each member of such group shall be jointly and severally liable for payment of such contributions. [I.R.C. § 412(b)]

### Q 19:93  What are the requirements to obtain a waiver from the minimum funding requirements?

Generally, the waiver must be for a business hardship. If an employer is (or in the case of a multiemployer plan, 10 percent or more of the number of employers contributing to or under the plan is) unable to satisfy the minimum funding standard for a plan year without temporary substantial business hardship (substantial business hardship in the case of a multiemployer plan), and application of the standard would be adverse to the interests of plan participants in the aggregate, the Treasury Department may waive the minimum funding requirements for such year with respect to all or any portion of the minimum funding standard. A plan sponsor may not receive more than 3 waivers out of any 15 (5 of any 15 in the case of a multiemployer plan) consecutive plan years. [I.R.C. § 412 (c)(1)(A)]

The application for a waiver must be received by the 15th day of the third month following the end of the plan year. [I.R.C. § 412(c)(5)(A)]

Notice must be provided of the filing for a waiver to each affected party. The notice must contain a description of the extent to which the plan is funded (only including benefits that are guaranteed by the PBGC) and for all benefit liabilities. [I.R.C. § 412(c)(6)]

If any amendment is made to the plan that increases liabilities during the waiver period, then the waiver will cease to apply. [I.R.C. § 412(c)(7)]

### Q 19:94  What are the effects of a waiver?

For a single-employer plan, the minimum required contribution under Code Section 430 for the plan year is reduced by the amount of the waiver and amortized over the next five years using the same segment rates as are used for funding. [I.R.C. §§ 412(c)(1)(B),§ 430(e)(2)(A)]

If the funding shortfall of a plan for any plan year is zero, then the waiver amortization bases are considered fully amortized and the installments are reduced to zero. [I.R.C. § 430(e)(5)]

If the plan is a multiemployer plan, the minimum required contribution under Code Section 431 for the plan year is reduced by the amount of the waiver and amortized over the next 15 plan years. (See Qs 19:119–19:126.) [I.R.C. § 431(b)(2)(C)]

### Q 19:95    What factors are considered by the IRS when determining whether a business hardship exists?

The factors taken into account in determining temporary substantial business hardship (substantial business hardship in the case of a multiemployer plan) shall include (but shall not be limited to) whether or not—

- The employer is operating at an economic loss;
- There is substantial unemployment or underemployment in the trade or business and in the industry concerned;
- The sales and profits of the industry concerned are depressed or declining; and
- It is reasonable to expect that the plan will be continued only if the waiver is granted.

[I.R.C. § 412(c)(2)]

If the employer is a member of a controlled group, the temporary substantial business hardship requirement is met if the requirements are met for both the individual employer and the controlled group. [I.R.C. § 412(c)(5)(B)]

### Q 19:96    Is security required in order to obtain a waiver?

It may be required. The Treasury Department may require security as a condition for granting or modifying a waiver from the minimum funding standards. This security may only be perfected or enforced by the PBGC. [I.R.C. § 412(c)(4)(A)]

### Q 19:97    Must the Treasury Department receive approval from the PBGC before granting a waiver?

Yes. The Treasury Department must provide the PBGC with:

- notice of the completed application for any waiver or modification, and
- an opportunity to comment on such application within 30 days after receipt of such notice, and consider:
  - any comments of the PBGC, and
  - any views of any employee organization (within the meaning of section 3 (4)) representing participants in the plan which are submitted in writing to the Secretary of the Treasury in connection with such application.

Information provided to the PBGC will be considered tax return information and subject to the safeguarding and reporting requirements of Section 6103(p) of the Internal Revenue Code of 1986. [I.R.C. § 412(c)(4)(B)]

### Q 19:98  Is permission required to change the funding method, valuation date, or plan year of a plan?

Yes. According to Code Section 412(d)(1) any such changes must be approved by the Treasury Department. Prior to the PPA, certain changes were given automatic approval. Current regulations have not yet been issued stating if these approvals will continue.

### Q 19:99  Can a plan be retroactively amended?

Yes, subject to certain criteria. Under Code Section 412(d)(2), if a plan adopts an amendment within two and a half months after year end and this amendment does not reduce the accrued benefits of any participants, then the plan administrator may elect to have the amendment apply as of the first day of the plan year to which it applies. This election is important in order to reflect this amendment in the funding; however, much of the effect of this amendment has been nullified by the fact that the minimum funding is now determined under a unit credit accrual method rather than being able to use a projected funding method.

### Q 19:100  What is the minimum required contribution for a single-employer defined benefit plan?

Minimum funding for single-employer defined benefit plans is now specified under Code Section 430. The minimum required contribution is either:

1. In the case of a plan in which the value of the plan assets (see Q 19:101) is less than the funding target (see Q 19:102) of the plan for the plan year, is equal to:

    a. The target normal cost (see Q 19:103) of the plan for the plan year, plus

    b. The shortfall amortization charge (see Q 19:104) of the plan for the plan year, plus

    c. The waiver amortization charge (see Q 19:105) of the plan for the plan year.

2. If the value of the plan assets equals or exceeds the funding target of the plan for the plan year, the target normal cost of the plan for the plan year is reduced by this excess (but not below zero).

[I.R.C. § 430(a)]

### Q 19:101  How is the value of the assets determined for purposes of determining the minimum funding requirement?

The assets in this circumstance are reduced by the amount of any prefunding balance and funding standard carryover balance. (See Q 17:XX) [I.R.C. § 430(f)(4)(B)]

### Q 19:102 What is the *funding target*?

The *funding target* is equal to the present value of all benefit liabilities accrued at the beginning of the plan year. [I.R.C. § 430(d)(1)] This present value is determined using the segment rates and a specific mortality table yet to be published (see Q 19:110).

**Example.** The Crazy For You Pension Plan needs to determine its funding target for the 2008 plan year. The sole participant, Mr. Batty, is 68 years old, reached the plan's normal retirement age at age 65, and has an accrued benefit of $12,000 per month. Assume that the first segment rate is 5.5 percent, the second segment rate is 6.0 percent, and the third segment rate is 6.5 percent. The funding target is determined as follows:

| Year | Age | Payment Amount | Vn (The Interest Discount for n Years) | Lx (The # Living at That Age) | Discount (Includes The Interest and Mortality Discount) | APR | Present Value |
|---|---|---|---|---|---|---|---|
| 2008 | 68 | 12,000.00 | 1.0000000 | 869328.9 | 1 | 125.725 | $1,508,698.25 |
| 2013 | 73 | 12,000.00 | 0.7651344 | 791373.8 | 0.6965227 | 107.737 | $ 900,492.74 |
| 2013 | 73 | 12,000.00 | 0.7472582 | 791373.8 | 0.6802495 | 104.374 | $ 852,004.77 |
| 2028 | 88 | 12,000.00 | 0.3118047 | 334821.6 | 0.1200914 | 52.173 | $ 75,186.13 |
| 2028 | 88 | 12,000.00 | 0.2837970 | 334821.6 | 0.1093043 | 51.338 | $ 67,337.41 |
| | | | | | | Total: | $1,452,361.56 |

The funding target for this plan at the beginning of the 2008 plan year is $1,452,362.

For at-risk plans the funding target is determined using the additional actuarial assumptions and, if the plan has also been at-risk for two out of the last four years, a loading factor. [I.R.C. § 430(i)(1)] In no event will the at-risk funding target be less than the regular funding target. There is a transition allowed for plans that have been in at-risk status for less than five years where a certain percentage to the deficiency is allowed to be added back in when determining the funding target based on the number of consecutive years the plan has been in at-risk status. [I.R.C. § 430(i)(5)]

### Q 19:103 What is the *target normal cost*?

The *target normal cost* is equal to the present value of the benefits accrued during the current year, including the increase in accrued benefit attributable to compensation increases. [I.R.C. § 430(b)]

**Example.** Betty Beep, age 37, is a participant in the Making Connections pension plan. She had an accrued benefit of $500 as of January 1, 2007, and now has an accrued benefit of $600 as of January 1, 2008. Since she is not scheduled to begin receiving benefits for another 28 years, only the third segment rate applies in determining the present value of the increase in her benefit. The target normal cost for her benefit is equal to the increase in benefit of $100 times the APR of 133.55 times a discount factor which includes interest and mortality of 0.1826 for a present value of $2,439.

The target normal cost for a plan in at-risk status for a year is equal to the present value of the benefits accruing for the year using the additional actuarial assumptions plus, if the plan has been at-risk for two out of the last four years, a loading factor. [I.R.C. § 430(i)(2)] In no event will the at-risk target normal cost be less than the regular target normal cost determined without regard to the plan's at-risk status. There is a transition allowed for plans that have been in at-risk status for less than five years where a certain percentage to the deficiency is allowed to be added back in when determining the target normal cost based on the number of consecutive years the plan has been in at-risk status. [I.R.C. § 430 (i)(5)]

### Q 19:104  What is the *shortfall amortization installment* and the *shortfall amortization base*?

The *shortfall amortization installment* is equal to the amount to amortize, with level payments, the shortfall amortization base for a plan year over seven years, amortized using the segment rates in effect in the year the base is established. [I.R.C. § 430(c)(3)]

The *shortfall amortization base* is equal to the funding shortfall for the year, less the present value of future shortfall amortization installments (due to prior shortfall amortization bases), less the present value of waiver amortization installments from prior years. All gains and losses are considered in the shortfall amortization. [I.R.C. § 430(c)(3)]

The funding shortfall for the year is the excess of the funding target for the year over the value of the plan's assets (as reduced by the amount of any prefunding balance and funding standard carryover balance). [I.R.C. § 430(c)(4)]

If there is no funding shortfall for a plan year, then in a later year any shortfall amortization bases and waiver amortization bases for all prior years are treated as fully amortized. There is no longer a full-funding limit, but this funding shortfall acts as a full-funding limit when it comes to fully amortizing existing bases. [I.R.C. §§ 430(c)(6), 430(e)(5)]

**Example.** The funding target of $1,452,362, in Q 19:102, is used in this example. The value of assets in the plan as of December 31, 2007 is $1,000,000. The plan had a funding standard carryover balance of $100,000. Therefore, the value of assets to use is $900,000. The transition rule from Q 19:105 is used, so the funding target is multiplied by 92 percent, or $1,336,173. The shortfall amortization base is equal to $1,336,173 less $900,000, or $436,173. This base is amortized over seven years using the segment rates in effect. Since there are two segment rates in effect over a seven-year period (the first segment rate is effective for the first five years, and the second is effective for the last two years), the calculation of the amortization is a little more complicated. The present value at each year must be calculated using the particular rate, and then added together.

| | | |
|---|---|---|
| 1 | Present value 1 year payments $= 1$ | 1.000000 |
| 2 | Present value 2 year payments $=$ line $1 + v1$ using segment 1 | 1.947867 |
| 3 | Present value 3 year payments $=$ line $2 + v2$ using segment 1 | 2.846320 |
| 4 | Present value 4 year payments $=$ line $3 + v3$ using segment 1 | 3.697933 |
| 5 | Present value 5 year payments $=$ line $4 + v4$ using segment 1 | 4.505150 |
| 6 | Present value 6 year payments $=$ line $5 + v5$ using segment 2 | 5.252408 |
| 7 | Present value 7 year payments $=$ line $6 + v6$ using segment 2 | 5.957369 |

The amortization installment for 2008 is equal to $436,173 divided by line 7, or 5.957369, which is $73,216.

### Q 19:105   Are there any transition rules applicable to determining the funding shortfall?

Yes. In the case of plan years beginning after 2007 and before 2011, only the applicable percentage of the funding target is taken into account in determining the funding shortfall for the plan year. The applicable percentage is determined in accordance with the following table:

| In the Case of a Plan Year Beginning in Calendar Year | The Applicable Percentage Is |
|---|---|
| 2008 | 92 |
| 2009 | 94 |
| 2010 | 96 |

This transition ceases to apply if the plan has a shortfall amortization base in any prior year. In addition, this relief is not available for plans that were not in effect for a plan year beginning in 2007 or were subject to DRC requirements in 2007. [I.R.C. § 430(c)(5)(B)]

### Q 19:106   What is the waiver amortization charge?

The waiver amortization charge (if any) for a plan for any plan year is the aggregate total of the waiver amortization installments for such plan year with respect to the waiver amortization bases for each of the five preceding plan years.

The waiver amortization installments are the amounts necessary to amortize the waiver amortization base of the plan for any plan year in level annual installments over a period of five plan years beginning with the succeeding plan year.

In determining any waiver amortization installment under this subsection, the interest rate used is the same as the segment rates which are used for determining the funding target.

The waiver amortization base of a plan for a plan year is the amount of the waived funding deficiency (if any) for such plan year.

In any case in which the funding shortfall of a plan for a plan year is zero, for purposes of determining the waiver amortization charge for such plan year and succeeding plan years, the waiver amortization bases for all preceding plan years (and all waiver amortization installments determined with respect to such bases) are reduced to zero. [I.R.C. § 430(e)]

### Q 19:107   When is a plan considered to be in *at-risk status*?

*At-risk status* means that a plan's funding target attainment percentage (FTAP) for the preceding year is less than 80 percent and the FTAP for the preceding year using the additional actuarial assumptions (but not the loading factor) is less than 70 percent. There is a phase-in to the 80 percent number where for 2008 it is lowered to 65 percent, for 2009 it is 70 percent, for 2010 it is 75 percent, and for 2011 and thereafter it is 80 percent. [I.R.C. § 430(i)(4)] Any plan with less than 500 participants on each day of the preceding plan year shall automatically be deemed to not be at-risk.

### Q 19:108   What is the *funding target attainment percentage*?

The *funding target attainment percentage* (FTAP) is the value of plan assets (as defined under Code Section 430(f)(4)(B)) expressed as a percentage of the funding target (without adjustment for at-risk status). [I.R.C. § 430(d)(2)]

**Example.** The FTAP for the plan in the example in Q 19:102 is equal to the assets of $900,000 ($1,000,000 less the funding standard carryover balance of $100,000) divided by the funding target of $1,452,362, or 61.97 percent.

### Q 19:109   What are the *additional actuarial assumptions* and *loading factor* that are applicable to at-risk plans?

The *additional actuarial assumptions* means that the actuary must assume that all employees who would be eligible to elect benefit payments during the next 10 years must be assumed to do so using the benefit form that produces the highest present value. For example, if there is a plan provision allowing for an immediate lump-sum distribution upon termination of employment, then the actuary must assume that the participant will terminate each year and elect the benefit form with the highest present value, which could be the lump sum based on the Code Section 417(e) rates.

The *loading factor* is equal to the sum of $700 times the number of participants in the plan plus 4 percent of the regular funding target for the plan year.

## Q 19:110   How are liabilities calculated?

All calculations are made as of the plan's valuation date. Except in the case of a small plan with 100 or fewer participants during the preceding plan year, the valuation date must be the first day of the plan year. For small plans, the valuation date may be any day during the plan year. For the first year of the plan, the determination of the number of plan participants is made during that first year. [I.R.C. § 430(g)]

In addition, certain actuarial assumptions used in determining liabilities are now prescribed while some are still left up to the actuary to determine. The assumptions that are prescribed are the interest rates and the mortality tables. Liabilities are valued using the applicable segment rate that corresponds to expected benefit payments during that time period. [I.R.C. § 430(h)(2)(B)] Optionally, the sponsor may elect to use the bond yield curve, without 24-month averaging, instead of the segment rate, but only for purposes of determining the required minimum contribution. Once this election is made, changing this would require Treasury approval. [I.R.C. § 430(h)(2)(D)]

The mortality table used in funding will also be prescribed but has not yet been issued. Instead of using the mortality table published by the Treasury Department, a plan sponsor may use a mortality table of their own as long as the plan is quite large and has been around for a long time in order to determine mortality experience. [I.R.C. § 430(h)(3)(C)]

Assumptions that are left to the actuary's professional judgment must each be reasonable (taking into account the experience of the plan and reasonable expectations) and which, in combination, offer the actuary's best estimate of anticipated experience under the plan. [I.R.C. § 430(h)(1)] For example, the actuary must assume that benefits will be paid in the optional forms provided under the plan, based on the plan's experience. [I.R.C. § 430(h)(4)]

## Q 19:111   What is the *segment rate*?

The *segment rate* is equal to the sum of the first, second, and third segment rates. The first segment rate is the single interest rate determined by the Treasury Department on the basis of the corporate bond yield curve with maturity during the next five years. The second segment rate is the single interest rate determined by the Treasury Department on the basis of the corporate bond yield curve with maturity between the fifth and twentieth years. The third segment rate is the single interest rate determined by the Treasury Department on the basis of the corporate bond yield curve with maturity beyond the twentieth year. [I.R.C. § 430(h)(2)(C)] The corporate bond yield curve reflects a 24-month average of the monthly yields of investment grade corporate bonds with varying maturities that are in the top three quality levels available. [I.R.C. § 430(h)(2)(D)] If the plan is in existence in 2007, then the segment rates may be blended with the old current-liability rates for a three-year phase-in (⅓ new to ⅔ old for 2008, ⅔ new to ⅓ old for 2009, 100 percent new in 2010). This phase-in is optional; a plan may elect not to use this transition rule. [I.R.C. § 430(h)(2)(G)]

## Q 19:112   How are assets calculated?

Under Code Section 430(f)(4)(A), the value of the assets is equal to the actuarial value of plan assets reduced by the pre-funding balance, but only if some portion of the pre-funding balance or funding standard carryover has been used to reduce the current year's contribution. This definition of assets is used when determining if a funding shortfall is incurred for the year.

Under Code Section 430(f)(4)(B), the value of the assets is equal to the actuarial value of plan assets reduced by the pre-funding balance and the funding standard carryover balance (unless there is a binding agreement with the PBGC to not use any portion of the pre-funding balance or funding standard carryover balance to reduce future contributions). This definition of assets is used in determining the amount of the funding shortfall.

Under Code Section 430(f)(4)(C), the value of the assets is equal to the actuarial value of plan assets reduced by the pre-funding balance. If this asset value is less than 80 percent of the funding target, then the credit balances cannot be used to satisfy the contribution but may be used to decrease the funding shortfall. [I.R.C. § 430(f)]

A plan may elect to reduce the pre-funding balance or funding standard carryover balance prior to determining the value of assets under Code Section 430(f)(4)(C) in order to avoid the rule when assets are less than 80 percent of the funding target.

Assets may be smoothed over a period not extending beyond 24 months, and the corridor must be between 90 percent and 110 percent of fair market value.

## Q 19:113   How are credit balances determined and maintained?

Credit balances are treated in different ways for different purposes, and it depends on if the credit balance was due to pre-2008 FSA credit balances (called funding standard carryover balance) or post-2007 credit balances (called the pre-funding balance).

The *funding standard carryover balance* is equal to the FSA credit balance as of the end of the 2007 plan year, increased with interest at a rate reflective of the plan's actual rate of return, decreased by any portion used to satisfy the minimum required contribution, and decreased by any additional amount as elected by the plan sponsor. [I.R.C. § 430(f)(7)]

The *pre-funding balance* is zero at the beginning of the 2008 plan year. It is increased by any portion of the excess of contributions over the minimum required contribution, increased by interest on the excess contributions at the effective interest rate, decreased by any portion used to meet minimum funding, decreased by any additional amount elected by the plan sponsor, and the balance from a prior year is credited with interest at the rate reflective of the plan's actual rate of return. [I.R.C. § 430(f)(6)]

The plan sponsor may elect to reduce by any amount the balance of the pre-funding balance and the funding standard carryover balance for any plan year (but not below zero). Such reduction shall be effective prior to any determination of the value of plan assets for such plan year under this section and application of the balance in reducing the minimum required contribution for such plan. The balance of the funding standard carryover balance must be used prior to any amount in the pre-funding balance. [I.R.C. § 430(f)(5)]

### Q 19:114   Are quarterly contributions required?

Maybe. If a plan has a funding shortfall for the preceding year, then the plan will be subject to quarterly installments for the current year equal to the lesser of 90 percent of the current year's minimum required contribution or 100 percent of the prior year's minimum required contribution. If the employer fails to make a required installment, then interest will be charged on the installment equal to the effective interest rate plus five percentage points for the period of the underpayment. [I.R.C. § 430(j)(3)]

### Q 19:115   What is the *effective interest rate*?

The *effective interest rate* is the single interest rate that would produce the same funding target as the funding target produced using the segment rate. This rate is used for crediting interest on the contribution requirement from plan year end-to-date contribution is deposited and is also used in determining the pre-funding balance. [I.R.C. § 430(h)(2)(A)]

> **Example.** Assume that the facts are the same as in Q 19:102. The funding target in that example generated a funding target of $1,452,362 based on a current age of 68 and a benefit of $12,000. The single interest rate that would provide that same present value is an interest rate of 6.21 percent.

### Q 19:116   How are contributions credited towards the minimum contribution?

If an employer makes any contribution to the plan after the valuation date for the plan year for which the contribution is made, and the contribution is for a preceding plan year, the contribution shall be taken into account as an asset of the plan as of the valuation date, except that in the case of any plan year beginning after 2008, only the present value (determined as of the valuation date) of such contribution may be taken into account. For purposes of the preceding sentence, present value is determined using the effective interest rate for the preceding plan year to which the contribution is properly allocable.

> **Example.** The plan sponsor makes a contribution for the 2008 plan year on September 15, 2009 of $100,000. The minimum required contribution is $96,000. The effective interest rate is 6 percent. The amount of the

contribution that is actually credited towards the minimum required contribution is $100,000 / (1 + (.06 × 8.5/12)) = $95,923. This contribution is not sufficient to meet the minimum funding requirements for 2008.

If any contributions for any plan year are made to or under the plan during the plan year but before the valuation date for the plan year, the assets of the plan as of the valuation date shall not include (1) such contributions and (2) interest on such contributions for the period between the date of the contributions and the valuation date, determined by using the effective interest rate for the plan year. [I.R.C. § 430(g)(4)]

### Q 19:117   What are the consequences of a plan being underfunded?

If a plan has an adjusted FTAP of less than 80 percent, then the plan sponsor may not make an amendment to the plan increasing benefits, unless:

1. Either the sponsor fully funds the cost of the increase due to the amendment, or,

2. Contributes enough to make the FTAP at least 80 percent (in addition to any other required contributions for the year).

This does not apply to a non-pay related benefit formula if the increase is solely to keep the benefits in line with the increase in the current average compensation of the participants of the sponsor. [I.R.C. § 436(c)] In addition, if this funding target is not reached then the credit balances may not be used to satisfy the minimum required contribution. [I.R.C. § 430(f)]

If the adjusted FTAP of the plan is 60 percent or greater, but less than 80 percent, the plan may only make a prohibited payment of the lesser of 50 percent of the present value of the total benefit or the PBGC guaranteed benefit. In addition, the participant may receive only one such payment during consecutive years while this restriction is in effect. [I.R.C. § 436(d)(3)]

If the plan sponsor is in bankruptcy or if the plan has an adjusted FTAP of less than 60 percent, then the plan may not make prohibited payments. It appears this applies to all plans, including one-participant plans. [I.R.C. § 436(d)] In addition, unpredictable contingent event benefits (UCEBs) may not be paid either. [I.R.C. § 436(b)] Benefit accruals must also cease as of the beginning of the plan year in which the adjusted FTAP is less than 60 percent, unless there is an additional contribution sufficient to make the adjusted FTAP at least 60 percent. [I.R.C. § 436(e)] After a benefit accrual restriction is removed due to an improved funding status, the plan does not need to provide the missed accruals. [I.R.C. § 436(i)]

If a plan was subject to a restriction in the prior plan year, the plan will remain restricted in the current plan year until the actuary certifies to the current adjusted FTAP. If the actuary has not certified to the current FTAP by the first day of the 10th month of the current plan year, then the plan will remain restricted through the end of that plan year. Even if a plan was not restricted from making benefit payments in the prior plan year, but was within 10 percentage points of being restricted, and if the actuary has not certified by the first day of the fourth month of the current plan year, then the plan will be considered restricted until the actuary certifies otherwise. The actuary has up until the first day of the 10th month to make this certification otherwise the plan will remain restricted until the end of that plan year. [I.R.C. § 436(h)]

A *prohibited payment* is a benefit payment whose value is (1) in excess of the monthly amount of a straight life-only annuity; (2) the amount of the payment to purchase an irrevocable commitment from an insurer; or (3) anything else determined by Treasury. [I.R.C. § 436(d)(5)]

Restrictions on benefit payments do not apply during the first five years of a plan. [I.R.C. § 436(g)]

Participants must be given a notice within 30 days of when a benefit becomes restricted. There is a monetary sanction under ERISA Section § 502(c)(4) for failure to provide the notice. [ERISA § 101(j)]

### Q 19:118    What is the *adjusted funding target attainment percentage*?

The *adjusted funding target attainment percentage* is the regular FTAP, adjusted by adding back in the value of any annuities purchased by the plan for non-highly compensated participants during the past two years. In addition, it is determined by adding in as an asset any security provided by the plan sponsor. [I.R.C. § 436(j)(2)]

## Multiemployer Pension Plans

### Q 19:119    How is a funding deficiency determined for a multiemployer plan after December 31, 2007?

For purposes of Code Section 412, the accumulated funding deficiency of a multiemployer plan for any plan year is (1) except as provided in paragraph (2), the amount, determined as of the end of the plan year, equal to the excess (if any) of the total charges to the FSA of the plan for all plan years (beginning with the first plan year for which this part applies to the plan) over the total credits to such account for such years, and (2) if the multiemployer plan is in reorganization for any plan year, the accumulated funding deficiency of the plan determined under ERISA Section 4243.

### Q 19:120    Does a multiemployer plan still maintain a FSA?

Yes. Unlike a single employer plan, a multiemployer plan is still required to maintain a FSA.

## Q 19:121   What charges are made to the FSA?

For a plan year, the FSA shall be charged with the sum of:

(A) the normal cost of the plan for the plan year;

(B) the amounts necessary to amortize in equal annual installments (until fully amortized):

   (i) in the case of a plan which comes into existence on or after January 1, 2008, the unfunded past service liability under the plan on the first day of the first plan year to which this section applies, over a period of 15 plan years,

   (ii) separately, with respect to each plan year, the net increase (if any) in unfunded past service liability under the plan arising from plan amendments adopted in such year, over a period of 15 plan years,

   (iii) separately, with respect to each plan year, the net experience loss (if any) under the plan, over a period of 15 plan years, and

   (iv) separately, with respect to each plan year, the net loss (if any) resulting from changes in actuarial assumptions used under the plan, over a period of 15 plan years;

(C) the amount necessary to amortize each waived funding deficiency (within the meaning of Code Section 412(c)(3)) for each prior plan year in equal annual installments (until fully amortized) over a period of 15 plan years;

(D) the amount necessary to amortize in equal annual installments (until fully amortized) over a period of 5 plan years any amount credited to the FSA under Code Section 412(b)(3)(D) (as in effect on the day before the date of the enactment of the PPA); and

(E) the amount necessary to amortize in equal annual installments (until fully amortized) over a period of 20 years the contributions which would be required to be made under the plan but for the provisions of Code Section 412(c)(7)(A)(i)(I) (as in effect on the day before the date of the enactment of the PPA).

## Q 19:122   What credits are made to the FSA?

For a plan year, the FSA shall be credited with the sum of:

(A) The amount considered contributed by the employer to or under the plan for the plan year;

(B) The amount necessary to amortize in equal annual installments (until fully amortized):

   (i) separately, with respect to each plan year, the net decrease (if any) in unfunded past service liability under the plan arising from plan amendments adopted in such year, over a period of 15 plan years;

(ii) separately, with respect to each plan year, the net experience gain (if any) under the plan, over a period of 15 plan years; and

(iii) separately, with respect to each plan year, the net gain (if any) resulting from changes in actuarial assumptions used under the plan, over a period of 15 plan years;

(C) The amount of the waived funding deficiency (within the meaning of Code Section 412(c)(3)) for the plan year; and

(D) In the case of a plan year for which the accumulated funding deficiency is determined under the FSA if such plan year follows a plan year for which such deficiency was determined under the alternative minimum funding standard under Code Section 412(g) (as in effect on the day before the date of the enactment of the PPA), the excess (if any) of any debit balance in the FSA (determined without regard to this subparagraph) over any debit balance in the alternative minimum FSA.

### Q 19:123   What happens to the amortization bases that were in existence prior to 2008?

There is a special rule in the case of any amount amortized under Code Section 412(b) (as in effect on the day before the date of the enactment of the PPA) over any period beginning with a plan year beginning before 2008 in lieu of the amortization under the new law such amount shall continue to be amortized under Code Section 412(b) as it was in effect prior to the law change.

### Q 19:124   Can the new amortization bases be combined as under old law?

Possibly. Regulations are yet to be issued regarding this, but the PPA provides that, as the case may be, bases may be combined into one amount under such paragraph to be amortized over a period determined on the basis of the remaining amortization period for all items entering into such combined amount, and may be offset against amounts required to be amortized under the other such paragraph, with the resulting amount to be amortized over a period determined on the basis of the remaining amortization periods for all items entering into, whichever of the two amounts being offset is the greater.

### Q 19:125   Is there any special rule regarding what interest rate must or may be used in determining costs and crediting to contributions?

It looks like the rule hasn't changed for multiemployer plans from the old law. The FSA (and items therein) shall be charged or credited (as determined under regulations prescribed by the Secretary of the Treasury) with interest at the appropriate rate consistent with the rate or rates of interest used under the plan to determine costs.

## Q 19:126   Is there a full-funding limit for multiemployer plans?

Yes. The term *full-funding limitation* means the excess (if any) of:

(1) the accrued liability (including normal cost) under the plan (determined under the entry age normal funding method if such accrued liability cannot be directly calculated under the funding method used for the plan), over

(2) the lesser of:

  (a)  the fair market value of the plan's assets, or

  (b)  the value of such assets.

In no event shall the full-funding limitation be less than the excess (if any) of:

(1) 90 percent of the current liability of the plan (including the expected increase in current liability due to benefits accruing during the plan year), over

(2) the value of the plan's assets.

If, as of the close of a plan year, a plan would (without regard to this paragraph) have an accumulated funding deficiency in excess of the full-funding limitation:

(1) the FSA shall be credited with the amount of such excess, and

(2) all amortization bases shall be considered fully amortized.

For purposes of determining the full-funding limit, assets shall not be reduced by any credit balance in the FSA.

# Chapter 20

# Deductibility of Employer Contributions

One of the many tax advantages an employer gains by sponsoring a defined benefit pension plan is the ability to deduct contributions to the plan from taxable income, thereby lowering the amount of federal income taxes paid by the plan sponsor. Contributions to defined benefit pension plans must be compared to several limitations, to make certain that it is appropriate for the deduction to appear on the plan sponsor's federal tax return. This chapter outlines these limitations and the applicable time frames for making a deductible contribution to a plan. The Pension Protection Act of 2006 (PPA) made extensive changes to these rules. The end of the chapter contains the deduction rules that will become applicable to plan sponsors in 2008. Depending on what type of taxable entity the plan sponsor is, determining what amounts are deductible and by whom can become very complicated and require the assistance of the plan sponsor's accountant.

## Deduction Limits

### Q 20:1  What is the maximum deduction for an employer that maintains a defined benefit plan?

In general, an employer can deduct contributions to a defined benefit plan to the extent the contributions are equal to an amount no greater than one of the following limits:

1. *Code Section 404(a)(1)(A)(i).* The amount necessary to satisfy the minimum funding standard under Internal Revenue Code (Code) Section 412(a), if that amount is greater than the amount in item #2 or item #3 below;

2. *Code Section 404(a)(1)(A)(ii).* The amount necessary to provide any un-funded past- and current-service credits for all employees determined as a level amount, or a level percentage of compensation, over the remaining future service of each employee; or

3. *Code Section 404(a)(1)(A)(iii).* The amount of the normal cost for the plan year, plus the amount necessary to amortize the unfunded accrued liability fully in equal annual payments over 10 years (see Q 20:11).

These amounts are subject to the full-funding limitation (see Q 20:4) for the plan year determined under Code Section 412. [I.R.C. § 404(a)(1)(A)(i), (ii), (iii)]

*Rules for limit 1.* The amount required to satisfy the minimum funding standard account is increased by any contributions that were made to satisfy the minimum funding standard account in the prior plan year, but were not deducted in the prior tax year solely because they were contributed to the plan's assets after the time allowed for the employer to take a deduction (see Q 20:22). These contributions are known as *includible employer contributions.* [Treas. Reg. § 1.404(a)-14(e)(1)(ii)] If a contribution was not deductible for any other reason in addition to its being made late, then it is not considered an includible contribution and cannot be deducted under this limit.

**Example.** Franz, a self-employed person, sponsors the Do-It-On-My-Own Defined Benefit Plan. The minimum required contribution for the 2000 cal-endar plan year is $50,000. Franz reports a loss on his Schedule C (Form 1040) for 2000 and files his 2000 tax return before April 15, 2001. The $50,000 contribution is funded on May 1, 2001, in order to meet the minimum funding requirement. This amount would not be considered an includible contribution for the 2001 plan year, because it would not have been deduct-ible even if it had been made on time; therefore, its being deposited late is not the sole reason for it not being deductible in 2000. (See also IRS Q&A 4 at 2000 ASPPA Annual Conference.)

For plans using the alternative funding standard account, limit 1 is deter-mined as if the employer switched back to the regular funding standard account in the current year and then is increased by any includible employer contribu-tions. [Treas. Reg. § 1.404(a)-14(e)(2)]

*Rules for limit 2.* This amount is the level amount or level percentage of compensation needed to fund the benefits under the aggregate, individual aggregate, or individual level-premium funding method. [Examination Guidelines for I.R.C. § 404, IRM 1.2.1.2(1)(a)] If 50 percent of the unfunded cost is attributable to any three employees, the unfunded cost for those employees must be distributed over at least five years. This limit does not otherwise reduce the amount deductible under limit 1, that is, fewer than five future years can be used in determining the cost for purposes of Code Section 412 and it will still be deductible under limit 1.

*Rules for limit 3.* The normal cost plus the amount necessary to amortize the unfunded accrued liability is equal to the normal cost for the plan year plus the sum of the limit adjustments (see Q 20:10).

## Q 20:2   Is interest added to the calculation of the deduction limits?

Yes and no. In computing the deduction limits under Code Section 404(a)(1)(A)(ii) and (iii) (see Q 20:7), the normal cost and limit adjustments are adjusted for interest from the valuation date to the earlier of the last day of the plan year or the last day of the taxable year. [Treas. Reg. § 1.404(a)-14(f)(3)] There is no corresponding offset of interest credited to contributions made prior to the plan- or tax-year-end.

**Example 1.** The Bed Rock Defined Benefit Plan has a plan year ending December 31, 2000. The corresponding fiscal year for which the plan sponsor will be taking the deduction for that plan year ends June 30, 2000. The level cost under Code Section 404(a)(1)(A)(ii) is $100,000 as of January 1, 2000, and the plan valuation rate is 7 percent. The maximum deductible amount under Code Section 404(a)(1)(A)(ii) is calculated with interest, only up to June 30, 2000, which is $103,500 ($100,000 × 1.035).

This adjustment for interest is allowable only when the deduction limit is calculated under Code Section 404(a)(1)(A)(ii) or (iii). If the deduction limit is determined under Code Section 404(a)(1)(A)(i), interest is added to the minimum required contribution from the valuation date to the end of the plan year, but interest is also credited on contributions made before the end of the plan year, thus reducing the deductible amount, because the amount required to meet the minimum funding requirement is reduced by the interest on the advance contributions. [1992 Enrolled Actuaries Meeting Gray Book, Q&A 33]

**Example 2.** Flat Rock Inc. sponsors a defined benefit plan, and the taxable year and plan year both end on December 31, 2000. The maximum deductible amounts calculated under Code Section 404(a)(1)(A)(ii) and (iii) are under $35,000. The amount necessary to satisfy the minimum funding standard account is calculated as follows:

| | |
|---|---|
| Normal cost | $10,000 |
| Amortization charge | $30,000 |
| Interest | $ 3,216 |
| Other | $    200 |
| Total charges | $43,416 |

| Contributions | $43,416 |
|---|---|
| Interest | $ 1,737 |
| Total credits | $45,153 |
| Closing credit balance | $ 1,737 |

The amount deductible to Flat Rock Inc. is the amount necessary to satisfy the minimum funding standard account such that there would be no credit balance in the funding standard account at the end of the year. Therefore, part of the $43,416 contribution will not be deductible. If the contribution is made on July 1, 2000, and the valuation rate is 8 percent, the amount deductible would be limited to $41,746 ($43,416 ÷ 1.04). This contribution credited with interest to the end of the year would be just enough to satisfy the minimum funding requirement.

### Q 20:3   Can the deductible amount be affected by an amendment made pursuant to Code Section 412(c)(8)?

Yes. Any amendment that is given retroactive effect pursuant to Code Section 412(c)(8) made for minimum funding purposes (see chapter 19) also applies in determining the maximum deduction under all three of the limits (see Q 20:1). [2001 Enrolled Actuaries Meeting Gray Book, Q&A 2]

This is consistent with Treasury Regulations Section 1.404(a)-14(d)(1) which states that the calculation of the deductible limit is based on the same funding methods, actuarial assumptions, and benefit structure as used for purposes of Code Section 412.

### Q 20:4   How is the full-funding limitation under Code Section 412 calculated for purposes of the Section 404 deduction limits?

The full-funding limitation is the lesser of the following amounts, calculated as of the end of the plan year (even when the deduction limits under Code Section 404(a)(1)(A)(ii) and (iii) are computed as of the end of the taxable year of the employer):

1. The excess, if any, of 150 percent of the Omnibus Budget Reconciliation Act of 1987 (OBRA '87) current liability including the expected increase in current liability due to benefits accruing during the plan year, over the lesser of the fair market value of the plan's assets or the actuarial value of the plan's assets; or

2. The excess, if any, of the Employee Retirement Income Retirement Act of 1974 (ERISA) accrued liability plus normal cost, over the lesser of the fair market value of the plan's assets or the actuarial value of the plan's assets.

For plan years beginning after December 31, 1998, 150 percent is replaced with the following percentages:

| Plan year beginning in: | Percentage: |
|---|---|
| 1999 or 2000 | 155 |
| 2001 | 160 |
| 2002 | 165 |
| 2003 | 170 |
| 2004 and thereafter | Repealed |

If a plan uses a funding method that does not directly calculate an accrued liability, it must use the accrued liability and normal cost under the entry age normal funding method. [I.R.C. § 412(c)(7)(A)(i)]

*Minimum full-funding limitation.* In no event is the full-funding limitation less than the excess (if any), as of the end of the plan year, of 90 percent of the Retirement Protection Act of 1994 (RPA '94) current liability, including the expected increase in such current liability due to benefits accruing during the plan year, over the actuarial value of the plan's assets. [I.R.C. § 412(c)(7)]

*Adjustments to assets.* Assets are valued using the same method as that used for purposes of the minimum contribution requirement under Code Section 412, except that the assets are reduced by any previously undeducted contributions made to the plan's assets that have been used to satisfy the minimum funding standard account, and increased by any contributions that were deducted in prior years, but have yet to be used to satisfy the minimum funding standard account (see Q 20:7).

*Plans with more than 100 participants.* Plans with more than 100 participants that are subject to the additional funding charge under Code Section 412(l) can, regardless of the full-funding limitations set forth above, deduct the amount required to achieve 100 percent funding using the RPA '94 current liability (see Q 20:5). This limitation will apply to all plans, regardless of their size, beginning in plan years that start after December 31, 2001.

**Example.** MSKJ Inc. sponsors a defined benefit pension plan with 50 participants. The following data are used to determine the maximum deductible contribution to the plan. All amounts are as of the end of the plan year, December 31, 2002. The value of the plan assets is projected to the end of the plan year at the assumed interest rate for funding; all current liability values are projected to the end of the year at the interest rate used to determine each current liability.

| | |
|---|---|
| The amount needed to satisfy the minimum funding standard at the end of the plan year | $ 88,275 |
| Normal cost plus limit adjustments at the end of the plan year | $120,000 |

| | |
|---|---|
| Actuarial value of plan assets at the end of the plan year at the valuation interest rate | $750,000 |
| Market value of plan assets at the end of the plan year at the valuation interest rate | $725,000 |
| OBRA '87 current liability plus expected increase due to benefits earned during the year valued at the end of the plan year at the OBRA '87 interest rate | $500,000 |
| ERISA accrued liability plus normal cost increased with interest at the plan's valuation interest rate at the end of the plan year | $900,000 |
| RPA '94 current liability plus expected increase due to benefits earned during the year valued at the end of the plan year at the RPA '94 interest rate | $916,667 |

The plan's market value of assets is less than the actuarial value. Therefore, the market value is used in computing the full-funding limitations applicable to this plan (except for the RPA '94 minimum full-funding limitation, which always uses the actuarial value of the plan's assets).

*Step 1.* The maximum deductible contribution before the application of any full-funding limitation is the greater of the amount required to satisfy the minimum funding standard account ($88,275) or the plan's normal cost plus limit adjustments ($120,000).

*Step 2.* The largest amount in Step 1, $120,000, is limited by the full-funding limitations under Code Section 412. The OBRA '87 full-funding limitation is the excess, if any, of 165 percent of the plan's OBRA '87 current liability over the plan's assets. If the limitation amount is calculated as of the beginning of the plan year, it must be projected to the end of the plan year. Because the plan's valuation date is the first day of the plan year, the limitation is carried forward to the end of the plan year with interest at the OBRA '87 interest rate. The full-funding limitation in Step 2 is $50,000, calculated as follows:

| | |
|---|---|
| 165 percent of OBRA '87 current liability ($500,000 × 1.65) | $825,000 |
| Market value of assets | ($725,000) |
| OBRA '87 full-funding limitation | $100,000 |

*Step 3.* The ERISA full-funding limitation is the excess, if any, of the plan's ERISA accrued liability plus normal cost over the plan's assets. If the valuation date is the first day of the plan year, the limitation is carried forward to the end of the plan year with interest at the plan's funding interest rate. The full-funding limitation in Step 3 is $175,000, calculated as follows:

| | |
|---|---|
| ERISA accrued liability plus normal cost | $900,000 |
| Market value of assets | ($725,000) |
| ERISA full-funding limitation | $175,000 |

*Step 4.* The RPA '94 full-funding limitation is the excess, if any, of 90 percent of the plan's RPA '94 current liability over the actuarial value of the plan's

assets. If the valuation date is the first day of the plan year, the limitation is carried forward to the end of the plan year with interest at the RPA '94 interest rate. The full-funding limitation in Step 4 is $75,000, calculated as follows:

| | |
|---|---|
| 90 percent of RPA '94 current liability ($916,667 × 0.90) | $825,000 |
| Actuarial value of assets | ($750,000) |
| RPA '94 minimum full-funding Limitation | $ 75,000 |

*Step 5.* The amount in Step 1, $120,000, is limited by the lesser of $100,000 or $175,000, but in no event can be less than $75,000. Therefore, $100,000 is the plan's full-funding limitation and the maximum deductible contribution.

### Q 20:5 Under what circumstances can an employer deduct contributions made in an amount equal to the unfunded RPA '94 current liability?

The deductible contribution can be greater than the deduction limits (see Q 20:1) and full-funding limitations (see Q 20:4) only in the case of a defined benefit plan (other than a multiemployer plan) that has more than 100 participants for the plan year and for all plans for plan years beginning after December 31, 2001. In determining whether a plan has more than 100 participants, all defined benefit plans maintained by the employer (or any member of the employer's controlled group within the meaning of Code Section 412(l)(8)(C)) are treated as one plan, but only employees of the member or employer are taken into account. [I.R.C. § 404(a)(1)(D)]

> **Example.** If the employer in the example in Q 20:4 had more than 100 participants, the maximum deductible contribution would be increased to $166,667 (($825,000 ÷ .90) – $750,000). That amount is determined by subtracting the actuarial value of the plan's assets without adjustment for any credit balance in the funding standard account from the RPA '94 current liability, all determined as of the last day of the plan year. [I.R.C. § 412(l)(8)(A)(i), (ii); Rev. Rul. 82-125, 1982-1 C.B. 64]

The Pension Funding Equity Act of 2004 changed how the RPA '94 current liability was calculated. However, for purposes of determining the maximum deductible amount under Code Section 404(a)(1)(D), an employer may elect to disregard these changes. In effect, this allows an employer to choose the method that will provide the greatest deduction for the 2004 and 2005 plan years. Although it is not clear, it appears you may use the lower end of the 30-year Treasury rate range to calculate the RPA '94 current liability in determining the maximum deduction under Code Section 404, even though this is a different rate than that used on the Schedule B in determining the RPA '94 current liability for Code Section 412 purposes.

The PPA made a further increase to this deduction limit for 2006 and 2007 plan years in anticipation of increased minimum funding requirements beginning in 2008 (see chapter 19). For these plan years, a single employer defined benefit plan may deduct contributions up to 150 percent (140 percent for multiemployer plans) of the unfunded current liability as determined under Code Section 412(l)(8)(A). [PPA § 801(d)]

In determining the current liability for this purpose for any plan year, in the case of a plan which has 100 or fewer participants for the plan year, the liability of the plan attributable to benefit increases for highly compensated employees (as defined in Code Section 414(q)) resulting from a plan amendment that is made or becomes effective, whichever is later, within the last two years shall not be taken into account. Officials at the IRS have given their opinion that this two-year measurement is measured from the first day of the plan year and the immediate two prior years. In addition, any amendment that is adopted or made effective within those last two years is considered. [IRS Greybook 2002-3] The IRS has also given their opinion that the adoption of a new plan is considered an amendment for this purpose. [IRS Greybook 2006-14]

> **Example.** The deductible limit is being determined for a 2006 calendar plan year. Any amendments, including an initial adoption of the plan, made or effective in 2004 or 2005 that increased benefits to highly compensated employees must be excluded from this computation (but not the increase to non-highly compensated employees). In addition, if there was a Code Section 412(c)(8) amendment that was adopted in 2004, but applicable to 2003, would be considered to be within the two-year time period as well.

### Q 20:6 What is the deduction limit if an employer has both defined benefit plans and defined contribution plans?

If amounts contributed to one or more defined contribution plans and one or more defined benefit plans would be deductible except for the fact that the employer sponsors one or more defined contribution plans and one or more defined benefit plans, the total amount deductible in a taxable year under these plans cannot exceed the greater of the following amounts:

1. 25 percent of the compensation (as limited by Code Section 401(a)(17)) otherwise paid or accrued during the taxable year to the beneficiaries under the plans; or

2. The amount of contributions made to or under the defined benefit plans to the extent those contributions do not exceed the amount of employer contributions necessary to satisfy the minimum funding standard provided by Code Section 412 with respect to any such defined benefit plans for the plan year that ends with or within such taxable year (or any prior plan year).

These limits do not apply, however, if no employee is a beneficiary under more than one of the plans. [I.R.C. § 404(a)(7)(C)] Pursuant to Code Section 404(a)(7)(C)(ii), if there is an employer contribution (excluding employee deferrals) made to the defined contribution to which at least one employee is a participant in both the defined contribution and the defined benefit plans, then the 25 percent limitation will apply. However, if no employer contribution is made, then the 25 percent limitation will not apply.

Contributions made to the employer's 401(k) plan pursuant to the employee's election count toward the 25 percent limitation and reduce the compensation used in calculating item #1 only for plan years that begin on or before December 31, 2001. After such date, those contributions no longer count against the 25 percent limitation and they do not reduce the compensation used in determining this limit.

In the event the defined benefit plan has more than 100 participants (or for all plans for plan years that begin after December 31, 2001), item #2 can be no less than the amount of the unfunded RPA '94 current liability (see Q 20:5). [I.R.C. § 404(a)(7)(A)(i), (ii)]

For the 2006 and 2007 plan years, the PPA made a change to allow all plan sponsors to deduct up to 6 percent of compensation in a defined contribution plan in addition to a full defined benefit plan deduction, even if the combined amount is in excess of 25 percent of compensation. [I.R.C. § 404(a)(7)(C)(iii)] In addition, beginning in the 2008 plan year, if the defined benefit plan is covered by the Pension Benefit Guaranty Corporation (PBGC), then Code Section 404(a)(7) does not apply at all. [I.R.C. § 404(a)(7)(C)(iv)]

**Example.** The Colleen Company sponsors two qualified retirement plans: a defined benefit plan and a 401(k) profit-sharing plan. Both plans cover the same employee group, whose total compensation paid for the 2000 plan year is $2,625,000. The employer contribution requirement to satisfy Code Section 412 for the defined benefit plan is $425,000. The employees have contributed $125,000 in 401(k) contributions and the employer has matched the 401(k) contributions with a total of $31,250. The employer would like to contribute a maximum profit-sharing contribution to the extent it will be deductible. The total maximum deductible contribution to both plans is 25 percent of total compensation, or $625,000 (25% × ($2,625,000 − $125,000)), because $625,000 is greater than the amount required to satisfy the minimum funding standard ($425,000). The remaining deductible contribution that the employer can allocate as a profit-sharing contribution is $625,000 less the contribution to the defined benefit plan and the 401(k) and matching contributions, or $43,750 ($625,000 − $425,000 − $125,000 − $31,250 = $43,750).

If the maximum profit-sharing contribution was to be determined instead for the 2002 plan year using the same numbers, the 401(k) contributions would not reduce the total deductible amount. The total maximum deductible contribution to both plans is 25 percent of total compensation, or $656,250 (25% × $2,625,000). The remaining deductible contribution that the employer can allocate as a profit-sharing contribution is $656,250 less the contribution to the defined benefit plan and the matching contributions (and is not affected by the 401(k) contributions), or $200,000 ($656,250 − $425,000 − $31,250). The change in law allows the Colleen Company to make a much greater deductible contribution to the profit-sharing plan than was previously allowed.

It is unclear at the time of this writing how the law change would impact this example for the 2006 and 2007 plan years. Some practitioners believe that an employer can contribute an additional 6 percent of compensation on top of the 25 percent limit. Others believe that only if the defined benefit contribution exceeds 19 percent of compensation can the defined contribution amount then be 6 percent. Further guidance is needed from the IRS in order to answer this question.

Because 401(k) contributions do not count against the deductible limit, a 401(k) plan that allows only salary reduction contributions can always be sponsored by an employer in addition to a defined benefit plan even if contributions to the defined benefit plan exceed 25 percent of total compensation. However, it should be noted that the actual deferral percentage (ADP) test applicable to a 401(k) plan may be a concern as qualified nonelective contributions (QNECs) may not be deductible. Therefore, distributions of excess deferrals may be required in order to correct a failed ADP test.

### Q 20:7   How are plan assets valued for purposes of determining the deduction limits under Code Section 404?

Plan assets are valued for purposes of determining the Section 404 deduction limits using the same method as that used for purposes of determining the required contribution under Code Section 412.

Excluded from the total assets of the plan is the amount of any plan contribution that has not been previously deducted, even though that amount may have been credited to the funding standard account in a prior year (i.e., an undeducted contribution). In the case of a plan using the frozen initial liability or attained age normal funding method, the undeducted contribution is included in the unfunded accrued liability. Therefore, such plans ignore completely any adjustments to the assets or unfunded accrued liability as a result of undeducted contributions. [Treas. Reg. § 1.404(a)-14(d)(2)(i)]

Included in the total assets of the plan is the amount of any plan contribution that has been deducted with respect to a prior plan year, even though that contribution is used to credit the funding standard account for the current year (i.e., a deductible contribution made after the prior plan year). A plan using the frozen initial liability or attained age normal funding method excludes from the unfunded accrued liability of the plan, the amount of the deductible contribution. Therefore, such plans ignore completely any adjustments to the assets or unfunded accrued liability as a result of contributions deducted in prior years. [Treas. Reg. § 1.404(a)-14(d)(2)(ii)]

### Q 20:8   What amortization bases are developed for purposes of determining the deductible contribution under Code Section 404?

A plan using a funding method that develops an unfunded accrued liability must establish and account for a 10-year amortization base for each of the following:

1. Establishment or amendment of the plan;

2. Changes in actuarial assumptions;

3. Experience gains or losses; and

4. Change in funding method.

A base is established only if it is required under Code Section 412 as a result of the funding method used. If the funding method does not maintain an unfunded accrued liability, no base is established. No base is established under Code Section 404 as a result of a current liability full-funding credit.

### Q 20:9  How are the 10-year amortization bases developed?

The 10-year amortization bases equal the expected liability minus the actual liability with regard to each amendment, change in assumption, experience gain or loss, and change in funding method. Each base is amortized over 10 years using the plan's valuation interest rate for determining plan costs. Each time a 10-year amortization base is established, generally it must be separately maintained to determine when the unamortized amount of the base is zero. (See Q 20:12 for a discussion of the rules relating to how 10-year bases may be combined.) The sum of the unamortized balances of all 10-year bases must equal the plan's unfunded accrued liability. [Treas. Reg. § 1.404(a)-14(h)]

### Q 20:10  What is the *limit adjustment*?

The *limit adjustment* is the lesser of the 10-year amortization amount or the amount necessary to amortize a 10-year amortization base fully. The deduction limit under Code Section 404(a)(1)(A)(iii) is the normal cost plus the sum of the limit adjustments for each 10-year amortization base plus interest on those amounts to the end of the plan year, or to the end of the taxable year if the taxable year ends earlier than the plan year.

The 10-year amortization amount is determined by dividing the 10-year amortization base at the time it is established by the present value of an annuity due of $1 for 10 years at the plan's funding interest rate. If, for instance, a 10-year amortization base of $10,000 is established for a plan using a 7 percent interest rate, the value of the annuity due would be 7.51523 and the 10-year amortization amount would be $1,331 ($10,000 ÷ 7.51523).

### Q 20:11  How are 10-year amortization bases determined on a year-to-year basis?

For the first year, each 10-year amortization base equals the unfunded accrued liability that results from past-service credits for a newly adopted plan. In subsequent years, each base equals the unamortized amount of the base as of the valuation date in the prior plan year, plus interest at the valuation rate to the current valuation date, minus the allocated contribution with respect to the base for the prior plan year. [Treas. Reg. § 1.404(a)-14(h)(3)]

The *valuation date* is the date as of which plan liabilities are valued under Code Section 412. If a valuation is performed less often than annually for purposes of Code Section 412, the amortization bases must be adjusted for purposes of Code Section 404 each year as of the date on which a Section 412 valuation would be performed if it was required on an annual basis. [Treas. Reg. § 1.404(a)-14(h)(3)]

The *allocated contribution* is the portion of the total contribution for the prior plan year allocated to each base. The portion allocated to each base equals the product of the total contribution and the ratio of the 10-year amortization amount to the total of all 10-year amortization amounts for all remaining bases. If, however, the result of this computation with respect to a particular base exceeds the amount necessary to amortize that base fully, the smaller amount should be deemed as the contribution made with respect to that base. The unallocated excess with respect to a now fully amortized base should be allocated among the other bases as indicated above, treating the unallocation excess as if it were an additional contribution. [Treas. Reg. § 1.404(a)-14(h)(4)]

The *total contribution* for purposes of determining the allocated contribution is the sum of the following reduced by the value of the prior year's normal cost as of the end of the prior plan year and interest on the normal cost to the current valuation date:

1. The total deduction, including any carryover deduction (see Q 20:28), for the prior plan year;
2. The interest on the actual contributions credited to the funding standard account for the prior plan year from the date they were credited to the funding standard account to the current valuation date; and
3. The interest on the carryover deduction (see Q 20:28) available as of the beginning of the prior plan year to the current valuation date.

The total contribution can be expressed as follows:

Total contribution  =  Total prior year deduction + Interest on Section 412 contributions + Interest on available carryover deduction – Normal cost as of end of prior plan year with interest to current valuation date

[Treas. Reg. § 1.404(a)-14(h)(6)]

**Example.** Ken Company sponsors a defined benefit pension plan that uses the unit credit funding method to determine plan costs. Three 10-year amortization bases are currently being maintained and amortized at an interest rate of 7 percent: an initial unfunded accrued liability, an unfunded accrued liability due to a plan amendment, and an actuarial gain. The total unfunded accrued liability as of the last valuation date was $266,000, the current year's normal cost is $18,000, and the total contribution as defined above was $60,000. To account for the amortization bases in the current year, the following steps are taken:

*Step 1.* The $60,000 total contribution is allocated in proportion to the 10-year amortization amounts (i.e., column B divided by the total of column B).

| | A<br>Initial<br>10-Year<br>Base | B<br>10-Year<br>Amortization<br>Amount | C<br>Total<br>Contribution | D<br>Ratio of<br>Total (as<br>Percentage) | E = C × D<br>Allocated<br>Contribution |
|---|---|---|---|---|---|
| Initial unfunded accrued liability | $400,000 | $53,225 | $60,000 | 88.89% | $53,334 |
| Plan amendment | $ 75,000 | $ 9,980 | $60,000 | 16.67% | $10,002 |
| Actuarial gain | ($ 25,000) | ($ 3,327) | $60,000 | −5.56% | −$ 3,336 |
| Total | | $59,878 | | 100.00% | $60,000 |

*Step 2.* The allocated contribution is subtracted from the prior year's outstanding balance of the 10-year amortization base increased with interest. That result is the current year's 10-year amortization base.

| | A<br><br>Prior Year's<br>10-Year Base<br>Unamortized | B = A × 0.07<br><br>Plus<br>Interest for<br>One Year | C<br><br>Less<br>Allocated<br>Contribution | A + B − C<br>Current<br>Year's<br>10-Year<br>Base<br>Unamortized |
|---|---|---|---|---|
| Initial unfunded accrued liability | $225,000 | $15,750 | $53,334 | $187,416 |
| Plan amendment | $ 60,000 | $ 4,200 | $10,002 | $ 54,198 |
| Actuarial gain | ($ 19,000) | ($ 1,330) | −$ 3,336 | −$ 16,994 |
| Total | $266,000 | $18,620 | $60,000 | $224,620 |

*Step 3.* The new 10-year base to be established as a result of changes in the unfunded accrued liability over the last year is determined. In this example, the actuary has determined that an actuarial loss of $5,000 occurred over the last plan year. This amount represents a new 10-year amortization base to be added to the unamortized bases in Step 2. Hence, the 10-year base as of the valuation date is $229,620 ($224,620 + $5,000).

*Step 4.* The 10-year amortization of $5,000 at 7 percent is determined. In this case, that amount is $665 ($5,000 ÷ 7.51523).

*Step 5.* The sum of the limit adjustments for the year is determined. The limit adjustment of each base is the lesser of the 10-year amortization amount or the remaining balance of the 10-year amortization base.

|  | A<br>Current Year's<br>10-Year Base<br>Unamortized | B<br>10-Year<br>Amortization<br>Amount | C<br>Lesser of<br>A or B Limit<br>Adjustment |
|---|---|---|---|
| Initial unfunded accrued Liability | $187,416 | $53,225 | $53,225 |
| Plan amendment | $ 54,198 | $ 9,980 | $ 9,980 |
| Actuarial gain | ($ 16,994) | ($ 3,327) | ($ 3,327) |
| Actuarial loss | $ 5,000 | $ 665 | $ 665 |
| Total | $229,620 | $60,543 | $60,543 |

*Step 6.* The plan's normal cost plus the limit adjustments for the unfunded accrued liability under Code Section 404(a)(1)(A)(iii) is $78,543 ($18,000 + $60,543). That amount as of the end of the year is $84,041, determined by adding interest at 7 percent of $5,498.

## Q 20:12   Other than separate accounting, what accounting methods are available for maintaining the 10-year amortization base and amount?

An employer can combine all of the 10-year bases that were previously accounted for separately into a single base (see Example 1) or start fresh by using, as the 10-year base and 10-year amortization amount, the unfunded accrued liability in the current year (see Example 2). [Treas. Reg. § 1.404(a)-14(i)]

**Example 1.** Combine all unamortized 10-year bases. The actuary for Ken Company in the example in Q 20:11 is asked to combine all of the 10-year amortization bases into a single base and amortization amount for purposes of determining the deduction limit under Code Section 404(a)(1)(A)(iii). To do this the actuary combines the bases as follows:

*Step 1.* The unamortized amount of the new single base equals the sum of all unamortized bases as of the valuation date. The total of the unamortized bases for Ken Company is $229,620, found in Step 5 of the example in Q 20:11.

*Step 2.* Based on the unamortized amount of each base, the actuary determines that if the current 10-year amortization amount is applied to each base until the base is fully amortized, each base would be fully amortized within 3.870 years, 6.488 years, 2.187 years, and 10 years, respectively. The years remaining are determined using the following formula:

$$\text{Years remaining} = \text{Ln}(1 - (i \times v \times A/B)) \div \text{Ln}(v)$$

where

$i$ = the plan's funding interest rate

$v = 1/(1+i)$

$A$  = unamortized 10-year base

B = 10-year amortization payment

Ln = natural logarithm of the amount in the parentheses

In the table that follows, 3.870 was determined as follows:

$$\text{Years remaining at 7\%} = \text{Ln}(1 - (0.07 \times 1/1.07$$
$$\times\ 187{,}416/53{,}225)) \div \text{Ln}(1/1.07)$$
$$= \text{Ln}(0.76964) \div \text{Ln}(0.93458)$$
$$= -0.26183 \div -0.06766$$
$$= 3.870$$

|  | A<br>Current Year's<br>10-Year Base<br>Unamortized | B<br>10-Year<br>Amortization<br>Amount | C<br>Years<br>Remaining |
|---|---|---|---|
| Initial unfunded<br>accrued Liability | $187,416 | $53,225 | 3.870 |
| Plan amendment | $ 54,198 | $ 9,980 | 6.488 |
| Actuarial gain | ($ 16,994) | ($ 3,327) | 2.187 |
| Actuarial loss | $ 5,000 | $ 665 | 10 |
| Total | $229,620 | $60,543 | |

*Step 3.* The absolute values of the unamortized bases are totaled, and the absolute values of the unamortized bases multiplied by the years remaining until the bases are fully amortized, are totaled.

| A<br>Years<br>Remaining | B<br>Absolute<br>Value<br>Unamortized | C = A × C<br>Step 3<br>Result |
|---|---|---|
| 3.870 | $187,416 | $725,300 |
| 6.488 | $ 54,198 | $351,637 |
| 2.187 | $ 16,994 | $ 37,166 |
| 10 | $ 5,000 | $ 50,000 |
| Total | $263,608 | $1,164,103 |

*Step 4.* The total result in Step 3, column C, is divided by the total result in Step 3, column B: $1,164,103 ÷ $263,608 = 4.416. This is the new amortization period for the single base calculated in Step 1. It can be expressed in fractional years or rounded off.

*Step 5.* The new 10-year amortization amount is calculated as the payment that would fully amortize the amount in Step 1 over the number of years determined in Step 4. In this case a payment of $58,161 would fully amortize $229,620 in 4.416 years at a rate of 7 percent ($229,620 ÷ 3.9480).

*Step 6.* The new 10-year amortization payment is the smaller of the total unamortized 10-year bases, $229,620, or the redetermined 10-year amortization amount in Step 5, $58,161. Hence, the new 10-year amortization amount or limit adjustment is $61,452.

The plan's normal cost plus limit adjustment for the unfunded accrued liability under Code Section 404(a)(1)(A)(iii) is $76,161 ($18,000 + $58,161). That amount as of the end of the year is $81,492 determined by adding interest at 7 percent of $5,331.

**Example 2.** Fresh start 10-year base and amortization amount. The simplest method for combining all 10-year amortization bases is to calculate the unfunded accrued liability as of the valuation date and amortize this amount over 10 years at the plan's interest rate. Based on the data from the example in Q 20:11, the unfunded accrued liability is $229,620 after adding the actuarial loss of $5,000 over the past year. This amount would be fully amortized at a rate of 7 percent over 10 years with a payment of $30,554. [Treas. Reg. § 1.404(a)-14(i)(5)]

The difference in the amount of the deductible contributions using the three different accounting techniques for the 10-year amortization bases should be noted.

| Example | Normal Cost | Limit Adjustment | Interest | Total |
|---|---|---|---|---|
| Example in Q 20:11 | $18,000 | $60,543 | $5,498 | $84,041 |
| Example 1 | $18,000 | $56,161 | $5,331 | $76,161 |
| Example 2 | $18,000 | $30,554 | $3,399 | $51,953 |

## Q 20:13   What happens to the accounting of the 10-year amortization bases and amounts if the funding interest rate is changed in the current plan year?

If the funding interest rate is changed in the current plan year, a new limit adjustment is calculated for all of the remaining 10-year amortization bases. The *new limit adjustment* is the lesser of the outstanding balance of the 10-year amortization base or the amount needed to amortize the outstanding balance of the 10-year amortization base at the new interest rate over the number of years remaining to amortize the base fully at the prior 10-year amortization amount. [Treas. Reg. § 1.404(a)-14(h)(8)]

**Example.** A plan with two 10-year amortization bases has changed its funding interest rate from 6 percent to 7 percent. The outstanding balances of the 10-year bases as of the beginning of the current plan year are $150,000 and $125,000, with the $125,000 base being the new base created at the beginning of the plan year. The 10-year amortization amount established at the time of the $150,000 base was $25,635 at 6 percent.

*Step 1.* Determine the years remaining to amortize the old 10-year amortization base fully, $150,000, at the old interest rate using the following formula:

$$\text{Years remaining} = Ln(1 - (i \times v \times A/B)) \div Ln(v)$$

where

> $i$  = the plan's old funding interest rate
>
> $v$  = $1/(1+i)$
>
> $A$ = unamortized 10-year base
>
> $B$ = Old 10-year amortization payment
>
> $Ln$ = natural logarithm of the amount in the parentheses

There are 6.9 remaining years for the $150,000 base, determined as follows:

$$\text{Years remaining at 6 percent} = Ln(1 - (0.06 \times 1/1.06$$
$$\times\ 150,000/25,635)) \div Ln(1/1.06)$$
$$= Ln(0.66879) \div Ln(0.9434)$$
$$= -0.40229 \div -0.05827$$
$$= 6.9 \text{ years}$$

*Step 2.* Determine the new 10-year amortization amount for each outstanding 10-year base at the new interest rate over the remaining years.

*$150,000 base.* The present value of an annuity due of $1 at 7 percent interest over 6.9 years is 5.70. Thus, the new 10-year amortization amount is $26,316 ($150,000 ÷ 5.70).

*$125,000 base.* Because this base was created in the current year, 10 years remain to amortize this amount fully. The present value of an annuity due of $1 at 7 percent interest over 10 years is 7.52. Thus, the new 10-year amortization amount is $16,622 ($125,000 ÷ 7.52).

*Step 3.* Determine the limit adjustment for each 10-year amortization base as the lesser of the outstanding balance of each 10-year amortization base or the 10-year amortization amount. Here, the 10-year amortization amounts are smaller in each case; hence, the limit adjustments will be $23,316 and $16,622 at the new interest rate.

[Treas. Reg. § 1.404(a)-14(h)(8)]

### Q 20:14  How do the unfunded accrued liability and the outstanding balance of the 10-year amortization payments relate to each other?

The unfunded accrued liability equals the present value of future benefits minus the present value of future normal costs minus the actuarial value of the assets. For purposes of the Section 404(a)(1)(A)(iii) limit, the unfunded accrued liability equals the net sum of the outstanding balance of the 10-year amortization bases minus any prior nondeducted contributions that are in the value of the assets plus deducted prior contributions that have not been included in the actuarial value of the assets for minimum funding purposes. [Treas. Reg. § 1.404(a)-14(h)(1)]

### Q 20:15   What happens to the 10-year amortization bases if the plan is subject to the full-funding limitation for the plan year?

If the deductible contribution for the plan year, inclusive of any prior carryover contributions (see Q 20:28), is limited by the ERISA full-funding limitation, all 10-year amortization bases are considered fully amortized and the deduction limit in the subsequent plan year is not adjusted to reflect the fully amortized bases. In the subsequent plan year, a new 10-year amortization base must be established for an experience gain or loss, and for any amendments or assumption changes in that year. [Treas. Reg. § 1.404(a)-14(k)]

### Q 20:16   Can an employer deduct contributions made to fully fund a plan on termination?

*For plan years that begin on or before December 31, 2001:*

Employer contributions to a defined benefit plan that are made in an amount sufficient to fully fund a plan on termination may be deductible depending on the level of the plan's benefits and the number of employees on the date of plan termination. Employers with more than 100 participants can contribute up to the unfunded RPA '94 current liability on a deductible basis. Generally, that amount is less than the plan's unfunded termination liability; therefore, only part of the contribution may be deductible. If benefits under a terminating plan are less than the amounts guaranteed by the PBGC as determined by ERISA Section 4022, a contribution to fully fund the plan may be deductible. [I.R.C. § 404(g)(3)(B)] If benefits under a plan are greater than the guaranteed benefits, the contribution made to fund the excess of those benefits will not be deductible under Code Section 404(g); however, it may be deductible under Code Section 404(a) (see Q 20:1).

If a contribution is made to fully fund all liabilities on termination and a portion of the contribution is not deductible, a 10 percent excise tax applies, but only for the year of the contribution (see Q 20:23). The portion that was nondeductible in the year of termination can be deducted ratably over the next 10 years. [Treas. Reg. § 1.404(a)-6(b)]

*For plan years that begin after December 31, 2001:*

Plans that are covered by the PBGC (see chapter 24) are allowed to contribute on a deductible basis that amount required to make the plan sufficient for all benefit liabilities. [I.R.C. § 404(a)(1)(D)(iv)] The IRS has informally stated that the plan may use the benefit liabilities as of the distribution date for determining the deductible limit under this provision, even if it is after the end of the plan year. [2004 ASPPA Annual Conference, IRS Q&A 5] Plans that are not covered by the PBGC are only allowed to make a contribution under the normal applicable limits regardless of whether the plan is terminating.

### Q 20:17   How are deduction limits determined for multiple employer plans?

For multiple employer plans established after 1988, the deduction limits in Code Section 404(a) are applied as if each employer were maintaining a separate plan. [I.R.C. § 413(c)(4)(A)] For plans established before 1989, the administrator of the plan could elect to have the plan treated as one maintained by separate employers. That election had to be made on the Schedule B of IRS Form 5500 filed for the first plan year beginning after November 10, 1988. Once such an election was made, it could not be revoked by the administrator without the consent of the Secretary of the Treasury.

### Q 20:18   Are there any special deduction limits for Section 412(i) plans?

Yes. Generally, an employer can pay and deduct premiums for an insurance contract described in Code Section 412(i). The premium (normal cost) for purposes of applying Code Section 404(a)(1)(A)(iii) and (2) cannot exceed a premium amount based on assumptions and methods that are reasonable in view of the provisions and coverage of the plan, the funding medium, reasonable expectations about the effects of mortality and interest, reasonable and adequate regard for other factors such as withdrawal and deferred retirement that can be expected to reduce costs materially, reasonable expenses of operation, and all other relevant conditions and circumstances. [Treas. Reg. § 1.404(a)-3(b)] Changes in methods, factors, and assumptions cannot be made in a subsequent tax year unless the changes are deemed proper or required by the Commissioner.

For a defined benefit plan that was subject to the minimum funding requirements of Code Section 412 and subsequently converted to a Section 412(i) plan, the employer's deduction limit with respect to the conversion year and succeeding plan years is the sum of the following:

1. The normal cost for the Section 412(i) plan established on the conversion date for post-conversion benefit accruals;
2. The lesser of the unamortized balance of any 10-year amortization bases or the 10-year amortization payments for any 10-year amortization bases remaining unamortized as of the conversion date that were maintained for purposes of Code Section 404(a)(1)(A)(iii) (see Q 20:9); and
3. The 10-year amortization payment, if any, for any 10-year amortization base created on account of treating the plan as if it terminated for purposes of Code Section 412 as of the last day of the plan year immediately preceding the conversion year (preconversion year).

The normal cost is based on the annual premiums for level annual premium contracts providing for the post-conversion benefit accruals (and any increases in benefits) that are reasonable in view of the funding medium and reasonable expectations as to the effects of mortality, interest, and other pertinent factors. [Rev. Rul. 94-75, 1994-2 C.B. 59]

## Timing of Contributions and Deductions

### Q 20:19   Does the plan need to be in existence before the end of the employer's fiscal year to take a deduction for that fiscal year?

Yes. The IRS in Revenue Ruling 81-114 [1981-1 C.B. 207] stated that a plan must be in existence as of the last day of the employer's taxable year to take a deduction for that taxable year.

> **Example.** Bed Rock Inc. has a fiscal year ending September 30, 2000, and adopts a defined benefit plan on December 30, 2000, with a plan year ending December 31, 2000. Bed Rock cannot take a deduction for the first plan year on its September 30, 2000, tax return.

### Q 20:20   Does the employer need to make a contribution before the end of the plan year to establish a valid trust?

No. A deduction is allowable under Code Section 404(a) for contributions paid after the close of the taxable year, but within the time prescribed for filing the employer's income tax return, even if the trust does not have a corpus at the close of the employer's preceding fiscal year. [Rev. Rul. 81-114, 1981-1 C.B. 207]

### Q 20:21   Can a cash-basis taxpayer deduct a contribution made after the fiscal year?

Yes. Cash-basis and accrual-basis taxpayers can deduct contributions made after the end of the fiscal year provided the contribution is on account of that taxable year and is made to the plan's assets no later than the due date for filing the employer's federal tax return with extensions. [I.R.C. § 404(a)(6)] For a contribution made after the close of the taxable year to be on account of that taxable year, the plan must treat the contribution as if it were made during that taxable year. In addition, the employer must either (1) designate in writing to the plan administrator or trustee that the contribution is on account of the employer's preceding taxable year, or (2) claim the contribution as a deduction on the tax return for that preceding taxable year. [Rev. Rul. 76-28, 1976-1 C.B. 106]

In Letter Ruling 200311036, the IRS ruled that, although an employer had designated in writing to the trustee that a particular contribution was on account of the current year, the employer could change this designation because the employer had not yet filed its tax return.

### Q 20:22  When must contributions be made in order to be deductible?

Contributions to a defined benefit plan can be deducted for a taxable year if the contribution is deposited to the plan's assets no later than the due date for filing the tax return for that taxable year (including extensions). [I.R.C. § 404(a)(6)] Although the deposit may be timely for deduction purposes, it may not be timely for purposes of satisfying the minimum funding standard. Conversely, a deposit may be timely for purposes of satisfying the minimum funding standard and may not be timely for deduction purposes.

> **Example.** Fred Flintrock is a sole proprietor and sponsors a defined benefit plan. If his tax return for 2000 is not on extension, he must make contributions by April 15, 2001, in order to deduct them on his 2000 tax return. If Fred makes the contributions after April 15, 2001, but before September 15, 2001, the contributions will be timely for purposes of satisfying the minimum funding standard for 2000 but must be deducted in 2001. Conversely, if Fred's tax return is on extension until October 15, 2001, and the contributions are made on this date, they will be timely for deduction purposes but not for purposes of satisfying the minimum funding standard for 2000.

If the employer files for an extension of time to file its tax return and then files its return before the original filing date, the due date for deductible contributions is the extended due date. [Rev. Rul. 66-144, 1966-1 C.B. 91] If, however the employer first files its tax return and then applies for an extension of time, the IRS has ruled that the extension is not valid for purposes of increasing the time for making deductible contributions to the plan. [Ltr. Rul. 8336006]

### Q 20:23  What is the penalty for contributing nondeductible amounts to a plan?

For any qualified employer plan, the penalty is a tax equal to 10 percent of the nondeductible contributions under the plan (determined as of the close of the taxable year of the employer). The term *nondeductible contributions* means the sum of the following amounts:

1. The excess, if any, of the amount contributed for the taxable year by the employer to or under the plan over the amount allowable as a deduction under Code Section 404 for such contributions; and

2. The amount of any prior year's nondeductible contributions, reduced by the sum of any nondeductible contributions returned to the employer during the taxable year and the portion returned of that amount so determined as deductible for the taxable year.

[I.R.C. § 4972(a), (c)(1)]

The tax is calculated on IRS Form 5330, Return of Excise Taxes for Employee Plans, and must be paid by the last day of the seventh month after the end of the taxable year.

**Example.** KL Banking makes a $200,000 contribution to its pension plan in 1998. The maximum deductible amount for 1998 is $175,000. In 1997 the bank made $15,000 in nondeductible contributions, and before the end of the 1998 tax year, $10,000 in nondeductible contributions were returned to KL Banking. The new nondeductible contribution to which the 10 percent excise tax applies for the 1998 taxable year is $30,000 (($200,000 − $175,000) + ($15,000 − ($10,000 + $0))). Hence the excise tax for 1998 is $3,000 ($30,000 × 10%).

*Exemption from excise tax for pre-1987 carryforward.* Any nondeductible contributions that existed as of December 31, 1986, are not subject to the 10 percent excise tax. Therefore, if any employer has been unable to deduct any of these amounts in any year since 1986, those amounts are not subject to the tax. [I.R.C. § 4972(c)(5)]

*Exemption from excise tax for terminating plan (for plan years that begin on or before December 31, 2001).* Any contributions made up to the RPA '94 unfunded current liability, even if the plan has less than 100 participants, to a plan that is covered by the PBGC plan termination insurance program in a plan year during which the plan is terminated under a standard termination procedure are not counted in determining nondeductible contributions for the taxable year. [I.R.C. § 4972(c)(6)(A)]

*Exemption from excise tax for employers with more than 100 participants sponsoring defined benefit and defined contribution plans.* If an employer sponsors both a defined benefit plan and a defined contribution plan and has more than 100 participants in the defined benefit plan, and contributions to these plans would be nondeductible because of the 25 percent of compensation limitation (see Q 20:6), the excise tax will not apply to nondeductible contributions to the defined contribution plan only if they do not exceed the greater of (1) 6 percent of compensation paid or accrued to beneficiaries under the plan, or (2) the sum of matching contributions and salary deferrals. [I.R.C. § 4972(c)(6)(B)]

*Exemption from excise tax for sole proprietors.* If a sole proprietor is required to make a contribution that is in excess of earned income for the taxable year in order to avoid a funding standard account deficiency, the excess will not be considered in determining nondeductible contributions. [I.R.C. § 4972(c)(4)]

*Exemption from excise tax for sound pension funding (for plan years that begin after December 31, 2001).* Contributions up to the ERISA full-funding limitation, even if they exceed the deductible limit, will not be considered in determining nondeductible contributions. The deductible limits under Code Section 404(a)(7) shall first be applied to amounts contributed to defined contribution plans and then to amounts described in this paragraph. If an employer makes an election to contribute up to the full-funding limit in the defined benefit plan using these rules, then the exemption provided under Code

Section 4972(c)(6) shall not apply to such employer for such taxable year. [I.R.C. § 4972(c)(7)] This Code Section was amended effective August 17, 2006, to apply the full-funding limitation cap only to multiemployer plans.

### Q 20:24   Under what circumstances can a plan return contributions from plan assets to an employer?

Contributions can be returned to an employer other than to one that participates in a multiemployer plan if the contribution was made by reason of mistake of fact, if the plan fails to qualify initially under Code Section 401(a), or if the contribution is not deductible under Code Section 404. [I.R.C. § 4980(c)(2)(B)(ii)(II), (III)] Nondeductible contributions can be returned to the employer by the last day that the employer could have made a deductible contribution to the plan. [I.R.C. § 4972(c)(3)]

Nondeductible contributions must be disallowed by the IRS before they can be returned to the employer. The plan administrator, sponsor, or authorized representative can make a request for a determination that the employer contribution be nondeductible if it is claimed as a deduction for purposes of determining whether it can be returned to the employer without adversely affecting the qualified status of the plan. There is a *de minimis* amount of $25,000 that can be reverted without specifically applying for a ruling as long as certain other requirements are met. [Rev. Proc. 90-49, 1990-2 C.B. 620]

### Q 20:25   Under what circumstances may excess contributions be returned to an employer in a multiemployer plan?

In a multiemployer plan, the employer making the contribution or withdrawal liability payment must demonstrate that an excessive contribution or overpayment has been made due to a mistake of fact or law. The contribution or payment must be returned within six months after the date on which the plan administrator determines that a mistake occurred, by filing a claim with the plan administrator.

The amount to be returned to the employer is the excess of the amount contributed or paid over the amount that would have been contributed or paid, had no mistake been made. Interest or earnings attributable to an excess contribution are not returned to the employer, and any losses attributable to an excess contribution must reduce the amount returned to the employer. The application of plan wide investment experience to the excess contribution would be an acceptable method of calculating losses.

Excess withdrawal liability payments, if in accordance with the PBGC regulations regarding the overpayments of withdrawal liability, may be returned to the employer with interest.

In general, if the amount of the excess contribution or overpayment was deducted by the employer in a prior year, then this amount must be included in gross income by the employer in the year it is withdrawn. Any interest credited or paid on the refund of mistaken withdrawal liability payments must also be included in gross income by the employer.

An excess contribution returned is charged to the funding standard account under Code Section 412 in the year in which the amount is returned. [Treas. Reg. § 1.401(a)(2)-1]

### Q 20:26 How does an employer have contributions disallowed by the IRS?

Revenue Procedure 90-49 [1990-2 C.B. 620] provides the mechanism to follow in order to have nondeductible contributions effectively disallowed by the IRS, thereby allowing the employer to distribute them from the trust and return them. This revenue procedure was developed in response to a plan having made quarterly contributions (see chapter 19), only to find out later that the full-funding limit applied for the year, making those contributions nondeductible. The following information needs to accompany this request:

1. The location of the office of the district director of internal revenue having jurisdiction over the plan, the employer identification number, the plan name and number, and the name and address of the plan administrator or plan sponsor.

2. A copy of the last actuarial valuation report, and a copy of the last Schedule B of Form 5500, including attachments thereto, that has been filed with the IRS.

3. The plan year for which the request is made (e.g., January 1, 2001, through December 31, 2001).

4. A list of the employer contributions actually paid in each month, from the 12th month before the beginning of the plan year for which the disallowance is requested through the date of the request and the plan year to which the contributions were applied.

5. A worksheet, signed by the enrolled actuary for the plan, following the format of the worksheet shown in Figure 20-1. This worksheet includes the calculation of the full-funding limitation, the amount of the reversion due to the employer as a result of the disallowance of the deduction of the employer contribution, and a certification by the enrolled actuary attesting to the accuracy of this information. The maximum amount that may be returned to the employer is the excess of (a) the amount contributed over (b) the amount that would have been contributed had the contribution been limited to the amount that is deductible. Earnings attributable to the excess contribution may not be returned to the employer, but losses attributable thereto must reduce the amount to be returned.

6. A copy of the current plan document, and a reference to the appropriate section in the plan document that permits the return of employer contributions.

7. Documentation that employer contributions are conditioned on deductibility. A copy of a board resolution will suffice for such documentation as

will plan language, provided employer contributions are conditioned on deductibility.

8. A statement as to whether the contributions for which a disallowance is being requested have been deducted on any tax return of the employer.

The request is mailed to the following address:

Internal Revenue Service
Attention: EP Letter Rulings
P.O. Box 27063
McPherson Station
Washington, DC 20038

[Rev. Proc. 2002-8, 2002-1 I.R.B. 252]

Within 90 days from the receipt of a complete request, the IRS will either contact the applicant to obtain more information or issue a form letter approving the request. A copy of this approval letter must be attached to the Schedule B of the Form 5500 that is filed for the plan year for which the disallowance is effective. The form letter will contain the caveat that the IRS has considered the disallowance of employer contributions solely for the purpose of applying Revenue Ruling 77-200. [1977-1 C.B. 98]

If the request for the disallowance of a nondeductible employer contribution is approved, and if the nondeductible contributions are returned to the employer before the Schedule B for the plan year in which the contribution was made is filed, the contribution is not reported on the Schedule B. If the nondeductible contribution is returned to the employer after the Schedule B for the plan year in question is filed, the contribution most be reported and credited under Code Section 412 on that Schedule B. However, the nondeductible contribution for which the funding standard account was credited under Code Section 412 creates an offsetting charge to the funding standard account on the Schedule B for the year in which the nondeductible contribution is returned.

### Figure 20-1. Actuarial Certification Worksheet

**Actuarial Certification**

Section 1. Full-Funding Limitation Calculation
Valuation Date: _____

I. ERISA Full-Funding Limitation

1.  Accrued liability:                                    _____
2.  Normal cost as of _____:                            _____
3.  Applicable interest on (1) and (2) to end of year    _____
    at valuation interest rate of _____%:
4.  (1) + (2) + (3):                                     _____
5.  Plan assets:                                          _____

6.     Applicable interest on (5) to end of year at valuation interest rate of _____%:       _____

7.     (5) + (6):       _____

8.     ERISA full-funding limitation ((4) − (7)):       _____

## II. Current Liability Full-Funding Limitation

9.     Current liability (including present value of benefit accruing during the current year):       _____

10.     Applicable interest on (9) to end of year at current liability interest rate of _____%:       _____

11.     Expected payments during current year:       _____

12.     Applicable interest on (11) to end of year at current liability interest rate of _____%:       _____

13.     (9) + (10) − (11) − (12):       _____

14.     Applicable percentage (165% for 2002) of (13):       _____

15.     Applicable interest on (11) to end of year at valuation interest rate of _____%:       _____

16.     (7) − (11) − (15):       _____

17.     Current liability full-funding limitation: ((14) − (16)):       _____

## III. RPA '94 Current Liability Full-Funding Limit

18.     RPA '94 current liability as of _____:       _____

19.     Expected current liability increase:       _____

20.     Interest on (18) and (19):       _____

21.     Expected benefit payments:       _____

22.     .90 × ((18) + (19) + (20) − (21)):       _____

23.     (7) − (21) − (22):       _____

24.     Section 412(c)(7)(E) full-funding limit amount:       _____

## IV. Full-Funding Limitation

25.     Lesser of (8) or (17), but not less than (24):       _____

## Section 2. Amount of Reversion to Employer

Plan Year Commencing:

1.     Employer Contributions:       _____

2.     Full-Funding Limitation:       _____

3.     Amount of Reversion due to Employer:       _____

      _____

## Section 3. Actuarial Certification

To the best of my knowledge and belief, the information supplied on this worksheet is true, correct and complete.

Signature: _____

Enrollment Number: _____

Date: _____

### Q 20:27   Is there a method for withdrawing nondeductible contributions without making an explicit request of the IRS?

Yes, but only if the amount of the withdrawn contributions do not exceed a *de minimis* amount. Under Revenue Procedure 90-49 [1990-2 C.B. 620], a plan may make a withdrawal of contributions that do not exceed $25,000 as these are considered *de minimis.* The following conditions, however, must be satisfied:

1. The terms of the plan must specifically allow for the return of contributions to the employer if they are determined by the IRS to be nondeductible.

2. Before or concurrent with, the date the nondeductible contribution is made to the plan, the contribution is specifically conditioned on deductibility in writing either (a) in the plan or (b) in the plan in combination with a certified corporate board resolution.

**Caution.** A contribution is not treated as specifically conditioned on deductibility unless the plan language or board resolution conditioning the contributions explicitly states that the contributions in question are conditioned on deductibility. For example, plan language stating that nondeductible contributions must or shall be returned to the employer meets this requirement. However, plan language stating that nondeductible contributions may be returned to the employer must be combined with a board resolution that specifically conditions the contributions on deductibility to meet this requirement.

In addition, the enrolled actuary for the plan must sign a worksheet that is prepared in the same manner as if the nondeductible contribution was not *de minimis* (see Q 18:25). This worksheet along with a copy of the applicable plan language or board resolution must be attached to the Schedule B of the Form 5500 that is filed for the plan for the year in which the nondeductible contribution is returned. Also, the employer who receives the return of contributions must also attach a certification to the Schedule B certifying that the contributions that are being returned have not been deducted on a tax return of the employer or, if deducted, an amended return has been filed.

The return of the nondeductible contribution must be made no later than one year from the date of the certification. If not returned by the employer's tax filing date, including extensions filed for and granted, the excise tax on nondeductible contributions will apply.

### Q 20:28   How are contributions made to the plan's assets in excess of the deduction limit handled?

Any contribution made to the plan's assets in excess of the deduction limit will become a carryforward contribution and will become deductible in a later year. Nondeductible contributions that are carried over into the next year are

first applied against the current deduction limit after reduction for any nondeductible contributions returned to the employer. (See Q 20:7 for an explanation
of accounting for nondeductible contributions in the plan's assets.) The carryforward in any plan year is equal to the contribution allocated to the taxable year
plus any prior carryforward less the deduction taken in the current taxable year.

> **Example.** In its 1996 plan year KL Banking made $5,000 in nondeductible
> contributions, which are carried over to its 1997 plan year. For the 1997 plan
> year it is determined that KL Banking's deduction limit is $100,000. The
> deductible contribution that KL Banking can make for 1997 is $95,000
> ($100,000 less the $5,000 carryover). Any contribution in excess of
> $95,000 would result in a new carryforward for 1997. For example, if
> $105,000 was allocated to the plan's assets in 1997, the new carryforward
> would be $10,000 ($105,000 + $5,000 − $100,000).

## Factors Affecting Deduction Limits

### Q 20:29    Can a plan take a deduction for benefits in excess of the Section 415 limits?

No. In computing any deduction limits, benefits in excess of the Section 415
limits cannot be taken into account. Further, anticipated increases in the cost-of-
living adjustments to the Section 415 limits cannot be considered for any year
before the adjustment takes effect. [I.R.C. § 404(j)]

> **Example.** Smith is the sole employee of a corporation sponsoring a defined
> benefit pension plan in 1997 and he has earned $140,000 in compensation for
> 1995, 1996, and 1997. The plan's benefit formula provides for a benefit of
> 90 percent of average compensation. In computing Smith's benefit and
> deductible contribution for the 1997 plan year, the benefit must be based
> on his benefit as limited by Code Section 415. Mr. Smith's retirement age
> under the plan and Social Security is 65; therefore, his maximum annual
> benefit under the Section 415 limit is the lesser of 100 percent of $140,000
> or $125,000. His benefit under the plan is 90 percent of $140,000, or $126,000.
> Since Smith's benefit under the plan formula would exceed the Section 415
> limit by $1,000, his benefit is reduced to $125,000 for purposes of the 1997
> maximum deductible contribution.

### Q 20:30    Are there any limits on the amount of compensation that can be taken into account?

Yes. In calculating accrued liabilities and normal costs for purposes of Code
Section 404(a)(1)(A)(i) through (iii), compensation in excess of $200,000 (as
adjusted by the IRS under Code Section 401(a)(17)(B)) cannot be taken into
account. In determining any full-funding limitations, adjustments to the
$200,000 limitation cannot be taken into account in any year before the year
the adjustment takes effect. [I.R.C. § 404(l)]

## Q 20:31   How do the plan's actuarial assumptions affect the amount of deductible contributions?

All deduction limits are affected by the actuarial assumptions used to determine plan costs because the actuarial assumptions are the basis used to set the limits under Code Section 404(a)(1)(A)(i) through (iii). In general, actuarial assumptions that use a low interest rate and a mortality table with a long life expectancy will generate the largest deduction limits. These are conservative assumptions, which anticipate that because of low investment returns and a longer payment period, more money is needed to fund retirement benefits. Conservative assumptions generate larger costs and are at the discretion of the plan's actuary, but the plan may have its contribution limited by the full-funding limitations. The actuarial assumptions for determining the OBRA '87 and RPA '94 full-funding limitations are set by the IRS and may preclude a contribution from being made to the plan.

## Q 20:32   Is there any restriction on the choice of actuarial assumptions used by a plan in relation to calculating the deduction limit?

For plan years beginning prior to January 1, 2008, the answer is no, there is no restriction on the choice of actuarial assumptions for determining the limits under Code Section 404(a)(1)(A)(i) through (iii), except that the choice must, in the opinion of the enrolled actuary, be reasonable in light of the actuary's expectation of the future experience of the plan. The actuary should be prepared to justify the choice of actuarial assumptions through the use of checklists, worksheets, or tables that review all relevant factors that make up the future experience of the plan. Such analysis can help users of the actuarial calculations understand the actuary's choice of assumptions. Members of certain actuarial organizations may choose to follow Actuarial Standards of Practice Statement 27, Selecting Economic Assumptions for Pension Obligations (see chapter 23), and determine a range of the actuary's best estimate of each economic assumption (e.g., the interest rate).

For plan years beginning after December 31, 2007, the same restrictions on actuarial assumptions that apply to the calculation of the minimum required contribution under Code Section 430 also apply to Code Section 404.

## Q 20:33   Can an additional deduction be taken for life insurance premiums?

Yes. The cost of life insurance protection, when added to the cost of retirement benefits, increases the contribution requirement for a defined benefit plan. As a result, the deduction limits under Code Section 404(a) are increased when the employer provides death benefits funded with life insurance. (See chapter 15 for further discussion regarding preretirement death benefits.) This does not apply for an owner-employee sponsored plan (see Q 20:35).

**Q 20:34  How are the deduction limits determined if an employer's plan year and taxable year are different?**

If an employer's plan year and taxable year coincide, the deduction limits are based on the plan year. If an employer's taxable year and plan year are different, the employer can choose one of three alternatives as long as the alternative is applied on a consistent basis. The alternative chosen cannot be changed unless consent is obtained from the IRS. The alternatives are as follows:

1. The deduction limit for the taxable year is the deduction limit for the plan year that begins within the taxable year;

2. The deduction limit for the taxable year is the deduction limit for the plan year that ends within the taxable year; and

3. The deduction limit for the taxable year is any weighted average of alternative 1 and alternative 2. Such an average can be based on the number of months of each plan year that fall within the taxable year, but the weighting does not have to be on that basis.

[Treas. Reg. § 1.404(a)-14(c)]

In computing the deduction limit under Code Section 404(a)(1)(A)(ii) and (iii), interest is computed from the valuation date to the earlier of the end of the plan year or the last day of the taxable year. [Treas. Reg. § 1.404(a)-14(f)(3)]

> **Example 1.** Extended Care Co. Inc. has a taxable year that runs from July 1, 1996, through June 30, 1997, and a plan year that runs from January 1, 1996, through December 31, 1996. The normal cost plus 10-year amortization (i.e., the sum of the limit adjustments) of the unfunded accrued liability as of January 1, 1996, equals $100,000. The valuation interest rate is 8 percent. Extended Care uses the limits for the plan year that ends within the taxable year. The plan year ends on December 31, 1996, which is within the taxable year that ends June 30, 1997. If the normal cost plus 10-year amortization of the unfunded accrued liability is the deduction limit, $108,000 ($100,000 × 1.08) would be deductible for the taxable year that ends June 30, 1997.

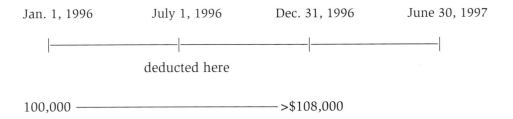

> **Example 2.** If Extended Care uses the limit for the plan year that begins within the taxable year, interest would be applied from January 1, 1996, through June 30, 1996 (six months), and would be deducted in the taxable year that ends June 30, 1996. Interest for half of a year would be 4 percent and result in a deduction limit of $104,000 ($100,000 × 1.04).

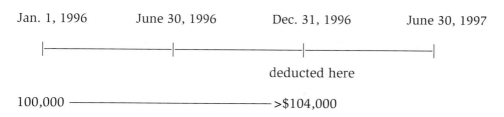

Jan. 1, 1996          June 30, 1996          Dec. 31, 1996          June 30, 1997

deducted here

100,000 ——————————————>$104,000

## Deductions for Owner-Employee Sponsored Plans

### Q 20:35   Do special deduction rules apply to owner-employee sponsored plans?

No. An *owner-employee* is a self-employed person who owns the entire interest in an unincorporated trade or business (a sole proprietor), or, in the case of a partnership, a partner who owns either more than 10 percent of the capital interest or more than 10 percent of the profit interest in a partnership. [I.R.C. § 401(c)(3)] The same deduction limits apply to owner-employee sponsored plans as to other plans. The compensation for an owner-employee, however, is based on earned income (see Q 20:36). Contributions allocated to the cost of life insurance are not deductible and contributions in excess of earned income (determined before reduction for contributions on behalf of the owner-employee individual) are not deductible, even if the contributions are required under Code Section 412. [I.R.C. § 404(a)(8)(C)]

### Q 20:36   What is *earned income*?

*Earned income* is net earnings from self-employment reduced for plan contributions required to fund all benefits for the plan participants and half of the self-employment taxes for the owner-employee individual.

**Example.** Jennette is the sole proprietor of an auto parts business. She has three employees who have met the service requirements to participate in her defined benefit pension plan. After paying all business expenses, other than the pension, Jennette has $100,000 of self-employment income. Her earned income for purposes of determining the deduction limit is $79,606 and her earned income for purposes of determining plan benefits is $34,606, calculated as follows:

| | |
|---|---|
| 1. Net profit before pension contribution | $100,000 |
| 2. Cost of employees' benefits | ($ 15,000) |
| 3. Half of self-employment taxes | ($  5,394) |
| 4. Earned income before pension contribution | $ 79,606 |
| 5. Required contribution for owner-employee | ($ 45,000) |
| 6. Earned income | $ 34,606 |

### Q 20:37    How are the partner's contributions deducted in a partnership?

Unless there is a special allocation in the partnership agreement, the deduction for the partner's contributions is taken in proportion to their profits interest in the partnership. [Treas. Reg. § 1.404(e)-1A(f)(2)] Therefore, in order for a partner to recognize the theoretical cost of his or her benefit for the year, it may be necessary to state this in the partnership agreement.

## Deductions of Plan Expenses and Fees

### Q 20:38    Can an employer receive a deduction for the administrative and actuarial fees incurred in the maintenance of a defined benefit plan?

Yes. Any expenses incurred by an employer in connection with the maintenance of a defined benefit plan that are not provided for by contributions under the plan are deductible by the employer under Code Section 162 or 212 to the extent they are ordinary and necessary. [Treas. Reg. § 1.404(a)-3(d)]

### Q 20:39    Can the plan pay these expenses directly?

Yes, it can, but the expenses do not increase the deduction limit as determined under Code Section 404(a). If the employer chooses to reimburse the plan for any expenses, the contribution is deductible only within the Section 404 limits computed without consideration of these expenses. In other words, the employer cannot deduct a contribution that was equal to the maximum amount computed under Code Section 404 and also deduct an additional contribution made to reimburse the trust for expenses paid.

### Q 20:40    Are brokerage commissions paid by the employer separately deductible to the employer?

No. Commissions paid to a broker are deductible only under the limits of Code Section 404. [Rev. Rul. 86-142, 1986-2 C.B. 60]

## Short Years

### Q 20:41    How is the deductible amount calculated when there is a short plan year?

When the employer changes the plan year, there must be a short year in transition to the new plan year end. With the change in plan year, there will be more than one plan year associated with the same taxable year of the employer or the sum of the number of months of each plan year associated with an employer's taxable year will be different from the number of months in the employer's taxable year. The deductible limit in all such cases must be adjusted.

The deduction limit for the employer's taxable year is adjusted by multiplying the sum of the deduction limits for the associated plan years by a fraction whose numerator, $t$, equals the number of months in the taxable year of the employer and whose denominator, $p$, is the aggregate number of months in the plan years associated with the taxable year.

The deductible amount for the short plan year is determined by ratably reducing the otherwise deductible amount for a 12-month plan year in proportion to the number of months in the short plan year. [Rev. Proc. 87-27, 1987-1 C.B. 769]

**Example 1.** Black Rock Inc. has a calendar taxable year and computes the deduction limit for its defined benefit plan on the basis of the plan year beginning October 1 within the calendar year. In 2000, the employer changes the plan year to a calendar year. This results in a short plan year beginning October 1, 2000, and ending December 31, 2000. The plan uses an aggregate funding method and the normal cost for the 12-month plan year beginning October 1, 2000, is $24,000. The deduction limit is not reduced by the full-funding limitation and is not increased by the amount required to meet the minimum required contribution.

The plan year associated with the 2000 calendar year of the employer is the plan year beginning October 1, 2000, and ending December 31, 2000. The deduction limit determined on the basis of this short plan year is $6,000 ($24,000 × $\frac{3}{12}$). The deduction limit applicable to the employer's 2000 taxable year is $24,000, the deduction limit for the short plan year, $6,000, multiplied by the fraction $t/p$ ($\frac{12}{3}$). For 2001 and subsequent taxable years, the deduction limit is the limit for the plan year coincident with the taxable year.

**Example 2.** The facts are the same as those in Example 1, except Black Rock creates a short plan year beginning October 1, 2000, and ending November 30, 2000, and subsequent plan years begin December 1. The normal cost for the 12-month plan year beginning December 1, 2000, is $38,000.

For the 2000 calendar year of the employer (taxable year), the plan year beginning October 1, 2000, and ending November 30, 2000, and the plan year beginning December 1, 2000, and ending November 30, 2001, are both associated with that taxable year. The number of months in the plan years associated with the taxable year is 14.

The deduction limit determined on the basis of the short plan year beginning October 1, 2000, is $4,000 ($24,000 × $\frac{2}{12}$). The deduction limit for the 12-month plan year beginning December 1, 2000, is $38,000. The deduction limit for the taxable year (calendar year 2000) is $36,000, obtained by multiplying the sum of the deduction limits, $42,000 ($4,000 + $38,000), by $\frac{12}{14}$. For 2001 and subsequent taxable years, the deduction limit is determined on the basis of the deduction limit for the 12-month plan year beginning December 1 within the taxable year (calendar year) of the employer. Thus, for the

2001 taxable year the deduction limit is determined by reference to the deduction limit for the plan year beginning December 1, 2001.

### Q 20:42    How is the deductible amount calculated when there is a change in the employer's taxable year creating a short taxable year?

In the case of a short taxable year, when the employer has consistently determined the deduction limit for each taxable year on the basis of the plan year beginning in the taxable year and when the plan year begins in the short taxable year, the employer can determine the deduction limit by the weighted average method or the special allowance method as described below.

Once a method is selected, the employer must consistently apply that method in determining the deduction limit.

*Weighted average method.* When the deduction limit claimed in the short taxable year is determined under Code Section 404(a)(1)(A)(ii) or (iii), the deduction limit is reduced by multiplying the deduction limit otherwise applicable under that section by the taxable year ratio (the number of months in the short taxable year divided by 12).

For subsequent taxable years, the deduction limit is the weighted average of the deduction limits for the plan year ending within the taxable year and for the plan year beginning in that taxable year. This amount is computed by adding the following amounts:

1. The deduction limit for the plan year ending within the taxable year multiplied by the difference between one and the taxable year ratio; and

2. The deduction limit for the plan year beginning within the taxable year multiplied by the taxable year ratio.

The deduction limit referred to in item #1 and item #2 above is the limit determined under Code Section 404(a)(1)(A)(i), (ii), or (iii), whichever is applicable.

When the deduction in the short taxable year is being claimed under Code Section 404(a)(1)(A)(i), the deduction limit in the short taxable year equals the sum of the following amounts:

1. The debit balance, if any, in the funding standard account as of the end of the previous plan year (without regard to the alternative minimum funding standard account) increased with interest to the end of the short taxable year; and

2. The taxable year ratio multiplied by the excess, if any, of the amount necessary to satisfy the minimum funding requirements for the plan year beginning in the short taxable year (including interest charges and credits only to the end of the short taxable year) over the amount determined in item #1.

For the first taxable year after the short taxable year, the deduction limit is the sum of the following amounts:

1. The amount that is necessary to satisfy the minimum funding requirements for the plan year beginning in the short taxable year, and that was not deductible in the short taxable year; and

2. The taxable year ratio multiplied by the deduction limit determined under Code Section 404(a)(1)(A)(i), (ii), or (iii) (whichever is applicable) attributable to the plan year beginning in the taxable year.

For subsequent taxable years, the deduction limit is the weighted average of the deduction limits for the plan year ending within the taxable year and for the plan year beginning in that taxable year. This amount is computed by adding the following amounts:

1. The deduction limit for the plan year ending within the taxable year multiplied by the difference between 1 and the taxable year ratio; and

2. The deduction limit for the plan year beginning within the taxable year multiplied by the taxable year ratio.

The deduction limit referred to in item #1 and item #2 above is the limit determined under Code Section 404(a)(1)(A)(i), (ii), or (iii), whichever is applicable.

*Special allowance method.* Under the special allowance method, the deduction limit under Code Section 404(a)(1)(A)(i), (ii), or (iii) for a short taxable year is the same as it is under the weighted average method. Under the special allowance method, however, the deduction limit in all of the taxable years following the short taxable year equals the sum of the deduction limit for the plan year beginning in the short taxable year plus (if the contribution for the short year exceeded the deduction limit for that year) a special allowance. The special allowance is 10 percent of the special allowance amount.

To compute the special allowance amount, the deduction limit determined under the special allowance method for the short taxable year is subtracted from the lesser of (1) the amount necessary to satisfy the minimum funding requirement for the plan year beginning in the short taxable year, or (2) the employer contribution made for the short taxable year. This special allowance can be used only for the first 10 taxable years after the short taxable year.

*End of plan year method.* With the approval of the Secretary of the Treasury as required under Code Section 446(e), the employer can determine the deduction limit under the end of plan year method. Under this method, the employer (1) takes no deduction for plan costs in the short taxable year and (2) changes the method for determining the deduction limit so that the limit is determined for the plan year ending within the taxable year. [Rev. Rul. 80-267, 1980-2 C.B. 139]

**Example.** For the taxable year beginning January 1, 2000, an employer has changed its annual accounting period from the taxable year ending

December 31, creating a short taxable year ending May 31. The employer has consistently deducted amounts contributed in a taxable year for the cost attributable to the plan year beginning in the taxable year. (The plan year begins April 1 and ends March 31.) For the short period January 1, 2000, to May 31, 2000, the employer intends to contribute the amount necessary to satisfy the minimum funding standard provided by Code Section 412(a) for the plan year beginning April 1, 2000.

The minimum required contribution for the plan year beginning April 1, 2000, is $100,000, and there is no debit balance in the funding standard account as of March 31, 2000. If the taxable year was not a short year, the deduction limit determined under Code Section 404(a)(1)(A)(ii) would be $110,000.

The deduction limit under Code Section 404(a)(1)(A)(i) for the short taxable year January 1, 2000, to May 31, 2000, is $41,667 ($0, the debit balance for the previous year + (($100,000, the minimum required contribution − $0) × $5/12$)). The deduction limit under Code Section 404(a)(1)(A)(ii) is $45,833 ($110,000 × $5/12$).

If the employer contributes $100,000 and the end of plan year method is not elected, the amount contributed in excess of the deduction limit in the short taxable year ($54,167) is considered a contribution carryover for a future taxable year.

For the plan year beginning April 1, 2001, the minimum required contribution is $110,000 and the deduction limit for the taxable year June 1, 2000, to May 31, 2001, determined under Code Section 404(a)(1)(A)(ii) (without regard to the fact that the previous taxable year was a short year) is $150,000; however, a special allowance amount is also calculated.

The special allowance amount ($54,167) is the excess of the lesser of (1) the amount necessary to satisfy the minimum funding requirement for the plan year beginning in the short taxable year ($100,000) or, (2) the employer contribution in the short taxable year ($100,000), over the deduction limit determined under the special allowance method for the short taxable year that is the greater of the deduction limit determined under Code Section 404(a)(1)(A)(i) ($41,667) or the deduction limit determined under Code Section 404(a)(1)(A)(ii) ($45,833). Therefore, the maximum deductible amount under Code Section 404(a)(1)(A)(ii) is determined using either of the following methods:

1. Weighted average method $126,667 (($110,000 × $7/12$) + ($150,000 × $5/12$)); or

2. Special allowance method $155,417 ($150,000 + (10% × $54,167)).

There is no official guidance on the calculation of the deductible amount for a short plan year when the limit has been consistently calculated on the basis of the plan year ending in the taxable year. It may be reasonable to assume, however, that a deduction would be allowed if it is computed on a proportional basis to its annual deduction. [1991 Enrolled Actuaries Meeting Greybook, Q&A 18]

### Q 20:43  How is the deductible amount determined when there is a short initial taxable year?

As long as the contribution to the plan, together with all other forms of compensation, does not exceed what would be considered reasonable compensation for the short initial taxable year of the employer, there is no proration required of the deduction limits. [Plastic Eng'g & Mfg. Co. v. Commissioner, 78 T.C. 1187 (1982)]

## Deduction Limits After PPA

### Q 20:44  What are the deduction limits applicable to single employer plans?

In the case of a defined benefit plan (other than a multiemployer plan), the amount determined under Code Section 404 for any taxable year shall be equal to the greater of:

1. The amount determined with respect to each plan year ending with or within the taxable year equal to the excess (if any) of—

   a. the sum of—

      (i)   the funding target for the plan year (see chapter 19),
      (ii)  the target normal cost for the plan year (see chapter 19), and
      (iii) the cushion amount for the plan year, (see Q 20:45) over

   b. the value (determined under Code Section 430(g)(2)) of the assets of the plan which are held by the plan as of the valuation date for the plan year or

2. the sum of the minimum required contributions under Code Section 430 for such plan years.

[I.R.C. §§ 404(o)(1), 404(o)(2)(A)]

However, if the plan is not subject to the at-risk rules of Code Section 430(i), the amount determined under item #1 above, can be no less than the sum of:

1. the funding target for the plan year (determined as if Code Section 430(i) applied to the plan), plus

2. the target normal cost for the plan year (also determined as if Code Section 430(i) applied).

[I.R.C. § 404(o)(2)(B)]

As of the date of publication of this material, it is not known exactly how these rules will be applied to a small defined benefit plan since Code Section 430(i) explicitly says that those rules do not apply to a small plan. For example, there are provisions for at-risk plans that require them to add a load and use additional actuarial assumptions in calculating the funding target, but do these provisions also apply to plans that are not at risk when calculating these amounts for Code Section 404?

### Q 20:45   What is the cushion amount for the plan year?

The cushion amount for any plan year is the sum of:

1. 50 percent of the funding target for the plan year, and
2. the amount by which the funding target for the plan year would increase if the plan were to take into account:
   a. increases in compensation which are expected to occur in succeeding plan years, or
   b. if the plan does not base benefits for service to date on compensation, increases in benefits which are expected to occur in succeeding plan years (determined on the basis of the average annual increase in benefits over the six immediately preceding plan years).

[I.R.C. § 404(o)(3)(A)]

In making the above computation, the plan's actuary must reflect the limitations under Code Section 404(l) (which provides the cap on compensation for the year) and Code Section 415(b) (which limits the amount of benefits which can be earned). [I.R.C. § 404(o)(3)(B)(i)]

In the case of a plan year during which a plan is covered by the PBGC, the plan's actuary may, notwithstanding Code Section 404(l), take into account increases in the limitations which are expected to occur in succeeding plan years. [I.R.C. § 404(o)(3)(B)(ii)]

In the case of a plan that has 100 or fewer participants for the plan year, the liability of the plan attributable to benefit increases for highly compensated employees (as defined in Code Section 414(q)) resulting from a plan amendment which is made or becomes effective, whichever is later, within the last two years cannot be taken into account in determining the target liability. [I.R.C. § 404(o)(4)] The IRS has informally opined that the establishment of a new plan is considered a plan amendment subject to this restriction.

### Q 20:46   Are there any special deduction rules applicable to plans that are terminating?

Yes. In the case of a plan that is covered by the PBGC terminates during the plan year, the deductible amount will be no less than the amount required to make the plan sufficient for benefit liabilities (within the meaning of ERISA Section 4041(d)). [I.R.C. § 404(o)(5)]

### Q 20:47   What actuarial assumptions are used in determining the deductible limit?

Any computation of the deductible limit for any plan year must use the same actuarial assumptions that are used for the plan year under Code Section 430. [I.R.C. § 404(o)(6)]

# Chapter 21

# Valuation of Liabilities and Assets

Defined benefit pension plans are kept financially sound by applying certain actuarial principles to quantify the plan's liability. Then assets are dedicated to provide the funds needed to pay the plan's liabilities. With the emergence of the Employee Retirement Income Security Act of 1974 (ERISA) and the numerous changes to the Internal Revenue Code (Code), the valuation of liabilities has become complex and confusing. The purpose of this chapter is to assist the reader in understanding the steps taken to value a plan's liabilities and assets.

## Actuarial Liabilities

### Q 21:1   What is an *actuarial liability*?

An *actuarial liability* is the value assigned to a future benefit payment based on factors that are relevant to the probability that the benefit will be paid taking into consideration an adjustment for the time value of money. This value is calculated, or determined, at a specific point in time, and the date of determination is often referred to as the *valuation date*.

> **Example.** Pension Plan *A* is required to pay to a participant's beneficiary a death benefit of $1,000 on the participant's death. If the valuation date occurs on the date the participant dies, the value of the liability is $1,000. If the participant is alive on the valuation date, however, actuarial principles of life contingencies and interest must be applied to the $1,000 benefit to determine its actuarial liability. If the Plan *A* participant is 60 years old and the

death benefit is payable one year from the valuation date, $1,000 is multiplied by the probability of death in the next year, discounted for one year of interest, to determine the actuarial liability. If the probability that a 60-year-old person will die before age 61 is 0.05, and the time value of money is measured at 5 percent, the actuarial liability of a death benefit of $1,000 payable one year from now is $47.62 ($1,000 × 0.05 × 1/1.05).

To get a clearer picture of the logic behind actuarial liabilities in general, assume that there is a pool of 10,000 60-year-old people who want to provide for a death benefit similar to the one in the example above. If each person deposited $47.62 in an investment paying 5 percent, the value of the investment at the end of the year would be approximately $500,000 (10,000 × $47.62 × 1.05). Five percent of the 10,000 60-year-olds are actuarially projected to die before age 61. The $500,000 pool will provide a $1,000 lump-sum payment to each of the 500 people who will die before attaining age 61.

The factors of probability used in measuring actuarial liabilities include historical studies that measure the rates of death, termination, retirement, disability, turnover, and other relevant factors that can be used to predict whether a payment or benefit will come due.

### Q 21:2  Is there more than one type of actuarial liability?

Yes. In general, there are two types of actuarial liabilities for defined benefit pension plans: *accrued liabilities* and *projected liabilities*.

An *accrued liability* is either the present value of accrued benefits or an accumulated accrued liability (see Q 21:7 for an explanation of the difference). An accrued liability represents the amount of money the plan should have in place to cover benefits that could have been funded in the past under various methods. If the assets are less than this amount, an unfunded accrued liability exists and must be funded over future years until it is eliminated.

A *projected liability* is the actuarial present value of all benefits now and those to be earned in the future. This type of liability takes into account projected service and benefits until the date benefits are to be paid. Generally, this type of liability is referred to as *the present value of future benefits*.

**Example.** The JP Law Firm is a sole proprietorship and JoAnn is the sole participant in its defined benefit pension plan. The plan's actuary determines that the accrued liability of the plan using the unit credit funding method is $150,000, taking into account JoAnn's current service and compensation. The actuary also determines that the plan's accrued liability under the entry age normal funding method is $75,000. These numbers differ significantly because of the methods used to determine accrued liability. The first is the value today of all benefits earned as of the valuation date; the second is what the trust fund would have accumulated to date if contributions had been made to the fund since the date JoAnn was hired. The first number requires no future contributions to the plan; the second assumes ongoing contributions. At retirement, both numbers will reach the same level.

### Q 21:3 Why do actuarial liabilities need to be valued in a defined benefit plan?

The determination of a defined benefit plan's actuarial liabilities helps the many parties interested in the continuation of the plan to determine its ability to pay benefits as they become due. Without a measure of the plan's future benefit obligations, no one would be able to determine how much money is sufficient to make good on promised benefits.

With the assistance of an enrolled actuary to make actuarial liability determinations for a pension plan, the plan sponsor will know how much to contribute to the trust fund each year, the governmental agencies will know to what extent a plan is funded, and the plan sponsor's creditors and advisors and plan participants will know how secure the pension benefits are.

## Valuation of Actuarial Liabilities

### Q 21:4 What are the individual elements of an actuarial liability?

An actuarial liability contains all of the amounts that represent the benefits to be paid, the probability that the benefit will be paid, and a discount factor for the time value of money.

Depending on the funding method used, the benefit portion of the liability may be a fraction of the total benefit, or in the case of a projected liability, 100 percent of the benefit. The factors used to determine the probability of payment and the time value of money vary depending on the provisions of the plan itself and the choice of actuarial assumptions used by the enrolled actuary to develop the liability.

A general actuarial liability formula follows:

Total actuarial liability = Benefit × Cost of benefit at assumed payment date × Interest factor × Probability that conditions for payment are satisfied

The total of this result for all participants would be the total actuarial liability for the plan. If the benefit could be paid as a result of a contingent event such as death, disability, or early retirement, the liability would be measured at each age the payment could occur and the sum total of each age would become the actuarial liability for the participant.

### Q 21:5 Can one defined benefit plan have more than one liability?

Yes. Several actuarial liabilities are developed for a defined benefit pension plan. Each liability is developed for certain disclosure, funding, and governmental reporting purposes. In general, most liabilities found in actuarial reports for defined benefit pension plans are of the accrued liability type, and the basic difference between each is the interest rate assumption used in accounting for the time value of money.

**Example 1.** The R&D Pension Plan is provided its actuarial accrued liability for purposes of determining the plan's current liability under Code Section 412. Its actuary determines that this amount, when using a 7 percent interest rate, is $350,000. For purposes of determining the value of the vested benefits for Pension Benefit Guaranty Corporation (PBGC) variable-rate premium purposes, the actuary determines that the plan's accrued liability, when using a 5 percent interest rate as required for the premium payment year, is $475,000. The plan's actuary also uses the unit credit funding method to determine that the plan's current accrued liability is $405,000 using a 6 percent interest rate assumption.

Certain liabilities may require the use of actuarial assumptions of decrement and salary scale; others do not. Whenever this occurs, the actuarial report discloses this difference.

**Example 2.** The R&V Company asks its plan's actuary to disclose the value of the plan's accrued liability for purposes of terminating the plan. The actuary determines that the plan has $1.5 million of actuarial liability on a termination basis. By coincidence, the interest rate for determining the plan's termination liability and funding liability is the same; however, the actuary notes that the actuarial liability on a termination basis is less than the plan's $1.75 million accrued liability for funding purposes. The $250,000 difference, as explained by the actuary, results from the fact that the termination liability does not take into account future increases in salary for the benefits earned to date, the cost of disability benefits, or preretirement death benefits that will no longer be payable after the plan terminates.

### Q 21:6    What actuarial assumptions are used in computing an actuarial liability?

The assumptions used in the determination of an actuarial liability are at the very least a factor for the cost of the benefit and an interest rate for the time value of money. There are many choices of assumptions that can be used for determining an actuarial liability, and they are the domain of the enrolled actuary hired to make the determination. It is useful to know that whatever the benefit being valued, one can be sure that the choice of actuarial assumptions will have some bearing on the rate of return on the assets providing the benefit payment and on the probability that the benefit will be paid in its entirety at the expected payment date.

**Example.** The Big Pension Plan asked its enrolled actuary to provide the amount of the actuarial liability for the disability benefit in the plan. The latest report indicates that the plan's total actuarial liability, inclusive of the disability benefit, is $2.5 million. The disability benefit is 100 percent of the accrued benefit at the date disability occurs, paid for the remainder of the participant's disability. The actuary indicates that the value of the disability benefit has been determined by assuming that a certain percentage of the employer's workforce will become disabled each year. This assumption is based on a table of probabilities that predicts the likelihood of a disability from one year to the next based on each participant's age. Furthermore, the actuary believes that any disability that occurs will cause the participant's life expectancy to change from that assumed for a normal retirement benefit. Therefore, there are three assumptions underlying the actuarial liability for the disability benefit. The first is the interest rate used to take into account the time value of money, the second is the assumed rate at which employees become disabled, and the third is how long the disability benefit will be paid on commencement of payments. The actuary reports to the employer that of the $2.5 million actuarial liability, $500,000 represents the value today of any disabilities that will occur in the future based on the current group of participants in the plan.

### Q 21:7　What is the difference between a *present value accrued liability* (also known as present value of accrued benefits) and an *accumulated accrued liability*?

A *present value accrued liability* represents the amount of assets needed today to provide the amount of the retirement benefit earned as of the valuation date based on the benefits earned for service as of that date. Sometimes, this liability is referred to as a *termination liability* because its value is based on the benefits that would be paid on termination of the plan or the participant. (See chapter 18 for detailed examples of the accrued liability under the unit credit funding method.)

An *accumulated accrued liability* represents what the value of the plan assets would be if contributions were made to the plan's trust fund over the entire careers of the employees. The accumulated accrued liability illustrates the level of assets required at a point in time if the annual contribution requirement developed by the funding method is paid into the trust fund each year. (See example in Q 21:2.)

> **Note.** An accumulated accrued liability takes into account benefits that will be earned in the future; a present value accrued liability looks at the value of the benefits if no additional service or benefits are granted after the valuation date. (See chapter 18 for detailed examples of the accrued liability under the individual entry age normal funding method.)

> **Example.** The JP Law Firm is a sole proprietorship and JoAnn is the sole participant in its defined benefit pension plan. The plan's actuary determines that the accrued liability of the plan using the unit credit funding method is $150,000, taking into account JoAnn's current service and compensation. The actuary also determines that the plan's accrued liability under the individual entry age normal funding method is $75,000. These numbers differ significantly because of the methods used to determine the accrued liability. The first is the value today of all benefits earned as of the valuation date; the second is what the trust fund would have accumulated to date if contributions had been made to the fund under that method since the date JoAnn was hired. The first number assumes no further benefits will be earned after the valuation date, and if they are, the plan would determine the value of those additional benefits earned and add that amount to the present value of accrued

benefits. The second assumes ongoing contributions of either a level dollar amount or percentage of annual compensation to fund the total benefit projected at JoAnn's retirement date.

### Q 21:8   What is the difference between the *present value of accrued benefits* and the *present value of vested accrued benefits*?

The *present value of the accrued benefits* is an actuarial liability that represents the value of the plan's benefits earned as of the valuation date before the application of the plan's vesting schedule. The *present value of vested accrued benefits* is an actuarial liability that reflects only those benefits that are nonforfeitable as a result of applying the plan's vesting schedule.

**Example.** The D&R Pension Plan has a vesting schedule of 100 percent after five years of participation in the plan with 0 percent vesting before the completion of five years of participation. Because D&R is a new company that has been in business for only three years, no employee has worked long enough to earn a nonforfeitable right to benefits in the plan. Therefore, the present value of the plan's vested accrued benefits is zero.

### Q 21:9   Is the sum of the individual participants' liabilities equal to the total plan liability?

Yes. Each participant represents an actuarial liability, and the sum total of the individual liabilities comprises the plan's total actuarial liability. Therefore, it is possible to know how much of the plan's total liability a participant, benefit, or group of participants represents. This can be useful in identifying where the actuarial liabilities exist for the employee group and who or what is causing the liability to increase or decrease from year to year.

**Example.** The Big Steel Construction Company sponsors a collectively bargained pension plan that offers early retirement benefits at age 55 without reduction for payment before normal retirement age. Currently, 25 percent of the plan participants are working beyond early retirement age, and the employer is considering a layoff of many workers. Fortunately, the plan's actuary has assumed that anyone working beyond age 55 will retire in the subsequent year with unreduced retirement benefits, and as a result the actuarial liability for these participants closely reflects what the plan's actuarial liability will be after a massive layoff. The employer is also considering offering lump-sum payments to those who retire as a result of the layoffs and wants to be sure the plan has sufficient cash assets to make these payments. A review of the actuarial liabilities of these potential retirees would be helpful in determining the amount of the lump-sum payments.

### Q 21:10   What is a *termination liability*?

When a defined benefit pension plan terminates, it no longer provides the plan participants the ability to earn an increase in their accrued benefit for service after the plan is terminated. The *termination liability* of a plan is the amount of money needed to cover the cost of all accrued benefits on the liquidation of the plan's trust fund. The cost of a plan's termination is the actuarial value of lump-sum payments and annuity contracts purchased to continue the payment of the accrued benefits after the plan is terminated. (See chapter 23 for a detailed discussion of the valuation of termination liabilities.)

> **Example.** The RM Company will terminate its defined benefit pension plan on December 31, 2002. After careful consideration of several insurance companies' programs, it is determined that the termination liability will be $5 million. Of this amount, $4.5 million will be paid to an insurance company to provide payment of the earned benefits under the plan to the retirees and certain deferred retirees who want to receive monthly payments of their accrued benefits, and $500,000 will be paid in lump sums to participants who elect a lump sum instead of an annuity.

## Calculation of Liabilities

### Q 21:11   How are actuarial liabilities calculated?

Depending on the type of actuarial liability and the purpose for its determination, the calculation method and assumptions vary; however, all calculations include only the benefits for the participants and beneficiaries at the time the valuation is made. It is sometimes mistakenly thought by users of actuarial reports that the liabilities include the value of benefits that may or will be earned by participants who have yet to be hired. For example, if an employer is told that the accrued liability for its plan is $1 million, the employer can be sure that this value is only for participants in the plan and not for a group of employees yet to be hired. Actuarial liabilities do not take into account the assumption that more participants will be hired over the next few years. An employer, however, can determine the impact that new plan participants will have on the plan's actuarial liabilities by asking the plan's enrolled actuary about the cost of new benefits for new employees.

Once the benefits for the participants and beneficiaries are determined, an actuarial liability can be developed by applying the plan's mortality table, interest rate or rates, and other relevant decrements chosen by the plan's enrolled actuary.

> **Example.** The R&D Pension Plan has three participants as of January 1, 2002. One of the participants is a 70-year-old retiree collecting $1,000 per month for life, the second has terminated employment and is scheduled to receive $500 per month for life in 10 years, and the third participant is actively working for R&D and is scheduled to retire in 15 years with a benefit of $2,000 per month for life. For the third participant's service to date, however, only $1,000 of the benefit has been earned. The actuary makes the following assumptions for developing an accrued liability for the plan:

1. The cost of the plan benefits at retirement will be $120 per dollar of benefit earned and $100 per dollar of benefit for a 70-year-old.

2. The trust fund will earn 6 percent per year compounded annually.

3. All participants will survive to retirement to collect their benefits.

The plan's accrued liability under the unit credit funding method would be determined as follows:

$$
\begin{aligned}
\text{Participant 1: } \$1{,}000 \times \$100 \times 1.0000 &= \$100{,}000 \\
\text{Participant 2: } \$500 \times \$120 \times 0.55839 &= \$\ 33{,}503 \\
\text{Participant 3: } \$1{,}000 \times \$120 \times 0.41727 &= \underline{\$\ 50{,}072} \\
\text{Total actuarial accrued liability} &= \$183{,}575
\end{aligned}
$$

### Q 21:12   How do benefits affect actuarial liabilities?

The benefits under a defined benefit pension plan have a significant influence on the magnitude of an actuarial liability because it is the value of the benefits that is represented by the liability. If a defined benefit pension plan provides other benefits beyond monthly payments at retirement, the value of those additional benefits will affect the plan's actuarial liability as well.

**Example 1.** Suppose the R&D Pension Plan in the example in Q 21:11 was amended on January 1, 2002, to provide a disability benefit for any active employee equal to the accrued benefit at the date of disability. The actuarial liability for the disability benefit would be added to the $183,575 accrued liability for the retirement benefits to develop the plan's new accrued liability taking into account the disability benefit. The benefit would be valued for the third participant only, because that participant is the only person currently eligible for the disability benefit.

For any change in benefits that increases or liberalizes the value of the benefits, there will be a corresponding increase in the value of the actuarial liability.

**Example 2.** The enrolled actuary of the BIG Company Pension Plan determines that the actuarial liability for the active participant group is $1 million using the unit credit funding method. The value of this actuarial liability is based on a benefit of $15 per month for each year of service for these employees. The employer has agreed that the benefit should be increased to $20 per month for all years of service. The plan sponsor should expect to see the actuarial liability for the plan increase to $1,333,333, which is the ratio of the new benefit to the old benefit multiplied by the actuarial liability for the old benefits (i.e., ($20 × $15) × $1,000,000).

### Q 21:13   Can changes in data affect liabilities?

Yes. Any change in the participants and beneficiaries of the employee group translates to a change in the data and affects the amount of the actuarial liability. A change in the actuarial liability from one year to the next can be calculated with precision if all actuarial assumptions for the plan meet the actual experience of the plan's data group over the one-year period. If they do not, a change in the liability over what was expected will result. This change is known as an actuarial gain or loss. Sometimes, an actuarial valuation is done using data that approximate the benefits. Then, when more precise data are used, a change in the actuarial liability will occur.

> **Example 1.** Suppose the Saxon Company Pension Plan has its actuarial liabilities valued using the base salaries for employees covered by the plan, and that Saxon Company has a policy of promoting employees within the company, and because of the nature of their work, certain promotions can double an employee's salary in one year. This would cause the actuarial liability for any such employee to double in a one-year period. This in turn would generate an actuarial loss if these data changes were not anticipated.

Similarly, if an employer keeps poor records of its employees, the plan's actuarial liabilities could be completely inaccurate.

> **Example 2.** The Mega Hotel Company sponsors a defined benefit pension plan and provides benefits for employees who have worked at any of its 1,000 hotels around the world. It has been the policy of the company to move management employees to different locations around the world for a period of at least three years. Unfortunately, there is no system in place to keep an accurate record of the years worked at each location, and every so often a transferred employee gets a new date of hire and service records for the previous location are lost. Fortunately, each year that the actuarial valuation for the plan is performed, the enrolled actuary requires that the date of hire for each person working for Mega Hotel be compared to the date on file in the previous year. Any such changes are pointed out to the actuary, and usually the old date of hire is maintained and confirmed with the employee and employer. If such steps were not taken, the data of the plan would become filled with duplications of benefits and lost service years, resulting in actuarial liabilities that are incorrect.

## Q 21:14   How does vesting affect liabilities?

A defined benefit pension plan's vesting schedule is applied to a plan's actuarial liabilities to illustrate the amount of benefit that would be payable on termination of a plan participant. A partial or full termination of a defined benefit pension plan may cause the plan to vest certain employees 100 percent in their accrued benefit.

If a plan uses a turnover table as part of the actuarial liability calculation, it is generally accepted practice to add into the plan's actuarial liability the value of the vested benefits expected to become payable on an employee's termination.

> **Example 1.** The Big Pension Plan has never had an employee who was hired between the ages of 18 and 25 work more than five years. In developing a turnover table for the plan, it is assumed that no employee in this age group will ever receive a retirement benefit, and therefore, the actuarial liability for this group is zero. The plan's vesting schedule, however, provides that after

three years of service, every employee will become 100 percent vested in his or her accrued benefit. Therefore, the actuarial liability is increased by the present value of the benefits that will be or are earned after completion of three years of service. The result is an actuarial liability greater than zero, but not nearly as large as it might have been if a turnover table had not been used.

### Q 21:15   Do actuarial liabilities change from one year to the next?

Yes. Actuarial liabilities change each year for changes in benefits, terminations, deaths, new participants, early and late retirements, and other such occurrences that affect the amount of benefit.

It is advisable and in some instances required for a plan to disclose the change in actuarial liabilities from one year to the next. Plans subject to the reporting requirements under Financial Accounting Standards Board Statements of Financial Accounting Standards No. 35 and No. 87 (see chapter 31) are required to disclose and account for changes in the plan's actuarial liability. Any plan using an immediate gain funding method should disclose the source of the plan's actuarial gain or loss by reconciling the change in the actuarial liability. Furthermore, if the required contribution is significantly different from one year to the next, the enrolled actuary should be able to illustrate how such a change occurred by reconciling the changes in the actuarial liability.

**Example.** The Gotham City Police Pension Plan had a significant change in the plan's funded ratio from 2001 to 2002. The city council wants to know how this happened when the plan's assets grew at the assumed rate and all actuarial assumptions were in line with the plan's experience for the plan year. The actuary points out that all assumptions were met with regard to all officers except Commissioner Gordon, who retired during the year. It turns out that the latest round of union negotiations changed the pay rate for the commissioner of Gotham City from $45,000 per year to $80,000 per year. The plan provides that benefits will be based on the pay rate in effect at the time the officer retires. In 2001 it was assumed that the liability for Commissioner Gordon would be $450,000 at retirement; however, the pay raise at the last minute caused his actuarial liability to increase to $800,000. The actuary shows how if the change in salary were not part of the commissioner's retirement benefits, the plan's funded ratio would not have changed so dramatically.

### Q 21:16   Do actuarial liabilities represent the exact value of a plan's benefits?

No. An actuarial liability is a subjective estimate of what the actuary, based on his or her choice of assumptions and funding method, believes the value of a plan's benefit to be on the valuation date; however, the calculated amount of actuarial liability is objective, and as such, the calculation is only an exact amount based on the assumptions and benefits used. The exact cost of a pension plan's benefits cannot be measured until the last benefit payment is made from the trust fund.

## Valuation of Assets

### Q 21:17   What is an *asset* of a defined benefit pension plan?

An *asset* of a defined benefit pension plan is any investment that is purchased on behalf of the plan and maintained in trust for the benefit of the plan's participants and beneficiaries. In making the purchase or sale of a plan asset, the plan's named fiduciary must act in accordance with certain standards outlined in ERISA and the Code (see chapter 27).

### Q 21:18   How are assets valued in a defined benefit pension plan?

Actuaries use several techniques for valuing assets in a defined benefit pension plan. When determining a contribution requirement for a plan, the enrolled actuary takes into account the value of the plan's assets on the valuation date. In making the funding determination, the plan's assets are valued actuarially. An actuarial value of a plan asset must meet certain criteria for it to be considered reasonable. The actuarial value of a plan asset must be determined under the following rules:

1. *Consistent basis.* The actuarial asset valuation method must be applied on a consistent basis. A method can satisfy the consistency requirement even though computations are based only on the period that has elapsed since the adoption of the method or on asset values occurring during that period. Any change in the asset valuation method is generally considered a change in the plan's funding method (see chapter 18).

2. *Statement of plan's method.* The method of determining the actuarial value (but not fair market value) of the assets must be specified in the plan's actuarial report. The method must be described in sufficient detail that another actuary employing the method described would arrive at a reasonably similar result. A deviation to include a type of asset not previously held by the plan is not a change in funding method.

3. *Consistent valuation dates.* The same day or days (such as the first or the last day of a plan year) must be used for all purposes to value the plan's assets for each plan year, or portion of a plan year, for which a valuation is made. For purposes of determining minimum funding requirements, each such day is a valuation date. A change in the valuation day or days used is a change in funding method (see chapter 18).

4. *Reflect fair market value.* The valuation method must take into account fair market value by making use of the fair market value (see Q 21:19) or average value (see Q 21:20) of the plan's assets as of the applicable asset valuation date. This is done either directly in the computation of their actuarial value or indirectly in the computation of upper or lower limits placed on that value.

5. *Results above or below fair market or average value.* The valuation method is not allowed if it is designed to produce a result that is consistently above or below the fair market value (see Q 21:19) and the average

value (see Q 21:20). A method designed to produce a result that consistently falls between fair market value and average value is allowed.

6. *Corridor limits.* Regardless of how the method reflects fair market value (see Q 21:19), the method must result in an actuarial value of the plan's assets that is not less than a minimum amount and not more than a maximum amount. The minimum amount is the lesser of 80 percent of the current fair market value (see Q 21:19) of plan assets as of the applicable asset valuation date or 85 percent of the average value (see Q 21:20) of plan assets as of that date. The maximum amount is the greater of 120 percent of the current fair market value of plan assets as of the applicable asset valuation date or 115 percent of the average value of plan assets as of that date. If, under a plan's method, the preliminary computation of the actuarial value falls outside these minimum and maximum amounts, the method can meet the corridor-limits requirement by adjusting the actuarial value to the nearest corridor limit applicable under the method. A plan can use an actuarial valuation method with a narrower corridor than those stated above; however, such an adjustment must be stated in the description of the plan's method. The Pension Protection Act of 2006 (PPA) changed the lower value of the corridor limit to 90 percent and the upper value of the corridor limit to 110 percent for plan years beginning after December 31, 2007. [I.R.C. § 430(g)(3)(B)(iii)]

[Treas. Reg. §§ 1.412(c)(2)-1(b)(1), 1.412(c)(2)-1(b)(6)]

### Q 21:19    What is the *fair market value* of a plan's assets?

The *fair market value* of a plan's assets is the price at which the property would change hands between a willing buyer and a willing seller, neither being under any compulsion to buy or sell and both having reasonable knowledge of relevant facts. [Treas. Reg. § 1.412(c)(2)-1(c)(1)]

### Q 21:20    What is the *average value* of a plan's assets?

The *average value* of a plan's assets is the average of the sum of the current fair market value of the assets plus the adjusted value of the assets (see Q 21:21) for each year of a stated period not to exceed the five (two, for plan years beginning after December 31, 2007) most recent plan years (including the current year). [Treas. Reg. § 1.412(c)(2)-1(b)(7)]

**Example.** The current fair market value of a plan's assets is $450,000, the adjusted values for the last two years are $425,000 and $430,000. This plan has an average asset value of $435,000 (($450,000 + $425,000 + $430,000)/3).

### Q 21:21    What is the *adjusted value* of a plan's assets?

The *adjusted value* of a plan's assets for a prior valuation date is the fair market value on that date with certain positive and negative adjustments. These adjustments reflect changes that occur between the prior asset valuation date and the current valuation date. No adjustment is made, however, for increases or decreases in the total value of plan assets that result from the purchase, sale, or exchange of plan assets or from the receipt of payment on a debt obligation held by the plan.

To determine the adjusted value of plan assets for a previous valuation date, the fair market value of the plan assets on that date is added to the sum of all additions to the plan assets since that date, excluding appreciation in the fair market value of the assets. These additions include contributions to the plan, interest or dividends paid to the plan, and any asset not taken into account in a prior valuation of assets, but taken into account for the current year, in computing the fair market value of plan assets. Amounts subtracted from the fair market value of the plan assets are reductions in plan assets since that date, excluding depreciation in the fair market value of the assets. Reductions include any benefits or expenses paid from plan assets. [Treas. Reg. § 1.412(c)(2)-1(b)(8)]

It appears that under the PPA any adjusted value that does not reflect full fair market value will not be allowed. [I.R.C. § 430(g)(3)(B)]

**Example.** The R&D Pension Plan is a calendar-year pension plan, and assets for funding purposes are valued as of the beginning of each year. The following chart shows the calculation of the average value of the plan assets as of 2002. The fair market value at the end of 2001 is $513,719 and becomes the fair market value as of January 1, 2002. The average value of the plan assets is determined to be $445,191.

|    |                                         | *1998*      | *1999*      | *2000*      | *2001*      |
|----|-----------------------------------------|-------------|-------------|-------------|-------------|
| 1  | Fair market value                       | $250,000    | $306,000    | $304,200    | $419,418    |
| 2  | Contributions                           | $ 50,000    | $ 45,000    | $ 60,000    | $ 55,000    |
| 3  | Interest and dividends                  | $ 15,000    | $ 15,300    | $ 27,378    | $ 20,971    |
| 4  | Benefits paid                           | ($ 25,000)  | ($ 27,000)  | ($ 30,000)  | ($ 27,000)  |
| 5  | Expenses                                | ($  4,000)  | ($  4,500)  | ($  $3,000) | ($  5,000)  |
| 6  | Gain or (loss)                          | $ 20,000    | ($ 30,600)  | $ 60,840    | $ 50,330    |
| 7  | Fair market value (sum of lines 1 through 6) | $306,000 | $304,200 | $419,418 | $513,719 |
| 8  | Net adjustments (sum of lines 2 through 5) | $ 36,000 | $ 28,800 | $ 54,378 | $ 43,971 |
| 9  | Fair market value                       | $250,000    | $306,000    | $304,200    | $419,418    |
| 10 | Net adjustment 1997                     | $ 36,000    | $       0   | $       0   | $       0   |
| 11 | Net adjustment 1998                     | $ 28,800    | $ 28,800    | $       0   | $       0   |
| 12 | Net adjustment 1999                     | $ 54,378    | $ 54,378    | $ 54,378    | $       0   |
| 13 | Net adjustment 2000                     | $ 43,971    | $ 43,971    | $ 43,971    | $ 43,971    |
| 14 | Adjusted value (sum of lines 9 through 13) | $413,149 | $433,149 | $402,549 | $463,389 |

| | | _1998_ | _1999_ | _2000_ | _2001_ |
|---|---|---|---|---|---|
| 15 | Total adjusted values | $1,712,236 | | | |
| 16 | Current market value | $ 513,719 | | | |
| 17 | Sum of market and adjusted | $2,225,955 | | | |
| 18 | Number of years in average | 5 | | | |
| 19 | Average value of assets | $ 445,191 | | | |

### Q 21:22  When must an asset be valued?

Plan assets must be valued on the same date each year, generally the plan's valuation date, which is the date on which all assets and liabilities are valued for purposes of preparing the annual actuarial report. Other dates may be required for certain disclosures on the employer's financial statement or other reports that are not part of the annual actuarial report.

### Q 21:23  Why are there different actuarial methods for valuing plan assets?

Because of the volatility of certain plan investments, the fair market value of the assets can increase or decrease over a one-year period at a rate much different from that assumed by the enrolled actuary. If the plan uses the fair market value of the plan's assets for determining its annual contribution requirement and there has been a substantial change in the value of the plan's assets over the last funding year, the next year's funding requirement could be substantially more or less than anticipated by the employer. Therefore, a plan may use an actuarial value of the plan assets other than fair market value to smooth the fluctuations in the plan's funding requirement from year to year.

### Q 21:24  What are some examples of asset valuation methods?

The following examples of asset valuation methods are taken directly from Treasury Regulations Section 1.412(c)(2)-1. The examples illustrate some commonly used asset valuation methods, one of which (Example 4) does not meet the requirements of the law.

**Example 1.** Plan _A_ considers the value of its assets to be initial cost, increased by an assumed rate of growth of _x_ percent annually. The method also requires that the actuarial value be adjusted as required to fall within the 110 percent to 80 percent corridor of the fair market value of the plan's assets.

**Example 2.** Plan _B_ computes the actuarial value of its assets by determining the fair market value of the plan assets, and then adjusting the fair market value to the extent necessary to make the actuarial value fall within a 5 percent corridor. This corridor is plus or minus 5 percent of the following amount: the fair market value of the assets at the beginning of the valuation period plus an assumed annual growth of 4 percent with adjustments for contributions and benefit payments during the period. If the 4 percent factor used by the plan is a reasonable assumption, this method is not designed to produce results consistently above or below fair market value. If in this instance this method results in an actuarial value outside the 110 percent to 80 percent corridor, the actuarial value of the assets must be adjusted to the nearest end of the corridor.

**Example 3.** Plan *C* values its assets by multiplying their fair market value by an *index number.* The use of the index results in the hypothetical average value that plan assets present on the valuation date would have had if they had been held during the current and four preceding years, and had appreciated or depreciated at the actual yield rates, including appreciation and depreciation, experienced by the plan during that period. The method requires an adjustment to the extent necessary to bring the resulting actuarial value of the assets inside the corridor described in the statement of the plan's actuarial valuation method. In this case, the stated corridor is 90 percent to 110 percent of fair market value.

**Example 4.** Plan *D* values its assets by multiplying their fair market value by 95 percent. Although the method reflects fair market value and the results of this method will always be within the required corridor, it is *not* acceptable because it consistently results in a value less than fair market value.

**Example 5.** Plan *E* values its assets by using a five-year-average method with appropriate adjustments for the period. Under the particular method used by Plan *E*, assets are not valued below 80 percent of fair market value or above 100 percent of fair market value. If the average produces a value that exceeds 100 percent of fair market value, the excess between 100 percent and 120 percent is recorded in a value reserve account. In years after one in which the average exceeds 100 percent of fair market value, amounts are subtracted from this account and added, to the extent necessary, to raise the value produced by the average for that year to 100 percent of fair market value. This method is permitted because it reflects fair market value by appropriately computing an average value, it produces a result that falls consistently between fair market value and average value, and it properly reflects the 110 percent to 80 percent corridor.

**Example 6.** Plan *F* computes the actuarial value of the plan assets as follows: The current fair market value of the plan assets is averaged with the most recent prior adjusted actuarial value. This average value is adjusted up or down toward the current fair market value by 20 percent of the difference between it and the current fair market value of the assets. This value is further adjusted to the extent necessary to fall within the corridor described in the statement of the plan's actuarial valuation method. The lower end of the corridor is the lesser of 80 percent of the fair market value of plan assets or 85 percent of the average value of plan assets. The higher end of the corridor is the greater of 120 percent of the fair market value of plan assets or 115 percent of the average value of plan assets. If the current fair market value of assets is $228,000 and the average value is $263,875, the actuarial asset value must not be less than $182,400 (80 percent of current fair market value, $228,000) nor greater than $303,456 (115 percent of average value, $263,875). This method is permitted because it reflects fair market value, it produces an actuarial value that is neither consistently above nor consistently below fair market or average value, and it is appropriately limited by the 110 percent to 80 percent corridor.

### Q 21:25 Can the method for valuing plan assets be changed?

Yes. Subject to certain restrictions imposed by the Treasury Department (see chapter 18), a plan may change the method for valuing its assets. Revenue Procedure 2000-40 [2000-42 I.R.B. 357] provides the methods and circumstances under which a plan can change its asset valuation method without seeking advance approval from the IRS. There are seven changes that can be made to the asset valuation method with automatic approval. (It is assumed that, for plan years beginning after December 31, 2007, if the plan's asset valuation method does not comply with changes required by the PPA then the plan will be required to change its asset valuation method and will have automatic approval to do so.) The changes listed below are taken directly from Revenue Procedure 2000-40. The terms *fair market value, average value,* and *adjusted value* are defined in Qs 21:19-21:21.

*Asset valuation change 1.* A plan can change the asset valuation method to fair market value.

*Asset valuation change 2.* A plan can change its asset valuation method to the average value (that does not have a phase-in), or to any alternative formulation that is algebraically equivalent to this average value. The asset value determined under the method must be adjusted to be no greater than 120 percent and no less than 80 percent of the fair market value. The stated averaging period cannot exceed five plan years.

For example, if the averaging period is five years, for the first year the average value is based on the fair market value of assets in the current year and the adjusted values of assets for the prior four years. An alternative formulation that is algebraically equivalent to this method is one in which the average value of assets is equal to the fair market value on the valuation date, minus decreasing fractions ($\frac{4}{5}$, $\frac{3}{5}$, $\frac{2}{5}$, and $\frac{1}{5}$, in this example) of the appreciation and depreciation of the assets in each of the four preceding years.

*Asset valuation change 3.* A plan can change its asset valuation method to the average value, modified to use the phase-in described below, or to any alternative formulation that is algebraically equivalent to this average value. The asset value determined under the method must be adjusted to be no greater than 120 percent and no less than 80 percent of the fair market value. The stated averaging period cannot exceed five plan years.

In the first year this method is used, the average value is calculated as it is in *asset valuation change 2* except that the adjusted values for all but the most recent prior year are replaced by the adjusted value for the most recent prior year. In the second year, the average is calculated as it is in *asset valuation change 2*, except that the values for all but the most recent two prior years are replaced by the adjusted value for the second most recent prior year. This process is continued until values for all prior years in the averaging period are phased in.

*Asset valuation change 4.* A plan can change the asset valuation date to the first day of the plan year.

*Asset valuation change 5.* A plan can change its asset valuation method to the smoothed market value (without phase-in) described below, or to any alternative formulation that is algebraically equivalent to this smoothed value. The asset value determined under the method must be adjusted to be no greater than 120 percent and no less than 80 percent of the fair market value. Under this method, the actuarial value of assets is equal to the fair market value of assets less a decreasing fraction (i.e., $(n-1)/n$, $(n-2)/n$, etc., where $n$ equals the number of years in the smoothing period) of the gain or loss for each of the preceding $n-1$ years. The stated smoothing period cannot exceed five plan years. Under this method, a gain or loss for a year is determined by calculating the difference between the expected value of the assets for the year and the fair market value of the assets at the valuation date. The expected value of the assets for the year is the fair market value of the assets at the valuation date for the prior year brought forward with interest at the valuation interest rate to the valuation date for the current year, plus contributions minus benefit disbursements, all adjusted with interest at the valuation interest rate to the valuation date for the current year. If the expected value is less than the fair market value, the difference is a gain. Conversely, if the expected value is greater than the fair market value, the difference is a loss.

For example, if the smoothing period is five years, the actuarial value of the assets will be the fair market value of the plan's assets, with gains subtracted or losses added at the following rates:

- $\frac{4}{5}$ of the prior year's gain or loss
- $\frac{3}{5}$ of the second preceding year's gain or loss
- $\frac{2}{5}$ of the third preceding year's gain or loss
- $\frac{1}{5}$ of the fourth preceding year's gain or loss

*Asset valuation change 6.* A plan can change its asset valuation method to the smoothed market value (with phase-in) described below, or to any alternative formulation that is algebraically equivalent to this smoothed value. The asset value determined under the method must be adjusted to be no greater than 120 percent and no less than 80 percent of the fair market value.

In the first year this method is used, the actuarial value of assets is equal to the fair market value as of the valuation date. In each subsequent year, the smoothed value is calculated in the same manner as it is in *asset valuation change 5*, except that the only gains or losses recognized are those occurring in the year of the change and in later years. The stated smoothing period cannot exceed five plan years.

*Asset valuation change 7.* A plan can change its asset valuation method to the average value, modified to use the alternative phase-in as described below, or to any alternative formulation that is algebraically equivalent to this average. The asset value determined under the method must be adjusted to be no greater than 120 percent and no less than 80 percent of the fair market value.

In the first year this method is used, the actuarial value of assets is equal to the fair market value. In the second year, the average value is calculated in the same manner as it is in *asset valuation change 2,* except that the averaging period is two years. In the third year, the average value is calculated in the same manner as it is in *asset valuation change 2,* except that the averaging period is three years. This process continues until the stated averaging period (not to exceed five years) is reached.

[Rev. Proc. 2000-40, 2000-42 I.R.B. 357, §§ 3.10-3.13, 3.15-3.17]

# Chapter 22

# Census Data and Demographics

Correctly determining pension benefit amounts requires the manipulation of an extraordinary number of details. Computations used by pension practitioners rely on detailed demographic information about a plan's population. Simple errors in the use of census data (e.g., transposing the numbers in a year of birth from 1937 to 1973) can have a huge impact on a plan's liability. This chapter examines how census data and mortality tables are used to arrive at accurate calculations of anticipated pension benefits, which in turn are used to assess necessary contributions and asset accumulation.

## Census Data

### Q 22:1  What is *census data*?

*Census data* of the employer is all the information regarding the employer's employees that is needed to determine the covered group, eligibility for benefits, the amount of benefits, and the payment form and duration. Such information includes the following:

- Name
- Date of birth
- Date of birth of spouse
- Date of hire
- Date of rehire (if applicable)
- Date or dates of termination

- Date of disability (if applicable)
- Date of retirement
- Date of death
- Hours worked
- Compensation paid
- Beneficiary and date of birth of the beneficiary
- Amount, form, and duration of benefits in pay status for retirees, beneficiaries, and disabled participants

Specific benefits may require additional information; for example, a disability benefit would require information about the date of disability and the duration of the disability period.

### Q 22:2    Should census data be reviewed?

Census data must be reviewed very carefully. Each year the data should be reconciled to ensure that the correct number of active participants is carried forward to the new year. The reconciliation should show new participants, terminations, deaths, disabilities, retirees, and end-of-period active participants. Terminated, vested, disabled, and retired participant counts should also be reconciled.

### Q 22:3    Are there different applications of census data results?

Yes. Normally a plan uses a *closed group*, that is, only employees currently employed by the employer. In a dynamic workforce environment, however, an *open,* or *projected,* method may be more appropriate for predicting the future costs of the plan. An actuary could estimate the number of new participants, retirees, terminations, deaths, and so forth based on the experience of the group and use the estimates to project future costs using an expansive, contractive, or stagnant model. Those projections allow the actuary to forecast contributions, asset accumulation, or benefit payouts.

### Q 22:4    How sensitive are actuarial calculations to census data changes?

The impact of demographic changes increases as the size of the group decreases. For example, the death of an owner in a top-heavy plan affects the benefits dramatically and jeopardizes the longevity of the plan. In larger populations, minor discrepancies have little or no impact on the result.

### Q 22:5    How does materiality affect the review of census data?

Although all census data must be reviewed, certainly the items that have the greatest impact on the benefit liabilities of the plan must be reviewed in greater detail. Such items include dates of birth, dates of employment, and compensation histories.

**Q 22:6   Is it necessary to obtain an employer's census data and demographic history before the establishment of a defined benefit plan?**

Yes. This information will be used to calculate accrued benefits and to determine the reasonableness of assumptions, including turnover, salary scale, mortality table, and so forth. In addition, this history may be important in testing benefits for discrimination.

## Mortality Tables

**Q 22:7   What is a *mortality table*?**

A *mortality table* is a set of probabilities of a person dying over the next year or years. It is established using a large (perhaps one million), select group, called the *radix*, and the group is measured from year to year to determine the number of people who live to the next year. The results are smoothed (because the radix may not be large enough to eliminate skewed frequencies) and provide the probability of living or dying to the next age.

When added to financial functions, the results provide the financial expectation of a stream of benefit payments, or an *annuity table.*

**Q 22:8   What is a *life expectancy table*?**

A *life expectancy table* is an annuity table with the interest rate set to zero. It represents the average future lifetime of a person from the current or starting age. Some tax tables use this concept (e.g., in the calculation of minimum required distributions), but life expectancy tables are rarely used in an actuary's work.

An actuary must apply the probability of living or dying beyond the age of life expectancy. If, for example, the life expectancy of a person of age 70 is 16 years, the actuary must determine the value of the benefits for a retiree who is age 87 even though the retiree will have passed his or her life expectancy at that age. Therefore, using a life expectancy table is never appropriate when determining the present value of an annuity stream of payments that will stop at death.

**Q 22:9   How do mortality tables differ?**

Mortality tables differ based on the group reviewed. For example, a disability mortality table is expected to have a greater rate of mortality than a healthy, working population table. A disability mortality table should also include the reduction of its population by recovery to healthy status.

An annuity table based on the population of those who are working and healthy at retirement age should show longer life expectancy than a life insurance table for the general population.

More payments are anticipated for longer life expectancies. More payments mean more reserves are required to provide those payments, and more required reserves translate to greater contributions.

### Q 22:10   Can a plan use different mortality tables for males and females in determining actuarially equivalent benefits?

No. A plan must use the same mortality table in determining actuarial equivalencies for male and female participants. The Supreme Court, in *Arizona v. Norris* [463 U.S. 1073, 1084–86 (1983)], held that the application of sex-distinct actuarial tables in calculating the amount of retirement benefits violated Title VII of the Civil Rights Act of 1964.

### Q 22:11   What is the *law of large numbers*?

The *law of large numbers* means that results can be predicted if the population studied is large enough. For example, if a coin is flipped 10 times (a small number), it could come up heads 10 times in a row. If, however, a coin is flipped one million times, heads will appear close to 50 percent of the time.

The law of large numbers is applied in actuarial work by using large radixes that provide reasonable probabilities of occurrences of such events as the number of people to become disabled or to die within a given time frame.

# Chapter 23

# The Role of the Enrolled Actuary

Actuaries place a value on risk. To compute this value, the actuary must first define the benefit or desired outcome and then apply assumptions on the probability of receiving the benefit or attaining the desired outcome. The benefit to be paid under a retirement plan may be different depending on the occurrence that triggers the payment. For example, on a participant's death, a beneficiary may receive 50 percent of the benefit that the participant would have received if the participant had not died. In computing the value of the death benefit, the actuary must include assumptions on the probability that the participant will die, the probability that the beneficiary will live, the timing of the benefit, and the duration of the benefit. The actuary must also assume an interest rate to determine the current value of the future benefit stream. This chapter covers various actuarial assumptions and the standards that an actuary can use in selecting those assumptions.

## Definition of Actuary

### Q 23:1   What is an *actuary*?

An *actuary* is one trained in evaluating the current financial implications of future contingent events.

Actuaries improve financial decision making by developing models to evaluate the current financial implications of uncertain future events and applying those models to problems of insurance and finance. Put simply, actuaries put a price tag on future risks.

Actuaries work in many industries, but mostly in the field of insurance, where their training is used in pricing products based on uncertain future events, such as death or accidents. In the pension field, actuaries are used to determine how much money is needed to provide a stream of retirement payments.

### Q 23:2 What is an *enrolled actuary*?

An *enrolled actuary* is an actuary in the field of pension plans licensed by the Joint Board for the Enrollment of Actuaries (JBEA) to practice before the government agencies responsible for administering the Employee Retirement Income Security Act of 1974 (ERISA). To be licensed, an actuary must satisfy experience and examination requirements specified by the board. Currently, the board requires three years of pension actuarial experience and successful completion of three examinations. [ERISA § 3042; I.R.C. § 7701(a)(35)]

### Q 23:3 How does one become an enrolled actuary?

First, to be licensed, an actuary must satisfy examination and experience requirements specified by the JBEA. Currently, the JBEA requires three years of pension actuarial experience and successful completion of two examinations, one of which has two parts (see Q 23:4). In addition, a candidate must submit a completed Form 5434, the JBEA Application for Enrollment. [ERISA § 3042; I.R.C. § 7701(a)(35)]

### Q 23:4 What examinations must be passed to become an enrolled actuary?

The JBEA administers two actuarial examinations that must be successfully completed by individuals to satisfy the actuarial knowledge requirement. The examinations are structured as follows:

1. The *Basic EA-1* tests knowledge of the mathematics of compound interest and practical financial analysis and the mathematics of life contingencies and practical demographic analysis.

2. The *Pension EA-2* examination consists of two segments. Segment A tests the selection of actuarial assumptions, actuarial cost methods, and the calculation of minimum required and maximum deductible contributions. Segment B tests knowledge of relevant federal pension laws as they affect pension actuarial practice.

The JBEA will grant a waiver of the EA-1 examination requirement to individuals who have successfully completed an academic program involving courses in actuarial mathematics or Course 2 or 3 of the Society of Actuaries Education and Examination Program.

### Q 23:5   What experience is required to become an enrolled actuary?

A candidate for enrollment must have satisfied certain responsible pension actuarial experience requirements. The candidate must have, within the 10-year period immediately preceding application for enrollment, completed either (1) a minimum of 36 months of responsible pension actuarial experience or (2) a minimum of 60 months of responsible actuarial experience, including at least 18 months of responsible pension actuarial experience. [20 C.F.R. § 901.13(b)]

*Actuarial experience* is the performance or direct supervision of services involving the application of principles of probability and compound interest to determine the present value of payments to be made at a certain time. *Responsible actuarial experience* means that the candidate has been involved in determining whether the methods and assumptions used are appropriate and has demonstrated a thorough understanding of actuarial principles. *Responsible pension actuarial experience* means responsible actuarial experience that also involves valuations of liabilities on pension plans using standard actuarial cost methods in determining normal cost, accrued liability, amortization of payments, and actuarial gains or losses. [20 C.F.R. § 901.1]

### Q 23:6   What are the requirements to renew enrollment?

An enrolled actuary's enrollment to practice is renewable every three years. To qualify for renewal of enrollment, the enrolled actuary must certify that he or she has satisfied the continuing professional education (CPE) requirements. Currently, a minimum of 36 hours of CPE are required during the three-year period. Of the 36 hours, at least 18 must comprise core subject matter; the remainder may be of a non-core nature. [20 C.F.R. § 901.11(e)(2)] The Form 5434-A, JBEA Application for Renewal of Enrollment, must be submitted on a timely basis with a $25 filing fee to ensure that the actuary's enrollment does not expire.

If an enrolled actuary belongs to an actuarial society (e.g., Society of Actuaries, American Academy of Actuaries, etc.), continuing education requirements for membership may vary from what is required by the JBEA and are often more stringent. In addition, the Actuarial Standards of Practice (ASOP) may require additional continuing education requirements in order to specialize in a particular field.

### Q 23:7   What qualifies as core subject matter?

Core subject matter is program content designed to enhance the knowledge of an enrolled actuary with respect to matters directly related to the performance of pension actuarial services under ERISA or the Internal Revenue Code (Code). Such core subject matter includes the characteristics of actuarial cost methods under ERISA, actuarial assumptions, minimum funding standards, Title IV of ERISA, requirements with respect to the valuation of plan assets, requirements for qualification of pension plans, maximum deductible contributions, tax treatments of distributions from qualified pension plans, excise taxes related to the funding of qualified pension plans, and standards of performance for actuarial services.

To qualify for continuing education credit, a course of learning must be a qualifying program that includes core and/or non-core subject matter conducted by a qualifying sponsor.

As stated in the Code of Federal Regulations, qualifying programs include:

1. *Formal programs.* Formal programs qualify as continuing education programs if they:

   a. Require attendance by at least three individuals engaged in substantive pension service in addition to the instructor, discussion leader, or speaker;

   b. Require that the program be conducted by a qualified instructor, discussion leader, or speaker, that is, a person whose background, training, education and/or experience is appropriate for instructing or leading a discussion on the subject matter of the particular program; and

   c. Require a written outline and/or textbook and certificate of attendance provided by the sponsor, all of which must be retained by the enrolled actuary for a three-year period following the end of the enrollment cycle.

2. *Correspondence or individual study programs (including audio and/or video taped programs).* Qualifying continuing education programs include correspondence or individual study programs completed on an individual basis by the enrolled actuary and conducted by qualifying sponsors. The allowable credit hours for such programs will be measured on a basis comparable to the measurement of a seminar or course for credit in an accredited educational institution. Such programs qualify as continuing education programs if they:

   a. Require registration of the participants by the sponsor;

   b. Provide a means for measuring completion by the participants (e.g., written examination); and

   c. Require a written outline and/or textbook and certificate of completion provided by the sponsor. Such certificate must be retained by the participant for a three-year period following the end of an enrollment cycle.

3. *Teleconferencing.* Programs utilizing teleconferencing or other communications technologies qualify for continuing education purposes if they either:

   a. Meet all the requirements of formal programs, except that they may include a sign-on/sign-off capacity or similar technique in lieu of the physical attendance of participants; or

   b. Meet all the requirements of correspondence or individual study programs.

4. *Serving as an instructor, discussion leader, or speaker.*

   a. Four hours of continuing education credit will be awarded for each contact hour completed as an instructor, discussion leader, or speaker at an educational program which meets the continuing education requirements of this section, in recognition of both presentation and preparation time;

b. The credit for instruction and preparation may not exceed 50 percent of the continuing education requirement for an enrollment cycle;

c. Presentation of the same material as an instructor, discussion leader, or speaker more than one time in any 36-month period will not qualify for continuing education credit. A program will not be considered to consist of the same material if a substantial portion of the content has been revised to reflect changes in the law or in the state of the art relative to the performance of pension actuarial service;

d. Credit as an instructor, discussion leader, or speaker will not be awarded to panelists, moderators or others whose contribution does not constitute a substantial portion of the program. However, such individuals may be awarded credit for attendance, provided the other provisions of this section are met; and

e. The nature of the subject matter will determine if credit will be of a core or non-core nature.

5. *Credit for published articles, books, films, audio and video tapes, etc.*

a. Continuing education credit will be awarded for the creation of materials for publication or distribution with respect to matters directly related to the CPE requirements of this section;

b. The credit allowed will be on the basis of one hour credit for each hour of preparation time of the material. It will be the responsibility of the person claiming the credit to maintain records to verify preparation time;

c. Publication or distribution may utilize any available technology for the dissemination of written, visual, or auditory materials;

d. The materials must be available on reasonable terms for acquisition and use by all enrolled actuaries;

e. The credit for the creation of materials may not exceed 25 percent of the continuing education requirement of any enrollment cycle;

f. The nature of the subject matter will determine if credit will be of a core or non-core nature; and

g. Publication of the same material more than one time will not qualify for continuing education credit. A publication will not be considered to consist of the same material if a substantial portion has been revised to reflect changes in the law or in the state of the art relating to the performance of pension actuarial service.

6. *Service on Joint Board advisory committee(s)*. Continuing education credit may be awarded by the Joint Board for service on (any of) its advisory committee(s), to the extent that the Board considers warranted by the service rendered.

7. *Preparation of Joint Board examinations*. Continuing educational credit may be awarded by the Joint Board for participation in drafting questions for use on Joint Board examinations or in pretesting its examinations, to

the extent the Board determines suitable. Such credit may not exceed 50 percent of the CPE requirement for the applicable enrollment cycle.

8. *Society examinations.* Individuals may earn CPE credit for achieving a passing grade on proctored examinations sponsored by a professional organization or society recognized by the Joint Board. Such credit is limited to the number of hours scheduled for each examination and may be applied only as non-core credit provided the content of the examination is non-core.

9. *Pension law examination.* Individuals may establish eligibility for renewal of enrollment for any enrollment cycle by:

   a. Achieving a passing score on the pension law actuarial examination offered by the Joint Board and administered under this part during the applicable enrollment cycle; and

   b. Completing a minimum of 12 hours of qualifying continuing education in core subject matter during the same applicable enrollment cycle.

   c. This option of satisfying the CPE requirements is not available to those who receive initial enrollment during the enrollment cycle.

[20 C.F.R. § 901.11(f)]

### Q 23:8  How is a credit hour measured?

A credit hour is 50 minutes of continuous participation in a program. Each session in a program must be at least one full credit hour, that is, 50 minutes. For example, a single-session program lasting 100 minutes will count as two credit hours, and a program comprised of three 75-minute sessions (225 minutes) constitutes four credit hours. However, at the end of an enrollment cycle, an individual may total the number of minutes of sessions of at least one credit hour in duration attended during the cycle and divide by 50. For example, attending three 75-minute segments at two separate programs will accord an individual nine credit hours (450 minutes divided by 50) toward fulfilling the minimum number of CPE hours. It will not be permissible to merge non-core hours with core hours. For university or college courses, each "semester" hour credit will equal 15 credit hours and each "quarter" hour credit will equal 10 credit hours. Measurements of other formats of university or college courses will be handled on a comparable basis. [20 C.F.R. § 901.11(h)]

### Q 23:9  What records must be maintained to prove compliance with the continuing education requirements?

Each individual applying for renewal must retain for a period of three years following the end of an enrollment cycle the information required with regard to qualifying CPE credit hours. This information must include:

- Name of the sponsoring organization
- Location of the program
- Title of the program and description of its content, for example, course syllabus and/or textbook

- Dates attended
- Credit hours claimed and whether core or non-core subject matter
- Name(s) of the instructor(s), discussion leader(s), or speaker(s), if appropriate
- Certificate of completion and/or signed statement of the hours of attendance obtained from the sponsor
- Total core and non-core credit

To receive continuing education credit for service completed as an instructor, discussion leader, or speaker, the following information must be maintained for a period of three years following the end of the applicable enrollment cycle.

- Name of the sponsoring organization
- Location of the program
- Title of the program and description of its content
- Dates of the program
- Credit hours claimed and whether core or non-core subject matter

To receive continuing education credit for a publication, the following information must be maintained for a period of three years following the end of the applicable enrollment cycle.

- Publisher
- Title of the publication
- A copy of the publication
- Date of publication
- Credit hours claimed
- Whether core or non-core subject matter
- Availability and distribution of the publications to enrolled actuaries

[20 C.F.R. § 901.11(i)]

### Q 23:10   What are the standards of performance for an enrolled actuary?

In general, an enrolled actuary is expected to undertake an actuarial assignment only if he or she is qualified to do so. In addition, the enrolled actuary is subject to the following duties as outlined in 20 C.F.R. Section 901.20(b) through (h):

1. *Professional duty.* An enrolled actuary shall not perform actuarial services for any person or organization that he or she believes or has reasonable grounds for believing may use his or her services in a fraudulent manner or in a manner inconsistent with law.

2. *Advice or explanations.* An enrolled actuary shall provide to the plan administrator, upon appropriate request, supplemental advice or explanation relative to any report signed or certified by such enrolled actuary.

3. *Conflicts of interest.* In any situation in which the enrolled actuary has a conflict of interest with respect to the performance of actuarial services, of

which the enrolled actuary has knowledge, he or she shall not perform such actuarial services except after full disclosure has been made to the plan trustees, any named fiduciary of the plan, the plan administrator, and, if the plan is subject to a collective bargaining agreement, the collective bargaining representative.

4. *Assumptions, calculations, and recommendations.* The enrolled actuary shall exercise due care, skill, prudence, and diligence to ensure that (a) the actuarial assumptions are reasonable in the aggregate and the actuarial cost method and the actuarial method of valuation of assets are appropriate; (b) the calculations are accurately carried out; and (c) the report, any recommendations to the plan administrator, and any supplemental advice or explanation relative to the report reflect the results of the calculations.

5. *Report or certificate.* An enrolled actuary shall include, in any report or certificate stating actuarial costs or liabilities, a statement or reference describing or clearly identifying the data, any material inadequacies therein and the implications thereof, and the actuarial methods and assumptions employed.

6. *Utilization of enrolled actuary designation.* An enrolled actuary shall not advertise his or her status as an enrolled actuary in any solicitation related to the performance of actuarial services and shall not employ; accept employment in partnership, corporate, or any other form; or share fees with any individual or entity who so solicits. However, the use of the term *enrolled actuary* to identify an individual who is named on the stationery, letterhead, or business card of an enrolled actuary, or of a partnership, association, or corporation, shall not be considered a violation of this requirement. In addition, the term *enrolled actuary* may appear after the general listing of an enrolled actuary's name in a telephone directory, provided that such listing is not of a distinctive nature.

7. *Notification.* An enrolled actuary shall provide written notification of the nonfiling of any actuarial document that he or she has signed upon discovery of the nonfiling. Such notification shall be made to the office of the Internal Revenue Service (IRS), the Department of Labor (DOL), or the Pension Benefit Guaranty Corporation (PBGC) where such document should have been filed.

### Q 23:11   What is the enrolled actuary's role in the administration of a defined benefit plan?

The enrolled actuary's primary function is to determine the amount of money needed by a defined benefit plan to pay future retirement benefits to plan participants. For plan years prior to the changes made by the Pension Protection Act of 2006 (PPA), the determination of this amount will depend on the assumptions and methods chosen by the actuary, and the selection of these will represent both his or her professional judgment and legislative constraints. The actuary must also certify the tax-deductible amount that can be contributed to the plan. With the passage of the PPA, Congress has taken away much of the professional judgment previously given to actuaries and now the assumptions and methods used in determining the minimum required and maximum deductible contributions are prescribed by law. (See chapters 19 and 20.)

## Selecting Actuarial Assumptions

### Q 23:12　What are *economic assumptions?*

*Economic assumptions* are primarily the investment return, discount rate, and compensation scale used in measuring obligations under defined benefit plans. Other economic assumptions are inflation, administrative expenses, cost-of-living increases, and cost of annuity conversions.

### Q 23:13　What are *demographic assumptions?*

*Demographic assumptions* are primarily the mortality, disability, voluntary and involuntary terminations, and retirement decrements used in measuring obligations under defined benefit plans. Other demographic assumptions are family composition; marriage, divorce, and remarriage rates; new entrants; leaves; layoffs; transfers and reinstatements; employment ages; and hours worked.

### Q 23:14　What other assumptions can an actuary use?

More limited assumptions are used to select the assumptions listed in Qs 23:12 and 23:13. Merit scales, that is, the component of compensation increases that is based on good performance, can be developed for compensation scales. Select and ultimate periods can be used to develop long-term interest projections, which are interest tables that use selected interest rates for a period of time and a singular rate for all years past the select period.

| Year | Percentage |
|------|------------|
| 1 | 7% |
| 2 | 6.75% |
| 3 | 6.5% |
| 4 | 6.25% |
| 5 and following | 6% |

For example, in the preceding table, the select period is years 1 through 4, and the ultimate period is year 5 and following. Productivity growth, real rate of return, risk-free rate of return, and risk premiums are used to determine interest and discount assumptions. *Productivity growth* is the realized and unrealized growth in a security. Real rate of return is the amount of the return over the risk-free rate of return. *Risk-free rate of return* is the short-term interest rate paid on U.S. Treasury bills. *Risk premium* is the additional return gained from investing in securities other than U.S. Treasury bills. The actuary can also apply hypothetical data to prepare models and illustrations to demonstrate the impact of a particular assumption.

### Q 23:15   What impact do legal requirements have on the selection of assumptions?

Under the law, specific liabilities, such as current liability (see chapters 19 and 21), must be computed using a specific interest rate or an interest assumption that lies within a specific range of rates (see Q 23:16). Actuarial standards that apply to the selection of assumptions do not apply to the use of assumptions that are mandated by law or regulation.

### Q 23:16   Can more than one interest rate be used in completing the valuation report of a defined benefit plan?

Yes. The actuary uses several rates. Following are descriptions of the more common interest rates.

*Funding interest rate.* The funding interest rate is normally the interest assumption that the actuary uses in computing the costs under Code Section 412. This rate is normally the same as the discount rate. For plan years beginning after December 31, 2007, this interest rate will be prescribed by law and will be equal to the segment rate in effect at that time.

*Interest rates for determining funding target.* For purposes of determining the funding target and normal cost of a plan for any plan year beginning after December 31, 2007, the interest rate used in determining the present value of the benefits of the plan, in the case of benefits reasonably determined to be payable during the five-year period beginning on the first day of the plan year, is the first segment rate with respect to the applicable month. The interest rate, in the case of benefits reasonably determined to be payable during the 15-year period beginning at the end of the period covered by the first segment rate, is the second segment rate with respect to the applicable month and the interest rate, in the case of benefits reasonably determined to be payable after the period covered by the second segment rate, is the third segment rate with respect to the applicable month.

*Segment rates (First, second, third segment rates).* For plan years beginning after December 31, 2007, segment rates are used for various purposes. The term *first segment rate* means, with respect to any month, the single rate of interest which is determined by the Secretary of the Treasury for such month on the basis of the corporate bond yield curve for such month, taking into account only that portion of such yield curve which is based on bonds maturing during the five-year period commencing with such month. The term *second segment rate* means, with respect to any month, the single rate of interest which shall be determined by the Secretary of the Treasury for such month on the basis of the corporate bond yield curve for such month, taking into account only that portion of such yield curve which is based on bonds maturing during the 15-year period beginning at the end of the period covered by the first segment rate. The term *third segment rate* means, with respect to any month, the single rate of interest which shall be determined by the Secretary of the Treasury for such month on the basis of the corporate bond yield curve for such month, taking into account only that portion of such yield curve which is based on bonds maturing during periods beginning after the second segment rate.

*Discount rate.* The discount rate is the rate used to compute the present value of benefits under a defined benefit pension plan. The actuary selects the discount rate based on the guidance provided in ASOP No. 27 (see Q 23:20). This rate is normally the same as the funding interest rate.

*Omnibus Budget Reconciliation Act of 1987 (OBRA '87) current liability rate.* The current liability interest rate is the rate used to compute the current liability of a plan. The interest rate used by the actuary is not subject to ASOP No. 27. It is a rate that must fall within a permissible range. The rate of interest must not be more than 10 percent above and not more than 10 percent below the weighted average of the rates of interest on 30-year Treasury securities during the four-year period ending on the last day before the beginning of the plan year. [I.R.C. § 412(b)(5)(B)] The actuary can select any point estimate (i.e., the exact interest rate selected within the range). This particular interest rate is no longer applicable.

*Retirement Protection Act of 1994 (RPA '94) current liability rate.* The RPA '94 current liability rate is the same as the OBRA '87 current liability rate except the corridor is no more than 5 percent above nor 10 percent below the weighted average of the rates of interest on 30-year Treasury securities during the four-year period ending on the last day before the beginning of the plan year. [I.R.C. § 412(b)(7)(C)] The actuary can select any point estimate within the range. This rate will no longer be applicable for plan years beginning after December 31, 2007.

*Mandatory employee contribution rate.* The mandatory employee contribution rate is the interest rate used in accumulating employee contributions to determine the amount of a participant's accrued benefit derived from employee contributions. The interest rate used is 120 percent of the federal midterm rate (as in effect under Code Section 1274 for the first month of the plan year). This rate must be used in conjunction with the Code Section 417(e)(3) rates (the rates for computing lump-sum benefits under defined benefit plans) for projecting values to normal retirement age.

*Actuarial equivalent interest rate.* The actuarial equivalent interest rate is the interest rate declared in the plan document to determine the alternate forms of benefit under a defined benefit pension plan or under the terms of the annuity contract.

*Maximum benefit computation rate.* Commonly referred to as the Section 415 rate, the maximum benefit computation rate is used for adjusting the maximum life annuity benefit payable at age 62 for other forms of benefit payments before, after, or at age 62. See chapter 12 for more details. [I.R.C. § 415(b)(2)(E)]

*Top-heavy interest rate.* The top-heavy interest rate is the rate used to compute the present value of accrued benefits under the plan to determine if the plan is top heavy. An actuary is not required to use the funding interest rate or the actuarial equivalent interest rate as specified by a plan; however, an interest rate not greater than 6 percent nor less than 5 percent will be considered reasonable if used with a reasonable mortality table. [Treas. Reg. § 1.416-1, Q T-26]

*Deficit reduction contribution rate.* The deficit reduction contribution rate is the same as the current liability rate except that the rate can be increased by the following percentages for the corresponding year:

| Year | Percentage |
|------|------------|
| 1995 | 109% |
| 1996 | 108% |
| 1997 | 107% |
| 1998 | 106% |
| 1999 and thereafter | 105% |

*Waiver from minimum funding standard rate.* In the case of a plan that is not a multiemployer plan, the interest rate used for computing the amortization charge of the waived amounts is the greater of 150 percent of the federal midterm rate (as in effect under Code Section 1274 for the first month of the plan year) or the rate of interest used under the plan in determining costs. In the case of a multiemployer plan, the rate is determined under Code Section 6621(b). In plan years beginning after December 31, 2007, the interest rate used in calculating the waiver amortization charge will be the same as the segment rates used for funding.

*Discrimination computation interest rate (Section 401(a)(4) rate).* In accordance with Code Section 401(a)(4), the standard interest rate used for discrimination testing is an interest rate that is neither less than 7.5 percent nor more than 8.5 percent. The person performing the discrimination testing selects the point estimate from within the range.

*Alternate forms of benefit for permitted disparity interest rate.* The interest rate used for computing alternate forms of benefit for permitted disparity is the same as the discrimination computation interest rate. The person performing the discrimination testing selects the point estimate from within the range.

*Statement of Financial Accounting Standards (SFAS) No. 87 interest rate.* The Financial Accounting Standards Board issues SFASs, standards by which accountants must practice. The interest rate used for SFAS No. 87 computations is the expected long-term rate of return on plan assets and is intended to be a long-term rate, suitable for projecting the return on plan assets. It reflects the expected return on plan assets on hand and new money to be received during the measurement year, as well as the reinvestment of those assets in future years. [SFAS No. 87-2.4(b)] The accountant preparing the financial statements is responsible for the selection of this assumption. This rate can and does change from year to year based on the accountant's opinion.

*SFAS No. 87 discount rate.* The discount rate for SFAS No. 87 computations is based on the currently available rates and is intended to be the rate at which the plan's obligations could be effectively settled on the measurement date. It is independent of the funding level and the plan's investments, and it is expected that the discount rate will change when interest rates in general change. The discount rate is used for all actuarial calculations under SFAS No. 87.

[SFAS No. 87-2.4(a)] The accountant preparing the financial statements is responsible for the selection of this assumption. This rate can and does change from year to year based on the accountant's opinion.

*SFAS No. 36 interest rate.* The interest rate used for SFAS No. 36 is normally either the actuarial equivalent interest rate or the funding interest rate. The actuary is responsible for selecting this rate.

*PBGC rates (old Section 417(e) rates).* The old Section 417(e) rates are the interest rates used by the PBGC for purposes of determining the present value of a lump-sum distribution on plan termination. These rates are no longer used for purposes of determining equivalent benefits under Code Section 417(e) for plan years beginning after 1999 when use of the GATT rate is required (see below).

*General Agreement on Tariffs and Trade of 1994 (GATT) rate.* The GATT rate, or applicable interest rate, is the annual rate of interest on 30-year Treasury securities for the month before the date of distribution or such other time that the secretary of the Treasury may by regulation prescribe. [I.R.C. § 417 (e)(3)(A)(ii)(II)]

### Q 23:17  If an interest rate or mortality table is listed in a plan document in the definition of actuarial equivalence, must an actuary use that rate or table for the assumptions in determining the costs of the plan?

No. An actuary must consider the effect that the definition of actuarial equivalence provided has on the benefits, but the actuary must use the assumptions that are, in the actuary's professional opinion, reasonable and reflect the actuary's best estimate of anticipated experience under the plan, except when these assumptions are prescribed by law. [I.R.C. § 412(c)(3)(B)]

### Q 23:18  Must each actuarial assumption selected be individually reasonable or can the assumptions be reasonable in the aggregate?

Actuarial assumptions must be individually reasonable, or must, in the aggregate, result in a total contribution to the plan equivalent to the contribution that would be determined if each assumption was reasonable. [I.R.C. § 412(c)(3)(A)] The PPA changed this language as well to the following:

> The determination of any present value or other computation . . . shall be made on the basis of actuarial assumptions and methods each of which is reasonable (taking into account the experience of the plan and reasonable expectations), and which, in combination, offer the actuary's best estimate of anticipated experience under the plan. [I.R.C. § 430(h)(1)]

ASOP No. 27 requires each assumption to be reasonable. [ASOP No. 27, § 3.9] Assumptions can be combined and used in the aggregate as long as the actuary has individual assumptions to back up the aggregation of assumptions. For example, in calculating the cost of a retirement plan, the actuary may assume that compensation increases will be approximately 3 percent per year. The actuary may also assume that the preretirement discount rate is 8 percent. The net effect is approximated by using a 5 percent preretirement discount rate.

Unlike other defined benefit plans, multiemployer plans are not legally required to use individually reasonable assumptions; however, the enrolled actuary must follow the provisions of ASOP No. 27 (see Q 23:20).

## Actuarial Standards and Code of Conduct

### Q 23:19   Are there any actuarial standards that apply in selecting actuarial assumptions for a defined benefit plan?

Yes. The Actuarial Standards Board (ASB) developed four actuarial standards that apply directly to pension actuaries, as follows:

1. ASOP No. 2: Recommendations for Actuarial Communications Related to Statements of Financial Accounting Standards Nos. 87 and 88;
2. ASOP No. 4: Measuring Pension Obligations (see Q 23:43);
3. ASOP No. 23: Data Quality (see Q 23:43); and
4. ASOP No. 27: Measuring Pension Obligations (see Q 23:20).

Copies of the standards can be obtained from the American Academy of Actuaries, 1100 Seventeenth Street NW, 7th Floor, Washington, DC 20036.

### Q 23:20   What are the basic provisions of ASOP No. 27?

The ASB's ASOP No. 27 provides guidance on the selection of economic assumptions in measuring pension obligations in defined benefit plans. Although the ASOP does not provide cookbook instructions, it illustrates the factors that an actuary may consider in determining materiality of an assumption, the components of an economic assumption, the development of a range of acceptable assumptions, and some of the weighting factors that the actuary may use in the selection of the point assumption (i.e., the specific interest rate the actuary picks within the range of assumption). It also provides suggested disclosure information.

### Q 23:21   What is meant by *materiality*?

*Materiality* refers to the magnitude of the impact of a particular benefit, feature, rate, or factor. For example, if all benefits are 100 percent vested on a participant's separation from service, termination rates to determine actuarial gains or losses would be meaningless and not material to developing estimates of the costs and values of the plan, because no benefits will be forfeited.

**Q 23:22   How does an actuary select an economic assumption?**

An actuary should consider the following factors in selecting economic assumptions:

1. The purpose and nature of the measurement for which the assumptions will be used;
2. The characteristics of the obligation to be measured;
3. Materiality of the assumptions to the measurement; and
4. Appropriate recent and long-term historical data.

To select the economic assumptions required for a particular measurement, the actuary first identifies the components of each assumption and evaluates relevant data. Next, the actuary develops a best-estimate range for each economic assumption required for the measurement. The *best-estimate range* is the narrowest range in which actual results compounded over the measurement period are more likely than not to fall. Finally, the actuary selects a point within the range on further evaluation of measurement-specific factors. [ASOP No. 27, §§ 3.3, 3.4]

**Q 23:23   How is an investment return assumption selected?**

The actuary first reviews current yields to maturity of government securities and corporate bonds, inflation forecasts, historical rates of return on asset classes, and historical plan performance, and then constructs the best-estimate range either by analyzing each component and combining them (building-block method), or by analyzing of future liabilities and matching a portfolio of bond investments needed to meet those liabilities (cash-flow matching method).

The range can be modified and/or a rate within the range can be selected after consideration of measurement-specific factors. [ASOP No. 27, §§ 3.6.2, 3.6.3] The actuary should document (at least annually) how the interest rate assumption was determined, as well as justification for any deviation from the ASOP.

**Q 23:24   What factors are included in the building-block method for selecting an interest rate assumption?**

Under the building-block method, the rate of return is viewed as a combination of various factors, including:

- "Real rate of return"
- Risk premium
- Inflation
- Investment expenses

The real rate of return is what a risk-free investment would receive as a rate of return without inflation, usually between 2 percent and 3 percent. The risk premium is the additional payment received by an investor to encourage them to take the risk. Investment expenses are the cost of managing the investment, as a percentage, including commissions.

### Q 23:25   What measurement-specific factors are used in selecting an investment return?

There are a number of measurement-specific factors to consider in selecting an investment return, including the following:

- Purpose of the measurement
- Investment policy
- Reinvestment risk
- Investment volatility
- Investment manager performance
- Investment expenses
- Cash-flow timing
- Benefit volatility
- Expected plan termination
- Tax status of the funding vehicle

[ASOP No. 27, § 3.6.3]

### Q 23:26   What impact does the purpose of the measurement have on the selection of an investment return?

The purpose of the measurement is a primary factor in the selection. For example, the interest rate selected for valuing lump-sum benefits in the year of termination may be very different from the interest rate selected for measuring the same plan's present value of benefits on an ongoing basis as the actuary must project the interest rate to be used in the future to satisfy these obligations.

### Q 23:27   What impact does investment policy have on the selection of an investment return?

Investment policy is one factor in predicting investment returns. For example, equity investments are more likely to have a higher return than investments in bonds. Therefore, an actuary will select a higher investment return if plan assets are invested more heavily in equities than he or she would if plan assets are invested primarily in bonds.

### Q 23:28   What impact does reinvestment risk have on the selection of an investment return?

Reinvestment of dividends and principal can affect future results. For example, dividends that are reinvested in the stock from which they came will generally outperform those that are reinvested in a money market fund.

**Q 23:29    What impact does investment volatility have on the selection of an investment return?**

Plans investing heavily in more volatile assets run the risk of liquidating those assets at depressed values to meet benefit obligations. In addition, other risks may be present, including risk of default or bankruptcy. The actuary may assume a lower investment return assumption in consideration of these extra risks.

**Q 23:30    What impact does the investment manager's performance have on the selection of an investment return?**

It may not be prudent to anticipate a continuation of past performance by an investment manager. Few money managers are able to sustain continued above-market returns, and poor managers are usually replaced. If the money manager is also the plan sponsor, however, it may be prudent to assume that he or she will not replace him or herself regardless of performance. Therefore, although past performance must be reviewed, it may or may not be reasonable to assume future performance will remain the same based on these factors.

**Q 23:31    What impact do investment expenses have on the selection of an investment return?**

If investment-related expenses are paid from plan assets, reduction in the investment return assumption may be necessary.

**Q 23:32    What impact does cash-flow timing have on the selection of an investment return?**

The actuary should analyze expected future contributions compared to the benefit payments that will be required to determine the plan's liquidity needs. If the plan is required to have more liquid investments than normal, a reduction in the investment return assumption may be prudent.

**Q 23:33    What impact does benefit volatility have on the selection of an investment return?**

Benefit volatility may be a primary factor in the selection of an investment return for small plans with unpredictable benefit payment patterns. In such cases, it is advisable to reduce the anticipated investment return to reflect the probability that the plan might be required to liquidate securities at depressed values to meet benefit obligations.

**Q 23:34    What impact does an expected plan termination have on the selection of an investment return?**

If it is projected that the plan will terminate at some future date (e.g., on retirement of the owner), the measurement period should be shortened. With a shorter, or defined measurement period, the actuary should be more conservative in selecting the investment return because the plan may not have sufficient time to recover from a year of poor performance.

### Q 23:35   What impact does the tax status of the funding vehicle have on the selection of an investment return?

If the plan is nonqualified, or disqualified, the income taxes due from the trust may reduce the plan's investment return and thus the actuary's selection of an investment return.

### Q 23:36   Can the ultimate form of benefit selected by participants affect the selection of the investment return assumption?

No. The amount of certain forms of benefit is based on rates defined by the plan document or the Code. For example, lump-sum benefits can be determined using Section 417(e) interest rates. These required interest rates should be reflected, however, in the determination of the amount of benefits expected to be paid, rather than in an adjustment to the investment rate of return used to measure the obligation. [ASOP No. 27, § 3.6.5]

### Q 23:37   Is there a formula that can be used to select economic assumptions?

No formula or worksheet exists that covers all circumstances. The following example is taken from a pension practice note prepared by the Pension Practice Council of the American Academy of Actuaries. This practice note was developed as an aid to actuaries in selecting and documenting the investment return assumption in complying with ASOP No. 27. It is not intended to be a definitive statement as to what constitutes generally accepted practice but merely describes an approach that may be used.

> **Example.** *Small Defined Benefit Plan.* This is a new plan covering a single participant currently aged 40 who is expected to retire at age 55, taking a lump-sum distribution from the plan. The plan has no investment experience, and the plan sponsor anticipates making investments in a conservative portfolio of stocks and bonds using his current broker. Given the capital-gain advantage of holding stocks outside the plan, the sponsor anticipates that plan investments could be 65 percent high-quality corporate bonds and 35 percent stocks. There is no anticipated cash-flow need for the estimated 15-year time horizon for the plan. Plan investment expenses, including brokerage commissions, are estimated to be 1 percent of plan assets.
>
> The 15-year historical rates of return for large company stocks and long-term corporate bonds are as follows:

|  | *Large-Company Stocks* | *Long-Term Corporate Bonds* |
|---|:---:|:---:|
| 25th Percentile | 7.1% | 2.6% |
| Median | 10.7% | 3.7% |
| 75th Percentile | 15.2% | 6.2% |

The actuary first determined that the historical range based on the 25th percentile to the 75th percentile results is as follows:

*25th percentile:*

$$0.35 \times 7.1\% + 0.65 \times 2.6\% = 4.18\%$$

*Median:*

$$0.35 \times 10.7\% + 0.65 \times 3.7\% = 6.15\%$$

*75th percentile:*

$$0.35 \times 15.2\% + 0.65 \times 6.2\% = 9.35\%$$

The actuary then verified that the range determined by this process (4.18% – 9.35%) was consistent with his expectation for inflation, 3 percent, and current government bond yields of 6 percent. Finally, given that all of the plan liability is tied to a single participant and considering the volatility of the plan benefits caused by interest rate fluctuations, as well as the anticipated level of investment expense, the actuary adopted a 5 percent investment return assumption.

With a larger plan, the actuary may use additional tools in selecting the investment return assumption, including a longer historical average and a comparison of historical plan returns to what has been achieved in the market.

### Q 23:38 What happens when government-mandated assumptions fall outside the range of reasonable assumptions as determined by the actuary?

The legal requirements always supersede the requirements of the ASOPs. There is no requirement that if there is a range of assumptions that can be used legally, the point estimate in the range must be the point that intersects or is closest to the actuary's best estimate. [ASOP No. 27, § 3.11]

### Q 23:39 Can an actuary change assumptions from year to year?

Yes. The best-estimate range should be reviewed each year to see if it is still appropriate. Although the range may not change significantly, the assumption within the range may change based on the actuary's professional judgment. [ASOP No. 27, § 3.12]

### Q 23:40 Is the actuary required to follow all steps outlined in ASOP No. 27 in selecting economic assumptions?

No. The actuary is not required to use a type of economic assumption or to select a more refined economic assumption when it is not expected to produce materially different results. In addition, if using a more refined approach will not produce materially different results, the actuary is not required to use it, if it cannot be done within a reasonable cost. [ASOP No. 27, § 3.14] However, if the actuary deviates from the requirements of ASOP No. 27, he or she may have an added burden of proof in the event that his or her assumptions are questioned.

### Q 23:41   How does the actuarial code of conduct enter into the selection of assumptions?

Precept 2 of the Actuarial Code of Professional Conduct indicates that an actuary must perform professional services with integrity, skill, and care. Precept 3 indicates that an actuary must perform services only when he or she is qualified to do so and meets applicable qualification standards. Precept 4 indicates that an actuary must ensure that professional services performed by, or under the direction of, the actuary meet applicable standards of practice. All three precepts indicate that the actuary must be knowledgeable regarding the standards of practice and must apply them in his or her work.

### Q 23:42   What if the plan sponsor demands the use of an assumption other than the one the actuary selects?

Actuarial assumptions are the domain of the actuary and must be determined by the actuary. The assumptions must represent the actuary's best estimate and judgment, not the judgment of his or her employer, the client, or another third party.

### Q 23:43   What standards apply to the selection of demographic assumptions?

ASOP No. 23, Data Quality, provides guidance to the actuary on selecting the data that underlie the actuarial work product: reviewing the data for appropriateness, reasonableness, and comprehensiveness; and making appropriate disclosures. [ASOP No. 23, § 1.1]

ASOP No. 4, Measuring Pension Obligations, provides guidance to the actuary on selecting all assumptions. This is the overall ASOP on selection of assumptions and cost methods. ASOP No. 27 provides guidance on selection of economic assumptions. Additional ASOPs are anticipated on the selection and use of actuarial cost methods and on the selection of demographic assumptions.

### Q 23:44   What must an actuary disclose concerning the assumptions used in a plan?

An actuary must fully disclose the assumptions used in the actuarial work product and any variances from the ASOPs that the actuary used. The work papers should provide supporting data for the selection of the assumptions. In addition, the actuary must report any possible conflicts of interest that may impact the professional opinions stated in any report. Any assumptions or methods used that are not in the control of the actuary, such as the discount rate in an SFAS No. 87 report or computation of current liability, should also be noted and disclosed.

### Q 23:45   How do changes in actuarial assumptions affect the results?

A modest change in assumptions may have a major impact on the results. For example, a 1 percent change in the discount rate could mean a 25 percent decrease in a plan's computed liability. A change in the mortality table used could mean a 6 percent to 12 percent change in liability.

### Q 23:46   Are there any other standards of practice that are applicable to enrolled actuaries?

Yes, there are standards of practice promulgated by any professional organizations (i.e., the Society of Actuaries, American Society of Pension Practitioners and Actuaries, Casualty Actuary Society, etc.) to which the actuary may belong and also standards that are promulgated by the Treasury Department and the IRS.

### Q 23:47   What are the standards of practice that are promulgated by the IRS?

In Circular 230, the IRS has outlined the standards of practice for those who may practice before the IRS. Enrolled actuaries in addition to attorneys, CPA's and enrolled agents are specifically mentioned as one of the four groups of individuals who may practice before the IRS. [31 C.F.R. § 10.3]

The IRS defines practice as:

> Practice before the Internal Revenue Service comprehends all matters connected with a presentation to the IRS or any of its officers or employees relating to a taxpayer's rights, privileges, or liabilities under laws or regulations administered by the IRS. Such presentations include, but are not limited to, preparing and filing documents, corresponding and communicating with the IRS, and representing a client at conferences, hearings, and meetings. [31 C.F.R. § 10.2(d)]

The general requirements of Circular 230 include:

1. A practitioner who, having been retained by a client with respect to a matter administered by the IRS, knows that the client has not complied with the revenue laws of the United States or has made an error in or omission from any return, document, affidavit, or other paper which the client submitted or executed under the revenue laws of the United States, must advise the client promptly of the fact of such noncompliance, error, or omission. The practitioner must advise the client of the consequences as provided under the Code and regulations of such noncompliance, error, or omission. [31 C.F.R. § 10.21]

2. A practitioner may not charge an unconscionable fee for representing a client in a matter before the IRS. [31 C.F.R. § 10.27]

3. In general, a practitioner must, at the request of a client, promptly return any and all records of the client that are necessary for the client to comply with his or her Federal tax obligations. [31 C.F.R. 10.28]

4. A practitioner shall not represent a client in his or her practice before the IRS if the representation involves a conflict of interest. [31 C.F.R. § 10.29]

5. A practitioner may not sign a tax return as a preparer if the practitioner determines that the tax return contains a position that does not have a

realistic possibility of being sustained on its merits (the realistic possibility standard) unless the position is not frivolous and is adequately disclosed to the IRS. [31 C.F.R. § 10.34]

6. A practitioner advising a client to take a position on a tax return, or preparing or signing a tax return as a preparer, must inform the client of the penalties reasonably likely to apply to the client with respect to the position advised, prepared, or reported. The practitioner also must inform the client of any opportunity to avoid any such penalty by disclosure, if relevant, and of the requirements for adequate disclosure. This paragraph applies even if the practitioner is not subject to a penalty with respect to the position. [31 C.F.R. § 10.34]

7. A practitioner advising a client to take a position on a tax return, or preparing or signing a tax return as a preparer, generally may rely in good faith without verification upon information furnished by the client. The practitioner may not, however, ignore the implications of information furnished to, or actually known by, the practitioner, and must make reasonable inquiries if the information as furnished appears to be incorrect, inconsistent with an important fact or another factual assumption, or incomplete. [31 C.F.R. § 10.34]

### Q 23:48 What activities of enrolled actuaries are covered by Circular 230?

It is unclear at this time what activities will and will not be covered under some amendments made in 2005. In general, it appears that the following activities are not covered:

1. The activity does not constitute giving advice.

2. There is no written advice (e.g., a telephone conversation regarding deductible contributions).

3. The advice does not concern a federal tax issue (e.g., fiduciary responsibilities).

4. The advice does concern a federal tax issue, but is not related to a listed transaction, a transaction whose principal purpose is the avoidance of tax, or a transaction whose significant purpose is the avoidance of tax.

5. The advice concerns a significant purpose transaction, but is not an opinion offering reliance or marketing and is not subject to confidentiality protections, or falls within a specific exception in the regulations.

Some officials in the Treasury Department have stated that they hope to provide further guidance regarding these rules in the future months.

# Chapter 24

# Pension Benefit Guaranty Corporation

The Employee Retirement Income Security Act of 1974 (ERISA) established the Pension Benefit Guaranty Corporation (PBGC) as a corporate entity within the Department of Labor (DOL). The purpose of the PBGC is to encourage the continuation and maintenance of voluntary private pension plans for the benefit of their participants, to provide for the timely and uninterrupted payment of pension benefits to participants and beneficiaries, and to maintain premiums established by the PBGC at the lowest level consistent with carrying out its obligations. The PBGC achieves these objectives by providing insurance coverage to certain defined benefit pension plans that meet certain criteria. In the event a plan is unable to pay benefits when they are due, the PBGC may take over the assets and liabilities of the plan to ensure continued payment of benefits.

## Coverage

### Q 24:1   Which plans are covered by the PBGC?

Only defined benefit pension plans that are qualified under Internal Revenue Code (Code) Section 401(a) are covered by the PBGC's plan termination insurance program. Certain defined benefit pension plans are exempted from coverage, however, if they are classified as any one of the following types of plans:

1. A governmental plan, including plans under the Railroad Retirement Act;
2. A church plan that elects not to be covered;
3. A non-U.S. plan for nonresident aliens;
4. An unfunded deferred compensation plan for a select group of management or highly compensated employees;
5. A plan that since the enactment of ERISA has not provided for employer contributions;
6. A plan that benefits only substantial owners, where a *substantial owner* is a sole proprietor or partner who owns 10 percent or more of the capital or profit interest in a business entity, or in the case of a corporation, a person who owns 10 percent or more of the voting stock or total stock of the corporation;
7. A plan of an international organization that is tax exempt under the International Organizations Immunities Act;
8. A defined benefit plan to the extent that it is operated as an individual account plan; or
9. A plan established and maintained by a professional service employer that did not have, at any time since the enactment of ERISA, more than 25 active participants.

[ERISA § 4021(b)]

### Q 24:2  What is an *individual account plan*?

A plan that provides benefits based solely on the amount available in an individual's account is an individual account plan. Therefore, a target benefit plan is an *individual account plan* and would not be covered by the PBGC. A cash balance plan, however, does not provide benefits directly through an individual account and is covered by the PBGC.

### Q 24:3  What is a *professional service employer* for purposes of PBGC coverage requirements?

A *professional service employer* is a sole proprietorship, partnership, or corporation that is owned or controlled by professional individuals. A professional service individual includes, but is not limited to, physicians, dentists, chiropractors, osteopaths, optometrists, other licensed practitioners of the healing arts, attorneys at law, public accountants, engineers, architects, draftsmen, actuaries, psychologists, scientists, and performing artists. [ERISA § 4021(c)(2)]

In addition, the PBGC generally defined a professional individual in PBGC Opinion Letter 76-106 [Sept. 3, 1976] as follows:

> In our view, a professional individual generally is one who provides services which require knowledge of an advanced type in a field of science or learning customarily acquired by a prolonged course of

specialized intellectual instruction and study, as distinguished from a general academic education and from an apprenticeship or from training in the performance of routine mental, manual or physical processes. The rendering of professional services generally requires the consistent exercise of discretion and judgment in its performance and would be predominantly intellectual in character.

### Q 24:4   When does a plan become covered by the PBGC?

A plan is covered by the PBGC at the time it is adopted or at the time it no longer meets any of the exceptions for excluded plans. As a result, the plan administrator must be certain of the plan's covered status at all times and be prepared to pay premiums to the PBGC at such time as the plan becomes covered.

**Example.** Smith & Smith is a law firm with 25 full-time employees who participate in a defined benefit plan sponsored by the firm. If at any time 26 or more participants are covered by the plan, the plan will become a PBGC-covered plan even if the participant count drops back to 25 or less in the future.

### Q 24:5   What can plan sponsors do if they are unsure whether the plan is covered by the PBGC?

If the plan sponsor is unsure whether the plan is covered by the PBGC, a request for a coverage determination should be mailed to the PBGC promptly. To respond to such a request, the PBGC will need to have certain information about the plan and the sponsoring organization, such as the benefits available, the type and ownership structure of the sponsoring organization, and the number of participants and beneficiaries in the plan. The request should be mailed to the following address:

Pension Benefit Guaranty Corporation
IOD/Technical Assistance Branch, Suite 930
1200 K Street, NW
Washington, DC 20005-4026

### Q 24:6   Can a plan sponsor appeal an initial determination of coverage?

Yes. A plan sponsor has the right to request a reconsideration of coverage under ERISA Title IV. The request must be made within 30 days of the original determination. It must be in writing, be clearly designated as a request for reconsideration, and state the grounds under which the reconsideration is requested. [PBGC Reg. § 4003.34] The request will be reviewed by an official in the PBGC with greater authority than the person who made the original determination. [PBGC Reg. § 4003.35]

### Q 24:7   When is a plan no longer covered by the PBGC?

Once a plan is covered by the PBGC, it continues to be covered until it is terminated under a standard termination filed on PBGC Forms 500 and 501. If the plan loses its tax-exempt status under the Code, any benefits accrued after the date the exemption is lost are not covered by the PBGC's termination insurance program. A plan that covers only substantial owners at the time the plan terminates is not covered by the PBGC even though the plan covered non-owner participants in the past.

### Q 24:8   Are frozen plans subject to PBGC coverage?

Yes. Although a plan may no longer accrue benefits for service or compensation earned after a certain date, the benefits already accrued are still subject to coverage by the PBGC.

## Premiums

### Q 24:9   What is the amount of premium a plan must pay?

The amount of premium is based on the number of plan participants on the premium payment date, usually the last day of the preceding plan year. If the plan is not a multiemployer plan and if it has any unfunded vested benefits, the plan is subject to a VRP in addition to a flat-rate premium.

The flat-rate premium for multiemployer plans is $2.60 per participant ($8 for plan years beginning in 2006); all other plans pay $19 per participant ($30 for plan years beginning in 2006 and $31 for plan years beginning in 2007). [PBGC Reg. § 4006.3(a)] These rates are subject to annual cost-of-living increases.

The VRP is $9 for each $1,000 of unfunded vested benefits. [PBGC Reg. § 4006.3(b)] For plan years beginning after December 31, 2006, there is a cap on the VRP for small plans with 25 or fewer participants on the first day of the plan year equal to the number of participants times $5 times the number of participants in the plan.

> **Example.** There are 10 participants in the Johnny Be Good defined benefit plan, prior to any cap on the variable-rate premium, the variable-rate premium for the plan year beginning in 2007 would be $2000. The cap is equal to 10 × 10 × $5 = $500. The flat-rate premium is 10 × $31 or $310. The total premium for the plan year beginning in 2007 is $810 ($500 + $310).

### Q 24:10   Who is a participant for PBGC purposes?

Employees who are actively earning or retaining credited service under the plan, nonvested participants, retirees and their beneficiaries collecting benefits, and terminated participants entitled to future benefits are participants for PBGC purposes. [PBGC Reg. § 4006.2]

For plan years beginning in 2001, individuals who do not have accrued benefits and for whom the law has no other benefit liability are no longer considered to be participants for premium purposes.

In addition, for pre-2001 plan years, terminated nonvested individuals cease to be participants for premium purposes when the individual incurs the greater of a one-year break in service under the plan or an absence of one full year. For plan years beginning after 2000, a terminated nonvested individual ceases to be a participant for premium purposes when the individual incurs a one-year break in service under the plan. If the plan provides for a *deemed cashout*, a terminated nonvested individual will be dropped from the participant count before incurring a break in service. [PBGC Reg. § 4006.6]

### Q 24:11   When is a plan exempt from paying the variable-rate portion of the premium?

A plan will not be required to pay the variable-rate portion of the premium if it meets one of the following exceptions:

1. *The plan has no vested participants.* A plan of any size with no vested participants as of the last day of the plan year preceding the premium payment year is exempt from the variable-rate portion of the premium as long as the plan administrator certifies to this fact.

2. *The plan is a plan described in Code Section 412(i).* A fully insured plan under Code Section 412(i) is exempt from the variable-rate portion of the premium as long as it is a Section 412(i) plan for the full plan year that precedes the premium payment year.

3. *The plan is a fully funded small plan.* A plan that has fewer than 500 participants may have the enrolled actuary certify (without disclosure of the computations) that the plan has no unfunded vested benefits when valued at the required interest rate. Such fully funded small plans are exempt from the variable-rate portion of the premium.

4. *The plan is terminating in a standard termination.* If the plan has filed a notice of intent to terminate in a standard termination that has a proposed date of termination that is on or before the last day of the plan year that precedes the premium payment year, the plan administrator may certify that this requirement is met and the plan will be exempt from the variable-rate portion of the premium. If the plan is unable to distribute benefits in a standard termination, this exemption will be revoked and the VRP owed will be due.

5. *The plan is at the full-funding limit.* A plan of any size may be exempt from the variable-rate portion of the premium if, on or before the earlier of the due date for payment of the variable-rate portion of the premium or the date that portion is paid, the plan's contributing sponsor or contributing sponsors made contributions to the plan for the plan year preceding the premium payment year in an amount not less than the full-funding limitation for such preceding plan year under ERISA Section 302(c)(7) and Code Section 412(c)(7). For a plan to qualify for this exemption, an

enrolled actuary must certify that the plan has met this requirement. The determination of whether contributions for the preceding plan year were in an amount not less than the full-funding limitation under ERISA Section 302(c)(7) and Code Section 412(c)(7) for such preceding plan year must be based on the methods of computing the full-funding limitation, including actuarial assumptions and funding methods, used by the plan (provided such assumptions and methods met all requirements, including the requirements for reasonableness, under ERISA Section 302 and Code Section 412) with respect to such preceding plan year. Any contribution that is rounded down to no less than the next lower multiple of $100 (in the case of full-funding limitations up to $100,000) or to no less than the next lower multiple of $1,000 (in the case of full-funding limitations above $100,000) is deemed to be in an amount equal to the full-funding limitation.

[PBGC Reg. § 4006.5(a), PBGC Technical Update 00-4]

**Example 1.** The Jumbo defined benefit plan has an ERISA full-funding limitation of $3,000, calculated as the excess of the plan's accrued liability of $30,000 over adjusted plan assets of $27,000 ($29,000 assets minus $2,000 credit balance). The plan's RPA '94 full-funding limitation is $900, calculated as the excess of 90 percent of the plan's current liability ($29,900) over the plan's full assets of $29,000. Thus, the plan's full-funding limitation is $3,000 (the greater of $3,000 or $900). The plan will qualify for the PBGC FFL (full-funding limit) Exemption if employer contributions equal or exceed $1,000, because the sum of the contributions and the credit balance will equal or exceed the $3,000 full-funding limitation.

**Example 2.** The Limbo defined benefit plan has an ERISA full-funding limitation of $3,000, calculated as the excess of the plan's accrued liability of $30,000 over adjusted plan assets of $27,000 ($29,000 assets minus $2,000 credit balance). The plan's RPA '94 full-funding limitation is $4,000, calculated as the excess of 90 percent of the plan's current liability ($33,000) over the plan's full assets of $29,000. Thus, the plan's full-funding limitation is $4,000 (the greater of $3,000 or $4,000). The plan will qualify for the PBGC FFL Exemption if employer contributions equal or exceed $2,000, because the sum of the contributions and the credit balance will equal or exceed the $4,000 full-funding limitation.

### Q 24:12    How is the value of the vested benefits determined each year?

The value of the vested benefits is determined as of the last day of the plan year that precedes the premium payment year based on the plan's provisions and population as of that date. For plan years beginning prior to 2008, a plan can use two methods for calculating the value of the unfunded vested benefits: the general rule or the alternative method.

The *general rule* calculates the value of the plan's vested benefits using the same actuarial assumptions and methods used to determine the additional funding requirement under Code Section 412(l); however, if the interest rate used for this purpose is greater than the required interest rate (see Q 24:14), the liabilities should be revalued at the required interest rate. In the event that the plan is not subject to the requirements of Code Section 412(l), any assumptions and methods that would be permitted if the plan were subject to those requirements may be used.

The general rule allows for the determination of the value of the vested benefits based on a valuation done on the first day of the premium payment year provided that the required actuarial assumptions and methods are used and that any material difference in the value of the vested benefits between the two valuation dates is reflected in the determination. Any plan using the general rule must have an enrolled actuary certify that the value of the vested benefits was determined in a manner consistent with generally accepted actuarial principles and practices. [PBGC Reg. § 4006.4(a)]

The *alternative method* allows the plan sponsor to use the current liability found on IRS Form 5500, Schedule B, for the plan year that precedes the premium payment year to determine the value of the vested benefits. Only plans with 500 or more participants must have an enrolled actuary certify to the calculations made using this method; plans with fewer than 500 participants can file PBGC Form 1 and PBGC Form 1, Schedule A, without an enrolled actuary's certification. Because the vested benefits on IRS Form 5500, Schedule B, are determined as of the first day of the plan year, an adjustment to those values is required to reflect the accrual of new benefits during the plan year and the use of the required interest rate.

To reflect accruals during the plan year, the total vested current liability for active and terminated vested participants not in pay status on Form 5500, Schedule B, is multiplied by a factor of 1.07.

To reflect the required interest rate adjustment, the value of the current liability on Schedule B is adjusted using the following formula:

$$VB_{adj} = VB_{pay} \times 0.94^{(RIR - BIR)} + (VB_{nonpay} \times 0.94^{(RIR - BIR)}$$
$$\times ((100 + BIR) \times (100 + RIR))^{(ARA - 50)})$$

where,

$VB_{adj}$    = adjusted vested benefits amount

$VB_{pay}$    = the plan's current liability for participants in pay status

$VB_{nonpay}$ = the plan's current liability for active and terminated vested participants multiplied by 1.07

RIR       = For 2004 and 2005, the applicable percentage (currently 85%) of the annual rate of interest determined by the Secretary of the Treasury on amounts invested conservatively in long-term investment-grade corporate bonds. For all other years, the applicable percentage (currently 85%) of the annual yield on 30-year Treasury constant maturities (i.e., the required interest rate)

BIR       = the interest rate for determining the plan's current liability

ARA     = the plan's assumed retirement age (should be the same as is entered on line 6b of Schedule B, Form 5500)

In lieu of using $0.94^{(RIR-BIR)}$, factors provided in the PBGC premium payment package may be substituted. [PBGC Reg. § 4006.4(c)]

For plan years beginning after 2007, the value of the vested benefits is equal to the funding target of the plan as determined under Code Section 436 using only vested benefits (see chapter 19) and a variation of the segment interest rates (see Q 24:14). [ERISA § 4006(a)(3)(E)(iii)]

### Q 24:13    Must any special adjustments be made to the value of the unfunded vested benefits if the plan sponsor is using the alternative method?

Yes. The alternative method calculates the value of the unfunded vested benefits as of the first day of the plan year that precedes the premium payment year; therefore, the value must be adjusted to the end of the plan year. Furthermore, if the plan has 500 or more participants, and a significant event (see Q 24:17) has occurred from the first day of the plan year to the end of the plan year, the alternative method cannot be used unless an enrolled actuary makes an adjustment to the value of the unfunded vested benefits to reflect the occurrence of that significant event and certifies the value of that adjustment.

The *adjusted unfunded vested benefit* is equal to the adjusted vested benefits (see Q 24:12) minus the adjusted value of the plan's assets. The *adjusted value of the plan's assets* is equal to the actuarial value of the plan's assets as of the first day of the plan year preceding the premium payment year without reduction for any credit balance in the plan's funding standard account. Any contributions made after the first day of the plan year preceding the premium payment year that are included in the value of assets as of such date must be discounted with interest at the required interest rate to such first day.

To adjust the unfunded vested benefits under the alternative method from the beginning of the plan year to the end, the following formula is used:

$$UVB_{adj} = (Vb_{adj} - A_{adj}) \times (1 + (RIR \div 100))^Y \text{ where,}$$

$UVB_{adj}$ = the amount of the plan's adjusted unfunded vested benefits

$VB_{adj}$ = the value of the adjusted vested benefits determined under the alternative method (see Q 24:12)

$A_{adj}$ = the adjusted value of the plan assets

$Y$ = one (1) year, unless the preceding plan year is a short plan year, in which case Y equals a fraction of one plan year expressed as a decimal

[PBGC Reg. § 4006.4(c)(5), (d)]

### Q 24:14    What is the required interest rate for valuing the plan's vested benefits?

For premium payment years that begin before July 1997, the required interest rate is 80 percent of the annual yield for 30-year Treasury constant maturities. For premium payment years after July 1997 and before January 2002, the required interest rate is 85 percent of the annual yield on 30-year Treasury constant maturities. For premium payment years that begin after December 2001 and before January 1, 2004, the required interest rate is 100 percent of the yield on 30-year Treasury constant maturities. The month that precedes the first day of the premium payment year is used to determine the yield on the 30-year Treasury constant maturities. For premium payment years that begin after December 31, 2003, and before January 1, 2008, the required interest rate is 85 percent of the composite corporate bond rate for the month preceding the month in which the plan year begins. [PBGC Reg. § 4006.4(b)(1); PBGC Tech. Update 02-1; Notice 2004-34; PPA § 301(a)(3)]

For premium payment years that begin after 2007, the required interest rate is equal to the first, second, or third segment rate for the month preceding the month in which the plan year begins, which would be determined under Code Section 436(h)(2)(C) if Code Section 436(h)(2)(D) were applied by using the monthly yields for the month preceding the month in which the plan year begins on investment grade corporate bonds with varying maturities and in the top three quality levels rather than the average of such yields for a 24-month period.

### Q 24:15  How are the assets valued for purposes of determining the unfunded vested benefits?

Under the general rule, for all plan years until the IRS changes the required mortality table under Code Section 412(l), the actuarial value of the plan's assets is used. For premium payment years after that date, the fair market value of the plan's assets will be used.

If the plan has 500 or more participants, contributions owed for any plan year that preceded the premium payment year must be included in the value of the plan's assets. To include such contributions, however, the contributions must have been paid into the plan before the due date for paying the variable-rate portion of the premium, or if earlier, the date the premium is actually paid. Any such contributions must be discounted to the last day of the plan year preceding the premium payment year using the plan asset valuation rate (on a simple or compound basis in accordance with the plan's discounting rules). Contributions for the premium payment year cannot be included in the value of the plan's assets. [PBGC Reg. § 4006.4(b)(2)]

Under the alternative method, the value of plan assets must be calculated as of the first day of the plan year preceding the premium payment year. For plans that use the first day of the plan year as the valuation date, the actuarial value of the plan's assets is the value as reported on Schedule B, line 1b(2), for the plan year preceding the premium payment year. If the valuation date is any date other than the first day of the plan year, the value of plan assets is the value reported on Schedule B, line 2a, for the same year.

The actuary must subtract from the above-calculated asset value the contributions receivable that were included in this asset value as of the first day of the plan year but were made after such date. For large plans that file Schedule H of Form 5500 for 1999, this amount is the sum of items 1b(1)(a) and 1b(2)(a) on

Schedule H. For small plans that file Schedule I of Form 5500 for 1999, the contributions receivable must be calculated as of the beginning of 1999, because they are not reported on Form 5500.

Under the alternative method, as under the general rule, plans with fewer than 500 participants may choose not to include any discounted contributions receivable in the value of plan assets. All contributions receivable subtracted from the value of assets and any other contributions paid for plan years before the premium payment year must be discounted to the first day of the plan year preceding the premium payment year using the required interest rate and then be added back to the asset value. These contributions must be discounted on a compound annual basis, except that simple interest can be used for any partial years. To include such contributions in this discount, the contributions must have been paid into the plan before the due date for paying the variable-rate portion of the premium, or if earlier, the date the premium is actually paid. Contributions for the premium payment year cannot be included in the value of the plan's assets. [PBGC Reg. § 4006.4(b)(2)]

> **Example.** The Red Rock Defined Benefit Plan, a calendar-year plan, has assets as of December 31, 1998, of $500,000, including a $50,000 contribution receivable deposited on March 31, 1999. As of December 31, 1999, the value of plan assets was $600,000, including a $45,000 contribution receivable deposited on March 31, 2000. The plan asset valuation rate is 8 percent and the required interest rate as of January 1, 2000, is 5.4 percent. To determine the value of plan assets for a 2000 premium payment, the plan sponsor has asked that assets be valued under both the general and alternative methods.
>
> Under the general method, the value of assets is determined as of the last day of the plan year preceding the premium payment year, or December 31, 1999, in this example. This value of $600,000 is reduced by discounting the contribution receivable (using either simple or compound interest) for the three months after the last day of the plan year. The $45,000 is reduced to $44,118 ($45,000/(1 + (0.08 × 3/12))). This makes the value of assets as of December 31, 1999, under the general rule equal to $599,118 ($600,000 − $45,000 + $44,118).
>
> Under the alternative method, the value of assets is determined as of the first day of the plan year preceding the premium payment year. The valuation date for this plan is also the first day of the plan year, and the actuarial value of assets as of the valuation date for the 1999 plan year as reported on Schedule B was $500,000. This value is reduced by discounting the contribution receivable for the three months after the first day of the plan year. Because the discount for this contribution is for less than a year, it can be reduced using simple interest. The $50,000 contribution is reduced to $49,334 ($50,000/(1 + (0.054 × 3/12))). The contribution receivable as of December 31, 1999, is also discounted, but this time using compound interest. The $45,000 contribution is reduced to $42,144 ($45,000/(1.054) (455/365)).

Subtracting the $50,000 contribution from the asset value of $500,000 leaves $450,000. The adjusted value of assets under this method is equal to $541,478 ($450,000 + $49,334 + $42,144).

### Q 24:16   How are vested benefits and assets valued in a new or newly covered plan?

For a new plan, all references to the last day of the plan year preceding the premium payment year with regard to the calculation of flat-rate premiums, VRPs, the number of plan participants, or exemptions are deemed to refer to the first day of the premium payment year, or if later, the date on which the plan became effective for benefit accruals for future service. [PBGC Reg. § 4006.5(d)]

### Q 24:17   What is a *significant event*?

A *significant event* is an event that causes the plan's liability to increase by an amount that may cause the value of the vested benefits to be undervalued when the alternative method is used. Therefore, if a plan has 500 or more participants, the plan can use the alternative method only if there has been no significant event from the beginning of the plan year preceding the premium-payment year to the end of such plan year. An enrolled actuary must either certify that no significant event has occurred, or if one has, the value of the unfunded vested benefits must be adjusted by the enrolled actuary to take this event into account.

A significant event may be any of the following:

1. An increase in the normal cost and amortization charges and credits due to a plan amendment, unless the increase is less than 5 percent of the actuarial costs absent the amendment;
2. Extension of coverage under the plan to a new group of employees that results in an increase of 5 percent or more in the plan's accrued liability;
3. A merger, spin-off, or consolidation that is not *de minimis* pursuant to the regulations under Code Section 414(l);
4. The shutdown of any facility, plant, store, or similar entity that creates immediate eligibility for benefits that would not otherwise be immediately payable for participants separating from service;
5. The offer by the plan for a temporary period (e.g., an early retirement window) to permit participants to retire at benefit levels greater than those to which they would otherwise be entitled;
6. A cost-of-living increase for retirees resulting in an increase of 5 percent or more in the plan's accrued liability; or
7. Any other event or trend that would result in a material increase in the plan's unfunded vested benefits.

[PBGC Reg. § 4006.4(d)]

### Q 24:18  What forms are filed with the PBGC to pay the premium, and when are they due?

For plans with fewer than 500 participants, the flat-rate and VRPs must be paid by the 15th day of the 10th full calendar month following the month in which the plan year began.

For plans with 500 or more participants, the flat-rate premium must be paid by the last day of the second full calendar month following the close of the preceding plan year. For such plans, the VRP must be paid by the 15th day of the 10th full calendar month following the month in which the plan year began.

If the filing deadline falls on a Saturday, Sunday, or federal holiday, the deadline is extended until the next day that is not a Saturday, Sunday, or federal holiday. If, however, the filing is late, interest and penalty charges are calculated including the Saturday, Sunday, or federal holiday.

The flat-rate portion of the premium is paid with PBGC Form 1 for plans with 500 or more participants. PBGC Form 1-ES (required of plans that reported 500 or more participants on their prior filing) is filed to pay the flat-rate portion of the premium by its due date if the plan sponsor has not yet determined the participant count or the value of the unfunded vested benefits by the due date for the flat-rate premium. PBGC Form 1, Schedule A, is used to determine the amount of the VRP, if any. All single-employer plans that are not exempt from the VRP must file PBGC Form 1 with the Schedule A. Single-employer plans that are exempt from the VRP should file PBGC Form 1-EZ. Having a variable-rate premium of zero is not the same as being exempt. Multiemployer plans file only PBGC Form 1.

> **Example 1.** The RCD Pension Plan has a calendar-year plan year and 1,000 plan participants. It is required to pay its flat-rate portion of the PBGC premium by the last day of February; the variable-rate portion of the premium is due by October 15. If the RCD Pension Plan had a plan year that ran from June 1 to May 31 each year, the due date of the flat-rate portion would be July 31, with the variable-rate portion due on or before March 15. [PBGC Reg. § 4007.11(a)]

> **Example 2.** The CAM Pension Plan has made contributions up to the full-funding limitation for the 2004 plan year. Because the plan has met one of the exemptions from paying the VRP, the plan administrator must file PBGC Form 1-EZ for the 2005 plan year.

Premium forms with payment (including amended fillings) are mailed to (if available prior to mandatory e-filing as described below):

Pension Benefit Guaranty Corporation
Department 77430
P.O. Box 77000
Detroit, MI 48277-0430

The address to use for delivery service (such as UPS or Federal Express) is:

Pension Benefit Guaranty Corporation
Bank One
9000 Haggerty Road
Department 77430, Mail Code: MI1-8244
Belleville, MI 48111

If payment is made by wire transfer, payment should be sent to:

Bank One, NA
Chicago, IL
ABA: 071000013
Account: 656510666
Beneficiary: PBGC
Reference: (give plan's EIN/plan number and the date the premium-payment year (PYC) commenced in the format: "EIN/PN: XX-XXXXXXX/XXX PYC: MM/DD/YY")

### Q 24:19  Are premium filings required to be made electronically?

Yes. In 2004, the PBGC introduced an online e-filing facility called "My Plan Administration Account," or My PAA, through which plan administrators can prepare and submit premium filings electronically. The use of My PAA for premium filings was optional up until July 1, 2006. It is now required for large plans having 500 or more participants during the prior plan year, and will be required for all plans beginning with the 2007 premium filings.

There are three methods available for meeting the new e-filing requirement:

1. The My PAA data entry method within the PBGC secure Web site (www.pbgc.gov). Filers enter their premium data directly into the system and then other service providers and/or the plan administrator certify to various portions of the filing.

2. The information is uploaded to the PBGC by use of private-sector software. The information is completed within the software and then uploaded to the PBGC, but this method does not allow for multiple certifications and these would still need to be made outside of the system and retained in a file for at least six years.

3. A combination of the previous two methods where special software is used that allows for multiple certifications and routing of the filing to the necessary individuals to sign off on the forms.

Payment is not currently required to be made within the My PAA system, but can be by using a credit card, electronic check, or ACH transfer. In addition, the premium can still be paid with a check; however, this method may be eliminated in the future.

This method of filing is required, except where the PBGC grants an exemption for good cause in appropriate circumstances. [PBGC Reg. §§ 4000.3(b), 4006.4, 4006.5, 4007.3]

### Q 24:20    When is a new or newly covered plan required to pay its PBGC premiums?

The required due date for PBGC premiums for newly covered plans is the same regardless of the number of participants in the plan. The flat-rate and VRPs are due on or before the latest of:

1.  The 15th day of the 10th full calendar month following the month in which the plan year began, or if later, the 15th day of the 10th full calendar month following the month in which the plan became effective for benefit accruals for future service;
2.  90 days after the date of the plan's adoption; or
3.  90 days after the date on which the plan became covered by ERISA Title IV.

[PBGC Reg. § 4007.11(c)]

> **Example.** Big Company adopted a pension plan on September 30, 2000. The first plan year began on January 1, 2001, and ended on December 31, 2001. Benefit accruals for future service began on January 1, 2001. The due date for the first premium payment is October 15, 2001.
>
> If Big Company adopted the plan on October 1, 2001, instead of September 30, 2000, the first premium due date would be December 30, 2001 (i.e., 90 days after the plan's adoption).
>
> If Big Company was a professional service corporation with 24 participants, it would not be covered by the PBGC termination insurance program. If, however, the pension plan had 26 participants on July 1, 2003, the first premium would be due on September 29, 2003 (i.e., 90 days after the plan became subject to ERISA Title IV).

### Q 24:21    How are premiums calculated in the first plan year?

Generally, premiums are calculated in the same way in the first year as in future plan years. However, a new plan that does not provide credit for service before the plan began will typically not have to pay a premium for its first plan year, but such a plan still must file PBGC Form 1-EZ. [PBGC Blue Book, 2001 Enrolled Actuaries Meeting Q&As 6, 10]

The premium snapshot date for a new plan can either be the plan effective date or the date of adoption. Either date can also be used in determining whether premium proration (see Q 24:22) is available (and what the proration fraction is). For plan years beginning before 2001, it is generally advantageous to use the date of plan adoption in order to prorate any premium due. For plan years beginning in 2001 and later, it is generally more advantageous to use the first day of the plan year unless the plan grants benefit service for years before the effective date of the plan. This is because the new PBGC definition of *participant* excludes those who have no accrued benefits; therefore, the plan would owe no premium for this first year (but would still need to file PBGC Form 1-EZ). Plans that grant past service may want to use the later date of plan adoption to prorate the premium that is due.

### Q 24:22   Are premiums prorated for a short plan year?

Yes. A short plan year exists in the following situations:

1. Creation of a new plan;
2. Change in the plan year;
3. Distribution of assets; and
4. Appointment of a trustee.

For a short plan year, the premium is prorated by the number of months in the short plan year, treating a part of a month as a full month. Alternatively, the plan sponsor may pay a full year's premium and request that the PBGC either calculate the correct amount and refund the difference or apply the difference to the subsequent plan year.

### Q 24:23   Will the PBGC accrue interest on late payment of premiums?

Yes. Any unpaid premium is subject to an interest charge compounded daily until the premium is paid in full. The interest rate is the same interest rate used for purposes of Code Section 6601(a). When calculating late payment interest charges, the PBGC counts Saturdays, Sundays, and federal holidays. The day that the premium was due is not counted, but the date it is paid is counted. If a bill from the PBGC is paid within 30 days after the date of the bill, however, interest will not accrue over that 30-day period. [PBGC Reg. § 4007.7]

### Q 24:24   What are the penalties associated with the late payment of a premium?

If a premium is not paid by the due date, the PBGC may impose a charge equal to the greater of 5 percent per month (or fraction thereof) of the unpaid premium, or $25. If the payment is made on or before the date when the PBGC issues a written notification indicating that there is or may be a premium deficiency, the penalty rate will be reduced to 1 percent per month of the unpaid premium. In no event will the late charge exceed 100 percent of the unpaid premium. [PBGC Reg. § 4007.8(a)]

### Q 24:25   Under what circumstances may the PBGC waive the penalty for a late premium?

There are instances in the PBGC regulations that allow for a waiver of the penalty for a late premium:

1. If payment was late by no more than 60 days, and the PBGC granted a waiver before the due date based on a substantial hardship on the part of the payer to make timely payment, no penalty will be charged.
2. If the sponsor of a plan with 500 or more participants fails to pay the full amount of the flat-rate premium by the first due date, and the amount of the premium that was actually paid was at least 90 percent of the amount that should have been paid or the amount paid was based on the per-participant rate and participant count for the preceding premium-payment

year, no penalty charge will be applied as long as the balance of the premium is paid as part of a reconciliation filing by the due date for the variable-rate portion of the premium on PBGC Form 1.

3. If there are any outstanding bills for PBGC premiums to reconcile amounts paid with amounts due and payment is made within 30 days of the bill, no penalty will be charged.

The PBGC has the authority to waive any and all late charges based on reasonable cause (see Q 24:26). Furthermore, it may choose to waive penalties on its own motion for any reason. [PBGC Reg. § 4007.8]

### Q 24:26   What does the PBGC consider reasonable cause for purposes of waiving premium penalties?

In general, there is reasonable cause for a failure to pay a premium on time if (1) the failure arises from circumstances beyond one's control and (2) one could not avoid the failure by the exercise of ordinary business care and prudence. Overlooking the requirement to file and pay the premium is not considered reasonable cause. In addition, individuals or firms that are outside the organization but that may be consulted for advice (e.g., attorneys, accountants, or actuaries) are considered part of the sponsoring organization. Therefore, if a failure could have been avoided by the exercise of ordinary business care and prudence by such members of the "outside organization," the PBGC does not consider there to be reasonable cause for the failure. [PBGC Reg. § 4007 Appendix, § 32]

### Q 24:27   May a plan request a refund of premium overpayments?

Yes. When a plan has overpaid a premium (e.g., the participant count reported on the final premium filing is lower than that reported on the estimated filing), the plan has the option of taking a credit on a subsequent year's premium filing form or requesting a refund. Prior to the PPA, ERISA regulations did not allow for the PBGC to pay interest on premium overpayments. However, the PBGC is now authorized to pay interest on periods beginning after August 17, 2006.

In the absence of a request for a credit or refund, PBGC will apply the overpayment toward any premium, penalty, and interest amounts that are owed for the current or any prior plan year. This may result in less of an overpayment available for a refund or credit.

## Participant Notification Requirements

### Q 24:28   Is the sponsor of a single-employer plan that has paid a VRP required to notify the plan participants that such a premium was paid?

Yes. Subject to an exemption for certain plans with minimum funded ratios, the plan sponsor of any single-employer plan must provide a 2006 Participant Notice to plan participants and beneficiaries that informs them of the funded status of the plan and the limits on the PBGC's guarantee of benefits if the plan terminates while it is underfunded, *unless* the plan meets one of the following three criteria:

1. No VRP is payable for the 2006 plan year;
2. The plan meets the DRC Exception Test for the 2006 plan year; or
3. The plan meets the DRC Exception Test for the 2005 plan year.

[ERISA § 4011(a), PBGC Tech. Update 06-3]

However, this notice is replaced with a different notice for plan years beginning after December 31, 2007. (See Q 24:41.)

### Q 24:29   How is it determined whether there was a VRP payable for the 2006 plan year?

A plan administrator is not required to issue a 2006 Participant Notice if a VRP is not payable for that plan year, either because (1) the plan has no unfunded vested benefits (determined on a premium basis), or (2) because the plan qualifies for at least one of five exemptions from the VRP contained in the PBGC's regulation on premium rates. One of these exemptions is for plans at the FFL under 29 Code of Federal Regulations Section 4006.5(a)(5).

The 2005 FFL required to be reported on the 2005 Form 5500, Schedule B, is used to determine whether the plan qualifies for the FFL exemption from the VRP for the 2006 plan year, based on contributions for the 2005 plan year.

The optional recalculation rule provided in the Pension Funding Equity Act of 2004 (PFEA) does not apply in this context. [PBGC Tech. Update 06-3]

### Q 24:30   Is a multiemployer plan required to provide participants with a notice of the plan's funding level?

Yes. Beginning with the plan year starting in 2005, each multiemployer plan must notify all interested parties of the funded status of their defined benefit plan. This notice must be provided to participants, beneficiaries, contributing employers, unions, and the PBGC.

This notice will be required to be issued within two months following the due date for the Form 5500 filing for the plan year (including extensions). Failure to provide the notice may result in a penalty of up to $100 a day per participant.

The DOL is to issue a model notice for multiemployer plans to use. This notice must provide the following information:

- Information about the plan and the plan administrator;
- The percentage funded if the plan is not 100 percent funded or an indication that the plan is 100 percent funded;
- The value of plan assets;
- The amount of benefits paid during the plan year;

- The ratio of assets to benefit payments;
- A summary of the rules governing insolvent multiemployer plans; and
- A general description of the benefits under the plan that are eligible for the PBGC guarantee.

In addition, the notice may include any other information the trustees of the plan deem appropriate, as long as it is not prohibited. [ERISA § 101(f)]

This notice is replaced with a different notice for plan years beginning after December 31, 2007, and is applicable to all defined benefit plans. (See Q 24:41.)

### Q 24:31    Is there an exemption that allows a plan sponsor to avoid the participant notice when a VRP has been paid?

Yes. In general, if a plan was not subject to the additional funding charge (also called the deficit reduction contribution or DRC) under Code Section 412(l) or ERISA Section 302(d) for the current or prior plan year, regardless of whether it has more than 100 participants, it will be exempt from the requirement to provide the participant notice in a plan year for which a VRP was paid.

A plan administrator is not required to issue a 2006 Participant Notice if the plan meets the DRC Exception Test for either the 2006 or 2005 plan year. Whether a plan meets the DRC Exception Test for a plan year depends on whether the plan's funded current liability (FCL) percentage is at or above various specified levels for several plan years. Specifically—

- A plan meets the DRC Exception Test for the 2006 plan year if the plan's FCL Percentage is—
  - At least 90 percent for the 2006 plan year, or
  - At least 80 percent for the 2006 plan year and at least 90 percent for either—
    - The 2005 plan year and the 2004 plan year, or
    - The 2004 plan year and the 2003 plan year.
- A plan meets the DRC Exception Test for the 2005 plan year if the plan's FCL Percentage is—
  - At least 90 percent for the 2005 plan year, or
  - At least 80 percent for the 2005 plan year and at least 90 percent for either—
    - The 2004 plan year and the 2002 plan year, or
    - The 2003 plan year and the 2001 plan year.

Plans with 100 or fewer participants on each day of the preceding plan year can make a determination as to whether the plan is exempt from the additional funding charge by using the current liability on IRS Form 5500, Schedule B, as of the beginning of the plan year and can substitute the market value of the assets for the actuarial value of the plan assets. Furthermore, if the interest rate used to determine the current liability is not the highest allowable, the current liability can be reduced by 1 percent for each 10th of a percentage point by which the highest rate exceeds the rate used.

Newly covered plans will be exempt from the notice for the first premium payment year. [PBGC Reg. § 4011.4(a), (b)]

The PBGC has also provided a worksheet to help in determining whether the notice is applicable (see worksheet). However, determining whether a participant notice is required for the 2006 plan year can be more complex than for past plan years. Three different interest rate bases can apply for determining the plan's FCL percentage for the years 2000 through 2006. In some cases plan administrators have the option of recalculating previous determinations of FCL percentages using a higher interest rate under the PFEA Optional Recalculation rule. Thus, plan administrators are encouraged to use the worksheet, paying particular attention to the various interest rates required or permitted to be used in determining the plan's FCL percentage for each plan year.

The worksheet presents one order of steps for determining whether a 2006 Participant Notice is required. However, a plan administrator may wish to use a different order, particularly if a plan's FCL percentages reported on prior Forms 5500, Schedule B, may be sufficient to satisfy the DRC Exception Test for the 2006 or 2005 plan years.

### Summary of Published Interest Rates for the DRC Exception Test for the 2006 Participant Notice

| For Plan Years Beginning in | 100% of the Weighted Average Corporate Bond Rate | 120% of the Weighted Average 30-year Treasury Rate | 105% of the Weighted Average 30-year Treasury Rate |
|---|---|---|---|
| Jan. 2002 | 7.34% | 6.85% | 6.00% |
| Feb. 2002 | 7.33% | 6.84% | 5.98% |
| Mar. 2002 | 7.32% | 6.83% | 5.97% |
| Apr. 2002 | 7.32% | 6.83% | 5.97% |
| May 2002 | 7.31% | 6.82% | 5.97% |
| June 2002 | 7.30% | 6.81% | 5.96% |
| Jul. 2002 | 7.28% | 6.80% | 5.95% |
| Aug. 2002 | 7.26% | 6.78% | 5.94% |
| Sept. 2002 | 7.23% | 6.76% | 5.91% |
| Oct. 2002 | 7.20% | 6.72% | 5.88% |
| Nov. 2002 | 7.17% | 6.70% | 5.86% |
| Dec. 2002 | 7.14% | 6.67% | 5.84% |
| Jan. 2003 | 7.11% | 6.65% | 5.81% |
| Feb. 2003 | 7.07% | 6.62% | 5.79% |
| Mar. 2003 | 7.03% | 6.58% | 5.76% |
| Apr. 2003 | 6.98% | 6.55% | 5.73% |
| May 2003 | 6.94% | 6.52% | 5.70% |
| June 2003 | 6.87% | 6.46% | 5.66% |

### Summary of Published Interest Rates for the DRC Exception Test
### for the 2006 Participant Notice (*cont'd*)

| For Plan Years Beginning in | 100% of the Weighted Average Corporate Bond Rate | 120% of the Weighted Average 30-year Treasury Rate | 105% of the Weighted Average 30-year Treasury Rate |
|---|---|---|---|
| Jul. 2003 | 6.80% | 6.41% | 5.61% |
| Aug. 2003 | 6.75% | 6.38% | 5.58% |
| Sept. 2003 | 6.72% | 6.37% | 5.57% |
| Oct. 2003 | 6.68% | 6.35% | 5.56% |
| Nov. 2003 | 6.63% | 6.33% | 5.54% |
| Dec. 2003 | 6.59% | 6.32% | 5.53% |
| Jan. 2004 | 6.55% | N/A | N/A |
| Feb. 2004 | 6.50% | N/A | N/A |
| Mar. 2004 | 6.45% | N/A | N/A |
| Apr. 2004 | 6.40% | N/A | N/A |
| May 2004 | 6.36% | N/A | N/A |
| June 2004 | 6.34% | N/A | N/A |
| Jul. 2004 | 6.32% | N/A | N/A |
| Aug. 2004 | 6.29% | N/A | N/A |
| Sept. 2004 | 6.25% | N/A | N/A |
| Oct. 2004 | 6.21% | N/A | N/A |
| Nov. 2004 | 6.17% | N/A | N/A |
| Dec. 2004 | 6.14% | N/A | N/A |
| Jan. 2005 | 6.10% | N/A | N/A |
| Feb. 2005 | 6.07% | N/A | N/A |
| Mar. 2005 | 6.03% | N/A | N/A |
| Apr. 2005 | 6.01% | N/A | N/A |
| May 2005 | 5.97% | N/A | N/A |
| June 2005 | 5.94% | N/A | N/A |
| Jul. 2005 | 5.90% | N/A | N/A |
| Aug. 2005 | 5.87% | N/A | N/A |
| Sept. 2005 | 5.84% | N/A | N/A |
| Oct. 2005 | 5.81% | N/A | N/A |
| Nov. 2005 | 5.79% | N/A | N/A |
| Dec. 2005 | 5.78% | N/A | N/A |
| Jan. 2006 | 5.77% | N/A | N/A |
| Feb. 2006 | 5.75% | N/A | N/A |
| Mar. 2006 | 5.75% | N/A | N/A |
| Apr. 2006 | 5.74% | N/A | N/A |
| May 2006 | 5.74% | N/A | N/A |
| June 2006 | 5.75% | N/A | N/A |
| Jul. 2006 | 5.77% | N/A | N/A |
| Aug. 2006 | 5.78% | N/A | N/A |

**VI. 2006 Participant Notice Worksheet**

**See above table for interest rates to be used to calculate FCL percentages.
(Note that for the 2003 and 2002 plan years,
there is a choice of interest rates that may be used.)**

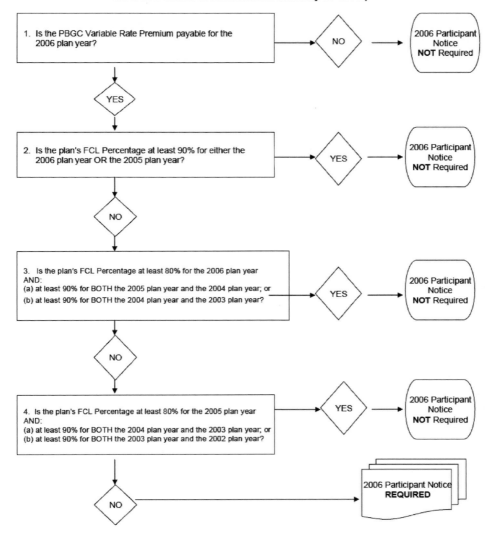

[PBGC Tech. Update 05-1]

> **Example.** For the 1997 plan year, the Kelly Plan had a funded ratio of 82.73 percent, based on plan assets of $4.55 million and a current liability of $5.5 million. Under this scenario, the employer would have to provide a participant notice. If, however, the plan has fewer than 100 participants and had

used an interest rate of 6.5 percent to determine its current liability, when the highest allowable current liability interest rate for 1997 was 7.36 percent, the plan's current liability could be reduced by the amount determined by taking the difference between 7.36 percent and 6.50 percent, and dividing the result by 10 ((7.36 ÷ 6.5%)/10 = 0.086). Multiplying the current liability of $5.5 million by 0.086 gives the amount by which the current liability can be reduced ($473,000). After subtraction of this amount, the plan's current liability is $5,027,000, and its funded ratio becomes 90.5 percent ($4,550,000/ $5,027,000). Accordingly, the plan would not be required to provide a participant notice.

### Q 24:32   What are the special rules applicable to small plans for calculating the FCL percentage?

A plan is considered to be a "small plan" for a plan year if it had 100 or fewer participants on each day during the preceding plan year. When determining whether a plan is a "small plan," its participants must be aggregated with the participants of all other defined benefit plans maintained by the same employer or any other member of the employer's controlled group in accordance with ERISA Section 302(d)(6)(C).

In calculating its FCL percentage for a plan year, a plan that is a small plan for that plan year may use one or both of the following rules:

1. The plan's FCL percentage may be calculated by using numbers that are required to be reported on the Form 5500, Schedule B, for the plan year for which the FCL percentage is calculated. Under this special rule, the FCL percentage is obtained by dividing—

    a. The market value of the plan's assets as of the beginning of the plan year by

    b. The plan's total current liability as of the beginning of the plan year.

2. When calculating current liability (whether or not the plan uses the special rule in item #1 above), if the plan's current liability required to be reported on Form 5500, Schedule B, was calculated using an interest rate lower than the highest allowable interest rate, the current liability at the highest rate may be determined by reducing the reported current liability by 1 percent for each 10th of a percent by which the highest allowable interest rate exceeds the interest rate used.

**Example.** Assume that a small plan's current liability as of January 1, 2004, is $250,000, based on an interest rate of 5.95 percent. The highest allowable interest rate for the 2004 plan year is 6.55 percent (the applicable 100 percent Weighted Corporate Rate). Because the highest allowable interest rate exceeds the interest rate used by six-tenths of a percent, current liability may be reduced by 6 percent to $235,000, as follows:

$$(1.00 - 06) \times \$250,000 = \$235,000.$$

[PBGC Tech. Update 04-4]

**Q 24:33 Are there special rules for calculating the plan's funded status for the 2002 and 2003 plan years?**

Yes. Section 405 of the Job Creation and Worker Assistance Act of 2002 (JCWAA) increases, for plan years beginning in 2002 or 2003, the maximum interest rate (from 105 percent to 120 percent of the specified weighted average of Treasury securities interest rates) that may be used to calculate current liability for purposes of calculating the additional funding charge. This change can affect both the requirement to issue the 2003 Participant Notice and the plan funding information required to be disclosed in the 2003 Participant Notice.

Under JCWAA, a plan will use the maximum current liability interest rate of 120 percent (rather than 105 percent) of the specified weighted average of Treasury securities interest rates to calculate the FCL percentage for the 2002 and 2003 plan years, but not for plan years 1999-2001.

The JCWAA maximum interest rate for the 2002 plan year is also used to determine whether a plan qualifies for the FFL exemption from the VRP (under 29 C.F.R. § 4006.5(a)(5)) for the 2003 plan year and therefore is not required to issue a 2003 Participant Notice.

**Example 1.** The Higher Up defined benefit plan's FCL percentage for the 2003 plan year is 90 percent or higher when computed using 120 percent of the specified weighted average of Treasury securities interest rates. This plan is not required to issue a 2003 Participant Notice.

**Example 2.** The Middle Road defined benefit plan's FCL percentage for the 2003 and 2002 plan years is less than 90 percent when computed using 120 percent of the specified weighted average of Treasury securities interest rates. The plan will use the 120 percent rate to determine whether it has an FCL percentage of 80 percent or more for the 2002 plan year or the 2003 plan year, but it may not use the 120 percent rate to compute the FCL percentage for any earlier plan year.

**Example 3.** Using the JCWAA maximum interest rate for the 2002 plan year, the Low Side defined benefit plan meets the FFL exemption from the VRP for the 2003 plan year. This plan is not required to issue a 2003 Participant Notice.

**Q 24:34 Are there special rules for determining whether a participant notice will be required for plan years beginning in 2004 or 2005?**

Yes. For plan years beginning in 2004 or 2005, it is allowable to recalculate the FCL percentages for previous years based on various interest rates. This is called the PFEA Optional Recalculation rule.

In general, a plan's FCL percentages for plan years prior to the 2004 plan year have been reported on Form 5500, Schedule B. In many cases, the FCL percentages calculated for one or more prior plan years will be sufficiently high that the plan meets the DRC Exception Test for the 2004 or 2003 plan year.

If the plan does not meet the DRC Exception Test for 2004 or 2003 using the FCL percentages that were originally calculated, the plan may recalculate the FCL percentages under the PFEA Optional Recalculation rule for the 2004 DRC Exception Test. Under this rule, the FCL percentages for the 2001, 2002, and 2003 plan years may be recalculated using the 100 percent Weighted Corporate Rate. Note that the PFEA Optional Recalculation will always result in a higher FCL percentage than the FCL percentage previously calculated (see Interest Rate Table below). The PFEA Optional Recalculation rule is *not* applicable to the DRC Exception Test for the *2003 plan year*. Thus, the FCL percentages for the 2001 through 2003 plan years used to determine whether the plan meets the DRC Exception Test for the 2004 plan year might be different from the FCL percentages for the 2001 through 2003 plan years used to determine whether the plan meets the DRC Exception Test for the 2003 plan year.

The following table provides a summary of which interest rate(s) must be used for various plan years to determine if a participant notice is required for the 2006 plan year.

### Interest Rate Table for 2006 Participant Notice

| Plan Year | Interest Rate for Determining FCL |
|---|---|
| 2006 | 100% Weighted Corporate Rate |
| 2005 | 100% Weighted Corporate Rate |
| 2004 | 100% Weighted Corporate Rate |
| 2003 | 120% Weighted Treasury Rate or 100% Weighted Corporate Rate |
| 2002 | 120% Weighted Treasury Rate or 100% Weighted Corporate Rate |

[PBGC Tech. Update 06-3]

**Example.** A VRP is payable for the Costs-A-Lot Plan for the 2004 plan year. Therefore, the plan administrator is required to issue a 2004 Participant Notice unless the plan meets the DRC Exception Test for the 2004 plan year or for the 2003 plan year. The following chart summarizes the plan's FCL percentages for relevant plan years:

### FCL Percentages for the Costs-A-Lot Plan

| Plan Year | 100% Weighted Corporate Rate | 120% Weighted Treasury Rate | 105% Weighted Treasury Rate |
|---|---|---|---|
| 2004 | 85% | N/A | N/A |
| 2003 | 75% | 70% | N/A |
| 2002 | 89% | 91% | N/A |
| 2001 | 91% | N/A | 80% |
| 2000 | N/A | N/A | 79% |

Following the steps in the Worksheet:

1. Is a variable-rate premium payable for the 2004 plan year?

   *Yes.*

2. Is the plan's FCL percentage at least 90 percent for either the 2004 plan year (determined using the 100 percent Weighted Corporate Rate) or the 2003 plan year (determined using the 120 percent Weighted Treasury Rate)?

   *No.* The plan's FCL percentage for the 2004 plan year is 85 percent (determined using the 100 percent Weighted Corporate Rate). The plan's FCL percentage for the 2003 plan year is 70 percent (as previously reported on Schedule B, determined using the 120 percent Weighted Treasury Rate).

3. Is the plan's FCL percentage at least 80 percent for the 2004 plan year (determined using the 100 percent Weighted Corporate Rate) and

   a. at least 90 percent for both

      i. the 2003 plan year (determined using the 100 percent Weighted Corporate Rate or the 120 percent Weighted Treasury Rate) and
      ii. the 2002 plan year (determined using the 100 percent Weighted Corporate Rate or the 120 percent Weighted Treasury Rate) *OR*

   b. at least 90 percent for both

      i. the 2002 plan year (determined using the 100 percent Weighted Corporate Rate or the 120 percent Weighted Treasury Rate) and
      ii. the 2001 plan year (determined using the 100 percent Weighted Corporate Rate or the 105 percent Weighted Treasury Rate)?

   *Yes.* The plan's FCL percentage is 85 percent for the 2004 plan year (determined using the 100 percent Weighted Corporate Rate).

Under item 3(b), the plan's FCL percentage for (i) the 2002 plan year is 91 percent (as previously reported on Schedule B, determined using the 120 percent Weighted Treasury Rate) and (ii) the 2001 plan year is 91 percent (determined using the 100 percent Weighted Corporate Rate, allowed by the PFEA Optional Recalculation rule).

Therefore, the plan administrator is not required to issue a 2004 Participant Notice.

### Q 24:35   What is the penalty for failure to provide the participant notice?

The PBGC can assess a penalty of up to $1,100 per day for failure to provide the participant notice for each day that the failure continues. [PBGC Reg. § 4011.3(c)] However, the PBGC is considering a new participant notice penalty policy that would tie the penalty primarily to the number of participants rather than the number of days the notice was delinquent. Under the new policy, if the failure is corrected on or before the date PBGC issues an audit notification, the penalty would be $5 per participant. If the failure is a repeat violation and is corrected preaudit, the penalty would increase to $20 per participant. If the failure is corrected postaudit, the penalty would be $40 per participant for first-time violations and $100 per participant for repeat offenders. In addition, the penalty rate would be prorated down for failures corrected within one year, and could be adjusted up or down by the PBGC based on facts and circumstances of each case.

The PBGC has instituted a Participant Notice Voluntary Correction Program (VCP) to encourage plan administrators to correct 2002 or 2003 compliance failures.

### Q 24:36   What is the Participant Notice Voluntary Correction Program (VCP)?

The VCP allows a plan administrator to correct recent failures to distribute a required participant notice. The VCP covers any 2002 or 2003 Participant Notice that was due before May 7, 2004, provided that it was not then the subject of a PBGC audit proceeding. According to the new program, the PBGC will not assess penalties for failure to provide a 2002 or 2003 Participant Notice if the plan administrator corrects the failure in accordance with the program guidelines. In addition, the PBGC will not pursue any failure to provide any pre-2002 Participant Notices unless there is a 2002 or 2003 failure that is not corrected. It is anticipated that many plan administrators will want to participate in the VCP as a precaution, even in the absence of a known participant notice failure.

In order to meet the requirements for penalty relief under the VCP, the plan administrator must:

1. Issue a timely VCP corrective notice; and
2. Notify the PBGC of the plan's participation in the VCP no later than 30 days after the due date for issuing the VCP corrective notice. The notification must include a copy of the VCP corrective notice and the name and telephone number of someone to contact with any questions.

If the failure was corrected prior to May 7, 2004, then the plan administrator will receive automatic penalty relief, and participation in the VCP is not necessary.

### Q 24:37   What are the requirements for a VCP corrective notice?

The plan administrator must issue a VCP corrective notice to those persons entitled to receive the plan's 2004 Participant Notice. If the plan is not required to issue a 2004 Participant Notice, then the notice will be issued to those persons who would be entitled to receive it if it was required. It is not necessary to issue a VCP corrective notice to those persons who were entitled to receive the missed 2002 or 2003 Participant Notice but who are not entitled to receive the plan's 2004 Participant Notice.

A VCP corrective notice must be issued by the due date of the plan's 2004 Participant Notice, or, if the plan is not required to issue a 2004 Participant Notice, the due date that would apply if the plan were required to issue it (for calendar year plans, generally October 4, 2004, November 15, 2004, or December 15, 2004).

The VCP corrective notice must include all the information required in the plan's 2004 Participant Notice (for example, current information on funding waivers, missed contributions, and limitations on our guarantee), or, if the plan is not required to issue a 2004 Participant Notice, all of the information that would be required in the plan's 2004 Participant Notice if it were required to be issued. However, there is a modification. Normally, a plan's 2004 Participant Notice would have to include the plan's "funded current liability percentage" for the 2003 plan year *or* for the 2004 plan year. Under the VCP, whether a plan administrator is correcting only a 2002 failure, both a 2002 and a 2003 failure, or only a 2003 failure, the plan's VCP corrective notice:

1. *Must* include the plan's "funded current liability percentage" for the 2002 plan year *and* for the 2003 plan year, and
2. *May* include as well the plan's "funded current liability percentage" for the 2004 plan year.

The notice does not need to contain information regarding participation in the VCP or that the information is being provided later than it should have been. There is a model notice available.

Issuing the VCP corrective notice may also satisfy the requirements for issuing a plan's 2004 Participant Notice.

### Q 24:38  What is the model VCP corrective notice?

The following is an example of a corrective notice that satisfies the requirements of the Participant Notice VCP when the required information is filled in. The PBGC has structured the VCP corrective notice to enable plans to issue a single notice that meets the requirements of the program and the 2004 Participant Notice.

#### NOTICE TO PARTICIPANTS OF [PLAN NAME]

The law requires that you receive information on the funding level of your defined benefit pension plan and the benefits guaranteed by the Pension Benefit Guaranty Corporation (PBGC), a federal insurance agency. [YOU MAY INCLUDE A STATEMENT TO THE EFFECT THAT THE PLAN HAD A PARTICIPANT NOTICE FAILURE FOR THE 2002 PLAN YEAR OR FOR THE 2003 PLAN YEAR (OR FOR BOTH). YOU MAY ALSO INCLUDE A STATEMENT TO THE EFFECT THAT THE PLAN IS PARTICIPATING IN THE PBGC'S PARTICIPANT NOTICE VOLUNTARY CORRECTION PROGRAM.]

YOUR PLAN'S FUNDING

As of [APPLICABLE DATE], your plan had [INSERT PLAN'S FUNDED CURRENT LIABILITY PERCENTAGE (AS DEFINED IN SECTION 302(d)(9)(C) of ERISA) FOR THE 2002 PLAN YEAR] percent of the money needed to pay benefits promised to employees and retirees.

As of [APPLICABLE DATE], your plan had [INSERT PLAN'S FUNDED CURRENT LIABILITY PERCENTAGE (AS DEFINED IN SECTION 302(d)(9)(C) of ERISA) FOR THE 2003 PLAN YEAR] percent of the money needed to pay benefits promised to employees and retirees.

[YOU MAY ALSO INCLUDE THE FOLLOWING STATEMENT:

As of [APPLICABLE DATE], your plan had [INSERT PLAN'S FUNDED CURRENT LIABILITY PERCENTAGE (AS DEFINED IN SECTION 302(d)(9)(C) of ERISA) FOR THE 2004 PLAN YEAR] percent of the money needed to pay benefits promised to employees and retirees.]

[SEE § 4011.10(c)(2) FOR SPECIAL RULES SMALL PLANS MAY USE TO DETERMINE THE PLAN'S FUNDED CURRENT LIABILITY PERCENTAGE.]

To pay pension benefits, your employer is required to contribute money to the pension plan over a period of years. A plan's funding percentage does not take into consideration the financial strength of the employer. Your employer, by law, must pay for all pension benefits, but your benefits may be at risk if your employer faces a severe financial crisis or is in bankruptcy.

[INCLUDE THE FOLLOWING PARAGRAPH ONLY IF, FOR ANY OF THE PREVIOUS FIVE PLAN YEARS, THE PLAN HAS BEEN GRANTED AND HAS NOT FULLY REPAID A FUNDING WAIVER.]

Your plan received a funding waiver for [LIST ANY OF THE FIVE PREVIOUS PLAN YEARS FOR WHICH A FUNDING WAIVER WAS GRANTED AND HAS NOT BEEN FULLY REPAID]. If a company is experiencing temporary financial hardship, the Internal Revenue Service may grant a funding waiver that permits the company to delay contributions that fund the pension plan.

[INCLUDE THE FOLLOWING WITH RESPECT TO ANY UNPAID OR LATE PAYMENT THAT MUST BE DISCLOSED UNDER SECTION 4011.10(b)(6):]

Your plan was required to receive a payment from the employer on [LIST APPLICABLE DUE DATE(S)]. That payment [has not been made][was made on [LIST APPLICABLE PAYMENT DATE(S)]].

PBGC GUARANTEES

When a pension plan terminates without enough money to pay all benefits, the PBGC steps in to pay pension benefits. The PBGC pays most people all pension benefits, but some people may lose certain benefits that are not guaranteed.

The PBGC pays pension benefits up to certain maximum limits.

The maximum guaranteed benefit is $3,698.86 per month or $44,386.32 per year for a 65-year-old person in a plan that terminates in 2004. [IF YOU ISSUE THIS NOTICE AFTER THE MAXIMUM GUARANTEED BENEFIT INFORMATION FOR PLANS THAT TERMINATE IN 2005 IS ANNOUNCED, YOU MAY ADD OR SUBSTITUTE THAT INFORMATION IN ORDER TO PROVIDE PARTICIPANTS

WITH MORE CURRENT INFORMATION. THE PBGC EXPECTS TO MAKE THAT INFORMATION AVAILABLE ON ITS WEB SITE AT WWW.PBGC.GOV IN EARLY NOVEMBER 2004.]

The maximum benefit may be reduced for an individual who is younger than age 65. For example, it is $1,664.49 per month or $19,973.88 per year for an individual who starts receiving benefits at age 55. [IN LIEU OF AGE 55, YOU MAY ADD OR SUBSTITUTE ANY AGE(S) RELEVANT UNDER THE PLAN. FOR EXAMPLE, YOU MAY ADD OR SUBSTITUTE THE MAXIMUM BENEFIT FOR AGES 62 OR 60. THE MAXIMUM BENEFIT IS $2,922.10 PER MONTH OR $35,065.20 PER YEAR AT AGE 62; IT IS $2,404.26 PER MONTH OR $28,851.12 PER YEAR AT AGE 60. IF THE PLAN PROVIDES FOR NORMAL RETIREMENT BEFORE AGE 65, YOU MUST INCLUDE THE NORMAL RETIRE-MENT AGE.][IF YOU ISSUE THIS NOTICE AFTER THE MAXIMUM GUARANTEED BENEFIT INFORMATION FOR PLANS THAT TERMINATE IN 2005 IS ANNOUNCED, YOU MAY ADD OR SUBSTITUTE THAT INFORMATION IN ORDER TO PROVIDE PARTICIPANTS WITH MORE CURRENT INFORMA-TION. THE PBGC EXPECTS TO MAKE THAT INFORMATION AVAILABLE ON ITS WEB SITE AT WWW.PBGC.GOV IN EARLY NOVEMBER 2004.][IF THE PLAN DOES NOT PROVIDE FOR COMMENCEMENT OF BENEFITS BEFORE AGE 65, YOU MAY OMIT THIS PARAGRAPH.]

The maximum benefit will also be reduced when a benefit is provided for a survivor. The PBGC does not guarantee certain types of benefits. [INCLUDE THE FOLLOWING GUARANTEE LIMITS THAT APPLY TO THE BENEFITS AVAIL-ABLE UNDER YOUR PLAN.]

- The PBGC does not guarantee benefits for which you do not have a vested right when a plan terminates, usually because you have not worked enough years for the company.
- The PBGC does not guarantee benefits for which you have not met all age, service, or other requirements at the time the plan terminates.
- Benefit increases and new benefits that have been in place for less than a year are not guaranteed. Those that have been in place for less than five years are only partly guaranteed.
- Early retirement payments that are greater than payments at normal retire-ment age may not be guaranteed. For example, a supplemental benefit that stops when you become eligible for Social Security may not be guaranteed.
- Benefits other than pension benefits, such as health insurance, life insur-ance, death benefits, vacation pay, or severance pay, are not guaranteed.
- The PBGC generally does not pay lump sums exceeding $5,000.

WHERE TO GET MORE INFORMATION

Your plan, [EIN-PN], is sponsored by [CONTRIBUTING SPONSOR(S)]. If you would like more information about the funding of your plan, contact [INSERT NAME, TITLE, BUSINESS ADDRESS AND PHONE NUMBER OF INDIVIDUAL OR ENTITY].

For more information about the PBGC and the benefits it guarantees, you may request a free copy of Your Guaranteed Pension by writing to Consumer Information Center, Dept. YGP, Pueblo, Colorado 81009. [THE FOLLOWING SENTENCE MAY BE INCLUDED:]"Your Guaranteed Pension" is also available on the PBGC's Web site at www.pbgc.gov.

Issued: [INSERT AT LEAST MONTH AND YEAR]

### Q 24:39   What must be included in the participant notice?

The PBGC has outlined in its regulations what must be included in the notice to comply with the notice requirement; however, because huge penalties may be imposed for failure to comply with the notice requirement, it may be best to use the following model notice, which is found in the regulations and updated annually, to meet the notice requirement.

**2006 Model Participant Notice**

The following is an example of a 2006 Participant Notice that satisfies the requirements of 29 C.F.R. Section 4011.10 when the required information is filled in.

### NOTICE TO PARTICIPANTS OF [PLAN NAME]

The law requires that you receive information on the funding level of your defined benefit pension plan and the benefits guaranteed by the Pension Benefit Guaranty Corporation (PBGC), a federal insurance agency.

YOUR PLAN'S FUNDING

As of *[month/day/year]*, your plan had *[insert Notice Funding Percentage determined in accordance with 29 C.F.R. section 4011.10(c)]* percent of the money needed to pay benefits promised to employees and retirees.

To pay pension benefits, your employer is required to contribute money to the pension plan over a period of years. A plan's funding percentage does not take into consideration the financial strength of the employer. Your employer, by law, must pay for all pension benefits, but your benefits may be at risk if your employer faces a severe financial crisis or is in bankruptcy.

*[Include the following paragraph only if, for any of the previous five plan years, the plan has been granted and has not fully repaid a funding waiver.]*

Your plan received a funding waiver for *[list any of the five previous plan years for which a funding waiver was granted and has not been fully repaid]*. If a company is experiencing temporary financial hardship, the Internal Revenue Service may grant a funding waiver that permits the company to delay contributions that fund the pension plan.

*[Include the following with respect to any unpaid or late payment that must be disclosed under 29 C.F.R. section 4011.10(b)(6):]*

Your plan was required to receive a payment from the employer on *[list applicable due date(s)]*. That payment [has not been made] [was made on *[list applicable payment date(s)]*].

PBGC GUARANTEES

When a pension plan terminates without enough money to pay all benefits, the PBGC steps in to pay pension benefits. The PBGC pays most people all pension benefits, but some people may lose certain benefits that are not guaranteed.

The PBGC pays pension benefits up to certain maximum limits.

- The maximum guaranteed benefit is $3,971.59 per month or $47,659.08 per year for a 65-year-old person in a plan that terminates in 2006. *[If you issue this notice after the maximum guaranteed benefit information for plans that terminate in 2007 is announced, you may add or substitute that information in order to provide participants with more current information. The PBGC expects to make that information available on its web site at www.pbgc.gov in early November 2006.]*

- The maximum benefit may be reduced for an individual who is younger than age 65. For example, it is $1,787.22 per month or $21,446.64 per year for an individual who starts receiving benefits at age 55. *[In lieu of age 55, you may add or substitute any age(s) relevant under the plan. For example, you may add or substitute the maximum benefit for ages 62 or 60. The maximum benefit is $3,137.56 per month or $37,650.72 per year at age 62; it is $2,581.53 per month or $30,978.36 per year at age 60. If the plan provides for normal retirement before age 65, you must include the normal retirement age.] [If you issue this notice after the maximum guaranteed benefit information for plans that terminate in 2007 is announced, you may add or substitute that information in order to provide participants with more current information. The PBGC expects to make that information available on its web site at www.pbgc.gov in early November 2006.] [If the plan does not provide for commencement of benefits before age 65, you may omit this paragraph.]*

- The maximum benefit will also be reduced when a benefit is provided for a survivor.

The PBGC does not guarantee certain types of benefits. *[Include the following guarantee limits that apply to the benefits available under your plan.]*

- The PBGC does not guarantee benefits for which you do not have a vested right when a plan terminates, usually because you have not worked enough years for the company.

- The PBGC does not guarantee benefits for which you have not met all age, service, or other requirements at the time the plan terminates.

- Benefit increases and new benefits that have been in place for less than a year are not guaranteed. Those that have been in place for less than five years are only partly guaranteed.

- Early retirement payments that are greater than payments at normal retirement age may not be guaranteed. For example, a supplemental benefit that stops when you become eligible for Social Security may not be guaranteed.
- Benefits other than pension benefits, such as health insurance, life insurance, death benefits, vacation pay, or severance pay, are not guaranteed.
- The PBGC generally does not pay lump sums exceeding $5,000.

WHERE TO GET MORE INFORMATION

Your plan, *[EIN-PN]*, is sponsored by *[contributing sponsor(s)]*. If you would like more information about the funding of your plan, contact *[insert name, title, business address and phone number of individual or entity]*.

For more information about the PBGC and the benefits it guarantees, you may request a free copy of "Your Guaranteed Pension" by writing to Consumer Information Center, Dept. YGP, Pueblo, CO 81009. *[The following sentence may be included:]* "Your Guaranteed Pension" is also available on the PBGC's Web site at www.pbgc.gov.

Issued: *[insert at least month and year]*

### Q 24:40   When must the notice be delivered to the plan participants and beneficiaries?

The plan administrator must provide the notice no later than 11½ months after the end of the plan year. Generally, this date is two months after the date for filing the annual report, Form 5500, for the plan (including extensions). [PBGC Reg. § 4011.8]

> **Example.** The R-Man Company was required to pay a VRP for the 2002 premium payment year. The plan was not exempt from the additional funding charge for the 2001 plan year and did not meet any other exception that would allow it not to provide the notice. The plan must provide its annual report by October 15, 2002, for the 2001 plan year with the extension. Therefore, the notice must be delivered no later than December 15, 2002.

### Q 24:41   What is the funding notice that must be provided for plan years beginning after December 31, 2007?

The PPA replaced ERISA Section 101(f), which contained the information that was required to be furnished to various parties for multiemployer plans, and made it applicable to all defined benefit plans that are covered by the PBGC (subject to Title IV of ERISA). This funding notice is provided on an annual basis to the PBGC, all participants and beneficiaries, each labor organization representing such participants and beneficiaries, and in the case of a multiemployer plan, to each employer that has a responsibility to contribute to the plan. A model notice is to be provided by the DOL by August 17, 2007, and can be distributed either in writing or electronically. It is to be distributed within 120 days after year end, unless the plan has 100 participants or fewer during the preceding year, then the notice is to be distributed when the annual Form 5500 is filed. The funding notice must contain the following information:

A. IDENTIFYING INFORMATION—Each notice must contain identifying information, including the name of the plan, the address and phone number of the plan administrator and the plan's principal administrative officer, each plan sponsor's employer identification number, and the plan number of the plan.

B. SPECIFIC INFORMATION—A plan funding notice must include:

1. In the case of a single-employer plan, a statement as to whether the plan's funding target attainment percentage for the plan year to which the notice relates, and for the two preceding plan years, is at least 100 percent (and, if not, the actual percentages), or

2. In the case of a multiemployer plan, a statement as to whether the plan's funded percentage for the plan year to which the notice relates, and for the two preceding plan years, is at least 100 percent (and, if not, the actual percentages);

3. In the case of a single-employer plan, a statement of—

   a. the total assets (separately stating the prefunding balance and the funding standard carryover balance) and liabilities of the plan, determined in the same manner as under code section 436, for the plan year for which the latest annual Form 5500 was filed and for the two preceding plan years, as reported in the annual report for each such plan year, and

   b. the value of the plan's assets and liabilities for the plan year to which the notice relates as of the last day of the plan year to which the notice relates determined using the asset valuation under subclause (II) of ERISA section 4006(a)(3)(E)(iii) and the interest rate under section 4006(a)(3)(E)(iv); and

4. In the case of a multiemployer plan, a statement of the value of the plan's assets and liabilities for the plan year to which the notice relates as the last day of such plan year and the preceding two plan years;

5. A statement of the number of participants who are—

   a. retired or separated from service and are receiving benefits,

   b. retired or separated participants entitled to future benefits, and

   c. active participants under the plan;

6. A statement setting forth the funding policy of the plan and the asset allocation of investments under the plan (expressed as percentages of total assets) as of the end of the plan year to which the notice relates;

7. In the case of a multiemployer plan, whether the plan was in critical or endangered status for such plan year and, if so—

   a. a statement describing how a person may obtain a copy of the plan's funding improvement or rehabilitation plan, as appropriate, and the actuarial and financial data that demonstrate any action taken by the plan toward fiscal improvement, and

     b. a summary of any funding improvement plan, rehabilitation plan, or modification thereof during the plan year to which the notice relates;

    8. In the case of any plan amendment, scheduled benefit increase or reduction, or other known event taking effect in the current plan year and having a material effect on plan liabilities or assets for the year (as defined in regulations by the Secretary), an explanation of the amendment, scheduled increase or reduction, or event, and a projection to the end of such plan year of the effect of the amendment, scheduled increase or reduction, or event on plan liabilities;

    9. In the case of a single-employer plan, a summary of the rules governing termination of single-employer plans covered by the PBGC, or

    10. In the case of a multiemployer plan, a summary of the rules governing reorganization or insolvency, including the limitations on benefit payments;

    11. A general description of the benefits under the plan which are eligible to be guaranteed by the PBGC, along with an explanation of the limitations on the guarantee and the circumstances under which such limitations apply;

    12. A statement that a person may obtain a copy of the annual report of the plan (Form 5500) upon request, through the Internet website of the DOL, or through an Intranet website maintained by the applicable plan sponsor (or plan administrator on behalf of the plan sponsor); and

    13. If applicable, a statement that each contributing sponsor, and each member of the contributing sponsor's controlled group, of the single-employer plan was required to provide the information under ERISA section 4010 for the plan year to which the notice relates.

  C. OTHER INFORMATION—Each funding notice shall include—in the case of a multiemployer plan, a statement that the plan administrator shall provide, upon written request, to any labor organization representing plan participants and beneficiaries and any employer that has an obligation to contribute to the plan, a copy of the annual report filed with the Secretary under section 104(a).

## Reportable Events

### Q 24:42  What is a *reportable event?*

A *reportable event* is an event that may affect a PBGC-covered plan's ability to pay benefits, or the plan's impending termination. Some events must be reported before the occurrence of the event; others must be reported after the occurrence of the event. Generally, unless a waiver is available or certain conditions are met, the event must be reported on PBGC Form 10 for events requiring a post-event notice and on PBGC Form 10-Advance for events requiring an advance notice.

## Q 24:43   What are the reportable events that require advance notice?

The following reportable events require a 30-day advance notice and must be filed on PBGC Form 10-Advance:

*Reportable event 1.* A person ceases to be a member of the controlled group, or the contributing sponsor has changed because of a change in the controlled group.

Advance notice is not required if the plan has 500 or fewer participants or the change in the controlled group is *de minimis*. For this purpose, *de minimis* means that the person or persons that cease to be part of the controlled group represent less than 5 percent of the plan's old controlled group for the most recent fiscal year or years ending on or before the effective date of the reportable event. [PBGC Reg § 4043.62]

*Reportable event 2.* A contributing sponsor or a member of a contributing sponsor's controlled group liquidates in a case under Title 11 of the U.S. Code, or under any similar federal law or law of a state or political subdivision of a state.

Advance notice is not required if the person who liquidates is a *de minimis* 5 percent segment of the controlled group for the most recent fiscal year or years ending on or before the effective date of the reportable event. [PBGC Reg. § 4043.63]

*Reportable event 3.* A contributing sponsor, or a member of a contributing sponsor's controlled group, declares an extraordinary dividend (as defined in Code Section 1059(c)) or redeems, in any 12-month period, an aggregate of 10 percent or more of the total combined voting power of all classes of stock entitled to vote or an aggregate of 10 percent or more of the total value of shares of all classes of stock of a contributing sponsor and all members of its controlled group.

Advance notice is not required if the person making the redemption is a *de minimis* 5 percent segment of the controlled group for the most recent fiscal year or years ending on or before the effective date of the reportable event. [PBGC Reg. § 4043.64]

*Reportable event 4.* In any 12-month period, an aggregate of 3 percent or more of the benefit liabilities of a plan maintained by a contributing sponsor or a member of its controlled group is transferred to a person that is not a member of the controlled group or to a plan or plans maintained by a person or persons that are not such a contributing sponsor or a member of its controlled group.

Advance notice is not required for this event if the transfer is complete and includes all assets and liabilities, the assets transferred equal the present value of the accrued benefits being transferred, and the assets represent less than 3 percent of the transferor's assets or if both plans involved in the transfer are fully funded. [PBGC Reg. § 4043.65]

*Reportable event 5.* A contributing sponsor has applied for a minimum funding waiver.

The deadline for advance notice is extended to 10 days after the event has occurred. [PBGC Reg. § 4043.66]

*Reportable event 6.* A contributing sponsor has defaulted on a loan with an outstanding balance of $10 million dollars or more.

Advance notice is not required if the default is cured or the lender waives the default within 10 days, or if later, by the end of any cure period. The deadline for filing advance notice is the later of (1) 10 days after default occurs; or (2) one day after (a) the cure period in the loan agreement (in the case of failure to make a required loan payment), (b) the date the loan is accelerated, or (c) the date the debtor receives written notice of default. [PBGC Reg. § 4043.67]

*Reportable event 7.* A member of the plan's controlled group commences a bankruptcy case, an insolvency proceeding, or an extension or settlement with its creditors.

The deadline for advance notice is extended to 10 days after the event has occurred. [PBGC Reg. § 4043.68]

### Q 24:44　Are all employers required to file advance notice of a reportable event?

No. Only non-publicly held companies with more than $50 million of aggregate unfunded vested benefits and a funded ratio of less than 90 percent are required to provide advance notice of a reportable event. [ERISA § 4043(b)] Unfunded vested benefits and funded ratios are generally determined under the same rules as the rules for determining the plan's VRP. However, although the JCWAA temporarily increased the required interest rate for calculating vested benefits for the VRP from 85 percent to 100 percent of the annual yield on 30-year Treasury securities for plan years beginning in 2002 or 2003, this statutory change did not apply for purposes of PBGC reporting and disclosure requirements that are tied to the VRP calculation such as this. In Technical Updates 02-1 and 04-2, the PBGC allowed usage of 100 percent of the Treasury yield to value vested benefits regardless of their plan year for reportable events with effective dates in calendar years 2002 or 2003, through May 31, 2004. [PBGC Tech. Update 04-2] Technical Update 04-3 expands the relief provided in Technical Updates 02-1 and 04-2 by allowing the further use of the JCWAA 100 percent Treasury Rate to value vested benefits in certain situations. Absent such further relief, the rate to be used for valuing vested benefits in these situations would be, depending on the plan year involved, either the pre-JCWAA 85 percent Treasury Rate or the PFEA 85 percent Corporate Rate. This relief is applicable to Information Years ending on or after June 1, 2004, where the last day of the plan year ending within the Information Year is on or before December 30, 2003.

The following chart shows the interest rates that may be used for valuing vested benefits for purposes of the $50 million and the 90 percent gateway tests, in light of JCWAA, PFEA, and the PBGC reporting relief provided in Technical Updates 02-1, 04-2, and 04-3:

### Section 4043(b) Advance Reporting Gateway Tests

| Event Year | Interest Rate for Advance Reporting Gateway Tests |
|---|---|
| 2002 or 2003 Plan Year | JCWAA 100% Treasury Rate |
| 2004 Plan Year: Events effective 1/1/04–5/31/04 | JCWAA 100% Treasury Rate or PFEA 85% Corporate Rate |
| 2004 Plan Year: Events effective on or after 6/1/04 | PFEA 85% Corporate Rate |
| 2005 Plan Year | PFEA 85% Corporate Rate |

**Example.** Two reportable events occur with respect to Plan *H*, which has an April 1-March 31 plan year. Event 1 is effective on April 30, 2004, and Event 2 is effective on September 30, 2004. For purposes of determining whether advance reporting is required:

- With respect to Event 1, vested benefits would be valued (as of the March 31, 2004, premium snapshot date) using either the JCWAA 100 percent Treasury Rate or the PFEA 85 percent Corporate Rate for the plan year that began April 1, 2004 (i.e., the March 2004 rate of 4.74 percent or 4.62 percent, respectively).

- With respect to Event 2, vested benefits would be valued (as of the March 31, 2004, premium snapshot date) using the PFEA 85 percent Corporate Rate for the plan year that began April 1, 2004 (i.e., the March 2004 rate of 4.62 percent).

A plan that meets this criterion may not be required to file advance notice if certain conditions exist at the time of the reportable event (see Q 24:43). [PBGC Reg. § 4043.61(b); PBGC Tech. Update 02-1]

### Q 24:45   What are the reportable events that require a post-event notice, and when is reporting of the event not required?

In general, a plan administrator and each contributing sponsor of a plan for which a reportable event has occurred must notify the PBGC on PBGC Form 10 within 30 days after he or she knows or has reason to know that the reportable event has occurred, unless a waiver or extension applies. Notice is waived for each of the following reportable events:

1. Tax disqualification of the plan or a determination that the plan is not in compliance with ERISA Title I [PBGC Reg. § 4043.21];
2. A plan amendment that decreases benefits [PBGC Reg. § 4043.22];
3. Termination or partial termination [PBGC Reg. § 4043.24]; or
4. Plan merger or consolidation, or the transfer of assets or liabilities. [PBGC Reg. § 4043.28]

The following reportable events *must* be reported to the PBGC on PBGC Form 10 within 30 days of the date of occurrence:

*Reportable event 1.* The number of active participants under a plan is reduced to less than 80 percent of the number of active participants at the beginning of the plan year or to less than 75 percent of the number of active participants at the beginning of the previous plan year.

The reporting of this event is waived if:

1. The plan has fewer than 100 participants as of the beginning of the current or previous plan year;

2. The plan was not required to pay a VRP for the year the event occurred, and the plan has less than $1 million in unfunded vested benefits as of the testing date or the plan would have no unfunded vested benefits if unfunded vested benefits were determined under the optional assumptions of PBGC Regulations Section 4010.4(b)(2); or

3. The reduction in active participants is caused by the cessation of operations at one or more facilities, and the fair market value of the plan's assets is at least 80 percent of the plan's vested benefits.

[PBGC Reg. § 4043.23]

*Reportable event 2.* The plan failed to meet the minimum funding standards of Code Section 412 or of ERISA Title I. These standards include a payment required as a condition of a previous funding waiver that is not made by its due date and a failure to make a required quarterly contribution under ERISA Section 302(e) or Code Section 412(m).

Notice is not required if the required minimum funding payment is made by the 30th day after its due date. [PBGC Reg. § 4043.25]

Reporting of missed quarterly contributions is waived if:

1. The employer had 100 or fewer participants in its defined benefit plans; or

2. The employer had 500 or fewer participants in its defined benefit plans and a participant notice for the plan under ERISA Section 4011 was not required for the plan year for which the quarterly contribution is owed or was not required for the prior plan year.

[PBGC Tech. Update 97-6]

*Reportable event 3.* The plan is currently unable to make benefit payments when due or is projected to be unable to make benefit payments when due.

A plan is currently unable to pay benefits when due if the plan has failed to provide any participant or beneficiary the full benefits to which the person is entitled under the terms of the plan. A plan is projected to be unable to pay benefits when due if, as of the last day of any plan year quarter, the plan's liquid assets are less than two times the amount of disbursements from the plan for such quarter. *Liquid assets* is defined as cash and marketable securities; *disbursements from the plan* means all disbursements from the trust, including purchases of annuities, payments of single sums and other benefits, and administrative expenses.

Notice is not required during a plan year in which the plan had no more than 100 participants. [PBGC Reg. § 4043.26]

*Reportable event 4.* The plan has made distributions to a substantial owner, and such distributions were not made by reason of the owner's death, the distribution exceeded $10,000, and immediately after the distribution the plan had unfunded vested benefits.

Notice is not required if:

1. The total of all distributions within the one-year period ending with the date of the distribution does not exceed the Section 415(b)(1)(A) limit (i.e., $135,000 for 2000);

2. No VRP is required to be paid for the event year; the plan would have no unfunded vested benefits if such benefits were determined under the assumptions of PBGC Regulations Section 4010.4(b)(2); or as of the testing date, the fair market value of the plan's assets is at least 80 percent of the plan's vested benefits amount; or

3. The sum of all distributions made to the substantial owner within the one-year period ending with the distribution is 1 percent or less of the end-of-year current value of the plan's assets (as reported on IRS Form 5500) for either of the two plan years immediately preceding the event year.

[PBGC Reg. § 4043.27]

*Reportable event 5.* A change in the contributing sponsor or controlled group has occurred as a result of a transaction causing one or more persons to no longer be members of the controlled group.

Notice is not required if:

1. The person or persons that will no longer be members of the plan's controlled group represent a *de minimis* 10 percent segment of the plan's old controlled group for the most recent fiscal year ending on or before the date the reportable event occurs;

2. Each person that ceases membership in the controlled group is a foreign entity other than a foreign parent;

3. No VRP is required to be paid for the event year;

4. The plan has less than $1 million in unfunded vested benefits;

5. The plan would have no unfunded vested benefits if such benefits were determined under the assumptions of PBGC Regulations Section 4010.4(b)(2); or

6. The plan's contributing sponsor, before the transaction, is a public company and the fair market value of the plan's assets is at least 80 percent of the plan's vested benefits.

[PBGC Reg. § 4043.29]

*Reportable event 6.* A member of the plan's controlled group is involved in any transaction to implement its complete liquidation, institutes a proceeding to be dissolved, or liquidates in a case under the Bankruptcy Code or similar law.

Notice is not required if:

1. The person or persons liquidating comprise a *de minimis* 10 percent segment of the plan's controlled group for the most recent fiscal year ending on or before the date of the liquidation, and each plan that was maintained by the liquidating entity is maintained by another member of the plan's controlled group after the liquidation;
2. Each person that liquidates is a foreign entity other than a foreign parent;
3. No VRP is required to be paid for the event year;
4. The plan has less than $1 million in unfunded vested benefits;
5. The plan would have no unfunded vested benefits if such benefits were determined under the assumptions of PBGC Regulations Section 4010.4(b)(2); or
6. The plan's contributing sponsor, before the transaction, is a public company and the fair market value of the plan's assets is at least 80 percent of the plan's vested benefits.

[PBGC Reg. § 4043.30]

*Reportable event 7.* A member of the plan's controlled group declares a dividend or redeems its own stock. Generally, these two transactions must result in a distribution in the form of cash or noncash that is in excess of 100 percent of the net worth of the member making the cash distribution or in excess of 10 percent in the case of a noncash distribution. If the distribution is in the form of cash and noncash, and the percentage of cash plus noncash exceeds 100 percent of the member's net worth the distribution is reportable.

Notice is not required if:

1. The member making the distribution is a *de minimis* 5 percent segment of the plan's controlled group for the most recent fiscal year ending on or before the date of the reportable event;
2. The distribution is made by a foreign entity other than a foreign parent;
3. The distribution is made by a foreign parent and made solely to other members of the plan's controlled group;
4. No VRP need be paid for the event year;
5. The plan has less than $1 million in unfunded vested benefits;
6. The plan would have no unfunded vested benefits if such benefits were determined under the optional assumptions of PBGC Regulations Section 4010.4(b)(2); or
7. The fair market value of the plan's assets is at least 80 percent of the plan's vested benefits.

[PBGC Reg. § 4043.31]

*Reportable event 8.* In any 12-month period, an aggregate of 3 percent or more of the benefit liabilities of a plan maintained by a contributing sponsor or a member of its controlled group is transferred to a person that is not a member of the controlled group or to a plan or plans maintained by a person or persons that are not such a contributing sponsor or a member of its controlled group.

Notice is not required if:

1. All of the plan's benefit liabilities and assets are transferred to one other plan;
2. The value of the asset being transferred equals the present value of the accrued benefits being transferred and is less than 3 percent of the assets of the transferor plan;
3. The transfer meets the requirements of Code Section 414(l); or
4. Following the transfer, the transferor and transferee plans are fully funded.

[PBGC Reg. § 4043.32]

*Reportable event 9.* A contributing sponsor has defaulted on a loan with an outstanding balance of $10 million or more.

Notice is not required if:

1. The default is cured, or notice is waived by the lender, within 30 days, or if later, by the end of the cure period stipulated in the loan agreement;
2. The debtor is a foreign entity other than a foreign parent;
3. No VRP need be paid for the event year;
4. The plan has less than $1 million in unfunded vested benefits;
5. The plan would have no unfunded vested benefits if such benefits were determined under the optional assumptions of PBGC Regulations Section 4010.4(b)(2); or
6. The fair market value of the plan's assets is at least 80 percent of the plan's vested benefits.

[PBGC Reg. § 4043.34]

*Reportable event 10.* A contributing sponsor has applied for a minimum funding waiver. Under no circumstances can a plan sponsor avoid the notice requirement for this event. [PBGC Reg. § 4043.33]

*Reportable event 11.* A member of the plan's controlled group commences a bankruptcy case, an insolvency proceeding, an extension, or settlement with its creditors; executes a general assignment for the benefit of its creditors; or undertakes to effect any other nonjudicial composition, extension, or settlement with substantially all of its creditors. [PBGC Reg. § 4043.35]

Notice is not required if the member of the controlled group involved in the bankruptcy or similar proceedings is a foreign entity other than a foreign parent. [PBGC Reg. § 4043.33]

### Q 24:46    What is the notice of failure to make required contributions under Code Section 412(n)?

A contributing sponsor of a single-employer plan is required to give notice to the PBGC on PBGC Form 200 whenever the unpaid balance of a required installment or any other payment required under ERISA Section 302 and Code Section 412 (including interest), when added to the aggregate unpaid balance of all preceding such installments or other payments for which payment was not made when due (including interest), exceeds $1 million. This notice must be filed with the PBGC no later than 10 days after the due date for any required payment for which payment was not made when due. [PBGC Reg. § 4043.81; PBGC Tech. Update 02-1]

### Q 24:47    What reporting requirements are applicable to underfunded plans of a controlled group?

The Retirement Protection Act of 1994 added Section 4010 to ERISA. ERISA Section 4010 requires certain controlled groups maintaining plans with large amounts of underfunding to submit financial and actuarial information annually to the PBGC (called a "Section 4010 Report").

Reporting is required (1) if the aggregate unfunded vested benefits of all defined benefit pension plans maintained by the controlled group exceed $50 million (for plan years beginning after 2007, this is changed to determining if the funding target attainment percentage at the end of the preceding plan year of a plan maintained by the contributing sponsor or any member of its controlled group is less than 80 percent.), (2) if the controlled group maintains any plan with missed contributions aggregating more than $1 million (unless paid within a 10-day grace period), or (3) if the controlled group maintains any plan with funding waivers in excess of $1 million and any portion is still outstanding (taking into account certain credit balances in the funding standard account).

The regulation requires the controlled group to file certain identifying information, certain financial information, each plan's actuarial valuation report, certain participant information, and a determination of the amount of each plan's benefit liabilities. The information submitted under the regulation allows the PBGC (1) to detect and monitor financial problems with the contributing sponsors that maintain severely underfunded pension plans and their controlled group members and (2) to respond quickly when it learns that a controlled group with severely underfunded pension plans intends to engage in a transaction that may significantly reduce the assets available to pay plan liabilities.

Reports are due 105 days after the end of the "information year" (generally the calendar year). [PBGC Reg. § 4010]

### Q 24:48    What information is required for a Section 4010 Report?

The following information must be included in a Section 4010 Report with respect to each member of the filer's controlled group and each plan maintained by any member of the controlled group:

- Identifying information (Q 24:49)
- Plan actuarial information (Q 24:50)
- Financial information (Q 24:51)

Previous filers that are not required to submit information for the current year must demonstrate why a filing is not required.

The PBGC may require any filer to submit additional actuarial or financial information that is necessary to determine plan assets and liabilities for any period through the end of the filer's information year, or the financial status of a filer for any period through the end of the filer's information year (including information on exempt entities and exempt plans). The information must be submitted within 10 days after the date of the written notification or by a different time specified therein.

### Q 24:49  What identifying information is required to be submitted in a Section 4010 Report?

Each filer is required to provide, in accordance with the instructions on the PBGC's Web site, the following identifying information with respect to each member of the controlled group (excluding exempt entities):

1. *Current members.* For an entity that is a member of the controlled group as of the end of the filer's information year—
   a. The name, address, and telephone number of the entity and the legal relationships with other members of the controlled group (for example, parent, subsidiary);
   b. The nine-digit Employer Identification Number (EIN) assigned by the IRS to the entity (or, if there is no EIN for the entity, an explanation); and
   c. If the entity became a member of the controlled group during the information year, the date the entity became a member of the controlled group.
2. *Former members.* For any entity that ceased to be a member of the controlled group during the filer's information year, the date the entity ceased to be a member of the controlled group and the identifying information required by paragraph (a)(1) of PBGC Regulations Section 4010.7 as of the date immediately preceding the date the entity left the controlled group.

In addition to the above information regarding the members, each filer is required to provide, in accordance with the instructions on the PBGC's Web site, the following identifying information with respect to each plan (including exempt plans) maintained by any member of the controlled group (including exempt entities):

1. Current plans. For a plan that is maintained by the controlled group as of the last day of the filer's information year—
   a. The name of the plan;
   b. The EIN and the three-digit Plan Number (PN) assigned by the contributing sponsor to the plan (or, if there is no EIN or PN for the plan, an explanation);

   c. If the EIN or PN of the plan has changed since the beginning of the filer's information year, the previous EIN or PN and an explanation;

   d. If the plan had not been maintained by the controlled group immediately before the filer's information year, the date the plan was first maintained by the controlled group during the information year; and

   e. If, as of any day during the information year, the plan was frozen (for eligibility or benefit accrual purposes), a description of the date and the nature of the freeze (e.g., service is frozen but pay is not).

2. Former plans. For a plan that ceased to be maintained by the controlled group during the filer's information year, the date the plan ceased to be so maintained, identification of the controlled group currently maintaining the plan, and the identifying information required by paragraph (b)(1) of PBGC Regulations Section 4010.7 as of the date immediately preceding that date.

[PBGC Reg. § 4010.7]

### Q 24:50  What actuarial information is required to be submitted in a Section 4010 Report?

For each plan (other than an exempt plan) maintained by any member of the filer's controlled group, each filer is required to provide, in accordance with the instructions on the PBGC's Web site, the following actuarial information:

1. The number of—

   a. Retired participants and beneficiaries receiving payments,

   b. Terminated vested participants, and

   c. Active participants;

2. The fair market value of the plan's assets;

3. The value of the plan's benefit liabilities, setting forth separately the value of the liabilities attributable to retired participants and beneficiaries receiving payments, terminated vested participants, and active participants, determined at the end of the plan year ending within the filer's information year;

4. A description of the actuarial assumptions for interest (i.e., the specific interest rate(s), such as 5 percent), mortality, retirement age, and loading for administrative expenses, as used to determine the plan's benefit liabilities; and

5. A copy of the actuarial valuation report for the plan year ending within the filer's information year that contains or is supplemented by the following information—

   a. Each amortization base and related amortization charge or credit to the funding standard account (as defined in ERISA Section 302(b) or Code Section 412(b)) for that plan year (excluding the amount considered contributed to the plan as described in ERISA Section 302(b)(3)(A) or Code Section 412(b)(3)(A)),

   b. The itemized development of the additional funding charge payable for that plan year pursuant to Code Section 412(l),

   c. The minimum funding contribution and the maximum deductible contribution for that plan year,

   d. The actuarial assumptions and methods used for that plan year for purposes of ERISA Section 302(b) and (d) or Code Section 412(b) and (l) (and any change in those assumptions and methods since the previous valuation and justifications for any change),

   e. A summary of the principal eligibility and benefit provisions on which the valuation of the plan was based (and any changes to those provisions since the previous valuation), along with descriptions of any benefits not included in the valuation, any significant events that occurred during that plan year, and the plan's early retirement factors,

   f. The current liability, vested and nonvested, calculated pursuant to Code Section 412, setting forth separately the value of the liabilities attributable to retired participants and beneficiaries receiving payments, terminated vested participants, and active participants,

   g. The expected increase in current liability due to benefits accruing during the plan year, and

   h. The expected plan disbursements for the plan year; and

6. A written certification by an enrolled actuary that, to the best of his or her knowledge and belief, the actuarial information submitted is true, correct, and complete and conforms to all applicable laws and regulations, provided that this certification may be qualified in writing, but only to the extent the qualification(s) are permitted under 26 Code of Federal Regulations Section 301.6059-1(d).

If any of the above information is not available by the due date for the filing, a filer may satisfy the requirement to provide such information by:

1. Including a statement, with the material that is submitted to the PBGC, that the filer will file the unavailable information by the alternative due date (15 days after the deadline for filing the plan's Form 5500 for the plan year ending within the filer's information year); and

2. Filing such information (along with the certification listed in item #6 above) with the PBGC by that alternative due date.

[PBGC Reg. § 4010.8]

For plan years beginning after December 31, 2007, additional information that is required include:

- The amount of benefit liabilities under the plan determined using the assumptions applied by the PBGC in determining liabilities;

- The funding target of the plan determined as if the plan has been in at-risk status for at least five plan years; and

- The funding target attainment percentage of the plan.

(See chapter 19 for definitions of funding target and funding target attainment percentage.)

### Q 24:51 What financial information is required to be submitted in a Section 4010 Report?

Each filer is required to provide, in accordance with the instructions on the PBGC's Web site, the financial information for each controlled group member included in the consolidated financial statements (other than an exempt entity), the member's revenues and operating income for the information year, and net assets at the end of the information year. [PBGC Reg. § 4010.9]

### Q 24:52 How does an employer file a Section 4010 Report?

For information years ending on or after December 31, 2005, the final Section 4010 regulations require that information be submitted using the PBGC's secure e-4010 Web-based application. The Web-based application:

- Offers a secure Web site for submitting confidential information;
- Reviews the filing and generates a list of omissions and inconsistencies prior to submission to ensure a filing is complete; and
- Enables filing coordinators to access and modify information entered in one year for a future year's filing.

Before using the Web-based application, the filer must establish an "e4010" account and select a user ID and password at www.pbgc.gov/e4010/. The Web-based application then walks the filer through the steps to complete Schedule G—General information, Schedule FG—Filing gateway, Schedule I—Identifying information, Schedule F—Financial information, and Schedule P—Plan actuarial information.

### Q 24:53 For what period is the required financial and actuarial information reported?

Financial information is reported for each member's fiscal year ending within the filer's "information year." The information year is the fiscal year of the filer, unless the members of the controlled group report financial information on the basis of different fiscal years, in which case the information year is the calendar year. Actuarial information is reported for each plan's plan year ending within the information year. [PBGC Reg. § 4010.5]

### Q 24:54 Must an entity or a plan be included in the annual information report if the entity or the plan is no longer in the controlled group as of the last day of the information year?

No. Controlled group members and their plans are determined as of a "snapshot" taken on the last day of the information year. [PBGC Tech. Update 96-3]

### Q 24:55 As of what date are unfunded vested benefits determined for purposes of the $50 million filing threshold?

Unfunded vested benefits for a plan are determined as of the last day of the plan year that ends within the filer's information year. If a controlled group has plans with different plan years, the unfunded vested benefits at the end of each plan's plan year are totalled to determine whether the controlled group has more than $50 million in unfunded vested benefits for the controlled group's information year. [PBGC Reg. § 4010.4(b)]

### Q 24:56  How are unfunded vested benefits calculated?

Vested benefits are calculated on a plan-by-plan basis as of the last day of the plan year that ends within the Information Year (the 4010 Gateway Testing Date). There are three possible methods for calculating unfunded vested benefits (the 4010 Gateway Test): (1) using the general method used to calculate the PBGC's variable-rate premium, (2) using the alternative calculation method used to calculate the PBGC's variable-rate premium, or (3) using the general method with optional assumptions (this option is only available for filings with respect to information years ending before December 31, 2005). [PBGC Reg. § 4010.4(b)(1)]

Under option 3 above, a plan may substitute the following assumptions for the standard assumptions used under the general method:

- An interest rate equal to 100 percent of the annual yield for 30-year Treasury constant maturities for the last full calendar month in the plan year;
- The fair market value of the plan's assets; and
- The same mortality table used for Code Section 412(l)(7)(C)(ii)(I).

[PBGC Reg. § 4010.4(b)(2)]

The following chart shows the interest rates that may be used for valuing vested benefits for purposes of the 4010 Gateway Test for 4010 Gateway Testing Dates on or after January 1, 2002, in light of JCWAA, PFEA, and the PBGC reporting relief in Technical Updates 02-1, 04-2, and 04-3:

**Section 4010 Gateway Test**
**For 4010 Gateway Testing Dates on or after January 1, 2002**

| *4010 Gateway Testing Date* | *Interest Rate for 4010 Gateway Test* |
| --- | --- |
| 1/1/02–12/30/03 | JCWAA 100% Treasury Rate |
| 12/31/03–12/30/05 | JCWAA 100% Treasury Rate |
| For Information Years Ending | or |
| 12/31/03–5/31/04 | PFEA 85% Corporate Rate |
| 12/31/03–12/30/05 | |
| For Information Years Ending on or after 6/1/04 | PFEA 85% Corporate Rate |

The rates shown below reflect changes made by the Pension Protection Act of 2006.

| | Plan Years | |
|---|---|---|
| *Ending on or After* | *and Before* | *Interest Rate to be Used for 4010 Gateway Test* |
| September 30, 2006 | October 31, 2006 | 5.06% |
| August 31, 2006 | September 30, 2006 | 5.19% |
| July 31, 2006 | August 31, 2006 | 5.36% |
| June 30, 2006 | July 31, 2006 | 5.36% |
| May 31, 2006 | June 30, 2006 | 5.35% |
| April 30, 2006 | May 31, 2006 | 5.25% |
| March 31, 2006 | April 30, 2006 | 5.01% |
| February 28, 2006 | March 31, 2006 | 4.87% |
| January 31, 2006 | February 28, 2006 | 4.80% |
| December 31, 2005 | January 31, 2006 | 4.86% |

For purposes of determining vested benefits for the 4010 Gateway Test for plan years ending on or after December 31, 2005, the PFEA 85 percent Corporate Rate no longer applies and instead would be required to use 85 percent of the annual yield on 30-year Treasury securities. However, the PBGC in Technical Update 06-1 granted filing relief to those employers that would be required to file if they used the proper rate but would not if they used the Corporate Rate. [PBGC Tech. Update 06-1.]

**Example.** A controlled group with an Information Year ending May 31, 2004, has two plans. Plan *A* has a 4010 Gateway Testing Date of September 30, 2003, and Plan *B* has a 4010 Gateway Testing Date of December 31, 2003. For purposes of the 4010 Gateway Test:

- Vested benefits in Plan *A* must be valued using the JCWAA 100 percent Treasury Rate for the plan year that began October 1, 2003 (i.e., the September 2003 rate of 5.14 percent).
- Vested benefits in Plan *B* could be valued using either the JCWAA 100 percent Treasury Rate or the PFEA 85 percent Corporate Rate for the plan year that began January 1, 2004 (i.e., the December 2003 rate of 5.07 percent or 4.94 percent, respectively).

[PBGC Tech. Update 04-3]

### Q 24:57   Must the same method be used for premium purposes and for Section 4010?

No. A filer may use a different method for calculating unfunded vested benefits for premiums and unfunded vested benefits for Section 4010.

### Q 24:58   May different methods be used for different plans?

Yes. There is no requirement that the method be consistent across all plans for the controlled group. [PBGC Reg. § 4010.4(b)]

### Q 24:59 May contributions paid after the end of a plan year be included in assets for purposes of determining whether the plan has more than $50 million in unfunded vested benefits?

The PBGC will permit a filer to include contributions made by the timely filing date, but only to the extent the contributions are attributable to the prior plan year for funding purposes under ERISA Section 302(c)(10) and Code Section 412(c)(10). Contributions used to satisfy quarterly contribution requirements for a plan year may not be included in plan assets as of the end of the prior plan year. [PBGC Tech. Update 96-3]

### Q 24:60 Does a filer have to discount the value of contributions paid after the end of a plan year?

Yes. The discount rate depends on the premium method used to calculate unfunded vested benefits for purposes of ERISA Section 4010. If unfunded vested benefits are determined under the general method, use the plan's asset valuation rate. If unfunded vested benefits are determined under the alternative calculation method, use the premium interest rate. [PBGC Tech. Update 96-3]

### Q 24:61 Are the other actuarial assumptions (other than interest rate and mortality) identical to those used to calculate the plan's current liability?

Generally, yes. Actuarial assumptions (other than interest rate and mortality) must be identical to those used to calculate the plan's current liability for funding purposes, unless different assumptions are required to reflect a significant event. [PBGC Tech. Update 96-3]

### Q 24:62 May plans use projected (rolled forward) census data for calculating unfunded vested benefits for purposes of the $50 million filing threshold?

Yes, provided the census data is rolled forward (consistent with generally accepted actuarial principles) to appropriately reflect the actual population as of the last day of the plan year ending within the information year. [PBGC Tech. Update 96-3]

### Q 24:63 What actuarial information is required to be submitted?

For each plan maintained by any member of the filer's controlled group, each filer is required to provide the following actuarial information:

1. The fair market value of the plan's assets;
2. The value of the plan's benefit liabilities at the end of the plan year ending within the filer's information year (see Q 24:65);
3. A copy of the actuarial valuation report for the plan year ending within the filer's information year (see Q 24:64); and

4. A written certification by an enrolled actuary that, to the best of his or her knowledge and belief, the actuarial information submitted is true, correct, and complete and conforms to all applicable laws and regulations, provided that this certification may be qualified in writing, but only to the extent the qualification(s) are permitted.

[PBGC Reg. Section 4010.8(a)]

### Q 24:64   What information is required to be included in the actuarial valuation report?

The actuarial valuation report must contain or be supplemented by the following information:

1. Each amortization base and related amortization charge or credit to the funding standard account for that plan year;
2. The itemized development of the additional funding charge payable for that plan year pursuant to Code Section 412(l);
3. The minimum funding contribution and the maximum deductible contribution for that plan year;
4. The actuarial assumptions and methods used for that plan year (and any change in those assumptions and methods since the previous valuation and justifications for any change); and
5. A summary of the principal eligibility and benefit provisions on which the valuation of the plan was based (and any changes to those provisions since the previous valuation), along with descriptions of any benefits not included in the valuation, any significant events that occurred during that plan year, and the plan's early retirement factors.

[PBGC Reg. § 4010.10(a)(3)]

### Q 24:65   How are benefit liabilities determined?

The value of a plan's benefit liabilities at the end of a plan year shall be determined using plan census data either as of the end of the plan year or as of the beginning of the next plan year, subject to a modification to use projected census data. In addition, the value of benefit liabilities shall be determined using the assumptions and methods applicable to the valuation of benefits to be paid as annuities in trusteed plans terminating at the end of the plan year. [PBGC Reg. § 4010.10(d)]

### Q 24:66   What if the actuarial information is not available by the filing due date?

Two types of actuarial information are required: (1) the values of each plan's assets and benefit liabilities, which must be filed by the due date, and (2) actuarial information related to the actuarial valuation report prepared for minimum funding purposes, which has an automatic extension to the extent not available by the due date. For the information eligible for the automatic extension, the filer should state in its initial filing what information is unavailable. The filer must submit the unavailable information by the alternative due date (15 days after the deadline, including extensions, for filing the plan's Form 5500 for the plan year ending within the filer's information year). [PBGC Reg. § 4010.10(b)]

### Q 24:67   May plans use projected (rolled forward) census data for calculating benefit liabilities?

Yes. Benefit liabilities are calculated as of the last day of the plan year ending within the information year, using the PBGC's termination assumptions in effect on that date. Thus, for calendar year plans, benefit liabilities would be calculated as of December 31. (The timing of the filing was designed so that most filers could calculate benefit liabilities at the same time and using the same census data used to determine pension obligations for financial statement purposes (as prescribed under SFAS 87)). The census data used to value benefit liabilities may be based on a roll forward of data (consistent with projections used for financial statement purposes) from any date within the plan year (including the first day) to the last day of the plan year (or, in certain circumstances, to the first day of the next plan year). Adjustments may need to be made to reflect the occurrence of significant events. [PBGC Reg. § 4010.10(d)(1)(ii)]

### Q 24:68   May the actuary use sampling techniques to determine a plan's population?

Yes. For calculating unfunded vested benefits or benefit liabilities, the actuary may determine the plan's population on the basis of either an actual census or a representative sample of the plan's population. The actuary shall determine, in accordance with generally accepted actuarial principles, what data to collect and what sampling techniques to use. [PBGC Tech. Update 96-3]

### Q 24:69   May a plan take into account changes in plan provisions that will become effective after the last day of the plan year but before the last day of the information year?

No. Both unfunded vested benefits and benefit liabilities should reflect only those plan provisions in effect on the last day of the plan year. [PBGC Tech. Update 96-3]

### Q 24:70   When are assets valued for purposes of reporting the fair market value of assets under ERISA Section 4010?

The fair market value of assets is determined on the last day of the plan year ending within the filer's information year, without regard to any contributions received by the plan after the end of the plan year. This should be the same value used for financial statement purposes. [PBGC Reg. § 4010]

### Q 24:71  What financial information is required to be submitted to the PBGC under ERISA Section 4010?

Each filer is required to provide audited financial statements for the fiscal year ending within the information year, unless they are not available. [PBGC Reg. § 4010.9(a)]

### Q 24:72  Are filers required to prepare and submit audited financial statements?

No. Although the filer must submit financial information, there is no requirement to prepare either audited or unaudited financial statements. However, if either audited or unaudited financial statements are prepared, they must be submitted. [PBGC Tech. Update 96-3]

### Q 24:73  If audited financial statements are not available by the due date, may unaudited statements be filed?

Yes. However, if unaudited financial statements are submitted, audited financial statements must be filed within 15 days after they are prepared. (Filers that routinely prepare audited financial statements later than 105 days after their fiscal year end may apply for an exemption that permits a later due date.) [PBGC Reg. § 4010.9(c)]

### Q 24:74  If neither audited nor unaudited financial statements are available by the due date, may copies of federal tax returns be filed?

Yes. However, if copies of federal tax returns are submitted, audited and/or unaudited financial statements must be filed within 15 days after they are prepared. [PBGC Reg. § 4010.9(c)]

### Q 24:75  What is considered an outstanding funding waiver?

A minimum funding waiver for a plan is considered outstanding if the statutory amortization period is still applicable, unless:

1. A credit balance exists in the funding standard account that is no less than the outstanding balance of all waivers for the plan;
2. A waiver condition or contractual obligation requires there to be a credit balance as described in (1) as of the end of each plan year; and
3. No portion of this credit balance is used to make any required installment applicable to the funding standard account for any plan year during the remainder of the amortization period.

**Q 24:76   Is the $1 million funding waiver reporting threshold applied on an aggregate controlled-group basis?**

No. The $1 million reporting threshold for funding waivers applies separately to each plan. If a plan has more than one funding waiver with outstanding balances, the amounts of the waivers, when granted, are aggregated. [PBGC Reg. § 4010.4(a)(3)]

**Q 24:77   If outstanding funding waivers of less than $1 million were granted to two separate plans but the plans subsequently merged, must the merged plan report if the waivers, when granted, totaled more than $1 million?**

Yes. [PBGC Tech. Update 96-3]

**Q 24:78   Can filers rely on an ERISA Section 4010 filing to comply with the reportable events requirements in ERISA Section 4043?**

No, filers may not substitute a Section 4010 annual information filing for a reportable event filing. A plan administrator or contributing sponsor filing a reportable event notice under Section 4043 is permitted, in lieu of submitting any required information to the PBGC, to refer to information previously submitted as part of a Section 4010 filing.

# Chapter 25

# Plan Termination

In the defined benefit plan market, it is often said that one does not understand how a defined benefit plan works until one understands the termination of a plan. Defined benefit plans are designed to provide benefits to covered participants. On termination, all of the participants and beneficiaries are paid their accrued benefits. This settlement of all benefits provides a thorough look at all features of a plan. An employer establishes a qualified retirement plan with the intention of maintaining it on a permanent basis; however, the law recognizes that no plan can last forever because the objectives and financial circumstances of employers change.

The plan document governs the termination of a plan. Unlike a defined contribution plan termination, a defined benefit plan termination has many complex features. The employer promised that an accrued benefit would be paid, and at plan termination all the accrued benefits must be funded. If there is a surplus of assets, it must be handled according to several rules. If there is a deficiency, the employer must generally make up the deficiency. Each of the various regulatory agencies has its own jurisdiction over certain aspects of plan termination. This chapter examines the methods of plan termination and the impact of plan termination on plan participants and the plan sponsor.

## Termination Procedures

### Q 25:1  Can a defined benefit plan be terminated?

Yes. A defined benefit plan can be terminated as long as the plan document provides for a plan termination. Some plans, like multiemployer plans or single-employer union plans, may require a special approval process, such as union and management agreement, to terminate. Collectively bargained plans may be tied directly to the collectively bargained agreement. Municipal and other governmental plans may need an act passed by the appropriate governing body or by a town or county referendum. Plans that are covered by Title IV of the Employee Retirement Income Security Act of 1974 (ERISA), that is, covered by the Pension Benefit Guaranty Corporation (PBGC), must comply with additional plan termination rules.

### Q 25:2  Are there any criteria a plan must satisfy to terminate?

Yes. In general, a plan must be fully funded and there must be a bona fide business reason for the plan termination. IRS Form 5310, Application for Determination Upon Termination, provides guidance on reasonable business reasons for plan termination. They are a change of ownership of the business by merger, the liquidation or dissolution of the employer, a change in ownership through sale or transfer, the existence of adverse business conditions, and the adoption of a new plan.

### Q 25:3  Who decides to terminate a plan?

The plan sponsor normally decides to terminate a plan. For a plan that is tied to a collectively bargained agreement, the decision may require agreement between representatives from the union and management.

The PBGC can terminate a covered defined benefit plan through the federal court system. The PBGC must show that the employer has not met minimum funding standards, that the plan is unable to pay benefits when due, that a distribution has been made to a substantial owner in excess of $10,000 within a 24-month period for reasons other than death and after such distribution there are unfunded vested liabilities, or that the possibility exists for liabilities to increase unreasonably if the plan is not terminated. [ERISA § 4042(a)]

### Q 25:4  What action must be taken to terminate a plan?

Numerous steps must be taken to terminate a plan. The first step is to establish a termination date. This is generally done by resolution of the plan sponsor's board of directors, and the termination date should be a date far enough in the future to allow for completion of other necessary administrative tasks before the termination becomes effective. For a plan that is subject to Title IV of ERISA, the termination date will be the date specified in the Notice of Intent to Terminate (NOIT). [ERISA § 4048(a)(1)]

A plan covered by ERISA Title IV must provide a notice to affected parties through a NOIT. This notice must be given at least 60 days, but not more than 90 days, before the proposed date of termination (see Q 25:15). In addition, an ERISA Section 204(h) notice is required for any termination, cessation, curtailment, or reduction of benefits. This notice must be provided for a reasonable period before the change (see Q 25:10).

Additionally, any amendments to the plan document for tax law changes that may not have been required as of the date of termination but will be retroactively effective must be made. The IRS must be notified that the plan is terminating. There is no legal requirement for a plan sponsor to obtain a favorable determination letter from the IRS. At a minimum, however, the plan sponsor must indicate on the IRS Form 5500 series that the plan has been terminated and all assets have been distributed to plan participants.

### Q 25:5   How quickly must assets be distributed after the termination date?

To properly terminate a qualified plan, all plan assets must be distributed to plan participants in accordance with the terms of the plan "as soon as administratively feasible" after the date of termination.

Whether a distribution is made as soon as administratively feasible is to be determined under all the facts and circumstances of the given case, but, generally a distribution that is not completed within one year following the date of plan termination will be presumed not to have been made as soon as administratively feasible. [Rev. Rul. 89-87, 1989-2 C.B. 81]

### Q 25:6   What are the ramifications of not distributing assets as soon as administratively feasible?

A plan under which all assets are not distributed as soon as administratively feasible is an ongoing plan and must meet the requirements of Internal Revenue Code (Code) Section 401(a) to continue its qualified status. This means that the plan will continue to be subject to such requirements as the minimum benefit and accrual rules of Code Section 416 (top-heavy requirements) and the minimum funding requirements of Code Section 412. Also, in any year in which the trust assets have not been distributed, the plan is subject to the information reporting requirements of Code Sections 6057, 6058, and 6059, which require continued filings of Form 5500 and Schedule B. [Rev. Rul. 89-87, 1989-2 C.B. 81]

## Reporting to the IRS

### Q 25:7   Should a favorable determination letter be obtained from the IRS with regard to a plan termination?

With rare exception, obtaining a favorable determination letter for the plan termination is the best approach. A plan termination is a fulfillment of the employer's promise to the employees up until the termination date. If operational or document errors are found on audit after all money has been distributed, the favorable tax status of the rollovers or the distributions can be jeopardized.

Ultimately, if a determination letter is not requested, the IRS will be notified of a termination through the IRS Form 5500 series reports indicating the return is a final return. The last actuarial report to be filed (IRS Form 5500, Schedule B, Actuarial Information) is for the plan year in which the plan is terminated. A Schedule B is not required for years following the year of termination.

### Q 25:8   What should a plan sponsor review before filing for a determination letter with regard to a plan termination?

The plan sponsor should carefully review several items before filing for a favorable determination letter. A self-audit is essential. Reviewing operational compliance and form compliance is also important.

The decision whether to file for a favorable determination letter should be documented in a board of directors' resolution.

Handling individual insurance policies can be difficult. The plan administrator should notify the participants as far in advance as possible of life insurance changes and provide participants with information on the allowable options. The normal options available include the following:

1. Cancel the policies and transfer the cash values to the other investments of the plan.
2. Allow participants to take a maximum policy loan and deposit the loan proceeds into the general investments of the plan.
3. Purchase the policies at net cash value.

The method of handling surplus assets should be determined in advance. If additional distribution options are desired, such as lump sums, amendments should be put in place first and then notices sent to employees.

### Q 25:9   What forms are filed with the IRS to obtain a favorable determination letter?

Listed below are the items normally presented to the IRS to obtain a favorable determination letter for a single-employer plan:

- IRS Form 5310, Application for Determination Upon Termination;
- IRS Form 2848, Power of Attorney and Declaration of Representative;
- IRS Form 6088, Distributable Benefits from Employee Pension Plans;
- Any amendments necessary for the termination process;
- The full plan document with any updates; and

- Sample election forms, that is, the forms provided to each participant for signature, that identify the amount of benefits and forms of distribution each participant is entitled to receive on termination approval, and help in closing the case earlier.

## Q 25:10   What is an *ERISA Section 204(h) notice*?

An *ERISA Section 204(h) notice* is a notice that must be provided to each participant in the plan, any alternate payee, and to each employee organization representing participants whose rate of future benefit accrual under the plan is reasonably expected to be significantly reduced, or for whom an early retirement benefit or retirement-type subsidy under the plan may reasonably be expected to be significantly reduced, by the ERISA Section 204(h) amendment. Whenever a plan is amended that either provides for a significant reduction in the rate of future benefit accrual or eliminates or significantly reduces an early retirement benefit or retirement-type subsidy, an ERISA Section 204(h) notice must be provided. This rule applies to all plans, except most profit-sharing–type plans. [Treas. Reg. § 54.4980F, Q&A 1] (See chapter 8 for more information regarding the Section 204(h) notice.)

## Q 25:11   What special filings are required for the year of termination?

The IRS Form 5500 series must be filed by the end of the seventh month from the month in which the last dollar of assets is distributed. This can hasten the filing deadline for most plans. IRS Form 1099-R must be prepared and sent to the plan participants and the IRS, and IRS Form 945 must be filed with the IRS to report any federal income tax withholding.

The plan administrator must keep track of all joint and survivor election forms. Monitoring proper execution may be difficult and a systematic method should be developed.

# Standard Terminations

## Q 25:12   What is a *standard termination*?

A *standard termination* is a termination processed by the PBGC, where assets are sufficient to meet liabilities. A single employer can terminate a plan under a standard termination only if the following criteria are satisfied:

1. The plan administrator provides a 60-day advance NOIT to all affected parties (see Q 25:15).
2. The plan administrator provides a notice of plan benefits to all affected parties on or before filing PBGC Form 500 with the PBGC (see Q 25:16).
3. The plan administrator files PBGC Form 500 with the PBGC on or before the 180th day after the proposed termination date.

4. The plan administrator distributes the plan's assets by the later of (a) the 180th day after the expiration of the PBGC's 60-day review period or (b) 120 days after receipt of a favorable determination letter from the IRS.

When plan assets are insufficient to meet projected liabilities, a plan may still be allowed to terminate in a standard termination if either the plan sponsor agrees to make a commitment to contribute any additional funds necessary (see Q 25:25), or a majority owner agrees to forgo benefits until all other liabilities are met (see Q 25:26).

The standard termination is completed for PBGC purposes as long as the PBGC does not issue a notice of noncompliance to the plan administrator. A notice of noncompliance is issued when the PBGC has reason to believe that the plan is not sufficiently funded for benefit liabilities or that the plan administrator did not follow the other requirements of a standard termination. [PBGC Reg. § 4041.21]

### Q 25:13  What are the procedural requirements of a standard termination?

The following steps must be taken to proceed with the termination of a single-employer plan in a standard termination:

1. Select a proposed termination date.
2. Issue a NOIT at least 60 days, and no more than 90 days, before the proposed termination date (see Q 25:15).
3. Issue a notice of plan benefits on or before filing PBGC Form 500 (see Q 25:16).
4. File PBGC Form 500, PBGC Schedule EA-S, and PBGC Schedule REP-S on or before the 180th day after the proposed termination date (see Q 25:14).
5. Issue a notice of annuity information, if applicable, no later than 45 days before the distribution date (see Q 25:18).
6. Distribute plan assets before the later of (a) 180 days after expiration of the PBGC 60-day review period or (b) 120 days after receipt of a favorable determination letter from the IRS.
7. Follow PBGC rules for finding missing participants, if any (see Q 25:28).
8. Issue a notice of annuity contract to participants receiving benefits in the form of an annuity no later than 30 days after all plan benefits are distributed.
9. File PBGC Form 501, Post-Distribution Certification, no later than 30 days after all plan benefits are distributed (see Q 25:27).

See the accompanying timeline for a graphical display of these requirements and deadlines:

### Standard Termination Timeline:
### Notice of Intent to Terminate to Distribution Deadline

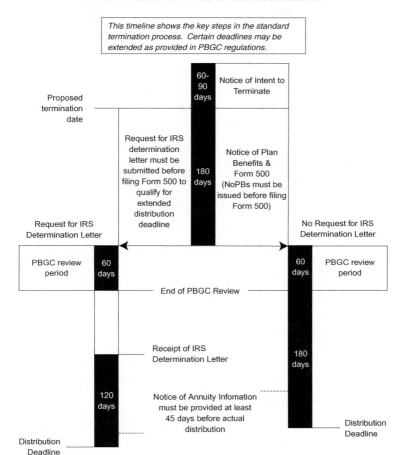

*This timeline shows the key steps in the standard termination process. Certain deadlines may be extended as provided in PBGC regulations.*

### Standard Termination Timeline:
### Post-Distribution Certification

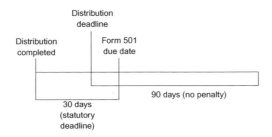

### Q 25:14   What forms are filed with the PBGC?

The following forms should be filed with the PBGC under a standard termination:

*PBGC Form 500, Standard Termination Notice Single-Employer Plan Termination.* PBGC Form 500 is required to be filed and signed by the plan administrator for the certification of information required for standard terminations and must be filed no later than 180 days after the proposed termination date.

*PBGC Schedule EA-S, Standard Termination Certification of Sufficiency.* PBGC Schedule EA-S must be completed by the enrolled actuary to certify that plan assets are projected to be sufficient to satisfy plan liabilities and must accompany PBGC Form 500.

*PBGC Schedule REP-S, Designation of Representative.* PBGC Schedule REP-S can be used by the plan administrator to designate another party to represent the plan before the PBGC. The plan administrator typically names the third-party administrator, attorney, or actuary as the designated representative.

### Q 25:15   What is included in a NOIT, and when must it be distributed?

At least 60 days and no more than 90 days before the proposed termination date, the plan administrator must issue a NOIT to each person who is an affected party as of the proposed termination date. Additionally, the plan administrator must issue the NOIT promptly to any person who becomes an affected party, as in the case of a beneficiary of a deceased participant or an alternate payee, within the time frame described above, or after the proposed termination date and on or before the distribution date. If the NOIT is issued early by a *de minimis* number of days through administrative error, the PBGC may consider the notice to be timely.

The NOIT must include the following:

- The name and plan number of the plan and the employer identification number of each contributing plan sponsor;
- The name, address, and telephone number of the person who may be contacted by an affected party with questions concerning the plan termination;
- A statement that the plan will be terminated in a standard termination as of a proposed termination date, and that each affected party will be notified if the proposed termination date is changed to a later date or if the termination does not occur;
- A statement that to terminate in a standard termination, plan assets must be sufficient to provide all plan benefits under the plan;
- A statement that benefit accruals ceased, in accordance with ERISA Section 204(h), as of a specified date before the NOIT was issued; will cease by plan amendment, in accordance with ERISA Section 204(h), as of the proposed termination date or a specified date before the proposed termination date, whether or not the plan is terminated; or will cease as of the termination date, but will continue if the plan does not terminate;

- A special annuity notice if annuities are to be purchased;
- A statement that each affected party entitled to plan benefits will receive a written notification regarding his or her plan benefits;
- A statement as to how a person entitled to receive a summary plan description (SPD) can receive it;
- For participants who are in pay status, an explanation that their benefit amounts will not be affected by the plan termination or that they will be affected and by how much; and
- A statement that after plan assets have been distributed in full satisfaction of all plan benefits under the plan with respect to a participant or a beneficiary of a deceased participant, either by the purchase of irrevocable commitments or by an alternative form of distribution provided for under the plan, the PBGC no longer guarantees the participant's or beneficiary's plan benefits.

[PBGC Reg. § 4041.23]

The PBGC's standard termination forms and instructions package, Appendix B, includes a model NOIT:

**Model Notice of Intent to Terminate (NOIT)**

Month/Day/Year

### NOTICE OF INTENT TO TERMINATE [PLAN NAME]

The [plan administrator] intends to terminate the [plan name] in a standard termination. The law requires that we provide you with written notice of the proposed termination.

In order for this plan to terminate, plan assets must be sufficient to provide all plan benefits. If the proposed termination does not occur, the [plan administrator] will notify you in writing.

**Name of Contributing Sponsor:**[Name]

**EIN/PN:**[#########/###]

**For Current Retirees:**[Include whichever statement applies]

- The proposed termination will not affect your [monthly] benefit amount.
- The proposed termination will affect your [monthly] benefit amount as follows: [explain]

**Proposed Termination Date:** MM/DD/YY

We will notify you in writing if the proposed termination date is changed to a later date.

**Contact Person:** If you have any questions concerning the plan's termination, contact:

[Name, Address, Phone Number]

**Cessation of Accruals:**[Include one of the following statements, whichever applies.]

- Benefit accruals will cease as of the termination date, but will continue if the plan does not terminate;
- A plan amendment has been adopted under which benefit accruals will cease, in accordance with Section 204(h) of ERISA, as of [insert either the proposed termination date or a specified date before the proposed termination date, whichever applies], whether or not the plan is terminated; or
- Benefit accruals ceased, in accordance with Section 204(h) of ERISA, as of [insert specified date before the NOIT was issued].

**Obtaining a Summary Plan Description:**

- If you wish to obtain a copy of the summary plan description for your plan, you may [call or write . . . ]

**Notification of Plan Benefits:**

- The [plan administrator] will provide you, at a later date, written notification regarding your benefits.

**Identity of Insurer(s):**[For all participants and beneficiaries except those who will receive benefits in the form of a nonconsensual lump sum, include whichever statement applies.]

- If you will receive a benefit in the form of an annuity, the [plan administrator] intends to purchase the annuity contract for your benefit from (one of) the following insurer(s) listed below. If we decide to select a different insurer, we will notify you in writing no later than 45 days before we purchase the annuity. [Insurer(s) Name and Address]
- If you will receive a benefit in the form of an annuity, the [plan administrator] intends to purchase an annuity contract for your benefit from an insurer to be selected at a later date. We will notify you in writing of the name and address of the insurer(s) from whom, or from among whom, we intend to purchase the annuity at least 45 days before we make the purchase.

**End of PBGC Guarantee:**

- After plan assets have been distributed to provide all of your benefits, either through the purchase of an annuity contract or in another form permitted by the plan, the PBGC's guarantee of your benefit ends.

**State Guaranty Association Coverage:**

[Required only if first time insurer(s) are identified]

- See enclosed notice.

[PBGC Standard Termination Filing Instructions, Appendix B]

## Q 25:16   What must be included in the notice of plan benefits?

The plan administrator must include the following information in the notice of plan benefits:

- The name and the plan number of the plan; the name and employer identification number of each contributing employer; and the name, address, and telephone number of an individual who may be contacted to answer questions concerning plan benefits.
- The proposed termination date given in the NOIT and any extension of the proposed termination date as allowed under the regulations.
- If the amount of plan benefits set forth in the notice is an estimate, a statement that the amount is an estimate and that plan benefits paid may be greater than or less than the estimate.
- Except in the case of an affected party in pay status for more than one year as of the proposed termination date, the personal data needed to calculate the affected party's plan benefits, along with a statement requesting that the affected party promptly correct any information believed to be incorrect.
- If any of the personal data needed to calculate the affected party's plan benefits is not available, the best available data along with a statement informing the affected party of the missing data and requesting the party to provide it.

For participants in pay status as of the proposed termination date, the statement should include the following:

- The amount and form of plan benefits, if any, payable to a beneficiary on the participant's death and the name of the beneficiary;
- The amount and form of plan benefits payable as of the proposed termination date; and
- The amount and date of any increase or decrease in the benefit scheduled to occur after the proposed termination date and an explanation of the increase or decrease, including a reference to the pertinent plan provisions.

For an affected party who, as of the proposed termination date, has validly elected a form and a starting date with respect to plan benefits not yet in pay status or with respect to whom the plan administrator has determined that a nonconsensual lump-sum distribution will be made, the plan administrator must include the following in the notice of plan benefits:

- The amount and form of the person's plan benefits payable as of the projected benefit starting date, and what that date is;
- The amount and form of plan benefits, if any, payable to a beneficiary on that participant's death and the name of the beneficiary;
- The amount and date of any increase or decrease in the benefit scheduled to occur after the proposed termination date and an explanation of the increase or decrease, including, where applicable, a reference to the pertinent plan provisions;

- The following items if the plan benefits will be paid in any form other than a lump-sum distribution and if the age at which, or the form in which, the plan benefits will be paid differs from the normal retirement benefit:
  - The age or form stated in the plan
  - The age or form adjustment factors
- The following items if the plan benefits will be paid in a lump sum:
  - An explanation of when a lump sum can be paid without the consent of the participant or the participant's spouse
  - A description of the mortality table used to convert to the lump-sum benefit and a reference to the pertinent plan provisions
  - A description of the interest rate to be used to convert to the lump-sum benefit and a reference to the pertinent plan provision and (if known) the applicable interest rate
  - An explanation of how interest rates are used to calculate lump sums, including a statement that the use of a higher interest rate results in a smaller lump-sum amount and a statement that the applicable interest rate may change before the distribution date

For any other affected party (i.e., those who are not in pay status or have not elected their benefit forms as of the date of the proposed termination), the plan administrator must include the following:

- The amount and form of the participant's benefits payable at normal retirement age in any one form permitted under the plan;
- Any alternative benefit forms, including those payable to a beneficiary on the participant's death either before or after benefits begin;
- If the person is or may be entitled to a benefit that would be payable before normal retirement age, the amount and form of benefit that would be payable at the earliest benefit commencement date and whether the benefit beginning on such date would be subject to future reduction; and
- If the plan benefits can be paid in a lump sum, a description of the mortality table to be used to convert to the lump-sum benefit, a description of the interest rate to be used to convert to the lump-sum benefit, the applicable interest rate, a statement that the use of higher interest rates results in a smaller lump sum, an explanation of how interest rates are used to calculate lump sums, and a statement that the applicable interest rate may change before the distribution date, including reference to pertinent plan provisions.

[PBGC Reg. § 4041.24]

### Q 25:17 After PBGC Form 500 is filed with the PBGC, when must the PBGC respond?

The PBGC must respond within 60 days of receiving a complete PBGC Form 500. The PBGC will notify the plan administrator in writing of the date that it received the standard termination notice and thus the date that the 60-day review period begins. If the PBGC does not issue a notice of noncompliance during its 60-day review period, the plan administrator can proceed with the distributions and close-out of the plan. The PBGC and the plan administrator may, before the end of the PBGC review period, agree in writing to extend the period beyond 60 days.

If the notice filed with the PBGC is incomplete, the PBGC may, based on the nature and extent of the omission, provide the plan administrator an opportunity to complete the missing information by the later of the 180th day after the proposed termination date or the 30th day after the date of the PBGC notice that the filing was incomplete. If the additional information is provided within that time frame, the PBGC Form 500 will be deemed to have been complete as of the original filing date, and the PBGC will determine whether this date will also hold as the start date of the 60-day review period.

The PBGC may require additional information relevant to the termination proceeding, and the additional information must be submitted within 30 days after the date of the written request from the PBGC. The PBGC can shorten the period at its discretion if it determines that the interests of the PBCG or the plan participants may be prejudiced by a delay in the receipt of the additional information. A request for additional information will suspend the running of the 60-day review period. The review period will restart on the date the additional information is received and will continue for the greater of the number of days remaining in the review period or five business days. [PBGC Reg. § 4041.26]

### Q 25:18   Who must receive a notice of annuity information, and what must it include?

The plan administrator must provide a notice of annuity information to each affected party entitled to plan benefits other than affected parties whose benefits will be distributed in the form of a nonconsensual lump sum.

The notice of annuity information must include the following as part of the NOIT:

- The name and address of the insurer or insurers from whom (if known) or (if not) from among whom the plan administrator intends to buy irrevocable commitments (annuity contracts);

- A statement that if the plan administrator later decides to select a different insurer, affected parties will receive a supplemental notice no later than 45 days before the distribution date; and

- The required information on state guaranty association coverage of annuities (the PBGC's standard termination forms and instructions package includes a model notice of annuity information).

If the identity of the insurer is not known at the time the plan administrator is required to provide it to an affected party as part of a NOIT, the plan administrator instead must provide it under a supplemental notice. The plan administrator must include a statement that irrevocable commitments may be bought from an insurer to provide some or all of the benefits under the plan, the insurer or insurers have not yet been identified, and the affected parties will be notified at a later date of the name and address of the insurer or insurers from which the annuities will be purchased. [PBGC Reg. § 4041.27]

### Q 25:19 What is the state guaranty association coverage information?

The state guaranty association coverage information that a plan administrator must provide to the affected parties consists of the following:

- That once the plan distributes a benefit in the form of an annuity bought from an insurance company, the insurance company takes over the responsibility of paying the benefit;
- That all states, the District of Columbia, and Puerto Rico have established guaranty associations to protect policyholders in the event of an insurance company's financial failure;
- That a guaranty association is responsible for all, part, or none of the annuity if the insurance company cannot pay;
- That each guaranty association has dollar limits on the extent of its guaranty coverage, along with a general description of the applicable dollar coverage limits;
- That, in most cases, the policyholder is covered by the guaranty association for the state where he or she lives at the time the insurance company fails to pay; and
- How to obtain the addresses and telephone numbers of guaranty associations from the PBGC.

[PBGC Reg. § 4041.27]

The following is the model notice as published by the PBGC in its Standard Termination Filing Instructions, Appendix C:

#### MODEL NOTICE OF STATE GUARANTY ASSOCIATION
#### COVERAGE OF ANNUITIES

Your pension plan may pay you your pension benefit in the form of an annuity purchased from a licensed insurance company. Once the plan purchases an annuity for you, the insurance company will be responsible for paying your benefit.

All states, Puerto Rico, and the District of Columbia have *guaranty associations*. The purpose of a guaranty association is to protect policyholders, up to specified limits, in the event the insurance company is financially unable to meet its obligations.

If you receive your pension benefits in the form of an annuity and the insurance company becomes unable to pay, a guaranty association may be responsible for all, part, or none of your annuity. Generally, where you live at the time the insurance company is unable to pay determines which guaranty association is responsible. In certain circumstances, other factors, such as where the insurance company is licensed to do business, determine which guaranty association may be responsible.

Each guaranty association has dollar limits on the extent of its coverage. In many states, guaranty association coverage limits are $100,000 for individual annuities and $300,000 for all insurance contracts with the same insurance company combined. However, state laws vary and can change over time, and different states may calculate the value of annuities differently.

This notice is to help you understand the general nature of the guaranty association protection of the annuity you may receive. It is only a summary. If you need information now or in the event the insurance company fails, you may obtain a list of the addresses and telephone numbers of guaranty association offices by contacting the PBGC's Customer Service Center at 1200 K Street N.W., Washington, D.C. 20005-4026 (telephone: (202) 326-4000) or by visiting the PBGC's website at www.pbgc.gov.

The following list of the guaranty associations with addresses and telephone numbers was published in October 2000 and August 2002.

Alabama Life and Disability Insurance Guaranty Association
6 Office Park Circle Suite
200 Birmingham, AL 35223
(205) 879-2202

Alaska Life and Disability Insurance Guaranty Association
P.O. Box 103415
Anchorage, AK 99510-3415
(907) 243-2311

Arizona Life and Disability Insurance Guaranty Fund 3443 North Central Avenue
Suite 1000
Phoenix, AZ 85012
(602) 248-0685

Arkansas Life and Disability Insurance Guaranty Association c/o Horne, Hollingsworth & Parker
401 W. Capital Suite 501
Little Rock, AR 72201
(501) 376-4731

California Life and Health Insurance Guaranty Association
P.O. Box 17319
8383 Wilshire Boulevard
Suite 810
Beverly Hills, CA 90209
(323) 782-0252

Colorado Life and Health Insurance Protection Association
475 17th Street Suite 1250
Denver, CO 80202
(303) 292-5022

Connecticut Life and Health Insurance Guaranty Association
130 Maple Street
Wethersfield, CT 06109
(860) 529-3495

Delaware Life and Health Insurance Guaranty Association
220 Continental Drive
Suite 309
Newark, DE 19713
(302) 456-3656

District of Columbia Life and Health Insurance Guaranty Association
1200 G Street, NW
Suite 800
Washington, DC 20005
(202) 434-8771

Florida Life and Health Insurance Guaranty Association
653-1 W. 8th Street
Suite 4060
Jacksonville, FL 32209-6511
(904) 355-6401

Georgia Life and Health Insurance Guaranty Association
2177 Flintstone Drive
Suite R
Tucker, GA 30084
(770) 621-9835

Hawaii Life and Disability Insurance Guaranty Association
1132 Bishop Street
Suite 1590
Honolulu, HI 96813
(808) 528-5400

Idaho Life and Health Insurance Guaranty Association
1327 South Five Mile Road
Boise, ID 83709
(208) 378-9510

Illinois Life and Health Insurance Guaranty Association
8420 W. Bryn Mawr Avenue
Suite 550
Chicago, IL 60631-3404
(773) 714-8050

Indiana Life and Health Insurance Guaranty Association
251 East Ohio Street
Suite 1070
Indianapolis, IN 46204-2143
(317) 636-8204

Iowa Life and Health Insurance Guaranty Association
c/o Nyemaster & Goode
700 Walnut Street
Suite 1600
Des Moines, IA 50309
(515) 283-3163

Kansas Life and Health Insurance Guaranty Association
2909 S.W. Maupin Lane
Topeka, KS 66614
(785) 271-1199

Kentucky Life and Health Insurance Guaranty Association
4010 Dupont Circle
Suite 232
Louisville, KY 40207
(502) 895-5915

Louisiana Life and Health Insurance Guaranty Association
451 Florida Street
North Tower, Suite 1400
Baton Rouge, LA 70801
(225) 381-0656

Maine Life and Health Insurance Guaranty Association
P.O. Box 881
Boothbay Harbor, ME 04538
(207) 633-1090

Maryland Life and Health Insurance Guaranty Association
9199 Reisterstown Road
Suite 216-C
Owings Mills, MD 21117
(410) 998-3907

Massachusetts Life and Health Insurance Guaranty Association
P.O. Box 3171
Springfield, MA 01101
(413) 744-8483

Michigan Life and Health Insurance Guaranty Association
c/o Colpean Associates P.C.
230 North Washington Square
Suite 316
Lansing, MI 48933-1312
(517) 487-2525

Minnesota Life and Health Insurance Guaranty Association
55 Fifth Street East
Suite 750
St. Paul, MN 55101
(612) 222-2799

Mississippi Life and Health Insurance Guaranty Association
330 North Mart Plaza
Suite 2
Jackson, MS 39211
(601) 981-0755

Missouri Life and Health Insurance Guaranty Association
520 Dix Road
Suite D
Jefferson City, MO 65109
(573) 634-8455

Montana Life and Health Insurance Guaranty Association
475 17th Street
Suite 1250
Denver, CO 80202
(303) 292-5022

Nebraska Life and Health Insurance Guaranty Association
1900 First Bank Building
Lincoln, NE 68508
(402) 474-6900

Nevada Life and Health Insurance Guaranty Association
One East First Street
Suite 1211
Reno, NV 89501
(775) 329-8387

New Hampshire Life & Health Insurance Guaranty Association
One Granite Place
Concord, NH 03301
(603) 226-9114

New Jersey Life and Health Insurance Guaranty Association
One Gateway Center
9th Floor
Newark, NJ 07102
(973) 623-3989

New Mexico Life Insurance Guaranty Association
2705 Juan Tabo B-2 NE
Albuquerque, NM 87112
(505) 237-9397

Life Insurance Company Guaranty Corporation of New York
c/o Financial Condition Life Bureau
New York Insurance Department
1 Madison Avenue
Area 10G
New York, NY 10010
(212) 578-5968

North Carolina Life and Health Insurance Guaranty Association
702 Oberlin Road
Suite 250
Raleigh, NC 27605-0218
(919) 833-6838

North Dakota Life and Health Insurance Guaranty Association
818 Main Avenue
Fargo, ND 58103
(701) 235-4108

Ohio Life and Health Insurance Guaranty Association
1840 Mackenzie Drive
Columbus, OH 43220
(614) 442-6601

Oklahoma Life and Health Insurance Guaranty Association
c/o Kerr, Irvine, Rhodes, Ables
201 Robert S. Kerr Avenue
Suite 600
Oklahoma City, OK 73102
(405) 272-9221

Oregon Life and Health Insurance Guaranty Association
c/o JBK & Associates
3541 Elderberry Drive South
Salem, OR 97302
(503) 588-1974

Pennsylvania Life and Health Insurance Guaranty Association
290 King of Prussia Road
Suite 218
Radnor, PA 19087
(610) 975-0572

Asociación de Garantía de Seguros de Vida e Incapacidad de Puerto Rico
Union Plaza Building
Suite 240
Hato Rey, PR 00918
(787) 765-2095

Rhode Island Life and Health Insurance Guaranty Association
c/o William L. Dixon
Suite 426
The Foundry
235 Promenade Street
Providence, RI 02908
(401) 273-2921

South Carolina Life and Accident and Health Insurance Guaranty Association
2926 Wexford Drive, NE
Orangeburg, SC 29115
(803) 536-9874

South Dakota Life and Health Insurance Guaranty Association
513 South Main Avenue
Sioux Falls, SD 57104
(605) 336-0177

Tennessee Life and Health Insurance Guaranty Association
1200 1st Union Tower
150 4th Avenue North
Nashville, TN 37219-2433
(615) 242-8758

Texas Life, Accident, Health & Hospital Service Insurance Guaranty Association
c/o LaShelle, Coffman & Boies, Ltd.
301 Congress
Suite 500
Austin, TX 78701
(512) 481-3000

Utah Life and Disability Insurance Guaranty Association
955 E. Pioneer Road
Draper, UT 84020
(801) 572-5066

Vermont Life and Health Insurance Guaranty Association
One National Life Drive
Suite M-480
Montpelier, VT 05604
(802) 229-3553

Virginia Life, Accident & Sickness Insurance Guaranty Association
8001 Franklin Farms Drive
Suite 328
Richmond, VA 23229
(804) 282-2240

Washington Life and Disability Insurance Guaranty Association
12514 S.E. 16th Street
Bellevue, WA 98005
(425) 562-3128

West Virginia Life and Health Insurance Guaranty Association
c/o Appalachian Life Insurance Co.
1124 Fourth Avenue
Huntington, WV 25707
(304) 529-4181

Wisconsin Insurance Security Fund
2445 Darwin Road
Suite 101
Madison, WI 53704
(608) 242-9473

Wyoming Life and Health Insurance Guaranty Association
475 17th Street
Suite 1250
Denver, CO 80202
(303) 292-5022

### Q 25:20   If the PBGC does not issue a notice of noncompliance, when is the plan required to close out?

The plan administrator must complete the distribution of plan assets in satisfaction of plan benefits by the later of 180 days after the expiration of the PBGC's 60-day review period, or if the plan administrator files for a favorable determination letter from the IRS at the same time as it files PBGC Form 500, 120 days after receipt of a favorable determination letter from the IRS.

If the plan administrator ever determines during the process that plan assets are insufficient to meet plan liabilities, the PBGC must be notified immediately and the close-out suspended.

Within 30 days after the last distribution date for any affected party, the plan administrator must file PBGC Form 501, Post-Distribution Certification. [PBGC Reg. §§ 4041.28, 4041.29]

### Q 25:21   What is a *notice of noncompliance*?

A *notice of noncompliance* is a notice issued by the PBGC that ends the standard termination process, nullifies all actions taken to terminate the plan, and renders the plan an ongoing plan. [PBGC Reg. § 4041.31(e)] The plan must continue, and benefit accruals can continue depending on the plan document and top-heavy status. A notice is to be issued to participants, if any of the requirements of a standard termination is not met.

### Q 25:22   Under what circumstances can the PBGC issue a notice of noncompliance?

The PBGC will issue a notice of noncompliance either for failure to meet certain predistribution requirements or for failure to meet distribution requirements.

The PBGC will issue a notice of noncompliance for any of the following predistribution requirement failures:

- Failure to issue a NOIT to all affected parties;
- Failure to issue a notice of plan benefits to all affected parties;
- Failure to timely file PBGC Form 500; or
- If, as of the proposed distribution date, assets will be insufficient to satisfy all liabilities.

The PBGC may decide not to issue a notice of noncompliance if it is not in the best interests of plan participants.

The PBGC has the discretion to issue a notice of noncompliance for failure to satisfy any of the distribution requirements, but will not issue a notice of noncompliance solely because benefits were distributed late if that fact is disclosed in PBGC Form 501 and more than 60 days has passed since the PBGC received that form.

### Q 25:23   What day-to-day functions can a plan carry out while it is in the process of terminating under a standard termination?

From the first day the plan administrator issues a NOIT to the last day of the PBGC review period, the plan administrator must continue to carry out the normal operations of the plan. During that period, however, the plan administrator cannot purchase irrevocable commitments to provide plan benefits or pay benefits attributable to employer contributions, other than death benefits, in any form other than an annuity. An exception to the above restriction is that the plan administrator can make payments to terminated participants if the plan permits and if the distribution is consistent with prior practice and the plan's funding sufficiency will not be jeopardized. PBGC premiums should continue to be paid. [PBGC Reg. § 4041.22]

### Q 25:24   When can a plan purchase irrevocable annuity commitments?

Unless there is a delay caused by waiting for receipt of a favorable determination letter from the IRS, the plan must purchase the irrevocable annuities within 180 days from the expiration of the 60-day (or extended) review period. If the plan has applied for and received the IRS favorable determination letter, the plan must purchase irrevocable annuities within 120 days after receipt of the favorable determination from the IRS. [PBGC Reg. § 4041.28]

### Q 25:25   Can an employer make a commitment to fully fund a plan for a standard termination?

Yes. If plan assets are projected to be insufficient to meet plan liabilities, the plan sponsor or a controlled group member can make a commitment to contribute any additional sums necessary to enable the plan to satisfy all plan benefits. The commitment must be in writing. [PBGC Reg. § 4041.21(b)(1)]

The PBGC's standard termination forms and instructions package, Appendix D, includes the following model commitment to make a plan sufficient for plan benefits:

**MODEL COMMITMENT TO MAKE A PLAN SUFFICIENT
FOR PLAN BENEFITS**

This agreement, by and between [name of company] (the "Company") and [name of plan] (the "Plan") shall be effective as of the last date executed.

Whereas, the Plan is an employee pension benefit plan as described in Section 3(2)(A) of the Employee Retirement Income Security Act of 1974 (ERISA), 29 U.S.C. 1001-1461; and

Whereas the Company is [describe entity, *e.g.*, corporation, partnership]; and

Whereas, the Company is a contributing sponsor of the Plan, or a member of the contributing sponsor's controlled group, as described in Section 4001(a)(13) and (14) of ERISA, 29 U.S.C. 1301(2) (13) and (14); and

Whereas, the Plan is covered by the termination insurance provisions of Title IV of ERISA, 29 U.S.C. 1301-1461; and

Whereas, the Plan administrator has issued or intends to issue to each affected party a notice of intent to terminate the Plan, pursuant to Section 4041(a)(2) of ERISA, 29 U.S.C. 1341(a)(2); and

Whereas, the Company wishes the Plan to be sufficient for plan benefits, as described in Section 29 CFR Section 4041.2; and

Whereas, the parties understand that if the Plan is not able to satisfy all its obligations for plan benefits, it will not be able to terminate in a standard termination under Section 4041(b) of ERISA, 29 U.S.C. 1341(b); and

Whereas, the Company is not a debtor in a bankruptcy or other insolvency proceeding.

Whereas, the Company is a debtor in a bankruptcy or other insolvency proceeding and the court before which the proceeding is pending approves this commitment.

Whereas, the Company is a debtor in a bankruptcy or other insolvency proceeding and this commitment is unconditionally guaranteed, by an entity or person not in bankruptcy, to be met at or before the time distribution of assets is required in this standard termination.

Now therefore, the parties hereto agree as follows:

1. The Company promises to pay to the Plan, on or before the date prescribed for distribution of Plan assets by the Plan administrator, the amount necessary, if any, to ensure that, on the date the Plan administrator distributes the assets of the Plan, the Plan is able to provide all plan benefits.

2. For the sole purpose of determining whether the Plan is sufficient to provide all plan benefits, an amount equal to the amount described in paragraph #1 shall be deemed a Plan asset available for allocation among the participants and beneficiaries of the Plan, in accordance with Section 4044 of ERISA, 29 U.S.C. 1344.

3. This Agreement shall in no way relieve the Company of its obligations to pay contributions under the Plan.

| Date: | Date: |
|---|---|
| By: | By: |
| Company: | Plan: |

### Q 25:26 Can a participant waive benefits to allow the plan to terminate in a standard termination?

Yes; however, only majority owners can do this. This waiver is not considered a waiver of benefits. It is an agreement to forgo receipt of benefits to the extent necessary to enable the plan to pay all other liabilities first. To be valid, this election must be in writing, have spousal consent if applicable, be made during the time period between the issuance of the NOIT and the date of the last distribution, and be consistent with any qualified domestic relations orders (QDROs) applicable to either the owner or the owner's spouse.

A *majority owner* is an individual who owns, directly or indirectly, 50 percent or more (taking into account the constructive ownership rules of Code Section 414(b) and (c)) of the plan (or contributing) sponsor. Unrestricted options are also considered under the constructive ownership rules. [PBGC Reg. § 4041.21 (b)(2)] The PBGC has stated that it interprets its regulations as limiting the ability of majority owners to elect this alternative treatment of receiving benefits to those who are majority owners at the time the election is made. This means that the owner's status could change subsequent to the election, or that the owner may not have been a majority owner as of the date of plan termination. Only the owner's status as of the date of the election matters. [2004 PBGC Blue Book, Q&A 5, Enrolled Actuaries Meeting]

### Q 25:27 Once all assets are distributed, how long does the plan sponsor have to notify the PBGC?

Within 30 days after the last distribution date for any affected party, PBGC Form 501 must be filed with the PBGC. The PBGC will assess a penalty for late filing of PBGC Form 501, however, only to the extent that the form is filed more than 90 days after the distribution deadline (including extensions). [PBGC Reg. § 4041.29]

## Missing Participants

### Q 25:28 What can a plan sponsor do if a participant cannot be located?

If a diligent search (see Q 25:30) is made for a missing participant but the participant cannot be located, the plan administrator must distribute benefits for the missing participant either by:

1. Purchasing from an insurer an irrevocable annuity on behalf of the missing participant; or
2. Paying the PBGC a designated benefit (see Q 25:31).

[PBGC Reg. § 4050.3]

### Q 25:29 What form is used to report missing participants and when is it due?

The plan sponsor must file PBGC Schedule MP and pay designated benefits by the time the PBGC Form 501, Post-Distribution Certification, is due, if there are any missing participants. [PBGC Reg. § 4050.6]

As with PBGC Form 501, no interest or penalties will be charged if the PBGC Schedule MP is filed no more than 90 days after the distribution deadline (see Q 25:27).

### Q 25:30  What is considered a diligent search?

A search is a diligent search only if the search:

1. Begins not more than six months before the issuance of the NOIT;
2. Includes an inquiry of any relatives of the missing participant who are known to the plan administrator; and
3. Includes the use of a commercial locator service to search for the missing participant.

[PBGC Reg. § 4050.4]

### Q 25:31  What is the amount of the designated benefit?

The amount of the designated benefit is the lesser of the maximum lump sum payable under Internal Revenue Code (Code) Section 415, or the amounts determined as follows (with all amounts computed as of the deemed distribution date):

1. *Mandatory lump sum.* If the participant was required to receive a mandatory lump sum and he or she is in pay status, the designated benefit is equal to the lump sum that would have been paid had the participant been located.
2. *De minimis lump sum.* If the lump sum payable is less than $5,000 and the participant is not in pay status, the designated benefit is equal to the lump-sum amount determined using the missing participant lump-sum assumptions (see Q 25:33).
3. *No lump sum.* The designated benefit of a participant who cannot elect an immediate lump sum is equal to the actuarial present value of the missing participant's benefit using the missing participant annuity assumptions (see Q 25:32).
4. *Elective lump sum.* The designated benefit is equal to the greater of the amounts determined under item #1 or #3 above.

[PBGC Reg. § 4050.5(a)]

### Q 25:32  What are the missing participant annuity assumptions?

To determine the designated benefit when required to use the missing participant annuity assumptions, the plan administrator must value the most valuable benefit. The most valuable benefit is determined using the interest rate assumptions found in Table I of Appendix B to ERISA Section 4044 for valuing a benefit to be paid by the PBGC as an annuity. The mortality table to be used is the 1983 Group Annuity Mortality Table, blended using 50 percent of the male mortality rates and 50 percent of the female mortality rates. In addition, $300 is added to each designated benefit in excess of $5,000 as an adjustment for expenses. These assumptions are applied as if the deemed distribution date was the termination date. [PBGC Reg. § 4050.2]

## Q 25:33    What are the missing participant lump-sum assumptions?

To determine the designated benefit when required to use the missing participant lump-sum assumptions, the plan administrator must value the most valuable benefit. The most valuable benefit is determined using the interest rate assumptions found in Table II of Appendix B to ERISA Section 4044 for valuing a benefit to be paid by the PBGC as a lump sum (this is the same as the old PBGC rate). The mortality rates to be used are those from Table 3 of Appendix A to ERISA Section 4044. These assumptions are applied as if the deemed distribution date was the termination date. [PBGC Reg. § 4050.2]

## Q 25:34    What is the *deemed distribution date*?

The *deemed distribution date* is the date on which all benefit distributions have been made (except to missing participants) or, if later, the last day of the period in which distributions may be made under a standard termination. [PBGC Reg. § 4050.2]

## Q 25:35    What is the most valuable benefit?

The most valuable benefit is dependent on whether the participant is in pay status. If the participant is in pay status, the most valuable benefit is the pay-status benefit. If the participant is not in pay status, then the most valuable benefit is the benefit payable:

1. At the age that generates the greatest present value;
2. Assuming that the participant is married to a spouse of the same age; and
3. With the form of payment being the qualified joint and survivor annuity benefit that would be payable under the plan.

[PBGC Reg. § 4050.5(b)]

> **Example.** The ACE defined benefit plan is terminating in a standard termination, but two participants are missing: Joseph and Gordon. The plan provides that any participant whose benefit has a present value of $5,000 or less will be paid a lump sum, and that no other lump sums will be paid.
>
> As of the deemed distribution date, the present value of Joseph's benefit is $4,000 under the plan assumptions. Because the present value is less than $5,000, the plan administrator pays the PBGC $4,000 as Joseph's designated benefit.
>
> The present value of Gordon's benefit is $6,000 under the plan assumptions and $4,500 under the missing participant lump-sum assumptions. Because the benefit is less than $5,000 under the missing participant lump-sum assumptions, it is considered to be *de minimis,* and the plan administrator pays the PBGC $4,500 as Gordon's designated benefit.

## Distress Terminations

### Q 25:36   What is a *distress termination*?

A *distress termination* is a termination that is filed under the PBGC regulations for a plan that does not have sufficient assets to meet plan benefit liabilities. [PBGC Reg. § 4041.41] A plan sponsor or the PBGC can initiate a distress termination.

### Q 25:37   Does the PBGC take any steps to prevent a distress termination?

Yes. In PBGC Technical Update 00-3, the PBGC introduced its Early Warning Program, which is designed to avoid having the PBGC force a plan termination. The program does so by working with plan sponsors to obtain protections before a business transaction significantly increases the risk of loss to the PBGC. The program generally focuses on transactions by two types of companies: (1) financially troubled companies and (2) companies with pension plans that are unfunded on a current liability basis.

The plan must meet the program's screening criteria, as follows:

1. The plan must have a bond rating that is below investment grade and current liability in excess of $25 million; or
2. The plan must have a current liability in excess of $25 million and an unfunded current liability in excess of $5 million.

Once these criteria have been met, the PBGC will inquire about business transactions that could substantially weaken the financial support for the pension plan. If the PBGC determines that a transaction could result in a significant increase in the risk of loss, the PBGC will try to negotiate with the company to obtain protections for the PBGC in lieu of terminating the plan.

### Q 25:38   What steps are required to initiate a distress termination?

The PBGC requires the following steps be taken to initiate a distress termination:

1. The plan administrator must issue a NOIT to all affected parties at least 60 days, and not more than 90 days, before the proposed termination date. The NOIT must also be distributed to all affected parties at or before the time the PBGC Form 600 is filed with the PBGC.
2. The plan administrator must file PBGC Form 600, Distress Termination (Notice of Intent to Terminate), for PBGC approval at least 60 days, and not more than 90 days, before the proposed termination date.
3. The plan administrator must file PBGC Form 601, Distress Termination Notice, Single Employer Plan Termination, with Schedule EA-D, Distress Termination Enrolled Actuary Certification, no later than 120 days after the proposed termination date.
4. The PBGC must determine that each contributing sponsor and each member of each sponsor's controlled group have substantial business hardship.

The PBGC can waive, at its own discretion, any of the rules with respect to notices if the PBGC believes that it will be more costly or administratively burdensome to the PBGC to maintain the requirements. [PBGC Reg. § 4041.41]

### Q 25:39  When does a substantial business hardship exist for purposes of a distress termination?

A substantial business hardship exists for purposes of a distress termination when each contributing sponsor and each member of each sponsor's controlled group satisfy at least one (but not necessarily the same one) of the following criteria:

- *Liquidation.* A person has filed, or has had filed against it, a petition seeking liquidation in a case under Title 11 of the U.S. Code or under a similar federal or state law and the case has not been dismissed.

- *Reorganization.* A person has filed, or has had filed against it, a petition seeking reorganization in a case under Title 11 of the U.S. Code or under a similar state law and the case has not been dismissed. Additionally, the person must notify the PBGC of any request to the bankruptcy court for the approval of the plan termination by concurrently filing with the PBGC a copy of the motion requesting court approval; the bankruptcy court must determine that unless the plan is terminated, such person will be unable to pay all its debts pursuant to a plan of reorganization and will be unable to continue in business outside the reorganization; and the bankruptcy court must approve the termination.

- *Inability to continue business.* A person demonstrates to the satisfaction of the PBGC that unless a distress termination occurs, the person will be unable to pay his or her debts when due and will be unable to continue in business.

- *Unreasonably burdensome pension costs.* A person demonstrates to the satisfaction of the PBGC that the person's costs of providing pension coverage have become unreasonably burdensome solely as a result of declining covered employment.

[PBGC Reg. § 4041.41(c)]

### Q 25:40  How must a plan be administered once a distress termination is filed?

After issuing a NOIT, the plan administrator must refrain from the following activities:

- Making loans to plan participants;
- Distributing plan assets or taking any other action to terminate the plan;
- Paying benefits attributable to employer contributions, other than death benefits, in any form other than an annuity; and
- Purchasing irrevocable commitments from an insurer.

Beginning on or after the proposed termination date the plan administrator must limit benefit payments to the benefits guaranteed by the PBGC (see Q 25:48). [PBGC Reg. § 4041.42]

### Q 25:41 What must be contained in a NOIT for a distress termination?

Much of the information required for a standard termination is required for a distress termination. In addition, a distress termination requires the plan administrator to report information regarding the distress nature of the termination. The items required to be sent as a written notice to each affected party at least 60 days and not more than 90 days before the proposed termination date are as follows:

- The name of the plan and the contributing sponsor;
- The employer identification number or numbers of the contributing sponsor or sponsors and the plan number;
- The name, address, and telephone number of the person who may be contacted for answering questions regarding termination;
- A statement that the plan administrator expects to terminate the plan in a distress termination;
- A statement that benefit accruals will cease with proper ERISA Section 204(h) notice if the amendment to cease benefit accruals is not simultaneous with the proposed plan termination date;
- A statement that an affected party is entitled to receive the latest SPD;
- A statement of whether plan assets are sufficient to pay all guaranteed benefits;
- A brief description of what benefits are guaranteed by the PBGC and a statement that participants and beneficiaries may receive a portion of the benefits to which each is entitled under the terms of the plan in excess of guaranteed benefits; and
- A statement that benefits may be subject to reduction because of the limitations on amounts guaranteed by the PBGC or because plan assets may not be sufficient to pay full benefits.

The PBGC will review the NOIT after it is filed with PBGC Form 600 by the proposed termination date and will notify the plan administrator of its determination. If the notice complies with the requirements for a distress termination, the distress termination can proceed. If the notice does not comply with the requirements, the proposed termination is null and void and the plan is considered ongoing. [PBGC Reg. §§ 4041.43, 4041.44]

### Q 25:42 What is included in a distress termination notice to the PBGC?

The plan administrator must file with the PBGC a PBGC Form 601, Distress Termination Notice, Single Employer Plan Termination, with Schedule EA-D, Distress Termination Enrolled Actuary Certification, by the 120th day following the proposed date of termination.

In addition, if the plan is insufficiently funded for the guaranteed benefits, all participant and benefit information must be filed by the later of 120 days after the proposed termination date or 30 days after receipt of the PBGC's approval for a distress termination. If the plan's enrolled actuary certifies that the assets are sufficient for guaranteed benefits or for benefit liabilities, no participant data need be supplied unless the PBGC requests the information. [PBGC Reg. § 4041.45]

### Q 25:43  Are there any additional premiums due for plans filing for a distress termination?

Maybe. Plans filing for a distress termination for the reasons of a reorganization in bankruptcy, an inability to continue in business, or an unreasonably burdensome pension costs will have an additional premium due equal to $1,250 times the number of participants with respect to each applicable 12-month period. [ERISA § 4006(a)(7)]

The term *applicable 12-month period* means the 12-month period beginning with the first month following the month in which the termination date occurs, and each of the first two 12-month periods immediately following. In the case of a plan termination that occurs in connection with a bankruptcy reorganization of the plan sponsor, the applicable 12-month period is the 12-month period beginning with the first month following the month which includes the earliest date as of which each such person is discharged or dismissed in the bankruptcy case.

The premium is due within 30 days following the beginning of each applicable 12-month period. In accordance with certain PPA provisions, if a commercial airline elects special funding requirements and terminates within a five-year period of such election, then the additional premium due upon a distress termination will be doubled to $2,500 per participant for each applicable 12-month period, and there will be no relief from this premium for sponsors in bankruptcy reorganization. [PPA § 402(h)(2)(B)]

### Q 25:44  When is a plan that files for a distress termination closed out?

The plan administrator, on receiving a distribution notice from the PBGC, must distribute plan assets in accordance with the rules of a standard termination (see Q 25:12) and file a PBGC Form 501, Post-Distribution Certification, that is modified according to PBGC Regulations Section 4041.50 to reflect the changes required for a distress termination. Those changes are as follows:

1. The term *plan benefits* is replaced with *Title IV benefits*.
2. The phrase "after the expiration of the PBGC's 60-day (or extended) review period under Section 4041.26(a)" is replaced with "the day on which the plan administrator completes the issuance of the notice of benefit distribution pursuant to Section 4041.48(a)."
3. The phrase "the requirements of Section 4041.25(c)" is replaced with "the requirements of Section 4041.48(d)."

### Q 25:45  What information can participants request to see in a distress termination?

For NOITs provided after August 17, 2006, participants may request to see all the information that was provided to the PBGC in the application for the distress termination, as long as no confidential information regarding participants is disclosed. This information must be provided within 15 days of the request. This information must also be provided upon request for plans that have been involuntarily terminated by the PBGC.

### Q 25:46  Can the PBGC involuntarily terminate an employer's defined benefit pension plan?

Yes. Under ERISA Section 4042 the PBGC has the right to institute termination proceedings whenever it determines that:

- The plan has not met the minimum funding requirements;
- The plan will not be able to pay benefits when due;
- There has been a distribution to a substantial owner that has caused the plan to become underfunded; or
- The possible long-run loss of the PBGC with respect to the plan may reasonably be expected to increase if the plan is not terminated.

## PBGC Benefits and Coverage

### Q 25:47  What pension plans are covered by the PBGC?

All qualified defined benefit plans that have been in effect for one year and are maintained by employers engaged in commerce or in an industry that affects commerce or by a labor union must be covered. The following types of plans, however, are excepted:

- Plans for governmental employees;
- Plans for church employees (unless the plan has made an election to be covered);
- Plans for societies or orders or associations under Code Section 501(c)(8), 501(a), or 501(c)(18) if no part of the contributions to or under the plan is made by employers of participants under the plan;
- Plans for which no employer contributions have been made;
- Plans that are unfunded and provide deferred compensation for a select group of management or highly compensated employees;
- Plans that are established and maintained outside the United States primarily for the benefit of individuals substantially all of whom are non-resident aliens;
- Plans that provide certain employees benefits in excess of the maximum limitations under Code Section 415;
- Plans that are maintained exclusively for substantial owners;

- Plans for international organizations that are exempt from taxation under the International Organization Immunities Act;
- Plans maintained solely for the purpose of complying with workers' compensation laws, unemployment laws, or disability laws;
- Plans that are considered individual account plans; and
- Plans that are established and maintained by a professional service employer that has not had, at any time since September 2, 1994, more than 25 active participants in its plan.

[ERISA § 4021(b)]

### Q 25:48    What benefits does the PBGC guarantee?

Even though accrued benefits become 100 percent vested on plan termination, the PBGC does not guarantee all vested benefits. [ERISA § 4022(a)] The PBGC limits benefit guarantees to specified amounts. The maximum amount guaranteed applies for the year of termination even if the participant does not retire for several years. For example, the maximum guaranteed benefit for 2006 of $3,971.59 applies to all participants of plans that terminated under a distress termination during 2005.

A plan amendment, including the adoption of a new plan, to increase benefits for participants other than substantial owners (this is changed to majority owners for NOITs after December 31, 2005) that is adopted within five years of termination is phased in by using the following formula: the number of years the amendment was in effect multiplied by the greater of $20 per month or 20 percent of the monthly increase in benefits. [PBGC Reg. § 4022.25] A plan amendment that increases benefits to substantial owners is subject to a 30-year phase-in rule (this has been changed to a 10-year phase-in for majority owners for NOITs after December 31, 2005). [PBGC Reg. § 4022.26] In computing the number of years, only complete 12-month periods shall constitute one year.

> **Example.** A plan was amended three years ago to increase benefits to participant Pat by $400 per month. Pat is entitled to $240 per month, which is three times the greater of $20, or $60 (3 × $20 = $60) or 20 percent of $400 (3 × (.20 × $400) = $240). If Pat was a substantial owner, she would be entitled to $40 per month ($400 × 3/30), plus the phase-in of the original benefit. If the termination was during 2007, and Pat was a majority owner rather than just a substantial owner, then she would be entitled to $120 per month ($400 × 3/30), plus the phase-in of the original benefit.

Benefits that are in pay status, or could have been in pay status, for a period of three years are guaranteed.

### Q 25:49    Under what circumstances does the PBGC provide payment to a participant of a PBGC-insured plan?

Generally, there are two circumstances under which the PBGC provides benefit payments: either the plan sponsor requests that the PBGC take over the plan's assets and liabilities or the PBGC forces the plan to terminate by instituting a plan termination.

When the plan sponsor is no longer able to maintain the plan, it can terminate the plan even if there are insufficient assets to cover all of the plan's benefit liabilities. In this case, the plan sponsor requests that the plan be terminated under a distress termination and the PBGC takes over the plan's assets and liabilities. For a plan to qualify for a distress termination, however, the plan sponsor must have instituted a distress termination procedure as outlined in ERISA Section 4041(c) and must have met certain hardship requirements (see Q 25:39).

The PBGC can, on its own accord, institute a plan termination if it believes termination is in the best interests of the plan participants and beneficiaries. This can occur as a result of any of the following events:

1. The plan has not met the minimum funding standards of Code Section 412.
2. The plan will be unable to pay benefits when due.
3. The plan has made a distribution to a substantial owner, and the plan is now underfunded after the payment.
4. A possible long-run liability to the PBGC on behalf of the plan will be created or increased unreasonably if the plan is not terminated.

[ERISA § 4042(a)]

### Q 25:50  What are the guaranteed maximum benefits that are paid to a plan participant on termination of a PBGC-covered plan?

Benefits are guaranteed by the PBGC only to the extent that they do not exceed the actuarial value of a benefit in the form of a life annuity payable in monthly installments, beginning at age 65, that is equal to the lesser of the following:

1. One-twelfth of the participant's average annual gross income from employment during (a) the five highest paid consecutive calendar years in which he or she was an active participant under the plan or (b) if the employee was not an active participant throughout that period, the lesser number of calendar years within that period as an active participant; or
2. $750 multiplied by the fraction $x/\$13,200$, where $x$ is the Social Security contribution and benefit base in effect on the date of plan termination.

[PBGC Reg. § 4022.22]

The maximum guaranteed benefit for the last 17 years is given in the following table:

| Year | Maximum Benefit |
|------|-----------------|
| 2006 | $3,971.59 |
| 2005 | $3,801.14 |

| Year | Maximum Benefit |
|------|-----------------|
| 2004 | $3,698.86 |
| 2003 | $3,664.77 |
| 2002 | $3,579.55 |
| 2001 | $3,392.05 |
| 2000 | $3,221.59 |
| 1999 | $3,051.14 |
| 1998 | $2,880.68 |
| 1997 | $2,761.36 |
| 1996 | $2,642.05 |
| 1995 | $2,573.86 |
| 1994 | $2,556.82 |
| 1993 | $2,437.50 |
| 1992 | $2,352.27 |
| 1991 | $2,250.00 |
| 1990 | $2,164.77 |

### Q 25:51 How does the PBGC reduce maximum benefits for form and age?

The guaranteed maximum benefit is reduced when received at an age younger than age 65 or in a form other than a life annuity. When reducing the benefit for an age younger than age 65, the benefit is reduced $7/12$ of 1 percent for each of the 60 months immediately preceding the 65th birthday, $4/12$ of 1 percent for each of the 60 months immediately preceding the 60th birthday, $2/12$ of 1 percent for each of the 120 months immediately preceding the 55th birthday, and for each succeeding 120 months, the monthly percentage reduction is $1/2$ of that used for the preceding 120-month period.

If the form of payment elected is other than a life annuity, the guaranteed maximum benefit shall be reduced as follows:

*Period certain and continuous annuity.* Benefit will be reduced by $1/24$ of 1 percent for each month up to 60 months of the continuous period that extends beyond the plan termination date, and $1/12$ of 1 percent for each month beyond 60 months.

*Joint and survivor annuity (contingent basis).* Benefit will be reduced by 10 percent plus $2/10$ of 1 percent for each percentage point in excess of 50 percent of the participant's benefit that will continue to be paid to the beneficiary. If the beneficiary is younger than the participant, there is an additional reduction equal to 1 percent for each year of age difference. If the beneficiary is older than the participant, add $1/2$ of 1 percent for each year of age difference. In computing the difference in ages, years over 65 years of age are ignored.

[PBGC Reg. § 4022.23]

## Q 25:52   What are the guaranteed maximum benefits for participants of multiemployer plans?

Participants of a multiemployer plan are guaranteed a maximum of 100 percent of the first $11 of the monthly benefit accrual rate and 75 percent of the next $33 for each year of service.

If the plan has received financial assistance from the PBGC within a one-year period ending on December 21, 2000, the maximum is limited to a participant's years of service multiplied by (1) 100 percent of the first $5 of the monthly benefit accrual rate and (2) 75 percent of the next $15.

> **Example.** The ER defined benefit plan is an insolvent multiemployer plan as of January 1, 2002. The plan had not received financial assistance previously from the PBGC. Peter is a participant in the plan with 30 years of service and had a benefit accrual rate under the plan of $23 per month. Peter's benefit under the terms of the plan is $690. The maximum guaranteed benefit by the PBGC is $600 ((100% × $11) + (75% × $12)) × 30 years.

If the plan had previously received assistance from the PBGC, Peter's maximum guaranteed benefit would be $487.50 ((100% × $5) + (75% × $15)) × 30 years.

## Q 25:53   What are the guaranteed maximum benefits for participants in the case of shutdown and other benefits?

The PBGC guarantee of shutdown and other unpredictable contingent event benefits (UCEB) is treated like other amendments and is phased in over five years from the date the UCEB occurred. [ERISA § 4022(b)(8)]

## Q 25:54   What date is used as the plan termination date for sponsors that have entered into bankruptcy proceedings?

Effective September 17, 2006, if a plan sponsor is in bankruptcy and terminates its defined benefit plan, then the date the sponsor entered bankruptcy is treated as the plan termination date for purposes of determining PBGC guarantees and who and what benefits are in asset allocation priority category 3 (those who retired or could have retired three years before the termination date). [ERISA §§ 4022(g), 4044(e)]

## Q 25:55   Is there a possibility of participants receiving greater than the PBGC maximum benefits if there are sufficient assets in the plan?

Yes. Assets are first allocated in accordance with the priority categories listed in ERISA Section 4044 (see Q 25:63). In addition, if the PBGC recovers assets from plan sponsors in a distress or involuntary termination, then additional benefits can be provided to participants who have lost a portion of their benefits due to PBGC guarantee limits. [ERISA § 4022(c)(3)]

## Surplus Assets

### Q 25:56   How do code provisions and the plan design affect plan terminations?

When there are surplus assets on plan termination, reallocation of the surplus can become a creative exercise. There are an infinite number of allocation methods; most of the considerations, for example, deciding who the plan sponsor wants to benefit, that are made in initial plan design must be followed on the reallocation of the surplus assets. The nondiscrimination regulations affect the design considerably (see Q 25:61). Past-service benefit accruals must be looked at carefully. In addition, maximum benefit limitations under Code Section 415, either as a percentage of pay or as a dollar amount, can become a problem.

Certainly, the anti-cutback provisions of Code Section 411(d)(6) play into plan design issues. Any subsidized benefit provided under the terms of the plan must be included in computing benefit liabilities on plan termination. [Rev. Rul. 85-6, 1985-1 C.B. 133]

### Q 25:57   What happens when a terminating defined benefit plan has surplus assets?

The plan document must define how surplus assets (the excess, if any, of plan assets over liabilities) are treated in the event of a plan termination. Surplus assets are used to increase benefits to plan participants or are reverted to the employer [Rev. Rul. 83-52, 1983-1 C.B. 87]. If the language in the plan document allowing for a reversion to the employer has not been in the document for at least five years or since the plan's effective date, whichever period is greater, the surplus assets must be allocated to participants in a nondiscriminatory manner. [Rev. Rul. 80-229, 1980-2 C.B. 133] If the surplus assets revert to the employer, a 50 percent excise tax is imposed on the reversion. The excise tax can be reduced to 20 percent if one of the following two events occurs:

1. The employer establishes or maintains a qualified replacement plan (see Q 25:58).

2. The plan provides benefit increases to participants in the terminating defined benefit plan (see Q 25:60).

[I.R.C. § 4980(d)(1)]

### Q 25:58   What is a *qualified replacement plan*?

A *qualified replacement plan* is a qualified plan established or maintained by an employer following the termination of a defined benefit plan that meets these three requirements:

1. At least 95 percent of the active participants in the terminated plan who remain employees of the employer after the termination are active participants in the replacement plan.

2. Before any amount is reverted to the employer, the replacement plan receives a direct transfer from the terminated plan in an amount exactly equal to the excess (if any) of:

   a. 25 percent of the maximum amount the employer could receive as a reversion; over

   b. The present value of benefit increases granted to participants in the terminated defined benefit plan.

3. In the case of a defined contribution qualified replacement plan, the amount transferred is either:

   a. Allocated to the accounts of plan participants in the year the transfer occurs; or

   b. Credited to a suspense account and allocated over a period not to exceed seven years.

[I.R.C. § 4980(d)(2)]

**Example.** Jim's Locksmith Inc. sponsors a defined benefit plan that will terminate effective December 31, 2002. The projected liabilities of the plan as of December 31, 2003, are $1 million. The projected assets are $1.2 million. A provision allowing for the reversion of surplus assets to the employer has been in place since plan inception. If Jim transfers $50,000 ($200,000 × 0.25) to a qualified replacement plan, he reduces the excise tax to 20 percent. This would allow the company to receive a reversion of $150,000 and to pay only a 20 percent excise tax on that amount, or $30,000 ($150,000 × 0.20), for a net of $120,000 returned to the company. If the entire amount is reverted to the company, the excise tax would be $100,000 ($200,000 × 0.50), and only $100,000 would be returned to the corporation.

### Q 25:59 Can more than 25 percent of the surplus assets be transferred to a qualified replacement plan?

Yes. Recently the IRS reversed its position taken in earlier Letter Rulings [Ltr. Ruls. 200227040, 200227041], and has stated that the employer may transfer more than 25 percent of surplus assets in a terminated defined benefit plan to a qualified replacement plan. In addition, this excess amount is treated in the following manner:

1. The amount transferred is *not* includible in the gross income of the employer;

2. No deduction is allowed with respect to the amount transferred; and

3. The amount transferred is not treated as an employer reversion for purposes of Code Section 4980.

The amount in excess of the 25 percent required to be transferred remains subject to the same allocation rules as the first 25 percent of the excess.

Any amount that reverts to the employer is still subject to the 20 percent excise tax under Code Section 4980(a) and is includible in the gross income of the employer. [Rev. Rul. 2003-85, 2003-32 I.R.B. 291]

**Example.** Jim Bob's pension plan is terminating in 2004, and the company is adopting a defined contribution plan. Ninety-five percent of the participants in the pension plan as of the termination date will be participating in the new defined contribution plan. After satisfaction of all liabilities in the pension plan, there remains $100,000 of surplus assets in the plan. Prior to taking a reversion, the pension plan transfers $60,000 to the defined contribution plan, which provides for receipt and immediate allocation of these excess assets. This transfer to a qualified replacement plan is at least 25 percent of the surplus assets in the plan; therefore the amount transferred is not includible in the income of the employer and is not treated as a reversion. The other $40,000 that reverts to the employer is subject to a 20 percent excise tax and is included in the gross income of the employer.

### Q 25:60  What requirements must be satisfied when participants' benefits are increased to qualify for the reduction in the excise tax?

The benefit increases must have an aggregate present value not less than 20 percent of the maximum reversion. In addition, the increases must take effect immediately on the termination date. [I.R.C. § 4980(d)(3)] The increase must be a pro rata increase, with each participant's accrued benefit increasing in the same proportion as the present value of the participant's accrued benefit bears to the aggregate present value of accrued benefits of all participants. [I.R.C. § 4980 (d)(3)(B)]

The allocation of the surplus assets must not discriminate in favor of highly compensated employees, and must not cause benefits to exceed the maximum benefit provisions of Code Section 415. [I.R.C. § 4980(d)(4)(A)]

**Example.** The facts are the same as those in the example in Q 25:58. Instead of establishing a qualified replacement plan to reduce the excise tax, Jim decides to increase benefits in the defined benefit plan. The amount required to be allocated is $40,000 ($200,000 − 0.20). This amount will be allocated pro rata to all participants in proportion to their accrued benefits unless doing so would be discriminatory. The present value of Jim's accrued benefit is $900,000; the present value of the only other participant's accrued benefit is $100,000. The excess would be allocated $36,000 to Jim ($40,000 − $900,000/$1,000,000) and $4,000 to the remaining participant.

### Q 25:61  How is it determined whether the allocation of excess assets is made in a nondiscriminatory manner?

One way to increase benefits in a nondiscriminatory manner is to amend the plan to provide a new benefit structure such that (1) the benefit structure would not be discriminatory if the plan were not terminated, and (2) the present value of the revised accrued benefits (whether or not nonforfeitable) as of the termination date equals the value of plan assets, and to distribute assets equal to the present value of the revised accrued benefits. The new benefit structure must satisfy other requirements of the law, such as Code Sections 411(d)(6) and 415.

**Example 1.** Plan *B* provides a benefit of 1 percent of average annual compensation up to the integration level plus 1.75 percent of average annual compensation in excess of the integration level, for each year of service up to 35. Plan *B* satisfies the requirements of Code Section 401(l). As of the termination date, the assets equal $100,000 and the present value of the accrued benefits (PVABs) (whether or not nonforfeitable) equals $80,000. The plan distributes the $100,000 by providing each participant with assets equal to 125 percent of the present value of the participant's accrued benefit (whether or not nonforfeitable).

Distributing assets equal to 125 percent of the present value of accrued benefits is tantamount to amending the plan by multiplying each of the terms of the benefit formula by 125 percent and distributing the PVABs. The revised formula would be 1.25 percent of average annual compensation up to the integration level plus 2.19 percent of average annual compensation in excess of the integration level, for each year of service up to 35. Because the excess benefit percentage (2.19 percent) exceeds the base benefit percentage (1.25 percent) by more than 0.75 percent, the revised formula is discriminatory in an ongoing plan. Accordingly, the distribution is discriminatory.

**Example 2.** The facts are the same as those in Example 1 except that the distribution is revised as follows: By a separate actuarial computation it is determined that a nonintegrated increase in the benefit formula of 1 percent of all compensation would increase the PVABs by $4,000. Plan B has surplus assets of $20,000 ($100,000 of assets as of the date of termination less $80,000, the present value of accrued benefits as of that date). Therefore, an increase of each of the terms of the benefit formula by 5 percent (a 1 percent increase in the benefit formula increases PVAB by $4,000; a 5 percent increase increases PVABs by $20,000) will produce a benefit formula that would be nondiscriminatory in an ongoing plan, and the PVABs (whether or not nonforfeitable) would equal the value of plan assets. Assets equal to the revised PVABs can be distributed without causing discrimination. [Rev. Rul. 80-229, 1980-2 C.B. 133]

## Underfunded Plans

### Q 25:62   Can a plan not subject to PBGC coverage terminate with insufficient assets?

Yes. Code Section 411(d)(3) allows a plan to terminate and pay benefits "to the extent funded." When a plan that is not covered by the PBGC terminates with insufficient assets, assets must be allocated in accordance with the priority categories established under ERISA Section 4044. [ERISA § 403(d)(1)] In addition, to prevent discrimination, the assets should be allocated so that the non-highly compensated employees receive from the plan at least the same proportion of the present value of their accrued benefits as highly compensated employees. [Rev. Rul. 80-229, 1980-2 C.B. 133]

### Q 25:63  What are the priority categories established by ERISA Section 4044?

When a single-employer plan that is not covered by the PBGC terminates, assets must be allocated to participants in the following order:

1. To that portion of each individual's accrued benefit that is derived from the participant's contributions to the plan that are not mandatory contributions;

2. To that portion of each individual's accrued benefit that is derived from the participant's mandatory contributions;

3. For benefits payable as an annuity:

   a. In the case of benefits in pay status three years before the termination date, based on the lowest benefit under the plan's provisions in effect during the five-year period ending on that date, and

   b. In the case of other benefits that would have been in pay status three years before the termination date if the participant had retired and started receiving benefits before the beginning of that three-year period, based on the lowest benefit under the plan's provisions in effect during the five-year period ending on the termination date;

4. To all other benefits of individuals guaranteed by the PBGC (disregarding the restrictions on benefits for substantial owners);

5. To all other nonforfeitable benefits under the plan; and

6. To all other benefits under the plan.

[ERISA § 4044(a)]

# Chapter 26

# Mergers and Acquisitions

*Corporate Transactions*

A defined benefit pension plan may be affected by a company acquisition or merger. A company contemplating acquiring another company that sponsors a defined benefit pension plan must conduct due diligence involving the plan. After the acquisition, there are a variety of actions that can be taken with respect to the plan, depending on economic and human resources factors.

*Plan Transactions*

If a company has more than one plan, it can merge one existing plan with another existing plan. An existing plan can also be divided into two or more plans. When a plan merger occurs, certain benefits of each prior plan must be retained. In a plan spin-off, a certain amount of assets must be transferred to the spun-off plan to ensure that plan participants do not lose accrued benefits.

This chapter identifies many issues that should be considered in the event of a corporate merger or acquisition and discusses the differences between plan transfers, mergers, and spin-offs and the actions required to retain qualified status.

## Corporate Transactions

### Q 26:1 What should a company be aware of when acquiring another company that maintains a defined benefit plan?

A company that is acquiring another company should conduct due diligence with respect to any qualified plans maintained by the seller. The buyer should obtain a copy of the plan, trust, plan policies and procedures, summary plan description (SPD), and the last three years' Internal Revenue Service (IRS) Forms 5500. It is important for the buyer to identify any potential qualification failures, such as defects in the plan and operational errors or omissions, and review actions taken by the plan administrator to correct past problems (see Q 26:4). Adequacy of funding should be reviewed.

The buyer will want to be assured that the plan has been amended to bring it into compliance with recent legislative and regulatory changes. The plan must be administered in accordance with the plan documents. No procedures or policies should have the effect of favoring highly compensated employees (HCEs). IRS determination letters should be reviewed to determine the impact of demographic changes.

Mergers, acquisitions, and other business combinations present a number of issues involving nondiscrimination testing for qualified plans. The HCEs must be identified and the plans must be reviewed before and after the merger to determine the impact of the change in census on coverage and nondiscrimination (see Qs 26:14 and 26:15).

### Q 26:2 Why is due diligence important?

The buyer may assume liabilities for problems associated with plan correction or disqualification. The loss of qualified status has serious consequences. The plan sponsor can lose deductions for contributions, the trust can lose its tax-exempt status, and vested participants may have to recognize income on the value of accrued benefits. Sanctions for noncompliance can be high.

Defects that affect plan qualification generally fall into one of three categories:

1. *Plan document failures (or form defects).* A document must include all provisions required under Internal Revenue Code (Code) Section 401(a). A plan that has not been amended to comply with legislative changes, such as the direct rollover rules or the limitation on compensation [I.R.C. § 401(a)(31), (17)], risks disqualification.

2. *Operational failures.* The plan must be administered in accordance with the plan document.

3. *Demographic failures.* The plan cannot discriminate in favor of HCEs.

Due diligence also provides valuable information regarding the financial condition of the plan. If the plan is overfunded, there may be a way to use the excess assets. Assumption of an underfunded plan may justify a reduction in purchase price. Liability for funding deficiencies or withdrawal liability (see chapter 5) can carry a significant cost.

The benefit program should be evaluated to determine whether it should be maintained.

### Q 26:3   Must any corporate events be reported to the Pension Benefit Guaranty Corporation?

Yes. The Pension Benefit Guaranty Corporation (PBGC) must be notified—either on an advance or post-event basis, depending on a variety of factors—of changes in a contributing sponsor or controlled group member; liquidation of a contributing sponsor or controlled group member; the payment of an extraordinary dividend or stock redemption; and a plan-to-plan transfer subject to the non-*de minimis* rules under Code Section 414(l) (see chapter 24). The filing enables the PBGC to evaluate recovery claims against members of a controlled group.

## Document and Operational Review

### Q 26:4   What representations and warranties are generally requested from the seller?

The buyer generally asks the seller to give certain representations and warranties about the plan and its administration. The seller will often be asked to make representations regarding the following:

1. All plans have been identified and complete copies of all plan documents have been provided.
2. The plan complies in form with the Employee Retirement Income Security Act of 1974 (ERISA) and the Code.
3. The plan has been administered in all material respects in accordance with its terms.
4. The plan has satisfied funding standards and all contributions have been made.
5. No unfunded benefit liabilities were shown on the most recent valuation report.
6. There have not been any recent changes in actuarial methods or assumptions.
7. No event has occurred that could adversely affect the qualified status of the plan.
8. There have been no prohibited transactions.
9. No lawsuits have been filed.
10. There have been no reportable events.
11. Plan liabilities are correctly reflected on the financial statements.
12. No contributions are due under a multiemployer plan.
13. IRS Forms 5500 have been filed on time.

### Q 26:5   What key documents should be reviewed?

Basic due diligence requires review of all important documents. It is helpful to look at these documents as early as possible to develop plan options. Important documents to review include the following:

1. Plan document;
2. IRS determination letter;
3. SPD;
4. IRS Form 5500 (for preceding three years);
5. Policies and procedures; and
6. Correspondence to or from the IRS, Department of Labor (DOL), or PBGC.

### Q 26:6   What documents are useful in assessing the financial strength of a plan?

Schedule B to IRS Form 5500 will provide some information regarding the funded status of the plan. Corporate financial statements will also indicate plan liabilities. Balance sheets will show unfunded liabilities based on projected benefits. The interest rate used for financial statement purposes does not, however, have to be the same as the rate used for funding purposes. Liabilities on plan termination may be even higher than liabilities reflected on the valuation reports or corporate financial reports because of use of General Agreement on Tariffs and Trade of 1994 (GATT) or PBGC rates or mortality tables (see chapters 19 and 25).

### Q 26:7   What liabilities may result from participation in a defined benefit pension plan?

A buyer should be aware of the following potential exposures:

1. IRS sanctions for noncompliance with the qualification requirements of the Code (loss of deductions, taxation of trust earnings, and taxation of participants) (see chapter 2);
2. Withdrawal liability (multiemployer plans) (see chapter 5);
3. Penalties for failure to file IRS Form 5500 [I.R.C. §§ 6652(e), 414(g)];
4. Prohibited transaction excise taxes (see chapter 27) [I.R.C. § 4975];
5. Liability for breach of fiduciary duty (see chapter 27);
6. Liability for a funding deficiency [I.R.C. § 412(n); ERISA § 302(f)];
7. Penalties for anti-cutback violations (see chapter 8); and
8. Penalties for coverage and participation violations (see chapter 6).

### Q 26:8   What types of administrative actions may create potential qualification problems?

A plan must be administered in accordance with the Code and ERISA in all respects. Because of extensive changes in the pension laws, the IRS allowed plans to be amended retroactively, in at least one case up to five years after the effective date of the changes in the law. Occasionally, benefit administration follows the language of the plan even though the plan provisions are effectively obsolete. Noncompliance with the law can jeopardize plan qualification or create liability to third parties. Typical administrative errors include the following:

1. Distribution options determined at the discretion of the plan administrator;
2. Prohibited in-service distributions;
3. Failure to provide notice of a qualified joint and survivor annuity (QJSA);
4. Payment of benefits in an optional form without appropriate consent;
5. Inadequate spousal consent or spousal consent granted out of the 90-day notice period;
6. Distribution of a lump-sum benefit without an explanation of direct rollover options;
7. Violation of Code Section 415;
8. Failure to provide top-heavy minimum benefits; and
9. Failure to apply top-heavy vesting schedule.

### Q 26:9 Are there any actions that can be taken to correct an error after discovery without risking disqualification?

Yes. The IRS has an extensive program designed to permit plan sponsors to correct plans without plan disqualification. Certain errors can be corrected without formal approval from the IRS. The Self-Correction Program (SCP) permits correction of an operational defect without IRS involvement. Other areas of noncompliance can be corrected with approval from the IRS. Under the Voluntary Correction with Service approval (VCP), a sponsor can obtain a compliance statement from the IRS approving a method of correcting an operational defect. More egregious problems and form defects must be resolved through the Closing Agreement Program. A complete description of the consolidated voluntary compliance program, known as the Employee Plans Compliance Resolution System (EPCRS), can be found in Revenue Procedure 2006-27. [2006-22 I.R.B. 945] Of course, if the problems are too serious, the buyer can require escrow of funds anticipated for correction or may choose not to become involved with the plan.

### Q 26:10 Must a determination letter be obtained?

No. Requesting a determination letter (an advance determination of a plan's qualified status issued by the IRS) is discretionary. In many instances, the acquiring company would be well advised to obtain a letter, particularly if a plan is being terminated or merged into a plan sponsored by the buyer. A determination letter will protect the recipient plan from IRS claims of form disqualification. Matters that are reviewed in the context of a determination letter request cannot be raised by the IRS at a later date. Of course, all material information about the plan must be included in the determination letter request. Plans must be updated to meet all technical requirements for qualification at termination. If a plan document has not been updated within the last few years, a letter should be obtained to ensure technical form compliance.

A determination letter does not resolve all issues related to a plan's qualified status. The letter does not address operational compliance or the reasonableness of actuarial assumptions. A change in demographics or a change in law may render the determination letter obsolete.

### Q 26:11    Are the pension implications of a stock sale different from those of an asset sale?

Yes. In a stock sale, the new owner merely "steps into the shoes" of the prior owner and automatically assumes liability for all pension matters.

Generally, a company that purchases the assets of another company does not assume the seller's liabilities. Under common law, this rule has been limited by four exceptions. Successors have been held liable when (1) there is an express or implied assumption of liability; (2) the transaction amounts to a consolidation, merger, or similar restructuring of the two corporations; (3) the purchasing corporation is a "mere continuation" of the seller; and (4) the transfer of assets to the purchaser is for the fraudulent purpose of escaping liability for the seller's debts. Although successor liability may exist in the context of multiemployer plans [Upholsterers Int'l Union Pension Fund v. Artistic Furniture of Pontiac, 13 Employee Benefits Cas. (BNA) 1138 (7th Cir. 1990)], it is not clear whether successor liability applies to single-employer plans in the absence of express assumption of liability.

If a multiemployer plan is involved (see chapter 5), the buyer and seller must consider possible withdrawal liability. Withdrawals or deemed withdrawals from multiemployer plans may present expensive withdrawal liability charges. A withdrawal does not occur solely because of a sale of stock, corporate reorganization, change in identity, or merger, consolidation, or spin-off of a company as long as the business change does not result in a change in the obligation to contribute to the plan. [ERISA § 4218]

On the other hand, a sale of assets will cause a withdrawal and trigger liability unless all of the following conditions are satisfied:

1. The sale is a bona fide arm's-length transaction between unrelated parties.
2. The buyer assumes the obligation to contribute to the plan for substantially the same number of contribution base units as those for which the seller had an obligation to contribute.
3. The buyer bonds or places in escrow an amount equal to one year of the seller's contributions (calculated as the greater of the average of the past three years or the last year).
4. The contract of sale provides that if the buyer withdraws within the next five plan years, the seller is liable for any liability that the seller would have incurred on the sale.

[ERISA § 4204(a)(1)]

## Ongoing Plan Considerations

### Q 26:12 What actions can a buyer take with respect to an existing defined benefit plan?

In many instances, matters relating to existing plans are addressed in the purchase agreement. After an acquisition, the plan can be:

1. Maintained as is;
2. Amended to take into consideration service, compensation, and so forth with the new employer;
3. Amended to fit any new benefits package;
4. Merged with a plan sponsored by the acquiring organization;
5. Frozen; or
6. Terminated.

### Q 26:13 How are HCEs identified after a business combination?

Under the general rules, an employee is an HCE if, in the determination year or the look-back year (the prior year, in most instances), the employee was a 5 percent owner of the business; or in the look-back year, the employee received compensation in excess of $80,000 (as indexed). [Temp. Treas. Reg. § 1.414(q)-1T, Q&A 13(c)] In determining an employee's compensation for purposes of determining HCE status, compensation received from the pretransaction employer can be considered. For the subsequent year, the determination depends on the nature of the transaction. In a stock sale, there is no change in employer; in an asset sale, there are two employers. There is no specific guidance from the IRS in this area.

### Q 26:14 How are the minimum coverage rules applied to a plan after a corporate change?

After the business change, the surviving plan may be significantly different from the plan maintained by the seller before the transaction. Or, for business reasons, it may be preferable to retain existing plans if at all possible. Each of the post-transaction plans must satisfy the minimum coverage rules under Code Section 410(b) (see chapter 6). A special transition rule provides extra time for compliance.

If an entity becomes a member of a new controlled group as a result of an acquisition or a change in corporate structure, the minimum coverage requirements are deemed satisfied during a one-year transition period. The deemed satisfaction rule applies if:

1. The minimum coverage rules were satisfied immediately before the change; and
2. Plan coverage is not significantly changed during the transition period (other than because of the controlled group change).

The transition period begins on the date of change in controlled group membership and ends on the last day of the first plan year beginning after the date of the change. [I.R.C. § 410(b)(6)(C)(ii)] The IRS has confirmed that this transition period applies through the end of the last day of that first plan year, meaning that changes would not be required until the following plan year. The transition period provides time to allow management to determine needed or appropriate changes to the benefit structure.

> **Example.** Dr. Patience has maintained a defined benefit pension plan for her small professional corporation for a number of years. Her practice will be merged into a much larger medical practice on April 1, 2003. After the merger, Dr. Patience's plan will not satisfy the minimum coverage or participation requirements. The plan may be retained during the transition period from April 1, 2003, to December 31, 2004 (the last day of the plan year beginning after the change). Something must be done for the plan year beginning January 1, 2005, to avoid loss of qualified status.

### Q 26:15   How can the nondiscrimination rules under Code Section 401(a)(4) be satisfied after a business acquisition?

After a business acquisition, there may be some problems passing the safe harbor test for nondiscrimination in amount of benefits (see chapter 10). This is often the case because the acquired business may have a completely different defined benefit pension plan or no plan at all. A plan must satisfy in both form and operation the three requirements described in the regulations to comply with the nondiscrimination rules of Code Section 401(a)(4):

1. Contributions or benefits under the plan must be nondiscriminatory.
2. Benefits, rights, and features available under the plan must be nondiscriminatory.
3. A plan amendment must not have the effect of discriminating significantly in favor of HCEs.

[Treas. Reg. § 1.401(a)(4)-1]

Most safe harbor formulas require the same benefit percentage of average compensation or the same benefit amount for all employees with the same number of years of service at normal retirement. Subsidized optional forms of benefit, early retirement subsidies, or more blatant differences will create difficulty in meeting the safe harbors.

Safe harbor plans can be restructured into component plans or can apply the general test for nondiscrimination (see chapters 10 and 11) to show that they are nondiscriminatory.

### Q 26:16   Can a special feature contained in the prior plan be retained for members of an acquired group only?

Yes. A benefit, right, or feature available under a plan exclusively to an acquired group of employees will be treated as satisfying the current availability and effective availability requirements of Code Section 401(a)(4) (see chapter 10) as long as the following conditions are satisfied:

1. The benefit, right, or feature satisfies the current and effective availability requirements as of a date selected by the employer to be the last date on which an employee could have been hired or transferred into the acquired group for that employee to be included in the acquired group of employees (the determination is made with reference to the current employer's plan and its nonexcludable employees).

2. The benefit, right, or feature is available under the plan of the current employer after the transaction on the same terms as it was available under the plan of the prior employer before the transaction.

[Treas. Reg. § 1.401(a)(4)-4(d)(1)(i)]

**Example.** ABC Company's plan permits an immediate lump-sum distribution option on termination of employment. XYZ acquires ABC and merges its plan into the XYZ plan. The XYZ plan provides a lump-sum option solely for former employees of ABC. The optional form of benefit satisfies the nondiscrimination requirements of Code Section 401(a)(4). [Treas. Reg. § 1.401(a)(4)-4(d)(1)(iii)]

### Q 26:17   How can potentially discriminatory rights, benefits, and features be addressed in the context of an acquisition?

Potentially discriminatory rights, benefits, and features can be:

1. Eliminated prospectively [Treas. Reg. § 1.401(a)(4)-4(b)(3)]; or
2. Carried to the new plan [Treas. Reg. § 1.401(a)(4)-4(d)(1)].

### Q 26:18   Can a plan grant service credit for service with the old business before the acquisition?

It depends. A plan cannot credit service in a discriminatory manner. [Treas. Reg. § 1.401(a)(4)-11(d)(2)] The surviving company's plan can provide credit for service with the old company before the acquisition (preparticipation service) if credit is extended to all similarly situated employees (see chapter 10). [Treas. Reg. § 1.401(a)(4)-11(d)(3)]

### Q 26:19   Is an employer required to recognize a participant's service in an older frozen plan for purposes of determining vesting service in a new plan after the two are merged together?

Yes. Treasury Regulations Sections 1.411(a)-(4) and 1.411(a)-5(a) provide that, in computing the period of service under a plan for purposes of determining the nonforfeitable percentage under Code Section 411(a)(2), all of an employee's years of service with the employer or employers maintaining the plan are taken into account subject to certain exceptions. These include an exception for years of service with an employer during any period for which the employer did not maintain the plan or a predecessor plan. In particular, Treasury Regulations

Section 1.411(a)-5(b)(3)(iii) provides that the period for which a plan is not maintained by an employer includes the period after the plan is terminated. For purposes of Treasury Regulations Section 1.411(a)-5, a plan is terminated at the date there is a termination of the plan within the meaning of Code Section 411(d)(3)(A) and the regulations thereunder. A partial termination, which occurs when a plan is frozen, is not a termination under these regulations. Therefore, after a merger of the two plans, service after the frozen plan was established must be taken into account for purposes of vesting in any benefit accruals under the new plan. [Rev. Rul. 2003-65, 2003-25 I.R.B. 1035]

### Q 26:20   Can the pension plan be terminated upon acquisition?

Yes. Generally the employer can terminate the plan at any time (see chapter 25). There are a number of questions that should be considered before making a decision to terminate the plan, including the following:

1. Will termination trigger withdrawal liability?
2. Are assets sufficient to meet liabilities on termination?
3. Are assets greater than liabilities?
4. What benefit commitments have been made to employees?
5. Are there any labor implications?

### Q 26:21   Must employees of an acquired company be covered under the defined benefit plan sponsored by the acquiring company?

Not necessarily. Any defined benefit pension plan must satisfy the minimum coverage and participation rules of Code Sections 410(b) and 401(a)(26) (see chapter 6). First, each plan must cover at least 50 employees or 40 percent of the entire workforce (considering the new "expanded" employer). [I.R.C. § 401(a)(26)] This is rarely an issue with a larger company, but may be a serious consideration when smaller companies are involved.

**Example 1.** Bytesize Inc., a company that employs 25 people, maintains a defined benefit pension plan for its employees. Bytesize Inc. is being acquired by Supersoft Inc., a company that employs 2,000 people, 100 of whom are HCEs. The Bytesize plan cannot be maintained after the acquisition without including the employees of Supersoft because it would cover fewer than 50 employees or 40 percent of the entire workforce.

Second, each plan must satisfy one of the two coverage tests described in Code Section 410(b):

1. The ratio percentage test (see chapter 6); or
2. The average benefit test (see chapter 6).

**Example 2.** Supersoft Inc., the company in Example 1, also maintains a defined benefit pension plan that covers all of its employees. It wants to exclude Bytesize employees from the plan. The exclusion is permissible because, even if all of the employees of Bytesize are non-highly compensated employees (NHCEs) (see chapter 6), the plan will satisfy the ratio percentage test of Code Section 410(b). The plan's ratio percentage is 98.7 percent (1,900 of the 1,925 NHCEs are covered under the plan, 98.7 percent, and 100 of the 100 HCEs are covered under the plan, 100 percent).

A separate line of business exception may apply in some cases for the minimum coverage requirements (see chapter 6).

### Q 26:22   What additional considerations apply when the demographics of the controlled group change?

Code Section 410(b) requires all pension plans to cover a certain percentage of nonexcludable employees (see chapter 6). When a new member of the controlled group is acquired or an existing member of the controlled group is sold, there is a grace period for satisfaction of the nondiscrimination rules. When a controlled group member is changed, a plan that satisfied Code Section 410(b) before the change will be treated as satisfying the coverage requirements of Code Section 410(b) until the second plan year starting after the date of the change. The grace period expires, however, if there is a material change in the plan. [I.R.C. § 410(b)(6)(C)]

### Q 26:23   Are there any limits on plan amendments after an acquisition?

Yes. Certain benefits, rights, and features are protected benefits under Code Section 411(d)(6) (see chapter 8). Accrued benefits, early retirement benefits, and optional forms of benefit, to the extent accrued, cannot be reduced or eliminated, or made subject to employer discretion. [I.R.C. § 411(d)(6); Treas. Reg. § 1.411(d)-4, Q-1]

If a plan is being amended to reduce the rate of future accruals, an ERISA Section 204(h) notice must be provided to participants, beneficiaries, alternate payees, and any involved unions at least 45 days (15 days for small plans with fewer than 100 participants) before the effective date of the amendment (see chapter 8).

### Q 26:24   Are there any implications if a substantial number of employees are terminated or laid off in connection with an acquisition?

An acquisition in and of itself does not result in a plan termination. If a substantial number or percentage of employees are terminated, however, a partial termination may result (see chapter 8). In this event, all affected employees must be 100 percent vested.

**Example.** Big Apple Co. acquires Appleseed and terminates all of the employees in the Macoun division. The Macoun division constituted 25 percent of the workforce. Macoun employees will become 100 percent vested in their accrued benefits.

**Caution.** Layoffs or terminations do not always result in partial termination. All the facts and circumstances should be considered (see chapter 8).

A partial termination results in 100 percent vesting only for affected employees, that is, the individuals whose employment was terminated. Employees who remain covered under the plan do not become 100 percent vested.

### Q 26:25  Can an existing defined benefit plan be maintained after an acquisition?

Yes. An existing plan can be maintained if it satisfies the coverage and participation requirements (see Q 26:21).

### Q 26:26  Can an existing defined benefit plan be merged into the buyer's plan after an acquisition?

Yes. Often plan merger is the simplest avenue after a corporate acquisition. In a plan merger, plan participants have no right to receive benefits merely because of the corporate change. Assets and liabilities are merely transferred to another plan. Benefits levels can be maintained or changed to fit the needs of the surviving company; protected benefits cannot be eliminated (see Q 26:23).

## Plan Transactions

### Plan Merger and Consolidation

### Q 26:27  What is a *plan merger or consolidation*?

A *plan merger* or *consolidation* occurs when two or more plans are combined into a single plan (see Q 26:30). Assets and liabilities are transferred from one plan to the surviving plan. After the merger or consolidation occurs, all assets are held by the one surviving plan, and all benefits are paid from the one surviving plan. The employer controls the transaction; that is, participants cannot elect to receive distributions from the plan.

### Q 26:28  Can two defined benefit plans be merged?

Yes, two or more defined benefit plans can be merged as long as each participant receives benefits on a termination basis from the plan immediately after the merger, consolidation, or transfer that are equal to or greater than the benefits the participant would receive on a termination basis immediately before the merger, transfer, or consolidation. [I.R.C. § 414(l)(1)]

If the sum of the assets of all plans is at least equal to the total present value of the accrued benefits for all plans, and the assets are combined and each participant's accrued benefit is preserved, the requirements of Code Section 414(l) will be satisfied. If the sum of the assets of all plans is less than the total present value of the accrued benefits for all plans, the accrued benefits could not be paid in full on plan termination. In this case, information regarding accrued benefits must be maintained to prevent any participant from receiving lower benefits if the plan is terminated than the participant would have received if the plan had terminated before the merger or consolidation. The plan administrator must maintain records to prioritize asset allocation if the plan is terminated. [Treas. Reg. § 1.414(l)-1(e)]

### Q 26:29   Why would an employer consider merging plans?

There are a number of reasons employers merge plans. The possible benefits of a merger include the following:

1. Consolidation of administration;
2. Creation of a holding facility for a terminating plan while another plan remains ongoing;
3. Benefit consolidation after a corporate acquisition;
4. Solving discrimination problems; and
5. Reduction of aggregate funding.

### Q 26:30   What is a *single plan*?

A plan is considered a *single plan* if all of the plan assets are available to pay benefits to participants and their beneficiaries. The critical factor is the availability of assets to pay benefits. A plan may be a single plan even if:

1. The plan has several different benefit formulas that apply to different participants;
2. The plan has several plan documents;
3. More than one employer, whether or not affiliated, contributes to the plan;
4. The plan assets are invested in a number of trusts; or
5. Separate accounting is maintained for purposes of cost allocation.

[I.R.C. § 414(1); Treas. Reg. § 1.414(l)-1(b)(1)]

### Q 26:31   What basic requirements apply in a plan merger?

Code Section 414(l) governs plan mergers, transfer of assets and benefits from one plan to another, and the division of one plan into two successor plans (spin-off). Generally, a merger, transfer, or spin-off of pension assets and liabilities should not adversely affect any of the plan participants. A plan participant must be entitled to a benefit immediately after the merger, consolidation, or transfer that is equal to or greater than the benefit he or she would have been entitled to receive immediately before the merger, consolidation, or transfer (if the plan then terminated) (see Q 26:40). [I.R.C. § 414(l)(1)]

Additionally, the surviving plan or transferee plan must include all of the benefit options and features applicable to benefits accrued as of the date of the merger that are protected benefits under Code Section 411(d)(6) (see chapter 8).

### Q 26:32  Must both plans be amended before a merger?

No. Each plan can be amended and submitted to the IRS for a determination of qualification; however, this is not required and can be a rather time-consuming and expensive process. It is possible to merge the plan documents into a single document, which serves as a successor plan document. Because the surviving plan is considered a continuation of both plans, the successor document could then be amended as necessary to ensure that each plan met the form requirements for qualification at every relevant time.

### Q 26:33  Can future service or salary increases affect benefits after a merger?

It depends on how the plan is drafted. If the pension benefit is based on final average compensation (see chapter 9), salary increases will increase benefits. Future service can also increase benefits.

**Practice Pointer.** If it is intended that benefits be frozen after an acquisition, an amendment to the plan should be prepared so that compensation and service after the merger are not recognized.

### Q 26:34  Can a church plan or governmental plan be involved in a plan merger?

Yes. Plans of tax-exempt employers and governmental plans (see chapter 5) can be involved in a merger. Occasionally, such a merger can result in loss of exemption from ERISA Title I and subject the plan to a number of unanticipated requirements. A merger with a for-profit company may expose the plan to potential excise tax liability (e.g., Code Section 4980A). Hospitals that enjoy church plan status should be particularly careful when business mergers occur. [Ltr. Rul. 9713021]

### Q 26:35  Can assets of a defined benefit plan be merged with assets of a defined contribution plan?

Yes. One of the plans should be converted into the other type of plan before the merger (i.e., the defined benefit plan converted into a defined contribution plan or the defined contribution plan converted into a defined benefit plan). If the defined contribution plan is converted to a defined benefit plan, the rules applicable to the merger of two defined benefit plans apply (see Q 26:28). [Treas. Reg. § 1.414(l)-1(l)]

Participants can also make a voluntary, fully informed election to transfer benefits from the defined benefit plan to the defined contribution plan. The participant must have the option to retain his or her guaranteed benefit. Notification and spousal consent are also required. [Treas. Reg. § 1.411(d)-4, Q&A 3] After the transfer, the guaranteed benefit feature of the defined benefit plan is lost unless the participant elects otherwise; the amount transferred to the defined contribution plan will be increased for investment gains and decreased for investment losses.

A direct transfer of excess assets from a defined benefit plan to a defined contribution plan would be considered a reversion of the assets to the employer, followed by a recontribution of the assets to the defined contribution plan, subject to the excise tax on reversions.

## Plan Division

### Q 26:36  Can benefits and liabilities associated with one plan be transferred to another plan?

Yes, benefit liabilities and plan assets can be spun off from one plan and transferred to another plan that assumes the liability for benefit payment. [I.R.C. § 414(l)(2)]

### Q 26:37  What is a *transfer of liabilities*?

A *transfer of liabilities* occurs when one plan reduces its assets and liabilities and another plan acquires the assets and assumes the liabilities of the first plan. All mergers and spin-offs involve a transfer of assets and liabilities from one plan to another. Transfers occur regularly when multiple plans are maintained within a controlled group for various subsidiaries or divisions and employees transfer among the various entities maintaining plans.

> **Practice Pointer.** Atlas Corp. maintains a number of plans for its various operating divisions. Alex is transferred from the Nuts & Bolts division to the Tooling division. Under the terms of the plans, when an employee is transferred to another division, the new division assumes liability for payment of benefits to the transferred employee under its plan, provided it receives assets from the plan that previously covered the employee. Accordingly, the Nuts & Bolts division plan transfers an amount equal to the present value of Alex's accrued benefits to the Tooling division plan. Thereafter, the Tooling division plan assumes liability for payment of all of Alex's benefits attributable to employment with Atlas Corp.

### Q 26:38  What is a plan spin-off, or split-off?

A plan spin-off, or split-off, occurs when an existing plan is divided into two or more plans. [Treas. Reg. § 1.414(l)-1(b)(4)] In a spin-off, the obligation to pay all of the accrued benefits for one or more participants is transferred from one plan to another, along with the amount of assets needed to satisfy the obligation. After the spin-off occurs, each participant is covered under one plan only; a participant's benefits cannot be divided between the two plans. [Treas. Reg. § 1.414(l)-1(n)(1)(i)] The primary difference between a spin-off and a transfer is that in the case of a spin-off, two new plans are created from one original plan. In the case of a transfer, benefits are transferred from one existing plan to another existing plan. A spin-off occasionally occurs in connection with a sale of a company or operating division. The new employer can maintain the benefit formula as is for the benefit of the employees employed by the acquired company or division, or the plan can be modified as determined by the acquiring entity.

**Example.** Red's Restaurant maintains a defined benefit pension plan for its employees. Red's Restaurant provides a separate medical plan for salaried employees and would like to separate the pension plan as well. It splits the existing plan into two plans—one for salaried employees and one for hourly employees. Assets are appropriately allocated to each plan. Thereafter, an hourly employee will receive pension benefits exclusively from the newly created plan for hourly employees, and a salaried employee will receive pension benefits exclusively from the newly created plan for salaried employees.

### Q 26:39  What requirements apply in a spin-off?

Plan spin-offs (see Q 26:38) (and transfers of assets and liabilities; see Q 26:37) must meet the requirements of Code Sections 401(a)(12) and 414(l). Accrued benefits of each participant must be allocated to only one of the spun-off plans. Immediately after the spin-off, each participant in each plan must be able to receive a benefit (if the plan terminated) equal to or greater than the benefit the participant would have been entitled to receive immediately before the spin-off if the plan had terminated then. [Treas. Reg. § 1.414(l)-1(n)(1)]

### Q 26:40  How much of the plan's assets must be transferred to the transferee plan in a spin-off?

When a defined benefit plan is spun off into two or more plans, benefits must be calculated on a termination basis before the spin-off (see Q 26:42). Each plan must provide benefits at least equal to these benefits if the spun-off plan is then terminated. *Benefits on a termination basis* means the benefits that would be provided by plan assets under ERISA Section 4044 if the plan terminated (see Q 26:42). [Treas. Reg. § 1.414(l)-1(b)(5)] In other words, the amount transferred must be sufficient so that each plan participant could receive (if the plan then terminated) a benefit that is greater than or equal to the benefit the person would have been entitled to receive immediately before the transfer date. [Treas. Reg. § 1.414(l)-1(b)(5)(i)] These rules are intended to protect benefits involved in a spin-off or transfer. The transferred assets must be sufficient to protect the benefits of the transferring participants, and the assets remaining in the original plan must be sufficient to protect the benefits of the participants who remain in that plan.

If a plan has sufficient assets to satisfy benefit liabilities on a termination basis, Code Section 414(l) can be satisfied by simply transferring the present value of each participant's accrued benefit to the other plan. If, after the merger, the plan is not fully funded for all accrued benefits, the plan must allocate assets to accrued benefits as of the day before the merger date, in accordance with ERISA Section 4044. [Treas. Reg. § 1.414(l)-1(e)]

### Q 26:41  Is there a way to transfer benefits and liabilities to another plan without maintaining protected benefits?

Protected benefits can be eliminated when a participant voluntarily transfers benefits to another plan. The transfer must satisfy the following requirements:

1. *Participant choice.* The participant must make a voluntary, fully informed election to transfer benefits to the new plan.

2. *Notice.* The participant must receive a notice of distribution options, including QJSA rights.

3. *Benefit rights.* The participant must have a right to an immediate distribution.

4. *Amount transferred.* The amount transferred must equal the present value of the accrued benefit using certain actuarial equivalencies.

[Treas. Reg. § 1.411(d)-4, Q&A 3]

## Asset Allocation

### Q 26:42   How does an actuary determine benefits on a termination basis?

The actuary must determine benefits on a termination basis for each affected participant in connection with the transfer of assets and liabilities from one plan to another. In making this calculation, an actuary must use reasonable actuarial assumptions. [Treas. Reg. § 1.414(l)-1(b)(9)] Although PBGC assumptions are identified as safe harbor reasonable assumptions for Section 414(l) calculations, other assumptions that need not be as favorable to the transferee plan can be used. Interest assumptions used by insurance companies in providing annuities to terminating plans or assumptions used in the plan for funding purposes or calculating actuarial equivalencies may also be appropriate for calculations under Code Section 414(l). Different assumptions will often produce remarkably different values.

As a general rule, all protected benefits under Code Section 411(d)(6)(B) (see chapter 8), such as retirement-type subsidies and optional forms of benefit must be included in the determination of benefits on a termination basis. [Rev. Rul. 86-48, 1986-1 C.B. 216]

### Q 26:43   What must be done if assets are insufficient to satisfy all liabilities upon termination after a merger?

In the event of a subsequent plan termination, the regular application of ERISA Section 4044 (see chapter 25) would be modified by using a different schedule of priority. This schedule is applied to prevent any participant from receiving a smaller benefit on a termination basis as a result of the merger. [Treas. Reg. § 1.414(l)-1(f)] This schedule can be developed at the time of the plan spin-off. In lieu of creating the schedule, the plan actuary can provide a certification indicating that all data necessary to determine the schedule as of the date of the merger will be maintained. [Treas. Reg. § 1.414(l)-1(i)(1)] This information must be maintained for five years after the date of merger. After five years have elapsed, the special schedule can be ignored. [Treas. Reg. § 1.414(l)-1(j)]

### Q 26:44   What can be done if assets exceed all liabilities?

The allocation of excess assets among plans involved in spin-offs depends on the circumstances and relationships of the plan sponsors. In many instances, excess assets in the transferor plan (assets in excess of the value of the benefits associated with the plan) do not have to be allocated to the benefits of participants being transferred to a spun-off or transferee plan, except to the extent such assets would be allocated to such benefits under ERISA Section 4044. When there are benefits attributable to employee contributions, a portion of the excess may have to be transferred to the transferee plan. [Jacobson v. Hughes Aircraft Co., 105 F.2d 1288 (9th Cir. 1997)] There is no fiduciary duty to transfer a proportionate share of surplus assets to a spun-off plan. [Bigger v. American Commercial Lines, 862 F.2d 1341 (8th Cir. 1988)] As long as the assets transferred meet the requirements of Code Section 414(l), the parties can negotiate the allocation of excess assets.

One of the requirements of Code Section 414(l) is that if the spun-off or transferee plan will be maintained by an employer in the same controlled group as the original plan's employer, and if neither plan is to be terminated as a result of the transaction causing the spin-off or transfer, a portion of the surplus must be allocated to each plan. [I.R.C. § 414(l)(2)(D)] As a general rule, excess assets must be allocated between the original plan and any spun-off plans by applying the applicable percentage to the excess assets. Each plan's *applicable percentage* is calculated by dividing:

1. The excess of the full-funding limitation determined under Code Section 412(c)(7)(A)(i) over the amount of the assets required to be allocated to the plan after the spin-off (without regard to excess assets); by
2. The sum of the excess amounts determined separately under item #1 for all the plans involved in the spin-off.

[I.R.C. § 414(l)(2)(B)]

The credit balance in the funding standard account (FSA) and the amortization bases of the FSA of the plan before the spin-off must also be allocated to each applicable plan. [Rev. Rul. 86-47, 1986-1 C.B. 215]

**Example.** Consolidated Holdings Inc. maintains a defined benefit pension plan for which costs are computed using the entry age normal funding method. Consolidated Holdings Inc. spins off its existing plan into two defined benefit plans—one for its hourly employees and one for its salaried employees. The allocations were made as follows:

|  | Original Plan | Hourly Plan | Salaried Plan |
|---|---|---|---|
| FSA credit balance | $ 20,000 |  |  |
| Market value of assets | $400,000 | $80,000 | $320,000 |
| Actuarial value of assets | $375,000 |  |  |
| Present value of plan benefits on a termination basis for Code Section 414(l) | $180,000 | $58,000 | $122,000 |

|                                        | *Original Plan* | *Hourly Plan* | *Salaried Plan* |
|----------------------------------------|-----------------|---------------|-----------------|
| Entry age normal accrued liability     | $425,000        | $200,000      | $225,000        |
| Outstanding balance and remaining period of amortization bases | $100,000 | $(30,000) | |
|                                        | (28 payments remaining) | (14 payments remaining) | |

Each of the spun-off plans must begin maintaining a separate FSA. The credit or debit balance of the single plan before the spin-off must be allocated to the FSAs of the spun-off plans on a reasonable basis, taking into account the assets and liabilities allocated between the plans.

When the fair market value of plan assets is greater than the present value of plan benefits on a termination basis, the credit balance of the original plan immediately before the spin-off should be allocated between the two plans resulting from the spin-off in the following manner:

1. Allocate an amount equal to the lesser of (a) the excess of the fair market value of the original plan's assets over its FSA credit balance, or (b) the present value of the original plan's benefits on a termination basis, between the two plans by applying the asset allocation rules in Treasury Regulations Section 1.414(l)-1(n).

2. Allocate the original plan credit balance between the hourly and salaried plans in proportion to the excess, for each spun-off plan, of the fair market value of assets actually allocated to that plan over the amount determined for that plan in step 1.

In this instance, the fair market value of the original plan's assets minus the plan's FSA credit balance is greater than the present value of plan benefits on a termination basis. Therefore, the amount to be allocated in the first step between the hourly and salaried plans is equal to the present value of the original plan's benefits on a termination basis (i.e., $180,000). The amount of $58,000 is allocated to the hourly plan and $122,000 is allocated to the salaried plan. The excess of the fair market value of the original plan's assets over the present value of benefits on a termination basis is $220,000. The excess of the fair market value of assets actually allocated to the hourly plan ($80,000) over the amount allocated to the hourly plan under the first step ($58,000) is $22,000. The corresponding excess for the salaried plan is $198,000 ($320,000 – $122,000). Under the second step, the original plan's credit balance ($20,000) is allocated between the hourly plan and the salaried plan in proportion to those excess amounts. Thus, a credit balance of $2,000 ($20,000 × ($22,000 ÷ $220,000)) is allocated to the hourly plan and a credit balance of $18,000 ($20,000 × $198,000 ÷ $220,000)) is allocated to the salaried plan.

The actuarial value of assets of the original plan ($375,000) should be allocated between the hourly plan and the salaried plan in proportion to the fair market value of assets allocated to the two plans.

Because the hourly plan has an unfunded accrued liability and the salaried plan has no unfunded accrued liability, all of the original plan's amortization bases should be allocated to the hourly plan and the remaining amortization period of each base should be retained. In addition, a new amortization base must be established for the hourly plan. For the salaried plan, the actuarial value of assets is greater than the accrued liability. No amortization bases of the original plan are allocated to the salaried plan and none should be established as a result of the spin-off. [Rev. Rul. 86-47, 1986-1 C.B. 215]

Excess assets do not have to be transferred to the transferee plan if the transferee plan is not sponsored by a member of the controlled group, assets are transferred out of a multiple-employer plan, or the plans involved are being terminated. [I.R.C. § 414(l)(2)(D)]

**Note.** The funding method will directly affect excess asset allocation.

### Q 26:45    How is plan funding affected after a merger with an overfunded or underfunded plan?

After a merger, two plans become a single plan. All assets, liabilities, and funding methods are considered in determining the funding requirements in transition and on an ongoing basis (see chapter 19). The merger of an underfunded plan with a significantly overfunded plan may eliminate the underfunding.

### Q 26:46    How can a company benefit from overfunding or excess assets?

It is possible to benefit, albeit often indirectly, from a plan that is overfunded or has assets in excess of liabilities. The excise tax on the reversion of assets (see chapter 25) often makes it cost prohibitive for a company to obtain excess assets from a plan. In some cases, employers have tried to recover surplus assets through a "spin-off termination." In this case, a plan is split into two or more plans, and one of the plans (with the excess assets) is terminated. This transaction will probably be treated as a termination of the original plan and the creation of one or more new plans, thereby subjecting excess assets to the reversion tax.

The excess assets can be used for the benefit of plan participants by amending the plan to increase or enhance benefits (see chapters 12 and 15). One option is to amend the plan into a cash balance plan (see chapter 13). Additions to the plan would thereafter come from surplus assets.

**Example.** Large Egg LLC has an overfunded defined benefit plan. It had considered adopting a 5 percent defined contribution plan. Large Egg LLC could convert the plan to a cash balance plan and credit a 5 percent allocation to each participant from existing defined benefit plan assets.

An overfunded pension plan can be merged with an underfunded plan for other employees, minimizing or eliminating the underfunding. Some plans are amended to provide "no cost" additional benefits, early retirement subsidies, or enhanced benefits.

## Administrative Requirements

### Q 26:47   What actions must be taken prior to a plan merger or transfer?

At least 30 days before a plan merger, consolidation, or transfer of plan assets or liabilities to another plan, the plan administrator must file an actuarial statement of valuation showing compliance with the requirement of Code Section 401(a)(12) that each plan participant will receive a benefit (if the plan were terminated after the merger, consolidation, or transfer) equal to or greater than the benefit he or she would have received if the plan were terminated immediately before such event. [I.R.C. § 6058(b); Treas. Reg. §§ 301.6058-1(e), 1.414(l)-1] This requirement is deemed satisfied by filing IRS Form 5310-A, or either IRS Form 5300 or 5303 if a determination letter is also desired. Form 5310-A must be filed for each plan involved in the transfer.

### Q 26:48   Must the IRS or DOL be notified of an anticipated plan merger or spin-off?

Yes. The sponsor or plan administrator of every plan involved in a plan merger, spin-off, or transfer of assets or liabilities must file IRS Form 5310-A, Notice of Merger, Consolidation, or Transfer of Plan Assets or Liabilities, at least 30 days before the date of the merger or transfer. [I.R.C. § 6058(b)]

*De minimis* defined benefit plan mergers, involving an amount that is less than 3 percent of the larger plan's assets, and *de minimis* spin-offs, less than 3 percent of the total assets for at least one day during that plan year, are exempt from filing when transferred assets are sufficient to satisfy benefit liabilities. [Treas. Reg. § 1.414(l)-1(n)(2)]

Failure to notify the IRS of a merger or transfer of assets results in a penalty of $1 per day of delinquency up to a maximum of $1,000. [I.R.C. § 6652(d)(2)]

A final IRS Form 5500 must be filed within seven months after the merger is effective for the plan that does not survive. The day of the merger is considered a day of operation for a plan. Therefore, if a calendar-year plan merged on January 1, 2002, Form 5500 would be required for both 2001 and 2002. If the merger had occurred on December 31, 2001, no Form 5500 for 2002 would be required.

### Q 26:49   What rights must be given to participants before defined benefit assets can be transferred to another plan?

Code Section 411(d)(6) prohibits any cutback in a participant's accrued benefit. Elimination of an optional form of benefit or other protected benefit rights with respect to pretransfer service is treated as a violation of Code Section 411(d)(6). In the context of a plan merger, both plans must be reviewed to ensure that no protected benefits, rights, or features are eliminated.

All protected benefits must be retained in the successor plan (see chapter 8).

**Example.** Alpha Corp has a defined benefit plan that permits a joint and survivor annuity benefit with an individual other than the participant's spouse permitted as contingent annuitant. Alpha's plan is merged into Mega Corp's plan, which does not contain this payment option. The special joint and survivor benefit must be retained for benefits accrued before the merger.

Even though Code Section 411(d)(6) protection applies only to accrued benefits, that is, benefits earned for service, compensation, and so forth before the merger, many plans maintain the protected feature for all benefits earned both before and after the merger to avoid administrative difficulty.

### Q 26:50   Must employees receive notice of a plan merger or spin-off?

No. There is no requirement that employees receive advance notice of a plan merger or spin-off, but plan participants must receive a revised SPD within 90 days of the event informing them of the name of the plan providing benefits, among other things (see chapter 28).

### Q 26:51   Can multiemployer plans be involved in plan mergers or spin-offs?

Yes. Special rules apply to multiemployer plans involved in a transfer of assets and liabilities. A plan sponsor generally cannot effect a merger involving multiemployer plans or transfer assets and liabilities to or from a multiemployer plan unless:

1. Accrued benefits are not reduced;
2. A special actuarial valuation is performed;
3. There is no reasonable likelihood that benefits will be suspended because of plan insolvency; and
4. The PBGC receives 120 days' advance notice.

[ERISA § 4231]

# Chapter 27

# Fiduciary Responsibility

Persons possessing certain powers with respect to the plan, or functioning in a discretionary capacity, are called fiduciaries. Under the Employee Retirement Income Security Act of 1974 (ERISA), fiduciaries are charged with a high standard of care in managing the plan and its assets. Fiduciaries may be personally liable for actions or omissions constituting breaches of fiduciary responsibility. This chapter explains who is treated as a fiduciary, the responsibilities imposed on a fiduciary, and the liabilities associated with a breach of fiduciary duty.

## The Basics

### Q 27:1  What is a *fiduciary*?

A *fiduciary* of a pension plan is anyone who

1. Exercises discretionary authority or control over management of the plan or management or disposition of its assets;

2. Renders or has authority or responsibility to render investment advice for a fee; or

3. Has discretionary authority or responsibility in the administration of the plan.

[ERISA § 3(21)(A); I.R.C. § 4975(e)(3)]

### Q 27:2   What is the significance of fiduciary status?

Fiduciaries are held to a high standard of conduct with respect to the plan. Fiduciaries are responsible for handling plan assets and can be liable in the event of improper investment of assets or breach of fiduciary responsibility. [ERISA § 404]

### Q 27:3   Are all plans subject to ERISA rules governing fiduciaries?

No. ERISA's fiduciary standards apply to all defined benefit pension plans except the following:

1. Governmental plans;
2. Church plans, except those electing to be covered under Internal Revenue Code (Code) Section 410(d); and
3. Plans maintained outside of the United States primarily for the benefit of nonresident aliens.

[ERISA §§ 4(b), 3(36), 401(a)(1)]

## Fiduciary Duties

### Q 27:4   What are a fiduciary's duties under ERISA?

ERISA Section 404 sets forth the basic duties of a fiduciary, as follows:

1. *Duty of loyalty.* A fiduciary must act for the exclusive benefit of plan participants and beneficiaries (see Q 27:5). [ERISA § 404(a)(1)(A)]
2. *Duty of prudence.* A fiduciary must act with care, skill, prudence, and diligence in matters relating to the plan (see Q 27:6). [ERISA § 404(a)(1)(B)]
3. *Duty to diversify investments.* A fiduciary must diversify plan assets so as to reduce the risk of loss (see Q 27:8). [ERISA § 404(a)(1)(C)]
4. *Duty to follow plan documents.* A fiduciary must act in accordance with the plan documents to the extent that they comply with ERISA (see Q 27:9). [ERISA § 404(a)(1)(D)]

### Q 27:5   What is the *exclusive benefit rule*?

Under the *exclusive benefit rule*, in discharging their duties, plan fiduciaries must act for the exclusive purpose of providing benefits to participants and their beneficiaries and defraying reasonable expenses of administering the plan. [ERISA § 404(a)(1)(A)] Fiduciaries must discharge all of their duties "solely in the interest" of the plan's participants and beneficiaries. Courts have interpreted this to mean that fiduciaries must act "with an eye single to the interests of the participants and beneficiaries" [Donovan v. Bierwirth, 2 Employee Benefits Cas. (BNA) 2145 (E.D.N.Y. 1981)] and "with complete and undivided loyalty to the beneficiaries." [Freund v. Marshall & Ilsley Bank, 1 Employee Benefits Cas. (BNA) 1898 (W.D. Wis. 1979)]

A fiduciary would violate the exclusive benefit rule if the fiduciary took an action that directly or indirectly benefited the fiduciary's own interests at the expense of the plan, its participants, or its beneficiaries. A few cases have questioned the application of the exclusive benefit rule to changes made to the plan by the employer. A program designed to encourage early retirement, and thereby reduce the workforce at overstaffed facilities, did not breach the exclusive purpose rule simply because the employer gained the consequential benefit of enhanced efficiency. [Trenton v. Scott Paper Co., 832 F.2d 886 (3d Cir. 1987)] The courts seem to have accepted situations in which the fiduciary receives an incidental benefit from a particular action. [Leigh v. Engle, 727 F.2d 113 (7th Cir. 1984); Donovan v. Walton, 609 F. Supp. 1221 (S.D. Fla. 1985)] A multiemployer plan considered investment with an insurance company on the condition that it invest in construction loans to projects employing union labor. In reviewing this matter, the Department of Labor (DOL) interpreted ERISA Section 404(a)(1) as prohibiting a fiduciary from subordinating participants' interests in retirement income to unrelated objectives. The proposed investment was to be evaluated based on its economic value to the plan as compared to other available investments. Fiduciaries would not violate the exclusive benefit rule if there was an incidental benefit to members (increased employment) as long as this incidental benefit was not the motivating factor in the investment decision. [DOL Op. Ltr. 85-036A]

### Q 27:6   What is the *prudent person rule*?

Under the so-called *prudent person rule,* a fiduciary must act with the care, skill, prudence, and diligence under the circumstances then prevailing that a prudent person acting in a like capacity and familiar with such matters would use in the conduct of an enterprise of a like character and with like aims. [ERISA § 404(a)(1)(B)]

In *Donovan v. Mazzola* [4 Employee Benefits Cas. (BNA) 1865 (9th Cir. 1983], one of the leading cases dealing with the prudence of plan investments, the court considered procedures used by the trustees and questioned whether the individual trustees, at the time they engaged in the challenged transactions, employed the appropriate methods to investigate the merits of the investment and to structure the investment. The court did not apply the "business judgment rule," but reviewed the trustees' actions under the prudent person rule contained in ERISA Section 404(a)(1)(B).

The regulations provide guidance for satisfying the prudence standard for investment of plan assets. [DOL Reg. § 2550.404a-1] A fiduciary must give appropriate attention to the facts and circumstances that the fiduciary knows, or should know, are relevant to the particular investment or investment course of action. A safe-harbor rule is included in the regulations. Compliance with the safe harbor presumes compliance with the prudence standard. Under the safe-harbor rule, the fiduciary must do the following:

1. Determine that the investment is reasonably designed as part of the portfolio to further the purposes of the plan, taking into account the possible risk of loss and opportunity for gain.

2. Consider the portfolio's composition with regard to diversification, liquidity, and current return relative to cash-flow needs, and projected return relative to funding requirements.

A trustee unfamiliar with an unusual or difficult investment decision is charged with making an independent inquiry into the merits of a particular investment rather than relying wholly on the advice of others. [Katsaros v. Cody, 4 Employee Benefits Cas. (BNA) 1910 (E.D.N.Y. 1983)] Failure of a plan to maintain a procedure for collecting delinquent employer contributions or to take steps to collect delinquent contributions violates the prudence standard.

### Q 27:7 Is an inexperienced fiduciary held to a different standard than a professional?

No. A fiduciary is not held to a lower standard because the fiduciary is not familiar with investments. The prudence required by the prudence standard of ERISA is not that of a prudent lay person, but rather that of a prudent fiduciary with experience in dealing with similar enterprises. [Marshall v. Snyder, 1 Employee Benefits Cas. (BNA) 1878 (E.D.N.Y. 1979)] The prudent person standard may be violated if a fiduciary who lacks the requisite education, experience, and skill to make investment decisions fails to consult an appropriate adviser before making such decisions. [Donovan v. Walton, 6 Employee Benefits Cas. (BNA) 1677 (S.D. Fla. 1985)] Trustees who may not understand the full details of a proposed investment are judged by the standard of one "familiar with such matters." The prudence standard is not a refuge for fiduciaries who are not equipped to evaluate a complex investment. [Marshall v. Glass/Metal Ass'n & Glaziers & Glassworkers Pension Plan, 2 Employee Benefits Cas. (BNA) 1006 (D. Haw. 1980)]

The prudence standard "measures the decisions of plan fiduciaries against the decisions that would be made by experienced investment advisers." [Joint Comm. on Taxation, 101st Cong, *Overview of the Enforcement and Administration of the Employee Retirement Income Security Act of 1974* (JCX-16-90) (1990)]

> ERISA does not require that all plan fiduciaries . . . be experts in all phases of plan administration. Nor does it require them to have expert knowledge in the whole range of activities carried on by a plan. Rather, they are encouraged to retain expert advisors to assist in making decisions that require special skills not normally possessed by laypersons[; however,][t]he mere retention of an expert cannot be permitted to act as a kind of talisman to protect a fiduciary against claims of failure to discharge their [sic] own fiduciary responsibilities. Expert advice must be considered as carefully as any other information that the trustees have available to them when making decisions to commit plan assets.

[Donovan v. Tricario, 5 Employee Benefits Cas. (BNA) 2057 (S.D. Fla. 1984)]

## Q 27:8   What is required to satisfy diversification requirements?

ERISA Section 404(a)(1)(C) requires fiduciaries to diversify the investments of the plan "so as to minimize the risk of large losses, unless in the circumstances it is clearly prudent not to do so." The diversification requirement cannot be stated as a fixed percentage, but depends on the facts and circumstances. Fiduciaries are cautioned against investing "an unreasonably large proportion" of plan assets in a "single security," in "one type of security," or in various types of securities "dependent upon the success of one enterprise or upon conditions in one locality."[H.R. Conf. Rep. No. 93-1280, at 304 (1974)]

The following factors are often applied in evaluating the adequacy of diversification:

- Plan purposes
- Amount of plan assets
- Financial conditions
- Type of investment
- Distribution as to geographic location
- Distribution as to industries
- Maturity dates

[H.R. Conf. Rep. No. 93-1280 (1974), reprinted in 1974 U.S.C.C.A.N. 5038]

A plan can invest all of its assets in a mutual fund without violating the diversification requirements. [DOL Op. Ltr. 75-93] Plan fiduciaries should spread the risk of loss to the plan. For example, the courts have ruled that a commitment of 23 percent of plan assets to a single loan in one instance subjected the plan to a risk of large loss and violated the diversification requirements. [Marshall v. Glass/Metal Ass'n & Glaziers & Glass Workers Pension Plan, 2 Employee Benefits Cas. (BNA) 1006 (D. Haw. 1980)]

## Q 27:9   What does a fiduciary have to know about the plan document?

ERISA Section 404(a)(1)(D) requires fiduciaries to administer the plan in accordance with the plan document and the law. To comply with this requirement, fiduciaries should be familiar with the terms of the plan, trust, and other governing documents. A limitation on investment powers contained in the plan is binding on trustees. [Marshall v. Teamsters Local 282 Pension Trust Fund, 458 F. Supp. 986 (E.D.N.Y. 1978)] A trustee is liable under ERISA for making an otherwise valid distribution of a participant's interest without his or her written consent when plan documents required written consent to distribution. [Franklin v. Thornton, 16 Employee Benefits Cas. (BNA) 1433 (9th Cir. 1993)] A fiduciary is not in breach of duty if the fiduciary fails to follow the plan because of an incorrect interpretation made in good faith. The trustees' misreading of the plan, resulting in its termination, did not create liability because the trustees "sought out the expert advice of counsel and an actuary, considered in good faith the three options presented to them, and implemented the option recommended by the experts." [Morgan v. Independent Drivers Ass'n Pension Plan, 15 Employee Benefits Cas. (BNA) 2515 (10th Cir. 1992)]

### Q 27:10 Is a fiduciary responsible for making sure benefit payments are accurate?

Yes, if the fiduciary does not act in the interest of plan participants. Because a fiduciary is required to act in accordance with plan documents under ERISA Section 404(a)(1)(D), a participant could argue that the fiduciary has breached its duty by permitting the payment of an incorrect benefit amount. Although the courts have imposed liability in some cases—for example, for paying benefits to individuals who were ineligible to receive benefits under the plan's terms [Donovan v. Daugherty, 3 Employee Benefits Cas. (BNA) 2079 (S.D. Ala. 1982)]—for the most part the courts have not assessed liability unless the fiduciary's decision was an abuse of the discretion granted to the plan administrator in the plan document. This standard was set in *Firestone Tire & Rubber Co. v. Bruch.* [10 Employee Benefits Cas. (BNA) 1873 (U.S. 1989)]

In a case involving the calculation of the present value of a participant's accrued benefit under a defined benefit plan, the court held that the plan administrator was not personally liable for damages associated with the benefit miscalculation because the calculation of benefits was not a fiduciary duty. [Joseph F. Cunningham Pension Plan v. Mathieu, 1998 U.S. App. LEXIS 15080 (4th Cir. 1998)] In a separate case, it was considered a fiduciary duty. [Pineiro v. PBGC, 1999 U.S. Dist. LEXIS 4691 (S.D.N.Y. 1999)]

In another case, the employer sent a distribution check to an address provided by the participant's estranged spouse. The estranged spouse fraudulently endorsed and cashed the check, and the employer refused to issue a new check to the participant. The participant took the employer to court and the court awarded the participant payment of benefits and attorneys' fees. [Gatlin v. National Healthcare Corp., 2001 U.S. App. LEXIS 3576 (6th Cir. 2001)]

In *Adams v. Brink's Co.* [372 F. Supp. 2d 854 (D. Va. 2005), a federal magistrate ruled that an administrative committee breached its fiduciary duty when it miscalculated a participant's benefit thereby causing him to make a decision to retire early. The court ruled that the participant should be allowed to rescind his earlier decision and have reinstated the full benefits that he would have been entitled to had he remained in employment until his normal retirement date.

### Q 27:11 What obligation does a fiduciary have when selecting an annuity provider?

Pursuant to ERISA Section 404(a)(1), fiduciaries must discharge their duties with respect to the plan solely in the interest of the participants and beneficiaries; they must also act for the exclusive purpose of providing benefits and must defray reasonable plan administration expenses (see Q 27:4). This requirement also applies to the selection of an annuity provider for purposes of a pension benefit distribution. There are certain steps that fiduciaries must take in selecting an annuity provider:

1. They must select the safest annuity available, unless under the circumstances it would be in the interests of the participants and beneficiaries to do otherwise.

2. They must conduct an objective, thorough, and analytical search for the purpose of identifying and selecting providers from which to purchase annuities. The types of factors that should be considered are as follows:

   a. The quality and diversification of the annuity provider's investment portfolio;

   b. The size of the insurer relative to the proposed contract;

   c. The level of the insurer's capital and surplus;

   d. The lines of business of the annuity provider and other indications of an insurer's exposure to liability;

   e. The structure of the annuity contract and guarantees supporting the annuities; and

   f. The availability of additional protection through state guaranty associations and the extent of their guarantees.

Selecting the safest annuity provider may not always be the most prudent if the cost of such provider is much greater than that of other providers but only marginally safer. It may also be in the interest of plan participants if selecting the less expensive provider increased the benefits of the participants. Conversely, if selecting a lower-cost provider only increases the size of a reversion to the plan sponsor, this would not be considered to be in the best interest of the plan participants. A riskier annuity provider should not be selected as a result of insufficient plan assets, but the fiduciary may condition the purchase of the annuities on additional employer contributions. [DOL Reg. § 2509.95-1]

In addition, participants and beneficiaries can bring an action for appropriate relief if the purchase of an annuity would violate fiduciary standards. [Pension Annuitants Protection Act of 1994]

## The Fiduciary

### Q 27:12   Who is a fiduciary?

The definition of fiduciary (see Q 27:1) confers fiduciary status on a person when that person is involved in management or administration of the plan, investment of plan assets, or providing investment advice. If a person exercises any of these functions or has the duty to exercise them, that person is a fiduciary of the plan.

Fiduciary status is based on function or authority. Therefore, it includes not only persons holding certain positions, such as a trustee, but also any person that in fact performs any of the functions described in the statutory definition, even if there is no title or identified relationship with the plan. [Lowen v. Tower Asset Mgmt., Inc., 8 Employee Benefits Cas. (BNA) 1289 (S.D.N.Y. 1987)]

Certain positions, such as that of a trustee, by their very nature confer fiduciary status. A position that is purely administrative in nature, however, does not confer fiduciary status. Individuals who have no power to make any decisions as to plan policy, interpretations, practices, or procedures, but who perform the following administrative functions for an employee benefit plan, within a framework of policies, interpretations, rules, practices, and procedures made by other persons, are not considered fiduciaries with respect to the plan:

- Application of rules determining eligibility for participation or benefits
- Calculation of services and compensation credits for benefits
- Preparation of employee communications material
- Maintenance of participants' service and employment records
- Preparation of reports required by government agencies
- Calculation of benefits
- Orientation of new participants and advising participants of their rights and options under the plan
- Collection of contributions and application of contributions as provided in the plan
- Preparation of reports concerning participants' benefits
- Processing of claims
- Making recommendations to others for decisions with respect to plan administration

Although such an individual is not a plan fiduciary, he or she may be subject to bonding requirements if the individual handles plan assets (see Q 27:43). [DOL Reg. § 2509.75-8, Q&A D-2]

### Q 27:13   What are the requirements regarding the number of fiduciaries a plan must have?

Each plan must have at least one named fiduciary, and if plan assets are held in trust, the plan must have at least one trustee. Except for this expressed minimum, there are no limits on the number of fiduciaries a plan can have. [DOL Reg. § 2509.75-8, Q&A FR-12]

### Q 27:14   What is the significance of the named fiduciary?

The plan must provide for one or more named fiduciaries to control and manage the operation and administration of the plan. [ERISA § 402(a)(1)] The plan instrument can actually designate the named fiduciary or can specify a procedure for the naming of one by the employer maintaining the plan. [ERISA § 402(a)(2)] The liability of a fiduciary that is not the named fiduciary, is often limited to the particular function that the party provides to the plan.

The primary responsibilities of the named fiduciary are

1. To establish a funding policy;
2. To direct trustees regarding investment of plan assets; and
3. To oversee the operation and administration of the plan.

Many plans designate the sponsoring employer as the named fiduciary. The plan document should indicate how the employer will specify particular persons to carry out certain fiduciary responsibilities under ERISA Section 405(c)(1)(B). [DOL Reg. § 2509.75-5, Q&A FR-3]

### Q 27:15   What role does a plan trustee serve?

The trustee is the party charged with the responsibility of holding and investing plan assets. Because the trustee has exclusive authority and discretion over the management and control of plan assets, the trustee is a fiduciary (see Qs 27:1 and 27:12). In some instances the trustee's powers are limited, such as when the plan expressly provides that the trustees are subject to the direction of the named fiduciary (a directed trustee) or the named fiduciary delegates management of plan assets to an investment manager (see Q 27:24). [ERISA § 403(a)]

### Q 27:16   Is the plan sponsor a fiduciary?

A plan sponsor becomes a fiduciary when it meets the definition in Q 27:1. The plan sponsor does not become a fiduciary merely because it established, amended, or terminated the plan. [Payonk v. HMW Indus., Inc., 11 Employee Benefits Cas. (BNA) 2198 (3d Cir. 1989); Amato v. Western Union Int'l, Inc., 6 Employee Benefits Cas. (BNA) 2226 (2d Cir. 1985)]

### Q 27:17   Can officers of a corporation be treated as fiduciaries?

Yes. If an officer, director, or employee of the employer sponsoring the plan exercises the authority, responsibility, or control described in ERISA Section 3(21)(A) or provides investment advice for a fee or other compensation, he or she will be a fiduciary. [DOL Reg. § 2509.75-5, Q&As D-4, D-5]

Generally, when a plan names a corporation as a fiduciary, the officers who direct the corporate acts are not, solely by virtue of their status as officers, themselves fiduciaries. Officers and directors of a plan sponsor are fiduciaries if they exercise control through the selection of the investment committee, administrative committee, or other plan officials. [Eaves v. Penn, 587 F.2d 453 (10th Cir. 1978); Marshall v. Dekeyser, 485 F. Supp. 629 (W.D. Wis. 1979)] A member of the board of directors of a corporation who selected plan fiduciaries was deemed to be a fiduciary. [Leigh v. Engle, 727 F.2d 113 (7th Cir. 1984)] The responsibility and consequently, the liability of the board or other selecting body, is limited, however, to the selection and retention of fiduciaries. In addition, if the directors are made named fiduciaries of the plan, their liability may be limited pursuant to a procedure provided for in the plan instrument for the allocation of fiduciary responsibilities among named fiduciaries or for the designation of persons other than named fiduciaries to carry out fiduciary responsibilities (see Q 27:24). [DOL Reg. § 2509.75-8, Q&A D-4] In one case, a court held that an employee of an institutional fiduciary who personally supervised and managed a plan's investment account was himself a fiduciary. [Dardaganis v. Grace Capital, Inc., 889 F.2d 1237 (2d Cir. 1989)] It appears, however, that if corporate officers are merely acting in their capacity as corporate officers, flow-through fiduciary characterization does not occur. [Confer v. Custom Eng'g Co., 952 F.2d 34 (3d Cir. 1991)]

### Q 27:18    Can lawyers, accountants, actuaries, or consultants be fiduciaries?

Generally, no. Attorneys, accountants, actuaries, and consultants generally are not considered fiduciaries, absent a showing of discretionary authority or control over plan assets. [Nieto v. Ecker, 9 Employee Benefits Cas. (BNA) 2153 (9th Cir. 1988); Yeseta v. Baima, 9 Employee Benefits Cas. (BNA) 1377 (9th Cir. 1988); Custer v. Sweeney, 20 Employee Benefits Cas. (BNA) 1569 (4th Cir. 1996)] An attorney, accountant, actuary, or consultant for a plan who neither exercises nor has any responsibilities, authority, or control described in ERISA Section 3(21)(A) and who does not provide investment advice to the plan for a fee or other compensation is not a fiduciary. [DOL Reg. § 2509.75-5, Q&A D-1]

The Ninth Circuit ruled in *Mertens v. Hewitt Associates* [14 Employee Benefits Cas. (BNA) 1973 (9th Cir. 1991)] that the mere provision of professional actuarial advice alone does not render a person an ERISA fiduciary. In this case, participants in a defined benefit pension plan claimed that an actuary violated its fiduciary duty by failing to modify actuarial assumptions to take into account increased costs of pension coverage. There were no claims that the actuary exercised control or authority over plan assets. ERISA fiduciary status focuses on function. An accounting firm was a fiduciary to the extent that it controlled whether contributions were returned to plan participants. [Blatt v. Marshall and Lasserman, 8 Employee Benefits Cas. (BNA) 1495 (2d Cir. 1987)]

### Q 27:19    Can investment advisers be fiduciaries?

Yes. An investment manager is a fiduciary by definition (see Q 27:25). The investment manager must acknowledge its fiduciary status in writing. [ERISA § 3(38)] A broker becomes a fiduciary when, without authorization and contrary to the trustee's instructions, he or she invests plan assets in highly speculative securities and disregards the trustee's instructions to liquidate. [Metzner v. D.H. Blair & Co., Inc., 8 Employee Benefits Cas. (BNA) 2159 (S.D.N.Y. 1987)]

### Q 27:20   Can someone be a fiduciary merely because of title?

Yes. Fiduciary status is based on function or authority (see Q 27:1). If a title carries with it certain responsibilities, the person is considered a fiduciary even if the person fails to act in a fiduciary capacity. The DOL has observed that some positions, such as plan administrator or trustee, may require any person who holds them to perform defined fiduciary functions and thereby undertake fiduciary status.

### Q 27:21   Can someone be a fiduciary merely because of an action?

Yes. Fiduciary status is based on function or authority (see Q 27:1). If a person exercises power or authority generally reserved to a fiduciary, the person will be considered a fiduciary even if the person fails to act in a fiduciary capacity. [DOL Reg. § 2509.75-8]

**Example.** Marty is responsible for processing claims for retirement benefits. When a plan participant is approaching retirement age, Marty provides information and benefit election forms to the participant. After the forms are complete, Marty forwards them to the insurance company that handles payment of benefits. Blair retired and returned his completed benefit election forms to Marty. Instead of forwarding the forms to the insurance company, Marty put the forms on the corner of his desk where they remained for almost two years. Because Marty's position was administrative in nature, he would not generally be viewed as a fiduciary (see Q 27:12). In this instance, however, Marty's failure to forward benefit election forms to the insurer prevented Blair from receiving his vested plan benefits for more than one and one-half years. Marty would be considered a fiduciary because he effectively exercised control over the disposition of plan assets. [See Blatt v. Marshall and Lassman, 8 Employee Benefits Cas. (BNA) 1495 (2d Cir. 1987).]

## Cofiduciaries

### Q 27:22   When can a fiduciary be held liable for the acts of another?

ERISA Section 405(a) makes a plan fiduciary liable for a breach of fiduciary responsibility by another fiduciary, even if he or she did not participate in the transaction, in the following three circumstances:

1. The fiduciary participates knowingly in, or knowingly undertakes to conceal, an act or omission of a cofiduciary that he or she knows constitutes a breach.
2. By the fiduciary's failure to comply with the prudence, diversification, or loyalty requirements or failure to follow plan documents in the course of

his or her own fiduciary duties, the fiduciary enables another fiduciary to commit a breach.

3. The fiduciary has knowledge of a breach of the other fiduciary and does not make reasonable efforts under the circumstances to remedy the breach.

Liability for a breach of fiduciary duty is extended to a cofiduciary only if that cofiduciary knowingly participated in the breach or had knowledge of the other's breach and made no effort to remedy the breach. [Davidson v. Cook, 4 Employee Benefits Cas. (BNA) 1816 (E.D. Va. 1983)] If a fiduciary has no knowledge of another's breach, he or she is not liable. [Chambers v. Kaleidoscope, Inc., Profit Sharing Plan, 7 Employee Benefits Cas. (BNA) 2628 (N.D. Ga. 1986)]

> **Example 1.** Bill and Bob are cotrustees. The trust prohibits investment in real estate. If Bill invests in real estate and tells Bob of this investment, Bob would be liable as well as Bill for the breach if Bob conceals the investment or makes no attempt to sell the real estate.

> **Example 2.** Bob allows his cotrustee, Bill, to control plan assets and does not review his actions. Bill sells plan assets and places the proceeds in his personal account. Bob is liable for a breach of fiduciary responsibility.

A fiduciary who violates ERISA Section 405(a) is jointly and severally liable for the damages caused by the cofiduciary's breach. [ERISA § 409(a)] Under the doctrine of joint and several liability, where two or more individuals together cause an injury, each one is liable to the victim for the total amount of damages. Joint and several liability can be rather expensive. In one instance, all partners of an accounting firm that served as investment manager to a profit-sharing plan were liable to the plan for losses caused by the embezzlement of plan funds by one of the firm's partners. Because the embezzling partner had been acting in the ordinary course of partnership business, the firm was liable for his acts under ERISA Sections 404 and 409. [Sheldon Co. Profit Sharing Plan v. Smith, 828 F. Supp. 1262 (W.D. Mich. 1993)] If one fiduciary is guilty of mere negligence and another is guilty of intentional misconduct, however, the court may consider relative fault in determining ultimate liability. [Chemung Canal Trust Co. v. Sovran Bank/Md, 14 Employee Benefits Cas. (BNA) 1169 (2d Cir. 1991); Cullen v. Riley, 14 Employee Benefits Cas. (BNA) 2569 (2d Cir. 1992)]

Indemnification may be applied as an equitable remedy when one fiduciary is significantly more at fault than another. [Donovan v. Robbins, 5 Employee Benefits Cas. (BNA) 2607 (7th Cir. 1985)] In this case the entire loss is shifted to the party who more justly deserves it.

Contribution among fiduciaries may also be recognized. Under the doctrine of contribution, a single fiduciary who is only partially responsible for a loss does not have to bear the cost of the entire loss, but instead shares the loss in an equitable fashion. [Chemung Canal Trust Co. v. Sovran/Bank Md, 14 Employee Benefits Cas. (BNA) 1169 (2d Cir. 1991)]

### Q 27:23 What should a fiduciary do to correct a breach of fiduciary duty by another fiduciary?

A fiduciary must make reasonable efforts to remedy a known breach by another fiduciary. [Davidson v. Cook, 4 Employee Benefits Cas. (BNA) 1816 (E.D. Va. 1983)] In ERISA Interpretive Bulletin 75-5 [DOL Reg. § 2509.75-5], the DOL provides guidance regarding remedial measures necessary to prevent cofiduciary breaches. Cofiduciaries must take all reasonable and legal steps to prevent the breach. These steps might include obtaining an injunction in federal court under ERISA Section 502(a)(3), notifying the DOL, notifying the plan sponsor, or publicizing the breach. Furthermore, all meetings concerning management and control of plan assets should be documented and any objections alleging potential violations of fiduciary responsibilities should be made part of the record. Resignation because of a breach by a cofiduciary will not generally discharge the duty to make reasonable efforts to remedy a breach. [DOL Reg. § 2509.75-5, Q&A FR-10]

### Q 27:24 Can a fiduciary delegate responsibility?

Yes. Fiduciary status does not confer absolute liability for all fiduciary functions. A fiduciary is liable only to the extent he or she performs a defined function or has power to do so.

A fiduciary can delegate responsibility in either one of the following instances:

1. *Allocation.* Named fiduciaries who allocate fiduciary responsibilities among themselves in accordance with a procedure set forth in the plan generally are not liable for acts of other fiduciaries carrying out such allocated responsibilities. [ERISA §§ 402(b), (c), 405(c)]

2. *Delegation.* If an investment manager has been appointed under ERISA Section 402(c)(3), a trustee escapes fiduciary liability for acts or omissions of the investment manager. [ERISA § 405(d)(1)]

Allocation or delegation can occur only under specific circumstances. A plan must explicitly allow allocation or delegation and supply a procedure for it. If the plan instrument does not describe such a procedure, any attempted allocation has no effect in relieving a named fiduciary from any liability. [ERISA §§ 402(b), (c), 405(c)] If directors of an employer sponsoring the plan are the named fiduciaries of the plan, their liability can be limited by procedures established in the plan document for allocating fiduciary responsibilities among named fiduciaries or for designating others to carry out fiduciary responsibilities. [DOL Reg. § 2509.75-8, Q&A D-4] Even if named fiduciaries allocate responsibilities or designate others to perform these functions, they are liable for breaches in the establishment and implementation of the allocation or designation procedure. [DOL Reg. § 2509.75-8, Q&As FR-13, FR-14]

ERISA Section 405(c)(1) does not allow named fiduciaries to delegate trustee responsibilities. Trustees must have exclusive authority and discretion to manage and control plan assets unless an investment manager has been appointed or the trustees are subject to the direction of a named fiduciary. A trustee can delegate a trustee responsibility to an investment manager (see Q 27:25). [ERISA §§ 403(a)(2), 402(c)(3)] If the trustee delegates investment management and control to an investment manager, the plan trustee has no further responsibility for managing the assets and incurs no liability for the acts or omissions of the investment manager. [ERISA § 405(d)(1)] After an investment manager is appointed, the investment manager cannot claim it had no power to control and manage the assets pursuant to an oral arrangement, thus relieving the manager of any liability. [Lowen v. Tower Asset Mgmt., Inc., 8 Employee Benefits Cas. (BNA) 2457 (2d Cir. 1987)]

### Q 27:25   What type of person or entity qualifies as an investment manager?

The term *investment manager* means any fiduciary, other than a trustee or named fiduciary, who:

1. Has the power to manage, acquire, or dispose of any asset of a plan;
2. Is registered as an investment adviser under the Investment Advisers Act of 1940; is a bank, as defined in that Act; or is a qualified insurance company; and
3. Has acknowledged in writing that he or she is a fiduciary with respect to the plan.

[ERISA § 3(38)]

A person who is not registered under the Investment Advisers Act of 1940 because of an exemption from registration (and who is not a financial institution) does not qualify as an investment manager. [DOL Reg. § 2509.75-8, Q&A FR-6] A person who is registered only as a broker-dealer under the Securities Exchange Act of 1934 cannot serve as an investment manager. [DOL Op. Ltr. 76-20]

### Q 27:26   What are the ongoing responsibilities of a fiduciary who engages an investment manager?

The fiduciary must exercise prudence in the selection of the investment manager and must properly monitor the manager. [Whitfield v. Cohen, 682 F. Supp. 188 (S.D.N.Y. 1988)] A named fiduciary has a duty to monitor the performance of the investment manager. [Brock v. Berman, 8 Employee Benefits Cas. (BNA) 1689 (D. Mass. 1987)] At reasonable intervals the performance of the manager should be reviewed by the appointing fiduciary in such manner as may be reasonably expected to ensure that the manager's performance has been in compliance with the terms of the plan and statutory standards and satisfies the needs of the plan. No single monitoring procedure will be appropriate in all cases; the procedure adopted may vary in accordance with the nature of the plan and other facts and circumstances relevant to the choice of the procedure. [DOL Reg. § 2509.75-8, Q&A FR-17]

### Q 27:27   What is ERISA Section 404(c), and can it be applied to a defined benefit plan?

ERISA Section 404(c) is a provision that offers relief from fiduciary responsibility for plan losses in individual account plans because each participant is responsible for managing the investments of their own accounts. [DOL Reg. § 2550.404(c)-1(a)] A defined benefit plan is not an individual account plan, and therefore this relief is not available to fiduciaries of defined benefit plans.

### Q 27:28   Can a nonfiduciary become liable as a fiduciary?

No. Until fairly recently courts had extended liability to nonfiduciaries who had knowingly participated in a fiduciary's breach of duty under ERISA. [Freund v. Marshall & Ilsley Bank, 1 Employee Benefits Cas. (BNA) 1898 (W.D. Wis. 1979)] In *Mertens v. Hewitt Associates* [948 F.2d 607 (9th Cir. 1991) aff'd, 113 S. Ct. 2063 (1993)] the Supreme Court held that ERISA does not permit monetary damages against nonfiduciaries. *Mertens* involved claims arising from the termination of Kaiser Steel Corporation's pension plan by the Pension Benefit Guarantee Corporation (PBGC) after the plan's assets became insufficient to meet its liabilities. Plaintiffs claimed that the actuaries, Hewitt Associates, improperly permitted the plan sponsor to select actuarial assumptions that reduced the funding obligation and ultimately resulted in insufficient assets.

### Q 27:29   Does a nonfiduciary have an obligation to alert the DOL or plan participants when it is aware of a breach of fiduciary duty?

No. Nonfiduciaries, such as third-party administrators (TPAs), actuaries, attorneys, accountants, and others who may be aware of a breach of fiduciary duty are not required to report it to the DOL or to the plan participants. [CSA 401 (k) Plan v. Pension Prof'ls, Inc., 195 F.3d 1135 (9th Cir. 1999)] The TPA should be very careful not to take any actions that would render it a fiduciary, and any service agreements should be clear that the TPA has no authority to make decisions, but has authority only to advise.

### Q 27:30   Can a successor fiduciary become responsible for acts of the prior fiduciary?

No. ERISA Section 409(b) provides that a fiduciary is not liable for any breach that occurred before he or she became a fiduciary or after he or she ceased to be a fiduciary. If, however, a successor fiduciary learns of a breach of duty and fails to take whatever action is reasonable and appropriate under the circumstances to remedy the breach, the failure to act may constitute a separate breach (see Q 27:22).

## Prohibited Transactions

### Q 27:31    What is a prohibited transaction?

A *prohibited transaction* is a transaction with a party-in-interest (see Q 27:33) that is prohibited under ERISA Section 406(a). A fiduciary cannot cause the plan to engage in any of the following transactions if the fiduciary knows or should know the transaction involves a party-in-interest:

1. Any sale, exchange, or leasing of any property between a plan and a party-in-interest [ERISA § 406(a)(1)(A)];

2. The lending of money or other extension of credit between a plan and a party-in-interest [ERISA § 406(a)(1)(B)];

3. The furnishing of goods, services, or facilities between a plan and a party-in-interest [ERISA § 406(a)(1)(C)];

4. Any transfer of any plan assets to a party-in-interest, any use of any plan assets by a party-in-interest, or any use of plan assets for the benefit of a party-in-interest [ERISA § 406(a)(1)(D)]; or

5. An acquisition or retention of employer securities or employer real property in violation of ERISA Section 407(a) [ERISA §§ 406(a)(1)(E), 406(a)(2)].

Transactions are prohibited if they are direct or indirect transactions with a party-in-interest. In *McDougall v. Donovan* [3 Employee Benefits Cas. (BNA) 2385 (N.D. Ill. 1982)], in which the trustees acquired a jet from a firm that had just acquired it from a union conference whose members were plan participants, the court found a prohibited transaction. The court noted that the "indirect transaction" prohibition could not be interpreted narrowly; otherwise virtually any transaction prohibited directly could be legitimized by insertion of a third party who could incidentally profit from its role.

### Q 27:32    Does ERISA prohibit other actions by fiduciaries?

Yes. In addition to the five specific prohibited transactions involving parties-in-interest under ERISA Section 406(a) (see Q 27:31), ERISA prohibits fiduciaries from engaging in various acts of self-dealing or conflicts of interest. A fiduciary cannot do the following:

1. Deal with plan assets in his or her own interest.

2. Act in a transaction involving a plan on behalf of a person whose interests are adverse to the interests of the plan, its participants, or its beneficiaries.

3. Receive any consideration for his or her own personal account from any party dealing with the plan in connection with a transaction involving the plan's assets.

[ERISA § 406(b)]

Trustees who negotiated a loan between two plans for which they served as trustees violated ERISA Section 406(b)(2) because the interests of borrower and lender are by definition adverse. [Cutaiar v. Marshall, 1 Employee Benefits Cas. (BNA) 2153 (3d Cir. 1979)]

### Q 27:33    Who is a *party-in-interest*?

A *party-in-interest* is:

1.  A fiduciary of the plan [ERISA § 3(14)(A)];
2.  A person providing services to the plan [ERISA § 3(14)(B)];
3.  An employer any of whose employees are covered by the plan [ERISA § 3(14)(C)];
4.  An employee organization any of whose members are covered by the plan [ERISA § 3(14)(D)];
5.  A 50 percent or more owner of an employer in item #3 or of an employee organization in item #4 [ERISA § 3(14)(E)];
6.  A spouse, ancestor, lineal descendent, or spouse of a lineal descendant of any of the persons listed above except an employee organization [ERISA § 3(14)(F), 3(15)];
7.  A corporation, partnership, trust, or estate 50 percent of which is owned directly or indirectly by the persons mentioned above (other than relatives) [ERISA § 3(14)(G)];
8.  An employee, officer, director, or 10 percent or more shareholder of any of the entities mentioned above except a fiduciary or a relative [ERISA § 3(14)(H)]; or
9.  A 10 percent or more partner or joint venturer of any entity listed above except a fiduciary or relative [ERISA § 3(14)(I)].

### Q 27:34    What is a *disqualified person*?

A *disqualified person* is the Code's counterpart to a party-in-interest (see Q 27:33). The Code imposes excise taxes on disqualified persons who participate in specific prohibited transactions with the plan. A disqualified person within the meaning of Code Section 4975(e)(2) includes generally the same group of individuals who would be considered a party-in-interest. An employee, however, is a disqualified person only if the employee is highly compensated (i.e., earning 10 percent or more of the total yearly wages of the employer). [I.R.C. § 4975(e)(2)(H)]

### Q 27:35    If an employer contributes property, such as marketable securities, to the plan, are there any implications under the prohibited transaction rules?

Yes. In *Commissioner v. Keystone Consolidated Industries, Inc.* [113 S. Ct. 2006 (1993)], the Supreme Court held that an employer's contribution of unencumbered real property to a defined benefit plan was a sale or exchange under Code Section 4975 where the stated fair market value of the property was credited against the employer's funding obligation to the plan.

An in-kind contribution to a defined benefit plan is considered a prohibited transaction by the DOL, regardless of whether the value of the contribution reduces the sponsor's funding obligation for the plan year in which the contribution is made, if the contribution is treated as a credit to a plan's funding standard account. The DOL prohibits such treatment because it would have the effect of reducing the sponsor's funding obligations in the future. [DOL Reg. § 2509.94-3(b)]

### Q 27:36   Do the prohibited transaction rules apply if fair market value is paid?

Apparently, yes. According to the court in *McDougall v. Donovan* [3 Employee Benefits Cas. (BNA) 2385 (N.D. Ill. 1982)], Congress did not intend to permit transactions that have independent business purposes, or that are fair under some independent measure. The congressional intent in enacting the prohibited transaction provision was to eliminate *all* transactions with the potential to bias the independent judgment of plan fiduciaries. It does not matter whether any harm results from the transaction. Congress wanted to prevent transactions that offered a high potential for loss of plan assets or for insider abuse. [Marshall v. Kelly, 1 Employee Benefits Cas. (BNA) 1850 (W.D. Okla. 1978); Cutaiar v. Marshall, 1 Employee Benefits Cas. (BNA) 2153 (3d Cir. 1979)]

### Q 27:37   What are the penalties for engaging in a prohibited transaction?

The Code imposes an excise tax on any disqualified person who participates in a prohibited transaction. Unlike the corresponding provision in ERISA, Code Section 4975 treats a transaction as prohibited regardless of whether the fiduciary authorizing the transaction on behalf of the plan knew or had reason to know that the transaction was prohibited. Currently, the initial tax is equal to 15 percent of the amount involved. The initial-level prohibited transaction tax was increased from 5 percent to 10 percent for prohibited transactions occurring between August 20, 1996, and August 5, 1997, and to 15 percent for prohibited transactions occurring after August 5, 1997. [Small Business Job Protection Act of 1996 (SBJPA), § 1453, Pub. L. No. 104-188]

If there is no correction of the transaction within the taxable period, there is an additional tax of 100 percent of the amount involved. [I.R.C. § 4975(b)]

The *amount involved* means the greater of the amount given or received, valuing any property involved at fair market value on the date of the transaction. *Correction* means undoing the transaction to the extent possible, but in any case placing the plan in a financial position no worse than it would have been in if the disqualified person had acted under the highest fiduciary standards. [I.R.C. § 4975(f)]

The ERISA prohibited transaction provisions focus on the fiduciary causing the plan to deal with a party-in-interest. In contrast, the excise taxes under the Code fall on the disqualified person.

### Q 27:38  Can penalties be waived?

Yes. If the transaction is corrected within 90 days of the mailing of the assessment of the second-tier (100 percent) tax, the tax is abated or refunded. [I.R.C. § 4961] When a plan actually made money (i.e., the transaction "corrected itself," since the returns exceeded those that would have been achieved if the investment had been of the highest fiduciary standard), the second-tier tax was abated. [Zabolotny v. Commissioner, 17 Employee Benefits Cas. (BNA) 1384 (8th Cir. 1993)]

### Q 27:39  Are there any exemptions or exclusions from the prohibited transaction rules?

ERISA Section 408 provides both administrative and statutory exemptions from the prohibited transaction provisions. In particular, ERISA Section 408(b) provides the following statutory exemptions:

1. Loans to plan participants or beneficiaries (see Q 27:41);
2. Contracts for office space or legal, accounting, or other services, provided that no more than reasonable compensation is paid;
3. Loans to an employee stock ownership plan (ESOP);
4. Investment of plan assets in deposits bearing a reasonable rate of return in a financial institution that serves as a plan fiduciary;
5. Purchase of life insurance from an employer maintaining the plan (see Q 27:42);
6. Provision of ancillary services by a financial institution that is a fiduciary provided that no more than reasonable compensation is paid for the services;
7. Exercise of a privilege to convert securities if the plan receives no less than adequate consideration pursuant to the conversion;
8. Transactions between the plan and a common or collective trust fund maintained by a party-in-interest that is a financial institution;
9. Distributions of plan assets in accordance with the terms of the plan and ERISA Section 4044;
10. Transactions involving withdrawal liabilities;
11. Merger of multiemployer plans;
12. Sale of certain stock that are not qualifying employer securities [I.R.C. § 4975(e)(8)];
13. Transfers of excess assets to a retiree health account qualified under Code Section 420;

14. Provision of investment advice to participants in an individual account plan;

15. Block trades between the plan and a party-in-interest;

16. Purchase or sale between the plan and a party-in-interest when the transaction is made electronically;

17. Certain transactions between the plan and a service provider, as long as adequate consideration is paid;

18. Foreign exchange transactions; and

19. Cross-trading of investments arranged by the same investment manager to different retirement plans.

Also, a 14-day grace period is allowed for correcting prohibited transactions once they are known to the fiduciaries, as long as it does not involve employer securities or employer property.

Under each of these circumstances, special conditions must be satisfied. [ERISA § 408(b)] For example, ERISA Section 408(b)(2) exempts contracts for office space from the prohibited transaction provisions if:

1. The office space is necessary for the operation of the plan;

2. The office space is furnished under a contract or arrangement that is reasonable; and

3. No more than reasonable compensation is paid for such office space or service.

DOL regulations indicate that a contract is not reasonable if it does not permit termination by the plan without penalty to the plan on reasonably short notice under the circumstances to prevent the plan from becoming locked into an arrangement that has become disadvantageous. [DOL Reg. § 2550.408b-2(c)]

Apart from statutory exemptions, ERISA Section 408(a) allows for administrative exemptions by the Secretary of Labor from all or part of ERISA Sections 406 and 407(a). Before granting an exemption, the Secretary must publish the proposed exemption in the Federal Register, provide an opportunity for a hearing so that interested persons can present their views, and make a determination on the record granting or denying the application.

### Q 27:40   Can the plan sponsor loan money to the plan if the plan is having liquidity problems?

Possibly, yes. Under an amendment to Prohibited Transaction Exemption 1980-26, a plan sponsor may loan money to the plan if certain criteria are met. The loan must be interest free, must involve a purpose incidental to the ordinary operation of the plan or to ordinary operating expenses, and is made to deal with the plan's liquidity problems. In addition, if the term of the loan extends 60 days or more, the loan must be made pursuant to a written loan agreement.

### Q 27:41   Under what conditions can a participant borrow money from a defined benefit plan?

Loans to participants are not treated as prohibited transactions if they meet the following conditions:

1. They are available to participants and beneficiaries on a reasonably equivalent basis.
2. They are not made available to highly compensated employees in an amount greater than the amount available to other employees.
3. They are made in accordance with specific plan provisions.
4. They bear a reasonable interest rate.
5. They are adequately secured.

[ERISA § 408(b)(1)]

Before the Economic Growth and Tax Relief Reconciliation Act of 2001 (EGTRRA), certain sole proprietors, partners, and owners of S corporations were prohibited from receiving participant loans. However, this restriction has been eliminated: now all participants are eligible to receive a participant loan without its being considered a prohibited transaction. [EGTRRA § 612]

### Q 27:42   Can a participant purchase insurance on his or her life from the defined benefit plan?

Yes. A plan can sell an individual life insurance contract to the insured participant, a relative of the participant who is the beneficiary under the contract, or another plan without violating the prohibited transaction rules. To satisfy the exemption the following conditions must exist:

1. The contract would, but for the sale, be surrendered by the plan.
2. With respect to a sale of a policy to the employer, a relative of the insured, or another plan, the participant insured under the policy is first informed of the proposed sale and is given the opportunity to purchase the contract from the plan; the participant also delivers a written document to the plan stating that he or she elects not to purchase the policy and consents to the sale by the plan of such policy to such employer, relative, or other plan.
3. The amount received by the plan as consideration for the sale is at least equal to the amount necessary to put the plan in the same cash position as it would have been in if it had retained the contract, surrendered it, and made any distribution owing to the participant of his or her vested interest under the plan.

[PTE 92-06, 57 Fed. Reg. 5189 (Feb. 12, 1992)]

## Fiduciary Liability

### Q 27:43   Are there any bonding requirements for fiduciaries?

Yes. ERISA Section 412 requires every fiduciary and every person who handles plan assets to be bonded. This bond, known as a *fidelity bond,* is intended to protect the plan in the event of loss due to fraudulent or dishonest acts of fiduciaries. A general bond for employee dishonesty may be sufficient to meet the bonding requirement.

The amount of the bond must be at least 10 percent of the plan assets as of the preceding plan year except that the bond cannot be less than $1,000 and generally need not exceed $500,000. The maximum bond is increased to $1 million for plans that hold employer securities for plan years after December 31, 2007. The Secretary of Labor can require a bond in excess of $500,000 after notice and providing an opportunity for a hearing. [ERISA § 412(a)] Plan assets can be used to purchase the bond. [DOL Reg. § 2509.75-5, Q&A FR-9] A bond is not required for any entity that is registered as a broker or a dealer if the broker or dealer is subject to the fidelity bond requirements of a self-regulatory organization. [ERISA § 412(a)(2)]

In addition, the amount of the bond may need to be increased for a small plan to avoid the requirement to engage an independent qualified public accountant (IQPA). One of the requirements to be eligible for this waiver is that either at least 95 percent of plan assets must constitute "qualifying plan assets" or any person who handles nonqualified plan assets must be bonded for at least this amount. [DOL Reg. § 2520.104-46(b)(1)(i)] In such a case, the bond is not limited to the $500,000 maximum. (See chapter 29 for more information.)

### Q 27:44   Who can sue a fiduciary?

ERISA Section 502(a) provides a broad range of possible civil enforcement opportunities. Plan participants or beneficiaries can sue to obtain benefits, enforce rights, or clarify rights to future benefits under the terms of the plan. Participants, beneficiaries, or fiduciaries can also sue to enjoin or obtain damages for any act or omission that violates ERISA or the terms of the plan. The DOL can also bring an action for violations involving the reporting, disclosure, or fiduciary responsibility parts of ERISA.

### Q 27:45   Can a fiduciary be held personally liable?

Yes. Under ERISA Section 409, a fiduciary must personally make good plan losses suffered by the plan as a result of a breach of any fiduciary duties. A fiduciary can also be required to restore to the plan any profits the fiduciary may have personally realized as a result of a misuse of plan assets. The fiduciary may be subject to other equitable or remedial relief as a court may deem appropriate, including removal from office. Either party may recover its attorneys' fee from the other party at the court's discretion. [ERISA § 502(g)(1)]

### Q 27:46 Can a fiduciary who is also a participant in a plan lose his or her benefit?

Yes. A participant's benefit can be reduced if a court requires payment because of:

1. A judgment or conviction of a crime involving the plan;
2. A civil action (or consent order or decree) entered by a court in an action for fiduciary breach; or
3. A settlement agreement entered into by the participant and the DOL or PBGC in connection with a breach of fiduciary duty.

[ERISA § 206(d)(4)]

A pension fund set off pension benefits due a former trustee when the trustee was convicted of engaging in a conspiracy to receive kickbacks in exchange for channeling $20 million of a fund's assets to a Florida mortgage company. [Coar v. Kazimir, 16 Employee Benefits Cas. (BNA) 1904 (3d Cir. 1993)]

### Q 27:47 Can additional penalties be imposed?

Yes. Courts have broad discretion in fashioning equitable relief to make the plan whole, including recision of unlawful transactions and recovery of moneys lost to the plan. [Marshall v. Snyder, 1 Employee Benefits Cas. (BNA) 1878 (E.D. N.Y. 1977)] Punitive damages are generally not considered other equitable or remedial relief; thus, a plan cannot recover punitive damages for a breach of fiduciary duties. [Sommers Drug Stores Co. Employee Profit Sharing Trust v. Corrigan Enters., Inc., 7 Employee Benefits Cas. (BNA) 1782 (5th Cir. 1986)]

The Secretary of Labor can impose a 20 percent penalty on the amount recovered from a fiduciary or any other person involved in a breach of fiduciary duty if the amount is recovered pursuant to a settlement agreement with the Secretary or is ordered to be paid to a plan or its participants by a court in proceedings instituted by the Secretary. [ERISA § 502(l)]

A criminal action can also be brought. A person can be fined or imprisoned for willful violation of reporting and disclosure requirements or embezzling or stealing plan assets. [ERISA § 501]

### Q 27:48 What type of insurance can a fiduciary get?

ERISA Section 410(b) allows the following:

1. A plan can purchase insurance for its fiduciaries or itself to cover liability or losses occurring by reason of the act or omission of a fiduciary if such insurance permits recourse by the insurer against the fiduciary in the case of a breach of a fiduciary obligation.
2. A fiduciary can purchase insurance for his or her own account.
3. An employer can purchase insurance to cover potential liability of persons who serve in a fiduciary capacity.

### Q 27:49  Can a plan sponsor indemnify a fiduciary?

Generally, no. Any agreement that purports to relieve a fiduciary from responsibility or liability for a duty imposed by ERISA is void because it is against public policy. [ERISA § 410(a)] Indemnification agreements are not prohibited if the fiduciary remains responsible and liable for his or her acts or omissions with the indemnifying party merely satisfying the liability. [DOL Reg. § 2509.75-4]

A plan provision indemnifying members of the board of directors, plan administrative committee, trustees, and others to whom fiduciary responsibility was allocated from liability for a breach of fiduciary duty, except for liabilities and claims arising from willful misconduct, was void. [Donovan v. Cunningham, 3 Employee Benefits Cas. (BNA) 1641 (S.D. Tex. 1982)]

### Q 27:50  Can a fiduciary voluntarily correct a breach of duty?

Yes. Under the Voluntary Fiduciary Correction Program (VFC) [67 Fed. Reg. 15,061], a fiduciary that voluntarily corrects a breach of duty can obtain a no-action letter from the Pension and Welfare Benefits Administration (PWBA) under which the PWBA agrees not to initiate a civil investigation under ERISA Title I regarding the applicant's responsibility for any transaction described in the no-action letter, or assess a civil penalty under ERISA Section 502(l) on the correction amount paid to the plan.

To be eligible for VFC relief, neither the plan nor the applicant can be under investigation by the PWBA, and the application must not contain evidence of potential criminal violations.

### Q 27:51  Is the relief granted under VFC available for all breaches of fiduciary duty?

No. Currently, VFC relief is available only for specific violations, which are listed in Section 7 of the procedure:

1. Delinquent participant contributions (including 401(k) contributions);
2. Loans at fair market value to a party-in-interest;
3. Below-market loans to a person who is not a party-in-interest;
4. Below-market loans to a party-in-interest with respect to the plan;
5. Below-market loans due solely to a delay in perfecting a plan's security interest;
6. Purchase of an asset by the plan from a party-in-interest;
7. Sale of an asset by the plan to a party-in-interest;
8. Sale and leaseback of real property to an employer;
9. Purchase of property from a person who is not a party-in-interest for a price other than the fair market value;

10. Sale of property to a person who is not a party-in-interest for a price other than the fair market value;

11. Payment of benefits without properly valuing the plan assets on which payment is based;

12. Duplicative, excessive, or unnecessary compensation paid by a plan; and

13. Payment of dual compensation to a plan fiduciary.

Guidance is provided in the procedure on fair market value determinations, correction amounts, and lost earnings. An application for relief must include a completed checklist, which is provided in Appendix B of the procedure.

Relief under VFC does not extend to criminal conduct.

### Q 27:52  Does the relief granted by VFC extend to relieving fiduciaries of any liability due to lawsuits brought by plan participants?

No. The no-action letter would not bar other persons (e.g., participants) from seeking redress under ERISA.

## Investments

### Q 27:53  Does a defined benefit plan need an investment policy?

Yes. Every plan must provide a procedure for establishing and carrying out a funding policy and method consistent with the plan's objectives. [ERISA § 402(b)]

### Q 27:54  Are directed investments permitted in a defined benefit plan?

No. The separate account feature is a feature of a defined contribution pension plan. Participant-directed investments are not permitted in defined benefit pension plans.

## Correction of Plan Defects

### Q 27:55  Can a plan correct errors in operation or documentation after the fact and still protect its qualified status?

Yes. In Revenue Procedure 2006-27 [2006-22 I.R.B. 945] the IRS has outlined the procedures that must be followed in their Employee Plans Compliance Resolution System (EPCRS). The components of EPCRS are the Self-Correction Program (SCP), the Voluntary Correction Program (VCP), and the Audit Closing Agreement Program (Audit CAP).

### Q 27:56   What is the Self-Correction Program (SCP)?

A plan sponsor that has established compliance practices and procedures may, at any time without paying any fee or sanction, correct insignificant operational failures under a defined benefit plan. In addition, in the case of a plan that is the subject of a favorable determination letter from the IRS, the plan sponsor generally may correct even significant operational failures without payment of any fee or sanction.

### Q 27:57   What factors are considered when determining if failures are insignificant?

The factors to be considered in determining whether or not an operational failure under a plan is insignificant include, but are not limited to:

1. Whether other failures occurred during the same period as the one being examined (for this purpose, a failure is not considered to have occurred more than once merely because more than one participant is affected by the failure);
2. The percentage of plan assets and contributions involved in the failure;
3. The number of years the failure occurred;
4. The number of participants affected relative to the total number of participants in the plan;
5. The number of participants affected as a result of the failure relative to the number of participants who could have been affected by the failure;
6. Whether correction was made within a reasonable time after discovery of the failure; and
7. The reason for the failure (for example, data errors such as errors in the transcription of data, the transposition of numbers, or minor arithmetic errors).

No single factor is determinative. Additionally, the IRS has stated that factors (2), (4), and (5) should not be interpreted to exclude small businesses. [Rev. Proc. 2006-27, 2006-27 I.R.B. 945 § 8.02 ]

### Q 27:58   What is the Voluntary Correction with Service Approval Program (VCP)?

A plan sponsor, at any time before audit, may pay a limited fee and receive the Service's approval for correction of a defined benefit plan. This program is open to correct most failures, even those available for correction under SCP. It is not available if the failure is identified under audit. Under VCP, there are special procedures for anonymous submissions and group submissions.

### Q 27:59   What is the Correction on Audit Program (CAP)?

If a failure (other than a failure corrected through SCP or VCP) is identified on audit, the Plan Sponsor may correct the failure and pay a sanction. The sanction imposed will bear a reasonable relationship to the nature, extent, and severity of the failure, taking into account the extent to which correction occurred before audit.

### Q 27:60   What kinds of errors may be corrected in a defined benefit plan through EPCRS?

The following are some of the errors that can be corrected:

- Failure to satisfy Code Section 415(b) (see Q 27:61)
- Failure to properly provide the minimum top-heavy benefit under Code Section 416 to non-key employees (see Q 27:62)
- Exclusion of an eligible employee from all contributions or accruals under the plan for one or more plan years (see Q 27:63)
- Failure to timely pay the minimum distribution required under Section 401(a)(9) (see Q 27:64)
- Failure to obtain participant and/or spousal consent for a distribution subject to the participant and spousal consent rules under Code Sections 401(a)(11), 411(a)(11), and 417 (see Q 27:65)

[Rev. Proc. 2006-27, 2006-22 I.R.B. 945]

### Q 27:61   How can a plan sponsor correct a Code Section 415(b) failure?

There are two possible ways to correct a Code Section 415(b) failure:

1. Return of overpayment method, or
2. Adjustment of future payments method.

Under the "return of overpayment method" the employer takes reasonable steps to have the overpayment (with appropriate interest) returned by the recipient to the plan and reduces future benefit payments (if any) due to the employee to reflect Code Section 415(b). If the amount returned by the recipient is less than the overpayment, adjusted for earnings at the plan's earnings rate, then the employer or another person must contribute the difference to the plan. In addition, the employer must notify the recipient that the overpayment was not eligible for favorable tax treatment accorded to distributions from qualified plans (and, specifically, was not eligible for tax-free rollover). (See Q 27:66 for more information regarding the tax treatment of overpayments.)

Under the "adjustment of future payments method," future payments to the recipient are reduced so that they do not exceed the Code Section 415(b) maximum limit and an additional reduction is made to recoup the overpayment (over a period not longer than the remaining payment period) so that the actuarial present value of the additional reduction is equal to the overpayment plus interest at the interest rate used by the plan to determine actuarial equivalence. If the employee is receiving payments in the form of a joint and survivor annuity, with the employee's spouse to receive a life annuity upon the employee's death equal to a percentage (e.g., 75 percent) of the amount being paid to the employee, the reduction of future annuity payments to reflect Code Section 415(b) reduces the amount of benefits payable during the lives of both the employee and spouse, but any reduction to recoup overpayments made to the employee does not reduce the amount of the spouse's survivor benefit. Thus, the spouse's benefit will be based on the previous specified percentage (e.g., 75 percent) of the maximum permitted under Code Section 415(b), instead of the reduced annual periodic amount payable to the employee.

**Example 1.** ErrorsRUs maintains a defined benefit plan funded solely through employer contributions. The plan provides that the benefits of employees are limited to the maximum amount permitted under Code Section 415(b), disregarding cost-of-living adjustments under Code Section 415(d) after benefit payments have commenced. At the beginning of the 1998 plan year, Jim retired and started receiving an annual straight life annuity of $140,000 from the plan. Due to an administrative error, the annual amount received by Jim for 1998 included an overpayment of $10,000 (because the Section 415(b)(1)(A) limit for 1998 was $130,000). This error was discovered at the beginning of 1999.

*Correction:* The employer uses the adjustment of future payments correction method to correct the failure to satisfy the limit in Section 415(b). Future annuity benefit payments to Jim are reduced so that they do not exceed the Code Section 415(b) maximum limit, and, in addition, Jim's future benefit payments from the plan are actuarially reduced to recoup the overpayment. Accordingly, Jim's future benefit payments from the plan are reduced to $130,000 and further reduced by $1,000 annually for life, beginning in 1999. The annual benefit amount is reduced by $1,000 annually for life because, for Jim, the actuarial present value of a benefit of $1,000 annually for life commencing in 1999 is equal to the sum of $10,000 and interest at the rate used by the plan to determine actuarial equivalence beginning with the date of the first overpayment and ending with the date the reduced annuity payment begins. Thus, Jim's remaining benefit payments are reduced so that he receives $129,000 for 1999, and for each year thereafter.

**Example 2.** The facts are the same as in Example 1, but Jim instead received a lump-sum distribution in 1998 that exceeded the Code Section 415 maximum by $110,000.

*Correction:* ErrorsRUs uses the return of overpayment correction method to correct the Code Section 415(b) failure. Thus, the employer notifies Jim of the $110,000 overpayment and that the overpayment was not eligible for favorable tax treatment accorded to distributions from qualified plans (and, specifically, was not eligible for tax-free rollover). The notice also informs Jim that the overpayment (with interest at the rate used by the plan to calculate the single-sum payment) is owed to the plan. The employer takes reasonable steps to have the overpayment (with interest at the rate used by the plan to calculate the single-sum payment) paid to the plan. Jim pays the $110,000 (plus the requested interest) to the plan. It is determined that the plan's earnings rate for the relevant period was two percentage points more than the rate used by the plan to calculate the single-sum payment. Accordingly, ErrorsRUs contributes the difference to the plan.

### Q 27:62  How does an employer correct an error in accruing minimum top-heavy benefits?

In a defined benefit plan, the minimum required benefit must be accrued in the manner provided in the plan. Therefore, non-key employees' accrued benefits are increased to the amount necessary to satisfy the minimum top-heavy requirements of Code Section 416.

### Q 27:63  How does an employer correct an omission of an eligible employee?

The permitted correction method is to provide benefit accruals for the employees excluded from a defined benefit plan. There are no earnings adjustments to make as the accrual is in the normal form of benefit payable at normal retirement age.

### Q 27:64  How does an employer correct a failure to make a minimum required distribution?

In a defined benefit plan, the permitted correction method is to distribute the required minimum distributions, plus an interest payment representing the loss of use of such amounts. The minimum should be calculated under the normal rules of the plan for such distributions.

### Q 27:65  How does an employer correct a failure to obtain proper participant or spousal consent to a distribution?

The permitted correction method is to give each affected participant a choice between providing informed consent for the distribution actually made or receiving a qualified joint and survivor annuity. In the event that participant and/or spousal consent (of whom the participant was married to at the time of the distribution) is required but cannot be obtained (because the spouse refuses to consent, does not respond to the notice provided, or cannot be located), the participant must receive a qualified joint and survivor annuity based on the monthly amount that would have been provided under the plan at his or her retirement date. This annuity may be actuarially reduced to take into account distributions already received by the participant. However, the portion of the qualified joint and survivor annuity payable to the spouse upon the death of the participant may not be actuarially reduced to take into account prior distributions to the participant.

**Example 1.** John, a married participant, retired and was entitled to receive a QJSA of $600 per month payable for life with $300 per month payable to his spouse, Jane, upon John's death. However, John elected to receive a lump-sum distribution of the present value of his straight life annuity. However, the plan did not receive proper consent for this distribution from Jane. The plan can either try to obtain consent now from Jane to the lump-sum distribution already made, or else it will be required to provide Jane with a survivor benefit of $300 per month payable for her life upon the death of John. (The $600 annuity benefit payable to John may be offset by the actuarial equivalent lump-sum distribution he already received.)

An alternative permitted correction method is to give each affected participant a choice between:

1. Providing informed consent for the distribution actually made;
2. Receiving a QJSA; or
3. Providing a single-sum payment equal to the actuarial present value of that survivor annuity benefit (calculated using the applicable interest rate and mortality table under Code Section 417(e)(3)).

**Example 2.** Assume the same facts as in Example 1. If the actuarial present value of a $300 per month annuity payable to the spouse for the spouse's life beginning upon the participant's death is $7,837 (calculated using the applicable interest rate and mortality table under Code Section 417(e)(3), and based on the assumptions that the participant is age 65, that the spouse is age 62, and that the applicable interest rate is 6 percent), then the single-sum payment under clause 3 above is equal to $7,837. If the spouse elects to receive the single-sum payment, then the payment is treated in the same manner as a distribution under Code Section 402(c)(9) for purposes of rolling over the payment to an IRA or other eligible retirement plan. [Rev. Proc. 2006-27, 2006-22 I.R.B. 945]

### Q 27:66   When there is a return of overpaid benefit payments to a plan from a participant, how are that participant's taxes calculated?

The IRS has addressed the availability of a deductible loss under three different situations.

Situation 1 involves a plan that paid too much to a participant in the form of an annuity and reduces future payments over a short time frame to recoup the loss.

**Example 1.** Fred retires in 2001 and begins receiving a single-life annuity benefit of $36,000 per year. These payments were included in Fred's gross income in 2001. In 2002, the plan determines that Fred's annual payments should have totaled $35,000 and reduces his 2002 payments to a total of $33,940 to reflect the $1,000 overpayment and applicable interest. In 2003, his payments of $35,000 per year resume.

Situation 2 involves a plan that paid too much to a participant, also in the form of an annuity, but reduces all future payments to recoup the loss.

**Example 2.** George retires in 1992 and begins receiving a single-life annuity benefit of $14,000 per year. In 2002, the plan determines that George was only entitled to receive benefit payments of $13,000 per year. The plan reduces all future annual payments to $12,100 in order to recoup the loss to the plan.

Situation 3 involves a plan that paid too much to a participant: however, the participant repays the excess to the plan, with interest.

**Example 3.** Lou retires in 2003 and receives a lump-sum distribution of $100,000. The plan determines in 2004 that he received $2,000 too much. Lou repays the plan $2,200 to cover the overpayment plus $200 in interest.

Under Situations 1 and 2, the participant is taxed on the amount actually received each year, so there is no change to prior year's taxes. Future year's taxes will be based on the amount actually received in each of those years.

Under Situation 3, a deductible loss is available to the participant in accordance with Code Section 165 if the repayment to the plan occurs in a year following the year of receipt of the benefit. Code Section 165 allows the participant to recognize a loss with respect to the excess amount that was taxable in a prior year. However, under Section 165, the participant must itemize deductions in the year of repayment in order to claim the loss, the 2 percent floor of Code Section 67(a) is applicable if the loss is $3,000 or less, and if the loss is greater than $3,000 the rules of Code Section 1341 apply. Code Section 1341 requires that the amount of tax imposed is the lesser of (a) the tax for the year computed with the deduction being claimed, or (b) the tax for the year computed without the deduction being claimed but minus the decrease in tax that would have been paid in the prior year had the benefit been paid correctly.

**Example 4.** The facts are the same as in Example 3. Lou is entitled to recognize a loss on his 2004 tax return as long as he itemizes deductions for this year, but it will be subject to the 2 percent floor under Code Section 67(a).

If the overpayment was repaid in the same year as the benefit was received, then the participant is only taxed on the net amount received during the year. [Rev. Rul. 2002-84, 2002-50 I.R.B. 1]

# Chapter 28

# Employee Communication

Under the Employee Retirement Income Security Act of 1974 (ERISA) and the Internal Revenue Code (Code), plan administrators must provide certain information to participants and beneficiaries. The disclosure of information allows a participant to be more aware of his or her benefits and rights under the plan. This chapter identifies the kinds of information that must be available to plan participants and beneficiaries.

## Benefits and Rights Under the Plan

### Q 28:1 What general disclosure rules apply to defined benefit pension plans?

Certain information and material relating to the plan must be provided to plan participants and beneficiaries. Disclosure basically takes three forms. First, the plan administrator must furnish certain information and materials to all participants and beneficiaries at stated times or if certain events occur. Second, the plan administrator must furnish certain information and materials to individuals on request. Third, the plan administrator must make certain information and materials available to participants and beneficiaries for examination at reasonable times and places. [DOL Reg. § 2520.104b-1(a)]

Participants and beneficiaries receive a number of items regarding benefits, rights, financial matters affecting the plan, and benefit distribution. The basic items of disclosure include the following:

- Summary plan description (SPD)
- Summary of material modifications (SMM)
- Summary annual report (SAR)
- Statement of benefits
- Statement of deferred vested pension benefits
- Explanation of qualified preretirement survivor annuities (QPSAs) or other preretirement death benefits
- Claims procedure
- Suspension of benefits
- Notice of Internal Revenue Service (IRS) filing requesting waiver of minimum funding standards
- Notice of failure to meet minimum funding standards
- Participant notice of payment of variable Pension Benefit Guaranty Corporation (PBGC) premium
- Explanation of qualified joint and survivor annuity (QJSA) and alternate forms of benefit payment
- Information about tax consequences of a distribution of benefits
- Notice of plan amendment that will reduce future benefit accruals
- Notice of intent to terminate
- Notice of benefit liabilities
- Notice of determination letter request

### Q 28:2 Must an employee be notified that he or she is eligible to participate in the plan?

There is no statutory obligation to inform an employee that he or she is eligible to participate in the plan. Once an employee is eligible, however, he or she must receive an SPD and other documents relating to the plan (see Q 28:3).

### Q 28:3 What documents must be given to participants?

The plan administrator must provide each participant and beneficiary with the following documents:

- SPD (see Q 28:22);
- SMM, which is a summary of any changes to the SPD (see Q 28:30);
- SAR (see Q 28:35);
- Statement of benefits (terminated vested employees) (see Q 28:60);
- Notice of failure to meet minimum funding standards (see Q 28:54); and
- Notice of transfer of excess assets to health benefit accounts.

[ERISA § 101(a), (d), (e)]

## Q 28:4  What other documents must be given to a participant on request?

The plan administrator must provide the following documents to a participant or beneficiary on written request:

- Statement of the participant's accrued benefits (see Q 28:6);
- Latest SPD (see Q 28:22);
- Latest annual report (see Q 28:35);
- Terminal report if applicable; and
- Documents under which the plan is established and operating.

[ERISA §§ 104(b)(4), 105(a)]

The participant or beneficiary must be fairly specific when requesting information. In *Haberern v. Kaupp Vascular Surgeons Ltd. Defined Benefit Pension Plan* [18 Employee Benefits Cas. (BNA) 1097 (3d Cir. 1994)], the court held that a participant's attorney's request for a meeting to discuss "troublesome" aspects of a plan's distribution to a participant and the plan's failure to indicate how distribution was calculated could not be construed as a written request for a statement of the participant's accrued benefits under ERISA Section 105(a). Although the letter complained that certain materials had not been supplied, it never requested that they be supplied. Although information must be supplied on request, the plan administrator is not obliged to meet with the participant to clarify or resolve issues unless the plan provides for such action.

Document disclosure can be fairly extensive. Disclosure applies to the plan, SPD, and other documents under which the plan is operated. These documents include the plan document and any trust agreement, collective bargaining agreement, or other contract or instrument under which the plan is established or operated, including written policies and procedures. The plan administrator does not have to provide documents unrelated to plan administration. In an advisory opinion relating to the disclosure of fee information in a health plan, the Department of Labor (DOL) expressed its opinion that any document or instrument that specifies procedures, formulas, methodologies, or schedules to be applied in determining or calculating a participant's or beneficiary's benefit entitlement under an employee benefit plan would constitute an instrument under which the plan is established or operated, regardless of whether such information is contained in a document designated as the "plan document." [DOL Adv. Op. 96-14A] This advisory opinion certainly reflects the DOL's position, but there is a difference of opinion among the courts regarding the release of actuarial reports. In one instance, the Sixth Circuit stated that actuarial valuation reports must be provided on request. [Bartling v. Fruehauf Corp., 29 F.3d 1062 (6th Cir. 1994)] To the contrary, the Second Circuit held that the disclosure provisions of ERISA Section 104(b)(4) did not extend to actuarial valuation reports. [Board of Trs. of the CWA/ITU Negotiated Pension Plan v. Weinstein, 20 Employee Benefits Cas. (BNA) 2510 (2d Cir. 1997)]

A plan administrator must mail the requested materials to the last known address of the party making the request within 30 days of the request. [ERISA § 502(c)] A reasonable amount can be charged to cover copying costs. [ERISA § 104(b)(4)] A copying charge is considered reasonable if it is equal to the plan's actual cost per page for the least expensive means of acceptable reproduction. The maximum charge, 25 cents per page, as established in the regulations, is often the charge assessed for copying. [DOL Reg. § 2520.104b-30]

Except for matters reasonably beyond their control, plan administrators can be personally liable to the participant or beneficiary for failing to provide the requested materials. Fines can be assessed in amounts up to $100 a day. [ERISA § 502(c)(1)]

### Q 28:5   What documents must be available for examination by participants?

The plan administrator must make copies of the following materials available for examination by any participant or beneficiary at the principal office of the plan administrator and other convenient locations:

- SAR
- Latest annual report
- Plan documents

[ERISA § 104(b)(2); DOL Reg. § 2520.104b-1(b)(3)]

### Q 28:6   What information can a participant obtain regarding his or her benefit entitlements?

ERISA Section 105(a) requires the plan administrator to furnish to any plan participant or beneficiary who requests it, in writing, a statement indicating, on the basis of the latest available information, the total benefits accrued and the amount of vested benefits that have accrued, or the earliest date on which benefits will become completely vested and nonforfeitable. In addition, ERISA Section 209(a)(1) requires the plan administrator to make a report to each participant who requests such a report. The report under ERISA Section 209 (a)(1) must be sufficient to inform the participant of his or her nonforfeitable accrued benefits. Under both of these sections, the participant is limited to making one request during any 12-month period. ERISA Section 209(a) requires similar reports to be provided to a participant who terminates employment or has a one-year break in service.

For plan years beginning after December 31, 2006, the Pension Protection Act of 2006 (PPA) modified ERISA Section 105(a) to require the administrator of a defined benefit plan to provide a pension benefit statement at least once every three years to each participant with a nonforfeitable accrued benefit and who is employed by the employer maintaining the plan at the time the statement is to be furnished, and to a participant or beneficiary of the plan upon written request. These statements must contain the following information:

1. The total benefits accrued;

2. The nonforfeitable pension benefits, if any, which have accrued, or the earliest date on which benefits will become nonforfeitable; and

3. An explanation of any permitted disparity under Code Section 401(l) or any floor-offset arrangement that may be applied in determining any accrued benefits.

The statements should be written in a manner calculated to be understood by the average plan participant, and may be delivered in written, electronic, or other appropriate form to the extent such form is reasonably accessible to the participant or beneficiary.

Information must be provided to a participant or beneficiary to help determine rights, eligibility, or benefit entitlements. A plan administrator must provide information about projected retirement benefits for an employee contemplating retirement in three, four, or five years because the information requested is fundamental and essential. [Roeder v. General Signal Corp., 1995 U.S. Dist. LEXIS 15530 (W.D.N.Y. 1995)] If requested, the benefit calculation worksheets must also be provided. [Bartling v. Fruehauf Corp., 29 F.3d 1062 (6th Cir. 1994)]

A participant is entitled to receive information regarding the formulas and calculations used to determine the amount of his or her accrued benefits. [Maiuro v. Federal Express Corp., 17 Employee Benefits Cas. (BNA) 2425 (3d Cir. 1994)] The court proposed guidelines for determining whether requested material must be provided, suggesting that material must be provided if

1. It is of such a character that would directly assist the requesting party in determining what his or her rights are under the pension plan;

2. It will directly assist the requesting party in determining where he or she stands (in terms of eligibility) with respect to the plan; or

3. It will directly assist the requesting party in determining the extent of his or her interest (provide monetary information) in the plan.

### Q 28:7 Is the plan responsible for incorrect benefits shown on a benefit statement?

If benefits shown on a benefit statement are incorrect and the benefits are calculated correctly at a later date, most courts will hold that the plan is not responsible for the incorrect benefits shown on the statement. [Miller v. Pension Plan for Employees of Coastal Corp., 780 F. Supp. 768 (D. Kan. 1991)]

A retiree who intentionally supplies false information to the plan administrator cannot force the plan to pay benefits based on the false information. [Fraser v. Central States, Southeast & Southwest Areas Pension Fund, 12 Employee Benefits Cas. (BNA) 1323 (C.D. Ill. 1990)] The statement provided to Fraser included the following language:

> The details we have given you with regard to your benefits are based on information we currently have in our files and on existing pension plan

provisions. Your eligibility to receive the benefit described in this letter is subject to change if we later find additional or conflicting information. . . .

When information disclosed to the participant is incorrect and the participant has taken actions based on his or her reasonable understanding to his or her detriment, some courts will enforce the participant's reasonable understanding.

### Q 28:8   In what form must documents be furnished to participants and beneficiaries?

Material must be distributed by any means reasonably calculated to ensure actual delivery of the material. Hand delivery of the documents at the employee's work site, mailing, or insertion in a company memorandum or periodical is permitted. If material is presented in a company memorandum or periodical, a prominent notice on the front page must state that the document includes important information about ERISA rights. [DOL Reg. § 2520.104b-1(b)]

### Q 28:9   How much can the plan charge for requested information?

The plan can impose a reasonable charge to cover the costs of copying the following documents if they are requested by the participant:

- SPD
- Latest annual report
- Plan documents
- Any terminal reports

[ERISA § 104(b)(4)]

The charge is not considered reasonable if it exceeds the least expensive copying cost. In no event can the copying cost exceed 25 cents per page. Other costs, such as mailing costs, cannot be passed on to the participant. [DOL Reg. § 2520.104b-30(b)]

No charge can be imposed for supplying other information for which disclosure is required under ERISA. [DOL Reg. § 2520.104b-30(a)]

### Q 28:10   Must the plan administrator release information to third parties?

As a general rule, only participants and beneficiaries are entitled to plan information. ERISA Section 104(b) requires the plan administrator to disclose certain documents "upon request of any participant or beneficiary." Statements or access to information regarding the plan do not have to be provided to a former employee who is not vested when employment is terminated [Nugent v. Jesuit High Sch., 2 Employee Benefits Cas. (BNA) 1173 (5th Cir. 1980); Weiss v. Sheet Metal Workers Local 544 Pension Trust, 4 Employee Benefits Cas. (BNA) 2273 (9th Cir. 1983)] or to a widow who was not a beneficiary. [Hernandez v. Southern Nev. Culinary & Bartenders Pension Trust, 662 F.2d 617 (9th Cir. 1981)]

On the other hand, if a participant authorizes the release of information to a third party in writing, the plan administrator must honor the request. [DOL Adv. Op. 82-021A] Information also must be provided to employees who are in covered employment, employees who can reasonably be expected to be in covered employment, and employees who can reasonably expect to return to covered employment, as well as employees who have a colorable claim to vested benefits. [Firestone Tire & Rubber Co. v. Bruch, 489 U.S. 101 (1989)]

### Q 28:11   When must an employee receive a statement of benefits?

A participant or beneficiary must receive a statement of benefits on request, but is entitled to receive only one statement of benefits during any 12-month period. [ERISA § 105(b)]

When a participant terminates employment, the plan administrator must provide an individual benefit statement showing the participant's deferred vested benefit. [ERISA § 105(c)] The statement must include the following:

- Name of the plan;
- Name and address of the plan administrator;
- Description of the amount and normal form of any deferred vested benefit to which the participant is entitled; and
- Description of any benefits that are forfeitable if the participant dies before a certain date.

The statement must be provided by the due date for Schedule SSA of IRS Form 5500 for the plan year following the plan year in which the participant terminated employment. [I.R.C. § 6057(e); Treas. Reg. § 301.6057-1(b)(2)]

For plan years beginning after December 31, 2006, a participant must receive a benefit statement at least once every three years. [ERISA § 105(a)(1)(B)]

### Q 28:12   Must a plan administrator provide information regarding accrued benefits for purposes of a qualified domestic relations order?

The plan administrator must provide the information identified above (see Qs 28:4 and 28:5) upon the request of a participant. Arguably, the potential alternate payee (see chapter 17) is not a participant or beneficiary, and therefore does not have the right to such information. In fact, it has been suggested that disclosure to an alternate payee may be a violation of a fiduciary's responsibility to administer the plan for the "exclusive benefit" of plan participant's and beneficiaries. The DOL's position is that prospective alternate payees—spouses, former spouses, children, and other dependents of the participant—should be afforded access to information sufficient to prepare a qualified domestic relations order (QDRO). As a "beneficiary," the alternate payee must be provided with copies of the SPD, latest annual report, plan document, and a number of other materials on request. [DOL QDRO Guidance Q 2-15 (July 1997)] Information must be furnished to third parties, such as alternate payees, when the participant has authorized the release in writing. [DOL Adv. Op. 82-021A]

### Q 28:13  Must a plan administrator provide any information regarding death benefits or any forms on which a participant can name a beneficiary?

It depends on the type of death benefit provided under the plan. Some plans provide preretirement death benefits only to the participant's spouse or another class of beneficiary that the participant cannot change. A plan can provide only the minimum preretirement death benefit required by law, a QPSA (see chapter 16), for married participants. In such case, the surviving spouse is automatically the designated beneficiary and the participant has no right to name another party to receive benefits in the event of death before retirement. An unmarried participant would have no right to designate a beneficiary because no death benefit is provided for unmarried participants. If, however, the plan charges for QPSA coverage or if the plan permits a participant to name another party as beneficiary in the event of death before retirement, the plan must provide a notice of the QPSA and offer the participant the opportunity to waive QPSA coverage or name another beneficiary (see Q 28:14).

If the plan gives the participant the right to name a beneficiary, the plan administrator should have beneficiary designation forms available for the participant's use. Some plans allow a participant to customize beneficiary designation forms to coordinate with estate plans.

### Q 28:14  What type of information must be provided regarding QPSAs or other preretirement death benefits?

Each participant must receive a written explanation of the following:

- The terms and conditions of the QPSA;
- The participant's right to waive the QPSA and the effect of a waiver;
- The rights of the participant's spouse to consent or not to consent to a waiver of the QPSA; and
- The right to and the effect of revocation of a waiver.

[I.R.C. § 417(a)(3); ERISA § 205(c)(3)]

### Q 28:15  When must the QPSA notice be provided?

A plan must provide a written explanation of a QPSA before the latest of the following:

1. The period beginning on the first day of the plan year in which the participant attains age 32 and ending with the close of the plan year preceding the plan year in which the participant attains age 35;
2. A reasonable period after the individual becomes a participant;

3. A reasonable period after the plan stops fully subsidizing the cost of the QPSA; or

4. A reasonable period after QPSA provisions become applicable to the participant.

If a participant separates from service before attaining age 35, a QPSA notice must be provided to him or her during the period beginning one year before the separation from service and ending one year after the separation. [I.R.C. § 417(a)(3)(B); ERISA § 205(c)(3)(B); Treas. Reg. § 1.401(a)-20, Q&A 35]

If the plan fully subsidizes the cost of the QPSA and the plan does not permit a participant to waive the benefit or designate another beneficiary, the plan does not have to provide the notice. [I.R.C. § 417(a)(5)(A); ERISA § 205(c)(5)(A)] *Fully subsidized* means that the participant's benefit is not reduced because of QPSA coverage and no charge is assessed to the participant to obtain the QPSA coverage. [I.R.C. § 417(a)(5)(B); ERISA § 205(c)(5)(B); Treas. Reg. § 1.401(a)-20, Q&A 38]

### Q 28:16   What action must a spouse take to consent to the waiver of the QPSA?

A spouse's consent to the participant's election to waive a QPSA, or to a designation of an alternative beneficiary, is not valid unless all of the following occur:

1. The spouse of the participant consents in writing to the participant's election.

2. The participant's election designates a beneficiary (or a form of benefit) that cannot be changed without spousal consent (or the consent of the spouse expressly permits designations by the participant without any requirement of further consent by the spouse).

3. The spouse's consent acknowledges the effect of such election and is witnessed by a plan representative or a notary public.

[I.R.C. § 417(a)(2)(A)]

Failure to obtain the requisite notarization or witness by a plan representative invalidates the consent.

Spousal consent is not required if the participant establishes to the satisfaction of the plan representative that there is no spouse or the spouse cannot be located. [I.R.C. § 417(a)(2)(B)] Spousal consent is not required if the spouse is legally separated or has been abandoned according to state law and the participant has a court order to that effect. [Treas. Reg. § 1.401(a)-20, Q&A 27]

### Q 28:17   Must a plan have any written procedures for participants and beneficiaries making a claim for benefits?

Yes. The SPD must include the procedures for making a claim under the plan and the procedures for appealing the plan administrator's determination if the claim has been denied.

For a claims procedure to be considered reasonable, these guidelines must be satisfied:

1. The claims procedure must be described in the SPD.

2. The claims procedure must not contain any requirements that unduly hamper or inhibit the filing or processing of claims.

3. The participant must receive, in writing, indication of the time limits for when a notice of claim denial must be furnished, when a request for review of a denied claim must be filed, and when review decisions must be completed.

4. The claims procedure must comply with the standards for notice of claim denial and for review procedures set forth in the regulations.

The SPD must describe the plan's procedures for presenting claims, the remedies available under the plan if claims are denied, and the review procedures required by the statute. [DOL Reg. § 2560.503-1(b)]

### Q 28:18   What must be included in a claim denial?

If a claim is denied, the affected party making the claim must receive notice in writing of the denial and have a reasonable opportunity for a "full and fair" review of the decision denying the benefit claim. [ERISA § 503(1)] The plan administrator must provide the claimant with a notice "written in a manner calculated to be understood by the claimant." [DOL Reg. § 2560.503-1(f)] The notice must provide the following:

1. Specific reasons why the claim was denied;

2. Specific reference to the plan provisions on which the denial is based;

3. A description of any additional material necessary for the claimant to perfect the claim; and

4. An explanation of the steps that must be taken if the participant or beneficiary wants to submit the claim for review.

[DOL Reg. § 2560.503-1(f)]

A short statement that a participant is not entitled to benefits does not satisfy the "specific reasons" requirement. [Short v. Central States, Southeast & Southwest Areas Pension Fund, 729 F.2d 567 (8th Cir. 1984)]

### Q 28:19   How quickly must the plan administrator respond to a claim for benefits?

If a claim is denied, notice of the decision must be provided to the claimant within a reasonable time after receipt by the plan of the claim. [DOL Reg. § 2560.503-1(e)] A period of time is deemed unreasonable if more than 90 days elapse after the plan receives the claim, unless special circumstances require an extension of time for processing the claim. If additional time is necessary to respond to the claim, the plan administrator must provide a written notice to the participant before the original 90-day period expires advising the participant that additional time is required. The extension cannot exceed 90 days. The notice of extension sent to the claimant must indicate the reason an extension is necessary and must give a date by which the plan expects to render a final decision. If a notice of a claim denial is not furnished within a reasonable period of time, the claim is deemed denied, and the claimant is permitted to proceed to the review stage. [DOL Reg. § 2560.503-1(e)(2)]

### Q 28:20   If a participant requests additional review of a benefit issue, when must the decision on review be made?

The decision on review must generally be made within 60 days after the plan receives the appeal request unless special circumstances (such as the need to hold a hearing) require additional time for review. [DOL Reg. § 2560.503-1(h)]

### Q 28:21   Must the plan administrator notify a participant when he or she must take certain actions to preserve rights under the plan?

No. The plan administrator has no duty to inform a plan participant that certain actions should be taken to preserve benefits or acquire rights under the plan. [Allen v. Atlantic Richfield Ret. Plan, 480 F. Supp. 848 (E.D. Pa. 1979)]

## Summary Plan Descriptions and Summary of Material Modifications

### Q 28:22   What is a *summary plan description*?

A *summary plan description,* or SPD, is a booklet provided to plan participants describing benefits, rights, and plan provisions. An SPD must be written "in a manner calculated to be understood by the average plan participant." [ERISA § 102(a)(1)] The SPD must be distributed to participants and beneficiaries at certain times (see Q 28:26) and must contain certain information (see Q 28:23).

### Q 28:23   What must be included in an SPD?

An SPD must contain information about the plan that is "sufficiently accurate and comprehensive to reasonably apprise . . . participants and beneficiaries of their rights and obligations under the plan." [ERISA § 102(a)(1)] In particular, the regulations require the following items to be included in the SPD:

- Legal name of the plan, as well as any other name by which it is commonly known to employees

- Name and address of the employer or employee organization sponsoring the plan (If the plan is sponsored by more than one organization, the SPD must include a statement that a complete list of sponsors can be obtained by written request and is available for inspection, or a statement that the participants and beneficiaries will be told, on written request, whether a particular organization is a sponsor, and if so, its address.)
- Plan sponsor's employer identification number
- Plan number
- Type of plan (i.e., defined benefit pension plan)
- Type of administration of the plan
- Name, address, and telephone number of the plan administrator
- Name, address, and telephone number of the agent for service of process
- Name, title, and business address of each trustee
- If applicable, a statement that the plan is governed by the terms of a collective bargaining agreement
- Description of the plan's participation and eligibility requirements
- Description of the normal retirement age and any conditions that must be satisfied to receive benefits
- Summary of plan benefits
- Description of the joint and survivor benefits, including any requirement that an election must be made to select or reject the joint and survivor annuity
- Description of circumstances that can result in the participant's ineligibility for, or denial, loss, forfeiture, or suspension of, any benefits that might otherwise be reasonably expected
- Statement as to whether plan benefits are insured by the PBGC and subject to ERISA Title IV, and if so, a summary of the guaranty provisions
- Description and explanation of the method of crediting years of service for eligibility, vesting, and benefit accrual, including information about the requirements for accrual of a full year of service and the method of proration for partial years of service
- Source of contributions to the plan and the method by which contributions are calculated (The plan may simply state that the contributions are actuarially determined.)
- Identification of the funding medium used to accumulate assets to provide benefits
- Plan's fiscal year
- Plan's procedure to present claims for benefits and obtain review of denied benefits
- Statement of rights under ERISA

[ERISA § 102(b); DOL Reg. §§ 2520.102-2, 2520.102-3]

### Q 28:24  Has the DOL issued model language for SPDs?

The DOL has issued model language describing ERISA rights, which should be included in every SPD. The DOL has also provided optional language describing whether a plan is covered by plan termination insurance. [DOL Reg. § 2520.102-3]

### Q 28:25  Must SPDs be translated into a foreign language for participants who do not speak English?

No. A plan does not have to issue multiple SPDs translated into various languages for its plan participants. If a significant percentage of participants do not speak English, the SPD must include a notice, in the language best understood by these participants, advising the participants that the plan administrator will provide assistance to them in understanding their rights and obligations under the plan. This assistance need not be in writing, but can be provided orally. [DOL Reg. § 2520.102-2(c)] To avoid confusion and misunderstanding, however, it is generally better to have some information available in writing.

### Q 28:26  When must SPDs be distributed?

SPDs must be provided to each participant and beneficiary no later than

1. 90 days after an employee becomes a participant; or
2. 120 days after the plan first becomes subject to ERISA's reporting and disclosure requirements.

[ERISA § 104(b); DOL Reg §§ 2520.104a-2(a), 2520.104b-2(a)]

A plan becomes subject to ERISA on the first day that an employee is credited with an hour of service under the plan. If a plan is adopted with a retroactive effective date, the 120-day period begins on the day after the day the plan is actually adopted. Many plans are adopted subject to IRS qualification. In this case, the 120-day period begins after the condition is satisfied, that is, after the determination letter is issued by IRS. [DOL Reg. § 2520.104b-2(a)(3)]

### Q 28:27  How often must the SPD be reissued?

The plan administrator must provide an updated SPD every five years if the plan has been amended. [ERISA § 104(b)(1); DOL Reg. § 2520.104b-2(b)(1)(ii)]

Even if no amendment has been made to the plan, a new SPD must be reissued every 10 years. [DOL Reg. § 2520.104-2(b)(2)]

### Q 28:28  Must retirees receive SPD updates?

Revised and updated SPDs do not have to be provided to retirees or terminated vested participants not yet in pay status if both of the following actions are taken:

1. When the participant retired, terminated employment, or began receiving benefits, the participant received a copy of the most recent SPD.
2. When the new SPD is issued, the plan administrator advises the retiree that benefits will continue in the same amount and mode elected by the retiree.

Vested terminated participants should receive a statement explaining any condition that could result in reduction, change, forfeiture, or suspension of benefits. [DOL Reg. § 2520.104b-4]

### Q 28:29  Are there special SPD requirements when a plan is merged with another plan?

Yes. After a merger, participants may still be eligible for benefits under the terms of the plan that has been merged into the new plan. The SPD for the surviving plan does not have to describe prior plan benefits if, within 90 days after the effective date of the merger, the plan administrator provides the following information to participants and beneficiaries receiving benefits under the merged plan:

- Copy of the successor plan's SPD and any SMMs
- Separate statement providing a brief description of the merger and the benefits provided by the merged and successor plans
- Notice that copies of the merger documents and successor plan documents are available for inspection and that copies can be obtained on request for a charge

After the merger, the SPD must include language clearly identifying participants and beneficiaries affected by the merger and explain how documents can be obtained that describe benefit entitlements. [DOL Reg. § 2520.104-4(b)(1)]

### Q 28:30  What is a *summary of material modifications*?

A *summary of material modifications,* or SMM, is an addendum, or insert, to the SPD summarizing changes to the plan that are not included in the SPD.

### Q 28:31  When must an SMM be provided?

An SMM must be provided within 210 days after the close of the plan year in which the plan is changed materially. Basically, whenever any information contained in the SPD is no longer correct, an SMM is necessary. [DOL Reg. § 2530.104b-3]

### Q 28:32  What is a material modification that would require distribution of an SMM?

Any change in the information required to be included in the SPD (see Q 26:23) is considered a *material modification* requiring an SMM. [ERISA § 102(b); DOL Reg. § 2520.104b-3]

### Q 28:33   What happens if there is a discrepancy between the plan and the SPD?

Although there is some difference of opinion in the courts, a plan may have to follow the provisions contained in the SPD if they are inconsistent with the operation of the plan, or the plan documents, even when the error is inadvertent. [Hansen v. Continental Ins. Co., 940 F.2d 971 (5th Cir. 1991)] In other instances, the courts have required an act of the participant taken in reliance on the express language of the SPD for the SPD to supersede plan provisions. [Bachelder v. Communications Satellite Corp., 837 F.2d 519 (1st Cir. 1988)] Most SPDs contain disclaimer language in an attempt to avoid claims based on conflicting provisions of an SPD and the plan documents. Typical disclaimer language would read as follows:

> In the event that there is any discrepancy between the terms of the Plan and the terms of this summary plan description, the Plan terms will govern.

### Q 28:34   Is a disclaimer valid?

Nothing in ERISA prohibits use of a disclaimer in SPDs. If a participant brings a claim based on a representation included in the SPD that is not present in the plan, a court can uphold the claim based on negligent misrepresentation despite the disclaimer, particularly when a participant acted in reliance on a statement in the SPD to his or her detriment. [O'Brien v. Sperry Univac, 458 F. Supp. 1179 (D.D.C. 1978); McKnight v. Southern Life and Health Ins. Co., 758 F.2d 1566 (11th Cir. 1985)]

## Summary Annual Reports

### Q 28:35   What is a *summary annual report*?

A *summary annual report,* or SAR, is a concise summary of the financial activity of the plan for the plan year as shown on the latest annual report.

### Q 28:36   Who must receive an SAR?

Each participant covered by the plan and each beneficiary receiving benefits under the plan must receive an SAR. However, due to the PPA, this requirement has been repealed for plan years beginning after December 31, 2007. It has been replaced, essentially, by an annual funding notice requirement. (See Q 28:42.) [ERISA § 104(b)(3)]

### Q 28:37   How often must SARs be distributed?

SARs must be distributed to all participants and beneficiaries annually, on or before the last day of the ninth month after the close of the plan year. [ERISA

§ 104(b)(3); DOL Reg. § 2520.104b-10(a), (c)] If the IRS grants an extension to file the annual report, distribution of the SAR can be delayed until two months after the close of the period for which the extension is granted. [DOL Reg. § 2520.104b-10(c)(2)]

### Q 28:38   What information must an SAR contain?

An SAR must include information to summarize the latest annual report fairly. The format prescribed by the DOL for the SAR is a fill-in-the-blank style. Variations are generally not permitted. Required information can be obtained from IRS Form 5500. If the information is not contained on Form 5500, it can be omitted. [DOL Reg. § 2520.104b-10(d)]

If the plan was funded at less than 70 percent of current liability, the funded percentage must be included in the SAR. [ERISA § 104(b)(3)]

For small plans (plans with fewer than 100 participants) to qualify for a waiver of the annual audit requirement (see chapter 29), the SAR must contain additional information. Effective for plan years that begin after April 17, 2001, the SAR for a small plan needs to contain the following:

- The name of each institution holding "qualifying plan assets" (excluding qualifying employer securities and participant loans) and the amount of such assets held by each institution as of the end of the plan year;

- The name of the surety company issuing the bond, if the plan has more than 5 percent of its assets in nonqualifying plan assets;

- A notice indicating that participants and beneficiaries may, upon request and without charge, examine, or receive copies of, evidence of the required bond and statements received from each institution holding qualifying assets that describe the assets held by the institution as of the end of the plan year; and

- A notice stating that participants and beneficiaries should contact the Regional Office of the U.S. Department of Labor's Pension and Welfare Benefits Administration if they are unable to examine or obtain copies of statements received from each institution holding qualifying assets or evidence of the required bond, if applicable.

[DOL Reg. § 2520.104-46(b)(1)(i)(B)]

### Q 28:39   What are *qualifying plan assets*?

The term *qualifying plan assets* means the following:

1. Qualifying employer securities;
2. Participant loans;
3. Any assets held by
   a. A bank or similar institution,
   b. An insurance company,
   c. A registered broker-dealer, or

   d. Any other organization authorized to act as an individual retirement
      account (IRA) trustee;

4. Shares issued by a registered investment company (RIC); or

5. Investment and annuity contracts issued by an insurance company.

[DOL Reg. § 2520.104-46(b)(1)(ii)]

### Q 28:40   Is an employee entitled to see IRS Form 5500?

Yes. Under ERISA, a participant must be provided with a copy of IRS Form
5500 and the financial report of the plan on written request. [ERISA § 104(b)(4)]

### Q 28:41   Does an employee have the right to know what a plan's investments are?

Yes. Plan administrators must furnish statements of assets and liabilities,
income and expenses, and notes accompanying such statements when requested
by a participant or beneficiary. [ERISA § 103(a)(1)(A), (b)(3)]

In addition, there are expanded disclosure requirements applicable to small
plans that want a waiver from the annual audit requirement (see Q 28:38).

### Q 28:42   What is the annual funding notice?

All defined benefit plans that are covered by the PBGC (i.e., subject to ERISA
Title IV) must provide a plan funding notice to the PBGC, to each plan participant
and beneficiary, to each labor organization representing such participants or
beneficiaries, and, in the case of a multiemployer plan, to each employer that has
an obligation to contribute to the plan.

### Q 28:43   What must the plan funding notice contain?

The plan funding notice must contain identifying information and specific
information regarding the plan.

The notice must contain the following identifying information:

1. The name of the plan;

2. The address and phone number of the plan administrator and the plan's
   principal administrative officer;

3. Each plan sponsor's employer identification number; and

4. The number of the plan.

The notice must also contain the following specific information regarding the
plan:

   1. In the case of a single-employer plan, a statement as to whether the plan's
      funding target attainment percentage (as defined in Code Section 436) for

the plan year to which the notice relates, and for the two preceding plan years, is at least 100 percent (and, if not, the actual percentages); or

2. In the case of a multiemployer plan, a statement as to whether the plan's funded percentage (as defined in Code Section 438) for the plan year to which the notice relates, and for the two preceding plan years, is at least 100 percent (and, if not, the actual percentages);

3. In the case of a single-employer plan, a statement of—

   a. The total assets (separately stating the prefunding balance and the funding standard carryover balance) and liabilities of the plan, determined in the same manner as under Code Section 436, for the plan year for which the latest annual report filed under Code Section 104(a) was filed and for the two preceding plan years, as reported in the annual report for each such plan year, and

   b. The value of the plan's assets and liabilities for the plan year to which the notice relates as of the last day of such plan year, determined using the asset valuation under subclause (II) of Code Section 4006(a)(3)(E)(iii) and the interest rate under Code Section 4006(a)(3)(E)(iv);

4. In the case of a multiemployer plan,—

   a. A statement of the value of the plan's assets and liabilities for the plan year to which the notice relates as the last day of such plan year and the preceding two plan years,

   b. A statement of the number of participants who are—

      i. retired or separated from service and are receiving benefits,
      ii. retired or separated participants entitled to future benefits, and
      iii. active participants under the plan,

   c. A statement setting forth the funding policy of the plan and the asset allocation of investments under the plan (expressed as percentages of total assets) as of the end of the plan year to which the notice relates;

5. In the case of a multiemployer plan, whether the plan was in critical or endangered status under Code Section 438 for the plan year to which the notice relates and, if so—

   a. A statement describing how a person may obtain a copy of the plan's funding improvement or rehabilitation plan, as appropriate, adopted under Code Section 438 and the actuarial and financial data that demonstrate any action taken by the plan toward fiscal improvement, and

   b. A summary of any funding improvement plan, rehabilitation plan, or modification thereof adopted under Code Section 438 during the plan year to which the notice relates;

6. In the case of any plan amendment, scheduled benefit increase or reduction, or other known event taking effect in the current plan year and having a material effect on plan liabilities or assets for the year, an explanation of the amendment, scheduled increase or reduction, or event, and a projection to the end of such plan year of the effect of the amendment, scheduled increase or reduction, or event on plan liabilities;

7. In the case of a single-employer plan, a summary of the rules governing termination of single-employer plans under Title IV of ERISA, or

8. In the case of a multiemployer plan, a summary of the rules governing reorganization or insolvency, including the limitations on benefit payments;

9. A general description of the benefits under the plan which are eligible to be guaranteed by the PBGC, along with an explanation of the limitations on the guarantee and the circumstances under which such limitations apply;

10. A statement that a person may obtain a copy of the annual report of the plan (Form 5500) upon request, through the Internet Web site of the DOL, or through an Intranet Web site maintained by the applicable plan sponsor (or plan administrator on behalf of the plan sponsor); and

11. If applicable, a statement that each contributing sponsor, and each member of the contributing sponsor's controlled group, of the single-employer plan was required to provide the information under ERISA Section 4010 for the plan year to which the notice relates.

In addition, a multiemployer plan must provide, upon written request, to any labor organization representing plan participants and beneficiaries and any employer that has an obligation to contribute to the plan, a copy of the annual report filed (Form 5500).

A model notice is to be provided by the DOL by the end of 2007.

### Q 28:44   When must the plan's funding notice be provided to interested parties?

In general, the funding notice must be provided not later than 120 days after the end of the plan year to which the notice relates. There is an exception for plans with 100 or fewer participants; the notice in this case must be provided by the time of the filing of the Form 5500.

### Q 28:45   How does a plan provide funding target attainment percentage or funding percentage in years when this specific calculation was not required?

There is a transition rule available that states that if the plan is required to report the funding target attainment percentage or funded percentage of a plan with respect to any plan year beginning before January 1, 2008, this requirement will be treated as met if the plan reports—

1. In the case of a plan year beginning in 2006, the funded current liability percentage (as defined in Code Section 412) of the plan for such plan year; and

2. In the case of a plan year beginning in 2007, the funding target attainment percentage or funded percentage as determined using such methods of estimation as the Secretary of the Treasury may provide.

## Suspension of Benefits Notice

### Q 28:46  When is a suspension of benefits notice appropriate?

If a retiree in pay status becomes reemployed, a plan can provide for suspension of the employer-derived portion of benefit payments while the former retiree is employed. When the employee retires (a second time), the benefit must be actuarially increased for the period of suspension unless special requirements are met. [Prop. Treas. Reg. § 1.411(b)-2(b)(4)(iii)]

Benefits can be permanently withheld during periods of employment, without actuarial adjustment when benefit payments later begin, if the individual meets minimum service levels, described as Section 203(a)(3)(B) service (see Q 28:47). [ERISA § 203(a)(3)(B); DOL Reg. § 2530.203-3] To permit this permanent forfeiture of benefits, the reemployed employee formerly in pay status must be issued a suspension of benefits notice (see Q 28:48) and be informed of the procedures relating to benefit suspension.

### Q 28:47  What is *Section 203(a)(3)(B) service*?

*Section 203(a)(3)(B) service* is defined by reference to the hours worked in a particular month or pay period. An employee is engaged in Section 203(a)(3)(B) service for each month the employee is employed for a minimum of 40 hours by the employer maintaining the plan. If the plan does not count hours of service for any reason—for example, if the plan credits service on an elapsed-time basis (see chapter 7)—the employee is engaged in Section 203(a)(3)(B) service for any month (or pay period) for which he or she is compensated for a minimum of eight days (or separate work shifts). [DOL Reg. § 2530.203-3(c)(1)]

### Q 28:48  What is a *suspension of benefits notice*?

A *suspension of benefits notice* is a notice provided to an employee who had retired and was receiving benefits under the plan informing the employee that his or her retirement benefits are being suspended and identifying the plan provisions that authorize the suspension of benefits. Many times an explanation of the suspension of benefits rules is contained in the SPD. In that case, the suspension of benefits notice can refer to the relevant portions of the SPD. If the plan provides for an offset of future benefits for benefits that are erroneously paid during periods of Section 203(a)(3)(B) service (see Q 28:47), the suspension of benefits notice must explain how the offset will work.

### Q 28:49  When must a suspension of benefits notice be given to a plan participant?

Reemployed employees who will have benefits suspended during a period of reemployment must be notified that their benefits are being suspended during the first payroll period or month of reemployment. Notification must be accomplished by personal delivery or first-class mail. [ERISA § 203(a)(3)(B); DOL Reg. § 2530.203-3(b)(4)]

### Q 28:50  What happens if a suspension of benefits notice is not provided when required?

If a suspension of benefits notice is not provided to a reemployed participant previously in pay status, his or her ultimate retirement benefits must be actuarially increased to reflect benefits lost during the suspension period. [Prop. Treas. Reg. § 1.411(b)-2(b)(4)(iii)]

### Q 28:51  May an employer change the types of employment covered by a suspension of benefits provision after an employee has already returned to work?

No. The U.S. Supreme Court ruled in *Central Laborers' Pension Fund v. Heinz* [124 S. Ct. 2230 (2004)] that an amendment to the plan's suspension of benefit rules that applied to a retiree's benefits earned before the amendment's adoption was subject to the anti-cutback limitations of Code Section 411(d)(6). In response to this ruling, the IRS issued Revenue Procedure 2005-23 (and extended the date required to comply in Revenue Procedure 2005-76) to limit the effect of the Supreme Court ruling to a prospective basis. This revenue procedure contains guidelines for those companies who had plans with provisions in conflict with the *Heinz* decision to correct their defects. [Rev. Proc. 2005-23, 2005-18 I.R.B. 991] This has also been added to the regulations in proposed form by Proposed Treasury Regulations Section 1.411(d)-3(a)(3).

## Funding

### Q 28:52  What notices must be provided to plan participants and beneficiaries when there are funding problems with the plan?

There are a number of notices that must be provided to participants and beneficiaries when funding is in issue. Participants and beneficiaries must receive the following notices regarding funding:

1. A *notice of funding waiver request* when the plan applies to the IRS for a waiver of the minimum funding standards (see Q 28:53);

2. A *notice of funding failure* when the plan sponsor misses an installment or payment needed to meet the minimum funding requirements (see Q 28:54); and

3. A *notice of funding status* when the plan becomes subject to a variable-rate PBGC premium (see Q 28:55).

### Q 28:53   What information must be provided to participants if the employer asks the IRS for a waiver from minimum funding standards?

The employer must provide notice of the filing of the application for the waiver to each employee organization representing employees covered under the plan and to each participant, beneficiary, and alternate payee. The notice must describe the extent to which the plan is funded for benefits guaranteed under ERISA Title IV (see chapters 24 and 25). [I.R.C. § 412(f)(4)]

### Q 28:54   Must employees be informed when an employer fails to meet minimum funding standards?

Yes. When an employer fails to make any payment required to meet the minimum funding standards (see chapter 19) before the 60th day following the due date of the payment, the employer must notify each participant and beneficiary (including an alternative payee) of the failure. [ERISA § 101(d)] There is no prescribed format for this notice.

No notice is required if a request for waiver of the funding standard is pending. If the waiver is denied, however, the notice must be provided within 60 days after the denial. [ERISA § 101(d)(2)]

### Q 28:55   Must employees be informed when the plan must pay the PBGC's variable premium?

Yes. An underfunded plan that is subject to the PBGC's variable-rate premium (see chapter 24) must notify plan participants of the plan's funded status and the limits on the PBGC's guarantee if the plan terminates while it is underfunded. [ERISA § 4011] This participant notice is not required if, in the current year or the prior year, the plan is exempt from making a deficit reduction contribution (DRC). Generally, a plan is exempt from making a DRC if it has a funded current liability of at least 90 percent. [PBGC Reg. § 4011.3] This notice has been repealed for plan years beginning after December 31, 2007, and is replaced, essentially, with an annual funding notice. (See Q 28:42.)

### Q 28:56   When must participant notices relating to funding be issued?

The plan administrator is required to issue participant notices relating to funding issues no later than two months after the deadline, including extensions, for filing IRS Form 5500 for the previous plan year. [PBGC Reg. § 4011.8]

### Q 28:57   What are acceptable ways of providing participant notices regarding funding to participants?

The participant notice must be given in a way reasonably calculated to ensure actual receipt by the persons entitled to receive it. The notice can be issued at the same time as another document, such as the SAR, but must be in a separate document. Posting a notice advising participants that the notice is available at work sites is not acceptable. Notice by electronic mail may be acceptable if potential recipients have access to and familiarity with electronic mail. [PBGC Reg. § 4011.9]

### Q 28:58  What information must be included in the participant notice?

The participant notice must contain information regarding the plan's funding status and an explanation of the PBGC's guarantee. Any outstanding funding waivers or missed funding contributions must be identified. The PBGC regulations contain a model participant notice that can be used to satisfy this notice requirement. If an employer prepares its own notice, the following data should be included:

1. Identifying information, including:
   a. Plan name and number,
   b. Employer name and employer identification number,
   c. Date of the notice,
   d. Identification of the person or persons who can provide information about the plan's funding;
2. A statement indicating that the notice is required by law;
3. Information about the plan's funding status (generally, the funded current liability percentage);
4. A statement to the effect that:
   a. To pay pension benefits, the employer is required to contribute money to the plan over a period of years,
   b. A plan's funding percentage does not take into consideration the financial strength of the employer, and
   c. The employer, by law, must pay for all pension benefits, but benefits may be at risk if the employer faces a severe financial crisis or is in bankruptcy;
5. A statement identifying any previous plan year (within the last five years) in which the plan was granted a minimum funding waiver that has not been fully repaid as of the end of the prior plan year;
6. A statement identifying the due date for any missed payment and noting that the payment has or has not been made, and if it has been made, the date of the payment;
7. A statement to the effect that if a plan terminates before all pension benefits are fully funded, the PBGC pays most persons all pension benefits, but some persons may lose certain benefits that are not guaranteed;
8. A summary of plan benefits guaranteed by the PBGC, with an explanation of the limitations on the PBGC's guarantee; and

9. A statement that further information about the PBGC's guarantee can be obtained by submitting a request for the booklet *Your Guaranteed Pension,* from No. 587G, Pueblo, Colorado 81009, along with the current price of the booklet.

[PBGC Reg. §§ 4011.10, 4011.11]

### Q 28:59  Who must receive the participant notices?

Plan participants, beneficiaries, alternate payees under a QDRO, and employee organizations that represent any group of participants for purposes of collective bargaining must receive the participant notices. [PBGC Reg. § 4011.7]

## Distribution

### Q 28:60  What notification must a participant receive regarding benefit distribution rights and options?

Distribution options and forms of benefit must be described in the plan document and SPD.

Benefits must normally be paid in the form of a QJSA. [I.R.C. § 401(a)(11)] Unless a plan fully subsidizes the cost of the survivor benefit and does not allow the participant to waive this form of benefit, the plan administrator must provide notices regarding the QJSA. [Treas. Reg. § 1.401(a)-20, Q&A 37] The notice must explain that the participant, with the consent of his or her spouse, can waive the QJSA form of benefit payment and elect an alternative form of payment. Generally, the notice must be provided within 90 days before a participant's annuity starting date. The election of an alternative form of payment is not valid, however, unless the participant receives a general description of the material features, and a general explanation of the relative values, of the optional forms of benefit available under the plan. [Treas. Reg. § 1.417-1(b)(2)(i)]

The plan administrator must provide information necessary for a reasonable employee to make an adequately informed decision. The explanation of benefit options should include an explanation that a joint annuitant designation is irrevocable if that is the case. [Law v. Ernst & Young, 14 Employee Benefits Cas. (BNA) 2710 (1st Cir. 1992)]

### Q 28:61  When must notice regarding benefit distribution rights and options be given to an employee?

In general, the participant must receive notice of rights and options under the plan no more than 90 and no less than 30 days before the annuity starting date (see chapter 14). Unless the plan provides for a waiver of the 30-day time period, these time period limitations (30 to 90 days) (see Q 28:62) must be strictly observed. If a participant, with the consent of his or her spouse, waives the joint and survivor annuity more than 90 days before the annuity starting date, the waiver is ineffective.

A plan may provide for a waiver of the 30-day time period as long as this is done with spousal consent, the participant is notified that he or she has at least 30 days to make this decision, and the distribution does not commence sooner than seven days after the explanation is provided. [I.R.C. § 417(a)(7)(B)]

### Q 28:62  Does the plan administrator have to provide information about the tax consequences of a distribution?

If a lump-sum option is available (see chapter 16), the plan administrator must notify the participant of the direct rollover option and other special tax rules. This notification is often referred to as the *402(f) notice*. [I.R.C. § 402(f); Treas. Reg. § 1.402(c)-2, Q&As 11-15]

The IRS has provided a model notice that can be used when a participant receives an eligible rollover distribution. [Notice 2002-3, 2002-2 I.R.B. 289] Plan administrators must notify plan participants receiving qualifying rollover distributions that such distributions can be rolled over, tax free, within 60 days to an IRA or other tax-qualified plan. If payment is made as a lump sum, plan administrators must also provide an explanation of income averaging options and capital gains treatment, if applicable, shortly after the distribution is made. Most plan administrators provide the tax notices before distribution.

## Plan Amendment and Termination

### Q 28:63  Must an employer notify employees of a plan amendment?

If a plan amendment results in a significant reduction in the rate of future benefit accruals or eliminates or significantly reduces an early retirement benefit or retirement-type subsidy, the plan administrator must notify all participants, certain beneficiaries, and any union representing plan participants. This notice is called an ERISA Section 204(h) notice.

### Q 28:64  How are participants to be notified of a significant reduction in the rate of future benefit accruals?

The ERISA Section 204(h) notice must be provided in writing in a manner calculated to be understood by the average plan participant. In addition, it must provide sufficient information to allow applicable individuals to understand the effect of the plan amendment. [ERISA § 204(h)(2)]

The ERISA Section 204(h) notice must be provided within a reasonable time before the effective date of the plan amendment. [ERISA § 204(h)(3)] In general, the notice must be provided at least 45 days before the effective date of any

ERISA Section 204(h) amendment. However, in the case of a small plan or a multiemployer plan, the ERISA Section 204(h) notice must be provided at least 15 days before the effective date of any Section 204(h) amendment. A small plan is a plan that the plan administrator reasonably expects to have, on the effective date of the Section 204(h) amendment, fewer than 100 participants who have an accrued benefit under the plan. Generally, the notice cannot be distributed until after the adoption of the amendment but can be distributed before adoption as long as there is no material modification of the amendment before it is adopted. [ERISA § 204(h)(5)]

### Q 28:65   What is considered a significant reduction in the rate of future benefit accruals?

Before the Economic Growth and Tax Relief Reconciliation Act of 2001 (EGTRRA), a significant reduction in the rate of future benefit accruals was defined as any amendment that was reasonably expected to change the amount of the future annual benefit commencing at normal retirement age. [Treas. Reg. § 1.411(d)-6, Q&A 5] For example, if the plan changed the definition of compensation in a way that would lower benefits, an ERISA Section 204(h) notice was required. [Davidson v. Canteen Corp., 957 F.2d 1404 (7th Cir. 1992)] In the *Davidson* case, the employer adopted an amendment to the plan that excluded from the plan's definition of compensation any income resulting from participation in the employer's stock option plan. Under the plan in question, benefits were based on the average of the 5 years of highest compensation in the 10 years immediately preceding retirement. Because the change in the definition of compensation would reduce the rate at which benefits would accrue in the future, the court held that the amendment was not valid until notice was given to employees.

In EGTRRA, Congress added a provision to specifically state that a plan amendment that eliminates or significantly reduces any early retirement benefit or retirement-type subsidy will be treated as having the effect of significantly reducing the rate of future benefit accruals. [ERISA § 204(h)(9)]

### Q 28:66   Must employers notify employees of a potential amendment to the plan?

Courts are beginning to recognize a duty to disclose information to participants about pending plan changes, such as an early retirement program under consideration. [Fischer v. Philadelphia Elec. Co., 994 F.2d 130 (3d Cir. 1993)] A plan fiduciary was not required to disclose voluntarily to a plan participant at the time the participant retired that the fiduciary was considering implementing a new early retirement plan absent an inquiry by the plan participant. [Pocchia v. Nynex Corp., 20 Employee Benefits Cas. (BNA) 1175 (2d Cir. 1996)] An employer does not breach its fiduciary duties by failing to notify employees nearing retirement that the company was considering an enhanced retirement offer to some of its employees, because the discussion of the plan was not yet being given "serious consideration" by the employer. [Muse v. IBM Corp., 20 Employee

Benefits Cas. (BNA) 2334 (6th Cir. 1996)] Once the plan sponsor gives serious consideration to an enhanced benefit package, it must respond truthfully to employee inquiries regarding the possibility of plan amendment. [Berlin v. Michigan Bell Tel. Co., 858 F.2d 1154 (6th Cir. 1988)] In response to this problem, some employers have attempted to construct a wall around supervisory and benefits personnel who had no actual knowledge that enhanced benefit amendments were under serious consideration. In *Mullins v. Pfizer, Inc.*, [23 F.3d 663 (2d Cir. 1994)], the court did not require disclosure as long as the company did not affirmatively mislead participants concerning future changes in benefits.

### Q 28:67  Who does not have to receive notice of a reduction in the rate of future benefit accruals?

Notice does not have to be provided to any participant or alternate payee whose rate of future benefit accrual is reasonably expected not to be reduced by the amendment. [ERISA § 204(h)(8)(A)]

### Q 28:68  What must be included in a ERISA Section 204(h) notice?

An ERISA Section 204(h) notice must include sufficient information to allow applicable individuals to understand the effect of the plan amendment, including the approximate magnitude of the expected reduction. If the effect of the amendment is different for different participants, the notice must either identify the general classes of participants to whom the reduction is expected to apply, or include sufficient information to allow each applicable individual receiving the notice to determine which reductions are expected to apply to that individual.

The information must be written in a manner calculated to be understood by the average plan participant and to apprise the applicable individual of the significance of the notice. If the amendment reduces the rate of future benefit accrual, the notice must include a description of the benefit or allocation formula before the amendment, a description of the benefit or allocation formula under the plan as amended, and the effective date of the amendment. If the amendment reduces an early retirement benefit or retirement-type subsidy (other than as a result of an amendment reducing the rate of future benefit accrual), the notice must describe how the early retirement benefit or retirement-type subsidy is calculated from the accrued benefit before the amendment, how the early retirement benefit or retirement-type subsidy is calculated from the accrued benefit after the amendment, and the effective date of the amendment.

**Example.** The Changes Inc. Plan has a normal retirement age of 65 but provides for an unreduced normal retirement benefit at age 55. The plan is amended to provide an unreduced normal retirement benefit at age 60 for benefits accrued in the future, with an actuarial reduction to apply for benefits accrued in the future to the extent that the early retirement benefit begins before age 60. The ERISA Section 204(h) notice states that and specifies the factors that apply in calculating the actuarial reduction (e.g., a 5 percent per year reduction applies for early retirement before age 60).

If the magnitude of the changes that result from the amendment are not reasonably apparent from the description provided by a narrative, additional narrative information may be required, as well as illustrative examples. Further narrative explanation of the effect of the difference between the old and new formulas or benefit calculation may be provided to make the approximate magnitude of the reduction apparent. In addition, if the magnitude of the reduction is still not reasonably apparent from the descriptions provided, the notice must include one or more illustrative examples showing the approximate magnitude of the reduction in the example. Thus, illustrative examples are required for a change from a traditional defined benefit formula to a cash balance formula or a change that results in a period of time during which there are no accruals (or minimal accruals) with regard to normal retirement benefits or an early retirement subsidy (a wear-away period).

These examples must illustrate the ranges of the reductions by showing examples that bound the possibilities. In addition, the examples generally may be based on any reasonable assumptions (e.g., about the representative participant's age, years of service, and compensation; any interest rate and mortality table used in the illustrations; and salary scale assumptions used in the illustrations for amendments that alter the compensation taken into account under the plan), but the ERISA Section 204(h) notice must identify those assumptions. If a plan's benefit provisions, however, include a factor that varies over time (such as a variable interest rate), the determination of whether an amendment is reasonably expected to result in a wear-away period must be based on the value of the factor applicable under the plan at a time that is reasonably close to the date the ERISA Section 204(h) notice is provided, and any wear-away period that is solely a result of a future change in the variable factor may be disregarded. For example, to determine whether a wear-away occurs as a result of a Section 204(h) amendment that converts a defined benefit plan to a cash balance pension plan that will credit interest based on a variable interest factor specified in the plan, the future interest credits must be projected based on the interest rate applicable under the variable factor at the time the Section 204(h) notice is provided. [Treas. Reg. § 54.4980F, Q&A 11]

### Q 28:69  How must an ERISA Section 204(h) notice be delivered to affected participants?

Under prior law, a plan administrator could use any method reasonably calculated to ensure actual receipt of the ERISA Section 204(h) notice, such as first-class mail to the party's last known address or hand delivery. [Treas. Reg. § 1.411(d)-6, Q&A 11] Posting a notice on a bulletin board is not sufficient. [Production and Maintenance Employees' Local 504 v. Roadmaster Corp., 954 F.2d 1397 (7th Cir. 1992)]

EGTRRA specifically authorizes the IRS to provide regulations to allow delivery of the notice by using new technologies. [ERISA § 204(h)(7)] In Letter

Ruling 200407021, the IRS ruled that a plan sponsor's Microsoft PowerPoint presentation at employee meetings satisfied the written notice requirement of ERISA Section 204(h). Although a letter ruling may not be relied upon by other taxpayers, it does show that the IRS is willing to accept this form of delivery. Some key points in the approval were that the plan sponsor did make available printed copies of the presentation, multiple employee meetings were held, and the plan sponsor took appropriate steps to ensure that all affected parties received the ERISA Section 204(h) notice.

### Q 28:70   What happens if the ERISA Section 204(h) notice is not provided to all participants?

Under EGTRRA, an excise tax equal to $100 per day per individual is applied to any failure to provide the ERISA Section 204(h) notice properly. There are limited exceptions to the application of the excise tax:

1. The excise tax will not be imposed if the plan administrator was not aware of the failure and exercised reasonable diligence in trying to satisfy the notice requirements.
2. The excise tax will not apply if the plan administrator exercised reasonable diligence in trying to satisfy the notice requirements and provides the ERISA Section 204(h) notice within 30 days of finding such failure.
3. The Secretary has the authority to waive the excise tax in full or in part for any failure that was due to reasonable cause to the extent that the payment of the tax would be excessive or be otherwise inequitable relative to the failure involved.

If the plan administrator exercised reasonable diligence in providing the ERISA Section 204(h) notice, the total excise tax imposed during the fiscal year of the plan sponsor will not exceed $500,000. [I.R.C. § 4980F]

If the failure to provide the ERISA Section 204(h) notice is egregious, all applicable individuals will be entitled to receive the greater of the benefits under the old or new plan formula. An egregious failure is defined as

1. An intentional failure; or
2. A failure, whether or not intentional, to provide most of the individuals with most of the information they are entitled to receive.

[ERISA § 204(h)(6)]

### Q 28:71   When must an employer notify employees of an employer's intent to terminate the plan?

ERISA Section 4041 requires plan administrators to provide two notices to participants, beneficiaries, employee organizations, and the PBGC before a pension plan is terminated:

1. A written notice of intent to terminate (NOIT) must be issued to "affected parties" at least 60, but not more than 90, days in advance of the proposed termination date. The plan termination can be invalidated by the PBGC if less than 60 days' notice is provided. The NOIT informs participants and beneficiaries of the sponsor's intent to terminate the plan and must include all of the following information:

   a. Name of plan and plan number;

   b. Name and employer identification number of the plan sponsor;

   c. Name, address, and telephone number of the person who may be contacted with questions regarding the termination;

   d. Statement that the plan administrator expects to terminate the plan in a standard termination on a proposed date that is set forth in the notice or a date after the occurrence of a specified event;

   e. If the termination is dependent on the occurrence of a future event, the nature of the event and when it is expected to occur;

   f. Statement that benefit and service accruals will continue until termination, or statement that benefit levels have been frozen;

   g. Statement that, to terminate in a standard termination, assets must be sufficient to satisfy benefit liabilities;

   h. Statement that the PBGC's guaranty will terminate after benefits have been satisfied;

   i. If benefits may be satisfied by the purchase of insurance, information regarding the potential insurers;

   j. Statement that affected parties will be notified if the termination does not occur;

   k. Statement indicating that each affected person will be receiving written notification of benefits that the person will receive; and

   l. For retirees, statement that benefits will not be affected by the plan termination. [PBGC Reg. § 4041.22(d)]

2. Notices of plan benefits must be provided to plan participants and beneficiaries no later than the date the standard termination notice is filed with PBGC.

(See chapter 25.)

## Miscellaneous

### Q 28:72   Must employees be notified if a plan is submitted to the IRS for a letter of determination?

Yes. The plan administrator must furnish a notice to interested parties to all such parties before a plan is filed with the IRS for a determination of qualification. The notice must be posted for current employees (or mailed to them) and mailed to retired and terminated vested participants and beneficiaries in pay status, at least seven days (10 days for mailing) before the date the plan is filed with the IRS.

### Q 28:73   What must be included in the notice to interested parties?

The notice advises plan participants that the plan is being filed and explains the means of commenting on the filing. [ERISA § 3001; Treas. Reg. § 1.7476-2] A model notice to interested parties is issued regularly by the IRS. [Rev. Proc. 2000-6, 2000-1 I.R.B. 187]

# Chapter 29

# Government Reporting and Disclosure

Each year, plan administrators must file certain reports and returns with the Internal Revenue Service (IRS), the Department of Labor (DOL), and the Pension Benefit Guaranty Corporation (PBGC). Some of the forms have dual purposes; they are used to collect information for more than one agency. Certain forms must be filed by the plan sponsor and others by the trustees. This chapter describes the forms required, the party required to file the forms, and the due date (with extensions) for filing the forms.

## Summary of Forms

### Q 29:1   To which government agencies must plan sponsors report?

The IRS, DOL, and PBGC all have certain reporting and disclosure requirements that apply to plan sponsors.

### Q 29:2   What are the IRS reporting requirements?

The IRS requires that each plan sponsor of a defined benefit plan file an annual report, the IRS Form 5500 series. The Form 5500 series must be filed for each year in which the plan has assets. [I.R.C. §§ 6058, 6059] The Form 5500 series has been streamlined and revised for plan years beginning in 1999 and later. Form 5500-C/R has been eliminated.

A defined benefit plan subject to the minimum funding standards of Internal Revenue Code (Code) Section 412 must file Schedule B, Actuarial Information, and attach it to Form 5500 (or to Form 5500-C/R for plan years beginning before 1999; see chapter 30 for more information on the Schedule B). Beginning with the

2005 plan year, the Schedule B (and any other applicable schedules, including Schedule P) is no longer required to be filed with the Form 5500-EZ. Filers, however, are still required to retain the completed and signed Schedule B. The Schedule B must be signed by an enrolled actuary who is licensed by the Joint Board for the Enrollment of Actuaries (see chapter 23). Forms 5500 and 5500-EZ must be signed by the plan administrator and the plan sponsor.

There are several other attachments to the Form 5500 series that may be required depending on various occurrences during the plan year:

*Schedule A, Insurance Information.* This schedule is required as an attachment if some or all of the benefits under the plan are purchased from or guaranteed by an insurance company, insurance service, or other similar organization. It must contain information prepared by the insurance organization and must be filed by the plan administrator.

*Schedule B, Actuarial Information.* This schedule is required as an attachment to Form 5500 and Form 5500-EZ for all defined benefit plans, except for fully insured plans [I.R.C. § 412(i)] and plans not required to file Form 5500-EZ (plans with less than $100,000 in assets).

*Schedule C, Service Provider Fees.* This schedule is required as an attachment to Form 5500 for large plans if (1) any person or entity received from the plan, either directly or indirectly, $5,000 or more in compensation for services rendered to the plan or (2) the plan terminated an accountant or enrolled actuary that was providing services to the plan. It must be filed by the plan administrator.

*Schedule D, DFE/Participating Plan Information.* This schedule must be attached to Form 5500 if the plan participated or invested in one or more common or collective trusts (CCTs), pooled separate accounts (PSAs), master trust investment accounts (MTIAs), or 103-12 investment entities (103-12 IEs) at any time during the plan year.

*Schedule G, Financial Schedules.* This schedule is required to report loans for fixed-income obligations in default or determined to be uncollectible as of the end of the plan year, uncollectible leases or leases in default, and nonexempt prohibited transactions.

*Schedule H, Large Plan Financial Information.* This schedule must be attached to Form 5500 to disclose a large plan's financial information for the plan year.

*Schedule I, Small Plan Financial Information.* This schedule must be attached to Form 5500 to disclose a small plan's financial information. It is an abbreviated version of Schedule H.

*Schedule P, Annual Return of Fiduciary of Employee Benefit Trust.* This schedule is an optional attachment to Form 5500 or Form 5500-EZ. Filing Schedule P begins the running of the statute of limitations on assessment and collection under Code Section 6501(a) for any Section 401(a) trust that is exempt from tax under Code Section 501(a). This statute of limitations applies to the taxes that may apply if the trust becomes retroactively disqualified or to unrelated business income taxes. This schedule must be signed by a trustee and submitted by the plan administrator.

*Schedule R, Retirement Plan Information.* This schedule is required as an attachment to Form 5500 for any plan that is subject to minimum funding requirements or had a distribution of benefits during the plan year.

*Schedule SSA, Annual Registration Statement Identifying Separated Participants with Deferred Vested Benefits.* This schedule must be attached to Form 5500 (or Form 5500-C/R for plan years beginning before 1999) to report information on separated participants entitled to deferred vested benefits, to remove participants who were previously reported and have since been paid, and to report changes in information on separated participants who were previously reported. This schedule must be filed by the plan administrator.

*Schedule T, Qualified Plan Coverage Information.* This schedule must be attached to Form 5500 to provide information concerning the plan's compliance with the minimum coverage requirements of Code Section 410(b). (This schedule is no longer required for 2005; the coverage information was moved to the Schedule R.)

### Q 29:3    Which schedules are filed for large plans and which schedules are filed for small plans?

A *large plan* is any plan with 100 or more participants as of the beginning of the plan year. The following schedules must be attached (if applicable) to the Form 5500 filing for the plan year: Schedules A, B, C, D, G, H, P, R, SSA, and T. In addition, large plans are required to attach an audit of the plan performed by an independent qualified public accountant (IQPA).

A *small plan* is defined as any plan with fewer than 100 participants as of the beginning of the plan year. The following schedules must be attached (if applicable) to the Form 5500 filing for the plan year: Schedules A, B, D, I, P, R, SSA, and T. Small plans are exempt from the audit requirement as long as certain requirements are met (see Q 29:4).

**Practice Pointer.** If the number of plan participants increases to 100 or more, or decreases to fewer than 100, from one year to the next, then, in general, different schedules must be filed than were filed in the previous year. Even if the number of participants changed, however, the filer may continue to file the same schedules as the previous year, provided that the plan had at least 80 participants but not more than 120 participants at the beginning of the plan year.

For plan years that began before 1999, large plans filed Form 5500 with Schedules A, B, C, G, P, and SSA (if applicable). Small plans filed Form 5500-C/R with Schedules A, B, P, and SSA (if applicable).

### Q 29:4    What requirements must be met for a small plan to be exempt from the requirement to engage an independent qualified public accountant (IQPA)?

To enhance the security of assets in small pension plans, the DOL amended the regulations that previously granted all small plans a waiver from the requirement to engage an IQPA. The amendments are effective for plan years beginning after April 17, 2001. There are three requirements to be eligible for the waiver:

1. At least 95 percent of the assets of the plan must constitute "qualifying plan assets" *or* any person who handles assets of the plan that do not constitute qualifying plan assets must be bonded for at least the amount of the value of the nonqualifying plan assets;

2. The plan must satisfy the additional disclosure requirements applicable to the summary annual report (SAR); and

3. The plan administrator must make available without charge each regulated financial institution statement and evidence of any bond as required by item #2 if these are requested from any participant or beneficiary.

[DOL Reg. § 2520.104-46(b)(1)(i)]

### Q 29:5   What are *qualifying plan assets*?

The term *qualifying plan assets* means the following:

1. Qualifying employer securities;
2. Participant loans;
3. Any assets held by
   a. A bank or similar institution,
   b. An insurance company,
   c. A registered broker-dealer, or
   d. Any other organization authorized to act as an IRA trustee;
4. Shares issued by a registered investment company (RIC); or
5. Investment and annuity contracts issued by an insurance company.

[DOL Reg. § 2520.104-46(b)(1)(ii)]

### Q 29:6   What are the disclosure requirements for the SAR?

In addition to the plan's having at least 95 percent of the assets be qualifying plan assets (or being bonded for the value of plan assets that are not qualifying), small plans (plans with fewer than 100 participants) are required to disclose certain financial information annually in the SAR. The SAR for a small plan will need to contain the following:

- The name of each institution holding *qualifying plan assets* (excluding qualifying employer securities and participant loans) and the amount of such assets held by each institution as of the end of the plan year.

- The name of the surety company issuing the bond, if the plan has more than 5 percent of its assets in nonqualifying plan assets.

- A notice indicating that participants and beneficiaries may, upon request and without charge, examine, or receive copies of, evidence of the required bond and statements received from each institution holding qualifying assets that describe the assets held by the institution as of the end of the plan year.

- A notice stating that participants and beneficiaries should contact the regional office of the DOL's Pension and Welfare Benefits Administration if they are unable to examine or obtain copies of statements received from each institution holding qualifying assets or evidence of the required bond, if applicable.

[DOL Reg. § 2520.104-46(b)(1)(i)(B)]

The SAR requirement has been repealed for plan years beginning after December 31, 2007. It has been essentially replaced by an annual funding notice. (See chapter 28.)

### Q 29:7 Are any attachments required to be filed with Schedule B?

Yes. There are various attachments required to be made to the Schedule B, depending on what types of disclosures are required for a specific plan. See chapter 30 for more information regarding these attachments. [ERISA § 103(d)]

All attachments must include the title of the attachments, the name of the plan, the plan sponsor's employer identification number (EIN), and the plan number (PN).

### Q 29:8 Does the IRS require defined benefit plans to file any other forms?

Yes, a defined benefit plan must file other forms if certain events occur:

*IRS Form 1099-R, Distributions From Pensions, Annuities, Retirement or Profit Sharing Plans, IRAs, Insurance Contracts, etc.* This form is required to report distributions from a defined benefit plan. Lump-sum, periodic, and nonperiodic payments are included. Rollovers to individual retirement accounts (IRAs) and other plans must also be included. Form 1099-R must be given to each participant who receives a distribution, and copies of these forms must be sent to the IRS along with transmittal Form 1096, unless Form 1099-R is filed electronically.

*IRS Form 945, Annual Return of Withheld Federal Income Tax.* This form is required to report withheld taxes from participant distributions during a calendar year. If semiweekly deposits are required, Form 945-A is required instead.

*IRS Form 5310, Application for a Determination of a Terminating Plan.* This form is optional for use by a terminating defined benefit plan to request a favorable determination letter on the termination of the plan.

*IRS Form 5310-A, Notice of Plan Merger or Consolidation, Spin-off, or Transfer of Plan Assets or Liabilities; Notice of Qualified Separate Lines of Business.* This form is required to inform the IRS about a merger, spin-off, consolidation, or transfer of plan assets or liabilities. It is also used if a plan sponsor uses separate lines of business for testing and coverage purposes.

*IRS Form 5330, Return of Excise Taxes Related to Employee Benefit Plans.* This form is required to report excise taxes due to prohibited transactions, failure to meet minimum funding standards, nondeductible contributions to a qualified plan, and reversions of plan assets to an employer.

*IRS Form 990-T, Exempt Organization Business Income Tax Return.* This form must be filed by Section 501(a) tax-exempt organizations that file the Form 5500 series and have gross income from an unrelated trade or business of $1,000 or more.

### Q 29:9   What determines which IRS Form 5500 report a defined benefit plan must file?

There are two alternatives in the IRS Form 5500 series: Form 5500 and Form 5500-EZ. The particulars of a plan determine which form and schedules apply to it. For plan years that began before 1999, small plans filed Form 5500-C/R.

*Form 5500 Annual Return/Report of Employee Benefit Plan.* Form 5500 must be filed annually by each pension benefit plan with various schedules depending on the size and features of the plan.

*IRS Form 5500-EZ, Annual Return of One-Participant (Owners and Their Spouses) Retirement Plan.* Form 5500-EZ should be filed by most one-participant plans. A *one-participant plan* is a pension plan that covers only an individual, or an individual and his or her spouse, who wholly owns a trade or business, whether incorporated or unincorporated, or a pension benefit plan for a partnership that covers only the partners, or the partners and the partners' spouses. The plan must meet the minimum coverage requirements of Code Section 410(b) without being combined with any other plan the sponsor may have that covers other employees of the business. The plan cannot cover a business that is a member of an affiliated service group, a controlled group of corporations, or a group of businesses under common control, and cannot cover a business that leases employees.

If a plan sponsor meets all the requirements above and has total plan assets of $100,000 ($250,000 for plan years after December 31, 2006) or less at the end of every plan year ending after January 1, 1994, or has two or more one-participant plans that combined have assets of $100,000 ($250,000 for plan years after December 31, 2006) or less at the end of every plan year ending after January 1, 1994, no Form 5500-EZ or other form has to be filed. Many actuaries feel uncomfortable not filing Form 5500, Schedule B, and request that the client file Form 5500-EZ with the Schedule B attachment, even though one may not be required. It may also be advisable to file Form 5500-EZ in order to file the Schedule P attachment and start the statute of limitations running on that tax year. Most actuaries complete Schedule B in plan years in which no Form 5500-EZ is required for their own records. The actuarial report needs to be completed each year regardless of the requirement for filing the forms.

*Simplified IRS Form 5500.* The Pension Protection Act of 2006 (PPA) authorized the IRS to develop a simplified Form 5500 for plans with fewer than 25 participants for plan years beginning after December 31, 2006, as long as the sponsor is not part of a controlled group or affiliated service group, is not required to be combined with any other plan in order to comply with Code Section 410(b), and use the services of any leased employees.

### Q 29:10   What forms does the DOL require?

The DOL has consolidated its reports with the IRS and the PBGC. The information supplied on the annual IRS Form 5500 series is sent to the DOL after the information is collected by the IRS.

### Q 29:11   Which forms must be filed with the PBGC?

*PBGC Form 1, Annual Premium Payment (including Schedule A, Single-Employer Plan Variable Rate Portion of the Premium).* This form must be filed by PBGC-covered defined benefit plans to report premiums due to the PBGC. Schedule A is used to determine the variable portion of the premium payment. A multiemployer plan is not required to complete or file Schedule A.

*PBGC Form 1-ES, Estimated Premium Payment.* This form is used by plan administrators to make premium payments for the flat-rate portion of the premium payment based on an estimated count of the participants covered and applies to plans with 500 or more participants.

*PBGC Form 200, Notice of Failure to Make Required Contributions.* This form must be filed by plan sponsors that fail to pay minimum funding amounts that, in the aggregate, exceed $1 million.

*PBGC Form 10, Post-Event Notice of Reportable Events.* This form must be filed within 30 days following the occurrence of certain reportable events.

*PBGC Form 10-Advance, Advance Notice of Reportable Events.* This form must be filed at least 30 days before the occurrence of certain reportable events.

*PBGC Form 500, Standard Termination Notice Single-Employer Plan Termination.* This form must be filed and signed by the plan administrator for the certification of information required for standard terminations and must be filed no later than 180 days after the proposed termination date.

*PBGC Form 500, Schedule EA-S, Standard Termination Certification of Sufficiency.* This schedule must be used by the enrolled actuary to certify that the plan is projected to be sufficient and must accompany PBGC Form 500.

*PBGC Form 501, Post-Distribution Certification.* The plan administrator must file this form within 30 days after the last distribution date for any affected party.

*PBGC Form 601, Distress Termination Notice.* The plan administrator must file this form with the PBGC by the 120th day following the proposed termination date for a plan with insufficient assets.

*PBGC Form 601, Schedule EA-D, Distress Termination Enrolled Actuary Certification.* This schedule must be used by the enrolled actuary to report the funding levels of the plan in a distress termination.

## Due Dates

### Q 29:12   When are the various forms due?

The following table outlines the forms and their due dates, including extended due dates and the means of obtaining an extension.

**Due Dates**

| Form | Due Date | Extended Due Date | Extension Request Form |
|---|---|---|---|
| IRS Forms 5500 and Form 5500-EZ and all schedules | Last day of seventh month following the end of the plan year | 15th business day of the 10th month following the end of the plan year or the extended due date of the employer's tax return, if the employer's tax year and the plan tear are the same | IRS Form 5558 or the Extension request for federal tax return of the corporation: the applicable extension request form for the employer's tax return |
| IRS Form 5310 | No required filing date | None | |
| IRS Form 5310-A | Filed at least 30 days before the event triggering the form | | |
| IRS Form 5330 | On or before the last day of the seventh month after the end of the taxable year of the employer for excess 401(k) contribution: last day of the 15th month after the close of the plan year to which the contribution relates | Up to the 13th month following the end of the taxable year of the employer (form filing only is extended, not payment of tax liability) | IRS Form 5558 |

| Form | Due Date | Extended Due Date | Extension Request Form |
|------|----------|-------------------|------------------------|
| IRS Form 5329 | Filed by the same due date as taxpayer's IRS Form 1040 | Due date of extended IRS Form 1040 | |
| IRS Form 1099-R | Participant receiving distributions must receive this form by January 31 following the year of distribution filed with IRS Form 1096 by the last day of February following the year of distribution | March 30 for IRS filing | IRS Form 8809 |
| IRS Form 990-T | April 15 following the year of occurrence of unrelated trade or business income | 15th business day of the 10th month following the end of the plan year | IRS Form 2758 |
| IRS Form 945 | January 31 following the year of distribution, or February 10 if less than $500 is due with the filing | None | |
| PBGC Form 1-ES | Last day of the second full calendar month following the close of the preceding plan year | None | |
| PBGC Form 1 & Form 1-EZ | 15th day of the eighth month following the month the plan year began | None | |
| PBGC Form 200 | Within 10 days from the due date of the required plan contributions | None | |
| PBGC Form 10 | Within 30 days after occurrence of the reportable event | None | |
| PBGC Form 10-Advance | At least 30 days before occurrence of the reportable event | None | |
| PBGC Form 500 | Within 180 days after the proposed termination date | None | |

| Form | Due Date | Extended Due Date | Extension Request Form |
|---|---|---|---|
| PBGC Form 500 schedule EA-S | With the PBGC Form 500 | None | |
| PBGC Form 501 | Within 30 days of the distribution of assets from the trust | No penalty will be charged if filed within 90 days | |
| PBGC Form 601 | Within 120 days after the proposed termination date | None | |
| PBGC Form 601, Schedule EA-D | With PBGC Form 601 | None | |

### Q 29:13   Does the government provide extensions when disasters occur?

Yes, depending on the circumstances. In the event of natural disasters, relief from the filing due dates is generally given to those in the affected areas. In the event of national disasters, relief may be provided to all filers. [I.R.C. § 7508A] For example, due to the events of September 11, 2001, general relief was provided to all filers and specific relief was provided to filers directly affected. [Notice 2001-61, 2001-40 I.R.B. 305; Notice 2001-68, 2001-47 I.R.B. 504] In addition, due to this specific disaster relief, an extension was provided to the due date for making required contributions under Code Section 412. [Ann. 2001-103, 2001-43 I.R.B. 375, Notice 2002-7, 2002-6 I.R.B. 489]

# Chapter 30

# Schedule B Issues

A defined benefit plan subject to the minimum funding standards of Internal Revenue Code (Code) Section 412 must file Schedule B, Actuarial Information, and attach it to Form 5500 or 5500-EZ each year. The Schedule B is completed by an enrolled actuary who is licensed by the Joint Board for the Enrollment of Actuaries. This chapter describes how to complete the 2006 Schedule B and discusses the issues that are encountered by enrolled actuaries in properly completing the Schedule B. Chapters 18 and 19 should be reviewed thoroughly for more information and examples regarding specific terms and calculations.

## What Must Be Filed

### Q 30:1   What is the *Schedule B*?

The *Schedule B* is the record of the funding standard account (FSA) for a certain plan year and details how the minimum required contribution is calculated.

### Q 30:2   Which plans are required to attach a Schedule B to the Form 5500?

The Schedule B is filed for all defined benefit plans [Treas. Reg. § 1.410(a)-2(c)] subject to the minimum funding standards of Code Section 412. Therefore, government plans are not required to file a Schedule B. In addition, although money purchase plans are subject to Code Section 412, they usually are not required to attach a Schedule B to their Form 5500 filing (see Q 30:4).

### Q 30:3   Is a terminating plan required to file a Schedule B?

Yes. A defined benefit plan is subject to the minimum funding standard account (MFSA) in the year of termination but not in the subsequent year. Revenue Ruling 79-237 [1979-2 C.B. 190] states that minimum funding standards apply until the end of the plan year that includes the termination date. Accordingly, the Schedule B is not required to be filed for any later plan year.

However, if a valid termination fails to occur—whether because assets remain in the plan's trust for, generally, longer than one year [Rev. Rul. 89-87, 1989-2 C.B. 81] or for any other reason (e.g., the Pension Benefit Guaranty Corporation (PBGC) issues a notice of noncompliance pursuant to 29 C.F.R. Section 4041.31 for a standard termination)—there is no termination date, and therefore, minimum funding standards continue to apply and a Schedule B continues to be required.

### Q 30:4   Are any other types of plans required to attach a Schedule B?

Generally, no. The only exception is for money purchase plans that have a waived funding deficiency. In this case, a money purchase plan must also attach a Schedule B to the Form 5500, but these plans are to complete only lines 3, 9, and 10 of the Schedule B (see instructions to Schedule R, Form 5500), and the Schedule B does not need to be signed by an actuary in this case. The administrator should review Revenue Ruling 78-223 [1978-1 C.B. 125] for guidance on special requirements if a waiver is in effect.

### Q 30:5   Are any defined benefit plans exempt from filing a Schedule B?

Yes. There are two exceptions to the requirement to file a Schedule B with the Form 5500:

1. Plans that have terminated in the prior year; and
2. Plans that are in compliance with Code Section 412(i).

In addition, the Schedule B does not have to be filed if Form 5500-EZ is not required to be filed for the plan year (e.g., if the employer meets the conditions to be exempt from filing because there is less than $100,000 in assets in all qualified plans of the employer as of the end of the plan year). However, the FSA for the plan must continue to be maintained, even if the Schedule B is not filed.

### Q 30:6 Are there different filing requirements for large and small plans?

Yes. The Schedule B is divided into two parts. Part I is to be completed by all defined benefit plans.

Part II (the Additional Required Funding Charge) is to be completed if the plan has 100 or more participants (active or nonactive) on *any* day of the prior plan year (i.e., a plan is exempt only if the plan did not have 100 or more participants on each day of the prior plan year). If the plan has 100 or fewer participants in the prior plan year, box F must be checked. This count takes into consideration all defined benefit plans of the employer, including any member of the employer's controlled or affiliated service group. Multiemployer plans are exempt from this section.

### Q 30:7 Can the signature of the enrolled actuary be made by stamping or be reproduced by a machine?

No. The signature of the enrolled actuary must be an original signature.

### Q 30:8 May an enrolled actuary qualify his or her signature to the Schedule B?

Yes. The enrolled actuary is permitted to complete and sign the Schedule B subject to qualifications as allowed under Treasury Regulations Section 301.6059-1(d). However, the filing requirement for the Schedule B is not satisfied if the actuary tries to "materially qualify such statement." Permitted qualifications include the following:

1. A statement that the report is based in part on information provided to the actuary by another person, that such information would customarily not be verified by the actuary, and that the actuary has no reason to doubt the substantial accuracy of the information (taking into account the facts and circumstances that are known or reasonably should be known to the actuary, including the contents of any other actuarial report prepared by the actuary for the plan);

2. A statement that the report is based in part on information provided by another person and that the actuary believes such information is or may be inaccurate or incomplete but that the inaccuracies or omissions are not material, the inaccuracies or omissions are not so numerous or flagrant as to suggest that there may be material inaccuracies, and that therefore the actuarial report is substantially accurate and complete and fairly discloses the actuarial position of the plan;

3. A statement that the report reflects the requirement of a regulation or ruling, and that any statement regarding the actuarial position of the plan is made only in light of such requirement;

4. A statement that the report reflects an interpretation of a statute, regulation, or ruling, that the actuary has no reason to doubt the validity of that

interpretation, and that any statement regarding the actuarial position of the plan is made only in light of such interpretation;

5. A statement that in the opinion of the actuary the report fully reflects the requirements of an applicable statute but does not conform to the requirements of a regulation or ruling promulgated under the statute that the actuary believes is contrary to the statute; or

6. A statement of such other information as may be necessary to fully and fairly disclose the actuarial position of the plan.

If the actuary has computed the funding requirements for the plan using qualification item #5 above, he or she must attach a statement (see Q 30:10) stating that he or she has not fully reflected any final or temporary regulation, revenue ruling, or notice in completing the Schedule B. This is required if, in his or her opinion, the actuary has complied with all applicable statutes but believes that a ruling or regulation is in conflict with a statute and that this interpretation may affect the deductibility of a contribution or cause a funding deficiency. This statement (labeled "Schedule B—Statement by the Enrolled Actuary") must indicate whether this interpretation would create either an accumulated funding deficiency or a nondeductible contribution if the actuary's belief is determined to be incorrect. In addition, the actuary must also check the box on the bottom of page 1 of the Schedule B.

## Attachments

### Q 30:9    Are attachments required to be made to the Schedule B?

Yes. Certain attachments are required in particular situations (see Q 30:10). All attachments to the Schedule B must include the following:

1. Name of the plan;

2. Plan sponsor's employer identification number (EIN);

3. Plan number;

4. Title at the top of each attachment stating that it is an attachment to the Schedule B and referencing the line to which the attachment relates; and

5. A descriptive phrase at the top of each attachment for ERISA Filing Acceptance System (EFAST) purposes.

When the package is assembled for filing, the attachments may be placed either directly behind the Schedule B or at the end of the filing.

### Q 30:10    What are some of the attachments that may be required to be made to the Schedule B?

The following is a list of possible attachments that may be required to be made to the Schedule B, with the "proper name" of each (according to the instructions to the Schedule B) that is to be listed at the top of the attachment:

1. Schedule B—Statement by Enrolled Actuary (see Q 30:8);
2. Schedule B, line 4a—412(m)(1) Lookback Rule (see Q 30:27);
3. Schedule B, line 4b—Liquidity Requirement Certification (see Q 30:29);
4. Schedule B, line 6—Statement of Actuarial Assumptions/Methods (see Q 30:32);
5. Schedule B, line 6—Summary of Plan Provisions (see Q 30:32);
6. Schedule B, line 6b—Description of Weighted Average Retirement Age (see Q 30:34);
7. Schedule B, line 6i—Estimated Rate of Investment Return (see Q 30:40);
8. Schedule B, line 8b—Alternative Minimum Funding Standard Account (see Q 30:44);
9. Schedule B, line 8b—Reorganization Status Explanation (see Q 30:44);
10. Schedule B, line 8b—Reorganization Status Worksheet (see Q 30:44);
11. Schedule B, line 8c—Schedule of Active Participant Data (see Q 30:46);
12. Schedule B, lines 9a through 9q—Development of Minimum Contribution Requirement for Each Individual Employer (see Q 30:48);
13. Schedule B, lines 9c and 9j—Schedule of Funding Standard Account Bases (see Q 30:49);
14. Schedule B, Line 9f—Alternative Deficit Reduction Contribution (see Q 30:53);
15. Schedule B, line 9h—Explanation of Prior Year Credit Balance/Funding Deficiency Discrepancy (see Q 30:54);
16. Schedule B, line 11—Justification for Change in Actuarial Assumptions (see Q 30:65);
17. Schedule B, line 11—Change in Current Liability Assumptions Approval Date (see Q 30:65);
18. Schedule B, line 12a—Change in Current Liability Applicable Condition (see Q 30:67);
19. Schedule B, line 12a—TRA '97 Transition Rule (see Q 30:67);
20. Schedule B, line 12a—Volatility Lookback Rule (see Q 30:67);
21. Schedule B, line 12j—Schedule of DRC Bases (see Q 30:72);
22. Schedule B, line 12m(4)—Alternative UCEB Calculation (see Q 30:73).

## Line-by-Line Instructions

### Q 30:11  What is the actuarial valuation date that needs to be entered on line 1a?

The actuarial valuation date is the date as of which all assets and liabilities are valued and as of which the funding requirements are determined for the plan. The valuation date for a plan year may be any date in the plan year, including the first or last day of the plan year. A valuation date can also be in a prior plan year as long as the assets of the plan exceed 125 percent of the current liability (defined in Code Section 412(c)(7)(B), the ERISA full-funding limit accrued liability) for the plan. In such case, the information used in the valuation must be actuarially adjusted to reflect any significant differences that occur in the plan year.

The valuation date is considered part of the funding method, and a change in the valuation date is considered a change in funding method. A change to the first day of the plan year has automatic approval, or, if the plan is terminating and is fully funded, the plan can change the valuation date to the date of plan termination.

### Q 30:12   What is included in the current value of assets for line 1b(1)?

The current value of assets is equal to the fair market value (FMV) of the assets as of the valuation date. The FMV does not include contributions for the year of valuation made before the valuation date and is not adjusted for credit balances or bases. Current assets do not include contributions for the current plan year. Rollovers or other assets that are not available to provide defined benefits are also excluded. Asset and liability amounts should be determined in a consistent manner each year, meaning that if a particular asset is excluded, the liability attributable to such asset should also be excluded.

**Example.** The Bedrock defined benefit pension plan purchases a whole life insurance policy to provide death benefits. The cash value of the policy is excluded for purposes of line 1b(1); therefore, the liability attributable to the death benefit should also be excluded for purposes of lines 1c(1), 1c(2), 1d(2), and 1d(3).

### Q 30:13   What is included in the actuarial value of assets for line 1b(2)?

The actuarial value of assets is determined in accordance with Code Section 412(c)(2). This requires the method used to be in compliance with the following:

1. The method must be applied on a consistent basis.
2. The method must be described and specified in the actuarial report.
3. The method must take into account the FMV or the average value.
4. The method cannot produce a result that is consistently above or below the FMV and the average value.
5. The actuarial value of the assets must fall within 80 percent of the FMV (or 85 percent of the average value) and must be no greater than 120 percent of the FMV (or 115 percent of the average value).

The actuarial value of assets is not adjusted for credit balances or amortization bases and does not include contributions for the year of valuation made before the valuation date. See chapter 21 for permissible methods of determining the actuarial value of assets.

### Q 30:14 What is the accrued liability for immediate gain methods as required for line 1c(1)?

ERISA Section 3(29) defines the term *accrued liability* as the excess of the present value measured as of a particular point in time (usually the valuation date) of the projected future benefit costs and administrative expenses for all plan participants and beneficiaries over the present value of future contributions (also known as the present value of future normal costs) of all applicable plan participants and beneficiaries. The accrued liability may be calculated differently for different types of funding methods. Immediate-gain funding methods include unit credit, entry-age normal, and individual-level premium. This line is not applicable for spread-gain funding methods.

### Q 30:15 What is the unfunded liability for methods with bases as required by line 1c(2)(a)?

This is applicable only for the frozen initial liability and attained-age normal funding methods. The *frozen initial liability method* determines the unfunded accrued liability using the entry-age normal funding method, while the *attained-age normal method* determines the unfunded accrued liability using the unit credit funding method (see chapter 18).

### Q 30:16 How is the entry-age normal accrued liability determined for line 1c(2)(b)?

Line 1c(2)(b) is completed only for spread-gain funding methods such as the aggregate, individual aggregate, frozen initial liability, and attained-age normal funding methods. The accrued liability in the entry-age normal funding method is what the value of the normal cost would be if the normal cost had been contributed to the plan each year from the employee's date of hire. If the present value of projected benefits is known as of the valuation date and the present value of all normal costs to be made to the plan in the future is subtracted from that amount, the remainder is how much money would have accumulated since the contributions began at each employee's hire date. The mathematical expression for the accrued liability is as follows:

Accrued liability = Present value of future − Present value of future normal costs

### Q 30:17 How is the entry-age normal cost determined for line 1c(2)(c)?

Like line 1c(2)(b) (see Q 30:16), line 1c(2)(c) is completed only for spread-gain funding methods. The entry-age normal funding method develops the normal cost by calculating what the contribution would have been starting from the earliest age at which the employee could have participated in a plan of the employer (generally, the employee's date of hire) if the plan had always been in existence. The mathematical expression for the normal cost for each participant would be as follows:

$$\text{Normal cost} = \frac{\text{Present value of future}}{\text{benefits at date of hire}} \div \frac{\text{Present value of annuity due of}}{\$1 \text{ over future working years}}$$

The plan's normal cost is the sum of the normal costs for all participants.

### Q 30:18 How is the amount excluded from current liability determined for line 1d(1)?

Code Section 412(l)(7)(D) allows certain preparticipation service to be disregarded in calculating the current liability for the additional funding charge under Code Section 412(l) and for determining current liability for the variable rate premium. [ERISA § 302(d)(7)] If the employer has made an election not to disregard such service, a zero must be entered on line 1d(1). Otherwise, the amount excluded from the Retirement Protection Act of 1994 (RPA '94) current liability should be entered.

The plan sponsor makes a one-time election to exclude a percentage of the benefits accrued before the time the participant entered the plan. Once made, this election cannot be revoked without the consent of the Secretary of the Treasury. The percentage that can be excluded is based on the number of years the participant has participated in the plan, as follows:

| Years of Participation | Percentage Excluded |
| --- | --- |
| 1 | 80% |
| 2 | 60% |
| 3 | 40% |
| 4 | 20% |
| 5 or more | 0% |

For the plan sponsor to disregard preparticipation service, the participant at the time of becoming a participant must

1. Not have accrued any benefits under any other defined benefit plan (whether or not terminated) maintained by the employer or a member of the same controlled group of which the employer is a member;
2. Not have participated in the plan before December 31, 1987; and
3. Have years of service greater than the minimum years of service necessary for eligibility to participate in the plan.

If there is a future amendment increasing benefits for preparticipation service, the then-current phase-in percentage is used. [1997 Gray Book from the Enrolled Actuaries Meeting, Q&A 11]

The rest of the current liabilities as calculated for lines 1d and 2b are adjusted for this election.

This election is not applicable in determining the full-funding limits.

### Q 30:19   How is the RPA '94 current liability determined for line 1d(2)(a)?

The RPA '94 current liability is calculated using the current liability interest rate within the 90 percent to 105 percent corridor. However, there was a special rule under Code Section 412(b)(5)(B)(ii)(II) which provided that for the 2005 and 2004 plan years, the interest rate used to determine current liability must not be above and must not be more than 10 percent below the weighted average of the rates of interest, as set forth by the Treasury Department, on amounts invested conservatively in long-term investment-grade corporate bonds during the four-year period ending on the last day before the beginning of the 2005 plan year. [Notice 2004-34, 2004-1 C.B. 848]

The RPA '94 current liability must be computed using the 1983 Group Annuity Mortality (GAM) (sex distinct) table from Revenue Ruling 95-28 [1995-1 C.B. 74] and, for disabled lives, the table from Revenue Ruling 96-7. [1996-1 C.B. 59]

All other actuarial assumptions used in calculating the FSA are also used for this purpose. However, no salary-scale assumption may be used. In addition, service is calculated through the end of the prior plan year, regardless of the valuation date.

### Q 30:20   How is the increase in the RPA '94 current liability determined for line 1d(2)(b)?

The increase in the RPA '94 current liability is the increase in the current liability assumed to occur due to increases in accrued benefits or salary during the plan year. For purposes of line 1d(2)(b), one year's salary scale may be assumed.

### Q 30:21   How is the current liability computed at the highest allowable rate determined for line 1d(2)(c)?

If required, the current liability for line 1d(2)(c) is determined in the same manner as for line 1d(2)(a), except that the highest interest rate allowed (105 percent of the weighted average interest rate on amounts invested conservatively in long-term investment grade corporate bonds during the four-year period ending on the last day before the beginning of the 2006 plan year) is used.

**Note.** Line 1d(2)(c) is not applicable for small plans (those with fewer than 100 participants on each day of the prior plan year) that do not complete Section II of the Schedule B, including multiemployer plans. In addition, this line does not need to be completed if the actuarial value of assets exceeds the

RPA '94 current liability (line 1b(2) divided by line 1d(2)(a)) by 90 percent or more. However, if this line is not completed, sufficient records should be retained so that the current liability amount that would otherwise have been entered on this line can be computed at a later time if required.

### Q 30:22  How are the expected plan disbursements determined for line 1d(3)?

The total amount of plan disbursements (including single-sum distributions) expected to be paid for the plan year after the valuation date is entered on line 1d(3). This total is determined as of the valuation date and adjusted with interest to the end of the plan year at the valuation interest rate. [Rev. Rul. 96-21, Q&A 8, 1996-1 C.B. 64]

### Q 30:23  How is the current value of assets determined for line 2a?

The current value of assets for line 2a is the same as the value entered on line 1(b)(1) (see Q 30:12), but is reported as of the beginning of the plan year. This is equal to line 11l, column a, of Schedule H; line 1c, column a, of Schedule I; or line 11a, column a, of Form 5500-EZ. Line 2a excludes, however, assets that are not available to provide defined benefits under the plan (e.g., certain types of rollovers) and contributions designated for the 2004 plan year.

### Q 30:24  How is the RPA '94 current liability calculated as of the beginning of the plan year for line 2b?

The same assumptions and methods are used in this calculation as are used for line 1d(2)(a) (see Q 30:19). Increases in current liability due to benefits accruing during the plan year are excluded. Three columns require answers on line 1d(2)(a):

*Column 1:*

The total number of participants as of the beginning of the plan year;

*Column 2:*

The portion of the liability attributable to vested benefits; and

*Column 3:*

The current liability attributable to all benefits, both vested and nonvested.

### Q 30:25  How are the total assets divided by total RPA '94 current liability determined for line 2c?

The amount in line 2c is equal to line 2a divided by line 2b(4). However, line 2c is completed only if the value is less than 70 percent; otherwise, it is left blank. [ERISA § 103(d)(11)]

### Q 30:26    How are contributions to the plan determined for line 3?

All employer and employee contributions made for that plan year are entered in the table for line 3. Only contributions deposited before the signing of the Schedule B should be entered. If the number of contributions exceeds the number of lines available, the actuary is allowed to total the contributions made by month. All contributions must be included on line 3 because attachments are not bar coded.

### Q 30:27    How is the funded current liability percentage determined for line 4a?

The funded current liability percentage is equal to the actuarial value of assets (line 1b(2)) divided by the RPA '94 current liability (line 1d(2)(a)) as reported on the prior year's Schedule B. [Rev. Rul. 95-31, 1995-1 C.B. 76] Plans with a current liability percentage of less than 100 percent are subject to the quarterly contribution requirements (see chapter 19).

For 2004, the funded current liability percentage for the preceding plan year is equal to line 1b(2) divided by line 1d(2)(a), both lines as reported on the 2003 Schedule B. If line 1d(2)(a) is zero for 2003 or if the plan is a new plan, enter 100 percent.

The Pension Funding Equity Act of 2004 (PFEA) provided a lookback rule for the purpose of applying Code Section 412(m)(1) for plan years beginning after December 31, 2003. If this lookback rule is used, a demonstration must be attached to the Schedule B, labeled "Schedule B, line 4a—412(m)(1) Lookback Rule."

### Q 30:28    What is the lookback rule provided by Section 101(d)(2) of the PFEA?

The lookback rule provides that for plan years beginning after December 31, 2003, the changes made by the PFEA may be applied as if such amendments had been in effect for all prior plan years.

### Q 30:29    How is the liquidity shortfall determined for line 4b?

If the plan is subject to the liquidity requirement, enter the liquidity shortfall (if none, enter zero) for each quarter of the plan year on line 4b. A liquidity shortfall is equal to the excess of three times the sum of the adjusted disbursements from the plan for the 12 months ending on the last day of the quarter over the plan's liquid assets. The term *adjusted disbursements* means disbursements from the plan reduced by the product of the plan's funded current liability percentage for the plan year and the sum of all disbursements made. The term *liquid assets* means cash, marketable securities, and other such assets.

The consequences of failing to meet the liquidity requirements are as follows:

1. There is an additional interest charge to the FSA under Code Section 412(m)(1);

2. The employer is treated as failing to make a required installment for purposes of Code Section 412(n)(1)(A);

3. A 10 percent excise tax under Code Section 4971(f) is applicable. File Form 5330 with the IRS to pay the 10 percent excise tax; and

4. Fiduciaries are prohibited from making certain payments from the plan under ERISA Section 206(e).

If the special rule for nonrecurring circumstances is used in the computation of the liquidity requirement, a certification by the enrolled actuary must be attached to the Schedule B, labeled "Schedule B, Line 4b—Liquidity Requirement Certification." [I.R.C. § 412(m)(5)(E)(ii)(II); Rev. Rul. 95-31, Q&A 13, 1995-1 C.B. 76]

The following plans are exempt from this computation:

1. Multiemployer plans;

2. Plans with a funded current liability percentage of 100 percent or more; and

3. Plans with 100 or fewer participants on every day of the prior year.

### Q 30:30  What is the actuarial cost method used by the plan for purposes of completing line 5?

The term *actuarial cost method* means the actuarial technique used in calculating the amount of the annual cost of pension plan benefits and expenses. [ERISA § 3(31)] The actuarial cost method to enter in this line refers to the primary funding method used by the plan (e.g., unit credit, aggregate).

If one method is used to establish an accrued liability for use under the frozen initial liability method for subsequent years, line 5 should be completed as if the frozen initial liability method was used in all years.

If the shortfall method is used, the appropriate box should be checked for the underlying method used to determine the annual computation charge.

### Q 30:31  What is a change in funding method for purposes of line 5i?

The funding method of a plan includes not only the specific type of funding method used by the plan but also all underlying computations used in applying the overall method. The funding method of a plan includes, for example, the date on which assets and liabilities are valued (the valuation date) and the definition of compensation that is used to determine the normal cost or accrued liability. A change in funding method is any change made to any aspect of the funding method, whether that be to the cost method, valuation date, or method used to determine the actuarial value of assets. [Rev. Proc. 2000-40, § 2.02, 2000-42 I.R.B. 357]

**Note.** If the change in funding method was made pursuant to Revenue Procedure 2000-40 [2000-42 I.R.B. 357], or Revenue Procedure 2000-41[2000-42 I.R.B. 371], "yes" should be checked on line 5j. If approval was granted by either an individual ruling letter or a class ruling letter for this plan, enter the date of the applicable ruling letter on line 5k.

**Note.** The plan sponsor's agreement to a change in funding method (made pursuant to Revenue Procedure 2000-40 or a class ruling letter) should be reported on line 7 of Schedule R (Form 5500). A separate attachment showing the plan sponsor's agreement need not be made.

(See chapter 18 for more information on changing the funding method of a plan.)

### Q 30:32   What are the actuarial assumptions used by the actuary and listed on line 6?

The actuarial assumptions include, for example, the valuation interest rate assumption, assumed retirement age, mortality table, rates of disability, salary scale, rates of turnover, and expense assumption. If line 6 does not fully describe the actuarial assumptions, the actuary must attach a statement labeled "Schedule B, line 6—Statement of Actuarial Assumptions/Methods" describing the actuarial assumptions and methods used to calculate the figures on the Schedule B (see Q 30:10).

In addition, the actuary must also attach a summary of the principal eligibility and benefit provisions on which the valuation was based, an identification of benefits not included in the valuation, a description of any significant events that occurred during the year, a summary of any changes in principal eligibility or benefit provisions since the last valuation, a description of plan early retirement factors, and any change in actuarial assumptions or cost methods and justifications for any such change. This attachment must be labeled "Schedule B, line 6— Summary of Plan Provisions" (see Q 30:10).

Also, the actuary should include any other information needed to disclose the actuarial position of the plan fully and fairly.

### Q 30:33   What are the current liability interest rates for line 6a?

The current liability interest rates are the current liability interest rates used in determining the RPA '94 current liability, computed to the nearest .01 percent (see Q 30:19). Generally, the interest rate used must not fall outside the corridor of 90 percent to 105 percent of the weighted average interest rate. [I.R.C. § 412(l)(7)(C)(i)] However, there was a special rule under Code Section 412(b)(5)(B)(ii)(II) which provided that, for the 2005 and 2004 plan years, the interest rate used to determine current liability must not be above and must not be more than 10 percent below the weighted average of the rates of interest, as set forth by the Treasury Department, on amounts invested conservatively in long-term investment-grade corporate bonds during the four-year period ending on the last day before the beginning of the plan year. [Notice 90-11, 1990-1 C.B. 319; Rev. Rul. 96-21, 1996-1 C.B. 64]

### Q 30:34   What is the weighted average retirement age for line 6b?

If each participant is assumed to retire upon attainment of the plan's normal retirement age (NRA), the plan's NRA is entered on this line. An age should be entered; do not enter "NRA." If the NRA differs for individual participants, enter a weighted NRA. Attach a page to the Schedule B labeled "Schedule B, line 6b— Description of Weighted Average Retirement Age" describing the methodology used, the weight applied at each potential retirement age, and the rate of retirement at each age. Otherwise, enter the assumed retirement age.

### Q 30:35   What are the mortality table codes that can be entered on line 6d?

Table 30-1 shows the allowable codes for various common mortality tables.

**Table 30-1. Allowable Codes for Mortality Tables**

| Mortality Table | Code |
| --- | --- |
| 1951 Group Annuity | 1 |
| 1971 Group Annuity Mortality (GAM) | 2 |
| 1971 Individual Annuity Mortality (IAM) | 3 |
| UP-1984 | 4 |
| 1983 IAM | 5 |
| 1983 GAM | 6 |
| 1983 GAM (solely per Revenue Ruling 95-28) | 7 |
| UP-1994 | 8 |
| Other | 9 |
| None | 0 |

**Note:** Code 7 is to be used *only* for the 1983 GAM table as published in Revenue Ruling 95-28 [1995-1 C.B. 74]. This was supposed to be the table that was blended 50 percent male and 50 percent female, but there was an error in the published rates. If a 1983 GAM table that is blended properly is used, code 9 (Other) must be entered.

If the female version of a table is used, an "F" must be added to the code.

If a setback or setforward is used, a "–" or a "+" must be added after the table code.

If a projection is used, a "P" must be added after the code with the year of projection.

### Q 30:36   What is the valuation liability interest rate to be entered on line 6e?

The valuation liability interest rate is the expected interest rate to be earned by the plan assets, both before and after retirement. If the assumed rate varies with the year, the weighted average over the following 20 years should be entered. This should be determined to the nearest 0.01 percent.

### Q 30:37  What is the expense loading assumption to be entered on line 6f?

The expense loading assumption is made by the plan actuary and is equal to what he or she believes is a reasonable expense assumption for the plan. If expenses are not payable from plan assets, it may be reasonable to enter zero here or, for example, when the investment return assumption is already adjusted to take into account expenses.

**Note.** The actuary should be careful not to violate Actuarial Standard of Practice (ASOP) No. 27, which may require the use of an explicit expense assumption (see chapter 23).

If there is only one expense loading assumption, this assumption should be entered as a preretirement rate, and "N/A" should be entered under "post-retirement." If expenses are assumed as a flat dollar amount (rather than as a percentage), it is necessary to calculate the preretirement assumption as a percentage of normal cost (or net amortization amounts if the normal cost is zero), and the postretirement assumption as a percentage of plan liabilities. The rate should be entered to the nearest 0.01 percent.

### Q 30:38  What are the annual rates of withdrawal for line 6g?

The annual rates of withdrawal are the turnover assumptions selected by the actuary. Certain rates of withdrawal applicable at ages 25, 40, and 55 need to be entered for males and females. If the actuary is using a *select table* (i.e., the rate of withdrawal for a new participant at the age shown is different for participants with the same age but longer service), he or she should enter an "S" before the rate. If the actuary is using an *ultimate table* (i.e., all participants of the age shown are assumed to experience the same withdrawal rates, regardless of service), he or she should enter a "C" before the rate if criteria other than service apply to the rates used. This rate should be computed to the nearest 0.01 percent. (See appendix E for various rates of turnover using standard tables.)

### Q 30:39  What is the salary-scale assumption to be entered on line 6h?

The rate entered must be a level rate of salary increase used for a participant from age 25 to assumed retirement age. If the rate is not level, it must be converted to a level rate. This rate must be calculated to the nearest 0.01 percent. If the benefit formula is not related to compensation, "N/A" should be checked.

### Q 30:40  How is the estimated investment return on the actuarial value of assets determined for line 6i?

The estimated investment return on the actuarial value of assets is measured over the one-year period ending on the valuation date. If the plan uses a beginning-of-year valuation, the estimated investment return is measured over the prior plan year. The rate of return is determined using the following formula:

$$2I/(A+B-I)$$

$I$ is the dollar amount of the investment return under the asset valuation method used for the plan. $A$ is the actuarial value of the assets one year ago. $B$ is the actuarial value of the assets on the current valuation date. The rate must be entered to the nearest 0.01 percent.

If there has been a change in the asset valuation method during the year of this measurement, the interest ($I$) is determined by ignoring the change in method. The asset value at year end ($B$) is determined using the new method. [2001 Gray Book of the Enrolled Actuaries Meeting, Q&A 8]

This formula must be used even if it does not represent very well the rate of return for the assets. However, the actuary may attach a statement showing a different rate of return along with the calculation of such rate. This attachment must be labeled "Schedule B, line 6i—Estimated Rate of Investment Return" (see Q 30:10).

### Q 30:41　How is the estimated investment return on the current value of assets determined for line 6j?

This estimate is done in the same manner as for line 6i, but using the current (fair market) value of the plan's assets for the one-year period ending on the valuation date.

### Q 30:42　How are the new amortization bases established for the plan year listed on line 7?

All new amortization bases established during that plan year are to be listed; even those that are considered fully amortized due to the application of the ERISA full-funding limit (line 9L(4)) should be listed. Table 30-2 shows codes that should be used when listing the types of amortization bases.

**Table 30-2. Codes for Amortization Bases**

| Code | Type of Amortization Base |
| --- | --- |
| 1 | Experience gain or loss |
| 2 | Shortfall gain or loss |
| 3 | Change in unfunded liability due to plan amendment |
| 4 | Change in unfunded liability due to change in actuarial assumptions |
| 5 | Change in unfunded liability due to change in actuarial cost method |
| 6 | Waiver of the minimum funding standard |
| 7 | Switchback from alternative funding standard account |
| 8 | Initial unfunded liability (for new plan) |

**Note:** A minus sign should be entered to the left of a credit base.

### Q 30:43 What is required to be entered for funding waivers and extensions for purposes of line 8a?

The enrolled actuary should enter the date of the ruling letter granting approval for a waiver of a funding deficiency or an extension of an amortization period for this plan year. If a waiver of a funding deficiency or an extension of an amortization period is pending, the Schedule B should be filed showing a deficiency. Once the request for waiver has been approved and received, the actuary should prepare an amended Schedule B and this amended Schedule B should be filed with page 1 of the Form 5500 to report the waiver or extension.

### Q 30:44 What alternative methods or rules can be used in calculating the MFSA for line 8b?

Alternative methods or rules are available to certain plans in calculating the MFSA. If one of these methods or rules is used, one of the codes noted in Table 30-3 should be entered.

**Table 30-3. Codes for Methods or Rules Used to Calculate Minimum Funding Standard**

| Code | Method or Rule |
|------|----------------|
| 1 | Shortfall method |
| 2 | Alternative Funding Standard Account (AFSA) |
| 3 | Shortfall method used with AFSA |
| 4 | Plan in reorganization status |
| 5 | Shortfall method used when in reorganization status |

The shortfall method can be used only by certain collectively bargained plans. Advance approval by the IRS is not required to use the shortfall method as long as it is first adopted for the first plan year to which Code Section 412 applies. (See chapter 19 for more information regarding the shortfall funding method.)

If the alternative MFSA is used (which can be used only if the plan uses the entry-age normal cost method), a worksheet must be attached and labeled "Schedule B, line 8b—Alternative Minimum Funding Standard Account" (see Q 30:10). The worksheet should show:

1. The prior year alternate funding deficiency (if any);
2. Normal cost;
3. Excess, if any, of the value of accrued benefits (excluding current year accruals) over the market value of assets (reduced by the amount of any contributions for the current plan year);
4. Interest on items #1, #2, and #3 above;
5. Employer contributions;
6. Interest on item #5 above; and

7. Funding deficiency: if the sum of items #1 through #4 above is greater than the sum of items #5 and #6 above, the difference should be entered.

In any plan year in which a multiemployer plan is in reorganization (see Q 30:45), the accumulated funding deficiency of the plan should be determined under Code Section 418B. If the plan is in reorganization for that plan year, the actuary must attach an explanation of the basis for the determination and label the explanation "Schedule B, line 8b—Reorganization Status Explanation." In addition, the actuary must attach a worksheet labeled "Schedule B, line 8b—Reorganization Status Worksheet," showing the following for that plan year:

1. The amounts considered contributed by employers;
2. Any amount waived by the IRS;
3. The development of the minimum contribution requirement (taking into account the applicable overburden credit, cash-flow amount, contribution bases, and limitation on required increases on the rate of employer contributions); and
4. The resulting accumulated funding deficiency, if any, which is to be reported on line 9p.

### Q 30:45   When is a multiemployer plan considered to be in reorganization status?

A multiemployer plan is in reorganization status for a plan year if the plan's reorganization index for that year is greater than zero. In general, a plan's reorganization index for any plan year is the excess of (1) the vested benefits charge for such year over (2) the net charge to the FSA for such year. The net charge to the FSA for any plan year is the excess (if any) of (1) the charges to the FSA for such year under Code Section 412(b)(2) over (2) the credits to the FSA under Code Section 412(b)(3)(B). The vested benefits charge for any plan year is the amount that would be necessary to amortize the plan's unfunded vested benefits as of the end of the base plan year in equal annual installments over 10 years (if the benefits are attributable to participants in pay status), or over 25 years (for any other benefits). [I.R.C. § 418]

### Q 30:46   What plans are required to attach a schedule of active participant data?

All plans covered by the PBGC (see chapter 24), other than multiemployer plans, are required to make an attachment labeled "Schedule B, line 8c—Schedule of Active Participant Data." This attachment must show the number of active participants in various age and service groupings. Plans with more than 1,000 participants must also show average compensation data for the active participants within each group. *Compensation* is defined as plan compensation (as limited by Code Section 401(a)(17)). No compensation information should be entered for groups of fewer than 20 participants. For purposes of this attachment, years of service are years of credited service under the plan's benefit formula. Partial years are rounded down.

If multiple employer plans are computing the funding requirements as if each employer maintained a separate plan, this attachment to the Schedule B should be completed in the same manner.

In addition to the age and service groupings, if the plan is a cash balance plan (or any plan using the characteristic code 1C on line 8a of the Form 5500) and is reporting 1,000 or more active participants on line 2b(3), the grid must also provide the average cash balance account of the active participants in that group, regardless of whether all active participants have cash balance accounts. It is not necessary to enter the average cash balance account in any grouping that contains fewer than 20 participants.

The attachment should look similar to the following:

**Schedule B, Line 8c—Schedule of Active Participant Data**

| Attained Age | YEARS OF CREDITED SERVICE | | | | | | | | | | | |
| | Under 1 | | | 1 to 4 | | | 5 to 9 | | | 40 & up | | |
| | No. | Average | | No. | Average | | No. | Average | | No. | Average | |
| | | Comp. | Cash Bal. | | Comp. | Cash Bal. | | Comp. | Cash Bal. | | Comp. | Cash Bal. |
| Under 25 | | | | | | | | | | | | |
| 25 to 29 | | | | | | | | | | | | |
| 30 to 34 | | | | | | | | | | | | |
| 35 to 39 | | | | | | | | | | | | |
| 40 to 44 | | | | | | | | | | | | |
| 45 to 49 | | | | | | | | | | | | |
| 50 to 54 | | | | | | | | | | | | |
| 55 to 59 | | | | | | | | | | | | |
| 60 to 64 | | | | | | | | | | | | |
| 65 to 69 | | | | | | | | | | | | |
| 70 & up | | | | | | | | | | | | |

In general, data to be shown in each age/service bin includes: (1) the number of active participants in the age/service bin, (2) the average compensation of the active participants in the age/service bin, and (3) the average cash balance account of the active participant in the age/service bin, using $0 for anyone who has no cash balance account-based benefit. If the accrued benefit is the greater of a cash balance benefit or some other benefit, average in only the cash balance account. If the accrued benefit is the sum of a cash balance account benefit and some other benefit, average in only the cash balance account. For both the average compensation and the average cash balance account, do not enter an amount for age/service bins with fewer than 20 participants.

In lieu of the above, two alternatives are provided for showing compensation and cash balance accounts. Each alternative provides for two age/service scatters (one showing compensation and one showing cash balance accounts) as follows:

1. Alternative A:

Scatter 1—Provide participant count and average compensation for all active participants, whether or not participants have account-based benefits.

Scatter 2—Provide participant count and average cash balance account for all active participants, whether or not participants have account-based benefits.

2. Alternative B:

Scatter 1—Provide participant count and average compensation for all active participants, whether or not participants have account-based benefits (i.e., identical to Scatter 1 in Alternative A).

Scatter 2—Provide participant count and average cash balance account for only those active participants with account-based benefits. If the number of participants with account-based benefits in a bin is fewer than 20, the average account should not be shown even if there are more than 20 participants in this bin on Scatter 1.

In general, information should be determined as of the valuation date. Average cash balance accounts may be determined as of either: (1) the valuation date, or (2) the day immediately preceding the valuation date.

Average cash balance accounts that are offset by amounts from another plan may be reported either as amounts prior to taking into account the offset, or as amounts after taking into account the offset. Do not report the offset amount. For any other unusual or unique situation, the attachment should include an explanation of what is being provided.

### Q 30:47 How is line 9 completed for plans using the shortfall funding method?

The normal cost entered on line 9b for a plan using the shortfall funding method is equal to the charge per unit of production (or per unit of service) multiplied by the actual number of units of production (or units of service) that occurred during the plan year. The amortization amounts entered on lines 9c and 9l are calculated in the same way.

### Q 30:48 How should line 9 be completed for multiple employer plans?

If the plan is a multiple employer plan subject to the rules of Code Section 413(c)(4)(A), all minimum funding requirements are calculated separately for each adopting employer. In such case, the actuary must attach a schedule for each employer showing the individually calculated amounts for lines 9a through 9q and must label this attachment "Schedule B, lines 9a through 9q—Development of Minimum Contribution Requirement for Each Individual Employer." These individual calculations should then be totaled for input on the appropriate lines on the Schedule B.

For purposes of the 100 percent of unfunded current liability deduction or the small-plan exemption from the additional funding charge, employees are counted on an individual-employer basis. [1997 Gray Book from the Enrolled Actuaries Meeting, Q&A 9] Therefore, the applicability of deficit reduction contributions (DRC), quarterly contributions, and so forth is determined separately for each employer.

## Q 30:49  What is required to be attached if there are amortization charges or credits on lines 9c or 9j?

If there are amortization charges or credits on lines 9c or 9j, the actuary must attach a maintenance schedule of FSA bases, and label the schedule "Schedule B, lines 9c and 9j—Schedule of Funding Standard Account Bases." The attachment should indicate the type of base, the outstanding balance of each base, the number of years remaining in the amortization period, and the amortization amount. If any bases were combined in the current year, the attachment must show information on the bases both before and after the combining of bases.

If an election was made under Code Section 412(b)(7)(F), applicable only to multiemployer plans, to defer a portion of an amount otherwise determined under Code Section 412(b)(2)(B)(iv), include an attachment describing this calculation and label the schedule, "Schedule B, line 9c—Deferral of Charge for Portion of Net Experience Loss."

## Q 30:50  How are funding waiver bases amortized for purposes of line 9c(2)?

All bases that are established due to a funding waiver are amortized using the mandated rate in Code Section 412(d). The mandated rate is equal to the following:

1. For plans other than multiemployer plans, the greater of (a) 150 percent of the federal midterm rate (as in effect under Code Section 1274 for the first month of such plan year) or (b) the valuation interest rate; or
2. For multiemployer plans, the federal short-term rate for the first month in each calendar quarter.

Funding waiver bases are amortized over five years if the base was established after 1988 (15 years for bases established before such date).

## Q 30:51  How is interest calculated to the last day of the plan year for purposes of line 9d?

Interest is calculated using the valuation interest rate in adjusting all charges to the end of the plan year, except that for a funding waiver, the mandated rate (see Q 30:50) is used to accumulate the interest on the amortization charge to the end of the year.

## Q 30:52  How is the additional interest charge due to late quarterly contributions determined for line 9e?

If the funded current liability percentage for the prior year (as reported on line 4a) was at least 100 percent, quarterly contributions are not required. Each quarterly contribution is equal to 25 percent of the lesser of (1) 90 percent of the current year's minimum required contribution, or (2) 100 percent of the prior year's minimum required contribution. If the prior plan year was a short plan year, only 90 percent of the current year's minimum required contribution should be used. [Notice 89-52, Q&A 4, 1989-1 C.B. 692] Quarterly contributions are due 15 days after the end of each plan quarter.

In determining the minimum required contribution for the prior year, an accumulated funding deficiency is included, but a waived minimum funding requirement is ignored. [Notice 89-52, Q&As 7, 8, 1989-1 C.B. 692] The minimum funding requirement for a plan year is determined without regard to any credit balance as of the beginning of such plan year. [Notice 89-52, Q&A 6, 1989-1 C.B. 692] A credit balance may be used to satisfy the quarterly installment *if* the contribution that creates the credit balance has been contributed before the due date of the installment. [Notice 89-52, Q&A 12, 1989-1 C.B. 692]

In determining the additional interest charge, interest is charged from the due date to the actual date of deposit. The interest rate used for this purpose is equal to the greater of:

1. 175 percent of the federal midterm rate at the beginning of the plan year;

2. The rate used to determine the RPA '94 current liability; or

3. The valuation rate.

If quarterly contributions are made and later determined to be nondeductible, Revenue Procedure 90-49 [1990-2 C.B. 620] provides rules for allowing a return to the employer of such contributions.

### Q 30:53   What is entered on line 9f?

The entry for this line is the required additional funding charge found on line 12q, or N/A if it is not applicable.

If an election was made under Code Section 412(l)(12) to reduce the amount of contributions required under Code Section 412(l)(1), determined without regard to Code Section 412(l)(12), an attachment must be included describing this calculation and labeled "Schedule B, Line 9f—Alternative Deficit Reduction Contribution."

### Q 30:54   How is the credit balance or funding deficiency determined for line 9h?

In general, the credit balance or funding deficiency as of the beginning of one year is equal to the ending credit balance or funding deficiency from the prior year. If these two amounts are not equal, the actuary must attach a statement, labeled "Schedule B, line 9h—Explanation of Prior-year Credit Balance/Funding Deficiency Discrepancy," and must fully describe the reason for the discrepancy.

### Q 30:55   How is the ERISA full-funding limitation determined for purposes of line 9l(1)?

The ERISA full-funding limitation is equal to the excess (if any) of (1) the accrued liability (including normal cost) under the plan over (2) the lesser of the

FMV of the plan's assets or the actuarial value of assets. [I.R.C. § 412(c)(7)] The accrued liability is determined under the method used to determine costs if the accrued liability can be directly calculated (the unit credit method), or under the entry-age normal funding method if such accrued liability cannot be directly calculated under the funding method used for the plan. [Rev. Rul. 81-13, 1981-1 C.B. 229]

The ERISA full-funding limitation can be calculated solely based on other entries on the Schedule B. It is equal to

1. *For plans using the unit credit funding method:* Line 1c(1) plus line 9b minus line 1b(1) or 1b(2) (whichever is smaller) minus line 9h. If the valuation date is not the end of the year, this total is accumulated to the end of the plan year at the valuation interest rate (line 6e).

2. *For all other funding methods:* Line 1c(2)(b) plus line 1c(2)(c) minus line 1b(1) or 1b(2) (whichever is smaller) minus line 9h. If the valuation date is not the end of the year, this total is accumulated to the end of the plan year at the valuation interest rate (line 6e).

### Q 30:56   How is the RPA '94 override (90 percent current liability full-funding limitation) calculated for purposes of line 9l(2)?

The RPA '94 override is equal to the excess (if any) of (1) 90 percent of current liability (including the expected increase in current liability due to benefits accruing during the plan year) over (2) the actuarial value of the plan's assets. [I.R.C. § 412(c)(7)] This is the RPA '94 definition of current liability (see Q 30:19).

This override can be calculated solely based on other entries on the Schedule B. It is equal to line 1d(2)(a) plus line 1d(2)(b), accumulated with interest to the plan-year end at the rate entered in line 6a(2), minus line 1d(4), with this total multiplied by 90 percent. From this is subtracted the lesser of line 1b(1) or 1b(2), accumulated to the end of the plan year at the valuation interest rate (line 6e). Then line 1d(4) is added back in.

The amount on line 9l(3) is used as an override to the other full-funding limitations to increase the full-funding limit to at least this value.

### Q 30:57   How is the waived funding deficiency calculated for line 9m(1)?

A credit for a waived funding deficiency for the current plan year is entered on line 9m(1). [I.R.C. § 412(b)(3)(C)] If a waiver of a funding deficiency is pending, the actuary should report a funding deficiency on Form 5500. If the waiver is granted after Form 5500 is filed, an amended Form 5500 should be filed with an amended Schedule B to report the funding waiver (see page 5 of the Instructions for Form 5500).

### Q 30:58  What other credits can be reported on line 9m(2)?

When a plan has used the alternative FSA and then switches back to the regular FSA, a credit is created in the plan year equal to the excess of the regular FSA charges over the alternative minimum FSA charges for the prior year.

### Q 30:59  How is the reconciliation account determined for line 9q?

The reconciliation account is made up of those components that upset the balance equation of Treasury Regulations Section 1.412(c)(3)-1(b). These components include the accumulation of charges to the FSA due to the additional funding charge, interest on late quarterly contributions, and the difference between the unamortized balance of a waived funding deficiency at the mandated interest rate and the outstanding balance at the plan's preretirement interest rate.

Valuation assets should not be adjusted by the reconciliation account balance when computing the required minimum funding. The reconciliation account balance is used only for purposes of reconciling the balance equation.

### Q 30:60  How is the portion of the reconciliation account due to additional funding charges determined for line 9q(1)?

The portion due to additional funding charges is equal to the sum of line 9q(1) (outstanding balance), increased with interest at the valuation interest rate to the first day of the current plan year, and line 9f (additional funding charge) from the prior year's Schedule B.

### Q 30:61  How is the portion of the reconciliation account due to additional interest charges from late quarterly contributions determined for line 9q(2)?

The portion due to additional interest charges from late quarterly contributions is equal to the sum of line 9q(2) (outstanding balance), increased with interest at the valuation interest rate to the first day of the current plan year, and line 9e (additional interest) from the prior year's Schedule B.

### Q 30:62  How is the portion of the reconciliation account due to a waived funding deficiency determined for line 9q(3)(a)?

This portion of the reconciliation account is applicable only if the interest rate used to amortize a waived funding deficiency is different from the valuation interest rate. Line 9q(3)(a) is equal to the prior year's reconciliation waiver outstanding balance, increased with interest at the valuation rate to the current valuation date and decreased by the year-end amortization amount based on the mandated interest rate.

### Q 30:63 How is the total reconciliation account determined for line 9q(4)?

The total reconciliation account is the sum of the reconciliation account items (adjusted at the valuation rate to the current valuation date, if necessary). The reconciliation account is wiped out in the plan year following the application of the ERISA full funding limit.

### Q 30:64 How is the contribution that is necessary to avoid a funding deficiency determined for line 10?

The contribution necessary to avoid a funding deficiency is equal to line 9p (accumulated funding deficiency), unless the alternative FSA is used. If the alternative FSA is used, the amount required under that method should be entered on line 10.

### Q 30:65 What is required for line 11 if the actuary has made a change to any actuarial assumptions?

If any of the actuarial assumptions have changed, the box for line 11 must be marked "yes." In addition, the actuary must attach a justification for any change made, labeled "Schedule B, line 11—Justification for Change in Actuarial Assumptions."

If the plan is covered by the PBGC and is not a multiemployer plan, it must request permission from the IRS to change the current liability assumptions unless the plan meets one of the following exceptions:

1. The change decreases the unfunded current liability by $5 million or less;
2. The aggregate unfunded vested benefits under the plan and for all plans of members of the employer's controlled group for the preceding year are $50 million or less; or
3. The change decreased the unfunded current liability by more than $5 million but less than $50 million, but the decrease equaled less than 5 percent of the current liability before the change in assumptions.

If a change in current liability assumptions requires IRS approval, an attachment stating the date of the ruling letter granting approval must be completed. This attachment should be labeled "Schedule B, line 11—Change in Current Liability Assumptions Approval Date."

If a change in current liability assumptions would have required IRS approval, but the plan met one of the exceptions to such requirement listed above, an attachment must be completed stating which exception the plan satisfies and the plan year for which it applies. The attachment should be labeled "Schedule B, line 11—Change in Current Liability Applicable Condition."

### Q 30:66  What is the additional funding charge requirement for Part II of the Schedule B?

The purpose of the additional funding charge is to bring the plan assets up to the level of the current liability. The additional funding charge is required *only* for plans with 100 or more participants on any day during the prior plan year, and only under certain conditions. Specifically, the additional funding charge is applicable to those large plans that do not meet certain funded liability ratios. This additional charge improves the funding of such plans by requiring larger contributions than would otherwise have been required.

### Q 30:67  How is the gateway percentage calculated for line 12a?

The gateway percentage is equal to the actuarial value of assets (line 1b(2)) divided by the RPA '94 current liability calculated at the highest allowable interest rate (line 1d(2)(c)).

If the gateway percentage is at least 90 percent, there is no additional funding charge, and the actuary should enter zero on line 12u.

If the gateway percentage is less than 80 percent, the actuary should proceed to line 12b.

If the gateway percentage is at least 80 percent but less than 90 percent, and if the gateway percentage for the prior two years or the two years before the prior year was at least 90 percent, the actuary should proceed to line 12u.

**Note.** Certain plans sponsored by companies engaged primarily in the interurban or interstate passenger bus service have gateway percentages that are greater than certain prescribed minimum percentages. If one of these transition rules is applicable, line 12a should be completed, and, if appropriate, a zero should be entered in line 12u. In addition, the actuary should attach a demonstration showing the use of the transition rule to the Schedule B and label the attachment "Schedule B, line 12a—TRA '97 Transition Rule."

In addition, PFEA '04 provided a lookback rule for the purpose of applying Section 412(l)(9)(B)(ii) for plan years beginning after December 31, 2003. If this lookback rule is used, attach a demonstration of the use of this lookback rule to the Schedule B and label the attachment, "Schedule B, line 12a— Volatility Lookback Rule."

### Q 30:68  What is the adjusted value of assets for line 12c?

This is equal to the actuarial value of assets minus the credit balance (line 1b(2) minus line 9h).

## Q 30:69   What is the liability attributable to any unpredictable contingent event benefit for line 12f?

A typical unpredictable event would be the layoff of several employees who, as a result of the layoff, begin receiving retirement benefits. These benefits and resulting liabilities must be isolated to determine the unpredictable contingent event benefit (UCEB), which is the greatest of the following:

1. The contingent event benefits (CEBs) paid during the plan year (including a payment for the purchase of an annuity contract);
2. The seven-year amortization of the unpredictable contingent event liabilities (UCEL); or
3. For plans with a funded ratio of less than 60 percent, 30 percent of the contingent event liabilities (for plans with a funded ratio greater than 60 percent, 30 percent is decreased by the product of 0.40 and the amount by which the funded ratio exceeds 60 percent).

[I.R.C. § 412(l)(5)]

The value of any UCEB that was included on line 12b (RPA '94 current liability) must be entered.

## Q 30:70   What is the outstanding balance of unfunded old liability for line 12g?

The outstanding balance of unfunded old liability is the same as the unamortized portions of the DRC amortization bases. This amount is equal to line 12(g) of the prior year's Schedule B reduced by the prior year's amortization amount and adjusted for interest at the prior year's current liability interest rate from the prior year's valuation date to the current valuation date.

The unfunded old liability (and therefore all its components) will be considered fully amortized in the first plan year that

1. The plan's funded current liability percentage (determined under Code Section 412(l)(9)(C)) is 90 percent or greater;
2. The plan is reestablished as a multiemployer plan; or
3. The plan has 100 or fewer participants on each day of the prior plan year.

[Rev. Rul. 96-20, Q&A 7, 1996-1 C.B. 62]

In the case of a collectively bargained plan, the outstanding balance of the unfunded old liability must be increased by the unamortized portion of any unfunded existing benefit increase liability in accordance with Code Section 412(l)(3)(C).

### Q 30:71   How is the unfunded new liability amount determined for line 12i?

To determine the unfunded new liability amount, the amortization percentage must first be calculated:

1. If line 12d (funded current liability percentage) is less than or equal to 60 percent, 30 percent is entered.

2. If line 12d is greater than 60 percent, 30 percent is reduced by the product of 40 percent and the excess.

**Example.** If the funded current liability percent is 75 percent, the amortization percentage is 24 percent, i.e., .24 (0.30 – (0.4 × 0.15)).

The unfunded new liability amount is equal to the product of the unfunded new liability (line 12h) and the amortization percentage.

### Q 30:72   How is the unfunded old liability amount determined for line 12j?

The unfunded old liability amount is the total amortization amount, based on the following:

1. The RPA '94 interest rate reported on line 6a(1);

2. The remaining amortization period of one year (for plan years beginning in 2006); and

3. The amortization amount for each DRC amortization base, which includes
   a. Unfunded old liability,
   b. Unfunded existing benefit-increase liability,
   c. Additional unfunded old liability, and
   d. The liability for unfunded mortality increase.

[Rev. Rul. 96-20, 1996-1 C.B. 62]

The actuary must make a separate attachment, labeled "Schedule B, line 12j—Schedule of DRC Bases," showing

1. The initial amount of each DRC amortization base being amortized (the unfunded old liability base and the additional unfunded old liability base do not need to be listed separately);

2. The outstanding balance of each DRC amortization base;

3. The number of years remaining in the amortization period; and

4. The amortization amount (with the valuation date as the due date of the amortization amount).

### Q 30:73  How is the amortization of all unpredictable contingent event liabilities determined for line 12m(4)?

The amortization of all UCEL is computed based on the following:

1. The RPA '94 interest rate (line 6a(1));
2. The valuation date as the due date; and
3. An amortization period of seven years.

In the first year of amortization, the employer may choose to override this calculation as 150 percent of line 12m(4). [I.R.C. § 412(l)(5)]

**Note.** An alternative calculation of an unpredictable contingent amount is available for the first year of amortization, as described in Code Section 412(l)(5)(D). If this alternative is used, the actuary must attach a statement describing this calculation. The attachment should be labeled "Schedule B, line 12(m)(4)—Alternative UCEB Calculation."

### Q 30:74  How is the RPA '94 additional amount determined for line 12m(5)?

The RPA '94 additional amount is equal to the unfunded current liability (line 12e) minus the outstanding balance of the unfunded old liability (line 12g), multiplied by the amortization percentage calculated in line 12i, minus the unfunded new liability amount (line 12i) (see Q 30:71).

### Q 30:75  How is the preliminary additional funding charge determined for line 12n?

The preliminary additional funding charge is equal to the excess of the DRC on line 12k over the unfunded new liability amount on line 12i, plus line 12m(6). This total is adjusted with RPA '94 current liability interest to the end of the plan year.

### Q 30:76  How are the contributions needed to increase current liability percentage to 100 percent calculated for line 12o?

This contribution amount is equal to the adjusted current liability minus the adjusted assets. [Ann. 96-18, 1996-15 I.R.B. 15]

Adjusted current liability is equal to the RPA '94 current liability plus the expected increase due to benefits accruing during the year minus the expected release from current liability for the plan year, with the total adjusted to the end of the year using the RPA '94 current liability interest rate. (Line 1d(2)(a) plus line 1d(2)(b) minus line 1d(2)(d), adjusted to the end of the year using the RPA '94 current liability interest rate.) [Rev. Rul. 96-21, Q&A 7, 1996-1 C.B. 64]

Adjusted assets are equal to the actuarial value of assets for the plan year adjusted by

1. Subtracting any credit balance (or adding any debit balance) in the plan's FSA as of the end of the before year, adjusted with interest to the valuation date at the valuation interest rate;

2. Subtracting from the plan assets the disbursements (including single-sum distributions) expected to be paid after the valuation date but before the end of the plan year;

3. Adding the charges (other than the additional funding charge under Code Section 412(l)) to the FSA for the plan year; and

4. Subtracting the credits (other than contributions and the amount of a waived funding deficiency) to the FSA for the plan year.

The actuarial value of assets and the adjustments described above are determined as of the valuation date, and each is appropriately adjusted with interest to the end of the plan year at the valuation interest rate. The result of this calculation may be a negative number. [Rev. Rul. 96-21, Q&A 8, 1996-1 C.B. 64]

### Q 30:77　How is the adjusted additional funding charge calculated for line 12q?

The adjusted additional funding charge is equal to a percentage of line 12p, depending on the number of plan participants. If the plan had 150 or more participants on each day of the preceding plan year, 100 percent should be entered. If the plan had fewer than 150 but more than 100 participants on each day of the prior plan year, take the greatest number of participants the plan had as of any day during the plan year, subtract 100 from this number, and multiply by 2 percent.

The adjusted additional funding charge is equal to the percentage computed above multiplied by line 12p. The actuary enters this number on line 9f as the adjusted additional funding charge that is added to the charges in the FSA.

## Other Schedule B Issues

### Q 30:78　What should an enrolled actuary do if he or she knows that a Schedule B that he or she prepared and signed was not filed?

An enrolled actuary is required to notify both the IRS and the Department of Labor when he or she is aware that a Schedule B that he or she prepared and signed for a plan was not filed. [20 C.F.R. § 901.20(h)]

**Q 30:79   May an enrolled actuary perform services for a client
            when there is a known conflict of interest with respect
            to the performance of such services?**

Yes. The actuary may perform services for a client when there is a known conflict of interest, but only after such conflict has been fully disclosed to all parties and each party has agreed to allow such service. [20 C.F.R. § 901.20(d)]

# Chapter 31

# Financial Accounting Standards

The Financial Accounting Standards Board (FASB, or the Board) provides guidance for the standards of practice in preparing and reporting financial accounting information. The FASB has released several standards of practice that are directly related to defined benefit pension plans. These statements affect the presentation of accounting and reporting by the employer and by the plan. FASB Statement of Financial Accounting Standards (SFAS) No. 87, Employers' Accounting for Pensions, provides the expense, asset, and liability disclosures used in preparation of employer financial statements. SFAS No. 35, Accounting and Reporting by Defined Benefit Plans, provides the standard for reporting assets and liabilities in the actuarial valuation of a defined benefit plan. SFAS No. 132(R) is an amendment of SFASs No. 87, No. 88, Employers' Accounting for Settlements and Curtailment of Defined Benefit Plans and for Termination Benefits, and No. 106, Employers' Accounting for Postretirement Benefits Other Than Pensions, and revises employers' disclosures about pension and other postretirement benefit plans. The FASB recently released Statement No. 158, Employers' Accounting for Defined Benefit Pension and other Postretirement Plans—an Amendment of FASB Statements No. 87, 88, 106, and 132(R). The changes are extensive, and the purpose of these changes is to better communicate the funded status of a sponsor's plans in a complete and understandable way to the users of the sponsor's financial statements.

## SFAS No. 87

### Q 31:1  Who is subject to the SFAS No. 87 reporting and disclosure rules and when are they effective?

An employer that offers pension benefits to its employees must follow the standards of accounting outlined in SFAS No. 87. For purposes of SFAS No. 87, a *pension plan* is a defined benefit pension plan offering payments to retired employees and/or their survivors either in the form of an annuity or lump sum. The Statement does not apply in the case of plans that provide only health benefits or life insurance to pre- or postretirement employees. State and local governments and federal executive agencies are not subject to the Statement and should follow the standards of the Government Accounting Standards Board. [SFAS No. 87, paragraphs 7, 8]

### Q 31:2  What is the purpose of SFAS No. 87?

SFAS No. 87 provides a standard method for accounting for an employer's pension-related costs. In the past, when no such standard existed, reported pension accounting was not comparable from one company to another and often was not consistent from one period to another for the same company. In addition, significant pension-related obligations and assets were not recognized in financial statements. [SFAS No. 87, paragraph 4]

### Q 31:3  What is SFAS No. 132?

SFAS No. 132 revises employers' disclosures about pension and other post-retirement benefit plans. It does not change the measurement or recognition of those plans but rather it standardizes the disclosure requirements for pensions and other postretirement benefits to the extent practicable. It also requires additional information on changes in the benefit obligations and fair values of plan assets that will facilitate financial analysis, and eliminates certain disclosures that are no longer as useful as they were when SFASs No. 87, No. 88, and No. 106 were issued. SFAS No. 132 suggests combined formats for presentation of pension and other postretirement benefit disclosures and permits reduced disclosures for nonpublic entities.

SFAS No. 132 is effective for fiscal years beginning after December 15, 1997. Restatement of disclosures for earlier periods provided for comparative purposes is required unless the information is not readily available, in which case the notes to the financial statements should include all available information and a description of the information not available. The FASB revised Statement 132 effective December 15, 2003, designating it as SFAS No. 132(R). This Statement retains the disclosures required by Statement 132, but adds additional disclosures in response to concerns expressed by users of financial statements; those disclosures include information describing the types of plan assets, investment strategy, measurement date(s), plan obligations, cash flows, and components of net periodic benefit cost recognized during interim periods. This Statement retains reduced disclosure requirements for nonpublic entities from Statement 132, and it includes reduced disclosures for certain of the new requirements. These new requirements are effective for plan years ending after December 15, 2003 for domestic plans, and June 15, 2004 for foreign plans and nonpublic entities.

### Q 31:4   What is SFAS No. 158?

This Statement improves financial reporting by requiring an employer to recognize the overfunded or underfunded status of a defined benefit postretirement plan (other than a multiemployer plan) as an asset or liability in its statement of financial position and to recognize changes in that funded status in the year in which the changes occur through comprehensive income of a business entity or changes in unrestricted net assets of a not-for-profit organization. This Statement also improves financial reporting by requiring an employer to measure the funded status of a plan as of the date of its year-end statement of financial position, with limited exceptions.

This Statement requires an employer that is a business entity and sponsors one or more single-employer defined benefit plans to:

1. Recognize the funded status of a benefit plan—measured as the difference between plan assets at fair value (with limited exceptions) and the benefit obligation—in its statement of financial position. For a pension plan, the benefit obligation is the projected benefit obligation (PBO); for any other postretirement benefit plan, such as a retiree health care plan, the benefit obligation is the accumulated postretirement benefit obligation.

2. Recognize as a component of other comprehensive income net of tax, the gains or losses, and prior service costs or credits that arise during the period but are not recognized as components of net periodic benefit cost pursuant to FASB Statement No. 87, *Employers' Accounting for Pensions,* or No. 106, *Employers' Accounting for Postretirement Benefits Other Than Pensions.* Amounts recognized in accumulated other comprehensive income, including the gains or losses, prior service costs or credits, and the transition asset or obligation remaining from the initial application of Statements 87 and 106, are adjusted as they are subsequently recognized as components of net periodic benefit cost pursuant to the recognition and amortization provisions of those Statements.

3. Measure defined benefit plan assets and obligations as of the date of the employer's fiscal year-end statement of financial position (with limited exceptions).

4. Disclose in the notes to financial statements additional information about certain effects on net periodic benefit cost for the next fiscal year that arise from delayed recognition of the gains or losses, prior service costs or credits, and transition asset or obligation.

This Statement also applies to a not-for-profit organization or other entity that does not report other comprehensive income. This Statement's reporting requirements are tailored for those entities.

This Statement amends Statement 87, FASB Statement No. 88, *Employers' Accounting for Settlements and Curtailments of Defined Benefit Pension Plans and for Termination Benefits,* Statement 106, and FASB Statement No. 132 (revised 2003), *Employers' Disclosures about Pensions and Other Postretirement Benefits,* and other related accounting literature. Upon initial application of this Statement and subsequently, an employer should continue to apply the provisions in Statements 87, 88, and 106 in measuring plan assets and benefit obligations as of the date of its statement of financial position and in determining the amount of net periodic benefit cost.

An employer with publicly traded securities is required to comply with most of the changes required by SFAS No. 158 for fiscal years ending after December 15, 2006. Employers without publicly traded securities are required to comply for fiscal years ending after June 15, 2007.

### Q 31:5   Why did the FASB issue Statement No. 158?

The Board issued this Statement to address concerns that prior standards on employers' accounting for defined benefit postretirement plans failed to communicate the funded status of those plans in a complete and understandable way. Prior standards did not require an employer to report in its statement of financial position the overfunded or underfunded status of a defined benefit postretirement plan. Those standards did not require an employer to recognize completely in earnings or other comprehensive income the financial effects of certain events affecting the plan's funded status when those events occurred.

Prior accounting standards allowed an employer to recognize in its statement of financial position an asset or liability arising from a defined benefit postretirement plan, which almost always differed from the plan's overfunded or underfunded status. Those standards allowed an employer to:

1. Delay recognition of economic events that affected the costs of providing postretirement benefits—changes in plan assets and benefit obligations—and recognize a liability that was sometimes significantly less than the underfunded status of the plan.

2. Recognize an asset in its statement of financial position, in some situations, for a plan that was underfunded.

Prior standards relegated information about the overfunded or underfunded status of a plan to the notes to financial statements. That information was in the form of a reconciliation of the overfunded or underfunded status to amounts recognized in an employer's statement of financial position. Presenting such information only in the notes often made it more difficult for users of financial statements to assess an employer's financial position and ability to satisfy postretirement benefit obligations.

The Board concluded that such reporting, together with other features of the existing standards, did not provide representationally faithful and understandable financial information and might lead to the inefficient allocation of resources in the capital markets. This Statement is the first step in a project to comprehensively reconsider Statements 87, 88, 106, 132(R), and related pronouncements.

### Q 31:6  How does SFAS No. 158 improve financial reporting?

This Statement improves financial reporting because the information reported by a sponsoring employer in its financial statements is more complete, timely, and therefore, more representationally faithful. Thus, it will be easier for users of those financial statements to assess an employer's financial position and ability to satisfy postretirement benefit obligations.

This Statement results in financial statements that are more complete because it requires an employer that sponsors a single-employer defined benefit postretirement plan to report the overfunded or underfunded status of the plan in its statement of financial position rather than in the notes.

This Statement results in more timely financial information because it requires an employer to recognize all transactions and events affecting the overfunded or underfunded status of a defined benefit postretirement plan in comprehensive income (or changes in unrestricted net assets) in the year in which they occur. Moreover, this Statement requires that plan assets and benefit obligations be measured as of the date of an employer's fiscal year-end statement of financial position, thus eliminating the alternative of a measurement date that could be up to three months earlier.

This Statement results in financial reporting that is more understandable by eliminating the need for a reconciliation in the notes to financial statements.

### Q 31:7  What does SFAS No. 87 require to be disclosed?

Employers sponsoring one or more defined benefit plans are required to disclose the following:

1. A description of the plan or plans, including employee groups covered, kinds of benefit formulas, funding policy, types of assets held, significant nonbenefit liabilities, and the nature and effect of significant matters affecting comparability of information for all periods presented.

2. The separate components of net periodic pension cost, which are service cost, interest cost, actual return on plan assets, and the net total of other components. (These other components are the net asset gain or loss during the period deferred for later recognition, amortization of the net gain or loss from earlier periods, amortization of unrecognized prior service cost, and amortization of the unrecognized net obligation or net asset existing at the date that SFAS No. 87 was first applied.)

3. A reconciliation of the funded status of the plan with amounts reported in the statement of financial position, which shows separately:

   a. Fair value of plan assets;

   b. Projected benefit obligation, accumulated benefit obligation, and vested benefit obligation;

   c. Unrecognized prior service cost;

   d. Unrecognized net gain or loss, including actual gains or losses not yet included in the market-related value;

   e. Unrecognized asset or obligation resulting at initial application of the Statement;

   f. Additional minimum liability, if any; and

   g. Amount of net pension asset or liability, which results if the employer's contribution to the plan exceeds periodic pension cost or if periodic pension cost exceeds the employer's contributions.

4. Weighted-average assumed discount rate and rate of compensation increase (if applicable) used to measure the PBO for each year presented.

5. Weighted-average expected long-term rate of return on plan assets for each year presented.

6. Amounts and kinds of securities of the employer and related parties included in plan assets.

7. Approximate amount of annual benefits of active employees and retirees covered by annuity contracts issued by the employer and related parties, if applicable.

8. Alternative methods used to amortize gains and losses and unrecognized cost of retroactive plan amendments, if applicable.

9. Existence and nature of an employer's commitments to amend the plan to provide benefits attributable to past service that are greater than the benefits defined by the written terms of the plan.

### Q 31:8   What does a typical SFAS No. 87 disclosure look like?

Several different disclosures are used, but all of them reconcile and substantiate the two most important disclosures: (1) the determination of the net periodic pension cost and (2) the reconciliation of the funded status.

**Example.** The Quilters Defined Benefit Plan presented the following disclosure to its accountant.

The determination of the net periodic pension cost, as of December 31, 2002, is as follows:

| | | |
|---|---|---|
| 1. | Service cost | $100,000 |
| 2. | Interest cost | $150,000 |
| 3. | Expected return on assets | $156,000 |
| 4. | Amortization of transition obligation/(asset) | $(25,000) |
| 5. | Amortization of prior service cost | $15,000 |
| 6. | Amortization of (gain)/loss: | $5,000 |
| 7. | Net periodic pension cost: (1+ 2 + 3 + 4 + 5 + 6) | $89,000 |

Reconciliation of the funded status as of December 31, 2002, is as follows:

| | | |
|---|---|---|
| 1. | Vested accumulated benefit obligation | $(2,000,000) |
| 2. | Nonvested accumulated benefit obligation | $(400,000) |
| 3. | Total accumulated benefit obligation (1 + 2) | $(2,400,000) |
| 4. | Effect of future salary increases | $(425,000) |
| 5. | Projected benefit obligation (3 + 4) | $(2,825,000) |
| 6. | Fair value of plan assets | $2,700,000 |
| 7. | Funded status (5 + 6) | $(125,000) |
| 8. | Unrecognized transition obligation | $(150,000) |
| 9. | Unrecognized prior service cost | $180,000 |
| 10. | Unrecognized net (gain)/loss | $375,000 |
| 11. | (Accrued)/prepaid pension cost (7 + 8 + 9 + 10) | $280,000 |
| 12. | Adjustment required to recognize minimum liability | - 0 - |
| 13. | Net pension (liability)/asset: (11 + 12) | $280,000 |

## Q 31:9   What is the measurement date?

SFAS No. 87 requires the measurement date of plan assets and obligations to be the date of the financial statements or, if used consistently from year to year, a date not earlier than three months before that date. SFAS No. 158 will require sponsors to measure the funded status of the plan as of the date of the year-end statement, with limited exceptions. In other words, sponsors have lost the ability to measure the funded status within three months of the year-end. Although measurements must be as of a particular date, information may be prepared before the measurement date and adjusted to account for subsequent events. The amount of the additional minimum liability presented in interim financial statements should be the same as the amount reported in the previous year-end statement of position, adjusted for accruals and contributions.

Net periodic pension cost for interim and annual financial statements should be measured on the basis of the assumptions used for measurements at the preceding year-end. If more current measurements of plan assets or of the pension obligation are available, or if measurements are affected by a significant event, such as a plan amendment, the most current measurements should be used.

### Q 31:10   What is meant by the term *unrecognized*?

SFAS No. 87 allows the employer to recognize only a portion of certain asset and/or liability figures on its financial statements; the others are *unrecognized*. The portion of the amounts that are not recognized are set up as accounts in the financial statement that will be recognized in later years. In general, all unrecognized amounts are amortized using straight-line amortization over the future benefit service of the plan's active employees.

### Q 31:11   What is the *net periodic pension cost*?

The *net periodic pension cost* is the amount recognized in the employer's financial statements as the cost of the pension plan for a period. In other words, this is the amount treated as the contribution required to maintain the plan for the accounting period. It does not have any bearing or relation to the amount determined for minimum funding purposes (see chapter 19) by the plan's actuary. In general, the two amounts may be close in terms of their quantity, but due to the methodology for determining each, the result is usually different.

### Q 31:12   What is the *projected benefit obligation* and the *accumulated benefit obligation*, and how do they differ?

The *projected benefit obligation* (PBO) is the present value (see chapter 18) of all benefits accumulated in the plan as of the date of the financial statement using the unit credit funding method *with* a salary scale (see chapter 18). It is the total cost to fund the plan on the measurement date based on the assumptions used in preparing the SFAS No. 87 statement, assuming no further additional benefits after the measurement date but including any increases in future compensation levels after that date. According to SFAS No. 158, the PBO is now the true measure of the plan's benefit obligation, rather than the *accumulated benefit obligation* (ABO) as in the past. The PBO takes into consideration the future compensation increases and the liability for benefits due to those increases. The Board felt that it was inconsistent to generate a cost (net periodic pension cost) based on the PBO and future compensation without recognizing the PBO and future compensation increases in the accrued liability as well.

**Example 1.** The Betsy Defined Benefit Pension Plan has two participants, one actively employed with 15 years until retirement and a benefit earned to date of 50 percent of salary, the other retiree collecting a monthly pension of $500. Using an annuity purchase rate of $120 per monthly benefit at retirement and $100 per month for the retiree, and a projected salary at retirement for the active employee of $75,000, the PBO is calculated as follows:

| Participant | Projected Salary | Monthly Benefit | APR | Discount Rate | Present Value (PBO) |
|---|---|---|---|---|---|
| Retiree | N/A | $500 | 100.00 | 1.00 | $50,000 |
| Active | $75,000 | $3,125 | 120.00 | 0.417265 | $156,474 |
| | | | | Total PBO | $206,474 |

The *accumulated benefit obligation* (ABO) is the present value of all benefits accumulated in the plan as of the date of the financial statement using the unit credit funding method *without* the use of a salary scale. It is the total cost to fund the plan on the measurement date based on the assumptions used in preparing the SFAS No. 87 Statement, assuming no further additional benefits, changes in compensation, or additional service after the measurement date.

**Example 2.** The facts are the same as in Example 1, except that the current salary for the active employee is $48,000, the ABO is calculated as follows:

| Participant | Current Salary | Monthly Benefit | APR | Discount Rate | Present Value (PBO) |
|---|---|---|---|---|---|
| Retiree | N/A | $500 | 100.00 | 1.00 | $50,000 |
| Active | $48,000 | $2,000 | 120.00 | 0.417265 | $100,144 |
| | | | | Total ABO | $150,144 |

In this example, the PBO exceeds the ABO by $56,330 ($206,474 – $150,144). When the plan uses a benefit formula unrelated to salary, the PBO and the ABO are the same. If the plan is pay related, and all benefits have been frozen, the ABO and the PBO will be the same.

**Note.** For this to occur, the plan would not be providing increases in benefits for salary earned after the freeze date.

## Q 31:13   What is the transition obligation/(asset)?

At the time an employer first applies SFAS No. 87, the plan may have benefits for which the plan has no assets. In other words, the plan may have an unfunded accrued liability. In this case, the employer would have a transition obligation if the assets were less than the PBO. If the assets exceed the PBO, the employer has a transition asset. The transition obligation/asset is determined upon the initial application of SFAS No. 87 in the employer's financial statements. The amount so determined, whether it is an obligation or an asset, is not fully recognized as a cost or an asset to the employer. It is unrecognized until such time as it is added to the periodic pension cost for the accounting year. The amount added to the periodic pension cost is a straight-line amortization of the transition obligation/asset.

**Example.** The Betsy Pension Plan had a transition obligation during the initial year the employer implemented SFAS No. 87. It was determined to be $1 million. The average remaining service years for the employee expected to receive benefits under the plan is 20. The employer elected to use 20 years to amortize the transition obligation. Thus the amount added to the net periodic pension cost is $50,000 ($1,000,000 ÷ 20 years).

### Q 31:14 What is the *prior service cost*?

After the employer implements SFAS No. 87, the plan may be amended from time to time to either increase or decrease benefits. If so, the change in the PBO as a result of the amendment must be accounted for as a separate cost component. The *prior service cost* equals to the excess of the PBO before the amendment and the PBO after the amendment. That amount is amortized over the remaining average service years of the employees expected to receive the amended benefits.

### Q 31:15 What is the (gain)/loss component in SFAS No. 87?

The (gain)/loss component of SFAS No. 87 is the sum of excess of the actual liability over the expected liability and the actual return on assets over the expected return on assets. The (gain)/loss is accumulated each year by adding the prior year's (gain)/loss to the current year's (gain)/loss reduced by the amortized portion of the (gain)/loss for the prior year. A negative result is a (gain), while a positive result is a loss.

Under SFAS No. 87, an employer will realize a (gain)/loss whenever actuarial assumptions are changed. Unlike the minimum funding standards of the Employee Retirement Income Security Act of 1974 (ERISA) and the Internal Revenue Code (Code), no liability or asset is created due to a reduction in liability (a gain) or increase in liability when actuarial assumptions are changed. Thus, when reading an SFAS No. 87 report, the user should not immediately assume that the entire (gain)/loss is attributable to the actuarial experience of the plan. Much of the (gain)/loss may be attributable to changes in assumptions.

### Q 31:16 How are unrecognized items amortized?

In general, unrecognized items are amortized using straight-line amortization. This method requires the unrecognized item to be divided by the average remaining service period of active employees expected to receive benefits under the plan. Three items are unrecognized at the time they are established. They are the transition obligation/(asset) (see Q 31:13), the prior service cost (see Q 31:14), and the (gain)/loss component (see Q 31:15). Each is amortized over average remaining service period of active employees expected to receive benefits under the plan. However, in the case of the transition obligation/(asset), if the average service years is less than 15, the employer may elect to use 15 years as the amortization period.

### Q 31:17 What is the *market-related value* of the plan's assets?

The *market-related value* is used to calculate the expected return on the plan's assets. The employer can use the fair market value of the plan's assets or a calculated value that recognizes changes in the fair value of the plan's assets in a systematic and rational manner over a period of not more than five years. The fair market value is defined as the amount that a pension plan could reasonably expect to receive for an investment in a current sale between a willing buyer and a willing seller, that is, other than in a forced or liquidation sale.

### Q 31:18   What is the (accrued)/prepaid pension cost?

The accumulated amount the employer has funded to the plan over the accumulated net periodic pension cost is known as the (accrued)/prepaid pension cost. If the employer has funded more than the periodic pension cost each year, the employer has prepaid the cost of the plan, at least according to these standards. If the contributions have been less than the periodic pension cost, the employer has an accrued cost to the plan.

**Example.** The Nantucket Whale Oil Traders Pension Plan, made effective 2000, had the following net periodic pension costs and contributions for the fiscal years 2000, 2001, and 2002.

| Year | Net Periodic Pension Cost | Contributions Made during Fiscal Year |
|---|---|---|
| 2000 | $150,000 | $125,000 |
| 2001 | $175,000 | $150,000 |
| 2002 | $160,000 | $250,000 |
| Total | $485,000 | $525,000 |

After three years the plan has received $40,000 in contributions in excess of the net periodic pension cost over the three-year period. Thus the employer would be showing a prepaid pension cost at the end of the fiscal year in the year 2002. Note that in the first year, the employer had an accrued pension cost of ($25,000). Note that the negative sign indicates an accrued pension cost, and a positive sign indicates a prepaid pension cost.

### Q 31:19   What is the adjustment to recognize additional minimum liability?

In the event the plan is underfunded when comparing the ABO to the market-related value of the plan's assets, the employer must make an adjustment to the (accrued)/prepaid pension cost by adding to it the amount of the underfunding. The sum of the two is the additional liability, recorded in the employer's statement of financial position. In addition, if the additional liability exceeds the sum of the unrecognized prior service cost and the transition obligation/asset, such excess is recorded as a charge to shareholder equity.

### Q 31:20   What assumptions are required for purposes of disclosure?

SFAS No. 87 requires each significant assumption used in determining the pension information to represent the best estimate for that specific assumption.

In other words, each assumption must be explicitly used, and not implied. Assumptions may include estimates of the occurrence of future events affecting pension costs such as mortality, withdrawal, disablement and retirement, salary scales, increases in benefit limitations, and discount rates to reflect the time value of money.

### Q 31:21    What are the *expected long-term rate of return* and the *discount rate*?

*Expected long-term rate of return* is an assumption about the average rate of return on the plan's assets. This rate is used to determine the expected return on plan assets in developing the net periodic pension cost and in determining asset gains and losses.

*Discount rate* is the rate used to adjust for the time value of money to determine the actuarial present value of the PBO and the ABO. In general, such rate is the rate at which the employer could reasonably expect to settle the plan's benefit payments. The employer could look at such rates as those offered by insurance companies for the purchase of an annuity, the annuity rates published by the Pension Benefit Guaranty Corporation (PBGC) and long-term rates of fixed interest obligations.

In SFAS No. 106, paragraph 187, the Board outlined how the discount rate should be determined (The Securities and Exchange Commission has stated that this concept that applies to the measurement of the postretirement benefit obligation would apply just as well to measuring the retirement benefit obligation.):

> The objective of selecting assumed discount rates is to measure the single amount that, if invested at the measurement date in a portfolio of high-quality debt instruments, would provide the necessary future cash flows to pay the accumulated benefits when due. Notionally, that single amount, the accumulated postretirement benefit obligation, would equal the current market value of a portfolio of high-quality zero coupon bonds whose maturity dates and amounts would be the same as the timing and amount of the expected future benefit payments. Because cash inflows would equal cash outflows in timing and amount, there would be no reinvestment risk in the yields to maturity of the portfolio. However, in other than a zero coupon portfolio, such as a portfolio of long-term debt instruments that pay semiannual interest payments or whose maturities do not extend far enough into the future to meet expected benefit payments, the assumed discount rates (the yield to maturity) need to incorporate expected reinvestment rates available in the future. Those rates should be extrapolated from the existing yield curve at the measurement date. Assumed discount rates should be reevaluated at each measurement date. If the general level of interest rates rises or declines, the assumed discount rates should change in a similar manner.

### Q 31:22   Are actuarial gains/losses recognized in SFAS No. 87?

Maybe. SFAS No. 87 does not distinguish between the sources of gains and losses and does not require the recognition of gains and losses in the periods in which they occur. The Statement uses what it calls a corridor approach for the recognition in net periodic pension cost of a minimum percentage of the cumulative amounts of gains and losses that have been recognized as part of periodic pension cost in previous years. If the cumulative unrecognized gain or loss exceeds 10 percent of the "greater of the projected benefit obligation or the market-related value of plan assets" at the beginning of the year, amortization is required. The amount to be amortized is that excess divided by the average remaining service period of active employees expected to receive benefits under the plan. The average remaining life expectancy of inactive participants should be used if all or almost all participants are inactive.

Instead of the minimum method suggested, SFAS No. 87 allows the use of any systematic method of amortization if the method (1) results in an amount equal to or greater than the minimum computed by the corridor approach, (2) is consistently applied, (3) is applied similarly to gains and losses, and (4) is disclosed. This corridor approach is used to reduce pension cost volatility and to allow gains or losses to be offset without affecting net periodic pension cost.

## SFAS No. 132

### Q 31:23   What disclosures are required to be made to be in compliance with SFAS No. 132?

The following disclosures are required (new disclosures added by SFAS No. 132(R) are marked with an *):

1. A reconciliation of beginning and ending balances of the benefit obligation showing separately, if applicable, the effects during the period attributable to each of the following: service cost, interest cost, contributions by plan participants, actuarial gains and losses, foreign currency exchange rate changes, benefits paid, plan amendments, business combinations, divestitures, curtailments, settlements, and special termination benefits.

2. A reconciliation of beginning and ending balances of the fair value of plan assets showing separately, if applicable, the effects during the period attributable to each of the following: actual return on plan assets, foreign currency exchange rate changes, contributions by the employer, contributions by plan participants, benefits paid, business combinations, divestitures, and settlements.

3. The funded status of the plans, the amounts not recognized in the statement of financial position, and the amounts recognized in the statement of financial position, including:

a. The amount of any unamortized prior service cost.

b. The amount of any unrecognized net gain or loss (including asset gains and losses not yet reflected in market-related value).

c. The amount of any remaining unamortized, unrecognized net obligation or net asset existing at the initial date of application of Statement 87 or Statement 106.

d. The net pension or other postretirement benefit prepaid assets or accrued liabilities.

e. Any intangible asset and the amount of accumulated other comprehensive income recognized pursuant to paragraph 37 of Statement 87, as amended.

4. Information about plan assets:

a. For each major category of plan assets, which shall include but is not limited to, equity securities, debt securities, real estate, and all other assets, the percentage of the fair value of total plan assets held as of the measurement date used for each statement of financial position presented.*

b. A narrative description of investment policies and strategies, including target allocation percentages or range of percentages for each major category of plan assets presented on a weighted-average basis as of the measurement date(s) of the latest statement of financial position presented, if applicable, and other factors that are pertinent to an understanding of the policies or strategies such as investment goals, risk management practices, permitted and prohibited investments, including the use of derivatives, diversification, and the relationship between plan assets and benefit obligations.*

c. A narrative description of the basis used to determine the overall expected long-term rate-of-return-on-assets assumption, such as the general approach used, the extent to which the overall rate-of-return-on-assets assumption was based on historical returns, the extent to which adjustments were made to those historical returns in order to reflect expectations of future returns, and how those adjustments were determined.*

d. Disclosure of additional asset categories and additional information about specific assets within a category is encouraged if that information is expected to be useful in understanding the risks associated with each asset category and the overall expected long-term rate of return on assets.*

5. For defined benefit pension plans, the ABO.*

6. The benefits (as of the date of the latest statement of financial position presented) expected to be paid in each of the next five fiscal years, and in the aggregate for the five fiscal years thereafter. The expected benefits should be estimated based on the same assumptions used to measure the company's benefit obligation at the end of the year and should include benefits attributable to estimated future employee service.*

7. The employer's best estimate, as soon as it can reasonably be determined, of contributions expected to be paid to the plan during the next fiscal year beginning after the date of the latest statement of financial position presented. Estimated contributions may be presented in the aggregate, combining (1) contributions required by funding regulations or laws, (2) discretionary contributions, and (3) noncash contributions.*

8. The amount of net periodic benefit cost recognized, showing separately the service cost component, the interest cost component, the expected return on plan assets for the period, the amortization of the unrecognized transition obligation or transition asset, the amount of recognized gains or losses, the amount of prior service cost recognized, and the amount of gains or losses recognized due to a settlement or curtailment.

9. The amount included within other comprehensive income for the period arising from a change in the additional minimum pension liability recognized pursuant to paragraph 37 of Statement 87, as amended.

10. On a weighted-average basis, the following assumptions used in the accounting for the plans: assumed discount rates, rates of compensation increase (for pay-related plans), and expected long-term rates of return on plan assets specifying, in a tabular format, the assumptions used to determine the benefit obligation and the assumptions used to determine net benefit cost.*

11. The measurement date(s) used to determine pension and other post-retirement benefit measurements for the pension plans and other postretirement benefit plans that make up at least the majority of plan assets and benefit obligations.*

12. The assumed health care cost trend rate(s) for the next year used to measure the expected cost of benefits covered by the plan (gross eligible charges), and a general description of the direction and pattern of change in the assumed trend rates thereafter, together with the ultimate trend rate(s) and when that rate is expected to be achieved.

13. The effect of a one-percentage-point increase and the effect of a one-percentage-point decrease in the assumed health care cost trend rates on (i) the aggregate of the service and interest cost components of net periodic postretirement health care benefit costs and (ii) the accumulated postretirement benefit obligation for health care benefits. (For purposes of this disclosure, all other assumptions shall be held constant, and the effects shall be measured based on the substantive plan that is the basis for the accounting.)

14. If applicable, the amounts and types of securities of the employer and related parties included in plan assets, the approximate amount of future annual benefits of plan participants covered by insurance contracts issued by the employer or related parties, and any significant transactions between the employer or related parties and the plan during the period.

15. If applicable, any alternative method used to amortize prior service amounts or unrecognized net gains and losses pursuant to paragraphs 26 and 33 of Statement 87 or paragraphs 53 and 60 of Statement 106.

16. If applicable, any substantive commitment, such as past practice or a history of regular benefit increases, used as the basis for accounting for the benefit obligation.

17. If applicable, the cost of providing special or contractual termination benefits recognized during the period and a description of the nature of the event.

18. An explanation of any significant change in the benefit obligation or plan assets not otherwise apparent in the other disclosures required by this Statement.

### Q 31:24   What are the disclosure requirements when an employer sponsors more than one defined benefit plan?

The disclosures required by this statement shall be aggregated for all of an employer's defined benefit pension plans and for all of an employer's other defined benefit postretirement plans unless disaggregating in groups is considered to provide useful information or is otherwise required by the statement.

### Q 31:25   How do the disclosures differ for nonpublic entities?

A nonpublic entity is not required to disclose the information required by paragraphs (1)-(3), (8), (13), and (15)-(18) of Q 31:23. A nonpublic entity that sponsors one or more defined benefit pension plans or one or more other defined benefit postretirement plans shall provide the following information, separately for pension plans and other postretirement benefit plans:

1. The benefit obligation, fair value of plan assets, and funded status of the plan.

2. Employer contributions, participant contributions, and benefits paid.

3. Information about plan assets:

   a. For each major category of plan assets, which shall include, but is not limited to, equity securities, debt securities, real estate, and all other assets, the percentage of the fair value of total plan assets held as of the measurement date used for each statement of financial position presented.*

   b. A narrative description of investment policies and strategies, including target allocation percentages or range of percentages for each major category of plan assets presented on a weighted-average basis as of the measurement date(s) of the latest statement of financial position presented, if applicable, and other factors that are pertinent to an understanding of the policies or strategies such as investment goals, risk management practices, permitted and prohibited investments including the use of derivatives, diversification, and the relationship between plan assets and benefit obligations.*

c. A narrative description of the basis used to determine the overall expected long-term rate-of-return-on-assets assumption, such as the general approach used, the extent to which the overall rate-of-return-on-assets assumption was based on historical returns, the extent to which adjustments were made to those historical returns in order to reflect expectations of future returns, and how those adjustments were determined.*

d. Disclosure of additional asset categories and additional information about specific assets within a category is encouraged if that information is expected to be useful in understanding the risks associated with each asset category and the overall expected long-term rate of return on assets.*

4. For defined benefit pension plans, the ABO.*

5. The benefits (as of the date of the latest statement of financial position presented) expected to be paid in each of the next five fiscal years, and in the aggregate for the five fiscal years thereafter. The expected benefits should be estimated based on the same assumptions used to measure the company's benefit obligation at the end of the year and should include benefits attributable to estimated future employee service.*

6. The employer's best estimate, as soon as it can reasonably be determined, of contributions expected to be paid to the plan during the next fiscal year beginning after the date of the latest statement of financial position presented. Estimated contributions may be presented in the aggregate, combining (i) contributions required by funding regulations or laws, (ii) discretionary contributions, and (iii) noncash contributions.*

7. The amounts recognized in the statements of financial position, including net pension and other postretirement benefit prepaid assets or accrued liabilities and any intangible asset and the amount of accumulated other comprehensive income recognized pursuant to paragraph 37 of Statement 87, as amended.

8. The amount of net periodic benefit cost recognized and the amount included within other comprehensive income arising from a change in the minimum pension liability recognized pursuant to paragraph 37 of Statement 87, as amended.

9. On a weighted-average basis, the following assumptions used in the accounting for the plans: assumed discount rates, rates of compensation increase (for pay-related plans), and expected long-term rates of return on plan assets specifying, in a tabular format, the assumptions used to determine the benefit obligation and the assumptions used to determine net benefit cost.*

10. The measurement date(s) used to determine pension and other postretirement benefit measurements for the pension plans and other postretirement

benefit plans that make up at least the majority of plan assets and benefit obligations.*

11. The assumed health care cost trend rate(s) for the next year used to measure the expected cost of benefits covered by the plan (gross eligible charges), and a general description of the direction and pattern of change in the assumed trend rates thereafter, together with the ultimate trend rate(s) and when that rate is expected to be achieved.

12. If applicable, the amounts and types of securities of the employer and related parties included in plan assets, the approximate amount of future annual benefits of plan participants covered by insurance contracts issued by the employer or related parties, and any significant transactions between the employer or related parties and the plan during the period.

13. The nature and effect of significant nonroutine events, such as amendments, combinations, divestitures, curtailments, and settlements.

### Q 31:26  What type of interim disclosures are required to be made of a public entity?

A publicly traded entity shall disclose the following information in its interim financial statements that include a statement of income:

1. The amount of net periodic benefit cost recognized, for each period for which a statement of income is presented, showing separately the service cost component, the interest cost component, the expected return on plan assets for the period, the amortization of the unrecognized transition obligation or transition asset, the amount of recognized gains or losses, the amount of prior service cost recognized, and the amount of gain or loss recognized due to a settlement or curtailment.*

2. The total amount of the employer's contributions paid, and expected to be paid, during the current fiscal year, if significantly different from amounts previously disclosed. Estimated contributions may be presented in the aggregate combining (i) contributions required by funding regulations or laws, (ii) discretionary contributions, and (iii) noncash contributions.*

### Q 31:27  What type of interim disclosures are required to be made of a nonpublic entity?

A nonpublic entity shall disclose in interim periods, for which a complete set of financial statements is presented, the total amount of the employer's contributions paid, and expected to be paid, during the current fiscal year, if significantly different from amounts previously disclosed. Estimated contributions may be presented in the aggregate combining (i) contributions required by funding regulations or laws, (ii) discretionary contributions, and (iii) noncash contributions.*

## Q 31:28   What are some examples of SFAS No. 132 disclosures?

The following three disclosures are from SFAS No. 132, as amended by SFAS No. 158, and present the annual disclosure for a publicly traded entity, an interim disclosure for a publicly traded entity and an interim disclosure for a nonpublicly traded entity.

### Illustration 1—Disclosures about Pension and Other Postretirement Benefit Plans in the Annual Financial Statements of a Publicly Traded Entity

(The financial statements of a nonpublic entity would be similarly presented but would not be required to include the information contained in paragraphs (1)-(3), (8), (13), and (15)-(18) of Q 31:23).

The following illustrates the fiscal 20X3 financial statement disclosures for an employer (Company A) with multiple defined benefit pension plans and other postretirement benefit plans. Narrative descriptions of the basis used to determine the overall expected long-term rate-of-return-on-assets assumption (paragraph 4(c)) (see Q 31:23) and investment policies and strategies for plan assets (paragraph 4(b)) (see Q 31:23) are not included in this illustration. These narrative descriptions are meant to be entity-specific and should reflect an entity's basis for selecting the expected long-term rate-of-return-on-assets assumption and the most important investment policies and strategies.

During 20X3, Company A acquired FV Industries and amended its plans. For one of the defined benefit pension plans, the ABO exceeds the fair value of plan assets, and Company A recognized an additional minimum liability in accordance with the provisions of paragraphs 36 and 37 of Statement 87.

### Notes to Financial Statements Pension and Other Postretirement Benefit Plans

Company A has both funded and unfunded noncontributory defined benefit pension plans that together cover substantially all of its employees. The plans provide defined benefits based on years of service and final average salary.

Company A also has other postretirement benefit plans covering substantially all of its employees. The health care plans are contributory with participants' contributions adjusted annually; the life insurance plans are noncontributory. The accounting for the health care plans anticipates future cost-sharing changes to the written plans that are consistent with the company's expressed intent to increase retiree contributions each year by 50 percent of health care cost increases in excess of 6 percent. The postretirement health care plans include a limit on the company's share of costs for recent and future retirees.

Company A acquired FV Industries on December 27, 20X3, including its pension plans and other postretirement benefit plans. Amendments made at the end of 20X3 to Company A's plans increased the pension benefit obligations by $70 and reduced the other postretirement benefit obligations by $75.

### Obligations and Funded Status At December 31

| | Pension Benefits | | Other Benefits | |
|---|---|---|---|---|
| | *20X3* | *20X2* | *20X3* | *20X2* |
| *Change in benefit obligation* | | | | |
| Benefit obligation at beginning of year | $1,246 | $1,200 | $742 | $712 |
| Service cost | $76 | $72 | $36 | $32 |
| Interest cost | $90 | $88 | $55 | $55 |
| Plan participants' contributions | | | $20 | $13 |
| Amendments | $70 | | $(75) | |
| Actuarial loss | $20 | | $25 | |
| Acquisition | $900 | | $600 | |
| Benefits paid | $(125) | $(114) | $(90) | $(70) |
| Benefit obligation at end of year | $2,277 | $1,246 | $1,313 | $742 |
| *Change in plan assets* | | | | |
| Fair value of plan assets at beginning of year | $1,068 | $894 | $206 | $87 |
| Actual return on plan assets | $29 | $188 | $5 | $24 |
| Acquisition | $1,000 | | $25 | |
| Employer contribution | $75 | $100 | $137 | $152 |
| Plan participants' contributions | | | $20 | $13 |
| Benefits paid | $(125) | $(114) | $(90) | $(70) |
| Fair value of plan assets at end of year | $2,047 | $1,068 | $303 | $206 |
| Funded status at year end | $(230) | $(178) | $(1,010) | $(536) |

**Note:** Nonpublic entities are not required to provide information in the above tables; they are required to disclose the employer's contributions, participants' contributions, benefit payments, funded status, and the net amount recognized.

Amounts recognized in the statement of financial position consist of:

| | Pension Benefits | | Other Benefits | |
|---|---|---|---|---|
| | *20X3* | *20X2* | *20X3* | *20X2* |
| Noncurrent Asset | $227 | $127 | $0 | $0 |
| Current Liabilities | $(125) | $(125) | $(150) | $(150) |
| Noncurrent Liabilities | $(332) | $(180) | $(860) | $(386) |
| | $(230) | $(178) | $(1,010) | $(536) |

Amounts recognized in accumulated other comprehensive income consist of:

|  | Pension Benefits | | Other Benefits | |
|---|---|---|---|---|
|  | 20X3 | 20X2 | 20X3 | 20X2 |
| Net loss (gain) | $94 | $18 | $(11) | $(48) |
| Prior Service Cost (credit) | $210 | $160 | $(92) | $(22) |
|  | $304 | $178 | $(103) | $(70) |

The ABO for all defined benefit pension plans was $1,300 and $850 at December 31, 20X3, and 20X2, respectively.

### Information for pension plans with an ABO in excess of plan assets

|  | December 31 | |
|---|---|---|
|  | 20X3 | 20X2 |
| Projected benefit obligation | $263 | $247 |
| Accumulated benefit obligation (ABO) | $237 | $222 |
| Fair value of plan assets | $84 | $95 |

### Components of Net Periodic Benefit Cost and other amounts recognized in other comprehensive income

|  | Pension Benefits | | Other Benefits | |
|---|---|---|---|---|
|  | 20X3 | 20X2 | 20X3 | 20X2 |
| Service cost | $76 | $72 | $36 | $32 |
| Interest cost | $90 | $88 | $55 | $55 |
| Expected return on plan assets | $(85) | $(76) | $(17) | $(8) |
| Amortization of prior service cost | $20 | $16 | $(5) | $(5) |
| Amortization of net (gain) loss | $0 | $0 | $0 | $0 |
| Net periodic benefit cost | $101 | $100 | $69 | $74 |

**Note:** Nonpublic entities are not required to separately disclose components of net periodic benefit cost.

### Other Changes in Plan Assets and Benefit Obligations Recognized in Other Comprehensive Income

|  | Pension Benefits | | Other Benefits | |
|---|---|---|---|---|
|  | 20X3 | 20X2 | 20X3 | 20X2 |
| Net Gain/(Loss) | $76 | $112 | $37 | $(48) |
| Prior Service Cost/(credit) | $70 | $0 | $(75) | $(27) |
| Amortization of prior service cost | $(20) | $(16) | $5 | $5 |
| Total recognized in other comprehensive income | $126 | $96 | $(33) | $(70) |
| Total recognized in net periodic benefit cost and other comprehensive income | $227 | $196 | $36 | $4 |

The estimated net loss and prior service cost for the defined benefit pension plans that will be amortized from accumulated other comprehensive income into net periodic benefit cost over the next fiscal year are $4 and $27, respectively. The estimated prior service credit for the other defined benefit postretirement plans that will be amortized from accumulated other comprehensive income into net periodic benefit cost over the next fiscal year is $10.

### Assumptions

**Weighted-average assumptions used to determine benefit obligations at December 31**

|  | Pension Benefits | | Other Benefits | |
|---|---|---|---|---|
|  | *20X3* | *20X2* | *20X3* | *20X2* |
| Discount rate | 6.75% | 7.25% | 7.00% | 7.50% |
| Rate of compensation increase | 4.25 | 4.50 | | |

**Weighted-average assumptions used to determine net periodic benefit cost for years ended December 31**

|  | Pension Benefits | | Other Benefits | |
|---|---|---|---|---|
|  | *20X3* | *20X2* | *20X3* | *20X2* |
| Discount rate | 7.25% | 7.50% | 7.50% | 7.75% |
| Expected long-term return on plan assets | 8.00 | 8.50 | 8.10 | 8.75 |
| Rate of compensation increase | 4.50 | 4.75 | | |

(Entity-specific narrative description of the basis used to determine the overall expected long-term rate of return on assets, as described in paragraph 5(d)(3) would be included here.)

**Assumed health care cost trend rates at December 31**

|  | *20X3* | *20X2* |
|---|---|---|
| Health care cost trend rate assumed for next year | 12% | 12.5% |
| Rate to which the cost trend rate is assumed to decline (the ultimate trend rate) | 6% | 5% |
| Year that the rate reaches the ultimate trend rate | 20X9 | 20X9 |

Assumed health care cost trend rates have a significant effect on the amounts reported for the health care plans. A one-percentage-point change in assumed health care cost trend rates would have the following effects:

|                                                   | *1-Percentage-Point Increase* | *1-Percentage-Point Decrease* |
| ------------------------------------------------- | :---------------------------: | :---------------------------: |
| Effect on total of service and interest cost      | $22                           | $(20)                         |
| Effect on postretirement benefit obligation       | $173                          | $(156)                        |

**Note:** Nonpublic entities are not required to provide the above information about the impact of a one-percentage-point increase and one-percentage-point decrease in the assumed health care cost trend rates.

**Plan Assets**

Company *A*'s pension plan weighted-average asset allocations at December 31, 20X3, and 20X2, by asset category are as follows:

**Plan Assets at December 31**

| *Asset Category*   | *20X3* | *20X2* |
| ------------------ | :----: | :----: |
| Equity securities  | 50%    | 48%    |
| Debt securities    | 30%    | 31%    |
| Real estate        | 10%    | 12%    |
| Other              | 10%    | 9%     |
| Total              | 100%   | 100%   |

(Entity-specific narrative description of investment policies and strategies for plan assets, including weighted-average target asset allocations (if used as part of those policies and strategies) as described in this statement would be included here.)

Equity securities include Company *A* common stock in the amounts of $80 million (4 percent of total plan assets) and $64 million (6 percent of total plan assets) at December 31, 20X3, and 20X2, respectively.

Company *A*'s other postretirement benefit plan weighted-average asset allocations at December 31, 20X3, and 20X2, by asset category are as follows:

**Plan Assets at December 31**

| *Asset Category*   | *20X3* | *20X2* |
| ------------------ | :----: | :----: |
| Equity securities  | 60%    | 52%    |
| Debt securities    | 30%    | 27%    |
| Real estate        | 5%     | 13%    |
| Other              | 5%     | 8%     |
| Total              | 100%   | 100%   |

Equity securities include Company *A* common stock in the amounts of $12 million (4 percent of total plan assets) and $8 million (4 percent of total plan assets) at December 31, 20X3, and 20X2, respectively.

**Cash Flows: Contributions**

Company *A* expects to contribute $125 million to its pension plan and $150 million to its other postretirement benefit plan in 20X4.

**Cash Flows: Estimated Future Benefit Payments**

The following benefit payments, which reflect expected future service, as appropriate, are expected to be paid:

|  | Pension Benefits | Other Benefits |
|---|---|---|
| 20X4 | $200 | $150 |
| 20X5 | $208 | $155 |
| 20X6 | $215 | $160 |
| 20X7 | $225 | $165 |
| 20X8 | $235 | $170 |
| Years 20X9-20Y3 | $1,352 | $984 |

### Illustration 2—Interim-Period Disclosures of a Publicly Traded Entity

The following illustrates the disclosures of a publicly traded entity for the first fiscal quarter beginning after December 15, 20X3.

**Components of net periodic benefit cost three months ended March 31**

|  | Pension Benefits | | Other Benefits | |
|---|---|---|---|---|
|  | 20X4 | 20X3 | 20X4 | 20X3 |
| Service cost | $35 | $19 | $16 | $9 |
| Interest cost | $38 | $23 | $23 | $14 |
| Expected return on plan assets | $(41) | $(21) | $(6) | $(4) |
| Amortization of prior service cost | $7 | $5 | $(3) | $(1) |
| Amortization of net (gain) loss | $2 | $0 | $0 | $0 |
| Net periodic benefit cost | $41 | $26 | $30 | $18 |

**Employer Contributions**

Company *A* previously disclosed in its financial statements for the year ending December 31, 20X3, that it expected to contribute $125 million to its pension plan in 20X4. As of March 31, 20X4, $20 million of contributions have been made. Company *A* presently anticipates contributing an additional $120 million to fund its pension plan in 20X4 for a total of $140 million.

### Illustration 3—Interim-Period Disclosures of a Nonpublic Entity in a Complete Set of Financial Statements

The following illustrates the disclosures for a nonpublic entity (Entity *A*) for the first fiscal quarter beginning after December 15, 20X3.

Entity *A* previously disclosed in its financial statements for the year ending December 31, 20X3, that it expected to contribute $125 million to its pension plan in 20X4. As of March 31, 20X4, $20 million of contributions have been made. Entity *A* presently anticipates contributing an additional $120 million to fund its pension plan in 20X4 for a total of $140 million.

## SFAS No. 88

### Q 31:29  When are the accounting standards under SFAS No. 88 applicable to a pension plan?

A "settlement" or a "curtailment" of defined benefit pension plan obligations requires the employer to incorporate the accounting standards under SFAS No. 88. If any of these events occurs, previously unrecognized items are recognized as part of the net periodic pension cost.

*Settlement.* A settlement is an irrevocable action that relieves the employer (or the plan) of primary responsibility for an obligation or eliminates significant risks related to the obligation and the asset used to effect the obligation. [SFAS No. 88 paragraph 3]

Examples of settlements are a purchase of a nonparticipating annuity contract for the payment of benefits, payment of lump sums in exchange for the right to annuity payments, or the termination of the plan in its entirety through a combination of both of these transactions.

*Curtailment.* A curtailment is an event that significantly reduces the future service of employees or eliminates the accrual of new benefits for future services.

Examples of curtailments include the closing of a facility employing participants benefiting under the plan or discontinuing a segment of a business. Termination or suspension of a plan that eliminates the ability to earn future benefits is also a curtailment.

### Q 31:30  What is the impact on the SFAS No. 87 calculations due to an SFAS No. 88 event?

In general, the amortization of the unrecognized prior service cost transition obligation and/or the gain/loss for the year SFAS No. 88 event occurs will be increased or decreased if the event creates a loss or a gain. The result is a change in the net periodic pension cost for the year of the event.

*Settlement.* In general, the employer will have to recognize in the net periodic pension cost a portion of the transition obligation and any unrecognized net gain or loss that existed on the date of settlement, based on the portion of the liability settled as it bears to the total liability prior to the purchase.

**Example 1.** The *Nantucket Whale Oil Traders Pension Plan* has purchased a nonparticipating annuity contract to cover the payment of benefits to the plan's retirees. At the time of the purchase, the PBO for the plan's retirees was $1 million. The cost of the settlement was $1.2 million. Thus, the plan realized an actuarial loss of $200,000 as a result of the purchase. In the calculation of the net periodic pension cost, the employer adds a portion of the transition obligation and any unrecognized net gain or loss that existed on the date of purchase. Suppose that the plan had a total PBO of $2 million, a transition obligation of $100,000 and an unrecognized loss of $200,000. The settlement of $1 million represented one-half the total PBO. SFAS No. 88 would require that half of the transition obligation and any unrecognized net loss be recognized in the periodic pension cost. In this case, $150,000 (one-half of $300,000) would be added to the net periodic pension cost.

*Curtailments.* When the PBO decreases as a result of a curtailment, it is a gain; an increase generates a loss. This gain or loss is recognized along with a portion of the prior service cost, the transition obligation, and any unrecognized gain or loss, depending on the pro-rata number of future years eliminated due to the curtailment.

**Example 2.** Nantucket Whale Oil Traders Pension Plan has decided to lay off a portion of its workforce. As part of that layoff, the employees may elect to receive the full value of their accrued benefits without a reduction for early retirement payment. As a result of this action, a curtailment loss occurs because the PBO for these employees will increase due to the benefit improvement. It is determined that these employees represent one-half of the future years for all employees. Thus one-half of the unrecognized service cost and unrecognized transition obligation in addition to any unrecognized gain or loss may be made part of the net periodic pension cost for the year. The exact computation of this amount depends on their relative value in comparison to others.

## SFAS No. 35

### Q 31:31   What is SFAS No. 35?

This statement, titled, "Accounting and Reporting by Defined Benefit Pension Plans," establishes standards of financial accounting and reporting for annual financial statements of a defined benefit pension plan. It applies both to plans in the private sector and to plans of state and local governmental units. It does not require the preparation, distribution, or attestation of financial statements for any plan.

### Q 31:32   What is the purpose of SFAS No. 35?

The primary objective of a defined benefit plan's financial statements is to provide information useful in assessing the plan's present and future ability to pay benefits as they become due. To accomplish that objective, the financial statements will include information regarding (1) the net assets available for benefits as of the end of the plan year, (2) the changes in net assets during the plan year, (3) the actuarial present value of accumulated plan benefits (APB) as of either the beginning or end of the plan year, and (4) the effects, if significant, of certain factors affecting the year-to-year change in the actuarial present value of APB. If the date as of which the benefit information ((3) above) is presented (the *benefit information date*) is the beginning of the year, additional information is required regarding both the net assets available for benefits as of that date and the changes in net assets during the preceding year. Flexibility in the manner of presenting benefit information and changes therein (items (3) and (4) above) is permitted. Either or both of those categories of information may be presented on the face of one or more financial statements or in accompanying notes.

Data regarding net assets should be prepared on the accrual basis. Plan investments should be presented at fair value. Contracts with insurance companies should be presented in the same manner as in the plan's annual report pursuant to ERISA.

### Q 31:33   When does SFAS No. 35 apply?

SFAS No. 35 applies to *annual* financial statements of a defined benefit pension plan that principally provides pension benefits. However, it applies to plans that also provide death, disability, or employment termination benefits. Interim statements are not covered. SFAS No. 35 applies to funded and unfunded plans and to plans that are subject to the provisions of ERISA as well as to those that are not.

SFAS No. 35 does *not* apply to plans expected to be terminated or to government-sponsored Social Security plans. For plans maintained outside the United States that are similar to plans in the United States, SFAS No. 35 applies only if financial statements of such plans are intended to conform with U.S. generally accepted accounting principles (GAAP).

Note that SFAS No. 35 does *not require preparation* of financial statements of a defined benefit plan (nor does it require distribution or attestation of the statements). It is applicable, however, when a plan's statements purport to be in accordance with GAAP.

### Q 31:34   What does SFAS No. 35 require to be included in the financial statements?

Annual financial statements should include the following:

- Information regarding (1) net assets available for benefits as of the end of the plan year and (2) changes in net assets during the year;
- Information about the actuarial present value of APB as of the beginning or end of the plan year; and
- Information about the effects, if significant, of certain factors affecting the year-to-year change in the actuarial present value of APB.

Additional supplementary information may be provided that helps users of a plan's financial statements assess the extent to which the plan itself is able to pay participants' benefits and the degree to which benefit payments are dependent on other factors (e.g., the commitment and capacity of the sponsor-employer and, for ERISA plans, the security provided by the PBGC).

Obviously, the usefulness of a plan's financial statements is enhanced when information about net assets and about the actuarial present value of APB is presented as of the same date. Similarly, information about both changes in net assets and changes in the present value of APB should be presented for the same period. Information as of the *end* of the plan year is preferable, but SFAS No. 35 permits presentation of data as of the *beginning* of the plan year.

Note that a statement of cash flows is *not* required to be presented, but it is encouraged when the statement would provide relevant information about the plan's ability to meet future obligations.

### Q 31:35   What information is required by SFAS No. 35 regarding the net assets?

Net assets available for benefits consist of contributions receivable and plan investments. Contributions receivable are amounts due to the plan from the following parties:

- Employers
- Participants
- Other sources of funding (e.g., subsidies or grants from federal or state agencies)

As to employers' contributions, evidence of a receivable due to the plan may include one or more of the following:

- A resolution by the employer's governing body (e.g., the board of directors) approving a contribution
- A consistent policy of funding the preceding year's amount
- A federal income tax deduction for a period ending on or before the plan's reporting date
- An accrued liability to the plan
- Receipt of formally committed amounts soon after the plan's year-end

Note that funds from federal revenue-sharing programs that are used for plan funding purposes at the employer's discretion are considered employer contributions.

Unfunded prior service costs do *not* represent a receivable due to the plan until the sponsor-employer formally makes a commitment to pay the plan. Similarly, any excess of the actuarial present value of APB over net assets is not a plan asset unless at the plan's reporting date the excess is legally, contractually, or by virtue of a formal commitment due to the plan.

As with other receivables, employers' contributions are subject to an appropriate allowance for uncollectible amounts.

Plan investments should be reported at fair value. *Fair value* is defined as the amount that the plan could reasonably expect to receive in a current sale between a willing buyer and seller. For investments with active markets, fair value is represented by the quoted market prices. If no active market exists for a specific type of investment but there is such a market for similar investments, selling prices in that market may be helpful in estimating fair value. If no market price is available, the use of discounted expected cash flows (at a rate commensurate with the attendant risk) or the use of independent qualified appraisers may be necessary to estimate fair value.

Contracts with insurance enterprises (whether or not the plan is subject to ERISA) should be presented at contract values.

Operating assets (e.g., furniture and equipment) should be valued at cost less accumulated depreciation or amortization.

### Q 31:36   What is required by SFAS No. 35 in presenting plan benefits?

APB represent future benefit payments that are attributable to employees' services rendered to the date as of which the actuarial present value of APB is determined (the benefit information date). APB comprise benefits expected to be paid to the following parties:

- Retired or terminated employees or their beneficiaries
- Beneficiaries of deceased employees
- Present employees or their beneficiaries

The best representation of benefits attributable to services already rendered is the combination of vested benefits and nonvested benefits expected to become vested (determined primarily in accordance with the benefit accrual provision and employees' history of pay and service up to the benefit information date).

To the extent possible, the plan's provisions should be applied in measuring APB. Note that even if the plan does not specify a benefit for each year of service, another of its provisions may imply how APB should be measured. The manner in which benefits for which the plan does not specify or suggest measurement should be considered to accumulate depends on whether the benefit is includible or excludable in vested benefits.

For includible benefits (e.g., a supplemental early retirement benefit that is vested after a given number of years of employment), the benefits should be considered to accumulate in proportion to the ratio of the number of years of completed service through the benefit information date to the number of years that will have been completed when the specific benefit first becomes vested.

For excludable benefits, the ratio to be used is the number of completed years of service to projected years of service upon anticipated separation of covered employment.

When measuring APB, the following guidelines should be followed:

- Whenever possible, APB should be based on employees' history of pay and service and other appropriate factors as of the benefit information date.
- Projected years of service should be a factor only in determining employees' expected eligibility for particular benefits, such as the following:
  - Increased benefits that are granted provided a specified number of years of service are rendered
  - Early retirement benefits
  - Death benefits
  - Disability benefits
- Automatic benefit increases specified by the plan (e.g., automatic cost-of-living increases) that are expected to occur after the benefit information date should be recognized.
- Benefits to be provided by means of contracts excluded from plan assets for which payments to the insurance enterprise have been made should be excluded.
- Plan amendments adopted after the benefit information date should not be recognized.
- If it is necessary to take future compensation into account in the determination of Social Security benefits, employees' compensation as of the benefit information date should be assumed to remain unchanged during their assumed future services. Increases in the wage base or benefit level pursuant to either the existing Social Security law or possible future amendments of the law should not be recognized.

When APB has been determined, the *actuarial* present value of APB is computed based on the following assumptions:

- The pension plan will continue in existence.
- Assumed rates of return should be based on rates reasonably expected to be earned on plan assets over the period during which benefit payments are deferred.
- Inflation rates should be reasonably estimated and should be considered in the assumption of rates of return.
- Administrative expenses of the plan (not of the sponsor) may be accounted for either by (i) adjusting the assumed rate of return or (ii) assigning such expenses to future periods and then discounting them back to the benefit information date.

As an alternative to the foregoing assumptions, the actuarial present value of APB may be determined by selecting assumptions inherent in the estimated cost (at the benefit information date) of obtaining insurance contracts that provide plan participants with APB.

### Q 31:37   How are changes in the actuarial present value of APB presented for SFAS No. 35?

Changes in actuarial assumptions to reflect actual experience are considered changes in accounting estimates. In accordance with Accounting Principles Board Opinion No. 20, the effects of such changes should be accounted for in the year of the change and prospectively.

Note that a change in assumed rates of return need not automatically occur when the mix of the investment portfolio changes. It may very well be that the risk of loss has changed as well, and thus the ultimate *overall* rate of return (i.e., after losses are considered) will remain relatively constant.

### Q 31:38   Can approximations be used in the presentation of the information required by SFAS No. 35?

In applying measurement principles, the use of averages or other methods of approximation is appropriate provided that the results are reasonably close to those that would have been otherwise obtained. Thus, "rolling back" to the beginning of the plan year or projecting to the end of the year of detailed employee service data may be appropriate.

### Q 31:39   How are postretirement medical benefit features reported for SFAS No. 35?

Some defined benefit pension plans provide postretirement medical benefits in addition to other retirement benefits. Such plans may fund a portion of their medical benefit obligations via a health benefit account (often termed a 401(h) account after that section of the Code). SOP 99-2 provides guidance on accounting and reporting of 401(h) features embedded in defined benefit pension plans.

- Because 401(h) net assets cannot be used to satisfy pension obligations, net assets available for pension benefits should not include assets held in a 401 (h) account; rather, 401(h) net assets should be presented as a single line item (i.e., as a liability) on the face of a defined benefit plan's statement of net assets and thus, deducted to arrive at the total of net assets available for pension benefits.

- The statement of changes in net assets should show only the changes in net assets of the pension plan itself, not including any components of the changes in net assets in the 401(h) account. Note, however, that the statement of changes in net assets should report qualified transfers to the 401(h) account and/or any unused or unspent amounts (including allocated income) in the 401(h) account at the end of the period that represent transfers of excess pension plan assets that should have been transferred back (but were not) to the defined benefit pension plans.

- Information regarding APB should relate only to pension obligations (i.e., obligations related to retiree health benefits should not be reported in the pension plan's statement of APB).

- Assets in 401(h) accounts used to fund health and welfare benefits (and the changes in those assets) should be reported in the financial statements of the health and welfare plan. Such information may be presented *either* as a single line item on the face of the statement *or* as components of individual line items (with accompanying footnote disclosure). Note that the method of presentation must be consistently applied in both the statement of net assets and the statement of changes in net assets. Claims paid through the 401(h) account should be reported in the statement of changes in benefit obligations, and 401(h) obligations themselves should be reported in the statement of benefit obligations.

### Q 31:40   What are the disclosures required by SFAS No. 35?

The following information should be disclosed:

- A description of the method(s) and significant assumptions used to determine the fair value of investments and the reported value of contracts with insurance enterprises.
- A description of the method and significant assumptions (e.g., assumed rates of return, inflation rates, and retirement ages) used to determine the actuarial present value of APB. (Any significant changes of method or assumptions between benefit information dates should be described.)
- A brief general description of the plan agreement including (but not limited to) vesting and benefit provisions.
- A description of significant plan amendments adopted during the year ending on the latest benefit information date. (If significant amendments were adopted between the latest benefit information date and the plan's year-end, that fact and the fact that the actuarial present value of APB does not reflect those amendments should be indicated.)
- A brief general description of (i) the priority order of participants' claims to the assets of the plan upon plan termination and (ii) benefits guaranteed by the PBGC, including a discussion of the application of the PBGC guaranty to any recent plan amendment.
- The funding policy and any changes in that policy during the plan year. (For a contributory plan, the disclosure should state the method of determining participants' contributions. Plans subject to ERISA shall disclose whether the minimum funding requirements of ERISA have been met. If a minimum funding waiver has been granted by the IRS or if a request for a waiver is pending before the IRS, that fact should be disclosed.)
- The policy regarding the purchase of contracts with insurance enterprises that are excluded from plan assets. (The plan's dividend income for the year, if that is related to excluded contracts, should be disclosed.)
- The federal income tax status of the plan, if a favorable letter of determination has not been obtained or maintained. (Disclosure of the plan's tax status can be disclosed in other circumstances as well.)

- Identification of investments that represent 5 percent or more of the net assets available for benefits.
- Significant real estate or other transactions in which the plan and any of the following parties are jointly involved: (i) the sponsor, (ii) the employer(s), or (iii) the employee organization(s).
- Unusual or infrequent events or transactions occurring after the latest benefit information date but before issuance of the financial statements that might significantly affect the usefulness of the financial statements when assessing the plan's present and future ability to pay benefits. (If reasonably determinable, the effects of such events or transactions should be disclosed. If the effects are not quantified, the reasons why they are not reasonably determinable should also be disclosed.)
- The significant effects of factors affecting the change in the actuarial present value of APB.
- The total actuarial present value of APB as of the benefit information date, categorized as follows:
  - Vested benefits of participants currently receiving payments
  - Other vested benefits
  - Nonvested benefits
- The following information regarding changes in net assets available for benefits:
  - The net appreciation (depreciation) in fair value for each significant class of investments, segregated between investments whose fair values have been measured by quoted prices in an active market and those whose fair values have been otherwise determined
  - Investment income
  - Contributions from the employer(s), segregated between cash and non-cash contributions
  - Contributions from participants, including those by the sponsor
  - Contributions from other identified sources (e.g., state subsidies or federal grants)
  - Benefits paid to participants
  - Payments to insurance enterprises to purchase contracts that are excluded from plan assets
  - Administrative expenses

Plan administrators are encouraged to supplement the plan's financial statements with a brief explanation that highlights those matters expected to be of most interest to participants. Presentation of a summary of financial information for a period of years or another form of trend disclosure may be helpful to users of plan financial statements.

Note that SFAS No. 35 does not resolve the issue of whether APB are liabilities or represent an equity interest in the plan. Accordingly, a certain amount of flexibility is permitted in the presentation of information regarding the actuarial present value of APB and of year-to-year changes in APB. Thus, relevant information about either or both of these amounts may be presented on the face of one or more of the separate plan financial statements or in the footnotes.

**Note.** Regardless of where it is presented, *all* such information should be presented in the same location and may *not* be shown as supplemental information outside the financial statements or notes thereto.

The following footnote disclosures are required of defined benefit pension plans providing 401(h) benefits:

- The nature of 401(h) account assets and the fact that such assets are available only to pay retiree health benefits
- A reconciliation of the net assets reported in the pension plan's financial statements with the net assets reported on Form 5500; the reconciliation should be accompanied by a discussion of the 401(h) account and by a clear explanation that assets held in the 401(h) account are not available to pay pension benefits

The following disclosures are required of health and welfare plans:

- A statement that retiree health benefits are partially funded through a 401(h) account of the defined benefit pension plan
- A statement that 401(h) account assets are available only to pay retiree health benefits
- Significant components of net assets and changes thereof in the 401(h) account
- A reconciliation of the net assets reported in the financial statements with net assets reported on Form 5500

The worksheets on the following pages provide detailed instructions for SFAS No. 87 and SFAS No. 132 accounting.

# Worksheets for SFAS No. 87 and SFAS No. 132 Accounting

Determination of Net Periodic Benefit Cost—Worksheet 1

_____ Defined Benefit Pension Plan

Pension Accounting for Fiscal Year Ending _____

1. Service cost
   a. Amount due at beginning of year _____
   b. Interest at _____ % for full year (discount rate) _____
   c. Total service cost (a + b) _____
2. Interest cost
   a. Projected benefit obligation (PBO) at beginning of year _____
   b. Expected disbursements, weighted for timing _____
   c. Average expected PBO (a − b) _____
   d. Discount rate _____ % _____
   e. Interest cost (c × d) _____
3. Expected return on assets
   a. Market-related value at beginning of year _____
   b. Expected disbursements, weighted for timing _____
   c. Expected receipts, weighted for timing _____
   d. Average market-related assets (a − b + c) _____
   e. Long-term rate of return _____ % _____
   f. Expected return on assets (d × e) _____
4. Amortization of transition (assets) or obligations (Schedule A) _____
5. Amortization of prior service cost (Schedule B) _____
6. Amortization of (gain) or loss (Schedule C) _____
7. Settlements or curtailments _____
8. Net periodic benefit cost (1c + 2e − 3f + 4 + 5 + 6+ 7) _____

Disclosure of Net Periodic Benefit Cost—Worksheet 2

Pension Accounting for Fiscal Year Ending _____

|  | *Fiscal Year Ending* | |
|---|---|---|
|  | *X + 1* | *X* |
| 1. Service cost (Worksheet 1, item 1c) | _____ | _____ |
| 2. Interest cost (Worksheet 1, item 2e) | _____ | _____ |
| 3. Expected return on plan assets (Worksheet 1, item 3f) | _____ | _____ |
| 4. Amortization of transition (assets) or obligations (Worksheet 1, item 4) | _____ | _____ |
| 5. Amortization of prior service cost (Worksheet 1, item 5) | _____ | _____ |
| 6. Recognized actuarial (gain) or loss (Worksheet 1, item 6) | _____ | _____ |
| 7. Recognized (gain) or loss due to settlement or curtailment (Worksheet 1, item 7) | _____ | _____ |
| 8. Net periodic benefit cost ($1 + 2 - 3 + 4 + 5 + 6 + 7$) | _____ | _____ |

Minimum Liability, Additional Liability, Intangible Assets—Worksheet 3

_____ Defined Benefit Pension Plan

Pension Accounting for Fiscal Year Ending _____

|  | *Fiscal Year Ending* | |
| --- | --- | --- |
|  | *X + 1* | *X* |

**Minimum Liability**

1. Accumulated benefit obligation projected to year end (See Schedule D-1 if projected to year end.)

2. Fair value of plan assets at year end (Use projected value to estimate; actual must be used for statements.)

3. Unfunded accumulated benefit obligation (1 – 2) (If zero or less, no minimum liability is required. Do *not* complete the remainder of this column.)

4. (Accrued)/prepaid benefit cost (Schedule E, line 4)

5. Additional liability (3 + 4) (not less than 0)

**Intangible Assets**

6. Unrecognized obligation from transition (If Schedule A indicates an (asset), enter zero.)

7. Unrecognized prior service cost (Schedule B, last column.)

8. Maximum intangible asset (6 + 7)

9. Actual intangible asset (lesser of 5 or 8)

**Net Amount**

10. Accumulated other comprehensive income (5 – 9, but not less than 0)

Funded Status and Reconciliation of Benefit Obligation
and Plan Assets—Worksheet 4

_____ Defined Benefit Pension Plan

Pension Accounting for Fiscal Year Ending _____

|  | | $X + 1$ | $X$ |
|---|---|---|---|
| **Change in Benefit Obligation** | | | |
| 1. | Benefit obligation at beginning of year (Schedule C, item 1) | _____ | _____ |
| 2. | Service cost (Worksheet 1, item 1c) | _____ | _____ |
| 3. | Interest cost (Worksheet 1, item 2e) | _____ | _____ |
| 4. | Plan participants' contributions | _____ | _____ |
| 5. | Amendments | _____ | _____ |
| 6. | Actuarial (gain) or loss during year | _____ | _____ |
| 7. | Acquisition or (divestiture) | _____ | _____ |
| 8. | (Disbursements paid) (Schedule F, item 2) | _____ | _____ |
| 9. | Settlement or curtailment | _____ | _____ |
| 10. | Benefit obligation at end of year | _____ | _____ |
| **Change in Plan Assets** | | | |
| 11. | Fair value of plan assets at beginning of year (Schedule C, item 2) | _____ | _____ |
| 12. | Actual return on plan assets (Schedule F, item 5) | _____ | _____ |
| 13. | Acquisition or divesture (Schedule F, items 3c – 2b) | _____ | _____ |
| 14. | Employer contributions (Schedule F, item 3a) | _____ | _____ |
| 15. | Plan participants' contributions (Schedule F, item 3b) | _____ | _____ |
| 16. | (Paid to participants) (Schedule F, item 2a) | _____ | _____ |
| 17. | Settlement or curtailment (Schedule F, item 2c) | _____ | _____ |
| 18. | Fair value of plan assets at end of year | _____ | _____ |
| **Amounts Recognized, Accrued, or Prepaid** | | | |
| 19. | Funded status (18 – 10) | _____ | _____ |
| 20. | Unrecognized transition amount (Schedule A, last column) | _____ | _____ |
| 21. | Unrecognized prior service cost (Schedule B, last column) | _____ | _____ |
| 22. | Unrecognized net actuarial (gain)/loss (Schedule C, line 6 EOY) | _____ | _____ |

23.  Net amount recognized in statement of
     financial position (19 + 20 + 21 + 22)            _____        _____

24.  Adjustments related to minimum liability          _____        _____

     a.   (Additional minimum liability)               _____        _____
          (Worksheet 3, line 5)

     b.   Intangible asset (Worksheet 3, line 9)       _____        _____

     c.   Accumulated other comprehensive             _____        _____
          income (Worksheet 3, line 10)

     d.   Total adjustments (a + b + c)                _____        _____

25.  (Accrued)/prepaid benefit cost (23 + 24d)         _____        _____

**Amounts Recognized in Statement of Financial Position**

26.  (Accrued)/prepaid benefit cost (25, above)        _____        _____

27.  Accrued benefit liability (24a, above)            _____        _____

28.  Intangible asset (24b, above)                     _____        _____

29.  Accumulated other comprehensive income            _____        _____
     (24c, above)

30.  Net amount recognized (26 + 27 + 28 + 29)         _____        _____

Amortization of (Gain) or Loss—Schedule C

_____ Defined Benefit Pension Plan

Pension Accounting for Fiscal Year Ending _____

|  | | *Beginning of Year* | *End of Year* |
|---|---|---|---|
| 1. | Projected benefit obligation (PBO) | _____ | _____ |
| 2. | Fair value of plan assets | | |
| 3. | Unrecognized transition obligation or (asset) (Schedule A) | _____ | _____ |
| 4. | Unrecognized prior service cost (Schedule B) | _____ | _____ |
| 5. | (Accrued) or prepaid benefit cost (Schedule E) | | |
| 6. | Unrecognized (gain) or loss (1 − 2 − 3 − 4 + 5) | _____ | _____ |
| 7. | (Gain) or loss not reflected in market-related value | | |
| | a. Fair value | _____ | _____ |
| | b. Market-related value | | |
| | c. Amount included in unrecognized transition obligation or (asset), not yet reflected in market-related value (Schedule C-2, column 1) | _____ | _____ |
| | d. Amount not reflected in market-related value | _____ | _____ |
| 8. | (Gain) or loss subject to amortization (6 + 7d) | _____ | _____ |
| 9. | Greater of 1 or 7b | _____ | _____ |
| 10. | 10% of 9 | _____ | _____ |
| 11. | (Gain) or loss subject to amortization (excess of 8 over 10) | _____ | _____ |
| 12. | Average future service of participants expected to receive benefits | _____ | _____ |
| 13. | Amortization amount (11 ÷ 12) | _____ | _____ |

Accrued or Prepaid Pension Expense—Schedule E

_____ Defined Benefit Pension Plan

Pension Accounting for Fiscal Year Ending _____

1.  (Accrued) or prepaid at beginning of year          _____
2.  Net periodic benefit cost for year          _____
3.  Contributions made during the year (Amounts not          _____
    segregated in a trust or otherwise restricted are not
    considered contributions even though they may be
    deemed contributions for Schedule B of Form 5500.)
4.  (Accrued) or prepaid pension expense at end of year          _____
    $(1 - 2 + 3)$

Asset (Gain) or Loss—Schedule F

_____ Defined Benefit Pension Plan

Pension Accounting for Fiscal Year Ending _____

| | | *Fiscal Year Ending* | |
| --- | --- | --- | --- |
| | | *X + 1* | *X* |
| 1. | Fair value at end of year | _____ | _____ |
| 2. | Actual disbursements | | |
| | a.  To participants | _____ | _____ |
| | b.  Divestiture, assets transferred out to other plan | | |
| | c.  Settlements and curtailments not included in item a | _____ | _____ |
| | d.  Total disbursements from plan | _____ | _____ |
| 3. | Actual receipts | | |
| | a.  From employer | _____ | _____ |
| | b.  From participants | | |
| | c.  Acquisition, assets transferred in from other plan | _____ | _____ |
| | d.  Total receipts by plan | _____ | _____ |
| 4. | Fair value at beginning of year | _____ | _____ |
| 5. | Actual return on assets (1 + 2d − 3d − 4) | _____ | _____ |
| 6. | Expected return (Worksheet 1, item 3f) | _____ | _____ |
| 7. | Asset (gain) or loss (6 − 5) | _____ | _____ |

# SFAS No. 132 Standard Pension Audit Confirmation Letter

SFAS No. 132—Standard Pension Audit Confirmation Letter

_____ Defined Benefit Pension Plan

Pension Accounting for Fiscal Year Ending _____

The following answers are submitted with respect to _____ Defined Benefit Pension Plan (the "Plan") related to the financial statements of _____ (the "Company") for the year of _____ .

**A. General Information**

1. The employee group covered:

2. The benefit provisions of the Plan used in calculations:

   a. The benefit provisions of the Plan used in calculating the net periodic benefit cost for the year and of the accumulated benefit obligation and the projected benefit obligation at the end of the year:

   b. Benefit provisions that had not taken effect in the year:

   c. Date of the most recent Plan amendment included in calculations:

   d. Participants or benefits excluded from the calculations, such as benefits guaranteed under an insurance or annuity contract:

3. The Plan sponsor's funding policy for the Plan:

4. Significant liabilities other than for benefits:

5. The method and amortization period used for the following:

    a. Calculation of market-related value of Plan assets:

    b. Amortization of any transition asset or obligation:

    c. Amortization of unrecognized prior service cost:

    d. Amortization of unrecognized net gain or loss:

6. Substantive commitments for benefits that exceed the benefits defined by the written plan that are included in the calculations:

7. Determination of the value of any insurance or annuity contract included in the assets:

8. Nature and effect of significant plan amendments and other significant matters affecting comparability of net periodic benefit cost, funded status, and other information for the current year with that of the prior year:

9. The following information relates to the employee census data used in calculating the benefit obligation and pension cost:

    a. The source and nature of the data and the date of collection:

b.   Participants:

|  | Number of Persons | Compensation (if applicable) |
|---|---|---|
| Currently receiving payments | _____ | _____ |
| Active with vested benefits | _____ | _____ |
| Terminated with deferred vested benefits | _____ | _____ |
| Active without vested benefits | _____ | _____ |
| Other | _____ | _____ |

c.   Attached is a listing of selected participants (by name or participant number) contained in the census and the following related census data for each: age or date of birth; sex; salary; and date of hire or years of service. The attached information agrees with the data used in the measurement except for:

## B. Net Periodic Benefit Cost

1.   Service cost _____

2.   Interest cost _____

3.   Expected return on plan assets: _____

4.   Amortization of transition (assets) or obligations _____

5.   Amortization of prior service cost _____

6.   Recognized actuarial (gain) or loss

7.   Recognized (gain) or loss due to settlement or curtailment _____

8.   Net periodic benefit cost _____

9.   The foregoing measurement of net periodic pension cost is based on the following assumptions:

Weighted-average discount rate _____ %

Weighted-average rate of compensation increase _____ %

Weighted-average expected long-term rate of return on plan assets _____ %

The basis on which the above rates were selected and whether the basis is consistent with the prior year:

The assumptions used in the measurement of net periodic pension cost:

10.   The calculations of the items shown in B1 to B8 are based on the following:

Asset information at _____

Census data at _____

Measurement date _____

11.   Adjustments made to project the census data forward to the measurement date or to project the results calculated at an earlier date to those shown in B1 to B8:

## C. Benefit Obligation Information

The following information relates to the benefit obligations for disclosure in the financial statements for the year referred to in the first paragraph of this letter:

*Change in benefit obligation*

|     |                                            |            |
| --- | ------------------------------------------ | ---------- |
| 1.  | Benefit obligation at beginning of year    | _____  |
| 2.  | Service cost                               | _____  |
| 3.  | Interest cost                              | _____  |
| 4.  | Plan participants' contributions           | _____  |
| 5.  | Amendments                                 | _____  |
| 6.  | Actuarial (gain) or loss during year       | _____  |
| 7.  | Acquisition or (divestiture)               | _____  |
| 8.  | (Disbursements paid)                       | _____  |
| 9.  | Settlement or curtailment                  |            |
| 10. | Benefit obligation at end of year          | _____  |

*Change in plan assets*

|     |                                                |           |
| --- | ---------------------------------------------- | --------- |
| 11. | Fair value of plan assets at beginning of year | _____ |
| 12. | Actual return on plan assets                   | _____ |
| 13. | Acquisition or divesture                       | _____ |
| 14. | Employer contributions                         | _____ |
| 15. | Plan participants' contributions               | _____ |
| 16. | (Paid to participants)                         | _____ |
| 17. | Settlement or curtailment                      | _____ |
| 18. | Fair value of plan assets at end of year       | _____ |

*Amounts recognized, accrued, or prepaid*

|     |                                                          |           |
| --- | -------------------------------------------------------- | --------- |
| 19. | Funded status                                            | _____ |
| 20. | Unrecognized transition amount                           | _____ |
| 21. | Unrecognized prior service cost                          | _____ |
| 22. | Unrecognized net actuarial (gain)/loss                   | _____ |
| 23. | Net amount recognized in statement of financial position | _____ |
| 24. | Adjustments related to minimum liability                 |           |
|     | a.  (Additional minimum liability)                       | _____ |
|     | b.  Intangible asset                                     | _____ |
|     | c.  Accumulated other comprehensive income               | _____ |
|     | d.  Total adjustments                                    | _____ |
| 25. | (Accrued)/prepaid benefit cost                           |           |

*Amounts recognized in statement of financial position*

|     |                                            |           |
| --- | ------------------------------------------ | --------- |
| 26. | (Accrued)/prepaid benefit cost             | _____ |
| 27. | Accrued benefit liability                  | _____ |
| 28. | Intangible asset                           | _____ |
| 29. | Accumulated other comprehensive income     | _____ |

30. Actuarial (gain) or loss during year       _____

31. The above amount of projected benefit obligation is measured based on the following assumptions:

    Weighted-average discount rate      _____ %

    Weighted-average rate of compensation increase   _____ %

    Description of the assumptions used in the measurement:     _____

32. (Disbursements paid)

    Asset information at      _____ %

    Census data at      _____ %

    Measurement date      _____ %

    Adjustments made to project the census data forward to the measurement date or to project the results calculated at an earlier date to those shown in C1 to C30:

33. Significant events noted subsequent to the current year's measurement date and as of the date of your reply to this request and the effects of those events, such as a large plant closing, which could materially affect the amounts shown in C1 to C30.

**D. Other Information**

1. An analysis for the year showing beginning amounts, additions, reductions, and ending amounts of the:

*Information Attached*

    a.   Projected benefit obligation    _____

    b.   Unrecognized prior service cost   _____

    c.   Unrecognized net loss or (gain)   _____

    d.   Unrecognized net transition obligation or (asset)   _____

2. Descriptions and summary calculations of gains or losses from settlements, curtailments, or termination of benefits during the year, such as from:

    a.   Purchases of annuity contracts:

    b.   Lump-sum cash payments to Plan participants:

    c.   Other irrevocable actions that relieved the Company or the Plan of primary responsibility for a pension obligation, and eliminated significant risks related to the obligation and asset:

     d.    Any events that significantly reduce the expected years of future service of employees:

     e.    Any events that eliminated for a significant number of employees the accrual of defined benefits for some or all of their future services:

     f.    Any special or contractual termination benefits offered to employees:

3.    Was all the information above determined in    Yes [ ]       No [ ]
accordance with SFAS No. 87 and No. 88
(including the FASB's Guides to
Implementation of Statement numbers 87 and
88, and the American Academy of Actuaries'
"An Actuary's Guide to Compliance with
Statement of Financial Accounting Standards
No. 87") as amended by FAS Statement No.
132, to the best of your knowledge?

Describe any differences.

4.    Describe the nature of your relationship, if any, with the Plan or the plan sponsor that might impair or appear to impair the objectivity of your work:

Actuarial Firm: _____

Certified By: _____

Signature: _____

Title: _____

Date: _____

# Appendix A

# 2007, 2006, 2005, 2004, 2003, 2002, and 2001 Covered Compensation Tables

## 2007 Covered Compensation Table
### Table II

| Calendar Year of Birth | Calendar Year of Social Security Retirement Age | 2007 Covered Compensation Table |
|---|---|---|
| 1907 | 1972 | $ 4,488 |
| 1908 | 1973 | $ 4,704 |
| 1909 | 1974 | $ 5,004 |
| 1910 | 1975 | $ 5,316 |
| 1911 | 1976 | $ 5,664 |
| 1912 | 1977 | $ 6,060 |
| 1913 | 1978 | $ 6,480 |
| 1914 | 1979 | $ 7,044 |
| 1915 | 1980 | $ 7,692 |
| 1916 | 1981 | $ 8,460 |
| 1917 | 1982 | $ 9,300 |
| 1918 | 1983 | $10,236 |
| 1919 | 1984 | $11,232 |
| 1920 | 1985 | $12,276 |
| 1921 | 1986 | $13,368 |
| 1922 | 1987 | $14,520 |
| 1923 | 1988 | $15,708 |
| 1924 | 1989 | $16,968 |
| 1925 | 1990 | $18,312 |
| 1926 | 1991 | $19,728 |
| 1927 | 1992 | $21,192 |
| 1928 | 1993 | $22,716 |
| 1929 | 1994 | $24,312 |
| 1930 | 1995 | $25,920 |
| 1931 | 1996 | $27,576 |
| 1932 | 1997 | $29,304 |
| 1933 | 1998 | $31,128 |
| 1934 | 1999 | $33,060 |
| 1935 | 2000 | $35,100 |
| 1936 | 2001 | $37,212 |
| 1937 | 2002 | $39,444 |
| 1938 | 2004 | $43,992 |
| 1939 | 2005 | $46,344 |
| 1940 | 2006 | $48,816 |
| 1941 | 2007 | $51,348 |
| 1942 | 2008 | $53,820 |
| 1943 | 2009 | $56,232 |
| 1944 | 2010 | $58,608 |
| 1945 | 2011 | $60,960 |

## 2007 Covered Compensation Table (*cont'd*)
### Table II

| Calendar Year of Birth | Calendar Year of Social Security Retirement Age | 2007 Covered Compensation Table |
|---|---|---|
| 1946 | 2012 | $63,276 |
| 1947 | 2013 | $65,556 |
| 1948 | 2014 | $67,680 |
| 1949 | 2015 | $69,732 |
| 1950 | 2016 | $71,664 |
| 1951 | 2017 | $73,524 |
| 1952 | 2018 | $75,300 |
| 1953 | 2019 | $77,004 |
| 1954 | 2020 | $78,660 |
| 1955 | 2022 | $81,780 |
| 1956 | 2023 | $83,280 |
| 1957 | 2024 | $84,684 |
| 1958 | 2025 | $86,004 |
| 1959 | 2026 | $87,264 |
| 1960 | 2027 | $88,464 |
| 1961 | 2028 | $89,604 |
| 1962 | 2029 | $90,660 |
| 1963 | 2030 | $91,704 |
| 1964 | 2031 | $92,700 |
| 1965 | 2032 | $93,612 |
| 1966 | 2033 | $94,440 |
| 1967 | 2034 | $95,160 |
| 1968 | 2035 | $95,760 |
| 1969 | 2036 | $96,252 |
| 1970 | 2037 | $96,612 |
| 1971 | 2038 | $96,912 |
| 1972 | 2039 | $97,188 |
| 1973 | 2040 | $97,404 |
| 1974 and later | 2041 | $97,500 |

## 2007 Rounded Covered Compensation Table

| Year of Birth | Covered Compensation |
|---|---|
| 1937 | $39,000 |
| 1938-1939 | $45,000 |
| 1940 | $48,000 |
| 1941 | $51,000 |
| 1942 | $54,000 |

## 2007 Rounded Covered Compensation Table (*cont'd*)

| Year of Birth | Covered Compensation |
|---|---|
| 1943 | $57,000 |
| 1944-1945 | $60,000 |
| 1946 | $63,000 |
| 1947 | $66,000 |
| 1948-1949 | $69,000 |
| 1950 | $72,000 |
| 1951-1952 | $75,000 |
| 1953-1954 | $78,000 |
| 1955 | $81,000 |
| 1956-1957 | $84,000 |
| 1958-1960 | $87,000 |
| 1961-1962 | $90,000 |
| 1963-1966 | $93,000 |
| 1967-1970 | $96,000 |
| 1971 and later | $97,500 |

[Rev. Rul. 2006-60, 2006-48 I.R.B. 977]

## 2006 Covered Compensation Table

| Calendar Year of Birth | Calendar Year of Social Security Retirement Age | 2006 Covered Compensation Table II |
|---|---|---|
| 1907 | 1972 | $ 4,488 |
| 1908 | 1973 | $ 4,704 |
| 1909 | 1974 | $ 5,004 |
| 1910 | 1975 | $ 5,316 |
| 1911 | 1976 | $ 5,664 |
| 1912 | 1977 | $ 6,060 |
| 1913 | 1978 | $ 6,480 |
| 1914 | 1979 | $ 7,044 |
| 1915 | 1980 | $ 7,692 |
| 1916 | 1981 | $ 8,460 |
| 1917 | 1982 | $ 9,300 |
| 1918 | 1983 | $10,236 |
| 1919 | 1984 | $11,232 |
| 1920 | 1985 | $12,276 |
| 1921 | 1986 | $13,368 |
| 1922 | 1987 | $14,520 |
| 1923 | 1988 | $15,708 |

## 2006 Covered Compensation Table (*cont'd*)

| Calendar Year of Birth | Calendar Year of Social Security Retirement Age | 2006 Covered Compensation Table II |
|---|---|---|
| 1924 | 1989 | $16,968 |
| 1925 | 1990 | $18,312 |
| 1926 | 1991 | $19,728 |
| 1927 | 1992 | $21,192 |
| 1928 | 1993 | $22,716 |
| 1929 | 1994 | $24,312 |
| 1930 | 1995 | $25,920 |
| 1931 | 1996 | $27,576 |
| 1932 | 1997 | $29,304 |
| 1933 | 1998 | $31,128 |
| 1934 | 1999 | $33,060 |
| 1935 | 2000 | $35,100 |
| 1936 | 2001 | $37,212 |
| 1937 | 2002 | $39,444 |
| 1938 | 2004 | $43,992 |
| 1939 | 2005 | $46,344 |
| 1940 | 2006 | $48,816 |
| 1941 | 2007 | $51,252 |
| 1942 | 2008 | $53,628 |
| 1943 | 2009 | $55,944 |
| 1944 | 2010 | $58,236 |
| 1945 | 2011 | $60,492 |
| 1946 | 2012 | $62,712 |
| 1947 | 2013 | $64,896 |
| 1948 | 2014 | $66,936 |
| 1949 | 2015 | $68,880 |
| 1950 | 2016 | $70,728 |
| 1951 | 2017 | $72,492 |
| 1952 | 2018 | $74,160 |
| 1953 | 2019 | $75,780 |
| 1954 | 2020 | $77,340 |
| 1955 | 2022 | $80,268 |
| 1956 | 2023 | $81,672 |
| 1957 | 2024 | $82,992 |
| 1958 | 2025 | $84,216 |
| 1959 | 2026 | $85,380 |
| 1960 | 2027 | $86,484 |

## 2006 Covered Compensation Table (*cont'd*)

| Calendar Year of Birth | Calendar Year of Social Security Retirement Age | 2006 Covered Compensation Table II |
|---|---|---|
| 1961 | 2028 | $87,540 |
| 1962 | 2029 | $88,500 |
| 1963 | 2030 | $89,436 |
| 1964 | 2031 | $90,336 |
| 1965 | 2032 | $91,164 |
| 1966 | 2033 | $91,896 |
| 1967 | 2034 | $92,520 |
| 1968 | 2035 | $93,024 |
| 1969 | 2036 | $93,420 |
| 1970 | 2037 | $93,684 |
| 1971 | 2038 | $93,900 |
| 1972 | 2039 | $94,080 |
| 1973 and later | 2040 | $94,200 |

| Year of Birth | Covered Compensation |
|---|---|
| 1937 | $39,000 |
| 1938-1939 | $45,000 |
| 1940 | $48,000 |
| 1941 | $51,000 |
| 1942 | $54,000 |
| 1943-1944 | $57,000 |
| 1945 | $60,000 |
| 1946 | $63,000 |
| 1947-1948 | $66,000 |
| 1949 | $69,000 |
| 1950-1951 | $72,000 |
| 1952-1953 | $75,000 |
| 1954 | $78,000 |
| 1955-1956 | $81,000 |
| 1957-1959 | $84,000 |
| 1960-1961 | $87,000 |
| 1962-1965 | $90,000 |
| 1966-1969 | $93,000 |
| 1970 and later | $94,200 |

[Rev. Rul. 2005-72, 2005-46 I.R.B. 944]

## 2005 Covered Compensation Table

| Calendar Year of Birth | Calendar Year of Social Security Retirement Age | 2005 Covered Compensation Table |
|---|---|---|
| 1907 | 1972 | $ 4,488 |
| 1908 | 1973 | $ 4,704 |
| 1909 | 1974 | $ 5,004 |
| 1910 | 1975 | $ 5,316 |
| 1911 | 1976 | $ 5,664 |
| 1912 | 1977 | $ 6,060 |
| 1913 | 1978 | $ 6,480 |
| 1914 | 1979 | $ 7,044 |
| 1915 | 1980 | $ 7,692 |
| 1916 | 1981 | $ 8,460 |
| 1917 | 1982 | $ 9,300 |
| 1918 | 1983 | $10,236 |
| 1919 | 1984 | $11,232 |
| 1920 | 1985 | $12,276 |
| 1921 | 1986 | $13,368 |
| 1922 | 1987 | $14,520 |
| 1923 | 1988 | $15,708 |
| 1924 | 1989 | $16,968 |
| 1925 | 1990 | $18,312 |
| 1926 | 1991 | $19,728 |
| 1927 | 1992 | $21,192 |
| 1928 | 1993 | $22,716 |
| 1929 | 1994 | $24,312 |
| 1930 | 1995 | $25,920 |
| 1931 | 1996 | $27,576 |
| 1932 | 1997 | $29,304 |
| 1933 | 1998 | $31,128 |
| 1934 | 1999 | $33,060 |
| 1935 | 2000 | $35,100 |
| 1936 | 2001 | $37,212 |
| 1937 | 2002 | $39,444 |
| 1938 | 2004 | $43,992 |
| 1939 | 2005 | $46,344 |
| 1940 | 2006 | $48,696 |
| 1941 | 2007 | $51,012 |
| 1942 | 2008 | $53,268 |
| 1943 | 2009 | $55,464 |
| 1944 | 2010 | $57,636 |
| 1945 | 2011 | $59,772 |
| 1946 | 2012 | $61,872 |

## 2005 Covered Compensation Table (*cont'd*)

| Calendar Year of Birth | Calendar Year of Social Security Retirement Age | 2005 Covered Compensation Table |
|---|---|---|
| 1947 | 2013 | $63,396 |
| 1948 | 2014 | $65,856 |
| 1949 | 2015 | $67,680 |
| 1950 | 2016 | $69,408 |
| 1951 | 2017 | $71,052 |
| 1952 | 2018 | $72,600 |
| 1953 | 2019 | $74,100 |
| 1954 | 2020 | $75,540 |
| 1955 | 2022 | $78,228 |
| 1956 | 2023 | $79,512 |
| 1957 | 2024 | $80,712 |
| 1958 | 2025 | $81,816 |
| 1959 | 2026 | $82,860 |
| 1960 | 2027 | $83,844 |
| 1961 | 2028 | $84,780 |
| 1962 | 2029 | $85,620 |
| 1963 | 2030 | $86,436 |
| 1964 | 2031 | $87,216 |
| 1965 | 2032 | $87,924 |
| 1966 | 2033 | $88,536 |
| 1967 | 2034 | $89,040 |
| 1968 | 2035 | $89,424 |
| 1969 | 2036 | $89,700 |
| 1970 | 2037 | $89,844 |
| 1971 | 2038 | $89,940 |
| 1972 and later | 2039 | $90,000 |

## 2005 Rounded Covered Compensation Table

| Year of Birth | Covered Compensation |
|---|---|
| 1937 | $39,000 |
| 1938-1939 | $45,000 |
| 1940 | $48,000 |
| 1941 | $51,000 |
| 1942-1943 | $54,000 |
| 1944 | $57,000 |
| 1945 | $60,000 |
| 1946-1947 | $63,000 |
| 1948 | $66,000 |

## 2005 Rounded Covered Compensation Table (*cont'd*)

| Year of Birth | Covered Compensation |
|---|---|
| 1949-1950 | $69,000 |
| 1951-1952 | $72,000 |
| 1953-1954 | $75,000 |
| 1955 | $78,000 |
| 1956-1958 | $81,000 |
| 1959-1961 | $84,000 |
| 1962-1965 | $87,000 |
| 1966 and later | $90,000 |

## 2004 Covered Compensation Table

| Calendar Year of Birth | Calendar Year of Social Security Retirement Age | 2004 Covered Compensation Table |
|---|---|---|
| 1907 | 1972 | $ 4,488 |
| 1908 | 1973 | $ 4,704 |
| 1909 | 1974 | $ 5,004 |
| 1910 | 1975 | $ 5,316 |
| 1911 | 1976 | $ 5,664 |
| 1912 | 1977 | $ 6,060 |
| 1913 | 1978 | $ 6,480 |
| 1914 | 1979 | $ 7,044 |
| 1915 | 1980 | $ 7,692 |
| 1916 | 1981 | $ 8,460 |
| 1917 | 1982 | $ 9,300 |
| 1918 | 1983 | $10,236 |
| 1919 | 1984 | $11,232 |
| 1920 | 1985 | $12,276 |
| 1921 | 1986 | $13,368 |
| 1922 | 1987 | $14,520 |
| 1923 | 1988 | $15,708 |
| 1924 | 1989 | $16,968 |
| 1925 | 1990 | $18,312 |
| 1926 | 1991 | $19,728 |
| 1927 | 1992 | $21,192 |
| 1928 | 1993 | $22,716 |
| 1929 | 1994 | $24,312 |
| 1930 | 1995 | $25,920 |
| 1931 | 1996 | $27,576 |
| 1932 | 1997 | $29,304 |
| 1933 | 1998 | $31,128 |

## 2004 Covered Compensation Table (*cont'd*)

| Calendar Year of Birth | Calendar Year of Social Security Retirement Age | 2004 Covered Compensation Table |
|---|---|---|
| 1934 | 1999 | $33,060 |
| 1935 | 2000 | $35,100 |
| 1936 | 2001 | $37,212 |
| 1937 | 2002 | $39,444 |
| 1938 | 2004 | $43,992 |
| 1939 | 2005 | $46,284 |
| 1940 | 2006 | $48,576 |
| 1941 | 2007 | $50,832 |
| 1942 | 2008 | $53,028 |
| 1943 | 2009 | $55,164 |
| 1944 | 2010 | $57,276 |
| 1945 | 2011 | $59,352 |
| 1946 | 2012 | $61,392 |
| 1947 | 2013 | $63,396 |
| 1948 | 2014 | $65,256 |
| 1949 | 2015 | $67,020 |
| 1950 | 2016 | $68,688 |
| 1951 | 2017 | $70,272 |
| 1952 | 2018 | $71,760 |
| 1953 | 2019 | $73,200 |
| 1954 | 2020 | $74,580 |
| 1955 | 2022 | $77,148 |
| 1956 | 2023 | $78,372 |
| 1957 | 2024 | $79,512 |
| 1958 | 2025 | $80,556 |
| 1959 | 2026 | $81,540 |
| 1960 | 2027 | $82,464 |
| 1961 | 2028 | $83,340 |
| 1962 | 2029 | $84,120 |
| 1963 | 2030 | $84,876 |
| 1964 | 2031 | $85,596 |
| 1965 | 2032 | $86,244 |
| 1966 | 2033 | $86,796 |
| 1967 | 2034 | $87,240 |
| 1968 | 2035 | $87,564 |
| 1969 | 2036 | $87,780 |
| 1970 | 2037 | $87,864 |
| 1971 and later | 2038 | $87,900 |

## 2004 Rounded Covered Compensation Table

| Year of Birth | Covered Compensation |
|---|---|
| 1937 | $39,000 |
| 1938-1939 | $45,000 |
| 1940 | $48,000 |
| 1941 | $51,000 |
| 1942-1943 | $54,000 |
| 1944 | $57,000 |
| 1945-1946 | $60,000 |
| 1947 | $63,000 |
| 1948-1949 | $66,000 |
| 1950-1951 | $69,000 |
| 1952-1953 | $72,000 |
| 1954 | $75,000 |
| 1955-1956 | $78,000 |
| 1957-1960 | $81,000 |
| 1961-1963 | $84,000 |
| 1964-1967 | $87,000 |
| 1968 and later | $87,900 |

[Rev. Rul. 2003-124, 2003-49 I.R.B. 1173]

## 2003 Covered Compensation Table

| Calendar Year of Birth | Calendar Year of Social Security Retirement Age | 2003 Covered Compensation Table II |
|---|---|---|
| 1907 | 1972 | $ 4,488 |
| 1908 | 1973 | $ 4,704 |
| 1909 | 1974 | $ 5,004 |
| 1910 | 1975 | $ 5,316 |
| 1911 | 1976 | $ 5,664 |
| 1912 | 1977 | $ 6,060 |
| 1913 | 1978 | $ 6,480 |
| 1914 | 1979 | $ 7,044 |
| 1915 | 1980 | $ 7,692 |
| 1916 | 1981 | $ 8,460 |
| 1917 | 1982 | $ 9,300 |
| 1918 | 1983 | $10,236 |
| 1919 | 1984 | $11,232 |
| 1920 | 1985 | $12,276 |

## 2003 Covered Compensation Table (*cont'd*)

| Calendar Year of Birth | Calendar Year of Social Security Retirement Age | 2003 Covered Compensation Table II |
|---|---|---|
| 1921 | 1986 | $13,368 |
| 1922 | 1987 | $14,520 |
| 1923 | 1988 | $15,708 |
| 1924 | 1989 | $16,968 |
| 1925 | 1990 | $18,312 |
| 1926 | 1991 | $19,728 |
| 1927 | 1992 | $21,192 |
| 1928 | 1993 | $22,716 |
| 1929 | 1994 | $24,312 |
| 1930 | 1995 | $25,920 |
| 1931 | 1996 | $27,576 |
| 1932 | 1997 | $29,304 |
| 1933 | 1998 | $31,128 |
| 1934 | 1999 | $33,060 |
| 1935 | 2000 | $35,100 |
| 1936 | 2001 | $37,212 |
| 1937 | 2002 | $39,444 |
| 1938 | 2004 | $43,968 |
| 1939 | 2005 | $46,236 |
| 1940 | 2006 | $48,492 |
| 1941 | 2007 | $50,724 |
| 1942 | 2008 | $52,908 |
| 1943 | 2009 | $55,008 |
| 1944 | 2010 | $57,096 |
| 1945 | 2011 | $59,148 |
| 1946 | 2012 | $61,152 |
| 1947 | 2013 | $63,132 |
| 1948 | 2014 | $64,968 |
| 1949 | 2015 | $66,720 |
| 1950 | 2016 | $68,352 |
| 1951 | 2017 | $69,912 |
| 1952 | 2018 | $71,376 |
| 1953 | 2019 | $72,780 |
| 1954 | 2020 | $74,136 |
| 1955 | 2022 | $76,656 |
| 1956 | 2023 | $77,856 |
| 1957 | 2024 | $78,972 |
| 1958 | 2025 | $79,992 |
| 1959 | 2026 | $80,952 |
| 1960 | 2027 | $81,852 |

### 2003 Covered Compensation Table (*cont'd*)

| Calendar Year of Birth | Calendar Year of Social Security Retirement Age | 2003 Covered Compensation Table II |
|---|---|---|
| 1961 | 2028 | $82,692 |
| 1962 | 2029 | $83,448 |
| 1963 | 2030 | $84,180 |
| 1964 | 2031 | $84,876 |
| 1965 | 2032 | $85,500 |
| 1966 | 2033 | $86,028 |
| 1967 | 2034 | $86,436 |
| 1968 | 2035 | $86,748 |
| 1969 | 2036 | $86,940 |
| 1970 or later | 2037 | $87,000 |

### 2003 Rounded Covered Compensation Table

| Year of Birth | Covered Compensation |
|---|---|
| 1937 | $39,000 |
| 1938-1939 | $45,000 |
| 1940 | $48,000 |
| 1941 | $51,000 |
| 1942-1943 | $54,000 |
| 1944 | $57,000 |
| 1945-1946 | $60,000 |
| 1947 | $63,000 |
| 1949-1949 | $66,000 |
| 1950-1951 | $69,000 |
| 1952-1953 | $72,000 |
| 1954 | $75,000 |
| 1955-1957 | $78,000 |
| 1958-1960 | $81,000 |
| 1961-1964 | $84,000 |
| 1965 and later | $87,000 |

[Rev. Rul. 2002-63, 2002-45 I.R.B. 803]

### 2002 Covered Compensation Table

| Calendar Year of Birth | Calendar Year of Social Security Retirement Age | 2002 Covered Compensation Table |
|---|---|---|
| 1907 | 1972 | $ 4,488 |
| 1908 | 1973 | $ 4,704 |

## 2002 Covered Compensation Table (*cont'd*)

| Calendar Year of Birth | Calendar Year of Social Security Retirement Age | 2002 Covered Compensation Table |
|---|---|---|
| 1909 | 1974 | $ 5,004 |
| 1910 | 1975 | $ 5,316 |
| 1911 | 1976 | $ 5,664 |
| 1912 | 1977 | $ 6,060 |
| 1913 | 1978 | $ 6,480 |
| 1914 | 1979 | $ 7,044 |
| 1915 | 1980 | $ 7,692 |
| 1916 | 1981 | $ 8,460 |
| 1917 | 1982 | $ 9,300 |
| 1918 | 1983 | $10,236 |
| 1919 | 1984 | $11,232 |
| 1920 | 1985 | $12,276 |
| 1921 | 1986 | $13,368 |
| 1922 | 1987 | $14,520 |
| 1923 | 1988 | $15,708 |
| 1924 | 1989 | $16,968 |
| 1925 | 1990 | $18,312 |
| 1926 | 1991 | $19,728 |
| 1927 | 1992 | $21,192 |
| 1928 | 1993 | $22,716 |
| 1929 | 1994 | $24,312 |
| 1930 | 1995 | $25,920 |
| 1931 | 1996 | $27,576 |
| 1932 | 1997 | $29,304 |
| 1933 | 1998 | $31,128 |
| 1934 | 1999 | $33,060 |
| 1935 | 2000 | $35,100 |
| 1936 | 2001 | $37,212 |
| 1937 | 2002 | $39,444 |
| 1938 | 2004 | $43,848 |
| 1939 | 2005 | $46,056 |
| 1940 | 2006 | $48,252 |
| 1941 | 2007 | $50,424 |
| 1942 | 2008 | $52,548 |
| 1943 | 2009 | $54,588 |
| 1944 | 2010 | $56,616 |
| 1945 | 2011 | $58,608 |
| 1946 | 2012 | $60,552 |
| 1947 | 2013 | $62,472 |
| 1948 | 2014 | $64,248 |

## 2002 Covered Compensation Table (*cont'd*)

| Calendar Year of Birth | Calendar Year of Social Security Retirement Age | 2002 Covered Compensation Table |
|---|---|---|
| 1949 | 2015 | $65,940 |
| 1950 | 2016 | $67,512 |
| 1951 | 2017 | $69,012 |
| 1952 | 2018 | $70,416 |
| 1953 | 2019 | $71,760 |
| 1954 | 2020 | $73,056 |
| 1955 | 2022 | $75,456 |
| 1956 | 2023 | $76,596 |
| 1957 | 2024 | $77,652 |
| 1958 | 2025 | $78,612 |
| 1959 | 2026 | $79,512 |
| 1960 | 2027 | $80,352 |
| 1961 | 2028 | $81,132 |
| 1962 | 2029 | $81,828 |
| 1963 | 2030 | $82,500 |
| 1964 | 2031 | $83,136 |
| 1965 | 2032 | $83,700 |
| 1966 | 2033 | $84,168 |
| 1967 | 2034 | $84,516 |
| 1968 | 2035 | $84,768 |
| 1969 or later | 2036 | $84,900 |

## 2002 Rounded Covered Compensation Table

| Year of Birth | Covered Compensation |
|---|---|
| 1935-1936 | $36,000 |
| 1937 | $39,000 |
| 1938-1939 | $45,000 |
| 1940 | $48,000 |
| 1941 | $51,000 |
| 1942-1943 | $54,000 |
| 1944 | $57,000 |
| 1945-1946 | $60,000 |
| 1947-1948 | $63,000 |
| 1949 | $66,000 |
| 1950-1952 | $69,000 |
| 1953-1954 | $72,000 |
| 1955 | $75,000 |
| 1956-1958 | $78,000 |

## 2002 Rounded Covered Compensation Table (*cont'd*)

| Year of Birth | Covered Compensation |
|---|---|
| 1959-1962 | $81,000 |
| 1963-1966 | $84,000 |
| 1967 and later | $84,900 |

## 2001 Covered Compensation Table

| Year of Birth | Table 1 | Table 2 | Table 3 |
|---|---|---|---|
| 1926 | $19,800 | $19,728 | $21,000 |
| 1927 | $21,000 | $21,192 | $21,000 |
| 1928 | $22,800 | $22,716 | $24,000 |
| 1929 | $24,600 | $24,312 | $24,000 |
| 1930 | $25,800 | $25,920 | $27,000 |
| 1931 | $27,600 | $27,576 | $27,000 |
| 1932 | $29,400 | $29,304 | $30,000 |
| 1933 | $31,200 | $31,128 | $30,000 |
| 1934 | $33,000 | $33,060 | $33,000 |
| 1935 | $35,400 | $35,100 | $36,000 |
| 1936 | $37,200 | $37,212 | $36,000 |
| 1937 | $39,000 | $39,312 | $39,000 |
| 1938 | $43,200 | $43,464 | $42,000 |
| 1939 | $45,600 | $45,540 | $45,000 |
| 1940 | $47,400 | $47,616 | $48,000 |
| 1941 | $49,800 | $49,656 | $51,000 |
| 1942 | $51,600 | $51,648 | $51,000 |
| 1943 | $53,400 | $53,568 | $54,000 |
| 1944 | $55,200 | $55,452 | $54,000 |
| 1945 | $57,600 | $57,312 | $57,000 |
| 1946 | $59,400 | $59,148 | $60,000 |
| 1947 | $61,200 | $60,936 | $60,000 |
| 1948 | $62,400 | $62,580 | $63,000 |
| 1949 | $64,200 | $64,140 | $63,000 |
| 1950 | $65,400 | $65,580 | $66,000 |
| 1951 | $67,200 | $66,960 | $66,000 |
| 1952 | $68,400 | $68,232 | $69,000 |
| 1953 | $69,600 | $69,444 | $69,000 |
| 1954 | $70,800 | $70,620 | $72,000 |
| 1955 | $72,600 | $72,756 | $72,000 |
| 1956 | $73,800 | $73,764 | $75,000 |
| 1957 | $75,000 | $74,700 | $75,000 |

## 2001 Covered Compensation Table (*cont'd*)

| Year of Birth | Table 1 | Table 2 | Table 3 |
|---|---|---|---|
| 1958 | $75,600 | $75,528 | $75,000 |
| 1959 | $76,200 | $76,296 | $75,000 |
| 1960 | $76,800 | $77,004 | $78,000 |
| 1961 | $77,400 | $77,664 | $78,000 |
| 1962 | $78,000 | $78,228 | $78,000 |
| 1963 | $78,600 | $78,780 | $78,000 |
| 1964 | $79,200 | $79,284 | $80,400 |
| 1965 | $79,800 | $79,704 | $80,400 |
| 1966 | $79,800 | $80,052 | $80,400 |
| 1967 | $80,400 | $80,280 | $80,400 |
| 1968 | $80,400 | $80,400 | $80,400 |

**Notes:**

1. Table 1 is the average (rounded to the nearest multiple of $600) of the taxable wage bases for the 35 calendar years ending with the year wherein an individual attains social security retirement age.
2. Table 2 is the average (rounded down to a multiple of $12) of the taxable wage bases for the 35 calendar years ending with the year wherein an individual attains social security retirement age.
3. Table 3 is the average (rounded to the nearest multiple of $3,000) of the taxable wage bases for the 35 calendar years ending with the year wherein an individual attains social security retirement age.

# Appendix B

## Annual Annuity Purchase Rates

Table 1—APR using 1994 GAR lists Annual Annuity Purchase Rates (APR) using the 1994 Group Annuity Reserving Table (94 GAR) from Revenue Ruling 2001-62, 2001-53 I.R.B. This table shows the value of the APR at various ages and interest rates.

(The monthly APR can be determined using the following formula:

(Annual APR $- {}^{11}\!/_{24}) \times 12)$

Table 2—Using 1983 GAR lists Annual Annuity Purchase Rates (APR) using the 1983 Group Annuity Mortality (GAM) table, blended using 50 percent male rates and 50 percent female rates. This table shows the value of the APR at various ages and interest rates.

(The monthly APR can be determined using the following formula:

(Annual APR $- {}^{11}\!/_{24}) \times 12)$

## Table 1—APR Using 1994 GAR

| x | 5% | 5.25% | 5.50% | 5.75% | 6% | 6.25% | 6.50% | 6.75% | 7% | 7.25% |
|---|---|---|---|---|---|---|---|---|---|---|
| 20 | 19.70 | 18.94 | 18.24 | 17.59 | 16.97 | 16.40 | 15.87 | 15.36 | 14.89 | 14.45 |
| 21 | 19.64 | 18.89 | 18.20 | 17.55 | 16.94 | 16.37 | 15.84 | 15.34 | 14.87 | 14.43 |
| 22 | 19.58 | 18.84 | 18.15 | 17.50 | 16.90 | 16.34 | 15.81 | 15.31 | 14.85 | 14.41 |
| 23 | 19.52 | 18.78 | 18.10 | 17.46 | 16.86 | 16.30 | 15.78 | 15.28 | 14.82 | 14.38 |
| 24 | 19.45 | 18.72 | 18.05 | 17.41 | 16.82 | 16.27 | 15.74 | 15.25 | 14.79 | 14.36 |
| 25 | 19.38 | 18.66 | 17.99 | 17.36 | 16.78 | 16.23 | 15.71 | 15.22 | 14.77 | 14.33 |
| 26 | 19.31 | 18.60 | 17.93 | 17.31 | 16.73 | 16.19 | 15.67 | 15.19 | 14.74 | 14.31 |
| 27 | 19.23 | 18.53 | 17.87 | 17.26 | 16.68 | 16.14 | 15.63 | 15.16 | 14.71 | 14.28 |
| 28 | 19.16 | 18.46 | 17.81 | 17.20 | 16.63 | 16.10 | 15.59 | 15.12 | 14.67 | 14.25 |
| 29 | 19.07 | 18.39 | 17.75 | 17.15 | 16.58 | 16.05 | 15.55 | 15.08 | 14.64 | 14.22 |
| 30 | 18.99 | 18.31 | 17.68 | 17.08 | 16.53 | 16.00 | 15.51 | 15.04 | 14.60 | 14.18 |
| 31 | 18.90 | 18.23 | 17.61 | 17.02 | 16.47 | 15.95 | 15.46 | 15.00 | 14.56 | 14.15 |
| 32 | 18.80 | 18.15 | 17.53 | 16.95 | 16.40 | 15.89 | 15.41 | 14.95 | 14.52 | 14.11 |
| 33 | 18.71 | 18.06 | 17.45 | 16.88 | 16.34 | 15.83 | 15.35 | 14.90 | 14.47 | 14.07 |
| 34 | 18.60 | 17.97 | 17.37 | 16.80 | 16.27 | 15.77 | 15.30 | 14.85 | 14.43 | 14.03 |
| 35 | 18.50 | 17.87 | 17.28 | 16.72 | 16.20 | 15.70 | 15.24 | 14.79 | 14.38 | 13.98 |
| 36 | 18.38 | 17.77 | 17.18 | 16.64 | 16.12 | 15.63 | 15.17 | 14.74 | 14.32 | 13.93 |
| 37 | 18.27 | 17.66 | 17.09 | 16.55 | 16.04 | 15.56 | 15.10 | 14.67 | 14.26 | 13.88 |
| 38 | 18.14 | 17.55 | 16.98 | 16.45 | 15.95 | 15.48 | 15.03 | 14.61 | 14.20 | 13.82 |
| 39 | 18.01 | 17.43 | 16.87 | 16.35 | 15.86 | 15.39 | 14.95 | 14.54 | 14.14 | 13.76 |
| 40 | 17.88 | 17.30 | 16.76 | 16.25 | 15.77 | 15.31 | 14.87 | 14.46 | 14.07 | 13.70 |
| 41 | 17.74 | 17.17 | 16.64 | 16.14 | 15.67 | 15.21 | 14.79 | 14.38 | 14.00 | 13.63 |
| 42 | 17.59 | 17.04 | 16.52 | 16.03 | 15.56 | 15.12 | 14.70 | 14.30 | 13.92 | 13.56 |
| 43 | 17.44 | 16.90 | 16.39 | 15.91 | 15.45 | 15.01 | 14.60 | 14.21 | 13.84 | 13.48 |
| 44 | 17.28 | 16.75 | 16.25 | 15.78 | 15.33 | 14.91 | 14.50 | 14.12 | 13.75 | 13.40 |
| 45 | 17.11 | 16.60 | 16.11 | 15.65 | 15.21 | 14.79 | 14.40 | 14.02 | 13.66 | 13.32 |
| 46 | 16.94 | 16.44 | 15.96 | 15.51 | 15.08 | 14.67 | 14.29 | 13.92 | 13.56 | 13.23 |
| 47 | 16.76 | 16.27 | 15.81 | 15.36 | 14.95 | 14.55 | 14.17 | 13.81 | 13.46 | 13.13 |
| 48 | 16.57 | 16.09 | 15.64 | 15.21 | 14.80 | 14.41 | 14.04 | 13.69 | 13.35 | 13.03 |
| 49 | 16.37 | 15.91 | 15.47 | 15.05 | 14.65 | 14.27 | 13.91 | 13.57 | 13.24 | 12.92 |
| 50 | 16.17 | 15.72 | 15.29 | 14.89 | 14.50 | 14.13 | 13.78 | 13.44 | 13.12 | 12.81 |
| 51 | 15.96 | 15.52 | 15.11 | 14.71 | 14.33 | 13.97 | 13.63 | 13.30 | 12.99 | 12.69 |
| 52 | 15.74 | 15.32 | 14.91 | 14.53 | 14.16 | 13.81 | 13.48 | 13.16 | 12.85 | 12.56 |
| 53 | 15.51 | 15.10 | 14.71 | 14.34 | 13.99 | 13.65 | 13.32 | 13.01 | 12.71 | 12.43 |
| 54 | 15.28 | 14.88 | 14.50 | 14.14 | 13.80 | 13.47 | 13.16 | 12.85 | 12.57 | 12.29 |
| 55 | 15.03 | 14.65 | 14.29 | 13.94 | 13.61 | 13.29 | 12.98 | 12.69 | 12.41 | 12.14 |
| 56 | 14.78 | 14.41 | 14.06 | 13.73 | 13.41 | 13.10 | 12.80 | 12.52 | 12.25 | 11.99 |
| 57 | 14.52 | 14.17 | 13.83 | 13.51 | 13.20 | 12.90 | 12.62 | 12.34 | 12.08 | 11.83 |
| 58 | 14.26 | 13.92 | 13.59 | 13.28 | 12.98 | 12.70 | 12.42 | 12.16 | 11.90 | 11.66 |
| 59 | 13.99 | 13.66 | 13.35 | 13.05 | 12.76 | 12.49 | 12.22 | 11.97 | 11.72 | 11.49 |
| 60 | 13.71 | 13.40 | 13.10 | 12.81 | 12.54 | 12.27 | 12.02 | 11.77 | 11.53 | 11.31 |

## Table 1—APR Using 1994 GAR (*cont'd*)

| x | 5% | 5.25% | 5.50% | 5.75% | 6% | 6.25% | 6.50% | 6.75% | 7% | 7.25% |
|----|-------|-------|-------|-------|-------|-------|-------|-------|-------|-------|
| 61 | 13.43 | 13.13 | 12.84 | 12.57 | 12.30 | 12.05 | 11.80 | 11.57 | 11.34 | 11.12 |
| 62 | 13.14 | 12.85 | 12.58 | 12.32 | 12.06 | 11.82 | 11.59 | 11.36 | 11.14 | 10.93 |
| 63 | 12.85 | 12.58 | 12.31 | 12.06 | 11.82 | 11.59 | 11.36 | 11.15 | 10.94 | 10.74 |
| 64 | 12.55 | 12.29 | 12.04 | 11.81 | 11.57 | 11.35 | 11.14 | 10.93 | 10.73 | 10.54 |
| 65 | 12.25 | 12.01 | 11.77 | 11.54 | 11.32 | 11.11 | 10.91 | 10.71 | 10.52 | 10.33 |
| 66 | 11.95 | 11.72 | 11.50 | 11.28 | 11.07 | 10.87 | 10.67 | 10.48 | 10.30 | 10.12 |
| 67 | 11.65 | 11.43 | 11.22 | 11.01 | 10.81 | 10.62 | 10.44 | 10.26 | 10.08 | 9.91 |
| 68 | 11.34 | 11.14 | 10.94 | 10.74 | 10.55 | 10.37 | 10.20 | 10.02 | 9.86 | 9.70 |
| 69 | 11.03 | 10.84 | 10.65 | 10.46 | 10.29 | 10.11 | 9.95 | 9.79 | 9.63 | 9.48 |
| 70 | 10.72 | 10.53 | 10.35 | 10.18 | 10.01 | 9.85 | 9.69 | 9.54 | 9.39 | 9.25 |
| 71 | 10.39 | 10.22 | 10.05 | 9.89 | 9.73 | 9.58 | 9.43 | 9.29 | 9.15 | 9.01 |
| 72 | 10.07 | 9.90 | 9.75 | 9.60 | 9.45 | 9.30 | 9.16 | 9.03 | 8.90 | 8.77 |
| 73 | 9.73 | 9.58 | 9.44 | 9.29 | 9.16 | 9.02 | 8.89 | 8.76 | 8.64 | 8.52 |
| 74 | 9.40 | 9.26 | 9.12 | 8.99 | 8.86 | 8.73 | 8.61 | 8.49 | 8.38 | 8.27 |
| 75 | 9.06 | 8.93 | 8.80 | 8.68 | 8.56 | 8.44 | 8.33 | 8.22 | 8.11 | 8.01 |
| 76 | 8.72 | 8.60 | 8.48 | 8.37 | 8.25 | 8.15 | 8.04 | 7.94 | 7.84 | 7.74 |
| 77 | 8.37 | 8.26 | 8.15 | 8.05 | 7.95 | 7.85 | 7.75 | 7.65 | 7.56 | 7.47 |
| 78 | 8.03 | 7.93 | 7.83 | 7.74 | 7.64 | 7.55 | 7.46 | 7.37 | 7.29 | 7.20 |
| 79 | 7.70 | 7.60 | 7.51 | 7.42 | 7.34 | 7.25 | 7.17 | 7.09 | 7.01 | 6.93 |
| 80 | 7.37 | 7.28 | 7.20 | 7.12 | 7.04 | 6.96 | 6.88 | 6.81 | 6.74 | 6.67 |
| 81 | 7.04 | 6.97 | 6.89 | 6.82 | 6.74 | 6.67 | 6.60 | 6.53 | 6.47 | 6.40 |
| 82 | 6.73 | 6.66 | 6.59 | 6.52 | 6.45 | 6.39 | 6.32 | 6.26 | 6.20 | 6.14 |
| 83 | 6.42 | 6.35 | 6.29 | 6.23 | 6.17 | 6.11 | 6.05 | 6.00 | 5.94 | 5.89 |
| 84 | 6.11 | 6.06 | 6.00 | 5.94 | 5.89 | 5.83 | 5.78 | 5.73 | 5.68 | 5.63 |
| 85 | 5.81 | 5.76 | 5.71 | 5.66 | 5.61 | 5.56 | 5.52 | 5.47 | 5.42 | 5.38 |
| 86 | 5.52 | 5.47 | 5.43 | 5.38 | 5.34 | 5.29 | 5.25 | 5.21 | 5.17 | 5.13 |
| 87 | 5.23 | 5.19 | 5.15 | 5.11 | 5.07 | 5.03 | 4.99 | 4.95 | 4.91 | 4.88 |
| 88 | 4.95 | 4.91 | 4.88 | 4.84 | 4.81 | 4.77 | 4.74 | 4.70 | 4.67 | 4.64 |
| 89 | 4.69 | 4.65 | 4.62 | 4.59 | 4.56 | 4.52 | 4.49 | 4.46 | 4.43 | 4.40 |
| 90 | 4.43 | 4.40 | 4.37 | 4.35 | 4.32 | 4.29 | 4.26 | 4.23 | 4.21 | 4.18 |

Table 2—APR Using 1983 GAR

| x | 5% | 5.25% | 5.50% | 5.75% | 6% | 6.25% | 6.50% | 6.75% | 7% | 7.25% | 7.50% | 7.75% | 8% |
|---|----|-------|-------|-------|----|-------|-------|-------|----|-------|-------|-------|----|
| 20 | 19.65 | 18.90 | 18.20 | 17.55 | 16.95 | 16.38 | 15.85 | 15.35 | 14.88 | 14.44 | 14.02 | 13.63 | 13.25 |
| 21 | 19.59 | 18.84 | 18.15 | 17.51 | 16.91 | 16.34 | 15.82 | 15.32 | 14.85 | 14.41 | 14.00 | 13.61 | 13.24 |
| 22 | 19.52 | 18.79 | 18.10 | 17.47 | 16.87 | 16.31 | 15.78 | 15.29 | 14.83 | 14.39 | 13.98 | 13.59 | 13.22 |
| 23 | 19.45 | 18.73 | 18.05 | 17.42 | 16.83 | 16.27 | 15.75 | 15.26 | 14.80 | 14.37 | 13.96 | 13.57 | 13.20 |
| 24 | 19.38 | 18.66 | 17.99 | 17.37 | 16.78 | 16.23 | 15.71 | 15.23 | 14.77 | 14.34 | 13.93 | 13.55 | 13.18 |
| 25 | 19.31 | 18.60 | 17.93 | 17.31 | 16.73 | 16.19 | 15.67 | 15.19 | 14.74 | 14.31 | 13.91 | 13.52 | 13.16 |
| 26 | 19.23 | 18.53 | 17.87 | 17.26 | 16.68 | 16.14 | 15.63 | 15.16 | 14.71 | 14.28 | 13.88 | 13.50 | 13.14 |
| 27 | 19.15 | 18.45 | 17.81 | 17.20 | 16.63 | 16.09 | 15.59 | 15.12 | 14.67 | 14.25 | 13.85 | 13.47 | 13.12 |
| 28 | 19.06 | 18.38 | 17.74 | 17.14 | 16.57 | 16.04 | 15.55 | 15.08 | 14.63 | 14.21 | 13.82 | 13.45 | 13.09 |
| 29 | 18.97 | 18.30 | 17.67 | 17.07 | 16.51 | 15.99 | 15.50 | 15.03 | 14.59 | 14.18 | 13.79 | 13.42 | 13.06 |
| 30 | 18.88 | 18.21 | 17.59 | 17.00 | 16.45 | 15.93 | 15.45 | 14.99 | 14.55 | 14.14 | 13.75 | 13.38 | 13.03 |
| 31 | 18.78 | 18.13 | 17.51 | 16.93 | 16.39 | 15.88 | 15.39 | 14.94 | 14.51 | 14.10 | 13.71 | 13.35 | 13.00 |
| 32 | 18.68 | 18.03 | 17.43 | 16.86 | 16.32 | 15.81 | 15.34 | 14.89 | 14.46 | 14.06 | 13.67 | 13.31 | 12.97 |
| 33 | 18.58 | 17.94 | 17.34 | 16.78 | 16.25 | 15.75 | 15.28 | 14.83 | 14.41 | 14.01 | 13.63 | 13.27 | 12.93 |
| 34 | 18.46 | 17.84 | 17.25 | 16.69 | 16.17 | 15.68 | 15.21 | 14.77 | 14.36 | 13.96 | 13.59 | 13.23 | 12.90 |
| 35 | 18.35 | 17.73 | 17.15 | 16.61 | 16.09 | 15.60 | 15.15 | 14.71 | 14.30 | 13.91 | 13.54 | 13.19 | 12.85 |
| 36 | 18.23 | 17.62 | 17.05 | 16.51 | 16.01 | 15.53 | 15.08 | 14.65 | 14.24 | 13.85 | 13.49 | 13.14 | 12.81 |
| 37 | 18.10 | 17.51 | 16.95 | 16.42 | 15.92 | 15.45 | 15.00 | 14.58 | 14.18 | 13.80 | 13.44 | 13.09 | 12.77 |
| 38 | 17.97 | 17.39 | 16.84 | 16.32 | 15.83 | 15.36 | 14.92 | 14.50 | 14.11 | 13.73 | 13.38 | 13.04 | 12.72 |
| 39 | 17.83 | 17.26 | 16.72 | 16.21 | 15.73 | 15.27 | 14.84 | 14.43 | 14.04 | 13.67 | 13.32 | 12.98 | 12.66 |
| 40 | 17.69 | 17.13 | 16.60 | 16.10 | 15.62 | 15.18 | 14.75 | 14.35 | 13.96 | 13.60 | 13.25 | 12.92 | 12.61 |
| 41 | 17.54 | 16.99 | 16.47 | 15.98 | 15.52 | 15.08 | 14.66 | 14.26 | 13.88 | 13.52 | 13.18 | 12.86 | 12.55 |
| 42 | 17.39 | 16.85 | 16.34 | 15.86 | 15.40 | 14.97 | 14.56 | 14.17 | 13.80 | 13.45 | 13.11 | 12.79 | 12.48 |
| 43 | 17.23 | 16.70 | 16.20 | 15.73 | 15.29 | 14.86 | 14.46 | 14.08 | 13.71 | 13.36 | 13.03 | 12.72 | 12.42 |

| | | | | | | | | | | | | | |
|---|---|---|---|---|---|---|---|---|---|---|---|---|---|
| 44 | 17.06 | 16.55 | 16.06 | 15.60 | 15.16 | 14.75 | 14.35 | 13.98 | 13.62 | 13.28 | 12.95 | 12.64 | 12.35 |
| 45 | 16.89 | 16.39 | 15.91 | 15.46 | 15.03 | 14.63 | 14.24 | 13.87 | 13.52 | 13.19 | 12.87 | 12.56 | 12.27 |
| 46 | 16.71 | 16.22 | 15.76 | 15.32 | 14.90 | 14.50 | 14.12 | 13.76 | 13.42 | 13.09 | 12.78 | 12.48 | 12.19 |
| 47 | 16.52 | 16.05 | 15.60 | 15.17 | 14.76 | 14.37 | 14.00 | 13.65 | 13.31 | 12.99 | 12.68 | 12.39 | 12.11 |
| 48 | 16.33 | 15.87 | 15.43 | 15.01 | 14.61 | 14.24 | 13.87 | 13.53 | 13.20 | 12.89 | 12.59 | 12.30 | 12.02 |
| 49 | 16.13 | 15.68 | 15.26 | 14.85 | 14.46 | 14.09 | 13.74 | 13.41 | 13.08 | 12.78 | 12.48 | 12.20 | 11.93 |
| 50 | 15.93 | 15.49 | 15.08 | 14.68 | 14.31 | 13.95 | 13.60 | 13.28 | 12.96 | 12.66 | 12.37 | 12.10 | 11.84 |
| 51 | 15.72 | 15.30 | 14.90 | 14.51 | 14.14 | 13.79 | 13.46 | 13.14 | 12.83 | 12.54 | 12.26 | 11.99 | 11.73 |
| 52 | 15.50 | 15.09 | 14.70 | 14.33 | 13.98 | 13.64 | 13.31 | 13.00 | 12.70 | 12.42 | 12.14 | 11.88 | 11.63 |
| 53 | 15.28 | 14.88 | 14.51 | 14.15 | 13.80 | 13.47 | 13.16 | 12.85 | 12.56 | 12.29 | 12.02 | 11.76 | 11.52 |
| 54 | 15.05 | 14.67 | 14.30 | 13.95 | 13.62 | 13.30 | 12.99 | 12.70 | 12.42 | 12.15 | 11.89 | 11.64 | 11.40 |
| 55 | 14.81 | 14.44 | 14.09 | 13.75 | 13.43 | 13.12 | 12.82 | 12.54 | 12.27 | 12.00 | 11.75 | 11.51 | 11.28 |
| 56 | 14.56 | 14.21 | 13.87 | 13.54 | 13.23 | 12.93 | 12.65 | 12.37 | 12.11 | 11.85 | 11.61 | 11.37 | 11.15 |
| 57 | 14.31 | 13.97 | 13.64 | 13.33 | 13.03 | 12.74 | 12.46 | 12.20 | 11.94 | 11.69 | 11.46 | 11.23 | 11.01 |
| 58 | 14.05 | 13.72 | 13.41 | 13.10 | 12.81 | 12.54 | 12.27 | 12.01 | 11.77 | 11.53 | 11.30 | 11.08 | 10.87 |
| 59 | 13.78 | 13.46 | 13.16 | 12.87 | 12.59 | 12.33 | 12.07 | 11.82 | 11.58 | 11.36 | 11.13 | 10.92 | 10.72 |
| 60 | 13.50 | 13.20 | 12.91 | 12.63 | 12.36 | 12.11 | 11.86 | 11.62 | 11.39 | 11.17 | 10.96 | 10.76 | 10.56 |
| 61 | 13.21 | 12.92 | 12.65 | 12.38 | 12.13 | 11.88 | 11.65 | 11.42 | 11.20 | 10.99 | 10.78 | 10.58 | 10.39 |
| 62 | 12.92 | 12.64 | 12.38 | 12.13 | 11.88 | 11.65 | 11.42 | 11.20 | 10.99 | 10.79 | 10.59 | 10.40 | 10.22 |
| 63 | 12.61 | 12.36 | 12.10 | 11.86 | 11.63 | 11.41 | 11.19 | 10.98 | 10.78 | 10.58 | 10.40 | 10.21 | 10.04 |
| 64 | 12.31 | 12.06 | 11.82 | 11.59 | 11.37 | 11.16 | 10.95 | 10.75 | 10.56 | 10.37 | 10.19 | 10.02 | 9.85 |
| 65 | 11.99 | 11.76 | 11.53 | 11.32 | 11.11 | 10.90 | 10.71 | 10.52 | 10.33 | 10.16 | 9.98 | 9.82 | 9.66 |
| 66 | 11.68 | 11.45 | 11.24 | 11.03 | 10.84 | 10.64 | 10.46 | 10.28 | 10.10 | 9.93 | 9.77 | 9.61 | 9.46 |
| 67 | 11.35 | 11.15 | 10.94 | 10.75 | 10.56 | 10.38 | 10.20 | 10.03 | 9.86 | 9.70 | 9.55 | 9.40 | 9.25 |
| 68 | 11.03 | 10.83 | 10.64 | 10.46 | 10.28 | 10.11 | 9.94 | 9.78 | 9.62 | 9.47 | 9.32 | 9.18 | 9.04 |
| 69 | 10.70 | 10.52 | 10.34 | 10.16 | 10.00 | 9.83 | 9.67 | 9.52 | 9.37 | 9.23 | 9.09 | 8.95 | 8.82 |
| 70 | 10.37 | 10.20 | 10.03 | 9.87 | 9.71 | 9.56 | 9.41 | 9.26 | 9.12 | 8.99 | 8.85 | 8.73 | 8.60 |
| 71 | 10.04 | 9.88 | 9.72 | 9.57 | 9.42 | 9.28 | 9.14 | 9.00 | 8.87 | 8.74 | 8.61 | 8.49 | 8.38 |

## Table 2—APR Using 1983 GAR (cont'd)

| x | 5% | 5.25% | 5.50% | 5.75% | 6% | 6.25% | 6.50% | 6.75% | 7% | 7.25% | 7.50% | 7.75% | 8% |
|----|------|------|------|------|------|------|------|------|------|------|------|------|------|
| 72 | 9.71 | 9.56 | 9.41 | 9.27 | 9.13 | 8.99 | 8.86 | 8.73 | 8.61 | 8.49 | 8.37 | 8.26 | 8.15 |
| 73 | 9.37 | 9.23 | 9.10 | 8.96 | 8.83 | 8.71 | 8.58 | 8.47 | 8.35 | 8.24 | 8.13 | 8.02 | 7.91 |
| 74 | 9.04 | 8.91 | 8.78 | 8.66 | 8.54 | 8.42 | 8.31 | 8.19 | 8.09 | 7.98 | 7.88 | 7.78 | 7.68 |
| 75 | 8.71 | 8.59 | 8.47 | 8.36 | 8.24 | 8.13 | 8.03 | 7.92 | 7.82 | 7.72 | 7.63 | 7.53 | 7.44 |
| 76 | 8.39 | 8.27 | 8.16 | 8.06 | 7.95 | 7.85 | 7.75 | 7.65 | 7.56 | 7.47 | 7.38 | 7.29 | 7.20 |
| 77 | 8.06 | 7.96 | 7.86 | 7.76 | 7.66 | 7.57 | 7.48 | 7.39 | 7.30 | 7.21 | 7.13 | 7.05 | 6.97 |
| 78 | 7.75 | 7.65 | 7.56 | 7.47 | 7.38 | 7.29 | 7.20 | 7.12 | 7.04 | 6.96 | 6.88 | 6.81 | 6.73 |
| 79 | 7.44 | 7.35 | 7.26 | 7.18 | 7.10 | 7.02 | 6.94 | 6.86 | 6.78 | 6.71 | 6.64 | 6.57 | 6.50 |
| 80 | 7.14 | 7.06 | 6.98 | 6.90 | 6.82 | 6.75 | 6.67 | 6.60 | 6.53 | 6.47 | 6.40 | 6.33 | 6.27 |
| 81 | 6.84 | 6.77 | 6.70 | 6.62 | 6.55 | 6.49 | 6.42 | 6.35 | 6.29 | 6.23 | 6.16 | 6.10 | 6.05 |
| 82 | 6.56 | 6.49 | 6.42 | 6.36 | 6.29 | 6.23 | 6.17 | 6.11 | 6.05 | 5.99 | 5.94 | 5.88 | 5.82 |
| 83 | 6.28 | 6.22 | 6.16 | 6.10 | 6.04 | 5.98 | 5.93 | 5.87 | 5.82 | 5.76 | 5.71 | 5.66 | 5.61 |
| 84 | 6.02 | 5.96 | 5.90 | 5.85 | 5.79 | 5.74 | 5.69 | 5.64 | 5.59 | 5.54 | 5.49 | 5.44 | 5.40 |
| 85 | 5.76 | 5.70 | 5.65 | 5.60 | 5.55 | 5.50 | 5.46 | 5.41 | 5.36 | 5.32 | 5.28 | 5.23 | 5.19 |
| 86 | 5.50 | 5.45 | 5.41 | 5.36 | 5.32 | 5.27 | 5.23 | 5.19 | 5.14 | 5.10 | 5.06 | 5.02 | 4.98 |
| 87 | 5.25 | 5.21 | 5.17 | 5.13 | 5.09 | 5.05 | 5.01 | 4.97 | 4.93 | 4.89 | 4.86 | 4.82 | 4.78 |
| 88 | 5.01 | 4.97 | 4.93 | 4.90 | 4.86 | 4.82 | 4.79 | 4.75 | 4.72 | 4.68 | 4.65 | 4.62 | 4.59 |
| 89 | 4.77 | 4.74 | 4.71 | 4.67 | 4.64 | 4.61 | 4.57 | 4.54 | 4.51 | 4.48 | 4.45 | 4.42 | 4.39 |
| 90 | 4.55 | 4.51 | 4.48 | 4.45 | 4.42 | 4.39 | 4.36 | 4.34 | 4.31 | 4.28 | 4.25 | 4.22 | 4.20 |

# Appendix C

## Rates of Turnover

# Rates of Turnover at Different Ages Using Various Tables

| Age | T1 Table 1 | T2 Table 2 | T3 Table 3 | T4 Table 4 | T5 Table 5 | T6 Table 6 | T7 Table 7 | T8 Table 8 | T9 Table 9 | TA Table 10 | TB Table 11 | TC Table 12 50% Withdrawal | TD Table 13 75% Withdrawal | TE Table 14 Male | TE Table 14 Female | TF Table 15 Male | TF Table 15 Female |
|---|---|---|---|---|---|---|---|---|---|---|---|---|---|---|---|---|---|
| 15 | 0.05447 | 0.05447 | 0.065861 | 0.05447 | 0.07947 | 0.07947 | 0 | 0.119478 | 0.17947 | 0.17947 | 0.24947 | 0.106972 | 0.130051 | 0.2 | 0.25 | 0.1 | 0.125 |
| 16 | 0.054456 | 0.054456 | 0.065847 | 0.054456 | 0.079456 | 0.079456 | 0 | 0.119456 | 0.179456 | 0.179456 | 0.249456 | 0.093798 | 0.117656 | 0.19 | 0.24 | 0.095 | 0.12 |
| 17 | 0.05444 | 0.05444 | 0.065831 | 0.05444 | 0.07944 | 0.07944 | 0 | 0.11944 | 0.17944 | 0.17944 | 0.24944 | 0.083175 | 0.107583 | 0.18 | 0.23 | 0.09 | 0.115 |
| 18 | 0.054423 | 0.054423 | 0.065814 | 0.054423 | 0.079423 | 0.079423 | 0 | 0.119423 | 0.179423 | 0.179423 | 0.249423 | 0.074426 | 0.099228 | 0.17 | 0.22 | 0.085 | 0.11 |
| 19 | 0.054405 | 0.054405 | 0.065796 | 0.054405 | 0.079405 | 0.079405 | 0 | 0.119405 | 0.179405 | 0.179405 | 0.249405 | 0.067095 | 0.09218 | 0.16 | 0.21 | 0.08 | 0.105 |
| 20 | 0.054384 | 0.054384 | 0.065775 | 0.054384 | 0.079384 | 0.079384 | 0.099384 | 0.119384 | 0.179384 | 0.179384 | 0.249384 | 0.060862 | 0.086148 | 0.15 | 0.2 | 0.075 | 0.1 |
| 21 | 0.054083 | 0.054113 | 0.062179 | 0.054113 | 0.078989 | 0.078989 | 0.098898 | 0.118807 | 0.178207 | 0.178207 | 0.24936 | 0.055496 | 0.080922 | 0.14 | 0.19 | 0.07 | 0.095 |
| 22 | 0.053344 | 0.053838 | 0.059081 | 0.053838 | 0.078587 | 0.078587 | 0.098398 | 0.118208 | 0.176903 | 0.176903 | 0.249334 | 0.060827 | 0.076346 | 0.13 | 0.18 | 0.065 | 0.09 |
| 23 | 0.052213 | 0.053552 | 0.056482 | 0.053552 | 0.078169 | 0.078169 | 0.097877 | 0.117584 | 0.175474 | 0.175474 | 0.249307 | 0.04673 | 0.072304 | 0.12 | 0.17 | 0.06 | 0.085 |
| 24 | 0.050732 | 0.053246 | 0.054379 | 0.053246 | 0.077723 | 0.077723 | 0.097331 | 0.11693 | 0.173919 | 0.173919 | 0.249276 | 0.043102 | 0.068808 | 0.11 | 0.16 | 0.055 | 0.08 |
| 25 | 0.048948 | 0.052917 | 0.052704 | 0.052917 | 0.077242 | 0.077242 | 0.096742 | 0.116242 | 0.172242 | 0.172242 | 0.249242 | 0.039869 | 0.065522 | 0.1 | 0.15 | 0.05 | 0.075 |
| 26 | 0.046904 | 0.052555 | 0.051387 | 0.052555 | 0.0767 | 0.076714 | 0.096114 | 0.115515 | 0.170413 | 0.170444 | 0.246364 | 0.036966 | 0.062854 | 0.092 | 0.14 | 0.046 | 0.07 |
| 27 | 0.044648 | 0.052156 | 0.050358 | 0.052156 | 0.075912 | 0.076132 | 0.095438 | 0.114745 | 0.168033 | 0.168526 | 0.243198 | 0.034348 | 0.060143 | 0.084 | 0.13 | 0.042 | 0.065 |
| 28 | 0.04222 | 0.051712 | 0.049547 | 0.051712 | 0.07489 | 0.075484 | 0.094704 | 0.113924 | 0.165174 | 0.166488 | 0.239742 | 0.031973 | 0.057503 | 0.076 | 0.12 | 0.038 | 0.06 |
| 29 | 0.039665 | 0.05122 | 0.048888 | 0.05122 | 0.073654 | 0.074766 | 0.093096 | 0.113046 | 0.16191 | 0.164332 | 0.235998 | 0.029808 | 0.054937 | 0.068 | 0.11 | 0.034 | 0.055 |
| 30 | 0.03702 | 0.050672 | 0.048312 | 0.050672 | 0.072219 | 0.073966 | 0.093031 | 0.112095 | 0.158305 | 0.162052 | 0.231996 | 0.027826 | 0.052446 | 0.06 | 0.1 | 0.03 | 0.05 |
| 31 | 0.034319 | 0.050063 | 0.047756 | 0.050063 | 0.070603 | 0.073077 | 0.092065 | 0.111053 | 0.154419 | 0.159644 | 0.227648 | 0.026004 | 0.050028 | 0.054 | 0.09 | 0.027 | 0.045 |
| 32 | 0.031593 | 0.049393 | 0.047165 | 0.049393 | 0.068731 | 0.072098 | 0.091 | 0.109903 | 0.150308 | 0.157103 | 0.223054 | 0.024322 | 0.047681 | 0.048 | 0.08 | 0.024 | 0.04 |
| 33 | 0.028866 | 0.048655 | 0.046488 | 0.048655 | 0.066916 | 0.071022 | 0.08982 | 0.108617 | 0.146011 | 0.154418 | 0.218187 | 0.022764 | 0.045402 | 0.042 | 0.07 | 0.021 | 0.035 |
| 34 | 0.02616 | 0.047853 | 0.045687 | 0.047853 | 0.064888 | 0.069851 | 0.088511 | 0.107172 | 0.141563 | 0.151581 | 0.213057 | 0.021317 | 0.043187 | 0.036 | 0.06 | 0.018 | 0.03 |
| 35 | 0.023492 | 0.046984 | 0.044736 | 0.046984 | 0.062764 | 0.068583 | 0.087062 | 0.10554 | 0.136986 | 0.148583 | 0.207669 | 0.019967 | 0.041029 | 0.03 | 0.05 | 0.015 | 0.025 |
| 36 | 0.020879 | 0.045878 | 0.043629 | 0.046058 | 0.060572 | 0.06723 | 0.085466 | 0.103702 | 0.132299 | 0.145419 | 0.202028 | 0.018705 | 0.038926 | 0.024 | 0.04 | 0.012 | 0.02 |
| 37 | 0.018335 | 0.043951 | 0.042376 | 0.045078 | 0.058332 | 0.0658 | 0.083717 | 0.101635 | 0.127508 | 0.142085 | 0.19613 | 0.01752 | 0.036871 | 0.018 | 0.03 | 0.009 | 0.015 |
| 38 | 0.015875 | 0.041388 | 0.041036 | 0.044052 | 0.056066 | 0.064302 | 0.081815 | 0.099328 | 0.122614 | 0.138578 | 0.189972 | 0.016402 | 0.034857 | 0.012 | 0.02 | 0.006 | 0.01 |
| 39 | 0.013518 | 0.038362 | 0.03969 | 0.042984 | 0.053786 | 0.062743 | 0.079756 | 0.096769 | 0.117612 | 0.134897 | 0.183551 | 0.015434 | 0.03288 | 0.006 | 0.01 | 0.003 | 0.005 |
| 40 | 0.011283 | 0.035035 | 0.038412 | 0.041878 | 0.051504 | 0.061129 | 0.077543 | 0.093957 | 0.1125 | 0.131043 | 0.176871 | 0.014612 | 0.030933 | 0 | 0 | 0 | 0 |
| 41 | 0.009186 | 0.031534 | 0.037229 | 0.04072 | 0.049206 | 0.059439 | 0.075151 | 0.090862 | 0.107238 | 0.126986 | 0.169918 | 0.013857 | 0.028992 | 0 | 0 | 0 | 0 |
| 42 | 0.00725 | 0.02797 | 0.036139 | 0.039496 | 0.046881 | 0.057652 | 0.072556 | 0.087459 | 0.101791 | 0.122695 | 0.162688 | 0.013033 | 0.02703 | 0 | 0 | 0 | 0 |
| 43 | 0.0055 | 0.024436 | 0.035048 | 0.038204 | 0.044533 | 0.055766 | 0.06976 | 0.083754 | 0.096155 | 0.118167 | 0.155213 | 0.011976 | 0.025047 | 0 | 0 | 0 | 0 |

| # | | | | | | | | | | | | | | | | | |
|---|---|---|---|---|---|---|---|---|---|---|---|---|---|---|---|---|---|
| 44 | 0.00396 | 0.020995 | 0.033784 | 0.036834 | 0.042159 | 0.053767 | 0.066758 | 0.079749 | 0.09033 | 0.113395 | 0.14752 | 0.010808 | 0.02304 | 0 | 0 | 0 | 0 |
| 45 | 0.002653 | 0.017686 | 0.032149 | 0.035372 | 0.039753 | 0.051633 | 0.06354 | 0.075447 | 0.084319 | 0.108377 | 0.139635 | 0.009524 | 0.021008 | 0 | 0 | 0 | 0 |
| 46 | 0.001595 | 0.014521 | 0.029962 | 0.033768 | 0.03727 | 0.049291 | 0.060053 | 0.070816 | 0.078098 | 0.103097 | 0.131549 | 0.00809 | 0.018947 | 0 | 0 | 0 | 0 |
| 47 | 0.000798 | 0.011515 | 0.0271 | 0.031954 | 0.03465 | 0.046643 | 0.056227 | 0.06581 | 0.071634 | 0.097539 | 0.123237 | 0.006429 | 0.016857 | 0 | 0 | 0 | 0 |
| 48 | 0.000274 | 0.008718 | 0.023544 | 0.029873 | 0.03185 | 0.043606 | 0.052 | 0.060394 | 0.0649 | 0.091694 | 0.114669 | 0.004539 | 0.014735 | 0 | 0 | 0 | 0 |
| 49 | 0.000015 | 0.0062 | 0.019386 | 0.027483 | 0.028841 | 0.040117 | 0.047337 | 0.054556 | 0.05789 | 0.08556 | 0.105825 | 0.002417 | 0.012574 | 0 | 0 | 0 | 0 |
| 50 | 0 | 0.004048 | 0.015245 | 0.024773 | 0.025627 | 0.036161 | 0.042247 | 0.048333 | 0.050645 | 0.079157 | 0.096712 | 0 | 0.010376 | 0 | 0 | 0 | 0 |
| 51 | 0 | 0.002343 | 0.011813 | 0.021787 | 0.02226 | 0.031803 | 0.036823 | 0.041842 | 0.043289 | 0.072492 | 0.087362 | 0 | 0.008131 | 0 | 0 | 0 | 0 |
| 52 | 0 | 0.001126 | 0.009082 | 0.018623 | 0.018837 | 0.027184 | 0.031228 | 0.035271 | 0.036029 | 0.065593 | 0.077785 | 0 | 0.005839 | 0 | 0 | 0 | 0 |
| 53 | 0 | 0.000385 | 0.006879 | 0.015407 | 0.015472 | 0.022489 | 0.025661 | 0.028834 | 0.029106 | 0.058501 | 0.068284 | 0 | 0.003491 | 0 | 0 | 0 | 0 |
| 54 | 0 | 0.000048 | 0.004987 | 0.012285 | 0.012288 | 0.017932 | 0.020347 | 0.022762 | 0.022778 | 0.051287 | 0.058806 | 0 | 0.001504 | 0 | 0 | 0 | 0 |
| 55 | 0 | 0 | 0.003344 | 0.009394 | 0.009394 | 0.013713 | 0.015488 | 0.017264 | 0.017264 | 0.044042 | 0.049572 | 0 | 0 | 0 | 0 | 0 | 0 |
| 56 | 0 | 0 | 0.002074 | 0.006847 | 0.006847 | 0.009995 | 0.011247 | 0.012499 | 0.012499 | 0.03689 | 0.040747 | 0 | 0 | 0 | 0 | 0 | 0 |
| 57 | 0 | 0 | 0.001172 | 0.004713 | 0.004713 | 0.006688 | 0.007718 | 0.008557 | 0.008557 | 0.029966 | 0.032483 | 0 | 0 | 0 | 0 | 0 | 0 |
| 58 | 0 | 0 | 0.000538 | 0.003024 | 0.003024 | 0.004414 | 0.004939 | 0.005464 | 0.005464 | 0.023415 | 0.024918 | 0 | 0 | 0 | 0 | 0 | 0 |
| 59 | 0 | 0 | 0.000161 | 0.001767 | 0.001767 | 0.00258 | 0.002879 | 0.003179 | 0.003179 | 0.017381 | 0.018172 | 0 | 0 | 0 | 0 | 0 | 0 |
| 60 | 0 | 0 | 0 | 0.000901 | 0.000901 | 0.001315 | 0.001465 | 0.001614 | 0.001614 | 0.012013 | 0.012348 | 0 | 0 | 0 | 0 | 0 | 0 |
| 61 | 0 | 0 | 0 | 0.000367 | 0.000367 | 0.000535 | 0.000594 | 0.000654 | 0.000654 | 0.007455 | 0.007539 | 0 | 0 | 0 | 0 | 0 | 0 |
| 62 | 0 | 0 | 0 | 0.000094 | 0.000094 | 0.000137 | 0.000152 | 0.000167 | 0.000167 | 0.003847 | 0.003831 | 0 | 0 | 0 | 0 | 0 | 0 |
| 63 | 0 | 0 | 0 | 0 | 0 | 0 | 0 | 0 | 0 | 0.00132 | 0.001295 | 0 | 0 | 0 | 0 | 0 | 0 |
| 64 | 0 | 0 | 0 | 0 | 0 | 0 | 0 | 0 | 0 | 0 | 0 | 0 | 0 | 0 | 0 | 0 | 0 |
| 65 | 0 | 0 | 0 | 0 | 0 | 0 | 0 | 0 | 0 | 0 | 0 | 0 | 0 | 0 | 0 | 0 | 0 |

# Internal Revenue Code Sections

*[References are to question numbers.]*

# Treasury Regulations

*[References are to question numbers.]*

## Temporary Treasury Regulations

## Proposed Treasury Regulations

# Revenue Procedures

*[References are to question numbers.]*

# Revenue Rulings

*[References are to question numbers.]*

# Notices, Letter Rulings, and Announcements

*[References are to question numbers.]*

## Notices

### Notice

### Notice

## Letter Rulings

### Ltr. Rul.

## Announcements

# ERISA Sections

*[References are to question numbers.]*

# DOL Regulations, Letters, Releases, etc.

*[References are to question numbers.]*

## DOL Regulations

## DOL Advisory Opinions

## DOL Opinion Letters

## DOL QDRO Guidance

# Pension Benefit Guaranty Corporation Regulations, Letters, Forms, etc.

*[References are to question numbers.]*

## PBGC Regulations

## PBGC Opinion Letters

### PBGC Op. Ltr.

## PBGC Forms and Schedules

## PBGC Technical Updates

### PBGC TU

# Accounting and Actuarial Standards

*[References are to question numbers.]*

## Actuarial Standards of Practice

### ASOP

### Enrolled Actuaries Meeting Blue Books

## Enrolled Actuaries Meeting Gray Books

## Financial Accounting Standards

### FASB

# Pension Protection Act of 2006

*[References are to question numbers.]*

# Table of Cases

*[References are to question numbers.]*

# Index

*[References are to chapters (Ch.), question numbers, and appendixes (App.). Alphabetization is letter-by-letter (e.g., "Schedule B" precedes "S corporations").]*

# O

# Q

# R

# S